Krzysztof Czarnecki Ileana Ober
Jean-Michel Bruel Axel Uhl
Markus Völter (Eds.)

Model Driven Engineering Languages and Systems

11th International Conference, MoDELS 2008
Toulouse, France, September 28 - October 3, 2008
Proceedings

Springer

Volume Editors

Krzysztof Czarnecki
University of Waterloo
Department of Electrical and Computer Engineering
200 University Ave., West Waterloo, ON, N2L 3G1, Canada
E-mail: czarnecki@acm.org

Ileana Ober
Université Paul Sabatier, IRIT - MACAO
118, route de Narbonne, 31062 Toulouse, France
E-mail: ileana.ober@irit.fr

Jean-Michel Bruel
Université de Pau et des Pays de l'Adour
Département Informatique
Av. de l'Université, B.P. 1155, 64013 Pau, France
E-mail: Jean-Michel.Bruel@univ-pau.fr

Axel Uhl
SAP AG, 69190 Walldorf, Germany
E-mail: axel.uhl@sap.com

Markus Völter
Independent Consultant
Grabenstrasse 4, 73033 Göppingen, Germany
E-mail: voelter@acm.org

Library of Congress Control Number: 2008935624

CR Subject Classification (1998): D.2, D.3, K.6, I.6

LNCS Sublibrary: SL 2 – Programming and Software Engineering

ISSN	0302-9743
ISBN-10	3-540-87874-2 Springer Berlin Heidelberg New York
ISBN-13	978-3-540-87874-2 Springer Berlin Heidelberg New York

Springer is a part of Springer Science+Business Media

springer.com

Printed in Germany

Typesetting: Camera-ready by author, data conversion by Scientific Publishing Services, Chennai, India
Printed on acid-free paper SPIN: 12534548 06/3180 5 4 3 2 1 0

Lecture Notes in Computer Science 5301

Commenced Publication in 1973
Founding and Former Series Editors:
Gerhard Goos, Juris Hartmanis, and Jan van Leeuwen

Preface

MODELS 2008 was the 11th edition of the series of conferences on Model-Driven Engineering Languages and Systems. The conference was held in Toulouse, France, during the week of September 28 to October 3, 2008. The local arrangements were provided by the Institut de Recherche en Informatique de Toulouse (IRIT).

The conference program included three keynote presentations, technical paper presentations, two panels, and several workshops and tutorials. The invited keynote speakers were Don Batory (University of Texas, USA), Jeff Kramer (Imperial College London, UK), and Patrick Rauhut (Airbus, Germany).

This volume contains the final versions of the papers accepted for presentation at the conference. The papers cover a wide range of topics from the field including model transformation, model management, domain-specific modeling, modeling language semantics, model analysis, and applications.

We received a record number of 271 full paper submissions from 40 different countries. Of these, 43 papers were submitted by authors from more than one country. The top three countries submitting papers were France (40), Germany (38), and Canada (24). A total of 58 papers were accepted for inclusion in the proceedings. The acceptance rate was therefore 21%, which is somewhat lower than those of the previous MODELS conferences.

At least three Program Committee or Expert Reviewer Panel members reviewed each paper. Reviewing was thorough, and most authors received detailed comments on their submissions. Conflicts of interest were taken very seriously. No-one participated in any way in the decision process of any paper where a conflict of interest was identified. In particular, PC members who submitted papers did not have access to information concerning the reviews of their papers.

We would like to thank everyone who submitted papers as well as proposals for workshops and tutorials. We would also like to thank the large number of volunteers who contributed to the success of the conference. Richard van de Stadt deserves special thanks for his prompt and gracious service in supporting special requests for CyberChairPRO, the conference management system used to manage papers submissions and the virtual PC meeting. Finally, we would like to thank our sponsors, ACM and IEEE Computer Society, for their support of the MODELS 2008 conference.

October 2008

Krzysztof Czarnecki
Ileana Ober
Jean-Michel Bruel
Axel Uhl
Markus Völter

Organization

Conference Chairs

Ileana Ober (IRIT, France)
Jean-Michel Bruel (LIUPPA, France)

Program Chair

Krzysztof Czarnecki (University of Waterloo, Canada)

Experience Track Chairs

Axel Uhl (SAP, Germany)
Markus Völter (Independent Consultant, Germany)

Technological Track Chair

Pascal Roques (Valtech Training, France)

Workshop Chair

Michel Chaudron (Technical University Eindhoven and Leiden University, The Netherlands)

Tutorial Chair

Xavier Blanc (University Pierre et Marie Curie, France)

Panel Chair

Sudipto Ghosh (Colorado State University, USA)

Research Project Symposium Chair

Iulian Ober (Toulouse University, France)

Doctoral Symposium Chair

Alexander Pretschner (ETH Zurich, Switzerland)

Educators' Symposium Chair

Michał Śmiałek (Warsaw University of Technology, Poland)

Publicity Chair

Benoit Baudry (IRISA, France)

Web Chair

Nicolas Belloir (LIUPPA, France)

Organizing Committee

Jean-Paul Bodeveix (France)
Pierre Bazex (France)
Nicolas Belloir (France)
Agusti Canals (France)
Maura Cerioli (Italy)
Xavier Crégut (France)
Patrick Farail (France)
Louis Féraud (France)
Geri Georg (USA)
Hervé Leblanc (France)
Michel Lemoine (France)
Thierry Millan (France)
Mario Paludetto (France)
Christian Percebois (France)

Program Committee

João Araújo (Portugal)
Uwe Aßmann (Germany)
Benoit Baudry (France)
Xavier Blanc (France)
Jean Bézivin (France)
Paulo Borba (Brazil)
Lionel Briand (Norway)
Betty Cheng (USA)
Shigeru Chiba (Japan)
Krzysztof Czarnecki (Canada)
Juergen Dingel (Canada)
Gregor Engels (Germany)
Alexander Egyed (Austria)
Jean-Marie Favre (France)
Bernd Fischer (UK)
Robert France (USA)
Harald Gall (Switzerland)
Dragan Gašević (Canada)
Geri Georg (USA)
Holger Giese (Germany)
Tudor Girba (Switzerland)
Martin Gogolla (Germany)
Aniruddha Gokhale (USA)
Orla Greevy (Switzerland)
Paul Grünbacher (Austria)
John Grundy (New Zealand)
Øystein Haugen (Norway)
Simon Helsen (Germany)
Robert Hirschfeld (Germany)
Heinrich Hussmann (Germany)
Jean-Marc Jézéquel (France)
Gabor Karsai (USA)
Jana Koehler (Switzerland)
Rainer Koschke (Germany)
Thomas Kühne (New Zealand)
Vinay Kulkarni (India)
Jochen Küster (Switzerland)
Ralf Lämmel (Germany)

Michele Lanza (Switzerland)
Michael Lawley (Australia)
Timothy C. Lethbridge (Canada)
Ed Merks (Canada)
Birger Møller-Pedersen (Norway)
Ana Moreira (Portugal)
Pierre-Alain Muller (France)
Richard Paige (UK)
Alexander Pretschner (Switzerland)
Gianna Reggio (Italy)
Bernhard Rumpe (Germany)
Andy Schürr (Germany)
Bran Selic (Canada)
Perdita Stevens (UK)
Eleni Stroulia (Canada)
Gabriele Taentzer (Germany)
Juha-Pekka Tolvanen (Finland)
Laurence Tratt (UK)
Axel Uhl (Germany)
Hans Vangheluwe (Canada)
Dániel Varró (Hungary)
Eelco Visser (The Netherlands)
Markus Völter (Germany)
Andrzej Wasowski (Denmark)
Thomas Weigert (USA)
Jon Whittle (UK)

Expert Reviewer Panel

Aditya Agrawal (USA)
Jean-Michel Bruel (France)
Nancy Day (Canada)
Sebastian Fischmeister (Canada)
Sébastien Gérard (France)
Jeff Gray (USA)
Ileana Ober (France)
Kasper Østerbye (Denmark)
Awais Rashid (UK)
Andreas Rummler (Germany)
Peter Sesoft (Denmark)

Steering Committee

Thomas Baar (Switzerland)
Jean Bézivin (France)
Lionel Briand (Norway)
Steve Cook (UK)
Gregor Engels (Germany)
Andy Evans (UK)
Robert France (USA)
Geri Georg (USA)
Martin Gogolla (Germany)
Heinrich Hussmann (Germany)
Jean-Marc Jézéquel (France)
Stuart Kent (UK)
Cris Kobryn (USA)
Ana Moreira (Portugal)
Pierre-Alain Muller (France)
Oscar Nierstrasz (Switzerland)
Gianna Reggio (Italy)
David Rosenblum (UK)
Bernhard Rumpe (Germany)
Douglas C. Schmidt (USA)
Bran Selic (Canada)
Perdita Stevens (UK)
Jon Whittle (Chair; USA)

Sponsors

ACM Special Interest Group on Software Engineering
(www.sigsoft.org)
IEEE Computer Society
(www.computer.org)

Additional Reviewers

Vasco Amaral
Carsten Amelunxen
Malte Appeltauer
Egidio Astesiano
Richard Atterer
Andrej Bachmann
Omar Bahy Badreldin
Florence Balagtas-Fernandez
András Balogh
Jan-Christopher Bals
Olivier Barais
Bruno Barroca
Thiago T. Bartolomei
Dominikus Baur
Basil Becker
Nelly Bencomo
Alexej Beresnev
Rodrigo Bonifacio
Phil Brooke
Erwan Brottier
Achim D. Brucker
Fabian Buettner
Sebastian Cech
Maura Cerioli
Franck Chauvel
Dan Chiorean
Fabian Christ
Peter J. Clarke
Michelle Crane
Arnaud Cuccuru
Akshay Dabholkar
Duc-Hanh Dang
Vegard Dehlen
Romain Delamare
Deepak Dhungana
Zinovy Diskin
Nikos Drivalos
Cedric Dumoulin
Huascar Espinoza
Johan Fabry
Fernando Castor Filho
Franck Fleurey
Alexander Foerster
Frédéric Fondement
István Forgács
Andrew Forward
László Gönczy
Christian Gerth
Giacomo Ghezzi
Thomas Goldschmidt
Pieter Van Gorp
Emanuel Grant
Danny Groenewegen
Hans Groenniger
Iris Groher
Lindsay Groves
Roy Grønmo
Thomas Gschwind
Baris Güldali
Ulrich Hannemann
Michael Haupt
Zef Hemel
Christoph Herrmann
Anders Hessellund
Thomas Hettel
Mark Hibberd
Stephan Hildebrandt
Otmar Hilliges
Berthold Hoffmann
Jippe Holwerda
Ákos Horváth
Michael Jackson
Mikoláš Janota
Cedric Jeanneret
Jendrik Johannes
Frédéric Jouault
Christophe Jouvray
Stefan Jurack
Markus Kaiser
Sven Karol
Lennart C. L. Kats
Nima Kaviani
Amogh Kavimandan
Dae-Kyoo Kim

Felix Klar
Florian Klein
Renate Klempien-Hinrichs
Patrick Knab
Imre Kocsis
Dimitrios Kolovos
Máté Kovács
Holger Krahn
Ingolf Krueger
Mirco Kuhlmann
Uirá Kulesza
Sabine Kuske
Elodie Legros
László Lengyel
Tihamér Levendovszky
Hongzhi Liang
Jens Lincke
Alexander De Luca
Christoph Lueth
Mass Soldal Lund
Tiago Massoni
Matthew J. McGill
Tom Mens
Kirsten Mewes
Gergely Mezei
Milan Milanovic
Dragan Milicev
Parastoo Mohagheghi
Brice Morin
Pieter Mosterman
Jean-Marie Mottu
Patrick Mukherjee
Freddy Munoz
Gunter Mussbacher
Stefan Neumann
James Noble
Jon Oldevik
Sebastian Oster
Cesare Pautasso
Luis Pedro
Gilles Perrouin
Claas Pinkernell
Eduardo Piveta
Fiona Polack
Ernesto Posse
Christopher Power
Rick Rabiser
Ansgar Radermacher
Oliver Radfelder
Y. Raghu Reddy
Dirk Reiss
Marko Ribaric
Márcio de Medeiros Ribeiro
Filippo Ricca
Sebastian Richly
Matteo Risoldi
David Roethlisberger
Jens Rommel
Louis Rose
Nilabja Roy
Suman Roychoudhury
Ahmad Saifan
Yavuz Sancar
Tim Schattkowsky
Marvin Schulze-Quester
Andreas Seibel
Sagar Sen
Steven She
Carla Silva
Karsten Sohr
Arnor Solberg
Christian Soltenborn
Jean-Sebastien Sottet
Jim Steel
Mark Stein
Matthew Stephan
Gerson Sunye
Eugene Syriani
Dániel Tóth
Safouan Taha
Gergely Varró
Sander Vermolen
Hendrik Voigt
Steven Völkel
Arild Waaler
Ksenia Wahler
Michael Wahler
Ingo Weisemoeller

Christian Wende
Bernhard Westfechtel
Gerd Wierse
Michael Wuersch
Jochen Wuttke
Andreas Wübbeke
Vadim Zaytsev
Olaf Zimmermann
Steffen Zschaler

Table of Contents

Keynote I

Model Transformation: Foundations

Requirements Modeling

Domain-Specific Modeling

Keynote II

Model Transformation: Techniques

Composition and Analysis of Behavioral Models

Model Comprehension

Keynote III

Model Management

Behavioral Conformance and Refinement

Metamodeling and Modularity

Constraints

Model Analysis

Service-Oriented Architectures

Adaptive and Autonomic Systems

Empirical Studies

Evolution and Reverse Engineering

Modeling Language Semantics

Dependability Analysis and Testing

Aspect-Oriented Modeling

Structural Modeling

Embedded Systems

Workshops, Symposia, Tutorials, and Panels

The Objects and Arrows of Computational Design

Don Batory[1], Maider Azanza[2], and João Saraiva[3]

[1] University of Texas at Austin, Austin, Texas, USA
batory@cs.utexas.edu
[2] University of the Basque Country, San Sebastian, Spain
maider.azanza@ehu.es
[3] Universidade do Minho, Campus de Gualtar, Braga, Portugal
jas@di.uminho.pt

Abstract. *Computational Design (CD)* is a paradigm where both program design and program synthesis are computations. CD merges *Model Driven Engineering (MDE)* which synthesizes programs by transforming models, with *Software Product Lines (SPL)* where programs are synthesized by composing transformations called features. In this paper, basic relationships between MDE and SPL are explored using the language of modern mathematics.

Note: Although jointly authored, this paper is written as presented by Batory in his MODELS 2008 keynote.

Keywords: Software product lines, model driven engineering, categories.

1 Introduction

The future of program design and development lies in automation — the mechanization of repetitive tasks to free programmers from mundane activities so that they can tackle more creative problems. We are entering the age of *Computational Design (CD)*, where both program design and program synthesis are computations [39]. By *design*, I mean "what are the steps to create a program that meets a specification" (i.e., do this, then this, etc.). Such a script is called a *metaprogram*. By *synthesis*, I mean "execute these steps to produce the program". This is metaprogram execution.

At the forefront of Computational Design are two complementary but different technologies: *Model Driven Engineering (MDE)* and *Software Product Lines (SPL)*. These technologies have much in common and may soon be hard to distinguish. But abstractly for this paper, I will refer to *"pure" MDE* as defining high-level models of an application, and transforming these models into low-level artifacts, such as executables. "Pure" MDE is a general paradigm for program synthesis. In contrast, I will refer to *"pure" SPL* as a domain-specific paradigm for program synthesis. It exploits the knowledge of problems in a particular domain, tried-and-tested solutions to these problems, and the desire to automate the construction of such programs given this knowledge. Both "pure" MDE and "pure" SPL are synergistic: the strengths of one are the weaknesses of the other. MDE and SPL are clearly not mutually-disjoint technologies, but I will present their strengths as such here.

K. Czarnecki et al. (Eds.): MoDELS 2008, LNCS 5301, pp. 1–20, 2008.

In a prior lifetime, I was a database researcher. My introduction to program synthesis was *relational query optimization (RQO)* [32]. The design of a query evaluation program was defined by a composition of relational algebra operations, a.k.a. a relational algebra expression. Expressions were optimized by applying algebraic identities called rewrite rules. Applying rules was the task of a query optimizer. It took me years to appreciate the significance and generality of RQO: it is a compositional paradigm for program synthesis and is a classic example of Computational Design. RQO fundamentally shaped my view of automated software development more than any software engineering course (in the 1980s and maybe even now) could have.

My research focusses on SPLs, where the goal is to design and synthesize any member of a family of related programs automatically from declarative specifications. The thrust of my early work was on language and tool support for SPLs. More recently, my interest shifted to elucidate the foundational concepts of SPL and MDE. Early on, I needed a simple modeling language to express program design and synthesis as a computation. I discovered that modern mathematics fit the bill.

Here's the reason: software engineers define structures called programs and use tools to transform, manipulate, and analyze them. Object orientation uses methods, classes, and packages to structure programs. Compilers transform source structures into bytecode structures. Refactoring tools transform source structures into other source structures, and metamodels of MDE define the allowable structures of model instances: transformations map metamodel instances to instances of other metamodels for purposes of analysis and synthesis. Software engineering is replete with such examples.

Mathematics is the science of structures and their relationships. I use mathematics as an informal modeling language (*not as a formal model*) to explain Computational Design. Certainly I claim no contributions to mathematics, but I do lay claim to exposing its relevance in informal modeling in SPLs. The foundation of my work rests on ancient ideas: that programs are data or values, transformations map programs to programs, and operators map transformations to transformations [11]. This orientation naturally lead me to MDE, with its emphasis on transformations.

Table 1. MDE, SPL, and Category Theory Terminology

Paradigm	Object	Point	Arrow
MDE	metamodel	model	transformation
SPL		program	feature

The goal of this paper is to expose a set of concepts on which MDE, SPL, and Computation Design are founded. Although the concepts come from category theory [25][30], a general theory of mathematical structures and their relationships, this paper is aimed at practitioners who do not have a mathematical background. I show how MDE and SPL ideas map to categorical concepts, and throughout this paper, I explain the benefits in making a connection. Table 1 summarizes the terminological correspondence. Basic concepts of category theory are in use today, but I suspect members of the SPL and MDE communities may not appreciate them. Also, as this conference is about modeling, it is worth noting that mathematicians can be superb modelers, and leveraging their ideas is largely what this paper is about. I begin by explaining a simple relationship between MDE and categories.

2 MDE and Categories

In category theory, an object is a domain of points (there does not seem to be a standard name for object instances — I follow Lawvere's text and use 'points' [25]).[1] In Figure 1a, an object is depicted with its domain of points, shown as a *cone of instances*. This diagram is familiar to the MDE community as a metamodel and its model instances (Fig.1b). "Pure" MDE focuses on a particular technology implementation (e.g., MOF, Ecore) of metamodels and their instances. However, the ideas of objects and instances are more general. This observation has been noted by others, e.g., Bézivin's technical spaces [24] and GROVE [34]. So one can think of a Java "object" whose instances are Java programs, a bytecode "object" whose instances are Java bytecode files, an XML "object" (XML schemata) whose instances are XML files, and so on.

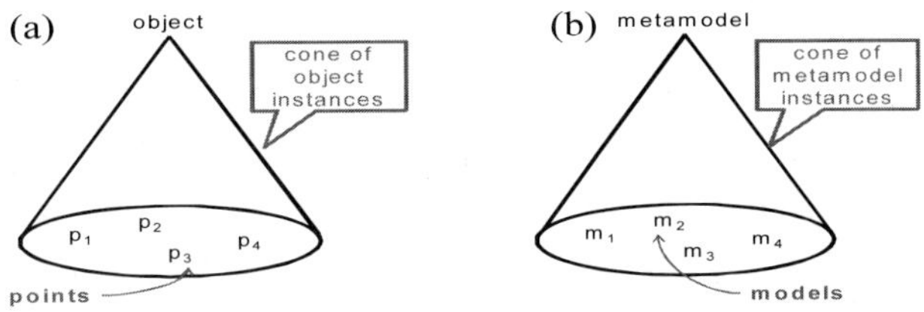

Fig. 1. Objects as Domains of points

Recursion is fundamental to category theory: a point can be an object. Fig. 2a depicts such a situation, which readers will recognize as isomorphic to the standard multi-level MOF architecture of Fig.2b:

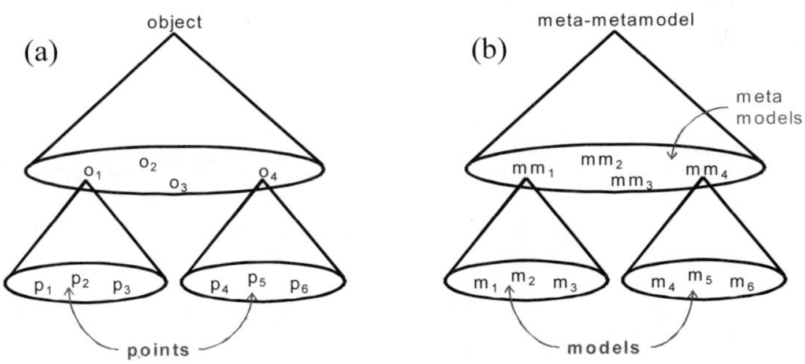

Fig. 2. Three-Level MOF Architecture

The MOF architecture is not interesting in category theory without arrows. An *arrow* is a *map* or *function* or *morphism* between objects, and whose implementation is unspecified.[2] Figure 3a shows an *external diagram* [25] that displays two objects, **s**

[1] I recommend Pierce's text on category theory [30] with concrete examples in [12] as illustrations; Lawvere's text is also quite accessible [25].

[2] A morphism is not necessarily a function; it can express a relationship, e.g., $\geq$.

and **J**, and an arrow **A** that maps each point of **S** to a point in **J**. (Arrows are always total, not partial, maps [30]). Figure 3b shows a corresponding *internal diagram* that exposes the points of every object of an external diagram and the mapping relationships among points. In general, there can be any number of arrows that connect objects; Figure 3c shows an arrow **B** that is different from **A**.

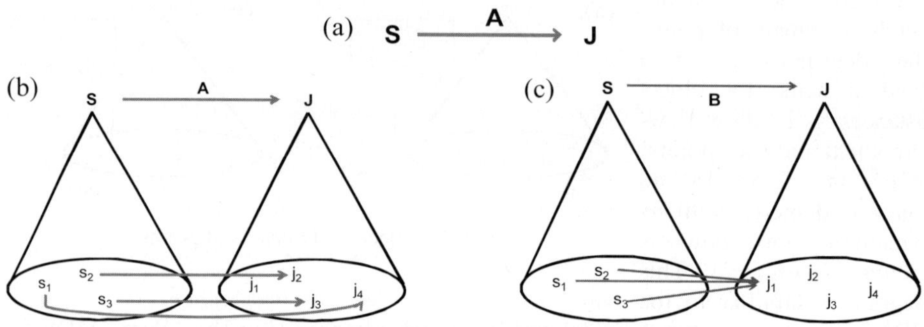

Fig. 3. External and Internal Diagrams

In this paper, I use the following terminology: an *arrow* is a mapping relationship, a *transformation* is an implementation of an arrow as expressed by an MDE transformation language (e.g., QVT [29], ATL [21], RubyTL [16], GReAT [1]), and a *tool* is any other (e.g., Java, Python) implementation of an arrow.

Now consider the following example: the external diagram of Fig. 4 shows that a message sequence chart (**MSC**) can be mapped to a state chart (**SC**) via a model-to-model transformation (**M2MX**). A state chart can be mapped to a Java program by a model-to-text transformation (**M2TX**). And a Java program is mapped to bytecode by the **javac** tool. Each arrow is realized by a distinct technology. In addition to these arrows, there are also identity arrows for each object.

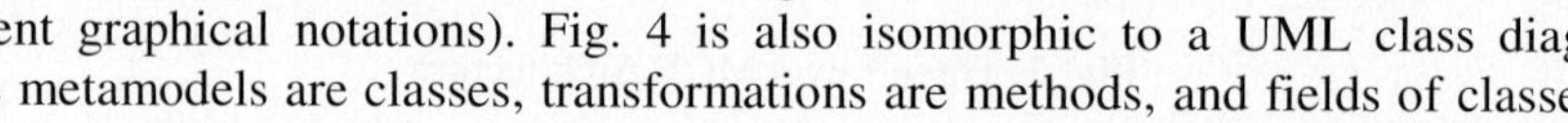

Fig. 4. Another External Diagram

There does not seem to be a standard name for such diagrams in MDE. Common names are tool chain diagrams [29] and megamodels [14] (both of which have slightly different graphical notations). Fig. 4 is also isomorphic to a UML class diagram, where metamodels are classes, transformations are methods, and fields of classes are private or hidden [10][34]. External diagrams are also standard depictions of categories. A *category* is a collection of objects and arrows, where each object has an identity arrow (i.e., identity transformation). Fig. 4 is an external diagram of a category of four objects and three non-identity arrows.

Besides objects and arrows, categories have the following properties [25][30]:

- Arrows are *composable*: given arrows **f:A→B** and **g:B→C**, there is a composite arrow **g•f:A→C**.

- Composition is *associative*: given arrows **f:A→B**, **g:B→C**, and **h:C→D** (with **A**, **B**, **C**, and **D** not necessarily distinct), **h•(g•f) = (h•g)•f**.
- For each object **A**, there is an identity arrow $\mathbf{id}_A$**:A→A** such that for any arrow **f:A→B**, $\mathbf{id}_B$**•f = f** and **f•**$\mathbf{id}_A$**=f**.

Identity and composed arrows are often omitted from external diagrams.

The above properties allow us to infer that there is an arrow **T:MSC→ByteCode** that maps message sequence charts to Java bytecodes, where **T=javac•MT2X•M2MX** (**T** is not displayed in Fig. 4). In general, there needs to be tool support for these abstractions, so that all arrows, regardless on how they are implemented, can be treated uniformly. GROVE [34] and UniTI [37] are steps in the right direction.

Category theory defines arrows that map one input object to one output object. But in MDE, it is common in model weaving to map multiple models as input and produce multiple models as output [15]. Category theory has an elegant way to express this. The idea is to define a tuple of objects (called a *product of objects* [25][30]), and this tuple is itself an object. Projection arrows are defined so that each component of a tuple can be extracted. Fig. 5 depicts an arrow **F:[O1,O2,O3]→[O4,O5]** which maps a 3-tuple of objects to a pair of objects, along with projection arrows.

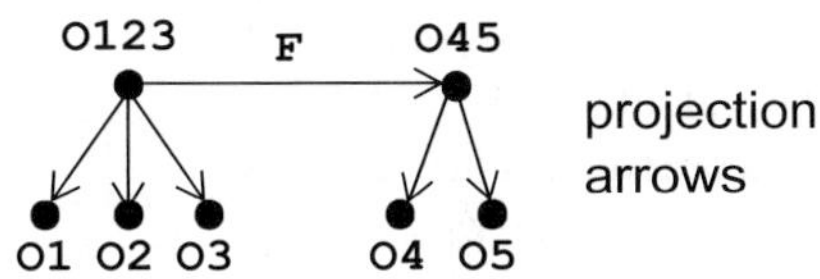

Fig. 5. Products of Objects

Now, let's look at Fig. 6, which depicts an internal diagram of Fig. 4. Although only one point is shown for each object, the relationships between these points ($\mathbf{m}_1$,$\mathbf{s}_1$,$\mathbf{j}_1$,$\mathbf{b}_1$) is also a category, sometimes called a *trivial category*, i.e., a category where each object represents a domain with a single point.

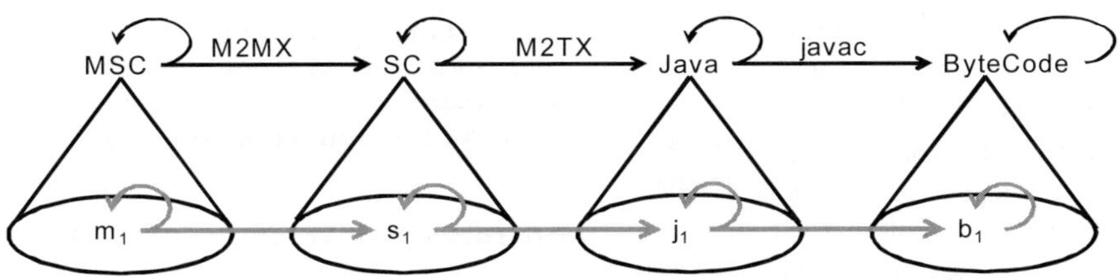

Fig. 6. An Internal Diagram of Fig. 4

In general, categories lie at the heart of MDE and can be found at all levels in a MDE architecture. Category theory provides an elegant set of ideas to express transformation relationships among objects that arise in MDE. The ideas are straightforward, if not familiar and have an elementary benefit: they may provide a clean foundation for MDE (e.g., such as a language and terminology to express MDE Computational Designs). A nice example of a formal use of categories in MDE is [19].

Now let's look at the connection between product lines and categories.

3 SPL and Categories

A software product line is a set of similar programs. Programs are constructed from features, which are increments in program functionality that customers use to distinguish one program from another. For example, program `P` is constructed from program `G` by adding feature `F`. This is expressed by modeling `F` as a function: `P=F(G)`.

The code of a product line of calculators is shown in Fig. 7. Associated with each line of code is a tag, which indicates the feature that adds that line. This makes it easy to build a preprocessor that receives as input the names of the desired features and strips off the code belonging to unneeded features. As can be imagined, this approach is brittle for problems of larger scale and complexity. Nevertheless, we use it as a reference to define what changes occur when a feature is added to a program.

The first program P_1 of the calculator SPL defines a `calculator` class and its `gui` class. The base calculator only allows numbers to be added. The second program P_2=`sub`(P_1), extends the base with a subtraction operation (both the `calculator` and `gui` classes are updated). The effect of the `sub` feature is to add new methods and new fields to existing classes, and to extend existing methods with additional code. More generally, features can add new classes and packages as well. The third program P_3=`format`(P_2) adds an output formatting capability to a calculator, where again new methods and new fields are added, and existing methods are extended. A fourth program, P_4=`format`(P_1), extends the base program with the `format` feature. One can push these ideas further, and say the base program is itself a feature, which extends the empty program `0`, i.e., P_1=`base(0)`. Feature `base` adds new classes (the base `calculator` class and the base `gui` class) to `0`.

```
base  class calculator {
base    int result;
base    void add( int x ) { result=+x; }
sub     void sub( int x ) { result=-x; }
base  }

base  class gui {
base    JButton add = new JButton("add");
sub     JButton sub = new JButton("sub");
form    JButton form = new JButton("format");

base    void initGui() {
base      ContentPane.add( add );
sub       ContentPane.add( sub );
form      ContentPane.add( form );
base    }

base    void initListeners() {
base      add.addActionListener(...);
sub       sub.addActionListener(...);
form      form.addActionListener(...);
base    }

form    void formatResultString() {...}
base  }
```

Fig. 7. Complete Code of the calculator SPL

These ideas scale: twenty years ago I built customizable databases (80K LOC each), ten years ago I built extensible Java preprocessors (40K LOC each), and more recently the AHEAD Tool Suite (250K LOC). All used the ideas that programs are values and transformations (features) map simple programs to more complex programs.[3]

Now consider the connection of SPLs to MDE. Fig. 8 shows a metamodel **MM** and its cone of instances. For typical metamodels, there is an infinite number of instances. An SPL, in contrast, is always a finite family of *n* similar programs (where *n* may range from 2 to thousands or more). So an SPL is a miniscule subset of a metamodel's domain. In fact, there is an infinite number of SPLs in a domain. If **MM** is a metamodel of state charts, it would not be difficult to find SPLs for, say, an IBM disk driver domain, a portlet flight booking domain, and many others.

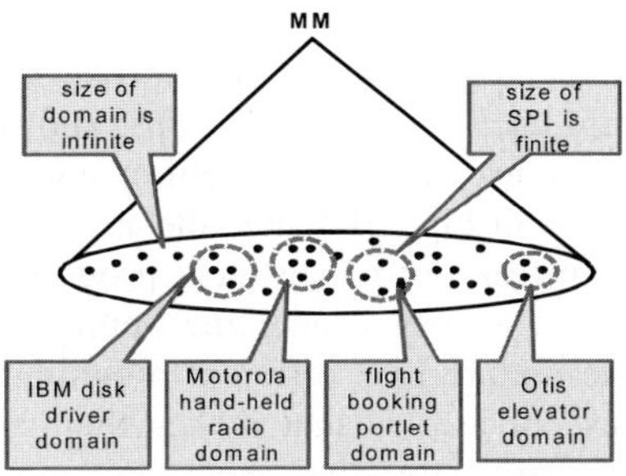

Fig. 8. SPLs and Metamodels

As mentioned earlier, SPLs define relationships between its programs. How? By arrows, of course. Fig. 9 shows the calculator product line with its four programs, along with the empty program **0**, which typically is not a member of an SPL. Each arrow is a feature. From the last section, it is not difficult to recognize that an SPL is itself a trivial category: each point is a domain with a single program in it, there are implied identity arrows and implied composed arrows, as required.

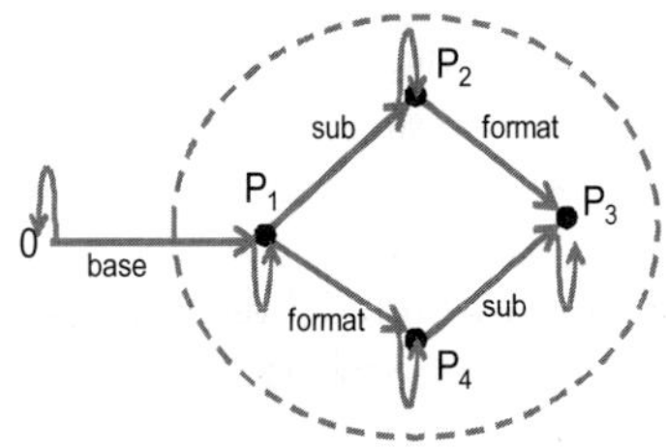

Fig. 9. Category of the Calculator SPL

Embodied in our description of SPLs is a fundamental approach to software design and construction, namely *incremental development*. Programs are built, step-by-step, by incrementally adding features. Not only does this control program complexity and improve program understandability, it also allows for the reuse of features (i.e., multiple programs in a product line could share the same feature). More on this shortly.

By composing arrows (features), the programs of an SPL are created. A program's design is an expression (i.e., a composition of arrows), and a program can have multiple, equivalent designs. For example, program P_3 has two equivalent designs: **P_3=format•sub•base(0)** (which we henceforth abbreviate to **P_3=format•sub•base**) and **P_3=sub•format•base**. Evaluating both expressions yields exactly the same program. Features **sub** and **format** are said to be *commutative* because they modify mutually disjoint parts of a program.

3.1 Pragmatics of Software Product Lines

If there are *n* optional features, there can be 2^n different programs. We see a miniature example of this in Fig. 9: there are 2 optional features (**format** and **sub**) and there are

---

[3] Readers who are familiar with the decorator pattern will see a similarity with features: a decorator wraps an object to add behaviors. Features can be dynamically composed, but in this paper, they are statically composed to produce programs. Another difference is scale: decorators wrap a single object, whereas features often modify many classes of a program simultaneously.

2^2=4 programs in the product line. A slightly larger and more illustrative example is Fig. 10. We want to create an SPL of many programs; we know the arrows that allow us to build each of these programs, and many programs use the same feature, e.g., the thick arrows of Fig. 10 denote the application of the green feature to 4 different programs, and the dashed arrows denote the application of the blue feature to 3 different programs. It is the reuse of arrows that makes them more economical to store than programs.

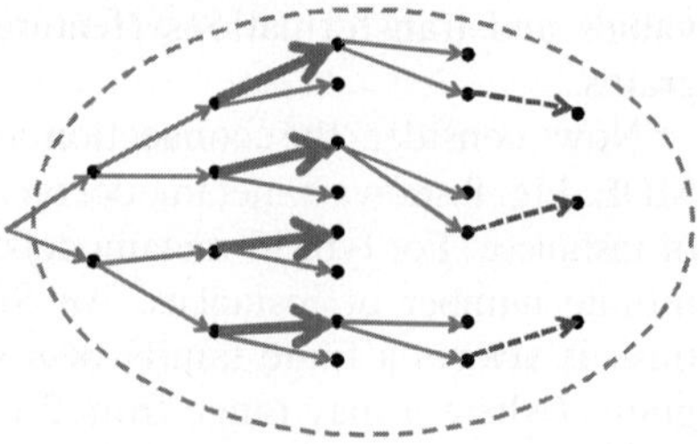

Fig. 10. Reuse of Arrows in SPLs

As an aside, features are like database transactions: they make changes to a program that are not necessarily localized: changes can appear anywhere in a program. But the key is that either all changes are made, or none are. Further, features can produce non-conforming programs (non-conforming models). Fig. 11 depicts an arrow **F** that relates programs P_3 and P_6, both of which conform to metamodel **MM**. But by arrow composibility, we see that **F=F3•F2•F1**. Applying **F1** to P_3 yields program P_4, and applying **F2** to P_4 yields program P_5, and P_6=F3(P_5). Note that programs P_4 and P_5 do *not* conform to **MM**. It is common for existing features to be decomposed into compositions of smaller features, the individual application of which does not preserve conformance properties of the resulting program or model.[4] The reason why these smaller arrows arise is that features often have a lot of code in common. Commonalities can be factored into small features (small arrows) that are shared in implementations of larger arrows. We will see examples of small arrows in the next section.

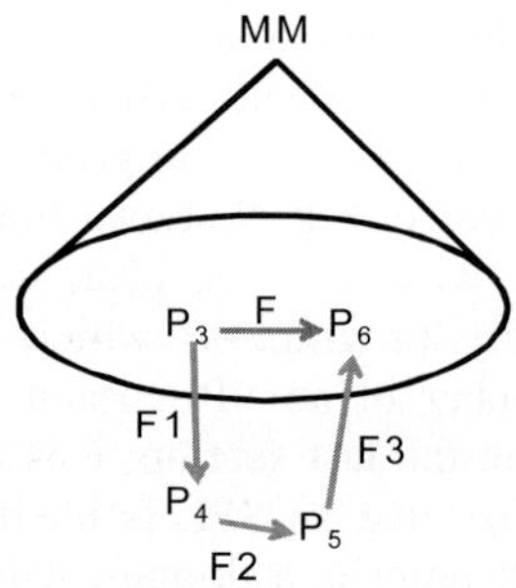

Fig. 11. F=F3•F2•F1

3.2 Arrow Implementations

There are two ways in which arrows are implemented. First is to implement arrows in the ATL, GReAT, etc. languages. The second and standard way for SPLs is that arrows are program or model *deltas* — a set of changes — that are superimposed on existing models (e.g., AHEAD [9], Scala [28], Aspectual Feature Modules [5], and AspectJ [22]). In effect, deltas can be viewed as a specific example of model weaving [15]. Which approach — writing modules that are to be superimposed or writing transformations— is "better"? This is not clear; I am unaware of any study to compare their trade-offs. In this paper, I focus solely on the use of deltas, so that core concepts in SPLs can be given their most direct MDE interpretation.

Here is an example. Fig. 12a shows the AHEAD representation of the `sub` feature of our calculator SPL. It states that the `calculator` class is extended with a "`void sub(int x)`" method, and the `gui` class is extended with a new field (`JButton sub`),

[4] Conformance for a program could be whether it type checks or not.

and its existing methods (`initGui()` and `initListeners()`) are wrapped (effectively adding more lines of code to these methods). We mentioned in the last section about decomposing a feature (arrow) into smaller features (arrows). Fig. 12b defines the AHEAD arrow (`subcl`) that changes only the `calculator` class, Fig. 12c defines the AHEAD arrow (`subgui`) that changes only the `gui` class. Composing `subcl` and `subgui` in either order produces `sub` (Fig. 12d). The `subgui` arrow could be decomposed even further, as a composition of arrows that introduce fields and wrap individual methods.

```
refines class calculator {
  void sub( float x ) { result=-x; }
}

refines class gui {
  JButton sub = new JButton("sub");

  void initGui() {
    SUPER.initGui();
    ContentPane.add( sub );
  }

  void initListeners() {
    SUPER.initListeners();
    add.addActionListener(...);
  }
}
```

(a) `sub=subcl•subgui=subgui•subcl`

```
refines class calculator {
  void sub( float x ) { result=-x; }
}
```

(b) `subcl`

```
refines class gui {
  JButton sub = new JButton("sub");

  void initGui() {
    SUPER.initGui();
    ContentPane.add( sub );
  }

  void initListeners() {
    SUPER.initListeners();
    add.addActionListener(...);
  }
}
```

(c) `subgui`

(d)

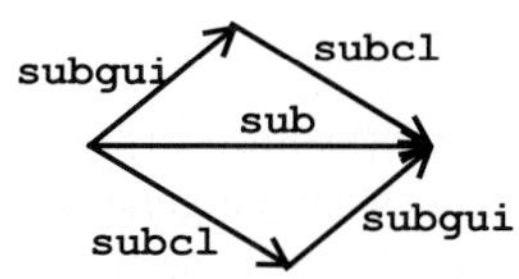

Fig. 12. AHEAD Arrow Implementations

The same ideas hold for MDE models. In two different product lines, fire support simulators [7] and web portlets [35], customized state machines were created by having features encapsulate fragments of state machines. By composing fragments, complete state machines were synthesized.

To me, the essential entities that programmers create in "pure" MDE are complete models (points); in "pure" SPLs they are features (arrows representing model deltas). Hence, there is discernible distinction between these paradigms, and exposing this distinction reveals an interesting perspective. Fig. 13a shows the metamodel **MM**, its cone of instances, and a particular product line **PL** whose members are $\mathbf{m}_1$, $\mathbf{m}_4$, and $\mathbf{m}_5$. The domain of a more general metamodel, called an *arrow metamodel* $\underline{\mathbf{MM}}$, is a superset of **MM**. Fig. 13b exposes the arrows that relate models in the **PL** product line, showing how models and features can be placed in the same cone of instances. Each model **m** is represented by an arrow $\mathbf{0}\rightarrow\mathbf{m}$. Fig. 13c erases **MM** and its cone to reveal that the instances of $\underline{\mathbf{MM}}$ are arrows. The subset of arrows that define **PL** is indicated in Fig. 13c, and so too are other sets of arrows (not necessarily disjoint) that are used to create other product lines. By combining a set of arrows with a feature model (i.e., a

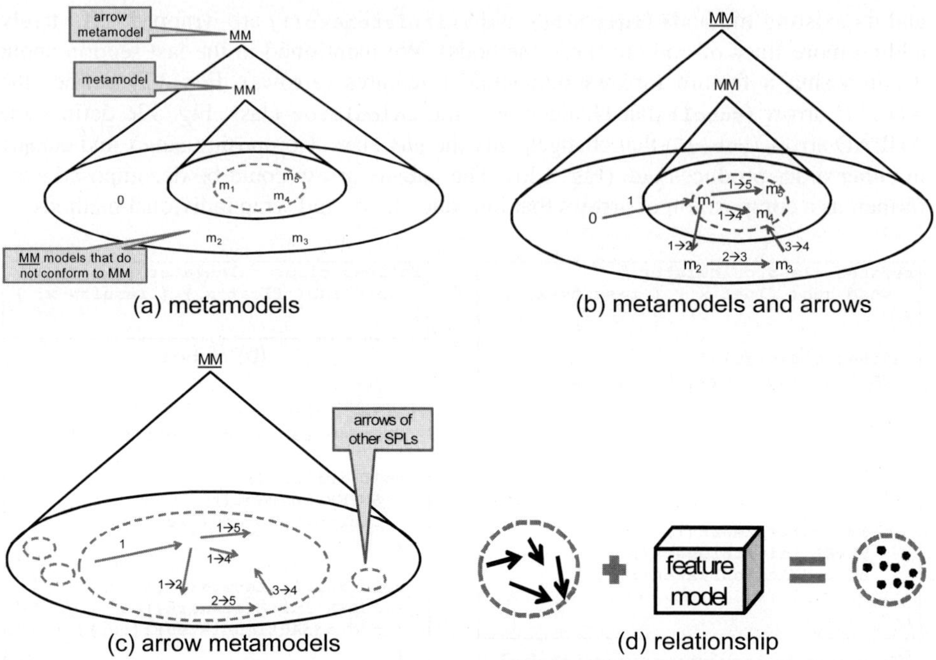

Fig. 13. Metamodels and Arrow MetaModels

specification that defines what composition of arrows are legal), the original product line **PL** within **MM**'s cone of instances can be generated (Fig. 13d).[5]

From a modeling perspective, the SPL approach to program construction recognizes a basic fact: all program artifacts — MDE models, Java programs, etc. — are not created spontaneously. They are created by extending simpler artifacts, and these artifacts come from simpler artifacts, recursively, until **0** is reached. The connection between successive artifacts is an arrow (from the simpler to the more complex artifact). By following arrows forward in time starting from **0**, an artifact (program, model, etc.) is synthesized. In effect, SPLs add a dimension of time to program or model designs. Proceeding forward in time explains how a program was developed in logical steps. Or stated differently, program synthesis is an integration of a series of well-understood changes.

3.3 Recursion

Product lines of models will be common, but product lines of metamodels, a form of product lines of product lines [8], will also be common. Fig. 14 depicts the MDE architecture. A product line of four metamodels is shown, along with the arrows that

[5] Support for deltas in conventional programming languages is largely absent. One can only define programs, *not* changes one wants to make to an existing program and encapsulate and compose such changes. It is as if one-half of a fundamental picture is absent.

connect them. Such arrows could be metamodel deltas (as we have described previously), or they could be refactorings [33][38]. Normally, when a metamodel is changed, one would like to automatically update all of its instances. The model-to-model transformation that is derived from a metamodel-to-metamodel transformation is called a *co-transformation* [33][38]. Co-transformations map product lines of one metamodel to product lines of other metamodels.

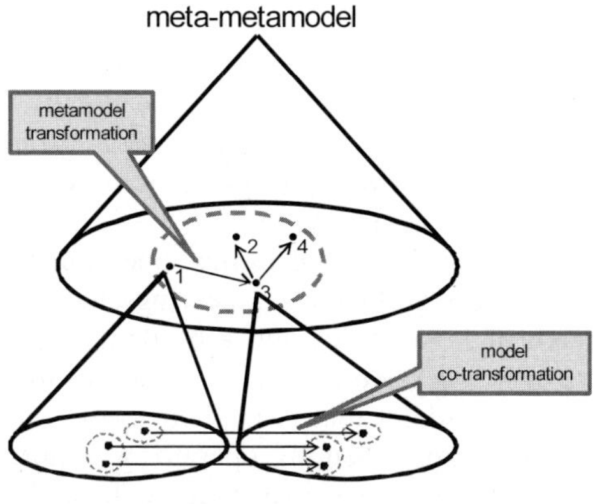

Fig. 14. Co-transformations

3.4 Recap

Categories lie at the heart of SPLs, and again the ideas are straightforward. Well-studied ideas in mathematics offers a clean language and terminology to express SPL Computational Designs. See [12] for an example. Now, let's see what happens when MDE and SPLs are combined into *model-driven software product lines (MDSPL)*.

4 MDSPL and Categories

A fundamental concept in category theory is the *commuting diagram*, whose key property is that all paths from one object to another yield equivalent results. The diagram of Fig. 15a is said to commute if $f_2 \bullet d_1 = d_2 \bullet f_1$. Commuting diagrams are the theorems of category theory.

Commuting diagrams arise in MDSPL in the following way. Consider Fig. 15b, which shows arrow **A** that maps object **S** to object **B**. A small product line of **S**

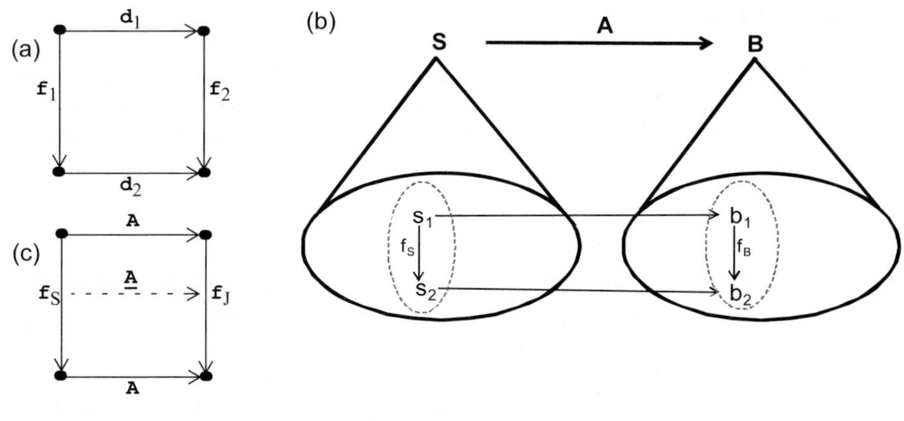

Fig. 15. Commuting Diagrams

instances is depicted, and these points are mapped by **A** to a corresponding set of points in **B**. In general, horizontal arrows are MDE transformations and vertical arrows are SPL features. Note that feature f_S that relates s_1 to s_2 is mapped to a corresponding feature f_B that relates b_1 to b_2. Mapping a feature (arrow) to another feature (arrow) is an *operator* or update translation [4]. Operator $\underline{A}$ relates features f_S and f_B in Fig. 15c by $f_B = \underline{A}(f_S)$.

From our limited experience, operators can sometimes be easy to write; generally they pose a significant engineering challenge. As a challenge example, let **S** be the domain of Java source and **B** be domain of Java bytecodes. Suppose feature f_S is a delta in source code that maps the source s_1 of program P_1 to the source s_2 of program P_2. f_B is the delta that is applied to the binary of s_1 to yield the binary of s_2 (i.e., $b_2 = f_B(b_1)$). Implementing operator $\underline{A}$ requires separate class compilation, a sophisticated technology that can compile Java files individually and delay complete type checking and constant folding optimizations until composition time [2]. In the next sections, we present examples of operators we have implemented.[6]

> **Note:** The generalization of metamodel **S** to the arrow metamodel $\underline{S}$ as explained in Section 3.2 also applies to the generalization of arrows. That is, the external diagram consisting of objects **S** and **B** and arrow $A{:}S \rightarrow B$ can be generalized to the external diagram with objects $\underline{S}$ and $\underline{B}$ and arrow $\underline{A}{:}\underline{S} \rightarrow \underline{B}$. This is the $\underline{A}$ operator discussed above.

> **Note:** $\underline{A}$ is a *homomorphism*: it is a mapping of $\underline{S}$ expressions (compositions of one or more $\underline{S}$ arrows) to a corresponding $\underline{B}$ expression (compositions of one or more $\underline{B}$ arrows). Let x and y be arrows of $\underline{S}$. The commuting relationship of a homomorphism is:
>
> $$\underline{A}(x \bullet y) = \underline{A}(x)\ \underline{A}(\bullet)\ \underline{A}(y)$$
>
> where $\underline{A}(\bullet)$ typically maps to function composition ($\bullet$). We talk about the practical benefits of such relationships next.

5 Benefits of Mapping Arrows

In the last two years, we discovered several uses for mapping arrows in MDE product lines: simplifying implementations [17], improving test generation [36], understanding feature interactions [23], explaining AHEAD [12], and improving the performance of program synthesis [35]. In the following sections, I briefly review two recent results.

5.1 Lifting

MapStats is an MDSPL where applications are written in SVG and JavaScript. MapStats applications display an SVG map of the U.S. where the map can be customized by adding or removing charts, statistics, and controls (Fig. 16).

---

[6] Gray has noticed that the kind of commuting diagrams shown here often require transformations that involve different technical spaces (using Bezivin's terminology). These are often hard to compose in practice, yet seem easy in these diagrams [18]. As mentioned earlier, there is a strong need for relating these tool chains [34][37].

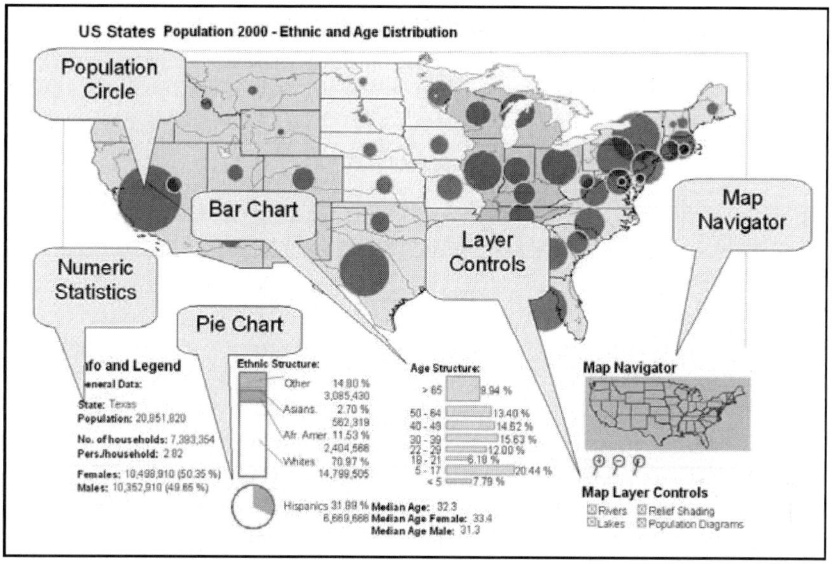

Fig. 16. A MapStats Application

The SPL design was a collection of MapStats features (arrows) and its feature model, which defined the legal combination of MapStats features. All MapStats features were implemented as XML documents or XML document deltas. By composing arrows using XAK, a general language and tool for refining XML documents [3], customized MapStats applications were synthesized. Early on, we discovered that a particular subset of arrows, namely those that implemented charts, were tedious to write. We used a basic concept of MDE to create a *domain-specific language (DSL)* to define charts and chart features. Each Chart feature was mapped to its corresponding and low-level MapStats feature by an operator (τ:`Chart`→`MapStats`). In effect, we "lifted" chart arrows from their MapStats implementation, to arrows in a Charts DSL (Fig. 17). By doing so, we simplified the writing of Charts arrows using the Charts DSL, and we automated the tedious implementations of their corresponding MapStats arrows.

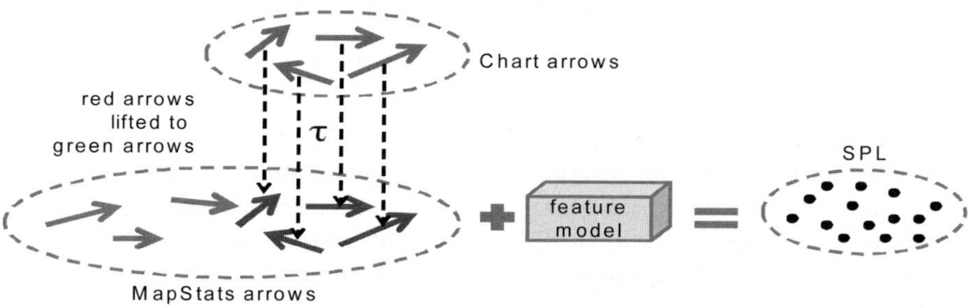

Fig. 17. Lifting Arrows

```
<chart data-type="age-population" type="pieChart" ...
  <item attr="AGE_30_39" color="green" name= ...
  <item attr="AGE_22_29" color="cyan" name=...
</chart>
```

(a) chart specification

```
<xr:refine xmlns:xr="http://www.atarix.org/xmlRef ...
  <xr:at select="//chart[@data-type='age-population' ...
    <xr:append>
      <item attr="AGE_18_21" color="blue" ...
    </xr:append>
  </xr:at>
</xr:refine>
```

(b) a Chart arrow

```
<chart data-type="age-population" type="pieChart" ...
  <item attr="AGE_30_39" color="green" name= ...
  <item attr="AGE_22_29" color="cyan" name=...
  <item attr="AGE_18_21" color="blue" name=...
</chart>
```

(c) a refined chart specification

```
<xr:refine ... >
  <xr:at select="//function[@data-type='age-population']
      [@parentId='ChartArea2'][@name='buildData']"...>
    <xr:append>
      <statement>
    this.chartAttrArray.push("AGE_18_21");
    this.chartNameArray.push("18-21");
    this.chartColorArray.push("blue");
      </statement>
    </xr:append>
  </xr:at>
</xr:refine>
```

(d) corresponding MapStats arrow

Fig. 18. MapStats and Chart Arrows

As an example, Fig. 18a shows a simple DSL spec **S** of a pie-chart that displays age population for the ranges **30-39** and **22-29**. Fig. 18b shows a specification of a chart arrow **R** that adds the range **18-21** to a Chart spec. The underlined code defines a pointcut that identifies nodes in an XML document, and the advice is to append the **18-21** range item to selected nodes. Applying **R** to **S** (evaluating expression **R(S)**) yields the Chart spec of Fig. 18c. The τ operator maps a Chart arrow to a MapStats arrow. The result of τ**(R)** is the MapStats arrow of Fig. 18d. Note that τ maps the

Chart pointcut to the corresponding MapStats pointcut, and maps the Chart advice to the corresponding MapStats advice written in JavaScript. τ was written in XSLT.

A homomorphism relates Chart arrows (S_k) to MapStats arrows (C_k):

$$\tau(S_i \bullet S_j) = \tau(S_i) \bullet \tau(S_j) = C_i \bullet C_j \tag{1}$$

We used (1) in two ways. First, when a particular MapStats application was specified as a composition of MapStats arrows, we used (1) to generate MapStats chart arrows. For example, let M_i denote non-chart arrows of MapStats. A MapStats application P is a composition of M arrows followed by C arrows. We translated P into equivalent expressions using (1) and evaluated either of these new expressions to synthesize P:

$$\begin{aligned} P &= C_2 \bullet C_1 \bullet C_0 \bullet M_1 \bullet M_0 && \texttt{// given} \\ &= \tau(S_2 \bullet S_1 \bullet S_0) \bullet M_1 \bullet M_0 && \texttt{// by (1)} \\ &= \tau(S_2) \bullet \tau(S_1) \bullet \tau(S_0) \bullet M_1 \bullet M_0 && \texttt{// by (1)} \end{aligned}$$

The second use of (1) was for verification: it defined a set of constraints that hold between pairs of Charts and MapStats features and their compositions. Here, as in previous experiences [35], our tools did not satisfy these constraints (meaning the equalities of (1) did not hold). This exposed bugs in our tools which we had to fix.[7] Now we have greater confidence in our tools as they implement explicit relationships in our MDSPL models. This is a win from an engineering perspective: we have insights into domains that we did not have before, and we have a better understanding, better models, and better tools as a result.

Lifting is a general technique that can be applied to many product lines. For more details, see [17].

5.2 Test Generation

Testing members of SPLs is a fundamental problem. We can synthesize different programs, but how do we know these programs are correct? In such cases, specification-based testing can be effective. Starting with a specification (or model) of a program, we want to derive its tests automatically. Alloy is an example of this approach [20].

Alloy works by translating an Alloy specification S into a propositional formula. A SAT solver finds the bindings that satisfy the formula, called a *solution*. Let I denote the set of all solutions for S. A test program is generated for each solution using the TestEra tool [26]. The set of all tests, T, is the output.

Alloy specifications can be developed incrementally by conjunction. That is, if program P_0 has specification S_0 and feature F has specification S_F, then the spec of F(P) is $S_0 \wedge S_F$. The conventional way to synthesize tests for a program is to compose the specifications of all of its features, and then use Alloy and TestEra to produce its tests. We know there is a commuting diagram behind this design, which Fig. 19 exposes. The left column of objects are Alloy specifications, the middle column are spec solutions, and the right column are tests. Horizontal arrows are the tools `alloy:S→I` and `TestEra:I→T`. Features are vertical arrows. The right-most column of vertical

[7] Although we could not prove the equivalence of (1), we could demonstrate equivalence by testing, as is done in conventional software development.

arrows are spec refinements. The middle column are solution refinements, and the right column are test refinements.

Only the conventional path, and no other, has ever been taken. The challenge is to determine how to implement an operator τ: $\underline{\mathtt{S}} \rightarrow \underline{\mathtt{I}}$ to map spec arrows to solution arrows and maybe another operator σ: $\underline{\mathtt{I}} \rightarrow \underline{\mathtt{T}}$ to map solution arrows to test arrows. Uzuncaova et al. discovered an elegant way to realize τ (for details, see [36]). This discovery exposed an alternative path, called the *incremental path*, that first derives the solutions for the base specification, and extends each solution to zero or more solutions of an incrementally more complicated specification. Once solutions to the target specification are found, the **TestEra** tool is used to produce the corresponding set of tests.

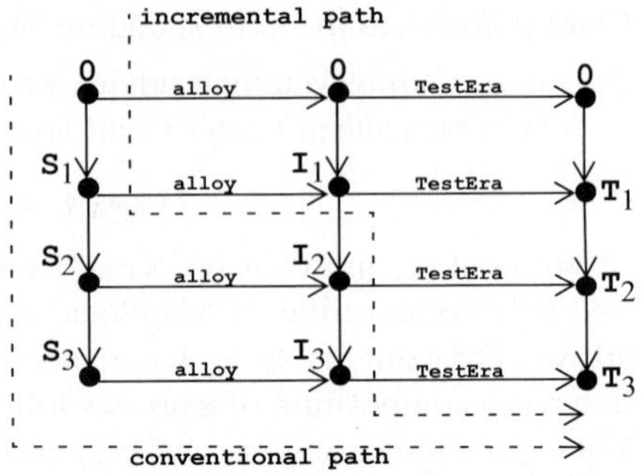

Fig. 19. Paths for Test Generation

Initial experiments revealed that in a majority of cases, the incremental path synthesizes test programs faster than the conventional path, and for some cases, the speedup was 30-50× faster. Not surprisingly, other paths were found to be even more efficient (i.e., extend a specification multiple times, then derive its solutions, then extend these solutions). Of course, we know that there are test arrows that relate tests for different programs, but here is a case where it is unlikely that creating an operator σ to map solution arrows to test arrows would be useful — all the work in extending tests seems to be in extending solutions.

In general, commuting diagrams reveal new ways to solve problems, and in some cases, these new solutions are better than existing solutions.

5.3 Recap of Benefits

Exposing commuting relationships in program synthesis, as illustrated in the previous sections, has revealed a set of interesting problems and novel perspectives that have lead to useful results. I expect many more applications of commuting diagrams in the future. An even more interesting, longer-term, and open question is whether mathematicians can leverage this connection of MDE and SPLs to provide deeper results.

6 Design Optimization

Design optimization is the most exotic part of Computational Design. If a program's design is an expression, then the expression can be optimized to produce an equivalent and improved design. In the last section, we saw commuting diagrams offered different paths to produce equivalent results. In the case of test generation, finding the right path could shorten generation time substantially. There is a counterpart in SPLs which originates from relational query optimization, that I now briefly describe.

Relational query optimization makes a clean distinction between functional requirements and non-functional requirements. A functional requirement is an arrow (e.g., relational operation); a non-functional requirement is a computable, estimatable, or measurable property of a composition of arrows (e.g., performance) [32].

Fig. 20 depicts an SPL of multiple programs, all of which are derivable from `0`. A subset of these programs satisfy the functional requirements of a program spec. (This is the inner set of programs in Fig. 20). Designers want a program of this inner set that also satisfies non-functional requirements and/or optimizes some quality metrics (e.g., performance). In principle, by enumerating this inner set, evaluating each point on its quality behavior, and selecting the point that exhibits the "best" quality (e.g., most efficient program w.r.t. some criteria), that is the program to build. Of course, how one enumerates or searches the inner set, how one evaluates or ranks points on the basis of quality metrics, and to do so efficiently, is often a challenging engineering problem. But this is the RQO paradigm: each relational algebra operation is an arrow, relational algebra expressions are arrow compositions, and relational query optimization is expression optimization with respect to performance.

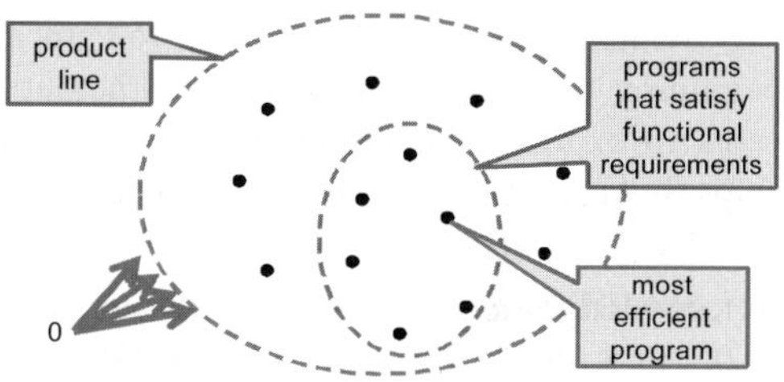

Fig. 20. Optimizing Program Designs

At present, I am aware of only a few examples of design optimization, among them are RQO [32], data structures [6], adaptive computing [27], middleware [40], and library synthesis [31]. A general technology for optimization may be constraint satisfaction [13]. The main challenge is finding domains where there are different ways of implementing the same functionality. Usually, most SPLs have only one implementation of a feature, and without multiple implementations, there may not be many opportunities for optimization a la RQO.

The key lesson is this: if you have a good conceptual framework, you will be able to recognize more easily the relationship among different and disparate areas of research. Much of what we do today as designers and implementors is to define and transform structures. By making these abstractions and distinctions clear(er), we will be that much closer to understanding the essence of MDE, SPLs, and Computational Design.

7 Conclusions

One of the key advances that brought database systems out of the stone age is relational query optimization. The relational model and the optimization of queries was rooted firmly in set theory, using elementary operations on sets (select, project, join, union). From a mathematical perspective, virtually nothing of set theory was used except for the first few pages in a set theory text. It was these simple ideas from set theory, not its deeper results, that made a lasting impact on databases.

The same may hold for category theory: its elementary ideas may find their way into the practice of MDE and SPL program design and synthesis. There is preliminary evidence that these ideas bring both pragmatic and pedagogical benefits. From an informal modeling viewpoint, the ideas I presented here are usable by engineers. Deeper results may be forthcoming.

How often will commuting diagrams arise in MDSPLs? This is not yet clear. One thing is clear: if you look, you will eventually find them. And if you don't look, you won't find them! Their utility will be decided on a per domain basis.

As mentioned in the Introduction, the future of software design and synthesis is in automation. Understanding fundamentals of Computational Design will tell us how to think about program design and synthesis in a structured and principled manner. It is clear that many ideas are being reinvented in different contexts. This is not accidental: it is evidence that we are working toward a general paradigm that we are only now beginning to recognize. Modern mathematics provides a simple language and concepts to express Computational Design and exposes previously unnoticed relationships that can be exploited for pragmatic benefit. This is a step in the right direction.

Acknowledgements. We gratefully acknowledge the helpful comments of K. Czarnecki, P. Kim, Z. Diskin, S. Apel, J. Gray, O. Diaz, and S. Trujillo on earlier drafts of this paper. This work was supported by NSF's Science of Design Project #CCF-0438786 and #CCF-0724979, the Portuguese Science Foundation (FCT) under grant SFRH/BSAB/782/2008, and the Basque Government under the Researchers Training Program.

References

[1] Agrawal, A., Karsai, G., Ledeczi, A.: An End-to-End Domain-Driven Software Development Framework. In: OOPSLA 2003 (2003)
[2] Ancona, D., Damiani, F., Drossopoulou, S.: Polymorphic Bytecode: Compositional Compilation for Java-like Languages. In: POPL 2005 (2005)
[3] Anfurrutia, F.I., Diaz, O., Trujillo, S.: On the Refinement of XML. In: ICWE 2007 (2007)
[4] Antkiewicz, M., Czarnecki, K.: Design Space of Heterogeneous Synchronization. In: Proc. Summer School on Generative and Transformational Techniques in Software Engineering (GTTSE) (2007)
[5] Apel, S., Leich, T., Saake, G.: Aspectual Feature Modules. IEEE TSE (April 2008)
[6] Batory, D., Chen, G., Robertson, E., Wang, T.: Design Wizards and Visual Programming Environments for GenVoca Generators. IEEE TSE (May 2000)
[7] Batory, D., Johnson, C., MacDonald, B., von Heeder, D.: Achieving Extensibility Through Product-Lines and Domain-Specific Languages: A Case Study. ACM TOSEM 11(2) (April 2002)
[8] Batory, D., Liu, J., Sarvela, J.N.: Refinements and Multi-Dimensional Separation of Concerns. In: ACM SIGSOFT 2003 (2003)
[9] Batory, D., Sarvela, J.N., Rauschmayer, A.: Scaling Step-Wise Refinement. IEEE TSE (June 2004)
[10] Batory, D.: Multi-Level Models in Model Driven Development, Product-Lines, and Metaprogramming. IBM Systems Journal 45(3) (2006)

[11] Batory, D.: Program Refactorings, Program Synthesis, and Model-Driven Design. In: ETAPS 2007, keynote (2007)

[12] Batory, D.: Using Modern Mathematics as an FOSD Modeling Language. In: GPCE 2008 (2008)

[13] Benavides, D., Trinidad, P., Ruiz-Cortes, A.: Automated Reasoning on Feature Models. In: Pastor, Ó., Falcão e Cunha, J. (eds.) CAiSE 2005. LNCS, vol. 3520, pp. 491–503. Springer, Heidelberg (2005)

[14] Bézivin, J., Jouault, F., Valduriez, P.: On the Need for Megamodels. In: Best Practices for Model-Driven-Software Development (2004)

[15] Bézivin, J., Bouzitouna, S., Del Fabro, M., Gervais, M.-P., Jouault, F., Kolovos, D., Kurtev, I., Paige, R.: A Canonical Scheme for Model Composition. In: ECMDA-FA 2006 (2006)

[16] Cuadrado, J.S., Molina, J.G., Tortosa, M.: RubyTL: A Practical, Extensible Transformation Language. In: ECMDA-FA 2006 (2006)

[17] Freeman, G., Batory, D., Lavender, G.: Lifting Transformational Models of Product Lines: A Case Study. In: ICMT 2008 (2008)

[18] Gray, J.: Private correspondence (July 2008)

[19] Ehrig, H., Ehrig, K., Ermel, C., Hermann, F., Taentzer, G.: Information Preserving Bidirectional Model Transformations. In: Dwyer, M.B., Lopes, A. (eds.) FASE 2007. LNCS, vol. 4422, pp. 72–86. Springer, Heidelberg (2007)

[20] Jackson, D.: Alloy: A Lightweight Object Modeling Notation. In: ACM TOSEM (April 2002)

[21] Jouault, F., Kurtev, I.: Transforming Models with ATL. In: Model Transformations in Practice Workshop at MODELS 2005 (2005)

[22] Kiczales, G., et al.: An Overview of AspectJ. In: Knudsen, J.L. (ed.) ECOOP 2001. LNCS, vol. 2072, pp. 327–353. Springer, Heidelberg (2001)

[23] Kim, C.H.P., Kaestner, C., Batory, D.: On the Modularity of Feature Interactions. In: GPCE 2008 (2008)

[24] Kurtev, I., Bézivin, J., Jouault, F., Valduriez, P.: Model-Based DSL Frameworks. In: OOPSLA 2006 (2006)

[25] Lawvere, F.W., Schanuel, S.H.: Conceptual Mathematics: A First Introduction To Categories. Cambridge University Press, Cambridge (1997)

[26] Marinov, D., Khurshid, S.: TestEra: A novel framework for automated testing of Java programs. In: ASE 2001 (2001)

[27] Neema, S.K.: System-Level Synthesis of Adaptive Computing Systems. Ph.D. Vanderbilt University (2001)

[28] Odersky, M., et al.: An Overview of the Scala Programming Language (September 2004), `http://scala.epfl.ch`

[29] Oldevik, J.: UMT: UML Model Transformation Tool Overview and User Guide Documentation (2004), http://umt-qvt.sourceforge.net/docs/

[30] Pierce, B.: Basic Category Theory for Computer Scientists. MIT Press, Cambridge (1991)

[31] Püschel, M., et al.: SPIRAL: Code Generation for DSP Transforms. Proc. IEEE 93#2 (2005); Special Issue on Program Generation, Optimization, and Adaptation

[32] Selinger, P., Astrahan, M.M., Chamberlin, D.D., Lorie, R.A., Price, T.G.: Access Path Selection in a Relational Database System. In: ACM SIGMOD 1979 (1979)

[33] Sprinkle, J., Karsai, G.: A Domain-Specific Visual Language for Domain Model Evolution. J. Vis. Lang. Comput. 15(3-4) (2004)

[34] Trujillo, S., Azanza, M., Diaz, O.: Generative Metaprogramming. In: GPCE 2007 (2007)

[35] Trujillo, S., Batory, D., Diaz, O.: Feature Oriented Model Driven Development: A Case Study for Portlets. In: ICSE 2007 (2007)
[36] Uzuncaova, E., Garcia, D., Khurshid, S., Batory, D.: Testing Software Product Lines Using Incremental Test Generation. In: ISSRE 2008 (2008)
[37] Vanhooff, B., Ayed, D., Van Baelen, S., Joosen, W., Berbers, Y.: UniTI: A Unified Transformation Infrastructure. In: Engels, G., Opdyke, B., Schmidt, D.C., Weil, F. (eds.) MODELS 2007. LNCS, vol. 4735, pp. 31–45. Springer, Heidelberg (2007)
[38] Wachsmuth, G.: Metamodel Adaptation and Model Co-Adaptation. In: Ernst, E. (ed.) ECOOP 2007. LNCS, vol. 4609, pp. 600–624. Springer, Heidelberg (2007)
[39] Wing, J.: Computational Thinking. In: CACM 2006 (March 2006)
[40] Zhang, C., Gao, G., Jacobsen, H.-A.: Towards Just-in-time Middleware Architectures. In: AOSD 2005 (2005)

Algebraic Models for Bidirectional Model Synchronization*

Zinovy Diskin

Department of Computer Science, University of Toronto
Department of Electrical & Computer Engineering, University of Waterloo
zdiskin@swen.uwaterloo.ca

Abstract. The paper presents several algebraic models for semantics of bidirectional model synchronization and transformation. Different patterns of model synchronization are analyzed (including view updates and incremental synchronization), and this analysis motivates the formal definitions. Relationships between the formal models are precisely specified and discussed. A new formal model of updates is proposed.

Introduction

By the very nature of modeling, a snapshot of an MDD-project appears as a diverse collection of interrelated models. If one of these models is modified, other related models must be also modified to maintain the relationships. In other words, updates to a model need to be propagated to the related models to keep the entire collection consistent.We will call this activity *model synchronization.*

Two main classes of synchronization scenarios can be distinguished. One is synchronization of overlapping models. For example, consider a behavioral model m (e.g., a UML sequence diagram) and a structural model n (a class diagram or a database schema) of the same domain. These models overlap in the sense that the structural part of m is normally a part of n, or a view to it. We may say that these two models have a common view/abstraction a and informally write something like $m \succ a \prec n$. If one of the models m, n is updated, its counterpart must be correspondingly updated too. Note that the consistency relation between models is not a (single-valued) *function*: given m, there may be many models n such that $m \succ a \prec n$, and symmetrically for n. However, a synchronization procedure must return a unique synchronized model, and hence some *synchronization policy* has to be adopted.

Another class of synchronization scenarios appears in model transformations (MT). Consider, for example, refinements of high-level models by more detailed ones, or implementation of UML models by Java programs. Synchronization procedures should be provided for both directions because either of the models, the source or the target one, can be modified. Consistency between models m

* Supported by Bell Canada through the Bell University Labs, by the Ontario Centres of Excellence and partially by the Ontario Research Fund (through Model-Integrated Software Service Engineering project).

K. Czarnecki et al. (Eds.): MoDELS 2008, LNCS 5301, pp. 21–36, 2008.

and n now means that n is a correct transform/implemetation of m. It is again a multi-valued rather than functional relation in both directions, e.g., the same UML model can be implemented differently, and different models can have the same implementation. Hence, in order to achieve uniqueness of synchronization, some synchronization policy is needed again.

As a rule, a reasonable policy is based on information contained in the old (before updates) models. Suppose we begin with two consistent models m and n, and then model n is modified to n'. To synchronize models and compute m', we may need (besides model n') information contained in models m and n, or perhaps only in m, or perhaps n' alone would suffice. Thus, we can distinguish *triple-model-*, *di-model-* or *single-model-based* synchronizations. In more detail, synchronization essentially depends on what data structures the models are (trees, XML documents, relational tables,...), and what operations over them are used in view definitions or in model transformations. The richer these structures and operations are, the more complex synchronization policies are. The issue is well known in the database community as the *view update problem*, and has been studied there since early 80s (see [10] for a survey). More recently, it has also been studied in the bi-directional programming community [14], and in replica synchronization, most notably, in work of the Harmony group [10]. The issue is also well-known to MDD practitioners, but its theoretical exploration in the modeling community only recently began [16, 1].

The goal of the present paper is to analyze a variety of synchronization patterns in an abstract semantic framework. We follow the *syntax-free* (or *metamodel-free*) style of formal modeling of model management procedures developed in [13, 10, 4, 16, 1] and also ignore metamodels and their mappings. In this approach, having a metamodel amounts to having a class of models M. Then, given two classes M and N, a forward triple-model-based synchronization policy appears as a function from $M \times M \times N$ to N, which takes a source model m, its updated version m' and the N-counterpart of m, n, as the arguments, and returns the updated version n' of model n. The backward synchronization is a symmetric mapping $N \times N \times M \to M$ returning the updated model m' for a triple (n, n', m). Similarly, a di-model synchronization is a pair of two-argument mappings sending (m', n) to n' (the forward synchronizer) and (n', m) to m' (the backward one). Since these mappings are interrelated, they should obey some constraints (*synchronization laws*). The latter can be algebraically expressed by identities, i.e., equations valid for all values of the variables involved, and we come to a typical algebraic setting. Somewhat surprisingly, interesting observations on the nature of synchronization can be made, and useful concepts emerge, even in this simple algebraic framework.

Nevertheless, having the diversity and complexity of concrete data structures involved in the synchronization scenarios, one may doubt the usefulness of abstract semantic considerations. These concerns are quite reasonable but not indisputable. A direct technical use of algebraic models is the possibility to verify consistency of bidirectional model transformation and synchronization w.r.t. synchronization laws. Indeed, the modern MT-languages are quite expressive and allow the designer to write unsafe transformation procedures (see [16] for a detailed discussion). Another problem is adequacy of the transformation program to what is really needed (validation). A conceptually transparent algebraic semantics cleared from unnecessary details can help here too. Finally, a well-designed declarative formulation can provide a useful guidance (the "what") for design and implementation (the "how") of transformation and synchronization tools. For instance, the replica synchronization programming language developed by the Harmony group [10] is entirely based on an abstract algebraic framework (of the so called *lenses*). Since declarative semantic foundations of the modern MDD tools are still under development, algebraic elaboration of the basic principles can be helpful. As it was noted in [16],

> ... it may seem foolhardy to write a paper which approaches semantic issues in bidirectional model transformations from first principles. However, ... the use of QVT-style bidirectional transformations has not spread fast, despite the early availability of a few tools, partly (we think) because of uncertainty among users over fundamental semantic issues.

In the paper we take the semantic argument for granted, and pursue the "foolhardy" syntax-free approach even further by analyzing and scrutinizing the first principles stated in [16]. We consider four groups of features that a synchronization tool can possess (see column names in Fig. 1), and formulate them algebraically via identities for three types of synchronization systems (row names). We will see that the same feature is realized and formulated differently for different systems; in addition, different features may overlap, especially for lenses and di-systems. Thus, having a precise formal description becomes a necessity to avoid confusion.

Related work and contributions of the paper. A long-standing tradition in modeling model synchronization can be referred to as *algebraic semantics* because synchronization procedures are considered as algebraic operations regulated by equational laws (identities). It can be traced back to early work on the view update problem (VU), particularly to seminal papers by Bancilhon and Spyratos [2] and Dayal and Bernstein [5]. This algebraic style was continued by Meertens in [13] in the context of constraint maintenance (CM) far more general than VU, and more recently was further elaborated in the works of the Harmony group on lenses [10] (but again within the VU-perspective). An adaptation of the CM-approach for bi-directional MT is developed by Stevens in [16]. A much broader and less formal perspective on model synchronization is presented by Antkiewicz and Czarnecki in [1], which aims to classify a wide spectrum of synchronization tools within a unified framework. The paper describes more than a dozen of different model synchronization patterns, including those that we will consider in the paper, but their precise algebraic treatment needs further work. The point is that only signatures of operations are discussed in [1] while identities (laws), which are central for algebraic theory, are not considered. In contrast to the syntax-free tradition, the work [7] presents an algebraic framework encompassing both syntax and semantics of MT but in the particular case of functional (rather than relational) transformations; model synchronization is not considered. Another approach encompassing both syntax and semantics is based on graph transformations, in which triple graph grammars [12] are especially relevant for model transformation [9].

The present paper is within the syntax-free algebraic approach, and its contributions are summarized in Fig. 1. Check-mark $\surd$ means that the cell was filled earlier (by the author named below the mark) while + denotes a contribution of the present paper, i.e., a precise formal definition and analysis of the concept. Combination of $\surd$ and + means that the notion was essentially modified to adapt it to our context.

Synch. pattern \ Synch. feature	Correctness: range	Correctness: domain	Hippocraticness	Evolution: history Ignorance	Evolution: Undoability	Invertibility
Lens	√	√+	√	√	√+	+
	The Harmony group				Stevens	
Diagonal system	√ Meertens Stevens	+	√ Meertens Stevens	+	√+ Stevens	+
Trigonal system	+	+	+	+	+	+

Fig. 1. Algebraic models of synchronization systems

It is worth mentioning that our version of undoability condition for di-system is more adequate to practical situations (see Remark 2 on p.8). Thus, we revise the notions of lens and di-system, introduce algebras for tri-systems and present a few results clarifying dependencies between synchronization systems and their features. We also present an important construction of building di-systems from lenses thus providing precise formalization and design guidance for synchronizing models having a common view $m \succ a \prec n$. Finally, our algebra of trigonal systems is based on a novel algebraic model of updates and update translation.

1 Updatable Views or Lenses

Models can overlap in different ways, which determine different types of synchronization procedures. Classification of possible overlapping scenarios/cases is an open issue but it is clear that the situation when one model presents a view to another model is important and widespread. For example, a structural or behavioral model n can be a view to another ("bigger") model m of the similar type. Or, the type of n can be more abstract than m, for example, m is a Petri net and n is a labeled transition system extracted from it. In such cases, model m is not only bigger but is also more conceptually refined than n. Or, m is a behavioral model (say, sequence diagram) and n is its structural view (the underlying collaboration diagram). Thus, we begin our comparative studies of synchronization patterns with synchronization of view systems, also known as the *view update problem*.

Given a *bigger* model m and a view definition, the *view* n is uniquely determined and we write $n = get(m)$ with *get* standing for *getView*. A view definition thus amounts to a totally-defined single-valued mapping $get\colon M \to N$ with M, N

denoting classes of big and view models respectively. Because views ignore or abstract away some information contained in big models, many different m's can be abstracted to the same view and the inverse mapping from views to big models is multi-valued. Making it single-valued is the famous *view update* problem: If the view model n was updated to n', we need to establish some *update policy* to propagate the changes back and build a unique big model m' such that $get(m') = n'$. A general solution proposed by the Harmony group is to analyze the structure of models and employ the old (before updates) big models for building update policies. That is, backward propagation of updates is considered to be a single-valued mapping of two arguments, $put: N \times M \to M$ (put stands for *putBack*), with the arguments being the updated view and the old big model respectively, and the value being the updated big model, $m' = put(n', m)$. Many examples of how it works for different data structures (trees and relational tables) can be found in works of the Harmony group, e.g., [10, 3]; see also Example 1 on page 6. Of course, getting the view of the updated big model should produce the updated view, $get(put(n', m)) = n'$, and putting back the original (not updated) view should not change the big model, $put(get(m), m) = m$ for all $m \in M, n' \in N$. In [10], these two identities are called the (PutGet) and (GetPut) laws respectively.

A delicate question is whether the mapping put is totally or partially defined. In applications, it is often more convenient to consider the space N of view models to be greater (or equal) than the range of get, $get(M) \subseteq N$. It may be even necessary like in our example of two-views system $M \xrightarrow{get_M} A \xleftarrow{get_N} N$ considered on page 1, if the ranges of get functions are different. By (PutGet)-law, non-surjectivity of get implies partiality of put because otherwise, for any $n' \in N$ we take any $m \in M$ and find that $n' = get(put(n', m))$. Thus, the N-domain of put must be a subset of get, $Dom_N(put) \subseteq get$. The exact equality would be an additional yet reasonable requirement: any real view can be propagated back. In this way we come to the notion of an *updatable* or *dynamic* view: it is a view definition (function get) equipped with a certain partial policy of update translation (put), which satisfy the identities above. The Harmony group calls such a pair (get, put), a *lens* (think of the mappings as being the top and bottom edges of a lens).

An important aspect of synchronization systems (emphasized in [16]) is their behavior with respect to undoing changes. For an updatable view, the typical undoing scenario is as follows: we start with a big model m and its view $n = get(m)$, then update the latter to n' and propagate changes back to $m' = put(n', m)$, afterwards we decide that update of n was not necessary and hence return view n' to its original state n. Now n can be considered as the updated state of n', and we expect that propagating the changes from n' to n back to M should undo the changes on the M-side too, $put(n, m') = m$. This condition is illustrated by diagrams (a) and (b) in Table 1, where arrows denote function applications. If the equality above holds for any m, n, n' 9and hence is identity), we call the system *undoable* (the term was coined in [16] but the notion introduced there is different).

Undoing is a particular case of the more general situation of applying a series of consecutive view updates $n_0 = get(m)$, $n_1 = n'$, $n_2 = n''$, $\ldots, n_k = n'_{k-1}$ and consecutive propagating them back, $m_0 = m$, $m_1 = put(n_1, m_0), \ldots$,

$m_k = put(n_k, m_{k-1})$. We say that synchronization is *history ignorant* if $m_k = put(n_k, m_0)$, that is, it is the final result/state of model n that matters rather than the way of evolution. When $n_k = n_0$, history ignorance means $m_k = put(n_0, m_0) = m_0$, i.e., undoability. Evidently, to ensure history ignorance for any integer k, it is sufficient to have it for $k = 2$. In terms of the Harmony group, the corresponding identity is called (PutPut) (see below).

Now accurate formal definitions and a few simple results are in order. Let M, N be two spaces of data structures (trees, lists, models, databases).

Definition 1 (Dynamic views or lenses)**.** A *lens* from M to N is a pair $\lambda = (get_\lambda, put_\lambda)$ of functions: total $get_\lambda\colon M \to N$ and partial $put_\lambda\colon N \times M \to M$. A lens is called *well-behaved* if conditions (Dom), (GetPut) and (PutGet) in Table 1 below are satisfied (the index λ is omitted; to shorten formulas, application of get is written with the dot-notation, $m.get$ for $get(m)$). Diagrams on the right visualize the identities.

If condition (PutPut) also holds (diagram (c)), the lens is called *very* well-behaved or *history ignorant.* A lens is called *undoable* if conditions (PutGet) and (Undo) hold (consider diagrams (a) and (b) together). Finally, a lens λ is called *total* if put_λ is a total function. Index λ is omitted if it is clear from the context.

Table 1. Conditions for lenses. All formulas are universally quantified for all their variables (m and n with primes). Symbol $\Downarrow$ means definability.

Condition:	View def. $get\colon M \to N$	Backward translation $put\colon N \times M \to M$
(Dom)	$put(m'.get, m) \Downarrow$	
(GetPut)	$m = put(m.get, m)$	
(PutGet)	$put(n', m).get = n'$	
(Undo)	$m = put(m.get, put(n', m))$	
history Ignorance		
(GetGet)	trivial	N/A
(PutPut)	N/A	$\dfrac{\text{let } m' = put(n', m)}{\text{then } put(n'', m') = put(n'', m)}$

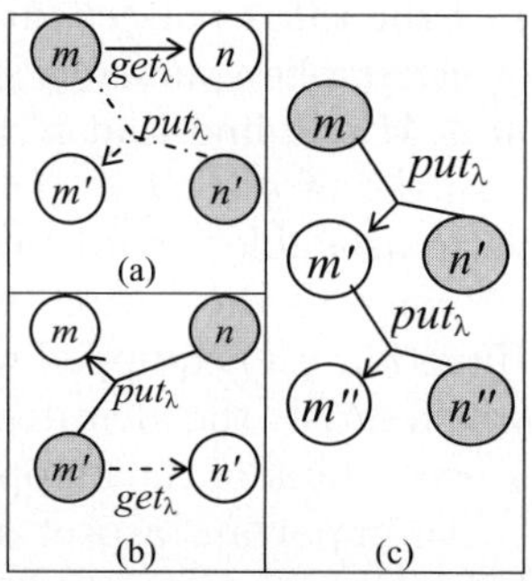

Remark 1. Definitions of lens and (very) well-behaved lens (but without condition (Dom)) were introduced by the Harmony group. The notion of undoable lens is new.

Proposition 1. Conditions (PutPut) and (GetPut) imply (Undo). Hence, a very well-behaved lens is undoable.

Proof. Write (PutPut) for $n'' = m.get$ and apply (GetPut) to the right part of the "then"-equality. □

Example 1. Suppose that the big model is a triple of rational numbers, $m = (x, y, z)$, and the view is defined by setting $n = (s, z)$ with $s = x + y$ (think of s as a query to the big model). If the view is updated to $n' = (s', z')$, computing the updated big model m' is problematic: we know that $x' + y' = s'$ but it is not enough to define x' and y'. To make the latter certain, we need one more condition for x' and y'. For example, we may assume that (a) $x' = x$ and then $y' = s' - x$, or that (b) $x' = x + \Delta s/2$, $y' = y + \Delta s/2$ where $\Delta s = s' - s$, or that (c) $x'/y' = x/y$. Each of these *update policies* uniquely determines an updated big model and hence a lens. For policies (a) and (b), the corresponding lenses are evidently very well-behaved (hence, undoable). For policy (c), these properties are followed from the distributivity laws of rational arithmetic.

Now consider another lens with view definition $get(x, y, z) = (x, y)$, i.e., n is just a projection of m, and the update policy $put(m, n') = (x', y', z + 1)$ so that the third component serves as a counter. For this lens, neither (PutPut) nor (Undo) hold.

2 Diagonal (Two-Model-Based) Synchronization

2.1 Preliminaries

Let M be a class of models (say, in UML), N a class of programs (say, in Java) and predicate mRn means that model m is implemented by program n. Importantly, relation R is not functional in either of the directions: there may be many implementations of the same model and different models can be implemented by the same program. In other words, mappings $\overset{\twoheadrightarrow}{R}\colon M \twoheadrightarrow N$, $\overset{\twoheadrightarrow}{R}(m) \overset{\text{def}}{=} \{n \in N \mid mRn\}$ and $\overset{\twoheadleftarrow}{R}\colon N \twoheadrightarrow M$, $\overset{\twoheadleftarrow}{R}(n) \overset{\text{def}}{=} \{m \in M \mid mRn\}$, are generally multi-valued. This is a typical situation for many cases of MT (cf. [16]). Another aspect is that mappings $\overset{\twoheadrightarrow}{R}$, $\overset{\twoheadleftarrow}{R}$ may result in empty sets (are partially defined), which is equivalent to having their inverses $\overset{\twoheadleftarrow}{R}$, $\overset{\twoheadrightarrow}{R}$ non-surjective. For example, not every Java program can be reverse engineered into UML due to the lack of expressiveness of the latter (e.g., [8] shows this for class diagrams). Thus, in general, the *(model) consistency* relation R is neither total nor surjective nor single-valued in either of the directions. Arguably, this schema is implicitly assumed by the QVT Relational Standard [15] (see [16] for a detailed discussion).

The following scenario is typical. Given first a pair of consistent models mRn, one of the models, say n, changes to n'. The goal is to synchronize models and find a suitable model $m' \in M$ consistent with n', i.e., $m'Rn'$. Formally, we have a single-valued mapping $M \xleftarrow{\overleftarrow{\delta}} N \times M$ called the *backward synchronizer*. Symmetrically, we need also a *forward synchronizer* $M \times N \xrightarrow{\overrightarrow{\delta}} N$ as illustrated by diagrams (a,b) in Table 2 (dashed arrows show the consistency predicate and solid arrows are for function applications). A principal distinction of this synchronization system from lenses is that now all three components of the system, the consistency relation and the synchronization mappings, must be defined independently while for lenses the consistency relation is derived from the mappings: mRn iff $n = get(n)$ for all models m, n. Thus, a diagonal synchronization system is a triple $\delta = (R_\delta, \overrightarrow{\delta}, \overleftarrow{\delta})$ as described above. Correspondingly, some synchronization laws that can be derived from lens axioms in Table 1 must be separately postulated for di-systems. Before presenting formal definitions, we will briefly discuss the underlying intuition.

A fundamental law of any synchronization is *correctness*: synchronization procedure must return consistent models, $m'R[\overrightarrow{\delta}(m',n)]$ and $[\overleftarrow{\delta}(n',m)]Rn'$ hold for all $m,m' \in M$,$n,n' \in N$. We call these conditions *range correctness*. Since we want to consider partial consistency relations ($\overrightarrow{\overrightarrow{R}}_\delta$ and $\overleftarrow{\overleftarrow{R}}_\delta$ may result in empty sets), range correctness implies that synchronizers must be only partially defined, otherwise we come to a contradiction: $[\overleftarrow{\delta}(n',m)]Rn'$ means that $n' \in \overrightarrow{\overrightarrow{R}}_\delta(M)$ for any $n' \in N$. Thus, to keep partiality of R in the direction from N to M, i.e., to have $\overrightarrow{\overrightarrow{R}}_\delta(M) \subsetneq N$, we must keep $Dom_N(\overleftarrow{\delta}) \subseteq \overrightarrow{\overrightarrow{R}}_\delta(M)$. It is reasonable to require the exact equality here: if $n' \in \overrightarrow{\overrightarrow{R}}_\delta(M)$ and hence $\overleftarrow{\overleftarrow{R}}_\delta(n') \neq \emptyset$, a suitable $m' = \overleftarrow{\delta}(n,m)$ can be found. In other words, if a model n ***can*** be synchronized, then the backward synchronization procedure is defined for n (and provides a correct synchronization by the range correctness). Thus, we postulate $Dom_N(\overleftarrow{\delta}) = \overrightarrow{\overrightarrow{R}}_\delta(M)$ and symmetrically $Dom_M(\overrightarrow{\delta}) = \overleftarrow{\overleftarrow{R}}_\delta(N)$ (*domain correctness*).

An important possible requirement is that if the updated model n' is still consistent with m, then synchronization does nothing, $m' = m$. Symmetrically, $\overrightarrow{\delta}(m',n) = n$ if $m'Rn$. In other words, synchronization does not affect ("harm") models that are already consistent, hence the name *Hippocraticness* adopted in [16] for this law. In section 3 we will argue that Hippocraticness should not be a necessary requirement for all synchronization systems. Still, for a non-Hippocratic system it makes sense to require a weaker form of "harmlessness": forward synchronization applied to the updated source model $m' = \overleftarrow{\delta}(n',m)$ (as the first argument) and the updated target model n' (the second one) does nothing on the target side, $\overrightarrow{\delta}(m',n') = n'$. Symmetrically, if $n' = \overrightarrow{\delta}(m',n)$, then $\overleftarrow{\delta}(n',m') = m'$. Another interpretation of these conditions is that the two synchronization mappings are mutually inverse in a special weak sense, hence the name, *weak invertibility*. Finally, we can formulate undoability and history ignorance laws in a way similar to lenses.

2.2 Formal Definitions and Results

Definition 2. A *diagonal synchronization system* (*di-system* in short) over $M \times N$ is a triple $\delta = (R_\delta, \overrightarrow{\delta}, \overleftarrow{\delta})$ with $R_\delta \subset M \times N$ a binary *consistency relation*, and $\overrightarrow{\delta} : M \times N \to N$ and $\overleftarrow{\delta} : N \times M \to M$ are two partial functions called the *forward* and *backward synchronizers* respectively (see diagram (a) below on the right). We call a di-system *well-behaved* if conditions (Corr) and (wInv) in Table 2 are satisfied. It is *very* well-behaved or *history ignorant* if, in addition, condition (hIgno) in the table holds (diagram (c)). The system is *undoable* if two (Undo) equations (with 's/t' standing for Undo on the source/target sides) hold (see diagrams (a,b) together). A di-system is *total* if both synchronizers are total functions.

Table 2. Conditions for diagonal synchronization systems. All formulas are universally quantified for all their free variables To ease reading formulas, we write $[m, n\rangle$ and $\langle m, n]$ for $\overrightarrow{\delta}(m, n)$ and $\overleftarrow{\delta}(n, m)$; diagrams on the right also help to visualize identities.

Condition: name and label	Forward synch. $\overrightarrow{\delta} = [*, *\rangle : M \times N \to N$	Backward synch. $M \leftarrow N \times M : \langle *, *] = \overleftarrow{\delta}$
Correctness (Corr):	// see discussion in sect. 2.1	
Domain (dmCorr)	$[m, n\rangle\Downarrow$ iff $m \in \overleftarrow{R_\delta}(N)$	$\langle m, n]\Downarrow$ iff $n \in \overrightarrow{R_\delta}(M)$
Range (rgCorr)	$mR_\delta[m, n\rangle$	$\langle m, n]R_\delta n$
weakInvert.(wInv):	// see diagram (a) on the right	
(wFB)	$m' = \langle m', [m', n\rangle]$	
(wBF)	$[\langle m', n], n\rangle = n$	
hist.Ignor.(hIgno) //see diagram (c)	let $[m', n\rangle = n'$ then $[m'', n'\rangle = [m'', n\rangle$	let $m' = \langle m, n']$ then $\langle m', n''] = \langle m, n'']$
Undoability (Undo)	// consider diagrams (a,b) together	
(tUndo)	$[\langle m', n], [m', n\rangle\rangle = n$	
(sUndo)	$m' = \langle\langle m', n], [m', n\rangle]$	
Hippocrat.(Hipp)	$mR_\delta n \Rightarrow [m, n\rangle = n$	$mR_\delta n \Rightarrow m = \langle m, n]$

Diagrams

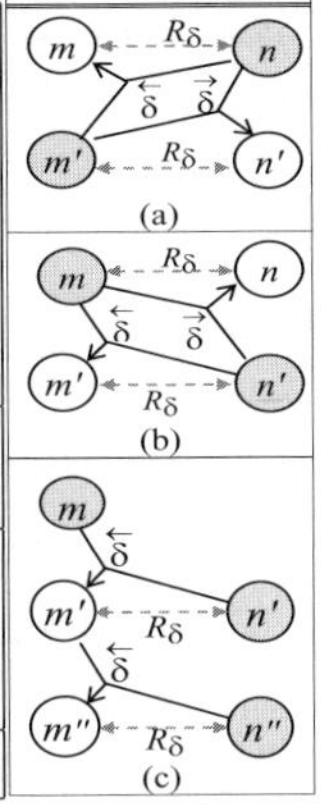

Remark 2. The idea of diagonal synchronization was proposed by Meertens [13] in the context of user interface design. What he called a constraint maintainer is a total di-system satisfying (rgCorr) and (Hipp). For model transformation, this notion was adopted by Stevens [16] and augmented with the following version of undoability: if $mR_\delta n$ and $n' = [m', n\rangle$, then $[m, n'\rangle = n$, and symmetrically for the backward direction. Because of the term $mR_\delta n$ in the antecedent, this is a very strong condition, which (as noted in [16]) "may be hard to meet". Our notion of undoability is weaker and more applicable to practical situations (see [6] for details).

Example 2. A few simple examples of undoable di-systems can be found in [16]. There are several interesting examples of di-systems in [13] but they are not history ignorant nor undoable. The reason is that Meertens considers di-systems in the context of *selective* synchronization for which history ignorance and undoability are somewhat unnatural: a detailed discussion can be found in [6]. Thus, existence of interesting examples of undoable di-systems is so far an open question. We will answer it affirmatively below in section 2.3.

Proposition 2. The following implications hold:

(i) (hIgno) and (wInv) imply (Undo)
(ii) (Corr) and (Hipp) imply (wInv)

Proof. (i) To prove (sUndo), write $\overleftarrow{\text{(hIgno)}}$ for $n'' = [m, n'\rangle$ and use (wFB). Symmetrically for (tUndo). (ii) is straightforward and observed in [16] □

The next result is proved in a straightforward way.

Lemma 3. Suppose that the consistency relation R_δ is functional from M to N, that is, there is a total function $f\colon M \to N$ such that $mR_\delta n$ iff $m.f = n$. Then for any $m \in M$, $n \in N$, $[m,n\rangle = m.f$ and a lens $\lambda(\delta) = (f, \langle *, *])$ is defined. The diagonal axioms specified in Table 2 then become lens axiom as specified in Table (a) in Fig. 2. Conversely, any lens λ determines a functional di-system $\delta(\lambda)$ as described above.

Corollary 4. Given a di-system δ with functional consistency relation, the lens $\lambda(\delta)$ is (very) well-behaved/undoable iff δ is (very) well-behaved/undoable. Similarly, given a lens λ, di-system $\delta(\lambda)$ is (very) well-behaved/undoable iff λ is such.

Thus, a di-system with functional consistency relation is nothing but a lens.

Condition of diagonal system δ	Corresponding lens $\lambda(\delta)$
Correctness	
$(\text{dmCor})^{\rightarrow}/(\text{dmCor})^{\leftarrow}$	trivial/(Dom)
$(\text{rgCorr})^{\rightarrow}/(\text{rgCorr})^{\leftarrow}$	trivial/(PutGet)
weak Invertibility	
(wFB)/(wBF)	(GetPut)/(PutGet)
history Ignorance	
$(\text{hIgno})^{\rightarrow}/(\text{hIgno})^{\leftarrow}$	trivial/(PutPut)
(tUndo)/(sUndo)	(PutGet)/(Undo)
Hippocraticness	
$(\text{Hipp})^{\rightarrow}/(\text{Hipp})^{\leftarrow}$	trivial/(GetPut)

(a) Di-systems vs. lenses

Condition of tri-gonal system δ	Corresponding lens $\lambda(\tau)$
Correctness	
$(\text{dmCor})^{\rightarrow}/(\text{dmCor})^{\leftarrow}$	trivial/(Dom)
$(\text{rgCorr})^{\rightarrow}/(\text{rgCorr})^{\leftarrow}$	trivial/(PutGet)
Identity	
$(\text{Idnt})^{\rightarrow}/(\text{Idnt})^{\leftarrow}$	trivial/(GetPut)
history Ignorance	
$(\text{hIgno})^{\rightarrow}/(\text{hIgno})^{\leftarrow}$	trivial/(PutPut)
(tUndo)/(sUndo)	(PutGet)/(Undo)
Invertibility	
(FwdBck)/(BckFwd)	(GetPut)/(PutGet)
Hippocraticness	
$(\text{Hipp})^{\rightarrow}/(\text{Hipp})^{\leftarrow}$	trivial/(GetPut)

(b) Tri-systems vs. lenses

Fig. 2. Correlations between identities in different synchronization algebras

2.3 Building Synchronization Systems from Lenses

In Introduction (page 1) we discussed the situation of two models having a common view, $m \succ a \prec n$. This is a quite general pattern having many instantiations in MDD, and the question is how to synchronize models m and n. In other words, what is a proper synchronization schema for this situation? The machinery developed above allows us to give a precise answer.

Construction 5. Let μ be a lens from M to some space A and ν be a lens from N to the same space A. Their *co-targetial composition* $\mu \bowtie \nu$ is a di-system over $M \times N$ defined as follows.

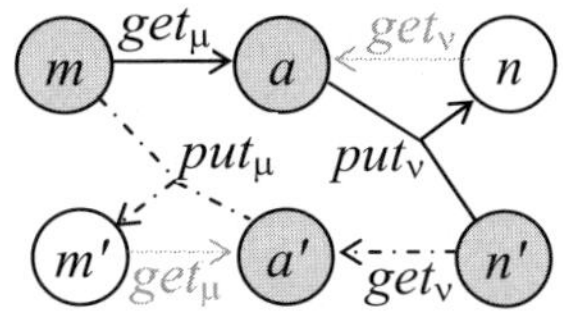

Consistency relation:: $R_{\mu\bowtie\nu}(m,n)$ iff $m.get_\mu = n.get_\nu$.
Forward synchronizer, $\overrightarrow{\delta}_{\mu\bowtie\nu} : M \times N \to N$::
$\overrightarrow{\delta}_{\mu\bowtie\nu}(m,n') \stackrel{\text{def}}{=} put_\nu(m.get_\mu, n')$.

Backward synchronizer, $\overleftarrow{\delta}_{\mu\bowtie\nu} : N \times M \to M$:: $\overleftarrow{\delta}_{\mu\bowtie\nu}(n',m) \stackrel{\text{def}}{=} put_\mu(n'.get_\nu, m)$.

Theorem 6. The co-targetial composition $(\mu \bowtie \nu)$ of lenses is a (very) well-behaved/undoable diagonal system as soon as both lenses are such. In addition, the system is Hippocratic.

Proof. Straightforward checking of the corresponding identities. □

Since the common-view relation between models is widespread in MDD, the theorem may have many applications. Particularly, it shows that the diagonal schema is instrumental for synchronizing behavioral and structural models. It also gives us a rich collection of non-trivial undoable di-systems, e.g., consider a UML behavioral model for m and a UML structural model for n.

3 Incremental Synchronization and Trigonal Systems

We consider the same synchronization scenario as above. Given consistent models mRn, model n changes to n' and we aim at finding its consistent counterpart m'. The idea of incremental synchronization is that if the changes from n to n' are not too significant, it is not reasonable to recompute the model $m' = \overleftarrow{\delta}(n',m)$ from scratch. Rather, having an update (an "edit sequence") v such that $n' = n.v$, we translate it back to the source side to obtain a source model update $u = \overleftarrow{\tau}(v)$ to be applied to the old source model, $m' = m.u$. In general, the update translation is multi-valued and we employ the previous version of the model m to make it certain. Thus, the update translation functions have the types $\overleftarrow{\tau} : V \times M \to M$, $\overrightarrow{\tau} : U \times N \to N$, where V, U are the spaces of updates on the target and the source sides respectively (cf. [1]).

In the context of incremental synchronization, Hippocraticness does not seem obligatory. Indeed, a model can contain some information that does not affect its consistency yet is useful. Hence, if even the updated model n' is consistent with "old" m, we may still want to update the latter to m' to make a better match with n'. As for history ignorance and undoability (foreign for selective synchronization [6]), they are quite natural requirements for incremental synchronization. We will consider them in more detail but first we need to make the notion of update more precise.

3.1 Modeling Updates

There are a few approaches in the literature: functional (in which updates are functions/procedures over the model spaces [5, 11, 1]), history-based (updates are edit sequences), state-based (an update is just a new state [10]). In the paper we present a new model, which can be classified as an abstract history-based one. We first consider a space of models M as a directed graph, whose nodes are models and arrows are updates. The latter can be thought of as edit sequences. Because there may be different updates leading to the same result, it would be a multi-graph (many arrows between the same nodes are allowed). Evidently, arrows-updates could be composed (just concatenate the sequences), and each node should have a loop arrow denoting the trivial "do-nothing" update (the empty sequence). The possibility to undo changes means that updates are invertible: for any arrow $u\colon m \to m'$ there is an arrow $u^{-1}\colon m' \to m$ such that $u; u^{-1} = 1_m$, where ; denotes update composition and 1_m denotes the "do-nothing" update for the node m. Similarly, $u^{-1}; u = 1_{m'}$.

Compatibility of update translation with undoing, i.e., undoability, is demonstrated by diagram below on the right, where bold arrows denote updates, thin arrows are translations and dashed arrows denote consistency. Given an update $u\colon m \to m'$ and a model n consistent with m, we translate u into an update $v = \overrightarrow{\tau}(u, n)\colon n \to n'$ on the target side. The inverse of u, arrow u^{-1}, is translated, in general, into $w = \overrightarrow{\tau}(u^{-1}, n')\colon n' \to n''$. Undoability of translation means that $w = v^{-1}$, that is, $n'' = n$ and $v; w = 1_n$. Evidently, if translation τ is compatible with both (i) update composition, $\overrightarrow{\tau}(u; u^{-1}, n) = \overrightarrow{\tau}(u, n); \overrightarrow{\tau}(u^{-1}, n')$, and (ii) "do-nothing", $\overrightarrow{\tau}(1_m, n) = 1_n$, then τ is undoable.

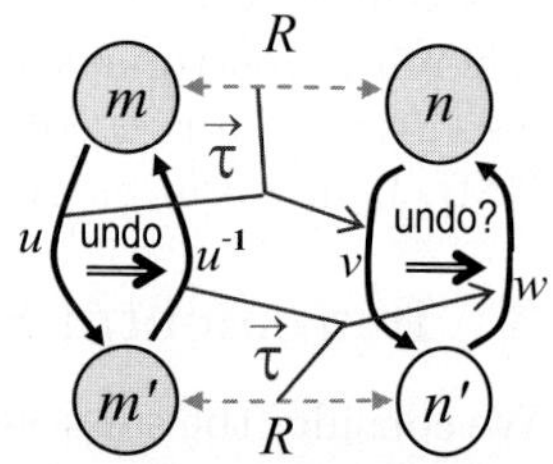

The two compatibility conditions (i,ii) were studied in [11] in the setting of functional updates. Our model is more adequate to practice than the functional one: an edit sequences is an artifact attached to a particular model – the source model of the sequence, rather than a function over the entire space of models. It is also technically simpler to work with. Yet we leave this model for a future work and in the present paper consider an even simpler notion closer to the framework of lenses [10] and coherent transformations of [16]. Namely, rather than considering updates themselves, we will deal with a binary *updatability* relation $U_M \subset M \times M$: $(m, m') \in U_M$ iff there is an update $u\colon m \to m'$. Relation U_M is reflexive (owing to "do-nothing" updates), symmetric (undoing) and transitive (update composition). Hence, updatability is an equivalence relations, and the model space is partitioned into classes of mutually updatable models. Assumption that there is more than one such class means that *not* any two model can be updated to each other. Thinking extensionally, this assumption may seem counter-intuitive: just entirely delete one model and then build the other one. However, if models embody some contextual information (e.g., authorship and authorization), the existence of mutually non-updatable models becomes reasonable.

Thus, a model space is a pair (M, U_M) with M a set and U_M an equivalence relation over M. Update translation is now modeled by a ternary function $\overrightarrow{\tau}\colon M \times M \times N \to N$ and undoability from M to N means that if $n' = \overrightarrow{\tau}(m, m', n)$ then $n = \overrightarrow{\tau}(m', m, n')$ as illustrated by diagrams (a1) and (b1) (adjoint to Table 3) to be considered together. Undoability from N to M is stated symmetrically – consider diagrams (a2) and (b2).

3.2 Trigonal Systems

Let (M, U_M) and (N, U_N) be two model spaces with updatability relations.

Definition 3. A *well-behaved trigonal synchronization system* over M, N (*tri-system* in short) is a triple $\tau = (R_\tau, \overrightarrow{\tau}, \overleftarrow{\tau})$ with $R_\tau \subset M \times N$ a binary *consistency relation*, $\overrightarrow{\tau}: M \times M \times N \to N$ and $\overleftarrow{\tau}: N \times N \times M \to M$ two partial functions called the *forward* and *backward synchronizers* resp., such that conditions (dmCorr), (rgCorr) and (Idnt) in Table 3 are satisfied. To ease reading formulas, for arguments $m, m' \in M$, $n, n' \in N$, we write $[m, m', n\rangle$ and $\langle m, n', n]$ for $\overrightarrow{\tau}(m, m', n)$ and $\overleftarrow{\tau}(n, n', m)$. A synchronization system is called *very well-behaved/undoable* if, in addition, conditions (hIgno)/(Undo) hold. If synchronizers are mutually inverse in the sense of conditions (Inv), the synchronization is called *invertible* – consider the pair of diagrams (a1)+(a2).

Table 3. Conditions for trigonal synchronization systems. All formulas are universally quantified for all their variables Expression $f(x)\Downarrow$ means that partial function f is defined at x. Diagrams under the table help to visualize the identities.

Condition: name and label	Forward increm. synch. $[*,*,*\rangle: M \times M \times N \to N$	Backward increm. synch. $M \leftarrow M \times N \times N : \langle *,*,*]$
Correctness: domain (dmCorr)	$[m, m', n\rangle\Downarrow$ iff $(mR_\tau n)$ & $(mU_M m')$	$\langle m, n', n]\Downarrow$ iff $(mR_\tau n)$ & $(nU_N n')$
range (rgCorr)	$\dfrac{\text{let } [m, m', n\rangle = n'}{\text{then } (m'R_\tau n') \,\&\, (nU_N n')}$	$\dfrac{\text{let } m' = \langle m, n', n]}{\text{then } (m'R_\tau n') \,\&\, (mU_M m')}$
Identity (Idnt)	$[m, m, n\rangle = n$	$m = \langle m, n, n]$
history Ignorance (hIgno)	$[m', m'', [m, m', n\rangle\rangle = [m, m'', n\rangle$	$\langle\langle m, n', n], n'', n'] = \langle m, n'', n]$
Undoability (Undo)	$[m', m, [m, m', n\rangle\rangle = n$	$m = \langle\langle m, n', n], n, n']$
Hippocraticness (Hipp)	$\dfrac{\text{if } m'R_\tau n}{\text{then } [m, m', n\rangle = n}$	$\dfrac{\text{if } mR_\tau n'}{\text{then } m = \langle m, n', n]}$
Invertibility (Inv): (BckFwd) (FwdBck)	$[m, \langle m, n', n], n\rangle = n'$ $m' = \langle m, [m, n, m'\rangle, n]$	

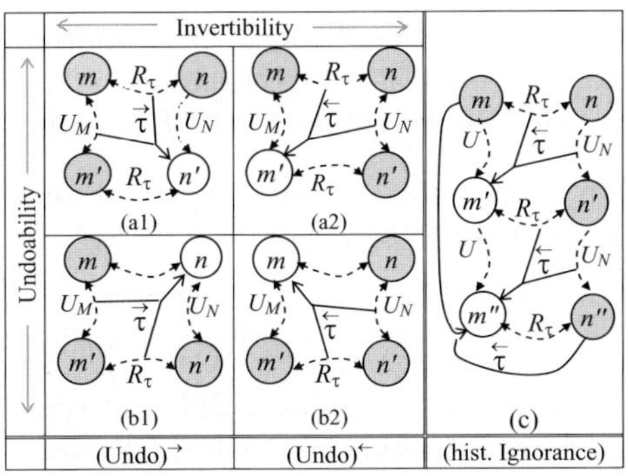

Proposition 7. The following implications hold: (i) (Hipp) implies (Idnt) and (ii) (hIgno) and (Idnt) imply (Undo).

Proof. (i) is straightforward. (ii) Assume $m'' = m$ in $\overrightarrow{\text{(hIgno)}}$ and $n'' = n$ in $\overleftarrow{\text{(hIgno)}}$.

Our next goal is to demonstrate that conditions of history ignorance, invertibility and Hippocraticness do not imply each other. We will build a series of examples.

Example 3. Suppose that R_τ, U_M, U_N are always true, i.e., $R_\tau = M \times N$, $U_M = M \times M$ $U_N = N \times N$, and synchronizers do not actually react to updates: $[m, m', n\rangle = n$, $m = \langle m, n', n]$. This tri-system is very well-behaved (hence undoable) but not invertible. It is trivially Hippocratic because it does nothing.

Example 4. Suppose that consistency relation is determined by a bijection $f\colon M \to N$ compatible with updatability: $mU_M m' \Rightarrow (m.f)U_N(m'.f)$. We define $R_f(m,n)$ iff $n = m.f$, $(m, m', n)\overrightarrow{\tau_f} \stackrel{\text{def}}{=} m'.f$ and $\overleftarrow{\tau_f}(n, n', m) \stackrel{\text{def}}{=} f^{-1}(n')$. Then the triple $\tau(f) = (R_f, \overrightarrow{\tau_f}, \overleftarrow{\tau_f})$ is very well-behaved and invertible. It is also trivially Hippocratic because any update destroys consistency.

Example 5. Let $M = N = \mathbf{R} \times \mathbf{R}$ with $\mathbf{R}$ denoting the set of real numbers. Then model are pairs of numbers, which we will write as ab for M and xy for N. We define updatability and consistency relation by $U_M = M \times M$, $U_N = N \times N$ and $abRxy$ iff $a = x$. Synchronizers are defined as follows: $[ab, a'b', xy\rangle = (x + \Delta a)(y + \Delta b)$ where $\Delta a = a' - a$, $\Delta b = b' - b$, and $\langle ab, x'y', xy] = (a + \Delta x)(b + \Delta y)$ where $\Delta x = x' - x$, $\Delta y = y' - y$. It is easy to check that this system is very well-behaved and invertible yet it is not Hippocratic. If $\Delta a = 0$ but $\Delta b \neq 0$, we have $a'b'Rxy$ yet $[ab, a'b', xy\rangle = x(y + \Delta b) \neq xy$. The cause of non-Hippocraticness is that model synchronization uses all information embodied in the models while their consistency is based on only a part of it.

Thus, (very) well-behavedness, invertibility and Hippocraticness are orthogonal concepts in tri-synchronization. Particularly, non-Hippocraticness is quite natural for incremental systems. On the other hand, (Idnt) laws can be regarded as a weak form of Hippocraticness and are always assumed to hold.

Lemma 8. Suppose that for a correct trigonal system τ the consistency relation R_τ is functional from M to N: there is a total function $f\colon M \to N$ such that $mR_\tau n$ iff $m.f = n$. Then for any $n, n' \in N$, $nU_N n'$ iff both $n, n' \in f(M)$, and for any $m, m' \in M$, , $[m, m', n\rangle = m'.f$ and$\langle m, n', n] = \langle m, n', m.f]$. This defines a lens $\lambda(\tau)$ with $get_{\lambda(\tau)} = f$ and $put_{\lambda(\tau)}(n', m) = \langle m, n', m.f]$. The trigonal axioms specified in Table 3 then become lens axiom as specified in Table (b) of Fig. 2. Conversely, any lens λ determines a functional tri-system $\tau(\lambda)$ as defined above.

Corollary 9. Given a correct tri-system τ with functional consistency relation, the lens $\lambda(\tau)$ is well-behaved (and undoable) iff τ is well-behaved (and undoable). Similarly, given λ, tri-system $\tau(\lambda)$ is very well-behaved/undoable iff λ is such.

This result together with Corollary 4 shows that when consistency relation is functional, both di- and tri-synchronization systems degenerate to lenses.

4 Conclusions

The paper presents an algebraic framework, in which semantics of different types of bi-directional model synchronization and transformation can be formally specified and analyzed. Three families of algebras for modeling synchronization were considered: lenses, di- and tri-systems, and four groups of algebraic laws representing four synchronization concepts were analyzed: (a) correctness (or well-behavedness), (b) Hippocraticness, (c) history ignorance and undoability, and (d) invertibility. The algebras can be seen as design schemas for synchronization tools, and the concepts as their possible features. Among these algebras, tri-systems present the most adequate and detailed model of incremental synchronization, and our analysis shows that they are also the most technically manageable: the optional concepts (b,c,d) are directly modeled and in fact are mutually orthogonal within the trigonal framework. For diagonal systems, these concepts partially overlap and mutually dependant. As for lenses, the same law, (GetPut) or (PutGet), plays multiple roles (Fig. 2), which makes the lens case of overlapping between the concepts the strongest amongst the three types of synchronization algebras. Importantly, for functional consistency relations, di- and tri-system degenerate into lenses (Corollaries 4, 9).

On a less technical side, the paper aims to emphasize the importance of the *view relationship* between models. It is widespread and appears as a basic unit from which other relationships can be built. Correspondingly, synchronization of models subjected to these complex relationships can be built from view synchronization systems, i.e., from lenses. The paper presents an important construct of this kind – composition of two well-behaved lenses with a common target, and shows that it results in a well-behaved di-system (Theorem 6). Further work is needed to explore the idea of assembling synchronization systems from lenses.

Acknowledgement. Comments of the anonymous referees were very helpful in restructuring the paper to its present form.

References

[1] Antkiewicz, M., Czarnecki, K.: Design space of heterogeneous synchronization. In: Generative and Transformational Techniques in Software Engineering (2008)

[2] Bancilhon, F., Spyratos, N.: Update semantics of relational views. TODS 6(4), 557–575 (1981)

[3] Bohannon, A., Pierce, B., Vaughan, J.: Relational lenses: a language for updatable views. In: PODS (2006)

[4] Brunet, G., Chechik, M., Easterbrook, S., Nejati, S., Niu, N., Sabetzadeh, M.: A manifesto for model merging. In: GaMMa 2006: Proc. Int. workshop on Global integrated model management. ACM Press, New York (2006)

[5] Dayal, U., Bernstein, P.: On the correct translation of update operations on relational views. TODS 7(3), 381–416 (1982)

[6] Diskin, Z.: Algebra of bidirectional model synchronization. Technical Report CSRG-573, Department of Compuitng Science, University of Toronto (2008), `ftp://ftp.cs.toronto.edu/pub/reports/csrg/573/TR-CSRG-573.pdf`

[7] Diskin, Z., Diengel, J.: A metamodel independent framework for model transformation: Towards generic model management patterns in reverse engineering. In: Favre, J.-M., et al. (eds.) 3rd Int.Workshop on Metamodels, Schemas, Grammas and Ontologies for Reverse Engineering (2006)

[8] Diskin, Z., Easterbrook, S., Dingel, J.: Engineering associations: from models to code and back through semantics. In: Paige, R., Meyer, B. (eds.) TOOLS Europe 2008. LNBIP 11, vol. 11. Springer, Heidelberg (2008)
[9] Ehrig, H., Ehrig, K., Ermel, C., Hermann, F., Taentzer, G.: Information preserving bidirectional model transformations. In: Dwyer, M.B., Lopes, A. (eds.) FASE 2007. LNCS, vol. 4422, pp. 72–86. Springer, Heidelberg (2007)
[10] Foster, J., Greenwald, M., Moore, J., Pierce, B., Schmitt, A.: Combinators for bidirectional tree transformations: a linguistic approach to the view update problem. In: POPL, pp. 233–246 (2005)
[11] Gottlob, G., Paolini, P., Zicari, R.: Properties and update semantics of consistent views. ACM TODS 13(4), 486–524 (1988)
[12] Königs, A., Schürr, A.: Tool integration with triple graph grammars - A survey. ENTCS 148(1), 113–150 (2006)
[13] Meertens, L.: Designing constraint maintainers for user interaction (1998), http://www.kestrel.edu/home/people/meertens/
[14] Mu, S., Hu, Z., Takeichi, M.: An algebraic approach to bi-directional updating. In: Chin, W.-N. (ed.) APLAS 2004. LNCS, vol. 3302. Springer, Heidelberg (2004)
[15] OMG, MOF QVT Final Adopted Specification. Formal/05-11-01 (2005), http://www.omg.org/docs/ptc
[16] Stevens, P.: Bidirectional model transformation in QVT: Semantic issues and open questions. In: Engels, G., Opdyke, B., Schmidt, D.C., Weil, F. (eds.) MODELS 2007. LNCS, vol. 4735. Springer, Heidelberg (2007)

An Invariant-Based Method for the Analysis of Declarative Model-to-Model Transformations

Jordi Cabot[1], Robert Clarisó[1], Esther Guerra[2], and Juan de Lara[3]

[1] Universitat Oberta de Catalunya (Spain)
{jcabot,rclariso}@uoc.edu
[2] Universidad Carlos III de Madrid (Spain)
eguerra@inf.uc3m.es
[3] Universidad Autónoma de Madrid (Spain)
jdelara@uam.es

Abstract. In this paper we propose a method to derive OCL invariants from declarative specifications of model-to-model transformations. In particular we consider two of the most prominent approaches for specifying such transformations: Triple Graph Grammars and QVT. Once the specification is expressed in the form of invariants, the transformation developer can use such description to verify properties of the original transformation (e.g. whether it defines a total, surjective or injective function), and to validate the transformation by the automatic generation of valid pairs of source and target models.

1 Introduction

Model-Driven Development (MDD) is a software engineering paradigm where models are the core asset. They are used to specify, simulate, test, verify and generate code for the application to be built. Most of these activities include the specification and execution of model transformations. The transformation of a model conformant to a meta-model into another one conformant to a (different) meta-model is called a model-to-model (M2M) transformation.

There are two main approaches to M2M transformation: *operational* and *declarative*. The former is based on rules or instructions that explicitly state how and when the elements of the target model should be created from elements of the source one. In declarative approaches, some kind of (visual or textual) patterns describing the relations between the source and target models is provided, rather than a program specifying how to create and link their elements. These patterns are complemented with additional information, e.g. to express relations between attributes in source and target elements, as well as to constrain when a certain relation should hold (frequently the OCL standard is used for this purpose [17]). Declarative approaches are higher-level than operational ones and they are inherently bidirectional because they do not specify any causality. Thus, they bring together in a single specification forward (i.e. source-to-target) and backward (i.e. target-to-source) transformations.

K. Czarnecki et al. (Eds.): MoDELS 2008, LNCS 5301, pp. 37–52, 2008.

Whereas several notations have been proposed for specifying M2M transformations [1, 14, 17, 19], there is a lack of methods for analysing the correctness of declarative M2M specifications in an integral way, taking into account the relations and constraints expressed by the transformation, as well as the meta-models and their well-formedness rules.

In this paper, we propose validation and verification techniques based on the extraction of implicit transformation invariants deduced from the declarative description of the transformations. These invariants state the conditions for a valid mapping between source and target elements and we express them in OCL. We call these invariants, together with the source and target meta-models, a *transformation model* [6]. To show the wide applicability of the technique, we study how to create this transformation model from two common notations for M2M transformations: QVT [17] and Triple Graph Grammars (TGGs) [19].

Once the transformation model is automatically derived we can determine several correctness properties of the original transformation by analyzing the transformation model with any available tool for the verification of static UML/OCL class diagrams (see [2, 7, 9, 21]). In particular, in this work we use our UMLtoCSP tool [9] for the analysis. The tool translates the transformation model into a constraint satisfaction problem that can be processed with constraint solvers to check different aspects of the model. For example, whether it is *satisfiable* (i.e. there is at least one valid pair of related source and target models), *total* (whether all valid source models have a valid related target model) or *deterministic* (whether a source model has just one valid target model).

We also use UMLtoCSP for validation, because the tool is able to automatically generate valid pairs of source and target models, or a valid target model for a given or partially specified source model. These generated pairs help designers in deciding whether the defined transformation reflects their intention.

Paper Organization. Section 2 introduces TGGs and the method for extracting invariants. Section 3 presents such method for QVT. Section 4 shows the use of the invariants for validation and verification of transformations. Section 5 compares with related work and Section 6 ends with the conclusions.

2 From TGG Rules to OCL Invariants

Triple Graph Grammars (TGGs) [19] were proposed as a means to specify transformations between two languages (i.e. meta-models) in a declarative way. TGGs build on the notion of graph grammar [18]. A graph grammar is made of a set of rules, each having graphs in their left and right hand sides (LHS and RHS), plus an initial graph (i.e. the model to be transformed). The application of a rule to a graph is only possible if an occurrence of the LHS (a *match* morphism) is found in it. Once such occurrence is found, it is replaced by the RHS. It may be possible to find several matches for a rule, and then one is chosen at random. The execution of a grammar is also non-deterministic: at each step, one rule is randomly chosen and its application is tried. The execution ends when no match is found for any rule. A M2M transformation by graph transformation has an operational style, as the rules specify how to build the target model assuming the source already exists or vice versa, thus being unidirectional.

TGGs are an attempt to increase the level of abstraction of a M2M specification, being more declarative and bidirectional. TGGs are made of rules working on triples graphs. These consist of two graphs called *source* and *target*, related through a *correspondence* graph. Any graph model can be used for these three graphs, from standard unattributed graphs $(V; E; s, t\colon E \rightarrow V)$ to more complex attributed graphs. The nodes in the correspondence graph (the *mappings*) have morphisms[1] to the nodes in the source and target graphs.

Definition 1 (Triple Graph). *A triple graph* $TrG = (G_s, G_c, G_t, cs\colon V_{G_c} \rightarrow V_{G_s}, ct\colon V_{G_c} \rightarrow V_{G_t})$ *is made of two graphs* G_s *and* G_t *called source and target, related through the nodes of the correspondence graph* G_c.

In the previous definition, V_{G_x} is the set of nodes of graph G_x. Morphisms cs and ct relate two nodes in the source and target graphs, such that $x \in V_{G_s}$ is related to $y \in V_{G_t}$ iff $\exists n \in V_{G_c}$ with $cs(n) = x$ and $ct(n) = y$. We often depict a triple graph by $\langle G_s \stackrel{cs}{\leftarrow} G_c \stackrel{ct}{\rightarrow} G_t \rangle$, and use $TrG|_x$ (for $x = \{s, c, t\}$) to refer to the x component of TrG. Next, we define triple graph morphisms as a triple of graph morphisms that preserve the correspondence functions cs and ct.

Definition 2 (Triple Graph Morphism). *A triple graph morphism* $f = (f_s, f_c, f_t) : TrG^1 \rightarrow TrG^2$ *is made of three graph morphisms* $f_x\colon TrG^1|_x \rightarrow TrG^2|_x$ *(with* $x = \{s, c, t\}$*) such that* $f_s|_V \circ cs^1 = cs^2 \circ f_c|_V$ *and* $f_t|_V \circ ct^1 = ct^2 \circ f_c|_V$*, where* $f_x|_V$ *is morphism* f_x *restricted to nodes.*

We use triple morphisms for three purposes: (i) to define the relation between the LHS and RHS of a TGG rule; (ii) to identify an occurrence (a match) of the LHS in the host graph and (iii) to type a triple graph.

A triple graph is typed by a *meta-model triple* [12] or TGG schema, which contains the source and target meta-models, and declares the types of mappings between the elements of both languages. Fig. 1 shows an example meta-model triple for a simplified translation between class diagrams and relational schemas. The class diagram meta-model includes the derived relation `AllParents` to navigate directly to all ancestors of a given class. The correspondence meta-model declares three classes: `C2T` is used to map classes and tables, whereas `A2Co` and `A2Ch` relate attributes and columns. This last mapping is used to relate an attribute from

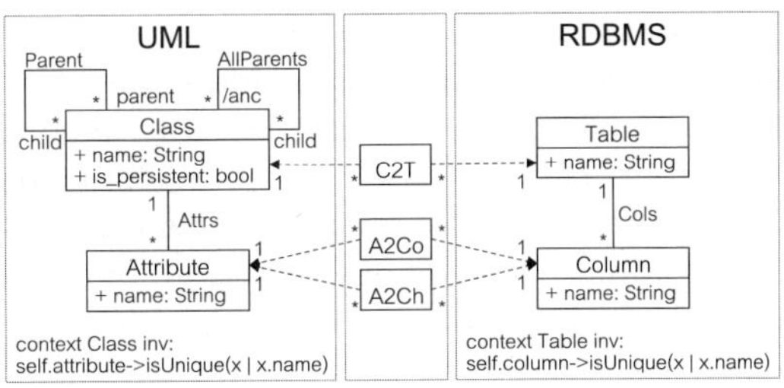

Fig. 1. Example meta-model triple

1 A morphism corresponds to the mathematical notion of (total) function between two sets, or in general between two structures (graphs, triple graphs, etc.).

a parent class to a column of a table associated with a child class. The dotted arrows specify the allowed morphisms from the correspondence to the source and target models. These can be treated as normal associations with cardinality 1 on the side of the source/target class and $*$ on the side of the correspondence class. The meta-model includes OCL constraints ensuring uniqueness of attribute names for each class, and similarly for tables.

A typed triple graph is represented as $(TrG, type\colon TrG \to MM)$, where the first element is a triple graph and the second a morphism to the meta-model triple. Morphisms between typed triple graphs must respect the typing morphism and can be so called *clan-morphisms* to take inheritance into account [12]. For simplicity of presentation, we omit the typing in the following definitions.

Besides a meta-model triple, a M2M transformation by TGGs consists of a set of declarative TGG rules that describe the synchronized evolution of two models. Thus, TGG rules have triple graphs in its LHS and RHS, so as to allow manipulating both models synchronously. We use OCL in TGG rules to define attribute conditions.

Definition 3 (Declarative TGG Rule). *A declarative TGG rule* $p = (r\colon \to \langle L_s \overset{cs^l}{\leftarrow} L_c \overset{ct^l}{\rightarrow} L_t\rangle\langle R_s \overset{cs^r}{\leftarrow} R_c \overset{ct^r}{\rightarrow} R_t\rangle, ATT_{COND})$ *is made of a triple morphism* r*, and a set* ATT_{COND} *of OCL constraints expressing attribute conditions.*

In the previous definition, the rule's LHS is $\langle L_s \overset{cs^l}{\leftarrow} L_c \overset{ct^l}{\rightarrow} L_t\rangle$, and the RHS is $\langle R_s \overset{cs^r}{\leftarrow} R_c \overset{ct^r}{\rightarrow} R_t\rangle$, as r is a triple morphism, the rule is non-deleting. Fig. 2 shows three example TGG declarative rules. They are shown using a compact notation where the LHS and the RHS are presented together, the elements created by the rule (RHS-LHS) are marked as `{new}`, and the elements of the LHS which are preserved are untagged. Rule `Class-Table` declares that every time a persistent class is created, a table with the same name is created simultaneously, and vice versa. `Attribute-Column` specifies that creating an attribute of a class which is already related to a table should create a related column with the same name in that table, and vice versa. Finally, `ParentAttribute-Column` creates a new column in the table associated to a child class for all attributes in each ancestor class. Note that a M2M specification by TGGs is declarative and bidirectional as rules do not specify any direction, but synchronously create and relate source and target elements.

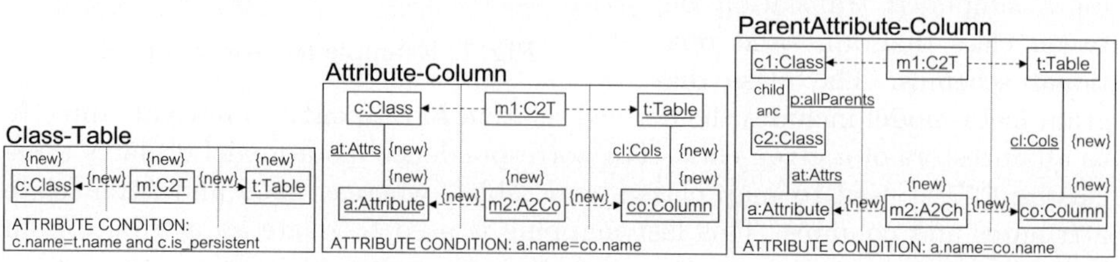

Fig. 2. Some TGG rules for the class-to-relational transformation

From this declarative specification, an algorithm was proposed in [19] to generate low-level *operational* TGG rules to perform forward and backward transformations, and to relate two existing graphs. The LHS of a forward rule is $\langle R_s \overset{cs^l}{\leftarrow} L_c \overset{ct^l}{\rightarrow} L_t \rangle$ and its RHS is equal to the RHS of the declarative rule. For example, the forward rule for rule `Attribute-Column` has objects `c`, `m1`, `t` and `a` in its LHS, and creates the `co` object related to `t` and mapped to `a` through the new mapping `m2`. Note that a causality has to be assigned to the expressions in the attribute condition section, so that the attribute values for the created objects can be derived from the ones in the LHS. This presents practical problems, which we avoid by compiling the TGG rules into OCL invariants and using a constraint solver, as shown in the next subsection.

2.1 From Declarative TGG Rules to OCL Invariants

The invariant extraction procedure enriches the transformation model with a set of invariants that capture the semantics embodied by the TGG rules. Intuitively, the invariants must guarantee that the target model is a valid transformation of the source according to the set of rules that can be applied on the source model, and similar for target. A rule is enabled source-to-target in any subgraph of the source model that matches the LHS of the forward operational rule and satisfies the attribute conditions for the source model, and similar for target-to-source. Rules can be fired whenever they are enabled. Thus, for each subgraph where the rule is enabled source-to-target, the invariants should make sure that (a) there is a subgraph of the target model which enables the same rule target-to-source, (b) there are mapping objects connecting both subgraphs as defined in the rule and (c) the union of both subgraphs satisfies any remaining attribute conditions. For each rule p, we call the invariant checking (a) and (b) for the source model $check_s^p$; the one checking (a) and (b) for the target model $check_t^p$; and the one checking (c) for both models $check_c^p$. The invariants capture this semantics using expressions like *"any subgraph matching the LHS of the forward/backwards rule is connected to the mapping objects"* or *"given a mapping object, the source/target models it connects must satisfy the attribute condition"*.

Next definitions describe our extraction procedure and the structure of the generated invariants. Our procedure makes two assumptions: (i) all rules create at least one element in the correspondence graph and (ii) each type of mapping is created by at most one rule.

Definition 4 (Invariant Extraction). *Given a declarative TGG rule* $p = (r\colon \langle L_s \overset{cs^l}{\leftarrow} L_c \overset{ct^l}{\rightarrow} L_t \rangle \rightarrow \langle R_s \overset{cs^r}{\leftarrow} R_c \overset{ct^r}{\rightarrow} R_t \rangle, ATT_{COND})$*:*

- $\forall n \in V_{R_x}$*, for* $x = \{s, t\}$*, s.t.* $\exists m \in V_{R_c} - r(V_{L_c})$ *with* $cs(m) = n$ *or* $ct(m) = n$*, add invariant* $\texttt{check}_x^p$ *to* $type(n)$*.*
- $\forall m \in V_{R_c} - r(V_{L_c})$*, add invariant* $\texttt{check}_c^p$ *to* $type(m)$*.*

Invariant $\texttt{check}_s^p$ checks the existence of triple graph $TrG^s = \langle R_s \overset{cs^l}{\leftarrow} L_c \overset{ct^l}{\rightarrow} L_t \rangle$, together with terms in ATT_{COND} consisting of elements in TrG^s only.

Similarly, invariant $\texttt{check}^p_t$ checks the existence of $TrG^t = \langle L_s \stackrel{cs^l}{\leftarrow} L_c \stackrel{ct^l}{\rightarrow} R_t \rangle$, and evaluates the terms in ATT_{COND} that consider elements in TrG^t only. Note the similarity with the pre-conditions for forward/backwards operational TGG rules. In addition, $\texttt{check}^p_c$ checks the existence of R and evaluates terms in ATT_{COND} made of elements in $R - r(L)$, not evaluated by previous constraints.

Definition 5 ($\textbf{check}^p_s$ Invariant). *Given TGG rule* $p = (r\colon \langle L_s \stackrel{cs^l}{\leftarrow} L_c \stackrel{ct^l}{\rightarrow} L_t \rangle \rightarrow \langle R_s \stackrel{cs^r}{\leftarrow} R_c \stackrel{ct^r}{\rightarrow} R_t \rangle, ATT_{COND})$*, then* $\forall n \in V_{R_s} - r(V_{L_s})$ *s.t.* $\exists m \in V_{R_c} - r(V_{L_c})$ *with* $cs(m) = n$*, the following invariant is generated:*

```
context type(n)     -- check_s^p invariant
 inv : if exists_n^p then self.cor_1->size() = 1 and ... self.cor_m->size() = 1
       else self.cor_1->size() = 0 and ... self.cor_m->size() = 0 endif
-------------------------------------------------------------------------------
context type(n)::exists_n^p ()   -- Helper for check_s^p: checks existence of TrG^s
 body: type(n_i) :: allInstances()->exists(n_i|...       } ∀n_k ∈ V_TrG^s − {n}
          type(n_j) :: allInstances()->exists(n_j|...    }

          n_i.role_j->includes(n_j) and...               } ∀e ∈ E_TrG^s s.t. n_i <-s- e -t-> n_j
            ...and ATT^s_COND)...)...)...)
```

where $cor_j = type(m_j)$ $(j = \{1...m\})$ *with* $m_j \in R_c - r(L_c)$ *and* $cs^r(m_j) = n$*,* $role_j$ *is the role in the meta-model allowing to navigate from* n_i *to* n_j *and* $ATT^s_{COND} \subseteq ATT_{COND}$ *is the biggest subset of constraints involving elements in* TrG^s *only. In* $exists^p_n$*, if some edge has* n *as source or target we use* $self$*.*

If association end $role_j$ has cardinality 1, then we do not use $n_i.role_j\!-\!\!> includes$ (n_j) but simply $n_i.role_j = n_j$ For all nodes $n \in L_s$ (instead of $R_s - r(L_s)$) that are connected to a newly created correspondence element, a similar invariant is generated with the form **if** $exists^p_n$ **then** $self.cor_1\!-\!\!>size() >= 1$ and $...self.cor_m\!-\!\!> size() >= 1$ **else** $self.cor_1\!-\!\!>size() = 0$ and $...self.cor_m\!-\!\!> size() = 0$ **endif**. This is necessary, as the node in the source graph already exists, so that it can be added further morphisms from the correspondence node. In the case of the invariant in Definition 5 it can receive just one morphism, as both nodes are created at the same time.

Invariants $\texttt{check}^p_t$ are generated in a similar way, but considering nodes $n \in V_{R_t} - r(V_{L_t})$ and then traversing the graph $TrG^t = \langle L_s \stackrel{cs^l}{\leftarrow} L_c \stackrel{ct^l}{\rightarrow} R_t \rangle$. For nodes created in the correspondence graph, invariants are generated as follows.

Definition 6 ($\textbf{check}^p_c$ Invariant). *Given TGG rule* $p = (r\colon \langle L_s \stackrel{cs^l}{\leftarrow} L_c \stackrel{ct^l}{\rightarrow} L_t \rangle \rightarrow \langle R_s \stackrel{cs^r}{\leftarrow} R_c \stackrel{ct^r}{\rightarrow} R_t \rangle, ATT_{COND})$*, then* $\forall n \in R_c - r(L_c)$ *the following invariant is generated:*

```
context type(n)     -- check_c^p invariant
 inv : type(n_i) :: allInstances()->exists(n_i|...      } ∀n_k ∈ V_TrG^c − {n}
         type(n_j) :: allInstances()->exists(n_j|...     }

          n_i.role_j->includes(n_j) and...               } ∀e ∈ E_TrG^c s.t. n_i <-s- e -t-> n_j
            ...and ATT^c_COND)...)...)...)
```

with $TrG^c = \langle R_s \stackrel{cs^r}{\leftarrow} R_c \stackrel{ct^r}{\rightarrow} R_t \rangle$ *and* $ATT^c_{COND} = ATT_{COND} - (ATT^s_{COND} \cup ATT^t_{COND})$ *the set of attribute conditions not evaluated by previous constraints.*

Lets consider the example rules. As all elements are created in rule `Class-Table`, an invariant is added to each one of the three involved classes. The one in the mapping checks that the source and target elements (a class and a table) it relates exist, and that the names match. The invariant for the class checks that it is persistent and, if (and only if) this is the case, a mapping object is connected to it. Finally, the invariant for tables checks that there is a mapping.

context C2T — $check_c^{Class-Table}$ *invariant*
inv : $Class :: allInstances()\text{->}exists(c|Table :: allInstances()\text{->}exists(t|$
$self.class = c \text{ and } self.table = t \text{ and } c.name = t.name))$

---

context Class — $check_s^{Class-Table}$ *invariant*
inv : **if** $self.is\_persistent$ **then** $self.c2T\text{->}size() = 1$
else $self.c2T\text{->}size() = 0$ **endif**

---

context Table **inv** : $self.c2T\text{->}size() = 1$ — $check_t^{Class-Table}$ *invariant*

Note that some invariants can be simplified, e.g. the one for `C2T` is equivalent to $self.class.name = self.table.name$. From `Attribute-Column` we generate invariants for the attribute, column and `A2Co` classes, as all are created. The one in the mapping checks that the attribute and the column it relates exist, that they belong to a related class and table, and that their names match. The invariant for the attribute checks that it is mapped to the corresponding mapping element. It does not have to check that the attribute is related to a table, as this is ensured by the association cardinality constraint in the meta-model. Finally, the invariant for the column checks only its relation to a mapping.

context A2Co — $check_c^{Attribute-Column}$ *invariant*
inv : $Attribute :: allInstances()\text{->}exists(a|Class :: allInstances()\text{->}exists(c|$
$C2T :: allInstances()\text{->}exists(m1|Table :: allInstances()\text{->}exists(t|$
$Column :: allInstances()\text{->}exists(co|$
$self.attribute = a \text{ and } a.class = c \text{ and } c.c2T = m1 \text{ and } m1.table = t$
$\text{and } self.column = co \text{ and } co.table = t \text{ and } a.name = co.name)))))$

---

context Attribute — $check_s^{Attribute-Column}$ *invariant*
inv : **if** $self.exists_a^{Attribute-Column}$ **then** $self.a2Co\text{->}size() = 1$
else $self.a2Co\text{->}size() = 0$ **endif**

---

context Attribute::$exists_a^{Attribute-Column^s}()$
body: $Class :: allInstances()\text{->}exists(c|C2T :: allInstances()\text{->}exists(m1|$
$self.class = c \text{ and } c.c2T = m1))$

---

context Column — $check_t^{Attribute-Column}$ *invariant*
inv : **if** $self.exists_{co}^{Attribute-Column}$ **then** $self.a2Co\text{->}size() = 1$
else $self.a2Co\text{->}size() = 0$ **endif**

---

context Column::$exists_{co}^{Attribute-Column}()$
body: $Table :: allInstances()\text{->}exists(t|C2T :: allInstances()\text{->}exists(m1|$
$self.table = t \text{ and } t.c2T = m1))$

3 From QVT-Relations to OCL Invariants

QVT-Relations is a declarative M2M transformation language part of the OMG QVT standard [17]. In this language, a bidirectional tranformation consists of a set of top-level relations between two models. Each relation defines two *domain patterns*, one for each model, and a pair of optional *when* and *where* arbitrary OCL predicates. These optional predicates define the link with other relations in the transformation: the *when* clause indicates the conditions under which the relation needs to hold and the *where* clause provides additional conditions, apart from the ones expressed by the relation itself, that must satisfied by all model elements in the relation.

Domain patterns can be viewed as graph patterns that must be matched to a set of model elements of the appropriate type, i.e. similar to the LHS/RHS of TGGs. However, there are differences in the matching process as patterns may contain *variables*, where some of them may be still *free* while others may be *previously bound* to model elements, e.g. resulting from the evaluation of when clauses or other expressions in the relation, depending on the execution direction of the transformation. Bound variables and constant expressions restrict the possible matches for the pattern. Instead, free variables become bound to the elements matching the pattern. These values may be used afterwards to constrain the value of further pattern expressions.

As an example, consider the rule *Class-Table* expressed as the QVT relation shown in Fig. 3. When executed in the UML→RDBMS direction the relation states that for each persistent class (i.e. each class satisfying the is_persistent condition imposed by the first domain pattern) there must exist a table with a name equal to the value of the *cn* variable. This variable has been initialized with the name of the class matching the first pattern. Additionally, to complete this part of the transformation, we require in the where clause that all attributes of *c* are mapped to table columns of *t* as stated in the relation *Attribute-Column* (inside *Attribute-Column*, variables *c* and *t* will be bound). When executed in the RDBMS→UML direction the variable *cn* takes the table name as a value and it is used to constrain the possible classes that can be a match for the first pattern. This variable binding process must be simulated by our generated invariants.

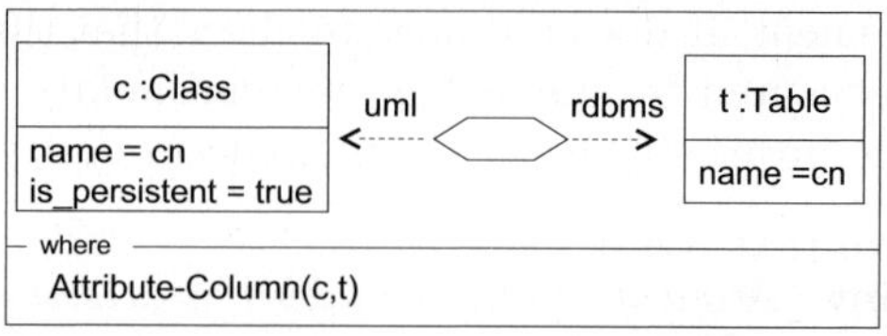

Fig. 3. Example of a QVT relation

3.1 Extracting the OCL Invariants

Many concepts of QVT-Relations resemble the elements appearing in TGG rules (see [11] for a comparison). Therefore, the procedure for extracting the implicit invariants in a QVT-Relations transformation is similar to that explained in the previous section for TGG rules. For our purposes, the two main differences are that in QVT-Relations related elements in both models are not linked by correspondence nodes and that relationships between different relations can be made explicit by invoking them in the when and where clauses. Due to space limitations, in this section we will focus on explaining these two aspects.

The absence of correspondence nodes forces us to integrate all conditions relating elements of both models into the $\texttt{check}_s^p$ and $\texttt{check}_t^p$ invariants. In TGG rules, these two invariants were mainly used to check that if the model contained a match for the LHS pattern of the operational forward/backwards rule, the required correspondence node existed. But here, the invariants must also take care of checking that when the LHS is a match, the RHS pattern is satisfied as well. To deal with the *when* and *where* clauses of a a relation r, we rewrite r as follows: *(when_clause and* r_{source}*) implies (*r_{target} *and where_clause)*, where r_{source} and r_{target} refer to the source and target patterns in r. Which domain is the source and which the target depends on whether we are generating the $\texttt{check}_s^p$ or the $\texttt{check}_t^p$ invariant. For each different relation r' referenced in any of these clauses, we create an auxiliary OCL query operation $r'(x_1, \ldots, x_n)$ that returns true iff the objects $x_1, \ldots, x_n$ passed as arguments to the operation would satisfy the relation r'.

Following these guidelines, the two invariants generated for the previous Class-Table relation are the following:

context Class — $check_s^{Class-Table}$ *invariant*
inv : self.is_persistent = true implies
    (Table::allInstances()−>exists(t | t.name=self.name and
        Attribute-Column(self,t)))

context Table — $check_t^{Table-Class}$ *invariant*
inv : Class::allInstances()−>exists(c | c.name=self.name and
    Attribute-Column(c, self))

4 Analysing the Extracted Invariants

The analysis of the OCL invariants extracted from a transformation specification can reveal insightful information regarding its correctness. In this section, we show how this analysis can be applied to two problems: (i) Validation of transformations: identifying transformations whose definition does not match the designer intent; and (ii) Verification of correctness properties of transformations: finding defects in the transformation, e.g. whether it is underspecified.

A key notion in our analysis will be the *transformation model*: the union of both the source and target metamodels, together with their integrity constraints (i.e. well-formedness rules), and the extracted OCL transformation invariants. The goal of this representation is leveraging existing UML/OCL verification and validation tools for the analysis of model transformations. For example, there are several tools addressing the *consistency* or *satisfiability* problem for UML/OCL models [2,9,21,7]: given a UML class diagram annotated with OCL constraints, decide whether there exists a legal instance of the model (i.e. an instance that satisfies all graphical and OCL constraints). Several approaches to this problem proceed constructively by automatically computing the legal instance, which is provided to designers as the output of the tool. As we will discuss in this section, many interesting problems on transformations can be reformulated as consistency problems on the transformation model.

4.1 Validation of Model Transformations

Validation tools clarify the question "*is it the right transformation?*" by allowing designers to test if the transformation behaves as expected.

The most basic level of validation for transformations is the ability to "execute" the transformation in one direction: given a source (target) model provided by the designer, generate the corresponding target (source) model. This execution is not trivial because declarative transformations define *what* is the target model corresponding to a source model, without focusing on *how* it is computed. Some relevant information like the order in which individual transformation rules should be applied is generally omitted.

Thanks to the extracted invariants, it is possible to execute the transformation without converting it into an imperative form beforehand. Intuitively, we will use a UML/OCL consistency checking tool to find an instance of the transformation model satisfying the source and target meta-model well-formedness rules, plus the transformation invariants, plus an additional constraint: that the instantiated source model is equal to the one provided by the designer. This way, we obtain a legal transformation model containing the initial source model plus a valid corresponding target model.

The input model can be described as an OCL invariant that restricts the possible set of legal instances to just one, the corresponding to that specific model. For instance, in our example, if the designer wants to execute the transformation using a source model with a single persistent class called "Company" with no attributes, in our validation process we would generate this additional invariant:

```
context Class inv:
Class::allInstances()->size() = 1 and Attribute::allInstances()->isEmpty() and
Class::allInstances()->exists ( cl | cl.name = "Company" and cl.is_persistent )
```

This invariant is passed to the solver along with the rest of the invariants. With this alternative, current tools do not need to be extended to cope with the automatic execution of model transformations. Computing an instance that satisfies both the source model invariant and the transformation invariants will yield the corresponding target model automatically. In a similar way, designers can check which source model/s would generate a specific target model.

A second validation level is the ability to transform partially specified models. For instance, in our running example a designer might want to know whether it is possible to generate a table with three columns without having to fully define an example model, a tedious and time-consuming task [20]. To help in this matter, we can use a similar approach to the one presented so far, but using a weaker invariant to specify the designer-provided input model. In this case, the UML/OCL consistency solver is free to add new elements to the input source model when searching for a legal target model.

As an example, we have used the tool UMLtoCSP [9] for UML/OCL model consistency checking to validate the TGG and QVT transformations defined as our running example. When validating different scenarios, we have identified two situations where the behavior might not be the one intended by a designer:

1. **Persistent classes without attributes:** These classes are translated into a table with no columns. Probably there should be an invariant stating that persistent classes should have at least one attribute. This scenario was found when using the following invariant as partial description of the source model:

```
context Class inv:
Class::allInstances()->exists( x | x.is_persistent and x.attr->isEmpty() )
```

2. **Persistent classes with non-persistent ancestors:** The third rule of the TGG generates a column for each attribute of each ancestor, regardless of whether they are persistent or not. Probably we should restrict columns to the attributes of persistent ancestors only. This scenario was detected using the model partially described by the invariant:

```
context Class inv:
Class::allInstances()->exists( x | x.is_persistent and not x.parent.is_persistent
and not x.parent.attr->isEmpty() )
```

Fig. 4 (2) and (3) show the instantiation which illustrates the problems in both scenarios, as computed automatically by the tool UMLtoCSP [9].

4.2 Verification of Model Transformations

The verification of transformations answers the question "*is the transformation right?*", e.g. are there any defects in the transformation? Up to now, existing methods for the verification of model transformations have focused on lower-level model transformation definitions (see Section 5) and thus, defects are not detected until later stages of the development process.

This verification problem can be expressed in terms of the transformation model because, like any other model, it is expected to satisfy several reasonable assumptions. For instance, it should be possible to instantiate the model in some way that does not violate any integrity constraint (including the OCL invariants). Moreover, it may be desirable to avoid unnecessary invariants in the model. Failing to satisfy these criteria may be a symptom of an incomplete, over-constrained or incorrect model, something which reflects potential defects in the original M2M transformation.

We can study quality notions of transformations at two levels: considering the role of individual rules within the transformation (**R**) or considering the transformation as a whole (**T**). Some properties can be studied at both levels, depending on where we place our focus, the entire model or an individual rule. The complete list of quality properties is the following:

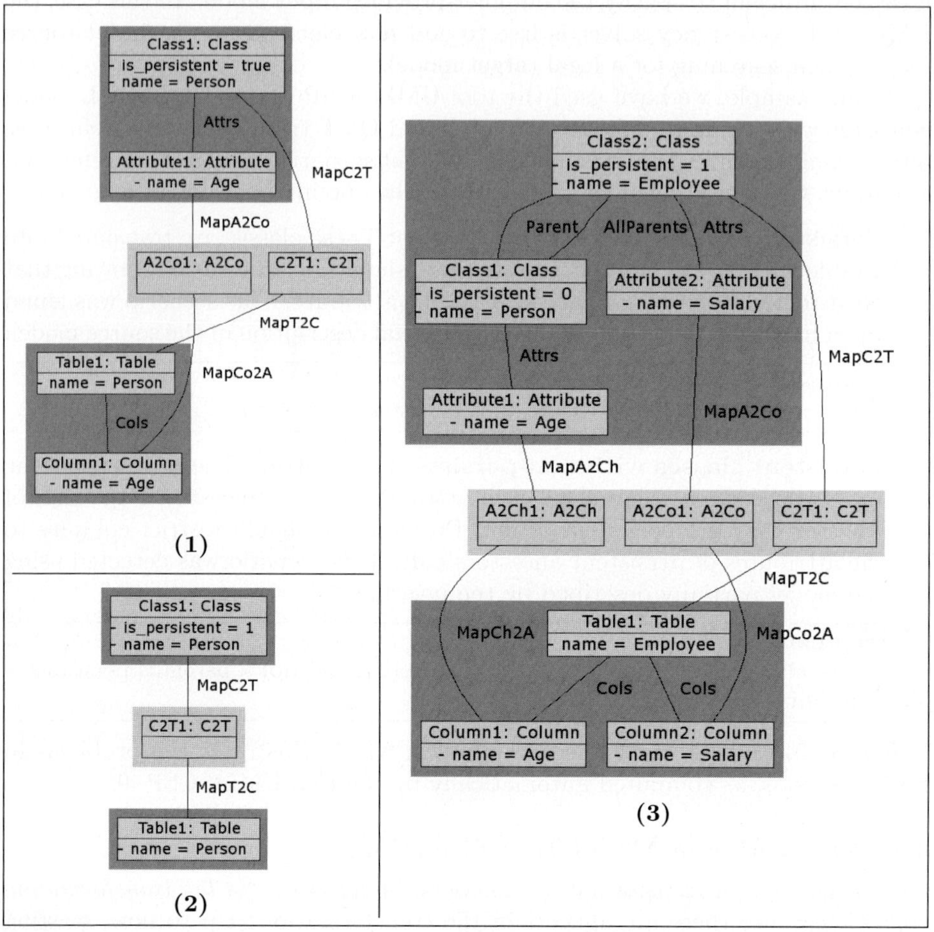

Fig. 4. Verification and validation using UMLtoCSP: (1) verifying satisfiability, (2) validating a scenario where a persistent class has no attributes, (3) validating a scenario where a persistent class has a non-persistent superclass

Satisfiable (T/R): There should be at least one source model with a target model satisfying the transformation invariants.

Total (T): Each source model has at least one corresponding target model.

Deterministic (T/R): Each source model has at most one corresponding target model.

Exhaustive (T): It is possible to generate each target model from at least one source model.

Injective (T): It is possible to generate each target model from at most one source model.

Non-redundant (R): Given a rule, there is at least one correspondence between source/target models that cannot be fulfilled if the rule is removed.

By rewriting these properties in terms of UML/OCL consistency, we can check them using existing tools. For example, satisfiability of the transformation is directly equivalent to the consistency problem, i.e. a transformation is satisfiable iff its transformation model is satisfiable. As an example, Fig. 4 (1) illustrates the verification of satisfiability on our running example using UMLtoCSP. The tool automatically proves the property by finding a legal pair of source and target models. The tool depicts a legal instance of the metamodel `Class` which is connected through the correspondance nodes to a legal instance of the metamodel `Relational`.

Other quality properties have to be decomposed into two or more consistency problems, affecting either only the source model, only the target model or the entire transformation model. For example, we can prove that a transformation is not total if we find a counterexample, a legal instance of the source model with no corresponding instance in the target model. To find the counterexample, first we need to generate a legal instance x of the source model. Then, we check if the entire transformation model is consistent when an additional invariant is added: the source model must be instantiated to x. If it is inconsistent, we have found our counterexample, otherwise, we keep generating new instances for x until we find our counterexample or we conclude no counterexample exists. A similar procedure can be used to check all the other quality properties.

If we are using a bounded verification tool like UMLtoCSP to generate legal instances, the search for counterexamples is limited to a bounded space. The designer defines this space by establishing the set of possible values for attributes and upper bounds to the number of objects and links to be considered. Bounding the search space ensures that the approach terminates (the tool always provides some answer) but as a consequence it becomes *incomplete* (when no counterexample is found, the result is inconclusive: there may be a counterexample outside the bounded search space). On the other hand, there are other UML/OCL verification approaches which are complete, like the theorem prover HOL-OCL [7], but may not terminate so they may require user assistance to complete proofs. Designers can select the tool which better fits their needs according to this trade-off.

5 Related Work

The term *transformation model* was coined in [6] where the authors described its benefits. The work of [1] presents a similar approach based on the mathematical concept of relation between the source and target models. In both works, transformation models are supposed to be manually specified by the designers. Our work can be seen as a continuation of these approaches, as we derive transformation models automatically from declarative M2M transformations, and show the feasability of such transformation models and which kinds of analysis can be done, in particular by using a constraint solver.

With respect to the analysis of transformations, our work offers new verification techniques. Current analysis techniques (especially for graph transformations [13, 18, 8]) were developed for standard (i.e. operational) rules and not declarative TGG rules. This implies that we could adapt them to operational TGG rules, but we cannot analyse declarative TGG rules with them. Besides, our method also opens the door to the verification of QVT transformations.

Our analysis approach, consisting in the translation of the M2M transformation to a formal domain is similar to other approaches: [5] and [3] transform the rules into Alloy; [4] translates them into Petri graphs and [22] into Promela for model-checking. However, again, these approaches are targeted to operational rules and/or present limitations with respect to the expressivity of the meta-models and the input transformation language.

The emphasis of MDD is revealing an urgent need to develop validation and verification techniques especially targeted for M2M transformations. For example, the work in [23] analyses meta-model coverage (i.e., which parts of the source/target model are not transformed) similar to our analysis of total/surjective transformations. There are also some works to develop frameworks for transformation testing, like [16] or to check the semantically equivalence between the initial model and the generated code [10]. We believe that our work can be regarded as a complementary contribution to this community effort.

6 Conclusions and Future Work

We have presented a new method for the analysis of declarative M2M transformations based on the automatic extraction of invariants implicit in the transformation definition. These invariants together with the definition of the source and target meta-models comprise a transformation model. Since this transformation model can be regarded as a standard UML/OCL class diagram, it can be processed with all kinds of methods and tools designed for managing class diagrams, spawning from direct application execution, to verification/validation analysis, to metrics measurement and to automatic code generation. The obtained results can then be interpreted in terms of the original transformation specification.

In particular, we have used our UMLtoCSP tool, to verify and validate declarative M2M transformations. This approach has the advantage that the M2M specification does not need to be operationalized for its analysis or execution.

Our method focuses on TGG and QVT but we believe it is feasible to extend it to cope with other similar transformation languages. Note that the extraction of invariants may serve as a means for the integration of different declarative M2M transformation languages, like QVT and TGGs.

In our future work, we will evaluate techniques to improve performance in the verification of complex transformations. We also plan to develop and adapt new techniques for transformation models that help us to perform an incremental execution of the model transformation and to detect and resolve inconsistencies due to simultaneous changes to both models.

Acknowledgments. Work supported by the Spanish Ministry of Education and Science, projects MOSAIC (TSI2005-08225-C07-06), MODUWEB (TIN2006-09678) and TIN2005-06053, and an UOC-IN3 research grant.

References

1. Akehurst, D.H., Kent, S., Patrascoiu, O.: A relational approach to defining and implementing transformations between metamodels. Journal on Software and System Modeling 2(4), 215–239 (2003)
2. Anastasakis, K., Bordbar, B., Georg, G., Ray, I.: UML2Alloy: A challenging model transformation. In: Engels, G., Opdyke, B., Schmidt, D.C., Weil, F. (eds.) MODELS 2007. LNCS, vol. 4735, pp. 436–450. Springer, Heidelberg (2007)
3. Anastasakis, K., Bordbar, B., Kuster, J.M.: Analysis of model transformations via Alloy. In: ModeVVa 2007, pp. 47–56 (2007)
4. Baldan, P., Corradini, A., König, B.: A static analysis technique for graph transformation systems. In: Larsen, K.G., Nielsen, M. (eds.) CONCUR 2001. LNCS, vol. 2154, pp. 381–395. Springer, Heidelberg (2001)
5. Baresi, L., Spoletini, P.: On the use of Alloy to analyze graph transformation systems. In: Corradini, A., Ehrig, H., Montanari, U., Ribeiro, L., Rozenberg, G. (eds.) ICGT 2006. LNCS, vol. 4178, pp. 306–320. Springer, Heidelberg (2006)
6. Bézivin, J., Büttner, F., Gogolla, M., Jouault, F., Kurtev, I., Lindow, A.: Model transformations? Transformation models! In: Nierstrasz, O., Whittle, J., Harel, D., Reggio, G. (eds.) MoDELS 2006. LNCS, vol. 4199, pp. 440–453. Springer, Heidelberg (2006)
7. Brucker, A.D., Wolff, B.: The HOL-OCL book. Technical Report 525, ETH Zurich (2006)
8. Cabot, J., Clarisó, R., Guerra, E., de Lara, J.: Analysing graph transformation rules through OCL. In: Vallecillo, A., Gray, J., Pierantonio, A. (eds.) ICMT 2008. LNCS, vol. 5063, pp. 225–239. Springer, Heidelberg (2008)
9. Cabot, J., Clarisó, R., Riera, D.: Verification of UML/OCL class diagrams using constraint programming. In: MoDeVVa 2008. ICST Workshop (2008)
10. Giese, H., Glesner, S., Leitner, J., Schfer, W., Wagner, R.: Towards verified model transformations. In: ModeVVa 2006 (2006)
11. Greenyer, J., Kindler, E.: Reconciling TGGs with QVT. In: Engels, G., Opdyke, B., Schmidt, D.C., Weil, F. (eds.) MODELS 2007. LNCS, vol. 4735, pp. 16–30. Springer, Heidelberg (2007)
12. Guerra, E., de Lara, J.: Event-driven grammars: Relating abstract and concrete levels of visual languages. Journal on Software and System Modeling, special section on ICGT 2004, 317–347 (2007)
13. Heckel, R., Küster, J.M., Taentzer, G.: Confluence of typed attributed graph transformation systems. In: Corradini, A., Ehrig, H., Kreowski, H.-J., Rozenberg, G. (eds.) ICGT 2002. LNCS, vol. 2505, pp. 161–176. Springer, Heidelberg (2002)
14. Jouault, F., Allilaire, F., Bézivin, J., Kurtev, I., Valduriez, P.: ATL: a QVT-like transformation language. In: OOPSLA Companion, pp. 719–720. ACM, New York (2006)
15. Küster, J.M.: Definition and validation of model transformations. Journal on Software and Systems Modeling 5(3), 233–259 (2006)
16. Lin, Y., Zhang, J., Gray, J.: A framework for testing model transformations. In: Model-driven Software Development, pp. 219–236. Springer, Heidelberg (2005)
17. OMG. MOF 2.0 Query/View/Transformation specification (2007)
18. Rozenberg, G. (ed.): Handbook of Graph Grammars and Computing by Graph Transformations. Foundations, vol. 1. World Scientific, Singapore (1997)
19. Schürr, A.: Specification of graph translators with triple graph grammars. In: Mayr, E.W., Schmidt, G., Tinhofer, G. (eds.) WG 1994. LNCS, vol. 903, pp. 151–163. Springer, Heidelberg (1995)

20. Sen, S., Baudry, B., Precup, D.: Partial model completion in model driven engineering using constraint logic programming. In: Proc. INAP 2007 (2007)
21. Straeten, R.V.D., Mens, T., Simmonds, J., Jonckers, V.: Using description logic to maintain consistency between UML models. In: Stevens, P., Whittle, J., Booch, G. (eds.) UML 2003. LNCS, vol. 2863, pp. 326–340. Springer, Heidelberg (2003)
22. Varró, D.: Automated formal verification of visual modeling languages by model checking. Journal on Software and System Modeling 3(2), 85–113 (2004)
23. Wang, J., Kim, S.-K., Carrington, D.A.: Verifying metamodel coverage of model transformations. In: ASWEC 2006, pp. 270–282. IEEE Computer Society, Los Alamitos (2006)

Precise Semantics of EMF Model Transformations by Graph Transformation

Enrico Biermann[1], Claudia Ermel[1], and Gabriele Taentzer[2]

[1] Technische Universität Berlin, Germany
{enrico,lieske}@cs.tu-berlin.de
[2] Philipps-Universität Marburg, Germany
taentzer@mathematik.uni-marburg.de

Abstract. Model transformation is one of the key activities in model-driven software development. An increasingly popular technology to define modeling languages is provided by the Eclipse Modeling Framework (EMF). Several EMF model transformation approaches have been developed, focusing on different transformation aspects. To validate model transformations wrt. functional behavior and correctness, a formal foundation is needed. In this paper, we define EMF model transformations as a special kind of typed graph transformations using node type inheritance. Containment constraints of EMF model transformations are translated to a special kind of EMF model transformation rules such that their application leads to consistent transformation results only. Thus, we identify a kind of EMF model transformations which behave like algebraic graph transformations. As a consequence, the rich theory of algebraic graph transformation can be applied to these EMF model transformations to show functional behavior and correctness. We illustrate our approach by selected refactorings of simplified statechart models.

Keywords: Model-driven software development, Eclipse Modeling Framework, model transformation, graph transformation.

1 Introduction

Model-driven software development is considered as a promising paradigm in software engineering. Models are ideal means for abstraction and enable developers to master the increasing complexity of software systems. Since models are central artifacts in model-driven software development, the quality of generated software is directly dependent on the quality of models. Modifying models (i.e. performing model refactoring [10]) to improve the understandability and refine the model structure is an important part of model development. Throughout this work, we use model refactoring as an example for precisely specifying model transformations.

The Eclipse Modeling Framework (EMF) [4] has evolved to one of the standard technologies to define modeling languages. EMF provides a modeling and code generation framework for Eclipse applications based on structured data models. The modeling approach is similar to that of MOF, actually EMF supports Essential MOF (EMOF) as part of the OMG MOF 2.0 specification.

K. Czarnecki et al. (Eds.): MoDELS 2008, LNCS 5301, pp. 53–67, 2008.

Containment relations, i.e. aggregations, define an ownership relation between objects. Thereby, they induce a tree structure in model instantiations. In MOF and EMF, this tree structure is further used to implement a mapping to XML, known as XMI (XML Meta data Interchange) [13]. Containment always implies a number of constraints for model instantiations that must be ensured at run-time. As semantical constraints for containment edges, the MOF specification states the following:

- *"An object may have at most one container."*
- *"Cyclic containment is invalid."*

As mentioned earlier, EMF provides full implementations of instance models. These implementations always ensure these constraints. A third constraint may be useful for storing EMF models: *"There is a distinguished object, the root object, which contains (transitively) all other model objects."*

Model-driven development relies heavily on model transformations. EMF models can be manipulated by several approaches to rule-based model transformations. A transformation framework for EMF models which follows the concepts of algebraic graph transformation [5] as far as possible, is presented in [2]. But EMF model transformation does not always behave like algebraic graph transformation. The main reason is the difficulty to always satisfy the containment constraints of EMF.

In this paper, we define EMF models as typed graphs with containment edges. We identify a kind of model transformation rules which lead to consistent EMF model graphs, if applied as normal graph transformation rules to consistent EMF model graphs. Thus, we identify a kind of EMF model transformations which behave like algebraic graph transformations. The advantage of this approach is that we can apply the rich theory of algebraic graph transformation to EMF model transformations for validation.

Our approach is illustrated by selected refactorings of simplified statechart models. The abstract syntax definition of statechart models mostly follows that in the UML2 EMF model [6], but does not consider regions, state actions, and structured transition inscriptions. Thus, we concentrate on the main statechart structure. Structural improvements of statecharts might comprise a number of refactoring steps. The theory provided by graph transformation helps us to identify a certain refactoring order by analyzing dependencies between refactoring rules. Moreover, refactoring steps might be in conflict to each other. Here, the graph transformation theory is helpful in analyzing potential conflicts between refactoring rules (see also [9]). Last but not least, a complex refactoring cannot be realized by just one rule. Therefore, termination is another issue which will be shown by checking sufficient termination criteria.

2 EMF Models as Graphs

In this section, we start to lay the basis for the application of graph transformation theory to EMF model transformations. As first step, we consider EMF instance models[1] as typed graphs with containment edges. Typing is expressed by a so-called type graph.

[1] Note that the EMF community uses the terms "EMF model" for metamodel and "EMF instance model" for a model conforming to a metamodel.

It has some similarities to a metamodel, but does not contain multiplicities and other constraints. Those have to be expressed by graph constraints, as done in [11].

Since containment plays a special role in EMF models, we distinguish a special kind of edge types defining containments. For being able to check for containment cycles later, we identify containment types (called *cycle-capable*) which may be part of containment cycles, summarized in C_{Cycle}[2]. Type graphs with containment types are called sound, if there is a root type which transitively contains all other concrete types.

Definition 1 (Graph). *A graph $G = (G_N, G_E, s_G, t_G)$ consists of a set G_N of nodes, a set G_E of edges, as well as source and target functions $s_G, t_G : G_E \to G_N$.*

Definition 2 (Type graph). *A type graph $TG = (T, I, A, C)$ consisting of graph $T = (N, E, s, t)$, a graph I, called* inheritance graph *sharing the same set of nodes N with T (but not the edges), a set $A \subseteq N$ of* abstract nodes, *and a set $C \subseteq E$ of* containment edges.

For each node n in I the inheritance clan *is defined by $clan_I(n) = \{n' \in N \mid \exists$ path $n' \xrightarrow{*} n$ in $I\}$ where path of length 0 is included, i.e. $n \in clan_I(n)$.*

Furthermore we define a containment relation[3]

$$contains_{TG} = \{(n,m) \in N \times N \mid \exists c \in C \wedge x, y \in N : s(c) = x \text{ with } n \in clan(x) \wedge t(c) = y \text{ with } m \in clan(y)\} \cup \{(x,y) \in N \times N \mid \exists z \in N : (x\ contains_{TG}\ z \wedge z\ contains_{TG}\ y)\}$$

Based on $contains_{TG}$ we create the equivalence relation
$equiv_{contains} = r(contains_{TG}) - \{(x,y) \in contains_{TG} | (y,x) \notin contains_{TG}\}$.
with r being the reflexive closure of $contains_{TG}$. Then we define
$C_{Cycle} = \{c \in C | \exists v_s \in clan(s(c)) \wedge \exists v_t \in clan(t(c)) : (v_s, v_t) \in equiv_{contains}\}$ *as a subset of cycle-capable containment edges that might be part of containment cycles.*

Type graph TG is called sound, *if there is a type node $r \in N - A$, called* root type, *such that the following holds: $\forall n \in N - A - \{r\} : (r, n) \in contains_{TG}$.*

Example 1 (EMF model for simplified statecharts). In the running example, we consider the refactoring of a simplified form of statecharts. In Fig. 1 an EMF model for a simplified statecharts variant is shown. Events, actions, and parallel regions are not shown. Nevertheless, this model is interesting from the containment point of view: The type graph is sound, since type $StateMachine$ contains all concrete types, i.e. is the root type. Type $Vertex$ is contained in $StateMachine$ as well as in $State$. Since $State$ inherits from $Vertex$, it is again contained in $State$. Due to the same reason, $Pseudostate$ is contained in $State$. Moreover, $Transition$ and $FinalState$ are contained in $State$. Please note that $NamedElement$ is abstract and does not have to be contained in the root type. The containment edge of types $superState\_subState$ can be part of containment cycles because a $State$ is either the source of the edge or it is in the clan of $Vertex$ (the target of the edge). Pairs $(State, State)$, $(State, FinalState)$, and $(FinalState, State)$ are in the equivalence relation. Thus, a $State$ (resp. $FinalState$) may contain $States$ (resp. $FinalStates$) and form containment cycles.

[2] Cycle-capable containment types would be containment loops in a flattened type graph without inheritance.

[3] If there is no confusion, we use infix notation for $contains_{TG}$, e.g. $(x\ contains_{TG}\ y)$ instead of $(x, y) \in contains_{TG}$.

Please note that the multiplicities shown in Fig. 1 are not formalized by type graphs, but have to be expressed by additional graph constraints [11] (not shown here).

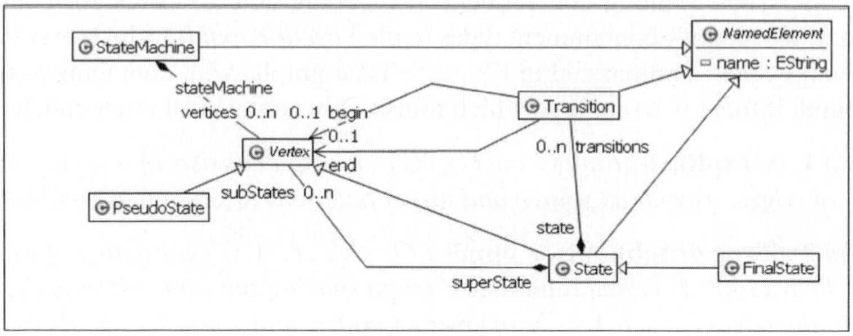

Fig. 1. EMF model for simplified statecharts

Now we define EMF instance models as typed graphs where each object node has at most one container and no containment cycles do occur. Graphs fulfilling these requirements are called *graphs with containment*. Although EMF instance models do not need to be rooted in general, this property is important for storing them, or more general, to define the model's extent.

Definition 3 (Typed Graph). *Given a type graph $TG = (T, I, A, C)$ and a graph G. Graph G is typed over TG, written type: $G \to TG$, if for all $e \in G_E$ holds*

$$type_{G_N} \circ s_G(e) \in clan_I(s_T \circ type_{G_E}(e)) \text{ and } type_{G_N} \circ t_G(e) \in clan_I(t_T \circ type_{G_E}(e)).$$

type is called a clan morphism. It is called concrete *if $\forall n \in G_N : type_{G_N}(n) \notin A$. Given a second clan morphism $type' : G \to TG$, $type'$ is* finer *than type, if*

$$type'_{G_N}(n) \in clan_I(type_{G_N}(n)) \text{ for all } n \in G_N \text{ and } type'_E = type_E.$$

Definition 4 (Graph with containment (C-graph)). *A graph with containment, short C-graph, is a graph G with a distinguished set of containment edges $G_C \subseteq G_E$. The containment edges induce the following transitive binary relation $contains_G$:*

- $contains_G = \{(x, y) \in G_N \times G_N \mid \exists e \in G_C : (s_G(e) = x \wedge t_G(e) = y)\} \cup$
  $\{(x, y) \in G_N \times G_N \mid \exists z \in G_N : (x \; contains_G \; z \wedge z \; contains_G \; y)\}$

All containment edges must fulfill the following properties (containment constraints):

- $e_1, e_2 \in G_C : t_G(e_1) = t_G(e_2) \Rightarrow e_1 = e_2$ *(at most one container).*
- $(x, x) \notin contains_G$ *for all $x \in G_N$ (no containment cycles).*

If G is typed over $TG = (T, I, A, C)$, there is a clan morphism type: $G \to TG$ which is consistent with containment, i.e. $\forall e \in G_C : type_{G_E}(e) \in C$

Please note that type graph TG is no C-graph.

Definition 5 (Rooted graph). *A C-graph G is called* rooted, *if there is a node $r \in G_N$, called* root node, *such that* $\forall x \in G_N$ *with* $x \neq r : r\ contains_G\ x$.

Example 2 (EMF instance model). Fig. 2 shows the main parts of a simple statechart modeling a phone. The containment can be well seen in the tree-like representation. However, source and target states of transitions are not shown in the tree view, but in a separate properties view (at the right bottom). It shows the properties of transition *caller hangs up* from state *DialTone* to state *Idle*. In addition, a purely graphical view of the same statechart is depicted on the right which is especially helpful to understand the transition structure inside of state *Phone*. This instance model fulfills both containment constraints and is rooted by a node of type *StateMachine*.

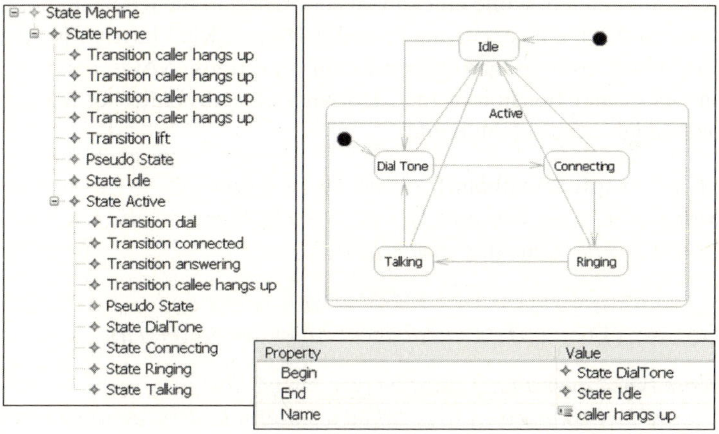

Fig. 2. EMF instance model of a simple phone

In this paper, we concentrate on the structural issues of EMF models and their formalization. Needless to say that objects also may have typed attributes. They can be formalized by attributed graphs as done in [5]. For the application of graph transformation theory presented in Section 5, attributes will play a minor role.

3 EMF Transformation Rules as Consistent Graph Rules

In this section, we start to define a special kind of graph transformation which formalizes a form of EMF model transformation leading always to EMF models consistent with typing and containment constraints. For that purpose, the form of allowed transformation rules has to be restricted. Consistent transformation rules allow the following kinds of actions which change containments:

1. Delete an object node with its containment relation.
2. Create a new object node and connect it immediately to its container.
3. Delete a containment relation together with its contained object node or change the container.

4. Create a containment relation with the contained object node or change the container.
5. Create cycle-capable containment edges only, if the old and the new container are both transitively contained in the same container.

Before we are able to precisely define consistent graph rules, we have to define relations between typed C-graphs, so-called C-graph morphisms. They define mappings of nodes and edges respectively, such that they are compatible with typing, source, and target functions. C-graph morphisms are needed to define graph rules such that the left (LHS) and the right-hand sides (RHS) are specified as well as the mapping from left to right. While the LHS defines the pattern to be found in the model, its relation to RHS formulates the actions to be performed. All object nodes and edges which occur in LHS but not in RHS are deleted, while all elements occurring in the RHS and not in the LHS are newly created. Elements occurring in both LHS and RHS have to be identified but are not changed. Moreover, negative application conditions (NACs) can be formulated. A NAC consists of an extension of the LHS where the structure not being part of the LHS is prohibited to occur in the model.

Definition 6 (C-graph morphism). *Given two C-graphs G, H, a pair of functions (f_N, f_E) with $f_N : G_N \to H_N$ and $f_E : G_E \to H_E$ forms a valid C-graph morphism $f : G \to H$, if it has the following properties:*

- $f_N \circ s_G(e) = s_H \circ f_E(e)$, $f_N \circ t_G(e) = t_H \circ f_E(e)$, *and*
- $\forall e \in G_C \Rightarrow f_E(e) \in H_C$ *(containment edges are preserved).*

If G and H are typed over TG, f must be type compatible, i.e. $type_G = type_H \circ f$. If f_N and f_E are inclusions, then G is called a subgraph of H, denoted by $G \subseteq H$.

The conditions in Def. 7 are due to the use of abstract types for rule elements and express that *1.* retyping of elements is not allowed, 2. newly created object nodes must be concretely typed, and *3.* node types occurring in NACs may be finer than in the LHS.

Definition 7 (Graph rule). *A graph rule typed over a type graph $TG = (T, I, A, C)$ is given by $p = (L \supseteq K \subseteq R,\ type,\ NAC)$, where L, K and R are C-graphs, type is a triple of typing clan morphisms $type = (type_L\colon L \to TG,\ type_K\colon K \to TG,\ type_R\colon R \to TG)$, and NAC is a set of pairs $nac_i = (N_i, type_{N_i}), i \in \mathbb{N}$ with $L \subseteq N_i$, and $type_{N_i}\colon N_i \to TG$ a typing clan morphism, such that the following conditions hold:*

1. $type_L \supseteq type_K \subseteq type_R$
2. $type_{R_N}(R'_N) \cap A = \emptyset$ *where* $R'_N := R_N - K_N$, *and*
3. $type_{N_i}$ is finer than $type_L$ *for all* $(N_i, type_{N_i}) \in NAC$

In the following definition, we formalize all actions that preserve consistent containment relations which have been described in the beginning of this section.

Definition 8 (Consistent graph rule). *Let $R'_C := R_C - K_C, L'_N := L_N - K_N$ and $L'_C := L_C - K_C$. A graph rule $p = (L \supseteq K \subseteq R,\ type,\ NAC)$* is consistent *wrt. containment if the following constraints are satisfied:*

1. *(node deletion)* $\forall n \in L'_N : \exists e \in L'_C$ *with* $t_{L'_C}(e) = n$,
2. *(node creation)* $\forall n \in R'_N : \exists e \in R'_C$ *with* $t_R(e) = n$,
3. *(containment edge deletion)* $\forall e \in L'_C$ *with* $t_L(e) = n$:
   $$n \in L'_N \quad \vee \quad (n \in K_N \wedge \exists e' \in R'_C \text{ with } t_R(e') = n)$$
4. *(containment edge creation)* $\forall e \in R'_C$ *with* $t_R(e) = n$:
   $$n \in R'_N \quad \vee \quad (n \in K_N \wedge \exists e' \in L'_C \text{ with } t_L(e') = n)$$
5. *(creation of cycle-capable containment edges)*
   $\forall e \in R'_C$ *with* $s(e) = n \wedge t(e) = m : \exists e' \in L'_C$ *with* $s(e') = o \wedge t(e') = m$:
   $$((o, n) \in contains_L \wedge (m, n) \notin contains_L) \vee (n, o) \in contains_L$$

Example 3 (Refactoring rules). In Figs. 3 to 5, we show three statecharts refactorings specified as EMF rules. Please note that object nodes with the same number mean that they are equal. The first one in Fig. 3 removes an isolated state from a composite state. Isolated means that no state or transition is contained and no transition starts or ends at this state. These constraints are guaranteed by the so-called *dangling condition* which allows the application of a graph transformation rule only if no edges are connected to nodes which are deleted by the rule (see Def. 9). This rule is consistent, since the isolated state node is deleted together with its containment edge.

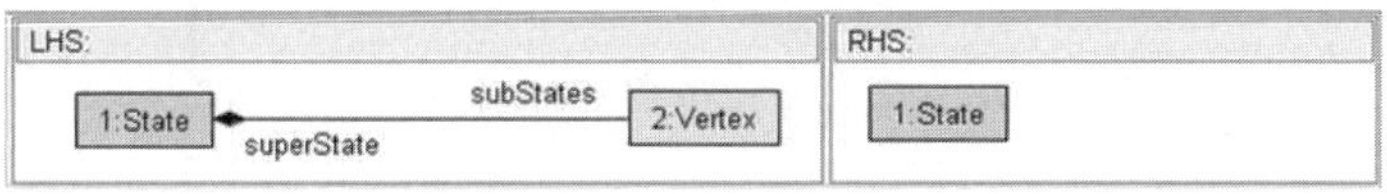

Fig. 3. Refactoring "Remove isolated state"

Two transitions with the same source, the same target, and the same name are considered as redundant and can be removed by the graph rule in Fig. 4. This rule is consistent, since the redundant transition node is deleted together with its containment edge.

The third refactoring folds two transitions with the same name if the original target states are contained in the same super state. This refactoring consists of two rules, depicted in Fig. 5 which are applied as long as possible. While the upper rule folds two transitions both going to substates, the rule at the bottom folds a transition to a substate with the transition to its superstate having the same name. The application of both rules together allows folding of an arbitrary number of such transitions. The upper rule in Fig. 5 has to be equipped with a NAC isomorphic to the right-hand side to be sure that

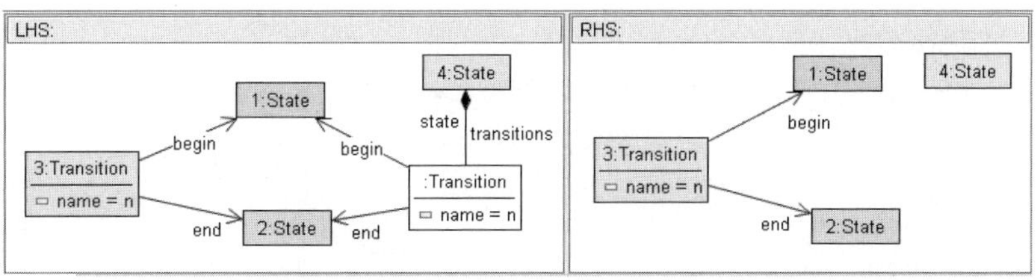

Fig. 4. Refactoring "Delete redundant transition"

a transition like the new one does not already exist. This rule is consistent, since both transitions are deleted with their containment edges, while the new transition comes along with a new containment edge. The rule at the bottom of Fig. 5 is also consistent, since a transition is deleted together with its containment edge.

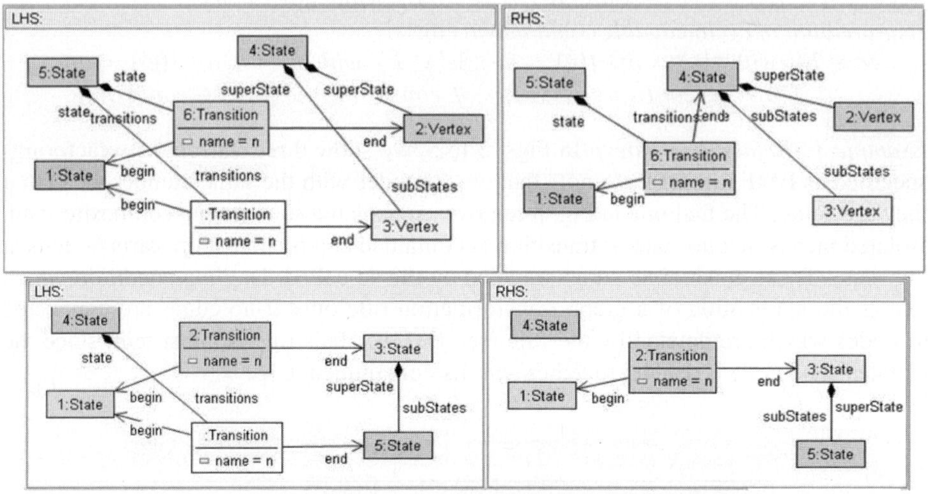

Fig. 5. Refactoring "Fold incoming transitions"

The last refactoring moves a state out of a composite state up to the surrounding one. This is possible, if all adjacent transitions already belong to the surrounding state. This condition is checked by two similar NACs, one of which is shown together with the rule in Fig. 6. The second NAC differs from the first one only in checking a similar condition for incoming transitions.

This rule changes the containment relation of a state, i.e. its containment edge is deleted and a new one is created. Therefore, cond. 3 and 4 of Def. 8 are fulfilled. Since *superState* is cycle-capable, Cond. 5 has to be checked, too. The edge from *State* 1 to 3 is newly created, thus there has to be a containment relation from *State* 1 to *State* 2 in LHS and no containment relation from *State* 3 to 1. These two conditions are fulfilled, thus this rule is also consistent.

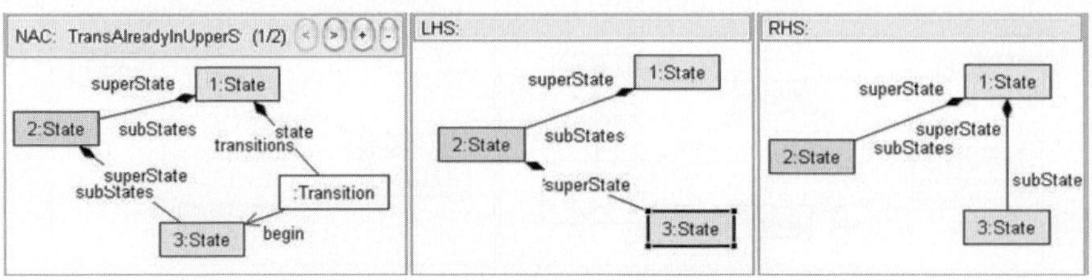

Fig. 6. Refactoring "Move State Up"

Summarizing, all refactorings can be formalized as consistent graph rules, since containment edges are deleted only if their corresponding containments are deleted. All newly created object nodes are created together with their containment edges. In the last refactoring rule, the container is changed consistently.

4 EMF Model Transformation as Consistent Graph Transformation Sequence

Having specified the kind of transformation rules which obey containment constraints, we define EMF model transformations as sequences of consistent graph transformation steps now. Thereafter, the main result of this contribution is presented. We show that each graph transformation step applying a consistent graph rule keeps the consistency of containment edges. Furthermore, we show that the application of consistent graph rules does not destroy roots.

A consistent rule may be applied to a graph (cf. Def. 9) if

1. Nodes are deleted only, if all adjacent edges occur in the rule as items to be deleted,
2. rule items may be matched with one and the same graph item if they are preserved,
3. more abstractly typed nodes may be mapped to finer typed nodes, and
4. all NACs are fulfilled where NAC-nodes may also be more abstractly typed than graph nodes.

Definition 9 (Matching and application of graph rules). *Let $p = (L \supseteq K \subseteq R, type, NAC)$ be a graph rule typed over TG, $(G, type_G)$ a typed C-graph with $type_G \colon G \to TG$ being a concrete clan morphism, and $m \colon L \to G$ a C-graph morphism. Then m is a match with respect to p and $(G, type_G)$, if*

1. m fulfills the so-called dangling condition, *i.e. $\forall n \in L'_N : \nexists e \in G_E - m_G(L_E)$ with $s_G(e) = m_N(n) \vee t_G(e) = m_N(n)$*
2. m fulfills the identification condition *for nodes, i.e. $\forall x_1, x_2 \in L_N$ with $m_N(x_1) = m_N(x_2) : x_1, x_2 \in K_N$ (analogously for edges)*
3. $type_G \circ m$ is finer than $type_L$.
4. m satisfies NAC, i.e. for each $nac_i = (N_i, type_{N_i}) \in NAC, i \in J$ there does not exists a C-graph morphism $o_i \colon N_i \to G$ such that $o_i|_L = m$ and $type_G \circ o_i$ is finer than $type_{N_i}$.

Given a match m, rule p can be applied to $(G, type_G)$ yielding a direct transformation $(G, type_G) \stackrel{p,m}{\Longrightarrow} (H, type_H)$ with concretely typed graph $(H, type_H)$ defined as in [5].

The transformation definition in [5] is based on the double-pushout construction in the category of typed graphs and graph morphisms which is unique up to isomorphism. Result graph H is constructed as by taking the original graph G, deleting all items in the LHS and not in the RHS, and then adding all RHS-items not being in the LHS, disjointly. That means all newly created items get new identifiers:

- $H_N = G_N - m_N(L_N - K_N) \uplus (R_N - K_N)$
- $H_E = (G_E - m_E(L_E - K_E) \uplus (R_E - K_E)$

- $s_H(e) = $ if $e \in G_E$ then $s_G(e)$ else: if $s_R(e) \in K_N$ then $m_N(s_R(e))$ else $s_R(e)$
- analogously for t_H
- $type_{H_N}(n) = $ if $n \in G_N$ then $type_{G_N}(n)$ else $type_{R_N}(n)$
- analogously for $type_{H_E}$

Example 4 (Result model). Fig. 7 shows the main parts of the simple statechart in Fig. 2 after applying refactoring *Fold incoming transitions*. All the transitions going to state *Idle* have been replaced by only one from state *Active*. This is possible, since all these transitions had the same name. Again the tree-like and the diagram view are shown, together with the properties view for the new transition *caller hangs up*.

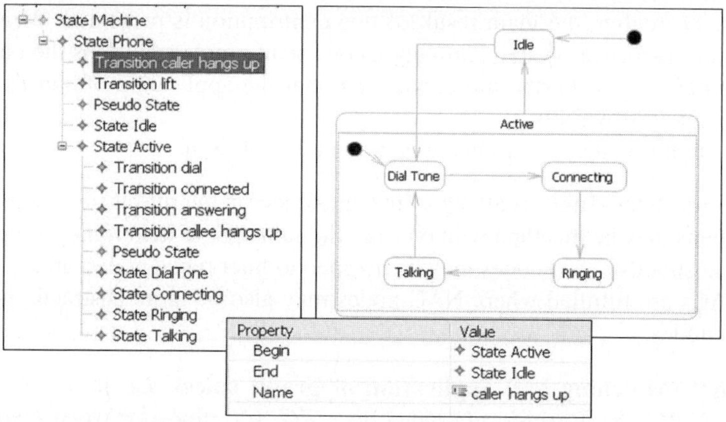

Fig. 7. EMF instance model of Fig. 2 after refactoring

Theorem 1 (Consistent graph transformation step). *Given a consistent graph rule* $p = (L \supseteq K \subseteq R, type, NAC)$ *and a match* $L \xrightarrow{m} G$ *to a C-graph G which is concretely typed by* $type_G \colon G \rightarrow TG$*. Then, the result graph* $(H, type_H)$ *of direct transformation* $(G, type_G) \overset{p,m}{\Longrightarrow} (H, type_H)$ *is a C-graph.*

Proof. See Section A.1 in the appendix.

Theorem 2 (Rooted graph transformation step). *Given a consistent graph rule* $p = (L \supseteq K \subseteq R, type, NAC)$ *and a match* $L \xrightarrow{m} G$ *to a rooted graph G which is concretely typed by* $type_G \colon G \rightarrow TG$ *and satisfies* NAC*. Then, the result graph* $(H, type_H)$ *of the direct transformation* $(G, type_G) \overset{p,m}{\Longrightarrow} (H, type_H)$ *is rooted.*

Proof. See Section A.2 in the appendix.

5 Towards Formal Validation of EMF Transformations

Having clarified the kind of EMF model transformations that can be formalized by algebraic graph transformation, we sketch how the rich graph transformation theory [5] can be applied to EMF model transformations. The theory is presented informally, just to give an idea how it can be applied in the context of EMF model transformations.

5.1 Conflicts and Dependencies

Graph transformation theory allows us to compute conflicts and dependencies of transformations by relying on the idea of critical pair analysis. The general-purpose graph transformation tool AGG [1] provides an algorithm implementing this analysis.

Critical pair analysis is known from term rewriting and can be used to check if a rewriting system contains conflicting computations. Critical pairs formalize the idea of showing a conflicting situation in a minimal context. From the set of all critical pairs we can extract the objects and links which cause conflicts or dependencies.

To construct minimal critical graphs, we basically consider all overlapping graphs of the left-hand sides of two rules with the obvious matches. If one of the rules contains NACs, extensions of the left-hand sides by parts of the corresponding NACs also have to be considered for the construction of overlapping graphs. The reasons why graph rules can be in conflict are threefold:

1. One rule application deletes a graph item which is in the match of another rule application (*delete-use* conflict).
2. One rule application produces a graph item that gives rise to a graph structure that is forbidden by a NAC of another rule application (*produce-forbid* conflict).
3. One rule application changes attributes being in the match of another rule.

AGG supports critical pair analysis for typed attributed graph transformations. As an important observation of the critical pair analysis, we can conclude that there is a preferred order for rule applications and reduce the number of actual conflicts in a transformation sequence. This is important for complex transformation sequences consisting of a number of steps to reach a certain goal. If all critical pairs can be resolved such that they can lead to the same result, the transformation system is called *locally confluent.*

Example 5 (Analyzing EMF model refactorings). Since all refactoring rules in the running example are consistent graph rules, the critical pair analysis is also available for EMF model refactorings. In [9], we have shown that critical pair analysis can be used to detect conflicts and dependencies between refactorings of class models. A formal specification of refactorings as graph transformation rules allows us to reason about dependencies between different types of refactorings. Due to the results presented in this paper, such an analysis is now available for EMF model refactorings.

Consider for example the application of refactoring rule *MoveStateUp* in Fig. 6 two times in parallel. It might happen that a state (2) which shall be moved out has a substate (6) that shall also be moved out. In that case, the substates relation between state (2) and its superstate (1) has to be deleted and is also used. Thus, we can identify a delete-use conflict here. Fig. 8 shows the critical pair for this conflict[4]. This conflict can be resolved by moving inner states up at first.

5.2 Termination Criteria

Besides conflicts and dependencies, we can also apply the developed termination criteria for graph transformation to consistent EMF model transformations. A locally confluent and terminating transformation system is confluent in general and thus shows a

[4] Note that rules and graphs are no longer shown as EMF instance models but as AGG graphs.

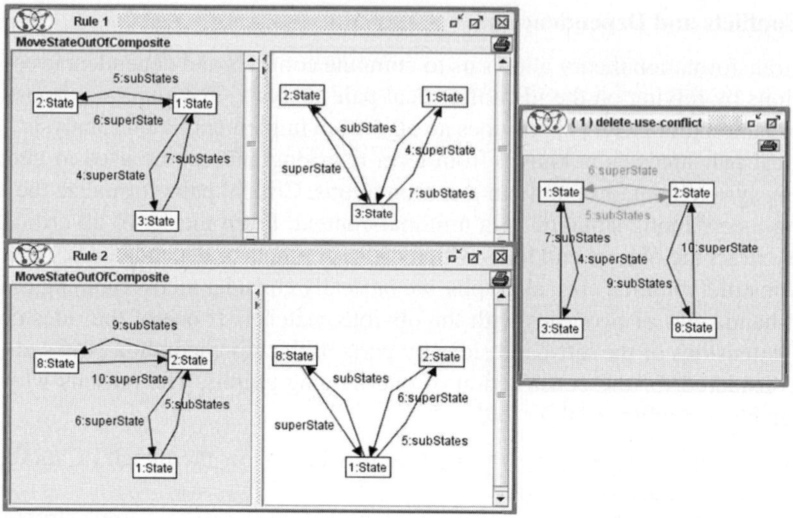

Fig. 8. Conflicting applications of Rule *MoveStateUp* two times

functional behavior. That means for each input there is a unique transformation result. In general, termination is undecidable for graph transformation systems. But if a system meets certain termination criteria, we can conclude that it is terminating.

The proof for termination of graph transformation systems [5] is based on layered graph transformation systems with deletion and non-deletion layers. Informally, the deletion layer conditions express that the last creation of a node of a certain type should precede the first deletion of a node of the same type. Furthermore, each rule application should delete more items of a certain type than it creates. Non-deletion layer conditions ensure that if an element of a certain type occurs in the LHS of a rule then all elements of the same type were already created in previous layers.

Termination of statechart refactorings. Considering again the refactoring rules in Section 3, we like to check if the first three refactorings can be applied automatically to optimize a statechart as far as possible. Since the first three rules are deleting ones and each rule decreases the number of model elements, the deletion layer conditions are satisfied and thus the refactoring is terminating. Refactoring rule "Move State Up" is of a different kind. It does not make sense to apply this refactoring automatically, since that would lead to statecharts where all states are contained in the uppermost state. Thus, we do not have to check the termination of applying this rule as long as possible.

6 Related Work and Conclusion

A precise specification of EMF model transformations can be advantageously used to validate important properties such as functional behavior. In this paper, we identified a variant of EMF model transformation that can be defined as algebraic graph transformation with node type inheritance. This result can be used to validate EMF model transformation based on the rich graph transformation theory available. These validation facilities are illustrated by selected model refactorings, formulated for a restricted form of statechart models.

The consistency constraints for transformation rules limit our approach, but not dramatically, since they mostly emerge directly from EMF containment constraints. However, the deletion of a containment relation without contained object might be attractive as it could lead to a detachment of a complete subtree. This kind of implicit deletion is not allowed, hence the deletion of an object tree has to be performed explicitly by applying rules which delete stepwise.

There are a number of model transformation engines which can modify EMF models: ATL [7], Tefkat [8], VIATRA2 [12], MOMEMT [3], etc. Each of these projects can be used to specify model transformations such as the statechart refactorings presented. In contrast to most model transformation engines, MOMEMT has a formal basis given by Maude which might be exploited for validation of EMF model transformations. But to the best of our knowledge, none of the existing transformation approaches supports confluence and termination analysis of EMF model transformations yet. The EMF Transformation Framework [2] currently supports the generation of transformation code in Java and the translation of EMF models and rules to AGG [1], a tool environment for algebraic graph transformation. However, a validation tool for EMF model transformations which seamlessly integrates analysis techniques provided by AGG, is left to future work.

Further valuable forms of quality assurance for EMF model transformation such as guidelines and refactoring as syntactical techniques as well as testing and debugging as semantical forms would make a comprehensive development environment for EMF model transformations perfect.

Acknowledgement. We would like to thank Hartmut Ehrig for his valuable comments on a previous version of this paper.

References

1. AGG Homepage, `http://tfs.cs.tu-berlin.de/agg`
2. Biermann, E., Ehrig, K., Köhler, C., Kuhns, G., Taentzer, G., Weiss, E.: Graphical Definition of In-Place Transformations in the Eclipse Modeling Framework. In: Proc. 9th International Conference on Model Driven Engineering Languages and Systems (MoDELS 2006), Genova, Italy (October 2006)
3. Boronat, A.: MOMENT: A Formal Framework for Model Management. PhD thesis, Universtat Politècnica de València (2007)
4. Eclipse Consortium. Eclipse Modeling Framework (EMF) – Version 2.4 (2008), `http://www.eclipse.org/emf`
5. Ehrig, H., Ehrig, K., Prange, U., Taentzer, G.: Fundamentals of Algebraic Graph Transformation. In: EATCS Monographs in Theoretical Computer Science. Springer, Heidelberg (2006)
6. Eclipse model development tools (2007), `http://www.eclipse.org/modeling/mdt`
7. Jouault, F., Kurtev, I.: Transforming Models with ATL. In: Proc. Workshop Model Transformations in Practice (at MoDELS 2005), Montego Bay, Jamaica (2005)
8. Lawley, M., Steel, J.: Practical Declarative Model Transformation With Tefkat. In: Proc. Workshop Model Transformation in Practice (at MoDELS 2005) (2005)

9. Mens, T., Taentzer, G., Runge, O.: Analysing refactoring dependencies using graph transformation. Software and System Modeling 6(3), 269–285 (2007)
10. Mens, T., Tourwé, T.: A survey of software refactoring. Transactions on Software Engineering 30(2), 126–139 (2004)
11. Rensink, A., Taentzer, G.: Ensuring structural constraints in graph-based models with type inheritance. In: Cerioli, M. (ed.) FASE 2005. LNCS, vol. 3442, pp. 64–79. Springer, Heidelberg (2005)
12. Varró, D., Balogh, A.: The model transformation language of the viatra2 framework. Sci. Comput. Program 68(3), 214–234 (2007)
13. MOF 2.0 / XMI Mapping Specification (2008), `http://www.omg.org/technology/documents/formal/xmi.htm`

A Proofs

A.1 Proof of Theorem 1

To be shown:
1. $\forall e_1, e_2 \in H_C : t_H(e_1) = t_H(e_2) \implies e_1 = e_2$
2. $(x, x) \notin contains_H$ for all $x \in H_N$

1. Assuming $\exists e_1, e_2 : t_H(e_1) = t_H(e_2)$ and $e_1 \neq e_2$

Case 1: $e_1 \in G_C$ and $e_2 \in G_C$:
Since G is C-Graph, we have $e_1 = e_2$. This contradicts the assumption.

Case 2: $e_1 \in G_C$ and $e_2 \in R'_C$:
Subcase 1: $t(e_2) \in R'_N$:
e_1 is in G and is preserved by p and $t(e_1)$ is preserved as well. So $t_H(e_1) = t_H(m'(e_2))$ contradicts $t(e_2) \in R'_N$.
Subcase 2: $\exists e'_2 \in L'_C$ with $t(e'_2) = t(e_2)$ (due to Cond. 3 and 4 in Def. 8):
$t(e'_2) = t(e_2) = t(e_1) \implies e_1 = e'_2 \in L'_C$ because L is a C-Graph. Therefore e_1 is deleted which contradicts its existence in H.

Case 3: $e_1 \in R'_C$ and $e_2 \in R'_C$.
Due to Cond. 1, 3 and 4 in Def. 8, we have three subcases:
Subcase 1: $t(e_1) \in R'_C$ and $t(e_2) \in R'_C$:
$t(e_1) = t(e_2) \implies e_1 = e_2$ because R is C-graph.
Subcase 2: $t(e_1) \in R'_C$ and $\exists e'_2 \in L'_C$ with $t(e'_2) = t(e_2)$
$t(e_2)$ is preserved by p and $t(e_1)$ is created. Therefore $t(e_1) \neq t(e_2)$ which contradicts the assumption.
Subcase 3 $\exists e'_1 \in L'_C$ with $t(e'_1) = t(e_1)$ and $\exists e'_2 \in L'_C$ with $t(e'_2) = t(e_2)$
R is a C-Graph and e_1 and $e_2 \in R_C$. So $t_R(e_1) = t_R(e_2)$ implies $e_1 = e_2$ and further implies $t_H(m'(e_1)) = t_H(m'(e_2))$

2. Assuming $\exists m \in H_N : (m, m) \in contains_H$. Then, there is a newly generated containment path $n \xrightarrow{*} m$ such that $(m, n) \in contains_G \wedge (n, m) \notin contains_G$. Due to Cond. 5 of Def. 8, we have to consider the following two cases for the creation of the last edge $e \in R'_C$ of the path $n \xrightarrow{*} m$, i.e. either an edge $e' \in L'_C$ is "shifted down" (Case 1), or it is "shifted up" (Case 2) in the containment hierarchy.

Case 1: $\exists e' \in L'_C$ with $s(e') = o \wedge t(e') = m : (o,n) \in contains_L \wedge (m,n) \notin contains_L$
$(m,n) \in contains_G \wedge (o,n) \in contains_L \wedge (o,m) \in contains_L \implies (m,n) \in contains_L$ because of the uniqueness of a containment path (since G and L are C-graphs). This contradicts the assumption $\lightning$.

Case 2: $\exists e' \in L'_C$ with $s(e') = o \wedge t(e') = m : (n,o) \in contains_L$
$(o,m) \in contains_L \wedge (n,o) \in contains_L \implies (n,m) \in contains_L \implies (n,m) \in contains_G$ contradicts the assumption $\lightning$.

A.2 Proof of Theorem 2

Assume that $G \overset{p,m}{\Longrightarrow} H$ with G being a rooted graph and H a non-rooted graph. Root node x of G is preserved by each consistent graph rule due to cond. 1 of Def. 8. Hence, $x \in D \implies x \in H$ with x being root node in H. Since H is non-rooted, there exists at least one other node $y \in H$ with $x \neq y$ and $(x,y) \notin contains_H$. There are two possible ways how this situation may result from applying rule p:

1. Node y is generated by p: $\exists y \in R'$.
2. The containment edge e_G with $t(e_G) = y$ is deleted: $\exists e_L \in L' : m(e_L) = e_G$.

Case 1: According to Cond. 2 in Def. 8, for the newly generated node y, there is a containment edge $e_R \in R'_C$ with $t_R(e_R) = y$. The source node of this newly generated containment edge is either another new node $z_R \in R'$ or an already existing node $n_K \in K$. Since only a finite number of new nodes can be generated by p, there is always one already existing node $n_K \in K$, which is the uppermost node of the newly generated containment path with y at the end, i.e. $(n_K, y) \in contains_R$. By comatch $R \overset{m'}{\longrightarrow} H$ we get $n = m'(n_K)$ and $(n,y) \in contains_H$. Since n is preserved by p, we have $m(n_K) = n$ such that $(x,n) \in contains_G \implies (x,n) \in contains_H$. From $(x,n) \in contains_H$ and $(n,y) \in contains_H$ we conclude that $(x,y) \in contains_H$ which contradicts the assumption $\lightning$.

Case 2:
Subcase 2.1: Target node $t(e_G) = y$ is deleted together with e_G. Due to the dangling condition, rule p may be applied only if y does not itself contain a node: $\nexists z : (y,z) \in contains_G$, or if all nodes contained recursively in y are also deleted by the rule: $\forall z : (y,z) \in contains_G : \exists z_L \in L'$ with $m(z_L) = z$. So, no nodes from the disconnected subtree (starting with y) remain in the graph which contradicts the assumption $\lightning$.

Subcase 2.2: Target node $t(e_G) = y$ is preserved by rule p, and by Cond. 3 of Def. 8, a new containment path $n \overset{*}{\longrightarrow} y$ is created. According to Def. 8, Cond. 3, the source node n of the first edge $e \in R'_C$ of path $n \overset{*}{\longrightarrow} y$ is a node preserved by rule p, i.e. $n_K \in K$ with $m(n_K) = n = m'(n_K)$. Hence, we have $(x,n) \in contains_H$ and $(n,y) \in contains_H$ and conclude that $(x,y) \in contains_H$ which contradicts the assumption $\lightning$.

A Formal Metamodel for Problem Frames

Denis Hatebur[1,2], Maritta Heisel[2], and Holger Schmidt[2]

[1] Institut für technische Systeme GmbH, Germany
d.hatebur@itesys.de
[2] University Duisburg-Essen, Faculty of Engineering, Department of Computer Science and Cognitive Science, Workgroup Software Engineering, Germany
{denis.hatebur,maritta.heisel,
holger.schmidt}@uni-duisburg-essen.de

Abstract. Problem frames are patterns for analyzing, structuring, and characterizing software development problems. This paper presents a formal metamodel for problem frames expressed in UML class diagrams and using the formal specification notation OCL. That metamodel clarifies the nature of the different syntactical elements of problem frames, as well as the relations between them. It provides a framework for syntactical analysis and semantic validation of newly defined problem frames, and it prepares the ground for tool support for the problem frame approach.

1 Introduction

It is a widely accepted opinion in the software engineering community that reusing software development knowledge helps to avoid errors and to speed up the development of a software product. One promising attempt that enables software engineers to systematically construct software using a body of accumulated knowledge are *patterns*.

Patterns have been introduced on the level of detailed object oriented design [13]. Today, patterns are defined for different software development activities. *Problem Frames* [20] are patterns that classify software development *problems*. *Architectural styles* are patterns that characterize software architectures [8]. They are also called “architectural patterns”. *Design Patterns* are used for finer-grained software design, while *frameworks* [11] are considered as less abstract, more specialized. Finally, *idioms* are low-level patterns related to specific programming languages [8], and are sometimes called “code patterns”.

It is also acknowledged that the first steps of software development are essential for the success of a software development project, because it is important to eliminate any source of error as early as possible. We believe that it is of particular importance to use patterns already in the requirements analysis phase of the software development life-cycle, as is also advocated by, e.g., Fowler [12] and Sutcliffe et al. [28, 29].

Jackson [19, 20] proposes the concept of problem frames for presenting, classifying, and understanding software development problems. A problem frame is a characterization of a class of problems in terms of the considered requirement, their main components (*domains*), and the connections between these components (*interfaces*, consisting

K. Czarnecki et al. (Eds.): MoDELS 2008, LNCS 5301, pp. 68–82, 2008.

of *shared phenomena*). Once a problem is successfully fitted to a problem frame, its most important characteristics are known.

Jackson defines five basic problem frames, as well as some variants of them. These frames are distinguished in the number and characteristics of the involved domains. Jackson does not claim that these frames are complete in the sense that each software development problem can be decomposed in such a way that all derived subproblems fit to one of his problem frames.

Several new problem frames have been developed, such as the frames presented in [10], architectural frames (combinations of architectural styles and problem frames) [24], a dynamic and a static information frame [21], security problem frames [15, 16, 17], frames for database-related problems [9], and *HCI*Frames [25, 27], which focus on usability problems.

Currently, the notation and semantics of problem frames are not defined *rigorously*. Under these circumstances, it is difficult to decide whether a new problem frame contains errors or contradictions. Some problem frames cannot make sense, e.g., because they would require users to be constrained, which contradicts their domain characteristics.

In this paper, we present a *formal metamodel for problem frames*, which contributes to an unambiguous comprehension of the problem frame approach. This metamodel is expressed in a *Unified Modeling Language* (UML) [31] class model, and the formal specification notation *Object Constraint Language* (OCL) [30]. It clarifies the nature of the different constituents of problem frames, as well as the relations between them.

As a consequence of formalizing the syntax of problem frames and their syntactical elements, the metamodel practically helps designing new problem frames. We equipped the metamodel with a number of *integrity conditions*, that allow one to verify that a frame is valid according to the metamodel. Furthermore, the metamodel provides a basis for *tool support* for the problem frame approach, and it prepares the ground for integrating a problem analysis phase based on problem frames into software development processes.

In the following Sect. 2, we present the problem frames proposed by Jackson [20]. In Sect. 3, we introduce our formal metamodel for the problem frame approach. In Sect. 4, we show how tool support for the problem frame approach can be provided using our formal metamodel, and in Sect. 5, we create and check two sample problem frames with the tool. Section 6 discusses related work, and we conclude in Sect. 7.

2 Problem Frames

Problem frames are a means to describe software development problems. They were invented by Michael Jackson [20], who describes them as follows: *"A problem frame is a kind of pattern. It defines an intuitively identifiable problem class in terms of its context and the characteristics of its domains, interfaces and requirement."* Problem frames are described by *frame diagrams*, which basically consist of rectangles, a dashed oval, and different links between them (see frame diagram in Fig. 1). The task is to construct a *machine* that improves the behavior of the environment in which it is integrated in.

Plain rectangles denote *domains* that already exist in the application environment. Jackson [20, p. 83f] considers three main domain types:

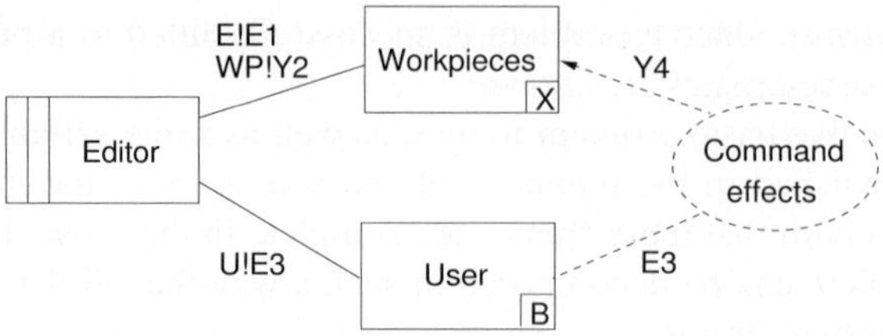

Fig. 1. *Simple workpieces* problem frame

Biddable domains. "*A biddable domain usually consists of people. The most important characteristic of a biddable domain is that it's physical but lacks positive predictable internal causality. That is, in most situations it's impossible to compel a person to initiate an event: the most that can be done is to issue instructions to be followed.*"

Biddable domains are indicated by B, and they are always *given*.

Causal domains. "*A causal domain is one whose properties include predictable causal relationships among its causal phenomena.*"

Often, causal domains are mechanical or electrical equipment. They are indicated with a C in frame diagrams. Their actions and reactions are predictable. Thus, they can be controlled by other domains. Causal domains can be *given* or *designed*.

Lexical domains. "*A lexical domain is a physical representation of data – that is, of symbolic phenomena. It combines causal and symbolic phenomena in a special way. The causal properties allow the data to be written and read.*"

Lexical domains are indicated by X. They are used for data representation purposes. This type of domains can be *given* or *designed*.

A rectangle with a double vertical stripe denotes the machine to be developed, and *requirements* are denoted with a dashed oval. The connecting lines between domains represent interfaces that consist of *shared phenomena*. Shared phenomena may be events, operation calls, messages, and the like. They are observable by at least two domains, but controlled by only one domain, as indicated by an exclamation mark. For example, in Fig. 1 the notation U!E3 means that the phenomena in the set E3 are controlled by the domain User.

A dashed line represents a requirement reference, and an arrow indicates that the requirement *constrains* a domain. If a domain is constrained by the requirement, we must develop a machine, which controls this domain accordingly. In Fig. 1, the Workpieces domain is constrained, because the Editor changes it on behalf of user commands to satisfy the required Command effects.

Software development with problem frames proceeds as follows: first, the environment in which the machine will operate is represented by a *context diagram*. Like a frame diagram, a context diagram consists of domains and interfaces. However, a context diagram contains no requirements, and it is not shown which domain is in control of the shared phenomena. Then, the problem is decomposed into subproblems. If ever possible, the decomposition is done in such a way that the subproblems fit to given problem frames. To fit a subproblem to a problem frame, one must instantiate its frame diagram, i.e., provide instances for its domains, interfaces, and requirement. The instantiated frame diagram is called a *problem diagram*. For example, a requirement such as "Online forms have to be provided that can be filled out by web users" can be used for instantiating the workpieces frame of Fig. 1.

Since the requirements refer to the environment in which the machine must operate, the next step consists in deriving a *specification* for the machine (see [22] for details). The specification describes the machine and is the starting point for its development.

3 A Formal Metamodel for Problem Frames

Based on Jackson's descriptions, we have developed a *formal metamodel for problem frames*. The benefits of such a metamodel are:

- Gain an *unambiguous comprehension* of the problem frame approach.
- *Clarify the syntax* of problem frames and their constituents.
- Provide a framework for *syntactical analysis and validation* of problem frames. This allows one to identify erroneous problem frames.
- Support the development of new problem frames.
- Provide a basis for *tool support* for the problem frame approach by an Eclipse [1] application (see Sect. 4 for details).
- Prepare the ground for integrating a problem analysis phase based on the problem frames approach into software development processes (see [16, 17] for details).

According to Jackson, the syntactical elements of a problem frame can be divided into several categories and subcategories. For example, a domain is either a biddable, causal, or lexical domain. For this reason, a formal method that supports object-orientation is appropriate to formalize problem frames and their syntactical elements. We use a UML [31] class model, and the formal specification notation OCL [30] to construct our formal metamodel for problem frames. The combination of a UML class model and a set of OCL expressions enables us to rapidly provide tool support for the problem frame approach.

In the following, we present the class model in Sect. 3.1, and the set of integrity conditions, expressed in OCL, in Sect. 3.2.

3.1 UML Class Model

In our class model, each syntactical element of a problem frame is represented as a class. Relations between the different elements are expressed using inheritance and associations. The associations are equipped with multiplicities, which express integrity conditions about the minimal or maximal number of occurrences of the syntactical elements in a problem frame. The association ends have names, so that OCL expressions about the objects that participate in an association can be specified (see Sect. 3.2).

Domains have **names** and **abbreviations**, which are used to define interfaces. Hence, the class Domain has the attributes name and abbreviation of type string. According to Jackson, domains are either **designed**, **given**, or **machine** domains. These facts are modeled by the boolean attibutes isGiven and isMachine in Fig. 2.

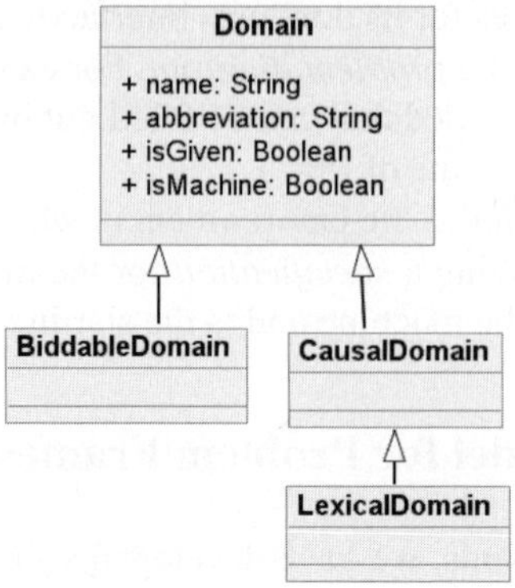

Fig. 2. Inheritance structure of different domain types

Jackson also distinguishes **biddable**, **causal**, and **lexical domains**. Therefore, we introduce the subclasses BiddableDomain, CausalDomain, and LexicalDomain of the class Domain. A lexical domain is a special case of a causal domain. This kind of modeling allows to add further domain types, such as *display domains* as introduced in [10].

Interfaces model connections between domains. The symbol "!" with a prefixed abbreviation of a domain name indicates that the domain *controls* certain **phenomena** contained in the interface. Therefore, we introduce the class Phenomenon, and its subclass InterfacePhenomenon in Fig. 3. Phenomena have **names**. Therefore, the class Phenomenon has an attribute name of type string. Jackson [20, 14] distinguishes **symbolic**, **causal**, and **event** phenomena. We model the different kinds of phenomena as an enumeration type PhenomenonType.

In frame diagrams, **interfaces** connect domains, and they contain phenomena. Therefore, we introduce the class Interface, which has associations to the classes InterfacePhenomenon and Domain. Interfaces connect (connects) at least two domains ([2..*]), and they contain (contains) at least one ([1..*]) phenomenon. Each domain is connected by at least one ([1..*]) interface (isConnectedBy), and each phenomenon is contained in exactly one ([1]) interface (isContainedInIf). An additional association between the class Domain and the class InterfacePhenomenon specifies that each interface phenomenon is controlled by (isControlledBy) exactly one ([1]) domain.

A problem frame contains a **requirement** that refers to certain domains via **requirement references**. A requirement **constrains** at least one domain. Hence, we introduce the classes Requirement, RequirementReference, and its subclass ConstrainingRequirementReference. Furthermore, we introduce associations between the class Requirement and the classes RequirementReference and ConstrainingRequirementReference. The latter two classes have also associations to the class Domain. A domain is either referred to (isReferredToByUsing) or constrained by (isConstrainedByUsing) a requirement reference or not ([0..1]). Each requirement reference is connected to (isConnectedToDomain) exactly one ([1]) domain. A requirement reference or a constraining requirement reference is connected to (isConnectedToReq) exactly one ([1]) requirement. A requirement refers to a domain using (refersToUsing) a requirement reference, and it constrains a domain using (constrainsUsing) at least one ([1..*]) constraining requirement reference.

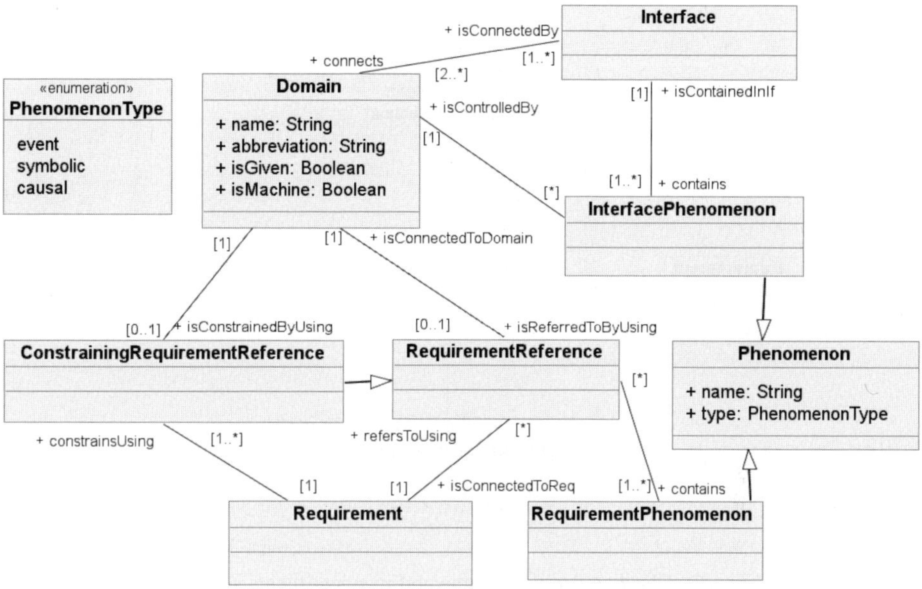

Fig. 3. Problem frames constituents and their relations

Since each (constraining) requirement reference contains phenomena, we introduce a subclass RequirementPhenomenon of the class Phenomenon, which has an association to the class RequirementReference. A (constraining) requirement reference contains (contains) at least one ([1..*]) requirement phenomenon.

According to Jackson, a **problem frame** consists of domains, a requirement, interfaces, and requirement references. Hence, we introduce a class ProblemFrame in Fig. 4. A problem frame consists of one machine domain and at least one additional domain (association end domains with multiplicity [2..*]), exactly one requirement (association end requirement with multiplicity [1]), at least one interface (association end interfaces with multiplicity [1..*]), and at least one constraining requirement reference (association end requirementReferences with multiplicity [1..*]).

3.2 Integrity Conditions

The class model presented in the previous Sect. 3.1 makes it possible to define *integrity conditions* on problem frames and their syntactical elements, which we express in OCL. The class model with its associated integrity conditions constitutes a formal metamodel for the development of new problem frames, as well as for validating and analyzing given problem frames with respect to the metamodel.

OCL is part of UML; it is a notation to describe constraints on object-oriented modeling artefacts such as class models. A constraint is a restriction on one or more values of an object-oriented model. For our metamodel, we make use of *invariants*, which are constraints that must always be fulfilled. Invariants are labeled with the keyword `inv`.

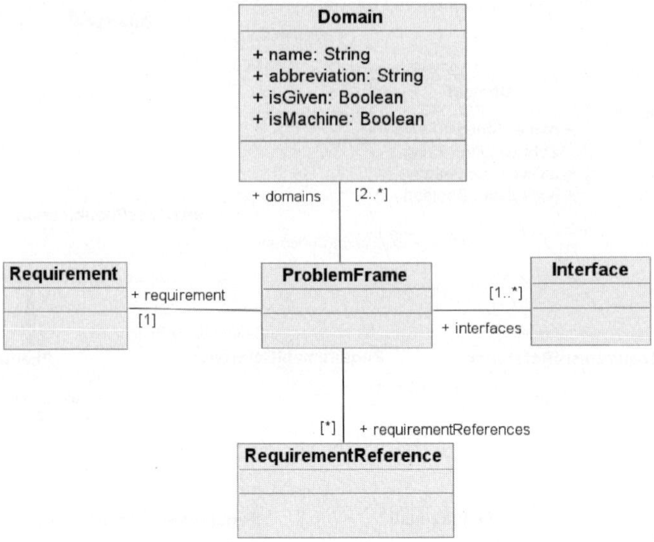

Fig. 4. A problem frame and its constituents

The `context` definition of an OCL expression specifies the model entity for which the OCL expression is defined. In our metamodel, this is usually a class defined in the class model depicted in Figs. 2, 3, and 4. In the following, a selection of the OCL integrity conditions are described, according to their context. The complete set of integrity conditions can be found in Appendix A. All integrity conditions have been checked using the *Octopus OCL Tool for Precise UML Specifications* [4]. The relatively high number of integrity conditions shows that the semantic integrity of problem frames is not trivial.

`context Domain`

A machine domain is always a designed domain. Therefore, a machine domain cannot be a given domain.

```
inv: self.isMachine implies not self.isGiven
```

`context BiddableDomain`

Biddable domains are always given domains.

```
inv: self.isGiven
```

A biddable domain cannot be constrained.

```
inv: self.isConstrainedByUsing->size() = 0
```

`context ProblemFrame`

A phenomenon contained in an interface is controlled by a domain connected by that interface.

```
inv: self.isContainedInIf.connects->includes(
  self.isControlledBy)
```

Each phenomenon contained in an interface is controlled by exactly one domain connected by that interface.

```
inv: self.contains->forAll(p: InterfacePhenomenon |
  self.connects->one(d: Domain |
   p.isControlledBy = d))
```

The machine domain is connected by an interface to a problem domain.

```
inv: self.interfaces->exists(i: Interface |
  self.domains->exists(d: Domain |
  self.domains->exists(m: Domain | m.isMachine and
  m.isConnectedBy->includes(i) and
  d.isConnectedBy->includes(i))))
```

The machine domain controls phenomena contained in an interface it is connected to.

```
inv: self.interfaces->exists(i: Interface |
  i.connects->exists(d: Domain | d.isMachine) and
  i.contains->exists(p: InterfacePhenomenon |
  p.isControlledBy.isMachine))
```

A domain is connected by interfaces, which are part of the problem frame.

```
inv: self.domains->forAll(d: Domain |
  self.interfaces->includesAll(d.isConnectedBy))
```

The names of domains must be unique.

```
inv: self.domains->forAll(d1: Domain |
  self.domains->forAll(d2: Domain |
  (d1.name = d2.name) implies (d1=d2)))
```

The requirement's constraining requirement references and requirement references are those contained in the problem frame.

```
inv: self.requirementReferences->includesAll(
  self.requirement.constrainsUsing)
```

4 Tool Support

Individual problem frames can be described as instantiations of the formal metamodel presented in Sect. 3. This formal metamodel constitutes the basis for the development of tool support for the problem frame approach.

We currently develop an Eclipse [1] application that supports generating newly defined problem frames for requirements analysis. This tool will be a rich graphical problem frame editor that allows one to draw and store problem frames, and will check the integrity conditions specified in the metamodel. We base this application on the open-source frameworks *Eclipse Modeling Framework* (EMF) [2], and *Graphical Editing Framework* (GEF) [3]. As an input for these frameworks, a metamodel specification in, e.g., *XML Metadata Interchange (XMI)* [6] (XML [7] storage format for UML diagrams) can be used. UML tools such as Papyrus UML [5] can generate these XMI files from the models presented in Figs. 2, 3, and 4. The XMI files serve as an input for EMF and GEF to automatically generate tool support for the problem frames approach. Additionally, for all integrity expressions from Appendix A, checks must be implemented or generated.

A a proof of concept, we have used the *Octopus OCL Tool for Precise UML Specifications* [4]. Octopus can check the syntax of the OCL constraints according to a corresponding UML class model. It can also import a class model from a tool supporting the XMI storage format. We used Octopus to check the OCL expressions presented in Appendix A, with the class diagram presented in Sect. 3.1, and to automatically generate a tool to create and edit instances of our formal metamodel for problem frames[1]. The generated tool can check whether a given problem frame is valid according to our formal metamodel[2]. It also generates a user interface prototype and an XML storage facility.

The approach of our formal metamodel and the automatic tool generation with Octopus (and also EMF and GEF) is comparable to the *model-driven architecture* (MDA) approach proposed by the *Object Management Group* (OMG). This approach is based on the metadata architecture including the XMI specification, called the *meta object facility*. A typical metamodels proposed by OMG is the UML metamodel, as it is described in the UML *superstructure* [31].

5 Formalizing and Checking Individual Problem Frames

We used the generated tool to check whether a given problem frame is valid according to our formal metamodel. With its user interface, all elements of a problem frame can be created and connected according to its graphical representation as an instance of the metamodel. The tool stores the instance in an XML file. In this XML file, the tool assigns an identification name to each instance of a class[3]. For each attribute of a class, the tool stores a value, and for each each navigable association end the tool stores the reference names of the connected class instances.

We validated our formal metamodel and the generated tool by instantiating Jackson's basic problem frames. The complete instance of the simple workpieces problem frame (see Fig. 1) can be found in [18]. The tool indeed shows that the instance is valid according to the formal metamodel, i.e., it is type correct and all OCL integrity conditions hold.

To demonstrate that the generated tool supports detecting errors, we consider the erroneous "problem frame" shown in Fig. 5. It is an incorrect variant of the simple workpieces problem frame shown in Fig. 1.

Figure 6 shows the domain *User* defined as a designed domain. According to the formalization of the class BiddableDomain in our metamodel, a biddable domain is always a given domain. Therefore, the generated tool finds an error when checking this OCL integrity condition.

The attribute isConstrainedByUsing has the value id_crr. According to the formalization of the class BiddableDomain in our metamodel, a biddable domain is never con-

[1] Download: http://swe.uni-duisburg-essen.de/en/members/schmidt/pftool/index.php

[2] For OCL expressions with `oclIsTypeOf` no code can be generated by the available version of Octopus.

[3] For better readability, we replaced the automatically assigned numbers by meaningful names in Fig. 6.

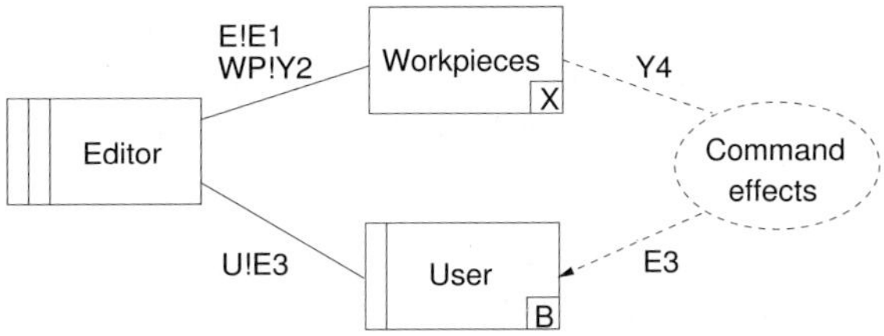

Fig. 5. Erroneous variant of the simple workpieces problem frame shown in Fig. 1

```
<instance id="id_U" class="PF.BiddableDomain">
    <attribute name="name" value="User" />
    <attribute name="abbreviation" value="U" />
    <attribute name="isGiven" value="false" />
    <attribute name="isMachine" value="false" />
    <attribute name="controls" idrefs="␣id_e3" />
    <attribute name="isConnectedBy" idrefs="␣id_i_e3" />
    <attribute name="isConstrainedByUsing" idref="id_crr" />
</instance>
```

Fig. 6. XML specification of the domain *User* of the simple workpieces problem frame shown in Fig. 1

strained. Therefore, the generated tool finds a further error when checking this OCL integrity condition.

The other parts of the erroneous "problem frame" shown in Fig. 5 are valid with respect to our formal metamodel.

6 Related Work

Not much work on providing the problem frame approach with a formal foundation can be found.

Lencastre et al. [23] define a metamodel for problem frames using UML. Their metamodel considers Jackson's whole software development approach based on context diagrams, problem frames, and problem decomposition. In contrast to our metamodel, it only consists of a UML class model. Hence, the OCL integrity conditions of our metamodel are not considered in their metamodel. The approach does not qualify for a metamodel in terms of MDA since, e.g., the class Domain has subclasses Biddable and Given, but an object cannot belong to two classes at the same time (c.f. Fig. 5 and 11 in [23]).

Hall et al. [14] provide a formal semantics for the problem frame approach. They introduce a formal specification language to describe problem frames and problem diagrams. As compared to our metamodel, their approach does not consider integrity conditions.

Seater et al. [26] present a metamodel for problem frame instances. In addition to the diagram elements formalized in our metamodel, they formalize requirements and specifications. Consequently, their integrity conditions ("wellformedness predicate") focus on correctly deriving specifications from requirements. In contrast, our metamodel concentrates on the structure of problem frames and the different domain and phenomena types.

7 Conclusions and Perspectives

In this paper, we have presented a formal metamodel for problem frames, which contains a number of integrity conditions. The metamodel with its integrity conditions constitutes a framework for the development of new problem frames as well as for the semantic validation and syntax checking of individual problem frames with respect to the metamodel. Additionally, it contributes to an unambiguous comprehension of the problem frame approach.

We have shown that such a metamodel with its integrity conditions can be used to automatically generate a tool according to the model-driven architecture approach. We used the metamodel and the generated tool to instantiate Jackson's basic problem frames and to check our own variations of the frames (e.g., [9]).

In the future, we intend to further elaborate our approach in the following directions:

- Apply the metamodel to context diagrams and instantiations of problems frames.
- Consider instantiations of formally defined problem frames, and use these formal descriptions to support the decomposition of problems into subproblems and the composition of the solutions developed for the subproblems.
- Build a more mature graphical problem frame editor based on GEF and EMF.
- Integrate the problem frame approach with object-oriented problem analysis methods and software development processes.

In summary, we believe that with this paper, we have prepared the basis for a more rigorous understanding of problem frames, which can also contribute to further maturing and enhancing the problem frame approach in practice.

References

[1] Eclipse - An Open Development Platform (May 2008), `http://www.eclipse.org/`
[2] Eclipse Modeling Framework Project (EMF) (May 2008), `http://www.eclipse.org/modeling/emf/`
[3] Graphical Editing Framework Project (GEF) (May 2008), `http://www.eclipse.org/gef/`
[4] OCL Tool for Precise UML Specifications (Octopus) (May 2008), `http://www.klasse.nl/octopus/`
[5] Papyrus UML (May 2008), `http://www.papyrusuml.org`
[6] XMI - XML Metadata Interchange (May 2008), `http://www.omg.org/docs/formal/05-09-01.pdf`
[7] XML - Extensible Markup Language (May 2008), `http://www.w3.org/XML/`
[8] Buschmann, F., Meunier, R., Rohnert, H., Sommerlad, P., Stal, M.: Pattern-Oriented Software Architecture: A System of Patterns. John Wiley & Sons, Chichester (1996)

[9] Choppy, C., Heisel, M.: Une approache à base de "patrons" pour la spécification et le développement de systèmes d'information. In: Proceedings Approches Formelles dans l'Assistance au Développement de Logiciels - AFADL 2004, pp. 61–76 (2004)
[10] Côté, I., Hatebur, D., Heisel, M., Schmidt, H., Wentzlaff, I.: A systematic account of problem frames. In: Proceedings of the European Conference on Pattern Languages of Programs (EuroPLoP), Universitätsverlag Konstanz (published, 2008)
[11] Fayad, M.E., Johnson, R.E.: Domain-Specific Application Frameworks. John Wiley & Sons, Chichester (1999)
[12] Fowler, M.: Analysis Patterns: Reusable Object Models. Addison Wesley, Reading (1997)
[13] Gamma, E., Helm, R., Johnson, R., Vlissides, J.: Design Patterns – Elements of Reusable Object-Oriented Software. Addison Wesley, Reading (1995)
[14] Hall, J.G., Rapanotti, L., Jackson, M.: Problem frame semantics for software development. Software and System Modeling 4(2), 189–198 (2005)
[15] Hatebur, D., Heisel, M., Schmidt, H.: Security Engineering using Problem Frames. In: Müller, G. (ed.) ETRICS 2006. LNCS, vol. 3995, pp. 238–253. Springer, Heidelberg (2006)
[16] Hatebur, D., Heisel, M., Schmidt, H.: A pattern system for security requirements engineering. In: Proceedings of the International Conference on Availability, Reliability and Security (AReS), pp. 356–365. IEEE Computer Society Press, Los Alamitos (2007)
[17] Hatebur, D., Heisel, M., Schmidt, H.: A security engineering process based on patterns. In: Proceedings of the International Workshop on Secure Systems Methodologies using Patterns (SPatterns), pp. 734–738. IEEE Computer Society Press, Los Alamitos (2007)
[18] Hatebur, D., Heisel, M., Schmidt, H.: A formal metamodel for problem frames (technical report). Technical report (2008), http://swe.uni-duisburg-essen.de/en/members/schmidt/index.php
[19] Jackson, M.: Software Requirements & Specifications: a Lexicon of Practice, Principles and Prejudices. Addison-Wesley, Reading (1995)
[20] Jackson, M.: Problem Frames. Analyzing and structuring software development problems. Addison-Wesley, Reading (2001)
[21] Jackson, M., Jackson, D.: Problem decomposition for reuse. Software Engineering Journal 11(1), 19–30 (1996)
[22] Jackson, M., Zave, P.: Deriving specifications from requirements: an example. In: Proceedings 17th Int. Conf. on Software Engineering, Seattle, USA, pp. 15–24. ACM Press, New York (1995)
[23] Lencastre, M., Botelho, J., Clericuzzi, P., Araújo, J.: A meta-model for the problem frames approach. In: WiSME 2005: 4th Workshop in Software Modeling Engineering (2005)
[24] Rapanotti, L., Hall, J.G., Jackson, M., Nuseibeh, B.: Architecture-driven problem decomposition. In: Proceedings of the 2004 International Conference on Requirements Engineering (RE 2004), Kyoto. IEEE Computer Society Press, Los Alamitos (2004), http://mcs.open.ac.uk/mj665/ArchDrvn.pdf
[25] Schmidt, H., Wentzlaff, I.: Preserving software quality characteristics from requirements analysis to architectural design. In: Gruhn, V., Oquendo, F. (eds.) EWSA 2006. LNCS, vol. 4344, pp. 189–203. Springer, Heidelberg (2006)
[26] Seater, R., Jackson, D., Gheyi, R.: Requirement progression in problem frames: deriving specifications from requirements. Requirements Engineering 12(2), 77–102 (2007)
[27] Specker, M., Wentzlaff, I.: Exploring usability needs by human-computer interaction patterns. In: Winckler, M., Johnson, H., Palanque, P. (eds.) TAMODIA 2007. LNCS, vol. 4849, pp. 254–260. Springer, Heidelberg (2007)
[28] Sutcliffe, A.: The Domain Theory, Patterns for Knowledge and Software Reuse. Addison-Wesley, Reading (2002)

[29] Sutcliffe, A., Maiden, N.: The domain theory for requirements engineering. IEEE Transactions on Software Engineering 24(3), 174–196 (1998)
[30] UML Revision Task Force. Object Constraint Language Specification. Object Constraint Language (OCL) (May 2006)
[31] UML Revision Task Force. OMG Unified Modeling Language: Superstructure (February 2007), http://www.omg.org/docs/formal/07-02-03.pdf

A The Complete Set of Integrity Conditions

context Domain

A machine domain is always a designed domain. Therefore, a machine domain cannot be a given domain.

```
inv: self.isMachine implies not self.isGiven
```

A machine domain cannot be referred to by a requirement using a requirement reference.

```
inv: self.isMachine implies
  self.isReferredToByUsing->size() = 0
```

A machine domain cannot be constrained.

```
inv: self.isMachine implies
  self.isConstrainedByUsing->size() = 0
```

context BiddableDomain

Biddable domains are always given domains.

```
inv: self.isGiven
```

Machine domains are always causal domains. Hence, biddable domains cannot be machine domains.

```
inv: not self.isMachine
```

A biddable domain cannot be constrained.

```
inv: self.isConstrainedByUsing->size() = 0
```

context LexicalDomain

Lexical domains cannot be machine domains since they represent data.

```
inv: not self.isMachine
```

context Interface

Each phenomenon contained in an interface is controlled by exactly one domain connected by that interface.

```
inv: self.contains->forAll(p: InterfacePhenomenon |
  self.connects->one(d: Domain |
   p.isControlledBy = d))
```

context InterfacePhenomenon

A phenomenon contained in an interface is controlled by a domain connected by that interface.

```
inv: self.isContainedInIf.connects->includes(
  self.isControlledBy)
```

context RequirementReference

Machine domains cannot be referred to by requirements (other direction of association).

```
inv: not(self.isConnectedToDomain.isMachine)
```

context ConstrainingRequirementReference

A machine domain cannot be constrained.

```
inv: not (self.isConnectedToDomain.isMachine)
```

A biddable domain cannot be constrained (other direction of association).

```
inv: not(self.isConnectedToDomain
  ->oclIsTypeOf(BiddableDomain))
```

context ProblemFrame

A problem frame has exactly one machine domain.

```
inv: self.domains->one (d: Domain | d.isMachine)
```

A phenomenon contained in an interface is controlled by a domain connected by that interface.

```
inv: self.isContainedInIf.connects->includes(
  self.isControlledBy)
```

The machine domain is connected by an interface to a problem domain.

```
inv: self.interfaces->exists(i: Interface |
  self.domains->exists(d: Domain |
  self.domains->exists(m: Domain | m.isMachine and
  m.isConnectedBy->includes(i) and
  d.isConnectedBy->includes(i))))
```

The machine domain controls phenomena contained in an interface it is connected to.

```
inv: self.interfaces->exists(i: Interface |
  i.connects->exists(d: Domain |
  d.isMachine) and
  i.contains->exists(p: InterfacePhenomenon |
  p.isControlledBy.isMachine))
```

Domains are connected by an interface to another problem domain.

```
inv: self.domains->forAll(d: Domain |
  self.interfaces->exists(i: Interface |
  d.isConnectedBy->includes(i)))
```

A domain can only control phenomena contained in those interfaces that are connected to it.

```
inv: self.domains->forAll(d: Domain |
  d.controls->forAll(p: InterfacePhenomenon |
  d.isConnectedBy->exists(i: Interface |
  i.contains->includes(p))))
```

A domain is connected by interfaces, which are part of the problem frame.

```
inv: self.domains->forAll(d: Domain |
  self.interfaces->includesAll(d.isConnectedBy))
```

A domain can be constrained by constraining requirement references, which are part of the problem frame.

```
inv: self.domains->forAll(d: Domain |
  not d.isMachine implies self.requirementReferences
  ->includes(d.isConstrainedByUsing)
  or d.isConstrainedByUsing->size()=0)
```

A domain can be referred to by requirement references, which are part of the problem frame.

```
inv: self.domains->forAll(d: Domain |
  not d.isMachine implies self.requirementReferences
  ->includes(d.isReferredToByUsing)
  or d.isReferredToByUsing->size()=0)
```

The names of domains must be unique.

```
inv: self.domains->forAll(d1: Domain |
  self.domains->forAll(d2: Domain |
  (d1.name = d2.name) implies (d1=d2)))
```

The abbreviations of domains must be unique.

```
inv: self.domains->forAll(d1: Domain |
  self.domains->forAll(d2: Domain |
  (d1.abbreviation = d2.abbreviation)
  implies (d1=d2)))
```

The names of problem domains and the phenomena names must be disjoint.

```
inv: self.domains->forAll(d: Domain |
  self.interfaces->forAll(
  i: Interface | i.contains->forAll(
  p: InterfacePhenomenon | d.name <> p.name)))
```

Each interface is connected to a domain contained in the problem frame.

```
inv: self.interfaces->forAll(i: Interface |
  self.domains->includesAll(i.connects))
```

Phenomena contained in an interface are controlled by exactly one domain that is contained in the problem frame and connected by the interface at hand.

```
inv: self.interfaces->forAll(i: Interface |
  i.contains->forAll(p: InterfacePhenomenon |
  self.domains->one(d: Domain |
  d.controls->includes(p) and
  i.connects->includes(d))))
```

The requirement's constraining requirement references and requirement references are those contained in the problem frame.

```
inv: self.requirementReferences->includesAll(
  self.requirement.constrainsUsing)
```

The requirement references are connected to the requirement of the problem frame (both directions of association).

```
inv: self.requirement.refersToUsing =
  self.requirementReferences
inv: self.requirementReferences->forAll(
  rr: RequirementReference |
  rr.isConnectedToReq = self.requirement)
```

The constraining requirement references and requirement references are connected to the domains of the problem frame.

```
inv: self.requirementReferences->forAll(
  rr: RequirementReference |
  self.domains->includes(rr.isConnectedToDomain))
```

Visualization of Use Cases through Automatically Generated Activity Diagrams

Javier J. Gutiérrez[1], Clémentine Nebut[2], María J. Escalona[1], Manuel Mejías[1], and Isabel M. Ramos[1]

[1] Department of Languages and Computer Systems,
University of Sevilla, Spain
{javierj,mjescalona,risoto,ramos}@us.es
[2] LIRMM, CNRS and university of Montpellier 2, France
nebut@lirmm.fr

Abstract. Functional requirements are often written using use cases formatted by textual templates. This textual approach has the advantage to be easy to adopt, but the requirements can then hardly be processed for further purposes like test generation. In this paper, we propose to generate automatically through a model transformation an activity diagram modeling the use case scenario. Such an activity diagram allows us to guess in a glimpse the global behavior of a use case, and can easily be processed. The transformation is defined using the QVT-Relational language, and is illustrated on a case study using a supporting tool.

1 Introduction

Requirement engineering is a crucial activity for a successful project. Among the different tasks to achieve in this activity is the writing of the elicited requirements in a given language (formal, semi-formal, or natural).

Structured use cases is a classical standard used in industry and taken as entry point of several research work [3][4][5][14]. By structured use cases, we mean use cases as defined in UML [22], enhanced with additional information like pre and post conditions, and scenarii. Such use cases usually follow templates like Cockburn one [3], defining in natural language usage scenarii, quality of service constraints, or graphical interface elements, like [4].

A UML use case model does not contain much information. It allows to define the frontier of the system, actors, name of use cases, and relations between the use cases, the actors, and linking actors and use cases. UML methodologies like RUP [23] or Catalysis [24] recommend to enhance this model with other UML artifacts like constraints to define contracts, and sequence diagrams to define system scenarii in a graphical way.

Both use case templates and UML methodologies thus incite the requirement writer to define scenarii, in a graphical or textual notation. Graphical notations for scenarii (system sequence diagrams [19] or activity diagrams [25]) have the advantage to give in a glimpse a good idea of the dynamic aspects of a use case (loops,

K. Czarnecki et al. (Eds.): MoDELS 2008, LNCS 5301, pp. 83–96, 2008.

alternatives, choices). Moreover, they can be easily used by a tool to be analyzed (for example for test generation purposes, also in [19]). On the other hand, they can be difficult to design, and domain experts cannot reasonably asked to draw them. On the opposite, textual scenarii are easy to write: the scenarii are composed of various steps, each one is described by natural language sentences, and linked with natural language connectors. Such textual scenarii do not give an immediate intuition of the behavior of the use case, and cannot easily be processed by a tool.

The original contribution of this paper is a process to generate in an automated way an activity diagram modeling use case dynamic from textual scenarii. The generation is performed by a model transformation, taking as input use case textual scenarii (conform to a metamodel defined in this paper), and producing an activity diagram (conform to a restricted part of the UML activity diagram metamodel). The transformation is defined using QVT-relational language and implemented in Java in a prototype tool.

This transformation allows to benefit both from graphical and textual scenarii advantages. Textual scenarii can be written. Then they can be transformed in a graphical view. This allows an easier integration to UML tools, and to use the activity diagram for further treatments like test generation for example.

The rest of this paper is organized as follows. Section 2 introduces the source and target metamodels, this means, the textual requirement metamodel and an excerpt of the UML activity metamodel. Section 3 describes the transformation to generate an activity diagram from a tabular requirement. Section 4 introduces a case study. Section 5 describes other related approaches and, finally, section 5 summarizes conclusions and ongoing works.

2 Functional Requirements and Activity Diagrams Metamodels

This section introduces the artifacts we deal with: functional requirements and activity diagrams. Both ones are described by metamodels: our own metamodel for functional requirements and a subset of the UML metamodel for the activity diagrams.

2.1 Functional Requirement Metamodel

There are many approaches to define textual requirements [3][4][5][14]. However the majority of the existing approaches are based on a common core of elements. These elements include the participants, preconditions, post-conditions, a set of main steps (to achieve the goal of the use case) and a set of exceptional steps (to manage alternative and erroneous scenarios). These common elements have been extracted from the cited approaches and modeled in the functional requirement metamodel introduced in figure 1 and briefly described in the following.

A *FRActor* element models an external actor who participates in the functional requirement performing the steps. The *FunctionalRequirement* element defines an interaction among the system and a set of external actors. The behavior of *FunctionalRequirement* is defined with three different sequences of steps. The main sequence defines the steps performed by *FRActor* elements and the system to achieve the goal of the functional requirement. The alternative steps indicate variants or additional behavior for the steps of the main sequence. The erroneous steps indicate erroneous scenarios after performing a step from the main sequence. Alternative and erroneous steps are modeled with *ExceptionalStep* element.

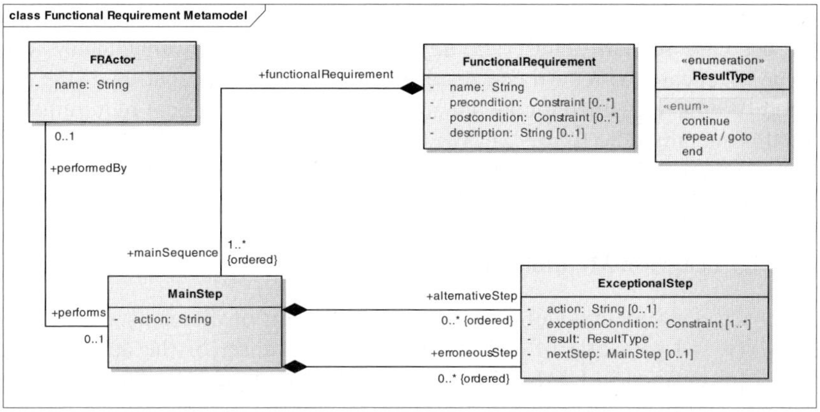

Fig. 1. Functional Requirement Metamodel

```
<useCase id="RF-01. Logging">
  <description> An user wants to access into the system.</description>
  <precondition>No.</precondition>
  <postcondition>System grants access to the user.</postcondition>
  <mainSequence>
    <step id="1"> User asks access into the system. </step>
    <step id="2"> System asks for a name and a key. </step>
    <step id="3"> User introduces a name and a key. </step>
    <step id="4"> System validates name and key. </step>
    <step id="4"> System allows access. </step>
 </mainSequence>
 <alternativeSteps>
  <astep id="2.1"> If the number of tries is greater than three,
  then the system shows an error message and this use case ends.
  </astep>
  </alternativeSteps>
  <errorSteps>
    <estep id="4.1"> If the name of the key size is less than
    four characters, then the system shows an error message and
    step 2 is repeated.
    </estep>
    <estep id="4.2">
        If the name or the key are not registered, the system
        shows and error message and step 2 is repeated.
    </estep>
   </errorSteps>
</useCase>
```

Fig. 2. Example use case (in XML format)

In this paper, the only relevant information for a *MainStep* element is the action performed (attribute *action*) and who performs the action. In an *ExceptionalStep* element, the action is not mandatory and the performer is the same one than the main step. The *exceptionCondition* attribute indicates a boolean expression that must be true to perform the step and the *result* attribute indicates the action to perform at the end of the exceptional step. Three possible results have been defined as the enumerated *ResultType* element: end the execution, continue the execution and repeat/go-to to another step. A continue result indicates that the execution of the functional requirement continues with the next step after the end of the alternative or erroneous step. The repeat or go-to result indicates that the execution of the scenario follows the execution of the step indicated in the *nextStep* attribute, and the end result indicates than the use case scenario ends. The *nextStep* attribute is only mandatory when the result type is repeat / go-to. An end result indicates that the execution of the scenario is finished. We have defined a concrete syntax to define functional requirements conform to this metamodel (figure 2). The concrete syntax is XML-based to make an approach available. One tool, available in [1], has been development to generate this XML for our modeling tool (described in section 4).

2.2 Activity Diagram Metamodel

The UML activities metamodel contains a vast amount of elements which improves the flexibility and semantic of activity diagrams. A subset of the activity diagrams metamodel (as defined in UML 2.0) has been selected (figure 3). This subset defines the elements automatically generated by the transformations introduced in next section. Indeed, after the automatic generation of the activity diagrams, additional elements, like data flow, may be added by hand.

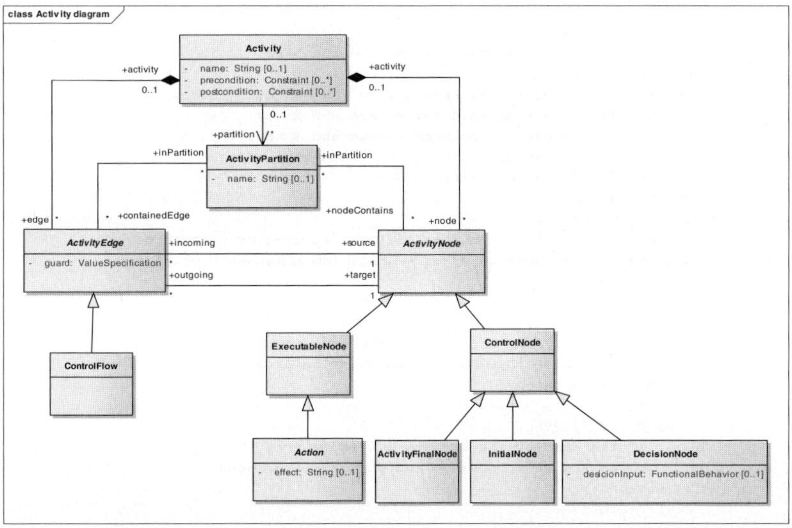

Fig. 3. Activity diagrams metamodel

Since UML 2.0, the activity diagram element has been replaced with the *Activity* metaclass. Indeed, this metaclass groups all the elements of an activity diagram: control flows, nodes and activity partitions. Activity partitions are groups of the elements of an activity diagram. Control flows indicate the incomings and outgoings of a node. Action nodes define a behavior. Decision node allows to select a flow as result of evaluating boolean predicates. Finally, the *InitialNode* and *ActivityFinalNode* elements indicate where the control flow begins and ends.

Next section, describes how these elements represents the concepts defined in the functional requirement metamodel.

```
2  transformation FR_2_AD (frm: FunctionalRequirementMetamodel,
3                          adm: ActivityDiagramMetamodel){
4
5  key Activiy(name);
6  key Action(effect, incoming, outgoing);
7  key ControlFlow(source, target);
8  key ActivityPartition(name);
9
10 top relation FunctionalRequirement_2_Activity {
11     checkonly domain frm fr: FunctionalRequirement {
12         name = fr_name,
13         precondition = pre,
14         postcondition = pos
15     };
16     enforce domain adm a: Activity {
17         name = fr_name,
18         precondition = pre,
19         postcondition = pos
20     };
21     where {
22         Actor_2_ActivityPartition (fr, a);
23     }
24 }
```

Fig. 4. From functional requirement to activity

3 Transformation from Textual Scenarios to Activity Diagrams

This section defines the transformation to generate an activity diagram (as an instance of the metamodel of figure 3) from a functional requirement (as an instance of the metamodel of figure 1). The objective of this transformation is to generate from a functional requirement an activity that models the whole functional requirement (with the same name, pre-conditions and post-conditions). In this activity, the activity partitions model the different actors implied in the functional requirement and the system under development, control flows model the execution paths or scenarios and actions and decision nodes model the steps and the exception conditions. Transformation performs next tasks:

1. generating an activity for each functional requirement,
2. generating an action for each main step and generate a decision node and additional actions for each exceptional step,
3. all elements in the activity diagram are connected using control flows.

All the tasks are defined using QVT-Relational [26]. We here present only the main ones in QVT-Relational; the whole transformation can be found in [1]. The steps are described in detail in next sections.

3.1 From Functional Requirements to Activity Diagrams

Initially, one activity is generated for each functional requirement. The related relation (called *FR_2_AD*), in QVT-Relational language, is showed in figure 4. The name, preconditions and post-conditions of the activity are the same than the ones in the functional requirement (lines 17, 18 and 19).

```
26 relation Actor_2_ActivityPartition {
27     checkonly domain frm fr: FunctionalRequirement {
28         performedBy = fra: FRActor {
29             name = fra_name
30         }
31     };
32     enforce domain adm a: Activity {
33         partition = ap: ActivityPartition {
34             name = actor;
35         }
36     };
37     where {
38         System_2_ActivityPartition (fr, a);
39     }
40 }
41
42 relation System_2_ActivityPartition {
43     checkonly domain frm fr: FunctionalRequirement {};
44     enforce domain adm a: Activity {
45         partition = ap: ActivityPartition {
46             name = 'System';
47         }
48     };
49 }
```

```
55 top relation MainStep_2_Action {
56     AP_name: String;
57     checkonly domain frm fr: FunctionalRequirement {
58         name = fr_name,
59         mainSequence = ms: MainStep {
60             action = ms_action,
61             AP_name = APName(performedBy);
62         }
63     };
64     enforce domain adm a: Activity {
65         name = fr_name,
66         node = act: Action {
67             effect = ms_action,
68             inPartition: ActivityPartition {
69                 name = AP_name,
70                 nodeContains = act: Action {}
71             }
72         }
73     };
74 }
75
76 function APName(pb: FRActor): String {
77     if (pb = oclUndefined) then
78         'System'
79     else
80         pb.name
81     endif;
82 }
```

Fig. 5. (a) From actor to activity partition. (b) From main step to action.

As seen in the previous section, one activity partition is also generated for each actor participant in the functional requirement (relation *Actor_2_ActivityPartition*, called in line 22) plus one additional partition for the system (as showed in figure 5(a), lines from 42 to 49). The next task is to transform the behavior, defined with three sequences of steps, of the functional requirement.

3.2 From Main Sequence to Actions

One action is generated for each step in the main sequence. The related QVT relation is given in figure 5(b). The attribute *effect* of the action is the attribute *action* of the step (line 67). The actions are included in the corresponding activity partition which may be identified using the *performedBy* attribute of the main step (lines 69, 70 and 71). However, if a step is performed by the system, this attribute is empty, so the action is classified in the system partition. This behavior is codified in the auxiliary function *APName* (line 76, figure 5(b)). The next step is to transform alternative and erroneous sequences in decision nodes and actions.

3.3 From Alternative and Erroneous Sequences to Actions

Two elements are generated from an alternative or an erroneous step. The QVT relation goes in figure 6.

The first element is a decision node (class *DesicionNode*, line 101), which evaluates the exception condition to allow or not the execution of the alternative or erroneous behavior. This exception condition is stored in the attribute *desicionInput*, which is generated with the auxiliary function *generatePredicate* (used in line 103). Due the exception condition was defined as constraints in the functional requirement metamodel (figure 1), this auxiliary function builds a string from a set of *Constraint* elements.

The second element is an action describing the additional behavior if any (as it has been seen in the functional requirement metamodel, an action attribute for exceptional steps is not mandatory). This action is generated by the auxiliary function *GenerateAction* (line 113). This function has been omitted from figure 7, but its code is quite similar to the QVT transformation *MainStep_2_*Action (figure 5(b)).

Then, every possible result has also a different representation in an activity diagram, so three different relations are called to generate the adequate elements for each type of results (only one, relation *GenerateEnd*, has been included in the *where* clause of figure 6, line 115).

```
87  top relation ES_2_DN {
88      AP_name: String;
89      checkonly domain frm fr: FunctionalRequirement {
90          name = nrf,
91          exceptionalSequence = es: ExceptionalStep {
92              action = es_action,
93              exceptionalCondition = ecSet: Set(Constraint) {},
94              mainStep = ms: MainStep {
95                  AP_name = APName(performedBy);
96              }
97          }
98      };
99      enforce domain adm a: Activity {
100         name = nrf,
101         node = dn: DesicionNode {
102             desicionInput = input: FunctionalBehavior {
103                 body = 'r='+GeneratePredicate(ecSet);
104             },
105             inPartition: ActivityPartition {
106                 name = AP_name,
107                 nodeContains = act: Action {}
108             }
109         }
110     };
111     where {
112         if not(es_action = oclUndefined) then
113             GenerateAction(es, a, es_action, AP_name);
114         else
115             GenerateEnd(es, a, dn, AP_name);
116         endif;
117     }
118 }
```

Fig. 6. From exceptional step to decision node

```
relation GenerateEnd {
    checkonly domain frm es: ExceptionalStep {};
    enforce domain adm a: Activity {
        edge = cf: ControlFlow {
            guard = '[r]',
            source = dn: DecisionNode {
                incoming = cf: ControlFlow {}
            },
            target = afn: ActivityFinalNode {
                outgoing = cf: ControlFlow {}
            },
            inPartition = ap: ActivityPartition {
                name = AP_name,
                containedEdge = cf: ControlFlow {}
            }
        }
    };
    primitive domain AP_name: String;
}
```

Fig. 7. Exceptional step of type end

With an end use case result, a new activity end node (class *ActivityFinalNode*) is added and it is linked with the decision (or action if any) generated in previous relation using a new *ControlFlow* (from line 124 to 136, figure 7).

For a continue use case, the action corresponding to the next step (in the main sequence) is obtained and linked with the decision (or action if any) using a control flow element. Finally, for a repeat/ go-to result type, the action corresponding for the next step attribute (see metamodel in figure 1) is obtained and linked with the decision (or action if any) using a control flow.

The last task is to add control flow elements among the elements that are still unlinked.

3.4 Linking Element with Control Flows

At this time of the transformation process, all elements have been created in the activity diagram, but only a few of them have been linked with other elements (the elements created in section 3.3). The final task is to link all the other elements with *ControlFlow* instances. No control flow may be added until all the elements are generated because the control flow source and target is different depending if the actions have been generated from main steps with or without alternative and erroneous steps (a step-by-step example is provided in next section).

This task is, mainly, an algorithmic task. However, it has been possible to define a set of relations to achieve every specific situation at the time to link the elements. These relations are briefly described in next points.

1 Initial node with first element and activity final node with last element
If the first main step of the functional requirement has not an alternative step, then, the initial node is linked with the action generated from the first step. In other case, the initial node is linked with the decision node generated from the exception condition of the first alternative. This relation is showed in figure 8. The same process is applied in the relation to link the last element in the activity diagram with an activity final node.

2 Decision nodes among them
As seen in the functional requirement metamodel (figure 1) all exceptional steps (alternative and erroneous steps) are ordered. So, the next task is to link the decision node generated from the first alternative step of a main step with the decision node generated from the second alternative step of the same main step, the decision node generated from the second one with the decision node generated from the third one, etc. This process is also done with the decisions nodes generated from the erroneous steps.

3 Decision nodes with activities
Next, the decision node generated from the last alternative step of a main step (if any) must be linked with the action element generated from this main step. In the same way, this action element must be linked with the decision node generated.

4 Nodes from one step with nodes from other step
Finally, the last decision node generated from the last erroneous step of the first main step is linked with the first decision node generated from the first alternative step of the second main step, and so on.

At this time, the activity diagram is finished.

```
top relation IN_a_FirstAlternative {
  predicate : String;
  checkonly domain FRM fr: FunctionalRequirement {
    name = nrf,
    mainSequence = sp: OrderedSet(MainStep),
    sp->first().action = acc,
    sp->first().alternativeStep.asOrderesSet() = as,
    if not(as->isEmpty())
      predicate = GenPred(as->first().exceptionCondition);
    else
      predicate = oclUndefined;
    endif
  };
  enforce domain ADM a: Activity {
    name = nrf,
    if (predicate <> oclUndefined)
      edge = cf: ControlFlow {
        guard = 'true',
        source = in: InitialNode {} ,
        target = dn: DesicionNode {
          desicionInput = predicate,
          incoming = cf: ControlFlow {},
          inPartition = ap: ActivityPartition {}
        },
        inPartition = ap: ActivityPartition {}
      }
    else
      edge = cf: ControlFlow {
        guard = 'true',
        source = in: InitialNode {},
        target = ac: Action {
          effect = acc,
          desicionInput = predicate,
          incoming = cf: ControlFlow {},
          inPartition = ap: ActivityPartition {}
        },
        inPartition = ap: ActivityPartition {}
      }
    endif
  };
}
```

Fig. 8. From initial node to first element

4 Case Study

This section describes a case study of the transformation defined in previous sections. The case study chosen is an incident report system. This system is running in a public organism in Spain. Use cases were written one year ago using NDT approach [5][6], which contains all the common elements of the metamodel in figure 1. No additional information was needed to apply our transformation. This system has 9 use cases, however, two of them have been discarded since they describe interactions among a concrete digital sign service that is not available for us. The total number of steps is 46. One activity diagram has been automatically generated from each use case. The total number of activity nodes is 41 and the total number of decision nodes is 15. The complete results of this case study can be found in [1]. One use case has been chosen (Login, from figure 2) to illustrate the transformations described in previous section.

To be able to apply our approach, we have first rewritten the use cases using our XML syntax. The transformations in previous sections have been implemented in a Java open-source tool (also available in [1]). The input is a XML file as the one showed in figure 2 (generated automatically from Sparx Enterprise Architect tool) and the output is a XMI activity diagram file. In following figures, the activity diagram has been loaded also with Sparx Enterprise Architect tool.

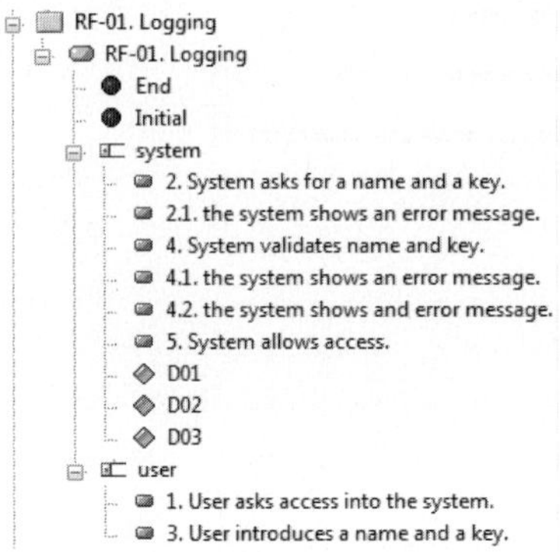

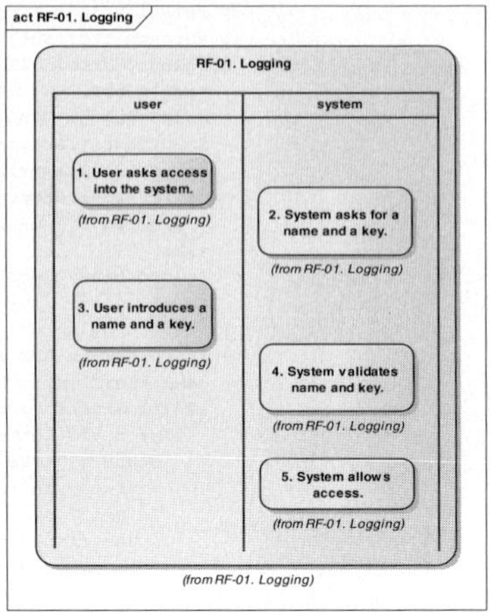

Fig. 9. (a) Elements generated from the functional requirement. (b) Actions from main step.

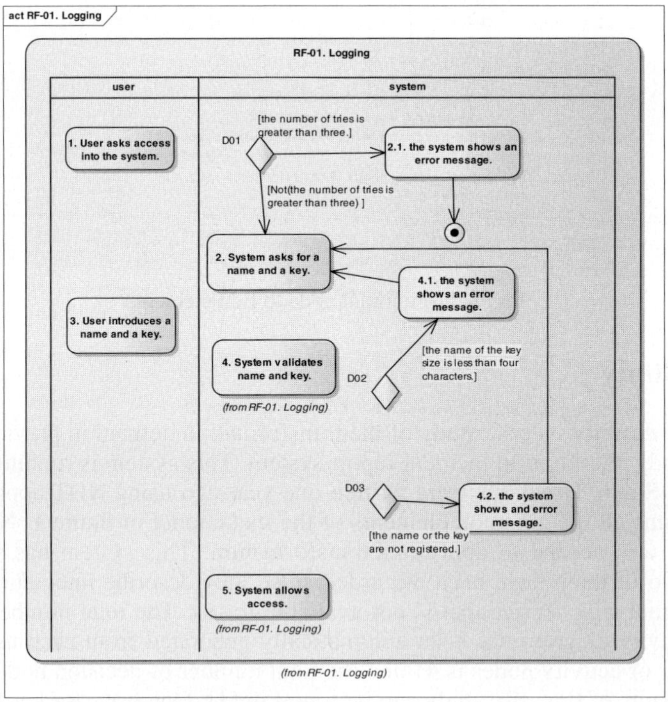

Fig. 10. From exceptional steps to decision nodes and actions

All the elements generated from the login functional requirement are showed in figure 9(a). The result of the relations introduced in sections 3.1 and 3.2 are showed in the incomplete activity diagram of figure 9(b). As described before, one activity, activity partitions and actions generated from main sequence have been added.

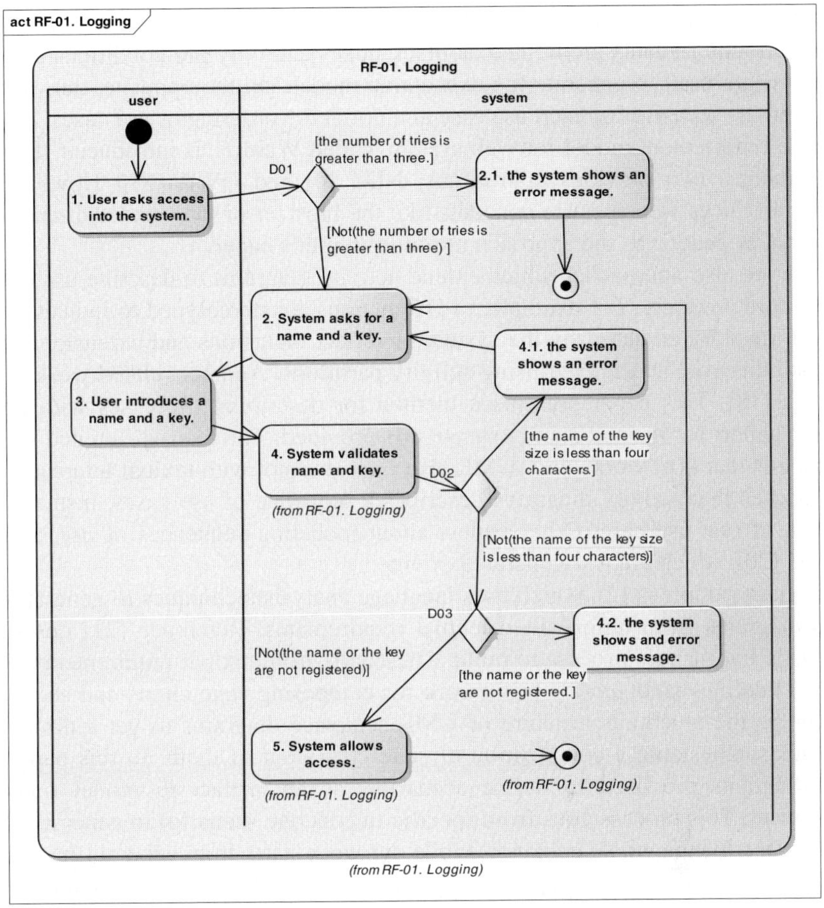

Fig. 11. Final activity diagram

The result of the relation introduced in section 3.3 is showed in the incomplete activity diagram in figure 10. As described before, a decision node and an action (if any) have been added for each alternative and erroneous step and some elements have been linked with control flows.

Finally, the result of relations described in section 3.4 is showed in the activity diagram in figure 11 and, now, this activity diagram is complete. As described before, all the elements of the diagram, plus an initial and final node, are linked using Control Flow element.

5 Related Works

At the time to write this paper, few works exists dealing with automatic processing of textual requirements from a model-based point of view. Reference [11] introduces a requirement metamodel and a set of transformations (in Kermeta language) to build an executable model from the requirements (defined as a labeled transition system). Functional requirements are treated as black boxes and only pre-conditions and post-conditions are used to generate the executable model. On the opposite, our approach focuses in the scenarios of each use case and not in the ordering of use cases. In [12] a complete requirement model for web system, called WebRE, is introduced. This new model merges two previous approaches: NDT [5] and UWE [13]. However, this model introduces web specific concepts like the browser or the links and navigation, so it is not as generic as the approach introduced in this paper.

There are also approaches which extend activity diagrams to describe use case behavior more precisely. For example, in [16] actions are stereotyped to indicate if they are performed by an actor, by the system or reflect inclusions and extensions. In our approach this goal is achieved using activity partitions. Another related work may be found in [18]. This paper presents a method for describing use cases with activity charts. Support for inclusion and extension is provided. The main difference with our approach is that [18] works with UML Use Case, but not with textual templates. This fact imposes that activity diagrams describes a sequence of use cases, instead of the behavior of one use case. Other papers about modeling sequences of use cases are [19] and [20], which are test-generated oriented.

Another example is [2], which uses language analysis techniques to generate state-charts diagrams from unformatted textual requirements. Reference [21] describes a systematic but manual process to build state-charts from textual requirements. Reference [17] defines an algebraic framework for composing state charts and shows how to leverage the algebraic structure of UML sequence diagrams to get a direct algorithm for synthesizing a composition of state charts out of them. In this paper, scenario diagrams are used to define scenarios, as an artifact to model functional requirement. This process goes from specific (a concrete scenario) to general (a state-chart to describe the whole behavior) while our work starts from general (the behavior of a whole scenario). In our approach, scenarios may be defined as a path obtained from the generated activity diagram.

6 Conclusions

This paper introduced a metamodel for functional requirements and a set of QVT relations to combine functional requirements in the form of use cases with activity diagrams (as described in UML 2.0) in an automatic way. These transformations allow requirement engineers and system users to work with the most valuable representation at any time. However, some drawbacks appear at the time of combining textual requirements with activity diagrams. The most obvious one is the loss of flexibility, for example at the time of adding new kind of result types. The task of adding a new result type implies add a new set of transformation for implementing the right activity diagram fragment for that new result and modify existing transformations for detecting the new result.

The representation of the functional requirement is not limited to XML. This paper has introduced a fragment of XML due it is the input of our supporting tool, as mentioned above. Other implementations may use different representations and it is even possible to design adapters. For example, in the supporting web site [1], a simple Java program to obtain XML from Enterprise Architect project file is provided.

As mentioned in previous sections, the functional requirement metamodel includes a common subset of the elements that may be found in existing functional requirements approaches. The main advantage is that the metamodel may be used with any of those approaches with very little or no changes. Furthermore this metamodel may be easily extended to include additional information like priority, stability of requirements, performing issues, traceability, etc.

Although the transformation process has been defined with QVT-Relational, it has been implemented in Java language. Java allowed us to implement a prototype (also available in [1]) in a shorter time than existing implementations of QVT-Relational or other transformation languages like ATL. However, one of our main ongoing works is to develop a stable version of the tool using one of the cited transformations languages.

Actually, we use the transformations described in this paper as a first step to generate test cases from use cases automatically. Transforming the textual requirements into activity diagrams allows us to apply graph coverage criteria, like covering all nodes or covering all flows, to generate concrete usage scenarios easily. Some papers describing our preliminary work (which was not formalized with metamodels and transformation) are [7][8][9]. Two additional case studies with empirical results are introduced in [10].

Acknowledgements

This work is partially supported by the Ministry of Science and Education (Spain) under the National Program for Researching, Development and Innovation, project QSimTec (TIN2007-67843-C06-03) and REPRIS (TIN2005-24792-E). Authors also wants to remark the help provided for the student who developed the system used in the case study.

References

[1] Supporting web site, `http://www.lsi.us.es/~javierj/`

[2] Boddu, R., Guo, L., Mukhopadhyay, S.: RETNA: From Requirements to Testing in Natural Way. In: 12th IEEE International Requirements Engineering RE 2004 (2004)

[3] Cockburn, A.: Writing Effective Use Cases, 1st edn. Addison-Wesley, Reading (2000)

[4] Dustin, E., Rashka, J., McDiarmid, D.: Quality Web Systems. Performance, Security, and Usability. Addison Wesley, Reading (2002)

[5] Escalona, M.J.: Models and Techniques for the Specification and Analysis of Navigation in Software Systems. Ph. European Thesis. University of Seville. Seville, Spain (2004)

[6] Escalona, M.J., Gutiérrez, J.J., Villadiego, D., León, A., Torres, A.H.: Practical Experiences in Web Engineering. In: 15th International Conference on Information Systems Development, Budapest, Hungary, 31 August – 2 September (2006)

[7] Gutiérrez, J.J., Escalona, M.J., Mejías, M., Torres, J.: Derivation of test objectives automatically. In: Fifteenth International Conference on Information Systems Development (ISD 2006), Budapest, Hungary, 31 August – 2 September (2006)

[8] Gutiérrez, J.J., Escalona, M.J., Mejías, M., Torres, J.: Modelos Y Algoritmos Para La Generación De Objetivos De Prueba. In: Jornadas sobre Ingeniería del Software y Bases de Datos JISBD 2006, Sitges, Spain (2006)
[9] Gutiérrez, J.J., Escalona, M.J., Mejías, M., Torres, J., Torres, A.: Generación automática de objetivos de prueba a partir de casos de uso mediante partición de categorías y variables operacionales. In: XIV Jornadas sobre Ingeniería del Software y Bases de Datos JISBD, Zaragoza, Spain (2007)
[10] Gutiérrez, J.J., Escalona, M.J., Mejías, M., Torres, J., Zenteno, A.H.: A Case Study for Generating Test Cases from Use Cases. Research Challenges in Information Science, Marrakech (2008)
[11] Baudry, B., Nebut, C., Le Traon, Y.: Model-driven Engineering for Requirement Analysis. In: Enterprise Distributed Object Computing Conference, Annapolis, MD, USA (October 2007)
[12] Koch, N., Zhang, G., Escalona, M.J.: Model Transformations from Requirements to Web System Design. In: Webist 2006. LNBIP, vol. 1. Springer, Heidelberg (2007)
[13] Koch, N.: Software Engineering for Adaptative Hypermedia Applications. Ph. Thesis, FAST Reihe Softwaretechnik, Munich, Germany, vol. 12. Uni-Druck Publishing Company (2001)
[14] Ben Achour, C.: Writing and Correcting Textual Scenarios for System Design. In: Natural Language and Information Systems Workshop, Vienna, Austria (1998)
[15] Roubtsov, S., Heck, P.: Use Case-Based Acceptance Testing of a Large Industrial System: Approach and Experience Report. In: TAIC-PART 2006, Windsor, UK (2006)
[16] Kösters, G., Six, H.-W., Winter, M.: Coupling Use Cases and Class Models as a Mean for Validation and Verification of Requirements Specifications. Requirements Eng. 6(1), 3–17 (2001)
[17] Ziadi, T., Hélouët, L., Jézéquel, J.-M.: Revisiting Statechart Synthesis with an Algebraic Approach. In: 26th International Conference on Software Engineering (ICSE 2004), Scotland, United Kindom (2004)
[18] Almendros-Jiménez, J.M., Iribarne, L.: Describing Use Cases with Activity Charts. In: Wiil, U.K. (ed.) MIS 2004. LNCS, vol. 3511, pp. 141–159. Springer, Heidelberg (2005)
[19] Labiche, Y., Briand, L.C.: A UML-Based Approach to System Testing. Journal of Software and Systems Modelling (SoSyM) 1(1), 10–42 (2002)
[20] Nebut, C., Fleurey, F., Le Traon, Y., Jézéquel, J.M.: Automatic Test Generation: A Use Case Driven Approach. IEEE Transactions on Software Engineering 32(3) (March 2006)
[21] Fröhlich, P., Link, J.: Automated Test Case Generation from Dynamic Models. In: Bertino, E. (ed.) ECOOP 2000. LNCS, vol. 1850, pp. 472–491. Springer, Heidelberg (2000)
[22] Object Management Group. The UML Superstructure (2007), `http://www.omg.org`
[23] Jacobson, I., Booch, G., Rumbaugh, J.: The Unified Software Development Process, USA. Object Technology. Addison-Wesley, Reading (1999)
[24] D'Souza, D.F., Wills, A.C.: Objects, Components, and Frameworks with UML: The Catalysis(SM) Approach, USA. Addison-Wesley Professional, Reading (1998)
[25] Hartmann, J., Vieira, M., Foster, H., Ruder, A.: TDE/UML: A UML-based Test Generator to Support System Testing. In: 5th Annual International Software Testing Conference, India (2005)
[26] Object Management Group. Meta Object Facility (MOF) 2.0 Query/View/Transformation Specification. Final Adopted Specification (2007), `http://www.omg.org`

Requirements Modeling and Validation Using Bi-layer Use Case Descriptions

Avik Sinha*, Matthew Kaplan, Amit Paradkar, and Clay Williams

IBM T J Watson Research Center, 19 Skyline Drive,Hawthorne, NY 10532
{aviksinha,mmk,paradkar,clayw}@us.ibm.com

Abstract. Extension of the modeling notations and formal languages for use case description are the commonly suggested solutions for adding precision to use case models. Practitioners have often argued against adoption of such techniques citing reasons like the steep learning curve for formal languages; and the quickness in using imprecise use case descriptions for communicating to different stake-holders of the system. In this paper we introduce the Archetest modeling environment, which through a unique bi-layer approach accepts use case descriptions in their imprecise form and then assists in adding precision through a wizard driven process. Thereby, it lends itself to both quick and precise modeling. Also the two forms of the use case models are self contained and cross-linked. This allows different modelers, the precise and the imprecise, to collaborate and also supports stake-holder specific feedbacks of the automated analysis. We describe the structure of Archetest's use case models, and show how these models are amenable to automated processing. We present a case study which reports on typical modeling times using Archetest and demonstrates its scalability.

1 Introduction

Graphical use cases along with their textual specifications are frequently used to model functional requirements of software applications [1,2,3,4,5,6,7]. Among the key stake holders in the use case based requirement modeling space are business analysts and requirements analysts. Business analysts with the help of subject matter experts write use cases in order to communicate effectively and efficiently to other stake-holders of the system. Requirements analysts are on the other hand, concerned with the ability to validate correctness and feasibility of the requirements. Therefore, while requirements analysts seek rigorously precise specification, business analysts value higher level description of systems and are less concerned with precision. In fact, some business analysts even believe that the overhead in formally specifying use cases make them difficult to use [8]. Due to these divergent needs, finding a software-modeling paradigm that has value both as a communication tool and as an aid to automatic validation has proven a serious challenge. This paper describes a use-case authoring system called

* Corresponding author.

K. Czarnecki et al. (Eds.): MoDELS 2008, LNCS 5301, pp. 97–112, 2008.

Archetest, that supports both descriptive and precise modeling and maintains strong relations between them. This dual approach aids business analysts in rapid elicitation and also allows requirements analysts specify with precision and perform useful analysis.

By descriptive modeling of requirements, we imply identification of the key use cases of a system and their high level textual specification[1]. By precise modeling of requirements, we mean precise description of the use cases' behaviors as relations between user inputs, system outputs and the internal states of the system. Some researchers arguably refer to this form of modeling as formalization of use cases. Many prior publications [9,10,11,12,13,14,15,16,17] have proposed techniques for formalization of use cases but only [15] among them can possibly support the dual form of modeling like Archetest. Even among the ones which could support the dual form, none of them maintain cross references between the two forms. Cross referencing of the descriptive and the precise model enables Archetest to maintain consistency and also to report analysis results to the different stake-holders in a form (abstract or precise) appropriate for them.

Through this paper we demonstrate how different stake-holders of requirements modeling can co-ordinate using the Archetest use case authoring environment. We demonstrate how precision can be added to descriptive requirements that may have been modeled by a different stake-holder. Further, this paper discusses how different validation analyses can be performed on a unified representation that combines and cross-references the information in the descriptive and the precise forms of use cases. To emphasize, the novel contributions of this work are:

1. the dual layered use case authoring approach.
2. the analysis techniques that maintain consistency in the overall model in spite of the different modes of information inputs.
3. the feedback mechanism that can filter messages to suit the needs of the appropriate stake-holder of the system.

2 The Archetest Modeling Paradigm

As mentioned in the introduction, the descriptive and the precise modeling of use cases in Archetest can be performed by different stake-holders. Precise modeling is optional if the use cases are needed only for communication purposes. The entire model is cross referenced and thus leads to consistent modeling by various stake-holders and is very flexible with regard to change.

2.1 Descriptive Use Case Modeling

Descriptive modeling in Archetest includes identification of the use cases and the actors of a system, followed by high-level description of the use case in terms of interactions between actors and the system.

[1] In principle, UML allows any notation for the description of a use case. However, use of templates to assign a structure to the description is a very common practice.

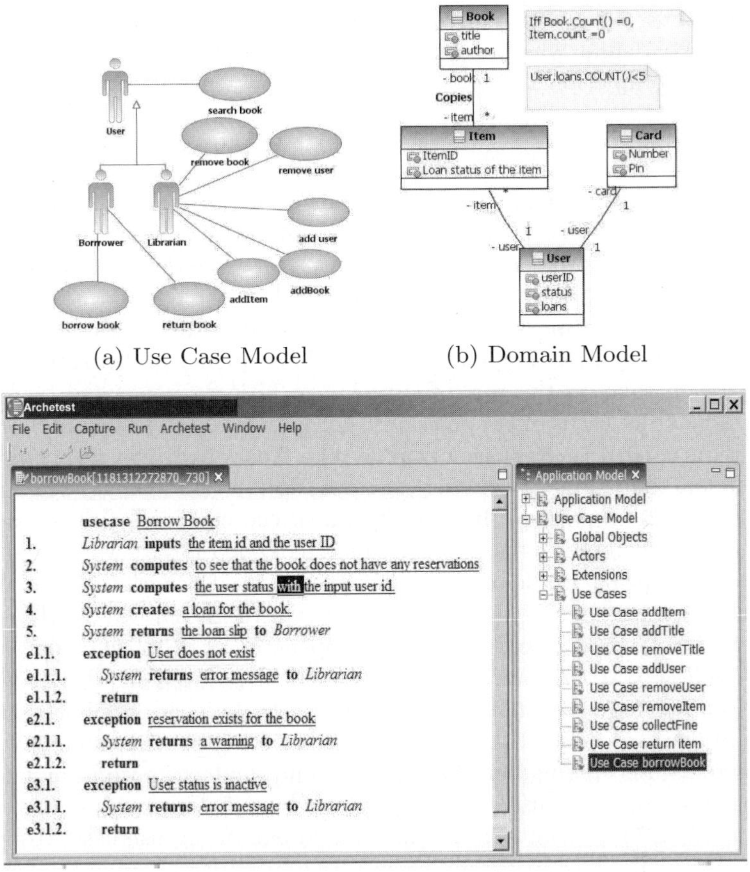

(a) Use Case Model (b) Domain Model

(c) Description of BorrowBook

Fig. 1. The Library System

This interaction is modeled via textual definition structured as series of use case steps, representing the events that occur during a use case[2]. The steps are ordered, and each has an associated sequence label. Use-case steps can define:

1. *input, output*: define information flow to or from an actor;
2. *system state update*: define how system state is changed as a result of the step;
3. *extension points*: identify locations where extensions defined in the global part of the use-case model may indicate invocation of another use case;
4. *inclusion* of another use case;
5. *exceptional conditions*: defining situations in which the ordinary flow of use-case steps must be interrupted, and replaced by some recovery sequence;

[2] This is similar in spirit to many existing use-case representations used in defining functional requirements [18,5].

6. *flow controls including return, retry,* and *continue*: used in recovery sequences to define whether and how to rejoin the interrupted main flow following completion recovery. Return indicates use case termination after recovery; retry models re-execution of the step giving rise to the exception, while continue models resumption at the following step.

For example, consider a model for a library reservation system that has use cases as shown in Figure 1(a). Textual description for a use case *Borrow Book* in Archetest may look like as shown in Figure 1(c). The description is composed of 5 main steps and 3 additional exception blocks.

Each kind of step in Archetest has one or more syntactic forms, loosely based on English syntax. The form consists of a sequence of descriptive free-text phrases, which take on the role of subjects or objects, separated by keywords that usually act as verbs or prepositions. For example, in statement 5 of the use case in Figure 1(c) `5. System returns the loan slip to Borrower`, "System","the loan slip" and "Borrower" are descriptive text strings, while **returns** ... **to** is a syntactic pattern. In order to make the use-case text as readable as possible a set of commonly-used synonyms are defined for keywords and in some cases alternate forms are defined for the same kind of use-case step.

The relationship between the use cases is established via UML identified constructs like "include" and "extension" operations. Both "include" and "extensions" follow UML semantics. *Include* identifiers are defined that when referenced in a use case the included use case will be invoked. Similarly, *extension point* identifiers are defined that, when referenced in use cases, define where extensions, guard permitting, will be invoked. The same extension point identifier can be used in numerous use cases. Separately from extension points, extensions are defined as a map from guard condition to extending use case. A single use case may participate as an extending use case in multiple extensions (with different extended use cases and/or guard conditions). Similarly, an extended use case may define extension points. We do not support use of a single extension point multiple times within a single use case at this time.

2.2 Precise Modeling

During precise modeling of requirements in Archetest the modeler first models the domain of interaction and subsequently, relates the steps in a use case description to concepts in domain model.

Domain Modeling. Domain modeling involves definition of domain classes and system invariants. Descriptive modeling and Domain modeling can be carried out independently of each other and, if needed, by different stake-holders of the system. Because the appropriate level for use case models is requirements, rather than design, domain model classes do not have associated methods. However, they do have attributes, typed by a pre-defined set of primitive types, including String, Real, Integer, and Boolean. Additional types may be lists or sets of types and the classes in the domain model. Generalization is supported. Attributes may have multiplicity and order defined, and optionally an initialization expression used to determine an attribute's initial value when objects of the containing class are created. Classes also include references, typed by the class of the target object. This is the primary means of expressing association between classes. In addition to the structural descriptions the domain model can have system wide constraints that we term *domain invariants.* Domain invariants can be modeled in Archetest via any of the following:

1. *Business Rules*: These are expressions on distinct universally quantified typed variables. For example a business rule may state that a borrower can borrow at most five books from the library: `User.loans.COUNT()`$<$ `5` . In this notation use of a class `User` as the basis of a term implies universal quantification. `COUNT()` is a method on sets that returns the cardinality of the set. We have avoided use of quantified variable notation in the interest of making the specification as widely understood as possible. Thus, a class used in a business rule refers to a universally quantified variable. In the event that a class is used more than once, all uses refer to the same variable.
2. *Key Invariants*: Key invariants describe features whose values are unique within a particular set of objects called a key context. For key contexts to be useful in practice, it is necessary that membership be changed only as a result of explicit state updates, and that contexts be readily determined as a result of these contexts. We have identified two kinds of context that satisfy this criterion: universal and feature. Universal-context keys must be unique among all objects of the same or conforming class. For example, a `User` object may have a universal key, `userId`. No two `Users` would have the same value for `userId`. That would include objects created as `Borrower`, of which `User` is a generalization. Feature-context keys are unique within the set of objects referenced via a particular multi-valued structural feature of an object. Thus, when modeling a hierarchical file system, in the context of a multi-valued attribute `Directory.files` of type `File`, attribute `File.name` need not be universally unique (i.e., unique among all `File` objects ever created), but must be unique within the `files` of a particular `Directory`.
3. *Association Invariants*: Another set of invariants is implied from the association between classes. These invariants constrain creation and deletion of objects. For instance, the class named *Book* has a one-to-many association to a class named *Items* (see Figure 1(b)), so anytime an instance of *Item* is created it has to be associated to "one and only one" instance of *Book*.

For many invariants, event flow for recovery from violation of a particular invariant is fixed regardless of the context in which the violation occurs. To support this situation, fixed use-case recovery behavior can be associated with invariants.

Adding precision to Use Case Steps. Adding precision to the descriptive model is a wizard driven process which may also be performed simultaneously. The use case steps are classified into the five types as identified in section 2.1.

Identification of the kind of use case step is performed by parsing them in accordance to a set of pre-populated patterns. Double clicking a parsed step in a use case model opens up a dialog box that is then used to define the precise behavior. An input or output step when double clicked pops up a parameter. Such a window lets the modeler define the name and the type of the input/output parameters. A drop down menu lists the types described in the domain model along with the primitive types. Thus the wizard ensures that the parameters' types are unambiguous. Additionally, for output parameters one can specify an associated update.

Updates can be defined using parameters and/or (created or queried) objects. Double clicking on any *state modification* step in a use case model will activate the update dialog box as shown in Figure 2. Using the dialog box one can

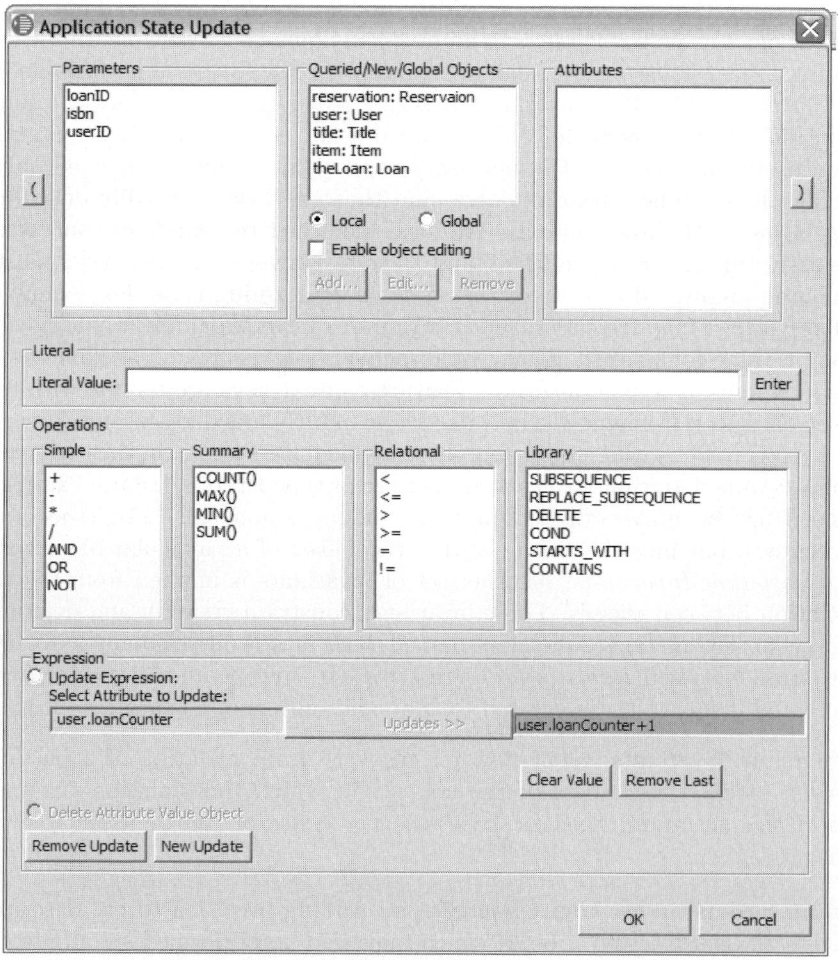

Fig. 2. Archetest wizard for adding precision to update statements

access created and queried objects, already defined parameters and a variety of operators and functions. One can define the update by identifying the attribute or parameter that gets updated and subsequently defining an update expression using a combination of pre-defined parameters, operators, attributes of objects and literals. For instance the figure elicits the precise modeling for the update statement `4.System` **`creates`** `a loan for the book`. The updated attribute is `user.loanCounter`. The update expression is set to `user.loanCounter+1`. Similar updates can be specified for all the update steps and output steps in the description. Also, a single step in the use case description can encompass multiple updates.

Specification of created or queried objects is facilitated by the object creation dialog box. A created object represents the process of instantiating a class in the domain model. A queried object, on the other hand, represents a directive that implies searching for an already created object for a given set of `<attribute, value>` properties. This way one use case can define updates to objects modeled as being created in a different use case.

3 Automated Analysis

Archetest transforms the precise information in the use case model to a unified flat representation in which each use case is represented by a set of guarded scenarios. The algorithm for transformation is presented in [19]. The algorithm takes into account special use case constructs like *included use cases* and *extension points*. The transformation algorithm also links elements of the unified representation to elements of the user created model. This is important to establish traceability.

In the unified representation, a guarded scenario is represented as a pair (g, U) where g is the guard condition (defined as predicate on domain attributes and use case inputs) and U is a set of update actions. Consider the example shown in Figure 1(c). The use case *BorrowBook* can be flattened to four equivalent scenarios as shown in Figure 3.

3.1 Ambiguity Analysis

Ambiguity errors in requirements modeling refer to requirements that cannot be clearly interpreted [20,21]. Archetest limits ambiguity in modeling by preventing common modeling errors. During descriptive modeling, all actors need to be defined before they can be accessed. Also, the *include* statement requires definition of the *included* use cases. An *extending* use case pre-empts the definition of the associated extension point. During domain modeling, Archetest prevents unwanted name conflicts. It does not allow one to arbitrarily specify the type of an attribute. The type of an attribute can only be set by a drop down menu, which is pre-populated with the pre-defined domain model types. Basic type checking prevents users from specifying bad initial values for the attributes and also ensures that the context for a key attribute be type consistent. Refinement

```
Use Case = borrowBook/{Actors:< Librarian , Borrower>}.
Parameters:
  input :<userID,itemID::String>
  output:<slip::returnSlip; errorMessage, warningMessage::String>

Success scenario
Guard: g1:
  ∃ book:(book.ItemID==itemId,book.reserved== false, Book(book)) &&
  ∃ user:(user.userId==userID, user.borrowPrivileges== true,
        user.type == userType.borrower, User(user))
Updates: u1:
  Created Objects -> {newSlip::returnSlip,theLoan::Loan}
  Created Links ->{<theLoan,user>;<theLoan,book>;<newSlip,theLoan>;
        <newSlip,book>}
  Parameter Updates-> slip := newSlip

Alternate Scenario 1
Guard: g2:
  ∃book:(book.ItemID==itemId, book.reserved== true, Item(book))
Updates: u2:
  Parameter Updates->warningMessage:= 'There is a reservation on the item'

Alternate Scenario 2
Guard: g3:
  ∃user:(user.userId== userID, user.borrowPrivileges==false,
        user.type == userType.borrower, User(user))
Updates: u3
  Parameter Updates -> errorMessage := 'User previleges are withdrawn'

Alternate Scenario 3
Guard: g4:
  ∀user,(user.userId != userID, User(user))
Updates: u4
  Parameter Updates -> errorMessage := 'No such user'
```

Fig. 3. Guarded Scenarios for Borrowbook

of use case steps in Archetest is GUI driven. This limits the expressions defining the precise behavior to use only the pre-populated domain model entities.

Nondeterminism in use case behavior could also lead to requirement ambiguities. Archetest analyzes the scenarios of a use case as represented in the unified representation and ensures that their guard conditions are mutually exclusive. Recall that in the unified representation a guard condition on scenario is defined as predicate on domain attributes and use case inputs. Two guard conditions are said to be mutually exclusive iff they cannot be simultaneously true for any system state and any value of the inputs. Non-determinism can also be caused by under-specification of delete actions. Domain models in Archetest lack distinction between composition and aggregation associations between classes.

Given a delete operation for an object in the absence of the exact nature of the association, it may not be clear whether or not to delete all the linked objects. Consequently, the exact behavior of a *d*elete object action may be not understood. To resolve this ambiguity Archetest prompts the user for further specification whenever it detects a *delete object*. The user is iteratively asked to choose between deleting or not deleting the linked objects (composition vs. aggregation).

3.2 Completeness Analysis

In order to find incomplete description of use cases, Archetest evaluates whether the set of guarded scenarios covers all possible situations. To start with, Archetest symbolically evaluates the expression $G = g_1 \cup g_2 \cup \ldots g_n$ where g_i is the guard condition on the ith scenario, s_i. If the result is a *tautology*[3] then we know that all the conditions of execution of a use case have been described. In the event that G is not a *tautology*, Archetest evaluates g^* such that $G \cup g^*$ is a *tautology*, i.e., $g^* \equiv \neg G$. For example, if we look into the example use case of *Borrow Book* in Figure 3 and compute $G = g_1 \cup g_2 \cup g_3 \cup g_4$. We find that G is not a tautology. In fact, $G \equiv$ ∃`user:user.type == userType.borrower`. Therefore, we compute the missing guard as $g^* \equiv$ ∃`user:user.type != userType.borrower`. Seeing, g^* we can say that the use case does not provide specification for the situations when a `User` exists with a *type* other than the `Borrower`.

3.3 Invariant Analysis

In a process called invariant analysis, Archetest analyzes the invariants and the use cases to determine whether the use case describes the behavior of the system when a certain related invariant is violated. Invariant analysis starts by first computing a *tripartite* graph, called `UCDMBRGraph`, in which the set of Use Cases, the set of Domain Model entities(Classes and Associations), and the set of Invariants each form a partition. For instance, consider the example business rule :`User.loans.COUNT()` $\leq$ `5`. The business rule can be affected by any of the three following ways: 1) by creating a loan; 2) by returning a book 3) by adding a user. Figure 4 illustrates a partial `UCDMBRGraph` for use cases `addItem`, `addBook`, the class `User`, and invariant `D1` from the Library example.

A use case node has an edge to a domain model entity if the use case manipulates (either *creates*, *updates* or *deletes*) the entity. Such an edge is labeled with 1) the nature of the manipulation (Create/Update/Delete), 2) attribute set of the entity being initialized/modified, and 3) the *navigation path* - the chain of class accesses - used to reach the instance being manipulated. Referring to the left hand side of Figure 4, an edge between use case `addUser` and class `User` exists and is labeled by `Create` action, {`userID`} attributes and an empty navigation path. Similarly, an edge exists between use case `BorrowBook` and class

[3] A tautology is a logical expression possibly containing more than one sub-expression, that is true regardless of the truth values of its parts.

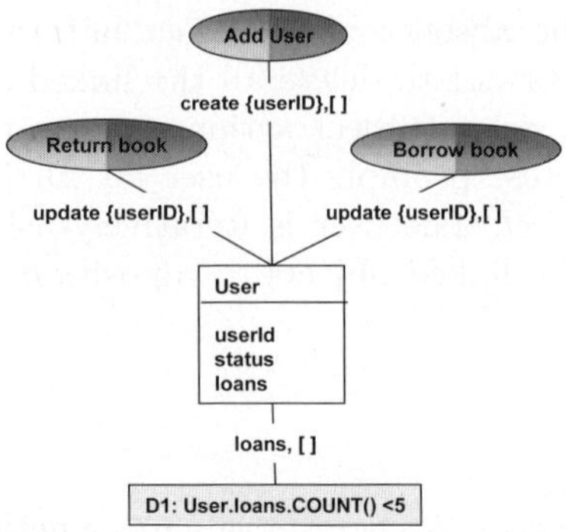

Fig. 4. UCDMBR Graph for Library

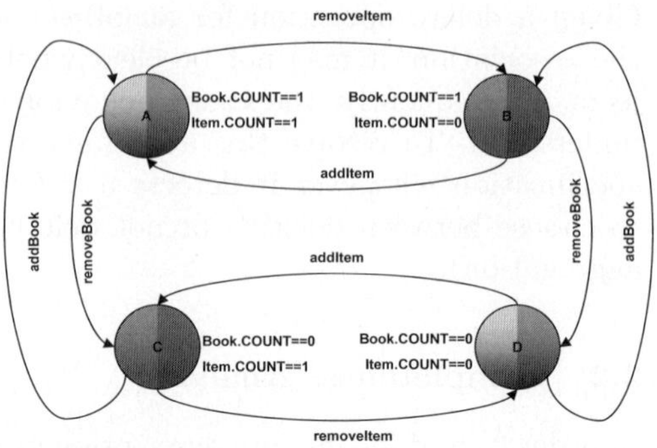

Fig. 5. Data State Graph

User and is labeled with Update action, {userID} attributes and an empty navigation path. An invariant has an edge to a domain model entity if the invariant refers to it. Such an edge is labeled with the referred attributes and the navigation path used to reach each attribute. Referring to the right hand side of Figure 4, an edge between invariant D1 and class User exists and is labeled with loans as the impacted attribute and an empty navigation path. Our analysis exploits the UCDMBRGraph to identify the set of potential use cases affected by an invariant. This is done by traversing the edge from an invariant to the domain model entities referred in it and then following the edges from the domain model entities to the use cases that modify those entities. Thus, invariant D1 refers to class User and attribute loans which in turn are modified by use cases addUser, borrowBook and returnBook. At this point, Archetest can evaluate the guard conditions for each of the affected use cases to evaluate whether the use case describes the behavior for violation of a business rule.

3.4 Consistency Analysis

An Archetest domain model can have invariants which can render certain data states not reachable. For example consider the example business rule that states Book.COUNT() == 0 $\iff$ Item.COUNT() == 0. This business rule states that number of books in the system cannot be zero unless the number of corresponding items is also zero. Therefore, the implication is that if a Book is removed from the Library, the list of Items needs to be simultaneously updated. Thus, the use case *removeBook* must always be accompanied by the use case *removeItem.* Since the use cases have no notion of concurrency, this may lead to inconsistencies in the system state. In order to identify such inconsistencies, Archetest constructs a system state graph based on the domain model and the unified representation, a subset of which is shown in Figure 5. The nodes represent various states of the system and the edges are annotated with the call of use case scenarios. For each node in the system state graph Archetest determines if it violates any of the system invariants, e.g.,states B and C in Figure 5. Archetest tags them as the "red-states". The remaining states are marked as "green states". A path to a "red state" produces a warning. Traversing the object graph if Archetest finds no exit path from a "red-state" to a "green state", it reports an error.

4 Error Feedback

For modeling errors Archetest provides immediate feedback via warning messages. All post-modeling analysis results are provided to the modeler as a set of suggestions once the analysis is complete. Archetest identifies a set of modeling locations that can lead to a particular modeling error. The error sources are identified by tracing back to the model location by making use of the information preserved during model transformations. A single error can originate from a number of model locations. Archetest suggests corrective action by listing each of the modeling locations.

Error feedback in Archetest can be filtered to the view chosen by stake-holders. The feedback could be filtered according to their origination location, according to their type and according to the contributor of the model. This not only helps narrow down the "to-do" list but also helps direct feedback to the appropriate stake-holders. For example, consider the result of completeness analysis as discussed in 3.2, viz., the use case *B*orrow Book does not provide behavioral specification for the situations when a `User` exists with a *type* other than the `Borrower`. For a business analyst, the message is translated to "Missing flow for use case `Borrow Book`: Describe flow when `User` has `userType` not equal to `Borrower`". The same error will have a much detailed view for a requirement analyst. Along with the message it will suggest the points of origination as: "Domain Model: User. userType", "Use Case: Borrow Book {steps 2,5,7}". Also it will print the diagnosis steps for him/her to understand the failure.

5 Case Study

As part of this case study, we used Archetest to model six different applications. Table 1 lists the various applications along with the number of use cases (UCs) the net number of scenarios (Scen), the net time to model in Archetest (tArch) in hours,the time to model descriptively in Archetest (tDesc), the time to add precision in Archetest (tPrec), the net time to model in a text editor using natural language (tOther) and the net number of requirements errors (Err). The choice of applications was guided by a desire to vary their size and complexity. As can be seen, between App_VM an App_SOA the sizes vary by almost of a factor of 10. App_OS represents a functional module of a file server system for a commercial operating system, App_SOA is an online repository of assets implemented via five interacting web-services, App_Lib is the loan management application for a library as previously described in the paper, App_ATM is an ATM application, App_DP is a department's project management application and App_VM is a use case description for a simple vending machine. As can be seen App_DP and

Table 1. Case Study Measurements

Application	UCs	Scen	tArch	tDesc	tPrec	tOther	Err
App_O/S	16	109	30	5	25	13	66
App_SOA	94	190	44	10	34	23	128
App_Lib	9	33	14	4	10	8	32
App_ATM	12	39	20	6	14	14	19
App_DP	7	12	1	0.2	0.8	0.8	8
App_VM	2	3	1	0.25	0.75	0.6	1

App_VM are considerably smaller than the rest. Also, App_SOA can serve as a representative industrial application.

The experiment was conducted for each system in three stages. In stage 1 the use cases were authored in plain English, based on verbal discussions with the code owners, by two independent modelers. The interviews were recorded. On completion the use case specifications were swapped between the modelers for cross validation. Once an agreement was reached, necessary corrections were made to the respective specifications. In stage 2 modeler 1 was asked to model use cases in Archetest and tArch, tDesc and tPrec were recorder while modeler 2 re-wrote the specification in plain English based on the recorded interviews and tOther was recorded. In stage 3 they swapped roles and times were re-recorded. Stage 1 was necessary to ensure that modelers understanding of the systems is complete. The use of two modelers was to reduce the effect of personal biases. Once stage 3 was complete, Archetest analyzed the models and computed errors. The case study results were then compiled based on the feedback from the modelers. The reported times are the averages of the two modelers. In all occasions the tArch exceeded tOther confirming the intuition that addition of precision has an associated cost. Also, tDesc was always considerably less than tPrec. This shows that majority of the time the modeler spent in Archetest was towards adding precision. But the time loss in adding precision is compensated by identification of modeling errors. The modeling errors that were prevented during the modeling phase were not recorded. We report in Table 1, the number of errors identified by Archetest analysis. Missing Requirements constituted the most frequently occurring requirement error. A deeper analysis showed that Missing Invariant-Handler requirements were the largest contributors to this class. This is probably because relations between requirements specified through use cases and domain-model invariants may not be evident to the modeler. A plot of requirement errors against the size (see Figure 6) shows that the number of requirement errors grows almost linearly with the number of use cases. This is an unexpected characteristic and may suggest that managing modeling errors remains tractable as model size increases.

In order to assess the scalability of the approach we measured the net time to model in Archetest and plotted it against the number of functions in an application (represented by scenarios). Figure 7 shows result of regression analysis between time to model and the number of scenarios. A best-fit minimizing sum of squared errors suggests a logarithmic fit. Hence, it can be said that

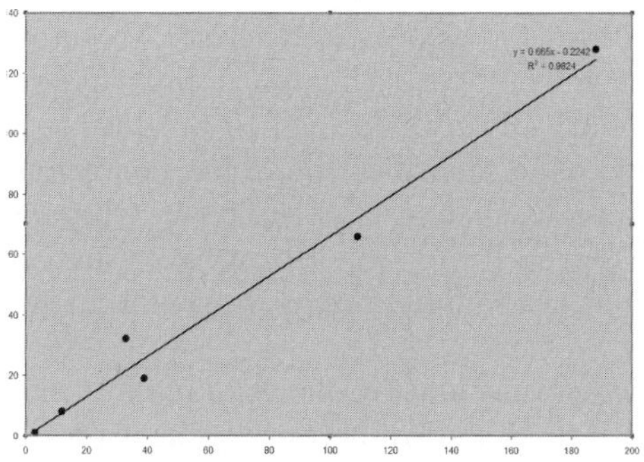

Fig. 6. Size vrs Errors

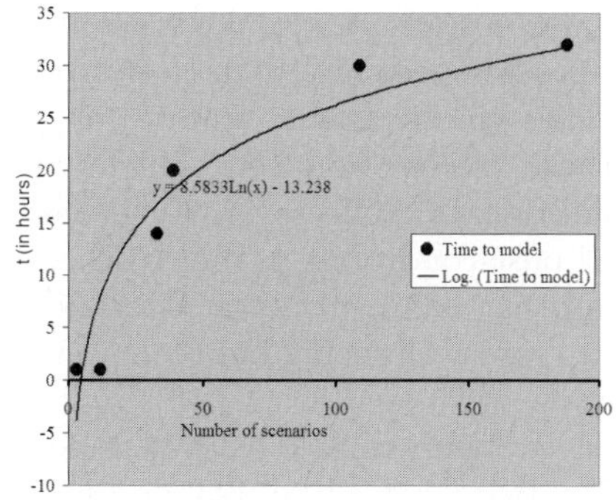

Fig. 7. Time / Size Regression

time_to_model $\propto$ ln(*size_of_app*). The logarithmic fit indicates that domain-modeling overhead is amortized across the set of all use cases. Thus, initial findings strongly suggest that, on a per-use-case basis, domain-model creation time decreases with increasing application size, implying greater than expected scalability of the modeling process. Present data are insufficient to fully characterize this relationship and more case studies will be required to substantiate these findings. However it will be interesting to investigate in detail how domain modeling overhead scales with respect to application size and complexity.

6 Related Work

Archetest is related to approaches that use a combination of use cases and class diagrams for functional requirement specification [18,13,22,10]. While, the use cases describe actor-system interactions, class diagrams are used to describe the domain / context of such interactions.

Our work is also related to the approaches that formalize use cases to identify system's state transition information with use case interactions. These formalization approaches can be classified into two broad categories:

- formalization by authoring use cases in a notation that has formal underpinnings such as use case charts [17], higher order logic [16], object calculus [14], petri nets [15].
- formalization by appending the use case description with additional models such as message sequence charts [9,12], activity flow diagrams [10,13], collaboration diagrams [13];

Among these, only Jorgensen in [15] discusses a multi-tier approach to formal analysis. His work however, fails to recognize the need to preserve the relation between the precise and descriptive forms of the model.

Additional related work focuses on requirements analysis using use cases. Hausmann et. al. use techniques based on graph transformation in [13] which is similar in spirit to Archetest. Unlike Archetest, their techniques require modelers to provide pre-conditions and post-conditions for use cases, whereas Archetest models specify input, update, output actions as expressions on domain model entities (see section 2.2), which are automatically transformed to produce pre-conditions and effects. Analysis based on explicit identification of pre-conditions and post-conditions in many other publications such as [16,15,11,14]. Glinz on the other hand proposes a semi-formal approach in [18]. He proposes extensive cross-referencing between scenarios and class model to reduce requirements errors.

Less closely related work includes consistency evaluation of design models such as by Briand et. al. in [23] and Egyed in [24]. While Archetest's focus is on use case models, these other techniques focus on design level models like state charts and sequence diagrams. Currently impact analysis and change management of models is not Archetest's objective. However, the ideas in this paper can be extended to incorporate change management for use cases.

7 Summary and Conclusions

This paper presented a use case authoring tool, Archetest, which supports use case definition in presence of a domain model. We showed how such a tool supports separation of two use-case concerns: informal definition for communication purposes and domain-expert use; and formal analysis for automated software engineering. Subsequently, we discussed requirement error detection techniques that Archetest supports. The paper concludes with a case study and analysis results on a set of applications of varying size and complexity.

In conclusion it can be said that by allowing use cases to be modeled in presence of a domain model and by allowing definition of behavioral predicates and expressions in terms of domain model elements, use cases can be captured with enough precision to run automated requirements analysis. We believe that such a tool will prove very valuable in most software engineering requirements collection activities. Apart from requirements analysis, Archetest is, at present, being used for Model Based Automatic Test Generation. In the future we intend to extend Archetest to other software engineering activities like use-case based cost estimation and software complexity analysis.

References

1. Carroll, J.M.: Five reasons for scenario-based design. In: HICSS (1999)
2. Firesmith, D.G.: Modeling the Dynamic Behavior of Systems, Mechanisms and Classes with Scenarios, pp. 32–36. SIGS Publication, New York (1994)
3. Hsia, P., Samuel, J., Gao, J., Kung, D., Toyoshima, Y., Chen, C.: Formal approach to scenario analysis. IEEE Softw. 11(2), 33–41 (1994)
4. Jacobson, I.: Object-oriented development in an industrial environment. In: OOPSLA 1987: Conference proceedings on Object-oriented programming systems, languages and applications, pp. 183–191. ACM Press, New York (1987)

5. Rosenberg, D., Scott, K.: Use case driven object modeling with UML: a practical approach. Addison-Wesley Longman Publishing Co., Inc., Boston (1999)
6. Rubin, K.S., Goldberg, A.: Object behavior analysis. Commun. ACM 35(9), 48–62 (1992)
7. Potts, C., Takahashi, K., Anton, A.: Inquiry-based requirements analysis. IEEE Software 11(2), 21–32 (1994)
8. Blain, T.: Use case series: Formal use case, `http://tynerblain.wordpress.com/2005/12/19/use-case-series-formal-use-case/`
9. Regnell, B., Kimbler, K., Wesslen, A.: Improving the use case driven approach to requirements engineering. re 00, 40 (1995)
10. Kösters, G., Pagel, B.U., Winter, M.: Coupling use cases and class models. In: BCS FACS/EROS Workshop on Making Object-oriented Methods more Rigorous (1997)
11. Lee, W.J., Cha, S.D., Kwon, Y.R.: Integration and analysis of use cases using mod- ular petri nets in requirements engineering. Software Engineering 24(12), 1115–1130 (1998)
12. Moreira, A., Jo a.A.: Generating object-z specications from use cases, pp. 43–50 (2000)
13. Hausmann, J.H., Heckel, R., Taentzer, G.: Detection of conicting functional requirements in a use case-driven approach: a static analysis technique based on graph transformation. In: ICSE, pp. 105–115 (2002)
14. Bures, F., Rysav, O.: Formal abstract architecture for use case specications. In: Proceedings of the 11th IEEE International Conference and Workshop on the Engineering of Computer-Based Systems, pp. 203–211. IEEE Computer Society Press, Los Alamitos (2004)
15. Jorgensen, J.B., Bossen, C.: Executable use cases: Requirements for a pervasive health care system. IEEE Softw. 21(2), 34–41 (2004)
16. Li, X., Liu, Z., He, J.: Consistency checking of uml requirements. In: ICECCS 2005: Proceedings of the 10th IEEE International Conference on Engineering of Complex Computer Systems (ICECCS 2005), Wasshington, DC, USA, pp. 411–420. IEEE Computer Society, Los Alamitos (2005)
17. Whittle, J., Jayaraman, P.K.: Generating hierarchical state machines from use case charts. In: Proc. of the 14th IEEE International Requirements Engineering Conference (RE 2006), Washington, DC, USA, pp. 16–25. IEEE, Los Alamitos (2006)
18. Glinz, M.: A lightweight approach to consistency of scenarios and class models. In: ICRE, pp. 49–58 (2000)
19. Sinha, A., Paradkar, A., Williams, C.: On generating efsm models from use cases. In: SCESM 2007: Proceedings of Sixth InternationalWorkshop on Scenario and State Machines, pp. 1–9 (2007)
20. Hayes, J.H.: Building a requirement fault taxonomy: Experiences from a nasa verication and validation research project. In: ISSRE 2003: Proceedings of the 14th International Symposium on Software Reliability Engineering, Washington,DC, USA, p. 49. IEEE Computer Society, Los Alamitos (2003)
21. Miller, L., Mirsky, S., Hayes, J.H.: Guidelines for the verication and validation of expert system software and conventional software. Technical Report NUREG/CR-6316, U.S. Nuclear Regulatory Commission and Electric Power Research Institute (March 1995)
22. Buhr, R.J.A.: Use case maps as architectural entities for complex systems. IEEE Trans. Softw. Eng. 24(12), 1131–1155 (1998)

23. Briand, L.C., Labiche, Y., O'Sullivan, L.: Impact analysis and change management of uml models. In: ICSM, Washington, DC, USA, p. 256. IEEE Computer Society, Los Alamitos (2003)
24. Egyed, A.: Fixing inconsistencies in uml design models. In: ICSE 2007: Proceedings of the 29th International Conference on Software Engineering, Washington, DC,USA, pp. 292–301. IEEE Computer Society, Los Alamitos (2007)

WebWorkFlow: An Object-Oriented Workflow Modeling Language for Web Applications

Zef Hemel, Ruben Verhaaf, and Eelco Visser

Software Engineering Research Group, Delft University of Technology, The Netherlands
Z.Hemel@tudelft.nl, rverhaaf@gmail.com, visser@acm.org

Abstract. Workflow languages are designed for the high-level description of processes and are typically not suitable for the generation of complete applications. In this paper, we present WebWorkFlow, an object-oriented workflow modeling language for the high-level description of workflows in web applications. Workflow descriptions define procedures operating on domain objects. Procedures are composed using sequential and concurrent process combinators. WebWorkFlow is an embedded language, extending WebDSL, a domain-specific language for web application development, with workflow abstractions. The extension is implemented by means of model-to-model transformations. Rather than providing an exclusive workflow language, WebWorkFlow supports interaction with the underlying WebDSL language. WebWorkFlow supports most of the basic workflow control patterns.

1 Introduction

Workflow is concernced with the coordination of *activities* performed by *participants* involving *artifacts* [9,19]. Workflow and business process modeling languages such as UML activity diagrams [5], BPEL [4], and YAWL [17], are designed for the high-level description of a wide variety of workflows or *business processes* ranging from the documentation of the operating procedures for a factory, the administrative processes involving (paper) documents of a business, or the procedures carried out by medical staff with patients in a hospital. Thus, participants in a workflow may be people, machines, or machines operated by people, and artifacts may be electronic data or physical artifacts. A worklow description may be just the documentation of a procedure to be carried out by humans, or it may be the specification of an interactive automated process. If automated, a workflow may be coordinated by a central machine (e.g. a web server), or it may consist of a network of collaborating (web) services. To cover this wide range of applications, workflow languages are restricted to modeling processes and not complete applications. That is, using a workflow engine for the execution of a process definition requires external applications or code to implement individual activities.

Web applications are concerned with presenting information to, and obtaining information from users interactively through a web browser. There are many types of web applications that contain workflow elements, i.e. the coordination

K. Czarnecki et al. (Eds.): MoDELS 2008, LNCS 5301, pp. 113–127, 2008.

of activities performed by participants. Consider for instance the following three examples. (1) An issue tracker coordinating the activities of the members of a project through registration, assignment and monitoring progress on issues. (2) A conference management system coordinating the activities of authors, program chairs, program committee members, external reviewers, meeting planners, and attendees to produce, review, select, and present a collection of scientific publications. (3) A user registration component, creating an account for a new user by subsequently registering, checking of credentials and confirming by email, involving a user and administrator. Thus, workflow concepts can be used as organizing principle for the engineering of many web applications, supporting the high-level implementation of the administration and monitoring of a process.

Rather than deriving an incomplete skeleton or boilerplate application from a process definition, a customized application with workflow requires *integration* of a workflow description language with a web engineering language.

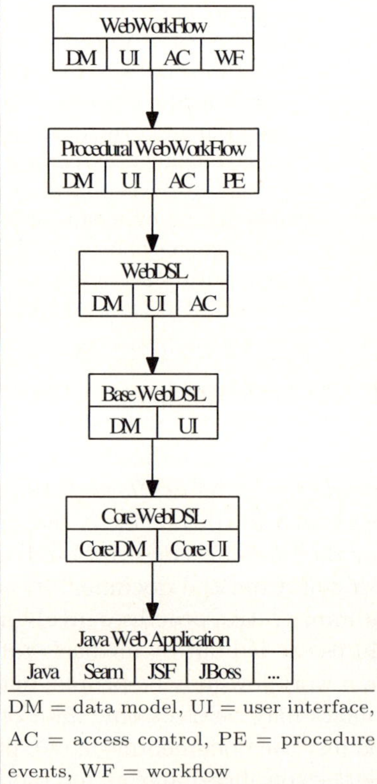

Fig. 1. WebWorkFlow is implemented as extension of WebDSL, which is itself implemented by means of model-to-model transformations to a core subset, which is transformed to code for the Java/Seam web platform

In this paper, we present WebWorkFlow, an object-oriented workflow modeling language for the high-level description of workflows in web applications. WebWorkFlow is an *embedded language* [3] extending WebDSL [18], a domain-specific language for web application development, with workflow abstractions (Figure 1). From the definition of procedures operating on objects, and a control flow description to connect these procedures, complete custom web applications can be generated.

The WebWorkFlow generator is designed and built using a number of best practices for *domain-specific language engineering* [18]. Rather than providing an exclusive workflow language, WebWorkFlow supports interaction with the underlying WebDSL language. This approach enables the use of workflow abstractions where possible, and the use of the regular web modeling facilities where needed. This practice is called *language integration and separation of concerns [7]*.

The target language (WebDSL) is a subset of the source language. The high-level language is more expressive (more concise models), but may not have the same coverage. For example, process expressions support only structured control-flow, while the underlying procedure event model supports unstructured control-flow. Thus, this approach makes it possible to use high-level abstractions where possible, but allows escaping to the next lower level where needed, thus increasing coverage of the language. This approach is called *compilation by normalization [10]* and is sketched in Figure 1. At the top level is WebWorkFlow, a rich DSL with sub-languages for data, user interface, access control and workflow modeling. WebWorkFlow is translated to lower-level procedural WebWorkFlow where workflow process descriptions have been translated to procedure events. Procedures are translated to a combination of data models, user interface elements and access control rules. This chain of transformations continues until all that is left is core WebDSL, a relatively low level model that can be easily mapped to the target platform, in this case Java/SEAM.

The rest of this paper is structured as follows. In the next section we introduce WebWorkFlow procedures by means of an example. In Section 3 we describe our implementation approach, explaining the procedure event model underlying the implementation of high-level process descriptions, the transformation of process expressions to procedure events, and the transformation of procedures to WebDSL, building on its high-level data model, user interface, and access control abstractions. In Section 4 we evaluate the coverage of WebWorkflow by examing the encoding of the control-flow patterns of Van der Aalst et al. [16]. In Section 5 we discuss the relation of WebWorkFlow to other process modeling approaches.

2 WebWorkFlow by Example

Workflows in WebWorkFlow are defined by means of *workflow procedures* that operate on *workflow objects*. In this section we introduce the high-level language constructs for defining objects and procedures, using as running example a simple workflow for organizing 'progress meetings' between managers and their employees. More precisely, rather than organizing the meeting itself, the workflow organizes the organization surrounding the meeting. Prior to the meeting, the manager and employee provide their own view on the progress of the employee. After the meeting the manager writes a `report` about the meeting. The employee may approve the report or may provide `comments` on the report, which may cause the manager to revise the report. When the report is approved, the manager finalizes it. The complete WebWorkFlow implementation of this `ProgressMeeting` workflow is defined in Figures 2 and 3.

```
entity User {
  username  :: String
  password  :: Secret
  name      :: String
  manager   -> User
  employees -> Set<User>
}
entity ProgressMeeting {
  employee      -> User
  employeeView :: Text
  managerView  :: Text
  report       :: Text
  approved     :: Bool
  comment      :: Text
}
```

Fig. 2. WebDSL data model for progress meeting workflow

Workflow Objects. WebWorkFlow is an *object-oriented* workflow language. Central to the definition of a workflow is a workflow object that accumulates the data produced in the process and documents its progress. Typically, a workflow object is a domain object in the domain model of the application. For example, in a conference management system natural workflow objects are `Paper` and `Review`. If the only purpose of a workflow is to schedule a number of steps without a natural domain object, a special entity can be created to represent the instances of the workflow.

Workflow objects are instances of entities described using WebDSL data models [18]. Figure 2 describes the data model for the progress meeting workflow. A data model consists of *entity declarations* such as `User` and `ProgressMeeting`.

```
procedure meeting(p : ProgressMeeting) {
  process {
    (writeEmployeeView(p)
                   |AND| writeManagerView(p));
    repeat {
      writeReport(p);
      (approveReport(p) |XOR| commentReport(p))
    } until finalizeReport(p)
  }
}
procedure writeEmployeeView(p : ProgressMeeting) {
  who  { principal = p.employee }
  view {
    derive procedurePage from p
       for (view(employee), employeeView)
  }
}
procedure writeManagerView(p : ProgressMeeting) {
  who  { principal = p.employee.manager }
  view {
    derive procedurePage from p
       for (view(employee), managerView)
  }
}
procedure writeReport(p : ProgressMeeting) {
  who  { principal = p.employee.manager }
  view {
    derive procedurePage from p
       for (view(employee), view(employeeView),
            view(managerView), report)
  }
}
procedure approveReport(p : ProgressMeeting) {
  who  { principal = p.employee }
  do   { p.approved := true; }
}
procedure commentReport(p : ProgressMeeting) {
  who  { principal = p.employee }
  view {
    derive procedurePage from p
       for (view(employee), view(report),
            commments)
  }
  do   { email(commentNotification(p));
  }
}
procedure finalizeReport(p : ProgressMeeting) {
  who  { principal = p.employee.manager }
  when { p.report != "" && p.approved }
}
```

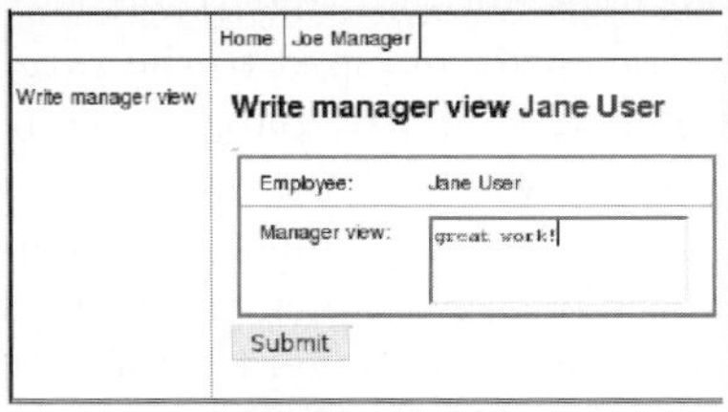

(a) `writeManagerView(p)`

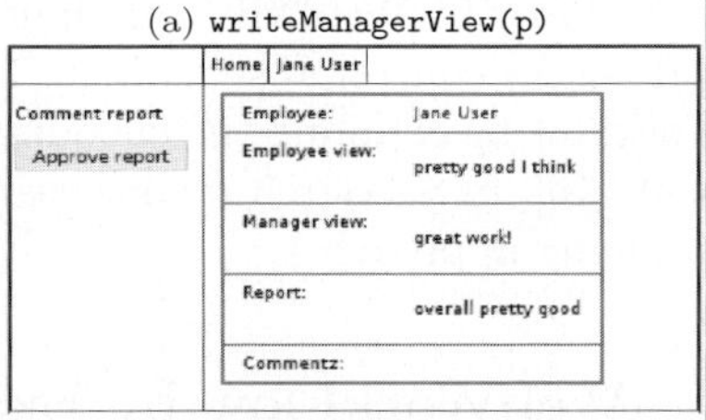

(b) `approveReport(p) |XOR| commentReport(p)`

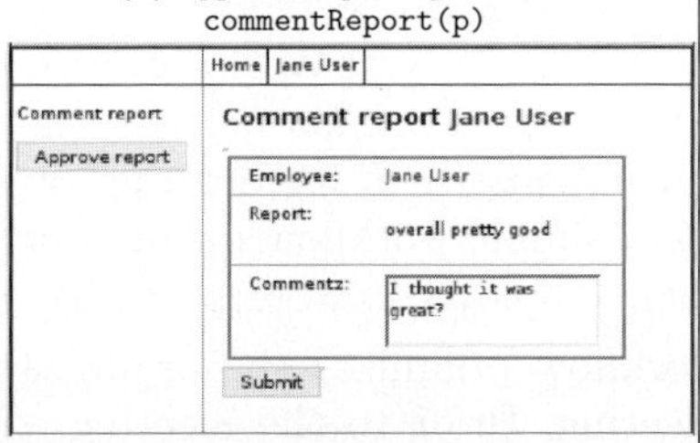

(c) `commentReport(p)`

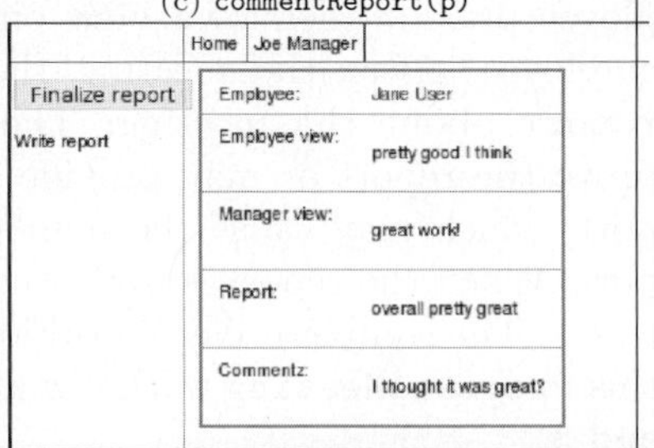

(d) `repeat{ writeReport(p) ... } until finalizeReport(p)`

Fig. 3. Progress meeting workflow procedure with screenshots

An entity declaration has *properties*, which associate data with entity instances. A property has a *name* and a *type*, which may be either a *value type* indicated by `::` (e.g. `String`, `Text`, `Secret`) or a reference type, indicated by `->`, referring to other entities or collections of entities (e.g. `Set<User>`).

Workflow Procedures. A workflow in WebWorkFlow is formalized by means of a *procedure*, which describes activities to be performed by one or more participants in a particular order. A procedure may consist of a single step, or may be a composition of procedures. A procedure may be automatic or may require a user to provide input, which may require a simple button click or filling in a complete form. Figure 3 defines the procedures for the progress meeting workflow. The `meeting` procedure defines the overall process of the workflow by composing the other procedures, which each define a single step. The screenshots on the right of Figure 3 are snapshots from a workflow conducted by 'Joe Manager' and 'Jane User'. The name in the menubar indicates the logged in user.

Figure 4 defines the syntax of high-level procedure definitions. Thus, a procedure definition has a *name* (`f`), exactly one typed parameter (`x:A`) indicating the workflow object to which the procedure applies, and a number of optional clauses, `who`, `when`, `view`, `do`, and `process`, which are discussed below. In the next section, the list of procedure clauses is extended to cater for the definition of *procedure events*.

```
procedure f(x : A) {
  who     { who }
  when    { when }
  view    { elem* }
  do      { stat* }
  process { pexp }
}
```

Fig. 4. Procedures

Actor. The `who` clause determines which participants can apply the procedure by means of an access control predicate, based on the declarative access control model of WebDSL [7]. The expression is a constraint on the current session and the workflow object, and any objects reachable from those via properties. The session includes a pointer to the *principal*, i.e. the logged in user associated with the session. For example, the `writeReport` procedure requires that the `principal` corresponds to `p.employee.manager`, that is, the manager of the employee for which the meeting is organized.

Activation. The `when` clause provides additional constraints on the applicability of a procedure. This is used for enforcing the ordering of procedures, as we will see in the next sections. However, in the high-level language, ordering of procedures is achieved by means of process expressions. Thus, further utility of the `when` clause is to test for preconditions on the workflow object. For example, the `finalizeReport` procedure tests that the `report` has actually been written by requiring that it is not the empty string, and that the report has been approved. Another application of the `when` clause is to test timing constraints, e.g. the deadline for a `submitPaper` procedure. A procedure is only applicable when the actor and activation constraints are satisfied. Thus, the page for applying a procedure and the links to that page are not accessible if these constraints are not satisfied.

User interface. The `view` clause defines the user interface for applying a procedure. This may be an arbitrary WebDSL page definition, allowing a completely customizable user interface [18]. The page definition can display any relevant information accessible through the workflow object and session, and will typically display a form for user input required by the procedure. It is often convenient and appropriate to derive a page definition from the data model. The WebDSL `derive` construct

```
derive style from e for (p1,...,pn)
```

provides a flexible mechanism for deriving a page from an entity declaration [8]. The `style` argument declares the style of the page, the expression `e` indicates the object and thus the type for which to generate the page, and the `pi` properties indicate which properties of the object should be displayed (`view`) and which should be edited. The `commentReport` procedure in Fig. 3 demonstrates how a `procedurePage` can be generated for two view properties (`employee` and `report`) and one edit property (`comments`).

Action. The `do` clause describes the action taken when the procedure is applied. Actions can be described using a simple imperative language. For a standard `procedurePage` the default action is to save the changes for the edit fields in the form, and no further action is needed. Additional actions may be taken to implement business logic, to send a notification email as in the `commentReport` procedure, or to create sub-workflows as described below.

Process. The `process` clause contains a *process expression* defining the composition of procedures to apply after invoking the containing procedure. For example, the `meeting` procedure in Figure 3 defines the composition of the individual steps in the `ProgressMeeting` workflow. Process expressions are composed from procedure invocations with several combinators. The sequential composition `e1 ; e2` of two expressions first applies `e1` and then `e2`. The parallel composition `e1 |AND| e2` applies `e1` and `e2` in parallel waiting for both to terminate. The iteration `repeat{e} until f(o)` applies `e` until procedure `f` is applied. The parallel composition `e1 |XOR| e2` enables the application of `e1` and `e2`, but cancels one if the other has terminated.

```
extend entity ProgressMeeting {
  meetings -> Set<ProgressMeeting>
}
procedure meeting(p : ProgressMeeting) {
  process {
    employeeMeetings(p);
    (employeeView(p) |AND| managerView(p));
    ... as before ...
  }
}
procedure employeeMeetings(p : ProgressMeeting) {
  who { principal = p.employee }
  do {
    for(u : User in p.employee.employeesList) {
      p.meetings
       .add(ProgressMeeting{employee := u})
    }
  }
  process {
    AND(q : ProgressMeeting in p.meetingsList) {
      meeting(q)
    }
  }
}
```

Fig. 5. Recursive workflow procedure

Recursive Procedures. The meeting example defines a workflow on a single workflow object `ProgressMeeting`. However, there can be multiple instances of this workflow in different stages of execution in parallel. For each user there can be a `ProgressMeeting` instance, or even several, say if an employee has more than one manager, or one for each year of employment. Thus, a workflow instance corresponds to an instance of the corresponding workflow object. Procedures can instantiate new sub-workflows by invoking procedures on linked objects (through properties). Such sub-workflows can also be *recursive* in the sense that a procedure may call itself on another workflow object. The example in Figure 5 illustrates recursion by extending the progress meeting example. In this workflow users do not only have managers, they can also *be* managers. Before evaluating the progress of a manager, all his or her own employees should be evaluated first. Thus, the `meeting` workflow procedure is adapted to invoke `employeeMeetings(p)`. In the `do` clause, a `ProgressMeeting` object is created and added to the set of `meetings` for each employee of the user. Then, in the `process` clause, the `meeting` workflow is initiated for each employee meeting in parallel so that all employees can start working on their `employeeView` simultaneously. The `employeeMeetings` procedure needs to be finished (all reports approved and finalized) before the managers meeting can proceed.

3 Transforming Procedures

In this section we explain how we implement the compilation by normalization approach to realize WebWorkFlow. We describe how WebWorkFlow procedures are implemented by means of model-to-model transformations to the underlying WebDSL language. The conceptual design of WebWorkFlow may suggest that it is an object-oriented language that can be directly translated to a regular object-oriented language such as Java. However, due to the statelessness of the HTTP protocol, state has to be kept in between requests. Traditionally, sessions have been used for this purpose, however sessions typically only last a few hours whereas a workflow can last years. Furthermore sessions are bound to one particular user, whereas many users can participate in a workflow. So rather than using sessions, the workflow state is persisted in the database through extension of the application's data model. Furthermore, page definitions are used to implement the user interface for applying a procedure, and access control rules to regulate the applicability of a procedure. The transformations rely on the data, user interface and access control modeling languages of WebDSL.

Procedures to Pages. The basic idea for the implementation of a procedure is illustrated in Figure 6 with the transformation of `procedure` *f*`(`*a*`:`*A*`){...}`. To record the state of a procedure, the workflow entity *A* is extended with a property with the name of the procedure referring to a `ProcedureStatus` object. The basic implementation of `ProcedureStatus` provides an `enabled` property, which indicates whether the procedure may be applied, and an `enable()` function, which can be used to set this property to true. The user interface for the procedure is realized by means of a page definition with the name of the procedure and the workflow object as argument. The *view* from the procedure is used as specification of the presentation and the do action is performed on submit and disables the procedure by resetting the enabled flag. Finally, an access control rule uses the *who* and *when* expressions to regulate access to the procedure. The enabled property of the status object is used as an additional requirement for applicability of the procedure.

Task Lists and Navigation. In addition to the basic page for applying a procedure, further elements for the user interface of an application can be derived from procedure definitions. In particular, a definition of a task list with links to pages for applicable procedures for a particular workflow object, or a list with all available procedures for a particular user. The access control mechanism of WebDSL ensures that links in such work lists are only displayed if the pages they point to are accessible. Thus, the user interface is dynamically adapted to the state of the application. This is illustrated in Figure 3, where links to applicable procedures can be seen in the sidebar.

```
procedure f(a : A) {
  who  { who }
  when { when }
  view { elem* }
  do   { stat* }
}
```

⇓

```
extend entity A {
  f -> ProcedureStatus
}
entity ProcedureStatus {
  enabled :: Bool
  function enable() {
    enabled := true;
  }
}
define page f(a : A) {
  elem*
  action do() {
    a.f.enabled := false;
    stat*
  }
}
access control rules {
  rule page f(a : A) {
    who && when && a.f.enabled
  }
}
```

Fig. 6. Transformation of procedure into access control rule, page definition, and entity declaration

Procedure Event Model. A procedure has a life cycle that starts with the creation of the workflow object it is associated with and ends with its destruction. WebWorkFlow provides an event model for observing the changes in the life cycle of a procedure. Observation of events is realized using the following event handling clauses in a procedure definition (Figure 7):

- enabled is triggered after a call of enable()
- disabled is triggered after a call of disable()
- done is triggered after the execution of the do clause
- processed is triggered after the procedure's process has terminated; in case a procedure has no process clause the processed event follows directly after the done event.

```
procedure f(a : A) {
  enabled   { stat* }
  who       { who }
  when      { when }
  view      { elem* }
  do        { stat* }
  done      { stat* }
  process   { pexp }
  processed { stat* }
  disabled  { stat* }
}
```

Fig. 7. Procedure events

To support modular subscription to the events of a procedure, the extend procedure mechanism can be used to add additional statements to an event handler. For example, the definition

```
extend procedure f(a : A) { processed { stat* } }
```

extends the processed event handler with the *stat** statements.

Encoding Procedure Dependencies. The procedure event model provides a general mechanism for encoding a wide variety of policies for ordering procedures. For example, the definition

```
extend procedure writeReport(p : ProgressMeeting){
  processed { p.approveReport.enable(); p.commentReport.enable(); } }
```

enables the procedures `approveReport` and `commentReport` after the `writeReport` procedure has terminated, which corresponds to a parallel split.

Process Expressions. While the procedure event handlers provide a flexible mechanism for composing procedures, it is also a rather tedious mechanism. A large number of procedure composition patterns can be captured using concise process expressions from which the correct event handling code can be generated automatically. For example, the sequential composition of two procedures can be encoded as in the `writeReport` definition above. That is, the sequential composition `f(x); g(x)` is encoded by calling `x.g.enable()` in the `processed` clause of `f`. This direct enabling of the successor of a procedure works fine provided that procedures are only called from one call site. Since workflow procedures are intended for human consumption, it is generally not a good idea to require the same activity in many different contexts. However, this constraint is typically violated in the case of recursion, which requires an initial call and the actual recursive call.

```
entity ProcedureStatus {
  caller      -> ProcedureStatus
  returnstate :: Int
  function enable(c : ProcedureStatus,
                  r : Int) {
    this.enabled := true;
    this.caller := c;
    this.returnstate := r;
    this.enabled(); }
  function disable() {
    this.enabled := false;
    this.disabled(); }
}
```

Fig. 8. Re-definition of `ProcedureStatus` for recording return address of procedure call

```
procedure f(a:A){ process{ g(a); h(a) } }
```

⇓

```
entity FStatus : ProcedureStatus {
  a -> A
  function next(state : Int) {
    if(state = 0) { a.g.enable(this, 1); }
    if(state = 1) { a.h.enable(this, 2); }
    if(state = 2) { this.processed(); }
  }
}
extend procedure f(a : A) {
  enabled { this.next(0); }
  processed {
    this.caller.next(this.returnstate);
  }
}
```

Fig. 9. Sequential composition with state machine

Dealing with multiple call sites requires a more dynamic approach to sequencing of calls. In order to return control to the proper callee, it is necessary to record the 'return address'. The return address of a workflow procedure call can be represented by the identity of the caller, i.e. its `ProcedureStatus` object, and its state. Figure 8 redefines `ProcedureStatus` with an `enable` function taking the caller identity and its state as arguments.

To determine the next step to take after a procedure returns, a process expression is transformed to a finite state machine encoded by the `next` function of the *F*`Status` entity, which specializes `ProcedureStatus` for a procedure *f*. To compute the state machine, all positions in the process expressions are assigned a unique number. For each combinator there are special rules for computing the transitions. We illustrate the computation with two examples, sequential composition (Figure 9) and parallel split (Figure 10). Procedure `f` in Figure 9 applies the sequential composition of `g` and `h`. It is transformed to the `next` function in the `FStatus` entity declaration and an extension of the procedure event handlers. When `f` is enabled, the transition from the start state (0) is taken, which will lead to `g` being enabled with state 1. When the `next` transition is taken from `g`, `h` is enabled with state 2. On return from `h` the process is completed and the `processed` event handler is called, which itself returns to the caller of `f`.

Figure 10 defines the implementation of the `e1 |AND| e2` combinator, which applies processess `e1` and `e2` in parallel and waits for both to complete before proceeding. The transformation assumes a normalized process expression in which the expression is preceded and succeeded by a simple procedure call. This assumption is also made for the branches of the split. Expressions that do not match this pattern (e.g. `(e1 |AND| e2); (e3 |AND| e4)` can be transformed to this form by insertion of automatic identity procedures. Note that the `[i]` expressions are state labels. When the split is reached (state 1), the heads of the two branches are enabled. When the first of the branches returns, the counter `count` is incremented. When the next branch returns the counter is 1 and the continuation `q` is enabled.

```
procedure f(a : A) {
  process {
   p(a); [1]
   ((g1(a); e1*; h1(a) [3])
    |AND| (g2(a); e2*; h2(a) [5]));
   q(a) } }
```

⇓

```
extend entity A { count :: Int }
extend entity FStatus {
  extend function next(state : Int) {
    if(state = 1) {
      a.g1.enable(this, 0);
      a.g2.enable(this, 0);
    }
    if(state = 3 || state = 5) {
      if(a.count = 1) {
        a.count := 0;
        a.q.enable(this, 0);
      } else {
        a.count := a.count + 1;
      } } } }
```

Fig. 10. Implementation of the split and join transitions of the `|AND|` parallel combinator

4 Encoding Patterns

A lot of research has been conducted on the assessment of workflow languages. Van der Aalst et al. [16] describe an extensive set of workflow patterns from the process perspective ranging from simple patterns such as sequential execution to complicated patterns such as loops and cancellation patterns. Recently, a revised version of these patterns was published [13]. Patterns have also been devised for the resource perspective [15] and the data perspective [14]. In this paper, we focus on the use of control patterns for evaluating workflow languages from the control perspective. Fig. 11 shows the coverage of these patterns for WebWorkFlow. In this table + means this pattern directly supported by WebWorkFlow, +/- means it is possible to implement through a workaround, and - means the pattern is not supported by WebWorkFlow. A number of patterns that are particularly noteworthy for WebWorkFlow are patterns 10, 12-15 and 22.

Although *arbitrary cycles (10)* are not often needed, they can be implemented using the lower-level procedure events `processed` or `done`, in which an arbitrary procedure can be enabled. This is an example of why it useful to have a high-level process description language, while at the same time still having access to a lower level of abstraction where not directly supported process features can be implemented.

Multiple instances (12-15) of procedures in WebWorkFlow are supported through multiple instances of the objects they operate on. One instance of a process can run on each object that the process is defined on. By creating new object instances, any number of instances of a process can be created. Multiple instances without synchronization (pattern 12) can be implemented by simply calling `enable()` on them, which instantiates them in a non-blocking manner. Synchronizing on a number of instances (pattern 13 and 14) can be realized by instantiating them using the `AND(a : A in o.aList){proc}` construct. Pattern 15 (Multiple instances without a priori runtime knowledge) can be implemented as follows:

Pattern	Support
1. Sequence	+
2. Parallel split	+
3. Synchronization	+
4. Exclusive Choice	+
5. Simple merge	+
6. Multi choice	+
7. Synchronizing merge	+
8. Multi-merge	+/-
9. Discriminator	+
10. Arbitrary cycles	+/-
11. Implicit termination	-
12-15. Multiple instance patterns	+
16. Deferred choice	+
17. Interleaved parallel routing	+/-
18. Milestone	+/-
19. Cancel activity	+
20. Cancel case	+/-
21. Structured Loop	+
22. Recursion	+
23. Transient Trigger	+
24. Persistent Trigger	+

Fig. 11. Control flow pattern coverage of WebWorkFlow

```
multiproc(o).enable(); stopmultiproc(o)
```

In the `done` clause of `multiproc`, the procedure instantly re-enables itself using `enable()`, creates a new object, and starts a process with `enable()`. Finally, `stopmultiproc` disables `multiproc` through a call to `multiproc.disable()`. To synchronize all processes created, a `when` clause can be added to the `stopmultiproc` procedure, to require for all instances that their processes are finished.

For *recursion (22)* we can distinguish three cases. First, tail recursion can be implemented using `repeat` and `while`. Second, recursion on properties of the object is supported by simply calling a procedure recursively on the property (e.g. Figure 5). Recursive self calls on an object `a` from a process defined on `a` are not supported. We have not yet found a use-case for non tail-recursive self recursion, so it does not seem much of an issue. (But examples are most welcome!)

Data Patterns. Rusell et al. in [14] discuss a number of workflow data patterns. WebWorkFlow defines its processes directly on top of data entities. This gives the procedures in the process direct access to the data entity and all the data that is linked from it. Through this mechanism many of the data patterns are naturally supported. WebWorkFlow is mostly lacking in data hiding, for which it provides no explicit support. Lack of space prevents us from providing a thorough evaluation of the data patterns that are supported by WebWorkFlow.

5 Discussion

During the design of WebWorkFlow a number of design decisions were made that distinguish it from other workflow systems. We compare our approach to other workflow approaches and discuss opportunities for future work.

Evaluation. Most workflow systems (YAWL, JBPM, BPEL) dynamically load a workflow description and *interpret* it. The advantage of this approach is the ability to adapt the workflow while the system is running. The workflow description can then simply be reloaded. This ability is often limited, however, to process descriptions, which means that no new tasks or procedures can be defined at runtime. In WebWorkFlow on the other hand, workflows are *compiled* to WebDSL (which in in its turn compiles to Java/JSF). As a consequence, run-time adaptations of the workflow process are not supported. However, the compiled application is much more light-weight than an interpreted worfklow management system.

The main concern of most workflow management systems is *controlling* the process. User interfaces and the rest of the application are handled in separate systems and are thus outside the scope of the workflow system. WebWorkFlow is an embedded DSL in WebDSL and therefore integrates well with the rest of WebDSL. This integration enables the developer to more easily develop and *generate* complete user interfaces, automated tasks and control flow. At the same time, it gives a maximum of flexibility as one can always resort to a lower level of abstraction in case the ultimate abstraction layer does not support a certain construction.

Following the tendency to design languages that are understandable by both business analysts and technical developers, and the shift from workflow to business process modeling, most workflow approaches use a *graphical language* for specifying processes. WebWorkFlow is specifically aimed at web developers and uses a *textual language*. The first reason to use a textual language is because it is an embedded DSL within WebDSL, which is a textual language. The second reason is that it turns out to be a very efficient and expressive way of expressing workflows.

Related Work. The approach that is taken by Brambilla et al. in [1], is that of adding workflow support to any domain model by performing a model transformation, by which the original model is extended with the necessary domain model elements to support workflow. WebWorkFlow applies these ideas to WebDSL. WebWorkFlow is more expressive than the approach discussed by Brambilla, because it does not cover nested sub-processes, which precludes recursion. Brambilla et al. themselves applied the ideas from [1] to WebML [2], where they describe how processes described in BPMN can be used to enact workflow processes in WebML applications. The authors envision that their explicit design styles in the future could be automated to generate skeleton applications based on process descriptions. WebWorkFlow realizes this vision; it does not only generate a skeleton application, but a complete application that can be *customized at the model level* to better suit application-specific needs.

YAWL is a graphical worklow language and system designed by Van der Aalst and Ter Hofstede, authors of the work on workflow patterns [13,15,14]. YAWL is designed to support almost every workflow pattern. Its formalization is based on high-level Petri nets [17]. Although YAWL is a graphical language, a lot of configuration needs to be done by setting parameters in property boxes. The process diagram does not always shows a complete picture because so much information is hidden inside properties. While YAWL is very expressive, it does not have the layered implementation that WebWorkFlow has, which allows to use lower level constructs to implement workflows not directly supported by the workflow language.

Panta Rhei [6] is a web-based workflow system that interprets workflows specified in a textual language. Workflow data in Panta Rhei is persisted in a database, which, like in WebWorkFlow, makes it possible to alter the execution of workflows at run-time by changing this data. A web browser is used as interface to the user. Communication with other systems is possible using an internal form representation, which remote systems must be able to interpret. Panta Rhei also has support for timing and transactional features, both of which are future work for WebWorkFlow.

WebWork is a web-only implementation of the workflow management system Meteor-2 [11]. It uses a graphical designer to specify a workflow, from which HTML and CGI scripts are generated. Automated tasks are performed using a socket connection with a web server and invoking CGI programs. WebWork is not as expressive as BPEL or BPMN, as only somewhat more than half of the first 20 workflow pattern are supported [16]. Also, the use of CGI adds flexibility, but a custom task is not easily constructed, as opposed to WebWorkFlow, where all code can be specified in one language.

BPMN (Business Process Modeling Notation) is a business process modeling notation language designed by the Business Process Modeling Initiative [20] and now maintained by the Object Management Group [12]. Its goal is to provide a notation for describing business processes understandable for both business analysts and technical developers. WebWorkFlow on the other hand is much more technical and mainly aimed at developers. In contrast to WebWorkFlow, BPMN is not directly executable. It is possible however, to derive executable workflow specifications from workflows specified using a subset of BPMN.

Future Work. An interesting area of research for WebWorkFlow is making procedures accessible through a web service interface (as opposed to the current HTML interface) and accessing procedures of remote servers. WebWorkFlow could then be used for web service orchestration, similar to BPEL.

Because of the user-initiated nature of WebDSL (and WebWorkFlow by extension), using timed events is not yet possible. Conceivable applications of timing features are scheduling tasks and using deadlines to automatically influence the execution of procedures.

As WebWorkFlow is used to generate a fully functional workflow system instead of specifying a workflow that is interpreted by a WFMS, regenerating and deploying the workflow system could potentially break ongoing workflows. This is a data model evolution problem and is future work. The automatically generated navigation based on procedure definitions is useful, but can still be enhanced. Process descriptions can be more fully utilized to generate navigation. Although it is possible to disable (parts of) procedures in the current version of the language, it is not straightforward to roll back the state of an application when errors occur. A transaction system similar to Panta Rhei might be helpful.

6 Conclusion

In this paper we introduced WebWorkFlow, an embedded DSL extending WebDSL with object-oriented workflow abstractions. Based on the definition of workflow procedures a full fledged executable application can be generated, including navigation and work lists. Following the 'compilation by normalization' [10] approach, WebWorkFlow achieves great flexibility and customizability by making the lower abstraction levels of the procedure event model and WebDSL web application modeling accessible next to the high-level workflow abstractions. WebWorkFlow covers most of the workflow control patterns. The patterns that are not directly expressible through the process expression language can often be implemented on the procedure event level, demonstrating the advantages of building a (workflow) language as an abstraction on a lower-level language.

Acknowledgments. This research was supported by NWO/JACQUARD project 638.001.610, *MoDSE: Model-Driven Software Evolution.*

References

1. Brambilla, M., Cabot, J., Comai, S.: Automatic generation of workflow-extended domain models. In: Engels, G., Opdyke, B., Schmidt, D.C., Weil, F. (eds.) MODELS 2007. LNCS, vol. 4735, pp. 375–389. Springer, Heidelberg (2007)
2. Brambilla, M., Ceri, S., Fraternali, P., Manolescu, I.: Process modeling in web applications. ACM Trans. Softw. Eng. Methodol. 15(4), 360–409 (2006)
3. Bravenboer, M., Visser, E.: Concrete syntax for objects. Domain-specific language embedding and assimilation without restrictions. In: Schmidt, D.C. (ed.) Proceedings of the 19th ACM SIGPLAN Conference on Object-Oriented Programing, Systems, Languages, and Applications (OOPSLA 2004), Vancouver, Canada, October 2004, pp. 365–383. ACM Press, New York (2004)
4. Curbera, F., Goland, Y., Klein, J., Leymann, F.: Business process execution language for web services, version 1.1. Technical report, IBM (2003)

5. Dumas, M., ter Hofstede, A.H.M.: Uml activity diagrams as a workflow specification language. In: Gogolla, M., Kobryn, C. (eds.) UML 2001. LNCS, vol. 2185, pp. 76–90. Springer, Heidelberg (2001)
6. Eder, J., Groiss, H., Liebhart, W.: The Workflow Management System Panta Rhei. In: Advances in Workflow Management Systems and Interoperability, Istanbul, Turkey, August, pp. 129–144. Springer, Heidelberg (1997)
7. Groenewegen, D., Visser, E.: Declarative access control for WebDSL: Combining language integration and separation of concerns. In: Schwabe, D., Curbera, F. (eds.) International Conference on Web Engineering (ICWE 2008), July 2008. IEEE CS Press, Los Alamitos (2008)
8. Hemel, Z., Kats, L.C.L., Visser, E.: Code generation by model transformation. In: Gray, J., Pierantonio, A., Vallecillo, A. (eds.) ICMT 2008. LNCS, vol. 5063, pp. 183–198. Springer, Heidelberg (2008)
9. Hollingsworth, D.: The Workflow Reference Model. Workflow Management Coalition, Document Number TC00-1003 - Issue 1.1 edn. (1995)
10. Kats, L.C.L., Bravenboer, M., Visser, E.: Mixing source and bytecode. A case for compilation by normalization. In: Kiczales, G. (ed.) Proceedings of the 23rd ACM SIGPLAN Conference on Object-Oriented Programing, Systems, Languages, and Applications (OOPSLA 2008), Nashville, Tenessee, USA, October 2008. ACM Press, New York (2008)
11. Miller, J.A., Palaniswami, D., Sheth, A.P., Kochut, K.J., Singh, H.: Webwork: $Meteor_2$'s web-based workflow management system. J. Intell. Inf. Syst. 10(2), 185–215 (1998)
12. Recker, J., Strategy, M.: Process Modeling in the 21 stCentury. In: BPTrends, pp. 1–8 (May 2006)
13. Russell, N., ter Hofstede, A.H.M., van der Aalst, W.M.P., Mulyar, N.: Workflow control-flow patterns: A revised view. Technical report, BPMcenter.org. (2006)
14. Russell, N., ter Hofstede, A., Edmond, D., van der Aalst, W.: Workflow Data Patterns. In: Delcambre, L.M.L., Kop, C., Mayr, H.C., Mylopoulos, J., Pastor, Ó. (eds.) ER 2005. LNCS, vol. 3716, pp. 353–368. Springer, Heidelberg (2005)
15. ter Hofstede, A., Edmond, D., van der Aalst, W.: Workflow resource patterns. BETA Working Paper Series, pp. 216–232 (January 2004)
16. van der Aalst, W.M.P., Hofstede, A.H.M.T., Kiepuszewski, B., Barros, A.P.: Workflow patterns. Distrib. Parallel Databases 14(1), 5–51 (2003)
17. van der Aalst, W.M.P., ter Hofstede, A.H.M.: YAWL: yet another workflow language. Information Systems 30(4), 245–275 (2005)
18. Visser, E.: WebDSL: A case study in domain-specific language engineering. In: Lammel, R., Saraiva, J., Visser, J. (eds.) GTTSE 2007. LNCS, vol. 5235. Springer, Heidelberg (2008)
19. WfMC. Terminology and glossary, 3rd edn. Document Number WFMC-TC-1011, Workflow Management Coalition (1999)
20. White, S.: Introduction to BPMN. In: IBM Cooperation (2004)

The Future of Train Signaling

Andreas Svendsen[2], Gøran K. Olsen[2], Jan Endresen[1], Thomas Moen[1], Erik Carlson[1], Kjell-Joar Alme[1], and Øystein Haugen[2]

[1] ABB, Bergerveien 12,
1375 Billingstad, Norway
{kjell-joar.alme,erik.carlson,jan.endresen,
thomas.moen}@no.abb.com
[2] SINTEF, Forskningsveien 1, Oslo, Norway
{oystein.haugen,goran.k.olsen,andreas.svendsen}@sintef.no

Abstract. Producing the source code for a railway interlocking system based on the description of a station has traditionally been a multistage manual process. We show how this process can be automated and made less error-prone by introducing model-driven development (MDD). This paper addresses the exp erience of developing a Domain Specific Language (DSL) to describe railway stations, Train Control Language (TCL), and tools to support this language. In the railroad domain where there are extreme safety requirements, it is essential to show that consistency and completeness can be assured. We address how the model is used to generate several different representations for different purposes. We look at advantages and challenges with our approach, and we discuss improvements to existing technologies to support our case better.

Keywords: Train, signaling, interlocking, DSL, model-driven development, MoSiS.

1 Introduction

A railway interlocking system is a system that prevents conflicting and dangerous train movements through a network of tracks and ensures that no clear signal is given to a train unless the requested route is safe. Normally the interlocking system gets a request to set a particular route for a particular train. It then checks if this is possible by reading the status of critical signals and track circuits to see if the track ahead is free. If all the conditions are satisfied, the necessary switches are locked in position and finally the clear signal is given to the train. The interlocking is a safety system of the highest classification.

In the old days the interlocking was mechanical, and was later replaced by relays. Today all new interlocking systems are computer based (CBI). One challenge is to configure the interlocking system for a particular station. Another challenge is that country specific rules must be handled. This work has been manual in nature and requiring multiple steps from creating and verifying the requirements (e.g. interlocking tables) to verifying the final code. This paper describes a Domain Specific Language (DSL) for specifying the stations and to allow automatic generation of interlocking tables and the

K. Czarnecki et al. (Eds.): MoDELS 2008, LNCS 5301, pp. 128–142, 2008.

code for the CBI etc. This Train Control Language (TCL) will improve the consistency and completeness of the specifications as well as reduce the human effort to implement new train stations.

2 The Manual Process of Creating Interlocking Source Code

ABB's Computer Based Interlocking is based on a 1oo2 programmable logic controller (PLC) configuration. "1oo2" means "1 out of 2" and it consists of two channels connected in parallel, such that either channel can process the safety function, [11]. A PLC is a digital computer used in industrial automation. The two PLCs have diversified code called A and B to enhance the safety of the system. The A and B codes are executed in parallel, each performing the same overall task. The results are compared continuously.

The current workflow for developing a specific CBI is illustrated in Fig. 1. Note that the figure shows the basic workflow and not all the details.

The input requirement specification is made up of two parts: One part is the generic CBI and the other is the customer's specification. These parts contain a drawing showing the structure of the station with its basic elements (tracks, track circuits, switches, signals, balises (radio transponders), derailers etc.) and an interlocking table for the station. The train routes are the total collection of possible routes that can be requested for a train. The interlocking tables are basically a set of Boolean equations for what needs to be true before allocating a route to a train. The national rules must also be incorporated into the CBI.

From the above inputs the functional specification for the CBI is created. This process is manual and hence it is susceptible to errors. The functional specification is a mapping of the interlocking tables into a set of logical equations. The logic of the CBI is directly linked to the tables. To ensure that the functional specification is correct it is formally reviewed often by the customers themselves. This review is also a manual process.

From the functional specification the design specification is developed. This specification is very close to the source code. The coding of the PLC is done by selecting parameterized functional blocks. The development of the design specification and the programming of the PLC are both manual operations. The development of the A and the B code are done by two separate teams with different tools and libraries in order to reduce the probability of common mode failure. The libraries incorporate the national rules and can be distinct for different countries. The formal review of the tools and libraries is normally only done once per country.

The formal reviews of the functional specification, tools and libraries are done according to Fagan inspection method, [9]. This is a structured process for finding errors in documents such as specifications, programming code and designs during various phases of the development process. The method is effective with respect to finding inconsistencies and errors, but rather time-consuming.

The PLC code is tested in three separate levels. The Integration tests reveal different interpretations by the two teams of the specifications. The Factory and Site Acceptance tests ensure the conformance to the input requirement specifications. The test cases are largely developed from the top level specifications.

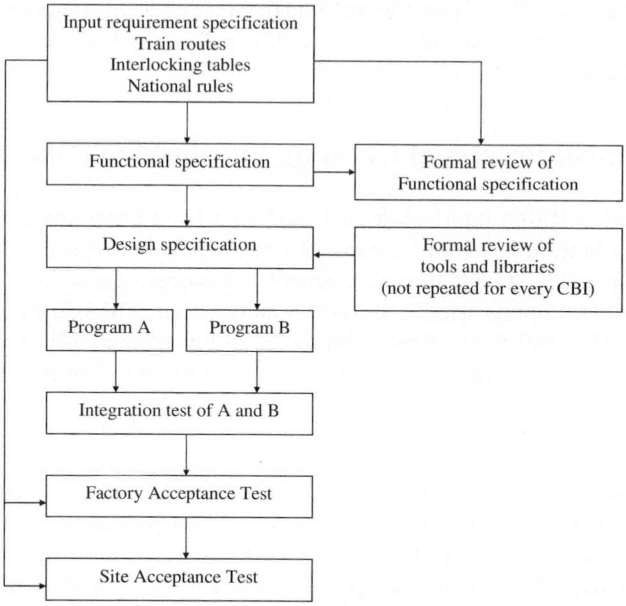

Fig. 1. Current workflow for developing a specific CBI

The vision for the future of CBI development is to be able to combine the station drawing with the train routes and interlocking tables in a DSL. From the models created in the TCL language, the PLC code and test cases should be automatically generated. Thus the formal review of the functional specifications can be eliminated, and the specification of factory and site acceptance tests requires no extra manual effort to produce.

3 TCL Language and Tools

The source code for the interlocking system is manually created from a given extended graphical representation of the station. The goal of TCL is to automate this process, and this can be achieved by using model-driven development (MDD) and transformations on the created models. The development of TCL has been driven by requests from ABB to improve the present process of creating source code for the interlocking system.

To be able to generate source code we need a formal representation of the stations. This has been achieved by creating a DSL for describing stations and their signals. The supporting tools include graphical and tree editors for creating stations, and model transformations to generate e.g. source code.

We will in this section give a brief description of the TCL language, the supporting editors and model transformations. A concise explanation of the tools used to develop the TCL tools is also given.

3.1 DSL Description

The TCL language is defined as an Ecore metamodel in the Eclipse Modeling Framework (EMF) [5]. EMF is a modeling framework that can be used to build modeling tools for a DSL. By specifying a metamodel for the TCL language, a tree editor for creating stations can be automatically generated by EMF.

A station consists of several basic elements, such as line segments, switches and signals. These elements are connected by endpoints to form what we visually know as a station. A simplified version of a station with two tracks is illustrated in Fig. 2.

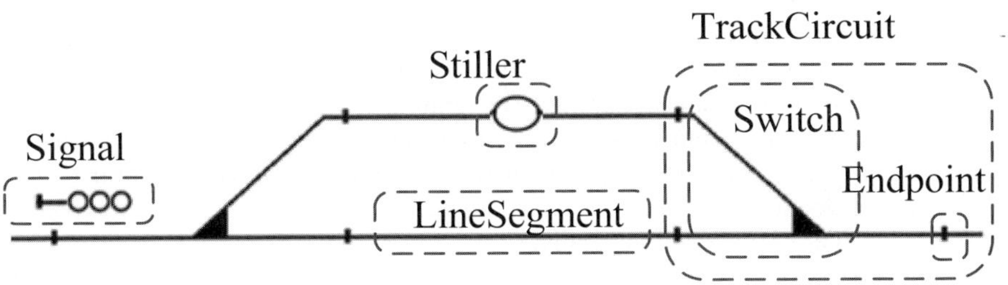

Fig. 2. TCL concrete syntax

This figure illustrates the basic elements *Signal, LineSegment, Switch, Stiller* and *Endpoint*. Endpoints are specialized into *TCEndpoint* and *MiddleEndpoint*, where the latter is used to connect LineSegments and Switches together (not shown in Fig. 2.). A *TrackCircuit* contains a number of LineSegments and Switches, and is separated by TCEndpoints. In local control mode a Stiller determines which direction a train can travel on a TrackCircuit. In remote control mode the Stiller has no function. A number of TrackCircuits constitute a part of a *TrainRoute*, which is a route between two MainSignals. An extract of the TCL metamodel that illustrates some of these concepts is shown in Fig. 3.

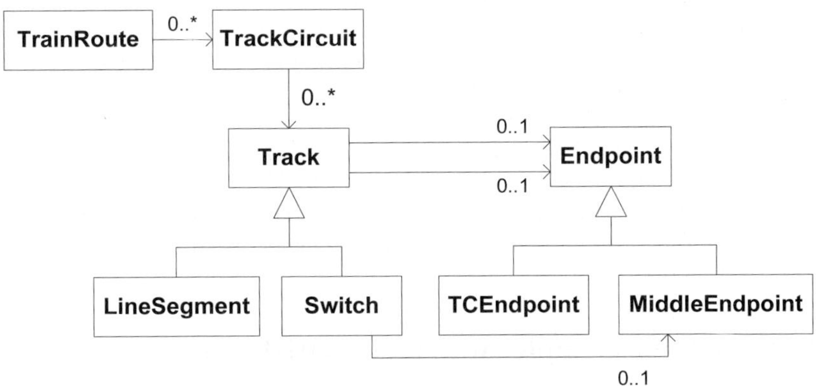

Fig. 3. TCL metamodel extract

To be able to secure the safety of a train route it is necessary to check that all the elements included in the train route are of an appropriate value (i.e. a TrackCircuit can not be occupied by another train). This can be achieved by traversing the station model created in TCL and checking that all necessary conditions for a train route are satisfied.

3.2 TCL Editors

The tree editor automatically generated by EMF is not very usable in larger station models. To improve this, we use the Graphical Modeling Framework (GMF) [4] in Eclipse to create a graphical editor. GMF is a framework for creating graphical editors based on EMF and GEF (Graphical Editing Framework).

A basic graphical editor can be created semi-automatically based on the metamodel for the DSL (in this case TCL). This process is divided into three parts: Graphical definition, tool definition and mapping. The graphical definition describes how the elements in the editor should look like, the tool definition describes the tool palette available for the user, and the mapping maps all this together. Basic editor code is automatically created, but in most cases, where we need some non-basic functionality, it is necessary to alter this code manually.

Consequently we have two editors for creating TCL stations, tree editor and graphical editor. Stations can be created in the tree editor by first creating a station object, and then adding every element as a child to this object. References between objects have to be set accordingly. When stations are created by the graphical editor, the elements in the station are drawn from a palette to a station canvas. References between objects are principally set by the editor since lines from one endpoint to another are drawn by the user.

Station models created by the tree editor and graphical editor are equivalent and can be processed by the same code generators. However, the graphical editor creates some extra meta-information in a separate file to store the locations of the elements.

3.3 Code Generation

To generate source code from the station models, we utilize MOFScript [7] to do model-to-text transformations. MOFScript is a model-to-text transformation engine that makes it possible to traverse instantiations based on any kind of metamodel and outputs any kind of text from the models. The format and fixed text are specified and hard-coded by the programmer, while information from the elements in the model is inserted into the proper places.

By using MOFScript we are able to traverse the station models to generate several representations, i.e. interlocking tables in HTML, logical equations which resembles source code that can be validated, and source code. The ability to create several different representations from one model is a big advantage by this approach, as we will see in the next section.

4 Using TCL for Completeness and Consistency

We have presented the various parts of TCL and the supporting tools. The intention is to use the graphical editor to create a model of a station. From this model source code and other representations can automatically be created, such that consistency and completeness are ensured.

4.1 TCL Procedure

When a new station is planned, the interlocking developer receives station drawings and a requirement specification from the customer. Based on the drawings for the station the developer designs the station in the TCL editor. A station is created by placing basic elements on a canvas and connecting them properly. The elements are named and given the proper values. An example station created in the graphical editor can be viewed in Fig. 4.

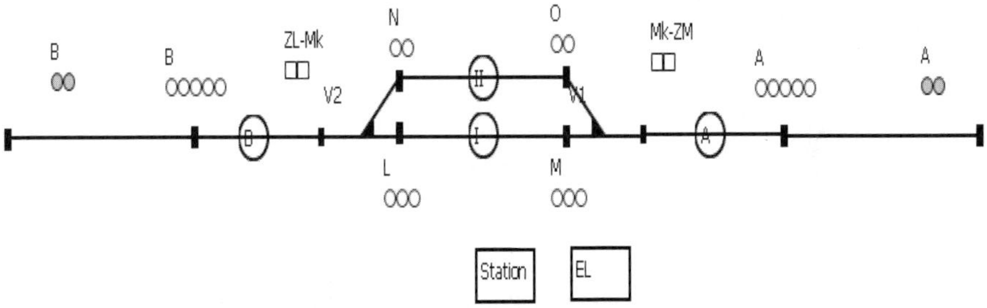

Fig. 4. A station named StationB created in TCL's graphical editor

The figure shows a double track with Signals, Stillers, Switches, Endpoints, Line-Segments and two Buildings. The appropriate names for the Signals, Switches and Stillers are listed in the figure. The editor supports automatically generation of various formats by simply pressing a button. This is illustrated in Fig. 5.

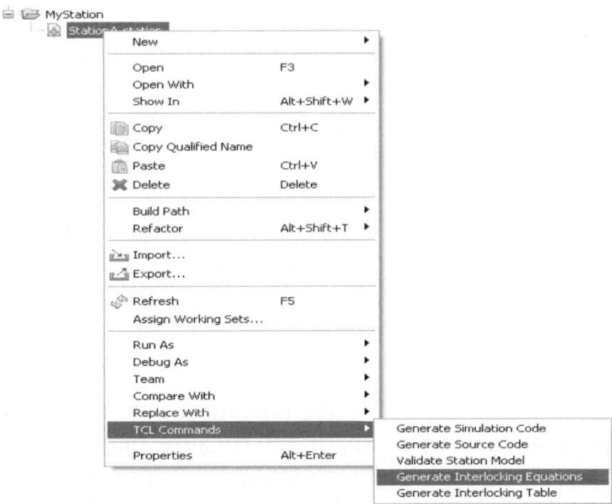

Fig. 5. Actions available in the TCL editors

From the model created in TCL an interlocking table is then generated. The interlocking table describes the conditions necessary to set a train route. The automatically generated interlocking table is compared to the interlocking table received from the customer. In advanced stations certain extensions may have to be added to the interlocking table based on local dependencies. This comparison also serves as a verification of the correctness of the station model created. An example of an interlocking table automatically generated from the TCL model in Fig. 4. is illustrated in Fig. 6.

Station: StationB

Interlocking Table:

Train Route Description	Train Route	Stiller B L/N B	Stiller I A/L B/M	Stiller II A/N B/O	Stiller A A M/O	Switch V2	Switch V1	Train Routes B2I B1II L2 N1 M2 O1 A2I A1II	Track Circuits L B 01 02 A M
From StationA to track 1	B2I	-	-			+		- + + + + + + +	= = =
From StationA to track 2	B1II	-		-		-		+ - + + + + + +	= = =
From track 1 to StationA	L2	-	-			+		+ + - + + + + +	= =
From track 2 to StationA	N1	-		-		-		+ + + - + + + +	= =
From track 1 to StationC	M2		-		-		+	+ + + + - + + +	= =
From track 2 to StationC	O1			-	-		-	+ + + + + - + +	= =
From StationC to track 1	A2I		-		-		+	+ + + + + + - +	= = =
From StationC to track 2	A1II			-	-		-	+ + + + + + + -	= = =

Fig. 6. Interlocking table automatically generated from TCL

The interlocking table describes necessary conditions for securing a train route. Fig. 4. illustrates StationB, assuming a StationA to the left and a StationC to the right. The train routes arriving and departing StationB are listed in Fig. 6. To secure the train route from StationA to track 1 (from Signal B to Signal M), Stiller B and Stiller I have to be set in the right positions. This is illustrated by the symbol "-" in Fig. 6. Switch V2 has to be in normal position, which is indicated by symbol "+". Track Circuits B, 01 and A also have to be unoccupied (symbol "="). If all these (and other) conditions are satisfied, the train route can be secured.

Based on the output of this design process and a generic description of the interlocking system that ABB already has developed, it is possible to automatically generate the various representations of the station. By the use of MOFScript a functional specification (equations) is generated. Based on the simple model *StationB* presented in (Fig. 4.), approximately 1500 lines of equations are generated (sample shown below).

```
Boolean expression:
x O.RB/RM
Hj.RB/RM    = Tu(x, t(Hj.RB/RM))
Signal function switch route(SR.RB/RM_45)
Sub function:
SR.RB/RM_45_1
```

The equations generated are identical to the equations that would have been manually created by a CBI engineer. This is important because the design process has to be formally verified. Based on the same method the PLC source code is generated. Generating both functional specification and source code from the same model assures a

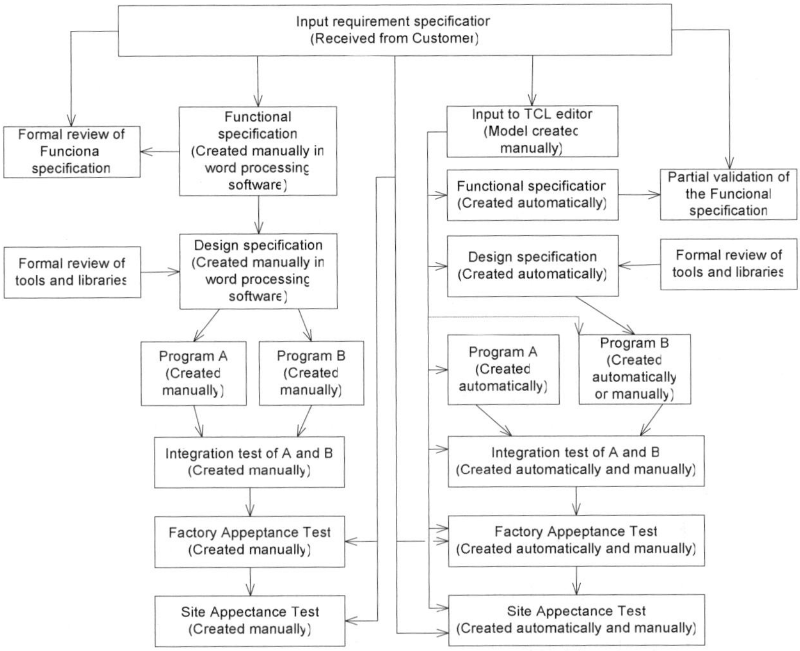

Fig. 7. Current and future (TCL) workflow

consistence between the two representations. If changes are required, they can be performed on the model, and the changes will be propagated consistently to all artifacts due to the completeness of the generated artifacts.

As a comparison to the previously described workflow, the future workflow using TCL is illustrated in Fig. 7. The current workflow is shown on the left and the workflow using TCL on the right. In the current process, every step from input requirement to source code and tests is done manually. Formal review of some of the steps is also required.

If TCL is utilized the workflow is automated. This process requires an extra step to create the station model in the TCL editor. However, it is feasible that the customer can use TCL instead of manually creating the input requirements and thus eliminate this step.

From the station models functional specification, design specification, source code and tests can be generated automatically. Since the TCL editor does not allow illegal station models, the formal review of the functional specification is not necessary. The key to ensure safety in this system is that Program A and Program B are developed by two separate teams. In the TCL approach we recommend to apply two teams to create two sets of generators. This will ensure the same tandem approach to safety.

Since the tests are supposed to find errors in the program produced, having independent tests is a good solution. However, there may be automatically generated tests as well to increase the safety of the system.

4.2 Completeness and Consistency

As we have seen in the current workflow, errors in the various steps are possible due to the manual procedure. Thus verification of each step is therefore required to ensure the safety of the system. Using TCL most of these steps are automatically created from a common model and by assuring that TCL and the generators are correctly implemented, consistency between the representations can be guaranteed. Thus the formal verification of some of the steps can be eliminated.

Several constraints are created to assure that stations are correctly created, and the editor makes sure that every necessary condition is taken into consideration. If the constraints are properly defined, the TCL editor guarantees completeness by not omitting any necessary elements. The most error-prone part of the current workflow is therefore avoided.

However, the constraints may not always be defined strict enough for ensuring a completely safe system. It is therefore important to still validate and test the results to minimize the probability of such errors.

5 Collected Experiences Developing TCL

During the development of TCL and its tools we gained various experiences. This was mainly from the development procedure of the DSL and its tools, and how necessary safety standards can be integrated into the system. A description of these parts is given in this section.

5.1 The Definition of TCL

The definition of Domain Specific Languages is not novel, and ample publications have described promising results [12]. During the development a number of already existing hypothesis have been strengthen and confirmed.

Importance of Domain Expertise. The importance of domain expertise is one such hypothesis that has proven to be vital during the specification of the TCL. An iterative and incremental process was followed and face-to-face meetings between the domain experts and the language engineers were arranged at a regular basis. Renaming and restructuring of domain concepts were often needed due to misconceptions. Even though the TCL is fairly small (approximately 25 metaclasses and their relations) the work required to create such a language should not be underestimated.

Both train specific and MDD technology knowledge were exchanged, e.g. training on MDD technologies was provided to the domain experts and vice versa. We believe that this has been a critical success factor to reach the common goal, namely a high quality DSL that can ease the development and reduce the time-to-marked (TTM).

Developing a DSL towards an Already Existing Framework. The source code for the PLC is defined as functional blocks with precise syntax. Since this source code resembles the logical equations, the task of generating source code is much the same thing as generating the equations. It can often be a challenge to transform elements in a DSL into variables and code with a previously defined syntax. However, MOF-Script turned out to be versatile and useful to transform models into specific source code. This task was therefore a lesser challenge than expected.

5.2 The Development of TCL Tool Support

The Graphical Editor. GMF has previously been used successfully to develop UML diagram like models [6] and is also the framework used to develop the TCL editor. The train station domain is special in its concrete syntax with its track circuits, switches and signals that should have two different directions. Although GMF allows automatic generation of graphical editors, we experienced some drawbacks.

Making connections between different diagram elements that are restricted to be glued onto specific places on these diagram elements is not possible to achieve using only predefined features of GMF. For instance when we are modeling a switch, we want the connecting tracks to be placed on the correct locations. However, this requires a manual update in the generated code. This is a feature that indeed should be supported in a DSL framework. Other commercial DSL tools, such as MetaEdit+ [13], provides a graphical icon editor where this is possible.

Making the diagram figure react to property change was also impossible to do using GMF configuration models. In the CBI domain both switches and signals have a direction property of type Enumeration: LEFT, RIGHT. Setting the property to RIGHT should be reflected in the editor. An alternative to manual changes in the generated code was to adjust the metamodel towards the GMF models supported features by introducing additional domain concepts, e.g. *LeftSignal* and *RightSignal*. This however was abandoned since there are several different signal types.

Model Transformations. The development of the model transformations has been done in close collaboration with the domain experts. To perform validation, the generation has used real stations as input, and the output has been compared to real life artifacts e.g. interlocking tables and equation documents.

Compared to using a standardized language like UML, the implementation of the transformation specifications became simpler. There are fewer meta-classes, and it was possible to map them directly to already existing framework components. MOFScript also provides extensive code completion based on the source model(s) meta concepts and this simplified the implementation.

Since we are generating different representations from the same source model it was also useful to have a well structured architecture that enabled reuse of specific transformation rules that performs complex navigation [14].

TCL Model Validation. From the formal definition of the language in the form of a metamodel, it is possible to validate the source model prior to executing the transformations. The language and its editor make sure that the systems conform to the way a station should be designed by adding constraints in the form of OCL (Object Constraint Language) expressions [15]. One such constraint is that for every manual switch it is also required to have at least one *derailer* on the incoming endpoint. Another such constraint is that we can only place certain kinds of signals at given locations.

5.3 Integration of Safety Critical Standards

The development of safety related systems for railway is governed by three CENELEC European Norms, EN 50126 [1], EN 50128 [2] and EN 50129 [3]. Collectively they are similar to the industrial standard IEC 61508 [11]. The norms advocate that a development shall be done according to the V-model with distinct phases with predefined activities. The V-model is a software development process where specification, design and development are on the left part of the V, and integration, test and validation are on the right part of the V. The verification of each phase consists of ensuring that the output from the phase is fulfilling the input requirements to the phase.

Using TCL does not significantly alter the V-model approach currently applied by ABB. TCL provides automatic generation of several different artifacts previously manually developed on the left part of the V. The integration, test and validation will still be preformed at the right side but in addition some automatic validation can be supported.

EN 50128 is specific for software development for railway control. The basic principles in the norm are based on the development of high quality software with extensive additions. However it is more formal and requires that evidence can be given that the process has been followed; all safety requirements have been validated through tests or analysis, and the norm specifies specific techniques and measures to be used in the different phases.

For the software design and implementation phase Table 1 is applicable:

Table 1. Software techniques

	Techniques / measures	SIL 4
1	Formal Methods including for example CCS, CSP, HOL, LOTOS, OBJ, Temporal Logic, VDM, Z and B	HR
2	Semi-Formal Methods	HR
3	Structured Methodology including for example JSD, MASCOT, SADT, SDL, SSADM and Yourdon	HR
4	Modular Approach	M
5	Design and Coding Standards	M
6	Analyzable Programs	HR
7	Strongly Typed Programming Language	HR
8	Structured Programming	HR
9	Programming Language	HR
10	Language Subset	HR
11	Validated Translator	HR
12	Translator Proven in Use	HR
13	Library of Trusted/Verified Modules and Components	HR
14	Functional/ Black-box Testing	R
15	Performance Testing	M
16	Interface Testing	HR
17	Data Recording and Analysis	M
19	Object Oriented Programming	R
M=Mandatory HR= Highly Recommended R= Recommended		

At software safety integrity level 4, the approved set of techniques shall include one of techniques 1, 2 or 3, together with one of techniques 11 or 12. The remaining techniques are treated according to their recommendations in the table, i.e. mandatory (M), highly recommended (HR) or just recommended (R). Normally a company will use all the M and HR and most of the R. However it is possible not to use the HR and R if it can be argued that something else will give the necessary level of safety. The choice will have to be accepted by the "assessor" who will review the overall safety of the system. The border between a formal and semi-formal method is open for debate but both are acceptable according to the norm for this phase of the development. Often UML is put in the class of semi-formal techniques. In the development of CBI, ABB uses all the techniques in Table 1 except numbers 1 and 11.

TCL and High Quality Software. All the above mentioned techniques (Table 1.) require an extensive amount of resources. One of the main goals of TCL is to integrate, and simplify the tasks as much as possible. Technique 1, *"Formal Methods"*, aims at the development of software in a way that is based on mathematics. The resulting descriptions should take a mathematical form and could be subject to analysis to detect inconsistency or incorrectness. Using TCL enables the CBI engineers to generate both interlocking tables and logical equations that address this requirement. The automatically generated interlocking tables could also be used when applying a *"Semi-Formal Method"* which often uses two dimensional decision tables to concisely describe the logical relationships between Boolean variables. The tabular nature makes the interlocking tables appropriate as a means of analyzing complex logical combinations expressed in code.

Utilizing a *"Modular Approach"* is another technique that according to EN 50128 is mandatory. This is already applied in ABB through the use of the interlocking code framework. However, the implementation of TCL and accompanying code generators has made it possible to hide even more details of the modules from the engineers.

Technique 5, "*Design and Coding Standards*", is used to ensure a uniform layout of the design documents and the produced code. It also includes guidelines on where and how to comment the code, and which language constructs that should be avoided (e.g. GOTO, exits and recursion). When followed, it can enforce egoless programming and a standard design method. As a consequence of using TCL and the automatic generation of code it becomes much easier to comply with these standards (they are implemented in the transformation specifications). This also concerns Technique 8, "*Structured Programming*", which aim is to design and implement the program in a way which makes it practical to analyze the program, e.g. complicated branching should be avoided. TCL combined with the interlocking framework ensures that the final implementation follows these recommendations.

Technique 11 and 12 are in traditional software development concerned with the source code compilers. Introducing code generation from models, the transformation engine and transformation specifications will also be subject to this validation, and therefore TCL introduces added complexity since more production software needs to be validated. Translators without operating experience or with serious known errors are prohibitive, however due to the nature of the process of defining a station in TCL, e.g. the intermediate results should be verified, and that one out of 11 and 12 is sufficient, it will be possible to validate TCL only through 12 (*"Translator Proven in Use"*).

During the development of TCL it has been shown that it is possible to integrate and simplify the handling of safety critical issues using a DSL. The added complexity due to MDD and safety critical issues is minimal and the advantages seem to be many and indeed promising.

6 Possibility of Adding Variability Handling

We have seen that TCL automates the procedure of creating interlocking source code for a station, which is advantageous when we want to create more than one station. However, by identifying the differences and similarities of the stations we are able to automate this process even further.

Haugen et al. [10] propose the use of a variability language to handle variations between stations. This method adds the possibility to automatically generate a station based on another previously created station, without increasing the complexity of TCL. The station repositories created from the TCL editors is used to perform the model-to-model transformations necessary to generate a new station. We have identified three scenarios where variability handling can be introduced:

- Simple variation: Stations with equal structure, where only names and attribute values are different.
- Simple structure variation: Stations with minor difference in structure (i.e. optional elements or substitution of an element with another of the same type).
- Advanced structure variation: Stations with differences beyond the substitution of simple elements (i.e. add or remove a track from the station).

Another case that is subject to change in the future is the functional level of the station. The European Rail Traffic Management System (ERTMS) has different functional levels, ranging from light signals used today to radio communication between the train and a central computer [8]. To ease the transition to a higher level, the variability language can be applied.

The basic idea in the approach described in [10] is to design variability and resolution models based on the base model. In this case the base model will be a station created in the TCL editor. A particular variability model is created to support one set of variations, i.e. variability between two stations or variability between two functional levels. The variability model describes which variations that can be applied to the base model and how this can be done. One or more resolution models are then created to describe the fixed values that the base model should be changed to.

The variability and resolution models only change the base model into another valid TCL model. Every concept needed in a station must therefore already exist in the base model on which we are applying variability. Furthermore, this approach does not require any changes made to the code generator or other transformations done to the stations models.

Since the variability language supports structural change to a base model, all the scenarios mentioned above can be solved by introducing the variability language. However, not all changes may be practical to model using this language. Thus having more than one basis station, and use the variability language to describe other stations that resembles these stations may be the best choice.

7 Conclusion and Future Work

This paper has presented the Domain Specific Language TCL and its tool support. We have seen the advantages of using MDD to automate the procedure of creating source code for a train interlocking system.

CBI development requires that the requirement, analysis, design and implementation documents are consistent and complete. The manual development process carried out today can lead to inconsistency between the different documents. TCL and a model-driven approach reduce the workload of keeping artifacts consistent and complete. Changes only have to be made on the station model, and the other artifacts can automatically be generated to preserve consistency and completeness.

During our development of TCL and tools, we experienced how well existing frameworks suits the development of editors and generators for the train domain. We found EMF and MOFScript powerful and easy to use, and we were able to generate the required results from the station models. Although GMF was able to generate a basic graphical editor and offer a great extensibility through source code alteration, the user interface could have been more powerful. GMF may therefore need some maturation.

MDD turned out to be a good approach for developing a safety critical system due to the preservation of consistency and completeness. By using automatic code generation the error-susceptible manual process is eliminated and we have seen how the safety standards are ensured by this approach.

Future Work. TCL has been developed as a prototype and has only been used to create small stations at the time being. The language should be extended with more primitives to support big stations, with as many as 50 tracks.

Adding variability handling to TCL by introducing the variability language described earlier would be a useful feature that requires more investigation. A case study should be initiated to see how big the advantages of this approach can be.

Acknowledgments. The work presented here has been developed within the MoSiS project ITEA 2 – ip06035. MoSiS is a project within the ITEA 2 – Eureka framework.

References

1. CENELEC, En 50126: Railway Applications - the Specification and Demonstration of Reliability, Availability, Maintainability and Safety (RAMS), CENELEC
2. CENELEC, En 50128: Railway Applications – Communication, Signaling and Processing Systems – Software for Railway Control and Protection Systems, CENELEC
3. CENELEC, En 50129: Railway Applications : Safety Related Electronic Systems for Signaling, CENELEC
4. eclipse.org, Eclipse Graphical Modeling Framework (GMF), `http://www.eclipse.org/modeling/gmf/`
5. eclipse.org, Eclipse Modeling Framework Project (EMF), `http://www.eclipse.org/modeling/emf/`
6. eclipse.org, Model Development Tools (MDT), `http://www.eclipse.org/modeling/mdt/?project=uml2tools`

7. eclipse.org, Mofscript, `http://www.eclipse.org/gmt/mofscript/`
8. ERTMS, European Rail Traffic Management System (ERTMS), `http://www.ertms.com/`
9. Fagan, M.E.: Design and Code Inspections to Reduce Errors in Program Development. IBM Systems Journal 15, 182–211 (1976)
10. Haugen, Ø., Møller-Pedersen, B., Oldevik, J., Olsen, G.K., Svendsen, A.: Adding Standarized Variability to Domain Specific Languages. In: 12th International Software Product Line Conference (SPLC), Limerick, Ireland (2008)
11. IEC, Iec 61508: Functional Safety of Electrical/Electronic/Programmable Electronic Safety-Related Systems
12. Kelly, S., Tolvanen, J.-P.: Domain-Specific Modeling: Enabling Full Code Generation. John Wiley & Sons, Inc., Chichester (2008)
13. MetaCase, Metaedit+ DSM Environment, `http://www.metacase.com/products.html`
14. Olsen, G.K., Aagedal, J., Oldevik, J.: Aspects of Reusable Model Transformations. In: ECMDA 2006 Workshop on Composition of Model Transformations: Proceedings of CMT 2006 (2006)
15. OMG, Object Constraint Language (OCL), `http://www.omg.org/technology/documents/formal/ocl.htm`

NAOMI – An Experimental Platform for Multi–modeling

Trip Denton, Edward Jones, Srini Srinivasan, Ken Owens, and Richard W. Buskens

Lockheed Martin Advanced Technology Laboratories, Cherry Hill NJ 08002
{ldenton,ejones,ssriniva,kowens,rbuskens}@atl.lmco.com

Abstract. Domain-specific modeling languages (DSMLs) are designed to provide precise abstractions of domain-specific constructs. However, models for complex systems typically do not fit neatly within a single domain and capturing all important aspects of such a system requires developing multiple models using different DSMLs. Combining these models into multi-models presents difficult challenges, most importantly those of integrating the various models and keeping both the models and their associated data synchronized. To this end, we present NAOMI, an experimental platform for enabling multiple models, developed in different DSMLs, to work together. NAOMI analyzes model dependencies to determine the impact of changes to one model on other dependent models and coordinates the propagation of necessary model changes. NAOMI also serves as a useful testbed for exploring how diverse modeling paradigms can be combined.

1 Introduction

Incomplete system specifications can lead to serious problems that do not manifest themselves until very late in the development lifecycle - when the costs to repair such problems may be astronomical. Model-driven design techniques can expose design flaws early in the project lifecycle, when the cost of a design change is minimal.

Invariably, multiple models are needed to comprehensively model all aspects of a system, encompassing system structure and behavior, and possibly other aspects as well (e.g., cost). As shown by Hessellund, Czarnecki, and Wasowski [1] large and complex systems can be accurately abstracted by the use of multiple domain-specific modeling languages (DSMLs). In fact, as noted by Greenfield, Short, Cook, and Kent [2], general-purpose modeling languages (e.g. UML, SysML) often lack the semantic precision required to model all aspects of a system.

The SysML and UML communities attempt to address this issue via domain specific extensions (e.g., the UML profile for Modeling and Analysis of Real-time and Embedded systems(MARTE) [3,4] and by providing explicit capabilities to describe dependencies on models implemented in other modeling languages (e.g., through the use of parametrics in SysML [5]).

Our vision of future model-centric systems engineering and development does not require or depend on the existence of a general-purpose modeling language. Instead, modelers construct multiple models using a suite of diverse domain-specific modeling languages (DSMLs), where each DSML allows specific aspects of a system to be precisely modeled. We refer to the interrelated compositions of the various models as

K. Czarnecki et al. (Eds.): MoDELS 2008, LNCS 5301, pp. 143–157, 2008.

multi-models. An overarching challenge, described in more detail in subsequent sections of this paper, is the complexity of integrating the various models in a cohesive manner. The root causes of this challenge are the diversity of the various modeling paradigms in both specification and implementation, the need for these models to share information about the system under design, and the need for model changes to be appropriately reflected in dependent models.

In this paper, we describe NAOMI, an experimental platform for enabling multiple models, developed using different DSMLs, to work together. NAOMI allows modelers to use any modeling languages they desire, and as new modeling languages and tools are developed, they can be integrated into the NAOMI infrastructure. NAOMI provides a standard way for linking the multiple facets of a system through a structured mechanism for specifying shared attributes of the system under design. Our approach is general and is not specific to any modeling paradigm, thus it may be used wherever multiple models need to be combined into a cohesive whole. Currently, the framework is targeted toward tools for the analysis of system behavior.

2 Key Multi-modeling Challenges

Successful integration of multiple interdependent models, where each model captures different aspects of a complete system specification, poses several difficult research challenges. In this section, we describe some of these challenges and derive a set of requirements that a generalized multi-model platform must meet to address these challenges.

2.1 Challenge 1: Capturing Multi-model Interdependencies

Previous work by Nuseibeh, Kramer, and Finkelstein [6], demonstrates the difficulty of capturing and expressing model interdependencies. In a multi-model, interdependencies can be identified by a sharing or exchange of data between models. As n integrated models may have an arbitrary amount of dependencies, for a multi-model composed of n constituent models, the number of dependencies can not necessarily be asymptotically bound with a polynomial function in terms of n. Therefore, as the number of models, the complexity of their interaction, and/or the size of the system being modeled increases, it becomes extremely difficult to manually keep track of these interdependencies. Even more difficult is tracking and analyzing the implications of these dependencies, both of which are necessary and challenging aspects of multi-model integration. As we will later demonstrate, in order to maintain consistency, it is important that these dependencies be explicit.

2.2 Challenge 2: Maintaining Multi-model Consistency

Hessellund et al. [1] demonstrated the need for maintaining consistency when modeling with multiple DSMLs. In a *consistent* multi-model, we believe there can be no unpropagated model changes. When a model in a consistent multi-model is modified, changes to the model must be correctly propagated to dependent models. Such changes may propagate through the entire set of models in the multi-model and even back to the original model itself. Not until the propagated changes converge so that no more change propagation is necessary, can we say that the multi-model is *consistent*. To reach multi-model consistency, model changes must be propagated in order with respect to their interdependencies. However, it may be difficult to determine such an ordering when the dependencies are cyclic. Even if a suitable ordering of change propagation can be determined, there is no way today to assess if the models will converge.

Additionally, constraints placed on models (e.g., performance or reliability bounds) further complicate the problem. Some changes may violate constraints and our notion of consistency must be extended to ensure that no constraints have been violated.

There is the practical consideration that multiple modelers must be allowed to make changes to their models simultaneously. Thus, propagation of model changes must be performed across compatible versions of the various models. Should particular changes not yield a consistent multi-model, rollback of the changes, again across compatible versions of the models, must be possible. An additional practical consideration is that the modeling tools themselves may evolve over time, in which the correct versions of the tools associated with the models must also be maintained to ensure that a consistent multi-model can be reconstructed.

2.3 Challenge 3: Semantic Precision of Inter-model Data Exchange

The fact that models are interdependent necessitates that they share or exchange data. The semantics of the data must be precisely known and understood by all models participating in the exchange. Achieving this precision is challenging given multiple models, expressed in different DSMLs. Model and meta-model transformation based approaches can allow for the preservation of semantics when data is exchanged between models [7,8], but this requires that the models either be described in languages derived from the same meta-model, or that experts specify the relationships between elements of the disparate meta-models. While syntactic transformation between languages may be possible and even potentially automatable, ensuring and/or preserving semantic correctness remains challenging.

2.4 Requirements

To address the challenges described in Sections 2.1, 2.2 and 2.3, a multi-modeling system must satisfy the following requirements:

1. The system must allow data exchange between models.
2. The system must support a means of specifying interdependencies between models.
3. The system must support a means of propagating changes from one model to all dependent models.
4. The system must be able to determine an ordering for propagation of model changes consistent with interdependencies among models.
5. The system must be able to identify when multi-models are consistent.
6. The system must support simultaneous updates of multiple models.
7. The system must be capable of supporting all of the above independently of modeling language or modeling tool.

8. The system must allow for the set of models and tools to vary over time.
9. The system must allow for multiple versions of models (and tools).
10. The system must support the ability to rollback to earlier versions of the models and tools.
11. The system must allow for transformations of data during inter-model exchanges.
12. The system must assure and enforce semantic correctness in inter-model data exchanges. (not addressed in this paper)

Requirement 1 follows from Challenges 1 and 3, requirement 2 follows from Challenge 1, requirements 3-11 follow from Challenge 2, and requirement 12 follows from Challenge 3. We present the design of NAOMI and show how it meets requirements 1 through 11 above. Requirement 12 will be addressed in future work.

3 NAOMI

NAOMI is an experimental platform for multi-model integration. NAOMI places no restrictions on the modeling languages or tools used to develop a multi-model of a system. It allows modelers to specify the models used to describe a system, along with their inter-dependencies, and uses this information to propagate changes to models.

Figure 1 shows a high level overview of NAOMI. Modelers edit models in DSMLs and use the Multi-Model Manager to construct the multi-model from individual models. Connectors isolate DSML specific interface code and interact with the Multi-Model Manager and the Sandbox, which provides modelers with a local copy of the Multi-Model Repository that holds the multi-model's artifacts under version control. The Execution Automation Engine determines an ordering of execution based on dependencies in the multi-model and orchestrates execution of the multi-model. The functionality provided by the system includes, model data exchange, constraint management, change propagation, model execution, and version management.

3.1 NAOMI Multi-model Repository

Various data items are stored in the Multi-Model Repository. We use the term *artifacts* to describe entities that define the multi-model. NAOMI artifacts include models, the

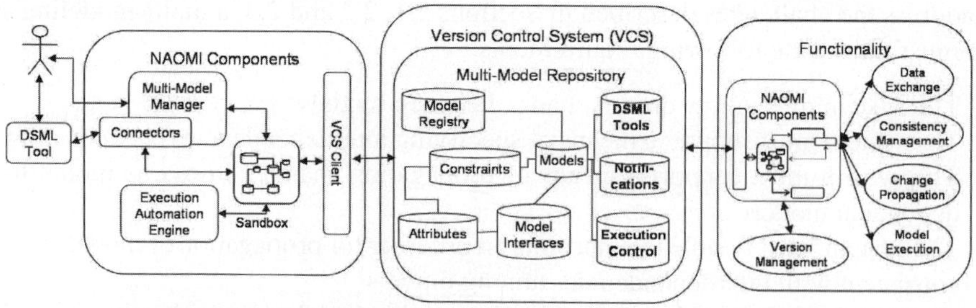

Fig. 1. High level overview of NAOMI, modelers edit models in domain specific modeling languages (DSMLs) and interact with NAOMI components which expose the multi-modeling functionality

model registry, model editing tools, interfaces, attributes, attribute constraints, and notifications. All of the NAOMI artifacts are stored in a *repository* that is under version control. This allows the entire multi-model to be reconstructed at any point during its evolution and for distributed collaboration via modifications to artifacts in the repository.

Model Attributes and Interfaces. In our notion of models, they can be grouped into two not necessarily exclusive groups, *Specification* and *Analytical* Models. *Specification* models help to define the system being modeled, for example UML may define the class hierarchy, valid system states or operational sequence diagrams. *Analytical* models, analyze aspects of the defined system, for example RT-Maude [9] may evaluate the safety parameters of the system, given a specific, state transition and component failure rate specification. Our concept of a model is a mapping written in some language, L_i, over a set of inputs, that produces a set of outputs. A model, M_j, is associated with a set of *attributes* that are inputs $I_j = \{a_1, a_2, \ldots, a_n\}$, which may be empty, and a set of attributes that are outputs $O_j = \{a'_1, a'_2, \ldots, a'_{n'}\}$, which may also be empty. We can represent the model, M_j by the tuple $M_j(L_i, I_j, O_j)$. This tuple is the interface that the model exposes to the system by adding it to the repository. A multi-model, M, can be defined as a set of models $M = \{M_1, M_2, \ldots, M_m\}$. To synchronize execution of the multi-model, we require that an attribute be owned by a single model and can only be written by the model that owns it. That is, if $a_i \in O_j$, then $a_i \notin O_n \forall O_{n \neq j} \in M$.

This input/output view of models works well where specification type models provide input for analytical models (sometimes the entire model itself serves as input for analysis), and the output of analytical models is used either as input to other analytical models or to further refine another specification model. There are cases however, where specification models only share parts of their specification. These shared parts, rather than being used "wholesale", sometimes only constrain or imply the existence of other specifications in other models. For example, in a UML model, state chart transition events may be limited to the methods defined in a specific class diagram. In the absence of specific model-to-model transformation tools, sharing this type of information in this input-output manner becomes difficult. In section 7 we discuss our plans for addressing this issue in our future work.

Model Registry. The model registry is used to determine membership in the multi-model; it is a simple list that enumerates the models in the multi-model. If a model is removed from the registry, the artifacts that correspond to that model remain in the repository, but that model will not participate in the multi-model.

Constraints. Models can have constraints associated with their inputs and outputs. These *attribute constraints* can be thought of as triggers on the value of the attribute. If a model has a constraint on input attribute a_i, the model is notified when the model that owns a_i outputs a value that violates this constraint. Output constraints are used by a model to ensure that the attributes written are valid from the point of view of the model that writes them.

Notifications. Notifications are messages sent to models to inform them of interesting events. For example, when a modeler edits a model which generates a change to an output attribute that violates some constraint, a notification is sent to the affected models.

Sandboxes. Modelers interact with NAOMI through local copies of the repository called sandboxes. Sandboxes allow modelers to work on local copies of their model without being affected by concurrent changes to the multi-model from other modelers. To interact with a project, modelers checkout local copies of the repository and make modifications. The modifications are communicated to other models by synchronization with the global version of the repository.

3.2 Functionality

Data Exchange. Data exchange between models is accomplished via attributes. The owner of an attribute writes the attribute and commits it to the multi-model repository. Readers synchronize their local sandbox with the repository and access the attribute to obtain the data output by the owner model.

Model Execution. In the context of NAOMI, model execution is the process whereby model inputs are read, the model is run, and the outputs are written. It is the combined action of reading the attributes from the repository, running the model (using the DSML tool), and writing the output attributes to the repository. For example, execution of an Excel spreadsheet model involves loading the spreadsheet, reading the input attributes into the spreadsheet, allowing the calculated cell values to be updated, and writing the output attributes. An underlying assumption is that the models are parametrized, and we distinguish between model *edits*, which are actual changes to the model, and attribute changes, which are changes to the values of attributes.

Change Propagation. When a model is modified, changes are propagated by controlled exchange of attributes between models. A multi-model may be thought of as a pseudo graph, $G(V, E)$ where each model is represented by a vertex such that $\forall M_i \in M | \exists v_i \in V$. Each edge, (u, v), represents data propagated from an output attribute of one model to the input attribute of another, that is

$$\forall (u, v) \in E | \exists M_i(L, I_i, O_i), M_j(L', I_j, O_j) : a_i \in O_i \wedge a_i \in I_j .$$

This definition admits parallel edges so E must be a multi-set. To propagate changes, we can perform a depth first search (DFS) on G and select the leaves to be executed first. We propagate changes from the leaves upward with respect to dependencies such that no model M_i is executed before another model M_j if $\exists a_i : a_i \in I_i \wedge a_i \in O_j$.

There are cases for which we can not know the order of execution based on our dependency graph. Some models, particularly nondeterministic models, may need to be executed for a specified number of iterations, or until their attributes meet some predetermined constraints. Also, when the dependency graph has strongly connected components composed of two or more models, we require some way to deal with cycles.

In both of these cases, we require expert input to successfully perform execution. We have provided a feature whereby modelers may enter rules that specify the systems behavior under these circumstances. Rules are of the form $R(M) \rightarrow S$, where R is a rule, mapping a match expression (a sequence of models participating in the execution), M, to a set of actions, S, which will be performed when M is encountered in the execution plan.

Consistency Management. In the context of a multi-model, we are interested in whether the composition of the constituent models is consistent. We assume that the individual models are consistent and define the following types of multi-model consistency.

Attribute Consistency: All attributes have been updated by their owner model since the last time their owner model's input attributes changed.

Constraint Consistency: The current values of all attributes do not violate any model specific constraints.

Attribute-Model Consistency: The modification times (time of last model edit) of all models are earlier than the modification times of their output attributes.

NAOMI Consistency: Multi-models that have the properties of attribute consistency, constraint consistency, and attribute-model consistency are defined as NAOMI consistent.

Attribute consistency indicates that all models have been executed with up-to-date input data. Therefore, there are no unpropagated attribute changes. For a specific version of the multi-model, this consistency property can be ensured by executing the multi-model. However, this assumes that the models are *deterministic*. We define a deterministic model as a model that always produces the same output for a given set of inputs, in absence of a model edit.

Constraint consistency indicates that the outputs of all of the models in the multi-model fall within acceptable ranges, and by attribute-model consistency we mean that models have not been edited since their outputs have been written. These consistency types are independent of each other, and achieving one does *not* imply achieving any other.

We say that multi-models that are attribute consistent, constraint consistent, and attribute-model consistent are *NAOMI consistent*. We believe that a NAOMI-consistent multi-model is coherent and represents a steady state of the multi-model. By steady state, we mean that executing *any* subset of the models in the multi-model in *any* order will not result in any changed attributes. Thus modelers can be confident that outputs from any model in the multi-model are reliable provided the models themselves are consistent and have been integrated such that the correct attributes are exchanged. Our notion of consistency in the context of a single model is purposely vague and intended only to convey the meaning that the individual model is correct according to its own definition.

Limitations are inherent in this approach. As previously indicated, the models must be deterministic, and there can be no cyclic dependencies in the multi-models. Also model execution must halt at some point, output must be written, and attributes must have a format that can be understood by models that read it.

Version Management. The version control system keeps all the artifacts under version control and is used to synchronize local sandboxes with the global repository. It provides modelers the capability to modify any version of an individual model or the multi-model as a whole. Changes can be rolled back, and the entire multi-model can be reconstructed at any time.

3.3 NAOMI Components

Connectors. Connectors are software components that connect individual models to the multi-model. They allow controlled information exchange between models. A primary design goal of NAOMI is to have simple, lightweight connectors, enabling the easy integration of new modeling languages and tools. Connectors are language and tool specific, but may be used for multiple tools if the tools provide equivalent interfaces to the connector. Connectors *must* provide the following:

1. A mechanism for reading attributes from local copies of attribute files and inserting the attribute contents in the appropriate model files.
2. A mechanism for extracting attributes from models and writing those attributes to local files.
3. A mechanism for writing an interface description. This capability ensures that the interface always reflects the actual inputs and outputs of the model.
4. A connector-independent, common mechanism to ensure that NAOMI can always determine when the value of an attribute has changed.

Multi-Model Manager. The Multi-Model Manager is the component responsible for assisting modelers in integrating and invoking connectors, performing consistency checks, constraining attributes, and generating automatic notifications. Additionally, the Multi-Model Manager allows modelers to visualize the repository and obtain an overall view of the multi-model.

Execution Automation Engine. The Execution Automation Engine is the component responsible for determining an order for the execution of individual models in the multi-model. This is obtained through analysis of the artifacts in the repository. The Execution Automation Engine uses this ordering to orchestrate the execution process which propagates dependencies.

3.4 Requirements Fulfillment

Table 1 maps the the NAOMI concepts to the design requirements from Section 2.4. Requirement 11 can easily be met by recasting a data transformation as a model in the normal NAOMI sense.

Table 1. NAOMI components and the requirements they fulfill

NAOMI Component	Requirement Implemented
Connectors	1, 2, 3, 7, 8, 11
Multi-Model Manager	1, 2, 3 , 5, 6, 8, 9, 11
Execution Automation Engine	3, 4, 5
Version Control System	6, 8, 9, 10

3.5 Scalability of Approach

We next address the issue of the scalability of our approach. The connectors parse the model files and insert/extract attributes. Parsing the model files can done in one pass for most types of files, so the runtime is $O(n)$ where n is the size of the model input files. We can assume that an attribute can be written in constant time, so the entire operation can be done in $O(n+m)$ where m is the number of attributes. Since $m \leq n$ the runtime is still $O(n)$.

The repository is managed by a version control system such as Subversion [10] which is designed to scale well and has been shown to work well with tens of thousands of files, i.e. Linux kernel source code trees. So the number of artifacts in the repository should not be a problem. Multiple repositories could be used to alleviate this, if it became a problem.

The Multi-Model Manager needs to keep certain artifacts in memory in order to manage the multi-model. While we have not tested it with large numbers of models, we believe it should scale to at least hundreds of models. If this became a problem, the models could be partitioned into groups, those groups could be represented by new models and a hierarchical system could be developed, mitigating this problem.

In order to propagate the model attributes throughout the multi-model, the models need to be executed (where applicable). While the execution can be distributed, the communication protocol used and the time to propagate changes could present issues if the number of models and their complexity increases. The runtime of this operation is difficult to predict given that the topology of the multi-model is a determining factor. More experiments need to be done in this area, and the existence of a platform for experimentation will make these measurements possible.

4 NAOMI Implementation

This section describes our implementation of NAOMI. An overview of the workflow is shown in Figure 2. Modelers use their modeling tool to edit DSML models. The Multi-Model Manager is used to (i) invoke the DSML connectors, (ii) browse the local sandbox, and (iii) commit model and artifact changes to the central repository. The Automated Multi-Model Execution Engine (AMMEE) is then used to analyze the central repository and prepare an execution plan, which is used to maintain multi-model consistency.

4.1 NAOMI Connectors

Connectors for NAOMI may be implemented in almost any language, as long as the connector requirements described in Section 3.3 are fulfilled. For example, an Excel connector can be written in Perl, and a UML connector can be written in Java. The integration mechanism is specific to the connector, and connector writers may implement the mechanism any way they choose. For example, an Excel connector might expect that Excel models are integrated by naming cells in a special way (e.g., a cell named `naomi_get.system.reliability` can instruct the Excel connector to retrieve the `system.reliability` attribute and place it in the cell).

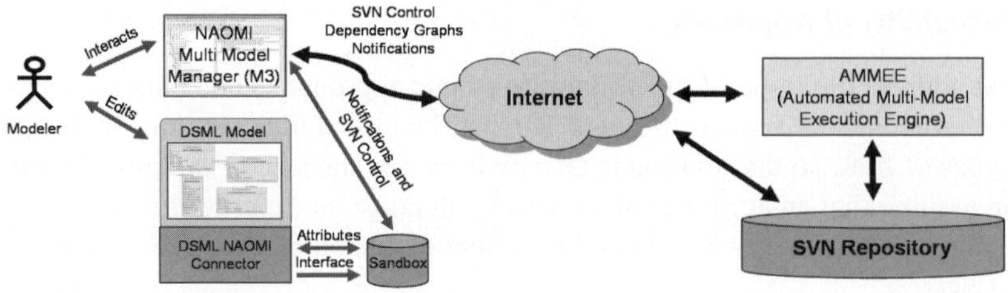

Fig. 2. NAOMI work-flow: modeler uses model tool to edit DSML model. Multi-Model Manager and connector are used to maintain sandbox files. M3 commits changes to NAOMI repository, which are analyzed by the Automated Multi-Model Execution Engine.

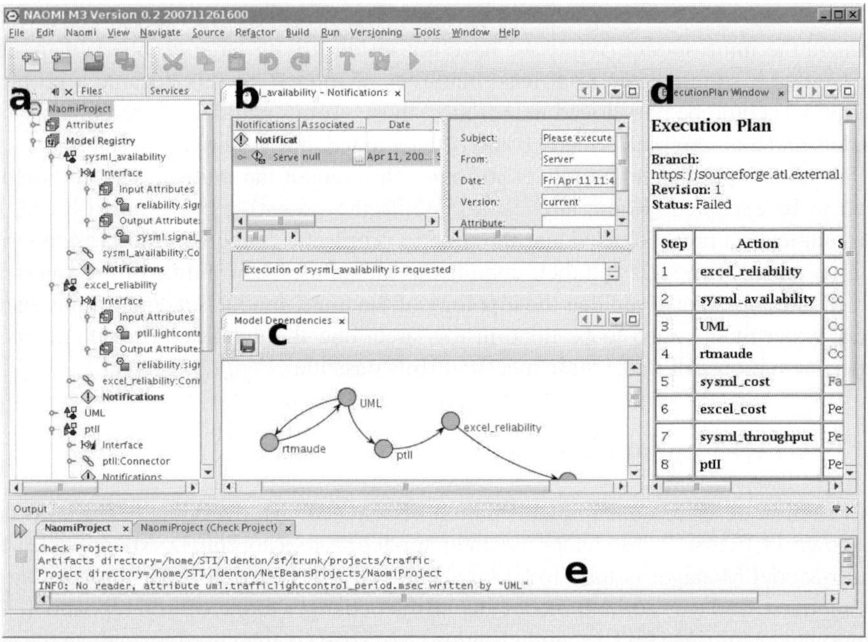

Fig. 3. M3 application showing a NAOMI project: (a) project node with DSML models, their interfaces, and connectors, (b) notification pane showing notification for the currently selected model, (c) model-dependency graph, (d) execution plan and status from AMMEE, (e) message area showing output from operation

4.2 Repository

The models and their corresponding editing tools reside inside the repository in their native forms. The repository is managed by the Subversion [10] version control system. Model interfaces, attributes, notifications, and the model registry are all implemented as XML [11] files, with defined XML schemas [12], stored inside the repository. Attribute constraints are defined as XML schemas that impose a restriction on an attribute file.

Every registered model is allowed one constraint schema per attribute, allowing each modeler to use a customized set of constraints. An XML schema validation engine is used to validate each attribute against the associated constraints.

4.3 NAOMI Multi-model Manager

The NAOMI Multi-Model Manager (M3) is implemented as a Netbeans [13] rich client to be used locally on modelers' machines to assist them in managing their sandboxes.

M3's user interface is shown in Figure 3. Section (a) of the figure shows the first level of repository visualization. Each registered model is shown as a node in an explorer-type view on M3. Expanding the model node reveals the interface, connector and notifications nodes. M3 also provides graph visualizations of the relationships between each model in the multi-model (shown in (c) of Figure 3). These visualizations allow modelers to see the full extent of the relationships between models and expose owner-less and reader-less attributes.

M3 automatically handles the sending and receiving of notifications and provides facilities for control of the SVN repository. Additionally, it works in conjunction with AMMEE to provide work flow management during model execution.

4.4 Automated Multi-model Execution Engine

The Automated Multi-Model Execution Engine (AMMEE) facilitates the generation of a workflow for integrated DSMLs in the context of a NAOMI project. When execution of a project is requested to resolve dependencies, AMMEE branches the project, queries the model registry for all registered models, and builds a dependency graph based on each model's inputs and outputs. A plan of execution, based on these dependencies, is stored in the repository. This plan is updated as execution progresses, and it allows modelers to examine the status of the multi-model's execution. AMMEE interacts with M3 to request the execution of each model until a consistent state is reached.

5 Experiments

We study model interactions in the context of a system for controlling traffic lights within a city. Our initial multi-model simply consists of requirements, partitioning, and interacting state machine algorithms for a single pedestrian light and single car light controller at the intersection of two streets. Our experimental multi-model consists of four models in four different DSMLs, which were chosen for simplicity of explanation:

- A structural model, developed in UML, that writes two attributes, "duration of red light" and "duration of green light" that specify how long the lights are on.
- An algorithmic model [14], developed in Ptolemy II, that reads the light durations and outputs a "light control failure time percent" attribute, which is the expected amount of time the two lights will be in a failure mode.
- A reliability model, developed in Excel, that reads the "light control failure time percent" attribute and writes a "signal availability percent" attribute, which is the percent of time the signal lights will be available.
- A requirements model, developed in SysML, that reads the "signal availability percent" attribute.

5.1 Experiment 1: Identifying Unanticipated Impacts

We demonstrate how NAOMI propagates changes in one model to dependent models and flags any unpropagated changes. When the "duration of red light" attribute is changed in the UML model, an attribute consistency check run in M3 fails on all models except the UML model. The reason for this can be seen by examining the model dependency graph in Figure 4; all of the other models are dependent either directly or indirectly on the output of the UML model. To resolve this problem, AMMEE defines the order of execution as visualized by the graph shown in the Figure 4. The Ptolemy II model is executed, propagating the aforementioned change in an attribute owned by the Ptolemy II model. The model execution continues in the prescribed order until the SysML model is executed, propagating the change to the SysML owned attribute, "signal availability percent." Upon completion, all attribute consistency checks pass, indicating successful attribute change propagation.

The change propagation we demonstrated shows how a seemingly simple change in one domain can cascade into others and how NAOMI can detect unpropagated changes.

Fig. 4. Model dependency graph for Experiment 1

5.2 Experiment 2: Tracking Violations of Design Intent

Next, we tested the capability to automatically alert modelers to constraint violations. We added a constraint to the input of the SysML model to ensure that "signal availability percent" is at least 90%. We then repeated Experiment 1: the change propagated to "signal availability percent," violated the constraint, and NAOMI automatically generated a notification to the SysML modeler that the constraint was violated. This shows that NAOMI is capable of attaching constraints to attributes which can be used to ensure models exchange valid data.

5.3 Experiment 3: Managing Model Coevolution

Lastly, we demonstrate managing model coevolution in a NAOMI project. The UML model is modified so that it no longer writes values to the "duration of green light" attribute. In Figure 5, a project consistency check shows an error because the Ptolemy model is reading an attribute that is no longer written by any model. This generates an alert to the modelers of the integration problem resulting from the evolution of the UML model. This type of error would be difficult to detect without the automated consistency checking that NAOMI provides.

6 Related Work

Previous approaches to multi-modeling often used a common representation that the various models are mapped to. For example, in the area of formal specification, Zave

```
Check Project:
Artifacts directory=/projects/traffic
Project directory=/NetBeansProjects/NaomiProject
ERROR: No writer for attribute duration_of_green_light read by Ptolemy II
```

Fig. 5. Example output from a project check that shows the Ptolemy II model is reading an attribute that is not written by any model

and Jackson [15] provided a compelling method for multi-paradigm formal specification. Using their method, partial specifications are produced with languages suited to the aspects under consideration. These partial specifications are converted to assertions in first order logic, and the multi paradigm specification is equivalent to the conjunction of these first order assertions.

Brooks, Feng, and Lee [14] described the construction of a hierarchical multi-model in Ptolemy II and showed how model based specification can be enriched by the incorporation of multiple distinct modeling formalisms. They also showed how actor-oriented classes enforce consistency across multi view models. Girault, B. Lee, and E. Lee [16] combined finite state machines with various concurrency models, each having different strengths and weaknesses, inside the Ptolemy framework.

Other approaches to multi-modeling have used meta-model-based integration techniques. Hardebolle, Boulanger, Marcadet, and Vidal-Naquet [7] describe ModHel'X, which was inspired by Ptolemy and implements a multi-formalism approach to computational modeling. The Open Tool Integration Framework (OTIF), described by Karsai, Lang,and Neema [8], addresses the data integration problem through meta-model-based transformations, and they present two architectures for the framework.

The Electronic Tool Integration (ETI) [17,18] framework is an example of using light-weight data exchange as a mechanism for tool integration using web-services. However, ETI does not address issues such as managed repositories, with built-in versioning and consistency management, which are critical for scalable application to projects.

Wimmer, Schauerhuber, Strommer, Schwinger, and Kappel [19] demonstrated a semi-automatic approach to bridging DSMLs based on the manual mapping of domain-specific meta-models and UML combining a dedicated bridging language, automatic generation of UML profiles and model transformations. In contrast, we follow a light-weight data exchange mechanism, without requiring an intermediate language.

Kappel, Kramler, Kapsammer, Reiter, Retschitzegger, and Schwinger [20] describe ModelCVS, which focuses on ontology-based meta-model integration via meta-model lifting. ModelCVS is built on the concurrent versions system, CVS [21] and recognizes the key role that versioning plays in multi-view modeling.

Our approach is different; we do not seek a common representation for the multi-model's constituent models, nor do we assume the meta-models of DSMLs will have sufficient semantic overlap to allow for a mapping. We remain tool and language agnostic by decoupling the implementation of a model from the interface it exposes to the multi-model and focus on the interactions between different DSMLs.

7 Conclusion

We have outlined key multi-modeling challenges and derived a set of requirements that a generalized multi-modeling system should fulfill. By adopting a language-neutral stance and representing models through interface abstractions, we showed how multi-models can be composed from diverse DSML models and kept consistent, avoiding limitations of previous methods that seek to transform models to a common representation. We presented NAOMI, an experimental platform that implements these concepts, and showed how this platform can assist modelers by propagating changes and data across domains, alerting them to violations of constraints and notifying them of failures in consistency. This work enables the construction of robust multi-models not possible without NAOMI.

For future work we wish to address the issue of ensuring the preservation of semantic meaning during the exchange of data between models as described by Challenge 3 in Section 2.3. Additionally we want to address the limitations in our input/output based view of models, particularly specification models as discussed in section 3.1. Our research in this area is ongoing, and we are looking at using approaches like that of Bräuer and Lochmann [22] to allow relevant specification information to be shared between different modeling languages. We are continuing to investigate ways of addressing the scalability issues associated with multi-model execution raised in section 3.5.

Acknowledgments

The authors would like to thank Edward A. Lee, Christopher Brooks, and Thomas Huining Feng of the University of California at Berkeley; Jose Meseguer, Peter Csaba Ölveczky, and Kyungmin Bae of the University of Illinois at Urbana-Champaign; Artur Boronat of the University of Leicester, Douglas Schmidt, Jules White, James H. Hill, and Sean Eade of Vanderbilt University for their helpful suggestions and their contributions to the NAOMI project.

References

1. Hessellund, A., Czarnecki, K., Wasowski, A.: Guided development with multiple domain-specific languages. In: Engels, G., Opdyke, B., Schmidt, D.C., Weil, F. (eds.) MODELS 2007. LNCS, vol. 4735, pp. 46–60. Springer, Heidelberg (2007)
2. Greenfield, J., Short, K., Cook, S., Kent, S.: Software Factories. Wiley, Chichester (2004)
3. OMG: Unified modeling language specification version 2.0 (2005), http://www.uml.org/
4. OMG: Modeling and analysis of real-time and embedded systems (MARTE) (2006), http://www.omgmarte.org/
5. OMG: Omg systems modeling language (sysml) specification version 1.0 (2007)
6. Nuseibeh, B., Kramer, J., Finkelstein, A.: Expressing the relationships between multiple views in requirements specification. In: ICSE 1993, pp. 187–196. IEEE Computer Society Press, Los Alamitos (1993)
7. Hardebolle, C., Boulanger, F., Marcadet, D., Vidal-Naquet, G.: A generic execution framework for models of computation. In: Fernandes, J.M., Machado, R.J., Khedri, R., Clarke, S. (eds.) MOMPES 2007, pp. 45–54. IEEE Computer Society, Los Alamitos (2007)

8. Karsai, G., Lang, A., Neema, S.: Design patterns for open tool integration. Software and Systems Modeling (SoSym) 4(2), 157–170 (2005)
9. Ölveczky, P., Meseguer, J.: Semantics and pragmatics of real-time maude. Higher-Order and Symbolic Computation 20(1), 161–196 (2007)
10. CollabNet: Subversion version control system (2006), `http://subversion.tigris.org/`
11. World Wide Web Consortium: W3C Extensible Markup Language (XML) (2006), `http://www.w3.org/XML`
12. World Wide Web Consortium: W3C XML schema (2006), `http://www.w3.org/XML/Schema`
13. Sun Microsystems: Netbeans (2008), `http://netbeans.org/`
14. Brooks, C., Feng, T.H., Lee, E.A.: Multimodeling: A preliminary case study. Technical Report UCB/EECS-2008-7, EECS Department, University of California, Berkeley (2008)
15. Zave, P., Jackson, M.: Where Do Operations Come From?: A Multiparadigm Specification Technique. IEEE Transactions on Software Engineering 22(7), 508–528 (1996)
16. Girault, A., Lee, B., Lee, E.: Hierarchical finite state machines with multiple concurrency models. IEEE Transactions on Computer-Aided Design of Integrated Circuits and Systems 18(6), 742–760 (1999)
17. Steffen, B., Margaria, T., Braun, V.: The Electronic Tool Integration platform: concepts and design. International Journal on Software Tools for Technology Transfer (STTT) 1(1), 9–30 (1997)
18. Margaria, T., Nagel, R., Steffen, B.: jETI: A Tool for Remote Tool Integration. In: Halbwachs, N., Zuck, L.D. (eds.) TACAS 2005. LNCS, vol. 3440, pp. 557–562. Springer, Heidelberg (2005)
19. Wimmer, M., Schauerhuber, A., Strommer, M., Schwinger, W., Kappel, G.: A Semi-automatic Approach for Bridging DSLs with UML? In: Proceedings of the 7th OOPSLA Workshop on Domain-Specific Modeling (2007)
20. Kappel, G., Kramler, G., Kapsammer, E., Reiter, T., Retschitzegger, W., Schwinger, W.: Modelcvs - a semantic infrastructure for model-based tool integration. Technical report, Johannes Kepler University of Linz and Vienna University of Technology (2005)
21. Grune, D., Berliner, B., Polk, J., Jones, L., Price, D.R., Baushke, M.: Concurrent versions system (2005), `http://ftp.gnu.org/non-gnu/cvs/`
22. Bräeuer, M., Lochmann, H.: Towards semantic integration of multiple domain-specific languages using ontological foundations. In: Proceedings of the 4th International Workshop on (Software) Language Engineering (ATEM) (2007)

Abstraction and Modelling — A Complementary Partnership

Jeff Kramer

Imperial College London, UK
j.kramer@imperial.ac.uk

Abstract. Why is it that some software engineers are able to produce clear, elegant designs and programs, while others cannot? Is it purely a matter of intelligence? One hypothesis is that the answer lies in abstraction: the ability to exhibit abstraction skills and perform abstract thinking and reasoning. Abstraction is a cognitive means by which engineers, mathematicians and others deal with complexity. It covers both aspects of removing detail as well as the identification of generalisations or common features, and has been identified as a crucial skill for software engineering professionals. Is it possible to improve the skills and abilities of those less able through further education and training? Are there any means by which we can measure the abstraction skills of an individual? In this talk, we explore these questions, and argue that abstraction and modelling are complementary partners: that abstraction is the key skill for modelling and that modelling provides a sound means for practising and improving abstraction skills.

K. Czarnecki et al. (Eds.): MoDELS 2008, LNCS 5301, p. 158, 2008.

Model Transformation as an Optimization Problem

Marouane Kessentini[1], Houari Sahraoui[1], and Mounir Boukadoum[2]

[1] DIRO, Université de Montréal
{kessentm,sahraouh}@iro.umontreal.ca
[2] Dept. d'Informatique, UQAM
boukadoum.mounir@uqam.ca

Abstract. Most of the available work on model transformation is based on the hypothesis that transformation rules exist and that the important issue is how to express them. But in real life, the rules may be difficult to define; this is often the case when the source and/or target formalisms are not widely used or proprietary. In this paper, we consider the transformation mechanism as a combinatorial optimization problem where the goal is to find a good transformation starting from a small set of available examples. Our approach, named model transformation as optimization by examples (MOTOE), combines transformation blocks extracted from examples to generate a target model. To that end, we use an adapted version of particle swarm optimization (PSO) where transformation solutions are modeled as particles that exchange transformation blocks to converge towards an optimal transformation solution. MOTOE has two main advantages: It proposes a transformation without the need to derive transformation rules first, and it can operate independently from the source and target metamodels.

1 Introduction

As for any new technology or paradigm, the widespread adoption of model-driven development (MDD) [1] depends strongly on the research community's capacity to produce pragmatic solutions to industry's day-to-day problems. In recent years, considerable advances have been made in modeling environments and tools, but there remain areas with room for improvement; such is the case of model transformation which is a central concern in the MDD paradigm. Model transformation allows concentrating the maintenance effort on models and using transformation mechanisms to generate code. In the literature, two kinds of transformations are identified: model-to-model and model-to-code [2]. In many cases, the latter type encompasses the first to reduce code generation complexity.

Most of the contributions in model transformation are concerned with defining languages to express transformation rules. Transformation rules could be implemented using (1) general programming languages such as Java or C#; (2) graph transformation languages like AGG [3] and VIATRA [4]; (3) specific languages such as ATL [5] and QVT [6]. Transformations are based sometimes

K. Czarnecki et al. (Eds.): MoDELS 2008, LNCS 5301, pp. 159–173, 2008.

on invariants, pre-conditions and post-conditions specified in languages such as OCL. Transformation rules are usually difficult to define or express, especially for proprietary or non-widely used formalisms. It is often easier for experts to show transformation examples than to express complete and consistent transformation rules [7]. This has led to the transformation by examples approach [13] where machine learning is used to derive rules from provided transformation examples. Machine learning algorithms can be very efficient when the training data has a good coverage of the studied phenomena (*i.e.*, when the training data is representative of the different transformation possibilities). However,or complex formalisms, the set of possibilities may be very large, and a large number of transformation examples may be required.

The question addressed in this paper is how to transform models in the absence of rules and an exhaustive set of examples? In such situations, the transformation can be viewed as an optimization problem in which a (partial) target model is automatically derived from the available examples. The transformation process of a source model becomes the solution of a search in multidimensional space where each dimension represents a model construct. Each point in the search space then represents a transformation possibility of the associated constructs, and a transformation solution will be a set of individual construct transformations. To explore the search space, we use Particle Swarm Optimization or PSO [8]. We chose PSO because it is well adapted to solve multimodal search problems and problems for which no easily implementable solution exists.

The approach we propose has many advantages. First, for any source model, it proposes a transformation without using or producing transformation rules. It also differs from case-based reasoning approaches in that all the existing models are used to derive a solution and not only the most similar one. Moreover, our approach is independent from source and target formalisms. Aside from the examples, no extra information is needed.

We evaluated our approach on the well-known case of the transforming UML class diagrams (CLD) into relational schemas (RS). The models obtained are comparable to those derived by transformation rules.

The remainder of this paper is as follows. Section 2 discusses related work and issues on model transformation. It particularly focuses on transformation by examples. An overview of our approach is given in Section 3. The heuristic (PSO) we use to search the solution space is described in Section 4. This section also gives details about our adaptation of this heuristic to the transformation problem. Section 5 presents the evaluation and discusses the results. Finally, conclusive remarks and future work directions are given in Section 6.

2 Model Transformation by Example

The approach proposed in this paper is meant to be generic to any pair of source and target metamodels (formalisms). However, to discuss the existing transformation approaches and to illustrate our contribution, we start by introducing the particular case of CLD-to-RS model transformation. This will help us describe the

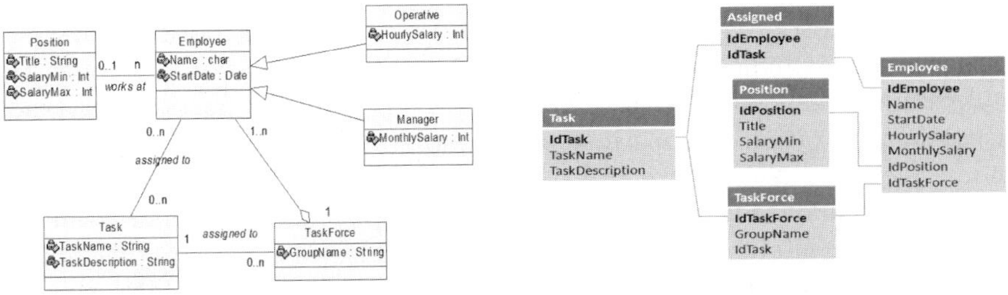

Fig. 1. Example of model transformation from (a) a CLD source model to (b) a RS target model

limitations of classical approaches to model transformation, and show how transformation by example may solve, in part, those problems when representativeness and coverage issues are properly addressed.

Figure 1 shows the example of a source model in the form of a CLD containing 12 constructs, 6 classes, 3 associations, 1 aggregation, and 2 generalization links. It shows also the associated target model expressed as a RS. 3 classes are mapped to tables (`Employee`, `Task`, and `TaskForce`). Association `assigned_to` is translated into a table because its multiplicity is $(0..N, 0..N)$. 2 other associations and the aggregation become foreign keys. Finally, attributes in subclasses are transformed into columns of the table derived from the parent class.

Many transformation approaches can be found in the literature. Czarnecki and Helsen [2], and Mens and Van Gorp [9] used various criteria to analyze those approaches. These criteria include the use or not of MDA as a basis for transformation, the complexity and scalability of the transformation mechanism, the use or not of annotations, the level of automation, and the used languages and implementation techniques. One of the conclusions is that the majority of existing approaches is based on rules that are often empirically obtained [10, 11]. As for any rule-based system, defining a set of rules is not an obvious task, and many unwanted limitations can comprise the results of this definition [12]. First, some transformations cannot be easily expressed in the form of rules. In addition, rule sets have to be complete, consistent, non redundant, and correct. It is difficult to ensure these properties in domains were little knowledge is available [7]. The difficulties are amplified when we consider that the rule sets may evolve. Adding new rules or changing existing one could compromise the abovementioned properties which make the adaptability and extensibility capabilities more complex to guaranty.

Another limitation is related to the subjective nature of some transformations. Experts may have divergent opinions on the transformation of some concepts [11]. For example, even in the well-known case of CLD to RS transformation, some authors propose to map a generalization link between two classes as two tables related by a foreign key, while others suggest creating a single table concatenating information from the two classes. Furthermore, experts may not master both source and target metamodels. For example, some are knowledgeable about UML, but are not database experts. Others are the opposite. In this context, it is difficult for them to easily speak both languages. It is recognized that experts can more easily give transformation examples than complete and consistent transformations rules [11]. This is particularly true in industrial organization where a memory of past transformation examples can be found.

To our best knowledge, what we propose is significantly different from what exists regarding model transformation by example (MTBE). In this domain, Varró and Balogh [14] introduce an automated process for MTBE using Inductive Logic Programming (ILP). The principle of this approach is to derive transformation rules semi-automatically from an initial prototypical set of interrelated source and target models. Similarly, Wimmer and al. [15, 16] derive ATL transformation rules from examples of business process models. Both works uses semantic correspondences between models to derive rules. One difference between the two approaches is that they respectively work at abstract vs. concrete syntax. Another is that Varró uses IPL when Wimmer rely on an ad hoc technique. Both models are dependent heavily on the source and target formalisms. Indeed, fine grained semantic correspondences have to be defined. Additionally, the problems mentioned above (consistency, etc.) still apply to the derived rules. Another limitation is the need to have representative sets of examples that cover well the transformation possibilities. In the context of complex formalisms, such example sets are difficult to obtain. Finally, the rules cannot be automatically derived. Expert intervention is needed during the whole process.

The alternative we propose makes an optimal use of the existing examples, without the need to produce transformation rules. It is similar to case-based reasoning with the difference that we do not select the most similar example and adapt its transformation. We alternatively take the best from all the examples. The next section details the foundation of our approach.

3 Approach Overview

We view a transformation example as a triple *<SMD, TMD, MB>*, where `SMD` and `TMD` are the source and target model descriptions, respectively , and where `MB` is a set of mapping blocks that relate subsets of `SMD` to their `TMD` equivalents.

A model description is a set of predicates that correspond to the contained constructs. Each construct can be represented by one or more predicates. For example, the class Employee in Figure 2 can be described as follows:

```
Class(Employee)
Attribute(Name, Employee,_)
Attribute(StartDate, Employee,_)
```

Predicate `Class(c)` indicates that c is a class. `Attribute(a, c, u)` indicates that a is an attribute of class c and potentially has a unique value ($u =$ "unique") or not ($u =$"_").

A mapping block gives the translation of a cohesive piece of a source model to its equivalent in the target model. We view a mapping block as the minimal set

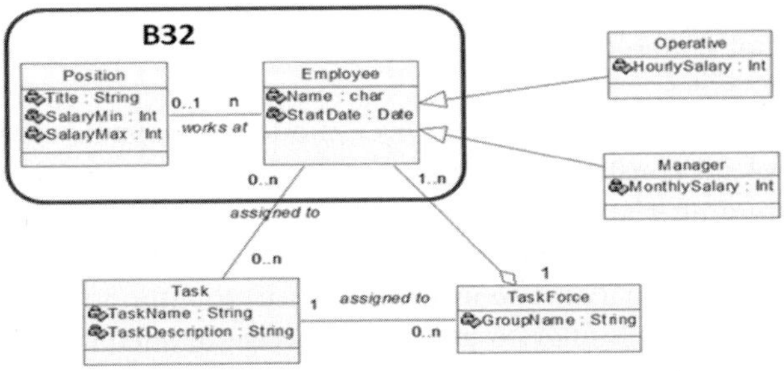

Fig. 2. Example of mapping block in the model of Figure 1(a)

of constructs in the source model whose transformations are interdependent. For example, association Works_at in Figure 2, cannot be transformed independently from classes Employee and Position. The associated mapping block, *B32*, is characterized as follows:

```
Begin b32
Class(Position) : Table(position).
Attribute(Title, Position,_) : Column(idPosition, position, pk), Column(title, position,_).
Attribute(SalaryMin, Position,_) : Column(salaryMin, position,_).
Attribute(SalaryMax, Position,_) : Column(salaryMax, position,_).
Class(Employee) : Table(employee).
Attribute(Name, Employee,_) : Column(idEmployee, employee, pk), Column(name, employee,_).
Attribute(StartDate, Employee,_) : Column(startDate, employee,_).
Association(0,1,_,n,_, Position, Employee) : Column(idPosition, employee, fk).
End b32
```

Classes Employee and Position are mapped to tables with the same names. Table columns are derived from the corresponding-class attributes. As no attribute has a unique value for both classes, primary keys (pk) idEmployee and idPosition are created. Finally, association Works_at is translated as foreign key (fk) idPosition in table employee.

A model M_i to transform is characterized only by its description SMD_i , i.e. a set of constructs. When transformation rules are not known, a construct can be transformed in a multitude of ways, each having a pertinence degree or quality. The latter depend on two factors: (1) the adequacy of the transformation, and (2) the coherence of the transformation with respect to the ones of other constructs. For example, consider a model with two classes, Car and Person, related by one-to-many association Belongs_to. Belongs_to could become a table, many tables, a column, a foreign key, or any other possibility. A possibility is considered to be adequate if there exists a mapping block in the examples that uses it for a similar construct; for example, the translation of Belongs_to to a foreign key is adequate because block *B32* uses a similar mapping for Works_at. At the same time, the transformation is coherent only if it is not in conflict with the ones of interdependent constructs. In the case of `Belongs_to`, its transformation as a foreign key is not coherent with respect to block *B32* if `Car` and/or `Person` are not mapped to tables.

The transformation quality of a source model is the sum of the transformation qualities of its constructs. Consequently, finding a good transformation is equivalent to finding the combination of construct transformations that maximizes global quality. As the number of combinations may be very large (several mapping possibilities) it can become difficult, if not impossible, to evaluate all of them. Heuristic search offers a good alternative in such situations.

We model the multi-dimensional space such that each dimension is associated with a construct. For instance, the transformation of the model in Figure 1 will generate a 12-dimensional space that accounts for the six classes and the 6 relationships. Each construct transformation possibility defines a new coordinate in the corresponding dimension to the construct. To explore the search space, we use the PSO heuristic search as explained in the next section.

4 Model Transformation Using PSO

In this section, we describe the general PSO algorithm and its application to MTBE. PSO has been successfully applied to various problems [17, 18]. But, it appears to only have been used for software testing in software engineering [19]. We start by describing the general PSO algorithm in the next subsection. Then, we show how it can be adapted to model transformation.

4.1 PSO Algorithm

PSO is a parallel population-based computation technique proposed by Kennedy and Eberhart [8]. It was originally inspired from the flocking behavior of birds, which emerges from very simple individual conducts. Many variations of the basic algorithm have been proposed, but they all share a common basis. First, an initial population (named swarm) of random solutions (named particles) is created. Then, each particle flies in the M-dimensional problem space with a velocity that is regularly adjusted according to the composite flying experience of the particle and some, or all, the other particles. All particles have fitness values, which are evaluated by the objective function to be optimized. Every particle in the swarm is described by its position and velocity. A particle position represents a possible solution to the optimization problem, and velocity represents the search distances and directions that guide particle flying. In this paper, we use the basic velocity and position update equations [8]:

$$V_{id} = W * V_{id} + C_1 \times rand\ (\ ) * (P_{id} - X_{id}) + C_2 * Rand() * (P_{gd} - X_{id}) \quad (1)$$

$$X_{id} = X_{id} + V_{id} \quad (2)$$

where, at each time (iteration), V_{id} represents the particle velocity and X_{id} its position in the search space. P_{id}, also called *pbest* (local best solution), represents the ith particle's best previous position, and P_{gd}, also called *gbest* (global best solution), represents the best position among all particles in the population. W is an inertia term; it sets a balance between the global and local exploration abilities in the swarm. Constants C_1 and C_2 represent cognitive and social weights and there are also two random functions *rand()* and *Rand()*(normally uniform in the interval [0, 1]) that represent stochastic acceleration during the attempt to pull each particle toward the *pbest* and *gbest* positions. For an M-dimensional search space, i^{th} particle in the swarm is represented by an M-dimensional vector, xid=(x_{i1},x_{i2},,x_{id}). The velocity of the particle, *pbest* and *gbest* are also represented by an M-dimensional vectors.

Algorithm 1. PSO algorithm

```
Initial population (particles) creating (initialization)
while Termination criterion not met do
   for each particle do
      Evaluate fitness
      Update local/global best (if necessary)
      Update velocity and position
   end for
end while
Return solution corresponding to the global best
```

Algorithm 1 shows the process of implementing the PSO algorithm. This process is repeated until user-defined stopping criteria are satisfied.

4.2 PSO for the Model Transformation Problem

In this section, we present our adaptation of the PSO algorithm to solve the model transformation problem.

Particle Representation. One of the key issues when applying PSO is how to encode a transformation between source and target models as a search solution, *i.e.*, how to find a suitable mapping between problem solution and PSO particle coordinates. As stated in Section 3, we propose to set up an M-dimensional search space to represent the M constructs of the source model. Each dimension has a finite and discrete set of values `b = {i| 1<=i<=N}`, where N is the highest index of the blocks extracted from the set of provided transformation examples. For instance, the CLD source model in Figure 1 defines a 12-dimensional space (see Table 1-top).

The PSO swarm is represented as a set of K particles, each defined by a position vector corresponding to the M constructs of the model to transform. For a particle position, the values of the vector elements are the mapping blocks selected for each construct. An example of particle position is given in Table 1-bottom. This solution suggests that *construct 1* will be transformed according

Table 1. An example of search space definition (top) and particle position in this space (bottom)

Construct in source model	The corresponding number
Position: class	1
Employee: class	2
Work at : assosiation	3
Assigned to 1: association	4
Task:class	5
TaskForce:class	6
Assigned to 2: association	7
Aggregation	8
Operative: class	9
Manager: class	10
Inheritance1	11
Inheritance2	12

Dimension : construct	1	2	3	4	5	6	7	8	9	10	11	12
Position : Block number	20	18	1	17	12	7	15	2	11	9	3	5

to *block 20*, *construct 2* according to *block 18*, etc. If a construct has no corresponding block with an applicable transformation, the fitness function defined in the next section penalizes the quality of the associated particle.

Our PSO algorithm starts (cf. Algorithm 1) by randomly generating the particle positions and velocities in the swarm. In our formulation, generating a particle position consists of affecting a random block number to each of the M constructs (dimensions in the search space). The initial population represents different possibilities (solutions) to transform the source model by combining a multitude of transformation examples. In the next section, we present the fitness function that measures the quality of each particle.

Fitness Function. Fitness is used to evaluate particle performance in the swarm. Generally, choosing a proper objective function as fitness function to represent the corresponding superiority of each particle is a key factors for successful completion of the PSO algorithm. A Euclidian distance is often used for the purpose. In our case, we defined the fitness function as follows:

$$f = \sum_{j=1}^{M} c_j \, * \, (t_j + m_j) \tag{3}$$

where, M represents the number of constructs in the model to transform,

$$c_j = \begin{cases} \textit{1, if the } j^{th} \textit{ construct can be transformed by the associated block} \\ \textit{0, otherwise} \end{cases}$$

$$t_j = \frac{\textit{number of matched parameters in the predicates of the } j^{th} \textit{ construct}}{\textit{total number of parameters in the predicates of the } j^{th} \textit{ construct}}$$

$$m_j = \frac{\textit{number of matched contructs related to the } j^{th} \textit{ construct}}{\textit{total number of constructs related to } j^{th} \textit{ construct}}$$

To illustrate the evaluation of the fitness function, let us come back to the example of Table 1. The association `work_at` defines the 3rd dimension of the space. Recall that this association is represented by the following predicate:

`Association (0,1,_,n,_,Position, Employee).`

The particle position showed in Table 1 associates the *block 1* to it. *Block 1* contains the following mapping:

```
Begin b1
Class(Client) : Table(client).
Attribute(N_Client, Client, unique) : Column(n_Client, client, pk).
Attribute(ClienName, Client,_) : Column(clienName, client,_).
Attribute(Address, client,_) : Column(address, client,_).
Attribute(Tel, client,_) : Column(tel, client,_).
Class(Reservation) : Table(reservation).
Attribute(N_reservation, Reservation, unique) : Column(n_reservation, reservation, pk).
Attribute(StartDate, Reservation,_) : Column(startDate, reservation,_).
Attribute(EndDate, Reservation,_) : Column(EndDate, reservation,_).
Attribute(Region, Reservation,_) : Column(region, reservation,_).
Association (1,1,0,n,_, Client, Reservation) : Column(n_Client, reservation, fk).
End b1
```

In *block 1 (b1)*, association between `Client` and `Reservation` is considered as similar to `works_at`. Over the 7 parameters that the association may have, `works_at` share 5 (1,x,x,n,_, origine and destination class names).

For this mapping, the part of the fitness associated to dimension 3 is calculated as follows. $c_3 = 1$ because it exists in *b1* an example transformation of the construct work_at, $t_3{=}5/7 = 0.71$, $m_3{=}2/2 = 1$ because the same `block 1` applies also to the related constructs of `work_at` (`Employee-Client` and `Position-Reservation`). The obtained values for the fitness function are normalized in order to obtain values in the range [0, 1]. Formally,

$$f_n = f/(2M) \tag{4}$$

We used the previous fitness function definition in order to maximize the completeness of the source model transformation and its consistency. Thus, the particle with the highest fitness will be superior to other particles and should be memorized (reserved) during the search process.

After the initial particle generation, the fitness function is used for updating PSO variables *gbest* and *pbest* (cf. Algorithm 1). The algorithm compares the fitness of each particle with those of the other particles in the population to determine the *gbest* position for each update. Then, for each particle, it compares its visited positions with the current one to determine its *pbest* position. The new positions affect the velocity of each particle according to Equation 1. The algorithm repeats itself until the particles converge to a good transformation solution of the source model. In our case, we mapped this criterion of convergence to a maximum number of generations (iterations).

Setting Parameters. The parameters in Equation 1 have an important effect on the search efficiency of the PSO algorithm. Acceleration constants C_1 and

C_2 adjust the amount of "tension" in the system. Low values allow particles to roam far from target regions before being tugged back, while high values result in abrupt movement toward, or past, target regions [20]. Based on past research experience, we set both constants C_1 and C_2 to 1.

Equations 1 and 2 may lead to large absolute values for V_{id} and X_{id}, so that a particle may overshoot the problem space. Therefore, V_{id} and X_{id} should be limited to a maximum velocity V_{max}, and a maximum position X_{max}, such that

$$X_{max} = N; X_{id} = \min(\max(0, X_{id} + V_{id}), X_{max}) \tag{5}$$

V_{max} serves as a constraint to control the global exploration ability of a particle swarm. It should take values in the interval [-N, N], N being the number of blocks in the existing transformation examples.

X_{id} represents the block number affected to a construct, it must be a positive integer. Hence, a real value for X_{id} is rounded to the closest block number by dropping the sign and the fractional part.

Inertia weight (W) is another important parameter of the PSO search. A proper value for W provides a balance between global exploration and local exploitation, and results in less iterations, on average, to find a solution. In practice, it is often linearly decreased through the course of the PSO, for the PSO to have more global search ability at the beginning of the run and more local search ability near the end. For the computational instances in this paper, W was set as follows [20]:

$$W = W_{max} - \left(\frac{W_{max} - W_{min}}{iter_{max}}\right) iter \tag{6}$$

Where W_{max} is the initial value of weighting coefficient, W_{min} is the final value of weighting coefficient, $iter_{max}$ is the maximum number of iterations, and $iter$ is the current iteration.

5 Evaluation

To evaluate the feasibility of our approach, we conducted an experiment with 10 small-size models. After describing our experimental setting, we will present the obtained results in the form of an execution example and a summary of the 10 model transformations. Finally, the results will be interpreted and discussed.

Experimental Setting. The PSO algorithm was implemented in JAVA. For the evaluation, we use 10-fold cross validation. We consider 10 examples of model transformation from class diagram to relational model, a single example is retained as the validation data for testing the model (source model to transform), and the remaining 9 examples are used as training data. For each fold, nine examples are used to create the initial swarm and the 10th as the model to transform. The obtained target model is then compared to the actual one. The precision of a model transformation is calculated as the ratio of correctly transformed constructs (Equation 7).

$$P = \frac{number\ of\ constructs\ with\ correct\ transformation}{total\ number\ of\ constructs} \tag{7}$$

For the algorithm, based on PSO-based experiences described in the literature and considering the particularities of the transformation problem, we used the following parameters:

- The inertia weight W is initially set to 1.3 and gradually decreases to 0.3 according to (Equation 7).
- The swarm is composed of 20 particles. This number is a good balance between population diversity and the quantity of available examples.
- As mentioned previously, C_1 and C_2 are both equal to 1 to give comparable weights to local and global search.
- The maximum number of iterations is set to twice the size of the population, i.e. 40. This is a generally accepted heuristic [20].
- Since two different executions of a search heuristic may produce different results for the same model, we decided, for each fold, to take the best result from 5 executions.

As mentioned in Section 4, the initial particle positions are randomly generated. The range of values for each element (construct) of a particle is defined as [0, *MaxBlocks*] where *MaxBlocks* is the total number of blocks extracted from the nine examples of the fold. The particle is confined within this range in each dimension. In our experiment *MaxBlocks* is less than 34, the maximum total number of the blocks in the ten examples.

Results and Interpretation. Before giving the global results of the evaluation, we start by detailing an example of execution for one of the used models.

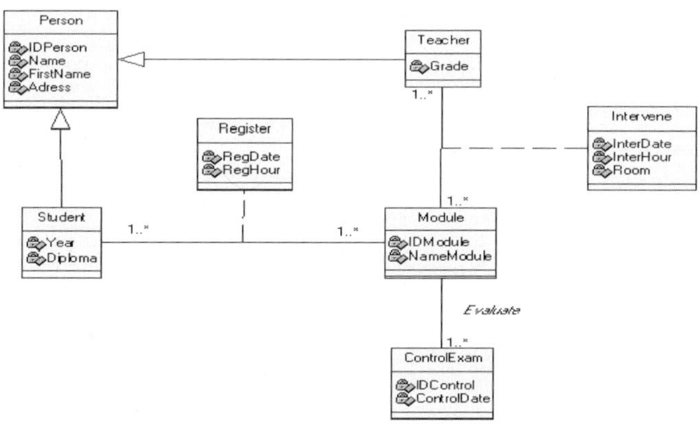

Fig. 3. One of the used models in the evaluation

Table 2. An execution trace of PSO algorithm

Generation	Best particle position by generation	Fitness
1	4 7 6 4 6 6 4 9 9 3 5 4	0.671
2	7 8 6 1 8 1 7 8 6 2 6 1	0.678
3	3 9 5 8 5 2 4 5 5 9 8 5	0.669
21	1 1 1 22 1 2 1 18 24 1 14 24	0.798
22	1 1 1 22 1 2 1 17 23 4 21 27	0.696
29	1 1 12 22 12 1 1 4 32 4 1 1	0.821
39	1 1 12 22 12 1 1 4 32 4 1 1	0.821
40	1 1 12 22 12 1 1 4 32 4 1 1	0.821

Table 2 shows a subset of the execution trace of the model of Figure 3. For each of the selected iterations, the position, i.e., the transformation blocks, and the fitness are given for the best particle (solution). Initially, particle positions and velocities are random. In the first generation, the best particle proposes to translate *construct1* (*class(person)*) by similarity with *block 4*, *construct2* (`class(Teacher)`) with *block7*, etc. This best solution has a fitness of 0.671 that can be explained by the fact that many constructs do not have adequate transformations. For the next iteration, PSO updates each particle velocity using Equation 1 to derive the new positions Equation 2. The new particle positions become new solutions to the model mapping. This is repeated for all the iterations until the maximum number of generation is reached (40 in our case). For some iteration, the obtained solutions can improve the global best gbest as in iteration 2 (0.671 to 0.678). No improvement can also be observed as in iterations 3 and 22 (respectively 0.678 to 0.669 and 0798 to 0.696).

The best solution for this example was found in the 29th iteration with a fitness of 0.821. After that, all the particles converged towards this solution. After determining the best transformation, *i.e.*, the best global particle found at the end of the run, the next step consists of actually transforming the model by applying the mappings of the associated blocks. Figure 4 gives the obtained

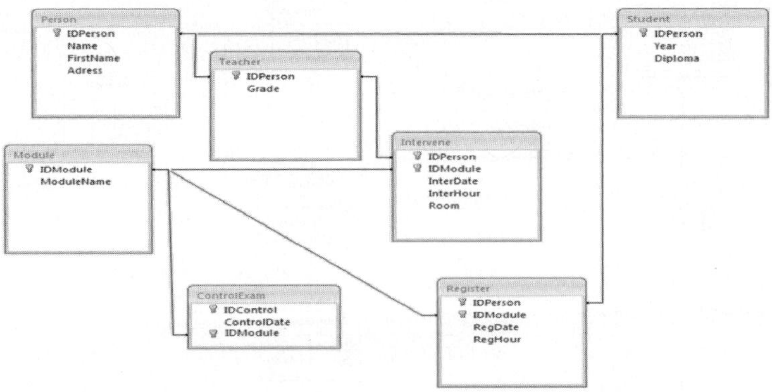

Fig. 4. Transformation result of the model in Figure 3

Table 3. 10-fold cross validation

Source Model	Best global fitness	Precision P (%)
1	0.830	100
2	0.865	100
3	0.754	91.6
4	0.785	87.5
5	0.910	100
6	0.821	100
7	0.935	100
8	0.814	87.5
9	0.636	75
10	0.802	90
Average precision		93.16
Standard deviation		8.86

relational schema for the class diagram of Figure 3). For example, `class(Person)` is transformed in the same way as `class(client)` that appears in *block1*.

Table 3 shows the precisions of the 10 generated transformations corresponding to the 10-folds. The average precision is more than 90% (93.16). Half of the models were perfectly transformed (100% precision). Model 9 has the lowest precision as 25% of the constructs had no or incorrect transformations.

The results also confirmed that our choice of fitness function is a good estimator of the transformation precision (correlation of 0.87). However, in some cases, a model can have a better fitness than another but a lower precision (case of models 3 and 4). This is due to the number of constructs in model. Indeed, unlike the fitness, precision is relative to the total number of constructs in the model.

Our approach proposes transformation solutions in situations where few examples are available. For some models partial transformation were suggested because they contain specific constructs. However, some constructs were transformed even if there were no similar constructs in the used examples. This was the case of an association with multiplicity $(1..N, 1..N)$. As the multiplicity elements are considered as parameters of the construct, the transformation of an association $(0..N, 0..N)$ was applied with a penalty in the fitness function. This adaptation can be more important if the coding takes into account the similarities between the source formalism concepts. It might be the case of aggregation, which can be considered as a more constrained $(1..N, 1..N)$ association. From a performance standpoint, all the experiments were conducted on a basic laptop computer, taking only few minutes. This illustrates again the simplicity and ease of use of PSO. The examples we used in the evaluation are relatively small. Thus, although we are confident in the validity of our approach, we cannot tell if larger and diagrams will be less or better transformed. Additional experiments with typical industrial software settings are needed to answer the question.

6 Conclusion and Future Work

This paper proposes the novel approach MOTOE to automate model transformation using PSO. MOTOE uses a set of transformation examples to derive a target model for a given source model. The transformation is seen as an optimization problem where different transformation possibilities are tried, and for each possibility a quality is associated depending on its conformance with the examples at hand. The proposed approach has the advantage that no rules are used or derived circumventing the representativeness and coverage problems of known transformation-by-example approaches.

We illustrated MOTOE with the transformation of UML class diagrams to relational schemas. In this context, we conducted an evaluation study. The experiment results clearly indicate that the derived models are comparable to those obtained by well-known rules. They revealed also that some constructs were correctly transformed although no transformation examples were available for them. This is possible because the approach use similarity between construct types.

Our approach has been experimented in the context of small-size examples with a well-known transformation mechanism. We are working now on larger models and with different meta-models (sequence diagrams to Petri nets for instance). This is necessary to more investigate the applicability of the approach but also the performance of the proposed algorithm when dealing with numerous large-scale models.

Regarding the search algorithm, PSO allows a good modeling of the transformation problem. However, the set of possible solutions that can be found bounds by the available examples. We plan to use other search-based algorithms that allow the discovery of unexpected possibilities through mutation such as Genetic Algorithms and Simulated Annealing. This work will need to refine the fitness function to evaluate what is not expected. More generally, the fitness function should be improved to give more importance to some construct types. For the moment, all constructs in the source model have equal importance.

References

[1] France, R., Rumpe, B.: Model-driven Development of Complex Software: A Research Roadmap. In: Briand, L., Wolf, A. (eds.) Intl. Conf. on Software Engineering (ICSE 2007): Future of Software Engineering. IEEE Computer Soceity Press, Los Alamitos (2007)

[2] Czarnecki, K., Helsen, S.: Classification of model transformation approaches. In: OOSPLA 2003 Workshop on Generative Techniques in the Context of Model-Driven Architecture, Anaheim, USA (2003)

[3] Taenzer, G.: AGG: a graph transformation environment for system modeling and validation. In: Proc. Tool Exihibition at Formal Methods 2003, Pisa, Italy (September 2003)

[4] Varro, D., Pataricza, A.: Generic and meta-transformations for model transformation engineering. In: Baar, T., Strohmeier, A., Moreira, A., Mellor, S.J. (eds.) UML 2004. LNCS, vol. 3273. Springer, Heidelberg (2004)

[5] Jouault, F., Kurter, I.: Transforming models with ATL. In: Proc. Of the Model Transformations in Practice Workshop at MoDELS 2005, Jamaica (2005)
[6] Object Management Group (OMG), Meta Object Facility (MOF) 2.0 Query/View/Transformation Specification Final Adopted Specification, ptc/05-11-01, http://www.omg.org/docs/ptc/05-11-01.pdf
[7] Behrens, U., Flasinski, M., Hagge, L., Jurek, J., Ohrenberg, K.: Recent developments of the ZEUS expert system ZEX. IEEE Trans. Nucl. Sci. NS-43, 65–68 (1996)
[8] Kennedy, J., Eberhart, R.C.: Particle swarm optimization. In: Proc. IEEE Intl. Conf. on Neural Networks, pp. 1942–1948 (1995)
[9] Mens, T., Van Gorp, P.: A Taxonomy of Model Transformation. In: Proc. Intl. Workshop on Graph and Model Transformation (GraMoT 2005) (2005)
[10] Egyed, A.: Heterogeneous Views Integration and its Automation, Ph.D. Thesis,Univ. of Southern California (2000)
[11] Egyed, A.: Automated abstraction of class diagrams. ACM Trans. Softw. Eng. Methodol. 11(4), 449–491 (2002)
[12] DuanCheung, Y., Fu, X., Gu, Y.: A metamodel based model transformation approach. In: Proc. ACIS Intl. Conf. on Software Engineering Research, Management and Applications, pp. 184–191 (2005)
[13] Varró, D.: Model Transformation By Example. In: Proc. ACM/IEEE Intl. Conf. on Model Driven Engineering Languages and Systems (MoDELS/UML) (2006)
[14] Varró, D., Balogh, Z.: Automating Model Transformation by Example Using Inductive Logic Programming. In: ACM Symposium on Applied Computing — Model Transformation Track (SAC 2007) (2007)
[15] Wimmer, M., Strommer, M., Kargl, H., Kramler, G.: Towards Model Transformation Generation By-Example. In: HICSS-40 Hawaii Intl. Conf. on System Sciences (January 2007)
[16] Strommer, M., Murzek, M., Wimmer, M.: Applying Model Transformation By-Example on Business Process Modeling Languages. In: Hainaut, J.-L., Rundensteiner, E.A., Kirchberg, M., Bertolotto, M., Brochhausen, M., Chen, Y.-P.P., Cherfi, S.S.-S., Doerr, M., Han, H., Hartmann, S., Parsons, J., Poels, G., Rolland, C., Trujillo, J., Yu, E., Zimányie, E. (eds.) ER Workshops 2007. LNCS, vol. 4802, pp. 116–125. Springer, Heidelberg (2007)
[17] Salman, A., Imtiaz, A., Al-Madani, S.: Particle swarm optimization for task assignment problem. In: IASTED Intl. Conf. on Artificial Intelligence and Applications (AIA 2001) (2001)
[18] Ai-ling, C., Gen-ke, Y., Zhi-ming, W.: Hybrid discrete particle swarm optimization algorithm for capacitated vehicle routing problem. Journal of Zhejiang University Science A 7(4), 607–614 (2006)
[19] Windisch, A., Wappler, S., Wegene, J.: Applying particle swarm optimization to software testing. In: Proc. Conf. on Genetic and Evolutionary Computation (GECCO 2007), pp. 1121–1128 (2007)
[20] Eberhart, R.C., Shi, Y.: Particle swarm optimization: developments, applications and resources. In: Proc. IEEE Congress on Evolutionary Computation (CEC 2001), pp. 81–86 (2001)

Example-Based Program Transformation

Romain Robbes and Michele Lanza

REVEAL @ Faculty of Informatics, University of Lugano, Switzerland
romain.robbes@lu.unisi.ch, michele.lanza@unisi.ch

Abstract. Software changes. During their life cycle, software systems experience a wide spectrum of changes, from minor modifications to major architectural shifts. Small-scale changes are usually performed with text editing and refactorings, while large-scale transformations require dedicated program transformation languages. For medium-scale transformations, both approaches have disadvantages. Manual modifications may require a myriad of similar yet not identical edits, leading to errors and omissions, while program transformation languages have a steep learning curve, and thus only pay off for large-scale transformations.

We present a system supporting example-based program transformation. To define a transformation, a programmer performs an example change manually, feeds it into our system, and generalizes it to other application contexts. With time, a developer can build a palette of reusable medium-sized code transformations. We provide a detailed description of our approach and illustrate it with examples.

1 Introduction

Software developers have to continuously adapt their systems to new requirements, frameworks, operating systems, or even programming languages. These changes, often performed manually, are cumbersome and error-prone, especially if applied repetitively and/or transversely on a system. Several approaches have been introduced to automate changes. The program transformation spectrum can be roughly divided in:

Refactorings are well integrated in many IDEs and –generally being one right-click away– easy to apply. They are safe due to their behavior-preserving nature. They are widely used, and part of many a developers' toolbox. They are however limited in scope: Only the handful of most common refactorings are available in IDEs. Implementing a new refactoring involves a significant coding effort.

Linked Editing refers to the ability of some code editors to change a code fragment and have the editor broadcast the changes to similar regions of code. The code regions can be either documented or detected by the tool. The impact of such tools is however limited since they usually work at the text level, not the syntactic level, thus only applicable to code fragments with a high degree of similarity. Parametrized edits are seldom supported. Refactoring and linked editing form the small end of the spectrum.

Aspect-Oriented Programming (AOP) allows crosscutting concerns to be abstracted and separated from the code base into aspects. As part of the compilation process, the program is transformed to include the aspects which were extracted. However using AOP involves learning a new language on top of the regular one, and adding a tool to the

K. Czarnecki et al. (Eds.): MoDELS 2008, LNCS 5301, pp. 174–188, 2008.

toolchain. If a project is not using AOP from the start, developers might be reluctant to add it later on. Also, developers must learn to metaprogram, i.e., consider their programs as data structures, which is neither evident nor immediate.

Program Transformation Languages are the most flexible and powerful approach, but they involve learning a new language and reasoning about the program at another, more abstract, level. Tranformations tend to deal directly with the AST of the program, while AOP uses special purpose (and more limited) constructs such as advices and pointcuts. Such languages are seldom integrated in a development process, and applied to the entire program as a separate step of the build process, making the use worthwhile only for large-scale, program-wide, transformations. AOP and transformation languages form the large end of the spectrum.

In the middle of the transformation spectrum we find manually performed small to medium-scale transformations. These are quite common: Kerievsky [1] describes how to combine refactorings and manual editing to introduce design patterns in an existing system, covering more than twenty-five patterns. Other examples of such transformations are repetitive tasks such as adaptations of the system to changes related to the problem domain, especially in the presence of duplicated code. These are not well covered by existing approaches. In many cases developers opt to perform the changes manually, leading to further decay in the system.

We present an *example-based* program transformation approach: To specify how a repetitive task should be automated, a programmer *records* a sequence of changes as an example of it. The rationale behind our approach is that highly abstract activities such as defining program transformations have less overhead when one is working on concrete instances of a problem. Starting from the example working in its particular context, the developer generalizes it to make it applicable in other contexts. During this process, we allow the developer to directly interact with the structure of the transformation and with the entities affected by it. Finally, the programmer can explicitly name and store the newly defined program transformation, and reuse it whenever/wherever it is needed. The contributions of this paper are:

- An example-based program transformation approach, based on (1) the recording of a sequence of changes to provide the initial transformation structure to be worked on, (2) a direct interaction with this structure to refine and generalize it, and (3) the interaction with example entities to set the scope of the newly defined transformation.
- A proof-of-concept of our approach through two distinct examples that demonstrate its versatility: The definition of an "informal" logging aspect, and the definition of the "extract method with holes" refactoring.
- An implementation of the approach in the form of a "Change Factory", enriching the Spyware platform that we built over the past few years.

Structure of the paper. Section 2 presents our approach in a nutshell, while Section 3 introduces the running example we use in the remainder of the paper. Section 4 to Section 8 detail the individual steps of our approach. Section 9 discusses our approach, including its applicability to other models than program ASTs, while Section 10 covers related transformation approaches. Finally, we conclude in Section 11.

2 Transforming Programs by Example

Example-based program transformation relies on IDE monitoring to record exemplar changes, i.e., concrete instances of transformations. Monitoring is implemented as part of our SpyWare[2] platform for the Squeak Smalltalk IDE. SpyWare monitors the programmer's activity, and converts it to changes stored in a repository. These changes are reified first-class objects used by our transformation tool, the Change Factory. Using a graphical interface, a change is refined into a general-purpose program transformation. To help in testing the transformation, the Change Factory supports a quick edit/try cycle: At any time, the transformation can be compared against the original example.

Defining and using example-based program transformations is divided in 6 steps, described alongside an example (in italics), the definition of an informal logging aspect.

1. **Record changes.** Record a concrete example of a transformation, by performing it manually on example entities. Our monitoring plugin automatically converts developer activity into first-class changes. *The example change for a logging aspect consists in introducing a logging statement at the beginning of a method.*
2. **Generalize changes in a transformation.** This process is performed automatically given a concrete sequence of changes. Each entity reference in the change is converted to a variable. Based on how each entity is created, modified or removed in the change sequence, the system deduces a role for it. Some will be parameters to the transformation, while others will need to be computed from these parameters. *From the example change, the generalization process deduces that the change applies to a parameter, X, which is a method, and that the location where the statement is inserted must be specified by the user.*
3. **Edit variable parts of the transformation.** Based on the roles of the variables deduced from the previous step, the developer uses the Change Factory to edit the transformation and to specify how variables are computed. *The developer specifies where to insert the statement in X (at the beginning), and specifies that the string printed in the logging statement should contain the name of X.*
4. **Introduce higher-level structures.** The developer can introduce high-level constructs such as iterations or conditionals to build larger changes from elementary building blocks. This allows us to exploit another ability of our approach, which is to record any number of elementary changes for a tranformation. *The developer specifies that to apply the logging transformation to a class, the previous change must be applied to all the methods of the class. He can also define variants of the change, depending on the number of arguments in the calling method.*
5. **Test the transformation on examples.** At any time during steps 3 and 4, the developer can test the effects of the modified transformation by running it repeatedly on the example entities. *The developer compares the results of the initial change and the specified transformation on the same targets.*
6. **Apply the transformation to the system.** Once the transformation is defined, it is saved and can be immediately used from the code browser of the IDE. This allows the transformation to be applied to one entity at a time. The transformation can also be applied to a larger number of entities at once. *The logging transformation is stored, ready to be applied at any moment to any program. The transformation can also be undone.*

3 Running Example

We present a more complex example that we use in the following sections. The goal is to create a custom refactoring, called "Extract Method with Holes", a more complex variant of "Extract Method". According to Fowler a refactoring tool featuring "Extract Method" is probably complex enough to implement most refactorings[1]. Refactoring tools featuring "Extract Method" are able to infer which local variables need to be passed as arguments to the extracted block of code (those that are referenced both in the code block that is being extracted and outside of it). A frequent situation however is that a constant expression in the block of code would need to be passed as a parameter to the new method that is being created. Since this expression is referenced only inside the code block that is extracted, it is not converted to a parameter (Figure 1, top). Another related situation is when a method is called on an extracted variable. The call becomes part of the extracted code, while sometimes it should stay in the calling method (Figure 1, bottom).

initial code and selection	"Extract Method" behavior	desired behavior
exampleMethod: argument argument + 42. ^ argument	**exampleMethod:** argument self addTo: argument. ^ argument **addTo:** argument argument + 42.	**exampleMethod:** argument self add: 42 to: argument. ^ argument **add:** value **to:** argument argument + value.
exampleMethod: arg1 **and**: arg2 arg1 + arg2 squared. ^ arg1	**exampleMethod:** arg1 **and**: arg2 self add: arg1 to: arg2. ^ argument **add:** arg1 **to:** arg2 arg1 + arg2 squared	**exampleMethod:** arg1 **and:** arg2 self add: arg1 to: arg2 squared. ^ argument **add:** arg1 **to:** arg2 arg1 + arg2.

Fig. 1. Default and desired behavior of "Extract Method'

In both cases, additional modifications are needed, using two possible alternatives:

1. **Extract Temporaries.** This is done by extracting the constant expression to a temporary variable, moving the temporary variable declaration out of code block, extracting the code block to the new method, and inlining the temporary again.
2. **Add Parameters.** This happens by extracting the code of the method, applying the "add parameter" refactoring to the newly created method, replacing the constant expression with the parameter in the body of the newly created method, editing the call site, and adding the constant expression in place of new parameter.

Both approaches require several steps and disrupt the flow of the programmer. In the following we show how, using our approach, we create the "Extract Method with Holes" refactoring: In addition to extracting a method, portions of constant code can be also extracted as parameters of the newly created method.

[1] See http://www.martinfowler.com/articles/refactoringRubicon.html

4 Recording the Example

Recording changes is based on our previous work on *Change-Based Software Evolution* [3,4,5], whose key concept is to view *change as a first-class entity* by modeling software evolution as a sequence of changes that take a system from one state to the next. These changes are inferred from the developer activity recorded by the IDE's event notification system, whenever the developer modifies the system. In short, we do not view a software system's history as a sequence of versions, but as the sum of *change operations* which brought the system to its actual state. This is conceptually similar to operation-based versioning [6], but at a much finer-grained level.

Program Representation. We model a system as an evolving abstract syntax tree (AST) containing nodes representing packages, classes, methods, variables and statements. Nodes have *properties*, which vary depending on the node type, such as: for classes, name and superclass; for methods, name, return type and access modifier; for variables name, type and access modifier, etc. The name is a property of entities since identity is provided by a unique identifier (ID). Each AST entity has a *change history* containing all changes applied to it during the system's evolution.

Change Operations. Change operations represent the evolution of the monitored system: All changes a programmer performs are captured and reified. They represent transitions between states of an evolving system, i.e., adding/removing/changing classes/methods, refactorings, etc. We support *atomic* and *composite* change operations.

Atomic Changes. An atomic change is an operation on a program's AST. It is executable, and can be undone, since it contains all the necessary information to update the model by itself, and to compute its opposite atomic change. By iterating on the list of changes we can generate all the states a program went through during its evolution.

Composite Changes. Change operations can be abstracted into higher-level composite changes having an intuitive meaning for a developer. For example moving a class from package *A* to package *B* consists in removing it from *A* and adding it to *B*. These two atomic changes can be grouped in a single *move class* change.

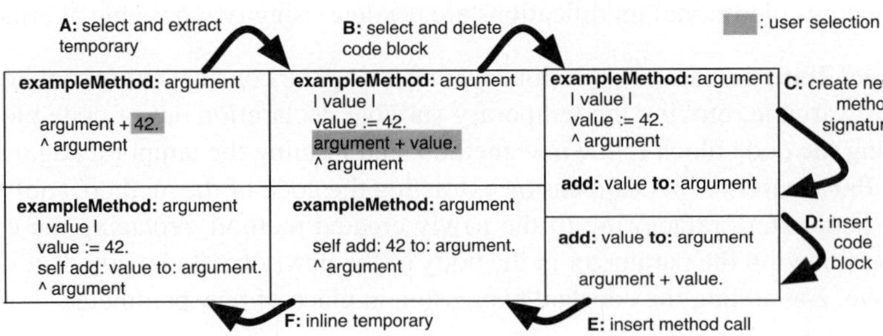

Fig. 2. Recorded changes for the running example

Recording Exemplified. For the "extract method with holes" refactoring, six composite changes (A - F) are recorded, as shown in Figure 2.

5 Generalizing the Example

Generalization is the process through which concrete changes are converted to transformations. In our system a transformation is a function that, given a set of parameters representing the entities to which the changes are applied, generates a new sequence of concrete changes similar to the example, but affecting arbitrary entities. To do this, we extended our change-based approach described previously with *generic changes*, which have the same structure as concrete changes, but their fields contain *variables*, instead of IDs of concrete entities. Whenever the variable is assigned an ID, all references to it are updated. To generalize an example, the developer looks into the change history, where the recent changes are stored, and selects the changes of interest.

Deducing the Role of Each Variable. Given the structure of a generic change, a role can be deduced for each variable, affecting how the programmer has to process it. For each variable *X*, these conditions are checked:

X is not created in the change. One of the changes affecting the variable is its creation. If X is not created in the change, its role is *parameter*. Otherwise, the variable does not belong to the parameters of the changes: A new, unique ID is generated for it each time the transformation is run.

X is an inserted/deleted statement. If X is inserted or deleted from the body of a method, a suitable location in the body of the method must be found when the transformation is run on a candidate method. X's role is thus *unlocated.*

X is inserted/deleted, but is not a subtree root. The location of X can be deduced from its parent's location. The programmer does not have to specify it, X is a *constant.*

Since changes can be composed, a given variable can play different roles in several parts of the change, e.g., it might be a parameter in some of the composite changes and a constant in another. At the transformation level, it will be a constant.

Generalizing Exemplified. Looking at the structure of the sequence of changes shown in Figure 2, the changes are affected the following way (the roles of variables are in italics):

Change A: The variable representing 42 is a *parameter*, which the user will set up via selection (see Section 6). The inserted statements (variable declaration and variable assignment), are *unlocated.*

Change B: The deleted block of code will also be a *parameter* of the transformation. Nodes under it are *constants.*

Change C: There are no parameters or variables needing a location, as every entity is created on the spot. They are *constants.*

Change D: The block of code is *unlocated* and needs a location (the very beginning of a method). The method which is a constant in C is a *parameter* in D.

Change E: The *unlocated* method call needs a location (the previous position of the selected code block).

Change F: The deleted statements (variable declaration, assignment and reference) are *unlocated*, while the value in the assignment (also *unlocated*) needs to be relocated where the variable reference was.

In the overall transformation, the only *parameter* is the method the refactoring is applied to.

6 Editing the Example

Editing the example is the first step requiring manual work through a user interface: Figure 3 shows the Change Factory interface, made of 4 panels.

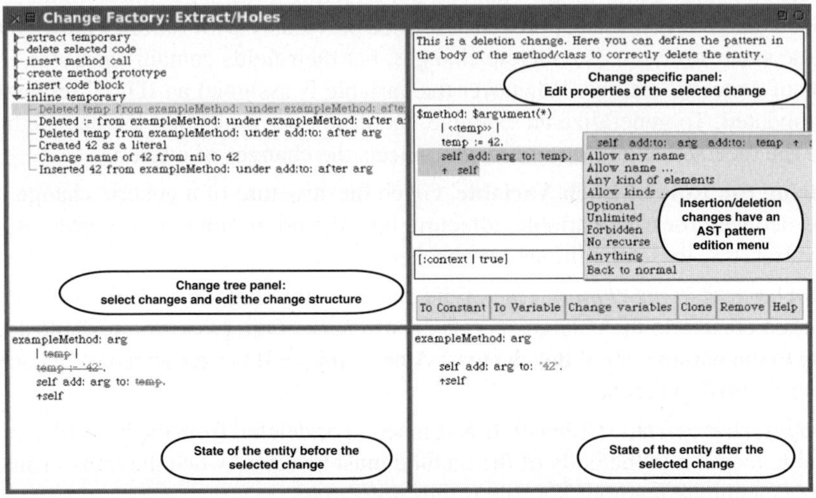

Fig. 3. The Change Factory's main interface, shown editing a deletion change

Using this interface, one can (1) change properties of variables such as their name, (2) specify the location of unlocated variables via user selection or pattern matching, (3) specify conditions which may prevent or modify the action of the change, (4) modify the structure of the change by adding, removing or reordering changes (next section), (5) add control structures such as iterations and conditionals (next section). Table 1 sums up what properties are editable for each atomic change.

Changing Properties. By default, a generic property change keeps the property of the original concrete change, but the Change Factory allows it to be either a computation or a demand for user input (e.g., the user might want to pick a name or a superclass for a given class). To compute properties, the change factory provides the user with a *context*

Table 1. The properties that can be edited for each change

Atomic Change	Aim	Possible actions
Creation	Create a new entity of a given type.	Change the kind of entity created. Remove to convert a constant or a variable to a parameter. Create one to do the opposite.
Addition or Removal	Add/Remove a method, variable, class, package from the class, package, system.	Define a condition for the successful addition of the current class, package, method or variable.
Property Change	Change a property (name, superclass, etc.) of an entity.	Change the kind of property set. Change the value of the property set (constant or function). Add a success condition.
Insertion or Deletion	Inserts/Remove a statement-level entity in a method body.	Define the insertion/deletion AST pattern for an unlocated variable. Add a success condition. Specify if a selection should be used.

object that can be queried for information during the change's application. Using the context, one can access the values of the parameters and variables during the change execution, as well as the entire state of the program. One can assume all the changes before the current change in the tranformation are instantiated and executed. The context has a convenient API to access the most useful queries, such as: current class or method, current method name etc. Identifiers can be bound to values in the context. Those values can be retrieved later on, to transmit information between changes.

Specifying Conditions. The context can be used to define conditions altering the behavior of the change depending on where it is applied (e.g., if the current method does not override another). Conditions can be either pre-conditions (tested before the change takes place) or post-conditions (tested on the modified entities after the change takes place). If these are not met during instantiation, the change *fails*: All the concrete atomic changes generated by the change so far are undone.

Locating Entities. When methods are involved, "Unlocated" entities must be found in the methods to which the transformation will be applied. However, dealing with the intricacies of ASTs is one of the overly abstract activities a programmer faces when transforming programs. In addition, building a mental representation is hard since example run-time ASTs are not easily accessible. It is not clear which nodes to look for in the AST, and where they should be located. We adress these problems by using the ASTs of the concrete entities to which the recorded changes were applied to as an initial *AST pattern* to be incrementally refined by the programmer. An *AST pattern* is an AST enriched with information to relax or constrain its comparison to other ASTs. Furthermore, we minimize the need for the programmer to consider the AST pattern structure by providing a *direct manipulation interface*. These two features work in concert: For each insertion or deletion of an unlocated entity, the programmer is presented with the state of the example just before (for a deletion) or after (for an insertion) the change was applied (Figure 3, top right). The variable inserted or deleted is highlighted to ease focusing. Behind the printed text, the programmer is interacting with a serialized AST pattern of the state of the original example method. When the transformation is applied to another method, the AST of the method will be retrieved and matched against the AST pattern in an attempt to find either a correct place in the AST for an inserted entity, or the ID of an entity in the AST to delete. If the ASTs do not match, the change fails.

Refining patterns with constraints. If no modification is made to the AST pattern, it will only match the initial method in its initial state. We allow the programmer to relax the constraints in the AST pattern by simply selecting a node or a range of nodes in the text. The tool maintains a mapping from text positions to AST nodes, sparing the programmer to manually locate every node. A context menu gives the available constraints for the selected nodes. Upon selection, the constraints are applied to the nodes, and the text in the panel is re-rendered to reflect the updated constraints. Several constraints can be put on the same node (name, kind, multiplicity, optionality, recursion). The constraints are listed in Table 2. Some common sets of constraints are provided as shorthands, such as "allow any method signature" (a method having any name, an unlimited number of arguments and an unlimited number of temporaries), or "any position in the body" (inserts nodes in the pattern matching other nodes in the relevant position).

Table 2. Available constraints in AST patterns

Constraint	Effect	Representation
None (default)	Same name and kind (entity type)	foo
Same kind	Same kind as original, any name is possible.	$temporary
Name matches	Same kind as original, name matches condition (e.g., the name must start with "set").	$temporary([n])
Kinds	Matches any set of kinds (e.g., any body statement).	$k1|k2 or $*
Optional	May be present.	foo(?)
Forbidden	May not be present. (e.g., specify a counter example).	foo(!)
Unlimited	May be present several times.	foo(+) or foo(*)
No recursion	Ignore any children of the entity (e.g., the presence of an *if* is important, not its contents).	foo(...)
Anything	Any nodes (possibly none)	...
Manual	Specified by the programmer with Smalltalk code	foo([])

Locating variables via selection. Some unlocated variables do not need an AST pattern to be found, but instead are selected by the user: When the change is instantiated, a window with the body of the method to which the insertion/deletion applies pops up, asking the user to select the relevant piece of code. One can also ask for the former position of a deleted selection (e.g., to substitute two pieces of code).

Editing Exemplified. Being selection-intensive, "Extract method with holes" does not need many property edits. The created variables in "Extract Temporary" (change A) need to be named, based on user input. In change C, the newly created method must be named –also via user input– based on the names of the arguments it takes. "Extract Method" must infer these arguments: It queries the context to get the set of arguments and temporaries which are referenced both inside and outside of the extracted block of code. The constant expressions and the extracted code block are user-selected. AST patterns need to be defined for the changes dealing with temporaries (A and F). Figure 4 shows how to refine the original AST to a satisfying AST pattern.

<table>
<tr><td>Original pattern</td><td>Change A: temporary location
exampleMethod: argument
| <<value>> |
value := 42.
^ argument</td><td>Change A: assigment location
exampleMethod: argument
| value |
value <<:=>> 42.
^ argument</td><td>Change F: temporary location
exampleMethod: argument
| <<value>> |
value := 42.
self add: value to: argument.
^ argument</td><td>Change F: assignment location
exampleMethod: argument
| value |
value <<:=>> 42.
self add: value to: argument.
^ argument</td><td>Change F: reference location
exampleMethod: argument
| value |
value := 42.
self add: <<value>> to:
argument.
^ argument</td></tr>
<tr><td>Constraints</td><td>any method signature
temporary in last position</td><td>any signature
first body statement</td><td>temporary named as parameter
in any position</td><td>any signature
assignment anywhere in body
match name in left hand side
the right hand side will be stored</td><td>any signature
position anywhere in the body
name matches parameter
replace with old right hand side</td></tr>
<tr><td>Refined</td><td>$method: $argument(*)
| $temporary(*) <<value>> |
...</td><td>$method: $argument*
| $temp* |
(...) <<:=>> (...)
...</td><td>$method: $argument*
| <<$temporary([n])>> |
...</td><td>$method: $argument*
| $temporary* |
...
$reference[n] <<:=>> ....
...</td><td>$method: $argument*
| $temp* |
...
<<$reference[n]>>
...</td></tr>
</table>

Fig. 4. Initial patterns and resulting constraints

7 Composing Changes

The transformation we specified only allows one "hole" to be defined in the selection. How can we allow an arbitrary number of "holes" to be defined? We need to operate at a higher level than atomic changes: The Change Factory can edit the change structure itself. It allows one to (1) alter the change structure, (2) repeat one or more changes, (3) define conditional and optional changes, or (4) call other transformations.

Altering the Structure of the Transformation. The recorded changes and their generalized counterparts have a tree structure. The Change Factory allows us to alter this structure by adding, removing, or reordering the changes. Composite changes can also be merged (two composite changes become one with the atomic changes of both), or split (one composite becomes two). These alterations can affect the behavior of the change: Removing a creation changes the role of the created unlocated variable or constant to a parameter. Splitting a change allows to decompose a composite change in smaller steps. Some of those might be wrapped in conditional structures afterwards.

Iteration. Transformations without loops are limited. For instance, our example works only with the case of a single "hole". We allow a generic composite change (or more) to be applied to a set of entities via a generic *iteration change*. An *iteration set* of entities has to be named and defined via an initializer expression, using the context. The *iteration set* is then stored in the context, and can be reused by other iteration changes operating on the same entities. When instantiated, the changes inside the iteration are applied to each element of the set, in sequence, by binding parameters of the changes to all members of the set. For instance, a change taking a method as parameter can be converted to an iteration change taking as parameter a class and as initializer a context query returning all methods of the class. Alternatively, the *iteration set* members might not be parameters of the change per se, but used in computation of properties inside the change (e.g., the name of entities created in the change depends on the name of the entity being iterated on). When instantiated, the change binds the current entity to a name in the context. Changes needing it in the computation of properties can query the context by name. Another kind of iteration consists in attempting a change for an unspecified number of times, until it fails to apply (this last part being undone). Changes needing to match a variable occuring several times in a method can thus be simplified.

Alternative and Optional Changes. Sometimes, the correct change to apply might not be known until instantiation-time: Conditional changes are implemented by non-deterministically applying a sequence of changes and choosing the first one to apply correctly. Previous failing changes are undone. If all changes inside it fail, the conditional itself fails. Alternatively, a context query returning an integer i can be executed during instantiation of the conditional. The change at index i inside the conditional will be selected and executed. Optional changes are similar to the first variant of conditional changes. They attempt to apply the changes inside them, but they will never fail themselves.

Calling Other Transformations. Transformations can call one another. The calling transformation specifies the values of the parameters to give to the callee. This allows reuse of commonly used transformations as building blocks of bigger ones.

Composing Exemplified. When we recorded the changes to define "Extract Method, with Holes", our first selection of the changes contained an extra change, the creation of "exampleMethod:" itself. This change had to be removed to allow "exampleMethod:" to become a parameter to the transformation. Also during recording, changes C and D were performed as one single change, which had to be split in two.

To specify that an unlimited number of holes can be defined, extracted into temporaries and subsequently inlined, we used several iteration constructs: A set of temporary names T is initialized in change A using as many selections and input names as the user wants. At the end of the transformation, T is reused in change F to inline all the "temporary" temporaries. Change A initializes the set of temporaries by asking the user for selections until he stops. Also, in changes C and E, a set of arguments computed from the context –mentioned in the previous section– is used to build the signature of the extracted method and the call to it in the original method: Each argument is inserted once. For the sake of reuse, the extracted and inlined temporary transformations should be defined separately. Extract temporary takes as parameter a method, and asks the user to select an expression inside it, while Inline temporary takes as parameter a method and a temporary before inlining all references to the variable.

An alternative iteration is to define a fixed number of "holes", by calling several times the "extract temporary" change. At the end of the transformation, the calls to "inline temporary" can be wrapped in optional changes. It is improbable that many holes will be needed in extracted code, making this "brute force" solution viable.

8 Testing and Applying Transformations

Due to the exploratory nature of our tool, the boundary between testing and applying a change is fuzzy: An applied change is one which has not been undone.

How Changes Are Instantiated. Instantiating the change works as follows: (1) Evaluate pre-conditions, (2) Give actual values (IDs) to parameters, (3) Instantiate the transformation, (4) Apply the resulting changes to the code base, and (5) Evaluate post-conditions.

Each change generated by the transformation is stored in the change repository, where it is explicitely linked to the transformation that produced it. This allows each transformation application to be documented and assesses the impact of each transformation to the system. Should a transformation need to be changed, all its applications could be undone, and then redone with the new definition.

Applying a Transformation to the System. Once defined, transformations can be applied on a case-by-case basis or in a system-wide fashion.

Case-by-case. The transformation is named and stored in a repository, and made accessible within the IDE through menus. When browsing code, the user can decide to apply it to the entities he is currently viewing. This is the preferred way to use a transformation such as "extract method with holes".

System-wide. Other transformations can be applied on several entities using a Change Applicator tool, with which one can select a larger set of entities in the system and display the result.

9 Discussion

Example-based program transformations have the following characteristics:

Example-based. Using our change representation on top of the AST we can infer from a single example which entities are parameters to the change and which ones need to have their location defined for the change to be generalizable. Furthermore, the programmer uses direct manipulation of serialized ASTs to work with the concrete syntax of the system, instead of having to learn a dedicated syntax to match entities. Since those ASTs are also extracted from examples, one does not have to start over, only abstract away from the concrete example which was given.

Exploratory. In our change-based model of software evolution, changes are executable and can be undone. Exploring alternatives while designing the transformation is natural and backtracking is provided.

Compositional. We allow *sequences* of changes to be recorded and specified. This allows us to raise the level of abstraction from other pattern-matching based tools which usually operate on a single pattern. Thanks to change composition we can pass variables between changes and define iterations, in order to transform code on a larger scale, allowing us to define medium-scale transformations.

Documentation and evolution. The generic changes are stored in the change repository to be reused. The concrete changes they generate are documented as coming from the generic change: The rationale for the change is known. It is possible to undo these changes if the transformation is no longer suitable or if it needs to be modified. In that case, the updated transformation could then be reapplied to the same entities.

Applicability to other programming languages. Our prototype is implemented in Smalltalk, a language with a simple and consistent syntax. Applying it to a more complex language like Java which is typed and includes generic types, might pose some issues. We think it is feasible, since many transformation tools exist for Java: The existence of such tools might help us porting our approach. However, whether the approach is as usable in such a context is still undetermined.

Applicability to modelling languages. We believe our approach is also applicable for models. We transform programs, but consider them as ASTs and not simple text. As such, we transform a particular kind of models. Adapting our process for models in a language such as UML might actually be simpler, as there should be less need for matching AST patterns, which are more frequent when dealing with source code. In addition, change-based representations of models start to appear. Blanc et al. use a change-based representation of model to check their consistency [7]. Kögel [8] implemented an operation-recording versioning system for models, which could be used as a basis for our approach.

Quality of the examples. When coding, programmers often make errors and backtrack. These digressions are recorded in our changes as well and are unnecessary when generalizing the change. To adress this one can use our change-editing facilities to remove undesired changes from the sequence. Alternatively, the example can be "replayed", i.e., re-recorded to avoid the quirks introduced the first time around.

Behavior preservation. Unlike refactorings, behavior preservation is not guaranteed. Our tool requires programmer supervision to ensure the results are correct.

10 Related Work

Program transformation. Several domain-specific programming languages and systems exist to transform programs, addressing the problems of how to locate entities to be changed in the program (by parsing or pattern matching), and actually performing the transformation: The Design Maintenance System (DMS) by Baxter et al. [9] includes the Transformation Control Language (TCL). The DMS is designed to handle large transformations on large source code bases. One documented use of the DMS was the port of a large component-based C++ application to CORBA [10]. To gather the requirements of this transformation, the authors first converted one module of the application by hand. Stratego/XT is another well-known tool [11] for program transformation, which has seen applications in defining language extensions. In [12], Visser argues that manipulating ASTs of programs is too complex for many applications, and proposes a scheme to instead use the concrete syntax of the programming language. The result is a transformation language with both Stratego and the concrete syntax. In the same vein, De Roover et al. [13] introduced a concrete layer on top of a logic programming language, similar to Java source code, with variables to be matched prefixed by question marks. The rationale is also to simplify matching structures by hiding the AST where possible. Due to its extensive IDE integration, the language-based approach closest to ours is iXj by Boshernitsan et al. [14], an interactive IDE extension to transform Java programs supported by a visual programming language. ASTs are represented graphically. The transformation still has to be written with only the starting state specified (via selection).

Refactoring. Refactoring [15,16] is a major feature of IDEs, which support the most common refactorings, first exemplified in the Smalltalk Refactoring Browser [17]. However the number of refactorings implemented in a refactoring engine is limited and covers only the most common cases. The same authors also implemented the Rewrite Tool [18] which uses pattern matching to implement arbitrary transformations. However the patterns defined in the transformations can only refer to one entity at a time and must be written from scratch in a dedicated language. Verbaere et al. have defined a dedicated scripting language [19], JunGL, to define new refactorings. JunGL is a hybrid functional/logic language whose logic layer eases writing queries on the AST. The "Extract Method" refactoring the authors describe still needs a few dozens of lines of code.

Model transformation. Transformation is a prominent concept in model-driven engineering. Several model transformation languages have been defined, such as MTL, Xion and Kermeta [20], or ATL [21]. However, they have a different target than our approach, since they transform abstract models of programs, and not the programs themselves.

While the approaches mentioned above are based on a program transformation language, a closer approach to ours is employed by Varró [22] to specify model transformations. His approach requires an example of a source model and a target model while we specifically consider changes between source-code entities. Another related approach has been documented by Wimmer et al. [23].

More lightweight approaches exist, such as regular expressions and keyboard macros in text editors. However, these techniques are text-based, losing the ability to easily query entities, and can be error prone.

Programming by example. The field of programming by example –or demonstration– (PBE) describes theories and provides tools which, from repetitive tasks performed by the user, infer a generalization of the behavior one wants to achieve. PBE aims for non-programmers to define simple automated tasks. PBE has been applied in a variety of areas [24]. In the same way, our system permits non-meta-programmers to define simple program transformations. However since the users differ, the approaches end up being quite different. Contrary to most PBE approaches, we do not wish to infer the action the user wants to do, but use the example to kick-start the generalization process. Since our users are programmers, they do not need a fully automatic process, but a sound basis to work with.

11 Conclusion

We presented an approach to specify program transformations which does not rely on a transformation language. Instead, its integration with the IDE and its underlying model of first-class changes allows programmers to define transformations by recording examples and subsequently generalize them. We defined a process supported by a tool, the Change Factory, to allow programmers to conveniently define transformations and where they should be applied in the system, based on the given examples. Several videos of the Change Factory in action are available at `http://romain.robb.es/spyware/`

We illustrated the feasibility of our approach through two examples, refactoring definition and informal aspect definition. Our approach is also applicable in the domain of linked editing and code clone management, although space lacks to describe this here. We described our approach on the restricted set of program models (ASTs), but think it can be applied to more general models. Change-based modelling tools are starting to appear as research prototypes.

Our approach so far uses only one example to start the process. Having more examples could help to infer variables with more accuracy, and partially automate the definition of the AST patterns as well as where to apply changes in the system. This belongs to future work.

Acknowledgments. We gratefully acknowledge the financial support of the Swiss National Science foundation for the project "REBASE" (SNF Project No. 115990).

References

1. Kerievsky, J.: Refactoring to Patterns. Pearson Higher Education, London (2004)
2. Robbes, R., Lanza, M.: Spyware: A change-aware development toolset. In: Proceedings of ICSE (30th International Conference in Software Engineering), pp. 847–850. ACM Press, New York (2008)
3. Robbes, R., Lanza, M.: A change-based approach to software evolution. Electronic Notes in Theoretical Computer Science (ENTCS) 166, 93–109 (2007)
4. Robbes, R., Lanza, M.: Characterizing and understanding development sessions. In: Proceedings of ICPC (15th International Conference on Program Comprehension), pp. 155–164. IEEE Computer Soceity Press, Los Alamitos (2007)

5. Robbes, R., Lanza, M., Lungu, M.: An approach to software evolution based on semantic change. In: Dwyer, M.B., Lopes, A. (eds.) FASE 2007. LNCS, vol. 4422, pp. 27–41. Springer, Heidelberg (2007)
6. Lippe, E., van Oosterom, N.: Operation-based merging. In: SDE 5: Proceedings of the fifth ACM SIGSOFT symposium on Software development environments, pp. 78–87. ACM Press, New York (1992)
7. Blanc, X., Mounier, I., Mougenot, A., Mens, T.: Detecting model inconsistency through operation-based model construction. In: Robby (ed.) ICSE, pp. 511–520. ACM, New York (2008)
8. Kögel, M.: Towards software configuration management for unified models. In: CVSM 2008: Proceedings of the 2008 international workshop on Comparison and versioning of software models, pp. 19–24. ACM, New York (2008)
9. Baxter, I.D., Pidgeon, C., Mehlich, M.: Dms: Program transformations for practical scalable software evolution. In: ICSE, pp. 625–634. IEEE Computer Society, Los Alamitos (2004)
10. Akers, R.L., Baxter, I.D., Mehlich, M., Ellis, B.J., Luecke, K.R.: Reengineering c++ component models via automatic program transformation. In: WCRE, pp. 13–22. IEEE Computer Society, Los Alamitos (2005)
11. Visser, E.: Program transformation with Stratego/XT: Rules, strategies, tools, and systems in StrategoXT-0. In: Lengauer, C., Batory, D., Consel, C., Odersky, M. (eds.) Domain-Specific Program Generation. LNCS, vol. 3016, pp. 216–238. Springer, Heidelberg (2004)
12. Visser, E.: Meta-programming with concrete object syntax. In: Batory, D., Consel, C., Taha, W. (eds.) GPCE 2002. LNCS, vol. 2487, pp. 299–315. Springer, Heidelberg (2002)
13. Roover, C.D., D'Hondt, T., Brichau, J., Noguera, C., Duchien, L.: Behavioral similarity matching using concrete source code templates in logic queries. In: Ramalingam, G., Visser, E. (eds.) PEPM, pp. 92–101. ACM, New York (2007)
14. Boshernitsan, M., Graham, S.L., Hearst, M.A.: Aligning development tools with the way programmers think about code changes. In: Rosson, M.B., Gilmore, D.J. (eds.) CHI, pp. 567–576. ACM, New York (2007)
15. Opdyke, W.F.: Refactoring Object-Oriented Frameworks. Ph.D. thesis, University of Illinois (1992)
16. Fowler, M., Beck, K., Brant, J., Opdyke, W., Roberts, D.: Refactoring: Improving the Design of Existing Code. Addison Wesley, Reading (1999)
17. Roberts, D., Brant, J., Johnson, R.E., Opdyke, B.: An automated refactoring tool. In: Proceedings of ICAST 1996, Chicago, IL (1996)
18. Roberts, D., Brant, J.: Tools for making impossible changes - experiences with a tool for transforming large smalltalk programs. IEE Proceedings - Software 152(2), 49–56 (2004)
19. Verbaere, M., Ettinger, R., de Moor, O.: Jungl: a scripting language for refactoring. In: Osterweil, L.J., Rombach, H.D., Soffa, M.L. (eds.) ICSE, pp. 172–181. ACM, New York (2006)
20. Muller, P.A., Fleurey, F., Vojtisek, D., Drey, Z., Pollet, D., Fondement, F., Studer, P., Jézéquel, J.M.: On executable meta-languages applied to model transformations. In: Model Transformations In Practice Workshop (2005)
21. Jouault, F., Kurtev, I.: Transforming models with atl. In: Bruel, J.-M. (ed.) MoDELS 2005. LNCS, vol. 3844, pp. 128–138. Springer, Heidelberg (2006)
22. Varró, D.: Model transformation by example. In: Nierstrasz, O., Whittle, J., Harel, D., Reggio, G. (eds.) MoDELS 2006. LNCS, vol. 4199, pp. 410–424. Springer, Heidelberg (2006)
23. Wimmer, M., Strommer, M., Kargl, H., Kramler, G.: Towards model transformation generation by-example. System Sciences. In: 40th Annual Hawaii International Conference on HICSS 2007, p. 285 (January 2007)
24. Lieberman, H.: Your Wish Is My Command – Programming by Example. Morgan Kaufmann, San Francisco (2001)

Detecting Patterns of Poor Design Solutions Using Constraint Propagation

Ghizlane El-Boussaidi and Hafedh Mili

Laboratoire de Recherches en Technologies du Commerce Électronique (LATECE)
Faculté des Sciences, Université du Québec à Montréal
B.P 8888, succursale Centre-Ville, Montréal (Québec) H3C 3P8, Canada
{el_boussaidi.ghizlane@courrier,hafedh.mili@}uqam.ca

Abstract. We are proposing an approach for applying design patterns that consists of recognizing occurrences of the modeling problem solved by the design pattern (problem pattern) in input models, which are then transformed according to the solution proposed by the design pattern (solution pattern). In this paper, we look at the issue of identifying instances of problem patterns in input models, and marking the appropriate entities so that the appropriate transformations can be applied. Model marking within the context of MDA is a notoriously difficult problem, in part because of the structural complexity of the patterns that we look for, and in part because of the required design knowledge-- and expertise. Our representation of design problem patterns makes it relatively easy to express the pattern matching problem as a constraint satisfaction problem. In this paper, we present our representation of design problem patterns, show how matching such patterns can be expressed as a constraint satisfaction problem, and present an implementation using ILOG JSolver, a commercial CSP solver.

Keywords: Marking models, constraint satisfaction problems, transformations, design patterns.

1 Introduction

Earlier transformational approaches described software development as a sequence of property-preserving transformations that are applied to a set of user requirements to produce functional software that satisfies a number of quality requirements [14]. Design choices made during the development process lead to different transformation chains. This idea was recently restored by the OMG' model driven architecture [11]. The basic idea behind MDA is to separate the specification of a system from its implementation on a specific platform. MDA proposes to specify a system as a platform-independent model (PIM), to specify platform models—models describing platforms—and, to transform the PIM to a platform-specific model (PSM) according to the chosen platform. Roughly speaking, the transformation from a PIM to a PSM is guided by a specification that provides the mapping between their entities. Generally these mappings are specified using a combination of model type mapping—defined on a meta-model level—and model instance mapping which uses a marking process where—depending on the target platform—the architect marks entities of the PIM.

K. Czarnecki et al. (Eds.): MoDELS 2008, LNCS 5301, pp. 189–203, 2008.

In practice, the transformations are not fully automated because the mapping between the source and target models is incomplete or non-deterministic [13] and, the marking process remains essentially a manual process. Consequently, a major challenge in MDA is: 1) to specify these mappings precisely to be able to encode them in systematic procedures, and 2) to support an automatic or semi-automatic marking process to guide these procedures when applied to other requirements. In this paper, we propose an approach for automatically marking models especially in the context of design patterns application. This approach consists of recognizing in input models instances of the design problem solved by a design pattern (problem pattern), which are then transformed according to the solution proposed by the design pattern (solution pattern). In this paper, we look at the issue of identifying instances of problem patterns in input models, and marking the appropriate entities so that the appropriate transformations can be applied. Our problem patterns representation enables to express the pattern matching problem as a constraint satisfaction problem.

The paper is structured as follows. Section 2 gives an overview of our approach to representing and applying design patterns. We describe the marking process in section 3. In sections 4 and 5 we show how the pattern matching problem is expressed as a constraint satisfaction problem. The implementation is presented in section 6 followed by a discussion in section 7 and the conclusion.

2 Overview of the Approach

Design patterns codify proven solutions to recurrent design problems. Design problems come in many shapes and forms, but a significant number of such problems can be expressed as poor solutions to modeling requirements. We represent such design patterns by triples (MP, MS, T) (see Fig. 1), where MP is a model describing the design problem solved by the pattern, MS is a model describing the solution proposed by the pattern, and T a transformation that transforms an input model exhibiting an instance of MP by replacing that instance with the corresponding solution. Both MP and MS are metamodels to the extent that their instances are models. We envision a catalog of such triples in a modeling workbench. Given an input model, a designer can try to detect potential instances of the problems solved by the patterns of the catalog in this model, i.e. matching the MP components of the patterns, to the input model. A successful match marks the entities of the input model by the roles they play in the model of the problem (MP), and suggests that the design pattern may be applicable to this model. The designer may then apply the transformation rules to the so marked model. The outcome is the input model where an instance of the design problem addressed by the design pattern has been replaced by the solution proposed by the pattern. In this paper we describe the matching and marking process.

Consider the example of a class hierarchy that represents a taxonomy of classes that implement the same behavior—same set of methods. A proverbial example of such a hierarchy is the class hierarchy representing the node types of an abstract syntax tree for some language X. Assume that the set of node types is stable—new constructs seldom get added to language X—but that new methods are regularly added to manipulate our abstract syntax trees in different ways. With the traditional <class,

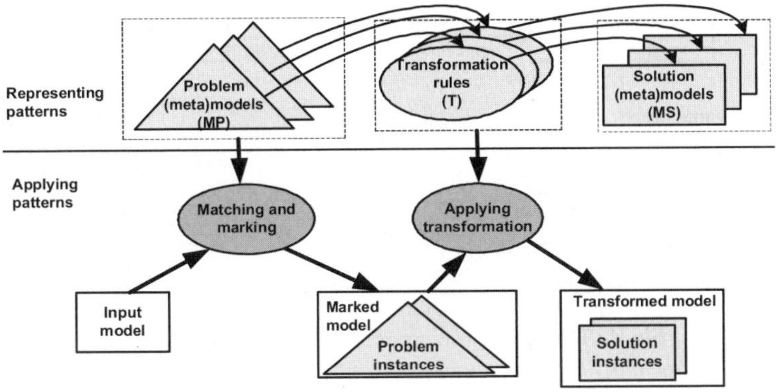

Fig. 1. Overview of the approach

method> organization, each time a new behavior is added (e.g. a method to pretty-print an expression in the language) we have to, potentially, change *every class* of the hierarchy by adding a node-specific implementation of that operation. The *visitor* design pattern proposes to make these changes more localized by grouping all of the implementations of a given operation in a single *visitor object* [7]. We now show how we represent the design problem solved by the visitor using our approach.Figure 2 shows a model of class hierarchies that implement the same behavior. The root of the hierarchy is represented by the metaclass ***AbstractClass*** which implements a number of ***AbstractOperation***'s (the 'has_message' link). This class has a number of concrete subclasses (***ConcreteClass***) which implement all of its ***AbstractOperation***'s—and possibly more—with ***ConcreteOperation***'s. To reflect the fact that every ***ConcreteClass*** has one ***ConcreteOperation*** (has_method) for each ***AbstractOperation*** supported by (has_message) its abstract superclass (***AbstractClass***), we use the homomorphism relation. To keep the model simple, we do not show the parameters and return types of the operations. We call this model the static problem model.

This, alone, does not represent typical situations where the visitor pattern applies; in fact, it represents a properly factored class hierarchy! What is missing is the kind of *future* evolution of the class hierarchy that the visitor pattern protects against, and that is, the number of methods defined by ***AbstractClass*** and implemented by its ***ConcreteSubclass***'es. In fact, most of GOF patterns can be understood in terms of making models more resilient to certain kinds of changes, and it is important to capture those changes. To this end, we extended our UML-based representation of problem models to represent time evolution. In particular, we have been able to represent all of the changes we came across in terms of changing (meta-level) association cardinalities. For example, if an abstract class can specify a changing (increasing) number of operations, the "has-message" association between ***AbstractClass*** and ***AbstractOperation*** will have a cardinality of 1 ↔ 0..*,++, where we added the "++" qualifier to indicate that cardinality will increase over time. Figure 3 shows the new problem model that shows time evolution. The evolving association end is called *time hotspot*. For further details about our language for modeling design problems see [12].

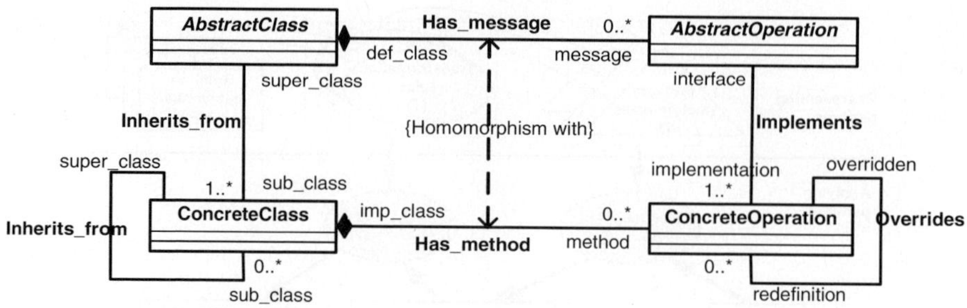

Fig. 2. The static problem model of the Visitor pattern

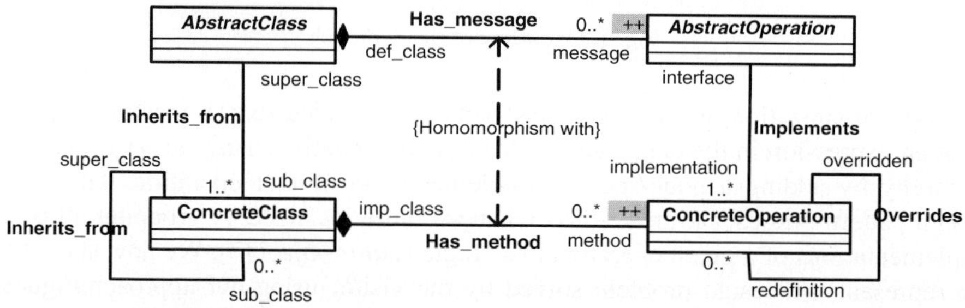

Fig. 3. The (complete) problem model = the static problem model + time hotspots

3 The Marking Process

The marking process is the process of recognizing instances of problem models in a given input model. As shown from the previous example, a problem model consists of a static component (Figure 2), which can be verified statically on input models, and evolution information (*time hotspots*), which is not implicit in input models, and will need to be somehow added to the input models. Accordingly, we break the problem model matching into three steps (Fig. 4).

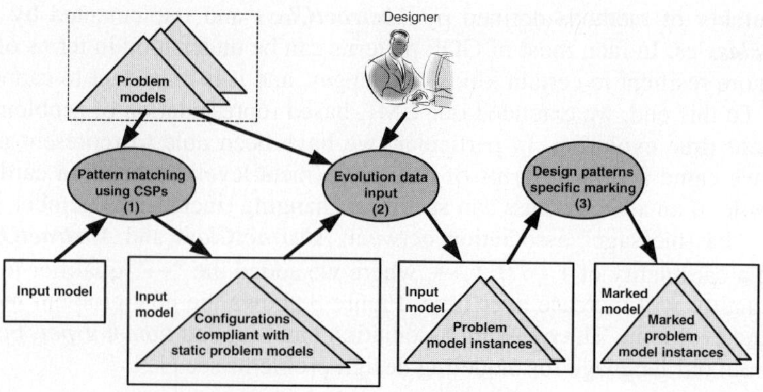

Fig. 4. The marking process

1. Static problem model matching: In this step we try to recognize in a given input model, structures that comply with some static problem models. This is basically a graph pattern matching problem, since models are typed graphs. To this end, we use constraint satisfaction techniques, explained in sections 4 and 5.
2. Evolution data input: a static problem model match does not mean that the corresponding design pattern applies. In fact, a model such as the one in Figure 2 characterizes several design patterns other than visitor (e.g. strategy and bridge). Evolution data can be input in one of two ways. If we have different versions of the system at hand, we can compare the class models of the different versions to see which parts have evolved between versions (see e.g. [16]). Alternatively, for new systems or for systems for which historical data is not available, we can prompt designers to identify *likely* variation points (e.g., the number of subclasses of a given class, the number of methods, etc.). Naturally, the accuracy of such variation points depends on the level of expertise of the designer and her/his experience with the problem domain.
3. Full problem model marking: In this step, the variation points—the time hotspots—complement the static problem match to ascertain the compliance of a fragment from the input model with the full problem model of a design pattern. Once such a fragment is found, we mark its elements (classes, methods, attributes, associations, inheritance relationships, etc.) with the roles they play in the pattern problem model. For the visitor problem model, a class will be tagged as ***AbstractClass***, its subclasses tagged as ***ConcreteClass***'s, its abstract methods tagged as ***AbstractOperation***, etc. Because different problem models may refer to the same roles (e.g. the notion of ***AbstractClass*** appears in many problem models), we need to qualify the roles by the pattern to which they refer. Thus, the same abstract class in the input model might be marked as Visitor.AbstractClass and Strategy.AbstractClass. Because the same input model may include different instances of *the same* problem model, the marks are further qualified by pattern instance number. Thus, a concrete class might be tagged as Strategy.1.ConcreteClass, Strategy.2.ConcreteClass, and Visitor.1.ConcreteClass. These tags are used by our transformation rules to make sure that different instances of design patterns do not interfere with each other.

4 Using CSPs for Pattern Matching

Models are graphs and recognizing a problem model in a given input model can be considered as a graph pattern matching problem. The latter is also known as the subgraph homomorphism problem, and was shown to be NP-complete [15]. Consider the graphs $L=(L_V, L_E)$ and $G=(G_V, G_E)$ shown in Fig. 5 where L_V and G_V represent the sets of vertices of L and G, respectively, and L_E and G_E represent their respective sets of edges. An homomorphism from L to G is a mapping M from L_V to G_V such that for each edge (A, B) in L_E, (M(A), M(B)) is an edge in G_E.

The graph homomorphism problem can be reformulated and solved as a constraint satisfaction problem [15]. First, we summarize the basic concepts of CSPs theory and then introduce an approach to solve the graph matching problem using CSPs.

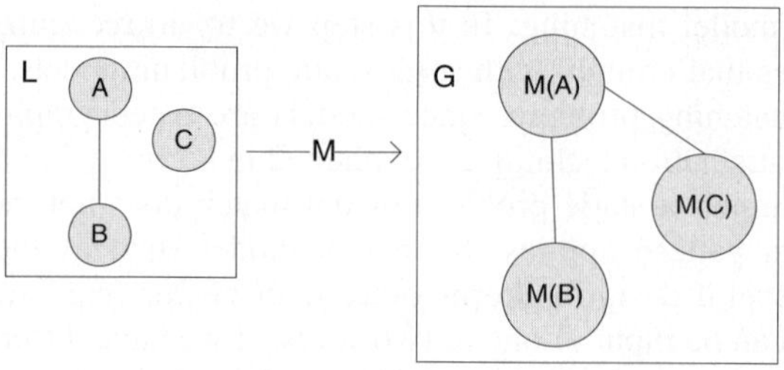

Fig. 5. A simple homomorphism example

4.1 CSP: Basic Concepts

A constraint satisfaction problem (CSP) is a problem that can be framed as finding values for a set of variables, within particular domains, under some constraints. Precisely, a CSP consists of [15] [3]:

- A finite set of variables $V=\{v_1,\ldots,v_n\}$
- Their corresponding domains (ranges of values); let D_i be the domain of the variable v_i,
- A set R of constraints, which is a finite set of restrictions on the variables of V. A constraint $C \in R$ defined over a tuple of variables $(v_1,\ldots, v_r)$ specifies how these variables can be assigned values from their domain. The constraint C can be seen as a relation from the tuple $\{v_1,\ldots, v_r\}$ to the cartesian product of these variables' domains, i.e. $C(v_1,\ldots, v_r) \subseteq D_1 \times \ldots \times D_r$. The size of this tuple is known as the *arity* of the constraint C.

A constraint C on a tuple of variables $(v_1,\ldots, v_r)$ is satisfied by a tuple of values $(d_1,\ldots, d_r)$ if and only if

1. $\forall(1 \leq i \leq r)\ d_i \in D_i$ (the domain of v_i) and,
1. $(d_1,\ldots, d_r) \in C(v_1,\ldots, v_r)$.

Much work in the literature focused on binary constraints since it has been proven that any n-ary discrete CSP can be translated into an equivalent binary CSP [3]. A solution to a CSP problem—when it exists– consists of a set of values $(d_1,\ldots, d_n)$ where each value d_i is assigned to a different variable v_i such that all the constraints in R are satisfied.

To illustrate these concepts let us consider the well known N-queen problem where we have to place N queens on an N by N chessboard such that no two queens are placed in the same row, in the same column, or in the same diagonal. One formalization of the N-queen problem as a CSP uses variables to represent the rows of the chessboard [17], where each variable can take values from 1 to N corresponding to the column position of the queen placed in that row. Hence:

$Dv_1 = Dv_2 = \ldots = Dv_N = \{1,2,\ldots,N\}$.

To ensure that no two queens are on the same column and no two queens are on the same diagonal, we use two constraints:

- $\forall i \# j\ v_i \# v_j$ and,
- $\forall i \# j$ if $v_i = a$ and $v_j = b$ then $|i - j| \# |a - b|$.

CSPs are generally solved using exhaustive search with backtracking. When a variable is assigned a value, all the constraints involving this variable are examined. This is known as *constraint propagation*, since the constraint reduces the domains of the related variables. In the N-queen problem, if we determine the column position of the queen on row *i* to be *j*, that removes *j* from the domains of all the other variables. During constraint propagation, if a variable's domain becomes empty, the algorithm backtracks to the last choice point where a value was assigned, and tries another *untried* value. If there are no other values to consider the algorithm backtracks to the preceding choice point, and so on. If there are no more choice points and a variable's domain is empty, the problem has no solution. When a variable's domain is reduced to one value, the variable is said to be bound [4].

4.2 The Graph Pattern Matching Problem as a CSP

Rudolf proposed to translate graph matching problems into equivalent CSP problems [15]. Using this approach for untyped graphs, each node and each arc of the pattern is mapped to a distinct variable where for each node variable, the domain is the set of nodes in the target graph, and for each edge variable, the domain is the set of edges in the target graph. The restrictions of a graph homomorphism are expressed using constraints.

Consider the following example from [15] where we look for occurrences of the graph L into the graph G (Fig. 6). In this approach, we have three variables x_1, x_2, x_3 whose domains are $D_1 = D_3 = \{d_1, d_3, d_4, d_6\}$ and $D_2 = \{d_2, d_5\}$ where D_i represents the domain of the variable x_i. The homomorphism properties are embodied in two constraints that state that when x_1, x_2 and x_3 are bound, then the value assigned to x_2—which is an edge—has a source equal to the value assigned to x_1 and a target equal to the value assigned to x_3:

- $C_{src}(x_2,x_1) = \{ (d_e,d_v) \in D_2 \times D_1 \mid source(d_e) = d_v\}=\{(d_2, d_1), (d_5,d_6)\}$[1]
- $C_{tar}(x_2,x_3) = \{ (d_e,d_v) \in D_2 \times D_3 \mid target(d_e) = d_v\}=\{(d_2, d_3), (d_5,d_6)\}$

These constraints reduce the domains of the variables, leading to two solutions, (d_1,d_2,d_3) and (d_6,d_5,d_6).

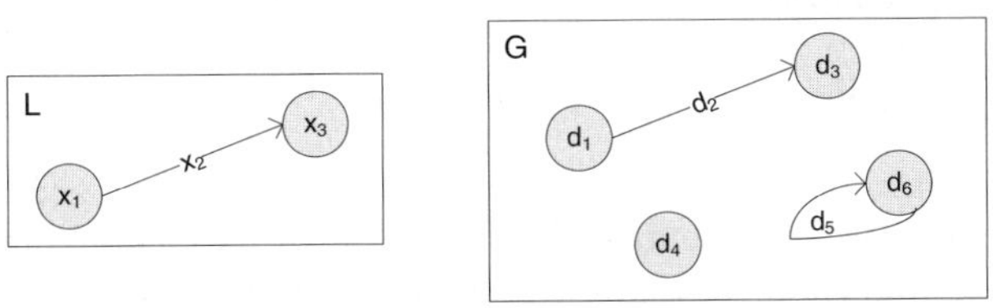

Fig. 6. A simple example of graph pattern matching

[1] e stands for edge and v stands for vertice, source and target are total mapings from the set of edges to the set of vertices.

5 Building CSPs from Problem Models

Our goal is to apply Rudolf's approach to find instances of a problem model in a given input model. Thus we need to translate our pattern matching problem into a CSP representation. Practically, this means generating a set of variables and a set of constraints for a given problem model and, computing the domains of the variables for a given input model. The process of generating CSPs from problem models and input models is illustrated in Fig. 7.

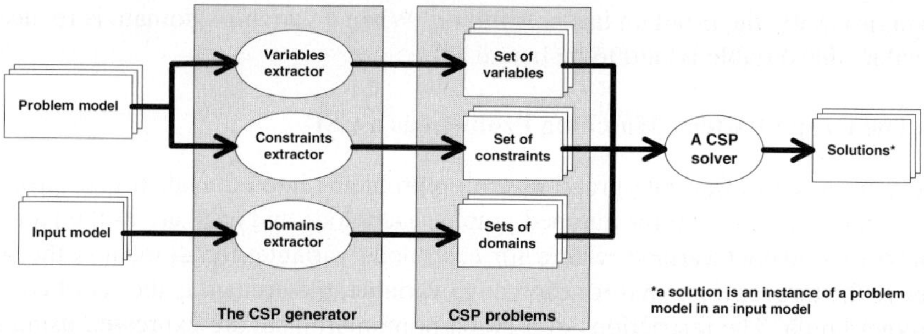

Fig. 7. The process of generating CSPs from problem models

5.1 Extracting Variables

For a given design pattern problem model, the variables consist of all the elements of the model, namely, its classes, operations, attributes, and all of the (meta-level) relationships between them (association, inheritance, etc.). For example, the problem model of the Visitor pattern (Fig. 3) yields the following variables, with self-explanatory names: var_AbstractClass, var_ConcreteClass, var_AbstractOperation, var_ConcreteOperation, var_inherits_from_1, var_inherits_from_2, var_has_method, var_has_message, var_implements, and var_overrides. The first four variables correspond to the entities of the problem model (its classes), and the last six represent associations between those entities. Note that we use two inherits_from variables to distinguish the inherits_from relationship between **ConcreteClass**'es and **AbstractClass**, from the inherits_from relationship between **ConcreteClass**'es.

5.2 Extracting Domains

Following our visitor example, given an input object model, we need to identify the domains for the ten variables mentioned above. Domain extraction raises an issue that is common to all CSPs, and has to do with the level of precision of domains—and the effort to expend for domain extraction. Consider the variable var_AbstractClass. We could define the domain for this variable to be the set of all the abstract classes in the input model, but then we have to develop an automated procedure to identify those in the input model. Alternatively, we could define the domain as all the classes of the input model, but then add a unary constraint to the set of constraints that identifies abstract classes among those. In fact, we could even use the entire input model as a domain, and have the unary constraint test for the "classness" and "abstraction" of the domain values. There is an advantage to having precise domains: the CSP solution process is more efficient, since there are fewer values to try. The disadvantage, from a representation point of view, is that some essential problem knowledge is buried in non-explicit, non-declarative procedures (domain extractors), as opposed to being expressed explicitly and declaratively in constraints.

Dealing with UML models is a mixed blessing: both "classness" and "abstractness" are represented explicitly[2], and thus computing the domains for var_AbstractClass and var_ConcreteClass is straightforward. Things are slightly more complicated with var_AbstractOperation and var_ConcreteOperation. UML does provide the **Operation** class, but the "abstraction" of operations is a programming concept. Thus, we can use all of the operations of the input model as domains for var_AbstractOperation and var_ConcreteOperation and add constraints to identify abstractness/concreteness, or, enrich the domain extraction procedure to make that distinction. Things get yet a bit more complicated with the variables var_inherits_from_1, var_inherits_from_2, var_has_method, var_has_message: these variables represent associations that are embodied/hardcoded in the UML metamodel, as opposed to being represented explicitly by entities. Indeed, in the UML metamodel, the association between a class and its methods is implicit in the definition of the class: it is not represented by an explicit entity of the UML metamodel. Idem for the inheritance relationship: it is an association in the UML metamodel itself (between classes), and not an entity[3]. Things get *yet* more complicated with the variable var_overrides—and the underlying "overrides" relationship between operations. This has no representation in UML metamodels in any shape or form (entity, attribute, association), and has to be computed from the ground up[4].

5.3 Extracting Constraints

Constraints represent relationships between the problem variables: they are what ties the problem model together. A number of such constraints are used to bind the various association ends to the associated entities. Figure 8 shows excerpts from the visitor problem model, and how the various components map to CSP components. As mentioned before, **AbstractClass**, **ConcreteClass**, and inherits_from are mapped to three variables var_AbstractClass, var_ConcreteClass, and var_inherits_from_1. The domains for these variables are *all* abstract classes, *all* concrete classes, and *all* inherits-from relationships in the input model, respectively. To match an "A inherits-from B" fragment in the input model, where A is an abstract class and B is a concrete class, we need two constraints that we call cons_inherits_1_src and cons_inherits_1_tar, defined as follows:

cons_inherits_1_src(var_AbstractClass,var_inherits_from_1) ≡
var_inherits_from_1.source = = var_AbstractClass
cons_inherits_1_tar(var_inherits_from_1,var_ConcreteClass) ≡
var_inherits_from_1.target = = var_ConcreteClass

---

2 In UML, the « abstractness » of a **Class** is represented by a boolean attribute (isAbstract) inherited from **Classifier**.

3 Such associations are usually represented as attributes of the UML metamodel classes. For example, **Class** has an attribute superClass, which can take a list of **Class**'es.

4 For example, by identifying operations that have the same signature, and leaving the inheritance aspect as a constraint.

Similar pairs of constraints are used to link the association ends for has_method, has_message, implements, and overrides.

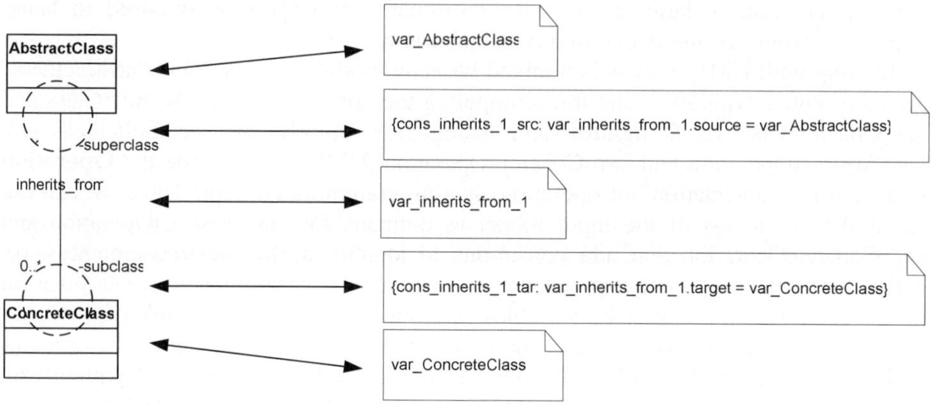

Fig. 8. An illustration of the mapping from problem model to variables and constraints

Finally, we define a constraint to represent the homomorphism between the has-message association between **AbstractClass**'es and **AbstractOperation**'s, on one hand, and **ConcreteClass**'es and **ConcreteOperation**'s, on the other.

6 Implementation

6.1 The Pattern Meta-model and the Transformation Rules

We implemented our language for representing patterns as a meta-model [12]. To do so, we used the Eclipse Modeling Framework™ (EMF) which includes a package called ECore that implements a lightweight version of MOF. Our meta-model was implemented as an extension to ECore. We also implemented our transformation rules using ILOG JRules. JRules is a hybrid object-rule system where the condition and action parts of rules refer to Java objects and methods. In our case, conditions and actions refer to elements of problem and solution models represented as instances of the ECore meta-model. The transformation rules are described in detail in [6].

6.2 The Pattern Matching Strategy with a CSP Solver

A major decision during the implementation of a CSP pattern matching strategy was to choose a solver. Having variables whose domains consist of objects—as opposed to scalar values—was a determining factor. We choose the ILOG JSolver™ toolset which is a constraint solver written in Java and designed to work against Java object models. Another significant advantage of JSolver in our context is its support for user-defined constraints coded in Java. This gives us the full power of the Java language to define new constraints. Indeed, we implemented our constraints as extensions to a generic user constraint class provided by JSolver. Practically the implementation of each constraint implied the implementation of domain reductions of its variables. To do so, JSolver provides domain modifiers (e.g. removeDomainValue) that we used in the propagation method of a constraint to eliminate the values that can not be part of a solution. When the domain of a variable is modified, the examination of the constraints on this variable is triggered [4].

We implemented the variables, the constraints and domain extractors in Java. The variables extractor module reads a problem model and maps its entities and their relationships into variables, as explained in section 5.1. The domain extractor module provides the necessary methods to extract the various domains from input models. As mentioned in section 5.2, we took advantage of the UML metamodel—as supported by EMF's ECore—to extract domains for the most common entity types (abstract classes, concrete classes, interfaces, etc.).The constraint extractor reads a problem model, identifies its associations, and generates the corresponding source and target constraints, as explained in section 5.3.

The process flow is as follows: the CSP generator (Fig. 7) instantiates the variable extractor, the constraints extractor and the domains extractor. Then it builds the CSP by retrieving the variables from the variables extractor, retrieving the corresponding constraints form the constraints extractor and setting the variables' domains by applying the domain extractor to the input model. Practically, we need to implement a CSP generator for each problem model, even though the different generators share a lot of functionality. So far, we coded CSP generators for four design patterns: the visitor, bridge, composite, and strategy.

6.3 Post-processing JSolver Output

Notwithstanding issues related to time hotposts (see section 3), the output produced by solver does not identify instances of design pattern problems as we would expect them. Given the model fragment show in Figure 9 (the proverbial example for the visitor pattern), and our codification of the problem model, JSolver will return four separate solutions delimited by the various dashed lines. This happens for two reasons. The first is a common problem in pattern matching, which we will illustrate with a simple example. Assume that we want to match the regular expression a^*b^* in some text. If my target string is cdfiaaabbxyz, then my expression a*b* will match ab, aab, aabb, aaab, and aaabb. A regular expression tool needs to be told, or coded in such a way, that it returns the longest matching sequence. JSolver returns all of the fragments that satisfy the set of constraints, and in those cases where we have recursive associations, it will generate paths with different lengths. This explains why it identified both Expression → Node and ArithmeticExpression → Expression → Node as solutions. Thus, we need to collect and collate such solutions to identify the largest model fragment that fits the pattern.

The second problem is a limitation of the version of JSolver™ that we used, which explains why we get Expression → Node, VariableRefNode → Node, and AssignmentNode → Node as separate solutions, as opposed to paths within the same solution. Indeed, to get *all* of the subclasses of a given class in one swoop, we need to be

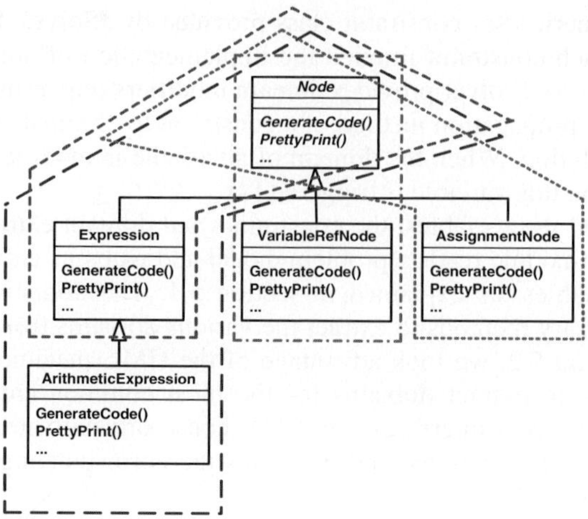

Fig. 9. JSolver produces problem model instance *fragments* which need to be collated into a single problem instance

able to define variables whose domains are *sets* of objects, as opposed to *individual objects*. The version of JSolver that we used supports only arrays of numbers, and requires us to specify the size of the array as part of the definition of variable, which is not practical, since we don't know the size before hand. We continue to explore ways around this limitation. For the time being, for a given problem model, we collect the solutions produced by JSolver and organize them in a "forest" based on common subpaths; once we are done, each tree in the forest represents a different problem instance.

We applied our approach to sample input models, and were able to detect instances of these patterns where appropriate. We are currently working on implementing a graphical user interface that enables us to highlight instances of the various design patterns within input models.

7 Discussion

7.1 Related Work

Our approach to detect instances of design problems solved by design patterns in models is related to the approaches that were proposed to tackle the problem of detecting patterns in object oriented systems. These approaches can be organized by the target application and by the technique used. Indeed, while the approaches in [1] and [5] aim at detecting design problems, the first uses metrics to evaluate the source code quality and, the second uses logic programming to do so. In both cases, design problems are defined as violations of object oriented heuristics and hence are of a lower level of abstraction than the design problems solved by design patterns. The approach in [2] uses logical functions to specify Java specific elemental patterns that compose design patterns. Elemental patterns are more suitable for automation but they do not provide as much design information as design patterns [9]. The approach in [8] uses constraint programming to detect design patterns in the source code. To the best of our knowledge, all these approaches focused on detecting instances or approximate instances of the solutions proposed by design patterns not the problems they are meant to solve. While [8] focuses on detecting solutions provided by design patterns, it is an interesting approach because it uses explanation-based constraints to detect approximate instances of these solutions. Although at the implementation level, there are some differences on how CSPs are used: relationships (e.g. composition) in [8] are considered as constraints over the variables, which requires to process the detected solutions (e.g. there could be more than one composition relationship between two classes and we need to retrieve all of them).

Recognizing a problem model in a given input model is a graph homomorphism problem. To tackle this problem, there are two main trends within model transformation approaches based on graph grammar. Indeed, approaches like [18] and [10] use search plans for the traversal of the LHS (left hand side) part of a rule while [15] uses constraint satisfaction techniques. The approach in [18] proposes to generate search plans using typical models of the system at hand. Depending on the graph pattern to be matched and the current model to be matched into, an optimal search strategy for the traversal of this graph pattern is derived from search plans. In the same trend, [10] proposes to represent search plan operations as cost-weighted predicates to achieve an adaptive ordering of these operations in particular the complex ones (e.g. negative application condition checking operation). This adaptive ordering enables to minimize the total cost of all the matching process. However, there is an overhead when calculating the cost of all possible search plans and the proposed representations of search plans are not intuitive.

Somehow graph matching strategies are based on some backtracking algorithms. The approach in [15] argues that most of the studies to optimize these algorithms are done in the context of CSPs. Hence to benefit from the research findings in CSPs, [15] proposes to translate the graph pattern matching problem into a CSP. Contrary to [18], this approach decouples the solution algorithm from the concrete model at hand. However, translating the graph pattern into a CSP representation involves a computation overhead which depends on the size of the graph pattern (i.e. the LHS of a transformation rule). In our context, this graph pattern is a problem model whose size is typically small as demonstrated by the Visitor problem model example, i.e. the average longest pattern path is three (aSubClass $\rightarrow$ aClass $\rightarrow$ aSuperClass).

7.2 Outstanding Issues

In our current implementation, we detect complete instances of a given problem model. However, some input models can include incomplete instances of some of our problem models. Our strategy to find these incomplete instances is to define, for a given design pattern, the minimum problem model and specify the set of transformation rules accordingly. To do so we need to specify which entities of the problem model are optional regarding the design problem specification, i.e. even if these entities are removed from the problem model, it still corresponds to the design problem solved by the given pattern. The set of mandatory entities and their relationships form the minimum problem model. Hence when no instance of a problem model is found, we remove from the corresponding constraint problem the variables representing its optional entities and we relax the constraints in which these variables are involved. We remove a variable at a time and if still no instance is found, we remove two variables at once, and so on. The retained instance is the one having the maximal size.

Another important problem to consider is the existence in an input model of overlapping instances of design problems. Indeed, we need to run tests on several larger models to check if there are any conflicts when different instances of the same pattern or different patterns apply to the same fragment of an input model. Design patterns relationships as described in [19] can help to implement an approach to solve these potential conflicts.

8 Conclusion

In this paper, we proposed a semi-automatic tool for marking models using constraint satisfaction techniques. This tool aims at providing a framework for recognizing design problems solved by design patterns and rewriting them according to the appropriate solutions. The key element of our approach is the explicit representation of design problems solved by design patterns. Indeed representing a design problem by an explicit model enables to recognize instances of this problem model and to specify declaratively the related design pattern's application by means of rules describing the transformation of this problem model into the corresponding solution model. Furthermore, our approach can be used to specify and apply other kind of patterns.

References

1. Alikacem, E., Sahraoui, H.A.: Détection d'anomalies utilisant un langage de description règle de qualité. In: Rousseau, R., Urtado, C., Vauttier, S. (eds.) LMO 2006, pp. 185–200 (2006)
2. Arcelli, A., Masiero, S., Raibulet, C.: Elemental Design Patterns Recognition In Java. In: 13th IEEE Int. Work. Software Technology and Engineering Practice, pp. 196–205 (2005)
3. Bacchus, F., van Beek, P.: On the Conversion between Non-Binary and Binary Constraint Satisfaction Problems. In: 15th Conf. on Artificial Intelligence, pp. 311–318 (1998)
4. Chun, A.: Constraint Programming in Java with JSolver. In: 1st Int. Conf. and Exhibition on the Practical Application of Constraint Technologies and Logic Programming (1999)
5. Ciupke, O.: Automatic Detection of Design Problems in Object-Oriented Reengineering. In: TOOLS 30, pp. 18–32. IEEE Computer Society Press, Los Alamitos (1999)
6. El-Boussaidi, G., Mili, H.: A Model-driven Framework for Representing and Applying Design Patterns. In: 31st COMPSAC, vol. 1, pp. 97–100 (2007)
7. Gamma, E., Helm, R., Johnson, R., Vlissides, J.: Design Patterns: Elements of Reusable Object-Oriented Software. Addison-Wesley, Reading (1995)
8. Guéhéneuc, Y.-G., Jussien, N.: Using Explanations for Design Patterns Identification. In: IJCAI 2001 Workshop on Modelling and Solving problems with constraints, pp. 57–64 (2001)
9. Gil, J., Maman, I.: Micro Patterns in Java Code. In: 20th conference on Object oriented programming systems languages and applications, OOPSLA 2005, pp. 97–116 (2005)

10. Horvath, A., Varro, G., Varro, D.: Generic search plans for matching advanced graph patterns. In: The 6th International GT-VMT Workshop (2007)
11. Model Driven Architecture Guide, http://www.omg.org/cgi-bin/doc?omg/03-06-01
12. Mili, H., El-Boussaidi, G.: Representing and Applying Design Patterns: What Is the Problem? In: Briand, L.C., Williams, C. (eds.) MoDELS 2005. LNCS, vol. 3713, pp. 186–200. Springer, Heidelberg (2005)
13. Mili, H., Mili, F., Mili, A.: Reusing software: Issues and research directions. IEEE Transactions on Software Engineering 21(6), 528–562 (1995)
14. Partsch, H., Steinbruggen, R.: Program Transformation Systems. Computing Surveys 15(3), 199–236 (1983)
15. Rudolf, M.: Utilizing Constraint Satisfaction Techniques for Efficient Graph Pattern Matching. In: Ehrig, H., Engels, G., Kreowski, H.-J., Rozenberg, G. (eds.) TAGT 1998. LNCS, vol. 1764, pp. 238–251. Springer, Heidelberg (2000)
16. Sahraoui, H., Boukadoum, M., Lounis, H., Ethève, F.: Predicting Class Libraries Interface Evolution: an investigation into machine learning approaches. In: The 7th APSEC (2000)
17. Tsang, E.P.K.: Foundations of Constraint Satisfaction. Academic Press, London (1993)
18. Varro, G., Friedl, K., Varro, D.: Adaptive Graph Pattern Matching for Model Transformations using Model-sensitive Search Plans. In: Karsai, G., Taentzer, G. (eds.) GraMot 2005. ENTCS, vol. 152, pp. 191–205 (2006)
19. Zimmer, W.: Relationships between design patterns. In: Pattern Languages of Program Design. Addison-Wesley, Reading (1994)

A General Approach for Scenario Integration*

Hongzhi Liang[1], Zinovy Diskin[2,3], Juergen Dingel[1], and Ernesto Posse[1]

[1] School of Computing, Queen's University, Canada
{liang,dingel,eposse}@cs.queensu.ca
[2] Department of Computer Science, University of Toronto
[3] Department of Electrical & Computer Engineering, University of Waterloo
zdiskin@swen.uwaterloo.ca

Abstract. An approach to integrating UML Sequence Diagrams is presented. It rests on a well-established theory, is generalizable to a large class of requirements engineering models, and supports many different kinds of scenario integration operations. An implementation of the approach as an Eclipse extension is described. Lessons learned from the implementation and during first, preliminary experiments to study the practical aspects of the approach, are discussed.

1 Introduction

The need to integrate software artifacts seems inherent to modern software development. On the one hand, the development may be distributed over several teams to leverage different expertise, experience or capabilities. On the other hand, breaking a task into smaller, more manageable pieces often is an effective means to deal with the kind of complexity that comes from, e.g., large numbers of stakeholders, views, features, or platforms. In each case, the separately developed artifacts need to be assembled as efficiently as possible into a consistent whole in which the parts still function as described.

While support for integration is required for a large variety of artifacts to, e.g., support separation of development or concerns, it appears particularly necessary for models of requirements. This is because requirements models are especially prone to change and evolution. This phenomenon is widely accepted within the software engineering community and much work has been done to address it.

Many approaches aimed at mitigating the effect of changing requirements appear to rely on some kind of integration. For instance, in [11] use case slices need to be composed, gradually refined and kept synchronized. Consequently, support for the integration of a different, possibly more detailed and separately developed, model into other models is required. In some situations this integration may be adequately realized through a simple kind of replacement operation; however, to achieve the traceability needed for large-scale, distributed development, a less destructive form of integration may be necessary. Moreover, the

* This work was supported by NSERC, the Ontario Centres of Excellence, IBM CAS Ottawa, Bell Canada through the Bell University Labs and partially by the Ontario Research Fund.

K. Czarnecki et al. (Eds.): MoDELS 2008, LNCS 5301, pp. 204–218, 2008.

refined part of a model may have complex relationships with its context that need to be preserved by the refinement.

Another class of approaches is based on role modeling, that is, the identification of the parts of an object that address a particular concern such as performing a task or maintaining an invariant. Changing requirements can then often be dealt with either by adding a role to an object or by modifying a single role without affecting the others. Role-based software development methodologies include Reenskaug's Object Oriented Role Analysis Method (OOram) [21] and VanHilst's Role-Oriented Programming (ROP) [27]. Both methodologies feature a "synthesis" step in which the implementation of an object is obtained from its roles. Again, possibly separately developed models of requirements describing the roles need to be integrated to produce a description of the overall behavior of the object. Typically, roles are not disjoint, that is, they can "overlap" in complex ways. For instance, two different collaborations may require the same interaction with an object. Indeed, a look at [21,27] shows it is exactly these kinds of relationship between roles that complicate the synthesis step. The integration must properly deal with these relationships and, for instance, avoid the creation of duplicated parts in the integrated model in case of overlap among the integration participants.

Despite the apparent need for the integration of models of requirements, relatively little concrete support for this activity seems to exist. A lot of the existing work on the topic of model integration either assumes a large degree of disjointness between models (e.g., the work on composition operations for UML Sequence Diagrams and Interaction Overview Diagrams), or targets very specific notations with no clear potential for a more general application. For instance, all three methodologies mentioned above remain relatively silent on how exactly the integration of the requirements models is to be achieved. In [11], the composition of use case slices is performed on the code level using, e.g., AspectJ. UML's package merge is mentioned as a mechanism to compose slices on the model level although package merge is currently not defined on interactions [5]. Moreover, no indication is given of how synchronization between separately evolving models can be accomplished. OOram cautions the developer to take care that the result of the synthesis model is "consistent with the meanings of all its base models" [21, page 124]. However, no exact definition of the synthesis operation is provided. In [27], the transparent composition of roles on the code level is discussed in detail, while the model level is discussed much more informally. For another example, consider the "combine" operation offered in IBM Rational Software Architect (RSA) V7.0 which is intended to support the integration of different models, but appears limited to class and object diagrams [15].

This paper describes our work towards filling this gap and pursues the following questions: How would an integration operation look like that properly deals with overlap between models and is generalizable to different kinds of requirements models? How could this operation be applied to a particular kind of model such as UML Sequence Diagrams? How could it be supported through tools? Which additional work is necessary to realize the vision of a general model integration operation? In particular, we present an approach to integrating a core subset of UML Sequence Diagrams which rests on a well-established theory, is generalizable to a large class of models, and supports many different kinds of scenario integration operations. Our approach uses category theory as a mathematical framework in which UML Sequence Diagrams are represented as *typed graphs* and integration is achieved through the explicit representation of the relationships between models via structure-preserving maps and a colimit construction. This construction results in an intuitive and versatile operation which not only provides traceability "for free" (the original models can easily be identified in the integration result), but also serves as an effective mechanism to structure the implementation and implement consistency checking. Moreover, the approach is generalizable to other diagrams used to represent requirements (e.g., Message Sequence Charts, Communication Diagrams). An Eclipse-based implementation of the approach is described. Lessons learned from the implementation and during first, preliminary experiments, e.g., to study different scenario integration patterns and the overall use of the approach, are discussed.

The remainder of this paper is structured as follows: The representation of UML Sequence Diagrams as typed graphs and the integration operation are described in Sections 2 and 3. The implementation is sketched in Sections 4. Related work is discussed in Section 5, while conclusions are given in Section 6.

2 Sequence Diagrams as Typed Graphs

In general, a scenario is a record of possible message exchanges between communicating objects. Figure 1(a) presents an example: a *Sale* scenario specified by a UML Sequence Diagram [18]. The *Sale*, and any other scenario has a structural base: a set of interacting objects and (implicitly) the types of messages they can exchange. Objects are explicitly specified in the boxes on the top of the lifelines. Messages are arrows from senders to receivers labeled with message names. In fact, some typing is implicit there. For example, it is reasonable to consider the two messages *initialOffer* and *counterOffer* as two different *occurrences* of the same message type *offer* between a *Seller* and a *Buyer*.

Sequence Diagrams have many advantages, but they are not directly amenable to formal manipulations. Since Sequence Diagrams (and an overwhelming majority of other modeling languages) are diagrammatic, a formalization based on graph-based structures seems to be advantageous. Fortunately, the graph-based formalisms possess other desirable properties: they (i) are amenable to effective algebraic manipulations, (ii) are expressive and provide a base for generic specifications, (iii) have solid theoretical support provided by *category theory* and by a large body of work in graph rewriting, (iv) have tool support. In this paper, we present an informal description of a formalization for the core subset of Sequence Diagrams. A more formal description can be found in [7].

In our formalization, a Sequence Diagram, as in Fig. 1(a), is represented as a typed graph, that is a chain of two type mappings between three graphs

$$G_0 \xleftarrow{\tau_1} G_1 \xleftarrow{\tau_2} G_2$$

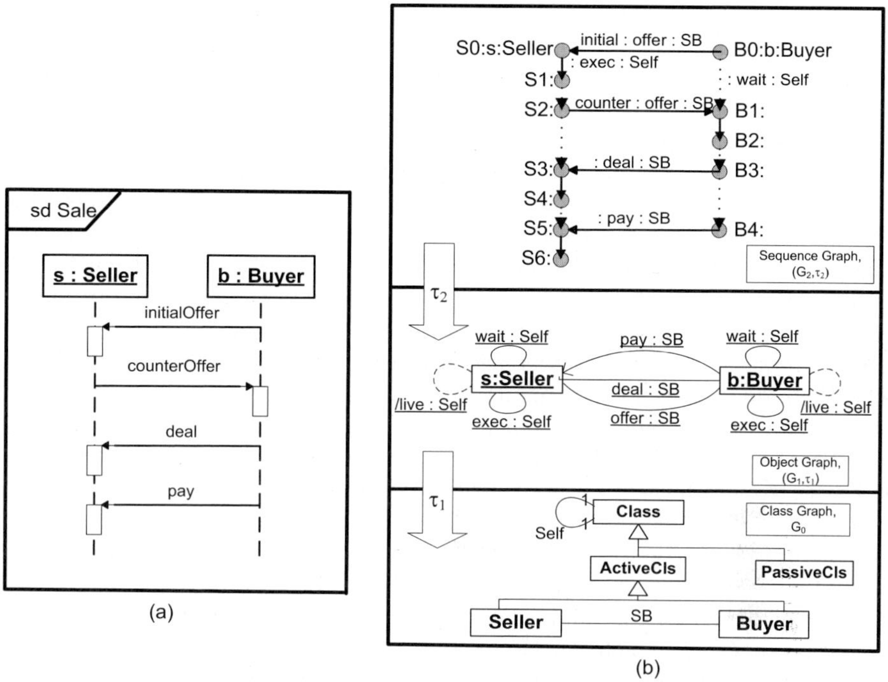

Fig. 1. A sample sequence diagram (a), and its typed graph (b)

as shown in Fig. 1(b). Graph G_0, or *class graph*, is shown in the bottom cell of Fig. 1(b) and is very similar to a UML Class Diagram, except that the edges represent *dynamic* rather than *static* associations [24]. We therefore interpret them as *message channels*, e.g., the *SB* message channel between *Seller* and *Buyer*. A root node called *Class* is contained in every class graph. A special message channel *Self* is represented as a self-association on *Class*. For concurrent systems, an object of a class may or may not own a thread of control. In other words, an object can be specified as either an *active object* having its own thread of control or a *passive object* without the control [22]. To distinguish these two different types of object, we introduce two sub-classes of the root *Class*, *ActiveCls* and *PassiveCls*. Inheritance is also used in our formalization to support sub-classing and association inheritance. For example, by introducing *ActiveCls* as a sub-class of *Class*, the message channel *Self* is inherited by *ActiveCls*.

Graph G_1, or *object graph*, whose nodes are objects participating in interactions and whose edges are *dynamic* links (instances of dynamic associations) or *message types* between objects, is shown in the middle cell of Fig. 1(b)[1]. Note that nodes and edges of this graph are typed (or labeled) by classes and

[1] More accurately, *buyer* and *seller* are roles (formal parameters in the interaction) that real objects could play. To simplify wording, we will call them objects when it will not lead to confusion.

message channels of Graph G_0 by mapping τ_1. We assume that an object of *ActiveCls* can be in one of two states: "executing" or "blocked and waiting for a response". To capture this, we introduce two special message types ***exec*** and ***wait*** as instances of self-association *Self*. Similarly, ***exec*** and ***rest*** (not used in Fig. 1) are introduced to capture the states of "executing" and "ready and really doing nothing" of an object of *PassiveCls*. A *derived* message type, */live*, is also shown in Fig. 1(b). A derived element is one that can be computed from other elements as a result of some algebraic operation. To be precise, we define $/live = \{\textbf{exec}|\textbf{\textit{wait}}\}^*$, i.e., any sequential composition of ***exec*** and ***wait*** arrows results in $/live$. In our formalization, although derived elements contain no new semantic information, they either facilitate the understanding of scenarios, or are even required for proper scenario integration. We borrow from UML and prefix the names of derived elements by "/".

Graph G_2, called *sequence graph*, is a partial order of *events* and *messages* typed over Graph G_1 by mapping τ_2, where nodes are event occurrences labeled by objects (to which these events happened) and arrows are message occurrences labeled by message types. The top cell of Fig. 1(b) shows the corresponding sequence graph of scenario in Fig. 1(a). Labels of all event occurrences besides S0 and B0 are omitted. If an arrow in G_2 is labeled by ***exec***, ***wait*** or ***rest***, then it will be attached to the lifeline of a single object (the one to which the self-association in G_0 is attached). For instance, all vertical arrows in our example sequence graph are labeled with either ***exec*** or ***wait***. Intuitively, labeling an arrow by ***exec*** or ***wait*** (***rest***) means, respectively, that in the time period between the source and target event occurrences the object is executing some procedure or doing nothing (is either blocked or ready). In the case of ***exec***, this is the procedure triggered by the message coming into the source event. To help us distinguish between arrows typed with ***wait*** (***rest***) or ***exec***, we use the following concrete syntax for them: the former are shown with dotted (e.g., between B0 and B1) and the latter with bold (e.g., between S0 and S1) arrows.

To summarize, we formalize Sequence Diagrams as three layers of directed, labeled graphs containing dynamic and static information, where lower layers serve as types for the higher layers. Such layered, typed structures are useful to support, e.g., consistency checking. Moreover, unlike formalizations based on, e.g., partially ordered multisets, our formalization retains the graphical nature of Sequence Diagrams. More precisely, there is an obvious similarity between the formalization and what is being formalized, which increases learnability.

3 Scenario Integration

We introduce scenario integration via a running example reminiscent of the role composition process required by OOram or ROP. Suppose we want to build a model (scenario) which integrates two copies of the Sale scenario into a brokered sale model: a BrokeredSale (*BS*) is a composition of two Sales, called the WholeSale (*WS*) and the RetailSale (*RS*). We want this integrated scenario to satisfy the following requirements:

(i) The *Retailer* is the *Buyer* in WholeSale, and it is the *Seller* in RetailSale.
(ii) The *Retailer*'s role requires two activities in addition to those of the sale transactions: a *Retailer* must do some *thinking* and some *banking*.

In order to integrate the two given scenarios we need to merge the corresponding class, object and sequence graphs. These three operations are in fact instances of the same generic operation of merging graphs, which we now sketch[2].

Given two typed graphs to be merged, we need to specify the overlapping elements (i.e., nodes and edges). That is, we need to establish a correspondence between these graphs of those elements which are supposed to be identified. To do this, a first approach, found in tools such as RSA [15], is to use heuristics like identifying elements by name. Such approach however, is not general enough. In particular it does not deal with requirements such as (i). A more general approach (arguably the most general approach) is to create a third graph, which we call the *head*, representing those common elements, and possibly containing new elements. We then specify how this third graph establishes the correspondence by defining a pair of maps which map elements of the head to elements of each of the original graphs. We call such maps *arms*. The head graph and the associated arms are called the *span* of the two original graphs. From the span, the merged graph will be generated.

Going back to the problem, we first look at how object graphs are merged, and then we consider sequence graphs. The merge of class graphs is obtained in an analogous manner.

Integration of object graphs. Fig. 2 shows the object graphs to be merged (WS_{OG} for the WholeSale and RS_{OG} for the RetailSale) together with the span (the head being the Retailer graph R_{OG} at the bottom) and the merged graph on top, satisfying the requirements (i) and (ii). The dashed arrows represent the correspondence mappings.

The head graph contains a new object *r:Retailer* with two self loops *thinking* and *banking*. There is a map from *r:Retailer* in R_{OG} to *b:Buyer* in WS_{OG}, representing the requirement that the retailer plays the role of buyer in WholeSale, and a map from *r:Retailer* in R_{OG} to *s:Seller* in RS_{OG}, representing the requirement that the retailer plays the role of seller in RetailSale. Hence, requirements (i) and (ii) are captured.

The merged object graph is BS_{OG}. Fig. 2 also shows how the elements of WS_{OG} and RS_{OG} are mapped to the elements of the resulting graph BS_{OG}. We now sketch how this graph is obtained. For full details, please see [7].

First, we form the disjoint union of the two original graphs and the head graph (WS_{OG}, RS_{OG} and R_{OG}.) Let us call this A. The mappings from the head graph (the arms) determine an equivalence relation on A where overlapping elements are identified. Then we partition the set of nodes of A according to this equivalence. That is, we group all equivalent nodes into sets. The collection of all these sets is the partition. In our example, we obtain three sets: A_1 =

[2] A detailed technical description of this operation can be found in many sources, e.g., [23] and our own technical report [7].

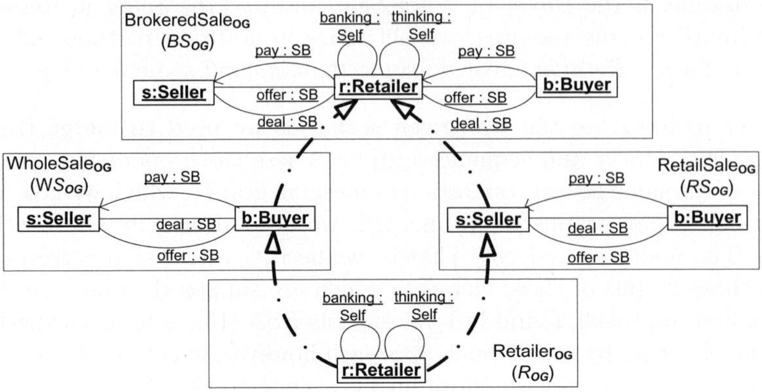

Fig. 2. The span of the WS_{OG} and RS_{OG} object graphs and the merged graph on top

$\{r{:}Retailer{::}R_{OG},\ b{:}Buyer{::}WS_{OG},\ s{:}Seller{::}RS_{OG}\}$, $A_2 = \{s{:}Seller{::}WS_{OG}\}$ and $A_3 = \{b{:}Buyer{::}RS_{OG}\}$, where we write $x : Class{::}Graph$ for the object x of type *Class* in graph *Graph*.

The merged graph consists of a node for each of these sets. Hence we have a node for the *Retailer*, one for the *Seller* from WS_{OG} and one for the final *Buyer* from RS_{OG}. Edges of the merged graph are obtained in a similar fashion. The merged graph will also contain all edges from the WS_{OG} and RS_{OG} graphs, as well as new edges from the head graph, such as *thinking* and *banking*, which are not present in the two original graphs. These edges are present in the corresponding node of the merged graph. With the merged graph, we also obtain mappings from WS_{OG} and RS_{OG} into BS_{OG}, describing how the former are embedded in the latter and providing useful traceability information.[3]

Integration of sequence graphs. Now suppose that we have some additional requirements for our BrokeredSale scenario:

(iii) The RetailSale follows the WholeSale.
(iv) After buying from the whole-seller, the *Retailer* does some thinking. After this, he/she begins the process of retail selling, which is followed by some banking.
(v) The *Retailer* pays the whole-seller after he/she receives payment from the retail *Buyer*.

These are behavioral requirements and so they are to be captured by the result of merging the sequence graphs for the WholeSale and RetailSale.

As with object graphs, to merge sequence graphs we need to specify the points of overlap, and we do this by providing a span, i.e. a head graph and the associated arms defining the correspondence.

---

[3] In the terminology of Category Theory, the merged graph and the associated mappings form a *pushout* of the span.

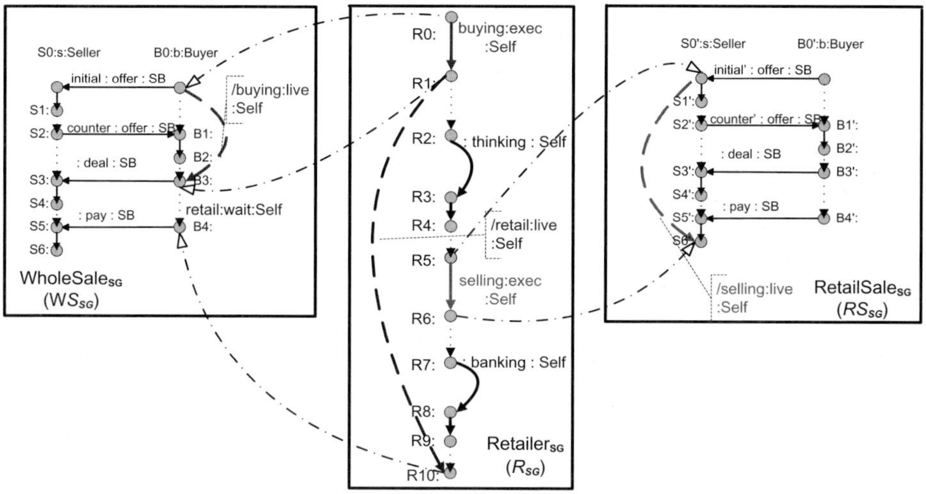

Fig. 3. The span of the sequence graphs WS_{SG} and RS_{SG} to be merged

Fig. 3 shows the sequence graphs to be merged with their span. The graph WS_{SG} is the sequence graph for the WholeSale, RS_{SG} is the sequence graph for the RetailSale, and R_{SG} is the sequence graph showing the lifeline of the *Retailer*, and thus it is the head of the span. Each graph is typed over its corresponding object graph.

By explicitly defining the correspondence between the two sequence graphs as a span in terms of the *Retailer*'s lifeline, we capture requirements (iii) - (v). In this graph, we are able to define new elements which where not present in either of the sale scenarios, such as the *thinking* and *banking* arrows. We also introduce arrows *buying* and *selling* which, while not present in the sale scenarios as individual arrows, correspond to a *composition* of arrows in their respective graphs. For example, the arrow *buying* in R_{SG} from R0 to R1 is mapped to the new derived arrow */buying* in WS_{SG}, which is the composition of the arrows from B0 to B3. Hence, the arrow *buying* can be seen, from the point of view of the retailer, as an abstraction of a sequence of actions that occur in the whole sale. Furthermore, we map a composition of arrows (*/retail*) in R_{SG} to a single arrow (*retail*) in WS_{SG}. Note that this composite arrow */retail* includes the *selling* arrow (which itself is associated to the composite */selling* in RS_{SG}.) This allows us to ensure that the RetailSale occurs within the retail process and before the *Retailer* pays the whole-seller, thus satisfying requirements (iii) - (v).

As with the object graph, we build the merged sequence graph by computing the equivalence relation induced by the span. This yields the sequence graph shown in Fig. 4(a). Note the derived (dashed-bold) arrows among the elements of this graph. When two arrows, where one is basic (in one graph) and the other is derived (in another graph) are glued together in the merge, the result is a derived arrow because it can be derived exactly in the same way as it is derived in its component graph. For example, the arrow *retail* was basic in

WS_{SG} but becomes derived in the merge after gluing it with the derived arrow */retail*, because all the operands for its derivation are present in the merged graph. Derived arrows in the merged graph are useful for traceability, but apart from that they can be safely removed. We call this last step of the integration *normalization*. In our example normalization is fairly trivial but it can be more complicated without posing any fundamental problems[4]. A sequence diagram equivalent to the merged graph without derived arrows is shown in Fig. 4(b).

General process. The example we have just considered suggests the following general process for scenario integration:

1. *Formalization*: We define a universe of typed graphs and specify the scenarios to be integrated (the *views*) as typed graphs in this universe.
2. *Specification of view correspondences*: We define the correspondence between views by providing *spans*, which consist of 1) *head graphs*, i.e., typed graphs which contain elements (nodes and edges) that represent the overlap of the views, and 2) *arms*, i.e., mappings specifying the roles that elements of a head graph play in each view. The head graphs can contain new information which was not present in the original views.
3. *Merge*: For each graph of the typed graphs (class, object, sequence) the merged graph is obtained by computing the equivalence induced by the span, and the corresponding partition of the (disjoint) union of the views.
4. *Normalization*: In each merged graph, we eliminate redundant arrows, i.e. arrows which can be derived from basic (non-composite) edges.

A fundamental property of the merge operation is that the resulting graph contains exactly all of the information from the original graphs and the head graph: nothing is lost because views are mapped into the merge, and nothing extra is acquired owing to the universal property of pushout. It is also worth noting that while the example described the integration of just two scenarios, this pattern is applicable to any number of scenarios to be merged[5].

Integration and refinement. Model refinement can be understood in terms of integration: given a model A, a refinement A' of A can be seen as the result of merging A with a model B specifying details of A. For example, the BrokeredSale scenario can be seen as a refinement of the WholeSale scenario, where the retail activity has been detailed by merging the RetailSale scenario via R_{SG}.

With such a view of refinement as integration, the relationships between the refined part of a model and its context are preserved by the operation of refinement. Nevertheless, this notion of refinement contrasts with the notion of refinement as proposed in, e.g., the STAIRS framework [9]. In STAIRS, the meaning of a sequence diagram is defined by the set of traces that any implementation must satisfy, and refinement is defined in terms of containment of sets of traces. We present an orthogonal view of refinement, where an action

[4] See [3,6] for more details.

[5] This is achieved by computing *general colimits*, of which pushouts are a particular example.

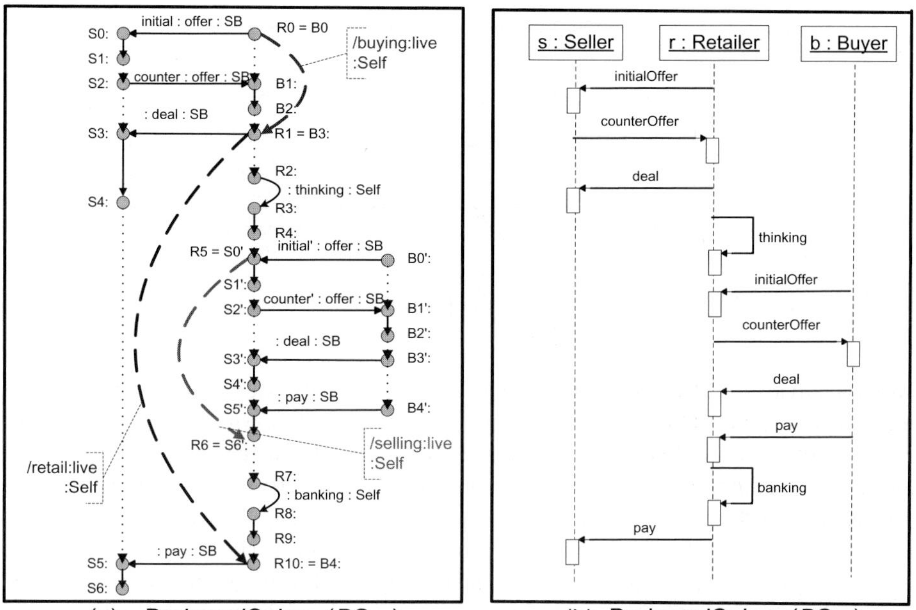

(a) BrokeredSale$_{SG}$ (BS_{SG}) (b) BrokeredSale$_{SD}$ (BS_{SD})

Fig. 4. Result of merge as a typed graph (a) and as Sequence Diagram (b)

or sequence of actions (and therefore the corresponding trace) is refined by a sequence of actions (resp. a trace) by expansion, i.e., an action (an arrow in the sequence graph) can by refined by a composition of actions (arrows.)

Our preliminary evaluations indicate that this view of refinement can be useful for model management in general and for the formalization and support for development methodologies that require the manipulation of requirements models (e.g., the methodology in [11] and OOram) in particular.

4 Implementation

A prototype implementation has been built as an Eclipse extension. This allows us to take full advantage of other existing Eclipse-based modeling tools (e.g., IBM RSA) which implement editing, visualization, import and export of Sequence Diagrams. We also rely on the EMF, UML2 and GMF frameworks.

The architecture of the prototype follows our general process described in Section 3. The main components of the prototype and the data flow among them are depicted in Fig. 5. Our prototype assumes that the Sequence Diagrams and the head of the merge are created by the user with the help of existing modeling tools, such as RSA. After importing the Sequence Diagrams, the *SD2TG Transformer* will automatically convert them into typed graphs. A variety of different existing transformation tools could have been used to develop this component. We have chosen TXL [25]. An Ecore-to-TXL grammar generator has been implemented to provide general support for writing TXL-based model-to-model

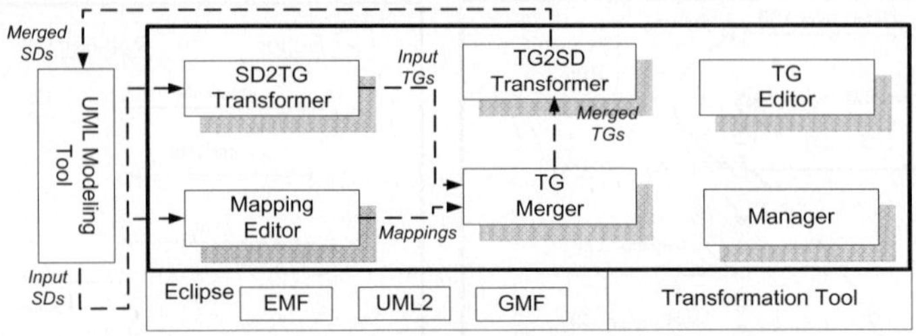

Fig. 5. The architecture of the prototype SD Integration Tool

transformations. The users interactively create mappings or correspondences between Sequence Diagrams with the help of the *Mapping Editor*. The correspondences between Sequence Diagrams are then translated to correspondences between typed graphs. Strictly speaking, a mapping editor operating on typed graphs directly rather than Sequence Diagrams would be more efficient, thus obviating the need for transforming mappings. Instead, the current implementation hides the typed graph representation from the users. As a consequence, it is likely more user-friendly as the users can work with familiar concepts, i.e., Sequence Diagrams. We are also working on an expert mode which allows users to work on typed graphs directly. In this expert mode, the similarity between a Sequence Diagram and its typed graph will be very helpful. Next, the *TG Merger* takes typed graphs and mappings between them, and produces a merged typed graph. Finally, before the merged result can be visualized by a UML modeling tool, the *TG2SD Transformer* transforms merged typed graphs back to Sequence Diagrams. Again, the transformation has been implemented in TXL.

An interactive graphical editor, *TG Editor*, based on the Eclipse Graphical Modeling Framework (GMF), is also provided. It allows for the creation, modification, and display of typed graphs. Moreover, it allows for the merge results to be validated through the examination of the typed graphs. To facilitate the overall Sequence Diagram integration process and to manage the data flows between components, the *Manager* has been implemented as an Eclipse wizard.

4.1 Evaluation and Observations

To evaluate the correctness of the implementation, we have run the prototype on a set of tests. The tests include, for instance, variations of the brokered sale. The merged results produced by the prototype were then visualized in RSA. Finally, the visualized results were manually inspected and compared with the expected results. These preliminary evaluation results show that the prototype was correctly implemented according to our general merge process. A more comprehensive evaluation involving different case studies and applications to some of the methodologies mentioned in the introduction are currently in progress.

We have made the following observations during the implementation and the evaluation of our prototype:

- An important step during integration is the discovery and specification of the correspondences between views. We agree with [2] that an explicit representation of these correspondences is unavoidable for a general and manageable notion of model integration. More work is necessary to alleviate the burden of discovering and specifying these relationships. A promising idea may be the use of high-level merge patterns. The identification of these patterns is subject of future work, but the brokered sale example, for instance, suggests that combinations and variations of, e.g., lifeline composition and refinement will be relevant here. By turning the identified patterns into user fillable templates, correspondences between views could be described in more high-level terms while the details are automatically generated. A complementary way to help identifying correspondences could be an activity similar to data schema matching [20].
- The UML Sequence Diagram syntax is slightly insufficient for the specification of the view correspondences. More precisely, it is impossible to select a portion of a lifeline between two occurrences that is not covered by an execution specification (in our formalization, the portion of the lifeline is a ***wait*** or ***rest*** message). A UML profile for typed graphs has been implemented as part of the prototype to remedy this situation. It can be optionally applied to Sequence Diagrams and allows a portion of a lifeline to be stereotyped as either a ***wait***, ***rest*** or derived message.
- The mathematical theory underlying our approach helped us structure our implementation, i.e., the prototype is clearly divided into several cohesive components and Java packages, each implementing a separate portion of the theory. Moreover, the prototype inherits some powerful properties from the theory. For instance, traceability between input and merged elements is easily achieved by our tool by following the span and the computed pushout. Finally, the typing information provided by typed graphs greatly facilitates consistency checking.
- Our approach to integration is quite general. Although we showed a two-way merge example, our merge process and prototype tool actually support multi-way merge with any number of scenarios and heads. Moreover, the merge process is not limited to Sequence Diagrams (or MSCs), but can be easily extended to other kinds of models, e.g., Communication Diagrams or Class Diagrams. In principle, every type of diagram representable as a directed, typed graph is amenable to our integration approach.

5 Related Work

The composition of behavior models has already been explored in different contexts. For instance, UML2 offers Interaction Overview Diagrams (IOD) [18], while MSCs have been generalized to high-level MSCs [10]. These diagrams are essentially graphs whose nodes represent scenarios and edges show the control flow between them. Thus, behaviors specified by nodes are considered non-overlapping. In contrast, we address the issue of how to specify overlap between scenarios, and then integrate them without duplication. A similar problem has been studied in semantic data modeling for a long time, where it is called *schema* or *view integration* (see the recent survey [1] and a widely cited paper [19]). Most work in view integration is non-generic in the sense that definitions and algorithms depend on the use of a particular modeling language. However, a general and data-model independent approach to the problem can be designed with category theory means [6]. The categorical framework has been used for schema merging in the contexts of database design [3] and metadata management [6], for early requirement engineering [23], and for software merge [17].

While view integration is well studied in the context of data modeling, only a few papers attempt to tackle the issue in behavior modeling [26,4], including a categorical approach to merging MSCs in [12]. The most important distinction of our approach is that we work with views augmented with derived elements because information considered basic in one view may be derived in another. This phenomenon is crucial to the integration problem and gives rise to an effective notion of refinement. Another distinction is that we allow for the specification of new information not captured by views during the identification of their overlap. In [12], categorical machinery is employed for merging partially-ordered multisets representing MSCs. Thus, the formalization in [12] is "string-based", rather than graph-based like ours. We argue that this change in representation makes the integration procedure less transparent and more difficult to learn. Finally, only injective morphisms are considered in [12], which might be a serious yet not relevant restriction. On the other hand, [12] considers also control structures in scenario modeling (high-level MSCs), which we leave for future work.

Recently, graph grammars have been proposed for the integration of aspects into different kinds of models (e.g., class diagrams, state machines, and sequence diagrams) [28,29]. A pattern language is used for the specification of the overlap between models and aspects. Compared to our work, the use of a pattern language to specify the relationships between models makes the approach more user-friendly. However, it also makes it less general and versatile because possibly quite different pattern languages need to be defined for different diagram types; since the pattern language needs to strike a delicate balance between expressiveness and usability, this step may not be straight-forward. Finally, our approach does not exclude the use of patterns and, moreover, may benefit from them. Yet we prefer to start with a general expression of model relationships and leave the identification of suitable patterns for a later stage of development.

Some work on the synthesis of state-based behavior models from scenarios involve the integration of scenarios as a by-product (see [16] for a survey). These approaches allow for complex forms of integration, and the labeling mechanism in [14] is clearly akin to our idea of explicit mappings ("arms"). However, our approach also allows us to include new information in the correspondence "head", which is not contained in any of the integrated models. As our brokered sale example illustrates, this new information can provide a new useful context into which the merged scenarios are placed. In addition, our approach inherits some useful properties from the underlying colimit operation (traceability and universality), which the majority of scenarios-from-state-machines procedures do not seem to offer.

Tools supporting tasks related to model management, particularly, model merging already exist, e.g., AMW [8] and Epsilon [13]. Conceivably, they could have been used to aid in the construction of our prototype. However, we chose to implement it without the use of existing merge tools because we wanted to study our approach in its purest form, unencumbered by the issues that can arise when encoding one theory in another. Moreover, we wanted to see to what extent the theory and its properties would be leveraged on the implementation level. We acknowledge, however, that the manual specification of mappings supported by AMW is similar to ours and could have been used for our mapping editor. In future work, it would be interesting to investigate the combination of AMW's automatic mapping generator or Epsilon's rule-based matching with our categorical approach.

6 Conclusions

We have presented an approach to integrating scenario-based models, particularly UML Sequence Diagrams, based on the colimit construction known from category theory. Our formalization of Sequence Diagrams as typed graphs retains the graphical nature of Sequence Diagrams, yet is amenable to algebraic manipulations and consistency checking. The approach provides traceability and guarantees that nothing is lost and nothing extra is acquired in the merge. Moreover, the algorithm is generalizable for other kinds of models and any number of models to be merged.

A prototype tool following the approach has been implemented. Initial evaluation has shown that the ideas presented in this paper represent promising steps towards more rigorous management of requirement models. However, the support for discovery and specification of model relationships needs to be improved.

References

1. Aleksandraviciene, A., Butleris, R.: A comparative review of approaches for database schema integration. Advances in Information Systems Development (2007)
2. Brunet, G., Chechik, M., Easterbrook, S., Nejati, S., Niu, N., Sabetzadeh, M.: A manifesto for model merging. In: 1st International Workshop on Global Integrated Model Management (GaMMa 2006), Shanghai, China (May 2006)
3. Cadish, B., Diskin, Z.: Heterogenious view integration via sketches and equations. In: Michalewicz, M., Raś, Z.W. (eds.) ISMIS 1996. LNCS, vol. 1079, Springer, Heidelberg (1996)
4. Desharnais, J., Frappier, M., Khédri, R., Mili, A.: Integration of sequential scenarios. IEEE Trans. Softw. Eng. 24(9), 695–708 (1998)
5. Dingel, J., Diskin, Z., Zito, A.: Understanding and improving UML package merge. Software and Systems Modeling (2008), doi:10.1007/s10270-007-0073-9
6. Diskin, Z.: Mathematics of generic specifications for model management. In: Encyclopedia of Database Technologies and Applications, Idea Group (2005)

7. Diskin, Z., Dingel, J., Liang, H.: Scenario integration via higher-order graphs. Technical Report 2006-517, Queen's University (2006), http://www.cs.queensu.ca/TechReports/Reports/2006-517.pdf
8. Del Fabro, M.D., Valduriez, P.: Semi-automatic model integration using matching transformations and weaving models. In: Sympos. on Applied Computing (2007)
9. Haugen, Ø., Husa, K., Runde, R., Stølen, K.: STAIRS: towards formal design with sequence diagrams. Software & Systems Modeling 4(4), 355–367 (2005)
10. ITU-TS. Recommendation Z.120: Message Sequence Chart (MSC) (2000)
11. Jacobson, I., Ng, P.: Aspect-Oriented Software Development with Use Cases. Addison-Wesley Professional, Reading (2004)
12. Klein, J., Caillaud, B., Hélouët, L.: Merging scenarios. In: 9th Int.Workshop on Formal Methods for Industrial Critical Systems. ENTCS, pp. 209–226 (2004)
13. Kolovos, D., Paige, R., Polack, F.: Merging Models with the Epsilon Merging Language (EML). In: Int. Conf. on Model Driven Engineering, Languages and Systems (MoDELS 2006) (2006)
14. Krüger, I., Grosu, R., Scholz, P., Broy, M.: From MSCs to statecharts. In: Int. Workshop on Distributed and parallel embedded systems, Norwell, MA, USA (1999)
15. Letkeman, K.: Ad-hoc modeling - Fusing two models with diagrams, http://www.ibm.com/developerworks/rational/library/07/0410_letkeman
16. Liang, H., Dingel, J., Diskin, Z.: A comparative survey of scenario-based to state-based model synthesis approaches. In: 5th International Workshop on Scenarios and State Machines, SCESM 2006 (2006)
17. Niu, N., Easterbrook, S.M., Sabetzadeh, M.: A category-theoretic approach to syntactic software merging. In: Int. Conf. on Software Maintainance (2005)
18. Object Management Group. Unified Modeling Language: Superstructure. version 2.1.2 Formal/2007-11-04 (2007)
19. Pottinger, R., Bernstein, P.: Merging models based on given correspondences. In: Proc. Very large databases, VLDB 2003 (2003)
20. Rahm, E., Bernstein, P.: A survey of approaches to automatic schema matching. VLDB Journal 10(4), 334–350 (2001)
21. Reenskaug, T.: Working With Objects: The OOram Software Engineering Method. Manning (1995)
22. Rumbaugh, J., Jacobson, I., Booch, G.: The Unified Modeling Language Reference Manual, 2nd edn. Addison-Wesley, Reading (2004)
23. Sabetzadeh, M., Easterbrook, S.: An algebraic framework for merging incomplete and inconsistent views. In: 13th Int.Conference on Requirement Engineering (2005)
24. Stevens, P.: On the Interpretation of Binary Associations in the Unified Modeling Language. Software and Systems Modeling 1(1) (2002)
25. TXL. About TXL (2007), http://www.txl.ca/nabouttxl.html
26. Uchitel, S., Chechik, M.: Merging partial behavioural models. In: 12th ACM SIGSOFT Int.Symposium on FSE, pp. 43–52. ACM Press, New York (2004)
27. VanHilst, M.: Role-Oriented Programming for Software Evolution. Ph.D. dissertation, Univ. of Washington, Dept. of Computer Science and Engineering (1997)
28. Whittle, J., Jayaramana, P.: MATA: A Tool for Aspect-Oriented Modeling based on Graph Transformation. In: Aspect-Oriented Modeling Workshop (2007)
29. Whittle, J., Moreira, A., Araújo, J., Rabbi, R., Jayaraman, P., Elkhodary, A.: An Expressive Aspect Composition Language for UML State Diagrams. In: Engels, G., Opdyke, B., Schmidt, D.C., Weil, F. (eds.) MODELS 2007. LNCS, vol. 4735. Springer, Heidelberg (2007)

Behavioral Modelling and Composition of Object Slices Using Event Observation

Iulian Ober[1], Bernard Coulette[1], and Younes Lakhrissi[1,2]

[1] Université de Toulouse - IRIT
118 Route de Narbonne, 31062 Toulouse, France
{iulian.ober,bernard.coulette,lakhriss}@irit.fr
[2] ACSYS, Faculté des Sciences de Rabat

Abstract. Some analysis and design methods for complex software systems lead to the specification of components (classes) by *slices*. It is the case of the use-case slicing technique proposed by Jacobson and Ng, and of view-based modelling proposed by Nassar et al. The composition of class slices is known from the literature to be closer to aspect composition than to traditional interface-based composition, but remains largely an open problem.

In this paper we propose a set of constructs to support the behavioral specification and composition of class slices, based on the idea of non-intrusive *event observation*. This allows slices to be specified separately – for example by different design teams – and to be integrated later without changes. The proposal is made in the context of VxUML, a language which supports view-based and use-case-driven separation of concerns.

1 Introduction

When tackling the complexity of large software systems, separation of concerns is essential for keeping the development process, the produced models and the code manageable. The separation of concerns can be done in different ways, but the objectives are always the same: being able to identify relatively independent "parts", so that they can be distributed to different actors of the process, be designed and built independently and, at the end, be integrated with the least possible effort and in a way which allows for future maintenance and evolution.

Traditional software decomposition methods rely upon a notion of *component*. A component is an entity which fulfills one or more functions in the overall system architecture and provides access to these functions via some form of *interface*. In general one end-user functional requirement is fulfilled by the collaboration of several components, and one component participates in fulfilling several requirements. In some extreme cases, small bits of functionality related to one requirement are spread over a very large number of components (a situation called *scattering*), and some components contain, beside their core functionality, bits of scattered functionality tightly interwoven (*tangling*). Such examples provided the motivation for aspect oriented programming [12].

K. Czarnecki et al. (Eds.): MoDELS 2008, LNCS 5301, pp. 219–233, 2008.

Recently there have been proposals for methods which aim to keep different concerns about end-user functional requirements separate throughout analysis, design and implementation. In general, this is done by superimposing a structure for functional decomposition over a (sufficiently resilient) component architecture. In this work, we concentrate on two related proposals: the use-case slicing approach of [9] and the view-driven approach of [15]. As we show in Section 2, both methods lead to designing objects (classes) as a composition of *slices*.

The subject of this work is the behavioral specification and composition of such object slices. The problem is known (see for ex. [9]) to be closer to aspect composition than to traditional interface-based composition. We propose a new behavior specification construct based on *event observation* and we show that this leads to good results in terms of slice coupling and support for incremental design (addition of slices).

The level of specification that we aim at is that of detailed, executable design models. We focus in particular on design models where state machines are used as operational behavior specifications for objects, something that is common in the design of reactive systems (e.g., embedded software, protocol layers, etc.). We integrate our proposal in VxUML, an executable UML profile which supports operational state machines and class slices (along the lines of [15]).

The paper is structured as follows: Section 2 discusses the motivation for this work, which comes from the necessity of flexible mechanisms for specifying and composing use-case slices and view-based slices. Section 3 describes the central concepts of our proposal: *events* and *probes*. Section 4 discusses (on an example) how these concepts are used for object slice specification and composition. We end the paper by comparing our proposal to some existing approaches (Section 5), and by drawing conclusions and the main lines of future work.

2 Object Slices: Background and Open Issues

In this section we briefly introduce the two design methods that we consider in this work, which both lead to the specification of classes as a composition of slices. We use as running example a hotel management system (the example also used throughout [9]). For brevity, we do not introduce the overall architecture and the whole set of requirements; we concentrate instead on the relevant aspects of one class, *Room*, which is involved in the realization of most of this system's use cases (reservation, customer check-in, check-out, maintenance, etc.)

We consider in particular the case of reactive objects, for which the behavior of slices is defined using state machines. Because slices can be cohesively attached to each-other, this leads to problems that are discussed at the end of the section on a motivating example.

2.1 Use-Case Slicing

Use-case slicing is an analysis and design discipline introduced in [9]. Its main prescription is that, for every identified use case of a system and for every component (class) participating in it, the aspects of the component pertaining to

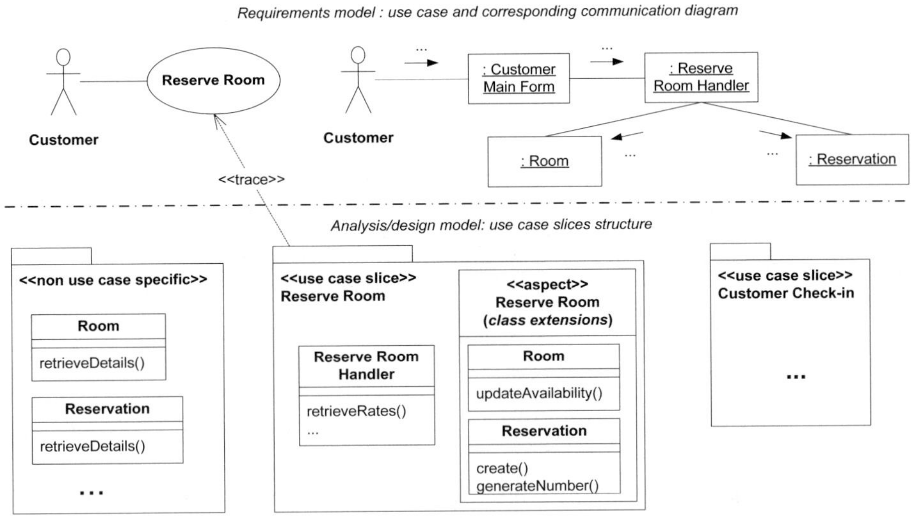

Fig. 1. Packaging of use case slices (as recommended in [9])

that use case are to be kept separate from the aspects pertaining to other use cases and from the aspects that are not use-case-specific. This prescription holds for analysis, design and implementation components. A *use-case slice* is a modelling element which contains the aspects specific to one use case, from all the involved classes.

Only the high-level principles for packaging slices are described in [9]. Figure 1 (extracted from the hotel management example) illustrates the main lines of the approach. For every use case identified in the requirements, there is a corresponding package in the analysis (and in the design) model, stereotyped as `<<use case slice>>`, containing the use-case-specific parts of every involved class (we call these *class slices*). Additionally, the analysis (design) model can contain component specifications limited to their non-use-case-specific features. Dependency relations (`<<trace>>`) allow to trace back from every slice to the originating use case from the requirements model.

The precise behavior specification and composition mechanisms for use-case slices are not further detailed in [9]. Moreover, executable object behavior descriptions based on state machines are not explicitly addressed. State machines are mentioned as a means to analyze object lifecycle, but they are left aside in detailed design.

2.2 View-Based Slicing

View-based slicing is an analysis and design discipline defined in [15]. It is based on the idea that a complex system usually has many external actors interacting with it, and that the concerns of the different actors can in general be separated and handled independently throughout system analysis and design.

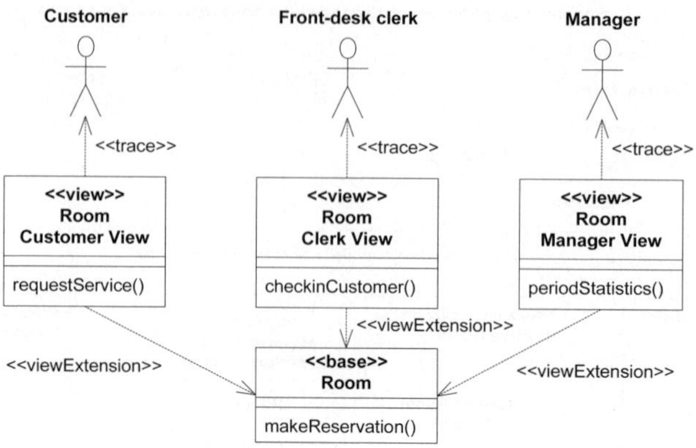

Fig. 2. Structure of a multi-view class in VUML [15]

While the separation lines are different from those recommended in use-case slicing, the principle of constructing each component (class) as a composition of slices containing distinct functionality remains the same. This is visible in the structure of the models (see the example in Figure 2): each *multi-view* class is specified via a *base* (grouping functionality that is not specific to any actor) and a set of actor-specific slices called *views*.

In the original view-based approach described in [15], only behavior specifications based on operations are discussed. Views are assumed to contain operations dedicated to a specific actor. This implies that the functionality captured in different views is strictly orthogonal, which is not always the case: the requests from different actors impact one another in general. Like for use-case slices, operational state machine specifications were not explicitly addressed.

2.3 State Machines: Semantic Choices

As we noted before, we are interested in the case where the complete executable specification of objects (slices) is given in terms of UML state machines. The UML standard [18] explicitly leaves open certain questions concerning the semantics of state machines, like *the concurrency model* (i.e. the semantics of active/passive objects, their relation to control threads), the precise semantics of *object interaction primitives* (how calls are handled by active objects, what is the relation between calls and state machine, etc.) or the *concrete syntax of actions* (used in transition effects and method bodies).

In order to have a semantically well-founded proposal, we have to make choices with respect to the aforementioned UML semantic variation points. In previous work we have participated to the definition of an executable profile for UML called Omega UML [6], for which we have developed execution and simulation tools [17]. The semantics of Omega UML is appropriate for the concepts proposed in this paper and convenient for rapid prototyping. Therefore we decided to integrate the same semantics into the VUML profile [15], resulting in an executable version of it to which we refer as VxUML.

For a complete definition of the Omega profile, we refer the reader to [6, 17]. Let us only note that the Omega concurrency and communication model corresponds largely to the semantics of UML in the Rhapsody tool [7] and that the concrete action syntax relies on conventions widely used in imperative object oriented languages (for example in Ada 2005).

2.4 Slices and State Machines: Problem and Motivating Example

As we already remarked, slices are closer to aspects than to stand-alone objects. This is because objects are loosely connected (in good designs), while slices are by construction tightly connected. A slice that extends the functionality of another slice cannot in general be specified based only on a black-box description of the extended slice, as it has to plug in at specific points of its behavior. However, it is desirable to be able to develop such slices independently, and in a way that allows integrating them without modifying the extended slice.

In the context of the hotel management system, we consider the example of a new view (and a corresponding use-case) being added to the requirements: the *room maintenance* view. We place the requirements on it:

- The maintenance can be triggered by various conditions (specific request from the manager or the front-desk clerk, elapse of a period, etc.). All the conditions are not specified a priori and it should be easy to add new ones.
- If the maintenance is triggered while the *Room* is unoccupied, a thorough check is performed.
- If the maintenance is triggered while the *Room* is occupied, maintenance is put on hold. If after N time units (days) the room is still occupied, a lightweight maintenance check is performed. A thorough check is performed only when the customer checks out.

These requirements can be realized by adding a *Room Maintenance* slice to the *Room* class. Figure 3 shows an informal analysis model of the state machine for *Room Maintenance*. The actual maintenance procedures are not detailed further.

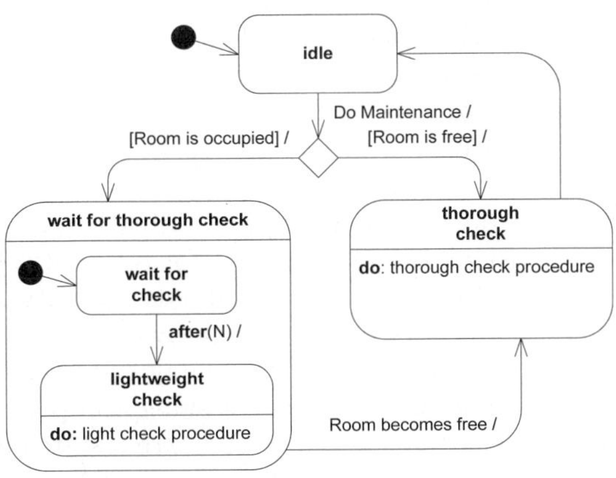

Fig. 3. Analysis state machine of the *Room Maintenance* slice

Explicit message-based communication is ill-adapted to specifying this type of slice: it implies modifying the other slices of *Room* (and possibly other classes) to introduce explicit calls for requesting maintenance (`Do Maintenance` trigger) and for signaling when the `Room becomes free`, as well as to ensure that check-in is delayed while the *Room* is in `thorough check`.

Our objective is to define the mechanisms allowing to write a self-contained executable specification of this slice without modifying the rest of the system. The idea is to let the slice specify precisely what *events* from the rest of the system it needs to *observe*, and how it reacts to them.

3 Behavior Specification Based on Event Observation

In this section we define the two essential notions of our proposal:

- *event*: a run-time entity which designates the occurrence of a particular condition in the execution of a software system/component, together with the relevant data for that occurrence.
- *probe*: a modelling construct which, for a given system execution, corresponds to an ordered set of *events* and allows to refer to these events in the system model (e.g., as triggers for some behavior).

While we introduce these notions in the context of VxUML, their definition is sufficiently generic so they can be appended to any language provided with a *structural operational semantics* (SOS, in the sense of [19]).

3.1 Events

We relate *events* to the smallest (i.e. indivisible) state changes described by the semantics of a model/language. In case of a structural operational semantics, events correspond to the transitions of the semantic *labeled transition system* (LTS) associated with a model.

SOS terminology. In SOS[19] the semantics of a program (or system model) is a labeled graph (LTS) whose vertices represent "*global states*" of the program, and whose edges (also called *transitions*) represent the smallest (atomic) steps executed by the program to go from one state to another. The graph paths which start in a global state identified as *initial* represent the possible *executions* of the program.

For a concurrent object-oriented language like VxUML, a global state includes the attribute values, states and request queues for all existing objects, as well as execution context (call stack, etc.) for all threads (activity groups). An LTS transition corresponds to the execution of an individual action by one object, such as: consuming an operation request from the queue, starting to fire a state machine transition, executing an assignment, issuing an operation request, etc. Note that an LTS transition is not to be confused with a state machine transition (from the state machine associated to a UML class): the latter is usually executed as a sequence of LTS transitions.

$$\frac{C : q \xrightarrow{[g]op(x)/\alpha} q', \begin{array}{l} \omega \in C \\ \omega.loc = q \\ \omega.v(g) = t \\ \omega.w = op(d).z \end{array}}{\Omega \xrightarrow{?op(d)} \Omega \begin{bmatrix} \omega.loc \mapsto \alpha \\ \omega.w \mapsto z \\ \omega.v \mapsto \omega.v[x \mapsto d] \end{bmatrix}}$$

Fig. 4. The *triggered operation input* transition rule

A *global state* is represented by an algebra whose signature obeys to some naming rules which give it a meaning. The LTS corresponding to a program/model is implicitly defined by a series of rules that may be used to construct it inductively. This means that *transitions* are not defined explicitly, but instead, a set of *transition rules* define the conditions under which a transition between two global states exists.

VxUML Events. In the case of VxUML, the semantics involves several types of atomic steps, each defined by a specific transition rule[1]. They include: object creation, object destruction, consuming an operation call, starting to fire a state machine transition, executing an assignment, issuing an operation call, returning a result from an operation, returning control from an operation, terminating a state machine transition (entering a state), and several others. Each LTS transition of one of the kinds mentioned above constitutes an event.

Event Data and Meta-Data. Every transition (event) in the SOS is defined in a particular context, and depends on a set of elements from the model (the program) and from the run-time that are specifically designated in the *transition rule* inducing it.

We take for example (Figure 4) the VxUML transition rule which defines an object performing a *triggered operation input* and subsequently firing a state machine transition. (For brevity, we do not include the whole VxUML SOS. Only the relevant elements of the rule are explained here, to the extent necessary for understanding the argument.)

The premise of the transition rule contains the contextual elements on which the application of the rule (and hence the *event*) depends. In particular, the *triggered operation input* event described here depends on:

– The existence of a class C *in the model*, containing a state machine, containing a transition from a state q to a state q', triggered by an operation

[1] In order to simplify the presentation, we consider here that the semantics of VxUML is directly defined as an SOS. This is in reality not the case, the semantics being given by a set of mapping rules to a different language (IF [3]), for which, in turn, SOS semantics is defined in [13].

op, guarded by a boolean expression g and having as effect a sequence of statements α. (This is the meaning of $C : q \xrightarrow{[g]op(x)/\alpha} q'$.)

- The existence at run-time, *in the global system state* Ω, of an object ω of class C ($\omega \in C$). ω should be precisely in state q ($\omega.loc = q$) and should have a request queue w containing in front position a request for op with a data parameter d ($\omega.w = op(d).z$). Moreover, the value of the guard g under the current attributes valuation v must yield true ($\omega.v(g) = t$).

Under these conditions, the transition rule states (in the bottom part) that a *triggered operation input* from the global state Ω is possible, and what the global state after this event is.

If the event is used as an interaction mechanism, i.e. it is *observed* by some other object, then the (model) *meta-data* and the (run-time system state) *data* mentioned above characterizes the event and needs also to be observable.

Note that the (meta-)data elements vary from one event type to another. For the operation input shown before, it includes: the concerned object (ω), its class (C), the machine state in which it was before the input (q), etc. For a different type of event, for example *object creation*, a different set of (meta-)data is relevant: the creator object, the class and reference of the created object, etc.

This context data constitutes what we call the *event parameters*. The *probe* construct, defined below as the language mechanism for manipulating events, offers access to these parameters.

3.2 Probes

A *probe* is a modelling construct which serves to identify and manipulate events that are relevant for a particular goal. In particular, we use probes for modelling implicit interaction between objects (see Section 3.3).

Analogy to Exception Objects. Probes must provide access to the event data and meta-data as outlined in Section 3.1. This is achieved by considering probes as being *objects* themselves. Their attributes store the relevant data of the last event matching them at any time during execution. A very good analogy from commonly used languages are *implicitly raised exception objects* in C++ or Java: they can be used for communication and for triggering behavior (when they are "caught"), and they are also objects themselves, with attributes carrying information about the context in which they were raised. The difference is that the activation of a probe by an event does not disrupt the normal execution if not used ("caught").

Elementary Probes. We argue that all interesting *probes* can be constructed based on (1) a limited number of *elementary probes* (roughly corresponding to the transition rules of the SOS) and (2) a set of *operations* derived from common set operations (union, intersection, complementing, projection).

We saw that events correspond to transitions from the semantic LTS. As such, each event has a *kind*, which is the *transition rule* of the SOS from which it is derived. We define *elementary probes* to correspond to these event *kinds*.

Since a model execution is a path $\mathcal{E} = (e_1, e_2, ...)$ in the semantic LTS, i.e. a sequence of events, a probe corresponds to a sub-sequence of these events. An *elementary probe* $\mathcal{P}$ corresponds to a *sub-sequence* $\mathcal{E}_\mathcal{P} = (e_{k_1}, e_{k_2}, ...)$ such that all e_{k_i} are of kind $\mathcal{P}$.

For example, in the case of VxUML, there will be an elementary probe $\mathcal{P}_{toinput}$ corresponding to the *triggered operation input* rule in Figure 4. This probe can be used to observe every event of type *triggered operation input*. We note that the number of SOS transition rules (and hence, the number of elementary probes) is usually quite small even for complex languages (around 15 for VxUML depending on how the semantics is defined).

Probe Operators. The semantic model of a probe is a *time-ordered sub-sequence* of the whole sequence of events generated in a system execution ($\mathcal{E}$). It is natural to allow probes to be composed using sequence operators: union, intersection, complement, projection.

The semantics of probe union, intersection and complement is self-explanatory. The projection operation allows to obtain from a probe $\mathcal{P}$ (with semantic model $\mathcal{E}_\mathcal{P}$) another probe $\mathcal{P}'$ whose semantic model $\mathcal{E}_{\mathcal{P}'}$ is a subsequence of $\mathcal{E}_\mathcal{P}$, based on a boolean condition on the event parameters.

Hereafter are two examples using the operators (for simplicity, we use the standard mathematical notations for probe operators):

- for identifying the triggered operation inputs that affect only a particular variable x one can take a projection of the elementary probe $\mathcal{P}_{toinput}$ (suppose the *.store* meta-data is a list of the attributes affected by an input):

$$\mathcal{P}_{toinput(x)} = \mathcal{P}_{toinput}\Big|_{x \in .store}$$

- for identifying the events that lead to modifying a particular variable x, one can take the union of $\mathcal{P}_{toinput(x)}$ (defined before) and of the probe matching *assignments* which affect x:

$$\mathcal{P}_{mod\,x} = \mathcal{P}_{toinput(x)} \quad \cup \quad \mathcal{P}_{assign}\Big|_{x \in .store}$$

Implicit Projections. In principle, the probe construct is orthogonal to all the other constructs of VxUML – in the sense that it serves a different purpose and it is not structurally related (contained into, etc.) to any other existing language construct. Therefore, in our model probes are defined as top-level constructs, on par with classes.

However, often one is interested in observing a particular kind of events only in a particular context (e.g., the *inputs* performed by one particular object). In principle, the projection operator presented before is sufficient for specifying the context, although in practice this may be syntactically awkward (for our example, one needs to explicitly designate the identity of the concerned object, raising the question of how this identity is referred to in the probe definition).

Therefore, it may sometimes be useful to define probes not as top-level constructs but within a context (e.g., inside a class), meaning that there is an implicit projection of the probe based on the context. This does not augment the expressive power of probes defined before, and is only syntactic sugar.

3.3 Behavior Specification and Composition with Probes

The purpose of introducing *probes* is to be able to identify *events* and use them for the behavioral specification of objects (slices). This is done by a construct allowing an object (slice) to *wait* for the arrival of an event e matching a probe $\mathcal{P}$. The natural place for such a construct is in the trigger of state machine transitions – therefore $wait(\mathcal{P})$ is defined as a new type of trigger.

Defining the semantics of *probe update* (i.e. the updating of $\mathcal{P}$'s attributes upon arrival of e) and *activation* (i.e. the triggering of a $wait(\mathcal{P})$ transition) implies making some choices. Among others, we have to decide whether the implicit communication that takes place between the object (slice) that produces the event and the one that *waits* for it is asynchronous (i.e. there is a memory of the activation status) or synchronous.

The semantics that we chose in VxUML is fully synchronous: e, the *update* of o, and the *activation* of subsequent transitions are executed atomically. In this semantics, the *wait* trigger works similarly to *condition variables* from Hoare's monitors [8] (also known from Java's `wait` and `notifyAll` primitives). For space reasons we refrain from further motivating our choices and from giving the complete SOS semantics.

3.4 UML Representation

This is a brief overview of the conventions employed for representing probes in VxUML (see examples in the next section):

- A probe defined in the context of a classifier is represented by a UML *Property* stereotyped as `<<probe>>`. If the probe is global (defined at top level) and there is no top level "system" class in the model, then the probe may be represented by an UML *InstanceSpecification*.

  In both cases, a probe is characterized by a name and a type. The type is either an elementary probe type like `OperationCallProbe`, or the abstract type `Probe` – when the probe may match events of different types, e.g., in case of unions.
- When the probe is defined by an expression with set operators, the expression is modeled as a constraint attached to the *Property* (or *InstanceSpecification*); in particular, the syntax for projection expressions is "`when` *boolean-condition*".
- A probe declaration can be placed inside a class (slice), meaning that there is one actual probe per instance of the class. In this case, the keyword `this` is used in the projection condition to denote the corresponding instance.

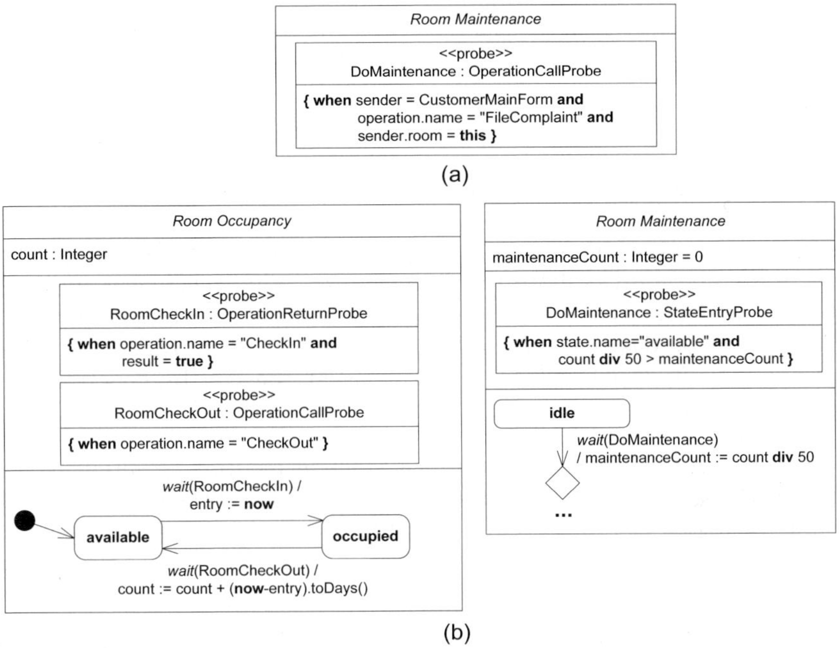

Fig. 5. Specification of the *Room Maintenance* slice with probes

4 Solution for Composition of Object Slices

The *probe* construct defined in the previous section is well-adapted for specifying use-case or view-based slices, as it allows to isolate the specification of the tight coupling between object slices in a way that the behavior specification of the slices themselves is not cluttered. We examine this on the *Room maintenance* example introduced in Section 2. As it was mentioned, the main problem is linking the behavior of this slice with that of other slices, in particular for triggering the `Do Maintenance` transition. We consider two examples:

- Room maintenance is triggered by a single event: whenever the Customer lodged in the Room files a complaint. In this case, one can simply use a `DoMaintenance` probe which monitors the operation call representing this action. Figure 5 (a) shows the declaration of the probe.
- Room maintenance is triggered by a more complex condition: whenever the *Room* is left by a customer, and it has been occupied for more than 50 days since the last maintenance. The test for this condition can be either embedded in the *Room Maintenance* slice, or it can be isolated in a separate slice specifically created for this purpose. In any case, the other slices need not be modified.

  Figure 5(b) shows the model corresponding to the second alternative. The new slice, called *Room Occupancy*, uses two *probes* for customer check-in and check-out, and counts the total occupation days in the `count` variable. The *Room Maintenance* slice, via the `DoMaintenance` probe, monitors whether the total occupation grows past a multiple of 50 when a customer checks out.

Note that in both examples, the executable (design) state machine of *Room Maintenance* slice remains very close to the analysis model from Figure 3 (the overall structure is the same, only the "informal" transition triggers are refined to probe triggers).

As it was mentioned in Section 2, one of the reasons for designing systems in slices is to be able to distribute the design tasks to independent actors/teams. Our experience shows that this type of process is well supported, since the slices may in general be designed based on undefined probes in a first time (using the abstract *Probe* type). Integration is done at the end by concretizing the definitions of probes.

A Note on Changing Requirements. In real projects requirements often change on the fly, and the design evolves with them. This means that slices can lately be added to a model, but also that the specification of existing slices may change over time (by adding new states, changing state names, adding transitions, etc.).

Probes provide support for the late definition of interfaces and bindings between object and/or slices (in the extreme case, at the very end of the development cycle, as suggested above). This form of modularity provides *isolation* in case of changing specifications. This means that the impact of a slice change on the rest of the system is often reduced to changing the definitions of the probes with which it interacts.

A Note on Spread Aspects. The *Room Maintenance* example is prototypical for what occurs in "localized" slices, i.e. slices that realize a functionality involving only a few objects (this is the case of functional use-case slices from [9] or of view-based slices).

In typical examples for aspect oriented programming, a functionality (usually an infrastructure-related one, like logging or access control) may be spread over a multitude of objects. Although there is no place for a full example, we maintain that our framework can be very effective for specifying such aspects. A logging functionality for example can be concentrated in a unique *logger* object, which observes all the relevant events throughout the system. In this case, probes are used for implicit communication between objects, instead of slices.

5 Related Work and Comparisons

Observation-Driven Specification. In [6] we defined an event-based framework for specifying execution timing constraints, using a dedicated *declarative* language. This work is a distant evolution of the ideas from [6], as the notions of event and probe defined here allow a generalized use of observation as object (slice) interaction mechanism.

Observation-driven behavior specification has to our knowledge not been proposed previously in the context of object-oriented modelling and programming languages. We took some inspiration in the concept of *observer*, introduced in [10] as a property specification formalism (and re-used in several other verification tools). Related ideas can also be found, under very different forms, in other domains like system tracing and debugging (see for example DTrace and the D language [14]) or autonomous agents.

Aspect-Oriented Programming. Although targeting the particular problem of designing systems by slices (view or use-case driven), our work has to be compared with results from the area of aspect-oriented modelling and programming. Indeed, designing systems by slices, like realizing cross-cutting concerns, inherently leads to tightly coupled components. Similarly to aspect-oriented frameworks, we are trying to cope with this by making part of the coupling *implicit*.

The body of literature dedicated to aspect models and languages is wide and growing rapidly. An important classification criterion for aspect frameworks concerns the constructs for defining *joinpoints* and their expressive power. In our framework, by combining event observation with the control structure of state machines, aspects can be triggered not only by individual events but by arbitrary patterns of events, with arbitrary conditions based on event data, etc. This is in general more expressive than what can be achieved in most "classical" aspect-oriented models, like the one of AspectJ [11], in which *joinpoints* are based mostly on syntactic conditions. However, a few recent proposals are closer to ours, in that they propose event (trace) based joinpoint models [20, 1], sometimes combined with a form of dynamic (run-time) weaving (e.g., [5, 16]).

In [20, 1, 16], joinpoints (sometimes called *tracecuts* because they are based on a multi-event trace) are defined in a declarative way, for example as a regular expression on events, and concern only sequential programs. The computational model that is closest to ours is the Concurrent Event-Based AOP (CEAOP) defined in [5], and which is based on the same principles of parallel composition of system components and aspects, and of event based synchronization. The main difference is that we define the characteristics of events and the probe construct, whereas in [5] events are just simple (uninterpreted) synchronization labels.

Aspects for state machine-based specifications are relatively less studied than their operation-oriented counterparts. SDMATA [21] is a transformation-based framework in which joinpoints are specified as state diagram patterns, and advices are specified as operations (element addition/deletion) on these patterns. The latest versions of the Motorola Weavr [4] introduce a similar framework, with a joinpoint model based on the structure of state machine diagrams and the possibility to modify this structure in aspects. Writing pattern-based aspects requires more than common programming skills and some knowledge of the structure of the UML state machines metamodel. Also, in our framework aspects are *interfaced* with the rest of the system based on a clearly determined set of *observable events*, whereas in SDMATA and in Veavr aspects are written in terms of the *structure* (i.e. *implementation*) of the state machines on which they are superposed. For this reason, we expect our observation-based aspects to be somewhat less sensitive to implementation changes in the rest of the system. On the negative side, these frameworks allow writing more intrusive aspects (by modifying and deleting elements – states, transitions, actions, etc.), while our framework offers only limited possibilities for this: for example, using the dynamic priority rules of Omega UML [6], one can give a higher priority to an aspect than to (a part of) the extended system, so that the extended system is blocked while the aspect executes, or use standard mechanisms in the aspect to terminate the execution of another object/slice.

Another framework that is somewhat related to ours is that of composition filters with superimposition [2]. Message filters are handlers which may intercept messages addressed to an object and perform some user-defined computation which can end by calling the corresponding method, by forwarding the message another object, or by taking any other course of action. However, in [2] filters only intercept messages that were explicitly sent to an object, and therefore there is no equivalent to the main feature of our proposal, which is to allow implicit communication between objects through observation.

6 Conclusions

This paper presents a modelling framework in which event observation is used as first-class object interaction mechanism. This is achieved mainly by formalizing the notion of *event* and its characteristics, and by defining a new modelling construct, the *probe*, which is used to match events and to manipulate event data.

The main (and motivating) application is the specification of tightly coupled components, such as those appearing in design methods based on use-case slicing or on view-based slicing. Frequently, the coupling between two components is unidirectional (*observed-observer*) and in such cases our framework reduces the burden of the designer by making part of this coupling implicit, and by avoiding most of the impact on the specification of the *observed* component.

We prototyped the constructs presented in this paper in a tool which translates (a subset of) VxUML to IF specifications [3]. This task was eased by the fact that IF is mainly dedicated to simulation and formal property verification, and it is easy to add a centralized event monitor to the platform. If the target is the final implementation, event observation must be done more efficiently, e.g. by code instrumentation based on a publish-subscribe pattern. We are currently experimenting with such an implementation. Among the difficulties we encounter, we note that the probe concept (in particular, access to event metadata) requires reflective support in the language in order to be fully satisfactory. Therefore, we orient our prototyping efforts on languages which offers such support (Java, Python).

References

[1] Allan, C., Avgustinov, P., Christensen, A.S., Hendren, L.J., Kuzins, S., Lhoták, O., de Moor, O., Sereni, D., Sittampalam, G., Tibble, J.: Adding trace matching with free variables to AspectJ. In: Proceedings of OOPSLA. ACM, New York (2005)

[2] Bergmans, L., Aksit, M.: Composing crosscutting concerns using composition filters. Commun. ACM 44(10), 51–57 (2001)
[3] Bozga, M., Graf, S., Ober, Il., Ober, Iu., Sifakis, J.: The IF toolset. In: Bernardo, M., Corradini, F. (eds.) SFM-RT 2004. LNCS, vol. 3185, pp. 237–267. Springer, Heidelberg (2004)
[4] Cottenier, T., van den Berg, A., Elrad, T.: Stateful aspects: The case for aspect-oriented modeling. In: Workshop on AOM at the 6th International Conference on AOSD, Vancouver (2007)
[5] Douence, R., Le Botlan, D., Noyé, J., Südholt, M.: Concurrent aspects. In: GPCE Proceedings, pp. 79–88. ACM, New York (2006)
[6] Graf, S., Ober, Il., Ober, Iu.: A real-time profile for UML. STTT 8(2), 113–127 (2006)
[7] Harel, D., Kugler, H.: The Rhapsody semantics of statecharts (or, on the executable core of the UML). In: Ehrig, H., Damm, W., Desel, J., Große-Rhode, M., Reif, W., Schnieder, E., Westkämper, E. (eds.) INT 2004. LNCS, vol. 3147, pp. 325–354. Springer, Heidelberg (2004)
[8] Hoare, C.A.R.: Monitors: An operating system structuring concept. Commun. ACM 17(10), 549–557 (1974)
[9] Jacobson, I., Ng, P.-W.: Aspect-Oriented Software Development with Use Cases. Object Technology Series. Addison-Wesley, Reading (2005)
[10] Jard, C., Monin, J.-F., Groz, R.: Development of Véda, a prototyping tool for distributed algorithms. IEEE Trans. Software Eng. 14(3), 339–352 (1988)
[11] Kiczales, G., Hilsdale, E., Hugunin, J., Kersten, M., Palm, J., Griswold, W.G.: An overview of AspectJ. In: Knudsen, J.L. (ed.) ECOOP 2001. LNCS, vol. 2072, pp. 327–353. Springer, Heidelberg (2001)
[12] Kiczales, G., Lamping, J., Mendhekar, A., Maeda, C., Lopes, C.V., Loingtier, J.-M., Irwin, J.: Aspect-oriented programming. In: Akşit, M., Matsuoka, S. (eds.) ECOOP 1997. LNCS, vol. 1241, pp. 220–242. Springer, Heidelberg (1997)
[13] Lakhnech, Y., Bozga, M.: IF-2.0 common language operational semantics. Technical report, VERIMAG (September 2002)
[14] McDougall, R., Mauro, J., Gregg, B.: Solaris(TM) Performance and Tools: DTrace and MDB Techniques for Solaris 10. Prentice Hall, Englewood Cliffs (2006)
[15] Nassar, M., Coulette, B., Crégut, X., Ebersold, S., Kriouile, A.: Towards a view based unified modeling language. In: ICEIS (3), pp. 257–265 (2003)
[16] Navarro, L.D.B., Südholt, M., Vanderperren, W., De Fraine, B., Suvée, D.: Explicitly distributed AOP using AWED. In: AOSD, pp. 51–62. ACM, New York (2006)
[17] Ober, Iu., Graf, S., Ober, Il.: Validating timed UML models by simulation and verification. STTT 8(2), 128–145 (2006)
[18] Object Management Group. Unified Modeling Language, `http://www.omg.org/spec/UML/`
[19] Plotkin, G.D.: A structural approach to operational semantics. J. Log. Algebr. Program 60-61, 17–139 (2004)
[20] Walker, R.J., Viggers, K.: Implementing protocols via declarative event patterns. In: SIGSOFT FSE Proceedings, pp. 159–169. ACM, New York (2004)
[21] Whittle, J., Moreira, A., Araújo, J., Jayaraman, P.K., Elkhodary, A.M., Rabbi, R.: An expressive aspect composition language for UML state diagrams. In: Engels, G., Opdyke, B., Schmidt, D.C., Weil, F. (eds.) MODELS 2007. LNCS, vol. 4735, pp. 514–528. Springer, Heidelberg (2007)

Scenario-Based Static Analysis of UML Class Models

Lijun Yu, Robert B. France, and Indrakshi Ray

Computer Science Department, Colorado State University, USA
{lijun,france,iray}@cs.colostate.edu

Abstract. Static analysis tools, such as OCLE and USE, can be used to analyze structural properties of class models. The USE tool also provides support for analyzing specified operations through interactive simulations in which users provide operation parameters, and manually assign values to state elements to reflect the effect of an operation. In this paper we describe an approach to statically analyzing behavior that does not require a user to manually simulate behavior. The approach involves transforming a class model into a static model of behavior, called a Snapshot Model. A Snapshot Model characterizes sequences of snapshots, where a snapshot describes an application state. A scenario describing a sequence of operation invocations can be verified against a Snapshot Model using tools such as USE and OCLE. We illustrate our approach by verifying a scenario against a Snapshot Model that describes the behavior of some operations in a role-based access control (RBAC) application.

Keywords: UML, Model Analysis, Behavioral Properties, Snapshot.

1 Introduction

Tool-supported rigorous analysis of design models can enhance the ability of developers to identify potentially costly design problems earlier. Correcting design problems early also reduces effort spent on implementing faulty designs. Our work on developing lightweight techniques for rigorously analyzing design-level class models focuses on providing answers to the following questions:

- How can we verify that a scenario (a sequence of object interactions) is valid with respect to behavior specified in a class model?
- How can we leverage existing UML static analysis tools when verifying scenarios?

Static analysis tools such as OCLE [Chiorean] and USE [Richters] [Gogolla07] can be used to analyze structural properties expressed in class models. These tools are used to check that object configurations conform to constraints expressed in class models. The USE tool also provides some support for checking operation specifications expressed in the Object Constraint Language (OCL) [OCL]. USE provides a facility that allows a user to interactively simulate the behavior of an operation by entering commands that change the states of objects. The state at the end of a simulation is checked by USE to determine if the operation's post-condition holds. Interactive simulation of operation behavior is useful, but can be tedious, time-consuming

K. Czarnecki et al. (Eds.): MoDELS 2008, LNCS 5301, pp. 234–248, 2008.

and error-prone when one has to manually simulate a number of operations in a scenario involving many interactions.

In this paper, we show how static analysis tools such as OCLE and USE can be used to support lightweight analysis of operation specifications without the need for manual operation simulations. In the approach, an application design model is transformed to a *Snapshot Model* that characterizes valid sequences of snapshots. A *snapshot* is an object configuration that describes a system state. A sequence of object interactions, called a *scenario*, is then checked against the invariants defined in the Snapshot Model.

In a previous paper we described an early version of the analysis technique that applied only to class models with operation specifications expressed in a highly-restricted form of the OCL [Yu]. In that version, each operation specification is converted to a parameterized invariant that is used to generate an invariant that is specific to a scenario under analysis. The parameters are operation arguments and references to before and after states of the object performing the operation (referred to as the target object). Before checking a scenario against a Snapshot Model, the parameterized invariants are instantiated with the actual arguments and references to target object states defined in the scenario to obtain Snapshot Model invariants. A modeler could then use OCLE or USE to check that the scenario conforms to the invariants expressed in the Snapshot Model.

The technique described in this paper improves upon the early version in the following ways: (1) There are no restrictions on operation specifications other than those imposed by tools such as USE and OCLE; (2) The operation specifications are directly transformed to Snapshot model invariants; there is now no need to instantiate parameterized invariants for each scenario; (3) Descriptions of scenarios, called *Scenario Models*, are used to generate sequences of snapshots that are checked against Snapshot Models. We also present a model verification process to support the use of the technique.

The rest of the paper is organized as follows. In Section 2 we give an overview of the process supporting systematic use of the lightweight analysis technique. In Section 3 we present the example used to demonstrate the technique. In Section 4 we provide an example application of the technique, and present an algorithm for producing Snapshot Models from design class models, and another for producing snapshot sequences from Scenario Models. In Section 5 we discuss related work, and in Section 6 we summarize our contributions and give pointers to future directions.

2 An Overview of the Verification Process

One way of leveraging static analysis tools in the analysis of scenarios is to build a class model, referred to as a Snapshot Model, which characterizes valid sequences of snapshots. This allows for the treatment of scenarios as instances (sequences of snapshots) that can be checked against a Snapshot Model. Tools such as OCLE and USE can be used without modification to check scenarios against Snapshot Models.

The technique described in this paper takes a design class model and transforms it into a Snapshot Model. *Scenario Object Models* describes sequences of snapshots and are generated from Scenario Models. A Scenario Model is a UML sequence model annotated with descriptions of operation effects. The operation effects are described using an action language called JAL (Java-like Action Language) [Dinh-Trong].

An overview of the process supporting the use of the technique is shown in Fig. 1. Two major roles are involved in the process: The *designer* and the *verifier*. The designer creates an Application Model consisting of a design-level class model with operation specifications written in OCL. Each class has fully defined attributes (that is, each attribute has a defined type, cardinality, and visibility) and each operation is associated with a specification consisting of pre- and post-conditions. The verifier creates Scenario Models describing scenarios that are to be verified against the behavior defined in an Application Model. Scenario Models are like test-cases in that they validate application model behavior.

A Scenario Model reflects the understanding a verifier has of how objects should interact in a scenario. The verifier must have access to the Application Model when creating a Scenario Model in order to determine the classes and the operations that can be called. A scenario described by a Scenario Model is classified by the verifier as either good or bad: A *good scenario* is one that the verifier claims is valid, and a *bad scenario* is one that the verifier claims is invalid.

The verification process consists of three major steps, as shown in Fig. 1.

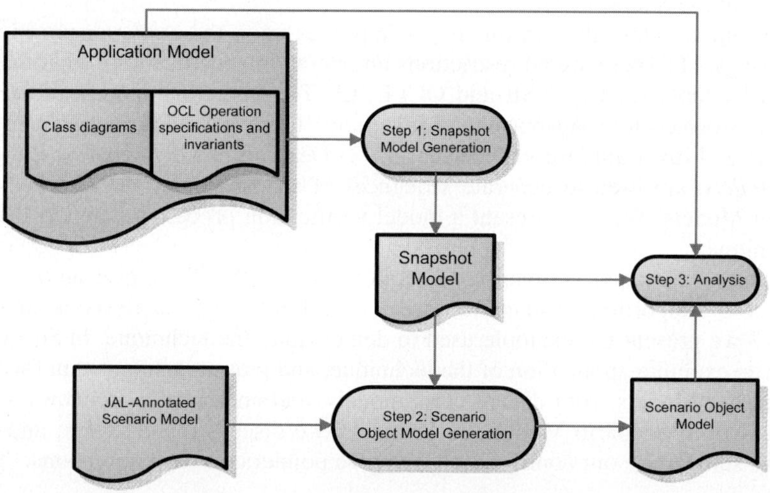

Fig. 1. Overview of the analysis process

In Step 1 a Snapshot Model is produced from an Application Model by introducing (1) a Snapshot class whose instance, called snapshots, represent states and (2) a hierarchy of Transition classes whose instances are pairs of snapshots, where a pair represents the before and after states of an operation execution (see Fig. 2). An instance of the Snapshot class is called a *snapshot object*. A snapshot object is a configuration of object states that describes a state of an application. It is important to note that a snapshot object consists of immutable instances of classes representing object states. A Transition class has a *before* and *after* association with the Snapshot class. Each specialization (derived class) of a Transition class corresponds to an operation in the

Application Model and it defines transitions triggered by the operation. The properties of a specialized Transition class (i.e., its basic attributes and associations) represent (1) the parameters of the corresponding operations, (2) the target object state in the before snapshot (i.e., the before state of the object performing the operation), and (3) the target object state in the after snapshot (i.e., the after state of the object performing the operation). The operation specification is transformed to an invariant defined in the context of the specialization.

An example of a Snapshot Model produced from a simplistic Application Model is shown in Fig. 2. The Snapshot Model shown in Fig. 2(b) shows a *Snapshot* class that consists of instances representing states of objects defined by classes in the Application Model. For example, the class A in the Snapshot Model represents states of the objects defined by the class A in the Application Model.

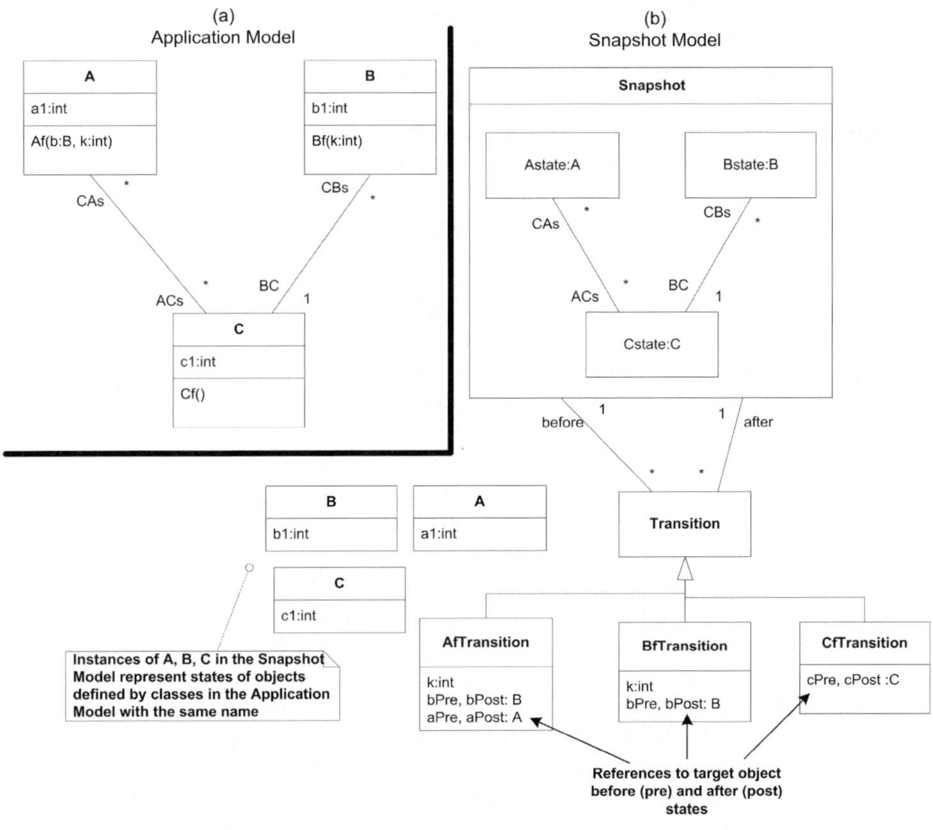

Fig. 2. Example of a Snapshot Model produced from an Application Model

The *Transition* class has three specializations: *AfTransition* represents transitions caused by the operation *Af()* in *A*, *BfTransition* represents transitions caused by the operation *Bf()* in *B*, and *CfTransition* represents transitions caused by the operation *Cf()* in *C*. The properties in each of these transition classes are the parameters and before and after states of the target objects of the corresponding operations. For example, the class *AFTransition* has (1) an attribute *k* representing the integer parameter of *Af()*, (2) two attributes, *bPre* and *bPost* representing the before and after states of the *B* reference parameter in *Af()*, and (3) two attributes, *aPre* and *aPost*, representing the before and after states of the operation's target object. Operation specifications and their corresponding invariants are not shown in this example. A more detailed example of a Snapshot Model is described in Section 4.

The technique is applicable to models of systems in which operations are executed sequentially, and thus a transition in the Snapshot Model is associated with only one triggering operation.

In Step 2, a Scenario Model developed by a verifier is used to produce a model of a sequence of snapshot transition instances. The Scenario Object Model consists of instances of Snapshot and Transition classes produced from the Scenario Model. An example of a Scenario Model and an algorithm for generating Scenario Object Models from Scenario Models are given in Section 4.

In Step 3, an OCL-based static analysis tool (e.g., USE, OCLE) can be used to verify the validity of the Scenario Object Model. If a good scenario is valid, or if a bad scenario is invalid with respect to a Snapshot model, then the Scenario Model and the Snapshot Model are consistent with each other. If a good scenario is found to be invalid, or a bad scenario is valid with respect to a Snapshot Model, then the Snapshot and Scenario Models have inconsistent descriptions of behavior.

3 A Role-Based Access Control Example

Role-based access control (RBAC) is the de facto access control model used in commercial organizations. In RBAC, users are assigned to roles, and roles are associated with permissions that determine what operations and data a user playing the role can access. The users initiate sessions in which they activate a subset of roles assigned to them. The operations that a user can perform in a session depend on the permissions associated with the activated roles. To simplify role management, roles are organized in the form of a hierarchy that reflects the organizational structure. The ordering relation is known as the dominance relation. The dominance relation is reflexive, transitive and anti-symmetric. A dominating role can have two types of hierarchy – permission inheritance hierarchy and role activation hierarchy. In permission inheritance hierarchy, a dominating role inherits the permission assigned to a dominated role. In role activation hierarchy, a dominating role can activate a dominated role. Constraints can be specified on the RBAC model to prevent conflict of interests occurring in an organization. Specifically, there are two types of constraints – Static Separation of Duties (SSD) and Dynamic Separation of Duties (DSD). These are defined as relationships between roles. SSD requires that conflicting roles should not be assigned to the same user. DSD imposes a more relaxed requirement – it allows conflicting roles to be assigned to the same user, but does not allow conflicting roles to be activated in the same session.

We use the RBAC example to illustrate our approach. Although we verified both the SSD and DSD properties, we show the analysis of SSD property only in this paper. Note that, the DSD property is more complex and is not shown in this paper for lack of space. The part of the RBAC model used in this paper is shown in Fig. 3. This partial RBAC model shows only the relationships admin, roles and users. The figure also does not show all the operations belonging to these classes, such as unassign roles. Missing from the model are the classes corresponding to sessions and permissions and their associated operations, such as, check access, activate and deactivate roles. We do not show these elements because they are not used in the scenario we analyze.

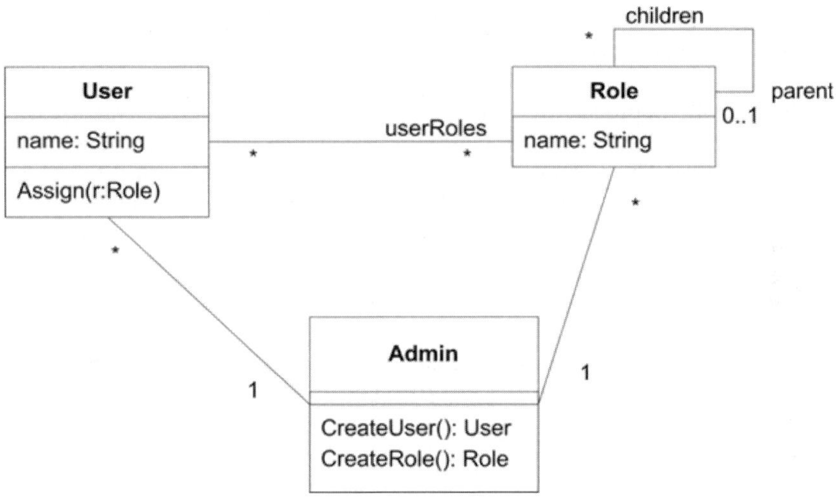

Fig. 3. Partial RBAC class model

The operation specifications of the RBAC model used later to demonstrate the generation of invariants on Transition classes in a Snapshot Model are given below:

```
  //pre- and post- conditions of the Assign method
  context User::Assign(role:Role)
  pre: self.assignedRoles->forAll(r | r.name <>
role.name)
  post: self.assignedRoles->exists(r | r.name =
      role.name)
     and self.assignedRoles@pre->forAll(r1 |
         self.assignedRoles->exists(r2 | r1.name =
         r2.name))
     and (self.assignedRoles->size() = self. as-
         signedRoles@pre->size() + 1)

  //Query method to check the role hierarchy relationship
  context Role::isDominating(roleName:String):Boolean
  pre:true
  post:
  if self.name = roleName then
      result = true
```

```
else
    if self.dominating->size() = 1 then
        result = false
    else result =
        (self.dominating.isDominating(roleName))
    endif
endif
```

The static separation of duty (SSD) property of RBAC restricts the assignment of conflicting roles to one user. This property is expressed as an invariant on the *User* class. The SSD property is one of the properties that we verify an example scenario against.

To illustrate the approach we will analyze a scenario involving two users, Alice and Bob, and the following roles: Cashier, Accountant, Senior Accountant, Senior Cashier and Teller. The Senior Accountant role dominates the role of Accountant. The SSD property in this application is the following: The role Accountant and Cashier cannot be assigned to the same user, and any role dominating the Accountant role and any role dominating the Cashier role cannot be assigned to the same user. The specification of this SSD property is given below:

```
context User
//Static separation of duty constraint
inv SSD: not (self.assignedRoles->exists(r | r.name =
       "Accountant")
   and self.assignedRoles->exists(r| r.name = "Cash-
    ier"))
//Static separation of duty with role hierarchies
inv SSD_RH: not (self.assignedRoles->exists(r |
       r.isDominating("Accountant"))
    and self.assignedRoles->exists(r |
       r.isDominating("Cashier")))
```

The scenario that will be analyzed is described by the following sequence of interactions (space does not allow us to show the sequence diagram but its form can be inferred from what follows): (1) user Bob is assigned Accountant role through a call to the *Assign()* operation, (2) Bob is then assigned SeniorCashier role through a call to the *Assign()* operation. This scenario is classified as a bad scenario, that is, it is a scenario that the verifier expects will violate a property in the Application Model (specifically, the SSD property).

4 Applying the Analysis Technique

In this section we describe, through an example, the verification process (see Fig. 1). We use the RBAC example described in the previous section to illustrate each step of the process.

Step 1: Snapshot Model generation

The Snapshot Model is formed by (1) creating a Snapshot class, (2) creating a hierarchy of Transition classes, and (3) converting operation specifications to invariants on instances of the Transition classes. In the following we outline the algorithm for creating a Snapshot Model. The RBAC application class model is used to illustrate the tasks outlined in the algorithm.

1.1. Create a Snapshot class:
The Snapshot class is a structured class that consists of a configuration of UML parts representing object states. Each part represents a set of object states and is thus associated with a class in the design class model. The configuration of parts is the same as the configuration of objects defined in the design class model. For example, the Snapshot class for the partial RBAC design model in Fig. 4 consist of a configuration of parts, where the *admin* part represents a state of the *Admin* object (*Admin* is a singleton class), the *users* part represents states of *User* objects and the *roles* part represents states of *Role* objects. The states are defined by classes in the Snapshot Model that have the same name as the corresponding classes in the design class model.

***1.2. Create a Transition class hierarchy with before and after associations to the Snapshot class*:** A Transition class is created for each operation in the design class model. A superclass called *Transition* that has before and after associations to the Snapshot class is also created (see the Transition class in Fig. 4). Given an operation, a Transition class with the name *ClassName_operationName_Transition*, where *className* is the name of the target object's class in the design class model and *operationName* is the operation's name, is created as follows:

- Create a Transition class property that references the before state of the operation's target object and another that references the after state of the target object. The property referencing the before state is named *classNamePre*, and the other property is named *classNamePost*. For example, in Fig. 4, the *Admin_CreateUser_Transition* class has attributes *adminPre* and *adminPost*, which are references to before and after states for the target *Admin* object of the *CreateUser()* operation.
- For each value (i.e., non-object) parameter in the operation, create a class property (attribute) with the same name and type in the Transition class. For each parameter that is an object reference, create two class properties with the same type as the object reference. One of the properties represents the before state of the object and is thus named *parameterNamePre*, and the other represents the after state of the object and is named *parameterNamePost*. For example, the operation *Assign()* in the *User* class has a reference to a role as a parameter, and this parameter is transformed to the attributes *rPre* and *rPost* in the *User_Assign_Transition* class shown in Fig. 4. The parameters that represent before and after object states are collectively referred to as *preState* and *postState* attributes.
- If there is a return parameter, create a property *ret* with the same type as the return parameter. For example, the *CreateRole()* operator in the *Admin* class returns a reference to a role object, and this return value is represented by the attribute *ret* in *Admin_CreateRole_Transition* class shown in Fig. 4.

***1.3. Generate Transition invariants from operation specifications*:** This critical task is also the most involved. We use the *Assign()* operator defined in the *User* class to illustrate the major aspects of the task. For each operation specification in the design class model, produce an invariant as follows:

- Replace all references to self in the pre-condition by the name of the Transition class attribute representing the target object before state (all references to self must be explicit in the operation specification for this to work). Also, replace all references to an object parameter in the pre-condition by the name of the attribute representing the before state of the object, and replace all references to the object in the post-condition by the name of the attribute representing the object's after state.
  EXAMPLE: The precondition of the *Assign()* operation,
  ```
  self.assignedRoles->
  forAll(r|r.name<>role.name)
  ```
  is transformed to (changes are in bold print)
  ```
  userPre.assignedRoles->
  forAll(r | r.name <> rPre.name)
  ```
- Replace all references to self in an expression involving @pre by the name of the attribute representing the before state of the object.
  EXAMPLE: The *Assign()* post-condition clause
  ```
  self.assignedRoles@pre-> ...
  ```
  is transformed to
  ```
  userPre.assignedRoles-> ...
  ```
- Replace all references to self in the post-condition that are not part of a @pre expression by the name of the attribute representing the after state of the target object.
  EXAMPLE: The *Assign()* post-condition clause
  ```
  self.assignedRoles->exists(...
  ```
  is transformed to
  ```
  userPost.assignedRoles->exists(...
  ```
- Add constraints that assert the existence of the object states referenced by preState attributes in the before states. The constrain has the form before.*partName* -> includes(*namePre*). Similarly, add constraints that assert the existence of the object states referenced by postState attributes.
  EXAMPLE: The following clauses assert the existence of the target user states in the before and after states of the snapshot respectively:
  ```
  before.users:User->includes(userPre)
  after.users:User->includes(userPost)
  ```
- Add constraints stating that objects which have not had their state changed in an operation have the same before and after state. These constraints can take two forms as illustrated in the examples given below:
  EXAMPLE: The constraint stating that the set of session objects is unchanged by the *Assign()* operation is stated below:
  ```
  after.sessions:Session = before.sessions:Session
  ```
  The constraint stating that the user objects not affected by the operation have the same before and after states is stated below:
  ```
  after.users:User->excluding(userPost)=
  before.users:User->excluding(userPre)
  ```

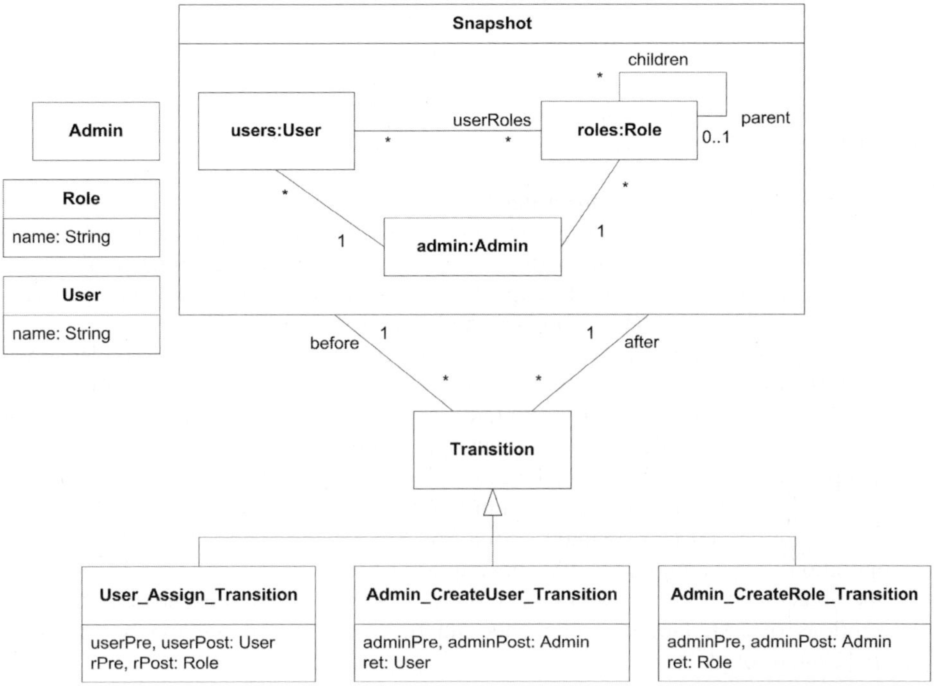

Fig. 4. RBAC snapshot model

The invariant for the User_Assign_Transition class is given below (the parts in bold are fragments added by the transformation process as discussed above):

```
context User_Assign_Transition
//From Assign() pre-condition
before.users:User->includes(userPre) and
before.roles:Role->includes(rPre) and
userPre.assignedRoles->
forAll(r | r.name <> rPre.name) and
//From Assign() post-condition
after.users:User->includes(userPost) and
after.roles->includes(rPost) and
  userPost.assignedRoles->
  exists(r | r.name = rPost.name) and
userPre.assignedRoles->
  forAll(r1|userPre.assignedRoles->
    exists(r2 | r1.name = r2.name)) and
  userPost.assignedRoles->size() =
      userPre.assignedRoles->size() + 1 and
after.users -> excluding(userPost) =
      before.users:User->excluding(userPre) and
after.roles:Role = before.roles:Role and
after.sessions:Session = before.sessions:Session and
after.admin:Admin = before.admin:Admin
```

In this RBAC model a system state is a configuration of user and role states that are linked as specified in the RBAC class model.

Fig. 4 shows the result of applying the process to the RBAC model. One subclass of Transition is populated for *Assign(), CreateUser(), and CreateRole()* operations and related parameters are created.

Step 2: Scenario Object Model generation

A Scenario Object Model describes a sequence of snapshot transitions, that is, it describes how a system state transits to a next system state as a consequence of an operation invocation. Sequences of snapshot transitions are generated from scenarios described using JAL-annotated sequence models called Scenario Models.

An example of a Scenario Model is shown in Fig. 5. The RBAC scenario described in Fig. 5 involves the activities performed in the order presented: Creation of a session, the creation of two roles (accountant and cashier), and then the assignment of the roles to a user identified by Bob. Each operation invocation in the scenario determines a pair of snapshot object: the before and after snapshots. The pair for one of the *Assign()* operation invocations is shown in Fig. 6.

Each operation call is associated with a JAL statement that describes the effect of the operation. For example, the JAL description of the *CreateUser()* operation states that the object *user* is created and added to the set of *users* linked to the *admin* object. Descriptions of JAL language elements can be found in our previously published papers [Dinh-Trong].

In a scenario, operation invocations may spawn calls to other operations. For example, a *Transfer* operation in a *Bank* class may call an operation *Withdraw* to take out money from the source account and then call an operation *Deposit* to add the

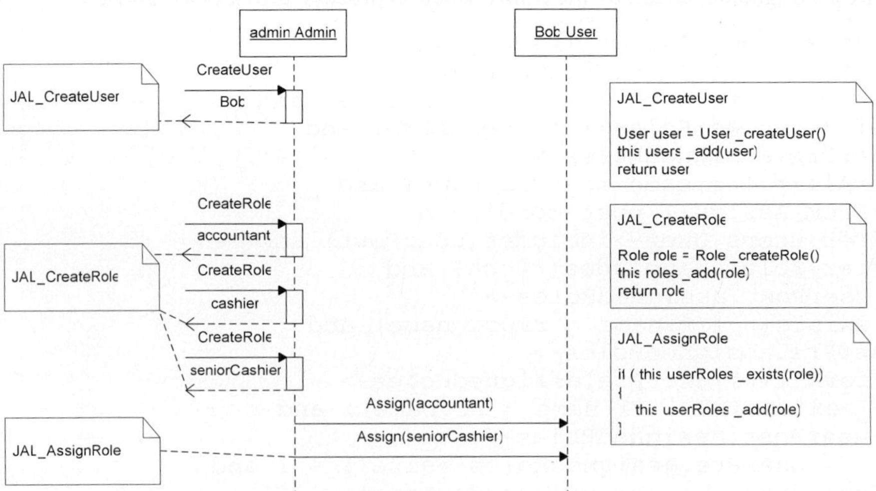

Fig. 5. A Scenario Model

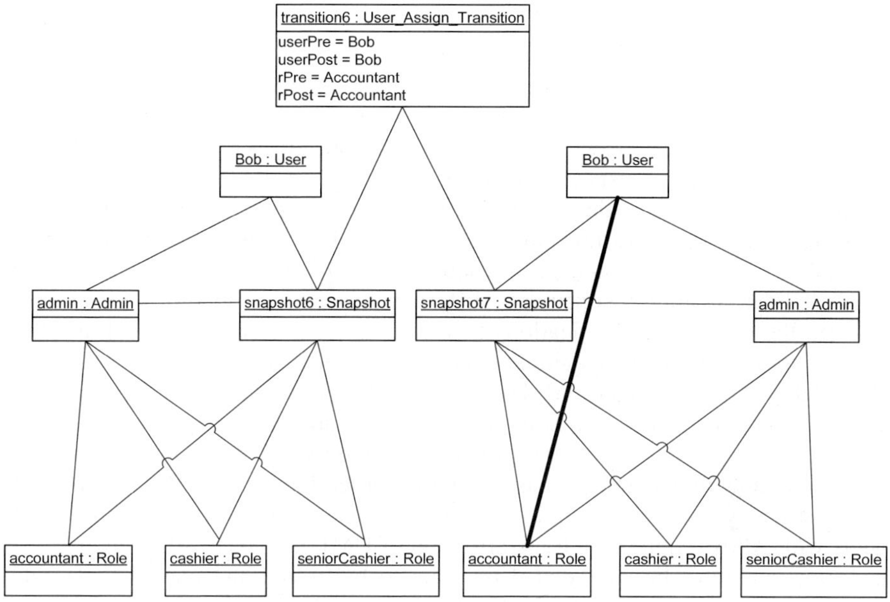

Fig. 6. Assign Accountant role snapshot transition

money to the destination account, before returning a result to the caller. In our approach we do not generate state transitions for each operation that is spawned from an encompassing operation. The operation specifications in OCL specify only the states before and after, and thus there is no need to build up the effect of an operation using the effects of the spawned operations. For this reason, spawned operations are treated as internal operation details that are hidden for analysis purposes and thus are not shown in Scenario Models.

A Scenario Object Model is obtained by executing the scenario and retaining the execution trace as a sequence of snapshot transitions. Animation tools such as UMLAnT [Dinh-Trong] can be used for this purpose.

Step 3: Check Scenario Object Model against the Snapshot Model

In this step the Scenario Object Model and the Snapshot Model are fed into a tool such as USE to determine if the sequence of transitions conforms to the invariants specified in the Snapshot model. For the RBAC example we analyzed scenario described in Fig. 5 against the Snapshot model shown in Fig. 4. We used the OCLE tool. The OCLE reported an error arising from the assignment of two conflicting roles to the same user: The *SeniorCashier* dominates *Cashier* and *Cashier* conflicts with *Accountant*. We also performed a second analysis involving a dynamic separation of duty (DSD) property which prohibits some roles assigned to a user to be activated at the same time in a session. As we expected OCLE reported an error arising from the activation of two conflicting roles in the same session created by *Bob*.

5 Related Work

Existing UML modeling tools like OCLE [Chiorean] and USE [Richters] provide support for validating syntactic and structural properties. OCLE [Chiorean] for example can detect syntactic errors in models and syntax errors in OCL specifications. OCLE also checks the consistency of OCL invariants on objects or object diagrams. A limitation of OCLE is that it currently does not support analysis of scenarios against operation specifications in class models. The latest version of USE tool [Gogolla07] validates pre- and post- conditions in interactive command mode. The way we validate operation constraints differs from how it is done in USE in that we transform the operation specifications to invariants of a Snapshot Model and thus a user does not have to manually simulate behavior to analyze a scenario.

The Alloy Analyzer [Jackson] developed by the Software Design Group of MIT generates examples or counter-examples of certain properties by exploring a search space given by limiting the number of entities in the model. Alloy models systems in a structural modeling language based on first-order logic. Alloy has been used to check abstract system designs and specification consistencies. The checking of UML models with Alloy requires the transformation of UML models to Alloy models. Such transformations must be validated if they are to be trusted and one must be able to trace errors in Alloys to errors in UML models. These are currently challenging problems.

Model checking has been applied to automate the verification of the safety and correctness of finite state-based systems [Clark]. There is research work that applies model checking techniques to the analysis of UML behavioral models. vUML [Lilius] is a tool to automatically convert UML statecharts to PROMELA specifications and invoke SPIN to verify the desired properties and inconsistencies. Eshuis [Eshuis] applied symbolic model checking to the analysis of UML activity models. The activity models are formalized and transformed to the input language of NuSMV. The translations are used to check the data integrity constraints of UML activity diagram and class diagrams in the workflow represented in the activity models. As with Alloy, a translation process is needed to convert the UML specifications into a model that can be verified by the model checker. The limitation of model checking techniques is that they suffer from state explosion problem. Compared with our approach that analyzes UML class models and constraints, model checking techniques are typically applicable to state-based models such as UML statecharts and activity models.

Static model analysis is useful in verifying design models. Ray et. al. [Ray] model RBAC and MAC access control policies with parameterized UML and compose the models. The static analysis on the composed models can find undesirable violations to the access control policies. However, the proposed approach is manual. The work on this technique was motivated by the problems we encountered with analyzing these types of models using existing techniques.

Testing techniques are applied to UML models to check design faults. Dinh-Trong [Dinh-Trong] proposed a systematic approach to testing UML designs. In the approach test cases are generated from a set of test adequacy criteria on the UML design model. Java is used to formally define execution semantics of UML. The design model is then transformed to executable models that exercise the test cases and evaluate the test results.

Model execution is another way to check dynamic model behaviors. Harel et. al. [Harel] propose a model execution framework Rhapsody that can translate class diagram and state charts into executable code and execute it. Our technique provides a lightweight alternative to checking scenarios against operation specifications.

6 Conclusions and Future Work

In this paper, we proposed a lightweight verification technique for checking scenarios against operational specifications. The approach consists of transforming a class model into a Snapshot Model that represents the static model of behavior. The Snapshot Model characterizes sequences of snapshots, where a snapshot represents an application state. We show how a scenario can be verified against this Snapshot Model using static analysis tools, such as OCLE and USE. The approach, applied on an example RBAC application, is able to detect inconsistencies between a given scenario and operation specifications.

We are implementing the algorithms in this paper in an Eclipse plugin which transforms the UML class models created with EMF (Eclipse Modeling Framework) plugin. The input scenario models are coded in JAL which is translated into executable Java code. The constraints are checked by USE plugin.

A lot of work remains to be done. The behavioral properties are analyzed with respect to given scenarios. We cannot claim that the property holds even when the results of analysis are positive with respect to the given scenarios. One future work aims at how to provide effective coverage of scenarios, to get higher assurance that the properties do indeed hold. The current work also assumes that the operations are executed sequentially. However, in complex real world applications, operations are often executed concurrently. In future, we plan to investigate how to extend our approach to handle concurrent execution of operations.

Acknowledgement

This work was partially supported by a grant from the AFOSR under Contract No. FA9550-04-1-0102.

References

[Chiorean] Chiorean, D., Pasca, M., Cârcu, A., Botiza, C., Moldovan, S.: Ensuring UML Models Consistency Using the OCL Environment. In: Electronic Notes in Theoretical Computer Science, vol. 102, pp. 99–110 (November 2004)

[Clark] Clark, E., Grumberg, O., Peled, D.: Model Checking. MIT Press, Cambridge (1999)

[Dinh-Trong] Dinh-Trong, T.T.: A Systematic Approach to Testing UML Design Models. In: Doctoral Symposium, 7th International Conference on the Unified Modeling Language (UML), Lisbon, Portugal (2004)

[Eshuis] Eshuis, R.: Symbolic model checking of UML activity diagrams. ACM Trans. Softw. Eng. Methodol. 15(1), 1–38 (2006)

[Ferraiolo] Ferraiolo, D.F., Sandhu, R., Gavrila, S., Kuhn, D.R., Chandramouli, R.: Proposed NIST Standard for Role-Based Access Control. ACM Transactions on Information and Systems Security 4(3) (August 2001)

[Gogolla05] Gogolla, M., Bohling, J., Richters, M.: Validating UML and OCL Models in USE by Automatic Snapshot Generation. Journal on Software and System Modeling 4(4), 386–398 (2005)

[Gogolla07] Gogolla, M., Büttner, F., Richters, M.: USE: A UML-based specification environment for validating UML and OCL. Sci. Comput. Program 69, 1–3 (2007)

[Harel] Harel, D., Gery, E.: Executable Object Modelling with Statecharts. IEEE Computer 30(7), 31–42 (1997)

[Jackson] Jackson, D.: Alloy: a lightweight object modeling notation. ACM Transactions on Software Engineering and Methodology 11(2), 256–290 (2002)

[Lilius] Lilius, J., Paltor, I.P.: vUML: a tool for verifying UML models. In: 14th IEEE International Conference on Automated Software Engineering, pp. 255–258 (October 1999)

[OCL] Object Management Group, Object Constraint Language Specification, Version 2.0

[Ray] Ray, I., Li, N., Kim, D.-K., France, R.: Using Parameterized UML to Specify and Compose Access Control Models. In: Proceedings of the 6th IFIP WG 11.5 Working Conference on Integrity and Internal Control in Information Systems, Lausanne, Switzerland (November 2003)

[Richters] Richters, M., Gogolla, M.: Validating UML Models and OCL Constraints. In: Evans, A., Kent, S., Selic, B. (eds.) UML 2000. LNCS, vol. 1939. Springer, Heidelberg (2000)

[UML2] Object Management Group, Unified Modeling Language: Superstructure, vers 2.0 Final Adopted Standard

[Yu] Yu, L., France, R.B., Ray, I., Lano, K.: A light-weight static approach to analyzing UML behavioral properties. In: Proceedings of the 12th IEEE international Conference on Engineering Complex Computer Systems, pp. 56–63 (July 2007)

Constructing Models with the Human-Usable Textual Notation

Louis M. Rose, Richard F. Paige, Dimitrios S. Kolovos, and Fiona A.C. Polack

Department of Computer Science, University of York, UK
{louis,paige,dkolovos,fiona}@cs.york.ac.uk

Abstract. We present an implementation of the OMG's Human-Usable Textual Notation (HUTN) [6] that provides a generic concrete syntax for MOF-based metamodels. The notation is summarised. Ways in which HUTN can be applied in order to improve the productivity of Model-Driven Engineering are identified. The use of HUTN to improve the quality of test suites for verifying model management operations (such as model-to-model transformation) is described. We also present a comparison of generic and domain-specific concrete syntax with HUTN.

1 Introduction

Whilst metamodel developers concentrate on the design of abstract syntax, the instantiation of a metamodel requires a concrete syntax. Concrete syntaxes can be classified as either *generic* or *domain-specific*. The former are defined at the level of metamodelling languages (e.g. MOF), while the latter are defined for specific metamodels. If a generic concrete syntax can be employed, then tool support can be provided for instantiating any metamodel, incorporating common features such as syntax highlighting and content assistance at no extra cost.

OMG's Human-Usable Textual Notation (HUTN) [6] defines such a generic concrete syntax, which aims to conform to human-usability criteria. However, we can find no current reference implementation of HUTN: the Distributed Systems Technology Centre's TokTok project (an implementation of the HUTN specification) seems to be inactive (the source code can no longer be found), whilst work on implementing the HUTN specification by Muller and Hassenforder [20] has been abandoned in favour of Sintaks [7], which operates upon domain-specific concrete syntax. Instead, metamodel developers use generation tools to derive specific syntax parsers and editors. Among these approaches, Eclipse technologies such as EMF [3] (and GMF [5]) can be used to generate tree-based (and graphical) model editors. Baar [1] introduces a formalisation of visual concrete syntax, and highlights its usefulness in analysis of correctness[1]. Text-to-model transformation tools such as xText [21], TCS [8] and TEF [25] can be used to define a custom concrete syntax for a metamodel and to generate a corresponding parser.

[1] For Baar, correctness means that each diagram (an instance of the visual concrete syntax) must correspond to only one model.

K. Czarnecki et al. (Eds.): MoDELS 2008, LNCS 5301, pp. 249–263, 2008.

HUTN can be used when a domain-specific concrete syntax is inappropriate or unnecessary. For example, if a metamodel is developed incrementally, use of a generic concrete syntax avoids the need for frequent revision that would apply if a domain-specific concrete syntax were used. Such revisions can significantly detract from the productivity of incremental development, as the domain-specific concrete syntax must be adapted each time the abstract syntax changes. A generic concrete syntax such as HUTN is also appropriate for iterative test-driven development (or rapid prototyping) of models.

We present an overview of our new implementation of the HUTN specification, developed atop the existing Epsilon model management platform. We discuss the ways in which we are employing the HUTN implementation for prototyping, for comparing models, and in testing – all important tasks in Model-Driven Engineering (MDE). First, we summarise HUTN.

2 Human-Usable Textual Notation

HUTN defines a generic concrete syntax for constructing instances of MOF-based metamodels. In this section, we introduce the core syntax and the key features of HUTN. The complete definition is available at [6]. To illustrate usage of the notation, we use the MOF-based metamodel of families in Figure 1. (A nuclear family "consists only of a father, a mother, and children." [19])

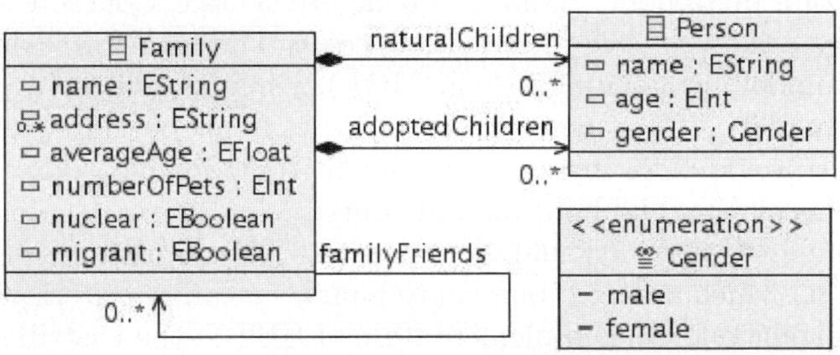

Fig. 1. Example metamodel: families and their children

2.1 Basic Notation

Listing 1.1 shows the construction of an *object* in HUTN, here an instance of the Family class from Figure 1. Line 1 specifies the package containing the classes to be constructed (`FamilyPackage`) and a corresponding identifier (`families`), used for fully qualifying references to objects (Section 2.3). Line 2 names the class (`Family`) and gives an identifier for the object (`The Smiths`). Lines 3 to 7 define *attribute values*; in each case, the data value is assigned to the attribute with the specified name. The encoding of the value depends on its type: strings are delimited by any form of quotation mark; multi-valued attributes use comma separators, etc.

The metamodel in Figure 1 defines a *simple reference* (familyFriends) and two *containment references* (adoptedChildren; naturalChildren). The HUTN representation embeds a contained object directly in the parent object, as shown in Listing 1.2. A simple reference can be specified using the type and identifier of the referred object, as shown in Listing 1.3. Like attribute values, both styles of reference are preceded by the name of the meta-feature.

```
FamilyPackage "families" {
   Family "The Smiths" {
      nuclear: true
      name: "The Smiths"
      averageAge: 25.7
      numberOfPets: 2
      address: "120 Main Street", "37 University Road"
   }
}
```

Listing 1.1. Specifying attributes with HUTN

```
FamilyPackage "families" {
   Family "The Smiths" {
      naturalChildren: Person "John" { name: "John" },
                        Person "Jo" { gender: female }
   }
}
```

Listing 1.2. Instantiation of naturalChildren – a HUTN containment reference

```
FamilyPackage "families" {
   Family "The Smiths" {
      familyFriends: Family "The Does"
   }
   Family "The Does" {}
}
```

Listing 1.3. Specifying a simple reference with HUTN

2.2 Keywords and Adjectives

While HUTN is unlikely to be as concise as a domain-specific concrete syntax, the notation does define a number of syntactic shortcuts in order to make model specifications more compact. These shortcuts can be used in place of more verbose (and more readable) full syntax. Shortcut use is optional, and their syntax is often intuitive [6, pg2-4]. Two example notational shortcuts are described here, in order to illustrate some of the ways in which HUTN can be used to construct models in a concise manner – a key concern when using HUTN to construct models for use in testing, as we will discuss in Section 3.

When specifying a *Boolean-valued attribute*, it is sufficient to simply use the attribute name (value `true`), or the attribute name prefixed with a tilde (value `false`). When used in the body of the object, this style of Boolean-valued attribute represents a *keyword*. A keyword used to prefix an object declaration is called an *adjective*. Listing 1.4 shows the use of both an attribute keyword (`~nuclear` on line 6) and adjective (`~migrant` on line 2).

```
1 FamilyPackage "families" {
2    nuclear ~migrant Family "The Smiths" {}
3
4    Family "The Does" {
5       averageAge: 20.1
6       ~nuclear
7       name: "The Does"
8    }
9 }
```

Listing 1.4. Using keywords and adjectives in HUTN

2.3 Inter-package References

To conclude our summary of the notation, we present two advanced features defined in the HUTN specification, which we have found to be useful when constructing large models. The first enables objects to refer to other objects in a different package, while the second provides means for specifying the values of a reference for all objects in a single construct (which can be used to improve the understandability of complex relationships in some cases). We conclude by discussing the way in which HUTN permits document customisation.

```
FamilyPackage "families" {
   Family "The Smiths" {}
}
VehiclePackage "vehicles" {
   Vehicle "The Smiths' Car" {
      owner: FamilyPackage.Family "families"."The Smiths"
   }
}
```

Listing 1.5. Referencing objects in other packages with HUTN

To reference objects between separate package instances in the same document, the package identifier is used in order to construct a fully qualified name. Suppose we introduce a second package to our metamodel in Figure 1. Among other concepts, this package introduces a Vehicle class, which defines an owner reference of type Family. Listing 1.5 illustrates the way in which the owner feature can be populated. Note that the fully qualified form of the class uses the names of elements of the metamodel, while the fully-qualified form of the object uses only HUTN identifiers defined in the current document.

The HUTN specification defines name scope optimisation rules, which allow the definition above to be simplified to: `owner: Family "The Smiths"`, assuming that (1) the VehiclePackage does not define a Family class, and (2) the identifier "The Smiths" is not used in the VehiclePackage block, or this HUTN document is configured to require unique identifiers over the entire document.

2.4 Alternative Reference Syntax

In addition to the syntax defined in Listings 1.2 and 1.3, the value of references may be specified independently of the object definitions. For example, Listing 1.6 demonstrates this alternate syntax by defining The Does as friends with both The Smiths and The Bloggs.

```
FamilyPackage "families" {
    Family "The Smiths" {}
    Family "The Does" {}
    Family "The Bloggs" {}

    familyFriends {
        "The Does" "The Smiths"
        "The Does" "The Bloggs"
    }
}
```

Listing 1.6. Using a reference block in HUTN

Listing 1.7 illustrates a further alternative syntax for references, which employs an infix notation.

```
FamilyPackage "families" {
    Family "The Smiths" {}
    Family "The Does" {}
    Family "The Bloggs" {}

    Family "The Smiths" familyFriends Family "The Does"
    Family "The Smiths" familyFriends Family "The Bloggs"
}
```

Listing 1.7. Using an infix reference in HUTN

2.5 Customisation Via Configuration

Some limited customisation of HUTN for particular metamodels can be achieved using *configuration files*. Customisations permitted include a parametric form of object instantiation (not yet implemented); renaming of metamodel elements; giving default values for attributes; and stating an attribute whose values are used to infer a default identifier. The HUTN specification [6] gives details of shortcuts and of the rules supported by configuration files.

In the next section, we motivate the need for a HUTN implementation in our development and testing of model management tools, reflecting on the shortcomings of other approaches, and deriving requirements for model specification.

3 Motivation: The Case of Model Construction for Testing

Generic concrete syntax can give benefit in a range of work with metamodels and model management, such as:

– rapid model production, used in investigating the appropriateness of metamodel design;
– visualisation of model comparisons; and
– provision of a model construction notation for testing model management tasks: e.g. model-to-model (M2M) or model-to-text (M2T) transformation.

Here, we focus on the last, the construction of models for testing operations of model management tools. We outline two non-HUTN approaches that we have used, and, in reflecting on their problems, motivate the use of HUTN, finally illustrating the sort of benefit that HUTN has brought to this work.

Model management is the discipline of managing assets involved in MDE. Model management tools both consume and produce models – for instance, a M2M transformation both produces and consumes models. Model management tools, like any software, are subject to rigorous testing. The test suite for a tool that consumes models requires sample models on which to run tests, whilst for a tool that produces models, models are needed against which to judge the test result (for a description of such verification, on model-to-model transformations, see [12,18]). Like any incremental and iterative development, changes in the tool being developed often requires change to the test suites. Equally, if a metamodel is updated, the models used by test suites require migration.

Before working with HUTN, we tried specifying test-suite models with EMF and in XMI. This caused problems when metamodels changed such that specified instances became invalid, as EMF's editor could not be used to migrate the specified models. Instead, the model migration involved hand-crafting changes in XMI.

A more successful approach (though, as we will see, not as flexible as HUTN) was to construct models programmatically. For instance, the code in Listing 1.8 constructs an instance of the Families metamodel, Figure 1, which has one family with two children.

```
@BeforeClass public static void constructModel() {
    final FamilyPackageFactory factory =
            FamilyPackageFactory.eINSTANCE;

    final Family family = factory.createFamily();
    family.setName("The Smiths");
```

```

    final Person john = factory.createPerson();
    john.setName("John");
    john.setGender(Gender.MALE);

    final Person jo = factory.createPerson();
    jo.setName("Jo");
    jo.setGender(Gender.FEMALE);

    family.getNaturalChildren().add(john);
    family.getNaturalChildren().add(jo);
}
```

Listing 1.8. A program to generate a model family using JUnit (Java)

Inclusion of the construction code for models as part of the test case reduces the number of files that needed to be edited when a test has to be updated. This simplifies the task of updating test cases. Also, in the programmatic approach, when changes to a metamodel render a model invalid, this is flagged by a compilation error on the test case. However, the inclusion of model construction code in the test case detracts from overall readability and conciseness.

In addition to wanting to improve the agility and responsiveness to change of our tool development we needed a way to specify model construction that was also also understandable, in order to improve maintainability. Therefore, the new approach to model specification needed to be:

- **concise**: to minimise the amount of code needed to construct a model;
- **readable**: by developers, so that they can easily understand test cases;
- **embeddable**: to support insular test cases (in which all the data needed to understand the test case is held in a single file), it must be possible to embed the model specification in the specification of a test case.

We now use HUTN for specification of test suite models: this provides human-usable, compact model code. For example, Listing 1.9 is the HUTN code for constructing the same model as that expressed programmatically in Listing 1.8.

```
FamilyPackage "families" {
  Family "The Smiths" {
    naturalChildren: male Person "John", female Person "Jo"
  }
}
```

Listing 1.9. Specifying a model using HUTN

As well as the obvious removal of Java code structures, the HUTN specification introduces helpful terminology to the test model, such as the `male` and `female` adjectives that specify values for the Gender type. Configuration rules were used to further reduce the size of the HUTN specification: the `name` attribute of Family and Person objects is assigned the value of the object's identifier.

Having demonstrated how HUTN supports our test-suite modelling requirements, we now turn to the HUTN implementation, which is essential for the realisation of non-manual test-suite model maintenance.

4 HUTN Implementation

Our implementation of HUTN makes extensive use of our Epsilon model management platform. We first summarise Epsilon and its component model management languages, before outlining the HUTN implementation itself.

4.1 The Epsilon Platform

Epsilon, the *E*xtensible *P*latform for *S*pecification of *I*ntegrated *L*anguages for m*O*del ma*N*agement [10], is a suite of tools for MDE. Epsilon comprises a number of integrated model management languages, supported by a common infrastructure, for performing tasks such as model merging, model transformation and inter-model consistency checking [11]. Whilst many model management languages are bound to a particular subset of modelling technologies [9], Epsilon is technology-agnostic – models written in any modelling language can be manipulated by Epsilon. Models implemented using EMF, MOF 1.4, pure XML, or CZT [23] are currently supported.

The core of the platform is the Epsilon Object Language (EOL) [14], a reworking and extension of OCL that includes the ability to update models, conditional and loop statements, statement sequencing, and access to standard output and error streams. The Epsilon task-specific languages are built atop EOL, giving highly efficient inheritance and reuse of features. Currently, these task-specific languages include support for model-to-model transformation (ETL [16]), model comparison (ECL), model merging (EML [13]) model-to-text transformation (EGL [24]) and model validation (EVL [15]).

4.2 Implementation of HUTN Using Epsilon

Our implementation of HUTN uses the task-specific languages of Epsilon. Although any languages for model-to-model transformation (M2M), model-to-text transformation (M2T) and model validation could have been used, Epsilon's existing domain-specific languages make the implementation a relatively simple exercise, and has the added advantage that the HUTN tool is directly compatible with the Epsilon model management facilities. Our implementation has been released as part of Epsilon, and includes development tools for Eclipse (a source code editor and builder).

Figure 2 outlines the workflow through our HUTN implementation, from HUTN source text to instantiated target model. The HUTN model specification is parsed to an abstract syntax tree using a HUTN parser specified in ANTLR [22]. From this, a Java postprocessor is used to construct an instance of a simple AST metamodel (which comprises two meta-classes, Tree and Node). Using

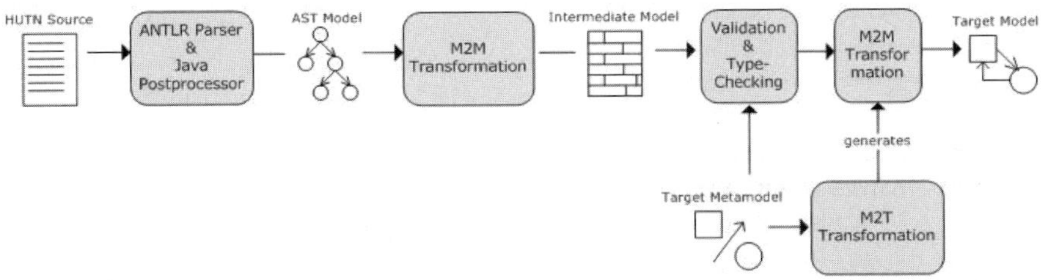

Fig. 2. The architecture of our HUTN implementation

ETL, M2M transformations are then applied to produce an intermediate representation from the AST model. Finally, a M2T transformation on the target metamodel, specified in EGL, produces a further M2M transformation, from the intermediate representation to the target model.

The workflow includes two M2M transformation stages, because the form of the AST metamodel is not suited to a one-step transformation. There is a mismatch between the features of the AST metamodel and the needs of the target model – for example, between the Node class in the AST metamodel and classes in the target metamodel. If a one-step transformation was used, each transformation rule would need a lengthy guard statement, which is hard to understand (and to verify). Instead, we designed a fine-grained representation of the HUTN AST as an intermediate: the instance of the AST metamodel is first transformed to this fine-grained representation (the *intermediate model*), and that representation is transformed in to the target model.

We now discuss the two M2M transformations in depth, along with a model validation phase which is performed prior to the second transformation.

AST Model to Intermediate Model. In the HUTN implementation, M2M transformation rules are written in ETL. An example transformation rule is shown in Listing 1.10. The rule transforms a name node in the AST model (which could represent a package or a class object) to a package object in the intermediate model. The guard (line 5) specifies that a name node will only be transformed to a package object if the node has no parent (i.e. it is a top-level node, and hence a package rather than a class). The body of the rule states that the type, line number and column number of the package are determined from the text, line and column attributes of the node object. On line 11, a containment slot is instantiated to hold the children of this package object. The children of the node object are transformed to the intermediate model (using a built-in method, `equivalent()`), and added to the containment slot.

```
1  rule NameNode2PackageObject
2      transform n : AntlrAst!NameNode
3      to p : Intermediate!PackageObject {
4
5      guard : n.parent.isUndefined()
6
```

```
    p.type := n.text;
    p.line := n.line;
    p.col  := n.column;

    var slot := new Intermediate!ContainmentSlot;
    for (child in n.children) {
       slot.objects.add(child.equivalent());
    }
    if (slot.objects.notEmpty()) {
       p.slots.add(slot);
    }
}
```

Listing 1.10. Transformation rule (in ETL) to convert AST nodes to package objects

Intermediate Model Validation. An advantage of the two-stage transformation is that contextual analysis can be specified in an abstract manner – that is, without having to express the traversal of the AST. This gives clarity and minimises the amount of code required to define of our constraints.

```
context ClassObject {
   constraint IdentifiersMustBeUnique {
      guard: self.id.isDefined()
      check: ClassObject.allInstances()
                .select(c|c.id = self.id).size() = 1;
      message: 'Duplicate identifier: ' + self.id
   }
}
```

Listing 1.11. A constraint (in EVL) to check that all identifiers are unique

We use EVL [15] to write verification statements to perform this analysis in our implementation of the HUTN specification, resulting in highly expressive syntactic constraints. An EVL constraint comprises a guard, the logic that specifies the constraint, and a message to be displayed if the constraint is not met. For example, Listing 1.11 specifies the constraint that every HUTN class has a unique identifier.

Intermediate Model to Target Model. Because the contextual analysis is performed on the intermediate model, we have assurance that this is a valid model before proceeding to the target model. In generating the target model from the intermediate model (Figure 2), the transformation uses information from the target metamodel, such as the names of classes and features. A typical approach to this category of problem is to use a higher-order transformation on the target metamodel to generate the desired transformation. In this case, we use a different approach, which we consider to be more readable: the transformation to the target model is produced by executing an EGL template on the target metamodel. EGL is a template-based text generation language. `[% %]` tag pairs are used to denote dynamic sections, which may produce text when executed. Any code not enclosed in a `[% %]` tag pair is included verbatim in the generated text.

Listing 1.12 is the EGL template for a M2T transformation on the target metamodel; it generates the M2M transformation used for generating the target model. The loop beginning on line 1 iterates over each meta-class in the metamodel, producing a transformation rule to generate target model instances of that meta-class from class objects in the intermediate model. The template guard (line 6) specifies that only class objects of the same type as the meta-class be transformed by the current rule. The template body is omitted from Listing 1.12 – it iterates over each structural feature of the current meta-class, and generates appropriate transformation code for populating the values of each structural feature from the slots on the class object in the intermediate model.

```
1  [% for (class in EClass.allInstances()) { %]
2  rule Object2[%=class.name%]
3    transform o : Intermediate!ClassObject
4    to t : Model![%=class.name%] {
5
6      guard: o.type = '[%=class.name%]'
7
8      -- body omitted for brevity
9    }
10 [% } %]
```

Listing 1.12. Initial sections of the template (in EGL) for generating rules (in ETL) to instantiate classes of the target metamodel

4.3 Discussion of HUTN Implementation

Like Muller and Hassenforder [20], we encountered a number of problems with the HUTN specification. Where we have encountered the same problem, we have employed their solutions.

A further problem encountered relates to the syntactic shortcut for HUTN adjectives. The HUTN [6] specification includes the grammar rules shown in Listing 1.13. The `AttributeName` and `ClassName` terminals produce the same token type. Therefore, the adjectival shortcut for a Boolean valued attribute with the value `true` is syntactically the same as the name of a class. For example, when parsing the expression, `nuclear`, it is not possible to determine whether to match an `AttributeName` or a `ClassName`.

```
ClassHeader ::= ClassAdjectives <ClassName> (ClassIdentifier)?
ClassAdjectives ::= (('~'? <AttributeName>) | DataValue)*
```

Listing 1.13. Extract from the HUTN grammar (taken from [6])

The solution that we adopt is to modify the HUTN grammar to require that such adjectives be prefixed with a colon. Thus, for example, the expression, `nuclear ~migrant Family "The Smiths" {}`, is rewritten as, `#nuclear ~migrant Family "The Smiths" {}`.

5 Discussion and Related Work

As noted previously, there are many tools that aid developers in constructing instances of a metamodel, including xText [21], TCS [8] and TEF [25]. Typically, these tools are used for model-specific concrete syntax; the initial overhead in generating editors and parsers, and designing the concrete syntax, is significant, and there is a further cost every time the metamodel or syntax is modified.

Some generated editors provide other model management facilities. For instance, oAW's text-to-model tool, xText [21] includes the Check language, which, in its approach to specifying domain-specific constraints on concrete syntax, is similar to our HUTN implementation's use of EVL (see Listing 1.11).

The Eclipse Modelling Framework (EMF) [3] provides an alternative to generated editors. EMF provides a reflective, tree-structure editor that can be used to instantiate a metamodel in a dynamic manner (the objects used to construct the model are not strongly-typed).

However, EMF's reflective editor does not provide any means for customisation. By contrast, Epsilon provides an enhanced reflective editor, Exeed, that permits such customisation via metamodel annotations. Our HUTN tooling provides an alternative reflective editor – one that recognises a textual, rather than a tree-structured, concrete syntax.

Epsilon's EOL can be used, with EUnit [17] – a task-specific language for testing built atop Epsilon – to perform unit testing of model management operations. To date, the models used in conjunction with eUnit have been specified using EMF editors. We have added a driver to the Epsilon Model Connectivity layer that connects EUnit and our HUTN implementation, so that Epsilon can support manipulation of models authored in HUTN. The driver allows Epsilon users to use eUnit to specify assertions in test cases and HUTN to construct models to be used in test suites alongside these assertions.

In relation to our use of HUTN in test suite development, Schuh and Punke [26] present an object-oriented programming pattern that describes a similar style of test model creation, called the ObjectMother pattern. They report that the standardisation of object creation improved the maintainability of test suites. They also note that by allowing tests to slightly change a fixture without defining a completely new object (e,g. use the Family, The Smiths, without the Person John as a child) it was possible to further improve the quality of test suites.

HUTN provides a generic concrete syntax for metamodels that conform to MOF. A generic concrete syntax provides a large degree of flexibility, and can be used as a notation for a number of distinct abstract syntax. It is useful where a domain-specific concrete syntax is inappropriate or unnecessary.

Notwithstanding the power of genericity, there are situations where a domain-specific concrete syntax is preferable. An example of where HUTN is unhelpful arose when developing a metamodel for the recording of failure behaviour of components in complex systems, based on the work of Wallace [27].

Failure behaviours comprise a number of expressions that specify how each component reacts to system faults, and there is an established concrete syntax for expressing failure behaviours. The failure syntax allows various shortcuts, such as the use of underscore to denote a wildcard. For example, the syntax for a possible failure behaviour of a component that receives input from two other components (on the left-hand side of the expression), and produces output for a single component is denoted:

$$(\{\_\}, \{\_\}) \rightarrow (\{late\}) \quad (1)$$

A failure behaviour can contain many expressions, and each component may be connected to many other components, so the metamodel for failure behaviours contains a large number of classes. In the generic concrete syntax, the specification of these behaviours is unhelpfully terse. For example. Listing 1.14 gives the HUTN syntax for failure behaviour (1), above.

```
Behaviour {
   lhs: Tuple {
      contents: IdentifierSet { contents: Wildcard {} },
                IdentifierSet { contents: Wildcard {} }
   }

   rhs: Tuple {
      contents: IdentifierSet { contents: Fault "late" {} }
   }
}
```

Listing 1.14. Failure behaviour specified in HUTN

In general, HUTN is less concise than a domain-specific syntax for metamodels containing a large number of classes with few attributes, and in cases where most attributes are used to define structural relationships among concepts. However, there might still be benefits from using HUTN in such cases, if the metamodel is likely to be modified frequently, or if the model does not yet have a formal metamodel.

6 Conclusion and Further Work

We have shown that OMG's HUTN is a valuable addition to the facilities available to metamodel developers, giving genericity and flexibility in modelling. We present our implementation of HUTN in the context of our primary motivation – of supporting models associated with test suites for tools associated with the Epsilon model management platform. We summarised the way in which our implementation has improved the quality of our test suites in MDE.

Future directions for our work with HUTN include improvements to our test-suite-model support, along the lines described by Schuh and Punke (above). We are also planning to aid a mechanism for specifying that an non-deterministic initialisation of features. Non-deterministic initialisation will permit features whose values are unimportant to the current test to be initialised automatically by the HUTN tooling.

We are also working on an extension of the HUTN implementation that supports *metamodel inference*. Currently, we have implemented the metamodel inference algorithm as a rudimentary transformation from the intermediate model to an Ecore [2] metamodel. We intend to use metamodel inference in prototyping model-centric systems.

Additionally, we are investigating other uses for HUTN, in particular: visualising the differences between versions of models: a HUTN view could be contributed to the EMF Compare platform [4]. We intend to use such visualisation to help identify categories of model and metamodel evolution.

Acknowledgement. The work in this paper was supported by the European Commission via the MODELPLEX project, co-funded by the European Commission under the "Information Society Technologies" Sixth Framework Programme (2006-2009).

References

1. Baar, T.: Correctly Defined Concrete Syntax for Visual Modeling Languages. In: Nierstrasz, O., Whittle, J., Harel, D., Reggio, G. (eds.) MoDELS 2006. LNCS, vol. 4199, pp. 111–125. Springer, Heidelberg (2006)
2. IBM Corporation. Ecore API Documentation (2006), `http://download.eclipse.org/modeling/emf/emf/javadoc/2.4.0/org/eclipse/emf/ecore/package-summary.html`
3. The Eclipse Foundation. Eclipse Modelling Framework Project (2008), `http://www.eclipse.org/modeling/emf/`
4. The Eclipse Foundation. EMF Compare (2008), `http://wiki.eclipse.org/index.php/EMF_Compare`
5. The Eclipse Foundation. Graphical Modelling Framework (2008), `http://www.eclipse.org/modeling/gmf/`
6. Object Management Group. Human-Usable Textual Notation Specification (2004), `http://www.omg.org/technology/documents/formal/hutn.htm`
7. IRISA. Sintaks (2007), `http://www.kermeta.org/sintaks/`
8. Jouault, F., Bézivin, J., Kurtev, I.: TCS: a DSL for the specification of textual concrete syntaxes. In: Proc. GPCE 2006, pp. 249–254. ACM Press, New York (2006)
9. Kolovos, D.S.: A Short Introduction to Epsilon (2007), `http://www.cs.york.ac.uk/~dkolovos/epsilon/Epsilon.ppt`
10. Kolovos, D.S.: Extensible Platform for Specification of Integrated Languages for mOdel maNagement Project Website (2007), `http://www.eclipse.org/gmt/epsilon`
11. Kolovos, D.S., Paige, R.F., Polack, F.A.C.: Epsilon Development Tools for Eclipse. In: Eclipse Summit 2006 (2006)
12. Kolovos, D.S., Paige, R.F., Polack, F.A.C.: Model comparison: a foundation for model composition and model transformation testing. In: Proc. GaMMa 2006, pp. 13–20. ACM Press, New York (2006)
13. Kolovos, D.S., Paige, R.F., Polack, F.A.C.: Merging Models with the Epsilon Merging Language (EML). In: Nierstrasz, O., Whittle, J., Harel, D., Reggio, G. (eds.) MoDELS 2006. LNCS, vol. 4199, pp. 215–229. Springer, Heidelberg (2006)

14. Kolovos, D.S., Paige, R.F., Polack, F.A.C.: The Epsilon Object Language (EOL). In: Rensink, A., Warmer, J. (eds.) ECMDA-FA 2006. LNCS, vol. 4066, pp. 128–142. Springer, Heidelberg (2006)
15. Kolovos, D.S., Paige, R.F., Polack, F.A.C.: On the Evolution of OCL for Capturing Structural Constraints in Modelling Languages. In: Workshop on Rigorous Methods for Software Construction & Analysis. LNCS, vol. 5115. Springer, Heidelberg (2008)
16. Kolovos, D.S., Paige, R.F., Polack, F.A.C.: The Epsilon Transformation Language. In: Vallecillo, A., Gray, J., Pierantonio, A. (eds.) ICMT 2008. LNCS, vol. 5063. Springer, Heidelberg (2008)
17. Kolovos, D.S., Paige, R.F., Polack, F.A.C.: Unit Testing Model Management Operations. In: Proc. MoDeVVa, ICST. IEEE, Los Alamitos (2008)
18. Lin, Y., Zhang, J., Gray, J.: A Framework for Testing Model Transformations. In: Model-driven Software Development, pp. 219–236. Springer, Heidelberg (2005)
19. Merriam-Webster. Definition of Nuclear Family (2008), `http://www.merriam-webster.com/dictionary/nuclear%20family`
20. Muller, P.-A., Hassenforder, M.: HUTN as a Bridge between ModelWare and GrammarWare. In: WISME Workshop, MODELS / UML 2005 (2005)
21. OpenArchitectureWare. openArchitectureWare Project Website (2008), `http://www.eclipse.org/gmt/oaw/`
22. Terence Parr. ANTLR Parser Generator (2008), `http://www.antlr.org/`
23. Community Z Tools Project. Community Z Tools (2007), `http://czt.sourceforge.net/`
24. Rose, L.M., Paige, R.F., Kolovos, D.S., Polack, F.A.C.: The Epsilon Generation Language. In: Schieferdecker, I., Hartman, A. (eds.) ECMDA-FA 2008. LNCS, vol. 5095, pp. 1–16. Springer, Heidelberg (2008)
25. Scheidgen, M.: Textual Modelling Embedded into Graphical Modelling. In: Schieferdecker, I., Hartman, A. (eds.) ECMDA-FA 2008. LNCS, vol. 5095, pp. 153–168. Springer, Heidelberg (2008)
26. Schuh, P., Punke, S.: ObjectMother: Easing Test Object Creation in XP. In: XP Universe (2001)
27. Wallace, M.: Modular architectural representation and analysis of fault propagation and transformation. Electr. Notes Theor. Comput. Sci. 141(3), 53–71 (2005)

X3D-UML: 3D UML State Machine Diagrams

Paul McIntosh, Margaret Hamilton, and Ron van Schyndel

RMIT University, GPO Box 2476V, Melbourne, VIC 3000, Australia
paul.mcintosh@internetscooter.com,
{margaret.hamilton,ron.vanschyndel}@rmit.edu.au

Abstract. X3D-UML utilises X3D (eXtensible 3D) to enable standards-based advanced 3D UML visualisations. Using X3D-UML, 3D UML State Machine Diagrams have been evaluated against actual user tasks and data, using the Sequential Evaluation methodology. The results of User Task Analysis, Heuristic Evaluation and Formative Evaluation phases provide clear evidence that the use of UML extended with 3D is a practical solution for visualising complex system behaviour. RoseRT model metrics show between 56%-90% of state machine diagram work would benefit from such 3D UML extensions; hence the 3D improvement can deliver considerable benefit to organisations.

Keywords: X3D-UML, 3D UML, X3D, 3D Software Visualization, VRML.

1 Introduction

Computers in current day software development houses are now capable of rendering quality real time 3D visualisations. In the past, 3D representations for UML have been suggested [1-4] and some research has been undertaken on specific aspects of 3D UML and related visualisations [5, 6]. Despite this, there has been no definitive research into the overall benefit of completing common and critical software engineering tasks with UML extended using 3D visualisations. If measurable benefit in 3D UML abstraction can be obtained for one task of note, then this suggests an area of potential lies untapped and idle in the graphics cards of engineers' computers.

Our research utilises the concept of X3D-UML, the presentation of UML in the Web3D ISO standard X3D (eXtensible 3D) [7], to test for benefit in the area of 3D UML state machine diagrams (also known as statechart diagrams). X3D-UML provides a standards-based approach to software visualisation, where the UML standard is presented through the X3D standard. This approach imposes constraints on the visualisation possibilities but those constraints enable the research results to be more broadly applicable to industry. X3D-UML is described further in section 2.

The reason that UML is chosen as the basis for 3D software visualisation research is that it is a current and accepted standard visual notation for software systems. Basing 3D software visualisation on an existing visual notation enables new visualisations to make use of the existing visual data such as layout, colour and other visual cues, which are already familiar to software engineers. Although in current implementations it is commonly thought of as a 2D notation only, it has been noted by Booch et al. that "*the UML allows you to create three-dimensional diagrams.*"[8]

K. Czarnecki et al. (Eds.): MoDELS 2008, LNCS 5301, pp. 264–279, 2008.

The reason that X3D, the successor to VRML (Virtual Reality Modelling Language), is chosen as the visualisation medium is that it is able to capture complete virtual environments containing 3D, 2D, animation, spatialised audio and video, user interaction, user defined objects, scripting and physical simulations[7]. However, this rich set of features only represents the visualisation possibilities, more importantly X3D is capable of rendering the types of visualisation currently found in UML, being large quantities of lines and text [9], and this capability provides the critical link between current UML and advanced UML visualisation.

For this research we have used IBM Rational Rose RealTime [10] and referred to here by its common name RoseRT. RoseRT makes extensive use of state machine diagrams for describing system behaviour and these descriptions generate code (i.e. "the model is the code"). The advantage for researching state machine diagram visualisations is that software engineers work extensively with them and must define them precisely to get the system to behave as required. Also implemented is the concept of separate substate diagrams, which is recommended practice for large hierarchies [11]. The screenshot below (Fig 1) shows an example of the current 2D RoseRT state machine diagram implementation, with substates appearing on different tabs and also accessible through clicking on superstates.

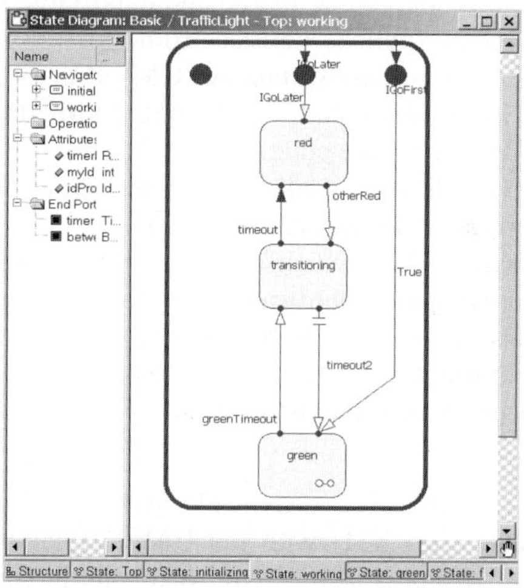

Fig. 1. RoseRT example of a complete state machine with substates displayed in different window tabs. The 'green' state contains an icon indicating that substates exist.

Substate levels do not provide a complete state machine view but they do aid the engineer in managing the layout of diagrams and the understanding the system behaviour from different levels of abstraction. Our hypothesis is that engineers would benefit from a 3D state machine diagram giving them "the best of both worlds", having advantages of separate substate diagrams but also the ability to view the state machine diagram as a whole.

The following sections describe X3D-UML, an overview of the methodology used to evaluate 3D UML state machine diagrams and the results so far of our research into this area. We also present some examples of future research in our conclusion.

2 X3D-UML

In this section we present X3D-UML as the means of defining and testing advanced 3D UML visualisations. We present the design rules, which form the implementation independent basis of X3D-UML. Also we describe the current implementation of X3D-UML based on the UML Diagram Interchange specification[12] and how this enables 3D extensions to UML to be clearly quantified.

The X3D-UML design rules provide constraints around the research undertaken. The reasons for these constraints are to focus the research results so they are as broadly applicable to industry as possible. The rules do not prevent novel areas being explored but they tether the underlying data back to existing UML development infrastructure. The constraints can be generalised to ensuring that visualisations are standards-based and that they will work with existing infrastructure, data and processes. These constraints are described below:

X3D – The visualisations shall be definable and exportable in the X3D standard[7].
UML - The visualisations shall be derived from existing standard UML notation and have the ability to be returned to standard UML diagrams.
Actual Data - The visualisation shall be generated directly from actual data, such as existing UML models or source code.
Actual Tasks - The visualisation shall be designed using and tested against actual user tasks that are derived from user task analysis.
Standard PC Hardware – The visualisations shall be usable and benefit measured on standard personal computer hardware used for software engineering (i.e. the equivalent computer hardware already being used for UML modelling).
Development Environment Imitation – The visualisation should imitate the look, "feel" and work processes of the existing UML tool implementation as closely as possible.

In past research we have used XSLT (eXtensible Stylesheet Language Transforms) to translate source code data into X3D with the UML visualisations predefined in an X3D "proto" library[9]. To apply X3D-UML with inbuilt functionality and to integrate it more easily with UML data, we have now developed a library, which is derived from the Diagram Interchange specification. According to the specification the goal "*is to enable a smooth and seamless exchange of documents compliant to the UML standard … between different software tools.*"[12], however it has been utilised in this research as a means of defining UML diagrams and further defining any extensions required to represent 3D visualisations.

With the Diagram Interchange, is provided the XMI (XML Metadata Interchange) model data for the specification[13]. To create the X3D-UML library, this XMI was imported into a UML tool and code generated directly from it. This code formed the basis of a UML diagram library, which was then adapted for use with X3D. For the research presented in this paper, only minimal changes are required to achieve a 3D state machine diagram. Simply adding a "z" value to the existing Diagram Interchange "point" class enables any graph element to be given a depth position (as well as "x" and "y"). This "z" value is then linked to state machine diagram depth as the UML model is processed, so that substate diagrams appear below their superstate.

3 Sequential Evaluation Methodology Overview

In this section we present the methodology applied to evaluating 3D state machine diagrams. *Sequential Evaluation* is a methodology for testing 3D user interfaces[14, 15] which uses a sequence of qualitative and quantitative useability techniques ordered so that low cost and generic techniques are applied first.

We have proposed refinements to this methodology for evaluating 3D UML[16] and further refinements are planned as a result of the study undertaken. In our application of *Sequential Evaluation* (Fig. 2) we start with the research question:

"Is there measurable benefit in a state machine diagram which makes use of 3D?"

We then answer the research question with results from the following stages:

(1) User Task Analysis - we first define the context of actual software development through analysis of actual users' goals, the tasks to achieve those goals and the importance of those tasks. This analysis is generated through accepted user task analysis techniques such as those described by Hackos and Redish[17].

(2) Heuristic Evaluation - the initial concept of the 3D state machine diagram is refined based on the results of user task analysis. This refined visualisation is then reviewed in the context of the defined user tasks by "Expert Evaluators" using "rule of thumb" and where possible, using documented guidelines (i.e. heuristics).

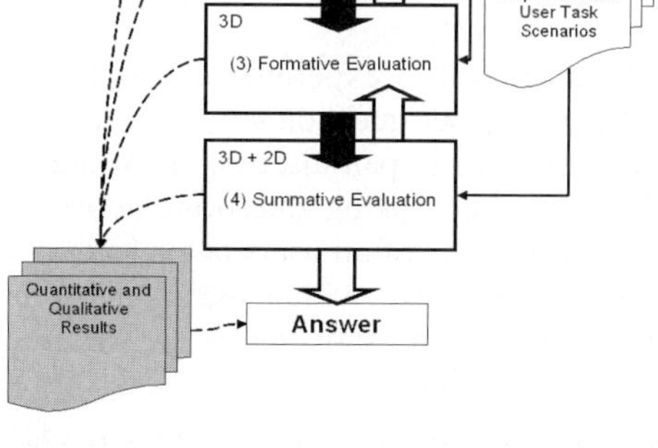

Fig. 2. *Sequential Evaluation* methodology [14, 15] as applied in researching 3D State Machine Diagrams [16]

(3) Formative Evaluation - the visualisation is refined based on expert feedback and then presented to users. Users are then walked through the user tasks of interest using the visualisation. With this information the visualisation is improved further.

(4) Summative Evaluation - the final 3D visualisation is tested against the existing 2D for achieving the defined user tasks. The aim of this evaluation is to provide empirical results that measure the benefit of the 3D UML extension.

These stages are further discussed with their results in the following sections.

4 User Task Analysis Results

In this section we present our findings from User Task Analysis. The purpose of this analysis is to capture the tasks related to state machine diagrams and the importance of those tasks, with supporting metrics where possible.

Part of this analysis is the understanding of the extent of substate usage in industry. To answer this, a survey of 1004 state machines, from four independent companies, was undertaken using a RoseRT model metrics script we developed. The results showed all models making extensive use of hierarchical state machines, with between 33.58% and 64.66% of all states existing at substate levels (Table 1).

Table 1. Substate survey of commercial RoseRT models, showing extensive substate usage. The results are from four industries and have been generalised to areas of "office equipment", "robotics control", "systems control" and "networking equipment".

Totals	Office	Robotics	Control	Network
State Machines	216	172	583	33
States	1576	411	3727	116
Level 1 States	780	273	1501	41
Level 2 States	567	90	1295	22
Level 3 States	208	48	617	22
Level 4 States	21	0	274	31
Level 5 States	0	0	40	0
Percentage of Substates	50.51%	33.58%	59.73%	64.66%

4.1 User Sessions

User sessions were undertaken with 3 experienced RoseRT users from a team of 5. The process is to walk through a set questionnaire with each user at their desk, then leading those closed questions to an open discussion. A later session involved observation of the users working while asking questions about their actions. From this study it was determined that the goal of all users is the same, the creation of a product subsystem. Each user owns a package within the model, which integrates to other subsystem packages. Even though the subsystems are different, the high level tasks were also the same and are as follows:

- Analysis + Design (pen + paper designs and "in the head" thinking)
- Creating Structure and Behaviour (translating design in to implementation)
- Refactoring (refining implementations, fixing bugs and adding new features)
- Test + Debugging (testing implementation)

In the refactoring task, users were required to refactor state machine diagrams 30%-40% of their week. These were deeply nested state machines and it was observed that while doing this task, users appeared to be compensating for a limitation in the UML representation of such diagrams. Each user had a different method for overcoming that limitation that did not involve the use of the diagram itself. The next sections explain the issue in more detail and the solutions proposed.

4.2 Cognitive Load in Considering State Machine Behaviour

The symptoms of the limitation in single level state machine views showed itself in users "thinking outside of the diagram". One user claimed to be often "*staring into space for 15 minutes*" trying to determine the consequences of deferring one event. Another used "find" functionality to find all items in the model with an event name so they could check them off individually. Yet, another stated that they took to drawing existing state machine diagrams on paper to be able to follow events through levels.

To explain this further, we consider a small hierarchical state machine diagram taken from the RoseRT help documentation on "Transition Selection Rules" (Fig. 3). This diagram is unusual as it displays the substate in the same diagram, which is not how RoseRT presents such diagrams; this gives some clue of the need to display the complete state machine when considering events, to enable better understanding.

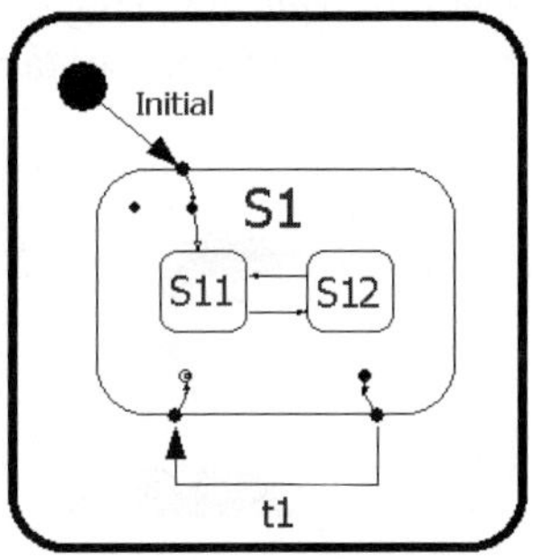

Fig. 3. Hierarchical state machine diagram from RoseRT documentation

State machines are driven by events which trigger transitions; however the visual notation is aimed at only representing the behaviour through notation such as states and the transitions between states. The presence of events may be indicated with text notation, either implicitly through transition names or explicitly through text adornment. For small state machines, this may be sufficient, however as the complexity of a state machine increases, the complexity of considering events increases dramatically. The cognitive load on the software engineer quickly becomes very large when considering the possible permutations of the state machine behaviour, especially for hierarchical state machines.

We now consider the following case study. Assume that this state machine (Fig. 3) is driven by only two events. Let us imagine that we are a software engineer who must make a change to S12. In order to implement this change we need to consider the impact of the possible incoming events on both S12 and S1, as S12 is a substate of S1, S1 must handle events "let through" by S12 (i.e. events not handled or deferred).

Now imagine that Fig.3 is two diagrams (Top and S1), as it would be in RoseRT and that we can only view one diagram at a time. In considering S12 we now have one extra "off-screen" diagram that needs to be thought about outside of the current view. If we were to add another substate level in S12 as part of that change (e.g. S123), we would have two "off-screen" diagrams to consider when working on S123.

As we see, the amount of "thinking outside of the diagram" is easily doubled, tripled or more depending on hierarchical depth.

4.3 Cognitive Off-Loading Using 3D and Event Notation

This section explains how 3D state machine diagrams and event notation may help the software engineer in cognition of hierarchical state machine diagrams. 3D allows the complete state machine to be viewed in one single view. Event notation is suggested as providing a visual summary of where events are handled. The figures 4-6 below summarise what information the UML presents to the software engineer and what they are required to imagine or think about to understand the effect of a single event on a state machine hierarchy. It must be stressed that at this stage of the evaluation process, neither the negative nor positive aspects of the visualisation have been tested. It is likely that aspects of the new visualisation may increase cognitive load in other areas of interpreting the information displayed. This section presents purely the proposed solution and how it has been derived from user task analysis.

Fig. 4. In the current situation the engineer is only able to view one state machine diagram at a time. In considering how a single event may be processed by the state machine, they must think about all superstates and how they may handle that event.

Fig. 5. With a 3D state machine diagram the engineer is able to view all state machine diagrams in the hierarchy and only needs to think about how each may handle that event

Fig. 6. With combined 3D and event notation the engineer need only think about the events that have impact on specific states levels, irrelevant diagrams can be ignored

4.4 Cognitive Load Metrics

The initial state machine survey (Table 1) only looked at state depth (i.e. individual states within a machine) and included "empty" non-behavioural state machines, however it is now understood that a better measure of complexity is state machine diagram depth. The software engineer is not merely interested in the states themselves, they are interested in the behavioural aspects of the diagram as a whole (states, transitions, choice points etc) and the state machine diagrams higher in the hierarchy which participate in that behaviour.

To analyse the extent of diagram hierarchies (as opposed to state levels), a new RoseRT script was created to count used diagrams and depth. In addition to this, the script calculated an "off-screen" metric based on the average number of additional diagrams that had to be considered for any given diagram in the hierarchy. To gather metrics, companies from the previous survey were contacted and the results of 664 state machines from 4 models are shown in Table 2.

The survey shows that hierarchical state machines are used a large amount of the time (37.2%-64.4%). This result is similar to the original substate usage survey; however with more detailed information it is now revealed that between 55.74%-89.85% of all used diagrams (either substate or superstate) form part of a hierarchical structure. This high number is due to hierarchical state machines containing more diagrams. For the most complex state machine found the software engineer had to consider, on average, 3.25 other diagrams for every diagram they worked on and that state machine contained 16 diagrams in total.

Table 2. New metrics for models from industries surveyed in Table 1 and a user task study subsystem. Off-screen diagrams is a cognitive measure of the average number of diagrams that need to be considered for any given diagram within a single hierarchical state machine.

Totals	Robotics	Robotics	Subsystem	Control
Single Layer State Machines	27	67	n/a	177
Hierarchical State Machines	16	54	3	320
Percentage Hierarchical	37.2%	44.6%	n/a	64.4%
State/Substate Diagrams	61	223	n/a	1743
Percent Diagrams Hierarchical	55.74%	69.96%	n/a	89.85%
Average Off-screen >= 2	0	1	2	26
Average Off-screen >= 1	1	12	3	129
Max. Average Off-screen	0.75	2	3.25	3.16
Max. Diagram Size	4	10	16	19

The survey clearly shows that any improvements in the area of understanding hierarchical state machine diagrams would be of great benefit to the software engineers work load. If other aspects of 3D visualisation (such as navigation issues etc) were known to be insignificant, then this survey would be evidence that 3D UML state machine diagrams would be of benefit to engineers by virtue of intuitively presenting them missing information required to do their tasks. Other aspects of 3D visualisation though are not insignificant; the question is how much benefit has been gained compared to what may be lost to other aspects such as navigation. The next phases of the research proceed to answer these questions.

5 Heuristic Evaluation Results

In this section we present the Heuristic Evaluation phase and results. The goals of this phase are to obtain feedback from expert evaluators so that the initial visualisation can be refined before more user intensive testing is undertaken as part of the Formative Evaluation phase. In addition to this, to mitigate the risk that the user tasks defined may have been unusual or company specific, feedback was also sought on how the tasks might compare with usage patterns in other companies.

Based on the user task analysis results, examples of 3D UML state machine diagrams were created with event notation, generated from the "Traffic Light" example model provided with RoseRT (Fig. 7). Event notation took the form of "event summaries" indicated at the top left of each diagram with a point and associated event name. If the same event was processed at different layers, the points were linked as a visual cue to which diagrams need to be considered for each event.

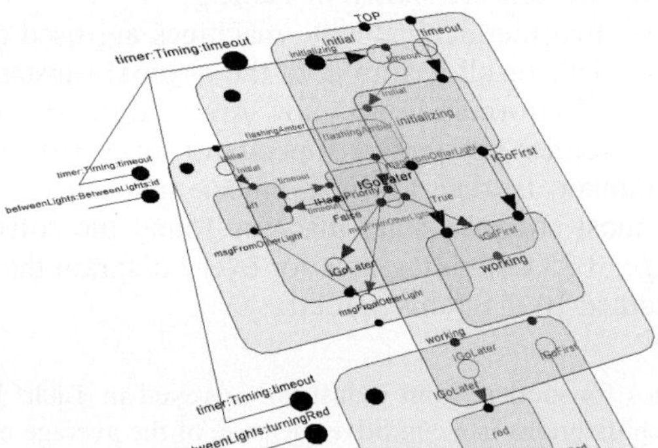

Fig. 7. 3D UML state machine diagram derived from user task analysis. The state machine diagram presents all diagrams in a hierarchy in a single 3D dynamic view and provides additional information about the events that drive the state machine behaviour.

Nine experts in the area of RoseRT and UML were contacted and provided with information on the defined user tasks, an evaluation report form to complete and the proposed 3D solution in the form of an X3D file which could be viewed with a browser. Evaluators were asked to *"evaluate the 3D state machine diagram examples given, against the task of refactoring existing state machine diagrams."*

In the time frame given to evaluators, two evaluation reports have been received to date. Evaluator 1, was a former IBM Senior Software Engineering Specialist with over 6 years experience *"with many (hundreds)"* of RoseRT customers and Evaluator 2, a Senior Software Engineering Consultant in real-time model driven development.

The overall opinion of the 3D state machine diagram from evaluator 1 was that *"Gestures for navigation and manipulation will be difficult, but the overall development experience would be served well I think."* Evaluator 2 was already of the opinion that *"a 3D view would be helpful"* and suggested the idea be taken further.

The results of the evaluation are summarised in the following sections.

5.1 User Task Question Responses

With the Refactoring task defined as, "refining implementations, fixing bugs and adding new features", the responses indicate that our user task analysis was indeed representative of industry and may also be applicable to the UML tool "Rhapsody".

Evaluator 1 User Task Responses Summary:
"Refactoring a state machine is indeed a problem and large hierarchies can quickly become difficult to manage" and *"This is mainly a problem with deep hierarchies or hierarchies that have been developed by someone else, e.g. a previous other, or teams"*. The estimate for weekly task percentages was *"30% structure 30% behavior (state machines), 30% design review"*.

Evaluator 2 User Task Responses Summary:
For refactoring state machine diagrams the *"experience is similar"*. For task percentages the estimate was that *"approx 30-45% of "normal/productive" modelling involves defining and refining behaviour and 30-40% defining and refining structure..."* however actual *"redesigning ... should not be >=20% of the effort"*.

5.2 3D State Machine Diagrams and Event Notation Question Responses

The following summarises common and specific responses given in relation to 3D useability issues and event notation questions from both evaluators:

Common Responses (In order of Evaluator 1 and Evaluator 2):

Layout - *"The lay-out needs to be applied in such a way that the 3D version of the diagram is usable"* and *"a new style of state diagram layout algorithm"* is required.

Navigation - *"The 3D browser doesn't really make navigation easy"* and *"an effective means to allow users to adjust to the optimal perspective"* is required.

Filtering - *"The 3D diagram contains a lot of information. State machines work well partially because the amount of information in a diagram is strongly reduced"* and *"eliding all of the states not "enclosed" by the chosen state... can hide a lot of unnecessary detail"*

Evaluator 1 Specific Responses:
Visual Connection between Layers - An enhancement would be a *"connection between a state at level N and the fold-out of it at level N+1"*

Evaluator 2 Specific Responses
Print Layout - *"printing 3D will be almost as important as on-screen visualization."*

Transition paths between State Layers – *"show the transitions between layers"*

Behaviour specific "Slices" – *"it would be nice to view "slices" of a hierarchical state diagram improve understanding the design of the state machine's behaviour."*

On the questions related to the benefit of event notation, evaluator 1 did not "*have a strong opinion*" either way. Evaluator 2 stated "*yes*" it would be of benefit.

6 Formative Evaluation Results

In this section we present the Formative Evaluation phase and results. The goal of this phase is to walk through the visualisation with the user to gain feedback required to refine the visualisation to a point where empirical testing can be undertaken in the Summative Evaluation phase. In this phase, two types of sessions were undertaken, an "off-site" session which was used to support the Heuristic Evaluation phase (due to the poor response rate) and "on-site" sessions with the refined visualisation.

6.1 Off-Site Formative Session

Prior to revisiting the site where the initial user task analysis was undertaken, a Formative session was undertaken with a former team member using the "Traffic Light" example (Fig. 7). The session was designed to provide additional information prior to refining the visualisation for on-site sessions. The user expressed that, as it was, the visualisation would be of benefit and suggested the following improvements:

- There needed to be a stronger visual link between substates and superstates.
- The event notation lines suggested incorrect relationships between states.
- Visually linking junction points between substates and superstates (as needed) would help when following transition paths.
- Showing (as needed) which transitions were triggered by each event would be useful (i.e. linking event notation points to their associated triggers).
- It would be useful to be able to exclude non-relevant state branches.
- There is even more potential benefit in 3D UML structure diagrams.

6.2 3D UML State Machine Diagram Refinements

From the Heuristic Evaluation results and the Off-Site Formative Evaluation session results the following conclusions have been made regarding the visualisation and the refinements needed to better suit users' tasks.

- There is definite and consistent perceived benefit in the 3D UML state machine diagram, prior to refinements.
- More precise user requirements are uncovered from walking through the 3D visualisation (i.e. user tasks become better defined).
- Layout of the diagram needs to be addressed.

- Navigation within the diagram needs to be addressed.
- Connections between substates and superstates needs to be clearer.
- Dynamic user controlled filtering of irrelevant data is required.
- Dynamic user controlled presentation of more data is required.
- Event notation links were not strongly desired and had negative aspects.

Based on these conclusions the visualisation (Fig. 8) was refined in the following ways:

- Event notation lines, junction point lines and other data enhancements were not implemented to determine through user feedback if these were indeed required for tasks (i.e. gain more precise user requirements in this area).
- Event notation summaries were listed at the bottom of diagrams.
- The user was provided with the ability to create and save a diagram layout.
- The ability to reposition the whole diagram in the view was introduced.
- Transparent connection "cones" visually linked superstates and substates.
- The ability to "shrink" branches to filter data was introduced.

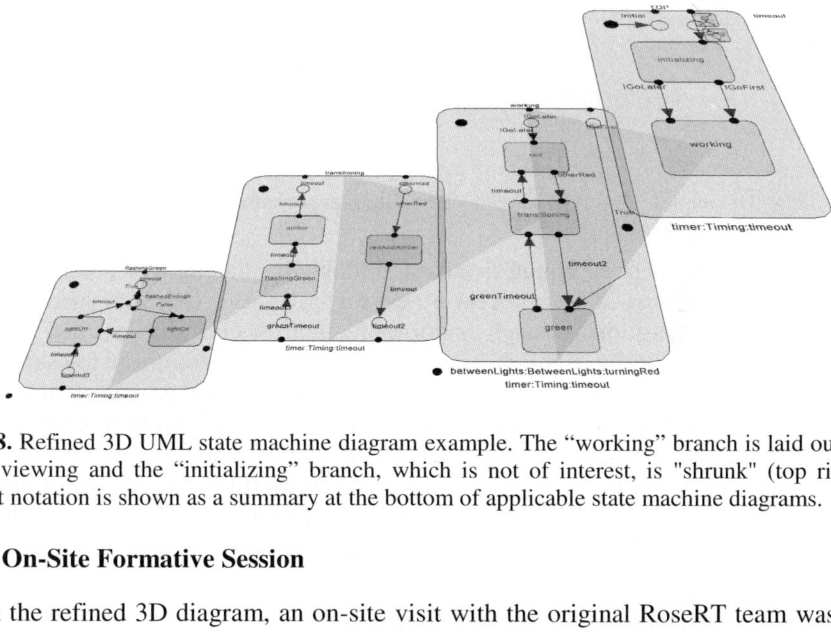

Fig. 8. Refined 3D UML state machine diagram example. The "working" branch is laid out for easy viewing and the "initializing" branch, which is not of interest, is "shrunk" (top right). Event notation is shown as a summary at the bottom of applicable state machine diagrams.

6.3 On-Site Formative Session

With the refined 3D diagram, an on-site visit with the original RoseRT team was arranged. In this session the users were individually taken through a 10 minute training session with the new visualisation based on the "Traffic Light" example model (Fig.8) and were taught basic X3D browser navigation techniques; such as how to centre the diagram, rotate and examine, layout the diagram and save that layout.

Users were then asked to pick an actual state machine diagram from a model they were working on and, from the chosen diagram, a 3D state machine diagram was generated. Users were then asked to walk through the diagram and comment on the features they need to do their job, as well as usability aspects. An example of the most complex state machine diagram generated is given in figure 9, with this diagram having an "off-screen" average of 3.25 diagrams (see 4.5 Cognitive Load Metrics).

All users stated that they saw benefit in the 3D UML state machine diagram and the event notation. The users stated this in strong terms with one user stating "*of course*" (it would be useful) as though it was such an obvious question it should not be asked, and another stating it would be "*definitely useful*".

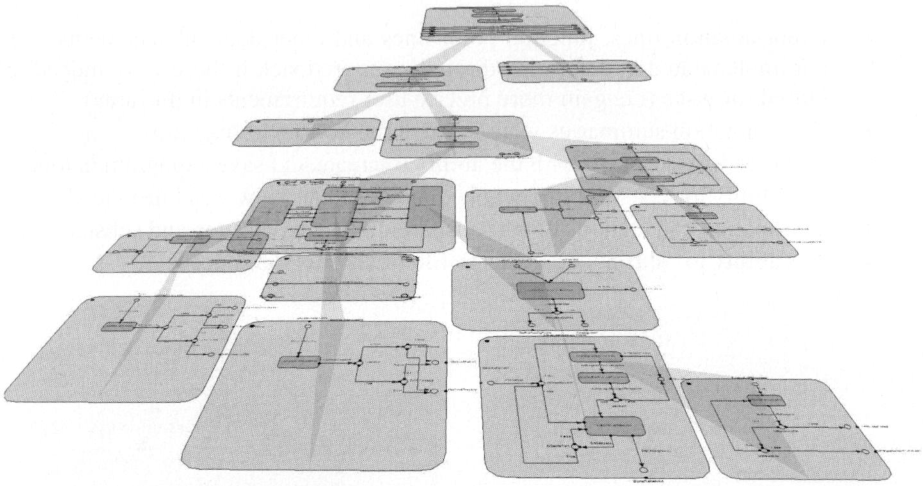

Fig. 9. Complete 3D UML state machine diagram generated from actual user data

The users each spent 30 minutes walking through the diagram and commenting on improvements. As part of this process a new low-level user task was uncovered related to tracing transitions through multiple diagram levels for a specific purpose. Users needed to logically highlight transition "chains" (i.e. groups of transitions) to analyse particular aspects of a state machine and these transition groups often spanned multiple levels of diagram. This user task was a logical extension to linking junction points between diagrams, as they form part of a transition chain.

The improvements suggested by the users are grouped together below in their respective categories and these are planned to be implemented before the Summative Evaluation (empirical testing) phase is undertaken:

Dynamic Features for Multi-Level Transition Tracing

- Highlight transition chains of interest.
- Link transition relationships at the same level in the hierarchy.

Essential Data

- Dynamic junction point linking between substate and superstates.

Navigation Improvements

- Restrict navigation options to prevent awkward views.
- Allow quick navigation to individual state machine diagrams.
- Hot-keys to navigate to different view aspects.

User Preferences

- Opacity configuration to suit user preferences and different graphics capabilities of machines.
- Ability to adjust layout diagram depth to suit diagram size.

7 Conclusions and Future Research

The results of our research to date present consistent evidence that there is benefit in 3D UML state machine diagrams. Though final empirical user testing will provide a more definitive answer and better quantify the benefit, the analysis so far highlights a common and critical software engineering task that benefits from an alternative UML visualisation provided by 3D. Both user and expert evaluation sessions provide qualitative evidence that benefit already exists in our 3D UML state machine diagram, however further refinements have been suggested to capitalise on 3D visualisation possibilities and improve navigation, to increase that benefit further.

The benefit of 3D UML state machine diagrams is in the area of understanding hierarchical state machine diagrams. Both user and expert responses show that this is an area of known concern and our analysis captures the extent. For RoseRT engineers, defining state machine behaviour is a task which occupies 30%-40% of their effort and our model metrics survey shows that between 56%-90% of that effort is likely to be related to hierarchical state machines. We further quantify the issue through a metric of "off-screen" information missing from the engineers' view which indicates the level of "out of diagram thinking" currently required.

The next phase of this research is Summative Evaluation, where the final refined 3D UML state machine diagram will be empirically tested for benefit on a larger user base. The generic benefit measures of speed and accuracy will captured from users completing typical tasks on the same model with both 2D and 3D UML state machine diagrams. The tests will make use of state machines with increasing complexity, so that we can chart performance of 2D vs. 3D diagrams over a range of complexity. This measure of "complexity benefit" will enable models to be analysed through our metrics script to predict overall benefit based on a complexity profile of each model.

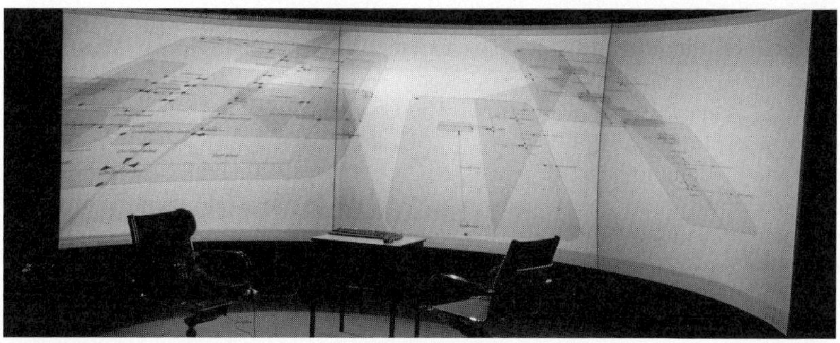

Fig. 10. Testing 3D UML visualisation at the RMIT Virtual Reality Centre

Due to the success of the 3D state machine diagram results, we have also commenced research into 3D UML system views. Based on user task analysis of teams collaborating on large software projects, these views will be able to capture the complete UML model in a single dynamic 3D view, allowing users to view the system as a whole, as well as filter data and highlight areas of interest. These views will be available to individuals through their standard workstations and are also being implemented for team use at RMIT's Virtual Reality Centre (Fig 10).

Acknowledgements

We would like to thank: RMIT for PhD scholarship funding; Expert Evaluators, Mark Hermeling and Tim Coddington; the anonymous users that volunteered their time; Garry Keltie for RMIT VR Centre assistance and Laura McIntosh for graphics.

References

1. Gil, J., Kent, S.: Three dimensional software modelling. In: Proceedings of the 20th international conference on Software engineering, Kyoto, Japan. IEEE Computer Society, Los Alamitos (1998)
2. Gogolla, M., Radfelder, O., Richters, M.: Towards Three-Dimensional Animation of UML Diagrams. In: France, R.B., Rumpe, B. (eds.) UML 1999. LNCS, vol. 1723. Springer, Heidelberg (1999)
3. Radfelder, O., Gogolla, M.: On better understanding UML diagrams through interactive three-dimensional visualization and animation. In: Proceedings of the working conference on Advanced visual interfaces, Palermo, Italy. ACM, New York (2000)
4. Thaden, U., Steimann, F.: Animated UML as a 3d-illustration for teaching OOP. In: ECOOP 2003 - Object-Oriented Programming. Proceedings of the 17th European Conference, Darmstadt, Germany. Springer, Heidelberg (2003)
5. Irani, P., Ware, C.: Diagrams based on structural object perception. In: Proceedings of the working conference on Advanced visual interfaces, Palermo, Italy. ACM, New York (2000)
6. Dwyer, T.: Three dimensional UML using force directed layout. in Australian symposium on Information visualisation, Sydney, Australia. Australian Computer Society, Inc. (2001)
7. Web3D Consortium. Extensible 3D (X3D) - ISO/IEC FDIS (Final Draft International Standard). 19775:200x (2004)
8. Booch, G., Rumbaugh, J., Jacobson, I.: The Unified Modeling Language User Guide. Addison-Wesley, Reading (1998)
9. McIntosh, P., Hamilton, M., Schyndel, R.v.: X3D-UML: Enabling Advanced UML Visualisation Through X3D. In: 3D technologies for the World Wide Web - Proceedings of the tenth international conference on 3D Web technology, Bangor, United Kingdom. ACM Press, New York (2005)
10. IBM, Rational Rose Technical Developer (2008), `http://www-306.ibm.com/software/awdtools/developer/technical/`
11. Ambler, S.W.: The Elements of UML(TM) 2.0 Style. Cambridge University Press, Cambridge (2005)
12. Object Management Group. Unified Modeling Language: Diagram Interchange - version 2.0 (2003)

13. Object Management Group. Diagram Interchange - XML file (2007), http://www.omg.org/cgi-bin/doc?ptc/05-06-07
14. Gabbard, J.L., Deborah, H., Swan, J.E.: User-Centered Design and Evaluation of Virtual Environments. IEEE Comput. Graph. Appl. 19(6), 51–59 (1999)
15. Bowman, D.A., et al.: 3D User Interfaces: Theory and Practice. Addison-Wesley/Pearson Education, London (2005)
16. McIntosh, P., Hamilton, M., Schyndel, R.v.: 3D UML State Machine Diagrams Evaluation Methodology (2008), http://www.x3d-uml.org/Publications/Technical_Reports
17. Hackos, J.T., Redish, J.C.: User and task analysis for interface design, p. 488. John Wiley & Sons, Inc., Chichester (1998)

Assessing the Influence of Stereotypes on the Comprehension of UML Sequence Diagrams: A Controlled Experiment

Marcela Genero[1], José A. Cruz-Lemus[1], Danilo Caivano[2], Silvia Abrahão[3], Emilio Insfran[3], and José A. Carsí[3]

[1] ALARCOS Research Group,
Department of Technologies and Information Systems,
University of Castilla-La Mancha
Paseo de la Universidad, 4
13071 Ciudad Real, Spain
{Marcela.Genero,JoseAntonio.Cruz}@uclm.es

[2] Department of Informatics
University of Bari
Via E. Orabona, 4
70126 Bari, Italy
caivano@di.uniba.it

[3] ISSI Research Group
Department of Information Systems and Computation
Universidad Politécnica de Valencia
Camino de Vera s/n
46022, Valencia, Spain
{sabrahao,einsfran,pcarsi}@dsic.upv.es

Abstract. The main goal of this paper is to provide empirical evidence, through a controlled experiment, of the influence of stereotypes when modelers, developers, and maintainers have to comprehend UML sequence diagrams. The comprehension of UML sequence diagrams with and without stereotypes was analyzed from three different perspectives: semantic comprehension, retention and transfer. The experiment was carried out with 77 fourth year undergraduate students of Computer Science from the University of Bari in Italy. The results obtained show a slight tendency in favor of the use of stereotypes in facilitating the comprehension of UML sequence diagrams, although it is not statistically significant. Further replications are needed to obtain more conclusive results.

1 Introduction

A wide use of models in software development has resulted in the creation of several modeling languages and notations with which to express graphical models. The most successful modeling language is the Unified Modeling Language (UML) [19], which is widely accepted in both industry and academia.

The main drawback of this language is that the set of general modeling constructs is not suitable for a specific purpose and hereafter the modeling might not be effective

K. Czarnecki et al. (Eds.): MoDELS 2008, LNCS 5301, pp. 280–294, 2008.

[27]. To address this drawback, several works propose the improvement of modeling with UML by customizing it with the extension mechanisms inherent in the language (e.g., stereotypes).

Stereotypes are used to clarify or extend the meaning of model elements and to introduce new modeling elements reusing the syntax of similar elements already available in the notation. However, does the use of stereotypes really lead to better models? In recent years, several studies through which to address this question have been conducted in the field of Software Engineering [24, 27]. These studies are focused on investigating the influence of stereotypes on the comprehension of UML class and collaboration diagrams. It is widely recognized that comprehension is one of the main factors to influence maintainability [9, 20, 23, 25], which must be assessed from the first steps of the software lifecycle, in the modeling phase (see related work in Section 2).

In our experience stereotypes are often used in industrial contexts and their use spans from use cases to class diagrams. Indeed industries use stereotypes within their development processes in order to specialize general processes to a particular technology in use, such as programming languages (C#, Java,...), application type (real time, web application, client-server, standalone, etc.), reusable components used (Microsoft Foundation Class Library, Enterprise Java Beans Library, etc.) or simply to give more detailed guidelines to the practitioners involved in the systems development processes. The use of stereotypes is also widespread in the academia in order to give students some practical instruments for guiding software design and to fill the information and representation gap of UML standard language. Well known stereotypes widely used in industry and academy are the Conallen's stereotypes [5] that are also supported by the most used UML Case Tool such as ARGO UML, Enterprise Architect and STAR UML. Today, these case tools are widely used in industrial contexts.

Nevertheless, the influence of stereotypes on the comprehension of requirements models, such as sequence diagrams has not yet been investigated. This fact has motivated us to develop the research presented in this work.

We focus on UML sequence diagrams since they are a widely used technique for reasoning about object interactions needed to realize a given scenario of functional requirement and on the comprehension of these diagrams since this is essential in the validation of requirements specifications among developers and stakeholders. A sequence diagram must be first comprehended before any desired changes to it can be identified, designed, or implemented.

In this paper, we present a controlled experiment to assess whether the use of stereotypes improves the comprehension of UML sequence diagrams. Specifically, we consider a set of stereotypes that have been proposed to enrich the semantics of interaction messages in UML sequence diagrams in the context of a Requirements Engineering approach for model-driven software development [10, 11]. The benefit of using these stereotypes is twofold. First, they can improve the comprehension of UML sequence diagrams, and second, they give specific information about how to deal with each individual source element in the transformation of UML sequence diagrams into conceptual models in the model-driven development process.

The controlled experiment was carried out by 77 fourth year of Computer Science undergraduate students at the University of Bari in Italy.

The structure of the paper is as follows. Firstly, related works on the empirical evaluation of UML diagram comprehension and specifically with regard to the use stereotypes are presented in Section 2. The definition of stereotypes for UML sequence diagrams is explained in Section 3. The description and execution of the experiment is described in Section 4. The data analysis and the interpretation of the experiment results are presented in Section 5. Finally, the conclusions and a discussion on future research work are presented in Section 6.

2 Related Work

The comprehension of UML diagrams has frequently been investigated (this list does not intend to be exhaustive, but simply illustrative):

- Purchase et al. [21, 22] report two experiments which take the perspective of human comprehension of UML class and collaboration diagrams considering five different notations in each study. In the case of class diagrams, they obtained that the best performing notation depends on the task for which the diagram was used, whilst for the collaboration diagrams, they concluded that a specification matches a diagram, but not when errors in a diagram can be identified.
- Cruz-Lemus *et al.* [6] present a family of empirical studies to investigate whether the use of composite states improves the understandability of UML statechart diagrams. The results, although not conclusive, show that the use of composite states does not improve the understandability of simple UML statechart diagrams.
- Genero *et al.* [9] present a family of experiments carried out to evaluate the relation between a set of measures for the structural properties of UML class diagrams and their understandability and modifiability. They also provide prediction models for such quality characteristics. They found that the measures related to associations and generalization seems to have more influence on the understanding and modification of UML class diagrams.
- Lange and Chaudron [15] use an experiment to validate whether there is a difference between a set of views which they propose to increase model understanding (MetaView, ContextView, MetricView, and UML-City-View), and the existing views with respect to comprehension correctness and effort. They conclude that correctness is improved and time needed is reduced when the proposed views are used.
- Xie *et al.* [30] present a study in which their proposed synchronization adorned UML sequence diagrams notation is used to verify whether it helps students towards a better understanding of concurrent executions and concurrency concepts. They finally find a statistically significant benefit.

To our knowledge, there are two recent works which are aimed at investigating the influence of stereotypes on the comprehension of UML diagrams:

- Staron *et al.* [27] have assessed the influence of stereotypes on the comprehension of models (UML class and collaboration diagrams) through a set of experiments. They found that stereotypes significantly helped both students and industrial programmers.

- Ricca *et al.* [24] describe a family of three experiments which were performed to assess the effectiveness of UML stereotypes in supporting comprehension tasks in class diagrams for Web design. They conclude that stereotypes significantly improve the performance of low ability/experience subjects.

The literature review described here reveals that comprehension is a principal concern in the context of UML modeling, but that the contribution of stereotypes with which to improve the comprehension of UML sequence diagrams has not yet been investigated.

3 Stereotypes for UML Sequence Diagrams

UML indicates that sequence diagrams are a means to model an aspect of the dynamic behavior of a system [12]. They can be used in the context of the whole system, of a subsystem, or they can be attached to a Use Case. Some authors indicate that at least one sequence diagram should be drawn per Use Case [7, 12]. When a sequence diagram is developed for a Use Case, the Use Case description can be used to develop at least the initial draft of the sequence diagram. Throughout the design process the Use Case diagram can be revised based on the results of the sequence diagram, and vice versa, until both models are appropriately tuned [16].

When using a sequence diagram at the type level, it represents a pattern interaction, which is a set of messages among object types with which to carry out a behavior. It has two dimensions: the vertical dimension represents time, and the horizontal dimension represents the different object types (classes). Time proceeds down the page and there is no significance to the horizontal ordering of the object types.

The emphasis in this type of diagrams is that of graphically representing the pattern interaction between object types by sending and receiving messages as time advances. In addition, when using sequence diagrams to realize a Use Case, the focus should not be on specifying detailed behavior with complex iterations and conditional messages (the *how*) but the interactions that are needed to perform the Use Case purpose (the *what*).

There is at least one sequence diagram per Use Case, one for the basic course of action, and another for each alternative course of action (if any). To build the sequence diagram for a Use Case, we analyze each Use Case at two levels:

- **Use Case diagram level:** actors that communicate with the Use Case;
- **Use Case specification level:** the set of steps or responsibilities to be performed in order to accomplish the Use Case.

At the Use Case diagram level, an actor can send and/or receive information to/from the Use Case. Every Use Case has at least one actor, which is the Use Case initiator and other collaborating actors. All the actors are potentially object types to be taken into account for the sequence diagram.

At the Use Case specification level, the main task is to obtain the set of responsibilities implied by the corresponding Use Case steps. Essentially, when the Use Case receives a stimulus (an external interaction), the system produces a set of interactions between its internal components (objects) as a response. These interactions are represented as messages in the sequence diagram. In [10, 11] they are classified according to their nature by using the following UML stereotypes:

- **«signal»** this is a message between an actor and the system.
- **«service»** this is a message that updates the state of an object. The properties new/destroy/update can be used if the object is to be created, destroyed or modified.
- **«query»** this is a message to query the state of a specific object or set of objects.
- **«connect»** this is a message which is used to indicate that an object from the sender object type needs to be connected (or related) to an object from the receiver object type.

Although the UML 2.1 standard [19] defines a set of general predefined stereotypes that can be used in UML depending on the L2 or L3 level of compliance, there are no specific stereotypes for sequence diagrams. For this reason, specific methods or tools should extend the notation and meaning provided by the standard UML features if they are to have a semantically richer modeling notation. In Figure 1, we present an example which shows the stereotyped interactions (messages) that are needed to realize a Use Case for items-sale in a conventional store. The explanation of the main interaction/messages is also given below.

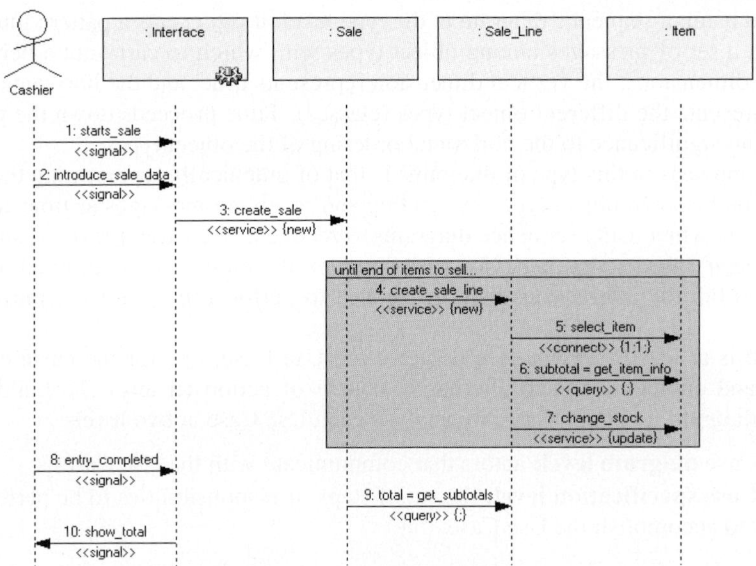

Fig. 1. An example of a sequence diagram with stereotyped messages

- **Message 1 and 2.** The cashier starts a sale. This message represents the commencement of communication between the Cashier and the Interface of the software system. The following message *introduce_sale_data* provides the data which is necessary to perform the operation.

- **Message 3.** The cashier creates a new sale. This message implies the responsibility of creating a new sale and registering its information. We have named this responsibility *create_sale* and allocated it to a new class called Sale.
- **Message 4.** The cashier records the identifier of each item to be sold. This action implies the responsibility of registering information about the items to be sold. We have named this responsibility *create_sale_item* and allocated it to a new class component called Sale-line.
- **Message 5.** The message *select_one_item* (with the stereotype **«connect»**) is identified because the analyst determines that a complete Sale-line must have one and only one Item (product) assigned to it.
- **Message 6.** The system determines the item price and adds this information to the current *sale_line*. This action implies the responsibility of querying an object that stores the item price. We have named this responsibility *get_item_info* with the stereotype **«query»**.
- **Message 7.** Another responsibility of the Use Case is that of updating the item stock when the item is sold. We have named this responsibility *change_stock* and allocated it to the previously detected class component Item.
- **Message 9.** The system calculates the total amount of the sale from the corresponding set of *sale_lines* and the system then shows the information concerning the complete sale to the Cashier (Message 10).

Note that at this level of specification, the details of the iteration or the control flow in the sequence diagram are not the main focus since we are mainly identifying and specifying *what* interactions are needed to realize the Use Case. This activity leads us to discovering classes and services and not to describing the complete behavior of the involved classes.

The process of specifying a Use Case as an interaction of collaborative objects continues thus until all the steps of the Use Case are defined in their corresponding sequence diagram. Developers should verify this specification looking for the satisfaction of the Use Case purpose and also validate it together with users during and after its construction. Comprehension is, therefore, a critical factor in the building of this type of diagrams.

4 Experiment Description

The main goal of this experiment is to assess whether the use of stereotypes improves the understanding of UML sequence diagrams. Therefore, by using the GQM template for goal definition [1, 3], the goal of our experiment is defined as follows:

"Analyze the use of stereotypes for the purpose of evaluating it with respect to the comprehension of UML sequence diagrams from the point of view of the researcher, in the context of fourth year undergraduate students in Computer Science from the University of Bari".

In order to run and report this experiment we followed the recommendations provided in several works [13, 29]. The design of the experiment presented in this paper is similar to those presented in [27].

We selected a balanced factorial design with group-interaction confounding [14]. The objects were UML sequence diagrams, with two possible values – stereotyped diagram and non-stereotyped diagram.

All the subjects were randomly assigned to 4 groups (1, 2, 3 and 4). The experiment consisted of two rounds. Two different diagrams were presented to every subject in each group. To avoid a possible learning effect, the diagrams came from different application domains (A and B). All diagrams and domains were similar in complexity and similarly common to all the subjects. More details about the experimental design are provided in the remainder of this section.

4.1 Planning

Various issues related to the planning of the experiment are introduced in this section.

- **Subjects.** The experiment was carried out by 77 fourth year Computer Science students who were taking a course in Empirical Software Engineering. The subjects had participated in two Software Engineering courses in which they had acquired training in UML diagrams. Their knowledge was sufficient for them to understand the given non-stereotyped diagrams, and they had roughly the same background. They had knowledge about the use of stereotypes in general, but they were taught about the stereotypes we proposed for UML sequence diagrams in a training session organized to take place the day before the experiment was carried out.

To avoid social threats due to evaluation apprehension, the students were not graded on their performance. On the contrary, the participants were granted 2 extra points in their final valuation at the end of the course

- **Experiment objects.** The experimental objects consisted of four diagrams, summarized below (these are presented fully at alarcos.esi.uclm.es/ExpStereotypes):

- DA-S: stereotyped diagram A and a general description of each type of stereotype.
- DA-N: non-stereotyped diagram A.
- DB-S: stereotyped diagram B and a general description of each type of stereotype.
- DB-N: non-stereotyped diagram B.

UML sequence diagram A-x describes a car rental domain. It describes an "Extras Rental" use case which may occur in addition to the car rental. Diagram B-x describes a hotel domain. It represents the sequence of interactions of the "Book room" use case. These experimental objects were presented in Italian.

- **Independent and dependent variables.** There are two independent variables in the experiment, the diagram type, with values: S (stereotyped) and N (non-stereotyped), and the diagram domain (A and B). By combining each level of the independent variables we obtain four treatments, as reflected by the four diagrams which are the objects of the experiment.

In accordance with certain suggestions concerning the measurement of comprehension [4, 6, 8], we have used the Cognitive Theory of Multimedia Learning (CTML) [18]. This choice was made on the basis of several reasons. First, it focuses on words and graphics, which are the elements in the UML sequence diagrams grammar. Second, it provides principles for the design of effective multimedia presentations which can be tested empirically. Third, it has evolved through years of work and development of experimental instruments and methods related to model comprehension [17, 18].

By following CTML, the comprehension of the UML sequence diagrams has been defined through three variables:

- **Semantic comprehension:** the ability to comprehend the semantics of the models.
- **Retention:** the comprehension of material being presented, and the ability to retain knowledge from it.
- **Transfer:** the ability to use the knowledge gained from the material to solve related problems which are not directly answerable from it.

It is expected that due to the use of stereotypes that enrich the meaning of the messages in the sequence diagram specification, the reader of a stereotyped sequence diagram will have additional key knowledge than a reader of a non-stereotyped one for comprehension, retention and transfer tasks.

For clearness, the quality model used (defined according to the GQM approach [1, 3]) is presented in Figure 2, which also points out the experimental hypothesis defined for each measure used.

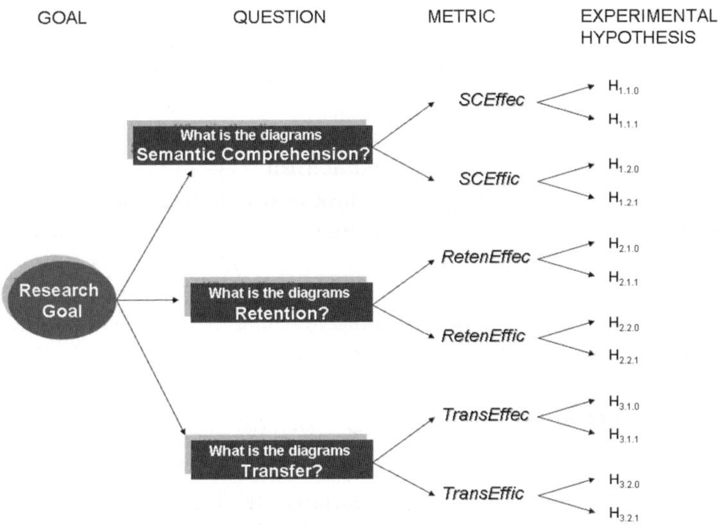

Fig. 2. Quality Model used and Experimental Hypotheses

In order to measure these variables, we have used three separate tests based on questionnaires. Each comprehension measure is computed as:

- Effectiveness: the proportion of correct answers provided in each test (number of correct answers / number of questions). This measure reflects the ability to understand the presented material correctly.
- Efficiency: the proportion of correct answers divided by time (Effectiveness / Time).

In this work, we call these values SCEffec/SCEffic (Semantic Comprehension Effectiveness and Efficiency), TransEffec/TransEffic (Transfer Effectiveness and Efficiency), and finally, RetenEffec/RetenEffic (Retention Effectiveness and Efficiency).

- **Hypotheses.** For Semantic Comprehension we wished to test the following hypothesis:
- Null hypotheses

  $H_{1.1,0}$: stereotypes do not improve the subjects' SCEffec when attempting to comprehend a UML sequence diagram.

  $H_{1.2,0}$: stereotypes do not improve the subjects' SCEffic when attempting to comprehend an UML sequence diagram
- Alternative hypotheses:

  $H_{1.1,1} = \neg H_{1.1,0}$

  $H_{1.2,1} = \neg H_{1.2,0}$

We analogously formulated a set of hypothesis H_2 for Retention measures (RetenEffec and RetenEffic), and another set H_3 related to the Transfer measures (TransfEffec and TransEffic) (see Figure 2).

We stated one-tailed hypotheses as we wanted to check if the use of stereotypes improved the way in which subjects comprehended UML sequence diagrams.

- **Instrumentation.** The instruments used in the experiment were three tests attached to each of the four treatments. In each test the subjects were asked to write down the time before starting to solve the tasks required in each test.

  The tests are described as follows:
- Test 1: contained 10 Yes/No questions concerning the semantic of the diagrams. This task was used to obtain SCEffec and SCEffic.
- Test 2: consisted of a 'fill-in-the-blanks' task in which the subjects had to complete a test describing the functionality of the diagrams. This task was used to calculate RetenEffec and RetenEffic.
- Test 3: the subjects had to name a set of new messages that had been attached to the original version of the diagrams, but were labeled only with the parameters. This task was used to calculate TransEffec and TransEffic.

4.2 Experiment Operation

The experiment consisted of two rounds. In each round, each of the groups was given a different treatment. In order to alleviate learning effect, as is previously mentioned, we divided the experimental subjects into 4 groups. We randomly assigned the corresponding diagrams to each group, but in different order. Table 1 presents the outline

Table 1. Experiment rounds

Round 1		**Diagram Type**	
		S	N
Domain	A	Group 1	Group 2
	B	Group 4	Group 3

Round 2		**Diagram Type**	
		S	N
Domain	A	Group 3	Group 4
	B	Group 2	Group 1

of the experimental operation. The description of each type of diagram has already been presented in section 4.1. This assignment of diagrams corresponds with the selected balanced factorial design with group-interaction confounding [14], which permits the alleviation of learning and fatigue effects.

The design of the experiment includes a previous three hour lecture which took place the day before the experiment was carried out. The lecture included various tasks:

- To introduce the students the stereotypes defined for UML sequence diagrams.
- To show the students an example, similar to the material used in the experiment. We solved the tasks in the example with the students.
- To perform a pilot study in order to assure that the students had understood the experimental material and tasks.

After this previous session, we checked the responses of the students, and we discovered that the students performed badly when solving the second task. Therefore, before the experiment was carried out, we carefully re-explained the tasks involved in Test 2.

4.3 Conducting the Experiment

The day after the training session, the experiment took place in a one and a half hour session. In the 30 first minutes we explained how to perform the experiment and randomly assigned the subjects to two balanced groups.

The experiment was conducted in a classroom, where the students were supervised and no communication among them was allowed. Both groups were located in the same room.

Each round (see Table 1) was performed in the following way:

1. The subjects received the material for Test 1 which included a UML sequence diagram and a questionnaire. After finishing this task, Test 1 was handed back to the supervisor.
2. The students received Test 2, which had to be solved without the UML sequence diagram. After completing the tasks, Test 2 was handed back to the supervisor.
3. The students received Test 3 and after solving it they returned it to the supervisor.

5 Data Analysis and Interpretation

All the statistical analyses presented in this section were performed using SPSS [26].

In this section, we present, for each variable, the descriptive statistics and the results of the ANOVA tests carried to test the formulated hypotheses. ANOVA is the most appropriate test with which to explore the results of a factorial design with interaction confounded [14, 28], i.e., the design used in our experiment.

All the tests in our study were carried out by using a statistical significance threshold of $\alpha = 0.05$. The null hypotheses were thus rejected if the statistical tests we used provided a statistical significance of the results that was not higher than 0.05.

Tables 2, 3, and 4 presents the descriptive statistics for the all the variables studied: Semantic comprehension, Retention and Transfer. Grey cells indicate the best subjects' performance.

Table 2. Descriptive statistics for the Semantic Comprehension

			SCEffec		SCEffic	
Diagram Type	**Domain**	**N**	**Mean**	**Std. Dev**	**Mean**	**Std. Dev**
S	A	38	0.756	0.1410	0.0020	0.00069
	B	39	0.782	0.1312	0.0027	0.00133
	Total	77	0.769	0.1360	0.0023	0.00112
N	A	39	0.761	0.1079	0.0022	0.00082
	B	38	0.741	0.1390	0.0024	0.00096
	Total	77	0.751	0.1242	0.0023	0.00089

For both the variables (SCEffec and SCEffic), the subjects obtained better global results in the stereotyped diagrams. Obviously this means that the stereotyped diagrams were more comprehensible, less error prone and required less time to understand than non- stereotyped diagrams.

Table 3. Descriptive statistics for the Retention

			RetenEffec		RetenEffic	
Diagram Type	**Domain**	**N**	**Mean**	Std. Dev	Mean	Std. Dev
S	A	38	0.636	0.1579	0.0029	0.0036
	B	39	0.784	0.1830	0.0035	0.0019
	Total	77	0.709	0.1854	0.0032	0.0029
N	A	39	0.637	0.1814	0.0024	0.0011
	B	38	0.807	0.1408	0.0036	0.0044
	Total	77	0.723	0.1823	0.0030	0.0032

Table 4. Descriptive statistics for the Transfer

			TransEffec		TransEffic	
Diagram Type	**Domain**	**N**	**Mean**	Std. Dev	Mean	Std. Dev
S	A	38	0.682	0.2501	0.0023	0.0011
	B	39	0.829	0.2404	0.0090	0.0058
	Total	77	0.755	0.2547	0.0056	0.0053
N	A	39	0.616	0.2248	0.0022	0.0013
	B	38	0.821	0.3139	0.0097	0.0064
	Total	77	0.719	0.2907	0.0060	0.0059

Table 3 shows that, related to Retention, the subjects obtained better results in effectiveness when they did not use stereotypes, while the scores were higher for efficiency when they worked with stereotyped diagrams. In addition, RetenEffec and RetenEffic values are significantly better for the diagrams of domain B. Therefore, the subjects who used non-stereotyped diagrams were able to recall a greater number of correct functionalities of the models, but the subjects with non-stereotyped diagrams performed better if we relate the number of correct answers with the time spent answering the test. This is probably due to the fact that stereotyped diagrams contain more information than those which are non- stereotyped and thus prove to be more difficult to remember (and not to understand!). It is interesting to note that effectiveness is calculated as the number of correct answers divided by the total number of expected answers. In our analysis, the unanswered questions are, at present, considered to be wrong answers. However, it is probable that if we consider effectiveness as the number of correct answers divided by the total number of given answers, the effectiveness would increase. The students were told not to fill in the blank if they did not remember the answer. The higher efficiency for the stereotyped diagrams seems to confirm this interpretation: the students answered what they remembered in a short time and did not consider the rest of answers.

The results for Transfer (Table 4) are the opposite of those for Retention. Better results were obtained for effectiveness when the subjects used the stereotyped diagrams, but they were worse for efficiency. Moreover, these results confirm that the stereotyped diagrams are more comprehensible and less error prone but that the quantity of information they include implies that more time is needed for diagram processing: in this case, and unlike the Semantic Comprehension, the students have to reconstruct the message flow in the sequence diagram and thus have to spend more time in understanding the semantic first and the syntactic of the diagrams later. This implies more time spent, which thus leads to lower efficiency.

Table 5 presents the results of the ANOVAs performed to check the hypothesis presented in Section 4.1. From this table, we can observe that in most cases, the domain significantly affects the comprehension of the diagrams (see bold cells). Table 2 evidences that the subjects performed worse with the diagrams of domain A (car rental). This could imply that the subjects found the car rental domain more difficult.

With respect to the use of stereotypes, there are no significant values in the table. Moreover, the powers of the tests, i.e. the ability to detect an effect if there is one, are low. This implies that we cannot reject the null hypotheses investigated in this work and accepting the alternative hypotheses could be risky and misleading. Furthermore we have results that might be a consequence of the treatment or be determined by an interaction effect between treatment and domain.

A similar data analysis which considered the data of each round separately was also carried out. The findings were worse. The order effect was also studied statistically, despite its being alleviated with the selected experimental design. As it was expected, no effect was found.

Table 5. ANOVAs results

Effectiveness		**SCEffec**			**RetenEffec**			**TransEffec**		
Source	**Df**	**F**	**sig.**	**Power**	**F**	**sig.**	**Power**	**F**	**sig.**	**Power**
Stereotypes	1	0.749	0.388	0.138	0.206	0.650	0.074	0.798	0.373	0.144
Domain	1	0.018	0.893	0.052	35.369	0.000	1.000	17.680	0.000	0.987
Efficiency		**SCEffic**			**RetenEffic**			**TransEffic**		
Source	**Df**	**F**	**sig.**	**Power**	**F**	**sig.**	**Power**	**F**	**sig.**	**Power**
Stereotypes	1	0.311	0.578	0.086	0.126	0.723	0.064	0.157	0.693	0.068
Domain	1	9.422	0.003	0.862	3.386	0.068	0.448	98.538	0.000	1.000

5.1 Threats to Validity

We must consider certain issues which may have threatened the validity of the experiment:

- Conclusion validity: The random heterogeneity of subjects is always present when experimenting with students and we are also conscious that they had no previous knowledge of the stereotypes used in the UML sequence diagram included in the experimental materials. Furthermore, if the knowledge of the students involved in the experiment could be assumed to be comparable to that of junior industry professionals, the working pressure and the overall environment in industry is different. We assumed a subjects' homogenous background, but this was not evaluated before the experiment was carried out.
- Construct validity: The hypothesis of equivalence between the complexities of the domains was not confirmed by data analysis and this has been one of the pitfalls of this work. In fact, there were relevant differences in the subject performances which can be attributed to the differences in the diagram domains: the car rental diagram was found to be much more difficult than that of the hotel.

6 Conclusions and Future Work

The main concern of this paper is to investigate the use of stereotypes in the context of UML sequence diagram from three different perspectives of the comprehension of UML sequence diagrams: Semantic Comprehension, Retention, and Transfer. This took place through a controlled experiment and, unfortunately the obtained results cannot be assumed to be final.

The p-values observed in the hypotheses test are non-significant and thus the null-hypotheses cannot be rejected. This implies that the stereotypes do not significantly improve comprehension in a statistical sense. Nevertheless, in 4 out of 6 cases the scores obtained by the subjects were higher when using stereotypes, which could imply that the use of stereotypes does, to some extent, help in the diagram comprehension.

Obviously these conflicting elements stimulate further investigation which we wish to carry out in the near future. We shall attempt to control the threats in a more effective manner and improve the experimental schema, addressing the following issues:

- The Domain effect must be eliminated before conclusions with regard to domains with a similar level of difficulty are drawn, or perhaps, a single domain should be used.
- We must confront the experience factor by attempting to point out the effect that the experience of using our stereotypes had on the subjects' performance. One possible way in which to do this might be to evaluate experience before the experiment and to consequently form the groups on the basis of blocking by experience;
- Data analysis must be improved by clarifying the difference between the non unanswered questions and the wrong answers and their impact on Effectiveness and Efficiency. In this work they are dealt with in the same way.

- According to Rica et al. [24], it may be advisable to investigate the possible existence of other relevant factors. This will be done by extending the definition of the actual quality model in use.

The present work is the first experiment within a planned family of experiments, and it considers not only students but also practitioners. In fact, as Basili et al. [2] note, families of studies are needed for knowledge building. We are already planning to replicate this experiment with fifth year students in Computer Science at the University of Castilla-La Mancha. The experience collected in this first study and in that of Castilla-La Mancha will allow us to refine the material and tasks with the objective of choosing the optimal configuration of the experiment and will make it possible to perform a case study in an industrial setting.

Acknowledgements

This research is part of the META project (TIN2006-15175-C05-05) financed by the "Ministerio de Educación y Ciencia (Spain)", the IDONEO project (PAC08-0160-6141) financed by "Consejería de Ciencia y Tecnología de la Junta de Comunidades de Castilla-La Mancha", and the Quality-driven Model Transformations project financed by the Universidad Politécnica de Valencia.

The authors would like to thank professors Giuseppe Visaggio and Maria Teresa Baldassarre (University of Bari) and their students for having cooperated in the performance of the experiment.

References

[1] Basili, V., Rombach, H.: The TAME Project: Towards Improvement-oriented Software Environments. IEEE Transactions on Software Engineering 14(6), 758–773 (1988)

[2] Basili, V., Shull, F., Lanubile, F.: Building Knowledge through Families of Experiments. IEEE Transactions on Software Engineering 25, 456–473 (1999)

[3] Basili, V., Weiss, D.: A Methodology for Collecting Valid Software Engineering Data. IEEE Transactions on Software Engineering 10(6), 728–738 (1984)

[4] Bodart, F., Patel, A., Sim, M., Weber, R.: Should Optimal Properties Be Used in Conceptual Modelling? Theory and Three Empirical Tests. Information Systems Research 12(4), 384–405 (2001)

[5] Conallen, J.: Building Web Applications with UML. Addison-Wesley Publishing Company, Reading (2000)

[6] Cruz-Lemus, J.A., Genero, M., Morasca, S., Piattini, M.: Using Practitioners for Assessing the Understandability of UML Statechart Diagrams with Composite States. In: Hainaut, J.-L., Rundensteiner, E.A., Kirchberg, M., Bertolotto, M., Brochhausen, M., Chen, Y.-P.P., Cherfi, S.S.-S., Doerr, M., Han, H., Hartmann, S., Parsons, J., Poels, G., Rolland, C., Trujillo, J., Yu, E., Zimányie, E. (eds.) ER Workshops 2007. LNCS, vol. 4802, pp. 213–222. Springer, Heidelberg (2007)

[7] Eriksson, H.E., Penker, M.: UML Toolkit. John Wiley and Sons, Chichester (1998)

[8] Gemino, A., Wand, Y.: Complexity and Clarity in Conceptual Modeling: Comparison of Mandatory and Optional Properties. Data and Knowledge Engineering 55, 301–326 (2005)

[9] Genero, M., Manso, M.E., Visaggio, A., Canfora, G., Piattini, M.: Building Measure-Based Prediction Models for UML Class Diagram Maintainability. Empirical Software Engineering 12, 517–549 (2007)
[10] Insfran, E.: A Requirements Engineering Approach for Object-Oriented Conceptual Modeling. In: DSIC 2003, University of Technology of Valencia
[11] Insfran, E., Pastor, P., Wieringa, R.: Requirements Engineering-based Conceptual Modeling. Journal of Requirements Engineering 7(2), 61–72 (2002)
[12] Jacobson, I., Christerson, M., Jonsson, P., Overgaard, G.: Object-Oriented Software Engineering, a Use Case-driven Approach. Addison-Wesley, Reading (1992)
[13] Juristo, N., Moreno, A.: Basics of Software Engineering Experimentation. Kluwer Academic Publishers, Dordrecht (2001)
[14] Kirk, R.E.: Experimental Design: Procedures for the Behavioral Sciences, 3rd edn. Brooks/Cole Publishing Company (1995)
[15] Lange, C.F.J., Chaudron, M.R.V.: Interactive Views to Improve the Comprehension of UML Models - An Experimental Validation. In: Proceedings of 15th IEEE International Conference on Program Comprehension (ICPC 2007), Banff, Canada, pp. 221–230 (2007)
[16] Larman, C.: Applying UML and Patterns. Prentice-Hall, Englewood Cliffs (1998)
[17] Mayer, R.E.: Models for Understanding. Review of Educational Research 59(1), 43–64 (1989)
[18] Mayer, R.E.: Multimedia Learning. Cambridge University Press, Cambridge (2001)
[19] OMG, UML 2.1 Unified Modeling Language (TM) (2006)
[20] Otero, M.C., Dolado, J.J.: Evaluation of the Comprehension of the Dynamic Modeling in UML. Information and Software Technology 46(1), 35–53 (2004)
[21] Purchase, H.C., Colpoys, L., McGill, M., Carrington, D.: UML Collaboration Diagram Syntax: an Empirical Study of Comprehension. In: Proceedings of 1st International Workshop on Visualizing Software for Understanding and Analysis (VISSOFT 2002), Paris, France, pp. 13–22 (2002)
[22] Purchase, H.C., Colpoys, L., McGill, M., Carrington, D., Britton, C.: UML Class Diagram Syntax: an Empirical Study of Comprehension. In: Proceedings of Australian Symposium on Information Visualisation, Sydney, Australia, pp. 113–120 (2001)
[23] Reinhartz-Berger, H., Dori, D.: OPM vs. UML - Experimenting with Comprehension and Construction of Web Application Models. Empirical Software Engineering 10, 57–79 (2005)
[24] Ricca, F., Di Penta, M., Torchiano, M., Tonella, P., Ceccato, M.: The Role of Experience and Ability in Comprehension Tasks supported by UML Stereotypes. In: Proceedings of 29th International Conference on Software Engineering (ICSE 2007), Minneapolis, USA, pp. 375–384 (2007)
[25] Selic, B.: The Pragmatics of Model-Driven Development. IEEE Software 20(5), 19–25 (2003)
[26] SPSS, SPSS 12.0, Syntax Reference Guide, Chicago, USA. SPSS Inc. (2003)
[27] Staron, M., Kuzniarz, L., Wohlin, C.: Empirical Assessment of Using Stereotypes to Improve Comprehension of UML Models: a Set of Experiments. The Journal of Systems and Software 79, 727–742 (2006)
[28] Winer, B.J., Brown, D.R., Michels, K.M.: Statistical Principles in Experimental Design. McGraw-Hill, New York (1991)
[29] Wohlin, C., Runeson, P., Hast, M., Ohlsson, M.C., Regnell, B., Wesslen, A.: Experimentation in Software Engineering: an Introduction. Kluwer Academic Publisher, Dordrecht (2000)
[30] Xie, S., Kraemer, E., Stirewalt, R.E.K.: Empirical Evaluation of a UML Sequence Diagram with Adornments to Support Understanding of Thread Interactions. In: Proceedings of 15th IEEE International Conference on Program Comprehension (ICPC 2007), Banff, Canada, pp. 123–134 (2007)

3D Parametric Models for Aeroplanes — From Idea to Design

Patrick Rauhut

Airbus Deutschland, Germany
Patrick.Rauhut@Airbus.com

Abstract. The early design phase of an aircraft is characterized by a large variation of studies in a short period of time. In order to support the variation of aircraft shapes, an approach is taken in which the different aircraft component models are defined by a limited set of parameters. The challenge lies in fulfilling numerous and partially conflicting engineering requirements. Models should be as flexible as possible so that virtually "any" aircraft shape can be represented, in parallel the model should address the needs of different engineering disciplines located on different sites and in different countries. On the other hand each engineering discipline re-quests simple models with the smallest set of parameters possible to address their specific need. Finally, aircraft design is not only geometric and interfaces with the numerical world need to be established. During this talk we will be exploring the challenges and identified solutions for abstracting the aircraft geometry in a set of parametric models that can be shared and commonly used; we will see how dedicated CAD tools support the engineer and how the geometric models can be linked with the numerical (e.g. systems) world.

K. Czarnecki et al. (Eds.): MoDELS 2008, LNCS 5301, p. 295, 2008.

MOOGLE: A Model Search Engine

Daniel Lucrédio[1], Renata P. de M. Fortes[1], and Jon Whittle[2]

[1] Institute of Mathematical and Computer Science - USP. Av. Trabalhador São-Carlense, 400 - Centro. Cx Postal 668 - CEP 13560-970 - São Carlos - SP - Brazil
lucredio,renata@icmc.usp.br
[2] Computing Department - InfoLab21, Lancaster University, Lancaster LA1 4WA UK
whittle@comp.lancs.ac.uk

Abstract. Models are becoming increasingly important in the software process. As a consequence, the number of models being used is increasing, and so is the need for efficient mechanisms to search them. Various existing search engines could be used for this purpose, but they lack features to properly search models, mainly because they are strongly focused on text-based search. This paper presents Moogle, a model search engine that uses metamodeling information to create richer search indexes and to allow more complex queries to be performed. The paper also presents the results of an evaluation of Moogle, which showed that the metamodel information improves the accuracy of the search.

Keywords: Model Search, Software Reuse, Model-Driven Development.

1 Introduction

With model-driven development (MDD) gaining importance, an increasingly large number of models is being produced and used by software organizations. As a result, some development methodologies, such as software factories [1], strongly rely on the *reuse* of models (as well as other artifacts) in order to take advantage of previously developed assets. In such an environment, model repositories play an important role (see, for example, [2]), and the ability to automatically search for models inside large repositories may be as critical as searching for code.

Model search also has an important educational value for students and teachers, allowing learners to find good (and bad) examples that can then be used to improve the acquisition of knowledge and provide hints at solutions [3].

To date, however, there are very few works in the model search and retrieval field. General-purpose search engines, such as Google code search, are not designed to search for models, and, in particular, are focused purely on text-based search. Although models are normally represented as text (using XMI [4]), in these search engines, the internal structure of the model – the metamodel – is not taken into account. Thus, it is only possible to perform simple text-based queries (such as "find book and price") and it is not possible to specify complex queries that incorporate the metamodel (such as "find book of type Class and price of type Attribute"). An additional shortcoming of existing search engines is

K. Czarnecki et al. (Eds.): MoDELS 2008, LNCS 5301, pp. 296–310, 2008.

that the only representation shown to the user is the actual model file, normally an XML file. Although some of the content is readable, most of it consists of machine-oriented tags and characters that have no meaning to a human reader. Section 2 presents more details about these works.

Moogle is a model search engine that helps in the process of finding models. Moogle's main contribution is the use of metamodeling information to create indexes that allow more complex queries to be performed. Moogle also formats the search results in a more readable way by removing irrelevant tags and characters from the actual model file. Finally, Moogle can search for models in any language, not only UML, as long as there is a well-defined metamodel which can be provided to Moogle. This feature makes it suitable for domain-specific modeling [5]. Section 3 describes Moogle's key features and its architecture.

An experimental evaluation was performed, comparing Moogle's advanced search – using metamodeling information – with simple text-based search. The results show that advanced search is more accurate, being more suitable for cases where the user has more details about the model s/he is looking for. However, it tends to retrieve fewer relevant models, and hence it is less suitable for when the user wants to retrieve a broader sample. Section 4 discusses the evaluation.

We conclude with the related work and final remarks (Sections 5 and 6).

2 Using Existing Search Engines for Model Search

Since models are normally represented as text, most search engines can be used to find models. A web search engine such as Google can retrieve models by using format-specific queries (e.g. the query "filetype:xmi customer" will retrieve all XMI files containing the word customer). Code search engines, such as Google code search, Koders and Krugle[1], allow programmers to search source code repositories. These can also be used to search models, based on their textual content.

However, these engines only consider the text inside the models. For example, it is not possible to search for a class named "Customer" or a sequence diagram whose participants are objects of the class "Registration". This lack of knowledge about metamodel information is their main missing feature.

Another drawback is that the results of existing search engines are only shown textually, i.e., an XMI file will be presented. Even for users familiar with the XMI format, the results are difficult to interpret. Thus, without actually downloading the model and opening it in a modeling tool, it is time-consuming to read its content. In the context of searching, where several models have to be inspected, downloading all of them is not practical.

There are also many XML-based search engines available[2]. These could be used to search models, using information from the XML structure, such as DTDs or XMLSchema. In this sense, it is possible to specify fine-tuned queries, such as searching only inside specific parts of the document. However, we are unaware of a XML search engine specifically devoted to model searching.

---

[1] www.google.com/codesearch, www.koders.com and www.krugle.com, respectively.

[2] See http://www.searchtools.com/info/xml-resources.html for a comprehensive list.

3 Key Features of Moogle and Its Architecture

Based on the strong and weak points of the related work, and on our previous experience [6,7,8], Moogle implements some key features related to model search:

- **Metamodel-based searching:** Moogle can process queries that use information from the metamodel. Model element types, attributes, and even the hierarchy between two model elements can be used as search criteria.

- **Different kinds of models:** Although UML is the most used modeling language, new languages are appearing for specific domains. Moogle supports different kinds of models, as long as a proper metamodel is provided.

- **Automatic indexing:** Models in Moogle are automatically indexed, so that no manual effort is needed in order to allow them to be searched.

- **Formatted results:** As discussed earlier, model files are not easily understood by most users without actually opening them in a modeling tool. Moogle tries to solve this issue by formatting the results in a way that XML tags and other unreadable characters are removed to improve readability.

- **Independence from storage media:** Moogle's core functionalities are independent from the storage media. Currently, Moogle works in the local file system, but its architecture was designed to be easily extended to other storage media, such as version control systems or web servers.

3.1 Using Moogle

Moogle offers three ways to search for models: **Simple Search**, **Advanced Search** and **Browse**. In simple search (Figure 1), general-purpose queries can be performed, using keywords. This is more suited for earlier stages of the development, when the developer is looking for models related to domain concepts.

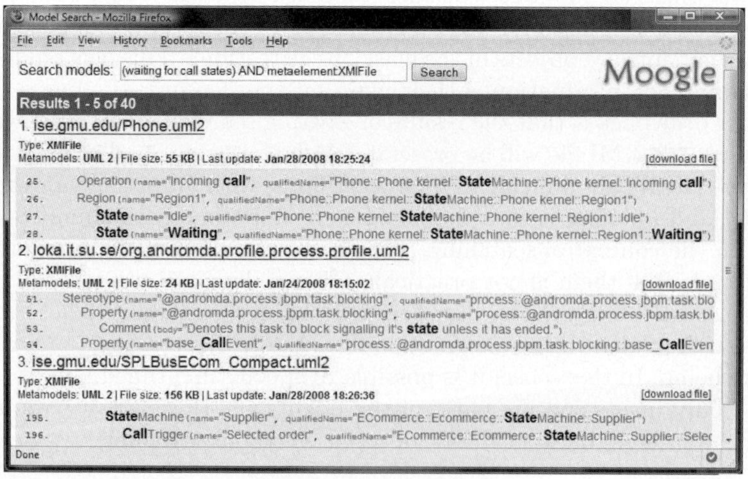

Fig. 1. Simple search

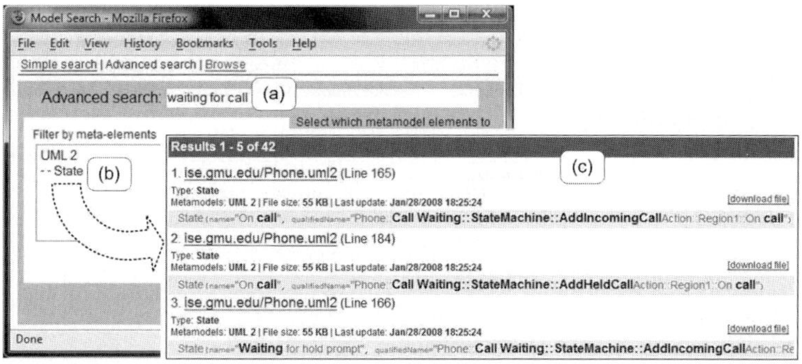

Fig. 2. Advanced search

For example, by searching for "waiting for call states" (Figure 1), all models containing these words will be found, irrespective of the type of the model elements. In the example in Figure 1, different types of model elements containing the words "waiting", "call" and "states" are returned, such as *Operations*, *States*, *StateMachines* and *Properties*.

In advanced search, the user can specify the types of model elements to be returned. For example, the query "waiting for call states" can be refined to retrieve only UML states. By specifying "waiting for call" as a query (Figure 2a), and filtering by "UML states" (Figure 2b), Moogle retrieves all UML states that contain the specified words (Figure 2c).

By clicking on a result, a formatted version of the model is presented. Figure 3 shows a comparison between the formatted preview provided by Moogle and the original XMI format. In the formatted version of this example, a package named "StateMachine" can be more clearly seen, containing a state machine named "Supplier", with four triggers and four operations. Also, the fonts of attribute values and element types are larger, to highlight the most important information.

Browsing (Figure 4) is similar to advanced search, but the developer does not specify keywords to be searched. Instead, all elements matching the specified filters are shown. The filters are organized into a faceted-based scheme [9]: there are five facets (Figure 4a): *Location*, *Metamodel*, *Metaelement*, *File size* and *Last update*. For each facet, the user can select one or more value, combining them freely. In this example, all UML2 Types located in files with size between 10 Kb and 100 Kb are being shown (Figure 4b).

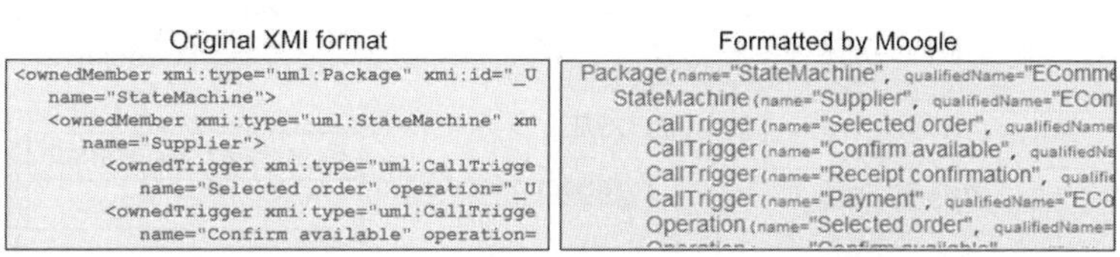

Fig. 3. Formatted preview vs original XMI format

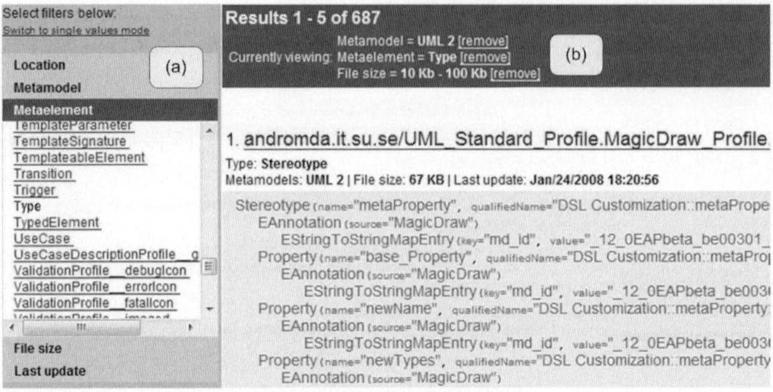

Fig. 4. Browsing

3.2 Architecture of the Search Engine

Except for the metamodel information, Moogle has the same functionalities as many existing web search engines. For this reason, its architecture uses an existing search engine, called Apache SOLR (lucene.apache.org/solr/). SOLR provides many functionalities, including keyword searching, search terms highlighting, paging of the results, filtering and facet-based browsing. It is an open source project, with an active community, and is very stable, being widely used.

Figure 5 shows the architecture of the model search engine. Moogle's GUI allows the user to interact with SOLR's functions. Queries are passed to SOLR through HTTP, and the responses (search results) are read in XML format.

To search for models, SOLR requires XML descriptors to be provided, containing all information to be searched, and all metadata used for the advanced filtering and browsing. In order to create such descriptors, an indexer component reads model files from a repository, interprets them, and extracts all the textual and metamodel information needed. Currently, Moogle is capable of interpreting XMI files, which are commonly used by most commercial modeling tools. It uses the Eclipse Modeling Framework (eclipse.org/emf) parser to read the XMI format. This parser can read any metamodel, as long as it is provided in the proper format (*jar* file). This feature makes Moogle capable of indexing and searching models in virtually any modeling language.

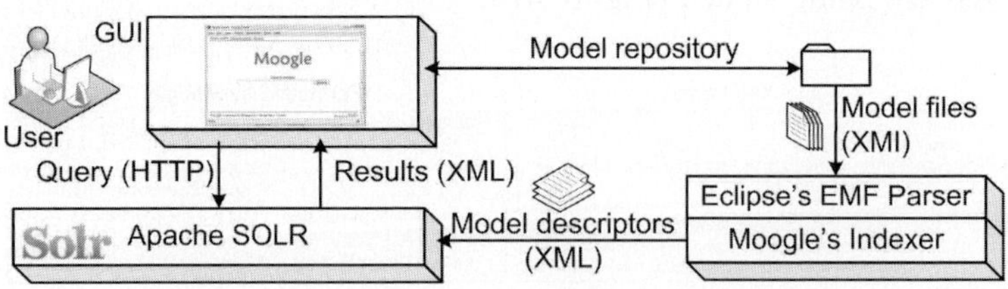

Fig. 5. Architecture of the model search engine

For each model, three actions are taken by Moogle's indexer:

- **Metamodels identification:** First, the indexer determines to which metamodels a model conforms, in order to correctly load the necessary contents into the EMF parser. To accomplish this, the indexer reads the first line of the file, which contains the namespace declaration for the metamodels being used [4]. A configuration file describes all metamodels supported by Moogle. The indexer then compares the namespace declaration with all metamodels contained in this configuration file. If one of the referenced metamodels is not found, then the model will not be indexed.

- **Metamodels loading:** After the metamodels are identified, the indexer loads their content (*jar* files) into the EMF parser. The locations of the *jar* files for each supported metamodel are also listed in the configuration file.

- **Model descriptor generation:** The indexer inspects the model file, extracts all textual content and creates a XML descriptor to be read by SOLR.

The following listing is an example of a model descriptor. Besides the basic metadata, such as the path of the model, the file size, etc., there is a field called "storedtext", containing every word of every element of the model, so that it will be found whenever one of these words is searched.

```
<doc> ... <field name="path">Phone.uml2</field>
   <field name="filesize">56628</field>
   <field name="lastupdate">2008-01-28T19:25:25:588Z</field>
   <field name="storedtext">
          Phone.uml2  Phone  http://www.eclipse.org/emf/2002/Ecore attributes
          kernel Hang up Incoming call Pick up Hang up Idle Waiting Phone </field>
</doc>
```

The previous descriptor allows whole model files to be searched. However, the indexer also adds one entry for each element inside a model. The following listing shows an example descriptor for a UML2 Operation, including its metamodel (*UML 2*), its type, or metaelement (*Operation*) and its attributes (*name*, *visibility*, *isAbstract*, etc) so that it can be found individually.

```
<doc> ... <field name="metamodel">UML 2</field>
   <field name="metaelement">Operation</field>
   <field name="path">Phone.uml2</field>
   <field name="name">Ring</field>
   <field name="visibility">public</field>
   <field name="isAbstract">false</field>
```

4 Evaluation of the Search Engine

The main difference between Moogle and other text-based search engines is its awareness of the underlying metamodels. This awareness has three advantages for model search: **(i)** The use of metamodel information optimizes the indexing process, by ignoring irrelevant tags and textual contents from the model files; **(ii)** The advanced search feature, where more complex filtering can lead to more powerful and expressive queries; and **(iii)** Better model previews, through metadata formatting. To assess these claims, an experiment to evaluate Moogle was designed with the following three goals in mind:

- G_1. **Effectiveness in retrieving models.** To determine if the use of metamodel information produces better indexes, and more effective searching;

- G_2. **Benefits of advanced search.** To determine if the advanced search is helpful to users, when compared with text-based search; and

- G_3. **Expressive power of the formatted preview.** To determine if the formatted preview is good enough so that the user does not need to download the file and open it in a tool in order to understand its contents.

4.1 Metrics

We used **recall** and **precision** metrics, which are the classic measures for search engines. **Precision** is the number of relevant results retrieved over the total number of results retrieved, and **Recall** is the number of relevant results retrieved over the number of relevant elements in the database [10]:

$$precision = \frac{relevantResults \cap retrievedResults}{retrievedResults}$$

$$recall = \frac{relevantResults \cap retrievedResults}{relevantElementsInDatabase}$$

In order to determine if the search engine has a good balance between precision and recall, we also used the **f-measure**, which is the harmonic mean of precision and recall [11]. The closer the f-measure is to 1.0, the better the mechanism is. But this will only occur if both precision and recall are high. The f-measure is calculated using the following formula:

$$F_\alpha = \frac{(1+\alpha) * (precision * recall)}{\alpha * precision + recall}$$

where α is used to weight the precision in relation to recall. We used $\alpha = 1$, which means that both precision and recall are equally important.

For goal G_1, these values were measured and compared with reference values from other experiences with reuse-oriented search engines in the literature. We found reports of precision and recall values close to 50% [12,13,8]. The f-measure for these values is also 50%. These were our benchmark values.

For goal G_2, we also measured precision/recall/f-measure, and compared the values obtained in simple search with the values obtained in advanced search.

Goal G_3 is more subjective, and thus more difficult to measure. We decided to use a combination of recall and the user's perception about having found the right model. If Moogle retrieved correct results and the user perceived these results as correct, then we posit that Moogle's output is understandable. If not, there is a problem with the comprehensibility of the output. During the experiment, for each query performed by the user, s/he would answer "yes" or "no" to the question: "Did you find the right model?". We then measured the number of queries where the user's perception about having found a model was inconsistent with the recall, i.e. a query had 100% of recall and yet the user claimed not to find a model. We believe, from our experience with search engines, that one of the main causes of this discrepancy is the lack of understanding about a model's content, caused by a bad textual representation. By measuring the number of queries that presented this discrepancy, we are, to some extent, measuring the quality of this formatted view. We found nothing to use as a benchmark value for this measure in the literature, so we considered that if more than 25% of the queries resulted in a wrong perception, the formatted preview was inadequate.

4.2 Preparation

The search engine was populated with 146 model files, gathered from publicly available repositories and samples. We developed a web crawler that automatically navigates through the results of a web search engine. We then used it with google.com to automatically find and download XMI files. The results are mostly model files published in open source repository systems, such as CVS and Trac[3]. We also got model samples used in research projects and classes, gathered from colleagues and students. These are random files, used in real projects, and therefore they represent a good sample of the kind of models that would exist in a models repository. The files comprise 82096 model elements, that can be individually searched using Moogle's advanced search features.

A set of eight problems/situations was defined, trying to cover different types of queries, geared towards both early lifecycle development, where the user has little idea about details of the domain (e.g. "find a UML model that describes a customer and its attributes"), and in later stages, where more detailed models are needed (e.g. "Which states and events should be considered in a state machine for a phone call?"). The problems were defined based on the experience of the authors and two modeling experts, both with academic and industrial experience: one of the experts had experience in creating and using UML models in software development as well as experience with automated transformations for recovering UML designs from legacy systems, and the other had some experience with domain-specific modeling in MDD projects. The definition of the problems also considered the availability of models that could solve the problem.

For each problem, we manually inspected the repository in search for relevant models. We considered as "relevant" any model that could contribute to a solution for the problem. For example, for the problem "Which states and events should be considered in a state machine for a phone call?", a model that has a class with a property named "phone number" is clearly irrelevant, while a model containing states and events named "phone", "call" and "waiting" is relevant. This process took approximately two hours for each problem. We found between 1 and 4 relevant models for each problem, each one containing 10 to 50 relevant elements.

An evaluation prototype was developed, to allow the experiment to be remotely performed by users in their own free time. The prototype consists of a web interface that presents the eight problems in sequence, to be solved using

[3] www.cvshome.org and trac.edgewall.org, respectively.

Moogle's interface. While the user is performing the queries and trying to solve the problems, the prototype registers every interaction. When the user finishes a problem, s/he clicks on a link to capture the user's perceptions whether or not s/he found a model. The next problem is then presented. After all problems have been completed, a short questionnaire is presented to gather other information from the user, including his/her impressions about the search engine and previous experience with search engines. The prototype also balances the queries between simple search and advanced search, so that half of the problems are solved using only simple search, and the other half using advanced search.

4.3 Results

The web evaluation prototype was sent to different people by e-mail, together with a short tutorial on how to use Moogle and how to perform the evaluation. The subjects were chosen by availability, and all had basic modeling skills. The evaluation was conducted over a two week period. At the end of the two weeks, thirteen subjects had completed the evaluation. Eleven had already used code search engines before, such as Google code search, Koders and Krugle, and thus had some experience in searching software for reuse. All of them had basic skills in modeling, but none had used a model search engine before.

The subjects performed a total of 200 queries, 129 using only simple search, and 71 using advanced search (the subjects were not forced to use advanced search). The precision/recall/f-measure was calculated for each query.

One problem we faced was that, in Moogle, each query results in one or more pages of results, each page containing up to five models. However, we noticed that users do not always browse through all pages. Our results have shown that in 80% of the queries, only the first page was visited, and in 95% of the queries, the user visited three pages or less. This means that if a model is retrieved, but appears only after page three, it is practically the same as not being retrieved at all. For this reason, our calculations consider pages one to three only. We also calculated the recall for an arbitrarily large number of pages (30), but only to verify if there are many relevant results appearing in later pages that are not normally visited. If the recall values considering three and thirty pages are similar, this means that there are not many models left unseen.

We also noticed that many queries found no models at all. A total of 58 queries had zero results, 27 using simple search and 31 using advanced search. Analyzing these queries, we found that in most of them (42), users were experimenting with different filters non-existent in the repository. In twelve of these queries, the advanced search features were being incorrectly used, with the user changing the query string directly in the text field, instead of the advanced search screen, or incorrectly placing characters such as quotes and double quotes, thus leading to invalid queries. In the remaining four queries leading to no results, the users specified the correct keywords and filters, and thus these were indeed the result of Moogle's inability to find the right model. We eliminated from the calculations the twelve queries where the users were using Moogle incorrectly.

Next, we present the results for each goal.

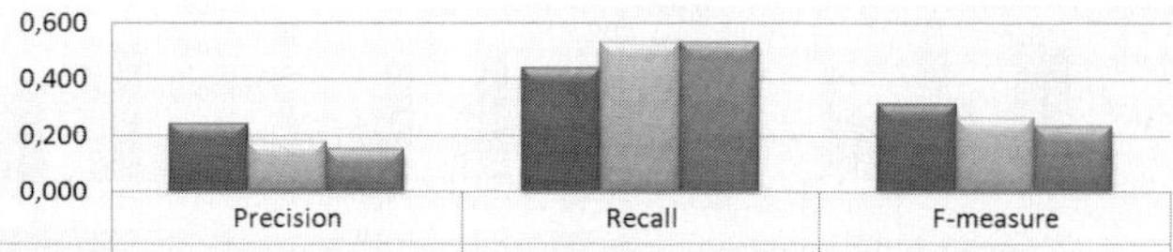

	Precision	Recall	F-measure
1st page	0,24	0,44	0,31
3 pages	0,17	0,53	0,26
30 pages	0,15	0,53	0,23

Fig. 6. Overall results

Goal G_1: Effectiveness in Retrieving Models. Figure 6 shows the overall results. The first observation is that, for each new page, precision decreases and recall increases. Precision goes down because more pages mean more irrelevant results. Recall goes up because, although there are more irrelevant results, there are also more relevant ones. Such a result coincides with intuition.

Recall varied from 44% to 53% for the 1st and 3 pages, respectively. These are similar to the reference value of 50% as reported in the literature. The precision varied from 24% to 17%, which is smaller than the reference value.

One positive result is that recall is exactly the same (53%), regardless of whether 3 or 30 pages are considered. This means that all relevant models retrieved are located in the first three pages. We thus concluded that Moogle's ranking policy, which is implemented by SOLR, is performing well.

Moogle performed worse than similar studies in terms of precision, but presented similar recall. A possible explanation is that the values of 50% refer to code search engines, with interfaces that are specific for searching code. For example, the engine tested by Frakes & Pole has a list of all keywords available for the user to choose [12]. Ye & Fischer use signature matching [13]. Although Moogle is closer to these in purpose, its architecture and interface are more similar to a document search engine, so we decided to additionally compare the precision and recall with document search engines.

Shafi & Rather present a study on precision and recall of five web search engines [14]. Their mean values of precision vary between 14% to 57%, with the most popular web search engines (AltaVista, Google and HotBot) presenting a precision rate around 28%. These values are closer to our results, indicating that Moogle could be behaving more like a document search engine.

However, a more plausible explanation is that the lower precision could be the result of the relatively small number of models in the repository. Although there were more than 80,000 indexed model elements, these corresponded to only 146 files. If we compare the number of files with the amount of components in the repositories of the reference works (between 2000 to 3000 components), and if we consider that only a small percentage of these files are relevant, precision would naturally be smaller, and recall would naturally be higher.

But we do not consider this lower precision as a major drawback, since this only means that the user will have to navigate through three pages to find the models. Considering that each page has 5 results, this is not very difficult.

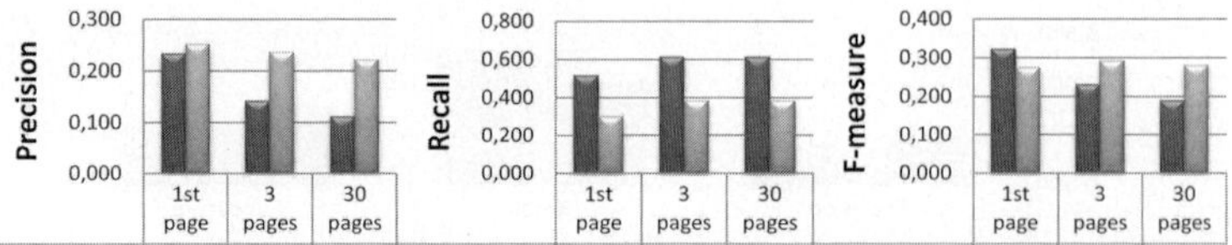

	1st page	3 pages	30 pages		1st page	3 pages	30 pages		1st page	3 pages	30 pages
Simple	0,233	0,142	0,111	Simple	0,516	0,612	0,612	Simple	0,321	0,230	0,189
Advanced	0,252	0,236	0,221	Advanced	0,302	0,384	0,384	Advanced	0,274	0,292	0,281
Improvement	7,79%	66,27%	98,53%	Improvement	-41,56%	-37,28%	-37,28%	Improvement	-14,64%	26,87%	48,87%

Fig. 7. Simple search vs advanced search

Goal G_2: Benefits of Advanced Search. Figure 7 summarizes the comparison between simple versus advanced search, which showed that advanced search is more accurate, with a small improvement of precision in the first page (around 8%), and a large improvement in the first three pages (around 66%). However, it has smaller recall, performing around 40% worse than simple search in the first three pages. The f-measure, which balances both precision and recall, shows that simple search is better in the first page (around 15%), but that advanced search performs better in the first three pages (around 27%).

Advanced search is more accurate, which means that it can lead to more relevant results when the right query is specified. However, it is not so good in retrieving a larger amount of models. In simple search, more generic queries can lead to more models being retrieved, but at the expense of more irrelevant results. We conclude that advanced search may be more suited for more skilled users, with more knowledge about what is needed, while simple search may help novice users in gaining knowledge about the engine and the repository.

Goal G_3: Expressive Power of the Formatted Preview. In 38% of the queries where users claimed not to have found a result, the recall was 100% in the first three pages, i.e. the users failed to see the result when it was there. This is larger than our reference value (25%), and could mean that the users were not able to understand the model contents, and thus a better preview is needed.

Qualitative Results. We did not perform a quantitative analysis on Moogle's performance. But even with more than 80000 index elements, the query results are returned in matter of seconds, often less than a second[4]. The indexing process is much slower. Indexing all 146 files takes approximately 15 minutes. This is mostly because the model interpretation process uses reflection to identify the meta-elements. However, a full reconstruction of the indexes is rarely necessary, since Moogle allows partial index updating.

The subjects reported some benefits when using Moogle: *the advanced search feature offers useful guidance in searching models*; *Moogle allows to find models in large repositories, where manual search is not possible*; *it is very accurate, helping to reduce false hits with the filters*; *it has a simple and easy to use interface*; *it offers different options to search for models*; and *it allows searching inside*

[4] Results given by SOLR interface, in a 2.2 Ghz processor with 2 GB of RAM.

complex XMI files. The noted benefits are in accordance with the quantitative data, because we verified that advanced search can indeed improve precision, and that Moogle can help in different ways when searching for models, both for novice and more skilled users.

Among the difficulties, almost all subjects reported the same drawbacks: *the lack of a graphical preview of the models*; and *the fact that the user needs to know the metamodel elements in order to properly use the advanced search engines*. The latter point is a consequence of the fact that Moogle uses UML2's metaelements, which do not always coincide with the commonly used name for a concept. For example, there is no "Attribute" metaelement in UML2. Rather, attribute filtering in Moogle must refer to "Property".

4.4 Threats to Validity

One of the main challenges of this experiment was to find a good quantity of models to populate the search engine, and to find a well-known subset of models that can be identified with a single query. If the number of models is too small, then the engine is not really being tested for effectiveness. We managed to find around 150 models, which correspond to more than 80 thousand searchable elements. However, the problems ended up having a small number of relevant models (1 to 4). We would like to test it with around 2000-3000 models, mainly to have more relevant models for each problem, and to better evaluate its accuracy.

Another threat is the determination of what is a "relevant" model. In this experiment, we extensively browsed the repository in searching for relevant models for each problem. However, a user's interpretation about what is relevant or not may be different. Although we think we reached a satisfactory consensus between the authors, a more unbiased selection process is desired.

The number of subjects is also important. Another study with search engines [12] involved 35 subjects, against 13 in our experiment. Although there were a large amount of queries (200), more subjects could lead to more solid results.

Finally, in our experiment, we did not force the users to use the advanced search features in a query. We did so because we wanted to determine the benefits of the advanced search as an additional feature, to be used together with simple search, and not separately. As a result, many queries that should have been performed using advanced search were performed only with simple search, which caused the imbalance between simple and advanced queries.

5 Related Work

Gulla et al. [15] argue that a model search engine should focus on the problem domain, using real-world terms that people are familiar with, and not on computer-related terms, such as tables, relationships and classes. The authors propose a search engine that uses linguistic techniques to translate user queries formulated using only real-world concepts into queries that use computer-related concepts. We agree with the authors, that it should be possible to search for models using only domain concepts. Moogle supports these kinds of queries, by relying on the existence of textual content describing the model, such as comments and notes. However, Moogle's advanced search uses UML2 metaelements, whose names do not always coincide with commonly used concepts.

Gomes et al. [16] present an environment for retrieving UML class models, using a keyword-based ontology, called WordNet. The search is performed based on similarity metrics, which take into consideration the relationship between the UML elements (packages, classes, interfaces, attributes, methods and relationships) and WordNet elements. Different metrics must exist, one for each type of UML element, and the use of the ontology allows more relaxed matching to be performed – using synonyms, for example. Moogle only supports similar word matching (e.g. "register" matches "registration", "registering", etc.), but it does not require metrics to exist for specific elements, and thus it can be used with any metamodel or modeling language, and not only UML class models.

Kozlenkov et al. [17] present a framework for discovering services. In order to formulate a query, the user specifies an interaction (a sequence diagram) where some messages should be realized by operations of the services to be discovered, and specifies constraints on these operations. The results are ranked according to the similarity with the specified query, measured by a distance function, which takes into consideration the semantic difference between the query and the services being queried. As the previous example, this work is well suited for a specific subset of models – namely, sequence diagrams – while Moogle is generic, and can be used with any kind of model.

The EMF Search project[5] provides the infrastructure for querying EMF-based models, focusing on the integration with the Eclipse Core Search API for end user tight integration. As in Moogle, the search engine takes into consideration metamodel elements, allowing the user to search for specific metamodel elements. It is very powerful, but it is not based on indexes, which means that a thorough introspection is performed each time a search is started, which is inefficient. This makes it more suitable for a single folder, or even a single file, while Moogle is more suitable for large repositories.

In Moogle we focused on other aspects of search, such as indexing and performance. As a result, it has some shortcomings regarding query formulation, mainly when querying more complex relations between model elements. The literature has some works to deal with this problem. For example, OCL can be used to query models [18]. In fact, the EMF project, cited above, uses OCL with this purpose. There are also template approaches, such as QVT [19] and graph queries [20], which could be used to formulate more powerful queries.

6 Conclusion and Future Work

This paper presented Moogle, a model search engine that uses metamodel information to enrich the indexing and querying tasks. Moogle allows simple and complex queries to be performed, considering not only the textual content of the

[5] http://www.eclipse.org/modeling/emft/?project=search#search

models, but also its internal structure. Moogle can be useful in two scenarios: in a development environment, providing a way to find and retrieve existing models for reuse, and in an educational environment, providing means to teachers and students to find examples of models during the learning process.

One of the main contributions of this paper is the evaluation, which showed that Moogle's advanced search and the use of metamodel information lead to more accurate results. When combined with the higher recall obtained in simple search, Moogle is suited to a wider range of users and activities. The evaluation has some threats to validity, as discussed in section 4.4, but we believe these do not invalidate the overall findings. Nevertheless, in future evaluations we intend to apply more "clinical" tests in order to obtain more solid results.

The evaluation also identified future enhancements for Moogle, such as providing a graphical preview, because the textual preview, although superior to the original model file, was not ideal. The use of synonyms for metaelements is also an open issue. The subjects had difficulties understanding the meaning of the metaelements because modelers typically do not have an in-depth knowledge of the UML metamodel. What is needed is richer semantic information associated with the models, and works from the semantic web area, such as [21], are good starting points for future work here.

Similarity search, where Moogle would find related models by similarity, was also mentioned by the subjects. Finally, in advanced search, when a model element is found, Moogle currently only shows the element isolated from the rest of the model. It would be good to show also its context, so that the user can better understand the element's place in the overall model.

We are planning to expand Moogle by plugging it into some common model repositories, such as the Atlantic Zoo[6]. We also plan to make Moogle available to the community, so that people will be able to upload their models and use it as a public model search tool. We think this has immediate applications, especially in an educational context.

Acknowledgments. This work was developed at the ISE department of George Mason University, USA, with the financial support from Brazilian institutions CAPES (process 0657/07-7) and CNPq (process 553066/2008-0). The authors would also like to thank the reviewers for the insightful suggestions.

References

1. Greenfield, J., Short, K., Cook, S., Kent, S.: Software Factories: Assembling Applications with Patterns, Models, Frameworks and Tools. Wiley, Chichester (2004)
2. Matheson, D., France, R., Beiman, J., Alexander, R., DeWitt, J., McEachen, N.: Managed Evolution of Model Driven Development Approach to Software-based Solutions. In: OOPSLA and GPCE Workshop, Vancouver, Canada (2004)
3. Isakowitz, T., Kauffman, R.J.: Supporting Search for Reusable Software Objects. IEEE Transactions on Software Engineering 22(6) (1996)

[6] http://www.eclipse.org/gmt/am3/zoos/atlanticZoo/

4. OMG: XML Metadata Interchange (XMI) Specification. Technical report, Object Management Group (2006)
5. Deursen, A.v., Klint, P., Visser, J.: Domain-Specific Languages: An Annotated Bibliography. SIGPLAN Notices 35(6), 26–36 (2000)
6. Lucrédio, D., Almeida, E.S.d., Prado, A.F.d.: A Survey on Software Components Search and Retrieval. In: 30th IEEE EUROMICRO Conference, Component-Based Software Engineering Track, Rennes - France, pp. 152–159. IEEE Computer Soceity Press, Los Alamitos (2004)
7. Lucrédio, D., Gavioli, A., Prado, A.F.d., Biajiz, M., Almeida, E.S.d., Meira, S.R.d.L., Yamamoto, C.H.: Component retrieval using metric indexing. In: The 2004 IEEE International Conference on Information Reuse and Integration (IEEE IRI-2004), Las Vegas - USA. IEEE Computer Society Press, Los Alamitos (2004)
8. Garcia, V.C., Lucrédio, D., Durão, F., Santos, E.C.R., Almeida, E.S.D., Fortes, R.P.: From Specification to Experimentation: A Software Component Search Engine Architecture. In: Gorton, I., Heineman, G.T., Crnković, I., Schmidt, H.W., Stafford, J.A., Szyperski, C.A., Wallnau, K. (eds.) CBSE 2006. LNCS, vol. 4063, pp. 82–97. Springer, Heidelberg (2006)
9. Prieto-Díaz, R.: Implementing Faceted Classification for Software Reuse. Communications of the ACM 34(5) (1991)
10. Grossman, D., Frieder, O.: Information Retrieval. Algorithms and Heuristics, 2nd edn. Springer, Heidelberg (2004)
11. Robin, J., Ramalho, F.: Can Ontologies Improve Web Search Engine Effectiveness Before the Advent of the Semantic Web? In: XVIII Brazilian Symposium on Databases, Manaus, Amazonas, Brazil, pp. 157–169 (2003)
12. Frakes, W.B., Pole, T.P.: An Empirical Study of Representation Methods for Reusable Software Components. IEEE Transactions on Software Engineering 20(8) (1994)
13. Ye, Y., Fischer, G.: Supporting Reuse By Delivering Task-Relevant and Personalized Information. In: ICSE 2002 - 24th International Conference on Software Engineering, Orlando, Florida, USA, pp. 513–523 (2002)
14. Shafi, S., Rather, R.A.: Precision and Recall of Five Search Engines for Retrieval of Scholarly Information in the Field of Biotechnology. Webology 2(2) (2005)
15. Gulla, J.A., Vos, B.v.d., Thiel, U.: An abductive, linguistic approach to model retrieval. Data and Knowledge Engineering 23(1), 17–31 (1997)
16. Gomes, P., Pereira, F.C., Paiva, P., Seco, N., Carreiro, P., Ferreira, J.L., Bento, C.: Using WordNet for case-based retrieval of UML models. AI Commun. 17(1), 12–23 (2004)
17. Kozlenkov, A., Fasoulas, V., Sanchez, F., Spanoudakis, G., Zisman, A.: A framework for architecture-driven service discovery. In: SOSE 2006: Proceedings of the 2006 international workshop on Service-oriented software engineering, Shanghai, China, pp. 67–73 (2006)
18. Akehurst, D.H., Behzad, B.: On Querying UML Data Models with OCL (2001)
19. OMG: Meta Object Facility (MOF) 2.0 Query/View/Transformation Specification. Technical report, Object Management Group (2008)
20. Furfaro, F.: Querying semi-structured data with graph grammars. In: International Conference on Information Technology: Coding and Computing (2002)
21. Gaspari, M., Guidi, D.: Towards an ontology-guided search engine. Technical report, Department of Computer Science - University of Bologna (2003)

Managing Model Conflicts in Distributed Development

Antonio Cicchetti, Davide Di Ruscio, and Alfonso Pierantonio

Università degli Studi dell'Aquila,
Dipartimento di Informatica
via Vetoio, Coppito I-67010, L'Aquila, Italy
{cicchetti,diruscio,alfonso}@di.univaq.it

Abstract. The growing complexity of current software systems naturally conveyed their development toward incremental and distributed approaches to speed up the process. Several developers update the same artefact operating concurrent manipulations which need to be coherently combined. The interaction among those changes inevitably involves conflicts which must be detected and reconciled.

This paper proposes a domain specific language able to define and manage conflicts caused by cooperative updates over the same model elements. The approach relies on a model-based representation of model differences and enables the specification and the detection of both syntactical and semantic conflicts.

1 Introduction

Software engineering projects are inherently cooperative, requiring many software engineers to coordinate their efforts to produce large systems [1]. With models becoming more and more commonplace, the collaboration among software developers in a distributed environment must increasingly consider also the management of models lifecycle [2]. For the collaboration based on software artefacts, version control systems are frequently used and play an important role among software engineers. However, the documents stored in these tools are almost code-level programs, and lack a reasonable organization and abstraction from designer's perspective. In this respect, merging documents representing modifications of models in a distributed environment is a challenging operation, both for its effectiveness and technical intricacy. In fact, every time modifications are merged, they may compete on the same resources giving place to conflict related issues. Conflicts can be distinguished into *syntactic* and *semantic* ones [3]. The former refers to modifications which interfere from a syntactic point of view, e.g. two modifiers give in parallel two different names to the same model element. The latter consists of collisions which are implicit and cannot be inferred from the structure of the performed modifications only.

A number of works have been proposed to deal with the problem of conflict management (see Sect. 4 for a discussion); nevertheless, they are usually based on implicit mechanisms for conflict detection, i.e. an *a priori* evaluation to understand which problems can arise and what are the ones to be checked. This makes impossible to find a technique capable of an arbitrary accuracy [3] and forces the designer to find a trade-off between *false-positive* and *false-negative* occurrences (in a similar way to e-mail spam filters).

K. Czarnecki et al. (Eds.): MoDELS 2008, LNCS 5301, pp. 311–325, 2008.

This work proposes a conflict definition technique consisting of a domain-specific language able to specify both syntactic and semantic conflicts endowed with associated resolution criteria. To this end, *difference models* (already presented in [4]) are used to represent modifications between subsequent versions of a model. Therefore, conflicts are formalized in terms of relations between difference models representing parallel and conflicting modifications. Arbitrary scenarios can be described enabling the identifications of semantics-related patterns usually neglected by the traditional structural-based methods. The aim is to pursue a flexible conflict management toward the support of domain specific versioning through customizable conflict sets.

The paper is organized as follows: Sect. 2 introduces the difference representation approach which underpins the proposed techniques. Next section illustrates the conflict specification metamodel and its application by means of a running example. Sect. 4 gives an overview of related works and finally, Sect. 5 draws some conclusions and presents possible perspective work.

2 Background

Increasingly, complex software systems are cooperatively designed in distributed environments and suitable techniques are required to detect and represent the various design modifications software systems undergo during their life-cycle. In the same way, changes performed in parallel need to be analyzed since they may cause conflicts which require to be managed.

This section recalls the technical background which underpins the approach proposed in this paper. In particular, Sect. 2.1 outlines the technique which is adopted in this work to represent model differences. The technique relies on suitable *difference models* which can be composed both in sequence and in parallel to represent more complex modifications as described in Sect. 2.2.

2.1 Representing Model Differences

The problem of model differences is intrinsically complex and requires specialized algorithms and notations [5]. Encoding the relevant information about modifications as

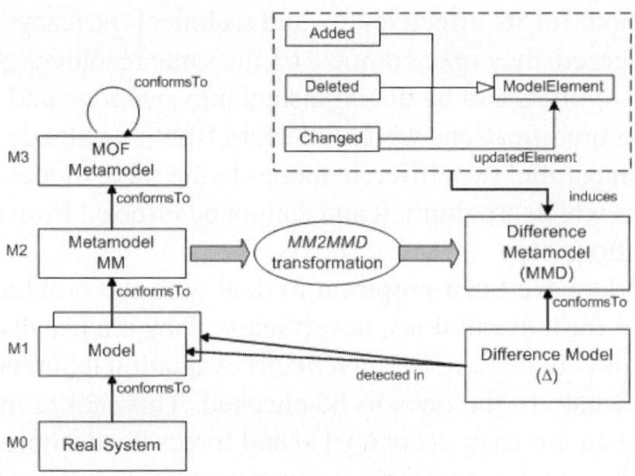

Fig. 1. Overall structure of the model difference representation approach

models allows the designer to derive from model differences powerful and interesting artefacts. In particular, they enable a wide range of possibilities, such as reconstructing the final model starting from an initial one, performing subsequent analysis, or detecting and manipulating conflicts. In this paper, model differences are represented according to the approach proposed in [4] and illustrated in Fig. 1: given two *base models* M_1 and M_2 which conform to an arbitrary *base metamodel MM*, their difference Δ conforms to a *difference metamodel MMD* derived from the former by means of an automated transformation `MM2MMD`. The approach does not impose any restriction over the metamodel *MM*, i.e. it is *metamodel-independent* and can be applied to any arbitrary modeling language as the simplified UML metamodel in Fig. 2. In particular, the metamodel extension implemented in the `MM2MMD` transformation consists of adding new constructs able to represent the possible modifications that can occur on models that are *additions*, *deletions*, and *changes*. For instance, the application of the `MM2MMD` transformation to the sample UML metamodel in Fig. 2 produces the difference metamodel in Fig. 3: essentially, for each metaclass `MC` of the source metamodel, the additional metaclasses `AddedMC`, `DeletedMC`, and `ChangedMC` are produced.

The generated difference metamodel is able to represent all the differences amongst models which conform to the base metamodel. For example, the instances of the new metaclass `AddedClass` in Fig. 3 can be used to represent additions of new classes in the initial model. In a similar way, the metaclasses which extend the `Deleted` one will be used to specify deletions of existing model elements. Interestingly, the difference metamodel is able to represent also model updates by means of instances of `Changed` elements. For instance, the visibility modification of the attribute `mouse` performed on the model M_1 in Fig. 4 leading to M_2 is represented in the upper side of the delta model in Fig. 5.a by means of `ChangedClass`, `ChangedAttribute`, and `ChangeOperation` elements. `Changed` elements are also used in the difference model in Fig. 5.b to represent the modifications performed in the model M_1 in Fig. 4 to obtain M_3. In particular, a `ChangedClass` instance is defined to represent the changes affecting the class `Mouse` in which a new constructor has been added.

The difference representation mechanism introduced above satisfies a number of properties, as illustrated in [4]. One of them is the *applicability*, i.e. difference models can be exploited to re-apply changes to arbitrary input models (see [4] for further details)

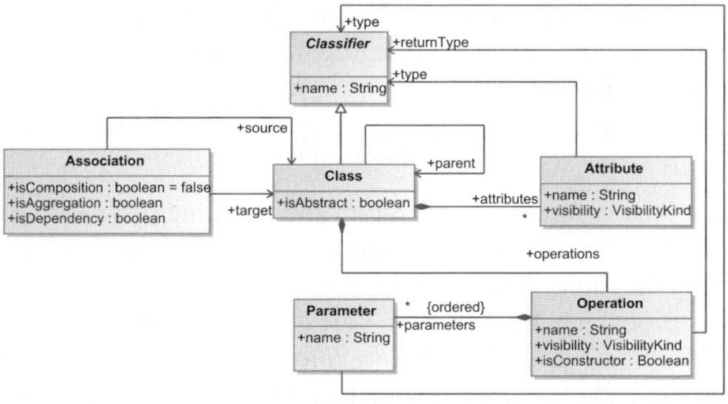

Fig. 2. Sample UML metamodel

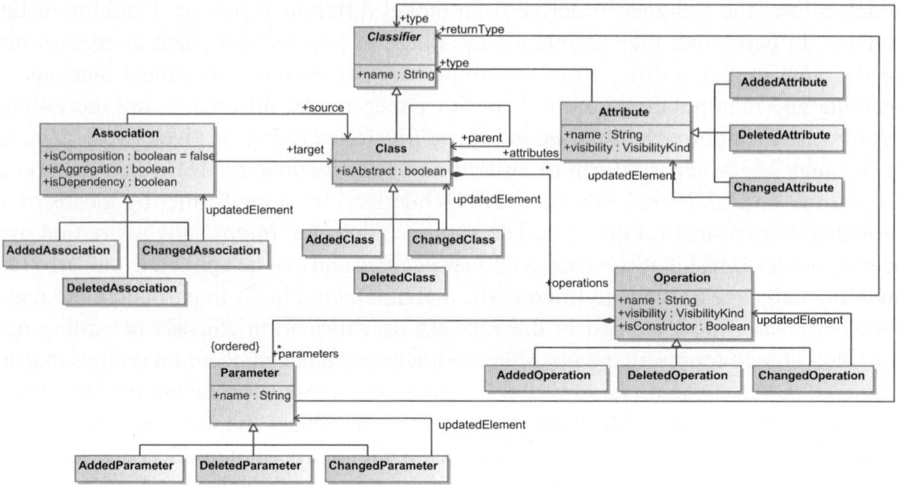

Fig. 3. Sample UML difference metamodel

and for managing model co-evolution induced by metamodel manipulations [6]. Another interesting property is the *compositionality*, that is the possibility to combine difference models by means of operators like the sequential and the parallel ones. This is crucial in cooperative environments where many software engineers have to coordinate their efforts to produce large software systems [1]. In this respect, combining difference models can give place to conflict issues which need to be resolved, as discussed in the rest of the section.

2.2 Composition of Model Differences

The evolution of a model consists of the initial specification and a number of difference models in such a way the final model can be obtained by applying all the modifications to the original one. In general, it can be convenient composing the difference models in order to obtain a unique one capturing all the occurred modifications. The composition can be performed in sequence and/or in parallel. In particular, if we consider only two subsequent modifications represented in the difference models Δ_1 and Δ_2, their sequential composition corresponds to merging the modifications conveyed by the first document with the second one, i.e.

$$\Delta = \Delta_1 \; ; \; \Delta_2 \tag{1}$$

with ";" the sequential composition operator. The resulting difference model contains a minimal difference set, i.e. only those modifications which have not been overridden by subsequent modifications. Interestingly, the representation technique has operators which are compositional, i.e. they are algebraically compatible with the induced transformations [4]. More precisely, the transformation $T_{\Delta_1\,;\,\Delta_2}$ induced by the composed difference model $\Delta_1 \; ; \; \Delta_2$ is completely defined by the transformations T_{Δ_1} and T_{Δ_2}, respectively, i.e.:

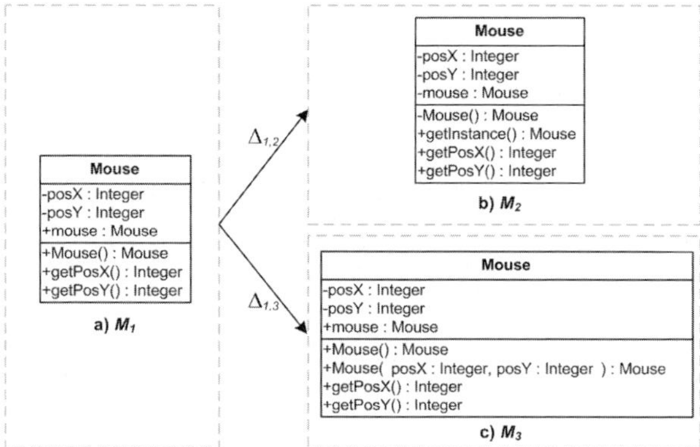

Fig. 4. Sample model modifications

$$T_{\Delta_1\ ;\ \Delta_2} = T_{\Delta_1} \cdot T_{\Delta_2} \tag{2}$$

with ";" as before and $\cdot$ an appropriate composition operator among transformation, i.e. the functional composition of transformations. Sequential compositionality is always assured by the sequential independence condition (see [3] for an extended discussion on the topic), i.e. when the modifications do not interfere with each other and can take place independently in any order.

Parallel compositions are exploited to combine modifications operated from the same ancestor in a concurrent way. In case both manipulations are not affecting the same model elements they are said to be *parallel independent* and their composition is obtained by merging the difference models. More formally, two difference models Δ_1 and Δ_2 are parallel independent if the following condition holds

$$\Delta_1 \mid \Delta_2 = (\Delta_1\ ;\ \Delta_2) + (\Delta_2\ ;\ \Delta_1) \tag{3}$$

where "+" denotes the non determinist choice. In essence, their application is not affected by the adopted order since they do not present any interdependencies. Otherwise, Δ_1 and Δ_2 are referred to as *parallel dependent* since conflict issues arise which need to be detected and eventually resolved. This is the case of the sample modifications $\Delta_{1,2}$, and $\Delta_{1,3}$ reported in Fig. 5. In particular, $\Delta_{1,2}$ represents the necessary modifications required to apply the *singleton* design pattern [7] (which will be considered throughout the paper as explanatory example) to the first version of the class `Mouse` reported in Fig. 4.a: the class constructor and the attribute `mouse` have been changed to private, and the new operation `getInstance()` has been added. The modifications represented in $\Delta_{1,3}$ consist of the addition of the new constructor `Mouse(posX: Integer, posY: Integer)` keeping the rest of the model unchanged (see Fig. 4.c).

According to (1) and (3), $\Delta_{1,2}$ and $\Delta_{1,3}$ in Fig. 5 are neither sequentially nor parallel independent. In fact, they interfere with the visibility of the attribute `mouse` and of the constructor `Mouse()`. In general, this kind of conflicts are called *syntactic conflict* (since the modifications interfere from a syntactical point of view) and there are a number of approaches which are able to detect them [3], even though their resolution generally requires manual interventions. For instance, according to [8] in order

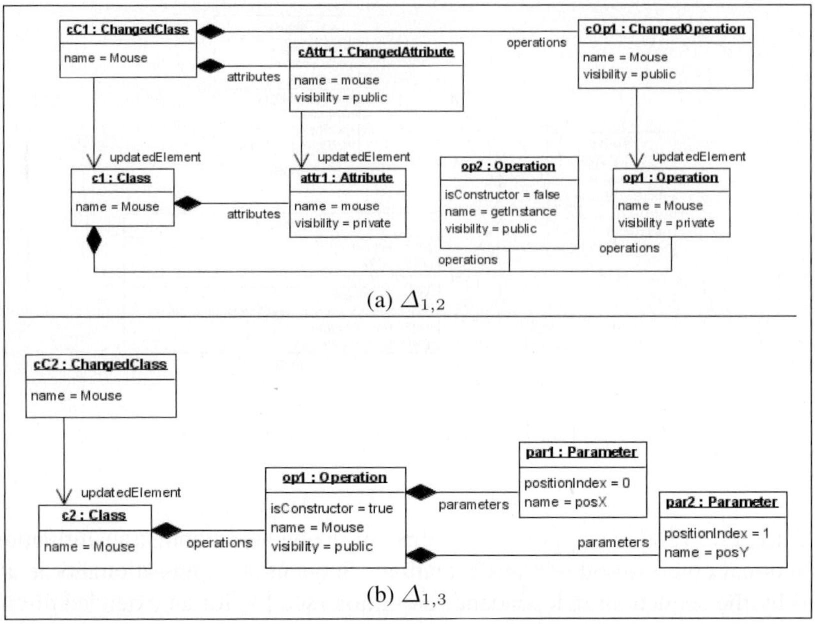

Fig. 5. Sample delta models

to maintain the singleton modification, the conflicts can be resolved by applying $\Delta_{1,3}$ and subsequently $\Delta_{1,2}$. In this way all the modifications are merged and the conflicting ones represented in $\Delta_{1,3}$ are overwritten by those in $\Delta_{1,2}$ leading to the target model in Fig. 6.

Although all the syntactic conflicts have been resolved, the obtained model in Fig. 6 does not adhere to the singleton design pattern prescriptions. In fact, taking into account the semantics behind the singleton, the accessibility of the new constructor `Mouse(posX:` Integer, posY: Integer) breaks that design pattern principles. This is due to parallel changes which interfere on a level which concerns the underlying pattern semantics and that are not syntactically detectable. In particular, the addition of the new constructor specified in the model $\Delta_{1,3}$ does not conflict with any modification represented in $\Delta_{1,2}$, even though it raises problems with respect to the semantic of the singleton

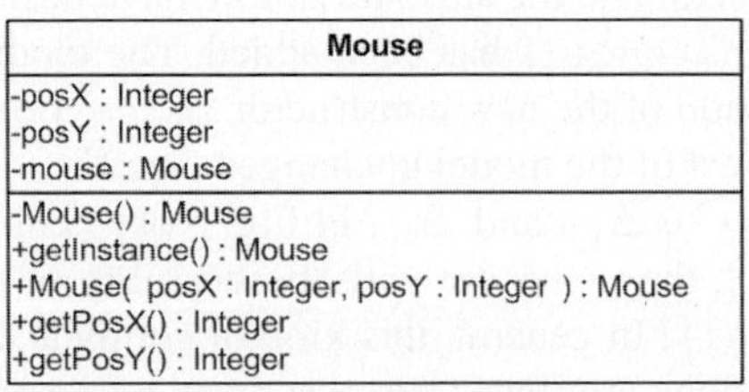

Fig. 6. Sample model $T_{\Delta_{1,3};\Delta_{1,2}}(M_1)$

design pattern. In general, this kind of conflicts are called *semantic conflicts* (according to the terminology in [3]) and demand explicit techniques to support their specification as advocated in [3].

The rest of paper proposes an approach able to support semantic conflicts. In particular, the proposal is based on a meta-model to specify conflicts and corresponding resolution criteria, and to (partly) automate their parallel composition.

3 A Metamodel for Conflict Management

The mechanism proposed in this paper is inspired by the work in [9], where the authors introduce the Join Point Description Diagrams (JPPDs) which are a mechanism to locate modification points in the source code (called *join points* according to aspect-oriented software development [10] terminology) from the model abstraction level. Each join point is defined through a set of UML model element patterns, which can be directly mapped toward OCL expressions. In order to minutely pick up source code points such descriptions must be fine-grained, which makes the resulting pattern definition very powerful. In this respect, OCL is widely accepted as a model query language, and its usability and scalability benefits are discussed in [9].

This paper extends and adapts the mentioned mechanism introduced in order to define a conflict specification formalism which relies on a model-based pattern language endowed with constructs for resolution criteria descriptions. In the following, the details of the conflict specification language will be explained together with its semantics given in terms of OCL expressions.

3.1 Representing Conflicts

Incompatibilities between parallel model modifications are precisely specified by means of *conflict models* relating left- and right- hand sides which represent not allowed contemporary matches. If one of them occurs, a conflicting situation has been found and needs to be solved. The reconciliation can be left to the manual intervention of developers, even if it could become a tedious and error prone task in the context of large systems. Besides, direct manipulation hides the rationale which guided the different choices. Therefore, we made it possible to attach resolution criteria by decorating the links between element patterns with reconciliation decisions.

An excerpt of the conflict specification metamodel is given in Fig. 7: a `Conflict Block` groups a number of pattern boxes and relations between them. In order to have a valid specification at least two patterns and one `ConflictRelation` between them are needed. In other words, conflict models must contain at least a left-hand side and a right-hand side visualizing an undesired scenario. A `PatternBox` contains a number of `DifferenceElements` each of which can have some related `MetaData`, i.e. general information which is not intrinsic to the specific difference model like the creation/modification date, the author and so on. Since a difference element represents a pattern, its properties can be used to narrow the matching set if specified; moreover, a variable can be declared which will be bound if there is at least one match (`boundVariableName`). The importance of this variable is that it can be referred to by other patterns through its

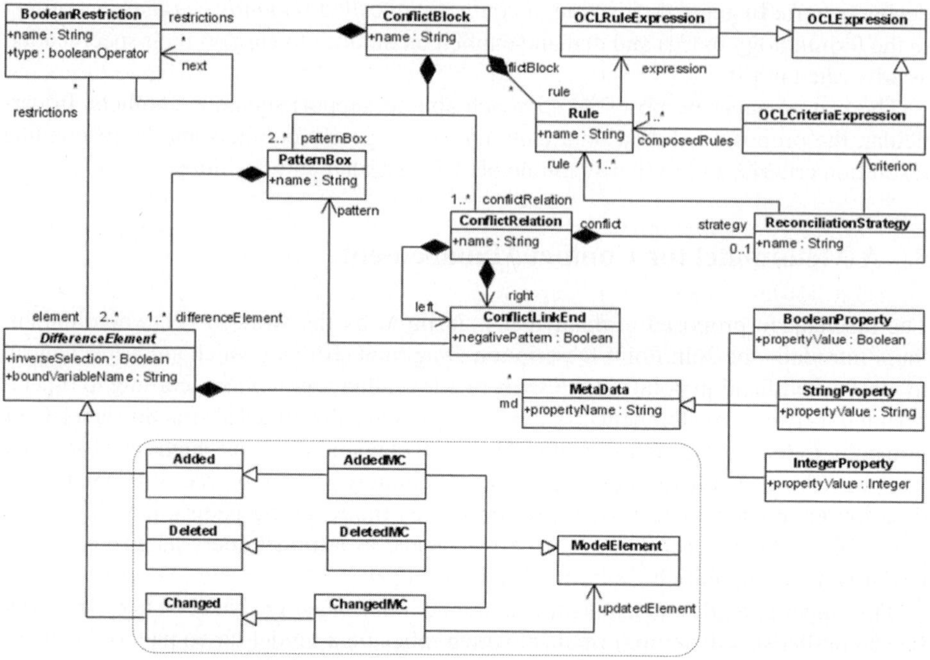

Fig. 7. The conflict specification meta-model

name; in this way, when a pattern is matched the variable is substituted with the current binding whenever it has been used.

Negative patterns can be specified by means of the `inverseSelection` flag, which can be considered as the `not` boolean operator. Moreover, two or more element patterns can be combined for refinement purposes; by default, they are joined through AND relations, i.e. they have all to be matched. Whereas, by means of `BooleanRestrictions` it is possible to compose patterns by using different boolean operators. In this respect, precedences between boolean operators are established through the `next` association. Finally, the `negativePattern` flag in each `ConflictLinkEnd` can be activated to negate the selection of the referred `PatternBox`. When `negativePattern` is enabled (i.e. set to true) an interesting collision management scenario takes place, since it means that there is a problem if a given modification has not been performed. Consequently, mandatory manipulations can also be prescribed through the proposed approach. The conflicting scenarios can be given corresponding resolution criteria through `ReconciliationStrategy`, which states how each conflict should be resolved. Criteria are expressed by means of `OCLExpressions` [11] and combine `Rules`, i.e. predicates in terms of `Metadata` information. In this paper, we focus on conflict specifications only, the interested reader can refer to [12] for a detailed discussion about the definition of reconciliation strategies.

As already mentioned, conflict definitions are based on `DifferenceElements`. In particular, elements to be related are selected through the corresponding delta metaclasses obtained by means of the automated meta-model generation procedure illustrated in Sect. 2.1. The dashed part in Fig. 7 shows how the current delta language is bound to the pattern. It has to be noted that `AddedMC`, `DeletedMC` and `ChangedMC` entities are used as placeholders of the current derived elements, as for example the `AddedClass`, `ChangedClass` and `DeletedClass` of the simplified UML metamodel shown in Fig. 2. Moreover, three new meta-classes have been added to match all instances of a certain kind of manipulation, that are `Added`, `Deleted` and `Changed`. In summary, delta elements can be selected at different levels of granularity, like the kind of manipulation they represent, the portion of input model entities involved in the modifications and the specific values used to perform the revision.

The definition of the conflict metamodel, as customized for the particular source metamodel taken into account, has been automated through a model transformation (currently implemented in ATL [13]) that takes as input the source metamodel and generates the corresponding conflict specification metamodel. For example, starting from the `SimpleUML` metamodel in Fig. 2 it is possible to automatically obtain the corresponding `SimpleUMLCSpec` metamodel, that is the appropriate conflict specification language. The description of the details of such transformation goes beyond the scope of this paper. However, it can be simply obtained by extending the mechanism for the difference metamodel derivation and the interested reader can find it for download at [14].

The obtained `SimpleUMLCSpec` conflict metamodel can be used to specify conflicts like the one depicted in Fig. 8 through the `ConflictBlock` element `cb`. For presentation purposes, the model is given as an object diagram which contains instances of the conflict metamodel even though alternative concrete syntaxes can be defined to have more human readable documents. The model specifies the singleton violation conflict which can be exploited to detect the semantic collision introduced in the previous section. In particular, it presents a collision in which two concurrent updates of a class (`cC1` and `cC2`) bound to the `cClass` variable, do not converge to compatible results. Going deeper, the left pattern (see the `pbLeft` element named `Singleton`) captures the minimal updates required to introduce the singleton design pattern that can be summarized as follows: *(i)* the modifications which involve the visibility of the attribute containing the instances of the class itself, and that of the constructor (see the elements `attr1` and `opt1`, respectively), and *(ii)* the addition of a new public operation which returns instances of the class (see the `op2` operation named `getInstance`).

The right-hand side of the conflict specification (see the pattern box `pbRight` named `Singleton violation`) specifies some modifications which corrupt the requirements prescribed for the singleton design pattern. Hence, neither the constructor should be made public (see the `cOp2` operation updated with the element `op3`), nor an additional public constructor should be added (see `op4`), nor the shared instance value should be made modifiable through a public attribute (see `attr2`). Such changes are grouped by means of the `OR` boolean operator represented by the `restriction` element. As said before, pattern entities are glued through an `AND` by default, which would require the contemporary matching of all the conditions. In this case it is sufficient that one of the three different updates is matched to violate the singleton pattern, or in other words to cause a collision with the left-hand side pattern box.

It is worth noting that this conflict definition abstracts from a particular class, whereas it refers to a generic situation where the singleton design pattern is introduced and in

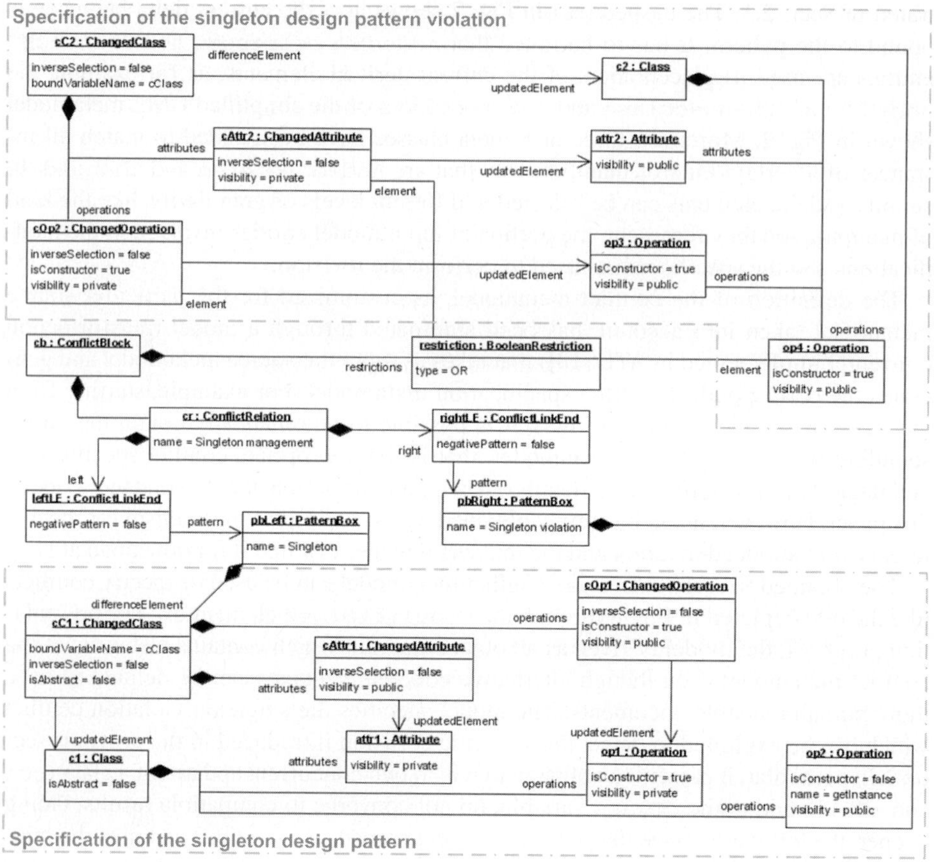

Fig. 8. A model specifying the singleton violation conflict

the mean time some concurrent delta corrupts that specific pattern. In this respect, it becomes evident the usefulness of bound variables, which can be exploited to refer to the particular values of the current matches (see the property `boundVariableName` of the elements `cC1` and `cC2`).

The application of the model in Fig. 8 to the difference models in Fig. 5 detects the occurrence of a semantic conflict consisting of the singleton violation introduced by the model $\Delta_{1,3}$ with respect to the differences represented in $\Delta_{1,2}$. In fact, by matching $\Delta_{1,2}$ with the left pattern box in Fig. 8 and $\Delta_{1,3}$ with the right one, a semantic conflict is identified and human interventions are required instead of generating models like the one in Fig. 6 (as current syntactical approaches do) which does not adhere to the singleton prescriptions.

The syntactic description of collisions has to be assisted by its semantics, in the same way difference metamodels induce transformations on input models. Therefore, in the following it is explained how to give precise meanings to conflict declaration models.

3.2 Interpreting Conflict Models

The interpretation of conflict models induces the verification of co-existing updates in the input difference models Δ_1 and Δ_2. Difference element patterns can be seen as model queries which are naturally expressed by OCL expressions, therefore, each model conforming to the metamodel shown in Fig. 7 can be translated into the corresponding OCL constructs (in a similar way to the approach given in [9]), which interrogate the couple of concurrent manipulations to detect collisions and eventually to give them a reconciliation. It has to be noted that the matching procedure has to be founded on a minimal set of expected entities and related properties, which are provided by the meta metamodel.

Let `ml` and `mr` be the instances for Δ_1 and Δ_2 models, respectively. Then the general OCL rule to match patterns against input models can be formulated as follows:

```
1  context ConflictRelation::
2    matchingPatternBoxes(ml: Sequence(DifferenceElement),
3                         mr: Sequence(DifferenceElement)) :
4    Sequence(TupleType(matchedL : Sequence(DifferenceElement),
5                       matchedR : Sequence(DifferenceElement)))
6  post: result =
7    self.matchPBL(ml,self.left)->
8      iterate(
9        lm; res = Sequence {} |
10         let rightMatches = self.matchPBR(lm,mr,self.right) in
11          if (rightMatches->notEmpty())
12          then
13            res->
14              append(Tuple{matchedL = lm, matchedR = rightMatches})
15          else
16            res
17        endif
18     )
```

Listing 1.1. The general OCL rule to match conflicting changes in parallel delta composition

The function `matchingPatternBoxes` returns a collection of conflicting situation pairs by means of tuples; in turn, each tuple contains a sequence of elements resulting either from the left pattern (`matchedL`) or from the corresponding right pattern selection (`matchedR`). Firstly, left pattern matches are detected through the `matchPBL` function (see line 6); then, this collection of elements is exploited to look for matches on the right-hand side of conflict specification (lines 7-14). In particular, `matchPBR` is iterated on left matchings to detect corresponding elements on the right; if the returned set of elements is not empty, the computed pair of changes is appended as an entry in the current result. In this way, left selections allow to resolve variable bindings which have been eventually exploited in the right part too, while the right pattern ones are computed autonomously and are not intended to be used on the left-hand side. For example, the `cClass` variable shown in Figure 8 is bound at the beginning of the matching process and then its value is exploited to find the remaining correspondences. In this respect, each time a variable is bound its value is resolved wherever it has been referred to.

Both the function `matchPBL` and `matchPBR` detect correspondences in the same way, by starting with variables which need to be bound (if there exist) and then resolving the remaining portion of correspondences. Listing 1.2 shows a key OCL function called by `matchPBL` and `matchPBR` for selecting entities which match against a given difference pattern.

```
1  context DifferenceElement :: matches(de :
2  Sequence{DifferenceElement}) :
3                                         Sequence(DifferenceElement)
4  pre : negate : Boolean = self.inverseSelection and
5        failed : Boolean = false
6  post: result =
7    de->
8        select(
9          mEl |
10           (mEl.oclIsTypeOf(self.oclType()) and
11           (mEl.isAbstract = self.isAbstract or
12            self.isAstract.oclIsUndefined) and
13           (mEl.name = self.name or
14            self.name = isUndefined)) xor
15           negate@pre
16       )->
17           iterate(
18             mEl; result = Sequence {} |
19               self.structuralFeatures->
20             iterate(
21               sF1; res = Sequence {} |
22                 if (sF1.oclIsTypeOf(Reference))
23                 then
24                   mEl.structuralFeatures->
25                     select(
26                       sF2 |
27                         sF2.oclIsTypeOf(Reference) and
28                         (sF1.matchReference(sF2) xor
29                          negate@pre) and
30                         (not sF1.opposite.oclIsUndefined() implies
31                         ((sF1.opposite.matchReference(sF2.opposite) xor
32                          negate@pre))) and
33                         (sF1.type.matches(sF2.type)->notEmpty())
34                     )->
35                       res->collect({sF2, sF1.type.matches(sF2.type)})
36                   and
37                     res->isEmpty() implies failed = true
38                 else
39                   res->collect(sF1.matches(de.structuralFeatures)) and
40                   res->isEmpty() implies failed = true
41             ) and
42               if (not failed)
43               then result->collect({mEl,res})
44               endif
45       )
```

Listing 1.2. The general OCL rule to match a delta element pattern

More precisely, given a difference element pertaining to the model specifying conflicts, the `matches` OCL function looks for possible correspondences in the input difference document provided as parameter. Therefore, firstly potential matching metaclasses are selected (lines 7-14) and then the related set of structural features needs to be met (lines 16-43). Going into more details, for each outgoing `Reference` both its properties and the linked element have to match (lines 21-35). In an analogous manner, the remaining structural properties (i.e. attributes) have to be considered as new patterns to be matched through recursive calls (lines 37-38).

At the end of the outlined process, a sequence is returned; if it is empty then the matching computation failed, i.e. no conflicts have been found, otherwise it contains entities in the difference document which correspond to the patterns depicted in the conflict model. In this respect, the binding of variables is preserved implicitly by means of the `DifferenceElement` meta-class which allows to enrich a delta element with the declared bound variable.

4 Related Works

This paper deals with colliding revisions of artefacts developed in parallel. Especially, it copes with interferences which can not be detected by means of syntactic analyses and are usually referred to as semantic conflicts [3]. Those issues are considered in few works, which tend to provide support only to a particular modeling language (see [15] for a detailed discussion). In this respect, the proposed technique can be considered as an extension of [16] to arbitrary metamodels.

In [15] the authors illustrate *SMoVer*, that is a model versioning tool able to deal with both syntax (structural) and semantic (behavioural) conflicts. In particular, the semantic issues are faced by exploiting appropriate view definitions toward which structural specifications are mapped. In other words, they use translational semantics in order to elicit particular interferences. With respect to our work, the mechanism in [15] requires new domain characterizations to customize the set of the identified interferences. Moreover, conflicts are detected by comparing the whole concurrent revisions, whereas here collisions are managed taking into account only difference documents, i.e. only the elements involved by changes.

Composition of differences is partly considered in few works which mainly focus on software refactoring like [8] and differences occurring on systems developed in parallel [17]. In [8] the authors propose a graph-based technique to discover couples of manipulation conflicts (*critical pairs*). Then, a set of conflict reduction heuristics is given, even if developers can not specify their own resolution criteria. The work in [17] deals with differences occurring on systems developed in parallel; through the use of program slicing and system dependency graphs, semantic interferences are detected. However, the level of abstraction is too low with respect to models. In this respect, we presented an approach to raise the level of abstraction by reformulating part of the knowledges and experiences of these works in a model-driven setting.

A number of efforts deal with the general problems of consistency management and model composition; as software systems are specified by means of disparate notations related to different points of view of the same application, keeping the different documents coherent with each others is an unavoidable issue to take care of [18,19]. In particular, consistency management is faced by defining a kind of conflicts between modifications occurring on the different views which are solved by propagating the changes toward newer coherent documents. However, in general these solutions are specifically designed for the problem domain they are applied in, like the UML diagrams and similar. Moreover, inconsistencies are always thought as existing between a pair of elements, while conflicts can be defined as ranging from a single and independent entity update to an arbitrary group of element manipulations. In summary, consistency management can be considered as a sub-problem of conflict issues.

In [20] a set of common definitions are provided to outline the key requirements of a model composition solution, in terms of language and tool support. Moreover, in [21] a number of operators for model integration are described and they have partially inspired the composition constructs proposed so far. Finally, other works take into account the specific issue of model merging, both in the case of different versions of a system design [22] and in a generic scenario, like [23,24] for example. However, those papers seem to focus on establishing correspondences between elements of the input models (matching phase), while conflict troubles are largely missed out.

5 Conclusions and Future Work

Increasingly, complex software systems are cooperatively designed in distributed environments and the interaction among concurrent manipulations inevitably causes conflicts which must be detected and reconciled.

This paper illustrated a model-driven conflict specification mechanism based on the declarative description of incompatibilities between competing difference models. In particular, a conflict metamodel has been proposed to specify conflict patterns between difference elements which cannot take place at the same time. This way, it is possible to introduce non-syntactical conflicts which usually would not be identified by merging approaches based on implicit conflict detection techniques. As a benefit, it is possible to improve conflict management adaptability to different application domains, since each domain has a set of its own semantic dependencies which need to be specified to obtain a useful detection and resolution method.

Future work will necessarily encompass further validation against large projects in order to evaluate the efforts demanded to the developer for managing model compositions. For example, the process could benefit of improved automation degree by taking into account heuristics and by-example approaches [15]. Finally, an enhancement of the conflict specification language will be investigated for supporting multi-view consistency, which demands the description of change interferences between models not necessarily conforming to the same metamodel, and hence inducing disparate difference metamodels.

References

1. Whitehead, J.: Collaboration in software engineering: A roadmap. In: FOSE 2007: 2007 Future of Software Engineering, Washington, DC, USA, pp. 214–225. IEEE Computer Society, Los Alamitos (2007)
2. Favre, J.M.: Meta-Model and Model Co-evolution within the 3D Software Space. In: Procs. of the Int. Workshop ELISA at ICSM (September 2003)
3. Mens, T.: A State-of-the-Art Survey on Software Merging. IEEE Trans. Softw. Eng. 28(5), 449–462 (2002)
4. Cicchetti, A., Di Ruscio, D., Pierantonio, A.: A Metamodel Independent Approach to Difference Representation. Journal of Object Technology 6(9), 165–185 (2007)
5. Lin, Y., Zhang, J., Gray, J.: Model Comparison: A Key Challenge for Transformation Testing and Version Control in Model Driven Software Development. In: OOPSLA Work. MDSD (2004)

6. Cicchetti, A., Di Ruscio, D., Eramo, R., Pierantonio, A.: Automating co-evolution in model-driven engineering. In: 12th IEEE International EDOC Conference (EDOC 2008), München (Germany) (to appear, 2008)
7. Gamma, E., Helm, R., Johnson, R., Vlissides, J.: Design Patterns. Addison-Wesley, Reading (1995)
8. Mens, T., Taentzer, G., Runge, O.: Detecting Structural Refactoring Conflicts Using Critical Pair Analysis. Electr. Notes Theor. Comput. Sci. 127(3), 113–128 (2005)
9. Stein, D., Hanenberg, S., Unland, R.: A Graphical Notation to Specify Model Queries for MDA Transformations on UML Models. In: Aßmann, U., Akşit, M., Rensink, A. (eds.) MDAFA 2003. LNCS, vol. 3599, pp. 77–92. Springer, Heidelberg (2005)
10. Filman, R., Elrad, T., Clarke, S., Aksit, M.: Aspect-Oriented Software Development. Addison-Wesley, Reading (2004)
11. Object Management Group (OMG): OCL 2.0 Specification, OMG Document formal/2006-05-01 (2006)
12. Cicchetti, A.: Difference Representation and Conflict Management in Model-Driven Engineering. PhD thesis, University of L'Aquila, Computer Science Dept. (2008)
13. Jouault, F., Kurtev, I.: Transforming Models with ATL. In: Bruel, J.M. (ed.) MoDELS 2005. LNCS, vol. 3844, pp. 128–138. Springer, Heidelberg (2006)
14. Cicchetti, A., Di Ruscio, D., Pierantonio, A.: Management of conflicts on the AMMA platform (May 2008), `http://www.di.univaq.it/cicchetti/conflictManagement.php`
15. Altmanninger, K., Bergmayr, A., Schwinger, W., Kotsis, G.: Semantically Enhanced Conflict Detection between Model Versions in SMoVer by Example. In: Procs of the Int. Workshop on Semantic-Based Software Development at OOPSLA 2007, Montral, Canada (October 2007) (to appear)
16. Cicchetti, A., Rossini, A.: Weaving models in conflict detection specifications. In: Procs of the ACM Symposium on Applied Computing (SAC 2007), Model Transformation track, pp. 1035–1036. ACM, New York (2007)
17. Thione, G.L., Perry, D.E.: Parallel Changes: Detecting Semantic Interferences. In: COMPSAC, pp. 47–56. IEEE Computer Society, Los Alamitos (2005)
18. Egyed, A.: Fixing Inconsistencies in UML Design Models. In: Procs. of the 29th ICSE 2007, pp. 292–301. IEEE Computer Society, Los Alamitos (2007)
19. Nentwich, C., Emmerich, W., Finkelstein, A.: Consistency Management with Repair Actions. In: Procs. of the 25th ICSE 2003, May 3-10, pp. 455–464. IEEE Computer Society, Los Alamitos (2003)
20. Bézivin, J., Bouzitouna, S., Fabro, M.D.D., Gervais, M.P., Jouault, F., Kolovos, D., Kurtev, I., Paige, R.: A Canonical Scheme for Model Composition. In: Rensink, A., Warmer, J. (eds.) ECMDA-FA 2006. LNCS, vol. 4066. Springer, Heidelberg (2006)
21. Reiter, T., Kapsammer, E., Retschitzegger, W., Wimmer, M.: Model Integration Through Mega Operations. In: Workshop on MDWE 2005 (July 2005)
22. Kolovos, D.S., Paige, R.F., Polack, F.: Merging Models with the Epsilon Merging Language (EML). In: Nierstrasz, O., Whittle, J., Harel, D., Reggio, G. (eds.) MoDELS 2006. LNCS, vol. 4199, pp. 215–229. Springer, Heidelberg (2006)
23. Engel, K.D., Paige, R.F., Kolovos, D.S.: Using a Model Merging Language for Reconciling Model Versions. In: Rensink, A., Warmer, J. (eds.) ECMDA-FA 2006. LNCS, vol. 4066, pp. 143–157. Springer, Heidelberg (2006)
24. Pottinger, R., Bernstein, P.A.: Merging Models Based on Given Correspondences. In: VLDB, pp. 826–873 (2003)

Metamodel Matching for Automatic Model Transformation Generation*

Jean-Rémy Falleri, Marianne Huchard, Mathieu Lafourcade, and Clémentine Nebut

LIRMM, CNRS and Université de Montpellier 2,
161, rue Ada, 34392 Montpellier cedex 5, France
{falleri,huchard,lafourcade,nebut}@lirmm.fr

Abstract. Applying Model-Driven Engineering (MDE) leads to the creation of a large number of metamodels, since MDE recommends an intensive use of models defined by metamodels. Metamodels with similar objectives are then inescapably created. A recurrent issue is thus to turn compatible models conforming to similar metamodels, for example to use them in the same tool. The issue is classically solved developing ad hoc model transformations. In this paper, we propose an approach that automatically detects mappings between two metamodels and uses them to generate an alignment between those metamodels. This alignment needs to be manually checked and can then be used to generate a model transformation. Our approach is built on the Similarity Flooding algorithm used in the fields of schema matching and ontology alignment. Experimental results comparing the effectiveness of the application of various implementations of this approach on real-world metamodels are given.

1 Introduction

The large success of Model-Driven Engineering leads to a relative abundance of metamodels, for various domains. Tools are developped to handle models conforming to the metamodels : code generators, model transformations and graphical editors. Inescapably, several metamodels for the same kind of applications are independently created. It is then quite natural to wish to use a tool-set adapted to a given metamodel for models conforming to another metamodel with the same purpose. For example, several metamodels exist to represent class models, and several tools exist to automatically refactor class models. The problem is to use a tool dedicated to a metamodel with a class model conforming to another metamodel allowing to express the same kind of class models. Even for the same application domain, various versions of the same metamodels usually exist, and the compatibility between the models conforming to the different versions has to be ensured. Usually, this problem is solved using manually written, ad hoc model transformations. Such model transformations are not difficult to write, but are numerous, and thus represent a large work load. In this paper, we propose

* France Télécom R&D has supported this work (CPRE 5326).

K. Czarnecki et al. (Eds.): MoDELS 2008, LNCS 5301, pp. 326–340, 2008.

to generate automatically an alignment between two similar metamodels. This alignment represents the correspondences between the elements of the source metamodel and those of the target metamodel. This alignment can then be used to generate the code of a model transformation.

The match operation is well-known in many application domains, such as semantic web, schema and ontology integration, data warehouses, e-commerce [1,2]. It takes as input two schemas and produces as output a set of relations (*e.g.*, equivalence and subsumption) between the entities of the two input schemas. Such an output is often called an alignment of two schemas. The notion of schema can appear as unclear since it highly depends on the concerned domain. Concretely, a schema can be an XML Schema, an ontology, a database schema or an object-oriented class model. Despite the variation between those formats, the mechanisms involved to perform the match operation are highly similar.

In this paper, we report experiments which evaluate and adapt the Similarity Flooding algorithm [3] to compute metamodel alignments. The context of our approach is the automated generation of model transformations. The input of the Similarity Flooding algorithm being two labeled directed graphs, part of our contribution is the proposal and assessment of several ways of encoding a given metamodel into a labeled directed graph (Section 3). In order to ensure the reproducibility of our experiments by readers of this paper, we present in detail the implementation choices we have taken for the Similarity Flooding algorithm (Section 4). Finally, the output is filtered and transformed into a metamodel alignment (Section 5).

2 Overview of the Approach

In this paper, we aim at generating a model transformation from an input model conforming to a metamodel MM_{source} to an output model conforming to a metamodel MM_{target}, aligning MM_{source} on MM_{target}. Such a transformation can be obtained using a schema matching approach.

The Similarity Flooding algorithm. Several surveys [1,2] describe the existing approaches concerning the matching problem. Those approaches could roughly be classified in two categories: schema level approaches that produce alignments using the schemas (e.g. an XML Schema), and instance level approaches that produce alignments using instances of the schemas (e.g. an XML document conforming to a given Schema). Our objective being to generate model transformations based on the metamodels, we focused on the first category. Among the many such approaches found in the literature, we chose to use the Similarity Flooding algorithm [3], for two main reasons. First, it takes as input directed labeled graphs representing the schemas to match, and converting metamodels to directed labeled graphs is an easy operation. Second, its generic design allows easy tuning in order to produce better results using information specific to the input format. The similarity algorithm works on directed labeled graphs. Those graphs are used in a fix-point computation process whose result tells us what

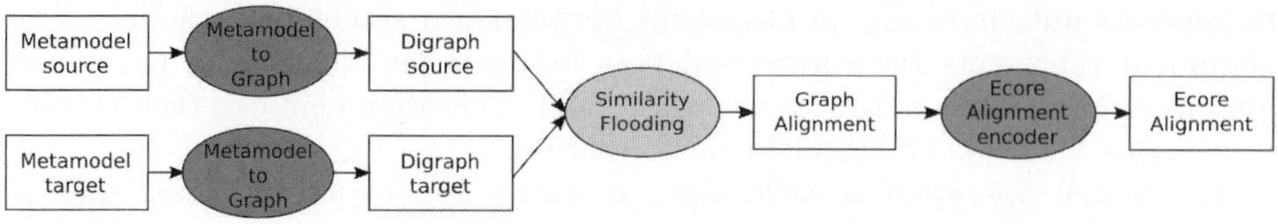

Fig. 1. Overview of the approach

nodes in one graph are similar to nodes in the second graph. This process is based on the following intuition: if a node is similar to another node, the neighbours of this node may be similar to the neighbours of the other node. We have the same intuition concerning metamodel alignment.

Overall approach. The approach we propose to compute a metamodel alignment between two metamodels MM_{source} and MM_{target} is three-phased (see Fig. 1):

1. Transformation of MM_{source} and MM_{target} to the directed labeled graphs G_{source} and G_{target}. There are several strategies to encode a metamodel into such a graph, and thus several graphs can be generated in a deterministic way from the same metamodel, depending on the chosen strategy. This step will be detailed in Section 3.
2. Application of the Similarity Flooding algorithm. To keep this paper self-contained, we explain this algorithm in Section 4.
3. Generation of an alignment between MM_{source} and MM_{target}. This step is described in Section 5.

We illustrate these three steps using the two metamodels $exMM_{source}$ and $exMM_{target}$ shown in Fig. 2. These two metamodels are both used to express class models, but the names of the elements and their structure are slightly different (one is UML-like and the other is Java-like).

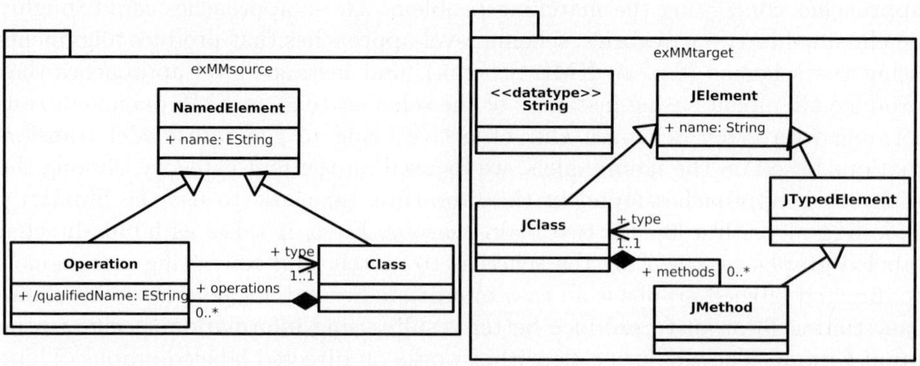

Fig. 2. Example $exMM_{source}$ (left) and $exMM_{target}$ (right) metamodels

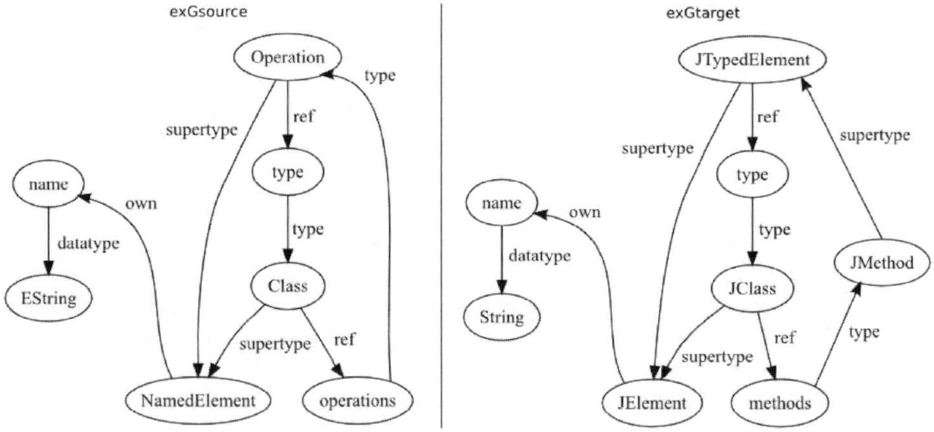

Fig. 3. Graphs generated using the example metamodels and the Minimal configuration

3 From Metamodels to Directed Labeled Graphs

In this section, we explain how to transform a metamodel into a directed labeled graph that can be exploited by the Similarity Flooding algorithm. This transformation has a crucial importance: it is in charge of extracting from the metamodels the information that will be used to compute the mappings between the metamodel elements. It also structures this chosen information: the structure of the graph is important since the Similarity Flooding algorithm computes the alignment based on the structure of the input graphs. In the following, we refer to the choice of the elements in the metamodel and the way to structure them in a directed labeled graph as a configuration.

To determine the most adequate configuration, we designed six possible configurations that explore the effects of derived elements (that may introduce redundancy and increases the complexity of the Similarity Flooding algorithm), of abstract classes, and of transitive closure on relations based on the inheritance relation. We describe below those six configurations, and how they impact the resulting alignment in the case study presented in Section 6. Our approach uses `Ecore` [4] as the meta-metamodel, thus the configurations refer to `Ecore` elements (*e.g.*, `EClass`, `EReference`).

The first configuration is called **Minimal**: it is the simplest and most intuitive one. It uses a small subset of elements included in the metamodel: it does not use any meta-attribute of the meta-classes. One labeled node is created for each `EClass`, each non-derived `EAttribute`, each non-derived `EReference`, each `EDataType`, each `EEnum` and each `EEnumLiteral` contained in the metamodel. The labels of those nodes are the names of the corresponding elements. A directed arc labeled *supertype* is created between two nodes that represent an `EClass` whenever those two `EClasses` are in an inheritance relationship. An *own* arc is created when an `EClass` owns an `EAttribute`. A *ref* arc is created when an `EClass` owns an `EReference`. A *type* arc is created when an `EReference` is typed by an EClass. A *datatype* arc is created when an EAttribute is typed by an EDataType or an EEnum. A *literal* arc is created when an EEnum owns an EEnumLiteral. Fig. 3 shows the graphs exG_{source} and exG_{target}, corresponding respectively to $exMM_{source}$ and $exMM_{target}$ metamodels, generated with this configuration.

The second configuration, called **Basic**, differs from the Minimal configuration by the way it represents the names of the elements. With the Minimal configuration, an element E (for example an Eclass) with name n is represented by a node N with label n, while with the Basic configuration, E is represented by a node N labeled by a unique identifier *#ID*, and linked to a node labeled n with an arc *label*. Fig. 4 shows the graph exG_{source} generated with this configuration. Such a configuration allows us to directly have the information on the frequence a name is used (we just have to count the number of arcs *label* entering a given node). This frequence can then be exploited by the Similarity Flooding algorithm.

The third configuration, **Standard**, extends the Basic configuration to obtain similarities not only inspecting the names of the elements, but also their types, and main attributes (abstract for the EClass, lowerBound and upperBound from EAttribute and EReference, and containment from EReference). In that purpose, a node representing an element E is linked by an arc labeled *kind* to a node N representing the type of the element E. N is labeled according to the type of the element E, removing the prefix "*E*" for all the elements of Ecore, and adding the suffix "*Element*" (e.g. *EClass* is turned into *ClassElement*). To deal with the main attributes, when an element E has for type a meta-class with an attribute A, then the node corresponding to E is linked with an arc labeled A to a node whose label is the value of the attribute A for E. For example, to represent an abstract EClass *myEClass*, the node representing *myEClass* is linked with an arc labeled *abstract* to a node labeled *true*. The left side of Fig. 5 shows an excerpt of the graph exG_{source} generated using the Standard configuration. The **Full** configuration extends the Standard configuration taking into account the derived EAttributes and EReferences. All the nodes representing an EAttribute or

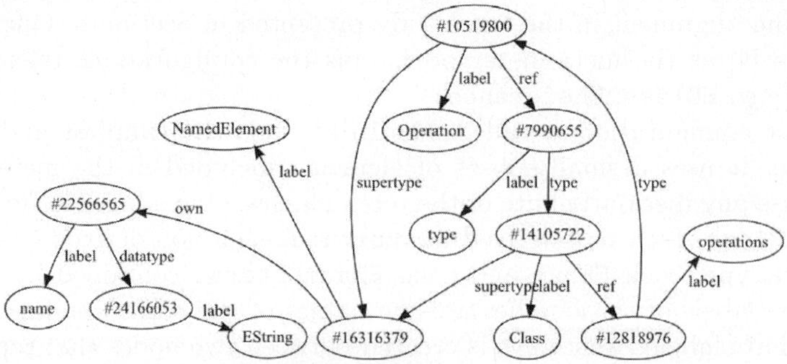

Fig. 4. Graph exG_{source} corresponding to $exMM_{source}$ using the Basic configuration (the name of the elements are in a dedicated node)

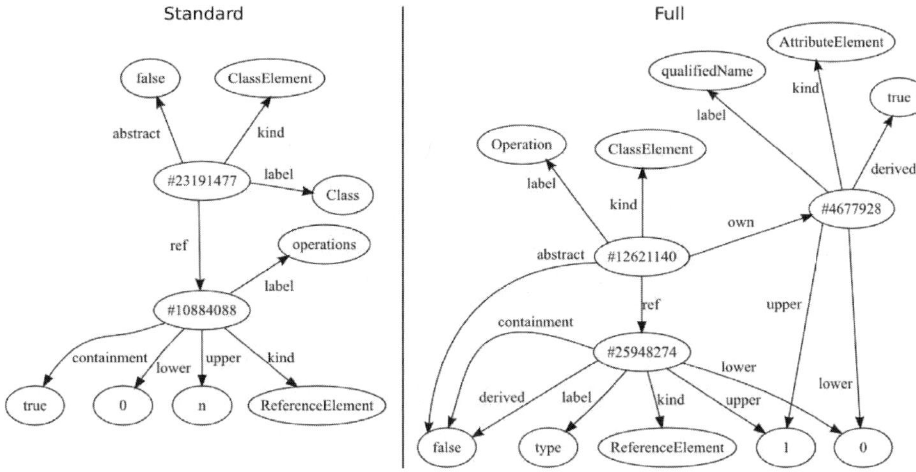

Fig. 5. Extracts of graph exG_{source} generated with the Standard and Full configurations

an EReference are added an arc labeled *derived* and leading to a node labeled *true* or *false* depending whether the element is derived. The right side of Fig. 5 shows an extract of the graph exG_{source} generated using this configuration.

The **Flattened** configuration is based on the Standard one, but with flattened inheritance. The nodes representing abstract EClasses and the arcs labeled *supertype* are deleted. Instead, arcs labeled *own* (resp. *ref*) connect nodes representing an EClass *Ecl* to nodes representing the EAttribute (resp. EReference) defined by *Ecl* and all its superclasses. Moreover, when an EReference *Eref* is typed by an abstract EClass *Ecl*, a *type* arc is created from the node corresponding to *Eref* to each non-abstract sub-class of *Ecl*.

The last configuration is called **Saturated** and is still based on the Standard one. Here, the transitive relations are saturated, like in [5]. EClass nodes are now connected by a *supertype* arc to the nodes representing all the super-classes of this EClass. EClass nodes are also connected by *own* (resp. *ref*) arcs to the nodes representing the EAttribute (resp. EReference) introduced and inherited by the EClass. Finally, for a node representing an EReference, *type* arcs are created to the node representing the EClass that types the EReference as well as all the nodes representing the super-classes of the EClass.

4 The Similarity Flooding Algorithm

This section describes the steps performed by the Similarity Flooding algorithm [3] to compute an alignment between two graphs G_{source} and G_{target}.

Step 1. The first step of this algorithm is the computation of a compatibility graph (called pairwise connectivity graph in [3]) between G_{source} and G_{target}.

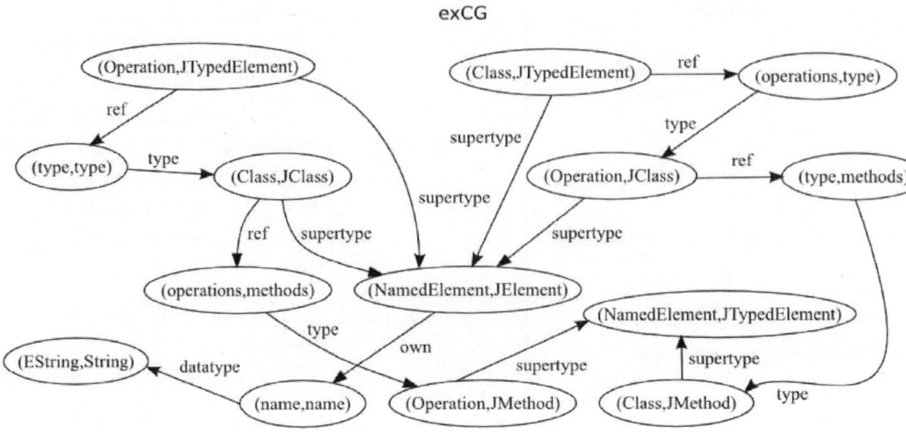

Fig. 6. The compatibility graph $exCG$ between exG_{source} and exG_{target}

A graph G_i is here a set of triples (x, r, y) with x and y two labeled nodes and r a labeled arc. The compatibility graph CG between two graphs G_{source} and G_{target} is built this way: $((x_1, x_2), r, (y_1, y_2)) \in CG$ iff $(x_1, r, y_1) \in G_{source}$ and $(x_2, r, y_2) \in G_{target}$. Therefore, a compatibility graph is a set of triples (s, r, t) such as $s = (x_1, y_1)$ and $t = (x_2, y_2)$ with x_1 and x_2 labeled nodes of G_{source}, y_1 and y_2 labeled nodes of G_{target}, and r a labeled arc. Nodes s and t are called compatibility nodes. Fig. 6 shows the compatibility graph built using the two sample graphs of Fig. 3.

Step 2. In this step, we compute a propagation graph using this compatibility graph. The labeled arcs of the compatibility graph created during the previous step are replaced by several weighted arcs. Different ways of computing the weights are compared in [3]. Here, we have chosen to use one that has proved to give good results. First, for each arc (s, r, t) of the compatibility graph, a reverse arc (t, r, s) is also created. Then, for each compatibility node n we compute O_l^n the number of arcs that start from n and are labeled by l. For instance, in Fig. 6, $O_{supertype}^{(NamedElement,JElement)} = 4$ and $O_{own}^{(NamedElement,JElement)} = 1$. For each triple (s, r, t) of the compatibility graph, a (s, v, t) triple is created in the propagation graph with $v = 1/O_r^s$. In Fig. 6 we can see that $(n_1, supertype, n_2)$ is replaced by $(n_1, 0.25, n_2)$ because $O_{supertype}^{n_1} = 4$, with $n_1 = (NamedElement, JElement)$ and $n_2 = (Class, JClass)$. Similarly, (n_1, own, n_3) is replaced by $(n_1, 1, n_3)$ because $O_{own}^{n_1} = 1$, with $n_3 = (name, name)$. Fig. 7 shows the propagation graph computed using the compatibility graph of Fig. 6.

Step 3. We dispose now of a propagation graph that indicates how the similarity values of the nodes will propagate through the graph. Before starting the fixpoint computation process, it is necessary to assign an initial similarity value to each node of the propagation graph. We chose to assign the initial value s_n^0 of a compatibility node $n = (x, y)$ with the following formula, similar to the one used

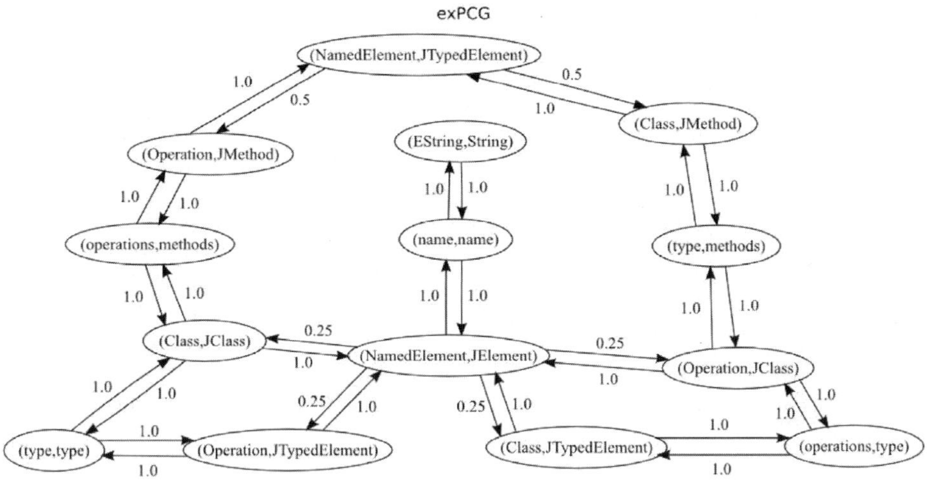

Fig. 7. The propagation graph *exPCG*

in [3]: if x or y is an identifier $s_n^0 = 0$, else $s_n^0 = 1 - lev(x, y)/max(len(x), len(y))$, with $len(x)$ the length of label x and $lev(x, y)$ the Levenshtein distance [6] between labels x and y. The Levenshtein distance between two labels is given by the minimum number of operations needed to transform one label into the other, where an operation is an insertion, deletion, or substitution of a single character. Table 1 shows the initial similarity value computed for each node of the propagation graph shown in Fig. 7. An iterative fix-point computation process will propagate these initial similarity values through the propagation graph. There are again many ways to propagate those similarity values. We chose the fix-point formula that has proved to give the best result and has the best convergence properties in [3]. This formula has the following definition. Let n be a compatibility node and I_n be the set of compatibility nodes that are connected to n by a weighted arc that ends at n, and let $w(s, t)$ be the weight of the arc between s and t. The similarity value s_n^{i+1} of node n at step $i+1$ is computed according to the following formula: $s_n^{i+1} = s_n^i + s_n^0 + \sum_{m \in I^n} w(m, n) \times (s_m^0 + s_m^i)$. At the end of a step of this iterative process, the similarity value of each compatibility node is normalized; i.e. divided by the greatest similarity value computed in the step. For instance, in the sample propagation graph shown in Fig. 7,

$$
\begin{aligned}
s_{n_4}^1 &= s_{n_4}^0 + s_{n_4}^0 + w(n_5, n_4) \times (s_{n_5}^0 + s_{n_5}^0) + w(n_6, n_4) \times (s_{n_6}^0 + s_{n_6}^0) \\
&\simeq 0.10 + 0.10 + 1 \times (0.11 + 0.11) + 1 \times (0.08 + 0.08) \simeq 0.58 \\
\text{with} \quad & n_4 = (operations, type),\ n_5 = (Operation, JClass), \\
& n_6 = (Class, JTypedElement).
\end{aligned}
$$

For this sample propagation graph, the best computed similarity value during the first step is $s^1_{(NamedElement,JElement)} \simeq 5.67$ hence at the end of the first

Table 1. Initial and final similarity value of each compatibility node

Compatibility node	Initial similarity value	Final similarity value
(NamedElement,JElement)	0.5833334	1.0
(name,name)	1.0	0.7771561
(EString,String)	0.85714287	0.5186626
(NamedElement,JTypedElement)	0.6923077	0.2985012
(Operation,JTypedElement)	0.23076922	0.44552472
(Class,JTypedElement)	0.07692307	0.13148126
(type,type)	1.0	0.63979846
(operations,type)	0.100000024	0.11389989
(Operation,JClass)	0.111111104	0.1868067
(Class,JClass)	0.8333333	0.7449572
(type,methods)	0.14285713	0.11238139
(operations,methods)	0.39999998	0.52174574
(Operation,JMethod)	0.3333333	0.3444618
(Class,JMethod)	0.0	0.14695258

step, $s^1_{(operations,type)} \simeq 0,10$ and $s^1_{(NamedElement,JElement)} = 1$. Let (S^i, S^{i+1}) be a vector of the similarity values computed at two successive steps i and $i+1$. This iterative fix-point computation process ends whenever the euclidean norm of this vector becomes less than ε for some $i > 0$. If the computation does not converge (it means that the euclidean norm of (S^i, S^{i+1}) never becomes less than ε), the process terminates after a maximal number of steps. More information on the complexity and the convergence properties of this algorithm are given in [3]. Table 1 shows the final similarity values of the compatibility nodes of the sample propagation graph shown in Fig. 7, with $\varepsilon = 0.05$. The set of tuples (n, v) with n a compatibility node and v a similarity value, corresponding to the columns *Compatibility node* and *Final similarity value* of Table 1, is called the multimapping between G_{source} and G_{target}.

Step 4. This last step filters the multimapping to produce a final alignment. We call R the multimapping and A the final alignment, with $A \subseteq R$. The method we use to filter the produced multimapping is called *SelectThreshold* in [3]. In the multimapping, a node of the source graph can be associated to several nodes of the target graph. Fig. 8 shows an extract of the multimapping produced with the sample graphs. In this extract, we can clearly see that the *type* node of the source graph can be associated to the *type* node or the *methods* node of the target graph. The *SelectThreshold* filter works as follows. For each couple (n, v) of the multimapping, with $n = (x, y)$, the best match for x (resp y) is looked for in the multimapping. The best match for x (resp. y) is a couple $(m, v) \in R$ such as $m = (x, z)$ (resp. $m = (w, y)$) with v the best similarity value for a node like m. We call s^{max}_x (resp. s^{max}_y) the similarity value for the best match for x (resp. y). For the previous couple (n, v), we compute $s^n_x = v/s^{max}_x$ and $s^n_y = v/s^{max}_y$. The couple $(n, v) \in A$ iff $s^n_x \geq threshold$ and $s^n_y \geq threshold$, with $threshold \in [0, 1]$. In the example of Fig. 8, we have $s^{max}_{operations} \simeq 0.52$ and $s^{max}_{type} \simeq 0.64$.

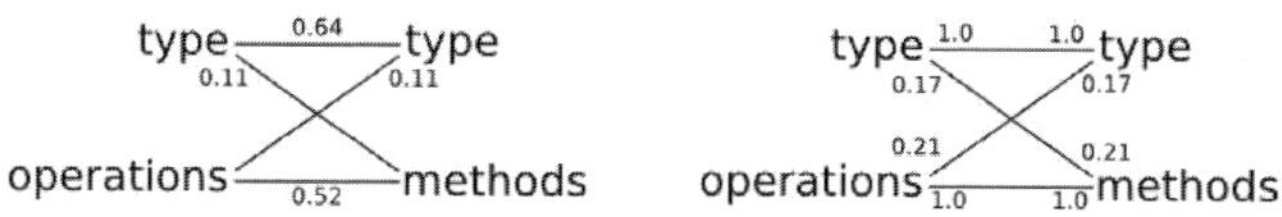

Fig. 8. Extract of the multimapping (left) and of the mutual multimapping (right)

Therefore, $s_{operations}^{(operations,type)} \simeq \frac{0.11}{0.52} \simeq 0.21$. Similarly, $s_{type}^{(operations,type)} \simeq \frac{0.11}{0.64} \simeq 0.17$. With $threshold = 0.2$, the couple $(operations, type)$ is discarded while with $threshold = 0.15$, it is included in the alignment. The choice of $threshold$ determines the alignment: a high value of $threshold$ will lead to $[0-1] \times [0-1]$ cardinality mappings (one element from the source metamodel corresponds at most to one element of the target metamodel). On the other hand, a low value of $threshold$ will create $[0-n] \times [0-n]$ cardinality mappings (a set of elements of the source metamodel corresponds to a set of elements of the target metamodel). Fig. 9 shows the alignment computed on the example graphs with $threshold = 0.95$. Each mapping of this alignment is correct, except the mapping between *Operation* and *JTypedElement*.

5 Computation of the Metamodel Alignment

In our approach, we consider a model transformation from a source metamodel MM_{source} to a target metamodel MM_{target} as a procedure that produces objects conforming to concrete classes of MM_{target} by the analysis of objects conforming to concrete classes of MM_{source}. Data used when analysing an object of the source model correspond to the non-derived attributes and references, because Ecore does not allow to express how an operation is computed or a derived feature. In the MDE technological space, many transformation languages exist. We did not want our approach to be tied to a particular language. To avoid that, we chose to build a language-independent alignment metamodel, inspired by the schema-matching metamodel given in [7]. Models conforming to this metamodel show how a metamodel is aligned to another metamodel. Such a model is built

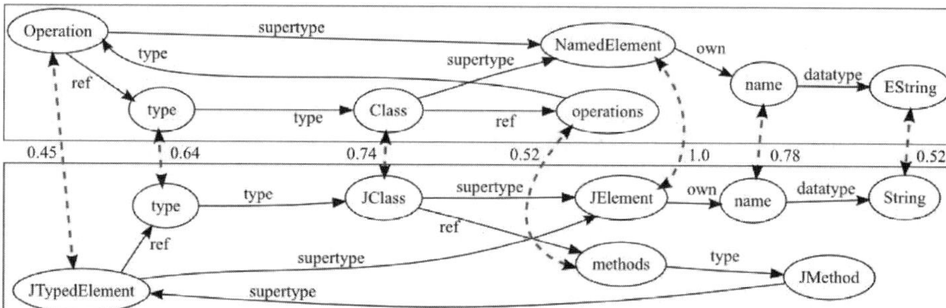

Fig. 9. Computed alignment between exG_{source} and exG_{target}

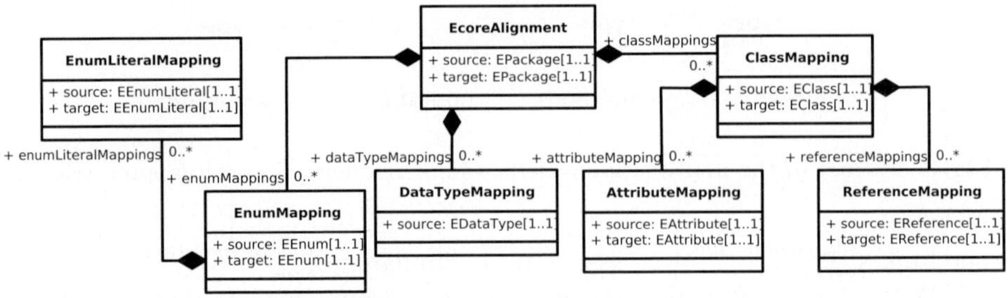

Fig. 10. Ecore alignment metamodel

by analysing and reorganizing the alignment produced by the Similarity Flooding algorithm. A transformation generator then reads an alignment model and generates the code of the transformation in a target language. Such an architecture allows to generate transformations in various languages. However, such code generators are out of the scope of this paper. The alignment metamodel is shown in Fig. 10. An Ecore alignment is composed of several class mappings, data type mappings and enumeration mappings. A class mapping is composed of several attribute and reference mappings. An enumeration mapping is composed of several enumeration literal mappings. Because we did not want to tackle complex element transformations (such as Class to Attribute or Attribute to Class mappings) in this paper, our metamodel only allows to express mappings between elements of the same kind. However, such cross-kind mappings can be found in the alignment produced by Similarity Flooding. According to our definition of a model transformation, we add the following constraints on our alignment metamodel: two mapped `EClass` are not abstract and two mapped `EReference` or `EAttribute` are not derived. The steps required to build such an Ecore alignment from a Similarity Flooding (SF) alignment are:

1. Search in the SF alignment all the mappings between two concrete `EClass` to buid the `ClassMapping` elements. Then for each such mapping:
   (a) When an `EAttribute` from the source `EClass` and its super-classes is mapped to an `EAttribute` contained by the target `EClass` or its super-classes, add an `AttributeMapping` element in the `ClassMapping`;
   (b) When an `EReference` from the source `EClass` and its super-classes is mapped to an `EReference` contained by the target `EClass` or its super-classes, add a `ReferenceMapping` element in the `ClassMapping`;
2. Search in the SF alignment all the mappings from a source `EEnum` to a target `EEnum` to build the `EnumMapping` elements. For each literal of a mapping source `EEnum` which matches on a literal of the target `EEnum`, add an `EnumLiteralMapping` element.
3. Search in the SF aligment all the mappings from a source `EDataType` to a target `EDataType` to build the `DataTypeMapping` elements.

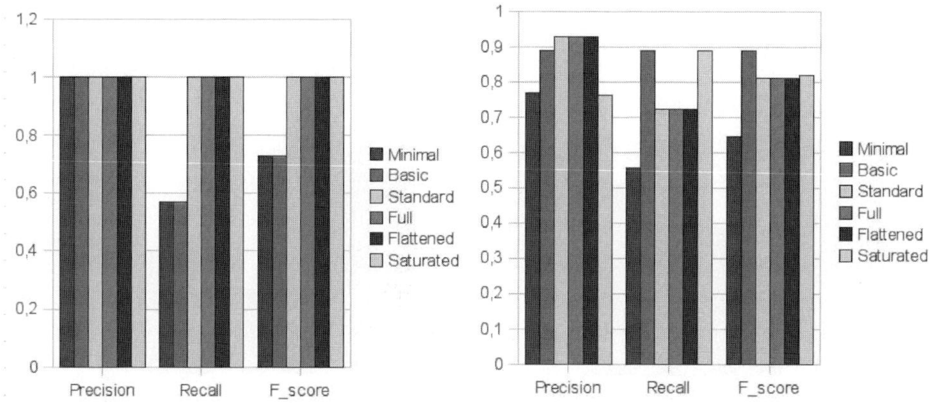

Fig. 11. Results of $exMM_{source} \leftrightarrow exMM_{target}$ (left) and $Ecore \leftrightarrow Minjava$ (right)

6 Case Study

This case study compares the results obtained on various metamodels with the different configurations proposed in Section 3. The parameters of the similarity flooding algorithm used in this case study are: $\varepsilon = 0.05$ and $threshold = 0.95$. Since many of the real world metamodels are designed to express class models, we chose to use those metamodels as a benchmark. The chosen alignment scenarios are: $exMM_{source} \leftrightarrow exMM_{target}$, $Ecore \leftrightarrow Minjava$, $Ecore \leftrightarrow Kermeta$ and $Ecore \leftrightarrow UML$. Ecore [4] is the meta-metamodel and hence a metamodel. Minjava [8] is a simple metamodel for the Java language, that allows to represent the structure of a Java program. Since Minjava imports the models from Java bytecode, it does not provide a way to describe how the methods of the different classes of a program are structured and thus is very similar to Ecore. Kermeta [9] is an extension of Ecore that allows to give a behavorial description of the operations and derived properties of a class model in addition to the structural description. UML [10] is a multi-purpose software modeling language that deals with class models (including behavioral description), use cases or statecharts. Since the elements from the metamodel used in the matching process are not the same for the different configurations of Section 3, we needed a common denominator between those configurations to compare them. This common denominator is the Ecore aligment model produced by the Ecore alignment encoder described in Section 5. This model only shows mappings between non abstract classes, non derived attributes and references, datatypes and enumerations. Those elements are included in all the different configurations. We compare the Ecore alignment model produced by the alignment encoder to an ideal alignment model designed by an expert (standard transformations such as Ecore to Kermeta have been used to build those ideal models). We evaluate our results with common metrics from the information retrieval field [11]. For each alignment, we compute $precision = \frac{\#correct\_found\_mappings}{\#total\_found\_mappings}$, $recall = \frac{\#correct\_found\_mappings}{\#total\_correct\_mappings}$

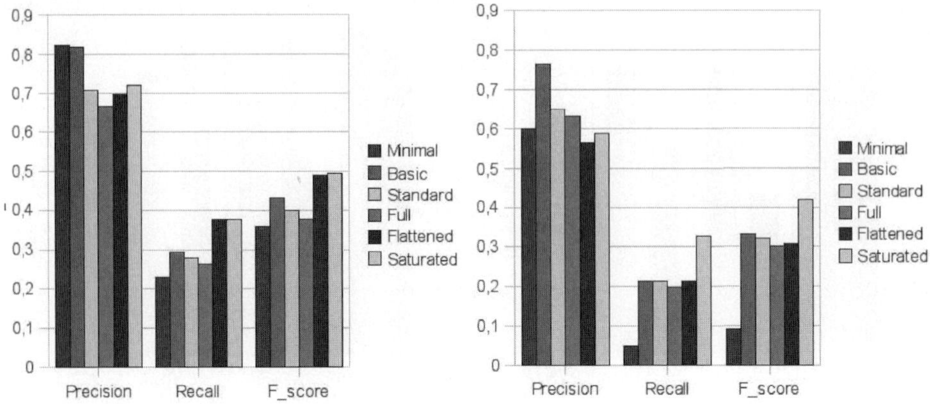

Fig. 12. Results of $Ecore \leftrightarrow Kermeta$ (left) and $Ecore \leftrightarrow UML$ (right)

and $f\_score = \frac{2 \times recall \times precision}{recall + precision}$. We have $precision \in [0,1]$. The higher is the *precision* value, the smaller is the set of wrong mappings. $recall \in [0,1]$. The higher is the *recall* value, the smaller is the set of the mappings that have not been found. *f_score* is the harmonic mean of *precision* and *recall*. $f\_score \in [0,1]$. It can be considered as a global measure of the alignment quality. A high value of *f_score* is obtained when the produced alignment has a good quality.

The results of our experiments are shown in Fig. 11 and 12. The results show that the best configuration is generally Saturated. On the other hand, the Minimal configuration gives very bad results. Full and Standard configurations, despite using more information from the metamodels, seem to produce slightly poorer results than the Basic configuration. The metamodels we used to match on Ecore vary in size. Minjava has more or less the same size as Ecore, Kermeta is a little bigger, and UML is very large. We can clearly see from the results that the alignment quality decreases when the size difference between the two matched metamodels is increasing. This is partly caused by the *SelectThreshold* filter that filters the alignment produced by Similarity Flooding. Results on $Ecore \leftrightarrow Minjava$ and $Ecore \leftrightarrow Kermeta$ show that good quality alignments can be produced by our approach.

7 Related Work and Conclusion

Related Work. Automating the discovery of mappings between schemas, ontologies, documents or (meta)models has been thoroughly investigated [1,2]. In the context of Model-Driven Engineering, several approaches for semi-automatic generation of transformations based on mapping have recently been proposed. In [12], model transformations are generated based on ontological information. The two metamodels are supposed to have a semantics given using a mapping onto a known ontology. Reasonning on the ontology then allows to generate a model transformation, adapting a bootstrap transformation that is whether automatically generated or existing. The transformation is written in the paper in QVT Relational. [13] studies the semi-automatic derivation of graph transformation rules based on manual set-up of prototype mappings between models. In another Model Transformation By-Example approach [14], users define a mapping directly on models in concrete syntax (M1 level), then, using a predefined known mapping between concrete and abstract syntaxes, ATL rules can be generated. Compared to these two approaches that are based on a given mapping (onto a pivot ontology or between examples), we focus on automatically determining the mapping on which is based the transformation generation.

In [7], the matching operation focuses on classes, datatypes and enumerations. The proposed class matching algorithm iterates until a fix-point is reached on evaluating if two leaf classes match. Characteristics including attributes, references and relationships (based on closure and composition of inheritance, association, agregation, type-of, etc.) are then used: if the number of matching characteristics is greater than a threshold average, the two classes are considered as similar. The exact computation of characteristic similarity is not much detailed in [7], but it is said that they used name, type and graph matching similarity. For datatypes, the possibility of representing a value of a type (*e.g.* int) by another type (*e.g.* float) is used. For enumeration, the numbers of identical litterals are compared. Experiments on partial UML and Java metamodels are shown in [15]. In [16], an architecture is proposed for semi-automating the generation of model transformations. A weaving metamodel describes the kinds of links generated by the matching engine and current transformation patterns. Matching is based on element to element and on structural similarities. Structural similarities computation is inspired by the Similarity Flooding approach. A configuration metamodel is introduced to tune the matching phase. Several case studies are conducted in [16]. Here we go deeper into the encoding of metamodels for applying Similarity Flooding. We detail and compare several configurations on known, available, full metamodels. These configurations are helpful for future case tool constructions. The whole process is detailed enough in order to be reproducible and compared to future metamodel matching approaches.

Conclusions and perspectives. In this paper, we have presented an approach that produces an alignment between two metamodels in an automated way. This approach is based on the application on metamodels of a well-known schema matching algorithm called Similarity Flooding. Our main contribution is the study on the various ways of encoding a given metamodel into a directed labeled graph that can then be exploited by the Similarity Flooding algorithm. We compared six strategies in a case study in terms of precision and recall of the computed mappings between metamodels. This case study points out that the more intuitive encoding strategy (Minimal) leads to poor results, and that the Saturated strategy is the best-suited in the majority of the cases. The generation of an Ecore alignement model (conforming to an Ecore alignment metamodel) from which model transformation code can easily be derived is our second main contribution. Future work will consist in designing code generators both for imperative and declarative languages. We also currently follow another perspective: we study how the Similarity Flooding algorithm can be tuned to our particular domain (metamodel matching). We are working on the way the initial similarity value of a compatiblity node is computed, and on the way we compute the weights of the arcs in the propagation graph.

References

1. Rahm, E., Bernstein, P.A.: A survey of approaches to automatic schema matching. VLDB J. 10(4), 334–350 (2001)
2. Shvaiko, P., Euzenat, J.: A survey of schema-based matching approaches. In: Spaccapietra, S. (ed.) Journal on Data Semantics IV. LNCS, vol. 3730, pp. 146–171. Springer, Heidelberg (2005)
3. Melnik, S., Garcia-Molina, H., Rahm, E.: Similarity flooding: A versatile graph matching algorithm and its application to schema matching. In: ICDE, pp. 117–128. IEEE Computer Society, Los Alamitos (2002)
4. Budinsky, F., Brodsky, S., Merks, E.: Eclipse Modeling Framework (2003)
5. Pottinger, R., Bernstein, P.A.: Merging models based on given correspondences. In: VLDB., pp. 826–873 (2003)
6. Levenshtein, V.: Binary codes with correction of deletions, insertions and substitution of symbols. Dokl. Akad. Nank. SSSR 163(4), 845–848 (1965)
7. Lopes, D., Hammoudi, S., Abdelouahab, Z.: Schema matching in the context of model driven engineering: From theory to practice. In: Advances in Systems, Computing Sciences and Software Eng., Netherlands, pp. 219–227. Springer, Heidelberg (2006)
8. Falleri, J.R.: Minjava (2008), `http://code.google.com/p/minjava/`
9. Triskell: Kermeta (2008), `http://www.kermeta.org`
10. Eclipse: UML2 EMF Plugin (2008), `http://www.eclipse.org/uml2`
11. Do, H.H., Melnik, S., Rahm, E.: Comparison of schema matching evaluations. In: Chaudhri, A.B., Jeckle, M., Rahm, E., Unland, R. (eds.) NODe-WS 2002. LNCS, vol. 2593, pp. 221–237. Springer, Heidelberg (2003)
12. Roser, S., Bauer, B.: An approach to automatically generated model transformations using ontology engineering space. In: Proceedings of Workshop on Semantic Web Enabled Software Engineering (SWESE) (2006)
13. Varró, D.: Model transformation by example. In: Nierstrasz, O., Whittle, J., Harel, D., Reggio, G. (eds.) MoDELS 2006. LNCS, vol. 4199, pp. 410–424. Springer, Heidelberg (2006)
14. Wimmer, M., Strommer, M., Kargl, H., Kramler, G.: Towards model transformation generation by-example. In: HICSS, p. 285. IEEE Computer Society, Los Alamitos (2007)
15. Lopes, D., Hammoudi, S., de Souza, J., Bontempo, A.: Metamodel matching: Experiments and comparison. In: ICSEA, p. 2. IEEE Computer Society, Los Alamitos (2006)
16. Fabro, M.D.D.: Metadata management using model weaving and model transformation. PhD thesis, Université de Nantes (2007)

Sufficient Criteria for Consistent Behavior Modeling with Refined Activity Diagrams

Stefan Jurack[1], Leen Lambers[2], Katharina Mehner[3], and Gabriele Taentzer[1]

[1] Philipps-Universität Marburg, Germany
{sjurack,taentzer}@mathematik.uni-marburg.de
[2] Technische Universität Berlin, Germany
leen@cs.tu-berlin.de
[3] Siemens, Corporate Technology, Germany
katharina.mehner@siemens.com

Abstract. In use case-driven approaches to requirements modeling, UML activity diagrams are a wide-spread means for refining the functional view of use cases. Early consistency validation of activity diagrams is therefore desirable but difficult due to the semi-formal nature of activity diagrams. In this paper, we specify well-structured activity diagrams and define activities more precisely by pre- and post- conditions. They can be modeled by interrelated pairs of object diagrams based on a domain class diagram. This activity refinement is based on the theory of graph transformation and paves the ground for a consistency analysis of the required system behavior. A formal semantics for activity diagrams refined by pre- and post-conditions allows us to establish sufficient criteria for consistency. The semi-automatic checking of these criteria is supported by a tool for graph transformation.

1 Introduction

Requirements engineering is the process of gathering, structuring, analyzing, and validating requirements of a software system. Requirements analysis and validation is needed to come up with a consistent requirements specification which provides the basis for all relevant development decisions. The detection of requirement errors late in the development process causes expensive iterations through all phases.

In object-oriented software development, the UML [1] has become the standard notation for software models at different stages of the life cycle and at different levels of abstraction, including the requirements specification. The result of the requirements analysis consists of a domain class diagram and a use case specification. The main scenario(s) of a use case are often specified with activity diagrams. The dynamic aspect—when something can be done—is captured by activity diagrams. The functional aspect—how it can be done—is described by pre- and post-conditions of activities which are first described in natural language. In particular, the functional aspect has not been formally integrated with the static domain model. The intended connections between domain classes and activity diagrams can mainly be indicated by giving meaningful names to activities.

K. Czarnecki et al. (Eds.): MoDELS 2008, LNCS 5301, pp. 341–355, 2008.

An early consistency check of activity diagrams taking into account pre- and post-conditions is difficult due to the informal nature of activity specifications. By consistency we mean that all flow paths of an activity diagram can be performed. In this situation, a more precise specification of each activity can pave the ground for a consistency analysis. We propose to refine activity diagrams by describing pre- and post-conditions of each activity by a pair of interrelated object diagrams as introduced in [2]. These object diagrams link formally the pre- and post-conditions with the domain model. The aim of the consistency analysis is to validate that control flow is consistent with pre- and post-conditions.

Graph transformation systems can be used to formalize this problem and to provide tool support for the analysis. A pair of pre- and post-conditions can be formalized as a graph transformation rule. The idea was first presented in [2] to analyze inconsistencies between activities during use case integration, however not taking into account the control flow. The idea was extended in [3,4] for analyzing inconsistencies during composition of an aspect-oriented extension of activity diagrams. The approach classified sources of inconsistencies taking into account the control flow. [5] provided sufficient applicability criteria for graph transformation rule sequences as formal foundation. This idea was employed in [6] to validate control flow structures for adaptable service-based applications. The structures are described by live sequence charts [7].

Based on our previous work cited above, this paper presents sufficient criteria for consistency analysis of activity diagrams. In order to apply the existing applicability criteria for graph transformation rule sequences from [5], we provide a semantics for activity diagrams refined with pre- and post-conditions. We also improve the existing applicability criteria and introduce new reduction mechanisms for the analysis phase. The automated checking of rule sequence applicability has been integrated into the graph transformation tool AGG [8]. We demonstrate the feasibility of our approach with an example.

The paper is organized as follows: Section 2 illustrates the use-case driven approach to requirements modeling and introduces the running example. In Section 3, we recall the concept of graph transformation, explain conflicts and dependencies of graph transformations, and present sufficient criteria for the applicability of graph transformation rule sequences together with two new reduction mechanisms for the applicability analysis of rule sequences. In Section 4 we present a graph transformation based semantics of refined activity diagrams, define consistency, and introduce an efficient way to analyze for consistency. We analyze our running example in Section 5. Related work is discussed in Section 6. Section 7 contains our conclusion and outlook.

2 Use Case-Driven Requirements Modeling

An use case diagram specifies a number of main scenarios by use cases, actors, and dependencies between them. UML activity diagrams can be used to model the behavior of each use case. In our approach we formalize activities by pre- and post-conditions based on a domain class diagram. In the following, we introduce this approach with a small case study of an online pizza service.

2.1 Use Cases and Domain Model

The center of our requirements analysis is an online service for a pizzeria offering pizzas and beverages. The pizzeria staff enters master data, e.g. different kinds of pizzas, toppings and beverages. Customers have to register before they are allowed to order food and beverages. As long as the order is not closed, further order items may be attached. Correspondingly, the system offers the use cases "create master data" and "take order" (cf. Fig. 1). The complex use case "take order" includes use case "add pizza to order". Further use cases are conceivable but not considered in the following due to space constraints such as requesting a voucher ("request voucher") or contacting the pizzeria staff ("write message").

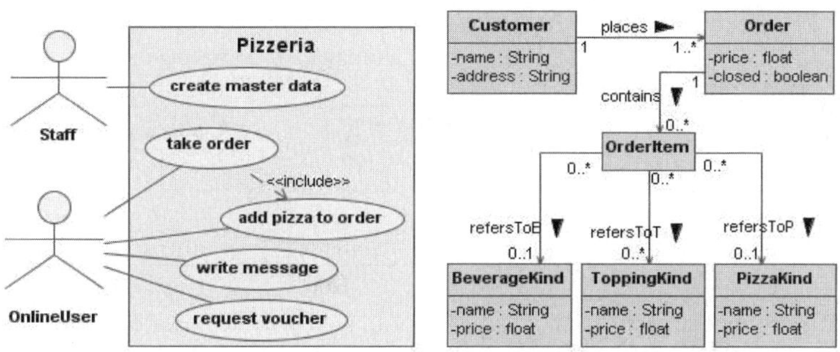

Fig. 1. Pizzeria example: Use cases (left), Domain model (right)

The corresponding domain model class diagram is shown in Fig. 1. It illustrates an *Order* placeable by a *Customer*. An order is constituted by a number of items (*OrderItem*), whereas each item may be associated with a kind of pizza (*PizzaKind*) and if desired multiple kinds of additional toppings (*ToppingKind*), or the item is associated with a *BeverageKind*. The structure of the domain model allows different pizza and/or beverages to be associated to the same order item, which is semantically undesired. To solve this constraint, an OCL expression could be formulated. In the following our refinements of the corresponding use cases prevent the occurrence of such links though.

2.2 Activities Refined by Pre- and Post-conditions

Fig. 2 shows the activity diagrams refining corresponding use cases as shown in Fig. 1. Use case "create master data" is refined in Fig. 2(a). It allows to create pizza, topping and beverage kinds. Fig. 2(c) shows the activity diagram refining use case "take order". It conditionally creates a customer followed by order creation. A Pizza or beverage can be added to the order in a loop. If all desired order items are added, the order is closed. The icon in the bottom right corner of activity "Add pizza to order" indicates a reference to the activity diagram shown in Fig. 2(b). It refines the use case "add pizza to order", whereas the corresponding *include* relation between the use-cases was already depicted in the use-case diagram (cf. Fig. 1).

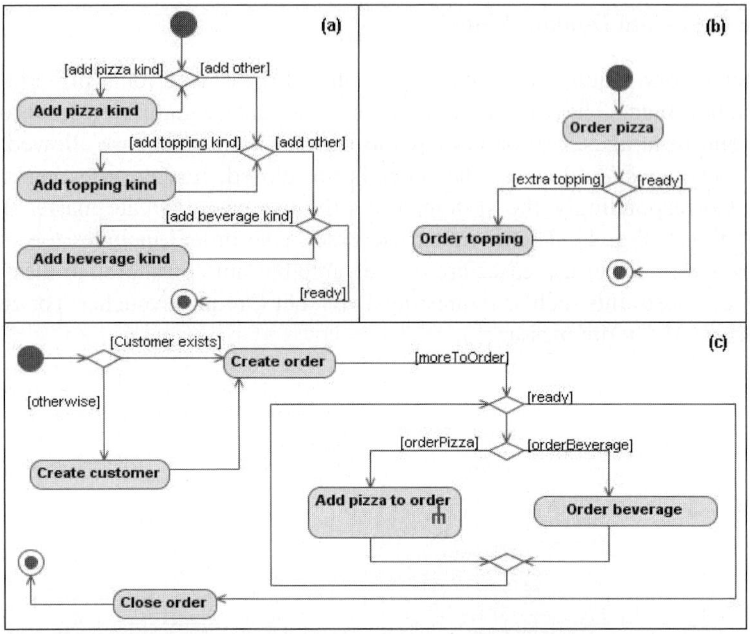

Fig. 2. Activity diagrams: Create master data(a), Add pizza to order(b), Take order(c)

Based on the domain model, the pre- and post-conditions of each activity can be specified using interrelated object diagrams extended by negative application conditions. The interrelation is expressed by numbers. Equal numbers refer to same instances. Object creation is specified by introducing a new element in a post-condition. Object deletion is specified by presenting it in the pre-condition only. A pair of pre- and post-conditions can be parameterized. Negative application conditions (NAC), depicted in red dashed (out)line, are used in pre-conditions to specify objects which must not exist.

Fig. 3 shows the pre- and post-condition pair of activity "Add pizza kind" of activity diagram "Create master data". A new *PizzaKind* object is created if a corresponding *PizzaKind* object does not exist. Input parameters *n* and *p* provide values for the *name* and *price* attributes. Conditions for activities "Add topping kind" and "Add beverage kind" are composed analogously.

Fig. 4 shows the pre- and post-conditions of the activities of activity diagram "Take order" where activity "Add pizza to order" has been replaced by its refinement. Note that the pre- and post-conditions of activity "Order pizza" and "Order beverage" ensure

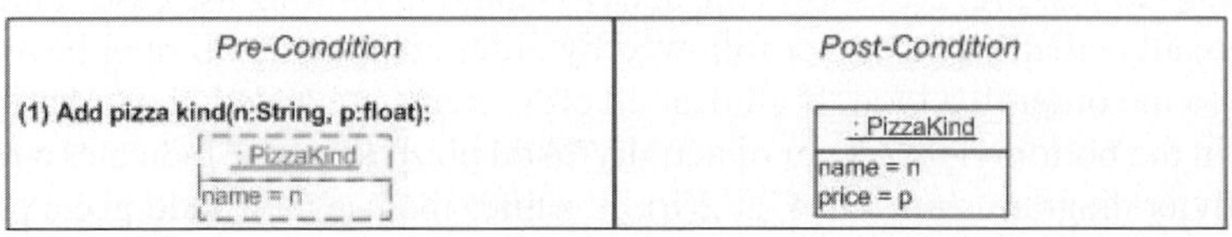

Fig. 3. Pre- and post-conditions for activity "Add pizza kind" of diagram "Create master data"

that each ordered pizza and/or beverage is associated to a different *OrderItem*. The pre- and post-conditions can be described as follows:

(1) A *Customer* is created with *name* and *address* set by input parameters *n* and *adr*, if an equally named customer does not exist already.
(2) An *Order* is created and linked to a *Customer* identified by parameter *n*, but only if no open order is already associated i.e. attribute *closed* is *false*.
(3) A new *OrderItem* is created and linked to an existing *PizzaKind* object. The pizza name is given as parameter.
(4) An existing *ToppingKind* is linked to the *OrderItem* related to a *PizzaKind*. The topping name is given as parameter.
(5) An existing *BeverageKind* is linked to an *Order* via a new created *OrderItem*.
(6) An *Order* is closed i.e. the attribute *closed* which must be *false* before is set to *true*.

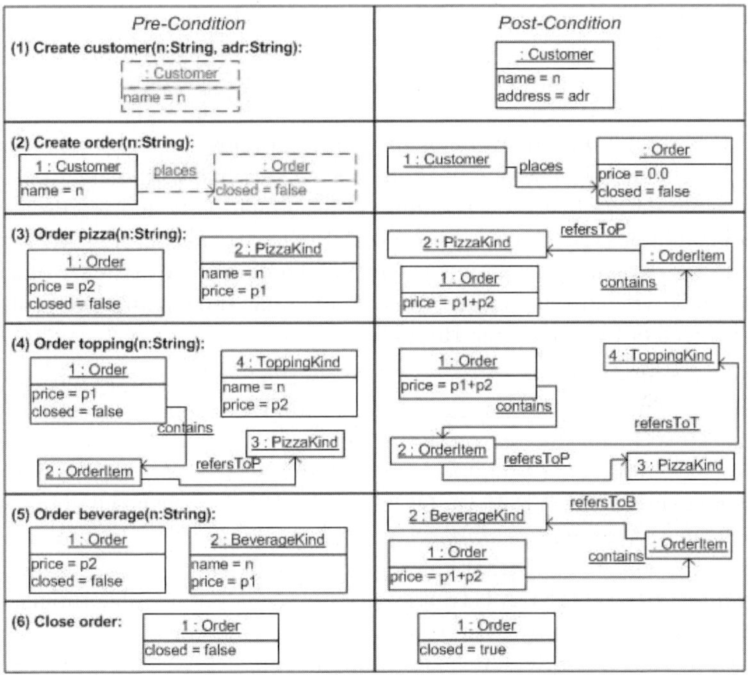

Fig. 4. Pre- and post-conditions for activities of activity diagram "Take order"

3 Formalization by Graph Transformation

The UML variant presented in Sect. 2 can be precisely defined by the theory of graph transformation [9]. While class diagrams are formalized by type graphs, activities with pre- and post conditions are mapped to graph rules. This serves as a basis for analyzing use case-driven requirement models precisely. Here, we summarize the main ideas.

3.1 Graphs and Graph Transformation

When formalizing object-oriented modeling, graphs occur at two levels: the type level (defined based on class diagrams) and the instance level (given by all valid object diagrams). This idea is described by the concept of *typed graphs*, where a fixed *type graph* TG serves as an abstract representation of the class diagram. Types can be structured by an inheritance relation. Multiplicities and other annotations are expressed by additional graph constraints. Instances of the type graph are object graphs equipped with a structure-preserving mapping to the type graph. A class diagram can thus be represented by a type graph, plus a set of constraints over this type graph.

Graph transformation is the rule-based modification of graphs. Rules are expressed by two graphs (L, R), where L is the left-hand side (LHS) of the rule representing the pre-condition and R is the right-hand side (RHS) describing the post-condition, and a mapping between objects in L and R. $L \cap R$ (the graph part that is not changed) and the union $L \cup R$ should form a graph again, i.e., they must be compatible with source, target and type settings, in order to apply the rule. Graph $L \setminus (L \cap R)$ defines the part that is to be deleted, and graph $R \setminus (L \cap R)$ defines the part to be created. Figure 4 shows pre- and post-conditions of the activities which can be interpreted as graph rules. Numbers indicate a mapping between left- and right-hand sides. Please note that the left-hand sides may contain two kinds of links, drawn by solid and dashed lines. Only the solid parts belong to the left-hand side and formulate a positive pre-condition while the dashed ones prohibit certain graph parts and represent negative application conditions (NACs). For example, rule *Create order* (cf. Fig. 4(2)) describes how an *Order* is created for a certain *Customer* and prohibits the existence of an already associated order with attribute *closed=false* at the same time i.e. the rule is applicable only, if all placed orders have been closed.

A *graph transformation step* $G \overset{r,m}{\Longrightarrow} H$ between two instance graphs G, H is defined by first finding a match m of the left-hand side L of rule r in the current instance graph G such that m is structure-preserving and type-compatible, and second by constructing H in two passes: (1) build $D := G \setminus m(L \setminus (L \cap R))$, i.e., delete all graph items that are to be deleted; (2) $H := D \cup (R \setminus (L \cap R))$, i.e., create all graph items that are to be created. A *graph transformation (sequence)* consists of zero or more graph transformation steps. A set of graph rules, together with a type graph, is called a *graph transformation system* (GTS). A GTS may show two kinds of non-determinism: (1) For each rule several matches may exist. (2) Several rules might be applicable.

The tool environment AGG (Attributed Graph Grammar System) [8] can be used to specify graph transformation systems and analyze their rules.

3.2 Conflicts and Dependencies

As discussed in the previous section, several rules may be applicable to a host graph. Either the results might be the same regardless of the application order, or if one of two rules is not independent of the second, the first one will disable the second. In this case, the two rules are in *conflict*. Conversely, two rules are said to be *parallel independent* if they do not disable each other. Instead, *sequential independence* guarantees that the order of application in a transformation sequence does not matter.

One of the main static analysis facilities for GTSs is the check for potential conflicts and dependencies between rules, both supported in AGG. This conflict and dependency analysis is based on critical pair analysis (CPA) [9,2]. A critical pair is a pair of transformation steps $G \stackrel{r_1,m_1}{\Longrightarrow} H_1$, $G \stackrel{r_2,m_2}{\Longrightarrow} H_2$ that are in conflict in a minimal context, identified through matches m_1 and m_2. The following conflicts can occur:

delete/use: The application of r_1 deletes an element used by the match of r_2.
produce/forbid: The application of r_1 produces an element that a NAC of r_2 forbids.
change/use: The application of r_1 changes an attribute value used by the match of r_2.

Critical pair analysis is also used to find potential dependencies between a transformation applying r_1 and another one applying r_2. This case is led back to critical pairs consisting of steps $H \stackrel{r_1^{-1},m_1'}{\Longrightarrow} G$ and $H \stackrel{r_2,m_2}{\Longrightarrow} K$. The inverse rule r_1^{-1} is obtained by exchanging LHS and RHS and translating the NACs into equivalent ones from LHS to RHS [9,5]. The following dependencies can occur:

produce/use: The application of r_1 produces an element needed by the match of r_2.
delete/forbid: The application of r_1 deletes an element that a NAC of r_2 forbids.
change/use: The application of r_1 changes an attribute value used by the match of r_2.

Rule r_2 *purely depends* on rule r_1 if the left-hand side of r_2 can be completely embedded into the right-hand side of r_1. This means that if rule r_1 has been applied then it delivered everything rule r_2 needs to be applied as well. Note that NACs belonging to r_2 are not necessarily satisfied though and still have to be checked.

If there are neither potential dependencies between transformations via r_1 and r_2 nor via r_2 and r_1 then rules r_1 and r_2 are sequentially independent. This leads to the fact that r_1 and r_2 can be switched if they occur next to each other in a rule sequence without any impact on the applicability of the rule sequence. We call such rule sequences in which sequentially independent neighbored rules are switched *shift-equivalent*.

3.3 Criteria for Applicability of Rule Sequences

In [5] sufficient criteria are introduced for the applicability of a rule sequence to a start graph. They describe which conditions a given rule sequence and some start graph G_0 should fulfill such that it becomes applicable to G_0.

Concurrent rules. For the applicability criteria we need the concept of a *concurrent rule* r_c which can be constructed from a sequence of single rules $r_1, r_2, \ldots r_n$. Such a concurrent rule r_c establishes in one transformation step the same effect as single rules $r_1, r_2 \ldots r_n$ would establish in consecutive transformation steps [10,9]. Thus, a concurrent rule summarizes in one rule which parts of the graph should be present, preserved, deleted and produced when applying the corresponding rule sequence to this graph. Thereby a concurrent rule fixes all interrelations between the summarized rule applications. Moreover we have a summarized set of NACs on the concurrent rule expressing which graph parts are forbidden when applying the corresponding rule sequence.

Applicability criteria. Given a rule sequence $s : r_1 r_2 ... r_n$, the applicability criteria[1] for s to some graph G_0 are defined as follows. Note that all criteria have to be fulfilled.

initialization: Rule r_1 is applicable to graph G_0.
no node deleting: Each rule in s must not delete object nodes.
no impeding predecessors: The predecessors of each rule r in s do not cause a conflict with r.
enabling predecessor(s): For each rule r in s:
- **pure:** There is a predecessor r' of rule r in s and r is purely dependent on r'. Moreover each NAC of r forbids a graph element of type t such that an element of type t is neither present in G_0 nor produced by any predecessor of r OR
- **nearest:** There exists a concurrent rule r_c of rule r and a (sequence of) predecessor rule(s) s' such that r_c is applicable to G_0, and all predecessors of r_c do not cause a conflict with r_c. Moreover r is not in conflict with each rule between s' and r OR
- **not needed:** Rule r itself is applicable to G_0.

Note that in order to fulfill the *enabling predecessor(s)* criterion it is important to check its three possibilities *pure, nearest* and *not needed*. It is recommended to follow this order to keep the set of conditions on graph G_0 minimal. Moreover note that as soon as a rule is enabled by reusing elements delivered by some predecessor rule, this dependency should be fixed while checking the criteria for all remaining rules. It is up to future work to integrate object flow in our activity diagrams in order to fix these dependencies from the beginning.

Reduction of Rule Sequences. A rule sequence s can be reduced before checking its applicability, i.e. sequence s is applicable to a graph G_0, if s can be reduced in one of the following ways to a rule sequence s' which satisfies the applicability criteria:

1. *Repeated element reduction [11].* Given a rule sequence $s : r_1 r_2 ... r_n$ such that two subsequent rules in s are equal. Sequence s can be reduced to s' by deleting one of these equal rules, if they are not in conflict with themselves and each subsequent rule has a pure enabling predecessor, is applicable to G_0, or is equal to a predecessor rule.
2. *Loop reduction [11].* Given a rule sequence $s : s_{start}(r_1 r_1 r_2 ... r_m)^n s_{end}$ with s_{start} and s_{end} being rule sequences and $m \geq 1, n > 2$. It is enough to execute $loop = (r_1 r_1 r_2 ... r_m)$ at most 2 times, if each rule r in s_{end} has a pure enabling predecessor, is applicable to graph G_0, or is equal to some rule in $loop$ or in s_{start}.
3. *Shift-equivalent reduction [5].* Rule sequences s and s' are shift-equivalent (as defined in Sect. 3.2).
4. *Summary reduction [5].* Rule sequence s' can be deduced from s by summarizing neighbored rules in s into concurrent rules.

[1] In addition to the criteria presented in [5] the criteria in this paper contain two improvements in the *enabling predecessor(s)* criterion (see motivation in [11]). In particular, we exploit in this paper the typing in the graph transformation system such that also rules with NACs are allowed to have a pure enabling predecessor. Moreover an enabling predecessor does not necessarily have to be direct if intermediate rules fulfill additional constraints.

4 Consistency Analysis with Refined Activity Diagrams

Activities are defined more precisely by pre- and post-conditions as explained in Sect. 2. They can be formalized by graph transformation rules as introduced in Sect. 3. This activity refinement enables us to analyze consistency of the required system behavior based on the applicability criteria presented in the previous section. In this section, at first we specify well-structured refined activity diagrams and define their semantics and consistency based on graph transformation. Then we present reduction techniques enabling the efficient analysis of refined activity diagrams for consistency.

4.1 Refined Activity Diagrams: Semantics and Consistency

We restrict our considerations to well-structured activity diagrams, i.e. those which consist of sequences, fork-joins, and loops only. A *well-structured activity diagram* A consists of a start activity s, an activity block B, and an end activity e such that there is a transition between s and B and another one between B and e. An *Activity block* is defined as follows:

- Simple: A simple activity is an activity block.
- Sequence: A sequence of two activity blocks connected by a transition form an activity block.
- Decision: A decision activity with two outgoing transitions going to an activity block each, and a merge activity with two incoming transitions from each of these blocks form an activity block.
- Loop: A decision activity followed by an activity block with an outgoing transition to the same decision activity form an activity block.
- Fork: A fork activity followed by two activity blocks followed by a join activity form an activity block.

A *refined activity diagram* A is a well-structured activity diagram such that each activity occurring in A corresponds to a graph transformation rule. Given an activity block B of a refined activity diagram A its corresponding set of rule sequences S_B is defined as follows.

- If B consists of a simple activity a, $S_B = \{a\}$.
- If B is a sequence of X and Y, $S_B = S_X \; seq \; S_Y = \{s_x s_y | s_x \in S_X \wedge s_y \in S_Y\}$
- If B is a decision block on X and Y, $S_B = S_X \; or \; S_Y = S_X \cup S_Y$
- If B is a loop block on X, $S_B = loop(S_X) = \bigcup_{i \in I} S_X^i$ where $S_X^0 = \{\lambda\}$ with λ being the empty sequence, $S_X^1 = S_X, S_X^2 = S_X \; seq \; S_X$ and $S_X^i = S_X \; seq \; S_X^{i-1}$ for $i > 2$.
- If B is a fork block on X and Y, $S_B = S_X || S_Y = \bigcup s_x || s_y$ with $s_x \in S_X \wedge s_y \in S_Y$ where $s_x || \lambda = \{s_x\}$, $\lambda || s_y = \{s_y\}$, and $xs'_x || ys'_y = \{x\} \; seq \; s'_x || ys'_y \cup \{y\} \; seq \; xs'_x || s'_y$.

Thus we define the *semantics* $Sem(A)$ of a refined activity diagram A consisting of a start activity s, an activity block B, and an end activity e as the set of rule sequences S_B generated by the main activity block B.

We define an activity diagram A to be *consistent* if there exists a non-empty set of graphs S such that each rule sequence in $Sem(A)$ is applicable to at least one of the graphs in S. Such a non-empty set of graphs S making an activity diagram A consistent is *without junk*, if for each graph in S at least one rule sequence in $Sem(A)$ exists such that it is applicable to this graph. Each graph in S without junk then represents a potential snapshot of the system to which an activity sequence in A can be applied consistently.

Finally, note that activity diagrams considered in this paper do not contain object flow. Integrating object flow is part of future work and promises to enable a more precise analysis. For now we restrict to *maximal object flow*. This means that each activity (resp. its corresponding rule) is expected to reuse as much as possible objects delivered or passed through by the former activity (resp. rule).

4.2 Analysis of Reduced Semantics

Based on the semantics and consistency definition of an activity diagram A we apply the criteria for checking the applicability of rule sequences given in Sect. 3 in order to check for consistency. The reductions presented in Sect. 3.3 allow to cut down the number of sequences in $Sem(A)$.

Thus we define a *reduced set of rule sequences* $Red(A)$ for a refined activity diagram A as follows: Reduce the set of rule sequences in $Sem(A)$ by applying to each sequence loop reduction, repeated element reduction, shift-equivalent reduction or summary reduction[2] (as defined in Sect. 3.3). It follows directly from [5,11] that if all sequences in $Red(A)$ satisfy the applicability criteria, then all sequences in $Sem(A)$ are applicable.

5 Example Analysis

Consider the pizzeria scenario in Sect. 2. First we analyze the use cases “create master data” and “take order” separately. Then we reason about the interrelation of both. In order to analyze the use cases the following steps are carried out: (1) Generate potential conflicts and dependencies of activity rules. (2) Examine all rule sequences defined by the activity diagram, and analyze their applicability according to criteria[3] by at first possibly reducing them. (3) Draw conclusions regarding the activities or activity diagrams, respectively.

5.1 Create Master Data

We consider at first use case ”create master data” and its activity diagram (cf. Fig. 2(a)). In order to be able to reason in a compact way about activity sequences, we use the

[2] Note that often it is desirable to apply more than one of the above reductions successively to the same sequence. Then it is necessary to verify that the satisfaction of the applicability criteria for the sequence to be reduced (instead of just applicability of this sequence) follows from the satisfaction of the criteria for the reduced sequence. Such kind of stronger reductions are important for automating consistency analysis and part of ongoing work.

[3] AGG [8] offers a new module for automatically checking the applicability criteria for given rule sequences and a start graph. Here we explain this check step by step.

following acronyms: AP=Add pizza kind, AT=Add topping kind, AB=Add beverage kind. Fig. 5 depicts the conflict and dependency matrices calculated by the tool AGG. The input data are rules corresponding to the pre- and post-conditions in Fig. 3. Note that each of these rules is parameterized. Consider e.g. rule *AP(n:String, p:float)*. It holds a parameter for the pizza name and another one for its price. This rule can only be applied if concrete values for its parameters are given. E.g. rule *AP("Margherita", 5)* can be applied whenever a Margherita pizza has not already been added. Otherwise, a produce-forbid conflict occurs which is shown in the conflict matrix computed by AGG. In particular, there is a conflict between *AP(n:String, p:float)* and *AP(n':String, p':float)* if the parameter values for *name* i.e. *n* and *n'* are the same. This holds analogously for the rules *AT* and *AB*. In all other cases there are neither conflicts nor dependencies. Considering again the activity diagram in Fig. 2(a), we start checking the applicability

Minimal Conflicts

first \ second	1: AddPizzaKind	2: AddToppingKind	3: AddBeverageKind
1: AddPizzaKind	1	0	0
2: AddToppingKind	0	1	0
3: AddBeverageKind	0	0	1

Minimal Dependencies

1: AddPizzaKind	2: AddToppingKind	3: AddBeverageKind
0	0	0
0	0	0
0	0	0

Fig. 5. Conflict and dependency matrix of "Create master data"

of all sequences in *Sem(Create master data)* according to the criteria. The first criterion to check is *initialization*. Its satisfaction depends on the first rule in each sequence only. Since each sequence in Sem(Create master data) starts with AP, AT or AB, by checking these three cases we cover the criterion for all sequences. Each rule's left-hand side (LHS) is empty i.e. no requirements concerning the existence of objects in the start graph are given. However, considering their negative application conditions (NAC) and the reasoning above, we conclude that the start graph may be empty or at least must not contain an object forbidden by a corresponding NAC, i.e. containing an object with a name according to the rule's parameter. Since all sequences contain rules with empty left-hand sides only, criterion *no node deleting* is obviously satisfied as well. As mentioned above there is one conflict between each rule with itself if their parameter values for *name* are the same. Thus all sequences with at most one occurrence of each rule satisfies the criterion *no impeding predecessor*. Otherwise, the parameters for attribute *name* of equal rules must differ in order to fulfill the criterion. The last criterion to check is *enabling predecessor(s)*. Since the dependency matrix in Fig. 5 does not show any dependencies, each rule after the first rule should be applicable to the start graph. Thus each rule fulfills the sub-item *not needed* of the enabling predecessor criterion. Summarizing, the refined activity diagram "Create master data" is consistent, if multiple occurring equal rules within a sequence do not use the same parameter values for their attribute *name* and the start graphs do not already contain objects forbidden by some rule in the sequence. If both constraints hold, the loops in the activity diagram can be run through as long as desired. Therefore pizza, topping and beverage kinds cannot occur twice with the same name in the menu.

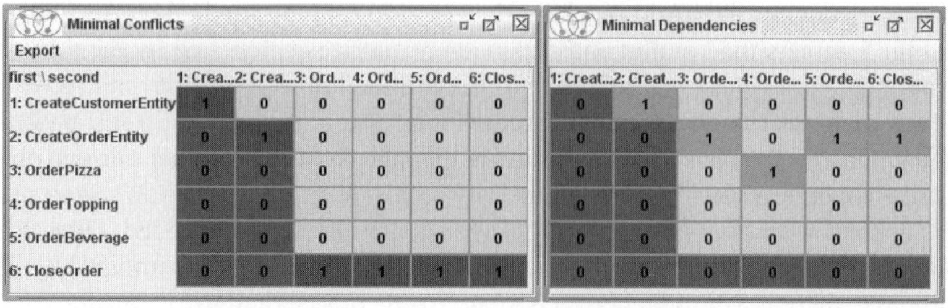

Fig. 6. Matrices with respect to the control flow

5.2 Take Order

Now we consider use case "take order" and its activity diagram (cf. Fig. 2(c)). As already addressed, an *include* reference to another use case "add pizza to order" is used. We deal with that situation by treating the activities of the corresponding activity diagram as part of the embedding one. We use acronyms again in the sequences for better readability: OP=Order pizza, OT=Order topping, OB=Order beverage, CC=Create customer, CO=Create order, CL=Close order. At first we take a look at the dependency and conflict matrices calculated by AGG (cf. Fig. 6). Irrelevant[4] entries have been colored gray. This is conceivable to be done automatically in the future. Considering again the activity diagram in Fig. 2(c), we start checking the applicability of all sequences in *Sem(Take order)* according to the criteria. We start our analysis with criterion *initialization*. Each sequence starts with CC or CO. For sequences starting with $CO(n)$ each start graph should have a *Customer* object named according to parameter n and additionally this object must not be linked to an *Order* with attribute *closed* being *false*. For sequences starting with $CC(n, adr)$ the start graph must not contain a *Customer* object named according to parameter n of rule CC. This ensures that two customers with the same name do not exist. Criteria *no node deleting* and *no impeding predecessor* are satisfied for all sequences, since no node is deleted by any rule and the conflict matrix (cf. Fig. 6) does not show any conflict between corresponding rules. The last criterion to check is *enabling predecessor(s)* where we reason about rules needing enabling predecessor(s) if they are not already applicable to the start graph. For rule sequences starting with CC, rule CO is the first one to be enabled. Now $CO(n2)$ is purely enabled by the preceding rule $CC(n1, adr1)$ if $n1 = n2$. By assuming maximal object flow (as explained in Sect. 4.1) it is clear that the customer which is created by CC is the one for which an order is created by CO. Moreover rule CL is purely enabled, namely by rule CO. Thus only for OP, OT and OB in the activity diagram we still have to check if they have enabling predecessor(s). Therefore at first we apply *summary reduction* (as defined in Sect. 3.3) to each OP with its corresponding successive OT's. Thus, each ordering of a pizza together with its toppings can be summarized in a concurrent rule which we call OPT. Independent of the number of toppings rules OB and OPT are not in conflict with each other and also not with themselves. This means that some pizza with toppings or beverage can be ordered without disabling the

[4] First only conflicts caused by (resp. dependencies on) some predecessor are relevant.

ordering of other items. Thus we conclude that each OPT as well as each OB has CO (resp. the sequence CC followed by CO for the case that a customer needs to be created) as nearest enabling predecessor(s), since it delivers the *Order* to which the pizza, topping, and beverage items should be added. Consequently the start graph should contain the corresponding *PizzaKind*, *ToppingKind* and *BeverageKind* objects in addition. Summarizing, *Sem(Take order)* contains two classes of sequences applicable to two different kinds of start graphs. The first one contains sequences without rule CC applicable to start graphs that already hold a *Customer* object. The other one contains sequences starting with rule $CC(n, adr)$ applicable to start graphs not already holding a *Customer* object with name n. Moreover the *PizzaKind*, *ToppingKind* as well as *BeverageKind* of ordered items should be available in the start graph.

As result we reveal the applicability of all given sequences in *Sem(Create order)* and *Sem(Take order)* with respect to specific sets of start graphs. This implies that the activity diagrams are consistent with respect to corresponding system snapshots. Finally we observe that almost every rule sequence of use case "take order" requires objects of type *PizzaKind*, *ToppingKind* and *BeverageKind* which are created by use case "create master data". This is meaningful since the pizzeria staff has to provide product information before a customer can order food and beverages. Only sequences $< CO, CL >$ and $< CC, CO, CL >$ do not require such objects as they do not order anything.

6 Related Work

The work presented in this paper is rooted in formal semantics and analysis of activity diagrams, model-based engineering, and graph transformation systems.

Eshuis [12] proposes denotational semantics for a restricted class of activity diagrams by means of labeled transition systems. Model checking is then used to check generic properties or model-specific properties. For reducing the state space it is assumed that a system will not forever stay in a loop. Stoerrle [13] defines a denotational semantics for control flow of UML 2.0 activity diagrams including procedure calls by means of petri nets. The standard petri net analysis provides analysis of generic properties, e.g. reachability or deadlock freeness. Our approach is dedicated to checking one property, namely consistency. The advantage of our approach is that we do not generate the whole state space like for model checking. Instead we provide sufficient criteria for statically checking if each run in the activity diagram can be completed. The disadvantage of our approach is that we cannot decide for every activity diagram whether it is consistent or not. It is unique to our approach that we refine activities with pre- and postconditions and that we use this refinement during the analysis.

Jayaraman et al. [14] use critical pair analysis to detect dependencies and conflicts between features modelled as a graph transformation modifying UML diagrams. This approach, however, is limited to a pairwise analysis of transformations. No control structure such as activity diagrams are considered for the analysis.

Fujaba [15] and Moflon [16] are mature graph transformation tools usable for specifying and executing transformations similar to AGG. Fujaba uses a kind of activity diagrams called story diagrams and integrates them with graph transformations similar to our approach. But AGG is the only graph transformation tool which supports critical pair analysis and the applicability checks on rule sequences as proposed in this paper.

7 Conclusion

In this paper, we present sufficient criteria for checking the consistency of activity-based behavior models in the context of requirements engineering. The additional effort of consistency checking pays off, if an early formal analysis is required. We check the consistency of refined activity diagrams. Activities are equipped with pre- and post-conditions which are formulated by interrelated object diagrams typed over a common domain model. This allows us to define the behavior of refined activity diagrams by graph transformation rule sequences. Sufficient criteria developed in the context of graph transformation can then be applied to check for consistency. Thereby one of the main new technical insights in this paper is that we are able to conclude applicability by analyzing sets of rule sequences in a static way.

Although the given criteria seem to apply often, there are applicable graph transformation rule sequences which cannot be examined by this new kind of static analysis. In that case, we can try to adapt our activity diagrams to the criteria, if sensible. Alternatively, stronger reduction mechanisms (their development is part of ongoing work) as the ones introduced in this paper should enable consistency analysis of a wider range of activity diagrams. Otherwise, a validation technique on execution level such as model checking should be used. For the time being, we assume that all rules do not delete object nodes. This criterion seems to be the most restricting one, however, it can be circumvented by just detaching an object node from the main object structure if it shall be deleted. For example, in use case "delete beverage order" an ordered beverage should be canceled. The corresponding *OrderItem* would be detached from its *Order*. Besides the small presented example of a pizza service, our criteria have been applied to the modeling of services and service orchestration [6] and need further evaluation in the future.

The graph transformation tool AGG offers a new analysis module for checking the presented applicability criteria for given rule sequences with dedicated start graph. We intend to extend this tool support by generating graph constraints to be fulfilled by start graphs of applicable rule sequences. For integrating this analysis with a UML CASE tool, it has to support the modeling of refined activities and has to provide a translation to graph transformation rule sequences. If a description of pre- and post-conditions by interrelated object diagrams is not offered, their definition by OCL constraints might be supported. Translating a restricted form of OCL constraints to graph rules could also enable an automated analysis based on AGG.

Our results are not limited to consistent behavior modeling for requirements engineering only. They help in identifying unintended imprecisions and may also be applied to the rigorous analysis of various kinds of work flow and business process models.

References

1. OMG: UML Resource Page of the Object Management Group, `http://www.uml.org/`
2. Hausmann, J., Heckel, R., Taentzer, G.: Detection of Conflicting Functional Requirements in a Use Case-Driven Approach. In: Proc. of Int. Conference on Software Engineering 2002, Orlando, USA. IEEE Computer Society, Los Alamitos (2002)

3. Mehner, K., Monga, M., Taentzer, G.: Interaction Analysis in Aspect-Oriented Models. In: Proc. 14th IEEE International Requirements Engineering Conference, Minneapolis, Minnesota, USA, pp. 66–75. IEEE Computer Society, Los Alamitos (2007)
4. Mehner, K., Monga, M., Taentzer, G.: Analysis of Aspect-Oriented Model Weaving. LNCS Transactions on Aspect-Oriented Software Development (to appear, 2008)
5. Lambers, L., Ehrig, H., Taentzer, G.: Sufficient Criteria for Applicability and Non-Applicability of Rule Sequences. In: Ermel, C., Heckel, R., de Lara, J. (eds.) Proc. International Workshop on Graph Transformation and Visual Modeling Techniques (GTVMT 2008), vol. 10, Electronic Communications of the EASST (2008)
6. Lambers, L., Mariani, L., Ehrig, H., Pezze, M.: A Formal Framework for Developing Adaptable Service-Based Applications. In: Fiadeiro, J.L., Inverardi, P. (eds.) FASE 2008. LNCS, vol. 4961, pp. 392–406. Springer, Heidelberg (2008)
7. Harel, D., Marelly, R.: Come, Let's Play - Scenario-Based Programming Using LSCs and the Play-Engine. Springer, Heidelberg (2003)
8. AGG: AGG Homepage, `http://tfs.cs.tu-berlin.de/agg`
9. Ehrig, H., Ehrig, K., Prange, U., Taentzer, G.: Fundamentals of Algebraic Graph Transformation. EATCS Monographs on Theoretical Computer Science. Springer, Heidelberg (2006)
10. Lambers, L., Ehrig, H., Orejas, F., Prange, U.: Parallelism and Concurrency in Adhesive High-Level Replacement Systems with Negative Application Conditions. In: Ehrig, H., Pfalzgraf, J., Prange, U. (eds.) Proceedings of the ACCAT workshop at ETAPS 2007. ENTCS. Elsevier, Amsterdam (to appear, 2008)
11. Jurack, S., Lambers, L., Mehner, K., Taentzer, G.: Sufficient criteria for consistent behavior modeling with refined activity diagrams: Long version. Technical Report 2008/11, Technische Universität Berlin (2008)
12. Eshuis, R., Wieringa, R.: Tool support for verifying UML activity diagrams. IEEE Trans. on Software Eng. 7(30) (2004)
13. Stoerrle, H.: Semantics of UML 2.0 Activity Diagrams. In: International Conference on Visual Languages and Human Centric Computing VLHCC. IEEE Computer Society, Los Alamitos (2004)
14. Jayaraman, P., Whittle, J., Elkhodary, A., Gomaa, H.: Model Composition in Product Lines and Feature Interaction Detection Using Critical Pair Analysis. In: Engels, G., Opdyke, B., Schmidt, D.C., Weil, F. (eds.) MODELS 2007. LNCS, vol. 4735. Springer, Heidelberg (2007)
15. Fujaba: Fujaba Homepage, `http://www.fujaba.de`
16. Moflon: Moflon Homepage, `http://www.moflon.org`

Implementation of the Conformance Relation for Incremental Development of Behavioural Models

Hong-Viet Luong, Thomas Lambolais, and Anne-Lise Courbis

Laboratoire LGI2P, École des mines d'Alès
Site EERIE, Parc Scientifique Georges Besse
30 035 Nîmes cedex 1, France
{Hong-Viet.Luong,Thomas.Lambolais,Anne-Lise.Courbis}@ema.fr

Abstract. In this paper, we show how to implement the conformance relation on transition systems. The computability of this relation relies on the composition of two operators: the reduction relation whose computability has been proven in our previous work, and the merge function of acceptance graphs associated with transition systems under comparison. It is formally demonstrated, and illustrated through a case study whose analysis is performed by a JAVA prototype we have developed. This research work is developed in order to be applied in a larger context: our goal is to support modelers to develop UML state machines through an incremental modelling method which is able to guarantee that model upgrading does not introduce inconsistencies. Hence, these works lead to a semantics for the specialisation relation between UML State Machines.

1 Introduction

Our area of interest concerns the build-up of UML behavioural models (state machines) according to an incremental approach. Such an approach is natural as it is based on a widely held mental process, because on the one hand, specifying a complex system requires a hierarchical and iterative approach, and on the other hand, initial specification cannot be considered as complete and must be updated all along the modelling process. The problem we address is to compare a model obtained at a given stage with models derived from previous stages: how is it possible to guarantee that updates do not introduce inconsistencies and preserve already modelled functionalities?

Few works deal with this problem in the context of UML modelling, despite the fact that the UML standard [1] is increasingly used in the industry. There are some UML simulation frameworks supporting behavioural model observation, but such intuitive and experience-based evaluations cannot be considered as systematic and reliable. Our goal is therefore to develop formal comparison techniques and tools ensuring consistency between behavioural models, taking into account the distinctive features of incremental modelling. As this problem is not much addressed in the literature [2,3], our first approach is to study tried and tested solutions of domains closely related to state machine modelling. Solutions have been found in works dealing with Labelled Transition Systems (LTS) and precisely on conformance, extension and reduction relations as well as may, must and testing preorders. We have demonstrated in a previous work [4]

K. Czarnecki et al. (Eds.): MoDELS 2008, LNCS 5301, pp. 356–370, 2008.

the extension and reduction relation computability. In this paper, we focus on the computability of the conformance relation. We demonstrate that it can be implemented. The proof is based on the composition of the reduction relation with a merge function applied on the acceptance graphs associated with the compared LTS. Applying this result on UML state machines [5,6] is not trivial and requires a long-term analysis, especially to deal with the complete standard. However, we illustrate the extension relation on a case study modelled both in LTS and its corresponding simplified UML model.

The paper is organised in three parts. At first, we give an overview of the main relations allowing LTS to be compared, and we give definitions useful to understand the demonstration of our theorem. The second part focuses on the conformance computability. For this purpose, we give the definition of acceptance graphs and their merging by reformulating existing works. In part three, we present the JAVA demonstrator we have developed to implement the conformance relation, and we give results obtained on a case study. Lastly, we make a conclusion and present our future work.

2 Definitions and Analysis of Existing Relations

In this part, we give fundamental definitions about Labelled Transition Systems (LTS) [7] and refusal sets [8] to understand the relations we have studied. We present the concept of acceptance sets [9] and some associated results. Before defining these concepts, we informally present existing relations allowing models to be compared at the different stages of the modelling, which should lead us to consider the problem of implementing the conformance relation.

2.1 State of the Art of Relations to Compare Behavioural Models

In the context of incremental development, existing relations defined to analyse and compare LTSs are **conf**, **red**, **ext** [10,11], as well as *may*, *must* and *testing* preorders [12].

The conformance relation has been formalised by Brinksma and Tretmans [8,11] to represent the notion of conformance between implementations and specifications (or between protocols and services) in telecommunication networks. Initial informal notion was proposed by the ISO standard ISO 9646 [13]. This standard specifies a general methodology for testing the conformance of products to OSI specifications which the products are claimed to implement. Tretmans formal definition translates the property stating that an implementation conforms to its specification, if any test that the specification *must* accept, *must* also be accepted by the implementation. Stated otherwise, any test that the implementation *may* refuse, *may* also be refused by the specification. These notions of "must accept" and "may refuse" tests, or experiments, are very similar to may and must preorders defined by Hennessy [9], except that Hennessy also takes into account the case of divergent processes. Divergent processes are those able to perform infinite internal transition sequences.

It appears that the conformance relation is not transitive. It is well suited to compare implementations with their specifications, but not to be used in refinement sequences. Combined with the notion of trace inclusion, it leads to extension and reduction relations. An extension guarantees the conformance relation with larger traces, whereas a reduction does the same but with fewer traces. Extension and reduction relations are, then, transitive relations. Moreover, for incremental construction of processes, the extension relation has the following interesting property:

$$S_2 \textbf{ ext } S_1 \Rightarrow (\forall I.\ I \textbf{ conf } S_2 \Rightarrow I \textbf{ conf } S_1) \quad (1)$$

This is the desired property for refinement construction, S_2 being a refinement of S_1. The **ext** relation is not the largest refinement relation [10], but it can be used for such purposes. As far as we know, the computability of these relations had not been demonstrated yet. Our first work has been to study a technique for implementing them. We demonstrated through a theorem that **red** and **ext** can be implemented as simulations between acceptance graphs [4].

The conformance relation and its variant (ioconf, ioco, ...) have been used in test generation and conformance testing tools [11]. However, no implementation of the conformance relation between LTS has ever been proposed. In section 3, we shall present a result which enables us to propose an efficient implementation of this conformance relation.

2.2 Formal Definitions of Conformance Relations

A LTS [7] is a graph consisting of states linked by labelled transitions. It models behavioural specifications as well as implementations.

Definition 1 (Labelled Transition Systems). *A LTS $P = (S, Act, \rightarrow, s_0)$ is a tuple consisting of:*
- *a non-empty finite set S of states;*
- *a set Act of actions;*
- *a transition relation $\rightarrow \subseteq S \times Act \times S$;*
- *an initial state $s_0 \in S$.*

$Act = L \cup \{\tau\}$ where τ represents any internal, unobservable actions, and L is the set of observable actions.

Before presenting the definitions of conformance relation, we give some usual notations:

$$s \xrightarrow{a} s' =_{def} (s, a, s') \in \rightarrow$$

$$s \xrightarrow{a_1 \cdots a_2} s' =_{def} \exists s_0, \ldots, s_n.\ s = s_0 \xrightarrow{a_1} \ldots \xrightarrow{a_n} s_n = s'$$

$$s \xrightarrow{a_1 \cdots a_2} =_{def} \exists s'.\ s \xrightarrow{a_1 \cdots a_n} s'$$

$$s \xRightarrow{\epsilon} s' =_{def} s = s' \text{or } s \xrightarrow{\tau \cdots \tau} s'$$

$$s \xRightarrow{a} s' =_{def} \exists s_1, s_2.\ s \xRightarrow{\epsilon} s_1 \xrightarrow{a} s_2 \xRightarrow{\epsilon} s'$$

$$s \xRightarrow{a_1 \cdots a_2} s' =_{def} \exists s_0, \ldots, s_n.\ s = s_0 \xRightarrow{a_1} \ldots \xRightarrow{a_n} s_n = s'$$

$$s \xRightarrow{\sigma} =_{def} \exists s'.\ s \xRightarrow{\sigma} s'$$

$$s \text{ after } \sigma =_{def} \{s' \mid s \xRightarrow{\sigma} s'\}$$

$$
\begin{aligned}
P \text{ after } \sigma &=_{def} s_0 \text{ after } \sigma \\
\text{Traces}: Tr(P) &=_{def} \{\sigma \in L^* \mid s_0 \stackrel{\sigma}{\Longrightarrow}\} \\
Out(p) &=_{def} \{a \in L \mid p \stackrel{a}{\rightarrow}\} \\
Out(p, \sigma) &=_{def} \cup_{p' \in p \text{ after } \sigma} Out(p') \\
Out(P, \sigma) &=_{def} Out(s_0, \sigma) \\
D(s, a) &=_{def} \{s' \mid s \stackrel{a}{\rightarrow} s'\}
\end{aligned}
$$

Definition 2 (Refusal set). *$Ref(P, \sigma)$, the refusal set of P after trace σ, is defined by:*

$$Ref(P, \sigma) =_{def} \left\{X \mid \exists p \in P \text{ after } \sigma.\ p \stackrel{e}{\not\Longrightarrow}, \forall e \in X\right\}$$

The refusal set is a set $Ref(P, \sigma) \subset \mathcal{P}(L)$. If $\sigma \notin Tr(P)$, $Ref(P, \sigma) = \emptyset$. The conformance relation is defined in the following way:

Definition 3 (Conformance relation conf). *Let P and Q be two LTS,*

$$Q \ \mathbf{conf}\ P \text{ if } \forall \sigma \in Tr(P).\ Ref(Q, \sigma) \subseteq Ref(P, \sigma).$$

Extension and reduction are defined as extending or reducing traces, while preserving the conformance.

Definition 4 (Reduction relation red). *Let P and Q be two LTS,*

$$Q \ \mathbf{red}\ P \text{ if } Tr(Q) \subseteq Tr(P) \text{ and } Q \ \mathbf{conf}\ P.$$

Definition 5 (Extension relation ext). *Let P and Q be two LTS,*

$$Q \ \mathbf{ext}\ P \text{ if } Tr(P) \subseteq Tr(Q) \text{ and } Q \ \mathbf{conf}\ P.$$

The relation **conf** is not a preorder relation: **conf** has not the transitivity property. But **red** and **ext** are reflexive and transitive.

2.3 Acceptance Sets

In this section, we present a definition of acceptance sets and their relation with refusal sets. This notion will be used in the next section to build up acceptance graphs associated to LTS.

Definition 6 (Acceptance set). *The acceptance set of P after σ is defined by:*

$$Acc(P, \sigma) = \{X \mid \exists p' \in P \text{ after } \sigma.\ X = Out(p', \epsilon)\}$$

The acceptance set represents the "sets of possible actions" of a process after a trace. Intuitively, the inclusion of acceptance set allows us to check whether a process is more deterministic than another.

Definition 7 (Set of sets inclusion). *Let $A, B \subseteq 2^{Act}$. $A \subset\subset B$ if:*

$$\forall S \in A.\ \exists S' \in B.\ S' \subseteq S.$$

The following theorem has been stated in [4].

Theorem 1. $\forall \sigma \in Tr(Q).\ Acc(P, \sigma) \subset\subset Acc(Q, \sigma) \Leftrightarrow Ref(P, \sigma) \subseteq Ref(Q, \sigma)$.

3 The Conformance Relation Computability

In this section, we present the definition of merging acceptance graphs [14] and demonstrate that the **conf** relation can be calculated through the merging acceptance graphs. Let us recall the definition of acceptance graphs.

3.1 Acceptance Graphs

An acceptance graph is the deterministic transition system corresponding to a LTS, where states are associated to their acceptance sets. Examples of acceptance graphs automatically generated by our JAVA prototype from LTSs are given in section 4.2, Figure 5.

Definition 8 (Acceptance graph). $\mathcal{A}(P) = \langle T, Act, \rightarrow_T, t_0\rangle$ *of the LTS* P *is a tuple where:*

- T *is the set of states.* $T = \{Q \in 2^S \mid Q = Q^\epsilon\}$*;*
- $\rightarrow_T$ *is the set of transitions;*
- *For* $t \in T$*, we define the acceptance set* $t.acc = \{X \mid X = Out(q, \epsilon) \wedge q \in t\}$*;*
- *For* $A \in t_1.acc$*,* $a \in A \Rightarrow \exists t_2 \in T$ *such that* $t_1 \xrightarrow{a}_T t_2$*;*
- $t_0 = (\{s_0\})^\epsilon$.

In this definition, the ϵ-closure is defined as follows:

Definition 9 (ϵ-closure). *The* ϵ*-closure of a set of states* Q *is:*

$$Q^\epsilon = \{p \mid \exists q \in Q.\, q \stackrel{\epsilon}{\Longrightarrow} p\}$$

This definition of acceptance graphs is similar to acceptance graphs of [12], except that acceptance sets do not take into account divergence states. It is also similar to the definition of acceptance graphs of Khendek [14], but Khendek uses a different definition of acceptance sets which is:

$$\begin{aligned} Acc(P, \sigma) &= \{Out(P, \sigma) - X \mid X \in Ref(P, \sigma)\} \\ &= \{X \mid \exists p' \in P \stackrel{\sigma}{\Longrightarrow} .\, Out(p') \subseteq X \subseteq Out(P, \sigma)\} \end{aligned}$$

The algorithm of acceptance graph construction introduced by [12] can be adapted to the construction of acceptance graphs as defined in this paper.

3.2 Merging Acceptance Graphs

The definition of merging acceptance graphs is introduced by Khendek [14]. The merging operation is defined as follows:

Definition 10 (Merge). *Let* P *and* Q *be two LTS, and* $\mathcal{A}(P)$ *and* $\mathcal{A}(Q)$ *their acceptance graphs:*

$$\mathcal{A}(P) = (T_1, Act, \rightarrow_{T_1}, t_{1_0})$$
$$\mathcal{A}(Q) = (T_2, Act, \rightarrow_{T_2}, t_{2_0})$$

The merging graph of the two above acceptance graphs is defined as follows:
$\mathrm{Merge}(\mathcal{A}(P), \mathcal{A}(Q)) = (T_3, Act, \rightarrow_{T_3}, \langle t_{1_0}, t_{2_0}\rangle)$

1. $T_3 = T_1 \times T_2 \cup T_1 \cup T_2$
2. *For each state* $t_{3_i} \in T_3$,
   if $t_{3_i} = \langle t_{1_i}, t_{2_j} \rangle$ *then* $t_{3_i}.acc = \{X_1 \cup X_2 \mid X_1 \in t_{1_i}.acc \wedge X_2 \in t_{2_j}.acc\}$,
   if $t_{3_i} \in T_x$ *then* $t_{3_i}.acc = t_{x_i}.acc$ *where* $x = 1, 2$.
3. *For each* $\langle t_{1_j}, t_{2_k} \rangle \in T_3$
   - $\langle t_{1_j}, t_{2_k} \rangle \xrightarrow{a}_{T_3} \langle t_{1_l}, t_{2_m} \rangle$ *if* $t_{1_j} \xrightarrow{a}_{T_1} t_{1_l} \wedge t_{2_k} \xrightarrow{a}_{T_2} t_{2_m}$
   - $\langle t_{1_j}, t_{2_k} \rangle \xrightarrow{a}_{T_3} \langle t_{1_0}, t_{2_0} \rangle$ *if* $(t_{1_j} \xrightarrow{a}_{T_1} t_{1_0} \wedge t_{2_k} \not\xrightarrow{a}_{T_2}) \vee$
     $(t_{1_j} \not\xrightarrow{a}_{T_1} \wedge t_{2_k} \xrightarrow{a}_{T_2} t_{2_0})$
   - $\langle t_{1_j}, t_{2_k} \rangle \xrightarrow{a}_{T_3} t_{1_l}$ *if* $t_{1_j} \xrightarrow{a}_{T_1} t_{1_0}, t_{1_l} \neq t_{1_0} \wedge t_{2_k} \not\xrightarrow{a}_{T_2}$
   - $\langle t_{1_j}, t_{2_k} \rangle \xrightarrow{a}_{T_3} t_{2_m}$ *if* $t_{2_k} \xrightarrow{a}_{T_2} t_{2_m}, t_{2_m} \neq t_{2_0} \wedge t_{1_j} \not\xrightarrow{a}_{T_1}$
4. *For each state* $t_{x_j} \in T_3$ *where* $x = 1, 2$
   - $t_{x_j} \xrightarrow{a}_{T_3} \langle t_{1_0}, t_{2_0} \rangle$ *if* $t_{x_j} \xrightarrow{a}_{T_x} t_{x0}$
   - $t_{xj} \xrightarrow{a}_{T_3} t_{x_l}$ *if* $t_{x_j} \xrightarrow{a}_{T_x} t_{x_l}, t_{x_l} \neq t_{x0}$

The operation Merge has some interesting properties. It is commutative and associative. Moreover, for any acceptance graph, there exists one LTS [14]. We write $\mathrm{Merge}(P, Q)$ the LTS of $\mathrm{Merge}(\mathcal{A}(P), \mathcal{A}(Q))$. The operation Merge guarantees the extension relation between the LTS of merging acceptance graphs and the initial LTS. In addition, the merging graph is always the least common cyclic extension of two initial graphs.

Proposition 1. *Let P, Q be two LTS.*

1. $\mathrm{Merge}(P, Q) = \mathrm{Merge}(Q, P)$
2. $\mathrm{Merge}(P, Q)$ **ext** $P \wedge \mathrm{Merge}(P, Q)$ **ext** Q.

3.3 Demonstration of the Conformance Relation Computability

This section gives the demonstration of the conformance relation computability through a reduction relation applied on the merging of acceptance graphs.

Theorem 2. *Let P and Q be two LTS,*

$$Q \textbf{ conf } P \Longleftrightarrow Q \textbf{ red } \mathrm{Merge}(P, Q).$$

Proof.

1. Let us prove $(\Rightarrow)$: Q **conf** $P \Rightarrow Q$ **red** $\mathrm{Merge}(P, Q)$

1.1. $\mathrm{Merge}(P, Q)$ **ext** $Q \Rightarrow Tr(Q) \subseteq Tr(\mathrm{Merge}(P, Q))$

1.2. Following the definition of merging graphs:

$$\begin{aligned} &\forall \sigma \in Tr(Q) \wedge \sigma \notin Tr(P).\ Acc(\mathrm{Merge}(P, Q), \sigma) = Acc(Q, \sigma) \\ \Rightarrow &\forall \sigma \in Tr(Q) \wedge \sigma \notin Tr(P).\ Acc(Q, \sigma) \subset\subset Acc(\mathrm{Merge}(P, Q), \sigma) \end{aligned} \quad (2)$$

With definition 3 and theorem 1, from Q **conf** P we know that:

$\forall \sigma \in Tr(Q) \cap Tr(P).\ Acc(Q, \sigma) \subset\subset Acc(P, \sigma)$,

Moreover, following definition 10:

$\forall \sigma \in Tr(Q) \cap Tr(P).$
$Acc(\mathrm{Merge}(P, Q)) = \{X_1 \cup X_2 \mid X_1 \in Acc(P, \sigma) \wedge X_2 \in Acc(Q, \sigma)\}$

It can be written as follows:

$$
\begin{aligned}
&\forall \sigma \in Tr(Q) \cap Tr(P). \\
&\quad \forall X_2 \in Acc(Q,\sigma).\ \exists X' \in Acc(P,\sigma).\ X' \subseteq X_2 \\
&\quad \Rightarrow \forall X_2 \in Acc(Q,\sigma).\ \exists X' \in Acc(P,\sigma).\ X' \cup X_2 \subseteq X_2 \\
&\quad \Rightarrow \forall X_2 \in Acc(Q,\sigma).\ \exists X \in Acc(\text{Merge}(P,Q),\sigma), X = X' \cup X_2.\ X \subseteq X_2 \\
&\quad \Rightarrow Acc(Q,\sigma) \subset\subset Acc(\text{Merge}(P,Q),\sigma) \qquad (3)
\end{aligned}
$$

With (2) and (3), we have: $\forall \sigma \in Tr(Q).\ Acc(Q,\sigma) \subset\subset Acc(\text{Merge}(P,Q),\sigma)$. So, with condition $Tr(Q) \subseteq Tr(\text{Merge}(P,Q))$ proven in 1.1., we have:

Q **conf** $P \Rightarrow Q$ **red** $\text{Merge}(P,Q)$

2. We prove ($\Leftarrow$): Q **red** $\text{Merge}(P,Q) \Rightarrow Q$ **conf** P

Since **conf** $=$ **red** $\circ$ **ext**, where $\circ$ is the composition between binary relations [10], we have:

Q **red** $\text{Merge}(P,Q) \wedge \text{Merge}(P,Q)$ **ext** $P \Rightarrow Q$ **conf** P. □

In [4], we have demonstrated that

$$Q \textbf{ red } P \Longleftrightarrow \mathcal{A}(Q) \lessapprox \mathcal{A}(P),$$

where $\lessapprox$ is a simulation relation defined over acceptance graphs. Hence, theorem 2 leads to

Corollary 1. *Let P and Q be two LTS,*

$$Q \textbf{ conf } P \Longleftrightarrow \mathcal{A}(Q) \lessapprox \text{Merge}(\mathcal{A}(P), \mathcal{A}(Q)).$$

This theorem and corollary allow us to implement the conformance relation between LTS. The tool we have developed strictly follows this result: it computes first acceptance graphs, then Merge, and then checks whether the reduction is satisfied or not. An example is presented in the next section.

4 Implementation and Results

This part gives an overview of the JAVA prototype we have developed to implement the conformance relation. We present a case study modelling a phone and the different models that may be set up during the incremental modelling approach. The conformance relation is computed to compare an implementation with a given specification. Intermediate steps and results of these computations are given to illustrate the application of theorem 2.

The relations being demonstrated on LTS, computation is obviously performed on LTS. Nevertheless, for every step of modelling, we present the UML state machine associated with LTS for two reasons: using UML model is more widespread than LTS, and this approach gives a quick outline of our future work consisting in applying results of LTS comparison on UML models.

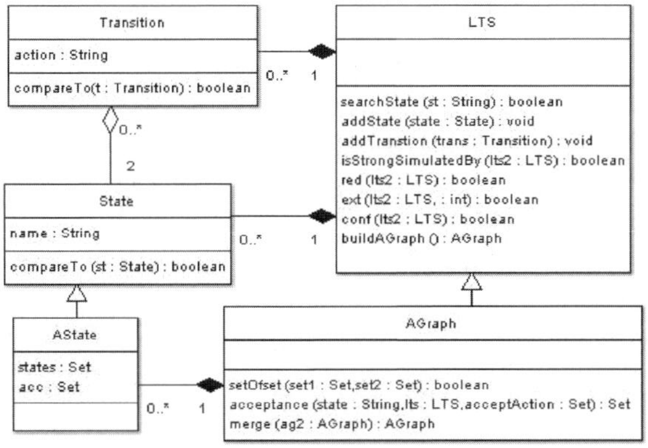

Fig. 1. The class diagram of the prototype

4.1 Implementation of the Conformance Relation

The JAVA prototype we have developed follows the computation approach of theorem 2. Consequently, the main implemented classes are *LTS* and *AGraph* (cf. Figure 1):

- *LTS* class implements a LTS as a set of states derived from the *State* class and transitions derived from the *Transition* class. As demonstrated in [4], relations *red* and *ext* have been implemented in terms of bisimulation (function *isStrongSimulatedBy*).
- *AGraph* class implements the acceptance graph associated with a LTS. It is itself a LTS, the state of which belongs to the *AState* class defined as a subclass of *State* class. The attribute *states* of the class *AState* defines the list of its associated states in the LTS. This attribute allows the relationship between acceptance graph nodes and LTS nodes to be established. Another fundamental attribute associated with a *AState* node is *acc* which is its acceptance set defined has a set of sets of actions.

In order to follow theorem 2, the conformance relation (function *conf*) has been implemented into three steps: build up of acceptance graphs associated with the reference LTS (the specification) and the LTS under analysis (the implementation), their merging into a new acceptance graph and at last, computation of the reduction relation between the acceptance graph of the reference LTS and the merging acceptance graph.

The following sections point out the results obtained by the JAVA prototype and present in details intermediate graphs automatically build up and analysed to demonstrate the conformance.

4.2 Case 1: Modelling a Simple Phone in Two Steps

This case study illustrates how to check the conformance relation between a phone and its specification defined from a user point of view. The phone is modelled to interact with a user, and *simulates* network activities (such as incoming calls) like internal treatments. A UML class diagram presenting phone classes and interfaces is shown in Figure 2. The specification provided interface (class *User_actions*) is composed of

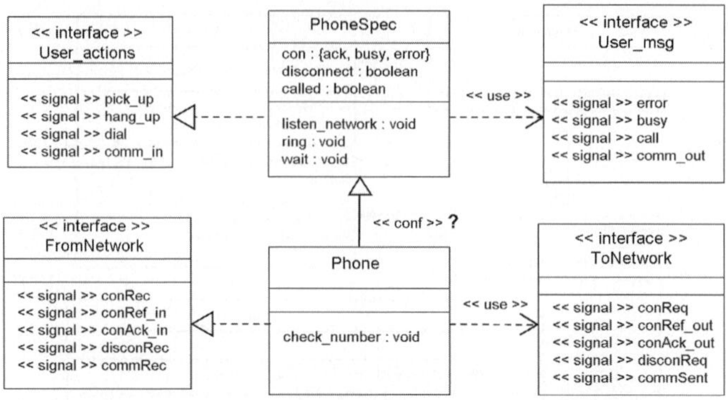

Fig. 2. Phone classes, with provided and required interfaces

signals sent by users: *hang_up*, *pick_up*, *dial* and *comm_in* (incoming communication). The specification required interface (class *User_msg*) is composed of signals sent by the phone: *error*, *busy*, *call* and *comm_out*.

The *Phone* is connected to a network. It uses and provides the same interfaces as its specification, plus network interfaces. Its provided interface is composed of signals sent by the network: connection received, incoming connection refused, incoming connection acknowledge, disconnection received and communication received. Its required interface is composed of signals sent to the network: connection request, outgoing connection refused, outgoing connection acknowledge, disconnection request and communication sent.

In UML, we distinguish between *actions* and *events*. There is no such distinction in LTS for which any transition label is an action. UML events can be signal events, call events, time events, change events and complete events. If the behaviour has to be observed according to a specific point of view, there is no simple means in UML to hide some events and actions. We will consider that UML change events, time events and complete events are internal. We also need to explicitly consider as internal some actions and signal events. UML tags can be used for such purpose.

Figure 3.a represents a UML state machine $SM_{PhoneSpec}$ of the phone specification. There are two functionalities: the user is called (right part of Figure 3.a) or the user is calling (left part of Figure 3.a).

We have not yet fully formalised the UML transformation into LTS, nevertheless main transformation rules can be expressed as follows:

- Change events, time events or complete events are modelled by the silent action τ;
- Call events, signal events and actions are translated into LTS actions;
- Any UML transition labelled by event and action (event / action), is split into two LTS transitions, separated by a state ($s_0 \xrightarrow{e} s_1 \xrightarrow{a} s_2$), where e is an action label which denotes the UML event, and a is an action label which denotes the UML action; if the UML action is not visible, it may be translated into a simple transition $s_0 \xrightarrow{e} s_1$;
- Non visible UML signal events, call events, and actions are modelled by the LTS internal action τ;

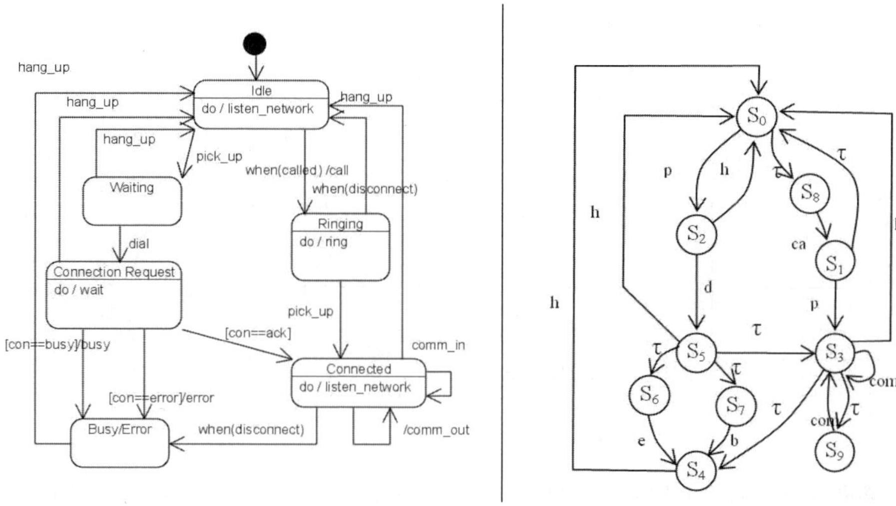

Fig. 3. (a) $SM_{PhoneSpec}$, *PhoneSpec* state machine. (b) $LTS_{PhoneSpec}$, associated LTS.

- UML activities inside states are considered like internal treatments and do not appear in LTS;
- UML hierarchical states are flattened and global transition from this state are distributed to every sub-states.

Note that the UML state machines we consider do not take into account signal or method parameters, neither other variables. Hence, UML guards are not taken into account in corresponding LTS, and systematically lead to nondeterministic transitions.

In order to have legible LTS, actions are named by the first letters of UML labels. UML signals which are both required and provided (such as *comm_in* and *comm_out*) are translated into a single LTS action (*com*). Figure 3.b shows $LTS_{PhoneSpec}$, the LTS associated with the state machine $SM_{PhoneSpec}$.

Let us consider the modelling of the phone state machine (Figure 4.a). Internal activities of $SM_{PhoneSpec}$ are refined: new network incoming and outgoing signals are used to build up new transitions or new sub-machines. For example, in the state *Idle* of $SM_{PhoneSpec}$, the *listen_network* activity and the associated change event $when(called)$, which only aims at detecting incoming calls, is replaced in SM_{Phone} by a transition triggered by the incoming signal event *conRec*.

The question is to verify if there is a conformance relation between the phone and its specification. It is automatically computed by our tool whose main intermediate results are given in details in the following figures. The first step performed by the JAVA prototype is to build up acceptance graphs associated with the two compared LTS and their merge.

The second step consists in verifying the simulation relation between the acceptance graph of LTS_{Phone} (Figure 5) and the merge (Figure 6).

This relation is computed by the JAVA prototype by verifying the simulation relation between the two graphs and the inclusion of acceptance sets. More precisely, two

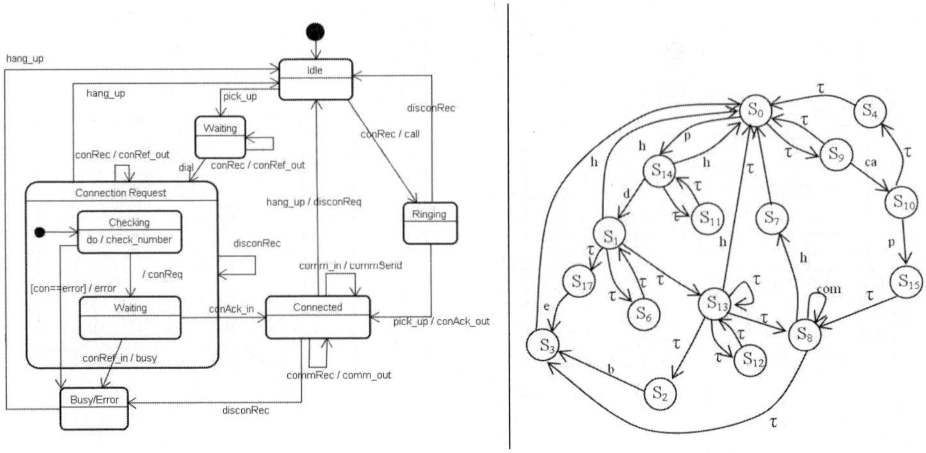

Fig. 4. (a) SM_{Phone}, the state machine of *Phone* class. (b) LTS_{Phone}, associated LTS.

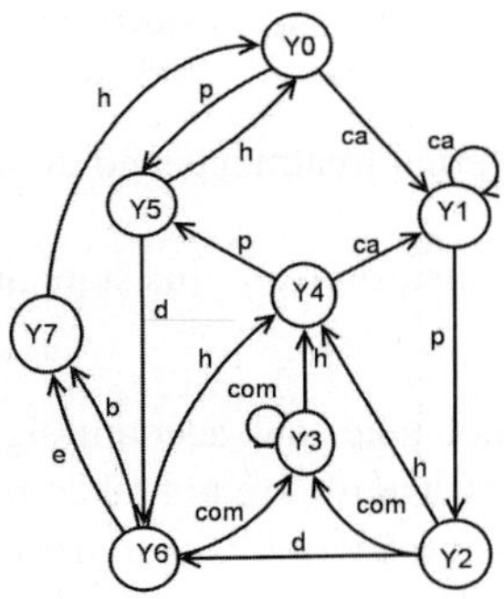

AState	Acceptance set
y_0	$\{\{ca, p\}\}$
y_1	$\{\{ca, p\}\}$
y_2	$\{\{com, h\}, \{d, h\}, \{h\}, \{com\}\}$
y_3	$\{\{com, h\}, \{h\}, \{com\}\}$
y_4	$\{\{ca, p\}\}$
y_5	$\{\{d, h\}\}$
y_6	$\{\{h\}, \{com, h\}, \{e\}, \{b\},$ $\{com, e, b, h\}, \{com, b, h\}, \{com\}\}$
y_7	$\{\{h\}\}$

Fig. 5. $\mathcal{A}(LTS_{Phone})$ graph and its acceptance sets

properties are automatically computed. The first one is that there exists, for each node of $\mathcal{A}(LTS_{Phone})$, a node of $\mathcal{A}(\text{Merge}(LTS_{PhoneSpec}, LTS_{Phone}))$ which simulates it.

The result of this first property is expressed by a set of pairs representing simulation relationships. In this case, it is: $\{(y_0, w_0), (y_1, w_1), (y_2, w_3), (y_3, w_5), (y_4, w_6), (y_5, w_2), (y_6, w_6), (y_7, w_7)\}$. The second property is that the acceptance set of each node of $\mathcal{A}(LTS_{Phone})$ is included in the acceptance set of its associated node in $\mathcal{A}$(Merge ($LTS_{PhoneSpec}$, LTS_{Phone})). This property is checked by analysing acceptance sets given in tables of Figure 5 and Figure 6 for each pair belonging to the simulation relation. The conformance relation is therefore verified and the phone is guaranteed to conform to its specification.

Next section deals with an extended specification of the phone.

4.3 Case 2: Modelling a Phone with Double Call

We are interested in modelling a phone able to accept a second call while the user is on the phone. The class *DoubleCallSpec* (Figure 7) is a specialisation of the *PhoneSpec*

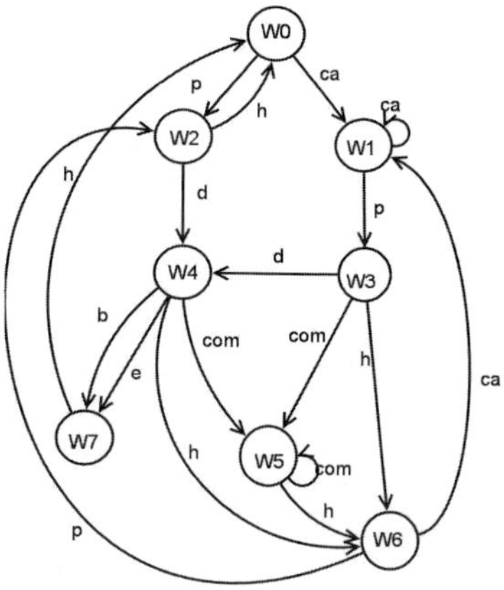

AState	Acceptance set
w_0	$\{\{ca, p\}\}$
w_1	$\{\{ca, p\}\}$
w_2	$\{\{d, h\}\}$
w_3	$\{\{d, h\}, \{h\}, \{com\}, \{com, h\}, \{d, com, h\}\}$
w_4	$\{\{e, h\}, \{com, e\}, \{e\}, \{com\}, \{b\}, \{com, e, b, h\}, \{com, b\}, \{b, h\}, \{e, b\}, \{com, h\}, \{h\}, \{com, b, h\}, \{com, e, h\}\}$
w_5	$\{\{h\}, \{com\}, \{com, h\}\}$
w_6	$\{\{ca, p\}\}$
w_7	$\{\{h\}\}$

Fig. 6. $\mathcal{A}(\text{Merge}(LTS_{PhoneSpec}, LTS_{Phone}))$ graph and its acceptance sets

class. It inherits *PhoneSpec* interfaces, and has its own required interface defining signals accepting or rejecting/stopping the second call. Figure 8.a represents the state machine of this new specification, called $SM_{DoubleCallSpec}$. The difference with the first specification is on state *Connected* since a *call* transition may occur on this state. Figure 8.b gives the corresponding LTS, named $LTS_{DoubleCall}$, obtained by the same informal transformation rules as in the previous case. The conformance relation between the phone and the double call specification has been computed according to the same steps as it has been shown in previous section.

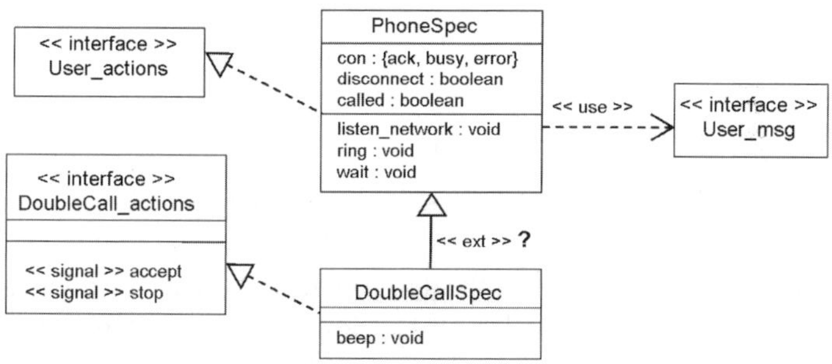

Fig. 7. Double call specification class, with provided and required interfaces

Again, the conformance relation is guaranteed. Moreover, there is an extension relation between the double call specification and the initial specification. Next modelling step consists in setting up the state machine of the implementation (*DoubleCall*) and verifying its conformance with *DoubleCallSpec*. Since the extension relation is a refinement relation (see property (1) in section 2.1), if *DoubleCall* conforms its specification, then it surely conforms to the initial phone specification. These results are summarised in Figure 9.

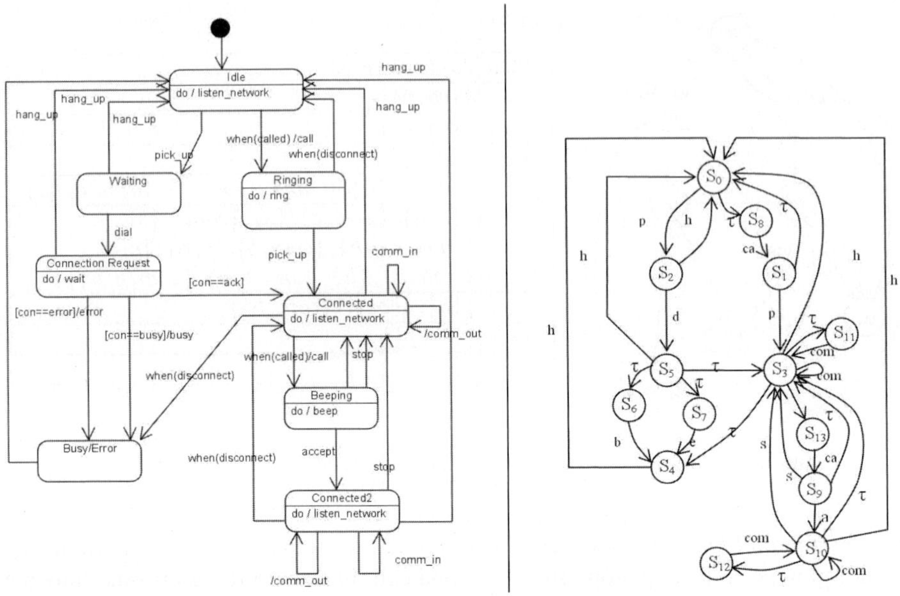

(a) $SM_{DoubleCallSpec}$, state machine (b) $LTS_{DoubleCallSpec}$, associated LTS

Fig. 8. Telephone with a second call

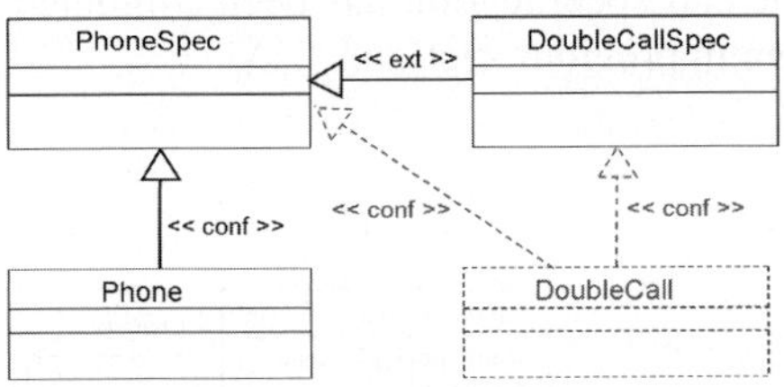

Fig. 9. Relations between phone specifications and their implementations

This case study shows two steps of the development of a state machine, with the second step including a new functionality, at two levels of abstraction (specification and implementation levels). The developed state machine is associated to a single class. Extensions of this class (specialisation or implementation) are then related to extensions of the state machine. For larger systems, we could consider developing state machines describing the behaviour of the whole system, and not only associated to a single class of the system. This would correspond to a *top-down* approach. Then, at a further development step, this would imply a decomposition of the whole state machine into several parts, involving communication between these parts. This approach of refinement through decomposition will constitute a research perspective. In the other direction, according to a *bottom-up* approach, the development of several state machines associated to different classes of the same system will lead us to consider the question of communication and resulting UML architecture involving these machines.

5 Conclusion and Future Work

Currently, the development of behavioural models following an incremental approach is hardly achievable. UML tools supporting state machines lack evaluation procedures, which could allow users to develop models step by step, and modify (change or extend) them according to evaluation results. We believe that a pragmatic development approach, such as ones adopted for program development, could be applied to behavioural modelling. Such an approach follows a simple repetitive cycle: construction, evaluation, correction. The evaluation means that we propose rely on model comparison. In previous works, we have presented how to compute extension and reduction relations and point out the use of the former one to verify model refinement. However, it is not adapted to verify, at the end of an incremental modelling process, if an implementation conforms to a specification.

In this article, we propose an implementation technique for conformance evaluation. The conformance relation defined over labelled transition systems, had never been implemented before. The technique we propose is based on model transformations into acceptance graphs and model merging. We have developed a tool which supports these steps on LTS models. We have proposed informal translation rules from UML State Machines to LTS. Hence, the conformance relation between LTS is a proposal for a semantics of UML state machine specialisation relation.

Our short term objectives are to automate the UML translation into LTS and integrate other state machine features such as concurrent sub-states and pseudo-states (e.g. choice, join and history) in order to be able to compare a large representative panel of state machines. We plan to integrate the extension and conformance relations into a UML CASE tool supporting incremental modelling processes. A complementary area of interest consists in comparing UML state machines with sequence diagram specifications. Such diagrams are largely used in first development steps. This will assist the modeler from early specification steps to detailed behavioural models, taking into account several modelling diagrams. A promising area of investigation, complementary to evaluation techniques, will consist in assisting the user during model construction with development schemes and patterns which would have been proved to preserve refinement or implementation relations.

References

1. OMG: Unified Modeling Language Specification. Object Management Group (2007)
2. Boiten, E., Bujorianu, M.: Exploring UML refinement through unification. In: Jürjens, J., Rumpe, B., France, R., Fernandez, E. (eds.) Critical Systems Development with UML - Proceedings of the UML 2003 workshop. Number TUM-I0323, Technische Universität München, pp. 47–62 (September 2003)
3. Beeck, M.V.D.: Behaviour specifications: Equivalence and refinement notions. Techreport 24/00-I, Universität Münster (November 2000)
4. Luong, H.V., Lambolais, T., Courbis, A.L.: Implementation of extension and reduction relations for incremental development of behavioural models. Technical Report RR-006-2008, EMA, Laboratoire LGI2P, École des mines d'Alès (2008)

5. Lambolais, T., Gout, O.: Using conformance relations to help the development of state-machines. In: ISSRE 2004, International Symposium on Software Reliability Engineering (November 2004)
6. Gout, O.: Développement incrémental de spécifications orientées objets. PhD thesis, École de mines d'Alès (2006)
7. Milner, R.: Communicating and Mobile Systems: The π Calculus. Cambridge University Press, Cambridge (1999)
8. Brinksma, E., Scollo, G.: Formal Notions of Implementation and Conformance in LOTOS. Technical Report INF-86-13, Dept. of Informatics, Twente University of Technology (1986)
9. Hennessy, M.: Algebraic theory of processes. The Foundations Of Computing. MIT Press, Cambridge (1988) ISBN:0-262-08171-7
10. Leduc, G.: Conformance relation, associated equivalence, and minimum canonical tester in lotos. In: PSTV XI. North-Holland, Amsterdam (1991)
11. Tretmans, J.: Testing concurrent systems: A formal approach. In: Baeten, J.C.M., Mauw, S. (eds.) CONCUR 1999. LNCS, vol. 1664. Springer, Heidelberg (1999)
12. Cleaveland, R., Hennessy, M.: Testing equivalence as a bisimulation equivalence. Formal Aspects of Computing 3 (1992)
13. ISO/IEC 9646-1: Information technology – Open Systems Interconnection – Conformance testing methodology and framework – Part 1: General concepts (1991)
14. Khendek, F., Bochmann, G.V.: Merging behavior specifications. Formal Methods in System Design 6, 259–293 (1993)

A Model-Based Framework for Statically and Dynamically Checking Component Interactions*

Guillaume Waignier, Prawee Sriplakich, Anne-Françoise Le Meur, and Laurence Duchien

Université Lille 1 - LIFL CNRS UMR 8022 - INRIA
59650 Villeneuve d'Ascq, France
{Guillaume.Waignier,Prawee.Sriplakich,
Anne-Francoise.Le_Meur,Laurence.Duchien}@inria.fr

Abstract. Building applications by assembling software components requires analyses of Architecture Description (AD) models for checking that component interactions respect the application and runtime context requirements. Most existing interaction model analyses are static: they do not take into account runtime information, e.g., parameter values.

This paper presents a model-based framework that enables architects to both specify component interaction and perform dynamic validation. Our framework analyses AD models to identify partially compatible interactions, which require runtime checking. Then, it instruments the application to reify runtime information for error detection. By using this framework in iterative software design processes, architects can get design feedback, *i.e.*, detected errors, and update the AD models accordingly. Moreover, our solution is generic regarding underlying platforms. This genericity is achieved through the mappings from the generic AD models to platform-specific API calls for constructing the running system.

1 Introduction

Component-Based Software Engineering (CBSE) is now a widely used paradigm for building complex software. In CBSE, a system is described by an assembly of components [1]. In the Model Driven Engineering paradigm, the specifications of components and their assembly may be considered as models, which we will refer to as Architecture Description (AD) models.

At design-time, AD models allow architects to reason about their application at a high level without considering implementation details. Concretely, architects care not only about specifying the composition of the required components to form the targeted system, but also about making sure that the resulting assembly is coherent in order to maintain system integrity. Mainly, system integrity relies on the compatibility of the components that interact together. It is common that this compatibility takes into account structural and behavioral component properties [2,3]. Other concerns may be considered, such as dataflow properties when architects need to reason about the value of the data exchanged through the entire assembly, or quality properties, such as timing and performance.

* This work was partially funded by the French ANR TL FAROS project.

K. Czarnecki et al. (Eds.): MoDELS 2008, LNCS 5301, pp. 371–385, 2008.

Checking the compatibility of component interactions at design-time corresponds to verifying not only that components directly connected with each other satisfy the various desired properties, but also that components that interact across the entire assembly respect these properties. The result of this static verification is of three types: *compatible*, when all the properties are satisfied, *incompatible*, when component interactions break the properties and finally *partially compatible* when the verification yields no error but can not be completed because some properties depend on values that can only be known at runtime.

In case of partial compatibility, architects may simply consider the assembly to be incorrect. Other solutions rely on dynamic checking, which involves adding assertions into the final application implementation. These assertions will be executed at runtime during the whole application execution to detect improper values that may break system integrity. An instance of this solution has been implemented by the Confract component model [4], which allows data values to be checked when they enter or leave a component. These solutions are not completely satisfactory because checks that are performed are not context sensitive. Indeed data value are considered locally without taking into account any control-flow information, which limits the cases that can be handled. Furthermore, if the targeted component platform does not provide any support for checking assertions at runtime, which is actually not a common component-platform feature, developers have no choice than to implement these assertions in their system. This may imply modifying components' code when source code is available, or adding in the architecture new components that have for function to execute the assertions. All of these modifications have to be applied for each platform the application may run on. Moreover, in existing approaches, the design and execution phases are not coupled. Consequently, if a runtime error occurs, the architect must first identify and fix the elements of the design that led to this problem and then manually load the system again.

In this paper, we propose CALICO, the Component AssembLy Interaction Control framewOrk to support the design and interaction checking of component-based systems in an iterative software design process. CALICO exhibits two levels : a model level and a platform level. At the model level, we provide architects with several models to specify their applications and properties. These models are statically checked and when a partial compatibility is detected, the framework automatically modifies the associated application at the platform level to enable context-sensitive monitoring of values. Accordingly, at the platform level, when the application is executed and tested in a given context, the monitored values are reified to the application model views and the corresponding partially compatible checks are completed. If an error is detected, the architect is notified and may then modify the architecture at the model level of CALICO, which triggers the verification of interaction compatibility and the propagation of the modifications to the running application. The architect can iterate this process until the design reaches a stable state in this specific execution context. Monitoring mechanisms are automatically removed before providing the final application to users.

Our approach takes full advantage of the model paradigm. Our framework can describe an application through several views, *i.e.*, structural, behavioral, and dataflow views. We propose metamodels for each view, as well as the modeling of the relationships between these views, which enables the views to remain consistent with each other.

Furthermore, creating a link between the running application and the application model views by reifying the runtime information, facilitates the architects task of interpreting application execution errors and identifying model elements that caused the errors. Finally, CALICO aims to alleviate shortcomings of several platforms in lacking validation support. Indeed, our interaction analyses are performed at the model level, which we have designed to be platform independent. We bridge the gap between the model-level analyses and the platforms, by proposing platform-specific mechanisms for instantiating the running application on a target platform and reifying runtime information. Overall our methodology enables reusing the model-level analyses on several platforms.

The rest of the paper is organized as follows. In Section 2 we illustrate with a running application example the need for performing checks at execution time and identify challenges that have to be addressed. Section 3 gives an overview of our framework and approach. The CALICO AD models and static interaction analyses are described in Sections 4 and 5, respectively. Section 6 presents our framework runtime support, which bridges the gap between the model and platform levels. Section 7 gives implementation details on our prototype. Finally, Section 8 provides some related work and Section 9 concludes.

2 A Running Example: Personal Health Record System

We illustrate the limits of static verification and thus the need for runtime checking through a simplified example of the French Personal Health Record system (PHR) [5]. PHR is a system that provides health-care professionals with the information needed for their patients care, such as biological analyses, X-rays, medications, *etc.* Such system has to be able to handle very heterogeneous medical information, going from lightweight text records to gigabytes of echographies. Furthermore, the devices used to display this information are also heterogeneous. They range from desktop computers with high-quality large-screen monitors and gigabyte network connections to simple PDAs with small screens and low-bandwidth GPRS network connection. Handling such data in a reliable way is critical: the system must be able to determine if a given data can be displayed appropriately with no loss of information.

2.1 Application Architecture and Properties

Figure 1 shows a subset of the PHR system, which contains four components. All medical information is stored in the component `Server`. A health-care professional can

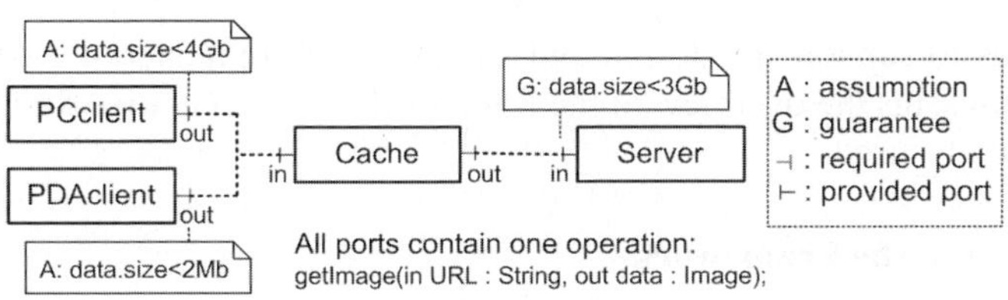

Fig. 1. Subset of the PHR architecture

consult medical data using a desktop PC, represented by the component `PCclient`, or a PDA, represented by the component `PDAclient`. To optimize data transfer, a component `Cache` is inserted between the clients and the server.

We propose to consider a dataflow property of this PHR system that the architect needs to verify. Component properties can be seen as *assumptions* and *guarantees*. For example, the component `PDAclient` (*resp.* `PCclient`) has been provided with the assumption that it will always receive data no larger than 2 Mb (*resp.* 4Gb). Satisfying this property will prevent out-of-memory errors. The component `Server` used in our system holds the guarantee that it will always send data no larger than 3Gb. In order to verify that the architecture will maintain system integrity, the architect must check that these assumptions and guarantees are compatible.

Both the `PDAclient` and `PCclient` components interact with the `Server` component. It can be statically checked that the assumption of `PCclient` will never be violated since `Server` guarantees to send smaller data. However, the static analysis of the interaction between `PDAclient` and `Server` leads to a partial compatibility because `Server` may send oversized data to `PDAclient`. Indeed, considering this architecture to be appropriate or not, completely depends on its execution contexts. In fact, a druggist will only request light-weight text prescriptions, whereas a radiologist will need oversized radiographies. Consequently, instantiating this architecture as-is will satisfy the druggist needs but another architecture will need to be designed for the radiologist.

2.2 Problems to Address

Statically determining if a given architecture may maintain system integrity is possible when all the property values are known. Nevertheless, several values are often not known before execution time and thus need to be discovered. Capturing runtime information to verify if a partially compatible architecture is in fact compatible (or not) in a given execution context requires more than intercepting the values exchanged between components of the running system. Indeed analyses of component interactions rely on control flow. For example, in the PHR system, to detect errors as early as possible, the detection should occur when `Server` responses to `Cache` with data that is larger than the `PDAclient` limit. This error must be detected only in the control flow issued from `PDAclient`. Furthermore, another challenge lies in the ability to provide the architect with a design process that can consider runtime information at the design level. This is what CALICO proposes to do.

3 The CALICO Framework

CALICO aims to support the design and validation of component-based assemblies. This section presents the overview of the framework and the iterative design process in which it should be used.

3.1 Overview of the Framework

CALICO is organized in two levels: a model level and a platform level, as shown in Figure 2.

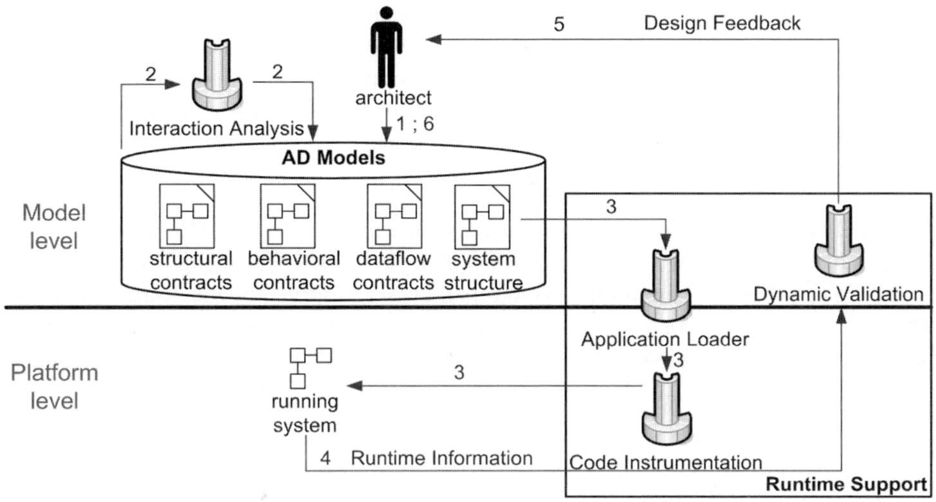

Fig. 2. Overview of CALICO

At the **model level**, CALICO provides architects with a set of metamodels to describe an application architecture and its properties through several views. A complete system specification is expressed across four AD models. The *system structure model* depicts the components and their connections to form the application architecture. The *structural contract model* describes structural properties of the component assembly. The *behavioral contract model* expresses the control flow going in and out of components. Finally, the *dataflow contract model* specifies the assumptions and guarantees on the values of the exchanged messages. These models form a basis for the component interaction analysis.

Static analysis of AD models is performed by the *Interaction Analysis* tool. This tool identifies interactions that are compatible, incompatible, or partially compatible. For each incompatible interaction, the tool notifies the architect who can then correct the application design. For each partially compatible interaction, the tool inserts a *validation point* in the system structure AD model to mark the location where a check at execution time is required.

The **platform level** holds the running system corresponding to the architecture described at the model level, as well as a set of runtime support tools, which bridge the gap between the model level and the platform level. The running system is loaded by the *Application Loader* tool, whose role is to automatically instantiate the running application from the specification of component assembly, *i.e.*, the system structure AD model.

The running application needs to reify all the runtime information required by the validation points, independently of the underlying platform. However, most platforms lack services for capturing runtime information, such as capturing control flow information. In our approach, the *Code Instrumentation* tool instruments the application code to add the missing functionalities required for reifying runtime information.

Once instrumented and loaded, the running system is capable of submitting runtime information to the model level. The *Dynamic Validation* tool receives this runtime information and completes the validation of the partially compatible interactions. If errors are detected, the tool provides design feedback to the architect at the model level.

3.2 An Iterative Design Process

CALICO supports iterative design processes. In each iteration, CALICO enables architects to alternate between design and checking activities. The design activity corresponds to updating the system models to repair errors identified by the design feedback. The checking activity consists in verifying component interaction compatibility. More precisely, the iterative process consists of the following steps (cf. Figure 2):

1. **Design:** Architects provide an initial design of the system, *i.e.*, the AD models.
2. **Interaction analysis:** The Interaction Analysis tool performs component interaction analysis on the models. For each partially compatible interaction detected, the tool inserts a validation point at the corresponding component port.
3. **Loading:** At the platform level, the framework instruments the application code and loads the system accordingly to the system structure AD model.
4. **Reification:** During its execution, the instrumented system submits the reified information to the model level.
5. **Feedback production:** The framework analyzes the reified information to detect runtime errors, and to produce design feedback to architects.
6. **Design update:** Accordingly to design feedback, architects can write an *update model*, which specifies changes of the AD models to fix the detected errors. The update model contains a sequence of operations for modifying the system structure, such as, adding/removing components and connectors to/from the system [6]. Once the models are modified, architects can repeat step 2 for identifying incompatible or partially compatible interactions that may have been introduced by the changes.

At the last iteration, when the architecture is stable, instrumented code is removed and the running system is separated from the model level.

4 Specification of AD Models

This Section presents the step 1 described in Section 3.2. At this step, the architect designs the structure and the properties of his/her architecture by specifying AD models conformed to the CALICO AD metamodels. This section describes the four CALICO metamodels: the system structure AD metamodel as well as the structural, behavioral and dataflow contracts AD metamodels.

4.1 Modeling System Structure

The system structure AD metamodel, shown in Figure 3, enables architects to describe the structure of their architecture, independently of any component platform. It contains metaclasses for representing components, ports and connector, which are common model elements that architects are familiar with. A `Component` is a computational

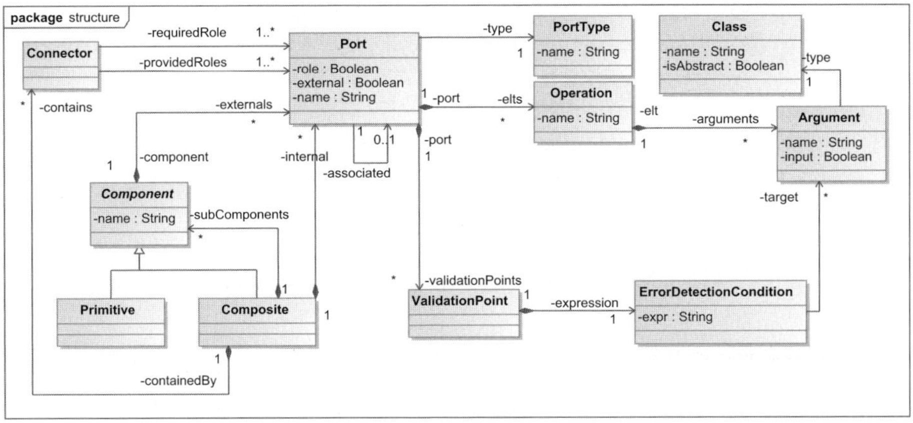

Fig. 3. System structure metamodel

element that provides or requires functionalities through its `Ports`. A functionality is represented by an `Operation` with input/output typed `Arguments`, which correspond to messages exchanged between components. A `Connector` describes the interactions between components, it can only connect required ports with provided ports.

Moreover, to capture the runtime context at the model level, we introduce the concept of `ValidationPoint`, which is dedicated to dynamic validation. Validation points mark the locations where runtime checks are required, they are placed at component ports where architects need to check messages that are sent and received. The condition to evaluate on the messages is expressed with the `ErrorDetectionCondition` of a validation point. Validation points are automatically inserted by the Interaction Analysis tool in order to observe partially compatible interaction. Furthermore, if needed, we provide architects with means to manually insert validation points.

Aside from validation points, our system structure AD metamodel is based on concepts common to all generic ADLs, such as Acme/Armani [7,8] and xADL [9]. Similarly to these ADLs, our metamodel allows meta-information to be associated with these concepts. However, the other ADLs lack means to reason about component interactions, *e.g.*, they consider ports as black-boxes. Thus, we have extended these ADL concepts to model messages exchanged through ports, in order to perform interaction analysis.

4.2 Modeling Component Contracts

CALICO contract metamodels allow architects to specify structural, behavioral, and dataflow properties for each component. In this article, we focus on dataflow properties, which depend on the behavioral properties and the structure of the application.

Structural Contract Metamodel. It enables architects to specify structural properties, in terms of OCL invariants [10], to constraint the structure of the application, *i.e.*, the component connections. For example, structural properties can express that each required port of a component must be connected with at least one provided port.

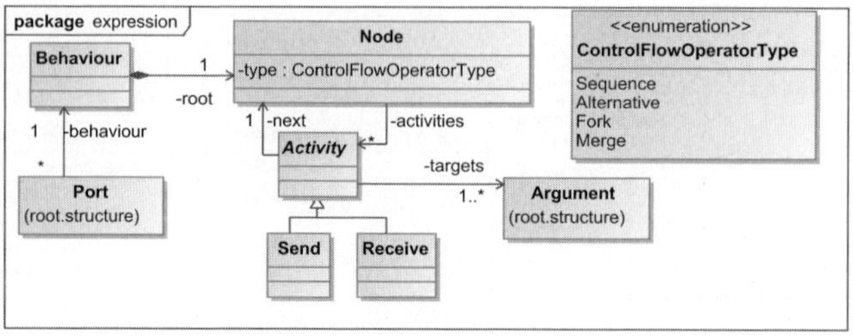

Fig. 4. Metamodel for specifying behavioral contracts

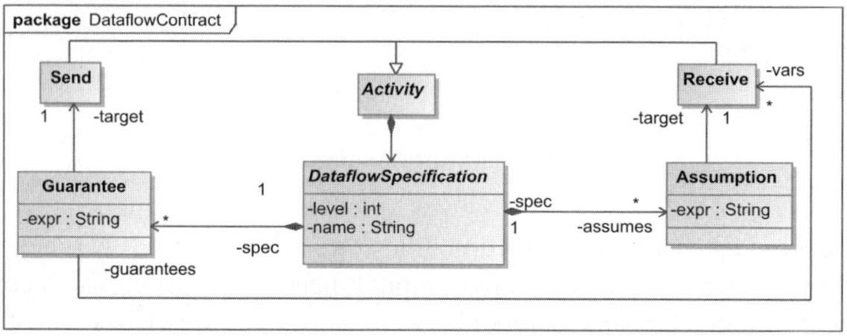

Fig. 5. Metamodel for specifying dataflow contracts

Behavioral Contract Metamodel. The specification of behavioral properties is based on a Control Flow Graph (CFG) [11]. A CFG is attached to each component. It specifies the order of the messages sent and received through the component ports. As shown in Figure 4, a CFG is composed of `Nodes` and `Activities`, which are directed edges. A node specifies a non structured control flow operator [12] (`ControlFlowOperator`), which can be either `Sequence`, `Alternative`, `Fork` or `Merge`. These operators are similar to the control nodes of UML2 superstructure: `DecisionNode`, `ForkNode` and `MergeNode` [13]. An activity corresponds to a message sending or a message reception, which represents states where a component respectively sends or waits for a message. In our approach, the CFG is context-sensitive since each node in the CFG contains the exchanged-message history, *i.e.*, the trace that brought the component to that state.

Our behavioral contract metamodel is strongly coupled with the system structure metamodel. This enables us to enhance the consistency between these two metamodels. For example, our behavioral metamodel prevents the architect from defining a sent activity of an incoming message in a provided port.

Dataflow Contract Metamodel. Dataflow properties specify the allowed ranges of values of incoming and outgoing messages, represented by the argument metaclass. To specify these properties, we propose an extension to CFGs. As shown in the metamodel of Figure 5, `Activities` in CFGs can be attached to `DataflowSpecification`. A `DataflowSpecification` describes an `Assumption` on a received argument or a `Guarantee` on a sent argument. The assumption and guarantee are expressed with

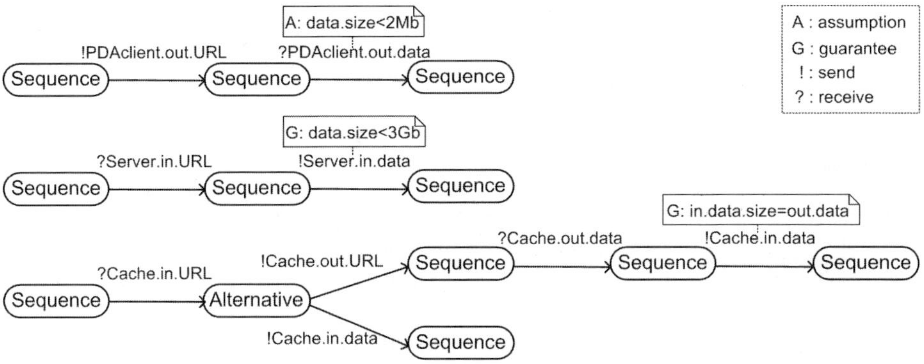

Fig. 6. Control flow and dataflow of `PDAclient`, `Server` and `Cache`

mathematical symbolic and numerical expressions. In our implementation, we use the algebra formalism proposed by the Maxima computer algebra system [14].

PHR Example. In Figure 6, we illustrate the specification of behavioral and dataflow properties with the PHR system shown in Figure 1. The CFGs of `PDAclient`, `Server` and `Cache` are represented with the activity diagram notation. For example, the component `Server` waits for a request (`?Server.in.URL`), then sends the medical data corresponding to the URL (`!Server.in.data`).

4.3 Platform Profiles

To make sure that an architecture designed at the model level can be loaded on a given platform, it is necessary to take into account the platform-specific constraints. For example, the compatibility rules between ports are platform-specific: in Fractal [15], they must have the same type whereas in CCM [16] they must have the same type and the same communication protocol (synchronous/asynchronous). To handle these platform-specific constraints, CALICO provides a means to define platform profiles that contains the set of contract models describing properties specific to a given platform. Once written, a profile may be reused to statically check that an application respects the platform specifications each time this application must be designed for this platform.

5 Static Interaction Analysis

This section presents the step 2 of Section 3.2. AD models are analyzed to detect incompatible, compatible and partially compatible interactions. The analysis is performed statically by the Interaction Analysis tool, which is independent of any platform. This paper focuses on the dataflow analysis, which depends on the behavioral analysis.

5.1 Behavioral Analysis

The goal of this analysis is to produce the CFG of the component assembly from the CFGs of each component. Its computation consists in synchronizing the CFGs of each

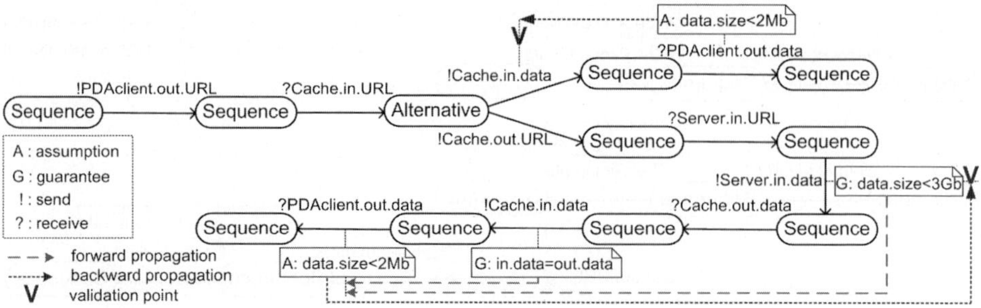

Fig. 7. Dataflow of the PHR system

connected component together. This synchronization is based on process algebras, such as CSP [2], FSP [3] or SFSP [17]. Our approach is different from existing approaches in that the computed CFG is context-sensitive. This context-sensitive characteristic enhances the dataflow validation by enabling the identification of dataflow paths.

5.2 Dataflow Analysis

Dataflow analysis relies on the global CFG computed by the behavioral analysis. Dataflow properties, attached on each node of the CFG, are propagated through the global CFG. This propagation is similar to constant propagation in partial program validation [18]. Since the edges in the CFG represent data transfer, a guarantee is propagated accordingly to the edge direction, *i.e.*, forward direction. On the contrary, an assumption is propagated backwards up to the first alternative or up to the last edge that transfers data involved in the guarantee. Accordingly to this forward/backward propagation, the guarantees and assumptions are propagated to edges in the CFG. These edges represent activities (message sending or reception) where the assumptions need to be checked against the guarantees. The checking can result in one of the following cases:

- the interaction is compatible if $guarantee \rightarrow assumption$.
- the interaction is incompatible if $guarantee \rightarrow \neg assumption$.
- the interaction is partially compatible.

In our approach, we aim to check partially compatible interaction as early as possible. Therefore, among all the activities involved in the error, the earliest activity in the dataflow will be chosen for checking the interaction. A validation point is inserted at the component port involved in this activity. The validation point's error detection condition corresponds to the partially valid equation produced from the resolution of the assumptions given the guarantees. The check will be performed only if the trace of the exchanged messages corresponds to the path of the CFG leading to this activity.

PHR Example. The dataflow graph computed from the assembly of `PDAclient`, `Cache`, and `Server` is shown in Figure 7. The guarantees of the `Cache` and the `Server` are propagated forward up to the end of the flow. The partially resolved assumption of the `PDAclient` is propagated backwards. In the control flow path involving the

`Server`, the propagation stops at the activity `!Server.data` since it is the last activity in which the argument `data` appears. Thus the analysis adds a validation point on the provided port of the component `Server`. The error detection condition is data.size<2Mb and the trace is !PDAclient.out.URL;?Cache.in.URL;!Cache.out.URL;?Server.in.URL; !Server.in.data . Similarly, a second validation point corresponding to the alternative flow path is added on the provided port of the `Cache` component.

6 Runtime Support

The runtime support of CALICO provides three tools to bridge the gap between the model level and the platform level: the Code Instrumentation tool, the Application Loader tool and the Dynamic Validation tool.

6.1 Code Instrumentation Tool

At the platform level, the running application needs to submit runtime information to the model level in order to complete the validation of partially compatible interactions. Nevertheless, not all existing platforms provide support for capturing the required runtime information. Consequently, the Code Instrumentation tool aims to automatically instrument the application code to enable the capture of the needed runtime information, independently of the underlying platform. We focus on the functionality for capturing the trace information since this information is required to check the dataflow properties and most component platforms do not provide tracing support.

To capture the trace, we need to collect the list of the messages going in and out of components through the entire control flow path that is been executed. To do so, component implementation, *i.e.*, source code or bytecode, must be modified. We propose an approach based on aspect weaving [19], which can be applied on any platform, as long as an aspect tool exists for the target programming language. Our tracing support relies on the generation and weaving of three aspects. These aspects are built from the information stored in the system structure AD model. The first aspect enables a component to receive a trace. It adds a `trace` parameter of type `List` to all operations in provided ports (cf Line 1 in Figure 8). It also stores in the list the activity corresponding to the reception of messages (cf Line 2). The second aspect enables a component to return a trace. It replaces the return type of all operations in provided ports by a new object type that encapsulates both the operation result and the trace (cf Line 1). It also creates a new instance `holder` of this new type (cf Line 5), adds to the list the activity corresponding to the send of the returned messages (cf Line 9) and returns the instance (cf Line 10). Finally, the third aspect enables components to send and receive the trace when they invoke provided operations of other components. Just before each call instruction, it adds to the list the activity corresponding to message sending (cf Line 4), then modifies each call to add the `trace` parameter (cf Line 5). Finally, after each call instruction, it stores in the list the activity corresponding to message reception (cf Line 7).

6.2 Application Loader Tool

The Application Loader tool instantiates the running application from the system structure AD model. It analyzes this model and generates the appropriate sequence of *system*

```
public DataProvider_getImage_Result getImage(String url, List<String>  trace) {
   addTraceRequestReception(trace, "getImage");
   ....
   addTraceRequestSending(trace, ref_server, "getImage");
   DataProvider_getImage_Result holder = ref_server.getImage(url, trace);
   trace = holder.getTrace();
   addTraceReponseReception(trace, ref_server,  "getImage");
   ....
   addTraceResponseSending(trace, "getImage" );
   return new DataProvider_getImage_Result(resultImage, trace);
}
```

Fig. 8. Instrumentalized `Cache` implementation

construction operations, such as creating/removing components and connectors. These operations are then translated into calls to the platform-specific API, to build the system. We have identified the correspondence between model-level concepts and concepts of a given target platform. The system construction operations for creating/removing components and connectors have direct corresponding operations in the API of any platform supporting runtime reconfiguration, which is the case of many recent platforms. However, the correspondence with the concept of validation point is not direct, since only a few platforms offer the concept of *interceptor*, which enables a port to intercept sent and received messages.

We propose a generic approach for creating and inserting interceptors in an application, independently of any underlying platform. An interceptor is realized as a component, which is placed between two interacting business components. This component has a pair of provided/required ports for forwarding calls. It intercepts messages, *i.e.*, the argument values and the trace added by the Code Instrumentation tool, and submits them to the Dynamic Validation tool.

6.3 Dynamic Validation Tool

The Dynamic Validation tool receives the runtime information sent by the interceptors. It analyzes it in order to check partially compatible interactions. This tool is decoupled from the underlying platform. It performs error detection at the model level, by evaluating the error detection condition specified in the validation points, against the reified runtime information. When the tool detects an error, it produces design feedback and notifies the architect.

For example in the PHR system, each time the `Server` sends a medical data to the `Cache`, the `Cache` interceptor provides the runtime information to the Dynamic Validation tool. The Dynamic Validation tool evaluates the error detection condition with respect to this information, which contains the data size and the trace. In this case an error occurs if the trace is issued by `PDAclient` and the data size is larger than 2Mb.

7 Implementation Status

We have implemented a Java prototype [1]. The Eclipse Modeling Framework (EMF) is used for generating an editor, which enables architects to visualize or edit the AD

[1] CALICO is available at http://calico.gforge.inria.fr

models. Consequently, architects can graphically manipulate their architecture and do not need to directly use the CALICO metamodels. EMF enables also the generation of model repository code, which offers programmatic support to manipulate the AD models. The EMF model repository code forms the core of all CALICO tools that require manipulating the AD models, *i.e.*, the Interaction Analysis and runtime support tools.

The aspect weaving mechanism to perform code instrumentation has been implemented with Spoon [20], which is a Java code transformation tool. However, this facility could have been implemented with any aspect weaving tools that support changes of both method contents and method arguments.

The Application Loader tool, which requires the ability to instantiate an application on a given platform, is organized into two parts: a generic part that generates system construction operations from a system structure AD model, and a *platform driver*, which translates the system construction operations into calls to the platform-specific API. This design choice allows the flexible support of different platforms. In our current prototype we have implemented the platform driver for the Fractal platform.

8 Related Work

Plastik is an ADL/Component runtime integration meta-framework [21]. Like our approach, Plastik combines a generic high-level view of a component-based architecture with a runtime platform. Their high-level view is based on an extension of Acme/Armani [7,8] and the runtime platform is OpenCom [22]. At the ADL level, Plastik allows the checking of Armani invariants expressed with a first order logic. Plastik is dedicated to support reconfiguration at both the ADL and platform levels. Nevertheless, the ADL level used in Plastik is less precise than the CALICO system structure metamodel. With Plastik, it is not possible to monitor the value of the arguments exchanged between the components. Indeed, the only runtime properties that can be reified at the ADL level correspond to dedicated operations. So, in Plastik, components must be implemented in a specific way so that they export their properties. In our approach, we can directly intercept data exchanged between components at the platform level and reify data at the model level without impacting the way of how components are implemented. Thus, our approach is completely transparent for the architect and developers.

Hein *et al.* [23] propose an approach to monitor and check a runtime system using models at runtime. To do so, they reify a runtime system by making a model snapshot and then check OCL constraints on the snapshot. In our approach, we reify the runtime information differently. First, our system structure model is kept during the execution of the system and we do not need to perform snapshot. Moreover, the architect can specify at the model level the runtime information that must be reified using the concept of validation point. Thus, only the needed exchanged data for performing validation at the model level is reified, whereas in [23] even useless runtime information is reified.

In some approaches, when validations can not be performed statically because of information that will only be known at runtime, tests are directly inserted in the runtime system. For example, [24] allows the architect to specify pre and post conditions on an architecture written with Acme/Armani. All of these conditions are transformed into executable assertions at runtime without performing partial validation. ConFract enables the architect to specify contracts, like our dataflow contracts, on components at the ADL level [4]. Nevertheless they are all transformed into runtime tests and no static validation is performed. In our approach, we perform a partial validation on the dataflow at the model level using backward and forward analysis like in [18]. The result of the partial validation is used to insert in the runtime system only the needed tests to check the partially valid interactions. Thus, these tests are inserted at the earliest in the dataflow, which facilitates the identification of the source of the error.

9 Conclusion

We have presented CALICO, a Component AssembLy Interaction Control framewOrk, to support the design and interaction checking of component-based systems in an iterative software design process. Our framework provides several metamodels to enable architects to specify a system architecture through several views. The models do not only serve for documenting the architecture but are associated with a set of mechanisms for reasoning on it, in particular, for verifying interaction compatibility. Our approach goes beyond traditional interaction verifications, which generally invalidate interactions whose compatibility is not determinable at design time. We introduce the notion of validation points, which specify interactions to be checked and conditions to be evaluated for detecting errors at execution time.

Another advantage of our approach is the coupling between the model level, where architects design the system, and the platform level, where the system prototype is executed to be dynamically validated for a given context. This coupling enables runtime information captured at the platform level to be reified and checked at the model level. Consequently, architects can easily locate model elements that could lead to runtime errors and adjust their design accordingly.

CALICO offers generic concepts that can be applied to multiple platforms. Those concepts concern both the design activity and the dynamic validation activity. Regarding the design activity, our framework offers modeling concepts that are platform-independent. The interaction validation mechanisms proposed at the model level can thus be used for checking applications on any component model platform. Regarding the dynamic validation activity, CALICO offers generic concepts for instrumenting an application so that its dynamic validation mechanism does not rely on platform-specific mechanisms for reifying runtime information.

Future work includes several extensions to the CALICO framework. First, we plan to develop several platform drivers to support other component model platforms than Fractal. Furthermore, we would like our framework to support QoS properties, such as response time, which will require the definition of a QoS metamodel and the update of the Code Instrumentation tool.

References

1. Medvidovic, N., Taylor, R.N.: A classification and comparison framework for software architecture description languages. IEEE Trans. on Software Engineering 26(1) (January 2000)
2. Hoare, C.: Communicating Sequential Processes. Prentice Hall, Englewood Cliffs (2004)

3. Magee, J.: Behavioral analysis of software architecture using ltsa. In: Proceedings of the 21st international conference on Software engineering, pp. 634–637. IEEE Computer Society, Los Alamitos (1999)
4. Collet, P., Rousseau, R.: Efficient Implementation Techniques for Advanced Assertion Languages. RSTI - Série L'Objet (RSTI-Objet) 5(3-4), 417–442 (1999)
5. Nunziati, S.: Personal health record, `www.d-m-p.org/docs/EnglishVersionDMP.pdf`
6. Sriplakich, P., Waignier, G., Le Meur, A.F.: Enabling dynamic co-evolution of models and runtime applications. In: Proceedings of the 1st IEEE International Workshop on Model-Driven Development of Autonomic Systems (MDDAS 2008), Turku, Finland, July 2008. IEEE Computer Society, Los Alamitos (to appear, 2008)
7. Garlan, D., Monroe, R.T., Wile, D.: Acme: Architectural description of component-based systems. In: Foundations of Component-Based Systems. Cambridge University Press, Cambridge (2000)
8. Monroe, R.T.: Capturing Software Architecture Design Expertise with Armani (2001)
9. Dashofy, E.M., der Hoek, A.V., Taylor, R.N.: A highly-extensible, XML-based architecture description language. In: Proceedings of the Working IEEE/IFIP Conference on Software Architecture (WICSA 2001). IEEE Computer Society, Los Alamitos (2001)
10. OMG: Object Constraint Language (OCL). 2.0 edn. (May 2006)
11. Allen, F.E.: Control flow analysis. SIGPLAN Not. 5(7), 1–19 (1970)
12. Russell, N., ter Hofstede, A.H., van der Aalst, W.M., Mulyar, N.: Workflow control-flow patterns: A revised view. BPM Center Report BPM-06-22
13. OMG: Unified Modeling Language (UML): Superstructure, v2.1.1 (August 2007)
14. Maxima: a computer algebra system, `http://maxima.sourceforge.net`
15. Bruneton, E., Coupaye, T., Leclercq, M., Quéma, V., Stefani, J.B.: An open component model and its support in Java. In: Crnković, I., Stafford, J.A., Schmidt, H.W., Wallnau, K. (eds.) CBSE 2004. LNCS, vol. 3054. Springer, Heidelberg (2004)
16. OMG: CORBA Component Model, v4.0, formal/06-04-01(April 2006)
17. Barais, O., Lawall, J., Le Meur, A.F., Duchien, L.: Safe integration of new concerns in a software architecture. In: Proceedings of the 13th Annual IEEE International Conference on Engineering of Computer Based Systems (ECBS 2006). IEEE Computer Society, Los Alamitos (2006)
18. Kildall, G.: A unified approach to global program optimization. In: 1st Annual ACM SIGACT-SIGPLAN Symposium on Principles of Programming Languages (1973)
19. Kiczales, G., Lamping, J., Mendhekar, A., Maeda, C., Lopes, C., Loingtier, J.M., Irwin, J.: Aspect-oriented programming. In: Akşit, M., Matsuoka, S. (eds.) ECOOP 1997. LNCS, vol. 1241. Springer, Heidelberg (1997)
20. Pawlak, R.: Spoon: Compile-time annotation processing for middleware. IEEE Distributed Systems Online 7(11) (November 2006)
21. Batistal, T., Joolia, A., Coulson, G.: Managing dynamic reconfiguration in component-based systems. In: Morrison, R., Oquendo, F. (eds.) EWSA 2005. LNCS, vol. 3527, pp. 1–17. Springer, Heidelberg (2005)
22. Coulson, G., Blair, G., Grace, P., Joolia, A., Lee, K., Ueyama, J.: Opencom v2: A component model for building systems software. In: IASTED Software Engineering and Applications (2004)
23. Hein, C., Ritter, T., Wagner, M.: System monitoring using constraint checking as part of model based system management. In: International Workshop Models@run.time (2007)
24. Jung, H., Rubio-Medrano, C.E., Wong, W.E., Cheon, Y.: Architectural Assertions: Checking Architecrural Constraints at Run-Time

Formal Definition of MOF 2.0 Metamodel Components and Composition

Ingo Weisemöller and Andy Schürr

Fachgebiet Echtzeitsysteme
Technische Universität Darmstadt
D-64283 Darmstadt, Germany
{weisemoeller,schuerr}@es.tu-darmstadt.de

Abstract. The Meta Object Facility (MOF) is one of the most frequently used languages for the definition of a DSL's abstract syntax. However, its lack of sophisticated modularization concepts in comparison to GPLs such as Ada or component-oriented ADLs makes it hard to maintain a large number of complex metamodels. MOF 2.0 packages can be used to a certain extent to define, refine, and compose language descriptions, but do not offer appropriate support for information hiding as well as for the specification of parametrizable metamodeling components. Motivated by a running example we, therefore, extend MOF 2.0 with concepts for the specification of proper metamodel components with provided export and required import interfaces. Furthermore, we present a formalization of a metamodel component composition operator based on graph morphisms. The resulting component-oriented version of MOF allows language developers to describe reoccurring, parametrizable sublanguages once and instantiate them differently in several metamodels.

Keywords: Metamodeling, MOF 2.0, software components, reusability.

1 Introduction

For the development of visual domain-specific modeling languages (VDSMLs), it is common practice to define their abstract syntax in a metamodel. Among others, the Meta Object Facility [8] (MOF) version 2.0 – as standardized by the OMG – is one of the most frequently used metamodeling languages. However, in comparison to modern general purpose languages (GPLs), it lacks sophisticated modularization concepts. This makes the definition of complex VDSMLs such as UML together with the maintenance of a large number of complex metamodels and reuse of metamodel fragments still rather inconvenient. MOF 2.0 packages and namespaces offer some support for the definition of metamodel components, but they neither distinguish between externally visible and internal structure of a component nor do they allow for the parametrization and instantiation of components with different parameter bindings. Furthermore, there is no way to describe the fact that one package relies on metamodeling elements from other packages, unless these elements are explicitly imported from a specific package.

K. Czarnecki et al. (Eds.): MoDELS 2008, LNCS 5301, pp. 386–400, 2008.

In comparison to MOF 2.0, programming languages such as Ada offer rather complex concepts for the definition and instantiation of generic, parametrized packages. The same is true for component-oriented architecture description languages (ADLs) or algebraic specification languages which introduced parametrized modules with export and import interfaces together with appropriate mapping morphisms more than 20 years ago. In this contribution we adopt the modularization concepts of algebraic specification languages and upgrade MOF metamodel packages to proper components with an arbitrary number of export and import interfaces: Export interfaces identify submodels of metamodel components that are visible to the outside world, whereas import interfaces identify parameter submodels that have to be instantiated and replaced by exported elements of other metamodel components. In the following we introduce a metamodel composition operator that creates new metamodel components by instantiating already defined components and by binding their required import interfaces to corresponding provided export interfaces of other components. Relying on a graph-transformation-based formalization of MOF 2.0 we define correct binding relationships between export and import interfaces as graph morphisms.

Since we present an approach to compose metamodels, our ideas are independent of a concrete syntax. However, most languages in of our areas of application use graphical notations. Therefore, we focus on visual modeling languages in the following chapters, which are organized as follows: In Section 2 we motivate our work based on some general remarks on reusability of visual modeling languages. We also discuss similar work from related domains including category-theory based modularization concepts for algebraic specification languages and graph grammars. A sample language from Section 3 is then used to illustrate the basic ideas of the definitions and theorems introduced in the remaining chapters. Section 4 introduces some basic definitions from another publication, where we presented a graph-transformation-based formalization of MOF 2.0 metamodels and metamodel transformations. We define our approach for metamodel composition in Section 5 and list some constraints for this composition in Section 6. Finally, we give a short summary of our work and outline some ideas for future enhancements in Sections 7 and 8.

2 Applicability and Related Work

Until today most VDSMLs and their abstract syntax and static semantics definitions in the form of metamodels are created from scratch. Nevertheless, when people start to study and compare existing VDSMLs and their metamodels they are able to identify a rapidly increasing number of reoccurring concepts and patterns. Based on our experiences in this area, we identified at least three categories or dimensions of reoccurring visual language definition concepts and patterns:

1. VDSMLs can be classified with respect to certain *structural properties*. For instance, most VDSMLs introduce named elements and namespaces. Others introduce type-instance-relations or provide modularization concepts. We often encounter a combination of multiple structural properties in a language.

2. A second dimension for the characterization of VDSMLs is determined by the *modeling paradigm* adopted by these languages. Among others, we can distinguish between control flow languages, data flow languages, rule based languages or languages dealing with entities and relations. Rather often, VDSMLs consist of sublanguages that adopt different modeling paradigms.
3. Furthermore, we can categorize VDSMLs by their *application domain*. For instance, languages from the area of business process modeling as well as languages designed to model software for supply and control units share a certain pool of common modeling concepts.

Previous scientific contributions have published similar observations and developed proposals how to increase the degree of reuse of metamodeling concepts, patterns, and fragments during the specification of new VDSMLs. For instance, Andreas Winter suggests some "reference meta schemes" for visual modeling languages in [11]. According to the categorizations described above, these schemes are basically components dealing either with modeling paradigms (such as control flow or data flow paradigm) or with structural properties such as type-instance-relations. Emerson and Sztipanovits suggest to instantiate templates to improve reusability of solutions to problems in language design [4]. Another template based approach to reusability of language components is presented by Amalio et al. in [2]. Indeed, templates for MOF seem to be a sensible and straight-forward realizable approach. They are similar to templates for UML class diagrams, which are supported by several CASE tools. The main drawback of a template-based reuse approach is that it neither supports information hiding (by means of export interfaces) nor comes with a precisely defined composition operator that takes a number of templates as input and produces another template as output. Moreover, multiple usages of a template will result in multiple instances of that template, which need to be maintained separately, whereas a single metamodel component may be reused for several languages.

To summarize, all publications we are aware of that study the problem of reusable VDSML definitions neither introduce proper metamodel components with provided export interfaces and required import interfaces nor present a precise formalization of interface binding or parameter instantiation and component composition operations as presented here. Our approach for the formal definition of metamodel components is inspired by category-based modularization concepts for algebraic specification languages that were invented about 20 years ago. For a detailed contribution on this, the reader is referred to [3]. Algebraic modularization concepts have been adapted in the past to handle the distribution of large graphs. For instance, Taentzer introduces a definition of network graphs in [10, pp. 103ff, 115ff], where parts of each local graph can be made available in interface graphs for other local graphs. In this way, a morphism between local graphs is defined, which allows to perform distributed graph transformations. When describing a transformation, it is transparent whether it runs on a local or a remote graph. The ideas behind this definition of distributed graphs are similar to our ideas how to compose metamodel components, but while Taentzer lies a main emphasis on the manipulation of a connected network of graph components we put the focus on the component composition operator itself.

Finally we have to mention approaches for the component-oriented development of textual domain-specific languages. For example, the MontiCore Framework allows to compose a language from several grammars [5]. However, these concepts are grammar-based and can, therefore, not be applied to metamodel fragments. Furthermore, the existence of reasonable concepts for the component-oriented definition of textual languages just underlines the fact that similar concepts for the design of metamodel based languages have to be developed urgently.

3 Running Example

As an example for the applicability of metamodel composition concepts we introduce the development of a language from the domain of document management (Fig. 1). It consists of three parts, which we have kept as small as possible:

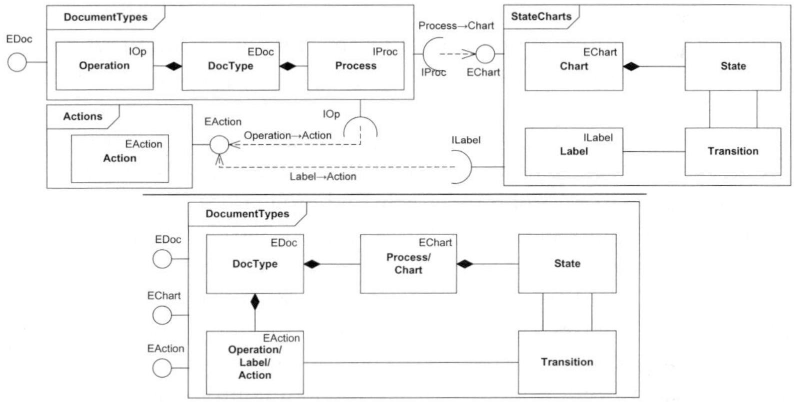

Fig. 1. Document Management Language: Components (top) and Composed Result

1. A document language, which is used to describe various types of documents. For these types, possible processes on the actual documents can be defined. In an insurance company for instance, there are applications for insurance and forms for the processing of damage event as document types. The steps from the receipt of a document to its archival storage will differ depending on its type, so it useful to define a different process for each document type.
2. A statechart language, which can be used to model processes in a state-based manner. It uses labels at the transitions to describe the concrete document manipulating operations between two states.
3. An action language, which is no closer specified here. In our example, it is intended to describe operations on certain kinds of documents. It is important to note that such a language should be replaceable by a different one, for instance depending on whether operations should be specified in a graphical or a text-based manner.

As shown in the example, metamodel components can have export (or provided) and import (or required) interfaces containing elements of the component. The interfaces a (meta-)class belongs to are shown in the upper right corner of the class. (Meta-)Associations, generalizations or other types of relations between classes may belong to export and import interfaces, too—but are neither imported nor exported in our running example.

When the parts of our document language are combined, each import interface is bound to an export interface of a different component, as indicated by the dashed arrows in the figure. The result of this composition of three components with the annotated renaming directives results in the metamodel component shown at the bottom of Figure 1. A concrete syntax and tools for a domain specific language could be developed on top of this resulting component.

A language developed on top of the new metamodel allows to describe several types of documents. For each type, a set of valid operations can be defined in the action language. Besides this, a document managing process can be defined in the statechart language. It is important to notice that the transition labels of the statechart language and the operations in the document language are mapped to the same metaclass of the action language. This represents the fact that the steps leading from one state to another are operations on the documents and will, therefore, be described in the language for document operations.

The composition of metamodel components, as shown in the example, is motivated for two reasons: First, a statechart language is *reusable* not only for the area of document management, but also for a variety of different domains. Second, several action languages could be used to describe document transformations; these languages should be *exchangeable* with each other, provided they are appropriate for the description of operations on documents.

Although we use a small and artificial language here, there are several larger examples of practical relevance where metamodel composition should be used. For instance, the UML infrastructure [6] is used by the UML superstructure [7] as well as by MOF [8]. Moreover, constraints written in OCL [9] can be embedded in either of these languages.

4 Previous Work and Preliminaries

In order to give a definition of metamodel components and their composition, we will obviously need an understanding of what a metamodel is. For the definition of metamodels, we use a simplified version of the one given in [1], which formalizes models and metamodels as graphs as well as the mapping between a model and its metamodel as graph morphism.

Definition 1 (Metamodel)
A metamodel MM is a four-tuple $MM := (C, A, first, second)$, where

C	*is the finite set of (meta-)classes,*
A	*is the finite set of (meta-)associations,*
$first : A \to C$	*is the mapping of associations to their first end,*
$second : A \to C$	*is the mapping of associations to their second end.*

The limitation to (meta-)classes and (meta-)associations—in the sequel simply termed classes and associations—makes metamodels much simpler than MOF models are. Nevertheless, we can argue that this limitation in the context of this paper is not too restrictive for the following reasons.

First, we get rid of packages due to the fact that they are replaced by the more expressive concept of metamodel components. Second, we ignore features of classifiers in a metamodel for the time being. We simply assume that the interfaces of our metamodel components contain classes and associations as atomic elements, which are imported respectively exported with all of their features. An appropriate extension of the definitions and theorems of this paper would be rather straight-forward handling features of classifiers like associations between classes. Third, primitive types, data types and enumerations are omitted. Concerning their occurrence in metamodels, components and interfaces and their reusability, these elements are very similar to classes, so they are left out here because they would have blown up our definitions unnecessarily. We also leave out generalization as well as property subsets or redefinitions in this first step to metamodel composition. Nevertheless, we are aware of the fact that these concepts will be of importance later on, and we discuss some of the problems related to their introduction informally in Section 7.

Although our definition of metamodels could be used to describe an arbitrary language consisting of entities and binary relations, we will limit our considerations to MOF in the following. A formal, MOF-compliant definition of metamodel instantiations and model transformations on these instances is given by Amelunxen et al. in [1]. We refer to this article for details, since our contribution is focused on composing metamodels, and therefore restricted to the M2 level.

5 Definition of MOF 2.0 Meta-modeling Composition

Our approach of metamodel composition is based on components with import and export interfaces. Such interfaces can be part of any metamodel component, and each import interface must be bound to an appropriate export interface at latest when the component is instantiated. An exported interface must obviously only contain classes and associations from the metamodel component it is provided by. We demand the same for import interfaces, since the classes and associations of such an interface should be present as placeholders before binding it to an export interface of a different metamodel. Therefore, we define a metamodel component with (export and import) interfaces as follows:

Definition 2 (Metamodel Component)
A metamodel component MMC is a six-tuple
$MMC := (C, A, first, second, Import, Export)$, *where*

$(C, A, first, second)$	*is a metamodel (cf. Definition 1)*
$Import$	*is the set of import (or required) interfaces and*
$Export$	*is the set of export (or provided) interfaces.*

An interface $i \in Import \cup Export$ *is a metamodel* $i := (C_i, A_i, first_i, second_i)$ *as introduced in Definition 1. The following properties must hold for* i*:*

$$
\begin{aligned}
&C_i \subseteq C \\
&A_i \subseteq A \\
&\forall a \in A_i \mid first_i(a) = first(a) \wedge second_i(a) = second(a) \ (*)
\end{aligned}
$$

A metamodel component is called *concrete* if it has no import interfaces and *generic* otherwise. Now that we have defined what import and export interfaces actually are, we have to introduce a way to bind elements in an import interface to elements in an export interface provided by a different metamodel component. Thus, the placeholders (the elements of the importing metamodel component contained in the import interface) are mapped to concrete implementations of the exporting component.

Definition 3 (Interface Binding)
Let $i = (C_i, A_i, first_i, second_i)$ *be an import and* $e = (C_e, A_e, first_e, second_e)$ *be an export interface. An interface binding* h *of* i *to* e *is a total morphism*

$$
\begin{aligned}
h &:= (h_c, h_a) : C_i \cup A_i \rightarrow C_e \cup A_e \ \textit{with} \\
h_c &: C_i \rightarrow C_e \ \textit{and} \\
h_a &: A_i \rightarrow A_e
\end{aligned}
$$

such that $h(first_i(a)) = first_e(h(a))$ *and* $h(second_i(a)) = second_e(h(a))$ *for all* $a \in A_i$*.*

An interface binding can be used to determine concrete implementation classes and associations for all placeholders in the import interface of a metamodel component. Thus, two components (such as the statechart and the action language in the example) can be combined to a single one by the following combination rules.

Definition 4 (Intermediate Result of Interface Binding). *Let*

$$
\begin{aligned}
MMC_i &= (C_i, A_i, first_i, second_i, Import_i, Export_i) \ \textit{and} \\
MMC_e &= (C_e, A_e, first_e, second_e, Import_e, Export_e) \ \textit{be metamodel components,} \\
i &= (C_{import}, A_{import}, first_{import}, second_{import}) \in Import_i, \\
e &= (C_{export}, A_{export}, first_{export}, second_{export}) \in Export_e \ \textit{and} \\
h &= (h_c, h_a) : C_{import} \cup A_{import} \rightarrow C_{export} \cup A_{export}
\end{aligned}
$$

be an interface binding from i *to* e*. The metamodel component*

$$
\begin{aligned}
MMC &= (C, A, first, second, Import, Export) \ \textit{with} \\
C &= C_i \cup C_e, \\
A &= A_i \cup A_e, \\
first(a) &= first_i(a), \ \textit{if } a \in A_i \ \textit{and} \\
first(a) &= first_e(a), \ \textit{if } a \in A_e, \\
second(a) &= second_i(a), \ \textit{if } a \in A_i \ \textit{and} \\
second(a) &= second_e(a), \ \textit{if } a \in A_e, \\
Import &= (Import_i \cup Import_e) \setminus \{i\} \ \textit{and} \\
Export &= Export_i \cup Export_e
\end{aligned}
$$

is called the intermediate resulting metamodel component of the interface binding h. This intermediate result contains both classes and associations from the import interface and the corresponding elements from the export interface. For these elements, we define the binary relations $\sim_C$ and $\sim_A$ on MMC as follows:

$$c_i \in C_{import} \sim_C c_{export} \in C_e \Leftrightarrow h_c(c_i) = c_e \textit{ and}$$
$$a_i \in A_{import} \sim_A a_e \in A_{export} \Leftrightarrow h_a(a_i) = a_e.$$

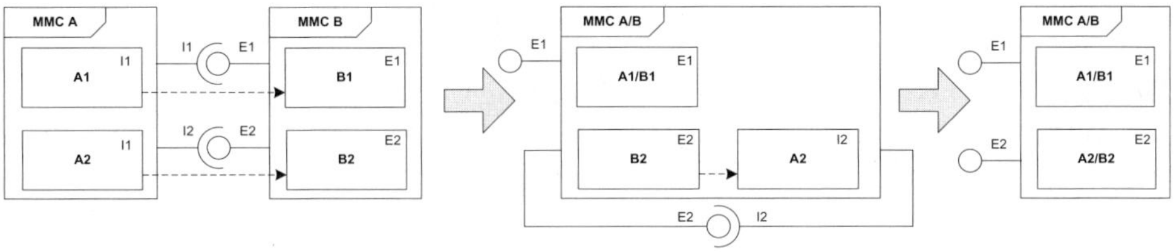

Fig. 2. Binding of Multiple Interfaces Between two Components

The composition described above can also be applied to multiple interfaces between two components. In this case, the interfaces can be bound sequentially as shown in Figure 2. Please note that classes mapped to each other (as indicated by the dashed arrows) are drawn as a single class in the resulting metamodel component. Obviously this is the desired result for the resulting language description. The underlying formalization of the identification of classes (and associations) from different metamodel components by means of equivalence relations is presented in Definition 5.

Complex languages will typically have multiple interfaces, and some of the export interfaces may provide classes or associations from import interfaces such as the class in *MMC*2 of Figure 3. The mapping between classes are indicated by dashed arrows in the figure that correspond to the previously introduced relation $\sim_C$. Based on the definitions of the relations $\sim_C$ and $\sim_A$ for all bindings of export to import interfaces in Figure 3 we construct equivalence relations $\equiv_C$ and $\equiv_A$ on the intermediate result $MMC = (C, A, first, second, Import, Export)$ as the symmetric, reflexive, transitive closure of all relations $\sim_C$ and $\sim_A$. These equivalence relations are needed to construct the final metamodel component that has equivalence classes of *MMC* as its own metamodeling elements.

Let us take a look at the classes of our sample language: The class Process is mapped to Chart, so these classes are in the same equivalence class. Both Operation and Label are mapped to Action, which results in an equivalence class with three elements. Altogether, we construct the following equivalence classes:

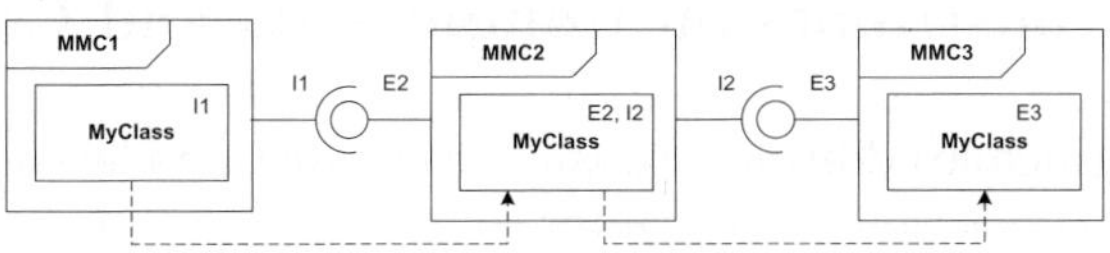

Fig. 3. Example of a Class Present in an Export and an Import Interface

$$\begin{aligned}
[DocType]_C &= \{\text{DocType}\}\\
[Chart]_C &= \{\text{Process, Chart}\}\\
[State]_C &= \{\text{State}\}\\
[Action]_C &= \{\text{Operation, Label, Action}\}\\
[Transition]_C &= \{\text{Transition}\}
\end{aligned}$$

Since associations do not occur in interfaces in this language, each association builds its own equivalence class. We can use the equivalence classes $[]_C$ and $[]_A$ to define the (final) resulting metamodel component.

Definition 5 (Result of Interface Binding)
Let $MMC = (C, A, first, second, Import, Export)$ be the intermediate result of interface bindings between an arbitrary (but finite) number of metamodel components. The (final) result of these bindings is a metamodel component, too:

$$\begin{aligned}
MMC_{red} &= (C_{red}, A_{red}, first_{red}, second_{red}, Import, Export) \text{ with}\\
C_{red} &= C \,/ \equiv_C,\\
A_{red} &= A \,/ \equiv_A,\\
first_{red} &: A_{red} \to C_{red}\\
&\quad [a]_A \mapsto [first(a)]_C \text{ for all } a \in A \text{ and}\\
second_{red} &: A_{red} \to C_{red}\\
&\quad [a]_A \mapsto [second(a)]_C \text{ for all } a \in A.
\end{aligned}$$

Lemma 1 (Well-Definedness of Interface Binding)
The result of interface bindings between metamodel components is well-defined.

Proof. We have to show that $first(a_i)$ maps to the same equivalence class $[c]_C \in C \,/ \equiv_C$ for all a_i in an equivalence class $[a]_A$. The proof for $second(a)$ is analogous, so we will skip it.

Let a_0, a_n be associations from the same equivalence class, i.e. $a_0 \equiv_A a_n$. Then we have a sequence of bindings $h_1, \ldots, h_n$ and a sequence of associations $a_1, \ldots, a_{n-1}$ with either $h_i(a_{i-1}) = a_i$ or $h_i(a_i) = a_{i-1}$ for all $1 \le i \le n$. If we can show $first(a_i) \equiv_C first(a_{i-1})$, then the lemma follows from the transitivity of $\equiv_C$. Without loss of generality, we can assume $h_i(a_{i-1}) = a_i$. Thus holds

$$\begin{aligned}
first(h_i(a_{i-1})) &= first(a_i)\\
\Leftrightarrow h_i(first(a_{i-1})) &= first(a_i) \text{ (by the definition of morphism } h_i)\\
\Leftrightarrow \quad first(a_{i-1}) &\sim_C first(a_i) \text{ (by the definition of } \sim_C)\\
\Rightarrow \quad first(a_{i-1}) &\equiv_C first(a_i) \text{ (by the definition of } \equiv_C)
\end{aligned}$$

6 Further Constraints on Components and Composition

In this section, we define additional constraints on metamodel components, interfaces and their composition to guarantee some important properties of composite metamodel components. We distinguish between properties for three levels of consistency:

1. *Static semantics compositionality constraints* ensure that the results of metamodel component composition are unambiguous and well-defined metamodel components with respect to the constructed metamodel element equivalence classes.
2. *Static semantics MOF consistency constraints* guarantee that applying our approach to valid MOF models results in valid MOF models again. Due to lack of space, we present a small number of possible violations of this kind of constraints rather than an exhaustive list of this category.
3. *Dynamic semantics compositionality constraints* finally deal with the compatibility of the metamodel component composition operator and the composition operator of their implementations as, e.g., generated by our metamodeling environment MOFLON. Once again, we will only present a subset of possible issues and solutions here.

Constraints of the first category are presented in this chapter. For the combination of components preserving these constraints we also show some important consequences for the resulting metamodel component. Properties of the second and third category are numerous, but can only be discussed briefly and informally in Section 7.

The first constraint to be introduced is required to ensure the above mentioned consistency of a composite component's equivalence classes of modeling elements. In the general case, a metamodel component may have an arbitrary number of import and export interfaces, and each metaclass and -association may be contained in an arbitrary number of export interfaces. As a consequence, it is possible to define interface bindings between a set of metamodeling component instances such that (1) a single placeholder metamodel element shared by two import interfaces is mapped onto more than one concrete metamodeling element or (2) a placeholder metamodel element shared by an export and an import interface is finally mapped onto itself through a cycle of export/import interface bindings. Both cases generate a metamodel component that is consistent from a syntactic and even MOF static semantics point of view, but contains equivalence classes with some undesired properties. The following constraint deals with issue (1) above, whereas the second constraint introduced below will address issue (2):

Constraint 1 (Disjoint Import Interfaces)
Let $MMC = (C, A, first, second, Import, Export)$ *be a metamodel component. The following property must hold:*

$$\begin{aligned} \forall\, I_1 &= (C_1, A_1, first_1, second_1) \in Import, \\ I_2 &= (C_2, A_2, first_2, second_2) \in Import \mid \\ I_1 &\neq I_2 \Rightarrow C_1 \cap C_2 = \emptyset. \end{aligned}$$

Remark 1. The associations in different import interfaces are disjoint if their classes are disjoint. This follows directly from property (∗) in Definition 2.

We also want to ensure that each element of a metamodel component is finally mapped to a concrete implementation. Therefore, let us take a look at the equivalence relations $\equiv_C$ and $\equiv_A$. The elements of each equivalence class and the mappings between them build the internal graph of the equivalence class:

Definition 6 (Internal Graph of an Equivalence Class)
Let $MMC = (\equiv_C, \equiv_A, first, second, Import, Export)$ *a metamodel component which results of mappings* $h_1, \ldots, h_n$. *For each* $[r] \in \equiv_C \cup \equiv_A$, *the internal graph of* $[r]$ *is the directed graph* $G_{[r]} = (V_{[r]}, E_{[r]})$ *with*

$$V_{[r]} = \{r\prime \mid r\prime \equiv r\}$$
$$E_{[r]} = \{(v1 \in V_{[r]}, v2 \in V_{[r]}) \mid \exists\, h_i : h_i(v1) = v2\}.$$

Constraint 2 (Acyclic Imports)
In a metamodel component $MMC = (\equiv_C, \equiv_A, first, second, Import, Export)$, *for each equivalence class* $[r] \in \equiv_C \cup \equiv_A$ *the internal graph* $G_{[r]}$ *must be acyclic.*

Theorem 1 (Existence of Unique Representatives)
Let $MMC_1, \ldots, MMC_n$ *be metamodel components with disjoint import interfaces and* $MMC = (\equiv_C, \equiv_A, first, second, Import, Export)$ *the result of interface binding for these components. For all equivalence classes* $[r] \in \equiv_C \cup \equiv_A$ *holds:*

$G_{[r]} = (V_{[r]}, E_{[r]})$ *is connected.* (1)
$deg^+(v) \leq 1\ \forall v \in V_{[r]}$. (2)
If $G_{[r]}$ *is acyclic, the graph has exactly one sink, called its* representative. (3)

Proof (sketch). The graph is connected by the definition of the equivalence classes. The outdegree of a vertex cannot be greater than 1 because of the disjointness of import interfaces. The existence of a sink can be proved by induction over the number of nodes. The idea for the induction step is that the n_{th} node of an equivalence class is connected to a subgraph with $n-1$ nodes. If the new node is a sink, then the old sink (from the subgraph) must be mapped to the new node because the outdegree of nodes must not be greater than 1.

Remark 2. The representative of an equivalence class in a compound metamodel is not bound to any other class. Thus, if the compound metamodel is completely bound (i.e. it has no unbound import interfaces), the representative must be a concrete element. This means, that for every bound placeholder, we have one and only one implementation: the representative of its equivalence class.

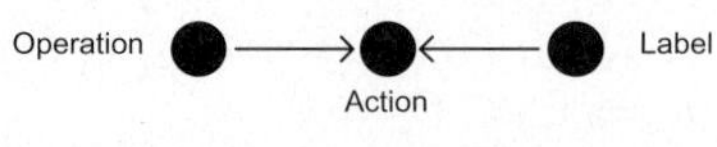

Fig. 4. Internal Graph of an Equivalence Class from the Sample Language

The internal graph of the equivalence class $[Action]_C$ from our sample language is shown in Figure 4. The classes Operation and Label are both mapped to Action, which is the representative of this equivalence class.

When a language definition is composed of multiple metamodeling components, which may in turn be composites, the order in which the interface bindings are processed might matter. We can show that, according to our construction, this order does not have an impact on the result.

Theorem 2 (Associativity of Interface Binding)
Let MMC_1, MMC_2, MMC_3 *be metamodel components, each of them with* $MMC_i = (C_i, A_i, first_i, second_i, Imp_i, Exp_i)$, *furthermore*

$h_1 : I_1 \in Imp_1 \rightarrow E_2 \in Exp_2$ *and*
$h_2 : I_2 \in Imp_2 \rightarrow E_3 \in Exp_3$ *be interface bindings and*
$MMC_i \circ MMC_{i+1}$ *be the result of composing* MMC_i *and* MMC_{i+1} *with interface binding* h_i.

Then the internal graphs (cf. Definition 6) of the equivalence classes in $(MMC_1 \circ MMC_2) \circ MMC_3$ *and* $MMC_1 \circ (MMC_2 \circ MMC_3)$ *are isomorphic.*

Proof (sketch). We only prove that the node sets of the internal graphs of a metaclass are equal; the edges do not differ according to the definition of the graph and the proof for associations is analogous. If $E_2 \cap I_2 = \emptyset$ the claim holds, because there is no sequence of mappings for which we need to show associativity. So let $c_1 \in I_1$, $c_2 \in E_2 \cap I_2$ and $c_3 \in E_3$ be classes with $h_1(c_1) = c_2$ and $h_2(c_2) = c_3$. We label the node set in the internal graph of an equivalence class of c in a component MMC as $V_{[c]_{MMC}}$. For $(MMC_1 \circ MMC_2) \circ MMC_3$ we get

$$V_{[c_1]_{(MMC_1 \circ MMC_2)}} = \{c_1, c_2\} \quad \text{(because } h_1(c_1) = c_2\text{) and}$$
$$V_{[c_1]_{(MMC_1 \circ MMC_2) \circ MMC_3}} = \{c_1, c_2, c_3\} \quad \text{(because } h_2(c_2) = c_3\text{).}$$

and for $MMC_1 \circ (MMC_2 \circ MMC_3)$ we get

$$V_{[c_2]_{(MMC_2 \circ MMC_3)}} = \{c_2, c_3\} \quad \text{(because } h_2(c_2) = c_3\text{) and}$$
$$V_{[c_1]_{MMC_1 \circ (MMC_2 \circ MMC_3)}} = \{c_1, c_2, c_3\} \quad \text{(because } h_1(c_1) = c_2\text{), so}$$
$$V_{[c_1]_{(MMC_1 \circ MMC_2) \circ MMC_3}} = V_{[c_1]_{MMC_1 \circ (MMC_2 \circ MMC_3)}}.$$

The last theorem we show for our definition of metamodel component composition is probably the most important one. For each component of a resulting language, we can map each class and association to its representative. This mapping is a total morphism, i.e. for the classes and associations of each component there are corresponding elements in the resulting language, and the structure of the components is preserved.

Theorem 3 (Total Morphism from Components to Result of Composition)
Let Let $MMC = (C, A, first, second, Import, Export)$ *be a metamodel component and* $MMC_{res} = (C_{res}, A_{res}, first_{res}, second_{res}, \emptyset, Export_{res})$ *be the result of binding all interfaces of* MMC *to other metamodels. Then the mapping*

$$h_{res} := (h_c, h_a)$$
$$h_c \quad : C \rightarrow C_{res} \text{ with } c \mapsto [c]_{C_{res}} \text{ for all } c \in C$$
$$h_a \quad : A \rightarrow A_{res} \text{ with } a \mapsto [a]_{A_{res}} \text{ for all } a \in A$$

is a total morphism.

Proof. The mapping is well-defined and total because of the definitions of interface binding and Lemma 1. To show that the mapping is a morphism we consider an arbitrary association a from an import interface in $Import$. Again, the proof for *second* is analogous to that for $first$, so it is sufficient to show that

$$h_c(first(a) = first_{res}(h_a(a)) \ (\star)$$

Because the binding of interfaces is associative, we can assume that h_{res} is the last binding to be applied. Then $(\star)$ follows immediately from the fact that h_{res} is a morphism.

7 Mapping the Formal Approach to MOF 2.0

The approach introduced in the previous sections allows for the definition and composition of MOF-compliant metamodel components. In contrast to the import and the package merge concept available in MOF, it is also possible to use different names for the same element in several components and to instantiate the same component multiple times with different import to export interface bindings, i.e. with different parameter instantiations. Due to lack of space the presented formalization of metamodel components focused on classes and simple associations only. Additional metamodeling concepts such as generalization can be added rather easily as shown in [1]. However, we have to stress the fact that the composition of valid metamodel components that make use of these additional concepts may not always result in a valid metamodel (component) according to the static semantics constraints of MOF. This problem also exists for the package merge concept of MOF [6, pp. 158ff], which could, for instance, be abused to create cyclic chains of generalization relationships.

When we extend the presented approach to all metamodeling concepts of MOF 2.0 then we have to introduce some additional metamodel composition constraints, too. For instance, it would be sensible to demand that generalization relationships on classes or redefinition or subsetting relationships on associations can always be lifted to their equivalence classes or that generalization relationships on equivalence classes do not form cyclic chains.

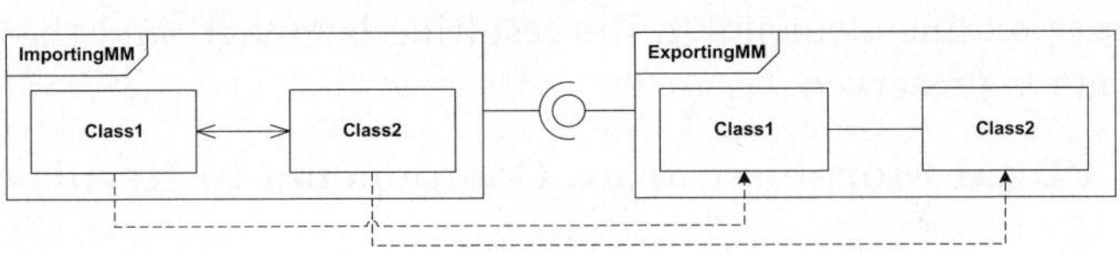

Fig. 5. Navigability of Associations in Metamodel Components

Another point of importance is the navigability of association ends. Consider the mapping indicated by the dashed arrows in Figure 5. The navigability of the association ends in the importing metamodel component would require get- and set-methods for the corresponding properties in the placeholder classes connected by the association. If there is no corresponding navigable association in the exporting metamodel component, such methods may not exist in the classes the placeholders are mapped to. Therefore, navigability of association ends will also result in additional properties that must hold for the components and the mapping. The solution of this issue may also have an impact on code generation: Let us assume that the binding of a component maps a placeholder element with some properties (like attached navigable association ends) onto a concrete metamodeling element that does not have these properties. In this case, the generated code of the concrete metamodeling element cannot be reused as it is, but has to be extended (with appropriate set and get methods). As a consequence we lose the possibility to create the implementation of a composite metamodel component by composing the generated implementations of all components (including the execution of some renaming operations).

In addition, we are aware of the fact that those concepts from MOF which had to be neglected here, may raise additional questions. This includes among other things like multiplicities of association ends, composite properties, and embedded OCL constraints. Some of the problems with the handling of still missing metamodeling concepts may be solved by adopting the solutions for rather similar problems that occur when MOF packages are merged. When dealing with OCL constraints belonging to export or import interfaces we have to use another source of inspiration: the formalization of modularization concepts for algebraic specification languages. The morphisms between different algebraic specification modules are already defined in such a way that they preserve the constraints (equations) associated with these modules. From a formal point of view we simply have to copy these definitions of morphisms in such a way that an import interface may only be bound to an export interface if the OCL constraints of the import can be verified using the OCL constraints of the export only (after renaming the affected metamodel elements).

8 Conclusions and Future Work

In this paper we have introduced a formal component-oriented metamodeling approach that (1) supports the definition of libraries of reusable metamodel components with an arbitrary number of export interfaces, (2) allows for the definition of parametrized (sub-)language descriptions by means of required import interfaces, (3) and comes with an appropriate metamodel composition operator. Some fundamental well-definedness properties of the defined metamodel composition operator and the resulting composite metamodel (components) were shown. But due to lack of space all presented definitions and theorems rely on a considerably simplified version of MOF 2.0 metamodels. Thus, further investigations and extensions of our approach are required until we can claim complete support for all MOF 2.0 metamodeling concepts. We have outlined some of the problems expected for future work on completely MOF 2.0 compliant metamodel composition in Section 7.

Besides these envisioned extensions, our approach could also be extended to instances of metamodels by putting the focus on objects and links rather than on classes and associations. If the ideas presented in this contribution are mapped to the M1 level successfully, this will result in a way to separate arbitrary instances (of MOF-compliant metamodels, of course) into components and reuse these components in different models in different ways. The result could be a significant improvement in reusability and maintainability of models, too.

Finally, it is a subject of future activities to study the impact of the component-oriented metamodeling approach on the code generation machinery of our metamodeling environment MOFLON in much more detail and to extend its implementation appropriately.

References

1. Amelunxen, C., Schürr, A.: Formalizing Model Transformation Rules for UML/MOF 2. IET Software Journal (accepted for publication, 2007)
2. Amlio, N., Stepney, S., Polack, F.: A Formal Template Language Enabling Metaproof. In: Misra, J., Nipkow, T., Sekerinski, E. (eds.) FM 2006. LNCS, vol. 4085, pp. 252–267. Springer, Heidelberg (2006)
3. Ehrig, H., Mahr, B.: Fundamentals of Algebraic Specification 2: Module Specifications and Constraints. Springer, Heidelberg (1990)
4. Emerson, M., Sztipanovits, J.: Techniques for metamodel composition. In: OOPSLA – 6th Workshop on Domain Specific Modeling, pp. 123–139 (October 2006)
5. Krahn, H., Rumpe, B., Völkel, S.: Efficient Editor Generation for Compositional DSLs in Eclipse. In: Proceedings of the 7th OOPSLA Workshop on Domain-Specific Modeling (DSM 2007), Montreal, Quebec, Canada (2007)
6. Object Management Group, Inc. Unified Modeling Language: Infrastructure(July 2005), http://doc.omg.org/formal/2005-07-05.pdf
7. Object Management Group, Inc. Unified Modeling Language: Superstructure (July 2005), http://doc.omg.org/formal/2005-07-04.pdf
8. Object Management Group, Inc. Meta Object Facility (MOF) Core Specification (January 2006), http://doc.omg.org/formal/2006-01-01.pdf
9. Object Management Group, Inc. Object Constraint Language (May 2006), http://doc.omg.org/formal/06-05-01.pdf
10. Taentzer, G.: Parallel and Distributed Graph Transformation: Formal Description and Application to Communication-Based Systems. PhD thesis, Technische Universität Berlin (1996)
11. Winter, A.: Referenz-Metaschema für visuelle Modellierungssprachen. Deutscher Universitätsverlag, Wiesbaden, Dissertation (in german), Institut für Informatik. Universität Koblenz-Landau (2000)

Interfaces and Metainterfaces for Models and Metamodels

Anders Hessellund and Andrzej Wąsowski

IT University of Copenhagen, Denmark
{hessellund,wasowski}@itu.dk

Abstract. Evolution and customization of component-based systems require an explicit understanding of component inter-dependencies. Implicit assumptions, poor documentation and hidden dependencies turn even simple changes into challenges. The problem is exacerbated in XML-intensive projects due to the use of soft references and the lack of information hiding. We address this with dependency tracking interface types for models and metamodels. We provide automatic compatibility checks and a heuristic inference procedure for our interfaces, which allows easy and incremental adoption of our technique even in mature projects. We have implemented a prototype and applied it to two large cases: an enterprise resource planning system and a healthcare information system.

1 Introduction

The challenge of evolving and customizing component-based systems is well-known in both academia and industry. The solution strategies devised by computer scientists, however, often fail to deliver due to an underlying misconception of what a *component* is. As Bosch [1, p.14] points out, the classic academic view is that a component is a small black-box asset with a narrow interface and a single point of access. The industrial view, on the other hand, is that components are large assets with no encapsulation and no distinction between interface and non-interface entities. A large class of model-driven systems exacerbates this problem by relying on XML-based domain-specific languages (DSLs) which use *soft references*—untyped, string-based references between XML documents.

XML-based DSLs are often used in a significant class of model-driven systems following an approach which we term *interpretative*. These systems use models expressed in XML as first-class artifacts. The models are not used by code generators in the development phase but rather by interpreters at load- or runtime. The DSLs are defined by an XML Schema and cover a range of concerns from simple configuration to full-blown programming. Typically, multiple such languages are used in concert, as described in [2], to address different concerns of an individual application. Components in such systems are often large, have blurred boundaries, and consist of a mixture of models conforming to various schemas, and of code snippets in a general-purpose language for custom functionality.

K. Czarnecki et al. (Eds.): MoDELS 2008, LNCS 5301, pp. 401–415, 2008.

The main advantage of using an XML-based language is the availability of generic tools for parsing and checking for schema conformance. However, there are also some serious problems. One of the most important of these problems is the use of soft references to tie together different XML models (possibly conforming to different metamodels). In order to refer to elements in other XML models, simple strings are used. The string references can not be checked by a standard schema conformance checker but rather by special tools such as SmartEMF [2] or Xlinkit [3] that require manual specification of every single reference in advance. Furthermore, since XML lacks an information hiding construct, there is no explicit definition of an interface between different XML models. To reveal dependencies between components implemented in such languages, one has to track every single reference instance, i.e., check every single XML model.

This paper presents an automatic, compositional approach to dependency tracking based on use of interfaces. The approach is applicable to a large class of model-driven systems, specifically *interpretative* systems using XML-based DSLs. Using a simple set of heuristics, we can infer interfaces for models and metainterfaces for metamodels. We discuss composition rules for model interfaces such that interfaces can be composed to create descriptions of larger units, like entire components. The approach is intended to be lightweight and easy to adopt. To validate this hypothesis, we have tested our approach on two existing industrial cases, an enterprise resource planning system [4] and a healthcare information system [5], and the results are promising. Our contributions are:

- A compositional approach to tracking soft dependencies based on interfaces
- An interface language for specification of interfaces and metainterfaces
- A notion of component interfaces via composition of model interfaces
- A lightweight bootstrapping procedure via inference for easy adoption
- An empirical evaluation in the form of two industrial case studies

Outline. A motivating problem selected from a case study is examined in Sect. 2. Sections 3–4 introduce interfaces for models and metamodels. Section 5 describes the interface inference implemented in our prototype, and Sect. 6 reports results of empirical validation. We address limitations and open problems in Sect. 7, and the related work in Sect. 8.

2 Dependencies and Soft References in OFBiz

We begin by demonstrating how hidden dependencies and soft references among models appear in actual systems. The Apache Open For Business (OFBiz) project [4], described in greater detail in Sect. 6, uses 17 different DSLs to define and implement various parts of its functionality. Two examples of these are: the *Screen Language* used to define user interface screens, and the *Entity Language* used to define business objects, their attributes and associations. A screen model usually refers to an entity model to render a business object in the user interface.

Figure 1 shows actual screen and entity models from the OFBiz project. The `ViewFXConversions` screen is located in the `Accounting` component and is used

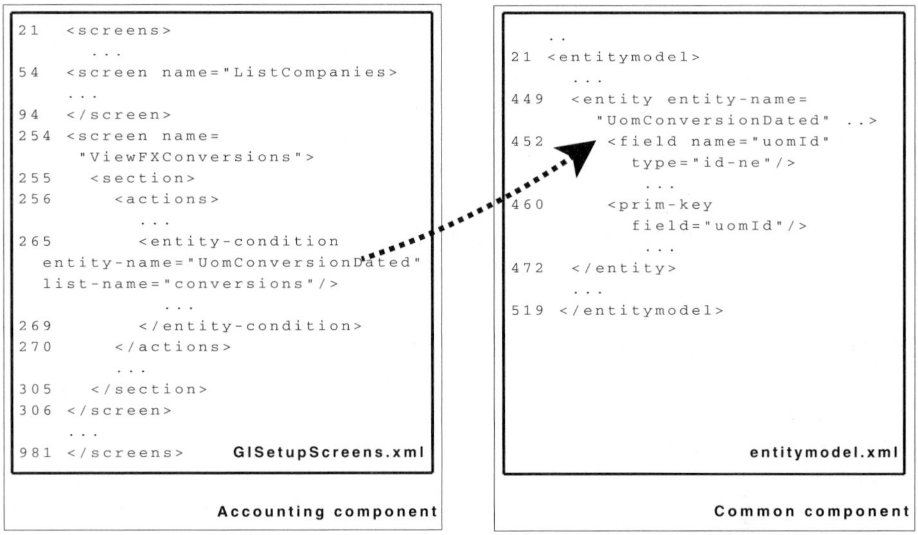

Fig. 1. The *GlSetupScreens.xml* contains general ledger screens, such as `ListCompanies` and `ViewFXConversions`, from the *accounting* component in OFBiz. The `ViewFXConversions` screen has a soft reference to the *common* component since it needs to render the `UomConversionDated` business object from the *entitymodel.xml*.

to display rates for foreign exchange conversions. The concept of a conversion rate is encapsulated in the `UomConversionDated` business object defined in the `Common` component. The `entity-name` attribute in the screen model is a reference to the entity model. When the interpreter encounters this attribute, it performs a lookup in the entity models and, in this case, renders the `UomConversionDated` object on the `ViewFXConversions` screen. This is a *soft reference*. Borrowing vocabulary from programming language theory, we call the attribute in the entity model the *name declaration* and the attribute in the screen model the *name use*. The reference must point to either an `entity` or a `view-entity` in the *Entity Language* but this is not checked until calltime when the screen is rendered. Developers must take care to manually update all references when they change the name declaration of a business object.

OFBiz is partitioned into a set of different components, such as Accounting and Inventory. In the example, the screen is defined in the Accounting component and the business object is defined in the Common component (that contains a library of basic, reusable objects and services). Since the screen refers to the entity model, the Accounting component has an implicit dependency on the Common component. XML does not have any language constructs for information hiding, so it is impossible to specify which elements of an XML model can be referred to. In other words, we can not state that the Common component provides `entity` and `view-entity` objects.

This means that replacing or updating an existing model or component in OFBiz requires a lot of work since every dependency must be revealed and checked manually. A previous study of OFBiz has shown that this is a significant cause of errors and a concern of the developers [2]. We address these difficulties by introducing an interface concept stating the provisions and requirements on three levels: First, on the metamodel level, we state which names are *provided*, i.e. declared for public access, and which external names are used in a metamodel, i.e. are *required* to exists. Second, on the model level, we state which exact (attribute instance,value)-pairs are provided and required. Third, a component is a collection of models, so on the component level, model interfaces should be composed to establish what a component requires and provides.

3 Interface Theory for Soft References

An *interface* is an abstract description of the way in which a *component* communicates with its *context*; It serves as a requirements specification for the developer of the component, a use specification for the user of the component, and a correctness specification for automatic verification. Our components are models stored in XML files at two levels of the modeling hierarchy: models and metamodels to which these models conform. A context for a model may be other models in the project. In this paper we restrict the communication between the model and a context to an ability to refer to, or being referred from, the context objects by means of soft references.

Since our interface theory for models only tracks soft references, our view of XML is grossly simplified. We define an *attribute instance* to be a fully qualified path to an attribute occurrence in an XML file, identifiable by an XPath expression. An attribute instance in a schema file is its conceptual counterpart. It corresponds to the `xs:attribute` notion in the XML Schema Specification. In our perspective, attribute instances, whether in XML files, or in schema files, are just abstract, distinct atomic units.

XML and schema files are just collections of attribute instances. For an XML file att_1 and a corresponding schema att_2 a many-to-one implementation relation $\mathcal{R}(\mathsf{att}_1 : \mathsf{att}_2) \subseteq \mathsf{att}_1 \times \mathsf{att}_2$ relates every attribute instance in att_1 to a single attribute instance in att_2. $\mathcal{R}$ is established by the standard XSD semantics.

Each model can potentially appear in multiple contexts. Since contexts are just sets of attribute instances from sets of model files, it seems natural to model them as unions of models. But a union of sets containing attribute instances is itself a set of attribute instances. So we define a context to be a set of attribute instances. Again in practice we distinguish contexts for models (other models) and contexts for meta models (other schema), but in our abstract view they are all just sets of distinguishable items. The interpretation is that if an attribute instance a is in some context ctx, so $a \in \mathsf{ctx}$, then ctx declares a, and it can be referred from other files using a soft reference. Such a generic treatment of contexts allows us to use interfaces both in small scale, where context can be fragments of models or entire models, and in the large, for collections of models, i.e., components.

Definition 1 (Interface). *An interface is a quadruple* $\mathcal{I} = (\mathsf{use}, \mathsf{decl}, \mathsf{req}, \mathsf{pro})$ *where* use *and* decl *are disjoint sets of attribute instances,* req *is a consistent propositional logic formula over* use*, and* pro *is a formula over* $\mathsf{use} \cup \mathsf{decl}$*. Moreover for every context* $\mathsf{ctx} \subseteq \mathsf{use}$ *we have that* $(\mathsf{req} \rightarrow \mathsf{pro})_{\mathsf{ctx}}$ *is consistent.*

Expression $(\varphi)_{\mathsf{ctx}}$ denotes a specialization of φ in the context ctx. Each occurrence in φ of a name $v \in \mathsf{use}$ is substituted with true if $v \in \mathsf{ctx}$ and with false otherwise.

Intuitively, the req formula expresses the necessary condition for a component to deliver its functionality; req must be formulated in terms of attribute instances that are found in the use set. In simple interfaces req just requires one attribute instance to exist. When a component refers to two or more attribute instances, then req is a conjunction of them. A reference to an abstract concept can be modeled as a disjunction of several references.

Consider the example in Table 1. On top, the signature (use and decl) of the interface is stated: four names might be used, and two might be guaranteed to be declared in this interface. The signature merely limits the symbols used in the remaining part of the interface. The *requires* block, which corresponds to req in Definition 1, states that this interface refers to an instance of attribute `entity-name` with value `'UomConversionDated'`, which can be either provided by an `entity` or a `viewentity`. A sum of the two XML scopes (`entity` and `view-entity`) effectively constitutes an abstract scope here, which is modeled by a disjunction in the interface. Similarly, this interface also requires an `entity` or a `view-entity` named `'PartyRole'` that is referenced from the `ListCompanies` screen. This entity has not been shown in Figure 1 for space reasons.

The formula pro, of Definition 1, describes ways in which the model can satisfy the interface. In the most common form of an interface pro is formulated in terms of declared names found in the decl set, and is just a simple conjunction, as in Table 1. In more sophisticated cases, general expressions can be used to express abstract interfaces—for example to summarize several similar components that differ slightly in what they provide. We allow use of names from use in the requires part in order to be able to express these more nuanced interfaces, for example when a part of the functionality is only available given a certain

Table 1. An interface for `GlSetupScreens.xml` (Ofbiz's general ledger UI)

```
names declared: /screens/screen[@name='ViewFXConversions']
                /screens/screen[@name='ListCompanies']
names used: /entitymodel/entity[@entity-name='UomConversionDated']
            /entitymodel/view-entity[@entity-name='UomConversionDated']
            /entitymodel/entity[@entity-name='PartyRole']
            /entitymodel/view-entity[@entity-name='PartyRole']
requires: (/entitymodel/entity[@entity-name='UomConversionDated']
            xor /entitymodel/view-entity[@entity-name='UomConversionDated'])
       and (/entitymodel/entity[@entity-name='PartyRole']
            xor /entitymodel/view-entity[@entity-name='PartyRole'])
provides: /screens/screen[@name='ViewFXConversions']
       and /screens/screen[@name='ListCompanies']
```

Table 2. An interface for `EntitityModel.xml`

```
names declared: /entitymodel/entity[@entity-name='UomConversionDated']
requires: true
provides: /entitymodel/entity[@entity-name='UomConversionDated']
```

precondition. This generalization creates a potential problem: we might write a *provides* block that is inconsistent with the associated *requires* block (for example require a and guarantee $\neg a$). Since such interfaces are obviously not useful, we restrict ourselves to *well formed* interfaces in the last sentence of Def. 1.

There are several kinds of verification to be considered in the presence of interfaces. First, a *conformance* procedure checks if a model obeys its own interface. Second, *refinement* or *subtyping* means that one interface properly strengthens another one, without breaking any other models, which might be using it. Third, the most central of these, *compatibility* of interfaces, means that for any two interfaces their composition models the composition of any two components implementing them in such a way that if the interfaces are compatible then there exist contexts that can use these two components combined.

The subtyping question is contravariant in nature: a subtype of an interface may relax the assumptions, and may strengthen the guarantees. Formally:

Definition 2 (Subtyping). *For two interfaces* $\mathcal{I}_1 = (\mathsf{use}_1, \mathsf{decl}_1, \mathsf{req}_1, \mathsf{pro}_1)$ *and* $\mathcal{I}_2 = (\mathsf{use}_2, \mathsf{decl}_2, \mathsf{req}_2, \mathsf{pro}_2)$ *say that* $\mathcal{I}_1$ *is a subtype of* $\mathcal{I}_2$*, written* $\mathcal{I}_1 \preceq \mathcal{I}_2$*, iff*

- $\mathsf{use}_1 \subseteq \mathsf{use}_2$ *and* $\mathsf{decl}_1 \supseteq \mathsf{decl}_2$,
- *and formulas* $(\mathsf{req}_2 \to \mathsf{req}_1)$ *and* $(\mathsf{pro}_1 \to \mathsf{pro}_2)$ *are valid.*
- *and* $(\mathsf{req}_1 \to \mathsf{pro}_1) \to (\bigvee_{\mathsf{decl}_2 - \mathsf{decl}_1} \mathsf{req}_2 \to \mathsf{pro}_2)$ *is valid.*[1]

Recall that req_i are interpreted as constraints on the contexts in which $\mathcal{I}_i$ may be used. The implication $\mathsf{req}_2 \to \mathsf{req}_1$ means that $\mathcal{I}_1$ constrains the environment no more than $\mathcal{I}_2$ does. Similarly pro_i are interpreted as resources guaranteed by $\mathcal{I}_i$, so $\mathsf{pro}_1 \to \mathsf{pro}_2$ means that any guarantee given by $\mathcal{I}_1$ must be stronger than the one given by $\mathcal{I}_2$. The final formula states that the interface refinement is conservative: it should not change the guarantees already specified in the part being refined. The refining interface can freely introduce constraints on new variables though.

Interface theories take an *existential* approach to compatibility: two interfaces are *compatible* if there exists a context in which they can be legally used.

Definition 3 (Compatibility). *Two interfaces* $\mathcal{I}_1 = (\mathsf{use}_1, \mathsf{decl}_1, \mathsf{req}_1, \mathsf{pro}_1)$ *and* $\mathcal{I}_2 = (\mathsf{use}_2, \mathsf{decl}_2, \mathsf{req}_2, \mathsf{pro}_2)$ *are compatible iff* $\mathsf{decl}_2 \cap \mathsf{decl}_1 = \emptyset$ *and there exists a context* $\mathsf{ctx} \subseteq \mathsf{use} = (\mathsf{use}_1 \cup \mathsf{use}_2) - (\mathsf{decl}_1 \cup \mathsf{decl}_2)$ *such that the formula* $[(\mathsf{req}_1 \vee \mathsf{req}_2) \wedge (\mathsf{req}_1 \to \mathsf{pro}_1) \wedge (\mathsf{req}_2 \to \mathsf{pro}_2)]_{\mathsf{ctx}}$ *is consistent.*

Let us elaborate on the above definition. First of all two compatible interfaces need to have disjoint sets of declared attribute instances, as otherwise it would

[1] Notation $\bigvee_V \varphi$ means elimination of variables in V from φ in propositional logic (a form of finite existential quantification): for one variable $\bigvee_v \varphi \equiv \varphi[0/v] \vee \varphi[1/v]$.

be impossible to resolve soft references to any shared name. Second, there must exists a context in which the composition can be legally used. Third, in this context one must be able to satisfy an assumption of one or the other of the interfaces (or both) while still being able to fulfill their obligations. Mind that a context ctx turns all the variables in use into constants, so satisfiability of the last two terms implies that it is possible to assign declared variables in $\mathsf{decl} = \mathsf{decl}_1 \cup \mathsf{decl}_2$ so that the original constraint of both interfaces is fulfilled.

Any two compatible interfaces can be composed, and we give rules to synthesize the interface for the composition. Assume names as in Definition 3. Then the result of composing $\mathcal{I}_1$ and $\mathcal{I}_2$ is an interface $\mathcal{I} = (\mathsf{use}, \mathsf{decl}, \mathsf{req}, \mathsf{pro})$, where $\mathsf{decl} = \mathsf{decl}_1 \cup \mathsf{decl}_2$, $\mathsf{req} := \bigvee_{\mathsf{decl}} .(\mathsf{req}_1 \vee \mathsf{req}_2) \wedge (\mathsf{req}_1 \to \mathsf{pro}_1) \wedge (\mathsf{req}_2 \to \mathsf{pro}_2)$, and $\mathsf{pro} = (\mathsf{req}_1 \to \mathsf{pro}_1) \wedge (\mathsf{req}_2 \to \mathsf{pro}_2)$.

Example 1. Consider a composition of the interface from Table 1 with the entity interface in Table 2. The entity interface fulfills the first assumption in the screen interface, but the second one remains to be pending. The two interfaces are compatible in the sense of Definition 3. The resulting composed interface is:

```
names declared: /screens/screen[@name='ViewFXConversions']
                /screens/screen[@name='ListCompanies']
                /entitymodel/entity[@entity-name='UomConversionDated']
names used: /entitymodel/view-entity[@entity-name='UomConversionDated']
            /entitymodel/entity[@entity-name='PartyRole']
            /entitymodel/view-entity[@entity-name='PartyRole']
requires: (not /entitymodel/view-entity[@entity-name='UomConversionDated'])
          or (/entitymodel/entity[@entity-name='PartyRole']
          xor /entitymodel/view-entity[@entity-name='PartyRole'])
provides: /entitymodel/entity[@entity-name='UomConversionDated']
     and ((not /entitymodel/view-entity[@entity-name='UomConversionDated']
          and (/entitymodel/entity[@entity-name='PartyRole']
               xor /entitymodel/view-entity[@entity-name='PartyRole']))
          implies (/screens/screen[@name='ViewFXConversions']
               and /screens/screen[@name='ListCompanies']))
```

We encourage the reader to perform the calculation herself. In practice, this synthesis can be performed using binary decision diagrams (BDDs) or a theorem prover, and further compatibility checking can also be automated. Observe that the synthesized interface promises to deliver the entity named `'UomConversionDated'` unconditionally. However delivery of `'ViewFxCompanies'` and `'ListCompanies'` depends on absence of a view named `'UomConversionDated'` (as this conflicts with the entity present in the interface), and availability of either an entity or a view named `'PartyRole'`. In order to use this interface (the requires section) you need to either refrain from providing the conflicting view, or make `'PartyRole'` available. Otherwise there is nothing this component can offer.

Other interesting uses of composition are possible. For example, an interface for a complicated file, can be created by treating parts of the file as separate models, specifying interfaces for them individually, and automatically synthesizing the interface for the entire file by applying the above composition rule. If you want to know what needs to be guaranteed to safely access `'ListCompanies'`, you can use the composition algorithm to get the answer, namely that `'UomConversionDated'` should be provided. Simply compose the interface that provides `'ListCompanies'`, with another one that requires it.

We admit that the synthesised interfaces are complex, even unsuitable to be read by humans. We should reiterate that these are not to be written manually, but synthesized and checked for compatibility automatically. In the long run the framework should incorporate an interactive exploration tool, which allows the user to investigate combinatorial spaces in the spirit of interactive product configuration [6]—without reading the specifications .

Last but not least, as any typical interface theory, ours also offers *substitutability* by design: for any two compatible interfaces $\mathcal{I}$ and $\mathcal{J}$, if $\mathcal{I}' \preceq \mathcal{I}$ and $\mathcal{J}' \preceq \mathcal{J}$ then $\mathcal{I}'$ and $\mathcal{J}'$ are compatible, allowing to safely substitute $\mathcal{I}'$ in place of $\mathcal{I}$ and, $\mathcal{J}$ in place of $\mathcal{J}'$ without introducing any obligation to recheck compatibility, as long as $\mathcal{I}'$ and $\mathcal{J}'$ do not *declare* any new names, which are already *used* in $\mathcal{I}$ or $\mathcal{J}$. This crucial property means that a developer can substitute a model without rechecking compatibility as long as the original and the new model implement the same interface.

4 Metainterfaces

Known interface theories do not explicitly distinguish between the meta level and the model level. They typically treat implementations uniformly, as completely refined specifications. Such interface frameworks are simpler to implement, and simpler to reason about. However since in development with DSLs, both models and metamodels are first-class artifacts that are being developed and evolved, it makes sense to exploit their co-existence and the special relation between the two kinds of models to obtain a more precise interface inference with less burden on users.

In Sect. 3, we have defined the schemas and XML files to be just sets of attribute instances at the two levels. Consequently the framework presented therein applies just as well to schemas as to the models, and all the definitions and claims are still valid (interfaces, subtyping, compatibility, composition, and substitutability). Even though at the metalevel we model associations between elements, as opposed to references between objects, at the plain logical level there is no difference between composing models and composing metamodels.

We show how metainterfaces together with metamodels can be useful in establishing conformance of models to interfaces. The correctness of a model is established in two steps: first the conformance of the XML file to its schema is checked using regular XML technology. Then the conformance of the XML file to its interface is checked, involving the schema interface. Why involve the schema? Ideally we would like to claim that if a model conforms to an interface, then it declares all the required names and does not use any names that are not mentioned in the `requires` block. While the former can be robustly checked, the latter cannot due to lack of information. Any attribute instance in the XML file can be a soft reference, but we do not know whether it is one and, if so, which attribute it uses. To provide a check for this conformance we enrich interfaces used for metamodels with additional information—links between the used names and the attribute instances (`xs:attribute`) that use them. This information, specified once per metamodel, can be efficiently reused for all conforming models.

Consider the example of a metainterface in Table 3. Note that the syntax is essentially the same, except that the names no longer include particular values, and we add `by` clauses to indicate the internal attributes responsible for the use. A formal definition of the metainterface follows.

Definition 4 (Metainterface). *A metainterface is a 6-tuple* $\mathcal{I} = (\mathsf{use}, \mathsf{decl}, \mathsf{req}, \mathsf{pro}, \mathsf{int}, \mathsf{by})$ *where* $(\mathsf{use}, \mathsf{decl}, \mathsf{req}, \mathsf{pro})$ *is an interface and* int *is a set of internal attribute instances disjoint with both* use *and* decl*, while* $\mathsf{by} \in \mathsf{int} \mapsto \mathsf{use}$ *maps internal attribute instances to external ones.*

An XML file att_1 conforms to its interface $\mathcal{I}_1$, iff (i) att_1 actually contains the attribute instances that are provided in $\mathcal{I}_1$ and (ii) the interface $\mathcal{I}_1$ declares the use of all the attribute instances used in att_1. Since (ii) cannot be checked automatically we approximate it using a metainterface. See the overview in Fig. 2. For every attribute instance $a \in \mathsf{att}_1$ (here a is `a = "softId"`) detect whether a makes an external reference by checking whether the corresponding attribute (here `a`) is mentioned in the metainterface $\mathcal{I}_2$, in a `by` clause. If so, we require that the corresponding used name, seen in the metainterface (here `b`), is declared as used in the interface with the same value as a (here `softId`).

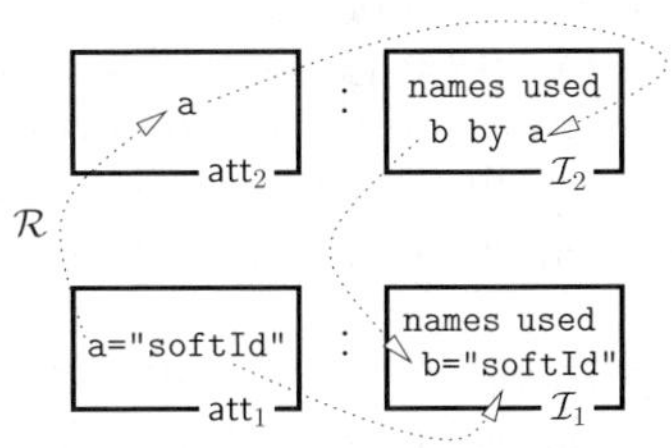

Fig. 2. Checking conformance of name uses

Definition 5 (Conformance). *Let* att_1 *be an XML file,* att_2 *be a schema file to which* att_1 *conforms, and* $\mathcal{R}$ *be an implementation relation between the two. Let* $\mathcal{I}_1 = (\mathsf{use}_1, \mathsf{decl}_1, \mathsf{req}_1, \mathsf{pro}_1)$*, and* $\mathcal{I}_2 = (\mathsf{use}_2, \mathsf{decl}_2, \mathsf{req}_2, \mathsf{pro}_2, \mathsf{int}_2, \mathsf{by})$ *be the corresponding interface and metainterface. We say that* att_1 *conforms to* $\mathcal{I}_1$*, written* $\mathsf{att}_1 : \mathcal{I}_1$*, iff* $(\mathsf{req}_1 \rightarrow \mathsf{pro}_1)_{\mathsf{att}_1}$ *is a valid formula and for every attribute instance* $a \in \mathsf{att}_1$ *such that* $\mathcal{R}(a) \in \mathsf{att}_2$ *and* by *is defined for* $\mathcal{R}(a)$ *in* $\mathcal{I}_2$*, we have that* $\mathsf{by}(R(a)) = value(a)$ *and* $(\mathsf{req}_1)_{\mathsf{att}_1} \rightarrow \mathsf{by}(R(a))$

Let us summarize the ingredients of our framework. We provide interfaces and meta-interfaces for models and metamodels, with algorithms for checking compatibility and subtyping and for computing compositions. For models we also allow conformance checking. Complete conformance checking for metamodels is impossible due to lack of knowledge on which attributes are soft references (unless a metametamodel is available). We do not think this is a large problem. Metainterfaces tend to be much simpler and smaller than interfaces and are specified by DSL designers. At the same time, interfaces, are used and written by regular users of DSLs, for whom the automatic support is much more valuable.

5 Interface Inference

We have seen how interfaces are specified, verified and composed. If this technology is to be useful in realistic development projects, we need to address another pressing question: how to easily specify a large number of interfaces? Below we propose a heuristic technique to automatically *infer* interfaces reflecting the current dependencies in a project. In Sect. 6, we evaluate the technique by applying its implementation to two large development projects.

The central idea is to discover associations between metamodels by heuristically mining all references between attribute instances in the available collection of models. Once metainterfaces are in place, a refinement procedure is applied to generate model interfaces. Our hypothesis is that this *bootstrapping* process, given a sufficiently large number of models, results in fairly precise approximations of the interfaces.

The inferred interfaces explicitly represent combinatorial dependencies, addressing the problems described in Sect. 1–2, allowing for safer evolution and customization of model-based components. Since we do not require any special conventions from the systems under analysis, the technique can be applied incrementally and for a large class of systems. Optional configuration files allow us to cater for domain-specific heuristics and coding conventions.

Identifying Potential Soft References. We begin with identifying all soft reference candidates in the models. A soft reference consists of a name declaration and a name use that are attributes with the same value. An attribute is a *potential name declaration* if it always takes unique values (so it can be used as a primary key). An attribute is a *potential name use* if all values it takes are a subset of the values taken by some potential name declaration attribute. Formally if ref and key are two different attributes, and ref_1 and key_1 their corresponding nonempty instance sets there is a potential simple soft reference with ref being the *name use* and key its name declaration if $ref_1 \subseteq key_1$.

In the example of Sect. 2, attribute `entity-name` on the `entity-condition` `element` refers to either an `entity` or a `view-entity`. This is because both `entity` and `view-entity` are subtypes of some implicit abstraction. The above simple inclusion check fails in such cases because the name declaration of a potential soft reference is really a union of all names participating in the abstraction;

Table 3. Metainterface for `widget-screens.xsd`, metamodel of `GlSetupScreens.xml`

```
names declared: /screens/screen[@name]
names used: /entitymodel/entity[@entity-name]
               by (/screens/screen/actions/entity-condition[@entity-name])
            /entitymodel/view-entity[@entity-name]
               by (/screens/screen/actions/entity-condition[@entity-name])
requires: /entitymodel/entity[@entity-name]
          or /entitymodel/view-entity[@entity-name]
provides: /screens/screen[@name]
```

here `entity` and `view-entity`. The values of a *name use* referring to such an abstraction will be a subset of this union and not of any of the individual sets. Mining uses of such abstractions is similar to mining for class hierarchies.

Let *ref* be an attribute, *keys* be a set of attributes from the same metamodel, and ref_1 and $key_{1..n}$ be their corresponding, non-empty pairwise disjoint instance sets. We identify a potential soft reference to an abstraction with *ref* as its name use and an abstraction over *keys* as its name declaration, if for each i we have that $ref \not\subseteq key_i$ while $ref \subseteq \bigcup_{i=1}^{n} key_i$.

Our prototype loads and parses all XML files in a project, identifying potential simple references and references to abstractions as defined above. After that a graph representing potential references is created. Every vertex in the graph represents either an attribute or an abstraction over attributes. There is an edge between every potential declaration and use, and between every abstraction and its members. Figure 3 shows a small fragment of the graph created for the example of Sect. 2 where an abstraction is created over `entity` and `view-entity` in the entity model. The `entity-condition[@entity-name]` attribute is shown to be a possible name use of a soft reference between itself and this newly formed abstraction. Effectively edges in this graph visualise cross-model references.

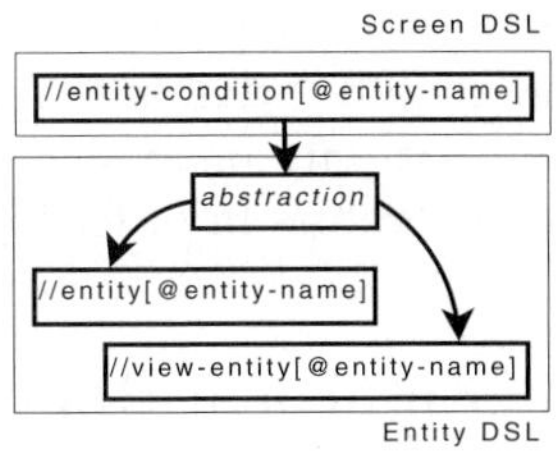

Fig. 3. A excerpt of the graph from the example

As the last step, all incoming edges of non-abstract vertices with both a positive in- and out-degree are removed, assuming that it is unlikely that an attribute can serve as both name declaration and name use at the same time.

Synthesize interfaces for metamodels. The next step in the process is the synthesis of an interface for each metamodel. The graph created above contains all the necessary information. For each metamodel, we simply have to locate vertices in the graph that corresponds to attributes or abstractions from that metamodel. For each of these vertices, we create an entry in the interface description of the metamodel. A vertex with an incoming edge results in a `provides` clause and a vertex with any outgoing edges results in a `requires` clause in the interface description. Synthesizing an interface for entity language based solely on the graph in figure 3 will give the following result:

```
names declared: n/a
requires: true
provides: /entitymodel/entity[@entity-name]
          /entitymodel/view-entity[@entity-name]
```

In other words, a metamodel provides a set of attributes that are name declarations of soft references. Similarly, a metamodel requires a set attributes that are name uses for each soft reference that originates in this metamodel. Interestingly, for abstractions we synthesize disjunctions in the metamodel where the name use is located. This is, for instance, shown in the *requires* clause of Table 3.

Refine interfaces from metamodels to models. We shall now generate interfaces for the models that were used to synthesize the graph and the metainterfaces. The synthesis forgoes by refining the metainterfaces.

Each entry in the interface description of a metamodel has a corresponding XPath expression. Evaluating such an XPath expressions results in a set of attribute instances. These instances are either name declarations or name uses of soft references as specified in the metamodel interface. The model interface entry is synthesized by taking an entry from the metamodel interface description and adding the concrete value of the attribute instance. Models do not just provide and require attributes but also attribute values. If two models are composed then not only must the correct attributes be present but these must also have specific values in order for the model interfaces to be compatible.

6 Empirical Report

In order to validate our claims we have tested the prototype on two industrial case studies—two *interpretative*, model-driven systems heavily relying on XML-based DSLs. We describe the nature of the two case studies now, before delving into a discussion of the results of experiments and limitations of our analysis.

Our main requirement when choosing the cases was to allow easy good access to code, so that our claims can be independently validated. Each case should furthermore be implemented in an *interpretative*, model-driven manner with XML based primary modeling languages. We selected one case which actually uses models more than regular code and another case which has the more common approach of using a 1:5 ratio between models and code.

The first case study is the Apache Open For Business (OFBiz) project [4]. OFBiz is an open source enterprise resource planning (ERP) system. It consist of a set of modules with basic ERP functionality such as accounting, manufacturing, e-commerce, inventory etc. It has been deployed in a large number of medium-sized companies. Larger users include United Airlines and British Telecom [7]. The implementation is in J2EE and XML and as a rough estimate of the size: the out-of-the-box solution consists of approximately 180 000 lines of Java code and 195 000 lines of XML.

The second case study is the District Health Information System (DHIS) [5] which is developed under the Health Information Systems Programme (HISP). DHIS is an open source healthcare information system which is developed as a joint project between participants in Cape Town and Oslo. It has been deployed in several African and Asian countries such as Mozambique, Malawi, Ethiopia, Nigeria, Vietnam and India. The implementation is in Java and XML and has a size of roughly 51 000 lines of Java code and 11 500 lines of XML.

We have implemented our approach in a Java-based program and tested it on the two cases. For each case, we ran a test with and without heuristic rules in order to see how performance and results were affected. We were interested in finding the number of inclusions and abstractions to see how many soft reference candidates were identified by our initial algorithm. Finally, the prototype cleans up the graph

Table 4. Results of testing the prototype on OFBiz and DHIS with and without heuristics. Columns, *#inclusions* and *#abstractions*, are the number of potentiel simple references and potential references to abstractions. The *edges* column corresponds to the final number of potential soft reference candidates after running all checks. The rightmost column, *result*, indicates the ratio between true and false positives for a sample language.

Setup	time	#models	#m.models	#inclusions	#abstractions	#edges	result
OFBiz, 8 rules	80.5s	609	14	61	12	46	29:1
OFBiz, 0 rules	81.3s	609	14	1112	39	391	n/a
DHIS, 3 rules	32.3s	176	6	58	7	73	8:1
DHIS, 0 rules	24.3s	176	6	245	8	106	n/a

as described in section 5 and produces a set of edges which form the basis for the synthesized interfaces. Table 4 shows the results of these experiments[2].

The heuristics that we have used are typically rather simple and fairly application-specific. For the OFBiz case, we were, as table 4 shows, able to reduce the number of edges, i.e., soft reference candidates, from 391 to 46 by 8 simple heuristics. An example of such heuristic is: *ignore all attributes from any metamodel if the value of an instance of this attribute contains the character sequence '${'.* The reasoning behind this heuristic is that the character sequence '${' indicates a reference to a java properties file as used in most localization schemes. The heuristics were devised in an incremental manner by looking at the produced graph and then writing heuristics to capture detected false positives. Table 4 clearly shows how especially the number of inclusions and edges decrease after the introduction of heuristics.

To evaluate our findings, we would ideally have to manually inspect all edges and check them against the documentation of the 20 DSLs involved in the experiment. This exercise would give us an exact ratio between false and true positives in the two experiments. Instead we have chosen a more limited evaluation where we approximate these figures by manually inspecting 1 sample language from each experiment. We used the Spring Beans Configuration language for DHIS and the Entity language for OFBiz, the results can be seen in the rightmost column in table 4. Further inspection of the remaining 18 DSLs will of course be necessary in order to completely ascertain the value of the approach. We do, however, claim that ratios 8:1 and 29:1 between true and false positives in the two case studies are very convincing results.

7 Discussion and Future Work

Identifying abstractions. Mining abstractions from attribute instances by means of searching for a partition built of all overlapping attribute instance sets was well-suited for our case studies (see Sect. 5). In general, the partition of the

[2] We excluded Minilang, entityconfig and serviceconfig DSLs from the setup for OFBiz.

reference value might be realized by a *selection* of overlapping sets, as opposed to all of them. A more general mining algorithm for abstractions could be devised by solving vertex cover problems [8, ch.6.3]. We have not attempted this so far.

Identifying false negatives. One of limitations of our approach is that results depend on the kinds of models that serve as input. If none of the models use a certain language feature, e.g., such as a soft reference, then this reference will not be detected. In terms of the evaluation that we described in section 6, these undetected soft references can be categorized as false negatives. An evaluation of the number of false negatives in the two cases remains future work.

Applicability to other systems. We assert that this approach is widely applicable to *interpretative* model-driven systems. Two XML-based DSLs, particularly interesting as test cases, are the XML User Interface Language (XUL) from the Mozilla Foundation and the Extensible Application Markup Language (XAML) from Microsoft. Both use a variant of soft references. On top of that XUL embeds JavaScript that poses an additional (static analysis) challenge, which we would have to address. Then using our prototype one could synthesize interfaces for libraries of user interface components in both languages in order to support evolution and upgrade of applications relying on such libraries.

8 Related Work

Our interfaces are mildly inspired by assume/guarantee interfaces of Alfaro and Henzinger [9], adapted to tracking soft references between models. Interface theories [9,10,11,12,13] have been so far developed using small scale case studies in embedded systems [14,15] and reliability engineering [16], but not in development of large scale software intensive systems. We are not aware of any attempts of interface inference in the interfaces community, or of exploitation of the relation between interfaces and metainterfaces.

The study of usage of multiple domain-specific languages in a single application has gained more interest in recent years. Work on static checking of models that span multiple DSLs can be found in tools such as Xlinkit [3] and SmartEMF [2]. These tools do, however, require manual specification rather than automatic extraction of the soft references before they can be checked.

Our approach can be seen as an attempt to uncover types in a set of untyped models similar to *soft types* in Scheme [17], JavaScript [18], and embedded DSLs in Java [19]. Our approach is different since our soft types are extracted through the automatic bootstrapping process described in Sect. 5.

9 Conclusion

We have offered a compositional approach to tracking soft dependencies based on interfaces. Using a new language for interfaces and metainterfaces, we can express complex dependencies and describe compositions of models into components. Our approach is lightweight and can be used to infer interfaces for existing systems. We have demonstrated this by implementing a prototype and applying it to two cases: an enterprise resource planning system and a healthcare information system. The approach and prototype are highly configurable and could be applied to a larger class of similar systems.

References

1. Bosch, J.: Design & Use of Software Architectures - Adopting and evolving a product-line approach. Addison-Wesley, Reading (2000)
2. Hessellund, A., Czarnecki, K., Wasowski, A.: Guided development with multiple domain-specific languages. In: Engels, G., Opdyke, B., Schmidt, D.C., Weil, F. (eds.) MODELS 2007. LNCS, vol. 4735, pp. 46–60. Springer, Heidelberg (2007)
3. Nentwich, C., Emmerich, W., Finkelstein, A.: Static consistency checking for distributed specifications. In: ASE, p. 115. IEEE Computer Society, Los Alamitos (2001)
4. The Apache Software Foundation: The Open For Business Project (OFBiz) (2008) (May 7th, 2008), `http://ofbiz.apache.org/`
5. Health Information Systems Programme (HISP): District Health Information Software (DHIS) (2008) (May 7th, 2008), `http://www.hisp.info/`
6. Junker, U.: Configuration. In: Rossi, F., van Beek, P., Walsh, T. (eds.) Handbook of Constraint Programming. Elsevier Science Inc., New York (2006)
7. Chen, S.: Opening Up Enterprise Software: Why Enterprises are Adopting Open Source Applications (2006), `http://www.opensourcestrategies.com/slides/`
8. Valiente, G.: Algorithms on Trees and Graphs. Springer, Heidelberg (2002)
9. Alfaro, L., Henzinger, T.A.: Interface theories for component-based design. In: Henzinger, T.A., Kirsch, C.M. (eds.) EMSOFT 2001. LNCS, vol. 2211. Springer, Heidelberg (2001)
10. Alfaro, L., Henzinger, T.A., Stoelinga, M.: Timed interfaces. In: Sangiovanni-Vincentelli, A.L., Sifakis, J. (eds.) EMSOFT 2002. LNCS, vol. 2491. Springer, Heidelberg (2002)
11. Alfaro, L., Henzinger, T.A.: Interface automata. In: 9th Annual Symposium on Foundations of Software Engineering (FSE), pp. 109–120. ACM Press, New York (2001)
12. Larsen, K.G., Nyman, U., Wąsowski, A.: Modal I/O automata for interface and product line theories. In: De Nicola, R. (ed.) ESOP 2007. LNCS, vol. 4421. Springer, Heidelberg (2007)
13. Larsen, K.G., Nyman, U., Wąsowski, A.: Interface input/output automata. In: Misra, J., Nipkow, T., Sekerinski, E. (eds.) FM 2006. LNCS, vol. 4085. Springer, Heidelberg (2006)
14. Chakrabarti, A., de Alfaro, L., Henzinger, T.A., Stoelinga, M.: Resource interfaces. In: Alur, R., Lee, I. (eds.) EMSOFT 2003. LNCS, vol. 2855. Springer, Heidelberg (2003)
15. Easwaran, A., Lee, I., Sokolsky, O.: Interface algebra for analysis of hierarchical real-time systems. In: Foundations of Interface Technologies (FIT) (2008)
16. Boudali, H., Crouzen, P., Haverkort, B.R., Kuntz, M., Stoelinga, M.: Rich interfaces for dependability: Compositional methods for dynamic fault trees and Arcade models. In: Foundations of Interface Technologies (FIT) (2008)
17. Wright, A.K., Cartwright, R.: A practical soft type system for scheme. In: LISP and Functional Programming, pp. 250–262 (1994)
18. Thiemann, P.: Towards a type system for analyzing javascript programs. In: Sagiv, M. (ed.) ESOP 2005. LNCS, vol. 3444, pp. 408–422. Springer, Heidelberg (2005)
19. Hessellund, A., Sestoft, P.: Flow analysis of code customizations. In: Vitek, J. (ed.) ECOOP. LNCS, vol. 5142, pp. 285–308. Springer, Heidelberg (2008)

Model&Metamodel, Metadata and Document Repository for Software and Data Integration

Nikola Milanovic, Ralf Kutsche, Timo Baum, Mario Cartsburg, Hatice Elmasgünes, Marco Pohl, and Jürgen Widiker

Technische Universität Berlin
{nmilanov,rkutsche,tbaum,mcartsbg,helmas,mpohl,jwidiker}@cs.tu-berlin.de

Abstract. Model-based software engineering (MBSE) projects require and generate numerous artifacts. While MBSE methodology and design tools have reached certain maturity level, the issue of artifact persistence and management has been somewhat left in the background. We present design and implementation of the repository that supports storing and managing of artifacts such as metamodels, models, constraints, metadata, specifications, transformation rules, code, templates, configuration or documentation, and their metadata.

1 Introduction

Model-based software engineering (MBSE) projects consume numerous artifacts, such as (meta)models, constraints, metadata, transformation rules, code or documentation. While MBSE methodology and modeling tools have reached a level of maturity, this is not the case with artifact persistence and management. The efficient management of the MBSE-artifacts is an important prerequisite for the adoption of the model-based paradigm. We present design and implementation of the repository that supports storing and managing artifacts and metadata in the model-based software and data integration process.

The repository is part of the BIZYCLE interoperability platform, a joint industry/academy R&D effort to investigate in large-scale the potential of model-based software and data integration methodologies, tool support and practical applicability for different industrial domains [1,2]. The consortium consists of six industrial partners and academia and is part of the program of the German government, the Berlin-Brandenburg Regional Business Initiative BIZYCLE (www.bizycle.de). The long-term goal is to create a model-based tool generation and interoperability platform, in order to allow for improved and partially automated processes in software component and data integration. These integration tasks are performed by experienced software engineers and application experts, manually programming the *connectors* i.e. *the glue* among software components or (sub)systems. This requires domain-specific as well as integration requirements' analysis skills. It is a very expensive procedure, estimated between 50 and 80 per cent of the overall IT investments (see e.g. [3]). In order to reduce this cost factor, the BIZYCLE initiative develops a methodology, tools and metatools for semi-automated integration according to the MDA paradigm.

K. Czarnecki et al. (Eds.): MoDELS 2008, LNCS 5301, pp. 416–430, 2008.

The BIZYCLE repository supports management and persistence of all complex artifacts generated during the BIZYCLE integration process. The main features of the BIZYCLE repository, that are focus of this paper, are artifact and metadata definition, repository architecture, and artifact management capabilities such as versioning, merging, and consistency control.

2 Related Work

The BIZYCLE repository is based on the Analytical Data on Artifacts and Models (ADAM) project, prototypically implemented at TU Berlin[4]. ADAM supports integration and development of software components by providing the possibility of storing artifacts, their metadata and relationships between artifacts. However, ADAM does not support some essential repository features required in large integration projects e.g., access and version control.

Since the early 90s several repository and SWE coordination approaches have been developed in the OOSWE community, their ideas are meanwhile part of all recent approaches. One of those is Fedora[5] which distinguishes between content and metadata persistence. Similar are OSCAR [6], enabling hierarchical management and artifact version control, and ADAMS [7], supporting distributed software engineering process by managing artifacts and relationships between them. Another open source repository tool, NetBeans Metadata Repository [8], is an extended implementation of MOF, which provides a JMI [9] based interface.

Repositories are also applied in commercial modeling and enterprise process management tools, such as Adaptive Repository, Aqualogic Enterprise Repository, ASG/Rochade etc. (detailed list can be found in [10]), but they are mostly used in runtime for documenting business metadata definitions and business rules/processes, monitoring and generating key performance indicators through data analysis, or performing risk analysis. Management of design-time artifacts is partially supported in modeling tools such as IBM Rational Asset Manager and MagicDraw Teamwork Server.

Repositories should address other aspects of content management like version control and model merging. In [11], the OMG Group provides an extension for MOF to attach versioning data to model elements. Alanen and Porres propose in [12] an algorithm for metamodel-independent difference calculation, merging of a model and union of two models. It is based on elementary transformation steps like creation, deletion or modification of model elements. On the metamodel-independent level merge conflicts cannot be resolved automatically, because the algorithm does not ensure the conformity of the resulting model to its metamodel. In the approach to the cross-language version management of models [13], Störrle formally defines version management by creating a common conceptual domain. Models are transformed into a common meta-metamodel for capturing differences. Additionally binding metrics are proposed for computing of similarity of two models. However, automatic merge conflict resolution is impossible. In [14], Hnětynka and Plášil propose distributed versioning model based on location identification for versioning support in distributed environments.

3 BIZYCLE Repository Information Model

The BIZYCLE repository has two principal roles: 1) to store and manage the artifacts produced in the context of the model-based software engineering project and 2) to store and manage metadata about the artifacts. In our terminology therefore, we distinguish between the content and its metadata, both of which are stored and managed in the repository (see information model in Figure 1).

Artifact is the most general abstraction concept and category whose content and metadata are managed in the BIZYCLE repository. The following artifact types are explicitly supported: metamodel, model, code, internal description and transformation rule. A model is an artifact representing any kind of modeling abstraction, created and managed by a modeling tool. In this implementation, models are limited to UML and DSL models and persisted in XMI format. Interfaces to our GMF-based custom modeling tools have been realized, effectively enabling these tools to use the BIZYCLE repository as model and metamodel persistent storage. Each model artifact is an instance of a metamodel artifact, which are also persisted. Transformation rules are artifacts describing how to transform one model into another, and are defined at the metamodel level. Currently we support transformations given in ATL. Code artifacts represent the code generated during the model-based engineering project, not limited to source code only but including e.g., platform-specific deployment descriptors. Finally, internal description refers to documentation manually or automatically generated during the project (it should not be confused with the external documentation which is provided up front). Each artifact may have its specific data associated with it (ArtifactSpecificData), which can be customized as a set of (key, value) pairs. For example, a user can define keys such as ToolName and ToolVersion to store the information about the modeling tool used to produce a model artifact. Artifacts are also annotated with external description, which is documentation about the artifact that is provided before the project has started. It can be stored in an external content-management system and just referenced, or physically stored (imported) in the BIZYCLE repository. External description covers documentation (e.g., requirements specification, interface list, manual), semantics (taxonomy, standards, thesaurus, ontology, glossary), component metadata and runtime data (log files, settings, statistics).

Each artifact has associated internal metadata as well as relational metadata. Internal metadata describe artifact name (label), identifier, creation/modification date, description, subject/keywords, status, creator and contributors. An artifact is furthermore owned by users, has permissions associated with it and belongs to one or more projects. More about user-, role- and project-management will be given in Section 5, Artifact Management.

Of more interest are the relational metadata that describe relations between the artifacts, as they build the foundation for the consistency checks. We define the following eight standard meta-relations. IsCopyOf marks an artifact which has been duplicated and saved into the BIZYCLE repository as a copy.

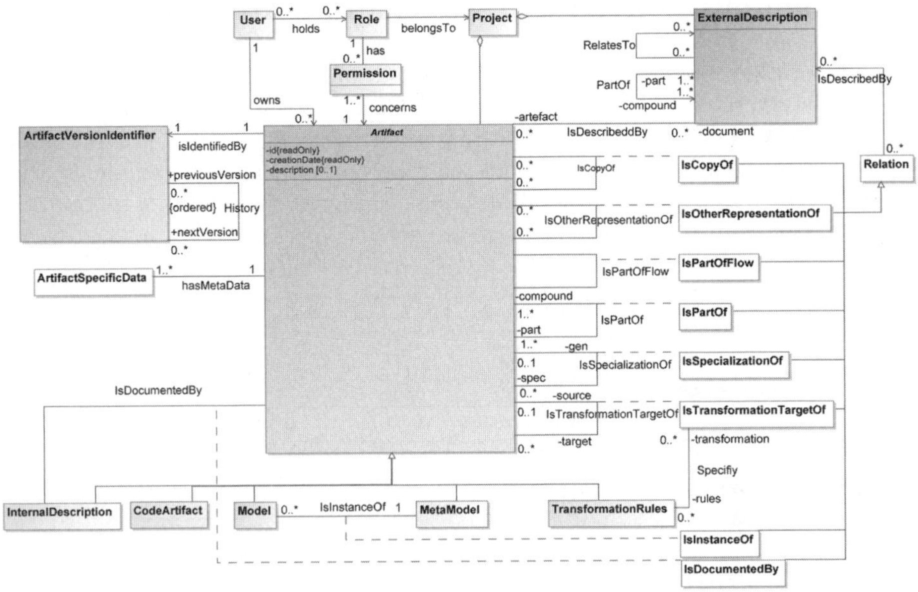

Fig. 1. BIZYCLE Repository Information Model (excerpt)

IsAnotherRepresentationOf denotes the identical artifacts which are persisted using different formats. An example is an artifact of the type Model which has been stored in XMI format, and then converted to another artifact of the same type and saved in RDF format. IsTransformationTargetOf groups artifacts which are required to perform model transformation, that is, binds source and target metamodels and models with the transformation rules used to perform the transformation. IsPartOfFlow is a meta-relation which is specific to the integration projects, and it groups artifacts that cooperate in a business process, described as activity (flow) diagram. IsPartOf marks artifacts that are parts of other artifacts using the subset semantics. For example, a complex metamodel or a model may be divided in parts that are managed separately. This relation plays an important role in the artifact locking and merging, as explained in Section 5.3. IsSpecializationOf denotes artifacts that are on the different level of abstraction, and orders them using generalization/specialization semantics. IsInstanceOf defines relationship between model and metamodel artifacts and is also used by the model checker to check consistency. Finally, IsDocumentedBy relation describes that artifact of the type Internal Description documents any other artifact type. Similarly, relation IsDescribedBy performs the analog for the external description documents. All meta-relations inherit from the generic Relation, which can be further extended according to the specific project needs. This is the way to customize meta-relations among the artifacts. Artifact version metadata, such as version number, history and lock status, are stored in the ArtifactVersion-Identifier, which will be detailed in the Section 5.3.

4 Design of the BIZYCLE Repository Architecture

The BIZYCLE repository architecture consists of several sub-components and two access layers. Tools that use the BIZYCLE repository access its API via the Remote Access Layer. External utility tools, such as theorem prover, model checker, user management and model merging components, communicate with the BIZYCLE repository via the Tool Access Layer. In the following section, the details of each sub-component or layer are given.

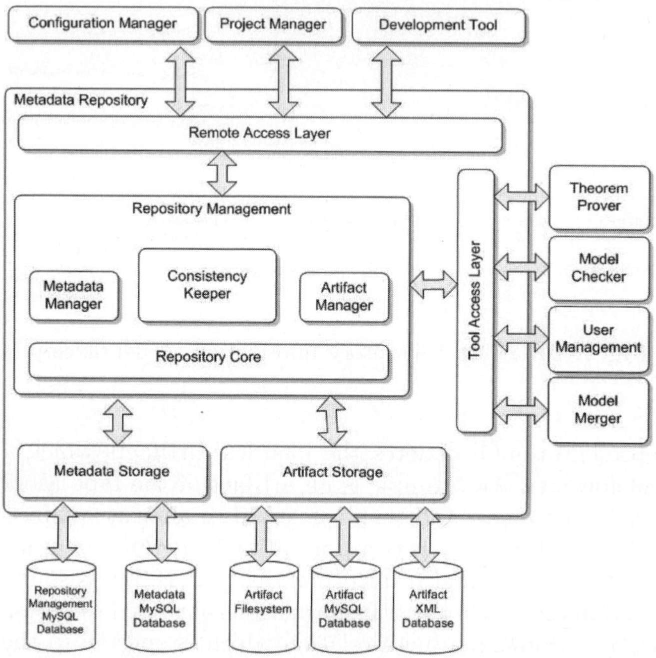

Fig. 2. BIZYCLE Repository Architecture

4.1 External Components and Remote Access Layer

The **Configuration Manager** is the configuration interface of the BIZYCLE repository. It makes use of the Artifact and Metadata Manager to define artifact type hierarchy, their metadata, constraints, consistency criteria and rules. It is possible to define an artifact type hierarchy in order to group metadata which are used for different artifact types.

The **Project Manager** is used to create and manage projects. This includes the management of users and their roles and authorization to access artifacts. It is also possible to import external artifacts that are created using tools that do not connect to the BIZYCLE repository via the Remote Access Layer (e.g., existing external descriptive documents).

The **Remote Access Layer** provides the interfaces to external tools such as model editors, transforation engines, conflict analyzers or code generators, allowing them to store and retrieve artifacts and their metadata. The BIZYCLE repository API is exposed at this layer. It features methods for transactional processing of the artifacts and allows for executing search and retrieval methods. Interfaces provided in this layer are exposed as J2EE session bean facade to Java clients and as WSDL endpoints (Web Services) to SOAP clients.

4.2 Core BIZYCLE Repository Components

The core BIZYCLE repository components provide the functionality needed to store and process artifacts and their metadata. Artifacts may contain metadata within their serialized form, e.g., an XMI file which contains extra information as annotations. They may also be provided together with metadata by external tools, e.g., use the BIZYCLE repository API to transmit an artifact and an extra piece of information containing the associated metadata. Some of the metadata are computable and have to be extracted by processing the artifact contents. To track and enable these artifact properties, any artifact type must be registered with the Artifact Manager component together with its consistency and metadata extraction policies.

The **Repository Management** component is responsible for the proper BIZYCLE repository operation. This includes providing extraction policies, metadata schemas, consistency rules and transactional processing of artifact and metadata updates. It makes use of the external **User Management** component to manage access to the artifacts based on rights. Sub-components of the Repository Manager are the Consistency Keeper, the Metadata Manager and the Artifact Manager.

The **Artifact Manager** is used to register the artifact types which may be stored in the BIZYCLE repository. For each artifact, there must be defined what MIME types are allowed, what metadata exist, how it can be generated, acquired and processed. These we call extraction policies for the metadata. Also, consistency rules are defined for each artifact and its metadata. Those rules are used by the Consistency Keeper. The Artifact Manager uses the Repository Core to access the Metadata and Artifact Storage sub-components. Consistency rules are repository-internal metadata for the artifacts and are stored using the Metadata Storage sub-component.

The **Metadata Manager** uses the extraction policies to process the metadata which have been either provided together with the artifact or have been derived by computational means. It uses the Metadata Storage via the Repository Core to save the extracted or provided metadata. The **Consistency Keeper** is an inference mechanism used for any repository transaction. It processes the consistency rules defined for each artifact type to examine the effect of the changes to the artifact in question. It may invoke external applications to validate the consistency of the artifact before committing the transaction, e.g., when a new version of a model is checked in to the BIZYCLE repository, a consistency rule defined for this artifact type might require checking whether the artifact is consistent with another artifact, namely its metamodel. The Consistency Keeper then calls a model checker via the Tool Access Layer to evaluate the rule and communicates the result.

The **Repository Core** component provides the basic persistence functionality which is used to store metadata and artifacts in the backend databases. This includes transactional processing of the database queries, managing referential integrity between the artifact and metadata databases and search functionality.

4.3 External Utilities

The **Tool Access Layer** is used to access external utility programs: theorem prover, model checker, user manager and model merger. **Theorem Prover** is an external tool used to verify consistency rules. It evaluates logical expressions which have been defined and stored using the Artifact Manager. **Model Checker** is used to check model artifact consistency by applying the common model checking methods, such as valid metamodel instantiation or integrity constraints. The **User Management** component is used for user authentication. It supports user and role management and performs authentication and authorization. Data access right within the repository are determined by assigning the roles within the Project Management component.

4.4 Persistence Layer

The persistence layer comprises Metadata Storage and Artifact Storage components. The **Artifact Storage** component manages the storage and retrieval of the artifacts. It encapsulates access to the underlying physical storage. The following storage mechanisms are supported: file system, relational database and XML database. The **Metadata Storage** component performs the storage and retrieval of metadata in the underlying databases. This includes metadata used for the operation of the BIZYCLE repository, e.g., which artifact types are allowed, what consistency rules are defined for them, all version information, as well as metadata about the artifacts that can be queried. The relational database is used for both types of metadata. The persistence layer enables transparent access as well as migration of the underlying content storage, e.g., a file system may be easily substituted with the relational database for storing content (model) data.

5 Artifact Management

The repository supports the following management options: project management, user control, artifact versioning, artifact merging and consistency preservation. These mechanisms are investigated in the following sections.

5.1 Project Management

The BIZYCLE repository is an important source of information for the management, development and maintenance of the MBSE artifacts and projects.

A project consists of a collection of various artifacts that are related to each other (Fig. 3). These artifacts are produced by the various development tools (e.g., model editor, code generator). The Configuration Manager component is used to define artifact types and their metadata schemas, so that the BIZYCLE repository is enabled to store the artifacts and their relations. Using the Project Manager component, projects as well as project-specific constraints and consistency criteria are defined. Furthermore, artifacts are selected and assigned to one or more projects. Roles and the associated access rights are defined according to the intended integration workflow. Project Manager also enables tracking of the integration workflow progress. It is possible to define project configurations based on labeling mechanisms, e.g., one configuration can be a certain project view or release. The User Management component is then used to create and modify user information and assign project-specific roles to users.

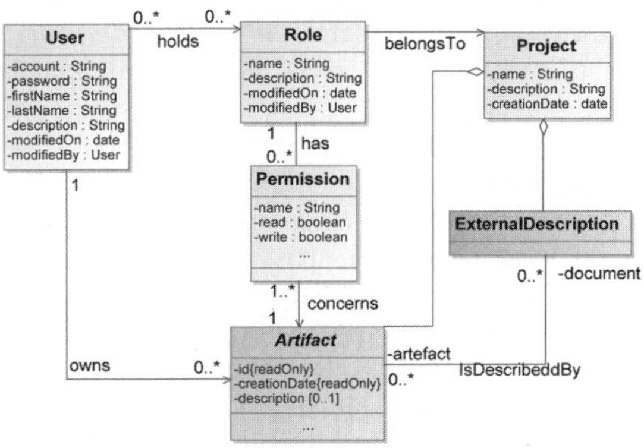

Fig. 3. Project Management and User Control

An artifact can belong to more than one project. An example is a shared metamodel or the common model transformation rules, which can be used in many scenarios, but still have to be kept consistent and centrally managed. Such shared artifact is created once (by its owner), and then can be imported into other projects by the creator or other user, depending on the rights. Non-shared artifacts have their owners, too.

5.2 User Management

Users are project members who are identified by their accounts and names. Users are assigned one or more roles which determine their access rights (permissions) in the BIZYCLE repository. Roles furthermore belong to projects and can be redefined on the project level. One user may have multiple roles in one or more projects. They define the activities and responsibilities and determine the allowed artifact access and manipulation level. For example, a user in a special role can make changes to particular artifacts (such as models), but he would have only read-only access to most artifacts (such as metamodels or transformations). The level of access for each role is defined by permissions. The management of users and artifact types are reserved for the BIZYCLE repository administrator. The project administrator can create projects, select artifact types, and assign roles and permissions. Other user roles (apart from repository and project administrator) are customizable and can be dynamically added.

5.3 Artifact Versioning

During their life cycle artifacts undergo a series of revisions. To reconstruct an old state of an artifact, applying versioning principles is essential. Katz [15] defines version as a semantically meaningful snapshot of a design object at a point in time and describes a design object as an aggregation of design data treated as a coherent unit by designers. Our design objects are artifacts like metamodels, models, transformation rules, generated code or documentation and therefore each version of an artifact represents one of the artifact's (historical) states. During the duration of an integration project, creating and maintaining a significant number of different versions of the same artifact is inevitable.

In order to support versioning, an appropriate version model is required. A version model defines which items in the BIZYCLE repository are to be versioned, which properties (attributes) are shared by all versions, how versions are to be organized and identified. It must also define operations for creating new versions and retrieving existing versions [16].

The versions are traditionally classified in revisions and variants. Revisions are versions of the same item which are created to supersede its predecessor and can be ordered along the time dimension. Variants (branches) are versions of the same item which can occur in parallel at a given time. While new revisions supersede old revisions, variants do not replace each other. The set of all revisions and variants is called a version group [16,17]. A trunk contains all revisions which represent the main line from the first version. Branches are used to represent the variants that exist in parallel. Sometimes two users have to concurrently make changes to an item. The concept of branch allows users to work in parallel on different versions of an item. A merge combines two versions from different branches into a new version in one of the branches.

All versions of an item which are often called a version group can be seen as "incarnations" of the same item. This requires a "sameness criterion" to decide whether two versions are versions of the same item [17]. The decision can be performed by using a unique identifier. All versions of an item must have the same unique identifier which identifies the versioned item. Within a versioned item, each version must be uniquely identifiable by a version identifier. With the prospect of having distributed repositories, items must also be globally identified. All versions of an item must carry item's identifier and a version identifier which must be unique in item's version history.

The version model supporting these requirements is illustrated in Figure 4. The number of potential versions of an artifact created during the integration process is clearly large, and the relationships between revisions (iterations) and variants may be complex. One of the important tasks of versioning is how to organize these versions within the BIZYCLE repository, and how to describe

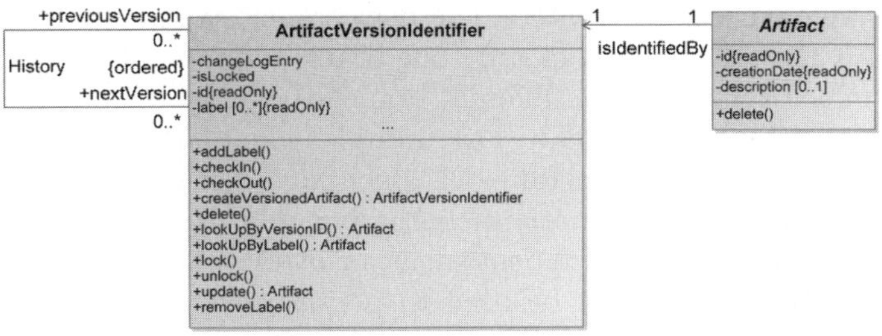

Fig. 4. Version Model

them so they can be properly found and understood by users. In our versioning model, each artifact is identified by a globally unique identifier id. Particular versions of an artifact are identified by the ArtifactVersionIdentifier which must be unique in artifact's version history. The artifact history is expressed by the History association. The complete history of a versioned artifact, including branches for artifact variants and merges, are described by storing the predecessors and successors. Labels may be used to mark certain artifacts, e.g., to allow developers to name and restore a particular state of a project.

Another important versioning facility is allowing the user to define version states which describe the lifecycles of artifacts. The possible states can be described in a taxonomy provided by project management and used to label certain versioned artifacts. The method lookUpByLabel allows users to retrieve an version by a given label.

Versioning is based on the checkout/checkin paradigm adopted in most of the current revision control tools. To perform changes to a specific version of an artifact the user must check out (checkOut method) this version to his workspace. He works usually on a local copy of the version. After performing his changes he checks in (checkIn method) the changed version as a new version of the artifact. A pessimistic approach to manage concurrency is adopted. It enables to lock the artifact by performing a lock operation and prevents conflicts due to editing the same artifact by different users. By locking an artifact a user indicates an intent to make changes. An artifact can be locked by just one user at a time.

5.4 Artifact Merging

In order to enable the cooperative development within an integration project team, the BIZYCLE repository supports branching and merging of artifacts. Whenever an artifact has to be changed by different users, each user must be able to create a new branch to work on the artifact. Each branch can be edited and versioned like the main trunk.

If the user *A* wants to work on a particular version of an artifact and this artifact is locked by the user *B* because he is changing the version, the user *A* must be able to check out this particular version and work on it. After his revisions the user *A* checks in the changed version, and a new branch from the checked-out version will be created. The new branch cannot be locked by user B anymore. A user is able to lock only one branch of an artifact.

Merging of the versions from different branches may be done either automatically (when possible), or manually. For example, when IsPartOf relation clearly marks parts of a model or a metamodel which have been processed in two different branches, a clean automatic merge is possible, assuming that the parts are independent. If the parts are dependent, or overlapping, external tools (referenced in the Section 2) may be used to perform syntactic merge. However, the results of such a merge, especially for models and metamodels, are not very good, since models and metamodels are used to capture semantics and pure syntax/text-based merge of XMI files produces conflicts and not very usable results. Source code artifacts, however, are the example of artifacts that can be merged using existing tools (such as cvs or svn) successfully.

5.5 Consistency Preservation

A repository that supports model-based software and data integration should be able to manage considerable amount of artifact versions, simple descriptive metadata and metadata that specify relations between the artifacts. Due to the complexity of maintaining relations and dependencies between the evolving artifacts, it is difficult but very important to guarantee integrity of the metadata. For this reason, one fundamental aspect of the repository is to preserve consistency.

The state of a database is consistent, if it does not contain any contradictory data. In the context of the BIZYCLE repository, many facets of consistency can be observed. We already introduced versioning methods to support distributed development, avoid concurrency problems and share artifacts, but there is also the need for intelligent handling of artifact and metadata changes during the continuous evolution of the artifacts. We consider two types of consistency that make up the repository consistency. The inner consistency is accomplished if the artifact is stored completely and its representation, like storage format or schema compliance, is free of errors (completeness and validity), which is mainly characterized by the artifact type. The outer consistency is achieved if its descriptive metadata is coherent and its relational metadata is non-contradictory.

Consistency Criteria and Inner Consistency. The consistency criteria consist of logical conditions and information about the evaluation and action procedures which are performed if criteria is triggered. The checking of consistency criteria conditions may also be performed by external tools, like XML validation engine for schema compliance, or model checker for model consistency. In case of a detected inconsistency, the preservation mechanism based on consistency preservation rules triggers detailed notifications of certain users, automated reconciliation or derivation of consistent versions of other affected artifacts.

Preservation of inner consistency is not a major point in our examination. We assume that the completeness of the artifacts is enforced by the transaction mechanisms of the BIZYCLE repository. Despite the fact that we pass the responsibility of enforcing validity to the tools that concentrate on artifact generation or transformation, e.g., modeling tools or code generators, it is also possible to check inner consistency within the BIZYCLE repository by taking advantage of corresponding applications like common schema validator, theorem prover, model checker or other services available at the external tool layer.

Outer Consistency: Criteria and Actions. Assuming the BIZYCLE repository is in a consistent state, changes of the metadata can violate the consistency criteria and set the repository in an ambiguous state. The consistency preservation process consists of activities controlled by the consistency keeper. It is a central entity of the BIZYCLE repository management, responsible for consistency preservation, when artifacts or metadata are created, updated or deleted. For each change request received by the remote access layer, the inner consistency of the concerned artifact has to be assured, which is the minimal requirement for artifact storage. This allows for extraction and derivation of its metadata by the metadata manager. Based on this information and already available metadata of previous versions, the consistency keeper investigates the applicability of outer consistency criteria. Consistency evaluation rules that guard the compliance of corresponding criteria are scheduled and executed, much like triggers that are commonly used in the relational databases. Using transactions, only those artifact-manipulating actions that are confirmed by the consistency keeper will be committed to the persistence layer, so results of the consistency evaluation process may lead to permission, denial or limitation of the persistent storage. Other processes may be initiated that are necessary to resolve consistency conflicts, such as asking for user assistance or launching automated conflict solvers.

If an artifact has been changed, the outer consistency with respect to the existing versions of related artifacts may be affected. Depending on the consistency rules the consistency keeper selects appropriate actions (Figure 5). An automated consistency preservation is the most desirable option, but in most situations missing formalisms lead to ambiguousness. Therefore, often only semi-automated or even manual inconsistency resolution is possible.

The given consistency actions illustrate automatic and manual actions. For example, if a transformation source changes (e.g., a model is modified which is related via IsTransformationTargetOf to another model), its corresponding transformation is automatically derived using the modified artifact instance as a source and reapplying the same transformation rule. Suppose however, that a metamodel has changed and that an appropriate transformation rule is no longer applicable – in this case a notification about inconsistency is signaled and manual intervention required. This holds for other relations, e.g., IsOtherRepresentationOf, where automatic consistency preservation is possible if a mapping between two representations, such as XMI and RDF, are known in advance. Finally, for some relations external tools perform consistency checks, e,g,. an external model checker is used to verify consistency of IsInstanceOf relation when either model or metamodel change. The propagation of changes may affect artifacts that do not directly relate to the artifact that originates the modification. Simply following all relations leads to inefficiencies. To avoid such problems, consistency keeper transforms the scheduled consistency actions into a directed,

Relation	Modification	Consistency preserving action
A IsCopyOf B	A/B	create a new copy
A IsDescribedBy D	A	propagate relation to new version
	D	propose versions of artifacts for possible relation assignment
A IsDocumentedBy D	A	if extraction policies exist: generate documentation; else: notify about artifact changes
	D	propose versions of artifacts for possible relation propagations
A IsOtherRepresentationOf B	A / B	if transformations/mappings exist: generate other representatio; else: notify about artifact changes (e.g. change log or metadata)
A IsSpecialisationOf B / A IsPartOf B / A IsPartOfFlow B	A / B	if transformations/mappings exist: update dependent artifact; else: notify about artifact changes (e.g. change log or metadata)
MA IsTranformationTargetOf T based on MMA and MMB using MB	T / MB	execute Transformation again
	MMA / MMB	notify about metamodel changes
M IsInstanceOf MM	M / MM	check conformance of M to metamodel MM using a model checker

Fig. 5. Consistency criteria and actions (excerpt)

acyclic graph. If this is not possible, e.g., there are cycles which would cause infinite loops of consistency checks and repairs, manual intervention is required.

6 BIZYCLE Repository Prototypical Implementation

The BIZYCLE repository has been prototypically implemented using J2EE technology and JBOSS as the application server. The parts that were developed are sketched in the implementation diagram (Figure 6).

A multi-tiered architecture is used, with facade, session, entity and physical persistence layers. The facade exposes BIZYCLE repository API as Java RMI interface to Java clients and as WSDL interface to SOAP clients. The realized clients are Eclipse GMF Model editors and MagicDraw. The session layer captures the BIZYCLE repository business logic and comprises session beans performing artifact processing (parsing XML/XMI and ATL content), metadata processing (deriving and managing artifact metadata), repository management (consistency, user and project related operations) and providing API to external tools (interfaces to XML schema validator, model checker and theorem prover). Session layer provides interfaces to both Facade and external tools. The entity bean layer provides data model abstraction, coarsely divided into Artifacts, Metadata and Project entity beans. Finally, behind the entity layer the persistent storage has been implemented, using a file system, relational database (MySQL) and an XML database (Berkeley XML DB) as storage for artifact content and the relational database (MySQL) for metadata storage. That way, storage is decoupled from both entity and session layers and can be dynamically reconfigured and its content migrated. The minimal configuration requires a file system for content storage and a relational database for metadata.

Instead of developing the repository from scratch, experiments have been made with integrating existing systems' functionality, especially in the field of artifact progression and versioning at the persistence level. Experiments have been performed with the common source control management software packages such as CVS, SVN and ClearCase. They provide different versioning models and support for collaboration, such as locking, variable merging models, transactional

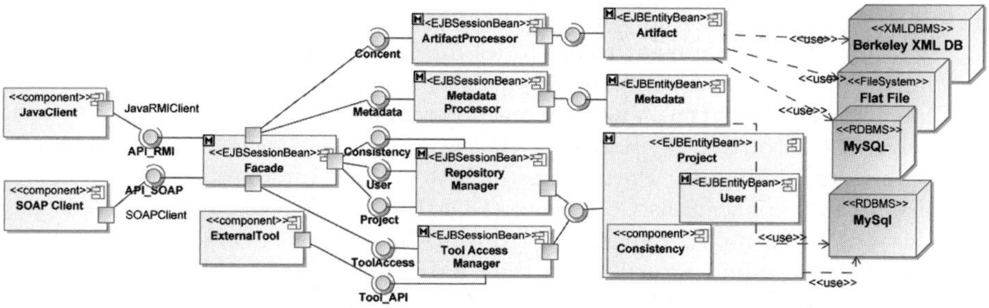

Fig. 6. Prototypical Implementation

behavior, enforcement of security aspects and storage of metadata for each artifact version. More advanced features of the repository concern project oriented artifact life cycle management, and Apache Maven has been investigated in this context. It standardizes the project structure by setting up conventions using certain project archetypes and simplifies the build behavior through unification of the build process. Furthermore, Maven handles project dependencies, provides features for documentation and reporting.

7 Conclusion and Future Work

For the complex MBSE (meta-)tool platform provided by the BIZYCLE frame, we have presented the information model, the software architecture, several methodological considerations and, finally, a prototypical implementation of the BIZYCLE repository. Particularly, the aspects of evolution, i.e. versioning, merging and consistency of the variety of (meta-)models, metadata, documents, and other artifacts, are challenges in this multi-user environment, and are still subject to research and development throughout the MDA community.

The flexible and open architecture of the BIZYCLE repository allows for plug-in integration of external tool support, such as consistency checkers, intelligent versioning and management support for different kinds of artifacts, as well as services to be found in the Eclipse framework. As we follow the paradigm of *continuous software engineering*, we are open to extend the repository with paradigm changes like other MOF metamodel level hierarchy, new modeling languages and their artifacts, new programming languages or middleware services, to be reflected in appropriate metadata sets.

References

1. Kutsche, R., Milanovic, N.: (Meta-)Models, Tools and Infrastructures for Business Application Integration. In: Kaschek, R., et al. (eds.) UNISCON 2008. LNBIP, vol. 5. Springer, Heidelberg (2008)
2. Kutsche, R., Milanovic, N., Bauhoff, G., Baum, T., Cartsburg, M., Kumpe, D., Widiker, J.: BIZYCLE: Model-based Interoperability Platform for Software and Data Integration. In: Proceedings of the MDTPI at ECMDA (2008)

3. Pulier, E., Taylor, H.: Understanding Enterprise SOA. Manning (2006)
4. Schmid, F.: Erstellung eines Repositories für die Verwaltung und Transformation von Komponentenmodellen (November 2004) (in German)
5. Fedora Repository, `http://www.fedora-commons.org/`
6. Boldyreff, C., Nutter, D., Rank, S.: Active artefact management for distributed software engineering. In: Proceedings of 26th Annual International on Computer Software and Applications Conference (COMPSAC 2002), pp. 1081–1086 (2002)
7. Lucia, A.D., Fasano, F., Oliveto, R., Tortora, G.: Adams: Advanced artefact management system. In: Proceedings of the CSMR, pp. 349–350. IEEE Computer Society, Los Alamitos (2006)
8. NetBeans Metadata Repository, `http://mdr.netbeans.org/`
9. MOF 2.0 / XMI Mapping Specification, v2.1.1, `http://www.omg.org/technology/documents/formal/xmi.htm`
10. 2008 metadata solutions report (December 2007), `http://www.gavsys.com/rptfiles/GavResearch-sample-report-pages-Nov2007.pdf`
11. Meta Object Facility (MOF) Versioning and Development Lifecycle Specification, v2.0, formal/07-05-01, OMG Group (May 2007)
12. Alanen, M., Porres, I.: Difference and Union of Models. Technical Report 527, Turku Centre for Computer Science (April 2003)
13. Störrle, H.: A formal approach to the cross-language version management of models. In: Proceedings of the NW-MODE 2007 (2007)
14. Hnětynka, P., Plášil, F.: Distributed Versioning Model for MOF. In: Proceedings of the Winter International Symposium on Information and Comunication Technologies (WISICT 2004), Trinity College Dublin, pp. 489–494 (2004)
15. Katz, R.H.: Toward a unified framework for version modeling in engineering databases. ACM Comput. Surv. 22(4), 375–409 (1990)
16. Westfechtel, B., Munch, B.P., Conradi, R.: A layered architecture for uniform version management. IEEE Trans. Softw. Eng. 27(12), 1111–1133 (2001)
17. Conradi, R., Westfechtel, B.: Version models for software configuration management. ACM Comput. Surv. 30(2), 232–282 (1998)

Model Construction with External Constraints: An Interactive Journey from Semantics to Syntax

Mikoláš Janota[1], Victoria Kuzina[2], and Andrzej Wąsowski[2]

[1] Lero, University College Dublin, Ireland
mikolas.janota@ucd.ie
[2] IT University of Copenhagen, Denmark
{victoria,wasowski}@itu.dk

Abstract. Mainstream development environments have recently assimilated guidance technologies based on constraint satisfaction. We investigate one class of such technologies, namely, interactive guided derivation of models, where the editing system assists a designer by providing hints about valid editing operations that maintain global correctness. We provide a semantics-based classification of such guidance systems and investigate concrete guidance algorithms for two kinds of modeling languages: a simple subset of class-diagram-like language and for feature models. Both algorithms are efficient and provide exhaustive guidance.

1 Introduction

Modern modeling and development environments, like Rational® Software Modeler, Visual Studio®, and Eclipse™ embrace interactive support. They offer context-sensitive hints of valid editing operations, such as name completion. These techniques are somewhat limited though. Proposed operations are locally correct with respect to a syntax definition, a metamodel, or a type system, but they do not guarantee global correctness, in the sense of satisfying more complex combinatorial constraints beyond the type system—a need more often seen in domain specific modeling languages (DSMLs). Recently, new techniques [24,11,22,20] have been proposed that increase adaptivity of guidance and strengthen the correctness guarantees.

All these techniques recognize the strength of interactive guidance as opposed to mere validation of constraints or batch synthesis of models without human intervention. Many constraints cannot be meaningfully validated on incomplete models. Effectively, validation provides feedback too late, when the model is ready, the errors are present and substantial revisions might be needed. Batch synthesis in turn favours purely mechanical constraint satisfaction, failing to uncover deep domain knowledge to achieve clarity characteristic to human-made artifacts. Interactive guidance is the midway path between the batch synthesis and validation. It is an incremental model transformation [6,19], which by providing early feedback eliminates the risk of inconsistencies. Still it puts the modeler in control, who shapes the model herself, striving for clarity and precision.

K. Czarnecki et al. (Eds.): MoDELS 2008, LNCS 5301, pp. 431–445, 2008.

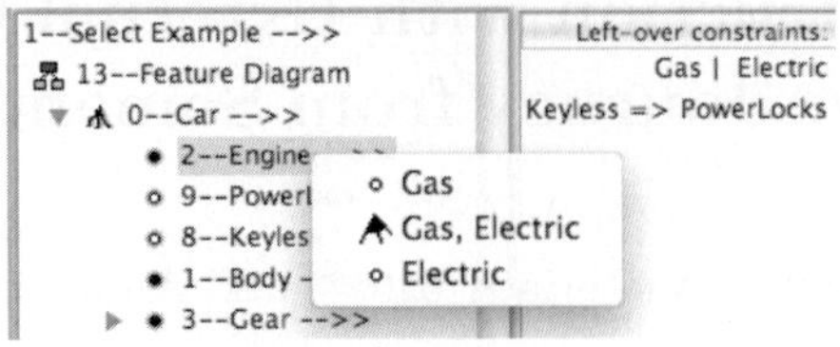

Fig. 1. Guidance with context menus (a screen from our prototype for feature models)

The aim of our work is twofold: 1) to advance the understanding of interactive model derivation from the semantics perspective and 2) to develop guidance algorithms for concrete modeling languages. Our contributions comprise:

– A rigorous definition of interactive model derivation, and a classification of derivation processes aligned with the conceptual modeling hierarchy.
– Identification of efficient and reliable existing technology supporting soundness preserving instantiation of a nontrivial subset of class diagrams.
– Novel algorithms for completeness-preserving and for semantics-preserving derivation of feature models. Crucially, our algorithms are terminating, complete and execute efficiently.
– A definiton of expressive power for guided derivation algorithms in general, and a corresponding evaluation of expressiveness for our new algorithms.

Our primary audience are builders of modeling tools in general and in particular of platforms for model driven engineering with DSMLs. We believe that the topic is also relevant for language designers and for researchers studying semantics of modeling languages and model transformation.

Outline. Section 2 introduces interactive model derivation, and its classification. Section 3 discusses soundness preserving derivation for class-diagram-like DSMLs. In Section 4 we recall basic background about feature models, used subsequently in Sections 5–6 to study completeness- and semantics-preserving derivation. We briefly describe our prototype in Section 6.3 and relate to existing literature in Section 7. We summarize and discuss future work in Section 8.

2 Interactive Model Derivation

Figure 1 shows a screen of our prototype model editor for feature models. A user has just asked for editing the Engine node and a list of suggestions has opened. Here, three choices are proposed, namely to create an or-group comprising Electric and Gas or append any of the features individually as an optional subfeature. In general, guidance is provided by offering valid editing steps. As the number of ways to proceed is typically large, the operations that are offered apply to a context determined by the user, e.g., a feature node, a class, or a state.

Figure 2 shows an overview of the process. The designer queries the editor for possible valid edit operations, the editor provides a list of such and the designer chooses one. The editor executes the operation and waits for the next input.

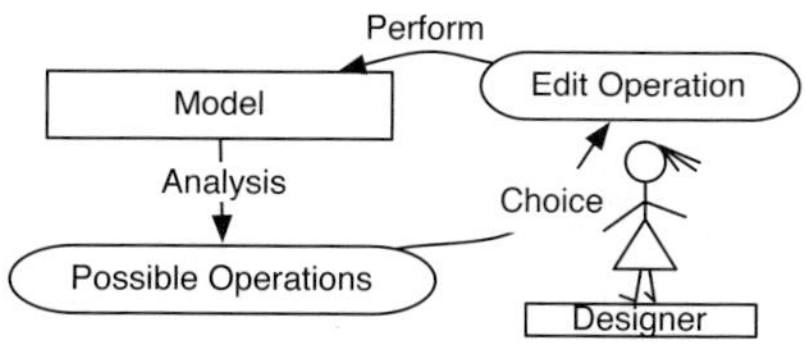

Fig. 2. An overview of the interactive model derivation process

How does the editor know which operations are valid? The operations are chosen so that they do not violate imposed constraints. The simplest constraints come from syntax and typing rules (well-formedness), the more intricate ones from combinatorial aspects of the domain, especially for DSMLs. A reasoning algorithm translates knowledge from constraints to an accessible form, such as a list of edit operations. Below we write VALID-OPERATIONS to denote such a reasoning algorithm. Naturally, even though we use a single name for all of them, the concrete algorithms differ depending on use cases and modeling languages.

Consider a modeling language $\mathcal{M}$ with the syntax defined using a metamodel. The semantics of $\mathcal{M}$ is given by assigning to each model $M : \mathcal{M}$ a logic description denoted $[\![M]\!]$. VALID-OPERATIONS returns a set of editing operations, which are mappings from models to models.

Naturally, a transformation applied to a model yields a change in the pertaining semantics. In this article we focus only on algorithms that identify transformations that *refine* the model. Semantically, a refinement is characterized by strengthening the semantics of the model (making the model more restrictive). Intuitively, any instance of the refined model is also an instance of the original one. More formally, for each $O \in$ VALID-OPERATIONS(M) the following implication holds: $[\![O(M)]\!] \rightarrow [\![M]\!]$.

Focusing on refinement is motivated by the goal of a *gradual* construction of the model. Hence we will be concerned with *sequences* of editing operations, most often with sequences that begin with an empty model and lead to a fully constructed one. A limit of such sequences of refinements is typically a point beyond which refinement is not desirable. For instance, for a model with semantics expressed as a set, a singleton set is a possible limit.

In general, we aim for guidance algorithms to propose enough operations so all such limits are attainable, not preventing the user from deriving any useful models. We will call this property *exhaustiveness of advice*. In a similar spirit we will require *validity of advice*, i.e., that *no* sequence of operations selected from the proposed choice is leading to an invalid model.

Apart from the refinement requirement, we also consider a constraint, φ, capturing additional domain knowledge. We have identified three different model derivation scenarios differentiated by what role the constraint φ has. The first scenario is mostly known under the term *modeling*: instantiation of metamodels. It aims at constructing a single instance of a metamodel, for example an object diagram, and can be seen as a gradual narrowing of a set of possible instances to a single instance of interest. We shall call such a process a *soundness-preserving*

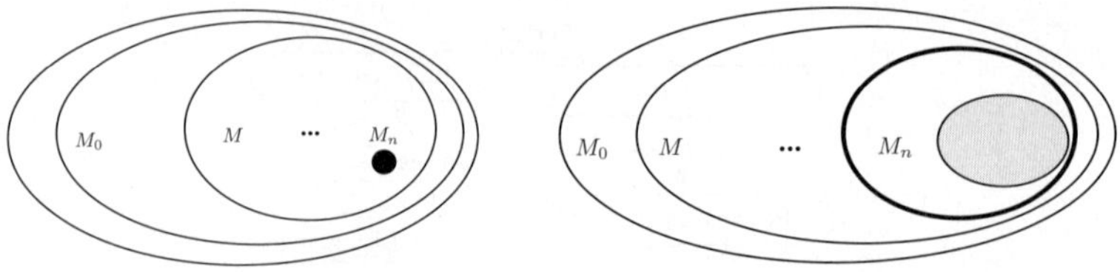

a. Soundness-preserving. **b.** Completeness-preserving.

Fig. 3. Limits of evolution in different classes of model derivation

model derivation. Consider the visualization in 3a. The designer seeks for a particular instance that satisfies φ and each of the transformations brings her closer to the desired solution. The ellipses represent intermediate models and the goal instance is depicted as $\bullet$. A very simple example of soundness-preserving derivation is interactive configuration [10,14] of feature-models [5], where one specific product, a configuration, from a domain is selected. Other applications include instantiation of highly combinatorial DSMLs as seen in [24].

We say that $\{O_i\}_{i=1..n}$ is a sequence of valid operations and $\{M_i\}_{i=0..n}$ is its associated sequence of intermediate models iff $O_i \in \textsc{Valid-Operations}(M_{i-1})$ and $M_{i+1} = O_{i+1}(M_i)$. For the derivation to be soundness-preserving all the intermediate models must be within the bounds of the constraint φ which represents the domain (φ can amount to a metamodel and a set of OCL constraints). More specifically, $[\![M_i]\!] \rightarrow \varphi$ holds for all i.

In soundness-preserving derivation any $\textsc{Valid-Operations}$ algorithm has the *exhaustive advice* property iff it enables deriving all valid instances, i.e., for any model M respecting the constraints ($[\![M]\!] \rightarrow \varphi$) there exists a sequence of valid operations and its associated sequence of models $\{M_i\}_{i=1..n}$ and $M = M_n$.

The second model derivation scenario takes us from modeling to metamodeling: modeling of domains, as opposed to single artifacts. Here the model derivation refines the entire universum of models to a *subset* that describes a certain domain as precisely as possible in the given language. We shall call such model derivations *completeness-preserving* since they focus not on finding a specific valid instance (as in soundness-preserving), but on *removing all unsuitable* instances. Figure 3b gives an intuition: The derivation starts with a very loose model M_0 and gradually approaches a model that tightly over-approximates φ.

Completeness-preserving model derivation is less common than the soundness-preserving one, in the same way as metamodeling is a less common activity than modeling. It can be used to reverse-engineer models from logic descriptions of constraints—a functionality particularly needed in modeling of non-software products, where designers are trained in product design but not in the kind of modeling commonly seen in IT. What is perhaps more interesting, it can be used to refine existing models of domains on which new constraints are being imposed. Such constraints may arise from the context of the model. For instance, in our previous work we have investigated how constraints in an architecture model propagate to constraints of the feature model [13].

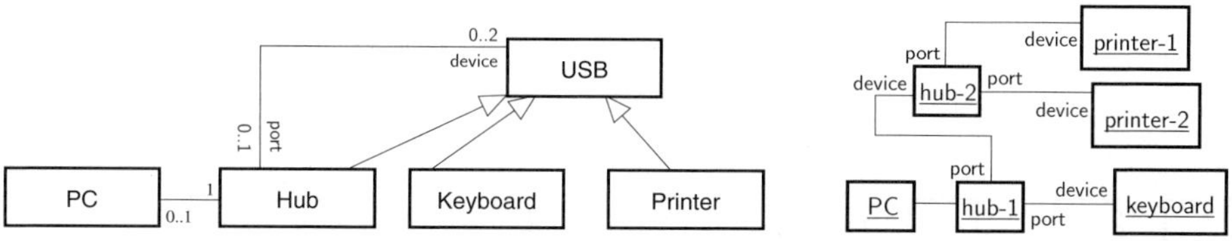

a. The USB metamodel **b.** A model of a USB bus

Fig. 4. The USB language and its instance. Inspired by [23]

Formally, for any sequence of valid operations $\{O_i\}_{i=1..n}$ and its sequence of intermediate models $\{M_i\}_{i=0..n}$ it holds that $\varphi \rightarrow [\![M_i]\!]$ for any i. We will say that a completeness-preserving VALID-OPERATIONS algorithm has the *exhaustive advice* property iff it enables to derive all the models that are weaker than φ, i.e., for any M, such that $\varphi \rightarrow [\![M]\!]$, there exists a sequence of valid operations and their associated intermediate models $\{M_i\}_{i=0..n}$ with $M = M_n$.

The final scenario is a very well known class of model transformations that lies in the intersection of semantics- and completeness-preserving cases: the class of *semantics-preserving* transformations or *refactorings*. Any refactoring O has the property that $[\![O(M)]\!] = [\![M]\!]$ and for any sequence of valid refactorings $\{O_i\}_i = 1..n$ with the intermediate models $\{M_i\}_{i=0..n}$ we have that $[\![M_i]\!] = [\![M_{i+1}]\!]$. We easily see that sequences of operations that satisfy this condition are both semantics- and completeness preserving.

Below we detail interactive derivation algorithms for concrete languages and corresponding use cases, one for each class out of the three defined above.

3 Soundness-Preserving Model Derivation

We have characterized soundness-preserving model derivation as an editing process proceeding via a sequence of models with decreasing space of possible completions, so that for any M_i we have that $[\![M_i]\!] \rightarrow \varphi$. Below we consider an instance of this problem for a DSML describing USB buses, defined by the metamodel in Fig. 4a. Each model in this language describes a USB bus comprising a PC to which a hub is connected. Each hub has two ports. Each port can be used as a socket to which another USB device is connected; either another hub, or a keyboard, or a printer. Figure 4b shows a simple model.

As it is often the case, the metamodel as such cannot fully express the syntactic restrictions on the model, so it is accompanied by a set of constraints. The constraints are typically formalized, but for the sake of simplicity we express them in plain English here: (C1) each model must contain exactly one instance of PC, (C2) every USB device is connected to a port or to the PC instance, and (C3) every bus has a keyboard connected or a free port to connect one. We want to assist the designer in creating USB models satisfying these constraints.

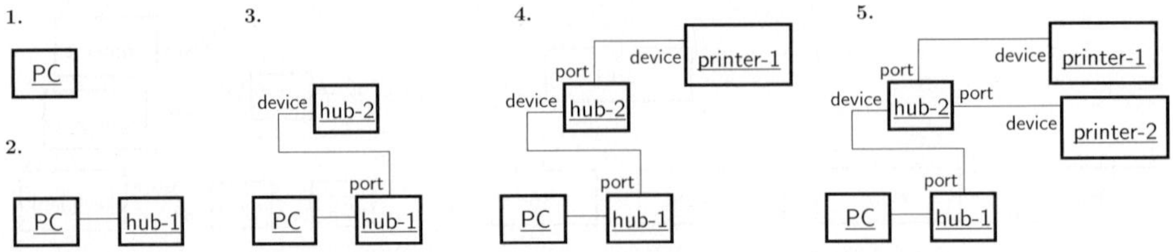

Fig. 5. Stages of editing the example from 4b

Out of many derivation processes possible, in this work we focus on syntactically monotonic ones, i.e., beginning with an empty model and refining the model syntactically by adding new elements step by step. The new elements must be added to the existing ones, which means that whenever we instantiate a new device on the bus, we need to connect it to one of the existing ports.

Figure 5 shows a derivation of a simple model. We start with an empty diagram. As a consequence of (C1) and (C2), the editor[1] proposes a single possible edit step: the instantiation of a PC node. Constraint (C2) yields a possible set of choices in the second step: instantiate and connect a hub (step 2). In step 3 the tool suggests instantiating and connecting a USB device object to any of the two ports of hub-1. All three types of devices are offered (a hub, a keyboard, and a printer). We choose the hub, and then similarly two printers in steps 4–5. The final step of the example is perhaps the most interesting one. We are in a state, in which only one port is free, in the hub-1 object. Possible edit steps for this port are to instantiate either a hub or a keyboard. Observe that a printer object cannot be suggested at this point as connecting a printer would exclude the possibility of connecting any other device to the bus. Consequently constraint (C3) would be violated. Selecting a hub is safe as it still leaves the possibility of connecting a keyboard later. Select a keyboard to obtaining the model in Fig. 4b.

3.1 Soundness-Preserving Derivation as Modular Configuration

Our USB language is in fact an instance of the *modular configuration problem.* In [23] algorithms for monotonic syntactic derivation of instances of these problems are presented, guaranteeing validity and exhaustiveness of advice.

Modular configuration problems can be equated to a decidable class of object-diagram-like languages with propositional constraints interpreted over associations. More precisely, a constraint associated with a class is interpreted separately for each of its objects, and can refer only to variables of the object itself, and to variables of objects directly reachable via a navigation step from that object. No quantification or iteration is allowed in constraints, and all associations have bounded multiplicity. While the metamodels can contain cycles, only acyclic and connected instances are allowed. As the constraints are interpreted over *instantiations* of associations they can encode many inductive properties normally reserved for first order logics—like having a keyboard on each bus.

[1] Such an editor is feasible, as [23] demonstrates.

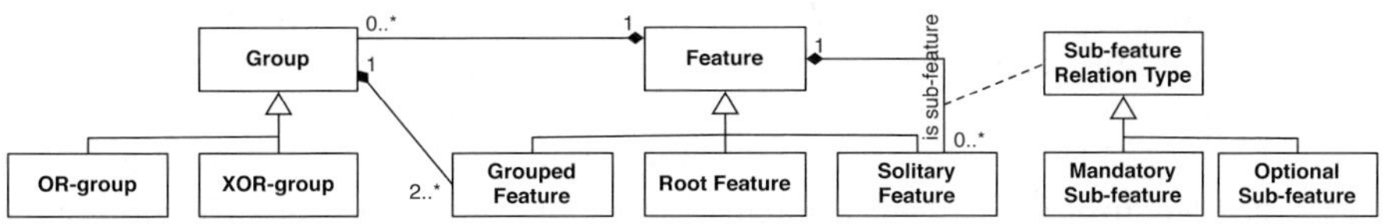

a. The metamodel

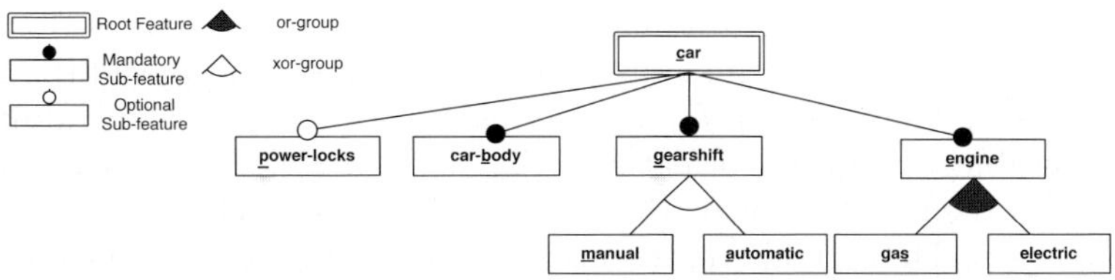

b. An example of a feature diagram, inspired by [7]

Fig. 6. The Language of Propositional Feature Diagrams

4 Background: Propositional Feature Models

Let us recall the language of feature models, exploited as an example in the upcoming sections. Feature models [15] are used to systematically describe variability and commonality in product line engineering [4]. In a nutshell, a feature corresponds to a specific functionality of a system. A feature model records available features, together with constraints and dependencies relating them.

A variety of feature diagram languages is found in the literature, mostly with propositional semantics [21]. We should note, however, that other semantics exist, for instance using grammars [2], higher-order [12] and probabilistic [8] logic. In this article we operate on the combinatorial core of feature models, the propositional models [7]. A propositional feature model comprises a *feature diagram* and a *constraint*. The diagram is the centerpiece. It records the features and dependencies in a graph-based notation. An additional constraint is appended if it cannot be expressed in the diagrammatic language itself.

A feature diagram organizes features in a tree, containing a node for each feature. A child node, or a *sub-feature*, is either *optional*, *mandatory*, or *grouped*. A grouped feature belongs either to an *or-group* or an *xor-group* with other sub-features of the same parent. Fig. 6a shows the metamodel of this language.

Apart from hierarchically organizing the features, the purpose of the diagram is to determine which combinations of features, so-called *feature configurations*, are permitted. The root feature must be present in all configurations. A sub-feature must not be selected into a configuration not containing its parent. A mandatory feature is required by its parent, whereas an optional one is not. From features grouped in an or-group (resp. xor-group) at least one (resp. exactly one) must be selected whenever the parent is selected. The feature diagram in Fig. 6b describes possible configurations of a car. Each car must have a body, gearshift, and engine; an engine is electric *or* gas (selecting both corresponds to a hybrid engine); a gearshift is *either* automatic or manual.

The semantics $[\![\cdot]\!]$ of a propositional feature diagram is defined as the set of permitted configurations. Symbolically such a set is identified with the set of satisfiable assignments of its characteristic formula in propositional logic. The formula is created by binding a single variable to each feature, and translating the syntax of a feature diagram in a natural manner. More specifically, the formula is a conjunction of the formulas yielded by the individual constructs, which are defined as follows. The root r is always selected, hence yields the formula r. Features $f_1, \ldots, f_n$ grouped in an or-group under the parent p yield the formula $f_1 \vee \cdots \vee f_n \leftrightarrow p$. An xor-group $f_1, \ldots, f_n$ yields $f_1 \vee \cdots \vee f_n \leftrightarrow p$ and additionally mutually disables the grouped features: $\bigwedge_{i \neq j} \neg(f_i \wedge f_j)$. Finally, each optional feature c with the parent p yields the formula $c \rightarrow p$ and each mandatory feature m yields $m \leftrightarrow p$. The formula representing the semantics of the model in Fig. 6b is: $c \wedge (p \rightarrow c) \wedge (b \leftrightarrow c) \wedge (g \leftrightarrow c) \wedge (e \leftrightarrow c) \wedge (g \leftrightarrow m \,\mathsf{xor}\, a) \wedge (e \leftrightarrow s \vee l)$. In order to obtain semantics of the entire feature model (M, ψ) we lift the semantics of the feature diagram M and conjoin it with the constraint ψ: $[\![(M, \psi)]\!] = [\![M]\!] \wedge \psi$.

Some authors extend the diagram language with *excludes* and *requires* edges that may cross the tree hierarchy. Such extended diagrams are technically fully expressive, in the sense that they can encode any propositional formula [21]. However, when it comes to expressiveness, there is little difference between the use of an explicit constraint (ψ) and the two additional constructs. Indeed, our results from Sections 5–6 can easily be extended to account for the two.

5 Completeness-Preserving Model Derivation

Section 2 characterizes completeness-preserving derivation as a sequence of transformations in which the semantics of intermediate models covers the given constraint at all times, so $\varphi \rightarrow [\![M_i]\!]$ for all intermediate M_i. In this section we develop a completeness-preserving Valid-Operations algorithm for a specific case—derivation of feature diagrams, or feature models without the constraint.

5.1 Analysis

Consider a scenario in which instead of a feature model of a car we are given a collection of constraints; for example that a car cannot have both manual and automatic gearshift. Let φ be a conjunction of such constraints. The constraints are proposed by various stakeholders involved in car development. Now a modeler needs to construct a feature diagram that faithfully captures φ.

How do we characterize a diagram that *faithfully* captures a constraint? On the one hand, the desired feature diagram should not be more restrictive than φ — otherwise it would have ruled out configurations that do not violate the constraints. On the other hand, the diagram should capture as much of the constraints as possible, ideally precisely those that are configurations of φ. In general, since a propositional feature diagram alone is not expressive enough to capture arbitrary constraints, we strive for capturing strongest possible overapproximations of φ, hoping that these would most clearly represent the intrinsic

VALID-OPERATIONS(M, n, φ) : set of operations

$\triangleright$ M is a (partially constructed) feature diagram

$\triangleright$ n is a node in M, present iff M is nonempty

1 **if** M is empty **then return** $\{\mathsf{Root}(r) \mid \varphi, M \models r\}$

2 *solitary* $\leftarrow \{\mathsf{Mandatory}(n, c) \mid \varphi, M \models c \leftrightarrow n$ and c not instantiated in $M\}$
$\cup \{\mathsf{Optional}(n, c) \mid \varphi, M \models c \rightarrow n$ and c not instantiated in $M\}$

3 *groups* $\leftarrow \{\mathsf{OrGroup}(n, m_1 \dots m_k) \mid n \leftrightarrow \varphi, M \models \bigvee_{i \in 1 \dots k} m_i,$
$k > 1$ and all m_i are not instantiated in $M\}$
$\cup \{\mathsf{XorGroup}(n, m_1 \dots m_k) \mid \varphi, M \models n \leftrightarrow \bigvee_{i \in 1 \dots k} m_i \wedge \bigwedge_{i \neq j} \neg(m_i \wedge m_j),$
$k > 1$ and all m_i are not instantiated in $M\}$

4 *refine* $\leftarrow \{\mathsf{RefineOR\text{-}group}(n, m_1, \dots, m_k) \mid$
$\{m_1, \dots, m_k\}$ is an or-group of p in M and $\varphi, M \models \bigwedge_{i \neq j} \neg(m_i \wedge m_j)\}$
$\cup \{\mathsf{RefineOptional}(n) \mid n$ is an optional child of p in M, and $\varphi, M \models n \rightarrow p\}$

5 **return** *solitary* $\cup$ *groups* $\cup$ *refine*

Fig. 7. Computing completeness-preserving operations for propositional feature models

combinatorial structure of φ. So we seek for a diagram M that conforms to the metamodel (Fig. 6a) and whose semantics is weaker than the provided constraints, so: $\varphi \rightarrow [\![M]\!]$, and which is refined as much as possible.

In another use case, a new constraint should to be imposed on an already existing feature model. Consider again the example of Fig. 6b. The designer adds a feature keyless-entry which requires power-locks. So an additional constraint keyless-entry $\rightarrow$ power-locks arises. The editor computes that the keyless-entry can be a sub-feature of power-locks and if the user opts for this operation, the implication can be removed. The editor also computes that keyless-entry can be made a sub-feature of car, due to transitivity of implication. However, if the user chooses this operation, the formula keyless-entry $\rightarrow$ power-locks is not captured in the diagram and must be appended as a new constraint to the model.

Similarly as in Sect. 3 we choose to work with syntactically monotonic derivations. For feature diagrams it means that our editing steps add new syntactic constructs to existing parts of the diagram, as opposed to modifying them. Strictly speaking, we do supply a few simple non-monotonic steps for usability reasons. These extensions however do not influence the expressiveness of the available transformations when it comes to validity and exhaustiveness of advice.

5.2 Completeness-Preserving Derivation of Feature Diagrams

The process starts with a feature diagram M satisfying $\varphi \rightarrow [\![M]\!]$. The algorithm VALID-OPERATIONS (see Fig. 7) suggests editing operations. As we do not want to overwhelm the user with an inundation of possible operations, the algorithm provides editing operations for a specific node, denoted n in Fig. 7.

For the sake of clarity, let us first assume that we have a magic oracle determining queries of the form $\varphi, M \models \psi$, meaning that assuming the constraint φ

and the semantics of diagram M, the proposition ψ holds: $\varphi \wedge [\![M]\!] \rightarrow \psi$. The algorithm mirrors, in a sense, the semantics of feature diagrams. For a given node n, it needs to find *all* possible mandatory sub-features, i.e., features c that are not in the diagram yet and for which the bi-implication $n \leftrightarrow c$ holds (line 2). Other primitives of the diagram meta-model are covered analogously.

Line 4 is somewhat different from the preceding ones. Whereas the previous lines *add* to the diagram, this one *modifies* the existing constructs. Any or-group may be refined to an xor-group if a sufficient constraint is provided, i.e., mutual exclusion of the grouped features. Analogously for the optional feature.

An implementation of the oracle $\varphi, M \models \psi$ is actually presented in [7], where a technique is developed for compiling a boolean formula into a so-called *feature graph.* When using a feature graph as an oracle, necessary queries can be evaluated in time polynomial in the number of features. Indeed, most of the queries used in the above algorithm can be established during a single traversal of the feature graph, which makes this algorithm very efficient. All this despite that most of the queries would require solving NP-complete problems, when applied to a textual representation of φ. Efficiency during derivation is possible, because the hardness of the problem is shifted to a startup phase, when the feature graph is generated (generation is NP-hard). The generation runs only once per an editing session (as opposed to at every editing step) and it can be efficiently implemented using binary decision diagrams [3].

Valid advice. The algorithm of Fig. 7 suggests only the operations that are completeness-preserving. More specifically, for any returned operation O and a model M s.t. $\varphi \rightarrow [\![M]\!]$ it holds that $\varphi \rightarrow [\![O(M)]\!]$. The proof of this fact proceeds by comparing the algorithm to the semantics defined in Sect. 4.

Exhaustive advice. This algorithm provides exhaustive advice, meaning that any feature diagram weaker than φ can be derived from the empty diagram in a finite number of steps by solely applying operations suggested by the algorithm. For the lack of space we do not provide the whole proof, but only illustrate the basic idea. Assume that an adversary gives us a diagram M and a constraint φ such that $\varphi \rightarrow [\![M]\!]$. Our goal is to re-construct M using the editor. We start at the root and descend towards the leaves. First, let us look at the root r: Because it is a root and $[\![M]\!]$ is weaker than φ, we have $\varphi \rightarrow [\![M]\!]$ and $[\![M]\!] \equiv r \wedge \psi$ for some ψ (see the definition of $[\![\cdot]\!]$ in Sect. 4). Together this yields that $\varphi \rightarrow r$, so r will be offered to the user (Line 1) as an option when she starts editing.

Let c be any optional sub-feature that has not been reconstructed so far and p be a re-constructed parent of c. We have $[\![M]\!] \equiv (c \rightarrow p) \wedge \psi$ and hence by the same reasoning as before $(\varphi \wedge p) \rightarrow c$, therefore c will be offered to the user as an optional child of p. The rest of the proof is carried out in an analogous fashion.

On the side, note that the algorithm enables us to start the derivation from an arbitrary diagram, not necessarily an empty one. Hence a stronger form of the exhaustive advice property can be shown for it: any diagram M' such that $([\![M]\!] \wedge \varphi) \rightarrow [\![M']\!]$ and that respects the parent-child relation imposed by M, can be derived from M using the suggested steps.

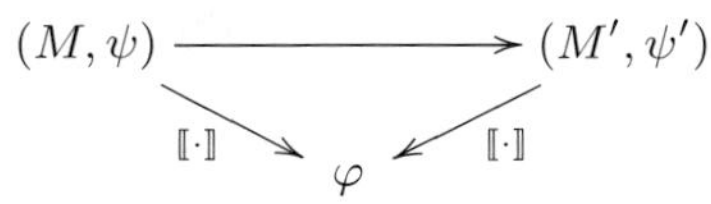

Fig. 8. A refactoring step for a feature model (M, ψ): $[\![M']\!] \rightarrow [\![M]\!]$, $[\![\psi]\!] \rightarrow [\![\psi']\!]$

6 Semantics-Preserving Editing Feature Models

Recall that a propositional feature model comprises a diagram and a boolean formula. The semantics of this pair is defined as a conjunction of the semantics of the diagram and the formula. For feature models, semantics-preserving transformations are those that preserve the satisfying assignments of that conjunction. One may imagine an amplitude of transformations that are semantic-preserving. Below we describe the type of transformation that we have targeted in our work.

6.1 Feature Diagram Refinement by Model Refactoring

Let us replay the scenario from Sect. 5.1, this time considering both a diagram *and* a constraint. As previously, the goal is to approximate the given constraint φ with a feature diagram, which is not likely to capture the constraint completely leaving a remainder in the second component of the model.

The editing process starts with the empty diagram and φ as the constraint component. The constraint is weakened gradually, whenever the diagram is refined. The semantics of the entire model is preserved throughout. Figure 8 schematically depicts what we expect from each single editing operation.

The algorithm in Sect. 5.2 lets us assist the user with refining the diagram while keeping its semantics weaker than φ. In here, the editor should also provide for automatic transformation of the constraint. For instance, if the constraint contains the formula $c \rightarrow p$ and the user makes c to be an optional sub-feature of p, one would predict that the formula in question will be removed from the constraints as the sub-feature relation already captures the implication (see Sect. 4). These simplifications are important for the user as they give her an intuition of how much of the left-over constraint is alread incorporated into the diagram.

We should note that there is no single obvious notion of simplification. Simplification cannot be defined as weakening. Changing $x \wedge y$ to x weakens and arguably simplifies, whereas changing x to $x \vee y$ weakens but hardly classifies as simplification. Hence, by simplification we mean an operation that reduces the size of the syntactic representation of the formula and keeps as much of the original structure as possible while preserving the pertaining semantics.

6.2 Adapting Constraint for Diagram Refinement

The diagram is refined by the user by choosing an operation from a set suggested by VALID-OPERATIONS (see Fig. 7). It is clear how these operations affect the diagram. Here we explain how to adapt the left-over constraint.

Our prototype accepts the input in the Conjunctive Normal Form (CNF) with enhancements that enable writing for instance IFF f_1 f_2 for the two clauses $\neg f_1 \vee f_2$ and $\neg f_2 \vee \neg f_1$. Each editing operation results in a set of clauses $\mathcal{C}$ that represents the constraints and a boolean formula ψ that corresponds to the semantics of the current feature diagram. Hence, the problem now is to simplify $\mathcal{C}$ under the assumption that ψ holds.

The first simplification we perform reduces $\mathcal{C}$ to such form that no clause $c \in \mathcal{C}$ is implied by the conjunct of the rest of the clauses and ψ, i.e., there is no $c \in \mathcal{C}$ such that $\bigwedge_{d \in \mathcal{C} \setminus \{c\}} (d \wedge \psi) \rightarrow c$. This reduction is implemented by repeatedly choosing and removing a clause that violates this property until no such clause exists[2]. Binary Decision Diagrams (BDDs) [3] are used to decide the individual implications but a SAT solver could be used as well.

Apart from performing the operations suggested by the algorithm VALID-OPERATIONS (Fig. 7), the user chooses the root of the feature diagram when the derivation process begins. A feature r can be chosen as a root if it is implied by all the other features while assuming φ. The choice of the root r corresponds to setting r to *true*. That lets us simplify $\mathcal{C}$ by repeatedly using the tautologies $(\mathit{true} \vee C) \leftrightarrow \mathit{true}$ and $(\mathit{false} \vee C) \leftrightarrow C$, a technique known as *unit propagation*.

Our motivation for using CNF was that it enables performing simplifications in a rather uniform manner while it is still fully expressive. Many useful constructs, e.g., f_1 *excludes* f_2, map directly to their clausal form ($\neg f_1 \vee \neg f_2$ in this case). Nevertheless, both types of simplification could be extended to operate on a general boolean form. Instead of operating on a set of clauses, one would operate on a set of boolean expressions. Then, the reduction of this set (first simplification) can be done in the same fashion. The unit propagation of the root would be replaced by substituting *true* for the root in each expression and subsequently applying standard boolean tautologies, such as $(a \wedge \mathit{true}) \leftrightarrow a$.

6.3 Implementation

We have embedded the algorithm VALID-OPERATIONS (see Fig. 7) into an Eclipse plug-in that lets the user load a file with a constraint and derive the desired feature diagram. The editing process follows the principles described in Sect. 2 and the simplification of the constraint is performed as described in Sect. 6.2. The constraint, in Conjunctive Normal Form, is translated to a BDD representation that is further used to compute the feature graph — a structure that answers queries for VALID-OPERATIONS (see [7] for details).

We have applied the implementation to models described in the literature, including the largest publicly available example known to us, a model of an ecommerce system from [18], for which the editor responded with imperceptible time delays. Details in [17]. The main bottleneck of our solution lies in the algorithm of [7], and its prime implicants computation. Preliminary experiments indicate that on typical formulae this algorithm scales up to 200-300 variables.

[2] Heuristics could be used for deciding which clauses should be removed first. For instance, one could start with the longer ones.

7 Related Work

The algorithm that compiles propositional constraints to a feature graph, which is used as an oracle in Sect. 5.2, originates in our previous work [7]. The present paper really completes the agenda of loc. cit.

Our work shares many goals with [24,11,22,20]. Still it differs significantly in several respects. First, they mostly focus on algorithms for concrete problems, while we also try to understand problems in a more general framework of preservation classes and advice properties. Second, the practical part of our work focuses on efficient terminating algorithms, with a particular performance gain in use of the offline compilation phase. In contrast, [24,11,22] rely on online query execution using Prolog, which does not even guarantee termination. We admit though that all report efficient execution times in practice, for the constraints they consider.

Third, we achieve exhaustiveness of advice, while the quality of advice is hard to assess in loc. cit. SmartEMF [11] provides a weak form of exhaustive advice, given that it terminates. The algorithm of Sen and coauthors [22] is a very good example of a solution which does *not* guarantee exhaustiveness of advice. In fact the latter algorithm has very little control over the kind of advice. It only provides a fixed number of hints, computed by running a Prolog engine several times on a constraint system representing valid choices. The constraints are permuted randomly in order to allow for finding different solutions.

Concrete modeling languages used in these works differ. While [24,11] focus on class diagram-like metamodels (e.g. Eclipse Modeling Framework), we work with modular configuration problems and feature models. The two languages we have chosen are less expressive than these in some sense, but this is what enables us to provide support that is more robust and automated. In [22] languages expressible using hyperedge replacement grammars are targeted.

SmartEMF [11] does not consider guidance beyond attributes. In particular, there are no hints given about the need to instantiate new objects in the model, which constitute most of the operations in our derivation processes.

Alves et al. [1] discuss refactorings of feature models, introducing a measure of quality for them. While we strongly disagree with this definition (which is basically a weakening relation) we state that semantics-preserving feature model derivation, as presented in here, falls under their definition of refactoring. In [1] a catalog of refactorings is proposed, but no firm claims of its exhaustiveness are made. In that sense our results are stronger, as we have argued that any models can be derived with our editing operations (exhaustiveness of advice). Being incremental, our operations do not enable refactoring *any* model to *any* model though. Such goal would require a mixture of both weakening and strengthening steps. We intend to explore this possibility in future.

Massoni et al. [19] have investigated refactorings that are done in two tiers: at the program (code) level and the object model level. The need for such refactorings arises in the evolution of projects developed under the model-driven paradigm. As in our work, the authors recognize the importance of formally sound refactorings and aim to establish such.

8 Summary and Future Work

Interactive model derivation is a process of constructing models and metamodels in the presence of automatic adaptive guidance on possible modeling steps. We have classified uses of model derivation into soundness-preserving, completeness-preserving and semantics-preserving, relating these classes to modeling and metamodeling activities. Then we have proposed guidance algorithms for two kinds of languages (pointing to existing work in one case). Our development was rigorous, exploiting logic constraints and reasoning algorithms. We have demonstrated the feasibility of such approaches by implementing a prototype for feature models and by testing it on existing examples.

While mainstream tools adopt interactive support technologies, the ultimate open problem in the field remains to be: how to generically and robustly provide exhaustive and valid guidance for an arbitrary language defined by a metamodel (for example in MOF or EMF) and a set of reasonably expressive constraints (like a large decidable subset of OCL). While others approached this problem by retaining an expressive language, but relying on a potentially nonterminating search, we have taken a different route. We considered simpler languages, but also more robust algorithms. In future we intend to investigate possibilities of supporting richer languages.

Even though we emphasize the importance of interactive support, in some cases it is still useful to automatically perform multiple editing operations. This desire poses several interesting problems ranging from HCI issues (how to present a choice of sequences of operations?) to optimization issues (how to efficiently discover sequences of interest?).

Acknowledgements. We thank Steven She for sharing with us the results of his scalability experiments with the algorithm presented in [7]. We also thank anonymous reviewers for constructive and invaluable feedback. This work is partially supported by Science Foundation Ireland under grant no. 03/CE2/I303_1.

References

1. Alves, V., Gheyi, R., Massoni, T., Kulesza, U., Borba, P., de Lucena, C.J.P.: Refactoring product lines. In: Jarzabek, S., Schmidt, D.C., Veldhuizen, T.L. (eds.) GPCE, pp. 201–210. ACM, New York (2006)
2. Batory, D.: Feature Models, Grammars, and Propositional Formulas. In: Obbink, H., Pohl, K. (eds.) SPLC 2005. LNCS, vol. 3714. Springer, Heidelberg (2005)
3. Bryant, R.E.: Graph-based algorithms for Boolean function manipulation. IEEE Transactions on Computers 35(8) (1986)
4. Clements, P., Northrop, L.: Software Product Lines: Practices and Patterns. Addison–Wesley Publishing Company (2002)
5. Czarnecki, K., Antkiewicz, M., Kim, C.H.P., Lau, S., Pietroszek, K.: Fmp and Fmp2rsm: eclipse plug-ins for modeling features using model templates. In: OOPSLA 2005: Companion to the 20th annual ACM SIGPLAN conference on Object-oriented programming, systems, languages, and applications, pp. 200–201. ACM, New York (2005)

6. Czarnecki, K., Helsen, S., Eisenecker, U.: Staged Configuration Using Feature Models. In: Nord, R.L. (ed.) SPLC 2004. LNCS, vol. 3154. Springer, Heidelberg (2004)
7. Czarnecki, K., Wąsowski, A.: Feature diagrams and logics: There and back again. In: Kellenberger [16]
8. Czarnecki, K., Wąsowski, A.: Sample spaces and feature models: There and back again. In: Proceedings of the 12th International Software Product Line Conference, SPLC 2008. IEEE Computer Society, Los Alamitos (2007)
9. Fundamental Approaches to Software Engineering. LNCS. Springer, Heidelberg (2008)
10. Hadzic, T., Jensen, R., Andersen, H.R.: Notes on calculating valid domains (2006), http://www.itu.dk/~tarik/cvd/cvd.pdf
11. Hessellund, A., Czarnecki, K., Wąsowski, A.: Guided development with multiple domain-specific languages. In: Engels, G., Opdyke, B., Schmidt, D.C., Weil, F. (eds.) MODELS 2007. LNCS, vol. 4735, pp. 46–60. Springer, Heidelberg (2007)
12. Janota, M., Kiniry, J.: Reasoning about feature models in higher-order logic. In: Kellenberger [16]
13. Janota, M., Botterweck, G.: Formal Approach to Integrating Feature and architecture Models. In: Fiadeiro, J.L., Inverardi, P. (eds.) FASE 2008. LNCS, vol. 4961, pp. 31–45. Springer, Heidelberg (2008)
14. Junker, U.: Configuration. In: Rossi, F., van Beek, P., Walsh, T. (eds.) Handbook of Constraint Programming. Elsevier Science Inc., Amsterdam (2006)
15. Kang, K.C., Cohen, S.G., Hess, J.A., Novak, W.E., Peterson, A.S.: Feature-oriented domain analysis (FODA), feasibility study. Technical Report CMU/SEI-90-TR-021, SEI, Carnegie Mellon University (November 1990)
16. Kellenberger, P. (ed.): Software Product Lines. IEEE Computer Society, Los Alamitos (2007)
17. Kuzina, V.: Interactive derivation of feature diagrams. Master's thesis, IT University of Copenhagen (to appear, 2008)
18. Lau, S.Q.: Domain analysis of e-commerce systems using feature-based model templates. Master's thesis, Dept. Electrical and Computer Engineering, University of Waterloo, Canada (2006), http://gp.uwaterloo.ca/files/2006-lau-masc-thesis.pdf
19. Massoni, T., Gheyi, R., Borba, P.: Formal Model-Driven Program Refactoring. In: Fiadeiro, J.L., Inverardi, P. (eds.) FASE 2008. LNCS, vol. 4961, pp. 362–376. Springer, Heidelberg (2008)
20. Mazanek, S., Meier, S., Minas, M.: Auto-completion for diagram editors based on graph grammars. In: IEEE Symposium on Visual Languages and Human-Centric Computing (VL/HCC). IEEE Computer Society, Los Alamitos (2008)
21. Schobbens, P.-Y., Heymans, P., Trigaux, J.-C.: Feature diagrams: A survey and a formal semantics. In: Proceeding of 14th IEEE International Requirements Engineering Conference (RE). IEEE Computer Society, Los Alamitos (2006)
22. Sen, S., Baudry, B., Vangheluwe, H.: Domain-specific model editors with model completion. In: Mosterman, P.J., Levandowszky, T., de Lara, J. (eds.) The 2nd International Workshop on Multi-Paradigm Modeling (2007)
23. van der Meer, E.R., Wąsowski, A., Andersen, H.R.: Efficient interactive configuration of unbounded modular systems. In: Haddad, H. (ed.) SAC, pp. 409–414. ACM, New York (2006)
24. White, J., Schmidt, D., Nechypurenko, A., Wuchner, E.: Domain-Specific Intelligence Frameworks for Assisting Modelers in Combinatorically Challenging Domains. In: GPCE4QoS (October 2006)

A Benchmark for OCL Engine Accuracy, Determinateness, and Efficiency

Martin Gogolla, Mirco Kuhlmann, and Fabian Büttner*

University of Bremen, Computer Science Department
Database Systems Group, D-28334 Bremen, Germany
{gogolla,mk,green}@informatik.uni-bremen.de

Abstract. The Object Constraint Language (OCL) is a central element in modeling and transformation languages like UML, MOF, and QVT. Consequently approaches for MDE (Model-Driven Engineering) depend on OCL. However, OCL is present not only in these areas influenced by the OMG but also in the Eclipse Modeling Framework (EMF). Thus the quality of OCL and its realization in tools seems to be crucial for the success of model-driven development. Surprisingly, up to now a benchmark for OCL to measure quality properties has not been proposed. This paper puts forward in the first part the concepts of a comprehensive OCL benchmark. Our benchmark covers (A) OCL engine accuracy (e.g., for the undefined value and the use of variables), (B) OCL engine determinateness properties (e.g., for the collection operations any and flatten), and (C) OCL engine efficiency (for data type and user-defined operations). In the second part, this paper empirically evaluates the proposed benchmark concepts by examining a number of OCL tools. The paper discusses several differences in handling particular OCL language features and underspecifications in the OCL standard.

1 Introduction

The Object Constraint Language (OCL) [1,2] is a central ingredient in modeling and transformation languages. Thus, approaches for Model-Driven Engineering (MDE) rely on it. OCL is supported in commercial tools like MagicDraw, Together, or XMF Mosaic and in open source tools like ATL [3] or Eclipse MDT OCL [4]. In many approaches, OCL is used as an assembler-like technology underlying model-centric software development. Of course, OCL has a higher degree of abstraction than conventional assemblers, but transformation technology is based on OCL like classical programming languages rely on assemblers.

The Object Constraint Language is employed for determining model properties, for checking the applicability of transformations, and in form of imperative OCL for performing transformations. For example, the QVT standard includes an important part on imperative OCL. Transformation approaches assume that

* In cooperation with Benjamin Büttelmann, Lars Hamann, Friederike Jolk, Bin Sun, Hui Wang, Lei Xia.

K. Czarnecki et al. (Eds.): MoDELS 2008, LNCS 5301, pp. 446–459, 2008.

the integrated OCL engine works correctly. The OCL core is also employed in language extensions like temporal OCL [5] or real-time OCL [6]. A correct and complete realization of OCL is essential for each single tool and indispensable in tool chains. Although the OCL standard offers two approaches for defining the semantics, the quality and conformance of concrete OCL implementations have to be guaranteed. Our experience proves that already basic OCL expressions are treated differently in different OCL engines.

In the first part of this paper we introduce the concepts of a comprehensive OCL benchmark. The benchmark is divided into several parts which treat accuracy, determinateness, and efficiency aspects. Our benchmark covers relevant features of the underlying modeling language and most features of OCL. It currently includes about 950 OCL expressions handling invariants and operation definitions as well as pre- and postconditions.

In the second part of this paper we will apply the benchmark to a number of OCL engines: ATL OCL [3], Dresden OCL [7], Eclipse MDT OCL [4], OCLE [8], Octopus [9], RoclET [10], and USE [11]. Further OCL engines like Kermeta OCL [12], KMF [13], OSLO [14], VMTS OCL [15] and other tools would have been possible candidates as well. The evaluation results are presented in anonymous form, because our aim is to show the applicability and validity of the benchmark concepts. We do not want to recommend or to discourage the use of a particular tool, but would like to emphasize the need for a benchmark which can help to build correct OCL implementations.

As indicated in Fig. 1, our OCL benchmark consists of 7 parts: The parts B1 to B5 treat accuracy, the part B6 deals with determinateness, and the part B7 handles efficiency. The parts B1, B2, and B3 include a UML model in order to check class and object diagram capabilities, invariants, pre- and postconditions, and state-dependent queries. B1 presents core features by checking invariants, B2 adds enumerations and pre- and postconditions, and B3 deals with advanced features like ternary associations and navigation therein. The parts B4 and B5 are based on state-independent queries covering the majority of OCL standard collection operations and their properties. B4 concentrates on the three-valued OCL logic, and B5 features laws between collections operations.

To give an impression of the different evaluations in the examined OCL engines, let us take some examples from the details discussed further down and consider the term `Set{1,2,3}->collect(i|Seq{i,i*i})` (`Sequence` abbreviated by `Seq`). We obtained three different answers from three OCL engines:

Accuracy	B1	Core (data types, invariants, properties, binary associations)
	B2	Extended core (enumerations, pre- and postconditions, queries)
	B3	Advanced modeling (ternary associations, association classes)
	B4	Three-valued logic (e.g., `1/0=1 or true`)
	B5	OCL laws (e.g., `select` versus `reject`)
Determinateness	B6	OCL features with non-deterministic flair (e.g., `any, flatten`)
Efficiency	B7	Evaluation for data type, user-defined and collection operations

Fig. 1. Overview on the 7 Parts of the OCL Benchmark

(A) `Bag{Seq{1,1}, Seq{2,4}, Seq{3,9}}`, (B) `Seq{Seq{2,4}, Seq{1,1}, Seq{3,9}}` and (C) `Bag{1,1,2,4,3,9}`. The answer (A) is the only correct representation of the expected result. Among the remaining three OCL engines, one engine could not handle two or more variables in iterate expressions, another engine did not treat nested variables with identical names correctly, and, for a given `SET` and an appropriate expression `EXPR`, the last engine calculated `SET=EXPR` correctly as `true`, but evaluated `SET->one(e|e)` to `true` and `EXPR->one(e|e)` to `false`.

The structure of the rest of the paper is as follows. Sections 2, 3, and 4 handle accuracy, determinateness, and efficiency, respectively. Section 5 presents the details of the empirical evaluation of the OCL engines. In Sect. 6 the paper is finished with a conclusion and future work. The technical details of the benchmark, i.e., all models, constraints, and queries, can be found in [16], and all details of the evaluation results are presented (partly in German) in [17].

2 OCL Engine Implementation Accuracy

Implementation accuracy is a measurement for the completeness and the correctness of the realization of OCL (and the needed modeling language features) in an OCL engine. Accuracy relates to syntactic and semantic features and is essential, because in tool chains each single tool must rely on the correct and complete OCL handling in the preceding tools. High accuracy is the premise for compatibility of OCL tools. Therefore situations like the following ones should be prevented: (1) The parser of the first tool does not accept the OCL expressions written with the second tool, or (2) the third tool accepts the syntax of the first tool, but shows different evaluation results.

2.1 Accuracy in the Modeling Language and in OCL

OCL constraints and queries refer to a context like a class or an operation. Therefore an OCL engine must provide support for a subset of the underlying modeling language. The most common features are class diagrams and object diagrams for state-dependent evaluation. Our benchmark assumes that central MOF resp. UML class diagram features are supported, e.g., classes, attributes, associations (binary, ternary, reflexive), roles, multiplicities, association classes, and enumerations.

All central OCL features must be available in an OCL engine and are therefore used in our benchmark. Central in this respect are, for example, object properties (attributes and roles), collection operations, and navigation with the collect shortcut. An OCL engine must be able to evaluate state-dependent expressions (e.g., `Person.allInstances()->select(age>18)`) and state-independent expressions (e.g., `Set{1..9}->collect(i|i*i)`). As indicated in the OCL standard, query evaluation by returning a result value and a result type is an important task of an OCL engine.

State-dependent expressions refer to objects, their attributes and roles. Typically these kinds of expressions are used in OCL pre- and postconditions specifying side-effected operations and OCL invariants. Our benchmark covers the mentioned OCL elements. The OCL standards 1.3 and 2.0 show minor differences for certain syntactic constructs. For example, according to OCL 1.3 all instances of a class are retrieved by `allInstances`, but in OCL 2.0 `allInstances()` is used. Our benchmark therefore formulates one constraint in particular syntactic variations in order to check for support of OCL 1.3 and OCL 2.0.

Beside checking for completeness of OCL features, a correct and consistent evaluation of OCL constraints and queries is required. The basis for an accurate evaluation of a complex expression is the correct implementation of every individual OCL operation. Such tests are put into practice by applying OCL collection operations, OCL data type operations and enumeration literals in complex terms. For OCL collection operations, the laws and relationships from [18] are our starting point.

2.2 Core Benchmark (B1)

The core benchmark checks rudimentary OCL and modeling language features. With regard to the modeling language, the applied model includes a class with simple attributes, a side-effect free user-defined operation and a reflexive binary association as shown in Fig. 2. The model is instantiated with an object diagram in order to check the capabilities of object creation, value assignment, handling of String, Integer and Boolean literals as well as link insertion and deletion. The core benchmark avoids special and advanced features like enumerations, empty collections and the undefined value and provides several different syntactic variations for the same expression.

Frequently used OCL operations and constructs are added to the model through the invariants, e.g., basic boolean predicates, the operations `collect` and `flatten`, `let` expressions, nested collections and navigation with the collect shortcut. Using the collect shortcut means to apply a property to a collection of objects which is understood as a shortcut for applying the

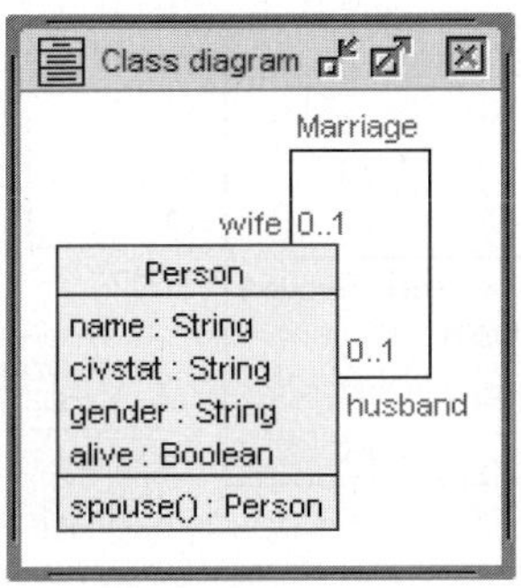

Fig. 2. Class Diagram of the Core Benchmark Model

property inside a `collect` call, e.g., `Person.allInstances().name` is a shortcut for `Person.allInstances->collect(name)`. Because not all considered OCL engines provide support for OCL queries, we restricted the core benchmark to invariants. Therefore, the core benchmark involves so-called query invariants which compare the query with the expected result in order to obtain a boolean expression.

Up to six different syntactic notations are provided for each invariant. Ideally the parser of an OCL engine accepts all variants, but at least one of them has to be accepted. Three choices arise from the naming and typing of variables in collection operations: Iterator variables can be explicitly defined (e.g., `Person.allInstances()->reject(p|p.gender='male')`); additionally they can be typed (e.g., `Person.allInstances()->reject(p:Person|p.gender='male')`), and several operations also accept implicit variables (e.g., `Person.allInstances()->reject(gender='male')`). The number of choices is doubled when we incorporate the notation of `allInstances()` without parentheses as it is permitted in OCL 1.3.

After the syntactic check the evaluation accuracy is identified with the aid of an example object diagram representing a snapshot of a valid system state. All core invariants are designed to be fulfilled in context of this system state.

2.3 Extended Core Benchmark (B2)

While the core benchmark only checks basic model elements, the extended core benchmark adds enumerations, side-effected operations with pre- and postconditions and state-dependent queries. Focus of the queries is object access (including cases treating the undefined value) and navigation as well as handling of enumeration literals and enumeration type attributes as shown in Fig. 3.

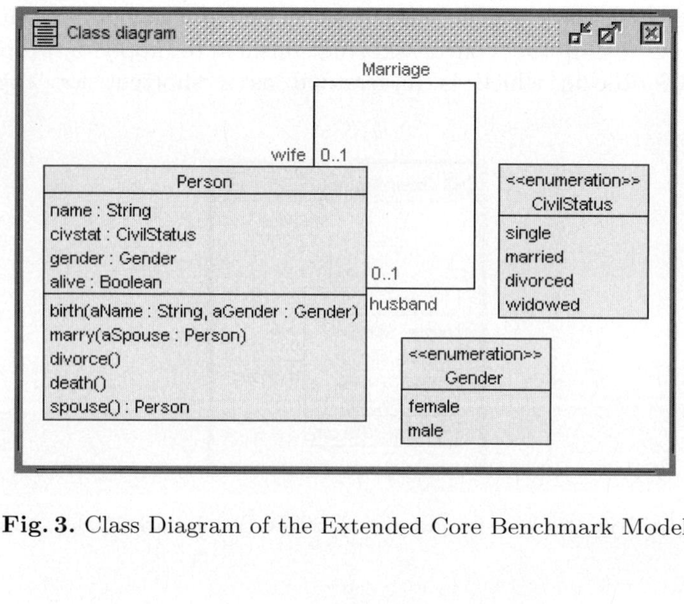

Fig. 3. Class Diagram of the Extended Core Benchmark Model

In this scenario several successive object diagrams are constructed to represent an evolving system. Each pair of successive states represents the execution of an operation specified in the extended model. We do not dictate whether user-defined operations should be directly executable, for example as Java methods, or whether they can be simulated on the modeling level. But in each case we demand the possibility to evaluate pre- and postconditions in context of one pair of system states.

2.4 Advanced Modeling Benchmark (B3)

Navigating ternary and higher-order associations and association classes is an advanced chapter in the OCL standard [1]. Higher-order associations are sometimes needed for concise modeling and are common in database modeling.

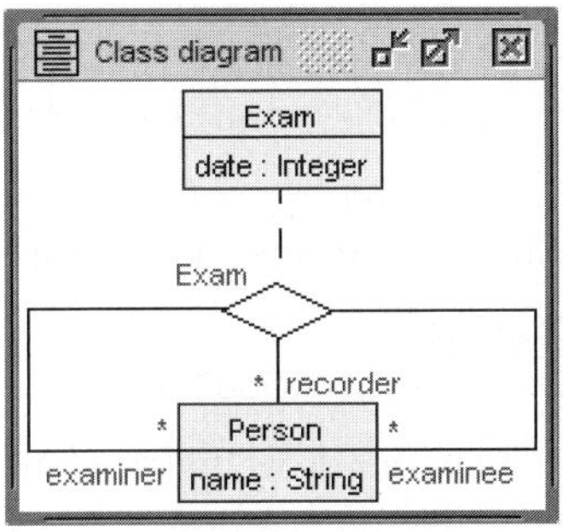

Fig. 4. Class Diagram of the Advanced Model

For this reason, the accuracy benchmark B3 is based on a model specifying a ternary reflexive association class. A link, i.e., an instance of the association class `Exam`, is identified by a triple of persons. Each person is allowed to attend exams in different roles. The following expression navigates within the ternary association.

```
let ada = Person.allInstances()->any(name='Ada') in
  ada.examiner[recorder]
```

The brackets indicate the direction from which an association is navigated. Therefore the above expression results in the set of examiners being present in an exam in which Ada is the recorder. In contrast, `ada.examiner[examinee]` results in all persons being an examiner of the examinee Ada.

2.5 Three-Valued Logic Benchmark (B4)

OCL offers a sophisticated handling of undefined values. This induces a three-valued logic which is tested in the fourth part B4 of the accuracy benchmark. Following the semantics defined in [1], B4 systematically checks the correct implementation of boolean OCL operations with context-free queries.

We emphasize that the OCL standard explicitly requires that, for example, 'True OR-ed with anything is True' and 'False AND-ed with anything is False'. This means that in these cases the undefined value is not allowed to be propagated.

2.6 OCL Laws Benchmark (B5)

Benchmark B4 was set up to check systematically the correct implementation of individual operations, with focus on collection operations. The analysis of semantic properties between OCL operations presented in [18] provides a basis for this benchmark. Each test case checks for the equivalence of two different OCL expressions, i.e., it tests whether the laws between two operations as exposed in [18] holds. If an OCL evaluation engine negates an equivalence, an erroneous implementation of at least one participating operation is indicated. The following example shows a law considered in the benchmark. The variable `e` represents a boolean OCL expression.

```
let c = sourceCollection in
c->exists(i|e) = c->select(i|e)->notEmpty()
```

Another important aspect is the use of the general collection operation `iterate` for substituting other operations. An example is shown below.

```
let c = sourceCollection in
c->exists(i|e) = c->iterate(i;r:Boolean=false|r or e)
```

For checking a law in the benchmark we have to substitute corresponding expressions by concrete source collections (`c`) and OCL subexpressions (`e`). In the case of boolean expressions a very simple form (`i<4`) is sufficient for testing, because we only need an expression which can result to true and to false depending on the value of the iterator variable. The complexity of the expression provoking the boolean value is irrelevant. A correct evaluation of the subexpressions has to be assured by other parts of the benchmark.

In contrast, the source collections have to be systematically chosen, because several inconsistencies do not occur until a particular element constellation is present. On this account each law is instantiated with (1) sets, bags and sequences, (2) empty collections, singleton collections and collections with many elements, (3) collections including the undefined value and excluding the undefined value as well as (4) collections including elements which fulfill the boolean expression and collections excluding these elements. In case of bags and sequences we additionally differentiate between (5) collections excluding equal elements and collections including equal elements which (6) fulfill or not fulfill the boolean expression. The combination of these six situations results in 29 cases for each equivalence. In some test cases like the one checking the law between the operations `collect` and `iterate` this number varies, because of the absence of a boolean expression, i.e., the cases 4 and 6 are not relevant. An example case is shown below.

```
let c = Set{-1,0,1,2} in
c->collect(i|i*i) =
c->iterate(i;r:Bag(Integer)=Bag{}|r->including(i*i))
```

3 OCL Engine Determinateness Properties (B6)

This part of the benchmark deals with OCL engine implementation properties for non-deterministic OCL features and operations for which the OCL standard allows a choice in the implementation like `any` or `flatten`. The aim of this benchmark is to reduce the freedom for implementation choice as far as possible.

In OCL there are at least five possibilities for converting sets and bags to sequences. Here, we will only discuss the ones for sets because the conversions for bags are analogous to the set conversions. Roughly speaking, sets can be made into sequences by using (1) `asSequence`, (2) `iterate`, (3) `any`, (4) `flatten` or (5) `sortedBy`. In the expressions below, `intSet` is an arbitrary OCL expression with type `Set(Integer)`, e.g., `Set{1..12}`.

```
(1) intSet->asSequence()
(2) intSet->iterate(e:Integer;
      r:Sequence(Integer)=Sequence{}|
      r->including(e))
(3) intSet->iterate(u:Integer;
      r:Tuple(theSet:Set(Integer),theSeq:Sequence(Integer))=
        Tuple{theSet:intSet,theSeq:Sequence{}}|
      let e=r.theSet->any(true) in
        Tuple{theSet:r.theSet->excluding(e),
              theSeq:r.theSeq->including(e)}).theSeq
(4) Sequence{intSet}->flatten()
(5) intSet->collect(e:Integer|Sequence{0,e})->
      sortedBy(s:Sequence(Integer)|s->first())->
        collect(s|s->last())
```

The first possibility is the direct conversion with `asSequence`. The second term uses an `iterate` over the integer set with an element variable and successively builds the sequence by appending the current element. The basic idea behind the third term is to choose an arbitrary element with `any` and to append this element to the result sequence. The fourth term calls `flatten` on a sequence possessing the integer set as its only element. The fifth possibility uses `sortedBy` to give an order to a bag of integer sequences. Each of the five terms represents a particular way to produce a sequence from a set. We are using the notion determinateness in this context because the OCL engine has to determine the order in the sequence. Our benchmark tests whether the orders produced by terms 2 to 5 coincide with the direct order given by `asSequence`. The benchmark part B6 checks also minor other points, for example, whether the following two properties hold which consider operation applications to a given set and its corresponding bag.

```
aSet->any(true) = aSet->asBag()->any(true)
aSet->asSequence() = aSet->asBag()->asSequence()
```

We understand such determinateness properties as points of underspecification in the OCL standard. Our benchmark gives the possibility to reduce this underspecification and with this the amount of freedom for the OCL engine implementor.

4 OCL Engine Efficiency (B7)

In this section we propose OCL expressions checking the evaluation efficiency in an OCL engine. The expressions are assumed to be evaluated in the different engines and the evaluation time has to be recorded. In order to have easily measurable and reliable evaluation times the expressions are usually evaluated in an iterate loop not only once but many times. The expressions in this section are divided on the one hand into expressions concerning the OCL standard data types Boolean, String, Integer and Real and on the other hand into expressions of a small model of towns and roads in between.

The expressions for the data types compute (A) the truth tables of the Boolean connectives available in OCL, (B) the inverse of a longer String value, (C) the prime numbers as Integer values up to a given upper bound, and (D) the square root of a Real number. As an example consider the following OCL expression for the prime numbers up to 2048.

```
Sequence{1..2048}->iterate(i:Integer;
  res:Sequence(Integer)=Sequence{}|
    if m.isPrime(i) then res->including(i) else res endif)
```

The operation `isPrime(i)` is defined in a singleton class MathLib as specified below. The operation is called on the singleton object m of class MathLib.

```
isPrime(arg:Integer):Boolean=
  if arg<=1 then false else
    if arg=2 then true else isPrimeAux(arg,2,arg div 2) endif endif
isPrimeAux(arg:Integer,cur:Integer,top:Integer):Boolean=
  if arg.mod(cur)=0 then false else
    if cur+1<=top then isPrimeAux(arg,cur+1,top) else true endif
  endif -- algorithm inefficiency irrelevant for benchmark
```

The expressions for the example model with towns and roads consider the underlying data structure as a graph with objects (nodes) and links (edges). They compute (A) the transitive closure, i.e., the directly and indirectly reachable nodes of a given node, and (B) the connected components of the graph, i.e., the maximal node sets in which all nodes are connected directly or indirectly. The example model has a single class and a single association as displayed in Fig. 5.

An example state with 42 towns and 42 roads is built up. The underlying graph has 5 connected components with 1, 2, 3, 13 and 23 nodes. In the example state the following OCL expression for the transitive closure is evaluated.

```
Set{1..1024*1024}->iterate(i:Integer;
  res:Bag(Set(Town))=Town.allInstances->collect(t|t.connectPlus())|
  res)
```

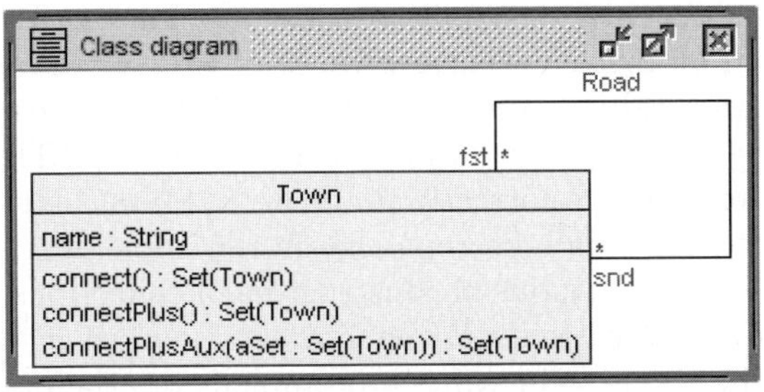

Fig. 5. Class Diagram for Towns and Roads

The operations `connectPlus()` computes all towns directly or indirectly reachable from the current node with the roles fst and snd. All details, i.e., models, invariants, and queries, of this part and the other parts of the OCL benchmark can be found in [16].

5 Empirical Evaluation of the Benchmark

The aim of this empirical evaluation of OCL engines is (A) to show the applicability of the benchmarks concepts developed before and (B) to make a contribution for improvements of current OCL engines. We want to emphasize the applicability of the benchmark and will therefore not go into details concerning the single tools. OCL engine developers can find all details in the cited material and are encouraged to perform our benchmark by themselves.

The OCL benchmark presented in this paper comprises 949 test cases, composed of 71 invariants and 878 query expressions. 121 expressions are state-dependent and 828 context-free. We checked 7 OCL evaluation engines including two code generators. One of the tools was only partly checked because of resource limitations. 401 accuracy and determinateness queries (46, 8%) were correctly evaluated by all engines except the aforementioned tool. All evaluation results of performed checks can be found in [17] (partly in German).

5.1 Core Benchmark (B1)

Even though benchmark B1 only includes very basic modeling language and OCL constructs and expressions, it reveals several problems. No evaluation engine accepts all syntactic variations. In general all tools except for one either demand parentheses for the operation `allInstances` or forbid them. Additionally 5 of 6 engines require typing of `let` variables.

Before checking the first OCL invariants one of the tools showed grave restrictions in context of the modeling language features, because no well-formedness rules of the UML metamodel are checked. Thus the tool, for example, does not require unique attribute names within a class definition.

If we disregard the syntactic variations the benchmark B1 checks 18 invariants. Assuming that an invariant is regarded as correctly evaluated when at least one notation is syntactically accepted and the corresponding expression results in true, only one tool evaluates all invariants correctly (18/18). The other tools evaluate from 6 to 16 expressions correctly (6/18, 6/18, 14/18, 14/18, 16/18). Responsible for these results are small discrepancies in the implementations. One parser does not accept range expressions in constructors of collections (e.g., `Set{1..9}`), another parser incorrectly treats string literals, because it handles quotation marks as part of the string. The same tool implements the operation `substring` with character numbers running from `0` to `self.size()-1`, while the OCL standard requires numbers from `1` to `self.size()`. Another noticeable problem is the general handling of iterator variables. Some tools do not permit equal variable names in nested collection operations (e.g., `c->select(p|...any(p|...)...)`). One of them additionally forbids implicit variables in case of nested operations (e.g., `c->select(...any(...)...)`). Even more demonstrative, more than half of the tested OCL engines do not have the ability to handle more than one iterator variable inside the operation `iterate` (e.g., `c->iterate(x,y|...)`) or other operations like `forAll`. On the other hand a tool which allows for more than one iterator variable evaluates the corresponding query incorrectly, because it implicitly flattens nested collections (e.g., `Bag{Sequence{'Ada',18}}` results in `Bag{'Ada',18}`). The latter example shows a sequence with elements having a different basic type. This constellation is however allowed, because both elements have the same super type `OclAny`. Three engines do not define a common super type and throw a type mismatch exception.

5.2 Extended Core (B2) and Advanced Modeling Benchmark (B3)

The extension of benchmark B1 uncovers further restrictions. Some of them are not profound, while others clearly decrease the accuracy of the respective tools. One tool does not provide for query expressions, so they have to be embedded as boolean expressions into invariants (e.g., `Set{1,2,3}->collect(i|i*i)` is transformed to `Set{1,2,3}->collect(i|i*i)=Bag{1,4,9}`). Another tool completely ignores postcondition definitions.

Many test cases directly access the identifiers of objects. Since no tool supports this feature except for one, the expressions can be adapted. The following example shows the adaption of a test case using the object identifier `ada` which represents the Person Ada.

`let o:OclAny=ada in o` is transformed to

```
let ada=Person.allInstances()->any(name='Ada') in
  let o:OclAny=ada in o
```

Although enumerations are lightweight extensions of a UML model, several tools have problems applying enumeration values. Whereas enumeration literals are generally correctly handled, enumeration type attributes eventually prevent a correct evaluation. In one case it is not possible to compare enumeration type attribute values among each other. In another case the comparison of enumeration type attribute values and enumeration literals fails.

A special bug emerges in one tool. Here the essential substitution property for equality is violated. An expression in the form of `SET->one(e|e)` results in true as well as `EXPR=SET`, but the expression `EXPR->one(e|e)` results in false.

Benchmark B3 discovers more obvious limitations and checks advanced modeling and OCL features. 6 of 7 tools do not support ternary associations and 3 tools do not provide for association classes at all.

5.3 Three-Valued Logic Benchmark (B4)

Benchmark B4 emphasizes a fact that already appeared in benchmark B2. Only one of the tested OCL engines sophisticatedly treats the undefined value. All other tools show in different ways a behavior which is not conformant to the OCL standard. One engine sometimes throws an exception if an operation is invoked on an undefined value, but the boolean operations are correctly implemented. Another engine does in some cases explicitly not allow for operation calls which result in an undefined value (e.g., the invocation of the operation `last` on an empty sequence). If, nevertheless, the undefined value occurs in a subexpression the whole expression will be undefined. A third engine does not allow undefined values in collections, i.e., it filters them out. So an expression like `Set{undefinedValue}->includes(undefinedValue)` results in false.

Especially the implementation of the boolean operations is analyzed in benchmark B4. In case of 4 tools we have to differentiate between the left hand side and the right hand side of a boolean operator. If the left hand side already determines the resulting value, the whole expression is correctly evaluated (e.g., `false and undefinedValue` results in false, `true or undefinedValue` results in true and `false implies undefinedValue` results again in true). Otherwise the expression is either not evaluable or results in undefined.

The inconsistent treatment of the undefined value continues in benchmark B5 and B6. Only 3 of 6 OCL engines evaluate all queries correctly in presence of the undefined value, but the other half produces at least partly wrong results. One tool completely refuses the evaluation if one or more undefined elements are included in a source collection. Another tool primarily fails in case of sequences including undefined values. A third tool only implements some operations like `iterate` and `collect` correctly. In contrast, operations like `exists` and `one` need at least one value which fulfills the boolean subexpression (e.g., `Sequence{undefinedValue,1,4}->exists(i|i<4)`). Other operations generate the undefined value in either case.

5.4 Laws (B5) and Determinateness Benchmark (B6)

Benchmark B5 and B6 discover additional problems. One tool, a code generator, does not support tuple types, and implements the `including` (as well as `iterate` and `forAll`) and `implies` erroneously. The former operation is transformed into a Java method which on the one hand declares primitive type parameters, on the other hand requires object type arguments in the methods body. An example extract of a corresponding method is shown below.

```
private Set including(..., boolean b1, boolean b2) {
  ...
  if ( !result.contains(new Boolean((b1.booleanValue() ||
       b2.booleanValue()))) ) { ... } ... }
```

The latter operation and its right hand side is simply unconsidered during the transformation process if the left hand side is not explicitly parenthesized (e.g., `expr1 and expr2 implies expr3` results in `expr1 and expr2`).

One tool does not regard the binding of boolean operations and predicates. They are evaluated from left to right (e.g., in case of (`expr1 implies expr2 and expr3`) the subexpression (`expr1 implies expr2`) is evaluated first). Another tool exhibits a bug which is easily overlooked. Collections used as components of tuples strangely include the `null` value falsifying several evaluation results. Yet another tool generally does not evaluate the operation size invoked on sequences, and additionally shows many unexplainable errors.

6 Conclusion

This paper proposes a comprehensive benchmark for OCL engines. OCL is employed as a basic technology in model-centric development approaches. The quality of an OCL engine is therefore crucial for the success of transformation-driven techniques. We have empirically evaluated our benchmark by considering a number of different OCL engines.

On the one hand, the results have shown incompatibilities following from different interpretations of the OCL standard. On the other hand, the benchmark has discovered faulty implementations of OCL features. The benchmark can help to harmonize the implementation of OCL features in different tools in order to allow for consistent modeling and transformation support. It can be applied as quality measure in OCL engine development.

After having carried out this benchmark, we can state a number of helpful preliminaries for performing OCL benchmarks in the future. An OCL engine should support (A) an import feature for class diagrams including operation definitions, invariants and pre- and postconditions as well as for system states in which evaluations are performed, (B) checking of boolean OCL expressions in the context of a system state, (C) evaluation of OCL expressions in the context of a system state and presentation of results, and (D) composition of the above steps in a single command line script so that comprehensive checks (our benchmark covers about 950 expressions) can be carried out in an automatic way.

Not all OCL engines considered in this paper offer the above functionality: RoclET does only allow to check invariants; ATL OCL concentrates on transformations with OCL conditions to be checked; both engines do not offer the direct evaluation of OCL expressions in a system state. Our goal is that OCL tool builders provide a suitable infrastructure with their tools and self-commit to perform a benchmark like ours on their own. Last, but not least, our benchmark has to be completed because not all relevant modeling language features (e.g., qualifiers) or all OCL features (e.g., ordered sets) are covered yet. Feedback from OCL engine users and developers will give us the possibility to improve and supplement our benchmark.

References

1. O.M.G. (ed.): Object Constraint Language 2.0 (formal/06-05-01). OMG (2006), http://www.omg.org
2. Warmer, J., Kleppe, A.: The Object Constraint Language: Precise Modeling with UML, 2nd edn. Addison-Wesley, Reading (2003)
3. ATL-Team: ATL Development Tools (2008), http://www.sciences.univ-nantes.fr/lina/atl/atldemo/adt
4. MDT-OCL-Team: MDT OCL (2008), http://www.eclipse.org/modeling/mdt/?project=ocl
5. Ziemann, P., Gogolla, M.: Extended with Temporal Logic. In: Broy, M., Zamulin, A.V. (eds.) PSI 2003. LNCS, vol. 2890, pp. 351–357. Springer, Heidelberg (2004)
6. Flake, S., Müller, W.: An OCL Extension for Real-Time Constraints. In: Clark, A., Warmer, J. (eds.) Object Modeling with the OCL. LNCS, vol. 2263, pp. 150–171. Springer, Heidelberg (2002)
7. Dresden-OCL-Team: Dresden OCL Toolkit (2008), http://dresden-ocl.sourceforge.net/
8. Chiorean, D.: OCLE-Team: Object Constraint Language Environment 2.0 (2008), http://lci.cs.ubbcluj.ro/ocle/
9. Kleppe, A., Warmer, J.: Octopus: OCL Tool for Precise UML Specifications (2008), http://octopus.sourceforge.net/
10. RoclET-Team: Welcome to RoclET (2008), http://www.roclet.org/
11. Gogolla, M., Büttner, F., Richters, M.: USE: A UML-Based Specification Environment for Validating UML and OCL. Science of Computer Programming 69, 27–34 (2007)
12. Kermeta-Team: Kermeta: Breathe Life into your Metamodels (2008), http://www.kermeta.org/
13. Akehurst, D., Patrascoiu, O.: KMF (Kent Modeling Framework) OCL Library (2008), http://www.cs.kent.ac.uk/projects/ocl/tools.html
14. Hein, C., Ritter, T., Wagner, M.: Open Source Library for OCL (OSLO) (2008), http://oslo-project.berlios.de/
15. VMTS-Team: Visual Model and Transformation System (VMTS) (2008), http://vmts.aut.bme.hu/
16. Gogolla, M., Kuhlmann, M., Büttner, F.: Sources for a Benchmark for OCL Engine Accuracy, Determinateness, and Efficiency, pages 242 (2008), http://www.db.informatik.uni-bremen.de/publications/Gogolla_2008_BMSOURCES.pdf
17. Büttelmann, B., Hamann, L., Jolk, F., Sun, B., Wang, H., Xia, L.: Evaluating a Benchmark for OCL Engine Accuracy, Determinateness, and Efficiency, pages 69 (2008), http://www.db.informatik.uni-bremen.de/publications/Buettelmann_2008_BMEVAL.pdf
18. Kuhlmann, M., Gogolla, M.: Analyzing Semantic Properties of OCL Operations by Uncovering Interoperational Relationships. In: Electronic Communications of the EASST, UML/MoDELS Workshop on OCL (OCL4ALL 2007) , vol. 9, pages 17 (2008), http://eceasst.cs.tu-berlin.de/index.php/eceasst

Contrary-to-Duties Constraints: From UML to Relational Model

Pedro Nogueira Ramos

ADETTI /ISCTE Computer Science Department
Av. Forças Armadas, Lisboa, 1649-026, Portugal
Pedro.Ramos@iscte.pt

Abstract. Sometimes, because of an atypical situation, an important mandatory association between classes in a UML Class Diagram must be replaced by an optional one. That semantic and functional impoverishment happens because the mandatory constraint must have a boolean value. In this paper we analyze the use of soft constraints in the UML Class Diagram, and their automatic repercussion in the corresponding Relational Model. The soft (deontic) constraints allow the formal representation of requirements, which ideally should always be fulfilled, but can be violated in atypical situations. In this paper we enrich a previous deontic approach, by introducing the ability to explicitly represent the so called Contrary-To-Duties requirements, i.e., domain integrity requirements that emerge as a consequence of an unfulfilled mandatory constraint. We support our approach with the UML/OCL language.

Keywords: UML, Contrary-To-Duties, Relational Model, Deontic Constraints.

1 Introduction

The paper addresses the formal representation of soft constraints in database applications. More specifically, the paper deals with a relational model enrichment that allows a flexible notion of the mandatory property in foreign key field. We have chosen to have a formal and a high level approach, and for that reason we have adopted the UML [1] notation together with the representation of OCL constraints [2].

In this paper we follow the intuitions and some of the work presented in [3]. In [3] the author has already proposed a relational model enrichment that allows a more flexible notion of mandatory fields (e.g., foreign keys fields). The motivation was to help the database designer in situations where a mandatory foreign key would be the natural solution, but cannot be implemented due to minor, although unavoidable, atypical situations.

The boolean mandatory attribute is adequate for requirements that must hold unavoidably, but is not adequate to deal with requirements that ideally should always be fulfilled, but can be violated in atypical situations. If those violable requirements are explicitly represented it is possible to maintain both the requirement and its violation and, consequently, recur to monitoring procedures for violation warnings. Without that explicit representation, the designer must always choose a non mandatory value if there is a chance, even if a small one, that in an atypical situation the field will not be filled.

K. Czarnecki et al. (Eds.): MoDELS 2008, LNCS 5301, pp. 460–474, 2008.

Consider the following real example[1] concerning the overtime hours control in an organization where sometimes the employees work for several days outside the organization (in the client's organization).

An organizational rule states that all overtime hours must be authorized by the employee hierarchic superior. Using a workflow system the employee fills in a requirement form that, if authorized by his superior, will be stored in a table record in which the ID of the superior must be filled in. However, sometimes the need for overtime hours is only detected when the employee is working outside the organization. A problem may arise if the employee is outside during a change of month (the problem is related with technical issues regarding the total amount of monthly overtime hours). When the employee is working outside with his superior the usual procedure consists of the employee sending a fax or an email (and then someone fills the requirement form for him) and his superior making a phone call or sending a fax authorizing the overtime hours. Due to security organizational procedures no one can electronically authorize overtime hours without a proper password. When the superior is outside and cannot access the system, the system cannot accept overtime hours. The solution adopted by the organization was to remove the requirement, which stated that all records of the overtime hour authorization table should always have the superior's ID.

The important aspect of the previous example is that, because of one atypical situation (which nevertheless happens several times) an important requirement was abandoned (the overtime authorization control is now made manually, where previously it was validated by the database). That happened because the requirement was inflexible. In [3] the flexible mandatory requirement is introduced in the Unified Modelling Language (UML) Class Diagram. The author also provides some guidelines about the automatic generation of the corresponding relational model (basically suggesting the utilization of triggers, but not providing guidelines on how to do it).

In this paper we strongly enrich the approach presented in [3] (deontic approach), enhancing its ability of application to real systems. The examples presented in [3] only consider situations where the violations of soft constraints (called deontic obligations) don't have consequences to the application behavior. When a soft constraint isn't fulfilled the system only has to report it. If we think in terms of the relational model, in those situations it is only necessary to maintain a set of views that reports the records where the "mandatory" fields aren't fulfilled. In this paper we present three new enrichments:

First we introduce in the UML Class Diagram the ability to explicitly represent the new constraints that emerge as a consequence of the violations of deontic obligations (Contrary-To-Duties constraints). We enrich the Class Diagram in order to allow the representation of sub-ideal states, i.e., situations where deontic obligations are violated and consequently new constraints (obligations) arise to deal with that undesired but tolerated situation.

Secondly we support our approach with the standard UML constraint language, the OCL language. In [3] the OCL representation of the constraints is completely missing and, consequently, a solid automatic mechanism to generate a corresponding relational model was impracticable.

---

[1] The author worked as a consultant in the organization where the example comes from.

Finally we provide some rules and objective guidelines for the automatic generation of trigger and views that support the database integrity maintenance.

The reason to focus our attention on the relational model is the fact that Object Database Management Systems aren't yet an efficient solution for demanding applications. The object-oriented paradigm is becoming the main background for system modeling, but unfortunately the object-oriented databases don't progress at the same speed, making relational databases the standard for data storing. The reason for choosing UML is the fact that it has become a standard language for design and conception of systems.

The paper is organized as follows: in section 2 we present and motivate the deontic approach presented in [3], providing also a corresponding OCL representation. In section 3 we present our extension, e.g., the ability to represent in a UML diagram (and using OCL) the domain integrity requirements that emerge as a consequence of an unfulfilled boolean mandatory constraint. In Section 4 we focus our attention on the Relational Model generation. Some concluding remarks are presented in the last section.

2 Deontic Constraints

In the relational model the attribute mandatory property is specified through a boolean value: *required* or *not required.* That binary representation is enough for most situations. The requirement that states that *all Invoices must have a date* means that the attribute date must be always fulfilled, i.e. it should be impossible to have an invoice without a date. That restriction is also valid in the real world, i.e., invoices without a date are illegal.

However, that simple approach is not always sufficient to capture some properties of the world. For example, let us consider the following requirement: "All students must have a zip code address". That requirement exists due to the fact that the university regularly needs to send correspondence to the student. However, is that a requirement that intends to capture an ideal situation or a requirement that the database should always fulfill? What will be the procedure if one student tries to register himself in the school and has forgotten his zip code? If we want to conditionally accept his registration (telling him that he must supply the zip code as soon as possible) then the requirement is about an ideal situation that sometimes doesn't happen (neither in the real world nor in the database). Blocking the registration could be a wrong choice because, apart from the fact that all data already inserted in the application form will be lost, the school will convey an unpleasant image of unnecessary bureaucracy. The zip code will be indispensable in the future, but during a short period of time the zip code is dispensable.

The previous example intends to distinguish two kinds of requirements:

i. requirements that ideally should always be fulfilled, but can be violated in atypical situations and;
ii. requirements that must hold unavoidably.

The boolean mandatory attribute is adequate for the requirements covered by the second situation, but is not adequate to deal with ideal but violable requirements.

Violable requirements, i.e., requirements that should hold but sometimes do not, must be represented differently from other requirements. Otherwise, the coexistence of the requirements and its violations will originate an inconsistent database state. If the violable requirement is explicitly represented it is possible to maintain both the requirement and its violation and, consequently, recur to monitoring procedures for violation warnings.

Consider the student/zipcode example in which the relational model is represented with predicate calculus sentences and zip code is a student attribute:

a) Requirement: $\forall_x \exists y$ (student(x)$\rightarrow$ zipcode(y,x))
b) Facts: student(ann), $\neg\exists$y zipcode(ann,y)

In order to avoid an inconsistent database (i.e., zipcode(ann,x) and $\neg$ zipcode(y,x)) a) should be replaced by:

a') Requirement: *Ideally* ($\forall_x \exists y$ (student(x)$\rightarrow$ zipcode(y,x)))

If we consider that a violation occurs if *Ideally(Φ) and* $\neg\Phi$, we can have a deduction system to automatically infer all the violations.

In the UML graphic notation the mandatory property is only represented in the associations' cardinality. In the UML Class Diagram, the cardinality lowest limit in a relation between classes usually takes the value 0 (Not Mandatory) or 1 (Mandatory). Consider the examples of Fig. 1.

In the first example the several zip codes are represented as objects of the Zip Code Class. In the situations described before the constraint may be too strong, i.e., all students must always have a zipcode.

In the second example of Fig. 1, regarding a DVD Store, given the cardinality relation, a DVD must always be associated to a Category (in order to be consulted by the clients in a computer). That relation represents a typical situation, i.e., all movies have at least a category. However, sometimes that strong restriction can be inconvenient, or even impossible to keep. Consider the situation where a set of movies has just arrived to the store. A plausible situation will be that an employee immediately registers the new movies in the database. Afterwards, another employee (probably someone with more knowledge about movies) updates the database in order to assign categories to the movies. In that scenario, during a period of time the movie isn't associated to any category. Blocking that situation could have unnecessary and undesirable consequences in the process flow (not allowing the immediate registration of movies in the database).

One may argue that, given the desired functionality, a different association should be chosen, i.e., cardinality with a zero lower limit (0...*). However, that solution can hide important properties of the reality (e.g., that a DVD has at least one category). Also, if that solution was to be adopted, it would be impossible to detect the "violations" of the desired situations.

In [3] it is proposed to incorporate the notion of ideality in the UML associations. By ideality we mean a constraint that is not mandatory, but whose violation must be registered in the database.

Going back to the examples of Fig. 1, the diagram should explicitly say that all DVDs must have a category (and students a zipcode), but that constraint can be violated. Also, it should become explicit that those violations must be registered.

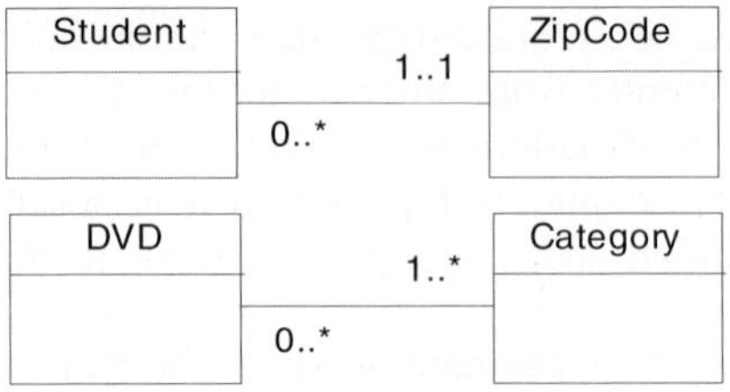

Fig. 1. Mandatory Relations

The reason why the registration of the violations should be explicit in the diagram is because that feature should be a database built-in feature and not implementation dependent. Like integrity constraints are part of the relational model, this notion of ideality became part of our automatically generated relational model mentioned in the last section.

To represent the ideality mandatory constraint (called "Obligation" in the figure label) the diagrammatic representation depicted in Fig. 2 is proposed. Notice that no new symbols or concepts are introduced in the UML diagram.

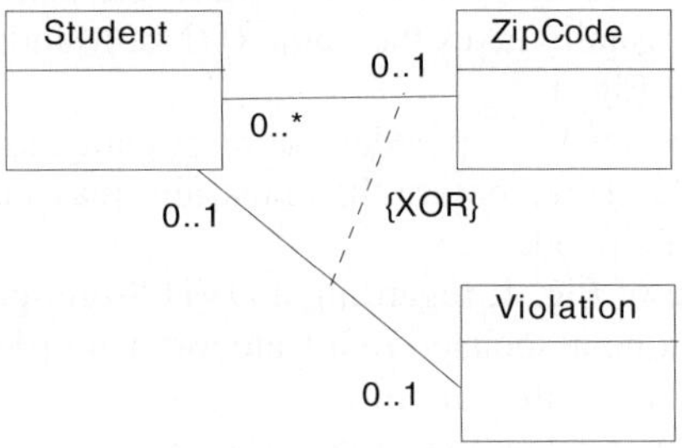

Fig. 2. Deontic Constraint (Obligation) Representation

The expression 'Obligation' comes from the deontic logic. There are already several works on deontic logic applied to databases [4]. In [5] and [6] the authors introduce the notion of Deontic Constraints (also called Soft Constraints). By deontic constraint they mean "constraints which express norms that indicate how things are in ideal worlds, how things ought to be. [...] such constraints are violable". In their approach all information and knowledge is represented through mathematical logic. They do not consider the relational model or diagrammatic representations of any kind.

In [3] the author doesn't present a clear semantics to the Class Violation of Fig. 2 (it's only presented as a set of violations). In this paper we adopt the approach first presented in [8]. Deontic rules are represented with violation constants: the previous expression *Ideally*(Φ) (or *Obligation*(Φ)) is represented as $\neg V_i \rightarrow \Phi$, in which V_i represents a violation constant. The authors consider a finite set of violation constants, each of them associated to one deontic rule. The semantics is intuitive: $\neg V_i \rightarrow \Phi$ means that if rule i isn't violated then Φ is a fact (in other words, rule i states that there is an obligation to ensure Φ). We consider that the Class Violation corresponds to the finite violation constants ΔV ($\forall_i\ V_i \in \Delta V$).

The disjunction (XOR) means that if the student does not have a zip code then a violation will be associated with the student[2]. Several classes can be associated with the Violation Class, as exemplified in Fig. 4 (ideally all students should have a zip code and all degrees should have a Coordinator Professor). Each violation object is associated only with one object.

In order to simplify the diagrams, in Fig. 3 and Fig. 5 an abbreviation is used to represent the Deontic Constraint (Deontic Association): the underlined zero represents the obligation / ideality concept[3].

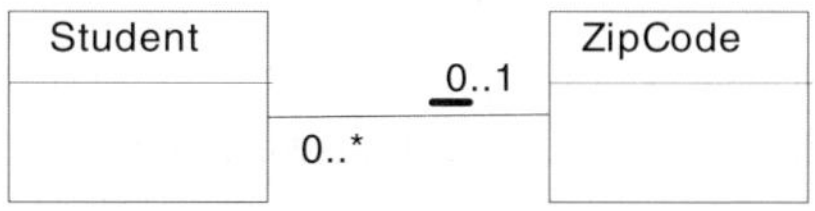

Fig. 3. Deontic Constraint Representation Abbreviation (Deontic Association)

In [3] the OCL representation of the constraints is completely missing and, consequently, a solid automatic mechanism to generate a corresponding relational model is impracticable. Object Constraint Language is a declarative language to describe constraint rules that apply to UML models. OCL syntax is intuitive enough, therefore we won't present its syntax in this paper.

Each OCL expression is written in the context of an instance of a specific class. Our deontic constraints can be represented as invariant conditions. An OCL expression is an invariant of the class and must be true for all instances of that class at any time.

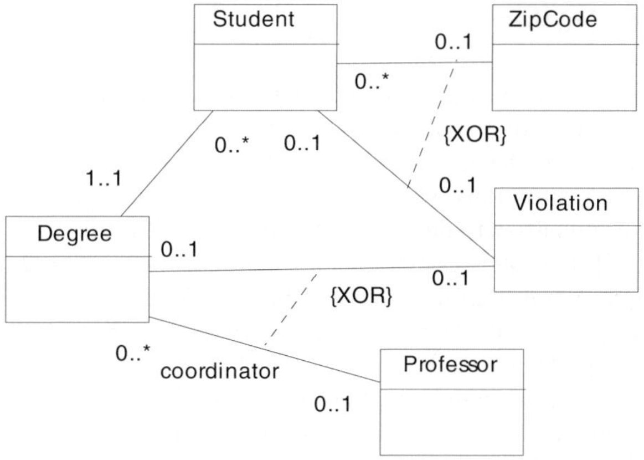

Fig. 4. More than one constraint representation in a diagram

[2] Notice that this representation is ambiguous. Since the relation is bidirectional, it may represent that there is an obligation to have a zipcode associated to all students (the intended meaning) or, there is an obligation to associate all zipcodes to students (a non intended meaning). This situation can be avoided with the UML navigation association name [1] or with OCL expressions like the one we present further on.

[3] As an alternative we could use a textual version like '0/1..1'.

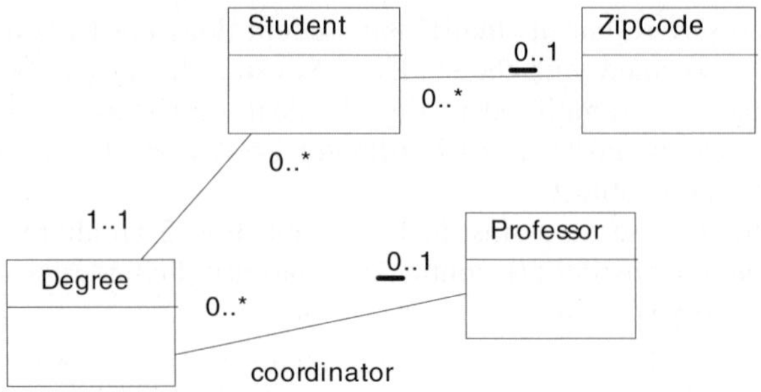

Fig. 5. Abbreviation of the diagram of Fig. 4

The following expression represents our proposal to model the obligation depicted in Fig. 3 (that is an abbreviation of Fig. 2). The context is the Student Class (ST_ZC and Viol-ST_ZC are the role names of the right side of the associations between Student and Zip Code and Student and Violation, respectively)

Inv Oblig-Sudent_ZipCode: ST_ZC->isEmpty() implies Viol-ST_ZC->notEmpty()

The previous representation is a specific instance of the more general schema: on the left side of the material implication we have the role of the 'deontic association end', and on the right side the violation-side role of the association between the class and the Violation Class.

3 Contrary-to-Duties

In this paper we introduce in the UML Class Diagram the ability to explicitly represent the new constraints that emerge as a consequence of the violations of deontic obligations. We enhance the Class Diagram in order to allow the representation of sub-ideal states, i.e., situations where deontic obligations are violated and consequently new constraints arise to deal with that undesired but tolerated situation. In the deontic literature [7] those new constraints are called Contrary-To-Duties constraints.

Consider an application that supports the budget control of a building company[4]. Every building project has its own budget. The budget is disaggregated into several items. When the project leader assigns a new work to a supplier, he fills in a Purchase Order (PO) (to be delivered to the supplier) and also fills in a Withhold Request (WR) (to ensure that the money will be available when the payment takes place). The Withhold Request (WR) is only allowed by the application if there is enough money in the corresponding budget item (a PO regards a specific item). In order to control the budget the following rule is implemented in the application: **every PO must be associated to a WR**. Consequently, POs are only allowed if there is enough money available in the budget item.

However there are situations where assignments must take place (the PO must be created) even if there is no budget (for example, unpredictable works). In such situations

[4] The example illustrates a real implementation done by the author for a building company.

the standard procedure is to request a budget rearrangement (for example, to exchange values between items). That request takes some time (even days) to be analyzed and sometimes the urgency of the work forces the project leader to *violate* the control rule (for example, an imminent land falling that requires a sustentation wall). In order to allow the violation of the rule, the application must accept that sometimes a PO is not associated to a WR. Given that flexible interpretation, what the rule really states is that **ideally every PO must be associated to a WR**.

In order to ensure a rigorous budget, when the rule is violated (a PO is not associated to a WR), apart from the Budget Rearrange Request (BRR), the project leader must organize a work meeting to elaborate a formal minute that justifies the decision to assign the new work (in this kind of meeting a third party entity – surveillance company - is always present). Notice that 'new obligation' (to have a minute signed by the three entities: the project leader, the supplier and the third party company) also represents an ideal situation. Sometimes (rare situations) the assignment must occur before the meeting takes place. So, when the first rule is violated (a PO is not associated to a WR) two new situations arise that can be expressed with two new rules:

1. If a PO is not associated with a WR then a BRR is necessary;
2. If a PO is not associated with a WR then the PO must be associated with a Minute Meeting (MM).

The first rule must always be fulfilled, which means that the application always rejects a PO that is not associated with either a WR or a BRR. The second one represents an ideal situation, which means that the application allows a PO that isn't associated either with a WR or with a MM. This second rule has the same semantics of the initial one; both represent obligations whose violation is accepted by the application.

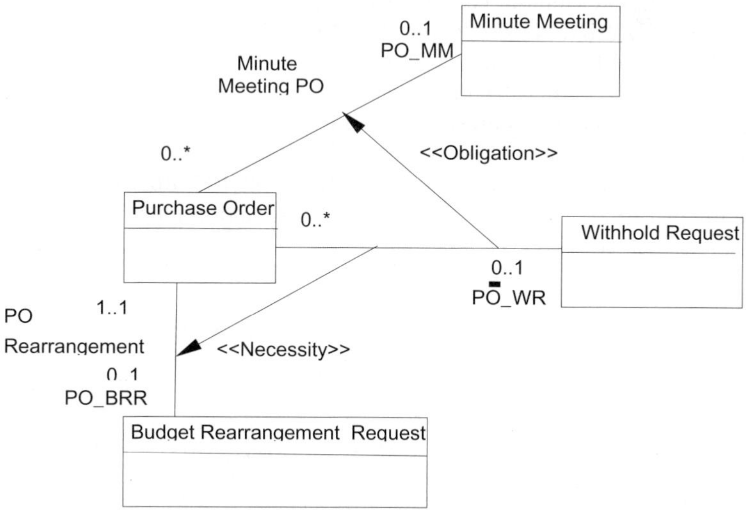

Fig. 6. Purchase Order Example

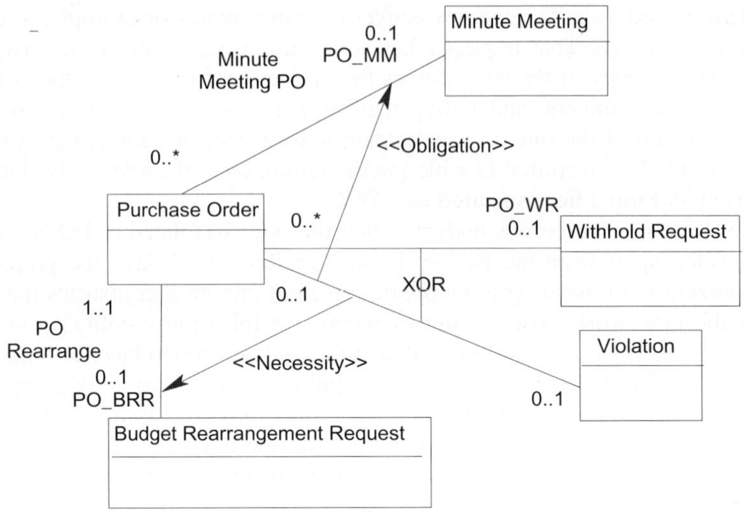

Fig. 7. Purchase Order Example (non abbreviated version)

Contrarily to the first example (Zip Code), in this example, from the violation of one obligation new constraints are derived. Those new constraints are called Contrary-To-Duties in the Deontic Logic Literature. Following this literature we will use the term Necessity to represent the first constraint of the example (situations that must necessarily occur). For the second constrain we will continue to use the term Obligation since it has the same meaning of the original rule (and the rule of the first example). In the diagram of Fig. 6 we propose the use of the UML Dependency Relation to capture the notions of Necessity and Obligation. The stereotypes must be read as follows: "the PO Rearrangement: PO_BRR Necessity and the Minute Meeting PO: PO_MM Obligation depends of the PO_WR violation". The OCL dependency constraint is described in Table 1. As we presented earlier, the diagram of Fig. 6 is an abbreviation of the diagram of Fig. 7 (in where we explicitly represents the Violation Class).

Notice that the derived obligation cannot be represented as illustrated in Fig. 8. That representation means the following: **ideally every PO must be associated to an MM**. But that isn't the case in the example. The association must only ideally occur if the PO isn't associated with a WR.

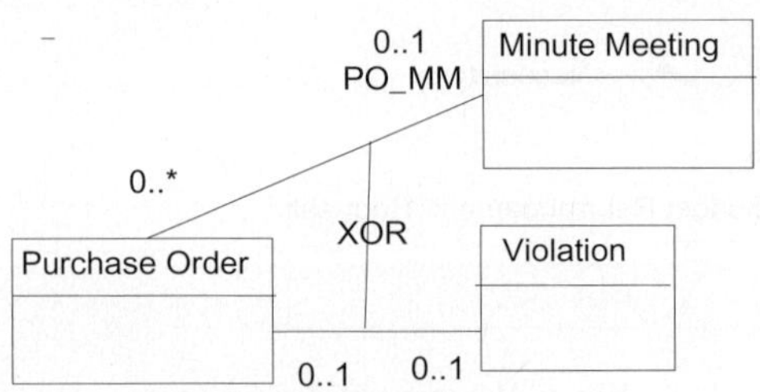

Fig. 8. An erroneous representation of the derived obligation

Table 1. OCL Constraints for the Purchase Order Example

```
Context: Purchase Order
Inv Oblig-PO_WR:
  PO_WR->isEmpty() implies Viol-PO_WR->notEmpty()
Inv CDutie_Necessity-PO:
  Viol-PO_WR->notEmpty() implies PO_BRR ->notEmpty()
Inv CDutie_Obligation-PO:
 Viol-PO_WR->notEmpty() implies  (PO_MM->isEmpty() implies
Viol-PO_MM->notEmpty())
```

In the current database domain, in the presence of Contrary-to-Duties scenarios, a different kind of constraint may arise: constraints, which state that a specific data association is **forbidden** until some constraint ('obligation') is fulfilled. We propose using a stereotyped dependency relation called Forbidden. Consider the following example:

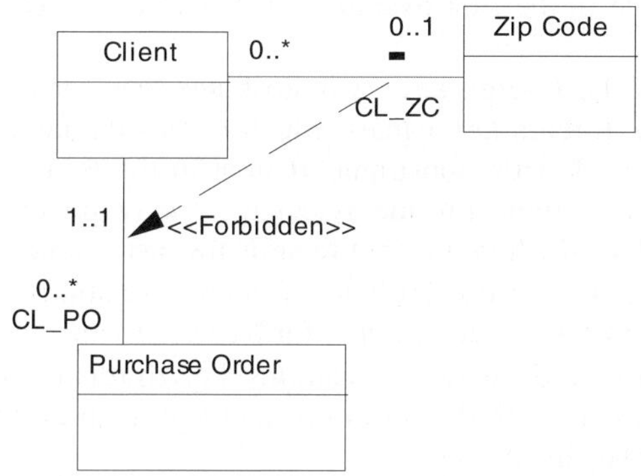

Fig. 9. Forbiddingness in a UML Class Diagram

The dependency relation stereotype called "forbidden" means that "the association 'Client P Order' cannot occur until the association 'Zipcode Client' happen (clients without the zip code cannot place orders). In OCL:

Table 2. OCL Constraints for the Client Purchase Order Example

```
Context: Client
Inv CDutie_Forbidden-ZC:
     Viol-CL_ZC->notEmpty() implies  CL_PO->isEmpty()
```

4 Mapping UML Deontic Constraints into Relational Ones

As mentioned earlier, our main goal is to adopt the UML Class Diagram as a starting point and automatically generate the corresponding relational model and its constraints.

Since we want to keep the deontic constraints in the database, triggers are the best choice to implement them. Using Before and After action triggers it is possible to ensure that all constraints are fulfilled. The procedure for monitoring the obligations fulfillment can be easily achieved using relational views. For each constraint (OCL invariant) we can generate a SQL view, which retrieves the records that don't satisfy it. That's, for example, what the Dresden Toolkit does (one of the few OCL-SQL generator, [9]). However, trigger and view generations aren't enough if we want to help the database administrator to maintain the data integrity. If the set of deontic constraints is only represented in code (SQL), it becomes very difficult to maintain it and understand it. We consider that, apart from trigger and view generation, a relational table should be created to store the obligations. That table would hold all the deontic associations (obligations) and the new constraints (dependency relations stereotypes) that arise as a consequence of their violation.

The Deontic Table has seven attributes:

- a distinctive identifier (the table primary key);
- the name of each table that implements the association (for example, Student and Zip Code in the first example, or, Client and Purchase Order in the last example);
- the name of the foreign key (two attributes, one for the table name and the other for the foreign key name), which relates the table that implements the class with the deontic constraint[5] (Client in the first example and Purchase Order in last example[6]) to the associated one (Zip Code in what regards the first example and Client in what regards the last example);
- one attribute to classify the kind of deontic relationship (i for Ideal[7], f for Forbidden, o for Obligatory and n for Necessity) and;
- a last one for the dependency relations, i.e., to relate a Forbidden or Obligatory or Necessity with the corresponding Ideal relation (the link is made using the primary key attribute).

In Fig. 10 we illustrate the data structure that supports the table and in Table 3 the previous examples are represented.

In the example, the second record means that there is an ideality (column 6) deontic relation between the tables Client and ZipCode (columns 2 and 3) that is implemented in the Client (column 4) Zipcode_fk (column 5) foreign key attributes. Notice that columns 2 and 3 are redundant because they can be obtained from columns 4 and 5. However, they are very useful to ensure an efficient and readable generation program.

The third record means that there is a forbidden (column 6) deontic relation between tables Client and Order (columns 2 and 3) associated to the previous ideality deontic relation (column 7).

[5] The table whose records are subject to constraints.

[6] The table Purchase Order is the owner of the foreign key that has the constraint. New POs can only be assigned to clients that have a zipcode (the constraint regards the Client ID in the PO table).

[7] The primary obligation.

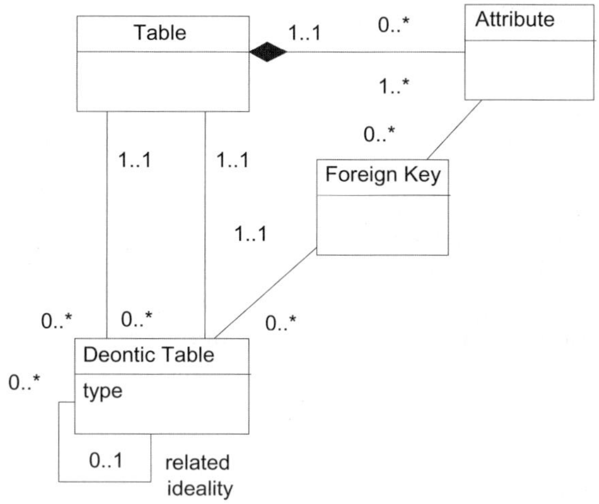

Fig. 10. The table structure

Table 3. Deontic Table: Examples of Deontic Table values

1	Student	ZipCode	Student	Zipcode_fk	i	
2	Client	ZipCode	Client	Zipcode_fk	i	
3	Client	Purchase Order	Purchase Order	Client_fk	f	2
4	Purchase Order	Withhold Request	Purchase Order	Withhold_fk	i	
5	Purchase Order	Minute Meeting	Purchase Order	minute_fk	o	4
6	Purchase Order	Budget Rearrange Request	Purchase Order	Budget_fk	n	4

Tables that implement the UML classes that are arguments of deontic associations (only classes located on the opposite side of the underlying zero abbreviation) will have a foreign key for each deontic association. The foreign key domain is the distinctive identifier of the Deontic Table (the foreign key represents the association between the class and the Violation Class). That foreign key will only assume a Null value when a violation occurs. For example, given the previous diagrams, the tables Student, Client and Purchase Order will have one foreign key each. Furthermore, each of the previous tables will also have one more foreign key for each <<Obligation>> dependency relation that represents a Contrary-To-Duties scenario of the previous deontic association. For that reason the Purchase Order table will have a second foreign key.

In order to facilitate the trigger generation and maintenance, the Foreign Key Referential Integrity Strategies for all foreign keys related to the Deontic Table should be Restricted. If we do so, we strongly restrict the number of triggers necessary to ensure all deontic constraints. Throughout the paper we present four different types of deontic constraints: Ideal, Obligatory, Forbidden, and Necessary. The first two constraints don't need any trigger support (Obligatory needs trigger support if arises as a consequence of a Contrary-To-Duties scenario). Views are sufficient to monitor violations.

Table 4. Examples of Triggers[8] and Views for OCL constraints in Table 1 and Table 2

a) Views for violation warnings

OCL Inv Oblig-PO_WR: (Ideal)

```
Select * from Purchase_Order, Deontic_Table where
Deontic_Table.idconstraint=
Purchase_Order.POWR_iddeonticconstraint
```

OCL Inv CDutie_Obligation-PO: (Obligation)

```
Select * from Purchase_Order, Deontic_Table As DT1,
Deontic_Table As DT2 Where
DT1.idconstraint=Purchase_Order.POMM_iddeonticconstraint and
DT2.idconstraint=DT1.CDTiddeonticconstraint
```

b) Trigger for integrity maintenance

Inv CDutie_Necessity-PO: (Necessity)

```
Before insert Purchase_Order
if (new.BRRID is null and new.POWR_iddeonticconstraint is
null) then return CancelEvent
```

Inv CDutie_Fordidden-ZC: (Fordidden)

```
Before insert Purchase_Order
Select ClientID from Client into ClientFlag where
new.ClientID=Client.ClientID and
Client.ZC_iddeonticconstraint is not nul
if (ClientFlag is not null) then return CancelEvent
```

OCL Inv Oblig-PO_WR: (Ideal)

```
After insert Purchase_Order
if (new.WHID is null) then POWR_iddeonticconstraint=4
```

OCL Inv CDutie_Obligation-PO: (Obligation)

```
After insert Purchase_Order
if (new.WHID is null and new.MMID is null) then
Purchase Order.POMM iddeonticconstraint =5
```

In order to ensure the Necessity constraint it will be necessary to generate a Before Insert trigger. That trigger will cancel the insertion if a violation associated with the new record exists and the 'necessary record' in the opposite table doesn't exist.

In order to ensure the Forbidden constraint it will be necessary to generate a Before Insert trigger. This trigger will cancel the insertion if a violation exists and the new record will be connected with a record of the forbidden table.

5 Final Remarks and Related Work

In this paper we have extended our previous work in order to introduce in a UML representation the ability to explicitly represent the so called Contrary-To-Duties requirements, i.e., domain integrity requirements that emerge as a consequence of an unfulfilled boolean mandatory constraint. We only used standard UML notation together with UML stereotypes (Obligation, Forbidden, Necessity) to capture all the notions we needed. We supported our approach with the standard UML constraint language, the OCL language.

[8] For the sake of clarity we use an informal and simple trigger syntax.

This approach, together with the deontic table and the SQL guideline generation presented in the last section, provides us with a framework that will support an automatic generation of the extended relational (deontic) model (based on the extended Class Diagram).

Borgida, in his work with exceptions in information systems (originally in [10] with further extensions, e.g., [11]) considers that exceptional situations arises when some constraints are violated, and that exceptions are considered as violations. In his proposal, the occurrence of a violation is signaled by the creation of an object in a class called ANY_VIOLATION. The author proposes an exception handling mechanism to specify failure actions. As Borgida, we also represent explicitly in the object model the constraints violations. Borgida uses two classes, one for the violations itself and another for the violation constraints. We only use the second one because the violations itself are represented by the foreign keys. Apart from these similarities, the approaches are considerably different. Borgida proposes a much more general mechanism to deal with exceptions handling in object oriented programming languages. Our approach, apart from been only oriented on one particular constraint (that Borgidas work doesn't treat), is focused on the database generation. Borgida, contrary to us, explicitly rejects triggers approached because he wants to maintain the control in a middleware software level. What we call Contrary-To-Duties constraints aren't treated by Borgidas work.

In the future it will be critical to automatically obtain the views and the triggers. In this paper we have provided some concrete guidelines, but we haven't yet implemented the automatic procedure.

Furthermore, in the near future it will be necessary to cover more complex situations like relations with more than two arguments and composite obligations like the ones depicted in Fig. 11.

Given the diagram we can infer that all courses should be associated to a degree and all courses should be associated to a coordinator. But it could be the case that the two obligations must only be treated as a conjunction and not separately (i.e., the obligation to be assigned to a coordinator disappears if the course isn't assigned to a degree).

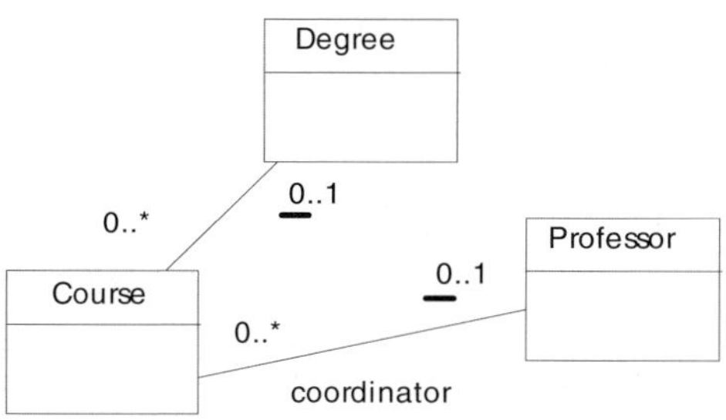

Fig. 11. Composite Obligations

References

1. Booch, G., Rumbaugh, J., Jacobson, I.: The Unified Modeling Language Reference Manual. Object technology. Addison-Wesley, Reading (1998)
2. Warmer, J., Anneke, K.: The Object Constraint Language: Getting Your Models Ready for MDA, 2nd edn. Object Technology. Addison-Wesley, Reading (2003)
3. Ramos, P.: Deontic Constraints: From UML Class Diagram To Relational Model. In: ECEIS, France (April 2003)
4. Wieringa, R.J., Meyer, J.: Applications of Deontic Logics in Computer Science: a concise overview. In: Meyer, J., Wieringa, R.J. (eds.) Procs. First Int. Workshop on Deontic Logic in Computer Science (1991)
5. Carmo, J., Demolombe, R., Jones, A.: An Application of Deontic Logic to Information System Constraints. In: Fundamenta Informaticae, vol. 46, pp. 1–17. IOS Press, Amsterdam (2001)
6. Meyer, J., Wieringa, R.J., Dignum, F.: The Role Of Deontic Logic in the Specifications of Information Systems. In: chomicki, J., Saake, G. (eds.) Logic for Database and Information Systems. Kluwer, Dordrecht (1998)
7. Carmo, J., Jones, A.: A New Approach to Contrary-To-Duty Obligations. In: Donald Dute, I. (ed.) Defeseasible Deontic Logic, Synthese Library (1996)
8. Tan, Y., der Torre, L.: Representing Deontic Reasoning in a Diagnostic Framework. In: ILCP 1994 Workshop on Legal Applications of Logic Programming, Genova, Italy (1994)
9. Dresden CL Toolkit, `http://dresden-ocl.sourceforge.net/`
10. Borgida, A.: Language features for flexible handling of exceptions. In: ACM Transactions on Database Systems (TODS) (1985)
11. Borgida, A., Murata, T.: Tolerating Exceptions in Workflows: A unified framework for Data and Process. In: Proc. International Joint Conference on Work Activities Coordination and Collaboration (WACC), USA (1999)

A UML/SPT Model Analysis Methodology for Concurrent Systems Based on Genetic Algorithms

Marwa Shousha[1], Lionel Briand[2], and Yvan Labiche[1]

[1] Carleton University, Software Quality Engineering Lab, 1125 Colonel By Drive
Ottawa, ON K1S 5B6, Canada
{mshousha,labiche}@sce.carleton.ca
[2] Simula Research Laboratory & University of Oslo, P.O. Box 134, Lysaker, Norway
briand@simula.no

Abstract. Concurrency problems, such as deadlocks, should be identified early in the design process. This is made increasingly difficult as larger and more complex concurrent systems are being developed. We propose here an approach, based on the analysis of specific models expressed in the Unified Modeling Language (UML) that uses a specifically designed genetic algorithm to detect deadlocks. Our main motivations are (1) to devise practical solutions that are applicable in the context of UML design without requiring additional modeling and (2) to achieve scalable automation. All relevant concurrency information is extracted from systems' UML models that comply with the UML Schedulability, Performance and Time profile, a standardized specialization of UML for real-time, concurrent systems. Our genetic algorithm is then used to search for execution sequences exhibiting deadlocks. Results on three case studies show that our approach can achieve efficient results.

Keywords: MDD, deadlocks, model analysis, concurrent systems, UML, SPT, genetic algorithms.

1 Introduction

Concurrency problems, such as deadlocks, should be identified early in the design process. This is made increasingly difficult as larger and more complex concurrent systems are being developed. With the recent trend towards Model Driven Development (MDD) [15], the choice of using Unified Modeling Language (UML) models and their extensions as a source of concurrency information at the design level, is natural and practical. The analysis of concurrency properties should not require additional modeling or a high learning curve on the part of the designers, or should at least minimize it. We hence propose an approach for the detection of concurrency problems that is based on design models expressed in UML [12]. Because extension mechanisms serve to tailor UML to various applications, when the UML notation is not enough to completely model a system for a given purpose, the notation is extended via profiles. Of particular interest here is the standardization of the Schedulability, Performance and Time (SPT) profile [19] that addresses domain specific

K. Czarnecki et al. (Eds.): MoDELS 2008, LNCS 5301, pp. 475–489, 2008.

aspects of real-time, concurrent system modeling. Our aim is to develop an automated methodology that can be easily tailored to all types of concurrency faults, and that can be easily integrated into a Model Driven Architecture (MDA) approach, the UML-based MDD standard by the OMG [15]. A tailored genetic algorithm (GA) uses information available in the UML design models to search for conditions under which threads can result into deadlocks. The proposed methodology is also geared towards large, complex systems characterized by large search spaces.

Our methodology begins by automatically collecting all information relevant to deadlocks (e.g., thread/lock interaction) from the system's UML design model extended with the SPT profile[1] [19]. This step can be easily automated using one of various existing UML tools and the underlying UML/SPT metamodel. The extracted information is then fed to a GA tailored to deadlock detection. The GA searches for execution sequences exhibiting deadlocks. If a deadlock sequence is found, it is immediately reported and the search ends.

The approach we adopt is meant to be general and can be adapted to a variety of concurrency faults by tailoring the fitness function of our specifically designed GA in order to address problems such as deadlocks, starvation, data races and data flow problems. The current paper, however, focuses on the detection of deadlocks. Future work will address other types of problems.

We next provide an overview about deadlocks, highlighting the information needed as input to our methodology. Section 3 introduces the SPT profile and discusses the mapping between the profile and deadlock concepts. Section 4 describes our methodology in detail, while Section 5 presents our tool support. Section 6 discusses the results of a number of case studies. Related work is presented in Section 7 and we conclude in Section 8.

2 Deadlocks

Concurrency introduces the need for communication between executing *threads*, which require a means to synchronize their operations. One of these means is shared memory communication, which ensures that shared resources are accessed individually and appropriately [7]. The most common techniques for shared memory communication are semaphores and mutexes. Semaphores, or counting semaphores, represent multiple access locks: at most `n` tasks (`n>1`) will have access to a shared resource [7]. The resource's *capacity* is the maximum number of threads executing within a shared resource. Mutexes are single access locks and are equivalent to a binary semaphore (`n=1`) [7]. Both types of shared memory communication will be referred to as *locks* in the remainder of this paper. Locks are first *acquired* before they are used, then later *released* when threads no longer need them. Threads waiting for access to a lock are placed in a conceptual *wait queue*. Wait queues define an *access policy*, e.g., FIFO, round robin, shortest-job-first, priority [2]. The various access policies require additional knowledge about threads. FIFO and round robin imply knowledge of *thread access times of locks*. These access times may be specified as ranges or definite values, although ranges are probably more common. Shortest-job-first implies

[1] The SPT profile has been replaced by Marte. The technique described was researched when Marte was yet a draft. However, the technique can easily be adapted to Marte.

knowledge of *thread execution times within locks* while the priority access policy implies knowledge of *thread priorities*.

Deadlocks occur when a thread is unable to continue its execution because it is blocked waiting for a lock that is held indefinitely by another thread [7]. In general, four conditions must be true before a deadlock occurs: 1. Threads share information that is placed under a lock, 2. Threads acquire a lock while waiting for more locks, 3. Locks are non preemptible, 4. There exists a circular chain of requests and locks (the circularity condition), as identified in a Resource Allocation Graph (RAG), i.e., a directed graph that depicts the allocation of resources to threads [2].

To proceed with our methodology, we must first map deadlock concepts, in particular those appearing in italics in this section, to UML and SPT concepts, as they form the input of the genetic algorithm.

3 SPT Profile to Deadlock Mapping

In UML, active objects have their own thread of control, and can be regarded as concurrent threads [12]. Only extensions of the UML standard, such as the SPT profile [19], provide mechanisms to model detailed information pertaining to concur-rency. We next describe the aspects of the SPT profile that are relevant to our work.

In the profile, concurrently executing entities are depicted with the `<<CRconcurrent>>` stereotype. As aforementioned, concurrency is also depicted in standard UML, but `<<CRconcurrent>>` enhances concurrent execution modeling. The profile also introduces two stereotypes that are of interest to us as they allow modeling the acquisition and release of resources: `<<GRMacquire>>` and `<<GRMrelease>>`, respectively. Protected resources, ones that are shared by concurrent threads, are stereotyped `<<SAresource>>`. Tags associated with this stereotype include `SAcapacity` (defines resource capacity) and `SAaccessControl` (access control policy, e.g., FIFO). During job execution, various actions take place that often have their own Quality of Service (QoS) characteristics. Stereotype `<<SAaction>>` depicts these actions, thereby allowing the specification of thread access times of locks, and thread execution times within locks. Tags for this stereotype include `SApriority` (the priority of the action), `RTstart` (the start time of the action), `RTend` (the end time of the action) and `RTduration` (the duration of the action). Start and end times, as well as durations could be specified as ranges.

The mappings between the deadlock concepts discussed in Section 2 and the profile are summarized in Table 1, illustrating the fact that we rely on three sub-profiles of the SPT profile. It is then clear that the information used by our GA can be automatically retrieved from UML/SPT models, in particular from sequence diagrams where those stereotypes and tags are used, as illustrated in Section 6 on an example.

4 Deadlock Detection

We proceed with describing how the input required for our methodology, as described in Section 3, is used for deadlock detection.

Table 1. Concept to SPT Mapping

Concept	SPT Stereotype/Tag	SPT sub-profile
Thread	<<CRconcurrent>>	RTconcurrencyModeling
Lock	<<SAresource>>	SAprofile
Lock acquire	<<GRMacquire>>	RTresourceModeling
Lock release	<<GRMrelease>>	RTresourceModeling
Wait queue access policy	<<SAresource>>/SAaccessControl	SAprofile
Thread priority	<<SAaction>>/SApriority	SAprofile
Lock execution time	<<SAaction>>/RTduration	SAprofile
Lock capacity	<<SAresource>>/SAcapacity	SAprofile
Lock access time range	<<SAaction>>/RTstart | RTduration	SAprofile

Because we aim at trying to find a sequence of access times that will result in the worst possible scenario of thread executions—namely deadlocks—our objective is a form of optimization. Hence, the values to be optimized to try to reach a deadlock situation are the access times of threads to locks. A number of techniques abound for solving optimization problems. Where the search space is large, GAs are the preferred choices [6, 17]. GAs are based on concepts adopted from genetic and evolutionary theories [10]. They are comprised of several components: a representation of the solution (referred to as the chromosome), a fitness of each chromosome (referred to as the objective or fitness function), the genetic operations of crossover and mutation which generate new chromosomes, and selection operations which choose chromosomes fit for survival [10].

A GA first randomly creates an initial population of chromosomes, then selects a number of these chromosomes based on a selection policy, and performs crossover and mutation to create new chromosomes. The fitness of the newly generated chromosomes is compared to others in the population. Depending on the replacement policy, individuals from the original population and children populations are merged into a single new population. The common replacement policy is elitism, whereby fitter individuals of the older population and newly created chromosomes are retained while less fit ones are removed. The process of selection, crossover and mutation, fitness comparison and replacement continues until the stopping criterion, such as a maximum number of generations [10], is reached.

We next introduce the various constituting components of our GA. It is important to note that these components are applicable to any concurrent system, as long as the input discussed previously is available. In other words, the GA components are only defined once. What varies from system to system are the input values.

4.1 Chromosome Representation

A chromosome is composed of genes and models a solution to the optimization problem. The collection of chromosomes used by the GA is dubbed population [10]. We want to optimize the access times of threads to locks. These are the values that will be altered by the GA to try to reach a deadlock situation. The access times must reflect schedulable scenarios. In other words, we need to ensure that all execution sequences represented by chromosomes are schedulable. This entails meeting system specifications of periods, minimum arrival times, etc. Thus, we need to encode threads, locks and access times, which are available in the input model: `<<CRconcurrent>>`, `<<SAresource>>` respectively (Table 1). A gene can be depicted as a 3-tuple (T, L, a), where T is a thread, L is a lock, and *a* is T's access time of L. A tuple represents the execution of a thread when trying to access a lock. Tuples are defined for a user specified time interval, i.e., a time range during which the user wants to study the system's behavior. The time interval controls how many times each thread attempts to access each lock: the greater the time interval, the more threads can access locks, hence adding more tuples/genes to the chromosome, thereby increasing its size. Without specifying a time interval, we cannot assume a fixed size for chromosomes, thus making crossover operations much more complex [13]. A heuristic for determining an appropriate time interval is given in Section 4.4. A special value of -1 is used to depict lock access times that lie outside this interval: (T, L, -1) represents a lock access that does not occur.

Because a chromosome models a solution to the optimization problem, it needs to be large enough to account for the scenario where all threads are accessing all locks during the time interval. Hence, the chromosome size (its number of genes) is equal to the total number of times all threads attempt to access all locks in the time interval. Notice that in this situation, a thread can appear more than once in the chromosome if it accesses more than one lock or if it accesses the same lock multiple times.

Three constraints must be met for the formation of valid chromosomes and to simplify the crossover operation discussed below. 1.) All genes within the chromosome are ordered according to increasing thread identifiers, then lock identifiers, then increasing access times. 2.) Lock access times must fall within the specified time interval or are set to -1. 3.) Consecutive genes for the same thread and lock identifiers must have access time differences equal to at least the minimum and at most the maximum access time range of the associated thread and lock, if start and end times are defined as ranges (Section 3).

Consider, for example, a set of three threads T1 (access range [23-25] time units), T2 (access range [15-22]) and T3 (access range [25-35]) each accessing lock L1. In a time interval of [0-30] time units, the chromosome length would be three since each of the threads can access L1 at most once during this time interval. The following is then a valid chromosome: (T1,L1,24) (T2,L1,20) (T3,L1,-1) where T1 accesses L1 at time unit 24, T2's access is at time 20 and T3 does not access the lock before time 30.

4.2 Crossover Operator

Crossover is the means by which desirable traits are passed on from parents to their offspring [10]. We use a one-point, sexual crossover operator: two parents are randomly split at the same location into two parts which are alternated to produce two

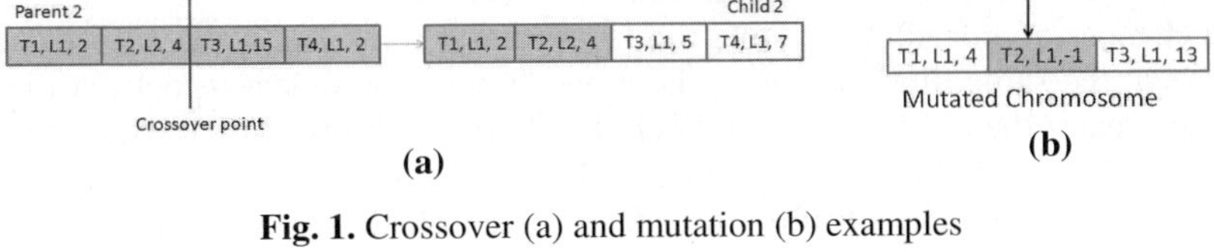

Fig. 1. Crossover (a) and mutation (b) examples

children. For example, the two parents on the left of Fig. 1(a) produce the offspring on the right. If, after crossover, any two consecutive genes of the same thread and lock no longer meet their lock access time requirements (constraint 3 is violated), the second gene's access time is randomly generated such that constraint 3 is met. This is repeated until all occurrences of this situation satisfy constraint 3.

4.3 Mutation Operator

Mutation introduces new genetic information, hence further exploring the search space, while aiding the GA in avoiding getting caught in local optima [10]. Mutation proceeds as follows: each gene in the chromosome is mutated based on a mutation probability and the resulting chromosome is evaluated for its new fitness. Our mutation operator mutates a gene by altering its access time. The rationale is to move access times along the specified time interval, with the aim of finding the optimal times at which these access times will be more likely to cause deadlocks. When a gene is chosen for mutation, a new timing value is randomly chosen from the range of possible access range values. If the value chosen lies outside the time interval, the timing information is set to -1 to satisfy Constraint 2. Similar to the crossover operator, if, after mutation, two consecutive genes no longer meet their lock access time requirements, the affected genes are altered such that the requirements are met. For example, assume threads T1, T2 and T3 attempt to access a target lock, L1 with access times T1[4-7], T2[20-30], T3[12-15] and time interval [0-25]. The first chromosome of Figure 1(b) is then valid. When the second gene of the chromosome is chosen for mutation, a new value (say, 27) is chosen from its access time range [20-30]. Because this falls outside the time range specified, the mutated gene has value -1.

4.4 Objective Function

The objective function calculates the fitness of chromosomes. In our methodology, we define an objective function that uses information about threads, locks, and thread access times of locks: one that is based on how close a given chromosome is to representing a deadlock. Yet, a deadlock can only be determined after threads acquire their needed locks. We thus first schedule thread executions according to arrival times specified in chromosome data (i.e., genes) for the time interval defined: i.e., genes indicate at what time threads access locks and this information, along with execution times available (for instance) from the UML/SPT model, is used by a scheduler to schedule thread executions within locks. Then we calculate the fitness by examining the state of threads and locks (threads waiting on and executing within locks) at the end of the time interval. Since a deadlock appears when the involved threads cannot proceed with their executions, any deadlock that occurs early during the time interval will propagate to the end of the interval; the objective function therefore examines the state of threads and locks at the end of the time interval.

The chances of a deadlocked situation increase when the number of threads accessing locks at the same time increases: the more threads try to access locks at the same time, the greater the chance of a deadlock. Furthermore, to account for the aforementioned circularity condition of deadlocks (Section 2), the probability of a deadlock increases with the number of times threads execute in locks and wait on them. We use these heuristics to develop an appropriate fitness function. Because a deadlock situation can only arise when there is a cycle of requests and locks, at least two threads must be executing within two locks that are full to capacity, while also waiting interchangeably for access of those locks.

This leads us to define a number of properties that the fitness function must possess: 1.) Because deadlocks involve at least two waiting threads, the fitness of scenarios where at least two threads are waiting on locks should always be superior than the fitness of scenarios where zero or one thread is waiting; 2.) The fitness function should be driven by the number of locks locked, i.e., an additional thread executing in a lock should increase the fitness; 3.) The fitness function should be driven by the number of threads waiting on locks, i.e., an additional thread waiting for access to a lock should increase the fitness. Property 1 ensures that situations where no deadlock is possible are penalized, whereas properties 2 and 3 guide the search towards situations where deadlocks are possible and increasingly likely.

Based on these premises, let us examine the fitness function of a chromosome c. Variables `#T` and `#L` represent the total number of threads and locks in the system, respectively. `threadsWaiting` is the total number of threads waiting on any lock. By definition, a thread waiting on a lock is blocked and its execution cannot resume until it gains access to the lock. Hence, this variable is in the range `[0-#T]`. `#LockExecs` is the total number of threads executing within all locks. It is the summation of the slots in all locks that are occupied. This variable is in the range `[0 -lockCapacities]`, where `lockCapacities` is the summation of all lock capacities. `threadsWaiting` and `#LocksExecs` are obtained after scheduling and are calculated at the end of the time interval, whereas `lockCapacities` comes from the UML/SPT input (Table 1).

Our fitness function for chromosome c gives higher fitness values to situations where more threads are executing and waiting on more locks; larger values are therefore indicative of fitter individuals.

$$f(c) = \begin{cases} \#LockExecs + threadsWaiting & \text{if } threadsWaiting < 2 \\ \#LockExecs + threadsWaiting + lockCapacities & \text{if } threadsWaiting \geq 2 \end{cases}$$

Showing that this fitness function satisfies the three aforementioned properties is straightforward and is omitted here due to space constraints (see [20]).

The fitness function is used by the GA after scheduling the threads according to their respective chromosomes. It is important to note that when there is a deadlock situation, the fitness function does not guarantee that the fitness value will be maximized. The fitness function is always a heuristic and cannot deterministically identify concurrency issues. For example, near deadlock situations where `threadsWaiting>2` may overshadow a deadlock situation where `threadsWaiting=2`. To ensure that a deadlock is detected when there is one, a RAG (Section 2) is built after scheduling, i.e., once we know the allocation of resources to threads according to chromosome data, to detect deadlocks when `threadsWaiting≥2`. Identifying cycles in such a graph is a well-known problem. Once a deadlock is detected from the RAG, the GA terminates and the chromosome yielding the deadlock is returned.

Consider the chromosomes of Figure 1(b). Recall the access times (T1[4-7], T2[20-30], T3[12-15]) and time interval ([0-25]). Further assume that lock execution times for each of the threads are 21, 5 and 10, respectively. L1 is assumed to have capacity 1 and a FIFO access policy. Figure 2 depicts the scheduling of both the

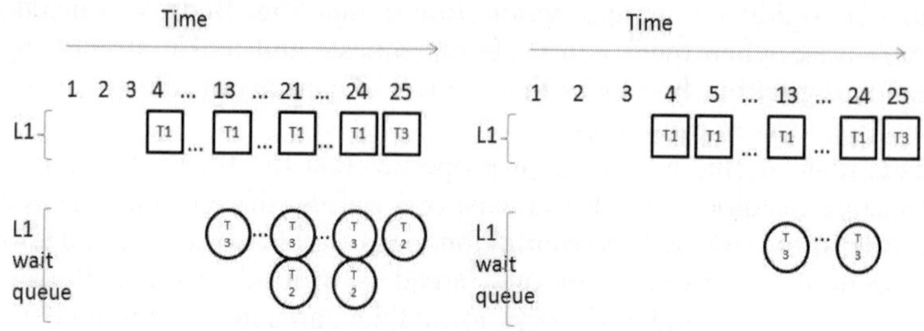

Fig. 2. Fitness Calculation Example

original chromosome (left) and the mutated chromosome (right): Threads accessing L1 are shown as squares and threads waiting in L1's wait queue are shown as circles. According to the original chromosome, T1 accesses L1 at time unit 4 until time unit 4+21-1=24. During this period, T2 and T3 are waiting on L1, starting at times 21 and 13, respectively. The fitness value of the original chromosome is 2 (`threadsWaiting<2`, hence `#LockExecs+threadsWaiting=1+1`). The mutated chromosome has fitness 1 (`#LockExecs+threadsWaiting=1+0` since `threadsWaiting<2`). Because in both situations `threadsWaiting<2`, no RAG check is needed. The original chromosome is thus closer to a deadlock situation than the mutated chromosome. This is logical since in the former case, one thread is waiting for access to the lock as opposed to the latter case where no thread is waiting.

For the fitness function to be effective, the time interval over which it is defined must be large enough so that deadlock situations have a chance to occur. Recall that the time interval determines the size of the chromosome. If the time interval is too large, chromosome size is affected and overall computation time of the GA increases. Hence, there is a tradeoff between having a long time interval to increase the likelihood of deadlock detection and overall GA computation time. A good range for the time interval is based on the longest thread execution time in all locks (`lt`) and the maximum lock access time of all threads (`ll`). These are obtained from the UML/SPT input, by looking at the `RTstart` and `RTduration` tags of all the threads stereotyped `<<SAaction>>` in sequence diagrams (Section 3). Our heuristic is to guarantee, using these two variables, that all thread accesses will occur at least twice, giving deadlocks a chance to occur. Therefore, the time interval equals: `[0-(lt+ll)*2]`.

5 Tool and GA Parameters

We have built a prototype tool, Concurrency Fault Detector (CFD), supporting our methodology. CFD is an automated system that identifies potential concurrency faults in any concurrent application. Currently, it can identify deadlocks, and work is in progress for the detection of other types of concurrency faults. CFD involves a sequence of steps. Users first input two categories of information: (1) UML/SPT sequence diagrams for the analyzed system, and (2) the execution time interval during which the system is to be analyzed. CFD then extracts the required information from the inputted sequence diagrams.

CFD is decomposed into three portions: a scheduler, a genetic algorithm, and a RAG evaluator. The GA, as described in Section 0, is used to determine whether an execution sequence exists that meets all input requirements and (potentially) results in a deadlock. CFD's scheduler emulates single processor execution. Deadlock detection is performed using a RAG whenever a chromosome results in at least two threads waiting on locks (Section 2). If a cycle is found, CFD outputs the details of the chromosome causing it and the corresponding RAG. If no deadlock is found after 1000 generations, CFD terminates, showing output details of the highest fitness chromosome found.

Since collecting input data is easy to automate from a UML case tool, and all the other phases are automated, CFD is meant to be used interactively: the user is expected to fix the design of the system when CFD terminates with a detected deadlock situation. This is the main reason why we developed a strategy that only reports one deadlock scenario at a time, i.e., per run of CFD, allowing designers to fix the system's design before running the modified design again on CFD.

CFD is used to investigate whether scenarios can be generated where deadlocks occur. If no such scenario is found, this does not guarantee that none exist. However, one can still feel more confident that such a case is unlikely.

Though various parameters of the GA must be specified, we can fortunately rely on a substantial literature reporting empirical results and making recommendations. Parameters include the type of GA used, population size, mutation and crossover rates and selection operator. We use a steady state GA, with a replacement percentage of 100%. The population size we apply is 200. This is higher than the size suggested in [10], but works more effectively for larger search spaces. The selection operator is rank selector, whereby chromosomes with higher fitness are more likely to be chosen than ones with lower fitness [18]. Mutation and crossover rates are $1.75/\gamma\sqrt{l}$ (where γ denotes the population size and l is the length of the chromosome) and 0.8, respectively. Both are based on the findings in [16] and [10], respectively.

All parameter values are based on findings reported in the literature, except population size, which was fine tuned after some experimentation. These parameter values have worked exceedingly well in all our case studies when considering both the detection rate and execution time to find a deadlock. The same parameter values can be used for other system designs, though further empirical investigation is required to ensure the generality of these parameter values in our application context. In the worst case, if one wants to be on the safe side and ensure fully optimal results, the parameters can be fine tuned once for each new system design: when the system design being checked is first analyzed. For further design modifications of the same system, the parameters need not be fine tuned.

6 Case Studies

Our case studies aim to evaluate the effectiveness and run-time efficiency of our GA at detecting deadlocks based on UML/SPT design models. We first describe the case studies and then discuss results.

6.1 The Dining Philosophers Problem (Phil)

The renowned n-dining philosophers problem has commonly been used to demonstrate deadlock detection and avoidance [8, 9]. The problem is summarized as follows: 40 philosophers are sitting at a round table either eating or thinking. Every two philosophers share one fork, yet only one can access a shared fork at a time. The forks are set so that each philosopher has one on their right and one on their left. When they are thinking, philosophers do not access forks. When they are hungry and attempt to eat, they pick up left forks first followed by right. When finished eating, forks are released in the same order. This solution can be deadlocked if all philosophers attempt to eat at the same time and all pick up their left forks. The search space is approximately $1.2 * 10^{19}$.

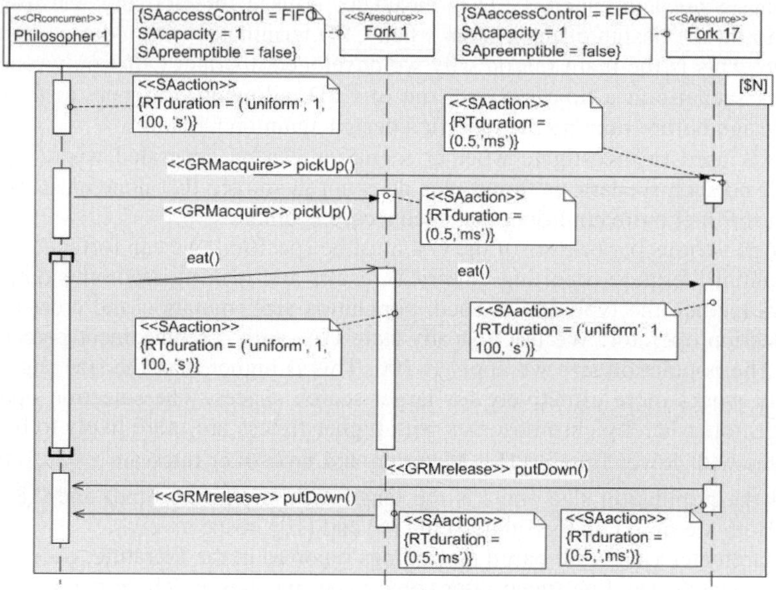

Fig. 3. Dining Philosophers Sequence Diagram

Concurrency aspects are depicted in Figure 3 for philosopher 1. This is an excerpt of the full sequence diagram. The complete sequence diagram would show the interactions of all philosophers and all forks. Philosopher 1 is depicted as a concurrently executing thread via `<<CRconcurrent>>`. It acquires two locks, Fork 17 and Fork 1, designated by `<<SAresource>>`. Fork 17 (left fork) and Fork 1 (right fork) each allow only one thread to execute at any given point in time, as indicated by `SAcapacity`. Each lock's waiting threads are accessed on a first come first served basis as specified by `SAaccessControl`. The philosopher's thinking time (access time range) is represented by `RTduration` in the first `<<SAaction>>`. Access times and lock execution times are both discrete uniform distributions between 1 and 100 seconds. The execution duration of Philosopher 1 (thread) in each of the locks is defined by `RTduration` on each lock's `SAaction`, i.e., between 1 and 100 time units.

Recall that CFD requires two inputs: sequence diagram and time interval. The first input for the case study is the complete sequence diagram. For the time interval, we used our heuristic (Section 4.4): the longest thread execution time is 100 (maximum eating time), and the longest lock access time (i.e., thinking time) is 100, hence the time interval is 400.

6.2 The Bank Fund Transfer Problem (Bank)

The bank fund transfer is based on a simple banking functionality: fund transfer between accounts, and simulates multiple threads transferring funds among different accounts [5]. Ten threads, representing 10 account holders, repeatedly transfer funds between any two randomly generated accounts out of 50 available accounts. When transferring from account A to account B, account A is first locked, then checks on the amount bounds of A are performed. If A can transfer the amount, account B is locked, then the amount is validated before the transfer is complete. Account B is released first, followed by account A. The corresponding sequence diagram is not shown here due to space constraints but can be found in [20]. Again, all the necessary information used by the GA, including the time interval, can be retrieved from the UML/SPT model (see [20]).

With this design, a deadlock can occur if one thread is transferring from account A to B, while another is simultaneously transferring from B to A.

The search space of this problem depends on the number of threads and the number of accounts, specifically $(n^2-n)^t$, where `n` is the number of accounts and t is the number of threads. For 10 threads and 50 accounts, the search space is approximately $7.7 * 10^{33}$.

6.3 The Cruise Control Problem (Cruise)

The cruise control problem emulates a car simulator along with its cruising controller. The system is divided into a number of classes: `CarSimulator` simulates the car engine, runs a thread while the car is started, and simulates car speed changes based on the throttle and brake settings as well as the controlled speed by the cruising system when it is enabled; `CruiseControl` is a container for both car simulator and cruise controller of the car. This is the entry class that receives commands and dispatches them to the car and the controller; `SpeedControl` is a thread that runs in the `Controller` to adjust car speed whenever cruising is enabled. When cruising is enabled, the current car speed is recorded and maintained for the duration of cruising time. When resuming cruising, the latest recorded speed is used as the speed to maintain during cruising; `Controller` simulates the cruise control of the car, disabling, enabling or resuming cruising according to the commands received by `CruiseControl`. It creates a new `SpeedControl` thread when cruising is enabled.

Unlike the other case studies, many different scenarios are available here for testing. Here, we limit it to the following test case scenario, as portrayed in the sequence diagram of [20]. This scenario tests a number of threads and locks:

```
engine on
repeat
  accelerate
  cruise control on
  brake
```

A deadlock can occur during breaking when the `CarSimulator` is executing the brake command and the `SpeedControl` is in its periodic run. Furthermore, in these particular states, a deadlock shows up only when the timing is just right so that both acquire two locks (`brakepedal` and `throttle`) at just the right times.

The search space here depends on the number of new `SpeedControl` threads created. For t new threads created, the search space is 6t+8. We create 2000 new threads in this case study.

6.4 Results

We first compare our results with randomly generated execution sequences (i.e., chromosomes). This is necessary in order to demonstrate that the detection of deadlocks is not easy in our case studies and that our GA really makes a useful contribution. In our GA, 200 sequences are first randomly generated as the initial population. Then, up to 200 new ones are generated using GA operations. These may replace up to all of the population. For 40 philosophers, the generation and replacement of sequences continues for 343 generations on average before a deadlock is detected. Hence, we randomly generated 68,800 sequences (200 + (200 * 343)) as a benchmark to assess the usefulness of our technique. (Note that in this case the evolution of the population is *not* driven by the fitness function.) Of the randomly generated sequences, none produced a valid sequence that leads to a deadlock situation. Similarly, 10,000 random sequences were generated for Bank and Cruise. The former produced no valid sequences yielding a deadlock, while the latter rarely did (roughly 0.05% of the time), owing to the significantly smaller search space in part compensated by more stringent requirements for a deadlock.

As GAs are a heuristic optimization technique, variance occurs in the results produced. To give an idea of the variability in results, each case study was run a number of times on an Intel Core 2 2.0 GHz processor. Results are presented in Table 2, with indications if a deadlock was detected (Error), the number of runs detecting the deadlock over the total number of runs, the total execution time, the average execution time per run, the search space, the number of random sequences generated and the percentage of time when random sequences detect a deadlock. The average execution time per run indicates, on average, how long it takes to execute any run, whether it finds the deadlock or not.

Table 2. Results

Case Study	Error found?	#Errors / #Runs	Total Runtime (hrs)	Average Execution Time per Run	Search Space	Number Random Sequences	Random Detects Deadlock (%)
Phil	Yes	12/25	02:27:23	1 min 27 sec	$1.2 * 10^{19}$	68,800	0
Bank	Yes	50/50	00:11:40	14 sec	$7.7 * 10^{33}$	10,000	0
Cruise	Yes	50/50	00:01:15	1.5 sec	$1.2 * 10^{4}$	10,000	0.05

CFD consistently detects deadlocks in two of the case studies. But for the 40 philosophers problem, CFD is unable to detect a deadlock in 13 runs out of 25, with each run taking a maximum of 10 minutes. However, when CFD is able to detect a deadlock (12/25 runs or 48% of the time), it does so in approximately a minute and a half. This implies that CFD can be run several times for a few minutes and then be very likely to detect a deadlock when there is one, in a short time. For example, 10 runs would take roughly 15 minutes and have a probability of less than 2/1000 not to detect a deadlock. Though not targeted to UML, the Phil case study is also addressed in [9] using a model checker: DELFIN$^+$. Because a heuristic is involved, we would expect some random variation in execution times and perhaps deadlock detection effectiveness across different runs, yet no mention is given as to how many runs were produced for 40 philosophers, implying that reports are for a single run [9]. It takes 10,000,000 msec for DELFIN$^+$ to detect a deadlock. This is drastically longer than the average time taken by CFD. Execution time differences between DEFLIN$^+$ and CFD may be *partly* explained by a difference in hardware (Intel Core 2 2.0 GHz processor versus Intel Pentium 4 2.80 GHz processor[2]). Though the way results are reported in [9] does not allow easy comparisons, such a large time difference still suggests CFD is comparatively very efficient.

It is interesting to note that CFD is able to detect a deadlock in all 50 runs of the Bank case study, even though it has a larger search space than that of the 40 philosophers. While the search space is smaller in the latter case study, the conditions for a deadlock are more stringent (all 40 philosophers must be accessing all left forks simultaneously, versus any two accounts with inverted source and destinations). This makes the search harder in the former case than the latter.

7 Related Work

A substantial amount of work aims at testing or verifying concurrent systems. They cover areas such as model checking and code-based static analysis. They are also diverse in their underlying technology, using GAs, dedicated languages, temporal logic, and automata theory, for example. GAs have also been used for various testing purposes in sequential systems - such as input data generation and integration testing - as well as real time systems - such as stress testing [21]. However, all these works lie out of the scope of the current paper.

Model checking has been used to test concurrent system requirements. Some checkers, such as UPPAAL [4], use models of the system under test while others, such as Verisoft [8], use the system's source code. Others, such as DELFIN+ [9], combine heuristic searches with model checking. In UPPAAL [4], a system is modeled as a network of timed-automata that execute in parallel and may synchronize with each other. The overall state of the system is determined by the combined states of each of the automata, clock constraints as well as values of variables. System specifications that are to be verified are inputted via UPPAAL's query language, which uses a version of Computation Tree Logic (CTL) [4]. Verisoft [8] relies on source code analysis and uses a GA, coupled with a model checker, to search for error states in the state space of a concurrent reactive system. The SPIN model checker [1] is based on automata theory where properties to be verified are expressed in Linear Temporal Logic (LTL) and the system under test is expressed using Process Meta Language (Promela) [1]. DELFIN+ [9] and HSF-SPIN [11] follow a directed model checking approach using heuristic searches (e.g., A*) to detect deadlocks in concurrent systems.

[2] DELFIN+ is not available for download, so we could not run it on our same environment.

With the current trend towards MDD [15], models are regarded as the essence of system development. While their development may be time consuming, they can be used to partially automate other activities. The methodology we propose is meant to be used in the context of the OMG MDA, hence our reliance on the UML standard and SPT profile, thereby reusing existing design models instead of developing specific models to be inputted to a model checker. As all information required by our methodology can be incorporated in the UML model of a system, this eliminates the need for additional modeling activities (e.g., using temporal logic). While the sequence diagrams required by CFD may not be as detailed as required when the system is initially designed, adding information to these pre-existing diagrams is easier than converting the whole model into a different model, such as timed-automata in the case of UPPAAL [4]. In essence, our methodology can be thought of as another user configurable model analyzer that is easier to use than a model checker because it does not require any additional knowledge than familiarity with UML/SPT. Moreover, our technique was shown in Section 6.4 to be effective in comparison to a model-checker for the 40 philosophers problem [9].

Another interesting and recent work that employs models to test concurrent systems is presented in [14]. The approach is to build a model - under the form of a UML state machine - that captures both the aspects of the system's behavior that one wants to test and the underlying programming language concurrency mechanisms, specifically Java. The Symbolic Analysis Laboratory (SAL) model checker derives test sequences from the model, which are then executed with Concurrency Analyzer (ConAn), a deterministic, run-to-completion testing tool [14]. This differs from our approach as our goal is to reuse of existing UML design models rather than UML models created specifically for testing language specific implementations.

In the context of MDD, a number of works also utilize the SPT profile (e.g., [3]), yet they mostly focus on performance analysis rather than the analysis of model properties.

8 Conclusions and Future Work

Concurrency abounds in many software systems. Such systems usually involve threads that access shared resources, and complex thread communication. If not handled properly, such accesses can lead to many problems, such as deadlock situations, which may hinder system execution. The earlier any problem is detected, the better. In this paper, we describe a methodology and a tool for detecting deadlocks based on the analysis of design representations in UML and SPT. Since our goal is to provide an automated test methodology that can be applied in the context of model-driven, UML-based development, the choice of UML/SPT was natural as it is the de facto standard for the object-oriented modeling of concurrent, real-time applications. This is also practical in reducing the need for complex tooling and training, and additional modeling to what is already required for UML-based development. Being geared towards systems characterized by large search spaces, our methodology uses a tailored genetic algorithm for searching deadlocks.

We presented three case studies that show very promising results. Even in the presence of large search spaces, our tool's running time is quite reasonable. Therefore, even in the worst-case scenario, when the GA detection rate is at its worst, it can be run several times for a few minutes and then be nearly certain to detect a deadlock if one exists.

Though we focus on deadlocks here, work is underway to tailor our fitness function to other concurrency problems associated with shared resources (namely data races, starvation, and livelocks) and thread communication. For example, the fitness function used for starvation is built on the assumption that the chances of starvation increase as the number of threads waiting for access to a lock increases.

References

1. Holzmann, G.J.: The Model Checker SPIN. IEEE Trans. Soft. Eng. 23(5) (1997)
2. Bacon, J.: Concurrent Systems – Operating Systems, Database and Distributed Systems: An Integrated Approach, 2nd edn. Addison-Wesley, Reading (1997)
3. Petriu, D.C.: Performance Analysis with the SPT Profile. Model-Driven Eng. Dist. Embed. Sys., 205–224 (2005)
4. Behrmann, G., David, A., Larsen, K.G.: A Tutorial on Uppaal (2004), `http://www.it.uu.se/research/group/darts/papers/texts/new-tutorial.pdf`
5. Yang, H.: Deadlock. Java Tutorials – Herong's Tutorial Notes, version 4.10 (2006), `http://www.herongyang.com/java/index.html`
6. Chinneck, J.W.: Practical Optimization: A Gentle Introduction. Draft (2007), `http://www.sce.carleton.ca/faculty/chinneck/po.html`
7. Downey, A.B.: The Little Book of Semaphores, 2nd edn. Green Tea Press (2008)
8. Godefroid, P., Khurshid, S.: Exploring Very Large State Spaces Using Genetic Algorithms. Intl. Journal Soft. Tools Tech. Trans. 6(2), 117–127 (2004)
9. Gradara, S., Sontone, A., Villani, M.L.: DELFIN+: An Efficient Deadlock Detection Tool for CCS Processes. J. Comp. System Sci. 72(8), 1397–1412 (2006)
10. Haupt, R.L., Haupt, S.E.: Practical Genetic Algorithms. Wiley-Interscience, Chichester (1998)
11. Edelkamp, S., Lluch-Lafuente, A., Leue, S.: Trail-Directed Model Checking. Proc. Soft. Model Check, Elec. Notes Theoretical Comp. Sci. 55 (2001)
12. OMG: Unified Modeling Language (UML). Version 2.1.2 (2007)
13. Jacob, C.: Illustrating Evolutionary Computation with Mathematica. Morgan Kaufmann, San Francisco (2001)
14. Kim, S., Wildman, L., Duke, R.: A UML Approach to the Generation of Test Sequences for JAVA-based Concurrent Systems. In: Proc. Austrl. Soft. Eng. Conf., pp. 100–109 (2005)
15. Kleppe, A., Warmer, J., Bast, W.: MDA Explained – The Model Driven Architecture: Practice and Promise. Addison-Wesley, Boston (2003)
16. Back, T.: Self-Adaptation in Genetic Algorithms. In: Proc. European Conf. Artif. Life, pp. 263–271 (1992)
17. Mahfoud, S.W., Goldberg, D.E.: Parallel Recombinative Simulated Annealing: A Genetic Algorithm. Parallel Comp. 21(1), 1–28 (1995)
18. Koza, J.R.: Genetic Programming: On the Programming of Computers by Means of Natural Selection. MIT Press, Cambridge (1992)
19. OMG: UML Profile for Schedulibility, Performance and Time Specification. Adopted Specification (2005), `http://www.omg.org/docs/formal/05-01-02.pdf`
20. Shousha, M., Briand, L., Labiche, Y.: A UML/SPT Model Analysis Methodology for Concurrent Systems Based on Genetic Algorithms. Technical Report SCE-07-06 Carleton University (2008)
21. Briand, L., Labiche, Y., Shousha, M.: Using Genetic Algorithms for Early Schedulability Analysis and Stress Testing in Real-Time Systems. Gene. Prog. and Evol. Mach. 7(2), 145–170 (2006)

Integrating Performance Analysis in the Model Driven Development of Software Product Lines

Rasha Tawhid[1] and Dorina Petriu[2]

[1] School of Computer Science, Carleton University, Ottawa, Canada
rtawhid@connect.carleton.ca
[2] Dept. of Systems and Computer Engineering, Carleton University, Ottawa, Canada
petriu@sce.carleton.ca

Abstract. The paper proposes to integrate performance analysis in the early phases of the model-driven development process for Software Product Lines (SPL). We start by adding generic performance annotations to the UML model representing the set of core reusable SPL assets. The annotations are generic and use the MARTE Profile recently adopted by OMG. A first model transformation realized in the Atlas Transformation Language (ATL), which is the focus of this paper, derives the UML model of a specific product with concrete MARTE performance annotations from the SPL model. A second transformation generates a Layered Queueing Network performance model for the given product by applying an existing transformation approach named PUMA, developed in previous work. The proposed technique is illustrated with an e-commerce case study that models the commonality and variability in both structural and behavioural SPL views. A product is derived and the performance of two design alternatives is compared.

Keywords: Software Product Line, Performance Analysis, Model to model Transformation, UML, MARTE, ATL.

1 Introduction

Software Product Line (SPL) engineering aims at improving productivity and reducing development time, effort, cost, and complexity by gathering the analysis, design and implementation activities of a family of systems. It is based on the reuse of core assets instead of working from scratch. An important challenge in the context of SPL approach is to model and manage variability between products and to support the derivation of specific products from the family assets.

Model-driven development (MDD) improves software development by capturing the key features of a system in models which are developed and refined as the system is created [18]. Many existing works have investigated ways of applying MDD to SPL development, with the goal of generating code for given products from the SPL model. In this paper, we propose to add another dimension to the model-driven development of SPL, by generating a performance model for a given product from the SPL model, in the early development phases. Early performance analysis allows developers to gain insight on the performance trouble spots for different design alternatives

K. Czarnecki et al. (Eds.): MoDELS 2008, LNCS 5301, pp. 490–504, 2008.

under different workload conditions. The goal is to help developers to evaluate the system performance and to choose better design alternatives as early as possible, so that the systems being built will meet their performance requirements.

Evaluating non-functional properties from UML models is possible by adding first additional information specific to the property to be evaluated, and then transforming the annotated UML model into a formal model which can be analyzed with known analysis techniques and tools [20]. Examples of formal models used for performance analysis are queueing networks, Petri nets, stochastic process algebras, etc. [3]. The "UML Performance Profile for Schedulability, Performance and Time" (SPT) standardized by OMG or its recent replacement, the "UML Profile for Modeling and Analysis of Real-Time and Embedded systems (MARTE)" [14] define quantitative performance annotations (such as resource demands made by different software execution steps, visit ratios, performance requirements, etc.) to be added to a given UML model, particularly to the architecture, behaviour and deployment views.

In literature there are many publications investigating the application of MDD to SPL, as discussed in section 2. Also, there is a body of work on software performance engineering aiming to build performance models from software specifications, which can be further used for early performance analysis [3]. However, to the best of our knowledge, our research is the first to propose an approach for integrating quantitative performance analysis in the early phases of UML-based model-driven development of SPL. The main research challenge stems from the mismatch between what a SPL model and a performance model represent. A SPL model is a collection of core "generic" asset models, which are building blocks for many different products with all kind of options and alternatives, while a performance model is an instance-based representation of a runtime system, focusing on how the system is using all kind of resources and how the competition for resources impacts the system performance (response time, throughput, utilization, etc.). Hence, a first research challenge is SPL-related: automating the derivation of a UML product model that contains all the views necessary for performance analysis (i.e., software architecture, key-performance scenarios and deployment) from a SPL model. A second research challenge is performance-related, due to the fact that a new dimension is added to the model transformation when dealing with performance annotations. The SPL model should have reusable generic parametric performance annotations, which will be bound to concrete values when generating the model of a specific product.

The approach proposed in the paper, illustrated in Fig.1, requires two transformations. The starting point is a UML model of a SPL with generic performance annotations, which uses two separate profiles: a "product line" (PL) profile similar to [10] for specifying the commonality and variability between products, and MARTE for performance annotations [14]. The first model-to-model transformation takes as input the SPL source model and a set of binding directives specifying the mapping between the generic and concrete performance annotations (in XML format). The *target model* of this transformation is a UML+MARTE model of a product, where the variability expressed in the SPL model has been analyzed and bound to a specific product, and the generic performance annotations have been bound to concrete values. This transformation uses the Atlas Transformation Language (ATL) [1] which is based on the Eclipse Modeling Framework (EMF).

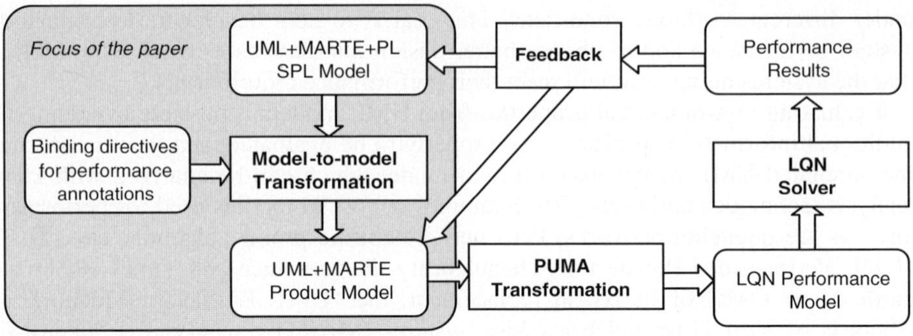

Fig. 1. Approach for integrating performance analysis with MDD of SPL

The second transformation takes as input the outcome of the first transformation and derives a Layered Queueing Network (LQN) performance model for the specific product, by using the PUMA transformation approach that has been previously developed in our research group [20][21]. After the performance model for a product was generated, it can be analyzed with existing LQN solvers and feedback regarding its performance properties will be given to the software development team. The focus of this paper is on the first transformation shown in the shaded area.

The proposed technique is illustrated with an e-commerce case study, which models the commonality and variability in both structural and behavioural views similar to the Product Line UML-based Software Engineering (PLUS) method [10]. (The differences between our approach and PLUS are discussed in section 2). The e-commerce web service is a high performance distributed application where several architectural questions arise. One of them is the location of data storage (centralized or distributed). We consider that this architectural decision is a *quality feature* (as opposed to a *functional* one) because it impacts non-functional requirements or concerns, such as performance, availability, security, reliability, etc. We propose to take into account quality features from the early phases of the SPL development process, and to represent their relationships with the functional features in the feature dependency diagram. Integrating performance analysis into SPL in the early development phases allows assessing the impact of different choices for the quality and functional features on system performance.

The paper is organized as follows: section 2 discusses related research, section 3 presents the transformation algorithm for product derivation, section 4 analyzes the performance effects of a case-study and discusses different design alternatives and section 5 presents the conclusions and future work.

2 Related Research

In this section, we discuss briefly related research on two topics: model-driven development of SPL, and performance analysis of UML models annotated with performance information (with SPT or MARTE) in early development phases.

A lot of work has been done in the area of integrating MDD into SPL to achieve the benefits of the two paradigms. The ultimate MDD objective in most of the cases is to generate code for a product from the SPL model; in some cases, however, a product model is also obtained.

In [5] is presented an approach for deriving the architecture of a product by selectively copying elements from the SPL architecture based on a product-specific feature configuration. Another approach in [13] describes the general architecture of the family and the variation configuration model. Variation points are specified in the SPL class view by using the stereotype <<vp>> implying a variation that needs to be resolved at configuration time. Based on these variation points, a graphical decision model is generated to configure the product architecture.

A domain-specific language called Model Template Transformation Language (MTTL) for specifying the transformations of model templates based on feature models is described in [2]. First, the product line model is developed by creating a feature model and a model template. Then, according to the selected feature, a feature configuration is created and an Atomic Transformation Code (ATC) is executed for specializing the model template.

In [18] aspect-oriented techniques are used to manage variability in SPL. In the problem domain, SPL is modeled using a DSL, where each variation needs to be configured with various options. In the solution domain, a component-based architecture is built starting with the minimal core and selectively adding additional parts by weaving aspects.

In [8] a feature-based model template is introduced, which consists of annotated models implementing the features. A template instance for a given feature configuration can be produced automatically. In [9] a generic two-phased product derivation process is presented. In the initial phase, a first configuration is created from the product family assets and modified in a number of subsequent iterations until the product satisfies all its requirements. In [15] the variability of a product line is modeled and realized by higher-order transformations using the MOFScript language. Generative programming is combined with aspects to represent the variability in SPL. A process to obtain a use case model for a specific application based on a feature configuration model is described in [6].

The work by Jézéquel et al. addresses product derivation at structural and behavioural levels [22][23]. An approach for deriving a product model based on a creational design pattern is proposed in [22]. A model derivation technique for static and behaviour views is proposed in [23]. The static derivation starts from a SPL class diagram and generates the product class diagram based on a decision model. An algebraic approach is proposed to derive statecharts for a specific product from the sequence diagrams of the product line, by transforming product scenarios given as a reference expression for SD into a composition of statecharts.

Another group addressing UML-based product derivation is Gomaa's group. In [10] a method called Product Line UML-based Software Engineering (PLUS) for modeling explicitly the commonality and variability in a SPL is presented. One of the few papers proposing tool support for multiple-view SPL models stored in a repository is [11]. Automated support for product derivation from the product line repository is also proposed in [11]. A modeling approach for dynamic reconfiguration of pattern-based software architectures is presented in [12].

It is worth mentioning that feature modeling is essential in SPL, yet the concept of "feature" is not a first-class model element in UML. Thus, we cannot use the traditional feature diagram in UML models. In order to overcome this problem, different stereotypes for representing features and feature dependency have been defined in literature (however, none is standard yet).

Our work is based on Gomaa's group work, especially on PLUS [10] for the following reasons: it is a well developed method applied to real-time systems, is concerned with the behaviour view needed for performance analysis, and uses a profile for extending UML with SPL concepts (which we use in this paper under the name "PL profile"). However, our approach has the following differences from PLUS: a) we deal with MARTE performance annotations both in the source and target models; b) we introduced the concept of "quality feature" described in section 3; c) we use sequence diagrams for behaviour representation instead of collaboration (communication) diagrams, taking advantage of their enhanced modeling power; d) we use deployment diagrams, also important for performance analysis; e) we modified slightly the PL stereotypes and tags in order to represent quality features.

Software Performance Engineering (SPE) is a methodology introduced in [17] that promotes the integration of performance analysis into the software development process from the early stages and continuing throughout the whole software life cycle. Since the introduction of SPE, there has been a significant effort to integrate performance analysis into the software development process by using different performance modeling paradigms: queueing networks, Petri nets, stochastic process algebras, simulation, etc. [3]. The performance modeling formalism used in this paper is the Layered Queueing Model (LQN) [19]. A good survey of transformations of software models into different performance models is given in [3]. Examples of such transformations are from UML to Layered Queueing Networks in [16], to Stochastic Petri Nets in [4], and to Stochastic Process Algebra in [7]. In this work we are using the transformation framework PUMA described in [20][21], which converts an annotated UML model of a concrete system into different performance models (Layered Queueing Networks, Queueing networks, Petri Nets). Usually, the interpretation of the performance model results is done by a performance analyst, who understands the formal performance model. Current research is being done to diagnose the performance problems automatically (by following a set of rules similar to the experts) and to suggest advice for improvement in terms that the software developers can easily understand.

3 Product Model Derivation

There are two major processes in SPL engineering: a) *domain engineering* for analyzing the commonality and variability between members of the product line and establishing reusable SPL models, and b) *application engineering* for deriving an individual product that is a SPL member from reusable SPL models.

In UML-based domain engineering, we represent SPL features as use case packages and feature dependency as stereotyped class diagram, describing all feature combinations possible with this SPL; also, we use a SPL class diagram, sequence diagrams, deployment diagram describing the overall views for this product line. To illustrate the proposed derivation process, we use an e-commerce case study similar to [10], with some modifications. The e-commerce SPL is a web-based product line that handles business-to-business (B2B) as well as business-to-consumer (B2C) systems.

For example in B2B, a business customer can browse and select items through several catalogs. Each customer has a contract with a supplier for purchases as well as bank accounts through which payments can be made. An operation fund is associated with each contract for fund availability. Optionally, a supplier may create a purchase order requesting new inventory supplies from the wholesaler.

3.1 Source Model

The source model is a SPL model that must contain, among other assets, structural and behavioural views which are essential for the derivation of performance models: a) structural description of the software showing the high-level classes or components, especially if they are distributed and/or concurrent; b) the deployment of software to hardware devices, and c) a set of key performance scenarios defining the main system functions frequently executed.

The use case diagram for the e-commerce SPL is given in Fig. 2. The kernel use cases required by all the family members are shown in white, the optional use cases that may be used by any member are drawn in light grey, and the alternative use cases used only by some members are shown in dark grey. The use cases are grouped by type in packages (not shown here due to space limitations). Each package corresponds to a feature bearing the same name as the package. For instance, the use cases from Fig. 2 can be grouped as follows: the kernel use cases in a package "E-Commerce Kernel", the optional use cases in "Purchase Order", the alternative use cases for B2C in "Home Customer", and the alternative cases for B2B in "Business Customer".

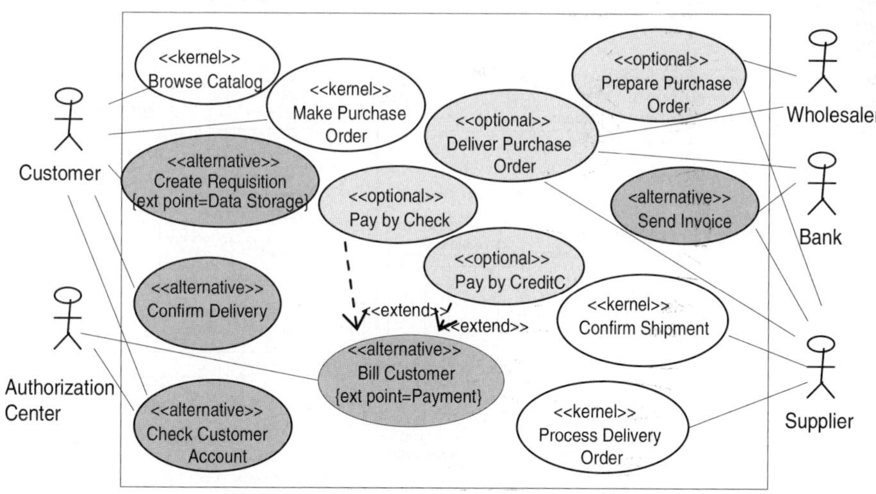

Fig. 2. Use case model of e-commerce SPL

Fig.3 illustrates the feature dependency represented as a class diagram with PL stereotypes, describing the way features can be combined within this SPL. For instance, the two alternative features "Business Customer" and "Home Customer" are mutually exclusive, hence they are grouped into an *exactly-one-of* feature group

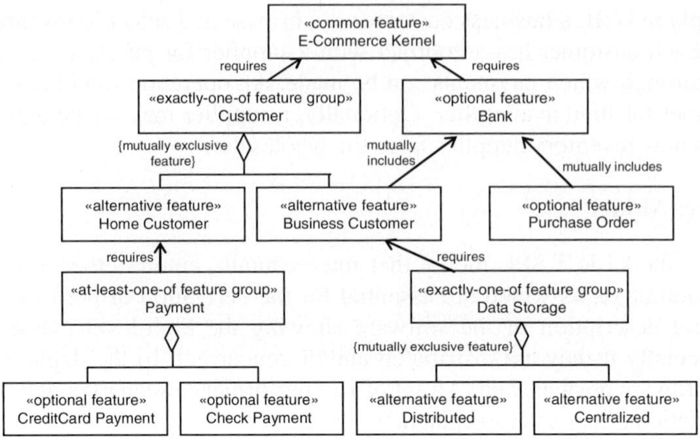

Fig. 3. Feature dependency in the e-commerce SPL

called "Customer". Beside the functional features, we add to the diagram so-called *quality features* characterizing design decisions that have impact on the non-functional requirements or concerns. For example the architectural decision related to the location of data storage (Centralized or Distributed) affects performance, and is represented in the diagram by two mutually exclusive quality features.

The class diagram for the e-commerce SPL in Fig. 4 shows that classes are stereotyped in three categories: kernel, variant or optional. The stereotypes for *variant* and

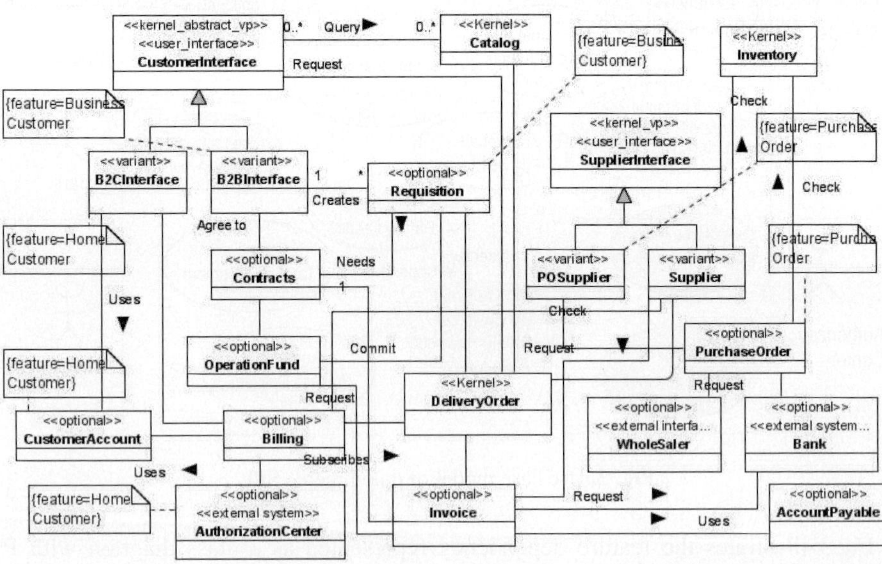

Fig. 4. Class diagram of e-commerce SPL

optional classes have a tag indicating the feature(s) requiring that class. A generalization/specialization hierarchy is used to model classes that behave differently in B2B and B2C systems (such as CustomerInterface and Supplier Interface).

For each scenario of each use case, at least a sequence diagram is created. Fig. 5 illustrates the scenario CreateRequisition, one of the 15 scenarios created for the case study. The sequence diagram itself is stereotyped as «GaPerformanceContext», indicating that this diagram is to be considered for performance analysis. This stereotype may have a set of parameters defining global properties of this analysis context, held by its tag contextParams. (In this example, the context has no global parameters).

Each lifeline is stereotyped as «PaRunTInstance», providing an explicit connection at the annotation level between a role in a behavior definition (a lifeline) and a run time instantiation of a process (active object). The tag {instance=Requisition} indicates which run-time instance of a process executes the lifeline role.

Conceptually, a scenario represented by a UML sequence diagram is composed of units of execution named steps. MARTE defines two kinds of steps for performance analysis: execution step (stereotyped «PaStep») and communication step (stereotyped «PaCommStep». «PaStep» may be applied to an ExecutionOccurence (represented as thin rectangle on the lifeline) or to the message that triggers it. For instance, in Fig.5, the message ContractQuery is stereotyped as an execution step:

«PaStep» {hostDemand=($ContD, ms)}

where the tag hostDemand indicates the execution time required by the step, which is given by the variable $ContD in time units of milliseconds. (In MARTE, the variables start with '$'). Note that using a variable for the execution time makes this a generic annotation that will be bound to a concrete value when deriving a given product. Both SPT and MARTE allow for variables and expression in annotations in order to raise the level of abstraction and make the annotations more reusable.

The same message ContractQuery is also stereotyped as a communication step:

«PaCommStep»{msgSize = ($ContQ,KB)}

where the message size is given by the variable $ContQ in KiloBytes.

The workload of a scenario is defined as a stream of events driving the system which can be open or closed. In our example:

«GaWorkloadEvent» {closed (population=$N2),(extDelay=$Z2)}

the workload is closed with a number of users $N1 and user think time for a user $Z2.

The alt fragments whose choices are based on the value of the quality feature DataStorage (which is represented as a scenario variation point) are stereotyped with the PL stereotype <<extension point>>{extension=DataStorage}.

Finally, the deployment diagram for the SPL is created assuming maximum distribution. It contains all the possible artifacts contained in all the products, even artifacts corresponding to optional or variant classes. Maximum distribution means providing the largest number of processors that might ever be used for any product of the SPL, it doesn't mean providing a processor for every artifact manifesting an instance of an active or passive class. If it is known that some instances have to run always on the same processor, they will be co-allocated on the same node.

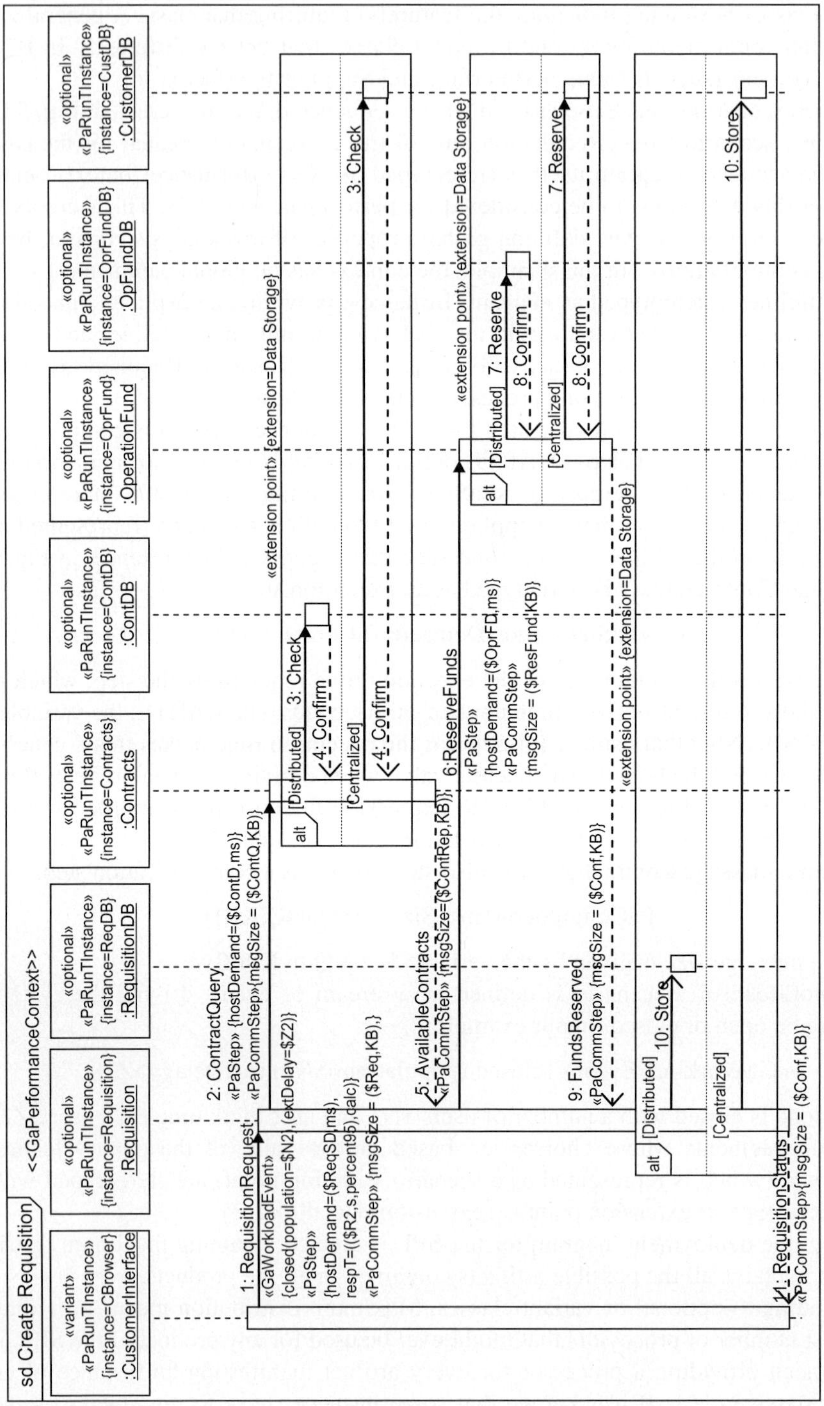

Fig. 5. SPL scenario CreateRequisition

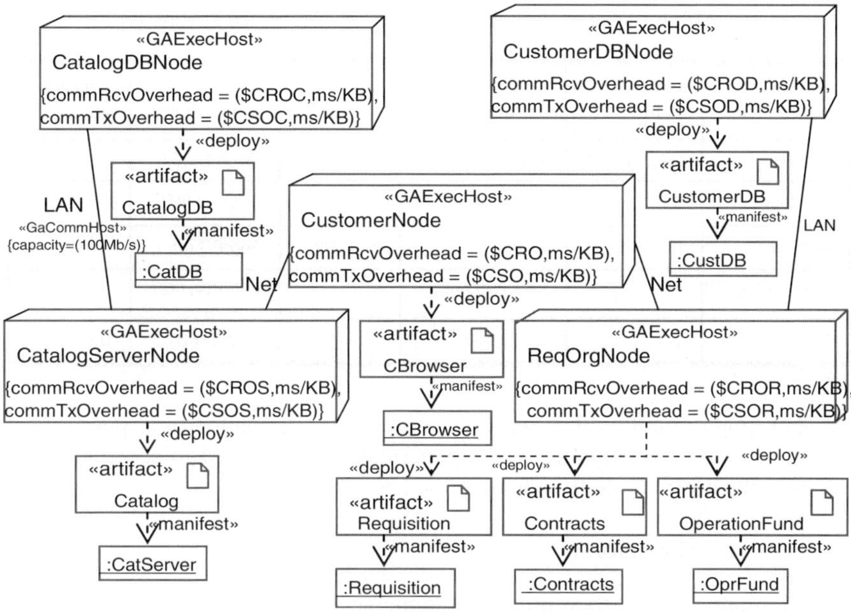

Fig. 6. Part of the SPL deployment diagram for the centralized architecture

Fig. 6 shows a part of the deployment diagram for the centralized architecture. Each processing node in the deployment diagram is stereotyped as an execution host with stereotype «GaExecHost». The node may be stereotyped with communication overheads. The attributes commRcvOverhead and commTxOverhead are the host demand overheads for receiving messages and sending messages, respectively.

3.2 Target Model

The target model represents a product, so it does not contain any PL profile extensions because the variability has been resolved. However, the product model contains performance annotations that have been bound to concrete values, as indicated by the user. The product model consists of a use case view, class diagram, sequence diagram for each scenario and deployment diagram.

Table 1 shows the mapping of the annotation variables to concrete values for two scenarios used in section 4, BrowseCatalog and CreateRequisition. Choosing the values to be assigned to the performance parameters from the SPL model is not a simple problem. In general, it is difficult to estimate quantitative resource demands for each activity in the design phase, when an implementation does not exist and cannot be measured yet. Several approaches are used by the performance analysts to come up with reasonable estimates in the early design stages: expert experience with previous versions or with similar software, understanding of the algorithm complexity, measurements of reused software, measurements of existing libraries, or using time budgets. As the project advances, early estimate can be replaced with measured values for the critical parts, increasing the model accuracy.

Table 1. Mapping of annotation variables to concrete values

generic parameters	concrete values	generic parameters	concrete values	generic parameters	concrete values
$N1	[10..1000]	$N2	0.1 * N1	$ContD (ms)	0.9
$Z1 (ms)	0	$Z2 (ms)	0	$ContQ (KB)	3
$R1 (s)	[0.7..67]	$R2 (s)	[0.9..56]	$oprFD (ms)	1.1
$CatSD (ms)	1	$ReqSD (ms)	1.1	$ContRep (KB)	2
$GetL (KB)	0.5	$Req (KB)	3	$Conf (KB)	0,5

Another kind of binding that takes place during the derivation of a specific product model from SPL is the binding of the generic roles associated to sequence diagram life-lines to the desired role for handling the chosen feature(s).

3.3 Model Transformation

This section presents briefly a prototype implementation for the derivation of a given product as a model transformation realized in the Atlas Transformation Language (ATL) [1]. The ATL transformation takes as inputs the source model described in section 3.1 as well as the PL profile and the MARTE profile and generates the target model for a product presented in section 3.2. The derivation process starts by selecting the features for the product we want to develop. The chosen features are checked against the feature dependency diagram from the source model to identify any inconsistencies between features. The steps of the proposed model transformation algorithm are presented in Fig. 7. Assume that the transformation is applied to the e-commerce case study to derive the business-to-business (B2B) model consisting of the use case, class, sequence and deployment diagrams from the e-commerce SPL model. Due to limited space, we discuss only the derivation of the product class diagram from the SPL class diagram (but the other diagrams are derived by following a similar approach of selectively adding only the elements required for the desired product). Since the SPL class diagram represents the union of all possible product class diagrams, the derivation can be done by selecting and copying the classes from the SPL class diagram to the product class diagram one by one. This derivation starts with the minimal core (in our case the kernel classes) and selectively adds additional classes based on the chosen features.

The ATL model transformation takes as inputs the SPL class diagram shown in Fig. 4. The source metamodel is the UML metamodel extended with the PL and MARTE profiles, and the target metamodel is the UML metamodel extended with MARTE only. The outcome of the transformation is the product model. From the SPL class diagram from Fig. 4, the kernel classes CustomerInterface, Catalog, SupplierInterface, Inventory, and DeliveryOrder are copied first into the product model, keeping the same name but removing the PL-related stereotypes. In the source model, each class is annotated with the feature that requires it. These annotations are represented as the values of the property in the stereotype for this class. The optional and variant classes are selectively copied to the target model according to the value of the property of the optional and variant stereotypes. For instance in this case the variant classes tagged with BusinessCustomer will be selected; the B2BInterface and Supplier classes are copied into the product model. Similarly, the optional classes will be copied. Finally the associations between these classes will be copied, if both classes attached to the association ends have been already copied.

Here we show an example of an ATL helper, hasStereotype, which defines how an element can be retrieved according to the name of its stereotype. This helper is called by the rule KernelClass which copies the classes stereotyped as kernel from the source to the target model, by keeping the same name.

```
BEGIN
1. Select the desired features for the product and check
   them for consistency.

2. Select use cases realizing the chosen features
   from the SPL use case diagram
   SWITCH
       CASE 1: Feature realized as use case package
               BEGINCASE
                    Select all use cases in the package;
               ENDCASE
       CASE 2: Feature realized as "extend" or "include"
               relationships between use cases
               BEGINCASE
                    Select the base use case and the
                    included or extended use cases;
               ENDCASE
       CASE 3: Feature realized as a variation point
               within a scenario realizing the use case;
               BEGINCASE
                    Select the respective use case;
               ENDCASE
   ENDSWITCH
3. Derive the product class diagram from the SPL
   class diagram.
        Select "kernel" classes;
        Select "optional" or "variant" classes
        corresponding to the chosen features;
        Select associations between selected classes;

4. FOR each scenario of the selected use cases
     Choose the corresponding sequence diagram;
     FOR each chosen sequence diagram
        Bind each generic role associated to a life-
        line to the desired role for handling the
        chosen feature;
        Bind the performance annotations to concrete
        values provided by the user;
     ENDFOR
   ENDFOR

5. Build the product deployment diagram from the SPL
   deployment
      Determine product artifacts;
      Bind generic processing nodes to actual ones;
      Bind generic performance annotations to
      concrete values;
END
```

Fig. 7. Steps of model transformation algorithm

```
helper context UML!Element def:hasStereotype(stereotype:String) :Boolean
= self.getAppliedStereotypes()-> exists (c |
c.name.startsWith(stereotype));

rule KernelClass{
        from
                s : UML!Class (s.hasStereotype('kernel'))
        to
                t : UML!Class (
                        name <- s.name,
                        ownedAttribute <- s.ownedAttribute,
                        ownedOperation <- s.ownedOperation
                        )  }
```

The following helper, which retrieves the value of the property with the specified name in the specified stereotype for this element, is used by the rules that copy the optional and variant classes:

```
helper context UML!Element def: getTaggedValue(stereotype : String,
        tag : String) : String =
        self.getValue(self.getAppliedStereotype(stereotype),tag);
```

4 Performance Analysis

After the target model of a concrete product is generated, it is further transformed into a LQN performance model using the PUMA transformation approach [20][21]. This section presents some performance analysis experiments conducted with the LQN models obtained for the B2B system for the centralized and distributed architectures.

Two key performance scenarios, BrowseCatalog and CreateRequisition, for the centralized B2B system are transformed together into the LQN models used for experiments. In the e-commerce application, it is important where the data is located in order to fulfill performance and security requirements. This location problem is examined in two different architectures: 1) distributed and 2) centralized.

In the centralized architecture, all customer data is contained in one database. Fig. 6 shows the centralized design with only one node, the CustomerDB Node that stores the customer database. The centralized architecture has the advantage that updating and maintaining the data consistency is easier, but has the disadvantage of becoming the system bottleneck for large system sizes (when both the number of customers and the amount of data go up). A distributed architecture represents a solution where several databases divide the data and the work among them. It has potential for faster response times and improved performance, but makes the updates and keeping data consistency more difficult.

We solved the LQN models for different numbers of users and compared the two B2B systems, which differ only in the choice of the Data Storage feature: Centralized and Distributed. The effects of the two architecture choices on the response time R1 perceived by a user who is browsing the catalog, and the response time R2 of a user placing a requisition are compared in Fig.8. We assumed that the system is used concurrently by N1 users who browse the catalog and N2 who place a requisition, where N1 is increasing from 10 to 1000 and N2 from 1 to 100, respectively. The LQN results show that the Data Storage feature has a considerable effect on performance as shown in Fig. 8, as the response time for the centralized architecture is significantly higher than for the distributed architecture for both user types.

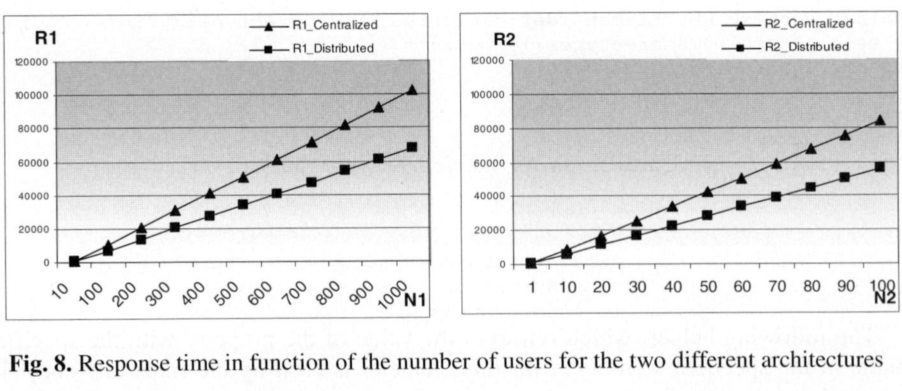

Fig. 8. Response time in function of the number of users for the two different architectures

This brief example illustrates the potential for performance analysis in early development stages, by allowing the developers to compare the performance effects of different design alternatives.

5 Conclusions

The Software Product Lines development process takes advantage of the reusability of a set of core assets shared among the members of a family of products, instead of building each product from scratch. In this paper, we propose to integrate performance analysis in the UML-based model-driven development process for SPL by adding generic performance annotations to the SPL model and reusing them when deriving a specific product.

To the best of our knowledge, our research is the first to tackle this problem. The main research challenges are rooted in the fact that a SPL model does not represent a clearly defined system that could be implemented, run and measured, so we cannot talk about analyzing its performance. A SPL model is instead a collection of core "generic" asset models, which are building blocks for many different products with all kind of options and alternatives. Hence, we need to derive first a concrete product with a well-defined structure and behaviour, and then we can consider analyzing its performance. The challenges of the proposed research are both SPL-related and performance-related.

Regarding the derivation of a product model from an SPL model, we are planning to consider in the future aspect-oriented modeling techniques for weaving new structural and behavioural elements into a product model. Regarding the challenge of dealing with performance annotations, we will investigate whether MARTE has all the necessary features to allow for expressing parametric generic reusable annotations. We also plan to devise a more user-friendly way than XML for expressing binding directives that handle a large amount of data.

Acknowledgments

This research was partially supported by Discovery grant from the Natural Sciences and Engineering Research Council of Canada (NSERC), and by the Centre of Excellence for Research in Adaptive Systems (CERAS).

References

1. Atlas Transformation Language (ATL), `http://www.eclipse.org/m2m/atl`
2. Avila-García, O., García, A.E., Sánchez Rebull, E.V.: Using Software Product Lines to Manage Model Families in Model-Driven Engineering. In: ACM symposium on Applied Computing, Seoul, Korea, pp. 1006–1011 (2007)
3. Balsamo, S., Di Marco, A., Inverardi, P., Simeoni, M.: Model-based performance prediction in software development: a survey. IEEE Transactions on Software Engineering 30(5), 295–310 (2004)
4. Bernardi, S., Donatelli, S., Merseguer, J.: From UML sequence diagrams and statecharts to analysable Petri net models. In: 3rd International Workshop on Software and Performance (WOSP 2002), Rome, pp. 35–45 (2002)
5. Botterweck, G., O'Brien, L., Theil, S.: Model-driven derivation of product architecture. In: 22nd IEEE/ACM international conference on Automated software engineering, Atlanta, Georgia, USA, pp. 469–472 (2007)

6. Braganca, A., Machado, R.J.: Automating Mappings between Use Case Diagrams and Feature Models for Software Product Lines. In: 11th International Software Product Line Conference (SPLC), Kyoto, Japan (2007)
7. Cavenet, C., Gilmore, S., Hillston, J., Kloul, L., Stevens, P.: Analysing UML 2.0 activity diagrams in the software performance engineering process. In: 4th International Workshop on Software and Performance (WOSP 2004), Redwood City, CA, pp. 74–83 (2004)
8. Czarnecki, K., Antkiewicz, M., Kim, C.H.P., Lau, S., Pietroszek, K.: Model-Driven Software Product Lines. In: OOPSLA, San Diego, California (2005)
9. Deelstra, S., Sinnema, M., Bosch, J.: Product derivation in software product families: A case study. Journal of Systems and Software 74, 173–194 (2005)
10. Gomaa, H.: Designing Software Product Lines with UML: From Use Cases to Pattern-based software Architectures. Object Technology. Addison-Wesley, Reading (2005)
11. Gomaa, H., Shin, M.E.: Automated Software Product Line Engineering and Product Derivation. In: 40th Hawaii International Conference on System Sciences (2007)
12. Gomaa, H., Hussein, M.: Model-Based Software Design and Adaptation. In: Int. Conference on Software Engineering for Adaptive and Self-Managing Systems, p. 7 (2007)
13. Haugen, O., MOller-Pedersen, B., Oldevik, J., Solberg, A.: An MDA-based framework for model-driven product derivation. In: Hamza, M.H. (ed.) Software Engineering and Applications, pp. 709–714. ACTA Press, Cambridge (2004)
14. Object Management Group, UML Profile for Modeling and Analysis of Real-Time and Embedded Systems, OMG Adopted Specification ptc/07-08-04 (2007)
15. Oldevik, J., Haugen, O.: Higher-Order Transformations for Product Lines. In: 11th Int. Software Product Line Conference (SPLC), Kyoto, Japan, pp. 243–254 (2007)
16. Petriu, D.C., Shen, H.: Applying the UML Performance Profile: Graph Grammar based derivation of LQN models from UML specifications. In: Field, T., Harrison, P.G., Bradley, J., Harder, U. (eds.) TOOLS 2002. LNCS, vol. 2324. Springer, Heidelberg (2002)
17. Smith, C.U.: Performance Engineering of Software Systems. Addison Wesley, Reading (1990)
18. Voelter, M., Groher, I.: Product Line Implementation using Aspect-Oriented and Model-Driven Software Development. In: 11th International Software Product Line Conference (SPLC), Kyoto, Japan (2007)
19. Woodside, C.M., Neilson, J.E., Petriu, D.C., Majundar, S.: The Stochastic Rendezvous Network Model for Performance of Synchronous Client-Server-like Distributed Software. IEEE Trans. on Computers 44(1), 20–34 (1995)
20. Woodside, C.M., Petriu, D.C., Petriu, D.B., Shen, H., Israr, T., Merseguer, J.: Performance by Unified Model Analysis (PUMA). In: WOSP 2005, Palma de Mallorca, Spain (2005)
21. Woodside, C.M., Petriu, D.C., Xu, J., Israr, T., Merseguer, J.: Methods and Tools for Performance by Unified Model Analysis (PUMA). Technical Report SCE-08-06, Carleton University, Systems and Computer Engineering, 35 pages (2008)
22. Ziadi, T., Jézéquel, J.M., Fondement, F.: Product line derivation with uml. In: Software Variability Management Workshop, University of Groningen Department of Mathematics and Computing Science, pp. 94–102 (2003)
23. Ziadi, T., Jézéquel, J.M.: Product Line Engineering with the UML: Deriving Products. In: Software Product Lines, pp. 557–586. Springer, Heidelberg (2006)

A Model-Driven Measurement Approach

Martin Monperrus[1,2], Jean-Marc Jézéquel[2], Joël Champeau[1], and Brigitte Hoeltzener[1]

[1] ENSIETA - Brest (Fr)
[2] INRIA & University of Rennes (Fr)

Abstract. Companies using domain specific languages in a model-driven development process need to measure their models. However, developing and maintaining a measurement software for each domain specific modeling language is costly. Our contribution is a model-driven measurement approach. This measurement approach is model-driven from two viewpoints: 1) it measures models of a model-driven development process; 2) it uses models as unique and consistent metric specifications, w.r.t a metric specification metamodel. This declarative specification of metrics is then used to generate a fully fledged implementation. The benefit from applying the approach is evaluated by two applications. They indicate that this approach reduces the domain-specific measurement software development cost.

1 Introduction

Model-driven engineering (MDE) [1] is an approach to software development that advocates the creation of domain-specific languages (DSL). Contrary to general-purpose programming languages, a domain-specific language addresses a limited range of applications. The main goal of DSLs is to reduce the product development cost by means of generative techniques [2]. From a MDE viewpoint, the DSL is specified with a metamodel; a program written in a DSL is called a model.

To address safety-critical concerns or quality assurance, models need to be measured. Ledeczi et al. state [2], that *another use of the models is design-time diagnosability analysis to determine sensor coverage, size of ambiguity groups for various fault scenarios, timeliness of diagnosis results in the onboard system, and other relevant* ***domain-specific metrics***. More recently, a similar point of view is expressed by Schmidt et al. [1]: *in the context of enterprise distributed real-time and embedded (DRE) systems, our system execution modeling (SEM) tools help developers, systems engineers, and end users discover,* ***measure****, and rectify integration and performance problems early in the system's life cycle.*

Contrary to general-purpose programming language measurement software, domain-specific measurement software is not a big enough niche market; that is to say there are no measurement software vendors for specific domains. Hence, companies have to fully support the development cost of the model measurement software.

K. Czarnecki et al. (Eds.): MoDELS 2008, LNCS 5301, pp. 505–519, 2008.

Conversely, generative techniques (e.g. [3]) are used to generate most of the modeling environment from an abstract definition of the domain, called a metamodel. These techniques allow a low-cost modeling environment. Systems are produced by means of model-driven code generation, as well as modeling environment. In this context, it is not conceivable to manually develop the measurement software. Indeed, the NASA recommends that *the cost of measurement should not add more than 2 percent to the software development or maintenance effort* [4].

Classical object-oriented program measurement software packages are complex and costly [5]. Similarly, the cost of a DSL measurement software comes from several requirements which are mainly: the automation of measurement, the integration into a modeling tool, the communication between the domain expert and developers, the need for extensibility and tailoring.

Our goal is to address the cost of a DSL measurement software by providing a generative measurement approach that can be applied to any kind of models. In other words, we would like to be able to generate a measurement software for design models, architectural models, performance models, requirements model, etc.

Our contribution is a model-driven measurement approach (we will use the expression *MDM approach* later in the paper). The core of the contribution is a metric specification metamodel. This measurement approach is model-driven from two viewpoints: 1) it measures models of a model-driven development process; 2) it uses models as unique and consistent metric specifications, w.r.t the metric specification metamodel. This approach consists of specifying metrics as instance of the metric specification metamodel. These metric specifications refer to a domain metamodel. The metric specifications are used to generate a fully fledged measurement software. The generated artifacts fully fullfill the requirements for measurement software presented above. The benefit from applying the MDM approach is evaluated with two applications.

The remainder of this paper is organized as follows. In section 2, we present the full process of model-driven measurement. Then, we present the metric specification metamodel (section 3). The instantiation of the whole approach is presented in two different contexts (section 4), including in an industrial one. We finally discuss related works in section 5 and conclude.

2 Overview of the MDM Approach

The measurement approach presented in this paper is intended to be applied to models of a MDE software development i.e.; applied to models fully described by a metamodel, which is later called domain metamodel. Our intuition was [6] that it is possible to generate a measurement software from an abstract and declarative specification of metrics. This abstract level for metrics can be defined by a metamodel as well. In other words, the measurement software is generated from a model of metric specifications.

Figure 1 presents our model-driven measurement approach as an UML activity diagram. The application of the MDM approach begins by considering a

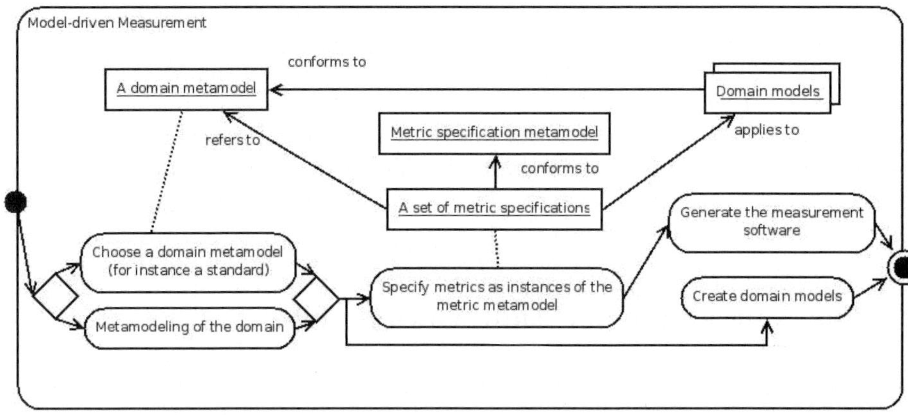

Fig. 1. Model-driven measurement: actions and artifacts

model space. This can be done into two ways. On the one hand, one can create a domain metamodel that exactly fits a given family of systems. On the other hand, one can choose an existing metamodel, for instance a standard one. Then, the MDM approach consists in specifying metrics as instances of a metric specification metamodel. This metric specification metamodel is the core of our contribution. It is presented in the next section. The metric metamodel is domain-indenpendent i.e.; does not contain concepts specific to a domain. It only contains concepts related to metrics. The next step of the MDM approach is to identify the models that will be measured. It is possible to measure models created for other engineering activities (e.g.; simulation) or to create new domain models. Eventually, the MDM approach allows to really measure models by means of generative techniques described below.

Figure 1 also sums up the artifacts involved in the approach. The metric specification metamodel is the core artifact, it remains unmodified in whatever applications of the MDM approach. A set of metric specifications is an instance of the metric specification metamodel. A metric specification refers to concepts of the domain metamodel. Domain models are created conforming to the domain metamodel and can be measured thanks to the metric specifications. Note that the same domain models can also ground other engineering activities such as code generation, verification and validation, or model transformations.

The MDM approach is a solution to the issue of the measurement software cost because all the models involved ground code generation. The metric specification metamodel is used to generate the metric specification editor. For this activity, the MDM approach is based on existing techniques [7,8,3]. The metric specification model is used to generate the measurement software itself. This generation activity is fully automated. The generator is implemented as methods of the metric specification metamodel. These methods output the corresponding Java code. To sum up, a metric specification model is taken as input to a generator which outputs a fully fledged measurement software integrated into the generated modeling environment. Hence, the MDM approach gives an enhanced modeling environment; where the enhancement consists of the measurement features.

To conclude this overview, the prototype that supports the MDM approach has been developed in the Eclipse (a generic development environment, see `www.eclipse.org`) and EMF [3] world. Metric specifications and domain models are EMF models w.r.t an EMF metamodel. The prototype generates an Eclipse plugin directly from the metric specifications. This plugin is a fully-functional software integrated into Eclipse.

3 The Metric Specification Metamodel

The MDM approach consists in specifying metrics as an instance of a metric specification metamodel. The metamodel is a definition of the metric concepts. It grounds the complete generation of the measurement software from an instance of the metamodel, called a metric specification model. The concepts of the metric specification metamodel can be applied to any domain models. For instance, the same concept can be instantiated as a metric for implementation models, real-time models, software architecture models or requirements models. In that sense, our metric specification metamodel is domain-independent [9]. It has been built following a bottom-up approach: from existing metrics to concepts of the metamodel. In regard to the application cases we studied, no other parts are needed.

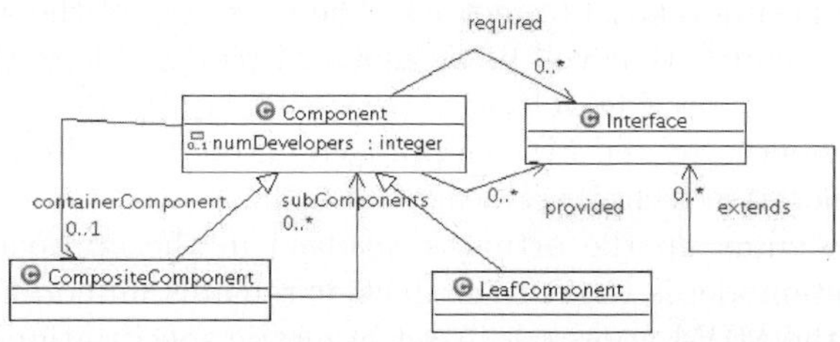

Fig. 2. The domain metamodel used for demonstration purposes

Supporting example and syntax: The presentation of the metric specification metamodel will be helped by several examples. Note that the concepts of the metric specification metamodel will be further called classes. Main ones will be emphasized as italic. Examples consists of instances of the metamodel. Illustrative metrics are for a simple domain metamodel for software architecture depicted in figure 2. In this domain metamodel, the concepts manipulated are Component and Interface, and their relationships. This example metamodel is presented for demonstration purposes only.

A proto-textual syntax is used to textually represent the metrics, because a XMI-based model is not readable. Since our approach is model-driven, the most important artifacts remains the metamodel and its conforming models. That's

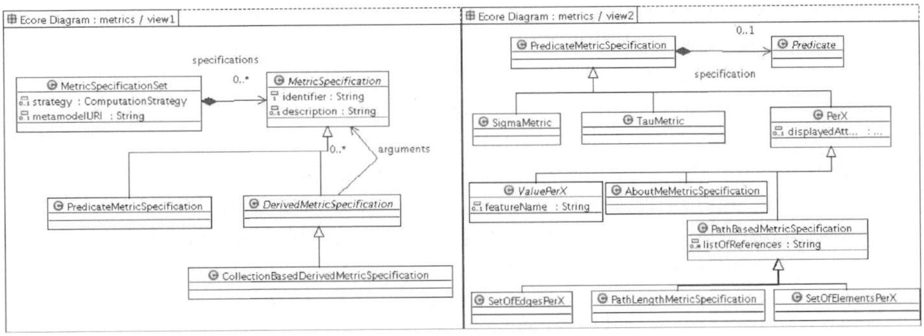

Fig. 3. The core of the metric specification metamodel

why we use a *proto*-syntax and do not further define and discuss it. However, for sake of understandability, we tried to define an intuitive one, with explicit cognitive links between keywords and the metric specification metamodel.

Figure 3 presents the classes that structure the metric specification metamodel. A class MetricSpecificationSet is the root element. It contains several MetricSpecification. A MetricSpecificationSet represents a set of domain metrics collected by a domain expert. They can come from the literature, existing tools, company quality plans, expert know-how.

A MetricSpecificationSet refers to a domain metamodel (attribute metamodelURI), and to a ComputationStrategy. A computation strategy defines which parts domain model are measured. This can be a file, a predefined list of model elements or a transitive closure on all model elements. A MetricSpecification is an abstract class that defines an atomic metric specification. Note that we use MetricSpecification and not Metric alone, to be able to differentiate a metric specification from a metric value. The modeling of measurement results i.e; metric values and their interpretation, is outside the scope of this metamodel. A MetricSpecification is subclassed. The DerivedMetricSpecification class handles arithmetic and based function based metrics (e.g.; addition, exponential): the subclassess of DerivedMetricSpecification are used to express complex metric formula. CollectionBasedDerivedMetricSpecification is the class that handles higher order metrics, mainly statistical operators, based on a set of metric values. It is subclasses as Sum, Average, Median, Stddev which are not represented in figure 3. The last subclass of MetricSpecification is PredicateMetricSpecification.

A PredicateMetricSpecification is an abstract class that contains a predicate. A predicate is a function from the set of model elements to the truth values. Predicate-related classes are presented later. Predicates are an important part of a metric specification since they precisely define the considered model elements for a given metric specification. We now consider the concrete classes that can be instantiated. The right part of figure 3 shows the classes that are instantiated as a metric specification for a given domain metamodel.

A SigmaMetric metric specification is the count of model elements that satisfy a predicate. The predicate can be as complex as needed. Similarly, the TauMetric is the count of model links; i.e. a link between two model elements. In this case, one has to specify the considered reference and if necessary, predicates for the link root and the link target. In the listing below, two instances of these classes considering the example domain metamodel of figure 2 are presented. A metric specification starts with the declaration of its type, a mandatory identifier, and an optional textual description. Then comes the declarative part of the metric. For instance, a SigmaMetric declares a predicate and a TauMetric a reference name. Note that the predicate is a textual syntax of predicate-based model elements, that will be presented later.

```
metric SigmaMetric NOCompComp is
  description "too complex components"
  elements satisfy "this.isInstance(Component)
          and this.required > 10
          and this.provided > 10
          and this.subComponents > 5"
endmetric

metric TauMetric NODeComp is
  description "The number of decomposition"
  link is "CompositeComponent:subComponent"
endmetric
```

The PerX class is an abstract class to specify metrics that are related to a given model element. By definition, the measurement of a domain model thanks to a PerX metric specification gives several values. The subclasses of PerX can be considered per se, or be given as input to a CollectionBased metric specification presented above, for instance the statistical operator average.

A ValuePerX metric specification represents metrics that can be obtained by considering only the model element satisfying a predicate. The ValuePerX class is abstract. It is subclassed as AttributeValuePerX, MultiplicityPerX. An AttributeValuePerX is a metric whose value is directly given by an attribute of the model element. A MultiplicityPerX metric is directly given by the actual multiplicity of a reference. Let us now consider two instances of these classes.

```
metric AttributeValuePerX NODev is
  description "The number of developers per component"
  elements satisfy "this.isInstance(Component)"
  value is "this.numDevelopers"
endmetric

metric AverageMetric ANORI is
  description "The average number of required
              interfaces per component"
  input metric MultiplicityPerX is
    elements satisfy "this.isInstance(Component)"
    multiplicity of "this.required"
  endmetric
endmetric
```

A SetOfElementsPerX metric specification is the number of model elements obtained after performing a transitive closure. The SetOfEdgesPerX class is similar to the SetOfElementsPerX class, except that it counts the number of edges considered during the transitive closure.

A AboutMeMetricSpecification is a metric that considers a given object as primary variable. This metric type is used each time the domain model contains derived relationships. That is to say, when a metric is the number of elements that has something to do with an object (symbolized by *me* in the name), but when there is not the corresponding reference is the domain metamodel.

A PathLengthMetricSpecification is the maximum path length of a set of path starting from a root model element to other model elements. PathLengthMetric-Specification class is used to specify metrics that are based on a domain distance. Let us now consider instance examples of these metrics.

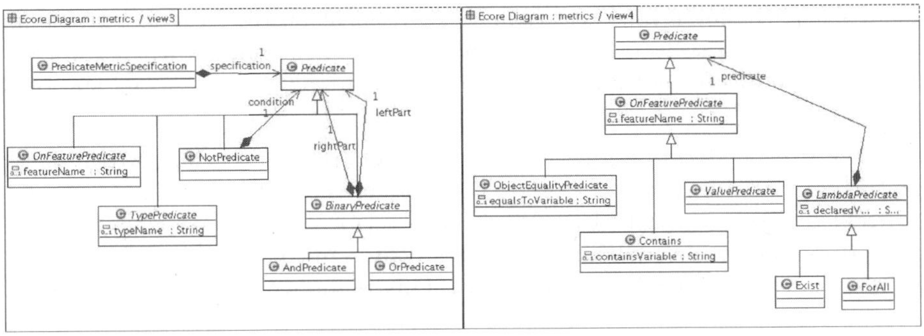

Fig. 4. Predicates in the metric specification metamodel

```
metric SetOfElementsPerX NOIT is
  description "The number of interfaces
             involved per component"
  x satisfy "this.isInstance(Component)"
  elements satisfy "this.isInstance(Interface)"
  references followed "required,provided,extends"
endmetric

metric AboutMeMetricSpecification COUPLING is
  description "coupling to this interface"
  elements satisfy "Interface.isInstance(self)"
  internal metric spec is metric SigmaMetric COUPLING_ is
  description "used for COUPLING"
  elements satisfy "this.provided == __me__ or this.required == __me__ "
endmetric

metric PathLengthMetricSpecification DD is
  description "Depth in decomposition"
  x satisfy "this.isInstance(LeafComponent)"
  references followed "container"
endmetric
```

Metric specifications heavily rely on predicate. We now present the definition of predicates in the metamodel. This presentation is supported by figure 4.

A predicate can be composed of an arbitrary number of subpredicates, in the same manner as a boolean function. Therefore, the metamodel contains the AndPredicate, OrPredicate, and NotPredicate. There are also classes to handle tests on the type of the model element. They are subclasses of the TypePredicate class. IsInstance tests the metaclass of a model element; IsDirectInstance tests the metaclass or one of its superclasses. The remaining class OnFeaturePredicate handles tests on features of a given model element. In this context, a feature means an attribute (e.g. a string "foo"), or a reference to another model element. OnFeaturePredicate class is further presented in the next paragraph.

The right part of figure 4 shows what are the possible tests on a given feature. ObjectEqualityPredicate enables us to test whether a reference points to a model element referred by a variable. ValuePredicate enables to test the value of an attribute (e.g. a boolean equals to "false" or an integer equals to "13"). LambdaPredicate enables us to apply a predicate to all elements of a collection. It is subclassed as Exists and ForAll to express first-order logic quantifiers. For sake of space, the following predicates do not appear on the figure. Contains us enables to test if a collection contains a model element referred by a variable. MultiplicityPredicate (not on the figure) enables us to test the actual size of a collection.

Limitations of the MDM approach: Since the metamodel is declarative, all metrics that are defined on top of explicit concepts of the metamodel can generally be specified within the MDM approach. The reciprocal statement is also true: any metrics that is composed of concepts not present in the metamodel cannot be expressed within the MDM approach. This point will be illustrated in the next section.

We have presented in this section the backbone of our model-driven measurement approach: the metric specification metamodel. An instance of this metamodel is a set of metric specifications formalized enough to generate the complete measurement software implementation.

4 Study of Instances of the MDM Approach

In this section we present the application of the MDM approach into two different contexts i.e.; the instantiation of the metric specification metamodel for two different domain metamodels.

4.1 Considering a Java Program as an Implementation Model

Let us consider Java programs as models conforming to Java metamodel. We can then specify Chidamber and Kemerer metrics [10] within the MDM approach. This viewpoint will help to demonstrate that 1) our metric specification metamodel encompasses with existing software metrics and 2) the code volume of the metrics implemented within the MDM approach is much smaller than the volume of the final executable code.

We have used the SpoonEMF (`http://tinyurl.com/spoonemf`) tool to transform a Java software to an Eclipse/EMF model. SpoonEMF is a binding between Spoon and EMF. Spoon [11] provides a complete and fine-grained Java metamodel where any program element (classes, methods, fields, statements, expressions, etc.) is accessible. SpoonEMF transforms a whole Java software into a single XMI model file.

We will now present the specification of the Chidamber and Kemerer metrics [10] as instance of our metric specification metamodel refering to the Spoon/Java metamodel. It is a fully declarative specification.

Weighted Methods per Class: We consider the Basili et al's [12] version of WMC, which is the number of methods defined in each class.

```
metric MultiplicityPerX WMC is
    description "Weighted Methods per Class"
    elements satisfy "this.isInstance(CtClass)"
    reference is "Methods"
endmetric
```

Depth in Inheritance Tree per Class: DIT is defined as the maximum depth of the inheritance graph of a class.

```
metric PathLengthMetricSpecification DIT is
  description "Depth in Inheritance Tree per Class"
  x satisfy "this.isInstance(CtClass)"
  references followed "Superclass"
endmetric
```

Number of Children of a Class: NOC is the number of direct descendants for each class. It is a typical use of the AboutMeMetricSpecification metric type: there is not the reference *children* in CtClass. AboutMeMetricSpecification fills this lack and enables us to correctly specify the metric.

```
metric AboutMeMetricSpecification NOC is
  description "Number of Children of a Class"
  x satisfy "this.isInstance(CtClass)"
  input metric SigmaMetric _NOC is
  elements satisfy "this.Superclass == __me__"
  endmetric
endmetric
```

Coupling Between Object Classes: CBO is the number of classes to which a given class is coupled.

```
metric AboutMeMetricSpecification CBO is
  description "Coupling Between Object Classes"
  elements satisfy "this.isInstance(CtClass)"
  input metric SetOfEdgesPerX _CBO is
  target satisfy "this.isInstance(CtTypeReference)
        and this.QualifiedName == __me__.SimpleName"
  endmetric
endmetric
```

Response For a Class: RFC is the number of methods that can be potentially executed in response to a message.

```
metric SetOfElementsPerX RFC is
  description "Response For a Class"
  elements satisfy "this.isInstance(CtClass)"
  x satisfy "this.isInstance(CtExecutableReference)"
  references followed "Methods,Body,Statements,
   Expression,AssertExpression,CaseExpression,
   ThenStatement,Condition,ElseStatement,Selector,
   Cases,Block,Finalizer,Catchers,AssertExpression,
   CaseExpression,Finalizer,Executable,
   DeclaringExecutable"
endmetric
```

Lack of Cohesion on Methods: Is is not possible to specify the LCOM metric of Chidamber and Kemerer as an instance of the metric specification metamodel. The reason is that it involves as the core metric component the concept of pair of functions. This concept is artificial w.r.t. the Java language and is not present in any form in the Java metamodel. However it still remains possible to manually develop the implementation of LCOM on top of the Java XMI model and the Java metamodel.

The benefits: The metric specification metamodel is rich enough to re-specify all but one Chidamber and Kemerer metrics with the MDM approach. In this context, the main artifacts are: a Java program considered as a model conforming to a Java metamodel, a set of metric specifications as a metric model instance of our metric specification metamodel.

The MDM approach is generative. The specification of Chidamber and Kemerer metrics is 24 lines of code with our textual declarative language. The generative step of the MDM approach generates a Java program of around 100 lines of code (LOC). This Java program uses a model measurement library of around 3000 LOC, that is not dedicated to Java but used in all the MDM approach instances. This library seats on top of SpoonEMF/EMF/Eclipse. It is not possible to estimate precisely the size of the actually used part of these software packages. By comparison, the *Metrics* (`http://metrics.sourceforge.net`) Java measurement tool is more than manually coded 20000 lines of code (its maturity and completeness has to be taken into account). Note that Java is a verbose language. With a more compact generated language like Smalltalk, this generated code volume would decrease but without the conciseness of pure dedicated declarative metric concepts.

4.2 Industrial Application: Metrics for Maritime Surveillance System Models

In this section, we present the application of the MDM approach in an industrial context. Our industrial partner, Thales Airborne Systems, is a world-wide company that designs and develops maritime surveillance systems. The MDM approach applied early in the system life cycle enables engineers to obtain: 1) metric values that estimate operational performance of the system; 2) architectural metric values that are used to dimension the system.

A maritime surveillance system (further called MSS) is a multi-mission system. It is intended to supervise the maritime traffic, to prevent pollution at sea, to control the fishing activities, to control borders. It is usually composed of an aircraft, a set of sensors, a crew and a large number of software artifacts. The number of functionalities, the relationships between hardware and software components and the communication between the system and others entities (base, other MSSs) indicate the complexity of the system.

Current system engineering process are mainly document-centric. Current MSS simulators are mainly code centric. During the system engineering activities, the problem is that it is very costly to develop a measurement software on top of both documents and code, in order to obtain operational metrics for MSS.

This context of system engineering metrics for MSS is a good candidate to apply the MDM approach. Therefore, we tried to obtain MSS domain metrics with our approach. In a previous paper [13], we presented a model-driven simulator for maritime surveillance systems. In this paper, we measure the models involved in the model-driven simulation with the MDM approach.

There is no standard metamodels for maritime surveillance systems. Consequently, we created a domain metamodel for maritime surveillance systems. The final metamodel is divided into three packages that address different concerns. More information on the models can be found in [13]. The MSS system architecture package contains architectural concepts. It is divided in five packages following a functional decomposition. The scenario package contains all the needed classes to represent a tactical situation. A model, instance of this metamodel, specifies the surveillance zone, the number and types of objects that are in the zone. For each object is specified a trajectory including the speed of the object. The operational event package contains classes that represent events that have a semantic with respect to a simulation at the system engineering level.

Domain metrics: To choose the domain metrics, we studied the legacy simulators and discussed with systems engineers of the company. We agreed on 16 metrics to be implemented with the MDM approach. The domain metrics in the context of the MMS development at the system engineering are of different types. The types follow the same functional decomposition as the packages.

System architecture metrics (5 metrics). These metrics are related to the architecture itself e.g.; the number of sensors in the system. These metrics are mostly dedicated to cost estimation and planning.

Scenario metrics (4 metrics). These metrics are related to the tactical operation in which the system will evolve. For instance, the number of boats in the surveillance zone. The system dimensioning depends on such domain metrics.

Simation trace metrics (7 metrics). These metrics are computed on simulation trace. They are estimations of the system properties; for instance the ratio of detected ships during the surveillance mission.

Each of these domain metrics has been specified as instance of the metric specification metamodel.

Conclusion: In the context of maritime surveillance system development at the system engineering level, we presented the application of the MDM approach. We presented the main components of the approach: the domain metamodels, models and metrics. The MDM approach enables engineers to obtain domain metric values for three different type of models used during the system engineering activities. This comprehensive and consistent way of measuring system models is an added value compared to costly ad hoc developments which consider either too document-centric or too code-centric artifacts.

We implemented 16 domain metrics for maritime surveillance systems using the MDM approach within 1 week (one day for the metrics, 4 days to solve bugs in the measurement software generator prototype). For comparison, a previous project that developed a similar set of domain metrics for an agent-based simulator took several months. However, this dramatic cost reduction factor has to be mitigated by the differences in maturity level and reliability of the obtained software. Still, it is clear that the MDM approach reduces the development cost by an order of magnitude (when creating the domain metamodel from scratch or to fit an existing DSL, the cost of its creation has also to be taken into account).

The success of this project is a first validation of the MDM approach. It also shows that measurement is not orthogonal to other engineering activities. The measured models, which give an estimation of the future characteristics of the system being built, are the same that are used for simulation. We assume that they could also be used for other model-driven activities such as model transformations, or model-driven testing.

5 Related Work

Links with the GQM: Compared to the Goal/Question/Metric (GQM) approach [14], ours is temporarily after in a measurement plan. To a certain extent, the MDM approach can be considered as an automated implementation of metrics obtained by the GQM approach.

Metrics on top of metamodels. Misic et al. [15] define a generic object-oriented metamodel using Z. With this metamodel, they express a function point metric using the number of instances of a given type. They also express a previously introduced metric called the system meter. Along the same line, [16] extends the UML metamodel to provide a basis for metrics expression and then use this model to express known metrics suites with set theory and first order logic. Tang and Chen address [17] the issue of model metrics early in the life cycle. Hence, they present a method to compute object-oriented design metrics from UML models. UML models from Rose are parsed in order to feed their own tool in which metrics are hard-coded. Similarly, El-Wakil et al. [18] use XQuery to express metrics for UML class diagrams. Metrics are then computed on XMI files of UML models. On the implementation issue, [19] exposes a concrete design to compute semantic metrics on source code. The authors create a relational database for storing source code. This database is fed using a modified compiler. Metrics are expressed in SQL for simple ones, and with a mix of Java and SQL for the others.

All these approaches differs from ours on crucial points. They are limited to models of object-oriented software. Hence, they do not address the growing amount of domain-specific languages. Metrics are manually implemented in a general-purpose programming languages. This kind of implementation can be considered complex and costly.

Baroni et al. [20] propose to use OCL to express metrics. They use their own metamodel exposed in a previous paper. Likewise, in [21], the authors use Java bytecode to instantiate the Dagstuhl metamodel and express known cohesion metrics in OCL. OCL, although initially designed to write constraints on UML class diagrams, can be easily extended to define metrics on any domain-metamodel.

OCL and the MDM approach are not disjoint, for instance, a part of the predicate package is similar to some OCL constructs. However, from a conceptual viewpoint, our metric metamodel define the right concepts for specifying model metrics. On the contrary, specifying model metrics with OCL involves the adaption of concepts from OCL to metrics. From a code reduction viewpoint [5] the

MDM approach enables to write shorter metric specifications. The implementation of the C&K metrics in OCL made in [22] are much longer to the one made here with the MDM approach. However, it is worth studying the mix of the MDM approach and the widely known OCL syntax and constructs to express the predicates.

Abstraction level for expressing metrics. Mens et al. define [23] a generic object-oriented metamodel and generic metrics. They then show that known software metrics are an application of these generic metrics. Marinescu et al. propose [5] a simplified implementation of object-oriented design metrics with a metric language called SAIL.

These contributions both explore the possibility of an abstraction level for expressing metrics. However, the domain of application of the abstraction level is limited to object-oriented software metrics. On the contrary, the MDM approach is domain-independent. It can be applied to any imperative or declarative modeling language specified by a metamodel (implementation metamodel, real-time system metamodel, software architecture metamodel, requirements metamodel, system of systems metamodel, etc.).

There are also previous contributions about a measurement-related metamodel. It is to be noted that a measurement-related metamodel can address three different concerns: the measurement process, the measurement results, and the metric specifications. The metamodel of [24] is more about the two first points (e.g.; classes InformationNeed, ScaleType, MeasurementResult). The OMG requested proposals for a Software Metrics Meta-Model [1]. Very recently, the unique submission was published [2]. This RFP was not very precise on which aspect the metrics metamodel is intended, but the proposed metamodel explicitely supports the three aspects.

Compared to these contributions, the MDM approach has a smaller scope: the metric specifications. Our declarative ways of specifying metrics are novel (except SigmaMetricSpecification and PathLengthMetricSpecification [23]) and are not dedicated to software metrics but to any artifacts specified by a metamodel. The main difference is that the MDM approach is fully thought in a generative way.

Domain specific metrics. The issue of domain specific metrics is a very new research field. As of today and to our knowledge, it has only been explored by Guerra et al. very recently in [25]. They propose to visually specify metrics for any DSL and introduce a taxonomy of generic metrics. Our approach is similar. We also create a metric specification in order to measure any domain models thanks to code generation.

Since their main goal, visual specification and redesign, is different, we explore different aspects of the issue and study different application cases. We consider metamodels in the EMOF context [26], whereas their metamodels are Entity-Relationships based. We propose new concepts to the metric specification metamodel which enable us more declarative metric specifications.

---

[1] OMG document adtmf/2006-09-03.

[2] OMG document adtmf/2008-02-01.

6 Conclusion

Our Model-driven Measurement Approach is a new technique in the field of measurement and model-driven engineering. Whatever the domain, whatever the maturity of the product during the development life cycle, it allows the effective measurement thanks to a complete generation of the measurement software from an abstract and declarative metric specification.

This generative approach cuts the development cost of measurement software. From a code volume viewpoint, the ratio between the final implementation and the abstract metric specifications is more than 10. At the system engineering level, it allows measurement not really made before.

On this basis, future research will be conducted to empirically measure the productivity enhancement achieved by a model-driven measurement approach. An important milestone will be to define an intuitive way of specifying metrics conform to the metric specification metamodel so as to let domain experts writing metrics by themselves.

References

1. Schmidt, D.C.: Model-driven engineering. IEEE Computer 39(2), 25–31 (2006)
2. Lédeczi, A., Bakay, A., Maroti, M., Vőlgyesi, P., Nordstrom, G., Sprinkle, J., Karsai, G.: Composing domain-specific design environments. IEEE Computer 34, 44–51 (2001)
3. Budinsky, F., Steinberg, D., Merks, E., Ellersick, R., Grose, T.J.: Eclipse Modeling Framework. Addison-Wesley, Reading (2004)
4. NASA Software Program: Software measurement guidebook. Technical report, National Aeronautics and Space Administration (1995)
5. Marinescu, C., Marinescu, R., Gîrba, T.: Towards a simplified implementation of object-oriented design metrics. In: IEEE METRICS, vol. 11 (2005)
6. Monperrus, M., Champeau, J., Hoeltzener, B.: Counts count. In: Proceedings of the 2nd Workshop on Model Size Metrics (MSM 2007) co-located with MoDELS 2007 (2007)
7. Sztipanovits, J.: Advances in model-integrated computing. In: Proceedings of the 18th IEEE Instrumentation and Measurement Technology Conference (IMTC 2001), vol. 3, pp. 1660–1664 (2001)
8. de Lara, J., Vangheluwe, H.: Atom3: A tool for multi-formalism and metamodelling. In: Kutsche, R.-D., Weber, H. (eds.) FASE 2002. LNCS, vol. 2306, pp. 173–188. Springer, Heidelberg (2002)
9. Monperrus, M., Jézéquel, J.M., Champeau, J., Hoeltzener, B.: Measuring models. In: Rech, J., Bunse, C. (eds.) Model-Driven Software Development: Integrating Quality Assurance. IDEA Group (2008)
10. Chidamber, S.R., Kemerer, C.F.: Towards a metrics suite for object-oriented design. In: Proceedings of OOPSLA 1991, pp. 197–211 (1991)
11. Pawlak, R., Noguera, C., Petitprez, N.: Spoon: Program analysis and transformation in java. Technical Report 5901, INRIA (2006)
12. Basili, V.R., Briand, L.C., Melo, W.L.: A validation of object-oriented design metrics as quality indicators. IEEE Trans. Softw. Eng. 22(10), 751–761 (1996)

13. Monperrus, M., Jaozafy, F., Marchalot, G., Champeau, J., Hoeltzener, B., Jézéquel, J.M.: Model-driven simulation of a maritime surveillance system. In: Schieferdecker, I., Hartman, A. (eds.) ECMDA-FA 2008. LNCS, vol. 5095, pp. 361–368. Springer, Heidelberg (2008)
14. Basili, V.R., Caldiera, G., Rombach, H.D.: The goal question metric approach. Encyclopedia of Software Engineering. Wiley, Chichester (1994)
15. Misic, V.B., Moser, S.: From formal metamodels to metrics: An object-oriented approach. In: Proceedings of the Technology of Object-Oriented Languages and Systems Conference (TOOLS 1997), p. 330 (1997)
16. Reissing, R.: Towards a model for object-oriented design measurement. In: ECOOP 2001 Workshop QAOOSE (2001)
17. Tang, M.H., Chen, M.H.: Measuring OO design metrics from UML. In: Proceedings of MODELS/UML 2002, UML 2002 (2002)
18. El Wakil, M., El Bastawissi, A., Boshra, M., Fahmy, A.: A novel approach to formalize and collect object-oriented design-metrics. In: Proceedings of the 9th International Conference on Empirical Assessment in Software Engineering (2005)
19. Harmer, T.J., Wilkie, F.G.: An extensible metrics extraction environment for object-oriented programming languages. In: Proceedings of the International Conference on Software Maintenance (2002)
20. Baroni, A., Braz, S., Abreu, F.: Using OCL to formalize object-oriented design metrics definitions. In: ECOOP 2002 Workshop on Quantitative Approaches in OO Software Engineering (2002)
21. McQuillan, J.A., Power, J.F.: Experiences of using the dagstuhl middle metamodel for defining software metrics. In: Proceedings of the 4th International Conference on Principles and Practices of Programming in Java (2006)
22. McQuillan, J., Power, J.: A definition of the chidamber and kemerer metrics suite for uml. Technical report, National University of Ireland (2006)
23. Mens, T., Lanza, M.: A graph-based metamodel for object-oriented software metrics. Electronic Notes in Theoretical Computer Science 72, 57–68 (2002)
24. García, F., Bertoa, M.F., Calero, C., Vallecillo, A., Ruiz, F., Piattini, M., Genero, M.: Towards a consistent terminology for software measurement. Information & Software Technology 48(8), 631–644 (2006)
25. Guerra, E., de Lara, J., Díaz, P.: Visual specification of measurements and redesigns for domain specific visual languages. Journal of Visual Languages and Computing, 1–27 (in press, 2007)
26. OMG: MOF 2.0 specification. Technical report, Object Management Group (2004)

Specifying Service Composition Using UML 2.x and Composition Policies

Judith E.Y. Rossebø[1,2] and Ragnhild Kobro Runde[3]

[1] Department of Telematics, NTNU, Norway
[2] Telenor R&I, Norway
[3] Department of Informatics, University of Oslo, Norway

Abstract. In the current and future service environment, service parts are being developed separately while being dynamically combined at runtime. In this paper we address the problem of defining a model-driven process for enabling dynamic composition of services. Composition policies are used to define choices in behaviour under which service roles involved in a composite service can be dynamically combined at runtime. We model policy-ruled choreography of collaboration components using a policy enforcement state machine (PESM). We also define transformation rules for translating a global PESM diagram into a set of local PESM diagrams, one for each role. As an example, we consider the case of dynamically composing an existing service with a set of authentication and authorization collaborations. The approach is supported by a formal syntax and semantics.

1 Introduction

Today, services are being developed and launched in a highly flexible and dynamic distributed environment. In this dynamic environment, service parts are being developed separately, but dynamically combined at runtime. For this, systems need to be able to adapt transparently to changes in the environment and add new services while adapting existing services with a minimum of user intervention. The overall goal of our work is to define a process for enabling dynamic composition of services. In this paper, we address this general problem in the special case of dynamically adding authentication and authorization to an existing service, as a means to ensure access to the service for authorized users only.

A service is an identified functionality involving a collaboration among entities that achieves some desired goals/effects for end users or other entities. One important aspect of services is that they normally are partial functionalities that cross-cut the component structure so that a service may involve several collaborating components while each component may participate in several services. We model a service in the context of UML 2.x [1], as a collaboration among roles with associated interactions behaviour. Service composition addresses the means of composing such collaborations and their roles services, both statically and dynamically.

K. Czarnecki et al. (Eds.): MoDELS 2008, LNCS 5301, pp. 520–536, 2008.

In [2], we described a framework for authentication and authorization patterns (AA-patterns), specified using UML 2.x collaborations. In [3], we introduced a policy-driven approach to service modelling, design, and implementation and we presented the concept of a policy enforcement state machine (PESM) for modelling the choreography of AA-patterns with services. The PESM diagram expresses graphically the ordering and policy decisions to be taken when collaborations are composed dynamically.

Essentially, the PESM is similar to a UML 2.x activity diagram in that a PESM is modelled as a graph defining the flow of invocations of elementary collaborations represented as nodes. Detailed behaviour associated with the collaborations is not shown, but is specified separately, e.g., using UML 2.x interactions. Choices in the PESM are governed by composition policies. This encompasses showing sequential dependencies, but also dependencies between concurrent behaviours and choices between different collaboration uses.

A policy rule is a rule that defines a choice in the (course of the) behaviour of a system [4]. The motivation for using policy to compose service composition is to enable collaborating roles to be dynamically composed together at runtime. The actual policy rules are specified separately from the roles and collaborations, allowing for changes to be made at runtime by changing the policy rules without changing the specification of the roles themselves.

Applying policy to service composition also makes it possible to connect the service specification to higher level strategies and goals, e.g., which may have been identified using the Goal-oriented Requirements Language (GRL) [5], as explained in [6]. This may include specifying policy that takes into account variables that are given by a higher level strategy, such as taking into account context parameters.

In this paper we take a closer look at the specification of the policy-based mechanism at the service and design model layers. The main contributions of this paper are: (1) a detailed exposition of global and local PESM diagrams and related concepts, (2) a precise syntax for composition policies, using Extended BNF, (3) transformation rules for translating global PESM diagrams and global composition policies into local PESM diagrams and local composition policies, and (4) a formal semantics for PESM diagrams (both global and local) and composition policies, based on the semantic model of STAIRS [7,8]. The semantics gives a precise understanding of the meaning of a PESM diagram, and is used to validate the transformation from global to local PESM diagrams and composition policies.

The rest of this paper is organized as follows: In Sect. 2, we introduce some basic terminology and present an example motivating the approach. Sect. 3 gives a brief introduction to the semantic model of STAIRS. Sects. 4 and 5 constitutes the main body of the paper, presenting first the global PESM diagrams at the service model layer, and then their transformation into local PESM diagrams, one for each composite role, at the design model layer. Related work is presented in Sect. 6, before concluding in Sect. 7.

2 Collaborations and Roles

For composing an existing service with a general AA-pattern, we assume that the service is described at the service model layer using a UML 2.x collaboration. Such an overview diagram describes the distributed parts involved in a service and which roles are to be played by the different service parts, providing a means of statically and structurally representing the binding of collaboration uses involved in a composed service to the actual service parts. Fig. 1 shows a collaboration overview diagram for a basic multimedia voice over IP (MMoIP) service.

An *elementary collaboration* is a service collaboration with exactly two elementary roles that collaborate on an interface to provide a service or a service feature [9]. Fig. 2 shows an elementary collaboration for a simple service that provides news headlines as running text on the screen. The visible interface behaviour associated with an elementary collaboration may be modelled using, e.g., UML 2.x interactions or semantic interfaces [9]. For ensuring correct dynamic composition in the runtime system, the visible interface behaviour between the two elementary roles should be validated with respect to safety and liveness properties [10,11].

An *elementary role* is the smallest modelling element. These are pre-defined behavioural specifications (elementary role state machines) that are not changed under dynamic composition. *Composite roles* are dynamic compositions of

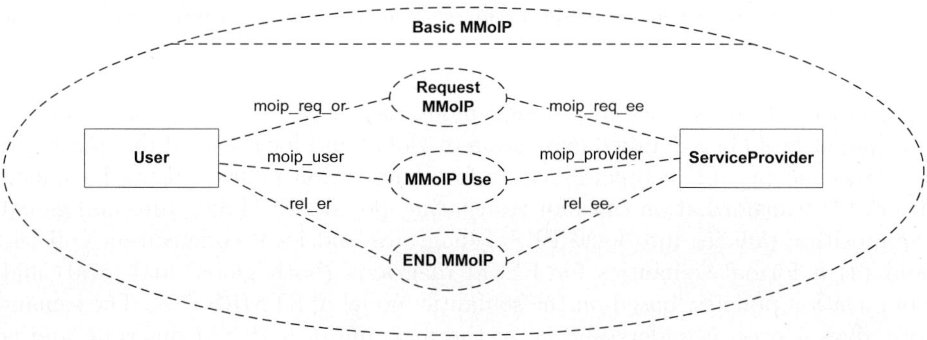

Fig. 1. Collaboration overview for a basic multimedia voice over IP service

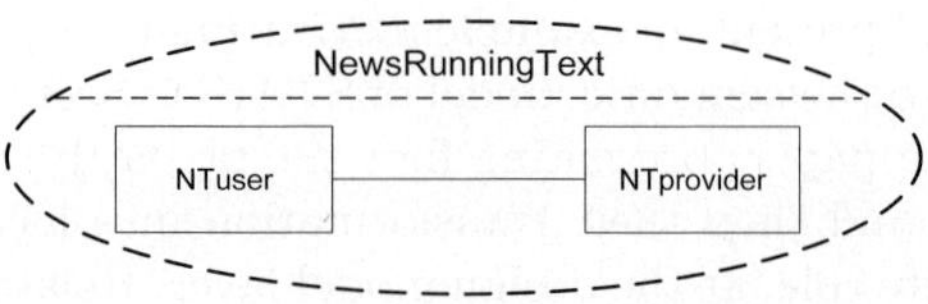

Fig. 2. Collaboration for a simple running text display service

elementary roles. Composite roles play elementary roles, governed by local composition policies as described in Sect. 5. In Fig. 1, each of the three sub-collaborations is an elementary collaboration for which the two elementary roles (e.g., `rel_er` and `rel_ee` in `END MMoIP`) are bound to the `User` and `ServiceProvider` composite roles, respectively.

To provide a MMoIP service that is enhanced with the news headlines text display service, we compose the `Basic MMoIP` composite service collaboration with the `NewsRunningText` elementary collaboration. In order to restrict service access to authorized users only, the MMoIP composite service is to be composed with AA-patterns. The resulting secure MMoIP composite service is then specified as a composition of AA-patterns and service collaborations, each of which is specified as an elementary collaboration. In Fig. 3, the MMoIP service is shown composed with the `NewsRunningText` elementary collaboration and the `User Pull` AA-pattern from [2].

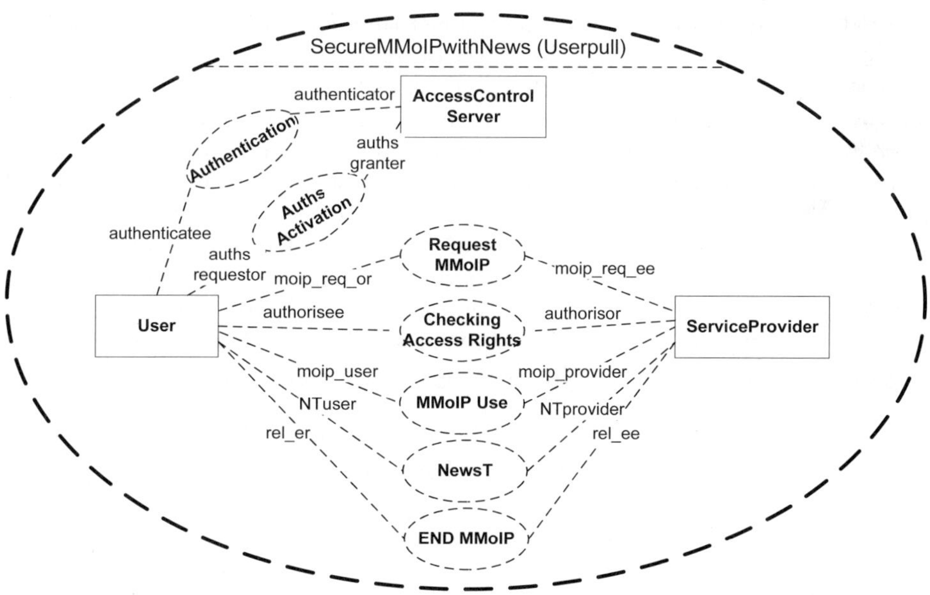

Fig. 3. Collaboration overview for composition of the MMoIP service with User Pull authentication and authorization

The collaboration overview diagram in Fig. 3 describes the elementary collaborations involved in the secure MMoIP service, but not how their associated behaviour should be composed in order to achieve the desired behaviour for the composed service. How this may be described is the main topic of this paper, and we will come back to this in Sect. 4. But first, we need to introduce the semantic model that we base our definitions on.

3 Introduction to the Semantics

In this section, we give an introduction to the denotational trace semantics of STAIRS [7,8], originally developed for UML 2.x interaction diagrams. The focus is on the parts necessary for understanding the semantic definitions in this paper.

A trace is a sequence of events, representing a system run. The most typical examples of events are the sending and reception of messages. Formally, a message is a triple (s, tr, re) consisting of a signal s (the content of the message), a transmitter tr and a receiver re. The send and receive event of a message m is denoted $!m$ and $?m$, respectively.

$\mathcal{H}$ denotes the set of all well-formed traces, i.e., traces where for each message, the send event is ordered before the corresponding receive event. An interaction obligation (p, n) is a pair of trace-sets where p represents positive (i.e., valid) system behaviour and n represents negative (i.e., invalid) system behaviour. Traces not described as either positive or negative, i.e., traces in $\mathcal{H} \setminus (p \cup n)$, are referred to as inconclusive, capturing the fact that specifications may be partial.

The complete semantic model is a *set* of interaction obligations. Intuitively, the (positive and inconclusive) traces within each interaction obligation represent underspecification, where the system may be able to produce only one of these traces. On the other hand, the different interaction obligations represent mandatory alternatives, in the sense that the system must fulfill each one of them.

STAIRS also defines the semantics of a number of composition operators, of which only sequential composition is directly used in this paper. Definition of other operators, including parallel composition, alternatives, negative behaviours, and looping, may be found in [8]. Sequential composition ($\succsim$) of two trace sets corresponds to point-wise interleaving of their individual traces, such that the ordering of events within each trace is maintained in the result, and for events on the same lifeline (i.e., role), all events from the first trace are ordered before the events from the second trace. Formally:

$$s_1 \succsim s_2 \stackrel{\text{def}}{=} \{h \in \mathcal{H} \mid \exists h_1 \in s_1, h_2 \in s_2 : \forall l \in \mathcal{L} : h \upharpoonright l = h_1 \upharpoonright l \frown h_2 \upharpoonright l\} \tag{1}$$

where $\mathcal{L}$ is the sets of all lifelines, $\frown$ is the concatenation operator on sequences, and $h \upharpoonright l$ is the trace h with all events not taking place on the lifeline l removed.

For interaction obligations, sequential composition is defined by:

$$(p_1, n_1) \succsim (p_2, n_2) \stackrel{\text{def}}{=} (p_1 \succsim p_2, (n_1 \succsim p_2) \cup (n_1 \succsim n_2) \cup (p_1 \succsim n_2)) \tag{2}$$

Notice that composing a positive and a negative trace always yields a negative trace, while the result of composing an inconclusive trace with a positive or negative trace is always inconclusive. Finally, for two diagrams d_1 and d_2 with semantics $[\![d_1]\!]$ and $[\![d_2]\!]$, their sequential composition is defined by:

$$[\![d_1]\!] \succsim [\![d_2]\!] \stackrel{\text{def}}{=} \{o_1 \succsim o_2 \mid o_1 \in [\![d_1]\!] \wedge o_2 \in [\![d_2]\!]\} \tag{3}$$

$$
\begin{array}{lll}
\langle\text{Policy rule}\rangle & \rightarrow & \texttt{T} : \langle\text{Trigger}\rangle \\
 & & \texttt{C} : \langle\text{Condition}\rangle \\
 & & \texttt{A} : \langle\text{Action}\rangle \\
 & & \texttt{G} : \langle\text{Goal}\rangle \\
\langle\text{Trigger}\rangle & \rightarrow & \langle\text{Event}\rangle \\
\langle\text{Condition}\rangle & \rightarrow & \texttt{Pred, C-role.Pred, C-role.Pred} \\
\langle\text{Action}\rangle & \rightarrow & \texttt{Cu (E-role} \rightarrow \texttt{C-role , E-role} \rightarrow \texttt{C-role) : C-name} \\
\langle\text{Goal}\rangle & \rightarrow & \texttt{C-role.Pred, C-role.Pred} \\
\langle\text{Event}\rangle & \rightarrow & \{\ \texttt{!}\ \mid\ \texttt{?}\ \}\ \langle\text{Message}\rangle \\
\langle\text{Message}\rangle & \rightarrow & \texttt{(Signal, C-role , C-role)}
\end{array}
$$

Fig. 4. Extended BNF syntax for global policy rules, with | denoting alternatives and { } as meta parentheses

In this paper, we also use constraints, which in the semantics is represented by the special event *check*:

$$[\![\ \mathsf{constr}(c) \ ]\!] \stackrel{\mathsf{def}}{=} \{(\{\langle check(\sigma)\rangle \mid c(\sigma)\}, \{\langle check(\sigma)\rangle \mid \neg c(\sigma)\})\} \tag{4}$$

where $c(\sigma)$ is true iff the constraint c holds in the state σ. Intuitively, this definition states that all traces where the constraint is evaluated to true are positive traces, while the traces are negative if the constraint does not hold.

4 Service Models

The collaboration overview diagram shown in Fig. 3 gives an overview of the elementary collaborations involved in the secure MMoIP service. In this section, we describe how composition policies and PESM diagrams may be used to describe how the associated behaviour should be composed in order to achieve the desired behaviour for the composed service.

4.1 Global Composition Policies

A *composition policy* is a set of policy rules specifying how a given set of elementary collaborations can be composed to obtain a given set of composite services. As such, a composition policy applies to a *family* of related services, where the number of possible services in the family depends on the choices governed by the policy rules. Choices are made to decide which set of collaboration uses will be composed in order to deliver the selected service.

In terms of the family of services defined by a composition policy, a UML 2.x collaboration overview diagram graphically represents a high level view of the service possibilities, where all or some of the elementary collaborations may have more concrete specializations as will be demonstrated in Sect. 4.2.

In Fig. 4, we define a BNF-grammar for policy rules. `Signal` represents the actual content of a message, `C-role` and `E-role` are names, representing composite and elementary roles, respectively. `Pred` is a boolean predicate, `C-name` is the name of a collaboration and `Cu` the name of a collaboration use.

As can be seen from the definition, a policy rule consists of four parts: trigger, condition, action and goal. The definition of these rules is derived from the event-condition-action rule paradigm of active database systems [12]. In order to ensure correct dynamic composition of a service, the system is obliged to execute the given action when a policy rule applies.

In a policy rule, the trigger T and condition C together define when the policy rule is applicable. The trigger is a receive or send event of a message sent to or from a composite role, which will then be the role discovering the trigger and responsible for enforcing the policy rule. For easier transformation from global to local policies, the condition is split in three parts, one condition for each of the two composite roles involved, and one condition relating the roles.

The action A defines the collaboration use to be performed when the trigger event has occurred, given that the constraints in the condition hold. The action also defines the necessary role bindings from elementary to composite roles.

The goal G defines the desired result of the action when the policy is applied and is a boolean predicate expressing when the goal is achieved from the perspective of the elementary collaboration as a whole. To allow for deriving the role goals for each of the policies that will follow the roles in the local PESMs, the goal of a composition policy rule is split in two, similarly to what is done for conditions. The goal provides flexibility of choice between different elementary collaborations with the same goal to provide options for ensuring that reaching the goal can be achieved so that the service can continue to execute correctly. For example, if one authentication pattern is not achievable, e.g., because constraints cannot be satisfied, another alternative with the same goal can be chosen so that the service can execute correctly.

Semantics. The elementary collaborations describe the visible behaviour of the two collaborating roles only, and the complete system may also exhibit behaviour not described in the elementary collaborations. In the composition policies, a trigger may either be an event described in another elementary collaboration, or an event not described at all. In the formal semantics, these two cases are handled in the same manner. We assume that for each composite role r, the last event to happen is stored as part of the state, and define the function $last(r)$ to return this event. The semantics of a trigger is then defined as a check of whether or not the trigger was the last event to happen:

$$[\![\texttt{T:}t]\!] \stackrel{\mathsf{def}}{=} [\![\mathsf{constr}(last(t.r) = t)]\!] \tag{5}$$

where $t.r$ is the sender of t if t is a send event and the receiver if t is a receive event.

As should be expected, the semantics of a condition is defined as a sequence of constraints requiring the given predicates to hold:

$$[\![\texttt{C:}c, a.c_a, b.c_b]\!] \stackrel{\mathsf{def}}{=} [\![\mathsf{constr}(c)]\!] \gtrsim [\![\mathsf{constr}(a.c_a)]\!] \gtrsim [\![\mathsf{constr}(b.c_b)]\!] \tag{6}$$

For the action part of the policy rule, we assume that $[\![$ `C-name` $]\!]$ is the semantics of the collaboration given by `C-name`. The semantics of a collaboration use is then found by replacing all occurrences of elementary roles with the corresponding composite roles. This corresponds to lifeline substitution in STAIRS, which is defined on events by:

$$subst(e, L) \stackrel{\mathsf{def}}{=} \begin{cases} k(s, L(tr), L(re)) & \textbf{if } e = k(s, tr, re),\ k \in \{!, ?\} \\ e & \text{otherwise} \end{cases} \tag{7}$$

where L is the mapping from elementary to composite roles. This definition may then be lifted to traces, trace sets, pairs of trace sets and sets of interaction obligations in standard pointwise manner.

The semantics of an action is then defined as:

$$[\![\ \texttt{A:Cu}(e \rightarrow a, f \rightarrow b) : \texttt{C-name}\ ]\!] \stackrel{\mathsf{def}}{=} subst([\![\ \texttt{C-name}\ ]\!], \{e \rightarrow a, f \rightarrow b\}) \tag{8}$$

Intuitively, the goal defines the desired result of the action, i.e., a constraint that should hold when the action has been performed. However, there may also be cases where the goal is not achieved, without this being a system error. In the formal semantics, this is reflected in two interaction obligations, one where the goal is required to hold, and one where it is also acceptable for the goal not to hold. As for constraints, the two parts of the goal are checked separately:

$$\begin{aligned}[\![\ \texttt{G:}a.g_a, b.g_b\ ]\!] \stackrel{\mathsf{def}}{=} & ([\![\ \mathsf{constr}(a.g_a)\ ]\!] \succsim [\![\ \mathsf{constr}(b.g_b)\ ]\!]) \cup \\ & ([\![\ \mathsf{constr}(a.g_a \vee \neg a.g_a)\ ]\!] \succsim [\![\ \mathsf{constr}(b.g_b \vee \neg b.g_b)\ ]\!])\end{aligned} \tag{9}$$

The semantics of a single policy rule formalises the fact that after the trigger t has occurred, then, if the condition c holds, action a should occur, and the goal g is the desired result afterwards. If the trigger does not occur, or the condition does not hold, the policy rule does not apply and the action a should not occur:

$$[\![\ \texttt{T:}t\ \texttt{C:}c\ \texttt{A:}a\ \texttt{G:}g\ ]\!] \stackrel{\mathsf{def}}{=} [\![\ \texttt{T:}t\ ]\!] \succsim [\![\ \texttt{C:}c\ ]\!] \succsim [\![\ \texttt{A:}a\ ]\!] \succsim [\![\ \texttt{G:}g\ ]\!] \tag{10}$$

4.2 Global PESM Diagrams

Graphically, a global policy enforcement state machine (PESM) is used to depict the dynamic composition of collaborations according to the composition policy. In Fig. 5, a PESM diagram for the secure MMoIP service is given. A global PESM diagram presents a graphical representation of the ordering of elementary collaboration uses from the collaboration overview diagram, possibly with some more concrete specializations. For example, in Fig. 3, only a generic elementary two party authentication collaboration is shown. The PESM diagram in Fig. 5 shows this collaboration specialized into three different choices: unilateral one pass authentication (`UOPA`), unilateral two pass authentication (`UTPA`) and mutual two pass authentication (`MTPA`).

As nodes, the PESM contains collaboration uses, each consisting of a collaboration use name (e.g., `UAs1a`), a collaboration name (e.g., `UOPA`), and the elementary roles as bound to composite roles (e.g., `authenticatee0` bound to

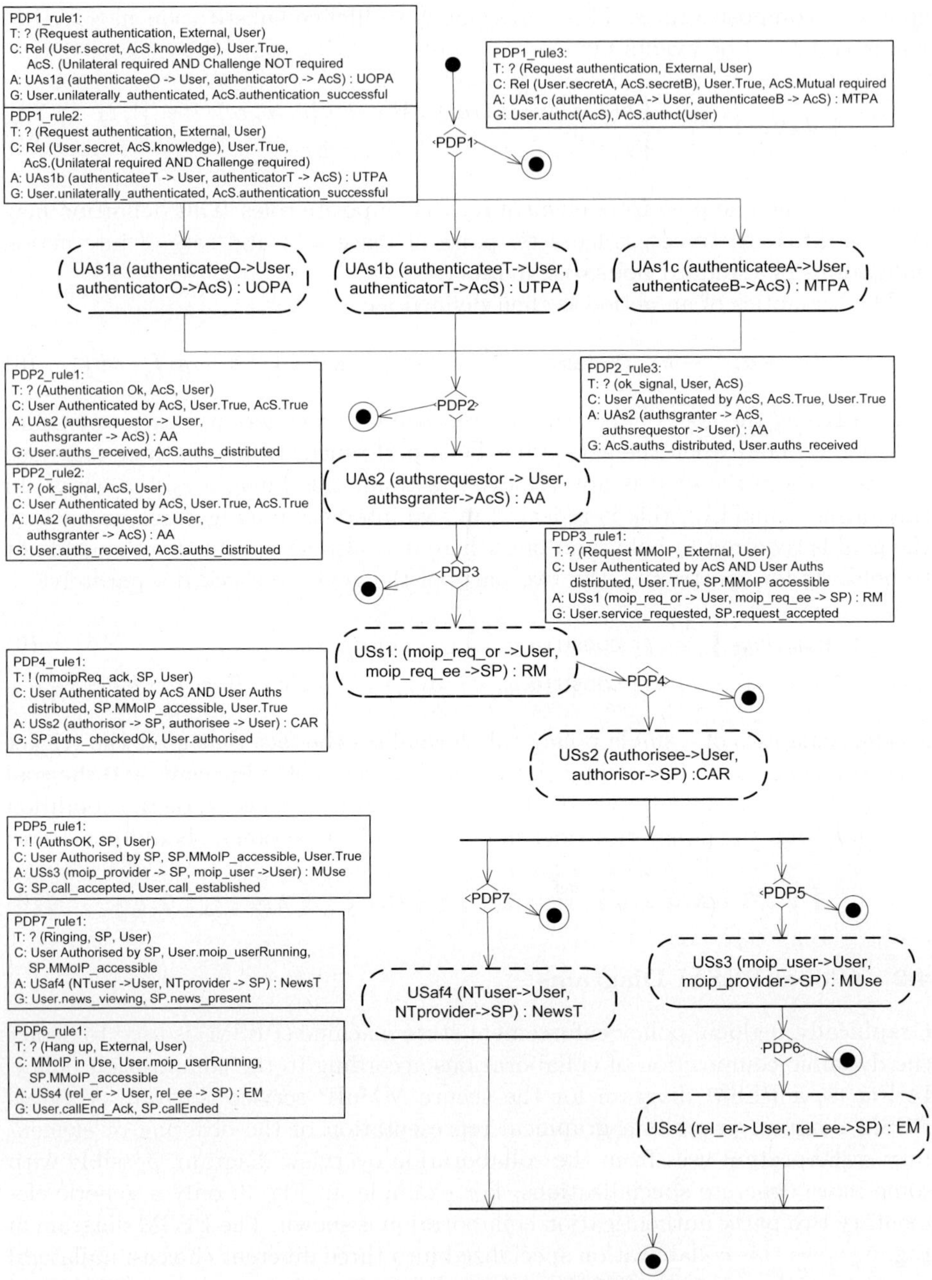

Fig. 5. Global PESM diagram for the SecureMMoIP collaboration

User and authenticatorO bound to AccessControl Server (AcS)). In Fig. 5, most of the names of the collaborations and composite roles from Fig. 3 are abbreviated to their intial letters, for instance AA for Auths Activation.

The collaboration uses are linked by transitions and choice nodes. The initial state represents the start of execution of the composite services represented by the PESM. The choice nodes are labeled as numbered policy decision points (PDP), so that policy rules can be defined with pointers to the PDP they apply to. At each PDP, policy ruled choice is evaluated, and the outgoing transition chosen is policy ruled. In Fig. 5, the first choice is made in PDP1, when the User composite role receives a request for authentication. This request is the trigger event for all three policy rules in PDP1, and which outgoing transition to be taken will then depend on the conditions in the policy rules. In this example, the Rel-predicates in the conditions state that there must be a relation between User.secret and AcS.knowledge/secret, but the exact nature of this relation is underspecified at this level of abstraction. If the condition of a rule is evaluated to true after the trigger event has occurred, the outgoing transition corresponding to the action part of the rule (e.g., UAs1a in the case of PDP1_rule1), is taken.

The final state is entered according to separate policy rules. For the example given in Fig. 5, these are rules where one of the given triggers occurs, but none of the other policy rules applies due to their conditions being false. For presentation purposes, these policy rules are not shown in the diagram in Fig. 5. The complete set of policy rules for this diagram may be found in [13]. Note that while final states are shown as exits from each of the PDP, these branches actually point to one final state. We have chosen, however, to represent the exit branches graphically in this manner to avoid an unreadable diagram.

The PESM along with the set of policy rules that apply, allow us to represent all the possible runs which allow achieving the overall goal for a family of services. One *service* (in the family) results when the choices have been made between the possible collaboration uses. This service consists of the selected collaboration uses to be composed, according to policy. Another service opportunity results when a different set of collaboration uses are selected, based on the policy rules. For each PDP, the actual execution of the service in the runtime system will follow one of the choices depicted in the PESM. For example, in Fig. 5, three different services result depending on which authentication collaboration is chosen. Additionally, the MMoIP basic collaborations are enhanced with the feature of presenting news as running text. This collaboration is also triggered according to policy, when the call set-up ringing signal is sent to the User by the ServiceProvider. From this point on, the user is able to view the news as running text on the screen in parallel to the MMoIP call.

While the PESM shows choice, the actual execution of a service in the runtime system will follow one of the possible choices depicted by the PESM. By specifying composition policies and service composition ruled by policy, we can enable dynamic composition in the runtime system. The composition policies may be specified prior to deployment of the composed services in the runtime system. This enables static composition with some dynamic composition allowed, depending on which policy rule is satisfied. It is also possible to alter the policy rules after deployment. For example, to require a stronger level of authentication in an already deployed service, a policy manager in the runtime system can govern dynamic changes so that a stronger authentication pattern is used in place of the weaker one. While, this is not directly addressed by our research, the Chisel framework could provide an environment for realizing this approach [14].

Semantics. For defining the semantics of a global PESM diagram, we treat the PESM as an interaction overview diagram, extended with PDPs and the corresponding policy rules. In Sect. 4.1, we defined the semantics of a single policy rule. The semantics of a PDP is then defined as the union of the semantics of all the corresponding policy rules:

$$[\![\ PDP \ ]\!] \stackrel{\mathsf{def}}{=} \bigcup_{p \in PDP} [\![\ p \ ]\!] \tag{11}$$

5 Design Models

At the design model layer, the behaviour of each elementary role is given as a UML 2.x state machine. Their coordination into composite roles is described using local composition policies and local PESM diagrams, one for each composite role. In the following, we present the syntax and semantics for local composition policies and PESM diagrams, and describe how they may be automatically derived from the global ones.

5.1 Local Composition Policies

Each global policy rule at the service model layer corresponds to two local rules, one for each of the composite roles involved in the collaboration specified in the action part. The role receiving the trigger is referred to as the *initiating role*, while the other is called the *participating role*. In addition to performing its role in the collaboration, the initiating role is responsible for sending a role request demanding the participating role to play *its* part.

Note that the initiating party is not necessarily the first one to act within the collaboration. For instance, in all three rules in PDP1 in Fig. 5, the composite role `User` is the initiating role receiving the trigger. As `authenticateeO`, the `User` is the first to send a message in unilateral one pass authentication (`UOPA`) whereas in unilateral two pass authentication (`UTPA`) it is the `AccessControl Server` as `authenticatorT` that sends the first message. Separating the initiating role from the collaboration to be initiated thus allows for greater flexibility in dynamic composition, as shown in Fig. 5, exemplified by the ability to change authentication pattern regardless of who makes the first move within the collaboration. For the full specification of these authentication patterns, see [2].

The local policy rules are similar to the global rules in that they consist of a trigger, a condition, an action and a goal. The main difference is that the actions

⟨Policy rule⟩	→	`T : `⟨Trigger⟩
		`C : `⟨Condition⟩
		`A : `⟨Action⟩
		`G : `⟨Goal⟩
⟨Trigger⟩	→	⟨Event⟩
⟨Condition⟩	→	`Pred` $\{$ `, Pred , C-role.Pred` $\}^?$
⟨Action⟩	→	$\{$ `!` ⟨Role-request⟩ `,` $\}^?$ `PlayRole(E-role)`
⟨Goal⟩	→	`Pred`
⟨Event⟩	→	$\{$ `!` | `?` $\}$ ⟨Message⟩
⟨Message⟩	→	`( Signal, C-role , C-role )` | ⟨Role-request⟩
⟨Role-request⟩	→	`( RoleReq(E-role), C-role, C-role )`

Fig. 6. Extended BNF syntax for local policy rules, with $\{\ \}^?$ denoting optional parts

to be performed are now given as state machines instead of collaborations. The global goal is distributed to the two roles, and similarly for condition, where the initiating role should be responsible for checking both its local condition and the condition relating the two roles.

The BNF-grammar for local policy rules is defined in Fig. 6, where `Pred`, `E-role`, `C-role` and `Signal` is as for global policy rules described in Sect. 4.1. `RoleReq(E-role)` should be understood as a special signal, namely a request for playing the elementary role given as parameter. This means that a role request is a special kind of message. The parts that are optional in the BNF-grammar, refer to elements that are present for the initiating role, but not for the participating role. For a given global policy rule, the corresponding local rules may be derived automatically following the pattern given in Fig. 7.

Global rule	Local rule, initiating role a	Local rule, participating role b
`T: t`	`T: t`	`T: ?(RoleReq(f),a,b)`
`C:` $c, a.c_a, b.c_b$	`C:` $c, c_a, b.c_b$	`C:` c_b
`A: Cu(e→ a,f→ b):C`	`A: !(RoleReq(f),a,b),` `PlayRole(e)`	`A: PlayRole(f)`
`G:` $a.g_a, b.g_b$	`G:` g_a	`G:` g_b

Fig. 7. From global to local policy rules

The semantics given to local policy rules is very similar to that of global policy rules, and is not repeated here. The only difference is with respect to the action part, where a role request is treated as any other message, and we assume that `E-role` is defined by an elementary role state machine with semantics $[\![$ `E-role` $]\!]$. The detailed semantics may be found in [13].

5.2 Local PESM Diagrams

Local PESM diagrams are used to graphically depict local coordination and enforcement of the local composition policies. From the global PESM diagrams at the service layer, it is possible to derive a number of local PESM diagrams, one for each composite role governed by the policy.

The transition is made by traversing the global PESM diagram by focusing on one composite role at a time. The collaboration uses, which the composite role participate in, are replaced by the corresponding elementary role state machine, while collaboration uses that do not involve the composite role are removed from the diagram along with the preceding PDP.

For the Secure MMoIP collaboration shown in Fig. 3, three local PESM diagrams may be derived from the global PESM diagram for the `User`, `Access-Control Server` (`AcS`), and `ServiceProvider` (`SP`) composite roles, respectively. The local PESM diagram for the `User` composite role is shown in Fig. 8, annotated with policy rules for each of the policy decision points. Policy rules for each of the PDP are shown alongside the diagram, for clarity. At PDP1_U, each of the three policy rules trigger `User` as initiating role and therefore it is required that a role request is sent to the `AcS`. In PDP2_U, however, two of the rules trigger `User` as initiating role, whereas PDP2_U_Rule3 requires that `User` plays the participating role, and the `AcS` in this case plays the initiating role, requesting that `User` play the `authsrequestor` role. For the specification of the `AcS` and `SP` composite role PESM diagrams, please see [13].

The notation for the local PESM is essentially as for the global PESM, however, each of the nodes represents an elementary role state machine. Semantically, there is no difference between global and local PESM diagrams.

6 Related Work

The collaboration-oriented approach presented in this paper builds on the work on composing services presented in [15,9]. In [16,17], the authors describe how UML collaborations can provide a framework for service modelling that enables service behaviours to be completely defined, and analysed for problems. Additionally, in [17], the authors provide a collaboration-oriented approach in which service models can be automatically translated to executable design models. However, the approach presented in [17] specifies collaboration coordination as UML 2.x activities with nested activities. The interfaces between activities (inter collaboration) is precisely defined, and is useful for the purpose of being able to generate state machines from the activities. However, such "hard-coded" interactions between reusable elements can restrict the possibilities for adaptation in a dynamic system. Our approach allows for dynamic adaptation by using policies to link together the separately specified collaborations. Adaptation is possible when triggered by an event or when policy rules are changed to allow for insertion of new behaviours.

A UML 2.x activity is commonly used to model a WEB services choreography, capturing interactions from a global perspective [18,19]. The PESM is similar, however, it allows us to define the overall choreography in a dynamic way. Policies and rules are used in [20] for discovering and finding compatibility to generate service flows in dynamic composition of web services. In automatic

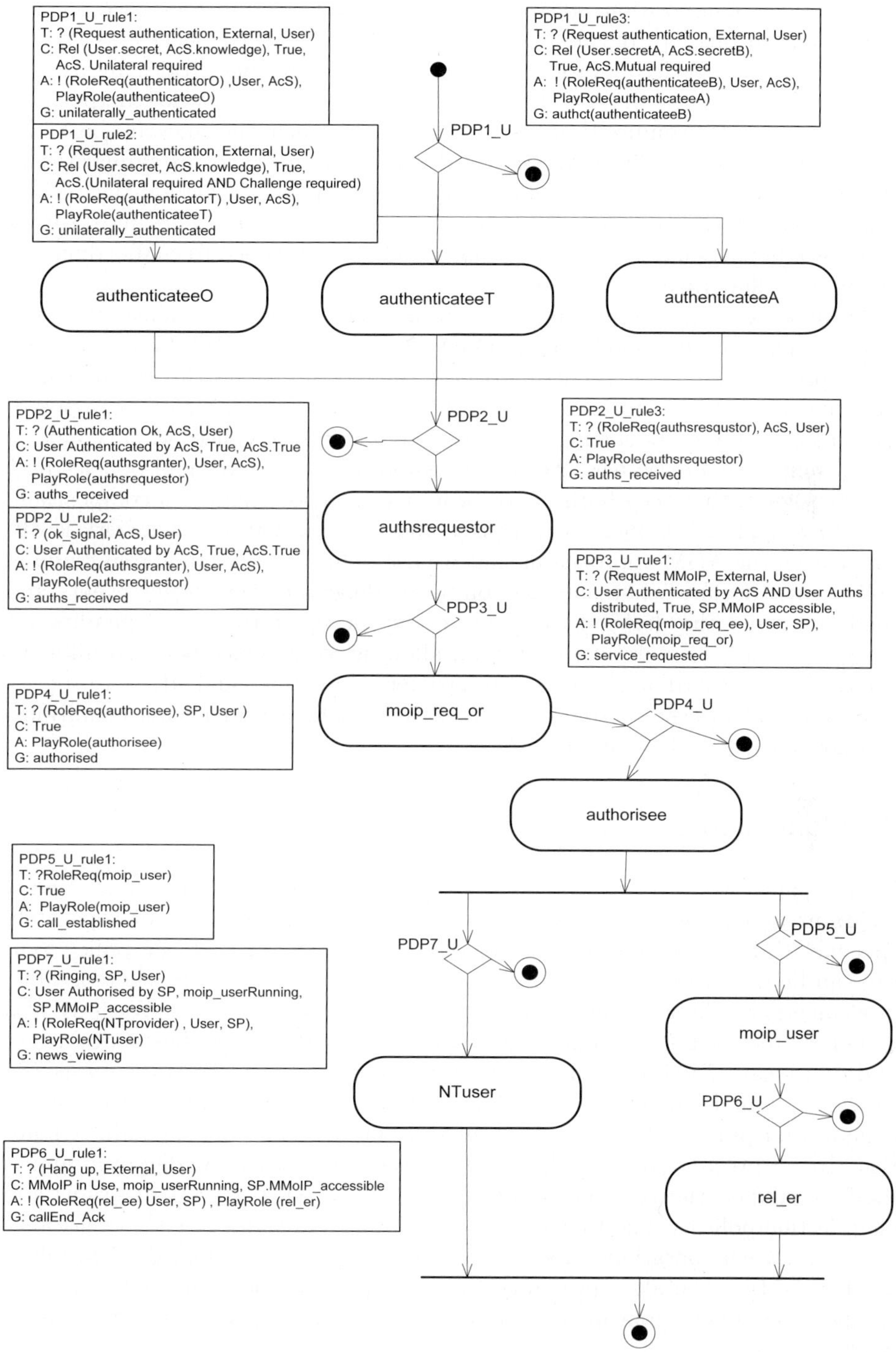

Fig. 8. Local PESM diagram for the User composite role

WEB services composition, software agents perform composition based on predefined algorithms [21]. In rule-based service composition approaches, constructs are provided for specifying processes by means of sets of rules. Rules are used in the web services composition approach to drive the process of service composition and govern service composition [22]. As in our approach, the rules are based on the so-called event-condition-action paradigm [12]. While there are similarities to our approach, we use policy rules to specify government of collaborative behaviour in multi-initiative collaborative services as opposed to modelling business processes. In particular, the composition policies are designed to enable dynamic linking of collaborative behaviour.

An area for which significant research has been done on composition is the area of aspect oriented modelling (AOM) [23,24]. Both the AOM approach and our approach address cross-cutting concerns, however, we do this by modelling roles and using policy to bind them and define how they are to be composed, whereas in AOM, cross-cutting aspects are woven into so-called primary models using composition directives. Although composition directives and policies play similar roles in that they both define ordering and coordination of composition, the AOM approach is more prescriptive and static in nature. Our work is different from the AOM approach in that we use policy and dynamic role-binding. Policy rules declare what may be composed depending on trigger events and conditions, and the decision to compose may occur at runtime depending on dynamic behaviour state of the system, allowing for a choice between different behaviours. Furthermore, we do not use patterns, pointcuts and advice to specify composition. However we specify more explicitly where, under what conditions, and how composition should occur.

7 Conclusions

In this paper we have presented an elaboration of our ideas on using PESM diagrams and composition policies to specify the coordination of separately specified UML2.x collaborations. We have demonstrated that the policy syntax can be used to specify composition policies for governing the choreography of elementary collaborations in dynamic composition of services. We have also demonstrated that local policy rules can be derived from global policy rules, and that local PESM diagrams can be derived from global PESM diagrams. We provide a formal semantics for PESM diagrams (both global and local) and for composition policies, based on the semantic model STAIRS [7,8]. The semantics gives a precise understanding of the meaning of a PESM diagram, and is used to validate the transformation from global to local PESM diagrams and composition policies. The PESM diagram allows us to emphasize the reusability of UML 2.x collaborations in service composition when combined with policy. We believe that the ideas presented in this paper may be easily generalized to composition of behaviour in general, but the exact details of this is left as future work.

Acknowledgements. The research on which this paper reports has been partly funded by the Research Council of Norway project SARDAS (152952/431). Thanks to the anonymous reviewers and to members of the SARDAS and ENFORCE projects for commenting on earlier versions of this paper.

References

1. Object Management Group: UML 2.1.2 Superstructure Specification, formal/2007-11-02 (2007)
2. Rossebø, J.E.Y., Bræk, R.: Towards a framework of authentication and authorization patterns for ensuring availability in service composition. Technical Report 332, Dept. of Inf., Univ. of Oslo (2007)
3. Rossebø, J.E.Y., Bræk, R.: Using composition policies to manage authentication and authorization patterns and services. In: Proc. Availability, Reliability and Security (ARES 2008), pp. 597–603. IEEE Computer Society Press, Los Alamitos (2008)
4. Damianou, N., Dulay, N., Lupu, E., Sloman, M.: The ponder policy specification language. In: Sloman, M., Lobo, J., Lupu, E.C. (eds.) POLICY 2001. LNCS, vol. 1995, pp. 18–39. Springer, Heidelberg (2001)
5. International Telecommunication Union: ITU-T Recommendation Z.150, User Requirements Notation (URN) – Language Requirements and Framework (2003)
6. Amyot, D., Becca, H., Bræk, R., Rossebø, J.E.Y.: Next generation service engineering. In: Proc. ITU-T NGN Kaleidoscope Conference. IEEE Computer Society Press, Los Alamitos (to appear)
7. Haugen, Ø., Husa, K.E., Runde, R.K., Stølen, K.: STAIRS towards formal design with sequence diagrams. Software and Systems Modeling 4(4), 349–458 (2005)
8. Runde, R.K.: STAIRS — Understanding and Developing Specifications Expressed as UML Interaction Diagrams. PhD thesis, Univ. of Oslo (2007)
9. Sanders, R.T.: Collaborations, Semantic Interfaces and Service Goals: a way forward for Service Engineering. PhD thesis, NTNU (2007)
10. Floch, J., Bræk, R.: A compositional approach to service validation. In: Prinz, A., Reed, R., Reed, J. (eds.) SDL 2005. LNCS, vol. 3530, pp. 281–297. Springer, Heidelberg (2005)
11. Engelhardtsen, F.B., Prinz, A.: Application of stuck-free conformance to service-role composition. In: Gotzhein, R., Reed, R. (eds.) SAM 2006. LNCS, vol. 4320, pp. 115–132. Springer, Heidelberg (2006)
12. Widom, J., Ceri, S. (eds.): Active Database Systems: Triggers and Rules For Advanced Database Processing. Morgan Kaufmann, San Francisco (1996)
13. Rossebø, J.E.Y., Runde, R.K.: Specifying service composition using UML 2.x and composition policies. Technical report, Dept. of Inf., Univ. of Oslo (to appear)
14. Keeney, J.: Completely Unanticipated Dynamic Adaptation of Software. PhD thesis, Trinity College, Univ. of Dublin (2004)
15. Sanders, R.T., Castejón, H.N., Kraemer, F., Bræk, R.: Using UML 2.0 collaborations for compositional service specification. In: Briand, L.C., Williams, C. (eds.) MoDELS 2005. LNCS, vol. 3713, pp. 460–475. Springer, Heidelberg (2005)
16. Castejón, H.N., Bræk, R., von Bochmann, G.: Realizability of collaboration-based service specifications. In: Proc. Asia-Pacific Software Engineering Conference (APSEC 2007), pp. 73–80. IEEE Computer Society Press, Los Alamitos (2007)

17. Kraemer, F.A., Herrmann, P., Bræk, R.: Synthesizing components with sessions from collaboration-oriented service specifications. In: Gaudin, E., Najm, E., Reed, R. (eds.) SDL 2007. LNCS, vol. 4745, pp. 166–185. Springer, Heidelberg (2007)
18. Kavantzas, N., Burdett, D., Ritzinger, G., Fletcher, T., Lafon, Y., Barreto, C.: WS-CDL version 1.0 (2005), `http://www.w3.org/TR/2005/CR-ws-cdl-10-20051109/`
19. Kramler, G., Kapsammer, E., Retschitzegger, W., Kappel, G.: Towards using UML 2 for modelling web service collaboration protocols. In: INTEROP-ESA 2005. Springer, Heidelberg (2005)
20. Chun, S.A., Atluri, V., Adam, N.R.: Policy-based web service composition. In: Proc. Research Issues on Data Engineering (RIDE 2004), pp. 85–92. IEEE Computer Society Press, Los Alamitos (2004)
21. Fujii, K., Suda, T.: Dynamic service composition using semantic information. In: Proc. Intl. Conf. on Service Oriented Computing (ICSOC 2004), pp. 39–48. ACM Press, New York (2004)
22. Yang, J., Papazoglou, M.P., Orriens, B., van den Heuvel, W.-J.: A rule based approach to the service composition life-cycle. In: Proc. Web Information Systems Engineering (WISE 2003), pp. 295–298. IEEE Computer Society Press, Los Alamitos (2003)
23. Reddy, Y.R., Ghosh, S., France, R.B., Straw, G., Bieman, J.M., McEachen, N., Song, E., Georg, G.: Directives for composing aspect-oriented design class models. In: Rashid, A., Akşit, M. (eds.) Transactions on Aspect-Oriented Software Development I. LNCS, vol. 3880, pp. 75–105. Springer, Heidelberg (2006)
24. Clarke, S., Walker, R.J.: Towards a standard design language for AOSD. In: Proc. Intl. Conf. on Aspect-Oriented Software Development (AOSD 2002), pp. 113–119. ACM Press, New York (2002)

A Model-Based Framework for Security Policy Specification, Deployment and Testing

Tejeddine Mouelhi[1], Franck Fleurey[3], Benoit Baudry[2], and Yves Le Traon[1]

[1] IT- Telecom Bretagne, France
[2] INRIA/IRISA, France
[3] SINTEF, Norway

Abstract. In this paper, we propose a model-driven approach for specifying, deploying and testing security policies in Java applications. First, a security policy is specified independently of the underlying access control language (OrBAC, RBAC). It is based on a generic security meta-model which can be used for early consistency checks in the security policy. This model is then automatically transformed into security policy for the XACML platform and integrated in the application using aspect-oriented programming. To qualify test cases that validate the security policy in the application, we inject faults into the policy. The fault model and the fault injection process are defined at the meta-model level, making the qualification process language-independent. Empirical results on 3 case studies explore both the feasibility of the approach and the efficiency of a full design & test MDE process.

Keywords: Metamodeling, Model-driven engineering methodology, Security.

1 Introduction

Security is not only a keyword, it is currently a critical issue that has to be embraced by modern software engineering (SE) techniques. From this SE point of view, having confidence in the implemented security mechanisms is the key objective when deploying a security concern. This objective can be reached by improving the design and implementation process via automation, such as security code generation from models, and by qualification criteria. Qualification criteria can be used for *a priori* verification of the specified security models' consistency, and for *a posteriori* validation of the quality of test cases executed on the final implementation. Qualification criteria should be independent of the many languages used to model security and – if possible – from the specificity of implementation languages. The same principles and same criteria should be applied to qualify the security mechanisms for various kinds of systems. Although such common principles and criteria are highly desirable, they are useless without the support of effective tools that make the qualification approach applicable in a final system implementation.

In this paper we focus on the confidence of an *access control policy* proposing a bi-dimensional approach, which is (1) an automated MDE process for deriving security components, (2) a qualification process which is security-language independent.

K. Czarnecki et al. (Eds.): MoDELS 2008, LNCS 5301, pp. 537–552, 2008.

The first dimension of the approach thus targets the automation of the process transforming a security policy into security components. This process is based on a standard architecture that involves designing a dedicated security component, called the policy decision point (PDP), which can be configured independently from the rest of the implementation containing the business logic of the application. The execution of functions in the business logic includes calls to the PDP (called PEPs – policy enforcement points), which grant or deny access to the protected resources/ functionalities of the system.

The proposed MDE process is based on a domain-specific language (DSL) in order to model security formalisms/languages as well as security policies defined according to these formalisms. This DSL is based on a generic metamodel that captures all the necessary concepts for representing rule-based access control policies. The process relies on several automatic steps in order to avoid errors that can occur with repeated manual tasks. This includes the automatic generation of a specific security framework, the automatic generation of an executable PDP from a security policy and the automatic injection of PEPs into the business logic using aspect-oriented programming.

In this context, the challenge for qualification is to offer some guarantee that the PDP is consistent and that it interacts with the business logic as expected (e.g. a hidden security mechanism may bypass some PEPs [1]). Since this interaction of the PDP with the business logic can be faulty, a second dimension is needed to improve the confidence in security mechanisms.

This second dimension consists of a qualification environment which provides (1) *a priori* verifications of security models before PDP component and PEP generation, (2) *a posteriori* validation of the test cases for the implementation of the policy. This qualification environment is independent of security policy languages and is based on a metamodel for the definition of access control policies. It provides model transformations that make the qualification techniques applicable to several security modeling languages (e.g. RBAC, OrBAC [2, 3]).

Section 2 presents the MDE process. Section 3 details the framework, while section 4 explains how we exploit this metamodel for security code generation and V&V certification. Section 5 presents the empirical results on three Java case studies.

2 MDE for Security

Errors in the security policy can have several causes. They can be caused by an error in the policy definition, by an error when translating the policy into an executable PDP or by an error in the definition of PEPs (calls to the PDP at the wrong place in the business logic, calls to the wrong rule, missing call, etc.). In order to increase the efficiency of the validation and verification tasks, we investigate an integrated approach based on two facets. First, we want to ensure as much quality as possible by construction. For that purpose we propose an MDE process based on a specific modeling language for security policies and automatic transformations to integrate this policy into the core application. Second, we develop generic verification and validation techniques that can be applied early in the development cycle and that are independent of any particular security formalism.

Figure 1 presents an overview of the proposed approach. From top to bottom, the process starts with the requirements for the system and ensures the integration of the security concerns in the running code.

The first step of the approach (1) is to build the security model for the application. The security model is a platform independent model which captures the access control policies defined in the requirements of the system. To allow security experts to create, edit and check this security model, it is modeled in a security domain specific modeling language. This language is based on a generic meta-model which allows several types of rule-based access-control policy to be expressed. In practice, the meta-model allows the type of rules to be modeled as well as the rules themselves.

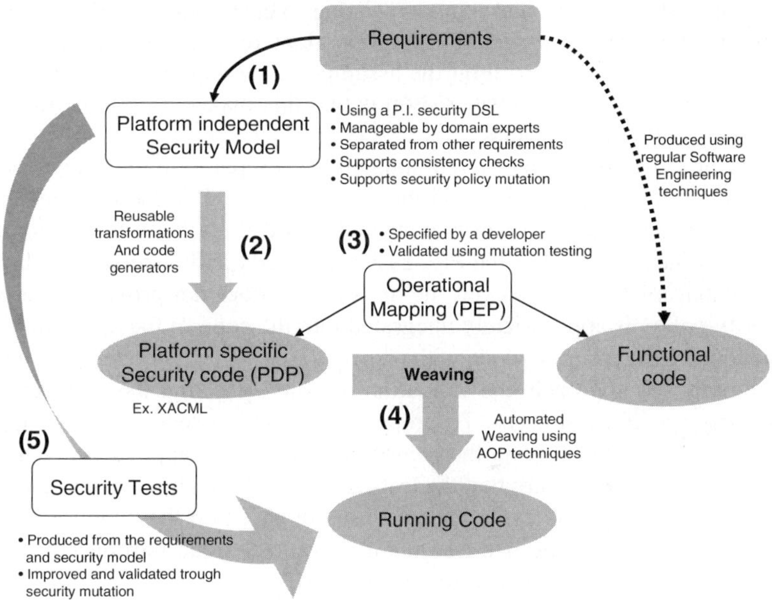

Fig. 1. Overview of the proposed approach

The main benefit of using a generic meta-model is that it allows the implementation of generic verifications and transformations and their application to all types of rule. Verifications are performed in order to check the soundness of the security policy and its adequacy with regards to the requirements of the application, in particular, the detection of conflicts between rules, which is a tedious task. A simple case of conflict occurs when a specific permission is granted by a rule and denied by another (possible with OrBAC language). These verifications also include checking that each business operation can be performed by at least one type of user or that a specific set of operations can only be performed by administrators. All these verifications are carried out by the security metamodel and are thus language independent.

After the platform independent security model has been validated, automated transformations are used to produce specific PDPs (2). The Policy Decision Point is the point where policy decisions are made. It encapsulates the Access Control Policy and implements a mechanism to process requests coming from the PEP and return a response which can be permit or deny In practice, the PDP is not usually fully generated but based on reusable security frameworks. These frameworks are configured with the specific security policy and connected to the application through the PEP. In the example presented in the figure, the output of the transformation is an XACML file that contains the security policy.

A critical remaining step for implementing the security of the application is to connect the security framework with the functional code of the application (3). In practice, this corresponds to adding the PEPs in the main code of the application. It is a critical step because any mistakes in the PEP can compromise the overall security of the application. To reduce the risk of mistakes, we use AOP, to make the security PEP introduction systematic (4), and mutation testing to ensure that the final running code conforms to the security model (5). An important reason to compose the security concern at the code level is to limit the assumptions on how the system is developed prior to this composition. Another reason is that this makes it possible to change the security policy after deployment.

The use of aspect-oriented programming allows a separation to be kept between the business logic of the application and the security code. The use of pointcuts allows calls to be introduced to the security code systematically without having to list all the specific locations. This makes the PEP easier to specify and understand, which avoids many potential mistakes. However, the use of AOP does not provide a warranty that the security policy is appropriately integrated into the code of the application. A careful validation of the resulting code with respect to the security model is required.

In the proposed approach, the validation is done by testing the final running code with security-specific test cases. To properly validate the security of the application, these test cases have to cover all the security features of the application. When testing, *test criteria* are used to ensure that the tests are "good enough" to assess the quality of the system under test. The test criteria we use are based on the mutation of the security model. Mutation testing is a test qualification technique introduced in [4] which has recently been adapted for security testing [5, 6].

The intuition behind mutation testing applied to security is that the security tests are qualified if they are able to detect any elementary modification in the security policy of the application (mutants). The originality of the proposed approach is to perform mutations on the platform independent security model using generic mutation operators. Since the transformation and weaving of the security policy in the application are fully automated, the tests can be automatically executed on the mutants of the application. If the tests are not able to catch a mutant then new test cases should be added to exercise the part of the security policy which has been modified to create this mutant. In practice the undetected mutants provide valuable information for creating new tests and covering all the security policies.

The objective of the test cases in a partly automated generation process (PDP and PEPs) is to check that the security policy of the application is fully synchronized with the security model. Indeed, in the mutation testing process, the model is modified and the tests are required to detect the modification in the running code. Thus, if any of the security rules are hard-coded in the application or if the application code bypasses the security framework, the modification will not be observable in the running code. In that case, the mutants corresponding to the hard-coded or bypassed security feature are not detected and the tester has to fix the application to make sure that all security rules are come from the security model.

Overall, the main benefit of the approach is to allow the security policy to be validated using verification on the security model and testing that the policy implemented in the application conforms to the security model. Because the testing is performed on the final running code it allows validation both that the PDP is according to the model but also that the PEP, i.e. the integration with the rest of the application, is correct. The following sections detail the main steps of the approach.

3 The Access Control Metamodel

In the literature, several access control formalisms such as RBAC or OrBAC are based on the definition of security rules. All these formalisms allow the definition of rules that control the access to data, resources or any type of entity that should be protected. The formalisms differ according to the type of rules and entities they manipulate. Since we want to provide validation mechanisms that can be used with various formalisms, we have defined a metamodel that captures the common concepts of rules and entities that are necessary to define these formalisms. The metamodel also captures the concerns for the definition of access control policies using these formalisms.

In this section we introduce this metamodel and illustrate how it supports the definition of RBAC and OrBAC

3.1 Generic Security Metamodel

The metamodel, shown Figure 2, is divided into two parts, that correspond to two levels of instantiation:

- It is possible to define a security policy formalism with the classes POLICYTYPE, ELEMENTTYPE and RULETYPE. A POLICYTYPE defines a set of element types (ELEMENTTYPE) and a set of rule types (RULETYPE). Each rule type has a set of parameters that are typed by element types.
- Based on a security formalism defined by instantiating the above classes, it is possible to define a policy using the classes POLICY, RULE and PARAMETER. A POLICY must have a type (an instance of POLICYTYPE) and defines rules and parameters. The type of a policy constrains the types of paramters and rules it can contain. Each parameter has a type which must belong to the element types of the policy type. If the *hierarchy* property of the parameter type is true, then the parameter can contain children of the same type as itself. Policy rules can be defined by instantiating the RULE class. Each rule has a type that belongs to the policy type and a set of parameters whose types must match the types of the parameters of the type of the rule.

These two parts of the metamodel have to be instantiated sequentially: first define a formalism, then define a policy according to this formalism.

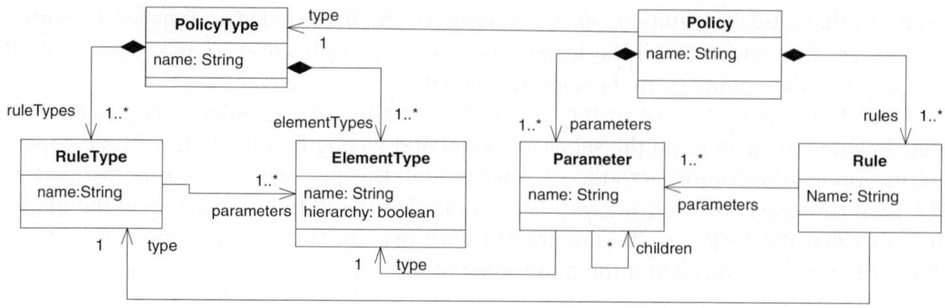

Fig. 2. The meta-model for rule-based security formalisms

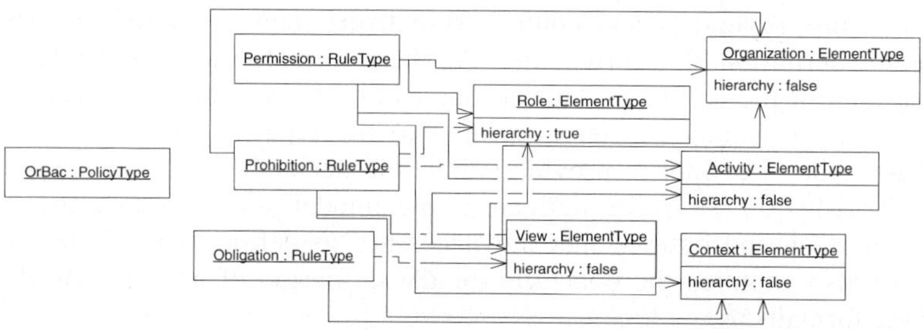

Fig. 3. The OrBAC security formalism

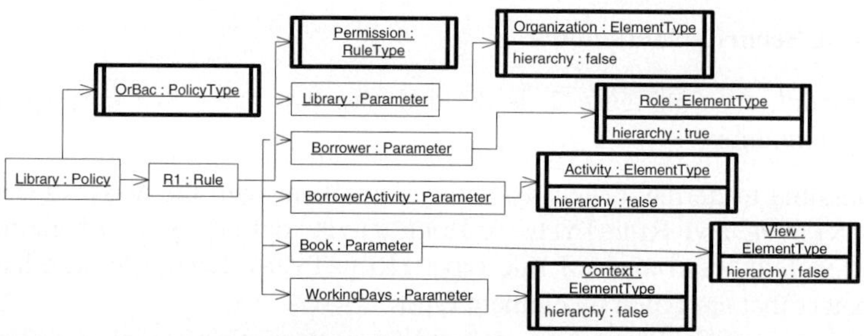

Fig. 4. Rule R1 for the library security policy

3.2 Instantiating the Metamodel

The two parts of the metamodel are instantiated at different moments and by different people. The classes that capture the concepts for a security formalism have to be instantiated first. They are instantiated by language engineers, and this instance defines a modeling language that can be used to model a security policy for a particular system. The classes that capture the concepts to define a policy can only be instantiated if a formalism has been modeled.

To illustrate this process, we redefine the OrBAC formalism as an instance of the generic metamodel and then we define an OrBAC security policy. In OrBAC there are five types of entities: organizations, roles, activities, views and contexts. OrBAC defines three types of rules: permission, prohibition and obligation. All three types of rule have the same five parameters: an organization, a role, an activity, a view and a context. Figure 3 shows how the metamodel was instantiated to model OrBAC security policies.

To illustrate our approach, we use the example of a library management system. This system defines three types of users: students, secretaries and a director. The students can borrow books from the library, the secretary manages the accounts of the students but only the director can create accounts. In the paper we use only a simplified version of the application with just a five security rules defined below:

```
POLICY LibraryOrBAC (OrBAC)
R1 -> Permission(Library Student Borrow Book
WorkingDays)
R2 -> Prohibition( Library Student Borrow Book Holidays )
R3 -> Prohibition( Library Secretary Borrow Book Default )
R4 -> Permission( Library Personnel ModifyAccount
UserAccount WorkingDays )
R5 -> Permission( Library Director CreateAccount
UserAccount WorkingDays )
```

Figure 4 shows an instance of the metamodel for rule R1. The objects in bold are objects that are defined by the OrBAC formalism in Figure 3. Rule R1 is well-formed because, as we can see in Figure 4, the rule has five parameters, each of them of the correct type: Organization, Role, Activity, View, Context. `Borrower` and `BorrowerActicity` are hierarchies of parameters. Rule R1 uses the sub-parameter `Student` defined in the `Borrower` hierarchy and `Borrow` in the `BorrowerActivity` hierarchy.

4 Exploiting the Security Metamodel

This section introduces two mechanisms that we have developed around the generic metamodel. First, we illustrate the fault models that we have defined at the meta-level and that can be executed to inject errors into security policies. Second, we detail how we transform a security policy, defined as an instance of the security metamodel, into a platform-specific security policy that can be 'hooked' onto the business logic.

4.1 Mutation Testing for Security

Mutation analysis involves qualifying a set of test cases for a program under test (PUT) according to the rate of injected errors they can detect. The assumption is that if test cases can detect errors that have been injected on purpose, they will be able to detect actual errors in the PUT. The validity of mutation analysis greatly depends on the relevance of faults that are injected. Faults are modeled as mutation operators that reflect typical faults that developers make in a particular language or domain. Several works (Xie et al. [5], Le Traon et al. [6]) have proposed mutation operators to validate test cases for security policy.

In this paper, we define five mutation operators for security policy testing, shown in Table 1. These operators are defined only in terms of the concepts present in the

Table 1. The mutation operators

Operator Name	Definition
RTT	Rule type is replaced with another one
PPR	Replaces one rule parameter with a different one
ANR	Adds a new rule
RER	Removes an existing rule
PPD	Replaces a parameter with one of its descending parameters

security metamodel, which means that they are independent of a specific security formalism. Thus, these operators can be applied to inject errors into any policy expressed with any formalism defined as an instance of our metamodel. The definition of mutation operators at this meta-level is critical for us since it allows the qualification of test cases with the same standard, whatever the formalism used to define the policy.

In order to generate faulty policies according to these operators, we have added one class to the metamodel for each operator.

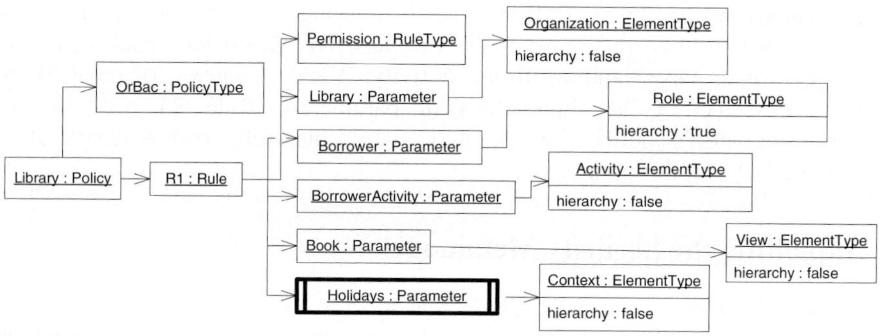

Fig. 5. Rule R1 mutated with PPR operator

RTT: Finds a first rule type that has the same parameter as the type of another rule type. Then it replaces the rule parameter of one rule having the first rule type with the other rule type.

PPR: Chooses one rule from the set of rules, and then replaces one parameter with a different parameter. It uses the knowledge provided by the metamodel (by ruleType and parameterType classes) about how rules are constructed.

ANR: Uses the knowledge about the defined parameters and the way rules are built. Then it adds a new rule that is not specified.

RER: Chooses one rule and removes it.

PPD: Chooses one rule that contains a parameter that has descendant parameters (based on the parameter hierarchies that are defined) then replaces it with one of the descendants. The consequence here is that the derived rules will be deleted and only the rule with the descendant parameter remains.

As an example, Figure 5 shows a mutant obtained by applying the PPR operator on rule R1 of the policy for the library system. In bold we can see the parameter that has been changed: the context has been changed form WorkingDays to Holidays.

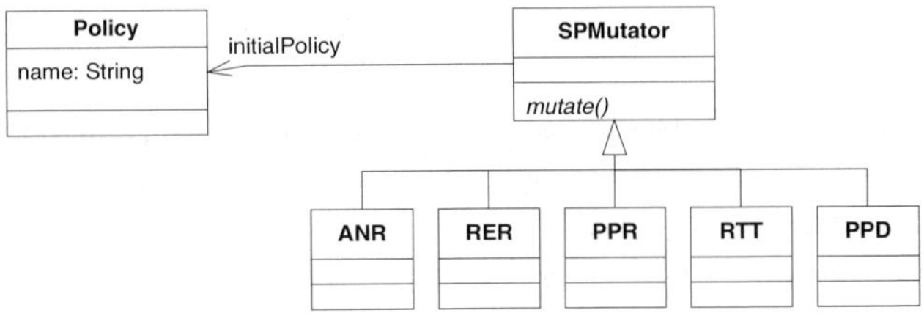

Fig. 6. The mutation operator classes

Figure 6 shows the operator classes. The `mutate()` method is implemented in Kermeta. What is important to notice in this method is that it is defined only using concepts defined in the metamodel. Thus, this method can generate a set of mutated policies, completely independently of the formalism they are defined with. It has to be noted that some mutant policies can be strictly equivalent to the initial policy. In that case no test case can detect the mutant. For mutation analysis, these equivalent mutants have to be removed.

The next section details the deployment of a security policy according to a particular formalism. Then this platform-specific policy is linked to the business logic through the PEPs. Thus, once a policy is mutated at the meta level, the injected error is automatically transformed into an error in the final system that can then be detected by a test case.

4.2 PDP XACML Code Generation from the Metamodel

We implemented a tool to generating XACML (Extended Access Control Markup Language) policies from our metamodel. The XACML file is added to the PDP. XACML is an OASIS standard dedicated to defining access control policies in XML files. There is a framework [7] that supports and helps to access, write and analyze XACML files. Writing XACML files manually is an error-prone task, due to the language complexity. In this paper, we used the existing XACML profiles for RBAC and OrBAC to generate XACML files from our metamodel. Due to space limitation, we do not detail these two profiles.

a) The PDP and the PEP

The PDP encapsulates the XACML policies and offers services to access the policy. The PEP is implemented in the applications and contains a mapping between the

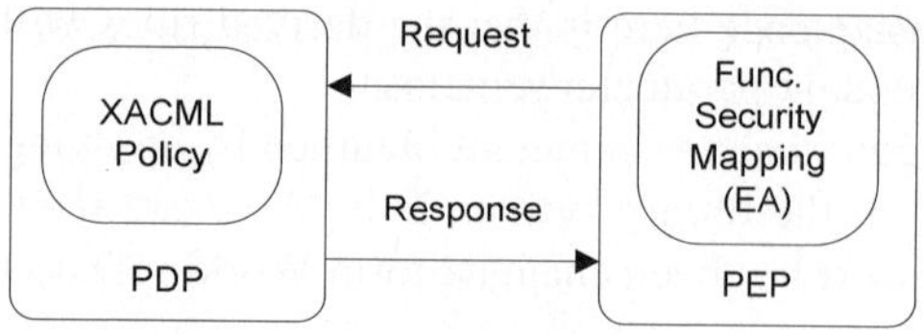

Fig. 7. PEP and PDP

application concepts (user roles, methods, resources and contexts) and the Or-BAC/RBAC policy concepts (roles, activities, views and contexts, or roles, permissions and constraints).

As shown in Figure 7, a PEP uses the mapping between the application concepts (user roles, methods, resources and contexts) and the OrBAC abstract policy (roles, activities, views and context) to get the OrBAC abstract entities. Then it sends a request to the PDP containing the role, the activity, the view and the context. The PDP responds with permit or deny.

b) Limitations

Depending on the underlying model (OrBAC or RBAC), the appropriate profile is used to generate XACML files. Therefore the XACML generator is not generic and a specific generator is needed for each model. However, it can be reused because it is defined at the model level and thus independent of the specified generic policy.

It is important to note that the tool allows XACML files to be generated for both the actual policy and the mutant policies. These mutants are generated at the generic level and the generator tool is used to create XACML files for these mutant policies. Thanks to this tool and the PDP architecture created, the mutation analysis becomes a 'push-button' technology. The mutants are automatically generated at the metamodel level. Then they are exported to XACML to be used by the PDP to evaluate the existing security tests. Therefore, our approach offers a powerful framework for evaluating security policy tests using mutation independently of the underlying access control language.

5 Case Studies and Results

We applied the Verification (V), the automated deployment of PDP and PEPs and the Validation (&V) on three systems:

LMS: A Library Management System.
VMS: A Virtual Meeting System.
ASMS: An Auction Sale Management System.

Table 2 gives the size of the 3 applications (the number of classes, methods and lines of code LOC).

Table 2. The size of the three applications

	# classes	# methods	LOC (executable statements)
LMS	62	335	3204
VMS	134	581	6077
ASMS	122	797	10703

5.1 The Process

In this section, we detail the verification step and the creation of PEP by aspect weaving. The results concerning the validation of the three case studies will be synthesized in the next subsection.

a) The verification step

The main verification is offered by construction, when the conformity of a security model to its metamodel is checked. In this way, we have a minimum consistency that is obtained with the conformance relationship of a model to its metamodel. We also add some extensible verification functions. They constitute preconditions which are checked before deploying the policy and generating the mutants. Two verification functions are implemented:

1. `policy_is_conform()`: the policy conformance to the underlying policy type (OrBAC or RBAC). In order to guarantee that the defined rules meet the types of parameters of rules defined by the policy type.
2. `no_conflicts()`: checks the absence of conflicts. It essentially involves checking that there are no rules having the same parameters and having different types.

The conformance verification function detects simple erroneous rules such as wrong parameters or wrong numbers of parameters.

b) Aspect weaving of the PEP

An aspect is composed of two main parts: (1) advice that implements the behavior of the cross-cutting concern, and (2) the pointcut descriptor (PCD) that designates a set of joinpoints in the base program where the advice should be woven. The weaving is performed automatically by a specific compiler. In the context of the development of secured applications, we propose to define PEPs as aspects, as shown in the following listing. The call to the PDP is weaved before the execution of the method. If the access is granted, the execution continues, otherwise a security exception must be raised. The PEPAspect aspect (implemented in AspectJ in the following listing) defines an advice that is woven before each execution of BookService.borrowBook. This advice calls the checkSecurity method that will then call the PDP by sending the role, activity, view and context given in the parameter. Note that the advice throws a SecurityPolicyViolationException. This exception is raised by checkSecurity when the PDP responds with a prohibition.

```
public aspect PEPAspect {
// PEP Joinpoint for borrow
before(User user,Book book) throws
SecuritPolicyViolationException :
borrowBookCall(user,book)  {

// Call to check for security rule
checkSecurity(user.getRole(), BORROWMETHOD
,BOOKVIEW, getTemporalContext());
        }
}
```

5.2 Validation Results

The validation of the PDP interacting with the business logic was done for the three case studies. The objective of these empirical studies is twofold:

1. Is the approach feasible and what results do we obtain when we modify the security policy language?
2. What are the differences between MDE and language specific approaches?

To answer both questions, we have an existing basis, which are the functional tests and the security tests which were generated to validate the specific OrBAC-based mutation approach [1, 8]. So we have two sets of test cases, which are *functional test cases* and *security policy test cases.*

System/functional tests: test cases generated based on the uses cases and the business models (e.g. analysis class diagram and dynamic views) of the system. Contrary to security tests, we call these tests functional.

Security policy tests: test cases generated specifically from a security policy. The objective of SP testing is to reveal as many security flaws as possible. In our case, the security test cases are generated from the OrBAC or RBAC policies. The test criterion we use requires that each access control rule must be tested by at least one test case. Since OrBAC requires more rules to specify a security policy equivalent to an RBAC one (prohibition rules can be explicitly specified), the test cases generated for OrBAC also satisfy the RBAC test criterion.

a) Process feasibility and results

For the first question, we applied the full generation process for the three case studies, with RBAC and OrBAC access control languages. The feasibility of the approach is thus demonstrated by these successful deployment and validation steps. The limit of this feasibility analysis is that the targeted systems are homogeneous, which means that the final execution platform is based only on Java. We believe that a sufficient number of systems are built with such platform assumptions, making the approach relevant at least for these systems. The number and categories of mutants that are generated for both security policy languages are given in Table 3. In this table we separate ANR mutants from non-ANR because they both generate very different types of mutant: non-ANR operators mutate the existing rules whereas ANR adds new rules. It is interesting to note that the number of mutants may vary significantly depending on the language chosen. However, based on this observation, we cannot conclude which language is likely to be error-prone.

Figure 8 presents the comparative mutation scores (percentage of mutants that are detected as faulty by the test cases) when we execute functional and security test cases on both implementations. We can thus compare how efficient each category of test generation is by using this qualification technique. Here, efficiency is evaluated by the ability of test cases at detecting specific types of faults. OrBAC non-ANR mutants (basic mutation operators) are more difficult to detect with functional test cases than RBAC mutants. This is interesting, since it shows that qualifying functional test cases using OrBAC may be a good choice. Clearly, security test cases are qualified for both languages. Second, concerning ANR mutants, which qualify whether the test cases exercise the "by default" policy of a system, it appears that functional test cases are not efficient, whatever the security policy language is. Circles pinpoint the very low mutation scores obtained especially with OrBAC policies. This is partly due to the fact that some ANR mutants we generate for OrBAC do not modify the behavior of the application, in other words, they are *equivalent mutants*. However, even after filtering equivalent mutants, both functional and security test cases obtain low scores. In the case of the LMS system, the differences in terms of quality between functional and security test cases for RBAC are quite visible (3% compared with 95 % mutation scores). Test cases sets that do not reach a high mutation score have to be completed to be qualified. In a previous work [1], we presented the real security faults we found in these cases studies, especially hidden security mechanisms. In summary, a same fault model leads to the injection of specific faults, which shows the interest of the technique.

b) MDE approach versus language-specific approach

Table 4 compares the number of mutants we obtain with OrBAC policies using a specific approach instead of the generic approach presented in this paper. Table 5 is more important since it presents the mutation scores, with functional and security test cases, obtained with the generic and the specific approach. The specific approach has

Table 3. Number of mutants generated for RBAC/OrBAC policies

	RBAC				OrBAC			
System\ mutants	rules	NON ANR	ANR	All	rules	NON ANR	ANR	All
LMS	23	437	257	694	42	330	714	1044
VMS	36	972	396	1368	106	426	1046	1572
ASMS	89	2937	647	3584	130	1138	1950	3088

Table 4. OrBAC specific mutants vs Generic mutants

System	generic mutants	specific mutants
LMS	1044	371
VMS	1572	1426
ASMS	3088	2056

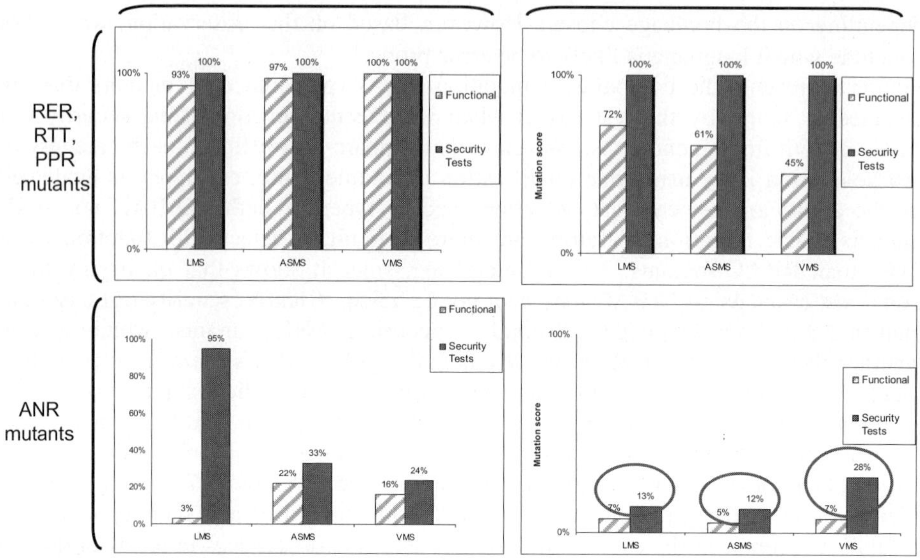

Fig. 8. Mutation scores per mutation operator and language

Table 5. OrBAC mutation results vs. Generic mutation results

Mutants	Basic Mutants (func. tests)			ANR mutants (sec. tests)		
System	LMS	VMS	ASMS	LMS	VMS	ASMS
Generic mutants	72%	61%	45%	13%	12%	28%
Specific mutants	78%	69%	55%	17%	19%	33%
Delta	-6%	-8%	-10%	-4%	-7%	-4%

been presented in [6, 8] and it benefits from the language and the dedicated platform (MotOrBAC tool associated with the language) to generate mutants. The delta reveals that, for all cases, the variation of mutation scores is lower than 10%. This delta is due to the generation of more mutants with the generic approach, and reflects the proportion of equivalent mutants when using the generic approach. The lack of quality of some mutants generated using the MDE process is counter-balanced by the interest of having a certification process that is language-independent. Moreover, this distance separating generic and specific can be reduced by the addition of a mutant filtering function at the language level.

6 Related Works

Previous work focused on providing model based methodologies for security. UMLsec [9] which is an extension of UML allows security properties to be expressed in UML diagrams. In addition, Lodderstedt et al. [10] propose SecureUML, which is close to our contribution, especially concerning the generation of security components from dedicated models. The approach proposes a security modeling language to define the access control model. The resulting security model is combined with the UML business model in order to automatically produce the access control infrastructure. More precisely, they use the Meta-Object facility to create a new modeling language to define RBAC policies (extended to include constraints on rules). They apply their technique in different examples of distributed system architectures including Enterprise Java Beans and Microsoft Enterprise Services for .net. The two processes differ since we do not merge the security and the business models but generate security components independently focusing on different aspects, even if SecureUML could be added for two reasons. First, we consider the functional design and the deployment of the access control model as independent processes which are finally merged. In addition, we consider the validation of the implementation and include it in our process. Moreover, our approach is generic and independent of the underlying access control model.

Previously, mutation has been applied to security policy testing. Xie et al. [5] proposed a mutation fault model specific to XACML policies. However, they had to deal with the problem of equivalent mutants due to the fact that mutants are seeded at code-level. Since Xie et al.'s work aims at testing the Policy Decision Point alone, implemented with XACML, their testing approach does not execute the business logic of the system. The same PDP-alone based testing approach is considered by Mathur et al. [11], who also mutate RBAC models by building an FSM model for RBAC and use strategies to produce test suites from this model (for conformance testing).

7 Conclusion

We have presented a new approach that uses a generic metamodel for security policy specification, deployment and testing. Our approach allows the access control model to be defined in a generic way, independently of the underlying access control language. The security policy is then exported to an XACML file that will be included in the PDP. Then, the PEP is implemented using AOP. Finally, we define mutation at a generic level and use it to qualify the security tests validating the implementation of the security policy. The feasibility of the approach and the interest of a common V&V are both illustrated by applying the approach to 3 case studies.

References

1. Le Traon, Y., Mouelhi, T., Pretschner, A., Baudry, B.: Test-Driven Assessment of Access Control in Legacy Applications. In: ICST 2008: First IEEE International Conference on Software, Testing, Verification and Validation (2008)
2. Ferraiolo, D.F., Sandhu, R., Gavrila, S., Kuhn, D.R., Chandramouli, R.: Proposed NIST standard for role-based access control. ACM Transactions on Information and System Security 4(3), 224–274 (2001)
3. Abou El Kalam, A., El Baida, R., Balbiani, P., Benferhat, S., Cuppens, F., Deswarte, Y., Miège, A., Saurel, C., Trouessin, G.: Organization Based Access Control. In: IEEE 4th International Workshop on Policies for Distributed Systems and Networks (2003)

4. DeMillo, R., Lipton, R., Sayward, F.: Hints on Test Data Selection: Help For The Practicing Programmer. IEEE Computer 11(4), 34–41 (1978)
5. Martin, E., Xie, T.: A Fault Model and Mutation Testing of Access Control Policies. In: Proceedings of the 16th International Conference on World Wide Web (2007)
6. Mouelhi, T., Le Traon, Y., Baudry, B.: Mutation analysis for security tests qualification. In: Mutation 2007: third workshop on mutation analysis in conjuction with TAIC-Part (2007)
7. Sun's XACML implementation, `http://sunxacml.sourceforge.net/`
8. Le Traon, Y., Mouelhi, T., Baudry, B.: Testing security policies: going beyond functional testing. In: ISSRE 2007: The 18th IEEE International Symposium on Software Reliability Engineering (2007)
9. Jürjens, J.: UMLsec: Extending UML for Secure Systems Development. In: Proceedings of the 5th International Conference on The Unified Modeling Language (2002)
10. Lodderstedt, T., Basin, D., Doser, J.: SecureUML: A UML-Based Modeling Language for Model-Driven Security. In: Proceedings of the 5th International Conference on The Unified Modeling Language (2002)
11. Masood, A., Ghafoor, A., Mathur, A.: Scalable and Effective Test Generation for Access Control Systems that Employ RBAC Policies (2006)

A Pattern Language Verifier for Web-Based Enterprise Applications

Bahman Zamani, Sahar Kayhani, and Greg Butler

Department of Computer Science and Software Engineering
Concordia University, Montreal, Canada
{b_zamani,s_kayha,gregb}@encs.concordia.ca

Abstract. The Pattern Language Verifier (PLV) is a process for verifying the application of a pattern language in a design. The PLV process focuses on a pattern language for the design of web-based enterprise applications. We show how PLV exploits the ideas of programming language compilers to detect the structural, syntactic, and semantic errors in a design model and then guides the designer in fixing the problems. To provide tool support, we integrate PLV into the ArgoUML modeling tool. We use the tool to design a simple student registration system as a case study, and show how the process finds the mistakes in the model and helps the designer in repairing the detected problems.

Keywords: Pattern Language, Model Driven Engineering, Profile.

1 Introduction

Models are the main artifacts that drive software development in Model Driven Engineering (MDE) [1]. Low quality models result in low quality software; hence, providing tool support for improving the quality of models is a central task in MDE. Pattern languages serve as domain-specific or issue-specific guides for the designers building software in the MDE approach. One benefit of using patterns is to help the designers to communicate their idea. The term "pattern language" refers to the fact that patterns create a vocabulary, i.e., a common language, used by designers [2]. However, two major issues in using a pattern language are "pattern selection" and "pattern application." These issues have direct impact on the quality of models. That means, selecting a wrong pattern or incorrect usage of a pattern could result in inconsistent and inefficient design and therefore low quality software. Hence, providing support for automatic verification of the models that have benefited from a pattern language will expedite the design process and result in better productivity.

In this paper, our goal is to present a process for verifying the application of a pattern language in a design. The process is called Pattern Language Verifier (PLV) and it focuses on Martin Fowler's *Patterns of Enterprise Application Architecture* [2] (henceforth, *PofEAA*). It should be noted that *PofEAA* is a pattern language in the domain of *designing* web-based enterprise applications; that means, while most of the Domain Specific Languages (DSLs) are defined

K. Czarnecki et al. (Eds.): MoDELS 2008, LNCS 5301, pp. 553–567, 2008.

for describing the *problem domain*, this pattern language should be considered as a DSL in the *solution domain* describing the architecture or *design* of the application. Typically, novice designers are vulnerable to making mistakes in using *PofEAA*.

In defining the PLV process, we have benefited from the analysis steps of the programming language compilers, i.e., we have defined three modules to detect the structural, syntactic, and semantic errors in a design model, along with a module that guides the designer in fixing the problems in a systematic manner. We have integrated the PLV process into an open source modeling tool, ArgoUML [3], and we have used the tool to design a simple student registration system as a case study. This case study shows the usefulness of the PLV process in assisting the designer to improve the design.

In Section 2, first we give our definition of a pattern language, then we introduce *PofEAA* and show how it can be considered as a pattern language. Section 3 describes the architecture of the PLV process, the *PofEAA* profile, and the technical details about the PLV modules. The implementation details of integrating PLV into the ArgoUML modeling tool is described in Section 4. Section 5 shows a case study of using the tool for designing a student registration system. Related works are discussed in Section 6. Section 7 concludes the paper and addresses some future works.

2 Pattern Language

Patterns have played an important role in software development in general, and in object-oriented approach in particular. As a simple anecdote, the seminal book on design patterns known as the "Gang of Four" (GoF) patterns [4] is used by many software experts and is cited by many researchers, e.g., its citation count on ACM is 1648 and on Google Scholar is 14608, and with 243 reviewers in amazon.com, it ranks 2nd in the Software Engineering Bestsellers category.

Software experts have borrowed the terms "Pattern" and "Pattern Language" from the architect Christopher Alexander. Alexander in [5] defines several *inter-related* patterns for architects who want to design buildings. Alexander expresses that "the link between the patterns are almost as much a part of the language as the patterns themselves" [5]. In this section, we aim to reach to a definition of the term "pattern language" and to discuss our justification for considering *PofEAA* as a pattern language.

2.1 Pattern Language Definition

In the software community, there are a few definitions for a pattern language [6,7,8,9]. By integrating the ideas of these sources, we consider a pattern language as *"a network of inter-related patterns with specific dependencies between patterns that lead the designer while designing a system using those patterns."* That means, selecting one pattern leads the designer to one or more patterns, and this process (or "structuring mechanism" [8]) continues until the whole system is designed.

By documenting patterns and the relationship among them, in fact the pattern author is defining a pattern language that could be used by designers in developing new software systems [9]. Pattern names play a crucial role in a pattern language, because designers can use those names as a vocabulary that helps them to communicate more effectively [2].

2.2 PofEAA Pattern Language

Our focus is on Martin Fowler's *PofEAA* patterns [2]. *PofEAA* contains over fifty patterns as solutions to recurring problems that designers encounter while *designing* a web-based enterprise application. We discuss how this set of patterns is qualified to be considered as a pattern language.

Despite the fact that the author of *PofEAA* does not force the designer to select one pattern after another, there exist several recommendations in the book that, from our point of view, for a novice designer can be considered a structuring mechanism that leads him/her in selecting appropriate patterns one after another. Furthermore, the set of patterns can be used to describe the design of an application as a whole. Therefore, we look at *PofEAA* as a pattern language for the *design* of web-based enterprise applications.

Based on the idea of three-tiered architecture for client-server platforms, the patterns in *PofEAA* are decomposed into three main layers: presentation, domain, and data source. The presentation layer is responsible for the user interface, the domain layer deals with application and domain logic and business rules, and the data source layer is related to communicating with the database. In addition to these three layers, there are some other categories of patterns, e.g., object-relational, basic, or distribution patterns.

We have selected a subset of *PofEAA* for our experiments. Figure 1 shows the placement of selected patterns in a three-layer architecture, in addition to a Service Layer pattern and some basic patterns. Due to lack of space we do not elaborate on the selected patterns here and refer the reader to the book [2]. The dependencies shown in the figure are based upon the recommendations (rules) given in the book. In the following, we briefly review these rules to convey the idea of Figure 1. Note that the PLV process uses these rules as a basis for detecting errors in a design (see Section 3.3).

Basically, there is no specific dependency between any of the patterns in the presentation layer and the layer beneath. However, if the designer decides to use the Service Layer pattern as an API for the application, this pattern usually works with a Domain Model or Table Module. This facts are reflected in Figure 1 by having two alternative dependencies, one from the presentation layer to either Service Layer or Transaction Script, the other from Service Layer to either Domain Model or Table Module.

Selecting patterns for the data source layer is more dependent upon the domain layer patterns. As it is indicated in Figure 1, if a Domain Model pattern is selected and the domain is rich, i.e., the structure of the domain model is complex, then the suggested pattern for the data source layer is Data Mapper, otherwise, Active Record is a better choice. In case a Transaction Script or Table

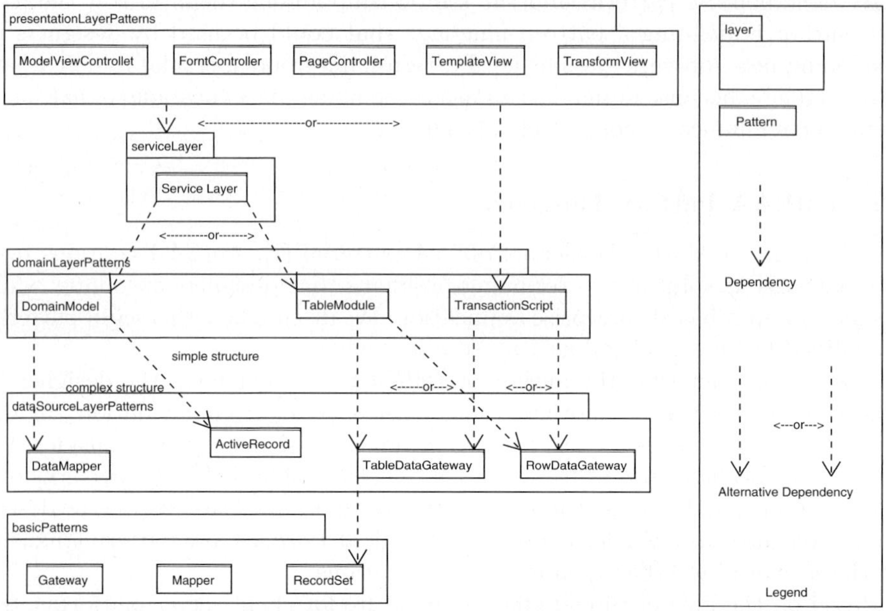

Fig. 1. Selected Patterns from *PofEAA* [2] in a Layered Architecture

Module is selected, then there are two options for data source layer, Table Data Gateway or Row Data Gateway. The last dependency is shown (in Figure 1) between Table Data Gateway and Record Set since these two work very nicely together. Note that according to the *PofEAA* book, Active Record is in the data source layer, therefore, in Figure 1, we kept Active Record inside that layer, however, to reflect the fact that it may contains some business logic, it should be considered on the boundary of the domain layer and the data source layer.

3 Pattern Language Verifier (PLV)

Due to the large number of patterns and the intrinsic complexity of the network (dependencies) of patterns in a pattern language, defining a process and providing tool support for verifying the application of a pattern language in the design model of a system would be a fruitful endeavor. We call our proposed process "Pattern Language Verifier," or PLV for short. To the best of our knowledge, most of the related work falls into the category of single pattern detection and those works do not focus on the pattern language aspects (see Section 6).

We believe that checking a model which is built using the patterns of a pattern language is similar to using a compiler for checking a source program which is written using a programming language. In compiler design, the compiling task is separated into two parts: analysis and synthesis. Analysis consists of three *phases* for detecting the lexical, syntactic, and semantic errors in a program based upon the *lexical*, *grammar*, and *semantic rules* of the underlying language. Synthesis deals with code generation and optimization. The information about variables and identifiers of the program are stored in a "Symbol Table" [10]. This similarity is the cornerstone of defining the PLV process. In the following, first we represent the architecture of PLV, then, we briefly introduce the profile as an important unit in the PLV, and finally, we will go to the details of PLV modules.

3.1 The PLV Architecture

Taking the three-phase *analysis* part of a compiler into consideration, we propose three main phases (or modules) for the PLV process. We need a phase for finding the patterns that are used in the model, because in designs which are made using a pattern language, patterns are the elements that a model is built upon. The module responsible for this phase is called Pattern Detector. In addition, we need a phase for checking the sequence or hierarchy of patterns used in the model and to see whether the pattern dependencies and layering is correct or not. We call the corresponding module Pattern Syntactic Checker. Finally, in the last phase, we should check the consistency and meaningfulness of the patterns considering the context information that is given by the designer. The related module is called Pattern Semantic Checker. In addition to the three main phases, we need a module for reporting the errors to the designer, displaying guidelines on how to fix the problem, and fixing the detected problems in the model. This module is called Pattern Advisor. Figure 2 shows the overall architecture of PLV.

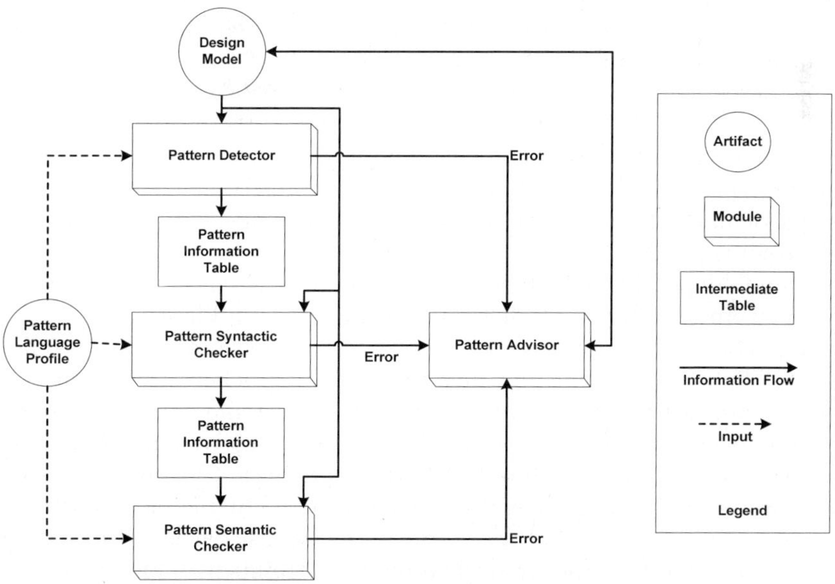

Fig. 2. The PLV Architecture

Note that, despite the similarities between the PLV process and the compiling process, there exist several differences too. The most important one is that the lexical, syntactic, and semantic rules used by a compiler are more formal and precise than the rules used by the PLV process. Another considerable difference is that in PLV, all the modules work on the same model and we cannot say that each phase changes the model from one representation to another, as it happens in the phases of a compiler.

3.2 Pattern Language Profile

As illustrated in Figure 2, the PLV process is based upon a profile that should already be defined for the underlying pattern language. According to [11], a UML profile is a package with stereotype «profile» that contains elements for a specific domain. For our process, we have defined a "*PofEAA* UML Profile," consisting of stereotypes and constraints. The stereotypes of the profile are particularly used by the Pattern Detector for finding patterns, and the constraints are used by all three main modules for checking the structure, syntax, and semantics of the underlying pattern language.

In *PofEAA* profile, we have four sub-packages corresponding to the layers shown in Figure 1 (except for Service Layer). Therefore, we have defined four stereotypes that extend the meta-class "Package" of the UML meta-model. Since each of our patterns consists of one or more classes, each pattern is associated with at least one stereotype that extends the meta-class "Class" of the UML meta-model. Only one of these stereotypes is considered, by the Pattern Detector, as the starting point for checking the structure of the pattern. Further, there are some stereotypes that extend the meta-class "Operation" of UML meta-model. These stereotypes are used for the operations that are mandatory for some of the patterns. All the constraints corresponding to the stereotypes are hard-coded into the PLV modules as explained in the following sections.

For instance, for pattern Front Controller (see Figure 3), we have three classes with stereotypes «handler», «command», and «concretecommand». These stereotypes (particularly the first one), when applied, show the designer's intention for using the corresponding pattern. Also, we need two operations with stereotypes «doget» and «dopost» in the Handler class. The structural constraints check the dependency, abstraction, and inheritance as indicated in Figure 3.

An important issue is to investigate "to what extent does a UML profile suffice for fulfilling the tasks of the PLV process?" We believe that if the profile constraints are rich enough to catch all the structural and syntactic errors in a design, then the profile facilitates the building of two corresponding modules of PLV. However, we think the duties of Pattern Semantic Checker are out of the scope of profile abilities, and therefore should be done by the module itself. One rationale is due to the fact that we consider "the inconsistencies with context information" as semantic errors, and the profile constraints have only access to the model elements, not the environment. Also the profile cannot help in building the Pattern Advisor because the profile constraints are not intended to perform model modifications.

3.3 PLV Modules

Similar to the compiler phases, each of the PLV modules uses a set of rules as the principles for checking the model to find errors. We have codified some structural, syntactic, and semantic rules from the *PofEAA* book. These rules are used by three corresponding modules of PLV. Table 1 is an excerpt from these rules. Note that selecting rule numbers and rule types is our choice and the rule descriptions are from the book. As it is noted earlier, these rules are not accurate enough, hence, in case of any imprecision (e.g., in R02: "The Table Data Gateway is *usually* stateless"), it is up to the developer of the PLV modules to decide how to code the rule into the process. In the following, we refer to the rules in Table 1 by the rule number; also we refer to Figure 5 (case study) in order to give a better perspective of each module.

Pattern Detector: As its name says, the responsibility of Pattern Detector is to find the patterns used in a model. This module checks the structure of the pattern. If the correct usage of a pattern is detected, pattern information is recorded in a Pattern Information Table to be used in the next phases. If there are problems in a pattern, the required information is passed to the Pattern Advisor to take the appropriate action.

This module has benefited from our previous work, the Sign/Criteria/Repair (SCR) process [12]. Sign is simply the presence of corresponding stereotype. This way, we eliminate the possibility of ambiguity in detecting patterns. Criteria is a set of structural rules which defines the correct application of a pattern. Repair

Table 1. Some Rules from *PofEAA* Book [2] used in the PLV Process

R#	Rule Type	Rule Description (*PofEAA* book page#)
R01	Structural	"A Front Controller handles all calls for a Web site, and is usually structured in two parts: a Web handler and a command hierarchy. The Web handler is the object that actually receives post or get requests from the Web server." (p.344)
R02	Structural	"A Table Data Gateway has a simple interface, usually consisting of several find methods to get data from the database and update, insert, and delete methods...The Table Data Gateway is usually stateless." (p.144)
R03	Syntactic	"A simple Domain Model can use Active Record, whereas a rich Domain Model requires Data Mapper." (p.117)
R04	Syntactic	"The fact that Table Data Gateway fits very nicely with Record Set makes it the obvious choice if you are using Table Module." (p.35)
R05	Semantic	"[for presentation layer] Your tooling may well make your choice for you. If you use Visual Studio, the easiest way to go is Page Controller and Template View. If you use Java, you have a choice of Web frameworks to consider. Popular at the moment is Struts, which will lead you to a Front Controller and a Template View." (p.99)
R06	Semantic	"If you have an environment like .NET or Visual Studio, then that makes a Table Module much more attractive." (p.30)

is a set of steps that helps the designer fix the problems. Note that in our PLV process, the repair part is the responsibility of the Pattern Advisor module.

For example consider the structural rule R01 in Table 1 that defines the criteria for the Front Controller pattern. To better see the logic behind this rule, consider Figure 3 that shows the structure of this pattern by a UML class diagram. Note that each rule in Table 1 is indeed a set of criteria. For instance, rule R01 consists of at least six conditions that need to be checked to show that the pattern is used correctly. Based on these criteria, Pattern Detector starts by finding a class with stereotype «handler». Then it looks for two operations with stereotypes «doget» and «dopost» in that class. The Handler class should be a client of an abstract class with stereotype «command» that has an operation with stereotype «process» and has at least one child class with stereotype «concretecommand». If all these checks are successful, we add a line in the Pattern Information Table and report the detected pattern to the designer (see Figure 5-B). Otherwise, we call Pattern Advisor to give an error message to the designer (see Figure 5-C) and guide him/her in fixing the problem (see Figure 5-D).

Pattern Syntactic Checker: This module checks both dependencies and layering of detected patterns. In case of any error or inconsistency, a call to the Pattern Advisor is made in order to report the problem to the designer and assist him/her repair the problem. Remember that a pattern language is a network of interrelated patterns. Hence, some patterns could be used only if another pattern has been used.

For instance, imagine that the Domain Model pattern is used in the domain layer and, while it is claimed that the domain is complex, for one of the domain objects, there is also an Active Record pattern in the data source layer. Based on the rule R03 in Table 1, these two patterns (considering the complexity) are inconsistent from the Pattern Syntactic Checker point of view. Therefore, an error message is shown to the designer by the Pattern Advisor along with guidelines on how to fix the problem (see Figure 5-F).

Pattern Semantic Checker: Sometimes, a model is syntactically correct, however, it does not comply with the best practices of the pattern language. The

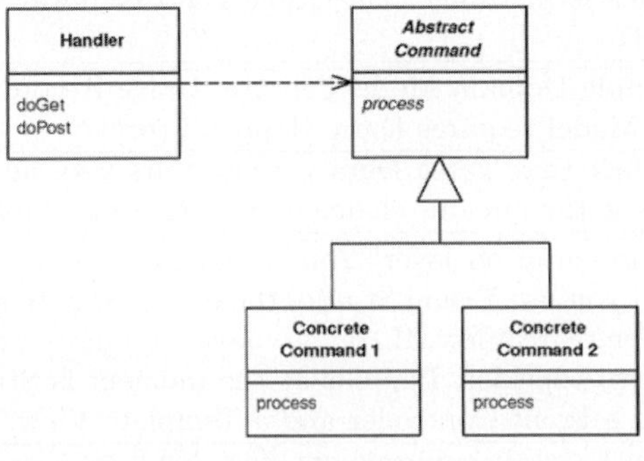

Fig. 3. The Front Controller Pattern [2]

Pattern Semantic Checker module is responsible to catch those mistakes. Conflict between the patterns in a layer, conflict between the context environment and the choice of patterns are some examples of the checks that this module performs. To do these kind of checks, we need to gather some information such as the tooling environment, complexity of the model, and expertise of the developers at the beginning of the modeling.

For example consider the case that the designer has selected .NET development platform (see Figure 5-A), then, we detect Domain Model pattern in the domain layer. This is contradictory with rule R06 in Table 1; hence, Pattern Advisor shows appropriate warning to the designer along with displaying the reasons that caused the error, and some suggestions for improving the design. For instance, it should recommend either using Table Module in the domain layer or to choose Java as development platform (see Figure 5-G).

Pattern Advisor: In addition to the main three phases (modules), Pattern Advisor is an important module which is responsible for reporting the errors, displaying the guidelines, and helping the designer in fixing the problems. For the cases that Pattern Advisor is able to perform automatic repair, it gives the opportunity to the designer, and upon designer's request, the required modifications are applied to the model. For problems that needs designer's decision, the guidelines for fixing the problem should be displayed and it is the designer's responsibility to modify the model.

Following are some of the modifications that are doable automatically by the Pattern Advisor: instantiating a pattern by creating required classes, adding missing operations or attributes to a class (See Figure 5-E), changing a class to abstract, and changing the navigability of an association.

Pattern Information Table: The Pattern Information Table is created by the Pattern Detector and contains basic information about the detected patterns, e.g., the pattern name and the layer in which the pattern is defined. This information is used by the second module (Pattern Syntactic Checker) which also adds more items to this table, e.g., list of patterns that the current pattern depends upon. This modified table will be used by the third module (Pattern Semantic Checker).

4 Integrating PLV into a Modeling Tool

In this section we briefly discuss how the PLV process is implemented into an open source UML modeling tool, ArgoUML [3] (see Figure 4). ArgoUML is a design critiquing system, i.e., it has predefined agents, called *Critics*, that are constantly investigating the current model and if the conditions for triggering a Critic hold, the Critic will generate a ToDo item (a *Critique*) in the ToDo list. A ToDo item is a short description of the problem, some guidelines about how to solve the problem, and, if it exists, a Wizard which helps the designer solve the problem automatically. The Critics are not intrusive, since the designer can completely ignore or disable them. The Critics and the Wizards are not user defined; they all are written in Java and are compiled as part of the tool.

In order to integrate the PLV process into ArgoUML, we have extended our previous implementations discussed in [12]. Since in ArgoUML 0.25 a new feature is added that allows us to apply a profile (only stereotypes) to a model, we define a profile that contains the stereotypes of our *PofEAA* profile (see Section 3.2). The constraints of the profile should be written in Java and are embedded into the Critics. Based on the critiquing idea of ArgoUML, for each kind of problem there should exist a Critic. Hence, for each pattern, we write a Critic class that checks the structural, syntactic, and semantic criteria of that pattern. That means, our three main modules (Pattern Detector, Pattern Syntactic Checker, and Pattern Semantic Checker) are built using Critic classes.

If any of the structural criteria is failed, the Critic is triggered and a ToDo item (a Critique) will be posted in the ToDo list under **Patterns of EAA**. By selecting a ToDo item, its description will be shown in the Details pane, and upon the user's request, the Wizard for the Critic will be executed and the problems found in the pattern usage will be fixed. If any of the syntactic or semantic criteria is failed, e.g., an error in the dependencies between patterns or an inconsistency of the design with context information is caught, the error along with the guidelines will be reported by the Critic itself in a separate tab in the Details pane of ArgoUML named **PofEAA Syntax and Semantics**. That means, the Pattern Advisor module is implemented in both Wizards and Critics which are written as Java classes.

5 Case Study: Student Registration System

In this section we show how the designer's actions are monitored by the PLV process, and how this process can assist the designer fix the problems in applying the *PofEAA* pattern language on a design model.

For our case study, we consider a simple *Student Registration System*. The system consists of students who register for courses that are offered by departments. Each course is taught by a professor and may have some prerequsites. Each professor works for a department and his/her job is to teach courses and to supervise students. For students and professors we keep their personal information in addition to their living address.

Figure 4 shows a screenshot of ArgoUML while the designer is designing the Student Registration System as a web-based application using *PofEAA* pattern language. We suppose that the design is not finalized yet. By applying the *PofEAA* UML profile to the model, the stereotypes are available for use (see part A). Selecting an appropriate stereotype, the designer shows his/her intention for using the corresponding pattern. The Front Controller pattern is chosen for the presentation layer with two commands: "register student" and "change department name" (see part B). The Domain Model pattern is chosen for the domain layer (see part C). In the data source layer, we see two patterns: Data Mapper is accessing student data and Active Record is selected for accessing department information (see part D).

In Figure 5 we see how the PLV modules check separate aspects of the design and guide the designer in solving the problems. This figure is a collection of partial screenshots from ArgoUML. We have tried to synchronize this section with the examples given in Section 3.3 for each module. Part A shows the designers' choices about the context of the design. Part B illustrates the outcome of Pattern Detector module. Patterns that are used correctly, along with their underlying layer and involved classes are shown in the **Detected Patterns** tab in the Details pane. Part C shows a ToDo item created by Pattern Advisor under **Patterns of EAA** due to an error ("missing insert operation") occurred in the Data Mapper pattern. By selecting this ToDo item, in part D, Pattern Advisor module gives guidelines to the designer on how to fix the problem. There is an automatic repair available for this problem. Part E is the result of automatic repair provided by Pattern Advisor; the missing operation is added to the class automatically. Syntactic and semantic errors are reported in a dedicated tab named **PofEAA Syntax and Semantics** in the Details pane. Part F shows a syntactic error. As the guideline explains, the error has occurred due to the inconsistency between the complexity of domain chosen by the designer (in part A) and the Active Record pattern which is used for accessing the Department data. The guideline suggests using Data Mapper instead of Active Record or changing the choice for complexity. Part G shows a semantic error reporting a conflict between the tooling environment selected in part A (.NET) and using Domain Model. The guideline recommends changing either the tool or the pattern.

6 Related Work

The ideas of PLV have roots in our previous works. In [13], we utilized the idea of defining stereotypes for detecting patterns and verifying the application of patterns in a design. Also, we compared the suitability of three modeling tools for integration of the detection process. In [12], the definition of a profile for *PofEAA* is started and a process called Sign/Criteria/Repair (SCR) was defined with focus on verifying the application of a *single* pattern in a design.

There exist several works on detecting GOF design patterns. Bergenti and Poggi [14], have built a tool which uses Prolog rules to detect GOF patterns (only eleven patterns are considered detectable). The tool is integrated into ArgoUML and is claimed to be extensible and customizable. Tsantalis et al. [15] have built an automatic design pattern detector based on a similarity scoring algorithm. They use a matrix format to capture the essence of each GOF pattern, and by converting the class diagram of the given system into a set of matrices, find pattern matches in the design.

In the area of model quality assessment, Breu and Chimiak-Opoka [16] have introduced a framework for quality assurance of models based on the concepts of Queries, Checks, and Views. Liu et al. [17] have introduced a classification for design inconsistencies, and then they have developed an expert system for detecting the inconsistencies in a given UML design. The system is able to give advice to the designer and fix the problems automatically.

The Epsilon Wizard Language (EWL), introduced by Kolovos et al. [18], is similar to OCL but enriched with model modification capabilities that enables the designer to write wizards for finding and fixing problems in UML models. Each wizard consists of three parts: title, guard, and body. If the guard is true, the title is displayed and the body is executed.

7 Conclusion

To verify the application of a pattern language for a domain, e.g., *PofEAA*, one should check the structure of each pattern that is used in the design model. Then, the dependencies between used patterns and the layering of patterns should be investigated. And finally, the design should be checked from the semantic point of view to find any conflict that can be caught between the choice of patterns and the context information, e.g., the tooling environment, the complexity of the domain, and the experience of the designers. These are the duties of three main modules of the PLV process that is proposed in this paper. Furthermore, the process is enriched with a Pattern Advisor which helps the designer in finding the roots of the problems and, if possible, provides automatic repair for the detected problems.

The PLV process supposes that we have already defined a UML profile for the underlying pattern language. The profile definition is a perfect solution for defining a DSL such as *PofEAA*. The stereotypes of the profile facilitate the detection of patterns and many of the pattern criteria, especially the structural and syntactic ones, can be checked via the constraints of each stereotype. However, the profile per se is not sufficient for the pattern language verification task since checking the criteria that need context information, e.g., semantic rules, are out of the scope of profile.

To evaluate the idea of PLV and its applicability and usefulness in current modeling tools, we did experiments with the ArgoUML modeling tool. We observed that the PLV process is able to be integrated in ArgoUML by writing Java code, and it helps designer in detecting problems early in the design process. However, hard coding the process into the tool is not a convenient way of tool extension and impedes the scalability of the process.

As part of our future work, we plan to extend the ideas and experiences found in this work and define a general framework for pattern language verification. For the experimental part of the current work, we need to extract more rules from *PofEAA* and embed them into the PLV modules; we should consider dynamic models too; also we should improve the Pattern Advisor to repair more problems automatically and be able to guide the designer for selecting the right pattern. Finally, we aim to validate the ideas by asking undergraduate students to use the tool and see if the tool can help them understand how far they are from a sound design, and how much progress they have made in fixing the problems.

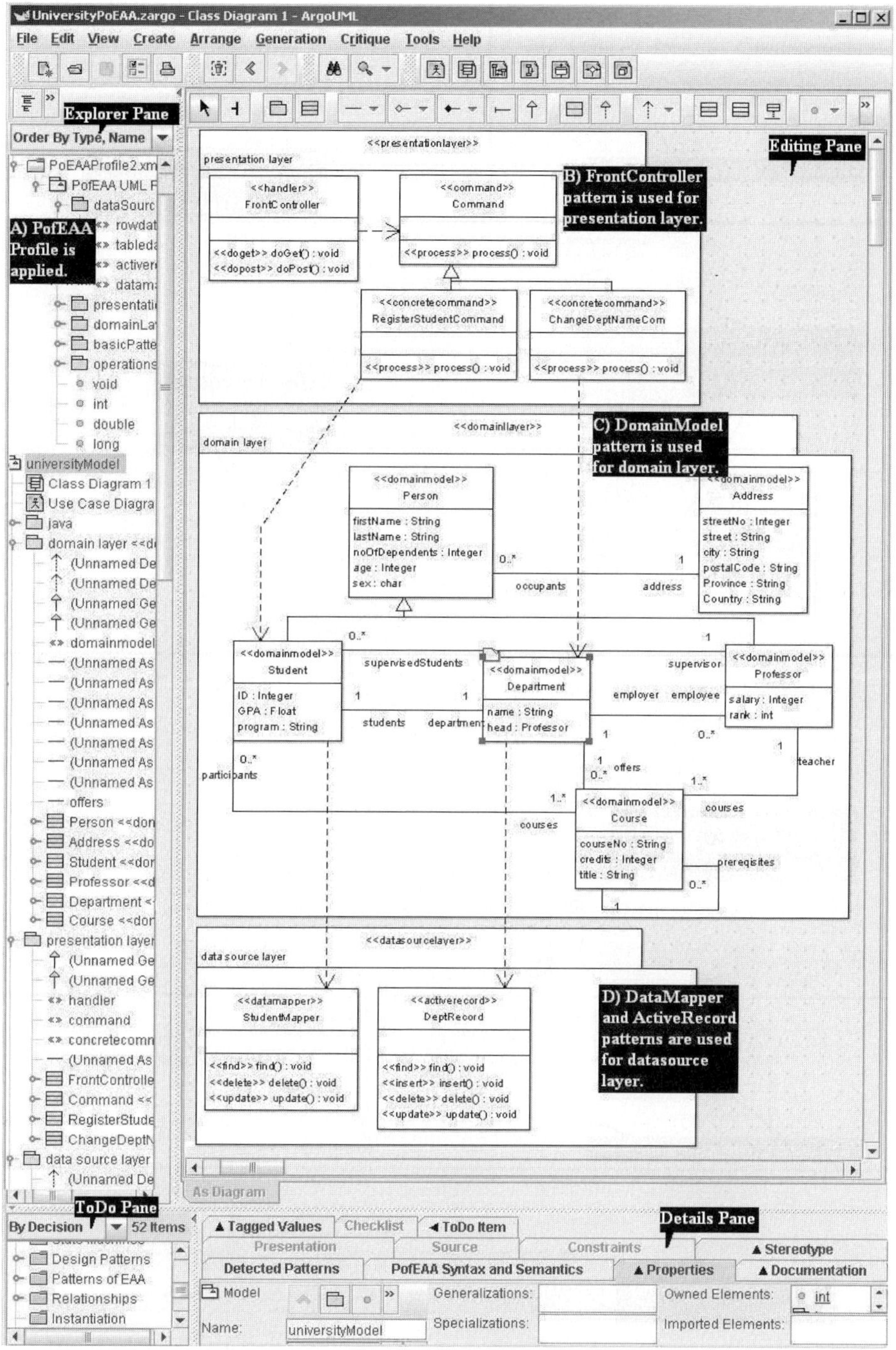

Fig. 4. Designing a Student Registration System in ArgoUML using *PofEAA*

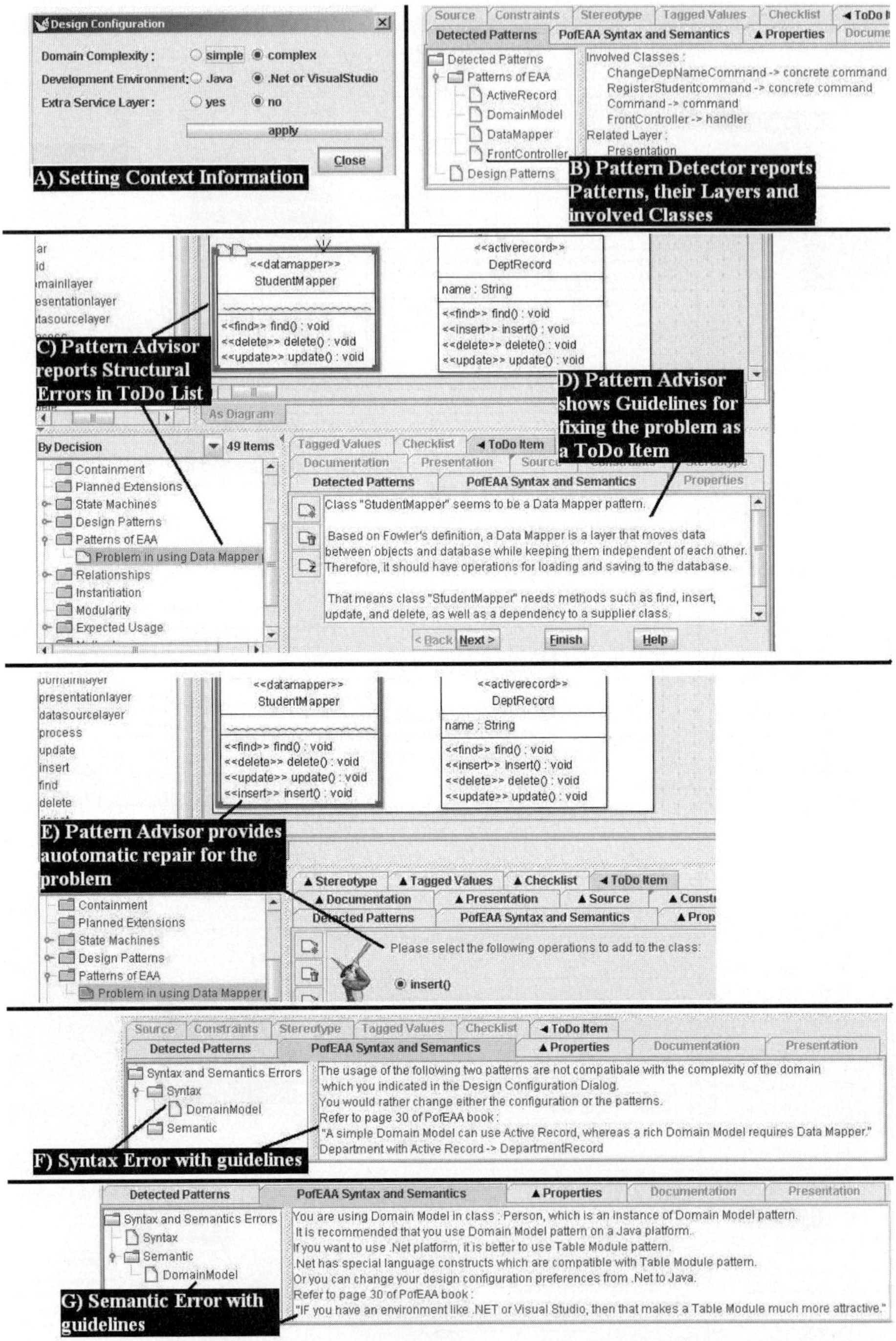

Fig. 5. Partial Screenshots of ArgoUML Showing how PLV is Verifying *PofEAA* Pattern Language in Designing a Student Registration System

References

1. Bézivin, J.: Model driven engineering: An emerging technical space. In: Lämmel, R., Saraiva, J., Visser, J. (eds.) GTTSE 2005. LNCS, vol. 4143, pp. 36–64. Springer, Heidelberg (2006)
2. Fowler, M.: Patterns of Enterprise Application Architecture, 1st edn. Addison-Wesley, Reading (2002)
3. Tigris.org: Argouml official web site (Retrieved on May 20, 2008), `http://argouml.tigris.org/`
4. Gamma, E., Helm, R., Johnson, R., Vlissides, J.: Design Patterns: Elements of Reusable Object-Oriented Software. Addison-Wesley, Boston (1995)
5. Alexander, C., et al.: A Pattern Language: Towns, Buildings, Construction. Oxford University Press, Oxford (1977)
6. Hillside.net: Patterns web site (Retrieved on May 20, 2008), `http://hillside.net/`
7. Schmidt, D.C., Fayad, M., Johnson, R.E.: Software patterns. Commun. ACM 39, 37–39 (1996)
8. Fowler, M.: Writing software patterns (2006), `http://www.martinfowler.com/articles.html`
9. Berczuk, S.: Finding solutions through pattern languages. Computer 27, 75–76 (1994)
10. Aho, A.V., Sethi, R., Ullman, J.D.: Compilers: principles, techniques, and tools. Boston. Addison-Wesley Longman Publishing Co., Boston (1986)
11. OMG: Unified Modeling Language: Specification, v1.4. OMG document formal/01-09-67 (2001)
12. Zamani, B., Butler, G., Kayhani, S.: Tool support for pattern selection and use. In: Second International Workshop on Software Quality and Maintainability, CSMR 2008 conference, ENTCS 2008, Athens, Greece (to appear, 2008)
13. Zamani, B., Butler, G.: Critiquing the application of pattern languages on uml models. In: Workshop on Quality in Modeling, MODELS 2007 Conference, Nashville, TN, USA, pp. 18–35 (2007)
14. Bergenti, F., Poggi, A.: Improving uml designs using automatic design pattern detection. In: 12th International Conference on Software Engineering and Knowledge Engineering (SEKE), pp. 336–343 (2000)
15. Tsantalis, N., Chatzigeorgiou, A., Stephanides, G., Halkidis, S.T.: Design pattern detection using similarity scoring. IEEE Trans. Software Eng. 32, 896–909 (2006)
16. Breu, R., Chimiak-Opoka, J.: Towards systematic model assessment. In: Akoka, J., Liddle, S.W., Song, I.-Y., Bertolotto, M., Comyn-Wattiau, I., van den Heuvel, W.-J., Kolp, M., Trujillo, J., Kop, C., Mayr, H.C. (eds.) ER Workshops 2005. LNCS, vol. 3770, pp. 398–409. Springer, Heidelberg (2005)
17. Liu, W., Easterbrook, S., Mylopoulos, J.: Rule-based detection of inconsistency in uml models. In: Workshop on Consistency Problems in UML-Based Software Development, Dresden, Germany, pp. 106–123 (2002)
18. Kolovos, D.S., Paige, R.F., Polack, F.A., Rose, L.M.: Update transformations in the small with the epsilon wizard language. Journal of Object Technology (JOT), Special Issue for TOOLS Europe 6, 53–69 (2007)

Automatically Generating Behavioral Models of Adaptive Systems to Address Uncertainty*

Heather J. Goldsby and Betty H.C. Cheng

Department of Computer Science and Engineering
Michigan State University, 3115 Engineering Building
East Lansing, Michigan 48824 USA
{hjg,chengb}@cse.msu.edu

Abstract. Increasingly, high-assurance applications rely on dynamically adaptive systems (DASs) to respond to environmental changes, while satisfying functional requirements and non-functional preferences. Examples include critical infrastructure protection and transportation systems. A DAS comprises a collection of (non-adaptive) target systems (represented as UML models) and a set of adaptations that realize transitions among target systems. Two sources of uncertainty inherent to DASs are: (1) predicting the future execution environment, and (2) using functional and non-functional trade-offs to respond to the changing environment. To address this uncertainty, we are inspired by living organisms that are astonishingly adept at adapting to changing environmental conditions using evolution. In this paper, we describe a digital evolution-based approach to generating models that represent possible target systems suitable for different environmental conditions, enabling the developer to identify the functional and non-functional trade-offs between the models, and then assisting the developer in selecting target systems for the DAS.

1 Introduction

Increasingly, high-assurance applications rely on *dynamically adaptive systems* (DASs) to react and respond to environmental changes, while continuing to meet functional requirements and make non-functional trade-offs. Examples include critical infrastructure protection and transportation systems. In an effort to promote separation of concerns, we consider a DAS to comprise a collection of (non-adaptive) *target systems* and a set of adaptations that realize transitions among target systems in response to environmental changes. We use the term *domain* to refer to a specific set of environmental conditions to be handled by a given target system (e.g., noisy network, sensor failure, and low battery could all be true for one domain). *Model-driven engineering*, which successively refines

* This work has been supported in part by NSF grants EIA-0000433, CNS-0551622, CCF-0541131, IIP-0700329, CCF-0750787, Department of the Navy, Office of Naval Research under Grant No. N00014-01-1-0744, Siemens Corporate Research, and a Quality Fund Program grant from Michigan State University.

K. Czarnecki et al. (Eds.): MoDELS 2008, LNCS 5301, pp. 568–583, 2008.

models from analysis to design and then automatically generates code [1], can be leveraged to support rigorous development of a DAS by modeling each of the target systems as a UML model (i.e., a class diagram and a *behavioral model* comprising a set of interacting state diagrams) and adaptations as transitions among them.[1] There are two key sources of uncertainty inherent to applications warranting adaptation: (1) predicting the future execution environment, and (2) using the trade-offs in non-functional characteristics and functional behavior to respond to the changing environmental conditions. To address these uncertainty issues, we can learn from nature. Living organisms are astonishingly adept at adapting to changing environmental conditions using evolution. In this paper, we harness the power of evolution [2] to automatically *generate* a suite of behavioral models that represent possible target systems suitable for a variety of combinations of environmental conditions not explicitly specified by the developer. We then automatically *identify* the non-functional characteristics and *latent functional properties* ("corner properties" or implicit, not required behavior) of the models [3], thereby assisting the developer in identifying trade-offs between the models in order to *select* the models to use as target systems.

Several architecture-based modeling approaches (e.g., [4, 5, 6]) capture the functional properties and non-functional characteristics of a DAS in architecture models that are used at run time to adapt the system, e.g., by adding, removing, or swapping a component. Although these approaches use a DAS to switch between different system configurations that have differing functional properties and non-functional characteristics, these system configurations must be modeled manually and do not support code generation. Additionally, several approaches manage imprecision during software development by having the developer manually create models that represent alternative interpretations of requirements (e.g., [7]) or by using fuzzy logic to represent requirements [8]. Lastly, several approaches are able to synthesize behavioral models from scenarios (e.g., [9, 10, 11]) and/or from formally specified properties (e.g., [11, 12]). Because these approaches were designed for non-adaptive systems, they do not explicitly address changing execution environments and do not assist the developer in making functional and non-functional trade-offs.

This paper introduces an approach to MDE for a DAS that explicitly address unpredictable execution environments and supports trade-off analysis to address the changing environmental conditions. First, in order to address the unknown execution environment, we automatically generate a suite of models, where each model satisfies the overall functional invariant, but has different functional and non-functional behavior that makes it more suitable for a potentially unique domain that was not explicitly specified. Next, to assist the developer in distinguishing the generated solutions and making informed trade-offs, we provide an automated means to explicitly identify the non-functional characteristics and latent behavior of the generated models. For example, our approach can be used to discover that one model is more fault-tolerant and energy efficient, whereas,

[1] Because UML is the *de facto* standard for object-oriented modeling languages, generating UML models facilitates their review and use by the MDE community.

another is more secure and resource intensive. The developer then selects the set of generated models to use as target systems for the DAS.

We use digital evolution-based techniques to support this process by generating a suite of models that represent possible target systems. *Digital evolution* [13] is a branch of evolutionary computation in which a population of self-replicating computer programs (i.e., digital *organisms*) exists in a user-defined computational environment and is subject to mutations and natural selection. To generate models, we constructed AVIDA-MDE (AVIDA for Model Driven Engineering),[2] which enables digital organisms to generate UML models that represent target system behavior. Mutations produce organisms that generate different behavioral models. Natural selection gives rise to a population of organisms that generate behavioral models that increasingly satisfy the functional system invariants with different behavioral characteristics that make it better suited for handling a particular domain.

We illustrate our approach by applying it to GridStix, an adaptive flood warning system [14]. The remainder of the paper is organized as follows. Section 2 presents relevant background information. Then Section 3 introduces GridStix as our running example and presents our approach. Section 4 describes AVIDA-MDE in detail. Section 5 describes results from applying AVIDA-MDE to GridStix. Section 6 discusses related work. Finally, in Section 7, we present conclusions and discuss future work.

2 AVIDA

AVIDA [13] is an evolutionary computation platform in which self-replicating digital organisms evolve in a fashion with more parallels to natural evolution than other forms of evolutionary computation (e.g., genetic algorithms and genetic programming). Specifically, whereas other evolutionary computation approaches, such as the genetic algorithm and genetic programming, evaluate each individual in the population and explicitly select individuals to move to the next generation, the evolution of digital organisms is more open-ended. The organisms are asynchronously evaluated; if an organism exhibits desirable behavior, then the relative amount of resources that the organism receives is increased. Because the evaluation is not used to explicitly select organisms to survive, poorly performing organisms may continue to exist in the population and could eventually produce a novel solution. Until recently, AVIDA has been used primarily to study biological evolution [13].

Figure 1 depicts an AVIDA population and the structure of an individual organism. Each digital organism comprises a circular list of instructions (its *genome*) that is executed atop its virtual CPU. The AVIDA instruction set is designed so that random mutations will always yield a syntactically correct program, albeit one that may not perform any meaningful computation. An AVIDA environment comprises a number of *cells*, where a cell is a compartment in which an organism can live. Each cell can contain at most one organism, and the size

[2] AVIDA is a digital evolution platform used to study biological evolution [13].

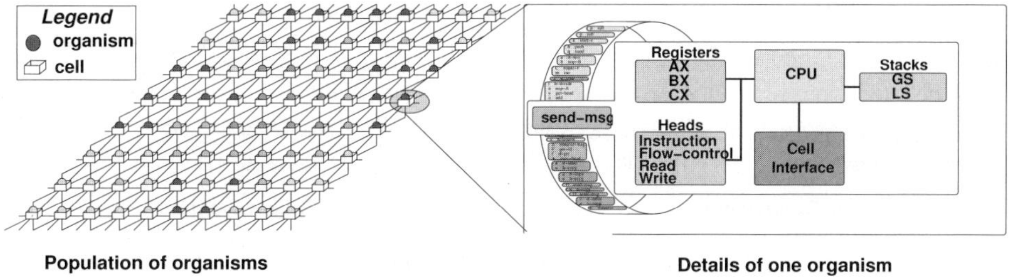

Fig. 1. Elements of AVIDA platform

of an AVIDA population is bounded by the number of cells in the environment. Organisms are *self-replicating*, that is, the genome itself must contain the instruction to create an offspring. Random mutations are introduced during replication. Mutation types include: replacing the instruction with a different one, inserting an additional, random instruction into the offspring's genome, and removing an instruction from the offspring's genome. For AVIDA-MDE, a mutation might change the label on a state diagram transition. When an organism replicates, a cell to contain the offspring is selected from the environment, and any previous inhabitant of the target cell is replaced (killed and overwritten) by the offspring.

Developers use *tasks* to describe desirable organism behavior. For example, we define a task that evaluates whether the generated behavioral models satisfy functional properties (e.g., invariant safety-critical properties). Performing a task increases an organism's *merit*, which determines how many instructions its virtual CPU is allowed to execute relative to the other organisms in the population. For example, an organism with a merit of 2 will, on average, execute twice as many instructions as an organism with a merit of 1. Because the population has a fixed maximum size, to have the best chance of surviving in the population, an organism must have as much merit as its peers. This competition for survival ensures that, over time, the population comprises organisms that increasingly satisfy more tasks.

3 Approach

To address uncertainty within the development of DASs, we propose a four step process with corresponding digital evolution-based tool support. We illustrate our approach using GridStix, an adaptive flood warning system [14].

3.1 Running Example: An Adaptive Flood Warning System

GridStix is an adaptive flood warning system deployed to monitor the River Ribble in Yorkshire, England [14]. Floods are an increasing and costly problem faced by the United Kingdom. The amount of damage caused by a flood is correlated with both the depth of the water and the amount of time between the flood

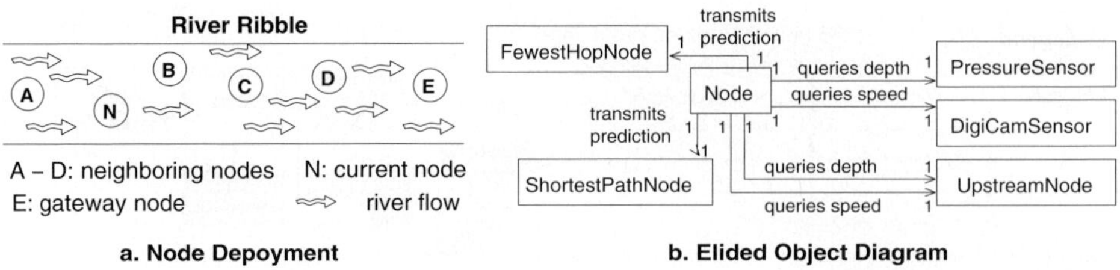

Fig. 2. GridStix Application

prediction and the flood. GridStix is a light-weight grid-computing flood monitoring system that comprises a set of nodes (e.g, A-E and N). Figure 2 provides an overview of GridStix and an elided portion of the corresponding object diagram. For this case study, we generate models that represent the target systems of one Node (N). A Node monitors the status of the river using its PressureSensor (depth sensor) and DigiCamSensor (digital camera river flow speed sensor). The node then queries an additional UpstreamNode (A) and uses the information from the UpstreamNode and the depth and speed it sensed to make a prediction. Lastly, the node transmits the prediction to a neighboring node (B, C, or D) that forwards it to a gateway node (E) that is connected to a modem and is responsible for sending the predictions off-site for additional processing. Three potentially conflicting non-functional objectives of a node are: (1) *energy efficiency* (EE) because a node has a limited power supply, (2) *fault-tolerance* (FT) because a node is deployed remotely, and (3) *prediction accuracy* (AC) because a node should avoid failures or false alarms. A node is able to adapt its behavior in a number of different ways that affect its non-functional attributes. In this case study, we enable a node to dynamically change its CPU speed, select a different routing algorithm to transmit information, e.g., shortest path (N→B→C→D→E) vs. fewest hop (N→D→E), and use a different physical network infrastructure to transmit predictions (e.g., bluetooth, wireless, GPRS – General Packet Radio Service, a packet-based wireless communication service).

3.2 Model-Driven Engineering for Dynamically Adaptive Systems

To provide context for our approach, we briefly describe the model-driven engineering process (depicted in Figure 3) for constructing a DAS [15]. At the Goal phase, the functional goals (e.g., Goal) of the dynamically adaptive system are identified [15]. At the Requirements phase, the domains (D_i and D_j), i.e., environmental conditions, and invariants (INV) of the DAS are identified. Additionally, adaptations among these domains are captured as dotted-line arrows. At the Design Models phase, design models (e.g., M_i, M_j, M_{ij}, M_{ji}) are constructed, where M_i and M_j represent designs for target systems, and M_{ij} and M_{ji} are design models capturing the behavior of the system during adaptation, where all of the models satisfy the invariants (INV). Each of the design models has a set of latent functional properties (e.g., LF_i, LF_j, LF_{ij}) and non-functional characteristics (e.g,. NF_i, NF_j, NF_{ij}) that make it more suitable for a specific domain. The

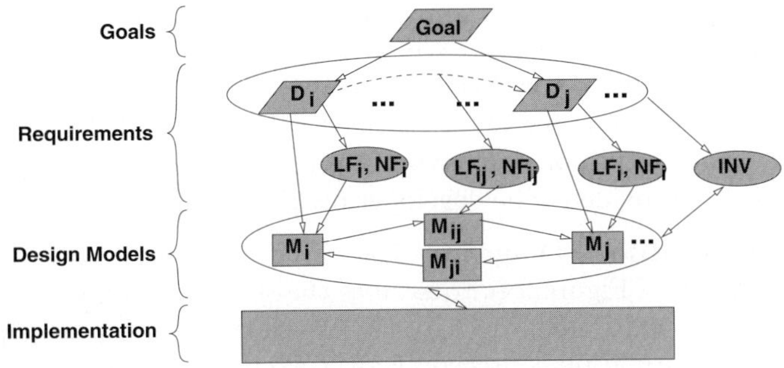

Fig. 3. MDE Process for a DAS

invariants and latent functional properties are specified as linear temporal logic (LTL) formulae and the non-functional characteristics are specified using a numeric value. At the Implementation phase, code can be automatically generated from the design models using code generators.

In this paper, we describe an approach to generating design models, M_i, of target systems. Each design model M_i should minimally satisfy INV, but it may also exhibit non-functional characteristics (NF_i) and latent functional properties (LF_i), all of which collectively make the behavior of M_i particularly well-suited to handle domain D_i. As a means to address uncertainty in execution environments, our approach also helps to discover additional domains based on viable, but not previously specified combinations of environmental conditions.

3.3 Process

Figure 4 provides a graphical depiction of our approach, where shading levels indicate different combinations of functional properties and non-functional characteristics. In the following, we provide additional detail about how the process addresses uncertainty within the development of DASs.

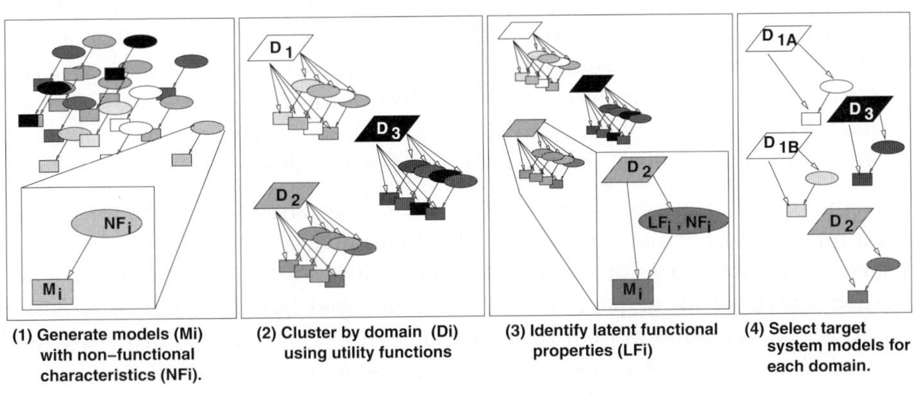

Fig. 4. Approach overview

Step 1: Generate models with non-functional characteristics. The model generation step addresses the uncertainty present in the unknown environment of the DAS. Specifically, AVIDA-MDE automatically generates a suite of models (e.g., M_i), each of which minimally satisfy the developer-specified invariants (INV), but may also contain additional behavior that makes it suitable for domains that were not explicitly provided. The developer provides the following inputs:

- **UML Class/Object Diagram:** The UML class/object diagram (e.g., a detailed version of Figure 2 b.) describes the structure of the system including the classes, attributes, operations, associations, and possible attribute values. This information is used by AVIDA-MDE to construct state diagram elements; for example, the class operations can be used as events and/or actions on the transitions, and boolean expressions involving the class attributes can express guards for the transitions.
- **UML State Diagrams:** For each class/object, the developer may optionally provide a state diagram describing existing behavior. In general, AVIDA-MDE can be used to generate new state diagrams or extend existing state diagrams [16].
- **Invariants:** Invariant functional properties (INV), specified in LTL, describe the desired behavior of the generated models. For example, a natural language representation of an LTL GridStix functional property [17] is *"Globally, it is always the case that if a node makes a prediction, then eventually the node will transmit the prediction to one of its neighbors."*
- **Scenarios:** Scenarios describe the possibilities for target system behavior. To account for the uncertainty in the execution environment, the developer specifies a set of *required functional scenarios* that must be supported by the generated models. Additionally, the developer specifies a set of *non-functional based scenarios*, where each one of the non-functional based scenarios specifies a different way to achieve the same functional objective (i.e., send prediction) with differing non-functional characteristics (i.e., send prediction using GPRS). One scenario from the non-functional based scenarios set must be supported by a generated model. For example, Figure 5 depicts a set of two non-functional based scenarios (**1, 2**) and one required scenario (**3**) for the GridStix system. The two non-functional based scenarios (**1, 2**) both set the CPU speed and query the PressureSensor. However, each scenario sets the CPU speed to different values and thus affects both energy efficiency (i.e., running slower conserves battery power) and accuracy (i.e., running faster is more accurate). The required scenario (**3**) probes the DigiCamSensor.

At a high level, the use of non-functional based scenarios enable AVIDA-MDE to automatically generate innovative behavioral models that address previously unspecified combinations of environmental conditions by integrating the behavior represented by all or parts of the non-functional based scenarios, required scenarios, and some additional behavior in such a way that the invariants are satisfied. Additionally, a model's potentially unique non-functional characteristics are calculated based on the non-functional based scenarios it supports and

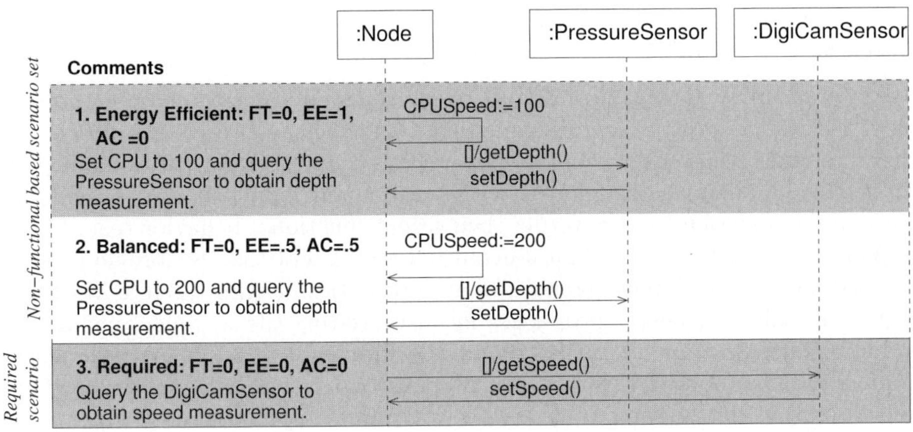

Fig. 5. GridStix Scenario Diagrams

also the number of states and transitions it uses. If Avida-MDE is unable to successfully generate any behavioral models, then this may indicate an inconsistency among the information provided by the developer.

Step 2: Cluster by domain using utility functions. To assist the developer in leveraging non-functional trade-offs between the models to address changing environmental conditions, we provide an automated means to cluster the generated models by a high-level description of the domains provided by the developer. Moreover, our key insight is that for each known high-level domain, a developer has a set of non-functional preferences that reflect their understanding of the domain's environmental conditions and can be used to identify a *domain model set*, a set of models whose non-functional characteristics make it suitable for a domain. To select models for a domain model set, we use a similar approach to that used by the Rainbow framework [18]. Specifically, we capture the developer's non-functional preferences for a given domain using a utility formula. The domain model set for a given domain comprises a set of models that maximize the utility function, but do so using different trade-offs between non-functional characteristics.

For example, the GridStix developers previously identified three high-level domains [14]: (1) normal conditions, (2) increased flow, and (3) flood. For the normal conditions, because the river is calm and a flood is unlikely, energy efficiency may be more important than fault-tolerance or accuracy, as captured by the following utility formula: $0.6*\mathsf{EE} + 0.2*\ \mathsf{FT} + 0.2*\ \mathsf{AC}$. Similarly, utility formulae are specified for the increased flow and flood domains. These utility formulae are used to cluster the generated models by domain. Models whose utility function evaluation are below a developer-specified and application-specific threshold do not reflect useful behavior, and hence are not an element of any domain model set and are therefore discarded. The coloring in Figure 4 indicates the non-functional characteristic differences between the models; as such, the models with light coloring are clustered in domain model set D_1, the models with moderate coloring are clustered for domain D_2, and the models with dark coloring are clustered for domain D_3.

Step 3: Identify latent functional properties. Within a domain model set, all of the models satisfy the invariants (INV), and their respective non-functional characteristics (NF_i) satisfy the developer's utility function for the domain (D_i). To further distinguish the models within a domain model set, we provide an automated approach to discovering their latent functional behavior (e.g., LF_i).

AVIDA-MARPLE [3] is a digital-evolution based tool that we previously developed to discover latent temporal logic properties. Within AVIDA-MARPLE, digital organisms generate properties by instantiating the five most commonly occurring specification patterns [19] in the form of LTL. The pattern placeholders are instantiated with boolean propositions created using class attribute and operation information from the class diagram (specified also as an input to AVIDA-MDE). During the AVIDA-MARPLE evolutionary process, organism mutations produce different LTL properties that may be satisfied by the UML model. Natural selection gives rise to a population of organisms that produce increasingly more relevant properties, where *relevancy* can refer to a type of property or the use of a specific attribute or operation. For the GridStix case study, we considered stronger properties more relevant because they revealed more information about the model; here, stronger means those properties that made stronger claims, such as universality, or those that contained conjunctive expressions. In essence, AVIDA-MARPLE discovers latent functional properties that developers may not otherwise specify or even consider. These latent functional properties may uncover unwanted behavior that could either be used to refine the requirements for generation or disqualify a model from representing a target system. For easier readability, these latent functional properties are presented to the developer in natural language [17].

Step 4: Select target system models for each domain. Using the non-functional characteristics and the latent functional properties, the developer identifies one or more models within each domain model set to use as a target system. This step has three parts. First, the developer eliminates models that have unwanted latent functional behavior (LF_i).[3] Second, the developer infers *sub-domains*, a fine-grained set of environmental conditions that were not explicitly specified by the developer, from the generated models. These sub-domains are indicated by clusters of models that use similar non-functional characteristics to satisfy the utility function of a domain model set. For example, within the Flood conditions domain, we identified two sub-domains that describe Node behavior when a neighboring node is submerged and when it is not submerged. Therefore, the identification of sub-domains addresses uncertainty in the execution environment by enabling the developer to identify combinations of environmental conditions that may not otherwise have been considered. In cases where there are no obvious sub-domains, then we consider that domain to be a *simple domain*.

[3] If all of the models have unwanted latent functional properties, then the developer should return to Step 1 and refine the input specifications accordingly.

Third, the developer selects one model within each simple domain or sub-domain to use as a target system. These selected models can be incorporated into the model-driven engineering process for DASs as inspiration for a human-created model, manually modified and then used to generate code, or used to generated code directly.

4 Using Digital Evolution to Generate Models

Avida-MDE enables developers to generate innovative behavioral models for target systems. Specifically, mutations produce behavioral models that developers might not otherwise discover, while natural selection pressures organisms to generate models that meet developer requirements, i.e., invariants. This blend of innovation and requirements satisfaction is especially pertinent for generating target systems that must respond to varying environmental conditions in a resilient and robust fashion. In previous work [16], we developed a preliminary version of Avida-MDE to generate behavioral models, but did not address non-functional model characteristics or look for latent properties to differentiate models. In the following, we describe the three major ways in which we extended the Avida platform to create Avida-MDE.

Configuration. Avida-MDE accepts the four configuration inputs specified by the developer, i.e., UML class diagram, UML state diagrams, invariants (in LTL), and scenarios (in a sequence diagram). These inputs serve three purposes: (1) The invariants and scenarios are requirements for the behavioral models. (2) The UML state diagrams describe existing behavior to be extended through generation. (3) The UML class diagram and scenario diagram provide the alphabet from which state diagram transitions are created. Specifically, for each scenario, the messages form a list of transition labels. In addition, for each class, a list of triggers (operations), a list of guards (expressions built using attributes), and a list of actions (the operations of classes related to it via associations) are extracted. Because the Avida-MDE alphabet includes triggers, guards, and actions (described by the class diagram), organisms are able to generate additional and potentially more interesting viable transitions, not otherwise considered by the developer.

New Instructions. To enable organisms to manipulate state diagrams, we developed a new set of Avida instructions that are reusable across all DAS applications specified by the configuration step. These instructions, when mutated into an organism's genome, are used to (1) *select* alphabet elements to use to create a transition, (2) *construct* a transition, and (3) *construct* a loop. Specifically, the selection instructions use different strategies for *selecting* alphabet elements to use to create a transition. The internal representation of an organism's alphabet is lists of states, transition labels, triggers, guards, and actions. Each list has an index that initially points to the first list element. (The list of states has two indices – one for the origin state and one for the destination state.) An organism selects an alphabet element by having the list index point to it. There are two transition construction instructions, where the first adds the transition described by the current origin state, destination state, and transition label, and the second, adds the transition described by the current origin state, destination state, trigger, guard, and action. When the parent organism replicates, its genome is mutated by randomly adding, deleting, and inserting these instructions at a pre-defined probability. Thus, it is likely that the model generated by an offspring is not the same as the model generated by its parent.

New Tasks. We defined a set of tasks to reward AVIDA organisms for generating a behavioral model that meets the developer-specified invariants and scenarios. Prior to replication, an organism and the model that it generates are evaluated by the tasks. An organism that performs these tasks will have a better chance of survival and will eventually dominate the population.

The scenario task (checkScenario) rewards an organism for generating a model that supports key scenarios defined by the developer. For each scenario, the developer must specify the messages between objects and may optionally include a start state for each object and specify whether the scenario should iterate. The reward for a required scenario is the percentage of the execution path supported by the state diagrams. Additionally, the reward for a non-functional based scenarios set is the maximum percentage of coverage of a given scenario among the scenarios used in the set. For example, using the non-functional based scenarios set in Figure 5, if an organism generated a behavioral model that supported 67% of the Energy Efficient scenario and 33% of the Balanced scenario, then the reward for this non-functional based scenarios set would be 67% of the maximum reward value.

A property task (checkProperty) rewards organisms that generate state diagrams that adhere to a formally specified property. These tasks constrain the behavior of the interacting state diagrams. To enable AVIDA-MDE to determine if the generated state diagrams satisfy a stated property, we extended AVIDA to use external third party tools. Specifically, the checkSyntax task uses Hydra, an existing UML formalization engine [20], to translate a UML model into Promela, the specification language for the model checker Spin [21]. Next, the checkWitness task uses Spin to verify that at least one execution path (i.e., a witness trace) through the Promela model satisfies the functional property specified by the developer in Linear Temporal Logic (LTL). Lastly, if the checkWitness for a given property passes, then the checkProperty task uses Spin to verify that the Promela specification satisfies the same functional property. Additional details on the external and previously developed analysis process can be found in [20].

5 Case Study

In this section, we provide further details about applying our approach to GridStix and discuss our results. The objective of our case study is to generate target systems that describe the behavior of the Node object as it interacts with its sensors, queries an upstream node, makes a prediction regarding the state of the river, and transmits information to a neighboring node.

Step 1: Generate models with non-functional characteristics. We provide the following information to use Avida-MDE to generate target systems for GridStix:

- **A detailed version of the UML Object diagram** (in Figure 2 b.); including operations, attributes, and attribute values to be used for the organism alphabet.
- **Functional invariant(s):** *"Globally, it is always the case that if a node makes a prediction, then eventually this prediction is transmitted to either its shortest path neighbor or its fewest hop neighbor."* This invariant, specified in LTL [17], is checked by the checkSyntax, checkWitness, and checkProperty tasks.
- **State diagrams** describe the behavior of all of the classes except Node. Because our case study focuses on the behavior of Node, these other state diagrams will not be extended by Avida-MDE.
- **Three required functional scenarios** describe: (1) querying the Node's DigiCam to monitor river speed, (2) querying the depth sensed by the UpstreamNode, and (3) querying the speed sensed by the UpstreamNode. Additionally, we specified two sets of non-functional based scenarios. The first set provides three computational speed alternatives (two of which are depicted in Figure 5). The second set provides six alternative ways to send data. The messages defined by these scenarios were used as a portion of the organism alphabet. Additionally, a checkScenario task was used to reward organisms for supporting the scenarios.

Using these inputs, forty Avida-MDE experiments were run in parallel to account for the stochastic nature of the evolutionary process. All of the experiments ran for 10 hours; we started the experiments at the end of a work day and the results were available by the beginning of the next work day. In total, 779 unique models were generated. For a given model, the value of a non-functional characteristic (i.e., energy efficient (EE), fault-tolerant (FT), or accuracy (AC)) is calculated by summing the values of that characteristic across the scenarios that it supports. For example, if a model supported scenarios **1** and **3** in Figure 5, then the value of EE would be 1.

Step 2: Cluster by domain using utility functions. Next, to manage the non-functional trade-offs, we partitioned the generated models into three domain model sets, one for each of the three high-level domains from the developer (i.e., normal conditions, increased flow, and flood). Specifically, we first specified a utility function for each domain:

- Normal conditions **utility** $= 0.6*$EE $+ 0.2*$FT $+ 0.2*$AC. We prefer that the nodes are energy efficient to preserve battery life.
- Increased flow **utility** $= 0.33*$EE $+ 0.34*$FT $+ 0.33*$AC. We prefer that the nodes are a balance of fault-tolerant, accurate, and energy efficient.
- Flood utility $= 0.2*$EE $+ 0.0*$FT $+ 0.8*$AC. We prefer that the nodes are accurate because the conditions are critical.

We then selected models that maximize the respective utility formula of each domain. Specifically, we selected 3 models from the normal conditions domain model set, 2 models from the increased flow conditions domain model set, and 3 models from the flood conditions domain model set. These models will be further evaluated to identify latent properties and possible sub-domains.

Step 3: Identify latent functional properties. Next, we used AVIDA-MARPLE to identify the latent functional behavior of the 8 selected models. For example, two of the discovered latent properties for one of the models in the normal conditions domain model set are:

1. *Globally, it is always the case that if Node.CPUSpeed < 100 holds, then FewestHopNode.received == 0 eventually holds.* (The shortest hop node always receives the prediction.)
2. *Globally, it is always the case that if Node.CPUSpeed > 200 holds, then FewestHopNode.received == 1 eventually holds.* (When the CPU speed is over 200, the fewest hop node receives the prediction.)

These properties together specify that the Node always sends its prediction to the ShortestPathNode, but also sends its prediction to the FewestHopNode if the CPUSpeed is greater than 200. This behavior implies that the Node is generally energy efficient (sending to the ShortestPathNode), but also has some innate fault-tolerance that is achieved by sending to the FewestHopNode only when the CPU speed is running quickly.

Step 4: Select target system models for each domain. Using the latent functional behavior identified as part of Step 3, we noted that 2 of the 8 models selected from the three domain model sets contained unwanted latent behavior. Thus, we eliminated them. The two models in the Increased Flow domain model set achieved the same utility value using similar non-functional characteristics; neither had unwanted latent behavior. To minimize model complexity, we selected the model with the fewest transitions. We repeated this evaluation process for the Flood domain model set, which also had two similar models. For the normal conditions domain model set, the two generated models satisfied their utility function similarly, but with differing non-functional characteristics. Specifically, based on the utility function parameters, we identified two sub-domains, where one sub-domain was more energy efficient and the other sub-domain was more fault-tolerant. The latent functional properties discovered for these two models reaffirmed our identification of sub-domains and explained why the models had differing non-functional characteristics. For example, the latent functional properties for the normal conditions - fault-tolerant sub-domain were previously described and indicate that it transmits predictions to both its shortest path and its fewest hop neighbor. Thus far, we have focused on functional and non-functional properties to illustrate the differences between the models generated by AVIDA-MDE to satisfy the same invariant requirements. These differences are, in fact, due to both the different transitions (i.e., guards, triggers, actions) that get generated for each diagram, as well as the different topological structures of the diagrams (e.g., number of states, number of

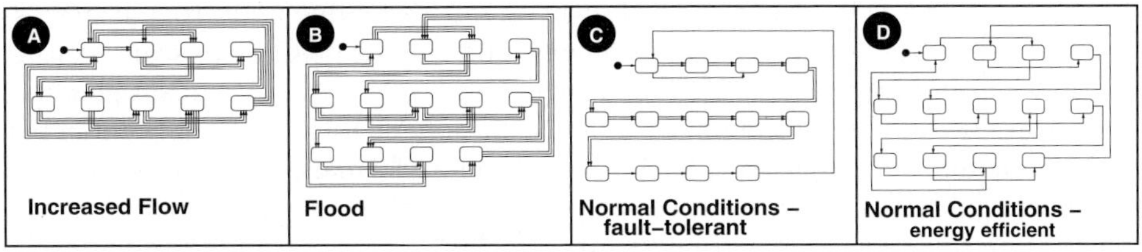

Fig. 6. Generated Target Systems

transitions, the connectivity between states, etc.). For example, Figure 6 highlights the amount of variation present in our generation process by depicting the varying topologies of the four generated models selected as target systems

6 Related Work

While there has been significant progress in synthesizing state diagrams from scenarios and/or properties, to the best of our knowledge, our approach is the only one to generate multiple solutions (in the form of models) for interacting objects, while considering functional properties and non-functional characteristics. In general, scenario-based synthesis techniques [9, 10, 11] accept a set of scenarios (i.e., a sequence diagrams) as input and produce a set of communicating state diagrams as output. The sequence diagram messages form the alphabet. Property synthesis techniques establish a one-to-one mapping between a formally specified property and a state diagram [12], where each state diagram represents all possible behaviors that satisfy the property.

Our approach addresses the uncertainty present in the development of DASs and thus differs from the synthesis approaches in three key ways: First, in addition to the alphabet formed by the scenario messages, Avida-MDE also uses an evolving alphabet that is created by combining the triggers, guards, and actions inferred from the class diagram (described in Section 4). One ramification of this alphabet is that Avida-MDE generates different transitions than those generated from the alphabets of other approaches. As a result, the generated behavioral model has the potential to be less intuitive and perhaps offer more resiliency than those created with traditional techniques. Second, in contrast to the synthesis approaches, Avida-MDE generates a suite of behavioral models that all satisfy the functional invariant, but have differing latent functional properties and non-functional characteristics. Third, to assist the developer in performing trade-off analysis, our approach clusters the models by non-functional preferences for a domain, identifies the latent functional properties, and infers sub-domains that identify unspecified combinations of environmental conditions.

7 Discussion

In this paper, we have presented an approach to addressing environmental uncertainty with a digital-evolution based approach to generating models for the development of a DAS. Next, we reflect upon our technique and provide suggestions for using it as part of the development process. It is possible to scale AVIDA-MDE to larger applications by increasing the length of the organism genome, increasing the number of organisms in a population, or by increasing the number of experiments run in parallel. Additionally, the performance of AVIDA-MDE is dependent upon many factors including the size of the model, number of experiments run, duration of experiments, and available computational resources. To use our approach effectively, developers should focus on describing *what* the DAS should do, rather than *how* the DAS should achieve this behavior. This strategy enables AVIDA-MDE organisms to have the most flexibility to generate innovative models that comply with developer requirements. However, determining the appropriate level of detail for the developer-specified requirements is frequently an iterative process (as is the case with traditional development techniques). If AVIDA-MDE generates too few models, then the topology information as specified by the scenarios should be relaxed. However, if AVIDA-MARPLE discovers unwanted latent behavior common to all of the generated models, then the invariant and/or scenario requirements should be refined.

Numerous directions for future work are possible. One possibility is to explore how digital-evolution based techniques can be used to identify the *quiescent states*, or states within the target system from which the DAS can adapt safely [22]. A second possibility is to enable organisms to instantiate design patterns and thus potentially create more modular and extensible designs. Another possibility is to use AVIDA-MDE to generate the adaptation logic (e.g., M_{ij}, M_{ji}) that describes how the DAS transitions between target systems.

References

[1] Schmidt, D.C.: Model-Driven Engineering. IEEE Computer 39(2) (2006)

[2] McKinley, P., Cheng, B.H., Ofria, C., Knoester, D., Beckmann, B., Goldsby, H.: Harnessing digital evolution. IEEE Computer 41(1), 54–63 (2008)

[3] Goldsby, H.J., Cheng, B.H.C.: An automated approach to detecting unwanted latent behavior in models of high assurance systems. Technical report, Michigan State University (May 2008) (submitted for publication)

[4] Garlan, D., Cheng, S.W., Huang, A.C., Schmerl, B., Steenkiste, P.: Rainbow: Architecture-based self-adaptation with reusable infrastructure. Computer 37(10), 46–54 (2004)

[5] Gorlick, M.M., Razouk, R.R.: Using weaves for software construction and analysis. In: ICSE 1991: Proceedings of the 13th International Conference on Software Engineering, pp. 23–34. IEEE Computer Society Press, Los Alamitos (1991)

[6] Magee, J., Dulay, N., Eisenbach, S., Kramer, J.: Specifying Distributed Software Architectures. In: Schafer, W., Botella, P. (eds.) ESEC 1995. LNCS, vol. 989, pp. 137–153. Springer, Heidelberg (1995)

[7] Noppen, J., van den Broek, P., Aksit, M.: Software development with imperfect information. Soft Computing 12, 3–28 (2008)

[8] Yen, J., Lee, J.: Fuzzy logic as a basis for specifying imprecise requirements. In: Second IEEE International Conference on Fuzzy Systems (1993)

[9] Whittle, J., Jayaraman, P.K.: Generating hierarchical state machines from use case charts. In: 14th IEEE International Requirements Engineering Conference (RE 2006), Washington, DC, USA, pp. 16–25 (2006)

[10] Harel, D., Kugler, H., Pnueli, A.: Synthesis revisited: Generating statechart models from scenario-based requirements. In: Formal Methods in Software and Systems Modeling (2005)

[11] Uchitel, S., Brunet, G., Chechik, M.: Behaviour model synthesis from properties and scenarios. In: ICSE 2007: Proceedings of the 29th International Conference on Software Engineering, pp. 34–43 (2007)

[12] Jobstmann, B., Bloem, R.: Optimizations for LTL synthesis. In: FMCAD 2006: Proceedings of the Formal Methods in Computer Aided Design (2006)

[13] Ofria, C., Wilke, C.O.: Avida: A software platform for research in computational evolutionary biology. Journal of Artificial Life 10, 191–229, International Society of Artificial Life (ISAL) (2004)

[14] Hughes, D., Greenwood, P., Coulson, G., Blair, G., Pappenberger, F., Smith, P., Beven, K.: An intelligent and adaptable flood monitoring and warning system. In: Proceedings of the 5th UK E-Science All Hands Meeting (AHM) (2006)

[15] Zhang, J., Cheng, B.H.C.: Model-based development of dynamically adaptive software. In: ICSE 2006: Proceeding of the 28th International Conference on Software Engineering, pp. 371–380 (2006) (Best Paper Award)

[16] Goldsby, H.J., Cheng, B.H.C., McKinley, P.K., Knoester, D.B., Ofria, C.A.: Digital evolution of behavioral models for autonomic systems. In: Proceedings of the 5th International Conference on Autonomic Computing (ICAC 2008), Chicago, Illinois (June 2008) (Best Paper Award)

[17] Konrad, S., Cheng, B.H.C.: Facilitating the construction of specification pattern-based properties. In: Proceedings of the IEEE International Requirements Engineering Conference (RE 2005), Paris, France (August 2005)

[18] Cheng, S.W., Garlan, D., Schmerl, B.: Architecture-based self-adaptation in the presence of multiple objectives. In: ICSE 2006 Workshop on Software Engineering for Adaptive and Self-Managing Systems, Shanghai, China (May 2006)

[19] Dwyer, M.B., Avrunin, G.S., Corbett, J.C.: Patterns in property specifications for finite-state verification. In: Proceedings of the 21st International Conference on Software Engineering, pp. 411–420 (1999)

[20] McUmber, W.E., Cheng, B.H.C.: A general framework for formalizing UML with formal languages. In: Proceedings of the IEEE International Conference on Software Engineering (ICSE 2001), Toronto, Canada (May 2001)

[21] Holzmann, G.: The Spin Model Checker, Primer and Reference Manual. Addison-Wesley, Reading (2004)

[22] Zhang, J., Yang, Z., Cheng, B.H., McKinley, P.K.: Adding safeness to dynamic adaptation techniques. In: Proceedings of ICSE 2004 Workshop on Architecting Dependable Systems, Edinburgh, Scotland, UK (May 2004)

Autonomic Management Policy Specification: From UML to DSML*

Benoît Combemale, Laurent Broto, Xavier Crégut,
Michel Daydé, and Daniel Hagimont

Institut de Recherche en Informatique de Toulouse (UMR CNRS 5505)
Université de Toulouse, France
first_name.last_name@irit.fr

Abstract. Autonomic computing is recognized as one of the most promizing solutions to address the increasingly complex task of distributed environments' administration. In this context, many projects relied on software components and architectures to provide autonomic management frameworks. We designed such a component-based autonomic management framework, but observed that the interfaces of a component model are too low-level and difficult to use. Therefore, we introduced UML diagrams for the modeling of deployment and management policies. However, we had to adapt/twist the UML semantics in order to meet our requirements, which led us to define DSMLs. In this paper, we present our experience in designing the Tune system and its support for management policy specification, relying on UML diagrams and on DSMLs. We analyse these two approaches, pinpointing the benefits of DSMLs over UML.

1 Introduction

Today's computing environments are becoming increasingly sophisticated. They involve numerous complex software that cooperate in potentially large scale distributed environments. These software are developed with very heterogeneous programming models which rely on their own specific configuration facilities. Moreover, software environments integrate components from different providers with proprietary management interfaces. Therefore, the management[1] of these software (installation, configuration, repair, etc.) is a much complex task which consumes a lot of human ressources.

A very promising approach consists in implementing administration features as an autonomic software. Such a software can be used to deploy and configure applications in a distributed environment. It can also monitor the environment and react to events such as failures or overloads and reconfigure applications accordingly and autonomously. Many works in this area have relied on a component model to provide such an autonomic system support [1,2,3]. The basic idea is to encapsulate the managed elements (legacy software) in software components (called wrappers) and to administrate the environment as a component architecture. We designed and implemented such a component-based autonomic management system (called Tune) and used it for the management of complex legacy software infrastructures.

* This work is supported by the SCORWARE RNTL project (contract ANR-06-TLOG-017).

[1] We also use the term administration to refer to management operations.

K. Czarnecki et al. (Eds.): MoDELS 2008, LNCS 5301, pp. 584–599, 2008.

However, we rapidly observed that the interfaces of a component model are too low-level and difficult to use. This led us to explore the introduction of higher level formalisms for all the administration tasks (wrapping, configuration, deployment, reconfiguration). Our main motivation was to hide the details of the component model we rely on and to provide a more abstract and intuitive specification interface (such specifications are called *management policies*). We mainly relied on UML diagrams for the modeling of management policies, but as we were not experts in modeling languages and were more focussed on middleware issues, we made use of UML diagrams which are very pragmatic and close to our needs, and we had to adapt/twist the UML semantics in order to meet our requirements. This naturally led us to define Domain Specific Modeling Languages (DSMLs) and their associated metamodels.

In this paper, we report on this experience which consisted in three steps: (1) designing a component-based autonomic system, (2) introducing management policy specification formalisms based on UML diagram and (3) defining several DSMLs for policy specification. And we motivate the transition between each step.

The rest of the paper is structured as follows. Section 2 describes the design and implementation of Tune, which provides a framework for component-based autonomic administration. Section 3 presents our experience in providing UML diagram based support for management policy specification. The DSML support introduced for policy specification is presented in Section 4. After an overview of related works in Section 6, we overview the lessons learned from these experiments in Section 5 and we conclude in Section 7.

2 An Autonomic Management System

2.1 J2EE Use Case

The Java 2 Platform, Enterprise Edition (J2EE) defines a model for developing web applications [4] in a multi-tiered architecture. Such applications are typically composed of a web server (e.g. Apache), an application server (e.g. Tomcat) and a database server (e.g. MySQL). Upon an HTTP client request, either the request targets a static web document, in which case the web server directly returns that document to the client; or the request refers to a dynamically generated document, in which case the web server forwards that request to the application server. When the application server receives a request, it runs one or more software components (e.g. Servlets, EJBs) that query a database through a JDBC (*Java DataBase Connection*) driver. Finally, the resulting information is used to generate a web document that is returned to the web client.

In this context, the increasing number of Internet users has led to the need of highly scalable and highly available services. To face high loads and provide higher scalability of Internet services, a commonly used approach is the replication of servers in clusters. Such an approach (Figure 1, *legacy layer*) usually defines a particular software component in front of each set of replicated servers, which dynamically balances the load among the replicas. Here, different load balancing algorithms may be used, e.g. Random, Round-Robin, etc.

This example is characteristic of the management of a distributed software infrastructure where very heterogeneous servers are distributely deployed, configured and interconnected in order to provide a global service. The management of the whole infrastructure can be very complex and requires a lot of expertise. Many files have to be edited and configured consistently. Also, failures or load peaks (when the chosen degree of replication is too low) must be treated manually.

2.2 Component-Based Autonomic Computing

Component-based management aims at providing a uniform view of a software environment composed of different types of servers. Each managed server is encapsulated into a component and the software environment is abstracted as a component architecture. Therefore, deploying, configuring and reconfiguring the software environment is achieved by using the tools associated with the used component-based middleware.

The component model we used in Tune is the Fractal model [5]. A Fractal component is a runtime entity that is encapsulated and has one or several interfaces (access points to a component that supports a finite set of methods). The signatures of interface can be described by a standard Java interface declaration. Components can be assembled to form a component architecture by binding components interfaces (different types of bindings exists, including local bindings and distributed RMI-like bindings). An (XML based) Architecture Description Language (ADL) allows describing an architecture and an ADL launcher can be used to deploy such an architecture. Finally, Fractal provides a rich set of control interfaces for introspecting (observing) and reconfiguring a deployed architecture, i.e. controlling components' attributes and bindings.

Any software managed with Tune is wrapped into a Fractal component which interfaces its administration procedures. Therefore, the Fractal component model is used to implement a management layer (Figure 1) on top of the legacy layer (composed of the actual managed software). In the management layer, all components provide a management interface for the encapsulated software, and the corresponding implementation (the wrapper) is specific to each software (e.g. the Apache web server in the case of J2EE). Fractal's control interfaces allow managing the element's attributes and bindings with other elements, and the management interface of each component allows controlling its internal configuration state. Relying on this management layer, sophisticated administration programs can be implemented, without having to deal with complex, proprietary configuration interfaces (generally configuration files), which are hidden in the wrappers. Here, we distinguish two important roles: (1) the role of the management and control interfaces is to provide a means for configuring components and bindings between components. It includes methods for navigating in the component-based management layer or modifying it to implement reconfigurations. (2) the role of the wrappers is to reflect changes in the management layer onto the legacy layer. The implementation of a wrapper for a specific software may also have to navigate in the component management layer, to access key attributes of the components and generate legacy software configuration files[2].

[2] E.g. for configuring an Apache, we need to access attributes from both the Apache component and the Tomcat components it is bound with.

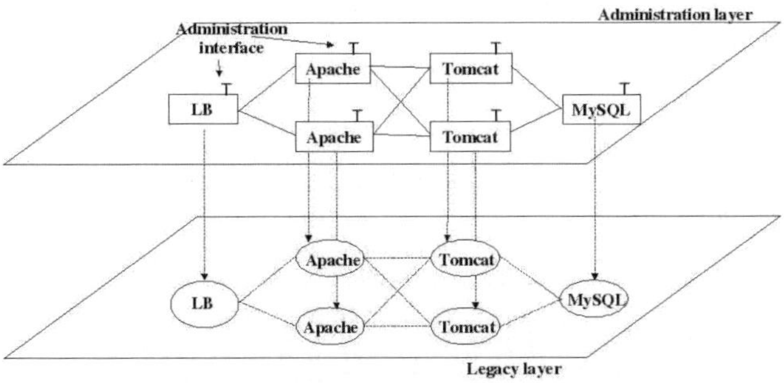

Fig. 1. Management layer for the J2EE application

2.3 Management Policy Specification

In a first prototype (Jade [2], a predecessor of Tune), the implementation of management policies was directly relying on the interfaces of the Fractal component model:

- A wrapper was implemented as a Fractal component, developed in Java, which main role is to reflect management/control operations onto the legacy software. For instance, if we consider the wrapper of the Apache software, the assignment of the port attribute of the wrapper is reflected in the *httpd.conf* file in which the port attribute is defined. Similarly, setting up a binding between an Apache wrapper and a Tomcat wrapper is reflected at the legacy layer in the *worker.properties* file.
- The description of a software architecture to be deployed was described in a Fractal ADL file. This ADL file describes in an XML syntax the set of components (wrappers) to instanciate (which will in turn deploy the associated legacy software components), their bindings and their configuration attributes.
- Reconfigurations were developed in Java, relying on Fractal APIs. These APIs allow invoking components' management interfaces or Fractal control interfaces for assigning components' attributes, adding/removing components and updating bindings between components.

Component-based autonomic computing has proved to be a very convenient approach. The experiments we conducted with this first prototype for managing J2EE infrastructures [2] (but also other distributed infrastructures such as Diet grid middleware [6]) validated this design choice. Figure 2 illustrates an experiment which consisted in automatically repairing (restarting) a failing Tomcat server (in the J2EE architecture of Figure 1). Initially, the load is balanced between the two replicas. When the failure occurs, all the load is addressed to the second replica. After repair, the load is again balanced between the two replicas.

3 UML-Based Autonomic Computing Policies Specification

As our system was used by external users (external to our group), we rapidly observed that the interfaces of a component model are too low-level and difficult to use. In order

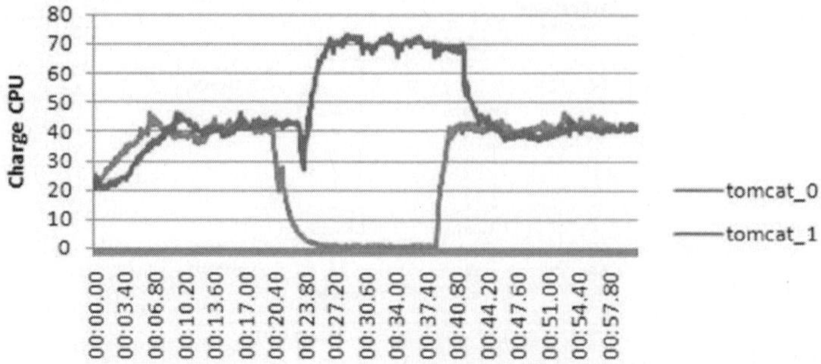

Fig. 2. Automatic restart of a Tomcat server on software fault

to implement wrappers (to encapsulate existing software), to describe deployed architectures and to implement reconfiguration programs, the administrator of the environment has to learn (yet) another framework, the Fractal component model in our case. More precisely, our previous experiments showed us that:

- Wrapping components is difficult to implement. The developper needs to have a good understanding of the component model we use (Fractal). Regarding wrapping, our approach is to introduce a Wrapping Description Language which is used to specify the behavior of wrappers. A WDL specification is interpreted by a generic wrapper Fractal component, the specification and the interpreter implementing an equivalent wrapper. Therefore, an administrator doesn't have to program any implementation of Fractal component.
- Architectures are not very easy to describe. ADLs are generally very verbose and still require a good understanding of the underlying component model. Moreover, if we consider large scale software infrastructure such as those deployed over a grid, describing an architecture composed of a thousand of servers requires an ADL description file of several thousands of lines. Our approach is to reuse UML formalisms for graphically describing architecture schemas. First, a UML based graphical description of such an architecture is much more intuitive than an ADL specification, as it doesn't require expertise of the underlying component model. Second, the introduced architecture schema is more abstract than the previous ADL specification, as it describes the general organisation of the application to deploy (types of software, interconnection pattern) in intension, instead of describing in extension all the software instances that may compose the architecture. This is particularly interesting for grid applications where thousands of servers have to be deployed.
- Autonomic managers (reconfiguration policies) are difficult to implement as they have to be programmed using the management and control interfaces of the management layer. This also requires a strong expertise regarding the used component model. Our approach is to reuse UML State Diagrams to define workflows of operations that have to be performed for reconfiguring the managed environment. One of the main advantage of this approach, besides simplicity, is that state diagrams

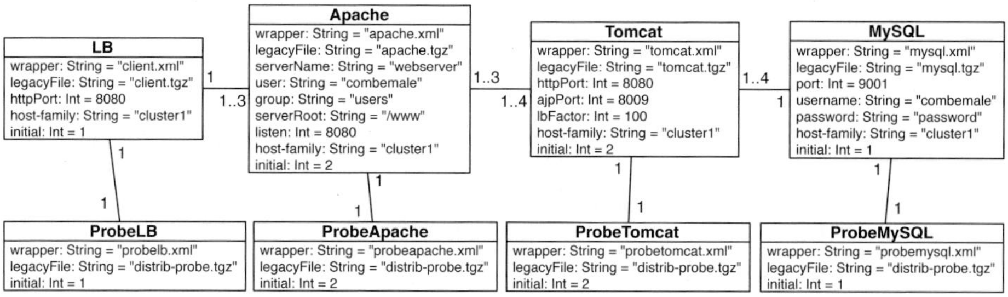

Fig. 3. Architecture schema for J2EE

manipulate the entities described in the deployment schema and reconfigurations can only produce a concrete architecture which comforms to the abstract schema, thus enforcing reconfiguration correctness.

We detail these three aspects in the next sub-sections.

3.1 UML-Based Formalism for Architecture Schemas

We adapted the UML class diagram formalism in order to allow specification of architecture schemas, as illustrated in Figure 3 where such a schema is defined for a J2EE organization. An architecture schema describes the overall organization of a software infrastructure to be deployed. At deployment time, the schema is interpreted to deploy a component architecture. Each element (the boxes) corresponds to a software which can be instantiated in several component replicas. A link between two elements generates bindings between the components instanciated from these elements. Each binding between two components is bi-directional (actually implemented by 2 bindings in opposite directions), which allows navigation in the component architecture in order to fetch any configuration attribute of the software infrastructure.

An element includes a set of configuration attributes for the software. Most of these attributes are specific to the software, but few attributes are predefined by Tune and used for deployment: *wrapper* gives the name of the WDL description of the wrapper, *legacyFile* gives the archive which contains the legacy software, *hostFamily* gives a hint regarding the dynamic allocation of the nodes where the software should be deployed, *initial* gives the number of instances which should be deployed.

The schema in Figure 3 describes a J2EE organization where one Load-Balancer, two Apaches, two Tomcats and one MySQL should be deployed. A probe is linked with each software, which monitors the liveness of the server in order to trigger a repair procedure. In this schema, a cardinality is associated with each link. It which constrains the interconnection of the deployed components. An intensional schema may be ambiguous, i.e. the actual deployed component architecture (bindings between components) will depend on the implemented deployment runtime. However, the user may describe a more extensional schema which will better fit his requirements.

The schema in Figure 3 deploys a component architecture as illustrated in Figure 1.

```
<?xml version='1.0' encoding='ISO-8859-1' ?>
<wrapper name='apache'>
  <method name="start" class="wrapper.util.GenericStart" method="start_with_linux" >
    <param ... /> <param ... /> </method>

  <method name="configure" class="wrapper.util.ConfigurePlainText" method="configure">
    <param ... /> <param ... /> </method>

  <method name="addWorkers" class="wrapper.util.ConfigurePlainText" method="configure">
    <param name="config-file" value="conf/worker.properties" />
    <param name="worker.list" value="Tomcat.nodeName" /> </method>

  <method name="stop" class="appli.wrapper.util.GenericStop" method="stop_with_linux" >
    <param ... /> <param ... /> </method>
</wrapper>
```

Fig. 4. A WDL specification

3.2 A Wrapping Description Language

Upon deployment, the above schema is parsed and for each element, a number of Fractal components are created. These components implement the wrappers for the deployed software, which provide control over the software. Each wrapper component is an instance of a generic wrapper which is actually an interpreter of a WDL specification.

A WDL description defines a set of methods that can be invoked to configure or reconfigure the wrapped software. The workflow of methods that have to be invoked in order to configure and reconfigure the overall software environment is defined thanks to a formalism introduced in Section 3.3. Generally, a WDL specification (illustrated in Figure 7) provides *start* and *stop* operations for controlling the activity of the software, and a *configure* operation for reflecting the values of the attributes (defined in the UML architecture schema) in the configuration files of the software. Notice that the values of these attributes can be modified dynamically. Other operations can be defined according to the specific management requirements of the wrapped software, these methods being implemented in Java.

The main motivation for the introduction of WDL are (i) to hide the complexity of the underlying component model (Fractal) and (ii) that most of the needs should be met with a finite set of generic Java methods implementations (that can be therefore reused). We covered the needs of our usecases with very few methods, plaintext and XML file accessors and a shell command launcher. A method definition includes the description of the parameters that should be passed when the method is invoked. These parameters may be String constants, attribute values or combinaison of both (String expressions). All the attributes defined in the architecture schema can be used to pass the configured attributes as parameters of the method invocations.

It is sometimes necessary to navigate in the deployed component architecture in order to configure the software. For instance, in a J2EE architecture, an Apache may be bound to several Tomcats. At the legacy layer level, the *worker.properties* configuration file of Apache must include the list of the nodes where the Tomcats have been launched. Therefore in Figure 7, the *addWorkers* method in the Apache wrapper must receive this list of nodes in order to configure the *worker.properties* file. The syntax of the method parameters in the wrapper allows navigating in the management layer in order to access the component attributes (in this case the *nodeName* attribute of each Tomcat), following the bindings between the Apache component and the Tomcat components. *Tomcat.nodeName* returns the list of *nodeName* attributes of the Tomcat components which are bound with the current Apache component.

3.3 UML-Based Formalism for (Re)configuration Procedures

Reconfigurations are triggered by events. An event can be generated by a specific monitoring component (e.g. probes in the architecture schema) or by a wrapped legacy software which already includes its own monitoring functions.

Whenever a wrapper component is instanciated, a communication pipe is created (typically a Unix pipe) that can be used by the wrapped legacy software to generate an event, following a specified syntax which allows for parameter passing. Notice that the use of pipes allows any software (implemented in any language environment such as Java or C++) to generate events. An event generated in the pipe associated with the wrapper is transmitted to the administration node where it can trigger the execution of reconfiguration programs (in our current prototype, the administration code, which initiates deployment and reconfiguration, is executed on one administration node, while the administrated software is managed on distributed hosts). An event is defined as an event type, the name of the component which generated the event and eventually an argument (all of type String).

For the definition of reactions to events, we reused the UML state diagrams formalism which allows specifying reconfiguration. Such a state diagram defines the workflow of operations that must be applied in reaction to an event. An operation in a state diagram can assign an attribute or a set of attributes of components, or invokes a method or a set of methods of components. To designate the components on which the operations should be performed, the syntax of the operations in the state diagrams allows navigation in the component architecture, similarly to the wrapping language.

For example, let's consider the diagram in Figure 5 (on the top) which is the reaction to a Tomcat (software) failure. The event (*fixTomcat*) is generated by a *probeTomcat* component instance, therefore the *this* variable references this *probeTomcat* component instance. Then:

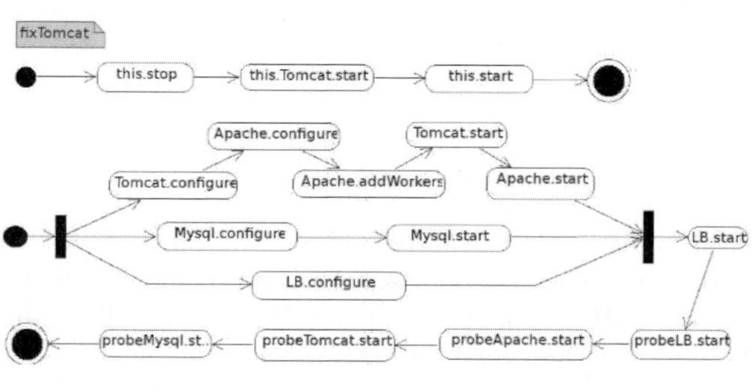

Fig. 5. State diagrams for repair and start

- *This.stop* will invoke the *stop* method on the probing component (to prevent the generation of multiple events),
- *This.Tomcat.start* will invoke the *start* method on the Tomcat component instance linked with the probe. This is the actual repair of the faulting Tomcat server,
- *This.start* will restart the probe associated with the Tomcat.

Notice that state diagram's operations are expressed using the elements defined in the architecture schema, and are applied on the actually deployed component architecture. The current version of Tune also provides operations which re-deploy components (change location or add component instances) while enforcing the defined abstract architecture schema.

A particular diagram is used to start the deployed J2EE environment, as illustrated in Figure 5 (on the bottom). In this diagram, when an expression starts with the name of an element in the architecture schema (Apache, Tomcat...), the semantics is to consider all the instances of the element, which may result in multiple method invocations. The starting diagram ensures that (1) configuration files must be generated, then (2) the servers must be started following the order Tomcat, Apache and LB (no constraint on MySQL). For each type of server, the server is started before its probe.

4 DSML-Based Autonomic Computing Policies Specification

Our first experiments with Tune focussed on the use of XML and UML to take advantage of well-known paradigms and of many existing open source tools. We used the UML2.0 graphical editors provided by the TOPCASED Eclipse-based toolkit [7] for the description of architectures and reconfiguration diagrams. However, the use of this unified language led us to specialize (pragmatically but sometimes awkwardly) its initial semantics in order to adapt it according to our needs. Because it is difficult to take into account this semantics specialization at the tools level, the user is let with all the freedom offered by UML.

For this reason, we are currently studying the possibility to define a dedicated metamodel for management policies definition. This allows us to define a constrained abstract syntax and a dedicated concrete syntax, relying on generic or generative tools, such as TCS [8] or Syntaks [9] for textual formalisms and TOPCASED [7] or GMF [10] for graphical formalisms. For each point of view that we have taken into account in Tune, we present the corresponding metamodel, offering a constrained, domain-specific and user-friendly languages.

4.1 The Configuration Description Language

The first language is the homogeneous definition of the application architecture. The UML-based formalism introduced in Section 3.1 was very close to the UML class diagram (rather than the UML component diagram, which can be quite confusing), reusing the concepts of classes, attributes and associations with multiplicities. However, the objective was mainly to reuse the expressiveness of the graphical notation, but with a domain specific semantic. The DSML we introduce here proposes a simple intentional

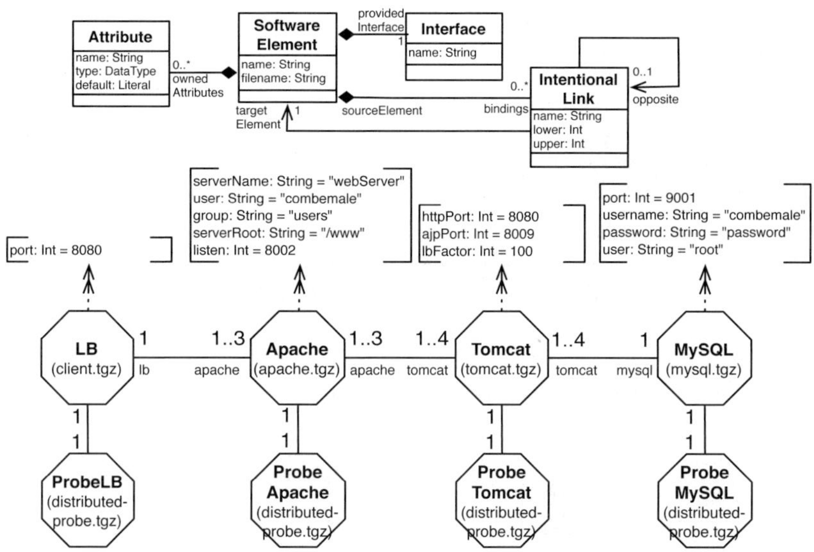

Fig. 6. The *Configuration Description Language*

architecture description language which allows to reify the heterogenous structural architecture of the legacy level. We call this language the *Configuration Description Language* (CDL). The main subset of the metamodel is depicted in Figure 6, also with an illustration with the model of the J2EE example of Section 3.

The main concept of this view is the *SoftwareElement* describing a particular type of software with its own configuration, management, and life cycle procedures. Each *SoftwareElement* is described by a set of properties (*ownedAttributes*), with an initial value (*defaultValue*), which are used by the administrator to reify the configurable attributes of the legacy software that the *SoftwareElement* represents. Note that a particular software can be reified by different *SoftwareElements* with different configuration properties.

The configuration language allows to describe an architecture in intension. This means here that each described *SoftwareElement* can be deployed into several instances. The architecture of the legacy level is intentionally reified through the definition of bindings (*IntentionalLink*), allowing to connect a *SoftwareElement* to another, and expressing a multiplicity (*lower* & *upper*) and a role (*name*). The multiplicity expresses the range of instances of the target *SoftwareElement* for each one of the source *SoftwareElement*. The role allows navigation with a query language relying on OCL [11]. It is also possible to define bi-directional *bindings* by defining an *opposite bindings*.

4.2 The Wrapping Description Language

The second language allows the definition of a wrapper and its relation with *SoftwareElements*. In the Wrapping Description Language introduced in Section 3.2, a wrapper was described in an XML dialect, only enabling runtime checks by the Tune machinery. With this DSML, it becomes possible to introduce static consistency checks

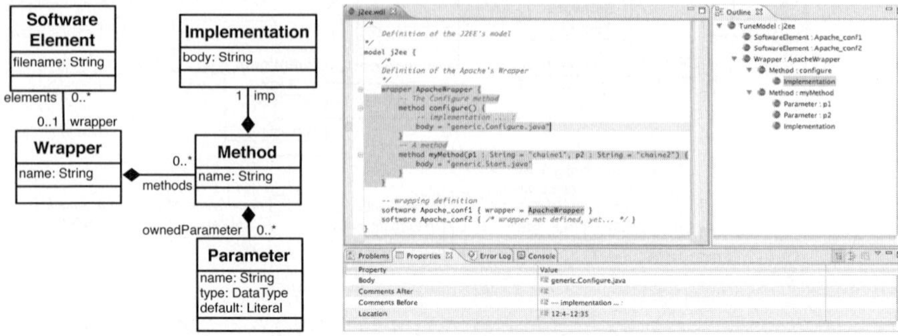

Fig. 7. The *Wrapping Description Language*

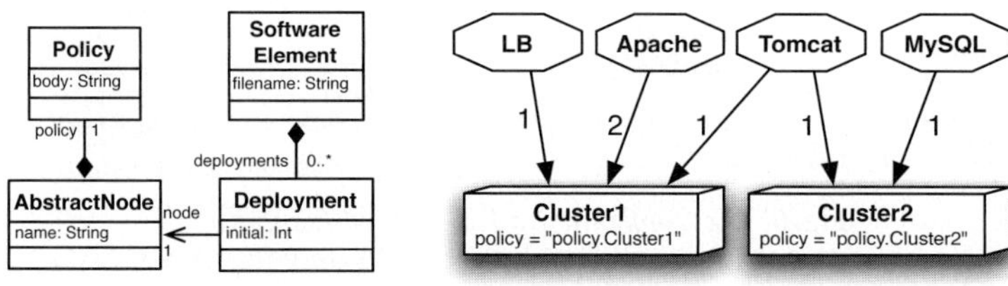

Fig. 8. The *Deployment Description Language*

regarding the architecture schema it may reference, especially for the navigation clauses included in method parameters.

The corresponding metamodel is presented in Figure 7, also with an illustration with a model defined with a specialized textual editor. A *Wrapper* describes *methods* which define actions that can be applied on the encapsulated software component. A wrapper may be referenced by different *SoftwareElements* (with different properties). A *Method* can be parametrized (*ownedParameter*) with any property (of the *SoftwareElement*) of the configuration description in which the wrapper is used, the OCL-based navigation language allowing to fetch the effective parameter values. The method implementations (*imp*) are given in the form of a reference to a program (currently a string referring to a Java class).

Note that this view must be consistent with the architectural view described with the CDL. We have thus defined OCL constraints to verify that the wrapper associated with a software element defines at least the methods provided by the interface.

4.3 The Deployment Description Language

The third language is used to define by intention or by extension, the real deployment of instances of each software component on system's nodes. In the UML-based formalisms described in Section 3.1, deployment policies were specified thanks to the *initial* and *host-family* attributes in the Architecture schema.

The introduced deployment DSML is described by the metamodel presented in Figure 8, also with the illustration with the J2EE example. For this, we define for each

SoftwareElement a set of *Deployments*, describing a real number of instances (*initial*) to be deployed on a node (*AbtractNode*). Nodes are known as "abstract" because they define a deployment policy (*policy*). Abstract nodes include the deployment information required to implement a deployment strategy, e.g. the physical address of a (single) real node on which instances should be deployed, or a list of physical addresses and an allocation function (for a cluster).

Note that this view must be consistent with the view described with the CDL. For instance, the number of deployed instances must be compatible with the multiplicities described in the configuration.

The clear separation of the deployment and architecture concerns allows to define several deployment orders for the same *SoftwareElement* (i.e. on different nodes), and to define different deployment models for the same architecture model. Finally, we clearly identify the concept of node.

4.4 The Reconfiguration Description Language

The last DSML allows the definition of reconfiguration policies. In the UML-based formalism introduced in Section 3.3, reconfiguration actions were expressed in terms of state diagrams, where we awkwardly inserted elementary actions as the state name. In accordance with the UML semantics, we decided to represent reconfiguration actions as activity diagrams in this DSML. Moreover, we introduced support in the DSML for the life cycle definition, allowing a clear description of links between events and reconfiguration actions, similarly to ECA (*Event/Condition/Action*) rules which typically used. This life cycle is expressed as a state diagram, where transitions are trigerred by events and execute reconfiguration actions defined as activity diagram.

We are inspired by the UML metamodel to express state diagrams (i.e. life cycles) and activity diagrams (i.e. reconfiguration policies). We don't reproduce this DSML metamodel since it is very similar to that of UML (with useless elements withdrawn).

5 Lessons Learned

5.1 Users'Viewpoint

Dealing with autonomic management policies, we have experienced the definition of **higher level formalisms** than the one used by the underlying Fractal components. The main motivation is to provide a formalism easier to understand and facilitating the definition of the views describing an application. These views are parsed by the Tune runtime in order to configure a Fractal component architecture. The first main benefit of this approach is to ease the learning and the adoption of the tool, for new users but also for experienced users. As an example, one student with no preliminary knowledge has been able to deploy his first application within two hours after a one hour seminar whereas several days were previously required.

In a first step, we have built our views by using UML diagrams, thus being close to a well-known and largely-adopted notation. Furthermore, it was possible to use the numerous available UML tools, providing the users with high level tools. Nevertheless, reusing the UML notation had one important drawback: we had to tailor the semantics of the diagrams we reused (the class and statemachine diagrams). Thus, we deviated from a standard UML model. For example, we used the name of a state to describe a method call rather that the UML behavior concept.

One solution, would have been to define a real UML profile rather than only reusing the graphical notation and tools but we would have also inherited the complexity of the UML metamodel. So, we investigated the use of DSMLs. It allows focussing on only the domain specific concepts and to define adapted views (as an example, the UML architecture schema has been split into two views, the configuration description language and the deployment description language). The semantics of the notation is well-founded because it is defined by a (MOF) metamodel completed by a set of OCL constraints to express constraints that are not captured by the metamodel itself.

Obviously, UML tools are not usable with our newly-defined DSMLs. So we had to develop new editors. The TOPCASED tool [7] has been used to generate the graphical editors. When sticking at the possibilities of this editor generator, some hours are sufficient to have a functional editor. If additional functionalities are required, the generated code has to be manually adapted. These adaptations may be time consuming but the base editor is really usable as is. We have also used TCS [8], a tool that permits to define a concrete syntax and the associated Eclipse editor (including colour, folding, name completion, etc). So we have been able to provide in a couple of hours a textual syntax for WDL that is easier to use that the XML like syntax.

Finally, the graphical and textual generated editors provide better **user assistance** than the UML editors because they **enforce the construction of coherent models** conforming to the DSML definition, including OCL constraints. So, users can see their mistakes before the Tune runtime reports them.

5.2 Correctness

The adopted approach favors correctness of managed applications for 3 main reasons:

- The definition of the management layer. Thanks to the management layer (composed of wrappers), the administrator of a software infrastructure does not have to manipulate complex configuration files, as in a J2EE clustered architecture. All the configurable entities (attributes, bindings, etc.) are reified in the management layer and can be homogeneously manipulated.
- The definition of an application pattern and its enforcement. The deployed application architecture is generated from the definition of a pattern (the architecture schema). Any reconfiguration described with the Reconfiguration Description Language can only result in an architecture which complies with this pattern.
- The definition of a user-friendly notation that favors the understanding of the users on their models is another step in the right direction. Indeed, the users are enforced to build coherent models, especially in the DSML approach, or are informed of possible mistakes without having to wait until their models are parsed by the Tune runtime. The application is then automatically generated.

6 Related Works

Autonomic computing is an appealing approach that aims at simplifying the hard task of system management, thus building self-healing, self-tuning, and self-configuring systems [12]. Management solutions for legacy systems are usually proposed as ad-hoc solutions that are tied to particular legacy system implementations (e.g. [13] for self-tuning cluster environments). This unfortunately reduces reusability and requires autonomic management procedures to be reimplemented each time a legacy system is taken into account in a particular context. Moreover, the architecture of managed systems is often very complex (e.g. multi-tier architectures), which requires advanced support for its management.

Relying on a component model for managing legacy software infrastructure has been investigated by several projects [1,2,3] and has proved to be a very convenient approach, but in most cases, the autonomic policies have to be programmed using the programming interface of the underlying component model (a framework for implementing wrappers, configuration APIs or deployment ADLs) which is too low level and still error prone.

Therefore, many projects explored model-driven approaches for designing autonomic management policies. Some of them proposed frameworks for modeling autonomic systems, e.g. a self-healing [14], a self-protecting [15], or a resource management system [16], the management system implementation being generated from the described management model. The modeling of such a system can still be quite complex and the integration within a legacy software organisation tricky. Some other projects proposed frameworks and runtimes for modeling the managed system and maintaining consistency between the managed system and its model at runtime [17,18]. The main advantage is well defined representation of the managed system, on which management policies can be applied. The tune system falls into this category, even if our management layer relies on the Fractal component model. Tune relies on DSML for the specification of a software architecture, its deployment and reconfiguration. These languages ensure that only consistent system states can result from deployment and reconfiguration.

Finally, some projects considered interactions between policies, mainly in order to deal with conflicts [19,20]. We are currently working on a DSML which should allow such coordinating between reconfiguration policies.

7 Conclusion and Perspectives

We are investigating the design and implementation of an autonomic system called Tune. Tune relies on a component model in order to administrate a legacy software infrastructure as a component architecture. Tune provides support for encapsulating (wrapping) software, describing the software architecture to manage and its deployment in a physical environment, and describing the dynamic reconfiguration policies to be applied autonomously. Our experiments with Tune led us to the conclusion that higher-level support was required for assisting administrators in policy description tasks.

For this purpose, our first experiments focused on the use of UML-based formalisms. These experiments confirmed the interest of raising up the abstraction level but we had to specialize the UML semantics according to the requirements of the considered field. It was difficult to take into account this specialization in the tools we reused. In a second step, we worked on the definition of a dedicated metamodel. The expected benefits are two-fold: to provide a formal definition of Tune's languages, and to statically and dynamically validate the policies described by administrators with customized editors.

This work opens many perspectives on which we are currently working. Although we already prototyped few specialized editors, we plan to provide editing tools for all the administration points of view considered by Tune. Also, the Tune developpers are currently extending the reconfiguration capabilities of Tune and the metamodel and the associated editing tools will evolve accordingly. In the longer term, we plan to revisit the design of the Tune system, considering that the management layer (illustrated in Figure 1) should be managed as a model (instead of a component architecture at the middleware level). This means that models would not only be used to describe policies, but would further be used to maintain the internal state of the Tune system. We refer to this new MDE field as *Model-Driven System Administration*. We are convinced that it is now essential to increase the abstraction level of software management, not only during the design but also during their development and administration.

References

1. Garlan, D., Cheng, S., Huang, A., Schmerl, B., Steenkiste, P.: Rainbow: Architecture-based self adaptation with reusable Infrastructure. IEEE Computer 37(10) (2004)
2. Hagimont, D., Bouchenak, S., Palma, N.D., Taton, C.: Autonomic Management of Clustered Applications. In: IEEE International Conference on Cluster Computing (2006)
3. Oriezy, P., Gorlick, M., Taylor, R., Johnson, G., Medvidovic, N., Quilici, A., Rosenblum, D., Wolf. A.: An Architecture-Based Approach to Self-Adaptive Software. IEEE Intelligent Systems 14(3) (1999)
4. Microsystems, S.: Java 2 Platform Enterprise Edition (J2EE), `http://java.sun.com/j2ee/`
5. Bruneton, E., Coupaye, T., Leclercq, M., Quéma, V., Stefani, J.B.: The Fractal Component Model and its Support in Java. In: Software - Practice and Experience, special issue on *Experiences with Auto-adaptive and Reconfigurable Systems* (September 2006)
6. Toure, M., Berhe, G., Stolf, P., Broto, L., Depalma, N., Hagimont, D.: Autonomic Management for Grid Applications. In: 16th Euromicro International Conference on Parallel, Distributed and network-based Processing (February 2008)
7. The TOPCASED Project, `http://www.topcased.org/`
8. Jouault, F., Bézivin, J., Kurtev, I.: TCS: a DSL for the specification of textual concrete syntaxes in model engineering. In: Proceedings of the 5th International Conference on Generative Programming and Component Engineering, October 2006, pp. 249–254. ACM Press, New York (2006)
9. Muller, P.A., Fleurey, F., Fondement, F., Hassenforder, M., Schneckenburger, R., Gérard, S., Jézéquel, J.M.: Model-driven analysis and synthesis of concrete syntax. In: Nierstrasz, O., Whittle, J., Harel, D., Reggio, G. (eds.) MoDELS 2006. LNCS, vol. 4199, pp. 98–110. Springer, Heidelberg (2006)
10. GMF: Graphical Modeling Framework, `http://www.eclipse.org/gmf/`
11. Object Management Group: UML Object Constraint Language (OCL) 2.0(June 2005)
12. Kephart, J.O., Chess, D.M.: The Vision of Autonomic Computing. IEEE Computer Magazine 36(1) (2003)

13. Urgaonkar, B., Shenoy, P., Chandra, A., Goyal, P.: Dynamic Provisiong of Multi-Tier Internet Applications. In: 2nd International Conference on Autonomic Computing (June 2005)
14. Jiang, M., Zhang, J., Raymer, D., Strassner, J.: A Modeling Framework for Self-Healing Software Systems. In: Workshop Models@run.time at the 10th International Conference on model Driven Engineering Languages and Systems (2007)
15. Pena, J., Hinchey, M.G., Sterritt, R., Ruiz-Cortes, A., Resinas, M.: A model-driven architecture approach for modeling, specifying and deploying policies in autonomous and autonomic systems. In: 2nd IEEE International Symposium on Dependable, Autonomic and Secure Computing, pp. 19–30. IEEE Computer Society Press, Los Alamitos (2006)
16. Barrett, K., Davy, S., Strassner, J., Jennings, B., van der Meer, S., Donnelly, W.: A model based approach for policy tool generation and policy analysis. In: Proc. 1st IEEE Global Information Infrastructure Symposium, pp. 99–105. IEEE, Los Alamitos (2007)
17. Sriplakich, P., Waignier, G., Le Meur, A.F.: Enabling Dynamic Co-Evolution of Models and Runtime Applications. In: 1st IEEE International Workshop on Model-Driven Development of Autonomic Systems, July 2008. IEEE Computer Society Press, Los Alamitos (2008)
18. Rohr, M., Boskovic, M., Giesecke, S., Hasselbring, W.: Model-driven Development of Self-managing Software Systems. In: Workshop Models@run.time at the 9th International Conference on model Driven Engineering Languages and Systems (MoDELS) (2006)
19. Agrawal, D., Lee, K.W., Lobo, J.: Policy-based management of networked computing systems. Communications Magazine 43(10), 69–75 (2005)
20. Davy, S., Barrett, K., Serrano, M., Strassner, J., Jennings, B., van der Meer, S.: Policy Interactions and Management of Traffic Engineering Services Based on Ontologies. In: Network Operations and Management Symposium, pp. 95–105 (September 2007)

Empirical Analysis of the Relation between Level of Detail in UML Models and Defect Density

Ariadi Nugroho[1], Bas Flaton[2], and Michel R.V. Chaudron[1,2]

[1] LIACS – Leiden University, Niels Bohrweg 1, 2333 CA Leiden, The Netherlands
[2] TU Eindhoven, PO Box 513, 5600 MB Eindhoven, The Netherlands
anugroho@liacs.nl, b.flaton@gmail.com, m.r.v.chaudron@tue.nl
http://www.liacs.nl/~anugroho, http://www.tue.nl/~mchaudro

Abstract. This paper investigates the relation between the level of detail (LoD) in UML models and defect density of the associated implementation. We propose LoD measures that are applicable to both class- and sequence diagrams. Based on empirical data from an industrial software project we have found that classes with higher LoD, calculated using sequence diagram LoD metrics, correlates with lower defect density. Overall, this paper discusses a novel and practical approach to measure LoD in UML models and describes its application to a significant industrial case study.

Keywords: Unified Modeling Language, Design Metrics, Quality Measure, Correlation Analyses.

1 Introduction

Understanding the impact of software models on downstream software development is important for delivering good quality software. This knowledge may help to avert software problems in an early stage of development and thus reduce the costs for solving software defects found after the construction phase. Taking this issue into consideration, much research has been done into analyzing how certain properties of software designs affect the quality properties of the final software product. The seminal paper of Chidamber and Kemerer [1] was aimed at identifying useful metrics from object-oriented designs. Further, assessments of design metrics and their implications on software defects have been reported in [2], [3], and [4]. Many more works ([5], [6], [7], [8]) are targeted at predicting fault-proneness of classes based on design metrics.

In this paper we propose a measure for UML models called level of detail (LoD) to investigate the relation between the quality of software models and the quality of the final implementation. We explain how this measure is determined based on both UML models (specifically on class and sequence diagrams) and source code. Subsequently, we analyze its relations with defect density as determined based on source code. Using data from an industrial project, we have found that classes that are modeled in sequence diagrams with a higher level of detail are found to have lower defect density than those modeled in sequence

K. Czarnecki et al. (Eds.): MoDELS 2008, LNCS 5301, pp. 600–614, 2008.

diagrams with a lower level of detail. Hence, this study shows how the LoD measure can be used for quantifying the level of detail of UML models. Additionally, the LoD measure is potentially useful as a predictor for software defect density.

This paper is organized as follows. In Section 2 the level of detail measure and the research hypothesis will be discussed. Sections 3 and 4 discuss data collection and data analyses respectively. Section 5 discusses the findings. Finally, conclusions and future work will be described in Section 6.

2 Level of Detail Measure

2.1 Hypothesis

In UML modeling, the level of detail can be measured by quantifying the amount of information that is used to represent a modeling element. For example, the modeling element 'message in a sequence diagram' may be represented by any of the following amount of information: an informal label, a label that represents a method name, a label that is a method name plus the parameter list.

In modeling class diagrams, many syntactical features are available to increase the level of detail: class attributes & operations, association names, association directionality, multiplicity and so forth. When the level of detail used in a UML model is low, it typically employs only a few syntactic features such as class-name and associations without specifying any further details or information about the class.

The way in which UML is used in general varies widely from project to project. This variation includes the level of detail and completeness used in the models. In this respect, the level of detail in UML models is important to assure that software developers can easily understand and implement them. This very notion of level of detail and its relation with comprehensibility form the main hypothesis of this study:

H_0: "There is no significant correlation between level of detail of UML classes and the defect density of the implementation classes"
H_{alt}: "UML classes that are modeled in a higher level of detail significantly correlate with a lower defect density in the implementation classes".

2.2 Metrics Definition

For classes, two methods for determining the LoD are explored. One LoD metrics is based on class-diagrams and one is based on sequence diagrams. The main reason of only using these two diagrams is because they are commonly used in practice. This decision is also supported by a survey finding reported in [9], which states that class, sequence, and use case diagrams are used most often in practice. Although use case diagrams are also commonly used in practice, they merely describe the required functionality, but not how to implement it.

Thus, except for missing requirements/functionality, other defect types are generally not related to use case diagrams.

Class Diagram LoD. The following metrics are used to measure the level of detail of classes in a class diagram.

- **NumAttrRatio** (CD_{m1})**.** Measures the ratio of the total number of attributes of a class in a model to the implementation.
- **AttrSigRatio** (CD_{m2})**.** Measures the ratio of attributes with signature to the total number of attributes of a class.
- **NumOpsRatio** (CD_{m3})**.** Measures the ratio of the total number of operations of a class in a model to the implementation.
- **OpsWithParamRatio** (CD_{m4})**.** Measures the ratio of operations with parameters of a class in a model to the implementation.
- **OpsWithReturnRatio** (CD_{m5})**.** Measures the ratio of operations with return (give return values) of a class in a model to the implementation.
- **AssocLabelRatio** (CD_{m6})**.** Measures the ratio of associations with label (e.g., association name) to the total number of associations of a class.
- **AssocRoleRatio** (CD_{m7})**.** Measures the ratio of associations with role name to the total number of associations attached to a class.

As can be seen from the above list, all the metrics are measured as ratios. Several of the above metrics are measured using both UML models and the implementation code (namely NumAttrRatio, NumOpsRatio, OpsWithParamRatio, and OpsWithReturnRatio). As an alternative, we considered the absolute numbers of attributes and operations. However, for class diagrams these metrics are a measure of the size, rather than the level of detail. We believe that the ratio between information present in the model and information present in the implementation is a good measure for the level of detail of the design.

Sequence Diagram LoD. The following metrics use information from sequence diagrams to measure the level of detail.

- **NonAnonymObjRatio** (SD_{m1})**.** Measures the ratio of objects with name to the total number of objects in a sequence diagram.
- **NonDummyObjRatio** (SD_{m2})**.** Measures the ratio of non-dummy objects (objects that correspond to classes) to the total number of objects in a sequence diagram.
- **MsgWithLabelRatio** (SD_{m3})**.** Measures the ratio of messages with label (any text attached to the messages) to the total number of messages in a sequence diagram.
- **NonDummyMsgRatio** (SD_{m4})**.** Measures the ratio of non-dummy messages (messages that correspond to class methods) to the total number of messages in a sequence diagram.
- **ReturnMsgWithLabelRatio** (SD_{m5})**.** Measures the ratio of return messages with label (any text attached to the return messages) to the total number of return messages in a sequence diagram.

- **MsgWithGuardRatio (SD_{m6}).** Measures the ratio of guarded messages (messages with conditional checking) to the total number of messages in a sequence diagram.
- **MsgWithParamRatio (SD_{m7}).** Measures the ratio of messages with parameters to the total number of messages in a sequence diagram.

In essence, the sequence diagram metrics cover two aspects of detailedness, namely object detailedness and message detailedness—the first two metrics belong to the former and the rest belongs to the latter. As with the class diagram LoD metrics, the sequence diagram LoD metrics are also measured using ratios.

None of the sequence diagram LoD metrics uses source code information although two of the metrics, namely MsgWithGuardRatio and MsgWithParamRatio, could have used code metrics as the denominators. Source code information was not used because it would be tricky and time consuming to calculate the metrics (especially for methods with guards) from class methods manually. Without source code comparisons, MsgWithGuardRatio and MsgWithParamRatio may not exactly measure detailedness because messages can be with or without parameters or guards, yet they are still syntactically and semantically correct. Nevertheless, our observation shows that many of the messages without parameter actually should have been modeled with parameter(s). The same holds for messages without guard. Based on this observation, we assume that sequence diagrams containing messages with parameters or guards generally have higher detail than those containing messages without parameter or guard.

The two methods in which we calculated a class' LoD will be discussed in the following passages. We start with the calculation using class diagram metrics.

Calculating LoD of a class from class diagrams was performed by measuring the class diagram metrics at the class level. Thus, the points of interest are classes in class diagrams. Consequently, the LoD value of a class is determined based on information that is related only to that particular class. We need to emphasize this because a slightly different approach was used to calculate LoD from sequence diagrams.

When calculating LoD from sequence diagrams, the LoD of a class was determined by calculating LoD metrics from the sequence diagram in its entirety (i.e., not limited to a class object in a given sequence diagram). This approach is an approximate measure to determine the LoD of class from the LoD of its surroundings because our data set did not contain object-level information. Further, since a class might appear as objects in more than one sequence diagrams, the sequence diagram LoD was calculated by taking into account all sequence diagrams where that particular class appears. To normalize the effect of a class' appearance frequency in sequence diagrams on its LoD score (LoD_{SD}), the LoD_{SD} score of a given class was calculated as an average of LoD scores of the sequence diagrams where it appears (see formula 3).

The calculations for the LoD measures based on class- and sequence diagrams are given in (1) and (3) respectively. Note that we have chosen to assign each of the composite metrics equal weight factors in the aggregate LoD measures. In the future we might experiment by varying these weights.

For implementation class x, corresponding design class x' and n sequence diagrams related to x':

$$LoD_{CD}(x) = CD_{m1}(x') + CD_{m2}(x') + CD_{m3}(x')... + CD_{m7}(x') \quad (1)$$

$$SeqLoD = SD_{m1} + SD_{m2} + SD_{m3}... + SD_{m7} \quad (2)$$

$$LoD_{SD}(x) = \frac{1}{n}\sum_{i=1}^{n} SeqLoD_i(x') \quad (3)$$

3 Empirical Data

This section describes the empirical data used in this paper, which includes the context of the system under study and the methods for collecting and preprocessing the raw data.

3.1 The System under Study

The system under study is an integrated healthcare system for psychiatrists in the Netherlands, hereafter referred to as IPS (not a real name). It was built as a web service using Java technology. IPS was chosen for this study because UML was used to model the system and because the version control system and bug tracking system were integrated with each other, allowing for fast tracing of source files that were modified to solve defects.

In the IPS project, RUP methodology was used, and this project involved off shoring to India. The modeling of the system was done in the Netherlands, while approximately 60 percent of the implementation and testing activities were done in India. For creating the UML models, the project used Rational XDE, and for the version control system and bug tracking system, the project used Rational ClearCase and Rational ClearQuest respectively. The summary of the IPS project is provided in Table 1.

In the IPS project, the UML models were used as a specification for the implementation. Thus, the models were created before writing the implementation code. The UML models were created by the designers and were later implemented by the developers in India and the Netherlands.

When this study was conducted, IPS project was already finished. The system was used by the client for sometime, but was later abandoned because of business economical reasons.

Table 1. Project Summary

Project size	# of staffs	Duration	Off-shored	Status	Model Size	SLOC
20 man-years	25 people	2.3 years	India	finished	104 use cases 266 classes 341 seq. diagrams	152,017

3.2 Defect Data Collection

The empirical data used in this study, including the defect data, was based on the latest version of IPS' project data. Besides actuality reason, the latest version was chosen because most of development activities were taking place in this version.

For now, the term finding, instead of defect, will be used to refer to the defects registered, because in fact the defect registration also contains many problems that are not defects. Further, only findings found during testing were taken into account. The statistics of the findings of the latest version recorded in ClearQuest are as follows:

- Test: 1546
- Review: 771
- Acceptance test: 212
- Integration test: 70

The findings analyzed in this study were those found during Test, which contained 1546 findings. The pre-processing of the finding data consisted of the following steps. First, the source files that were corrected/modified to solve each finding were extracted from the ClearCase repository (these files hereafter referred to as faulty classes). A Perl script was employed to perform this activity automatically. Second, the number of times a file was corrected due to distinct findings was calculated as a measure of defect-count of that file (note: only Java files that were not interfaces were taken into account). Thus, a Java file that was corrected more than once under the same finding will be counted as having only one defect-count. Finally, the findings were analyzed to determine whether they could be categorized as defects. For this purpose, in-depth analyses were performed, which include categorizing the defects into different types by inspecting how the defect was solved in the source files.

Due to the large number of findings, the analysis was applied to a sample of the total findings. The sampling approach will be further discussed in the Data Analysis section.

3.3 Metrics Data Collection

The class metrics, both from the UML models and from (reverse engineered) code, were calculated using a tool called SDMetrics [10]. This tool supports definition of custom metrics; therefore it has been very useful to calculate the LoD metrics. Nevertheless, the calculation of sequence diagram metrics could not be performed automatically because Rational XDE does not export the sequence diagram information in the XMI exporting process (note that SDMetrics requires an XMI file of a UML model to calculate metrics). Hence, manual inspection of the sequence diagrams in Rational XDE was performed to calculate the sequence diagram metrics.

All gathered data, both metrics and findings, were stored in a MySQL database. This database was designed to store all project information so that queries could be performed easily. A front-end was also developed to enable data analyses and entries from and to the database.

4 Data Analysis

4.1 Data Sampling

Out of 1546 findings reported in Test, only 566 were traceable to the modified source files. The fact that there was a large number of findings that was not traceable to the modified source files might be due to the following reasons. First, there were findings that were solved without modifying source files, which include changes in the database or application server. Second, it is possible that a finding was solved indirectly, i.e., by solving other findings. Finally, it is often the case that findings were rejected for some reasons, for instance because they could not be reproduced. In these cases, no source file was corrected to solve the findings.

Since defect-source traceability was a prerequisite for the analyses, findings without this traceability had to be excluded; thus, the target population for the analysis was 566 findings. Out of these 566 findings a random sampling was performed. The sample size was initially targeted at 100, but later increased to 164. The sampling was performed by assigning a random number to each finding and then sorting the findings based on the random numbers. The sample was taken from the first 164 findings from the sorted list.

4.2 Descriptive Statistics

Defect Type Distribution. Each finding from the sample space was inspected by looking at both its description and the corrected source files. Based on this inspection, the findings were categorized into seven general defect types. These defect types were based on various sources in the literature (e.g., [11], [12], [13]) and were selected because they were most relevant and frequently encountered in our study. The sample's defect type distribution is shown in Figure 1.

As can be seen from Figure 1, a large number of the findings falls into the category of UI-related defects (28 percent), followed by user data I/O (17 percent) and data handling (16 percent)—the rest being equal to or lower than 10 percent of the sample size. Also note that a considerable number of findings falls into non-defect category (27 percent). In this respect, we have observed that many of the findings categorized into non-defect were those related to change requests. Additionally, five percent of the analyzed findings could not be categorized into any of the defect categories (undetermined).

Except for the UI-related, undetermined, and non-defect, all defect types were considered for further analyses. UI-related and undetermined defects were excluded because they are of a type for which UML modeling could not have prevented their occurrence. After having excluded these three defect types, we were left with 83 usable defects for further analyses.

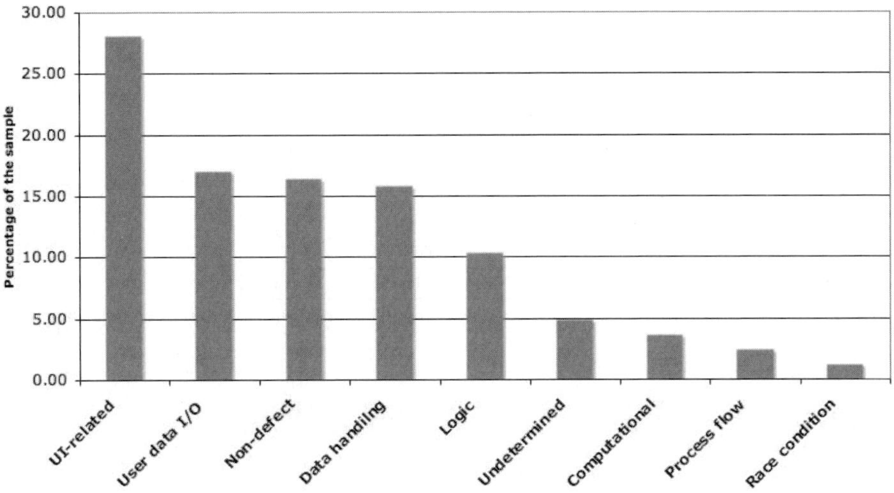

Fig. 1. Sample defect type distribution

Faulty Classes. As discussed previously, faulty classes are Java classes that were corrected to solve defects. We found 142 faulty classes that were corrected due to the 83 defects discussed in the previous section. However, eight of the faulty classes were found to be missing from the actual source code. These missing classes might have been deleted or merged with other classes after the corrections; hence they could not be found in the last source code version. In fact some of the classes also changed in names, but we managed to trace them manually in the actual code. At the end there remained 134 faulty Java classes.

Of 134 faulty classes, only 43 were found to be modeled as UML classes (hereafter referred to as design classes). The matching process between faulty classes and design classes was performed using database query and based on name similarity. The profile of the 134 faulty classes with respect to their presence in the UML model is as follows.

- 27 classes were modeled as classes in the class diagrams.
- 30 classes were modeled as objects in the sequence diagrams.
- 14 classes were modeled as both classes and objects in the class- and sequence diagrams.
- 91 classes were not modeled at all.

Table 2 shows the distribution of defects across the faulty classes. Note that data in Table 2 also includes classes that were not modeled. As Table 2 shows, more than 77 percent of the faulty classes (104 of them) contain one defect, and slightly more than 13 percent (18 of them) contain two defects. The rest of the classes (12 of them) contain between three to seven defects.

Figure 2 shows the distribution of lines of code (in KLOC) and defect density of the faulty classes, in defects per KLOC. From the KLOC boxplot, we can see

Table 2. Distribution of defects across faulty classes

# of classes	Percentage	Defect-count
104	77.60	1
18	13.40	2
5	3.70	3
3	2.20	4
1	0.70	5
2	1.50	6
1	0.70	7
134	100.00	191

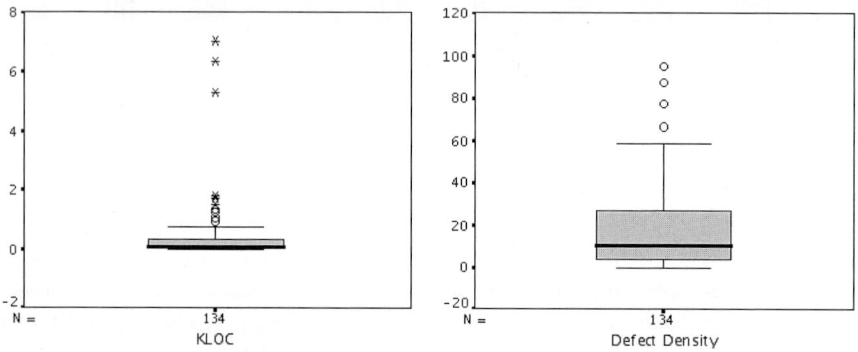

Fig. 2. Boxplots of the faulty classes' KLOC and defect density

that the class size is ranging from 0.01 to 7.0 KLOC, with the median value of 0.10. The defect density of the faulty classes, however, is ranging from 0.16 up to 95.24 defect/KLOC, with the median value of 10.87 (indicated by the horizontal line in the box). Besides their skewness to the bottom, also note the presence of outliers and extreme values in both boxplots. These outliers and extreme values were not due to wrong data entry; hence, no data point was deleted.

In total, there were 266 design classes, out of which 27 matched to faulty classes from our defect sample. On the other hand, 341 sequence diagrams were modeled, out of which 238 were related to 30 faulty classes (the identification of sequence diagrams in which the faulty classes were modeled as objects was done manually). The statistics of the LoD metrics for both class and sequence diagrams that are related to faulty classes are summarized in Figure 3.

As can be seen from the boxplots in Figure 3, the distribution of the class LoD is skewed. The bottom 50% scores fall around zero value and the top 50% of the scores are spread over a wider range. However, note that LoD scores of the sequence diagrams are symmetrically distributed—the minimum and maximum scores are 3.5 and 6.5 respectively, while the median value is 5.

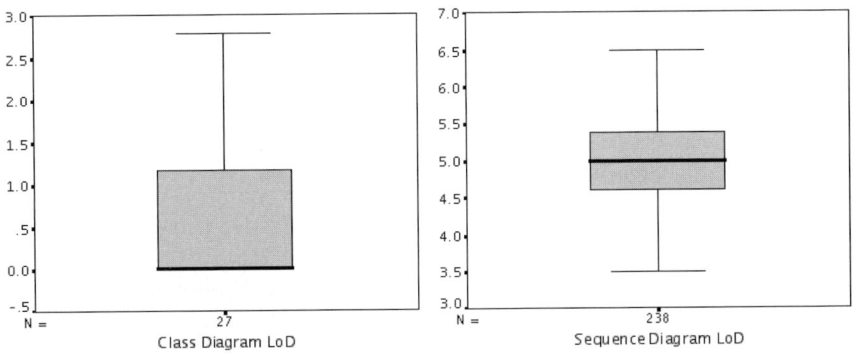

Fig. 3. Boxplots of class and sequence diagram LoD

4.3 Correlation Analyses between LoD and Defect Density

In this section two correlation analyses will be performed to investigate the relation between the level of modeling detail of classes and their defect density. We first consider LoD_{CD} and then LOD_{SD}.

Using Class Diagram Metrics. This analysis aims to explore if there is a significant correlation between LoD_{CD} and defect density. To answer this question, the LoD_{CD} scores of the 27 faulty classes were determined using the class metrics. The descriptive statistics of the LoD_{CD} scores are shown in Figure 4.

Since there were outliers in the defect density data (See Figure 4), an area transformation was performed to reduce the effects of the outliers and to achieve a normal data distribution. The transformation was applied to both the LoD_{CD} score and the defect density data sets so that their relative differences are maintained. However, having transformed the data, a normal distribution for the LoD_{CD} metrics data set still could not be achieved. Because the assumption of

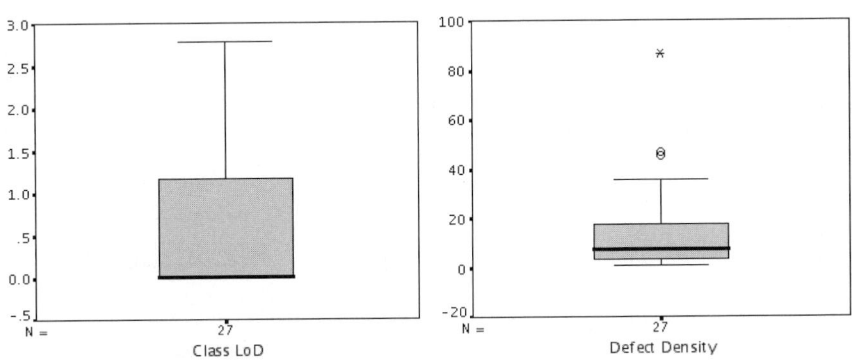

Fig. 4. Boxplots of class LoD (using class diagram metrics) and defect density

Table 3. Spearman's correlation coefficient between class LoD (using LoD_{CD}) and defect density

	Defect Density
Class LoD	-.222
Significance (2-tailed)	.265

normal data distribution was violated, a non-parametric test was used, namely Spearman's correlation test. The result of the analysis is shown in Table 3.

As Table 3 shows, the correlation analysis does not reveal a significant correlation between LoD_{CD} and defect density ($R = -.222$ and significance value of .265). The correlation coefficient R reveals a true significance when the significance value is lower or equal to 0.05. Hence, we have to reject the H_{alt} hypothesis when LoD is measured using LoD_{CD}.

Using Sequence Diagram Metrics. In this analysis we use the LoD_{SD} metrics to quantify level of detail. The LoD_{SD} metrics were used to measure the LoD of the 30 faulty classes that were modeled as objects in sequence diagrams. The summary of the LoD scores and defect density of the 30 faulty classes is presented in Figure 5. Please refer to Figure 3 for the summary of LoD_{SD} scores of the 238 sequence diagrams related the faulty classes.

As with the previous analysis, the same data transformation procedure was undertaken to normalize the data sets prior to the correlation analysis (the relation between the two variables after normalization is shown in Figure 6). Having transformed the data, a normality test confirmed that the data sets were normally distributed. Hence, for this analysis Pearson's correlation analysis was used instead of Spearman's. The result of the analysis is shown in Table 4.

As can be seen in Table 4, Pearson's correlation analysis resulted in a negative (R = -.540) and significant correlation between the two variables. Hence, classes

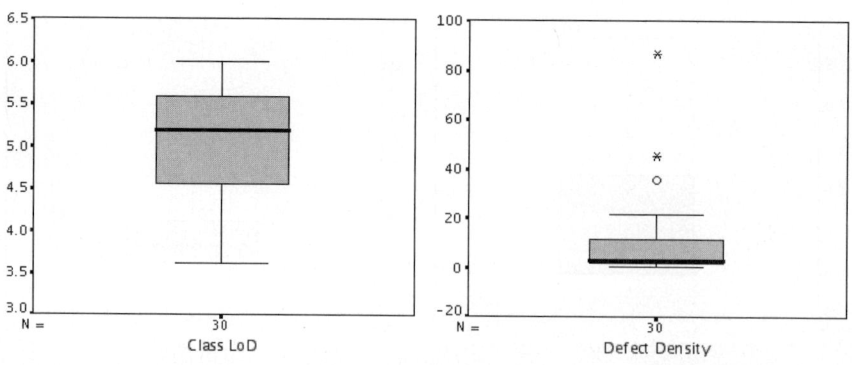

Fig. 5. Boxplots of class LoD (using sequence diagram metrics) and defect density

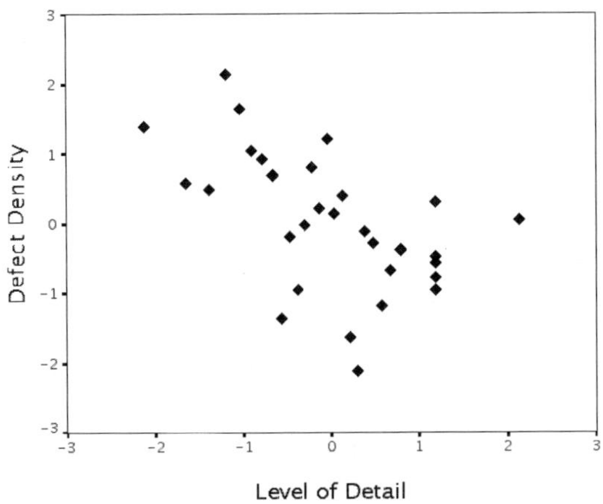

Fig. 6. Scatterplot showing the relation between LoD and defect density (using normalized data)

Table 4. Pearson's correlation coeff. of LoD scores (using LoD_{SD}) and defect density

	Defect Density
Class LoD	-.540**
Significance (1-tailed)	.001

**indicates significance at 0.01 level (1-tailed)

appearing in sequence diagrams with a low LoD_{SD} tend to have higher defect density than those appearing in sequence diagrams with a high LoD_{SD}. Further, the value of R^2, which measures the amount of variability of defect density that is accounted by LoD_{SD}, equals 0.29. This means that LoD_{SD} accounts for 29 percent of the variability of defect density. Hence, the correlation analysis confirmed the H_{alt} hypothesis; thus, the H_0 hypothesis can be rejected.

The above correlation suggests that as the LoD of classes decreases, the correctness of the implementation of those respective classes also decreases accordingly. This might be due to an increase in erroneous interpretations caused by the lack of information in the sequence diagrams.

5 Discussion

5.1 What Does the Correlation Actually Mean?

The significant correlation between LoD_{SD} and defect density indicates that classes modeled in sequence diagrams with high LoD have lower defect density than those modeled in sequence diagrams with lower LoD. This result essentially confirms the H_{alt} hypothesis stated earlier in this paper.

We should note, however, that the value of LoD_{SD} of a class is measured at the diagram level instead of at the instance level. While this approach may be less precise than using instance level information, it still provides sufficient ground to determine the LoD of a class using sequence diagram LoD metrics. Therefore, we are confident that the result confirms a strong indication of significant correlation between class LoD and defect density.

Note that the correlation analysis using class diagram LoD metrics did not result in a significant correlation. This result might suggest the followings. First, the class diagrams were less developed, which in turn results in class diagrams with equally low LoD. Second, the class diagrams were not as much consulted in the implementation as the sequence diagrams. Each of these factors is influential to the presence of a significant correlation between class LoD and defect density.

Although there is a correlation between LoD_{SD} and defect density, at some point increasing model detailedness will no longer be effective to reduce defect density. This circumstance poses an important question about the notion of level of detail in modeling: at what level of detail should UML models be developed?

5.2 Some Remarks for Modeling Practices

The awareness for developing UML models with an appropriate level of quality for the problems at hand has been the subject of many studies. For instance, the risks of defects in UML models and an approach to minimize them have been discussed in [14]. Our case study reported in [15] also reveals why level of detail and completeness in UML models are often sacrificed in practice. Furthermore, a survey reported in [16] captures the opinions of software developers on how level of detail should be applied in UML models: more details should be applied to components that are critical, important, or pertain to concepts that are new to the developers. Apart from these studies, an experimental study reported in [17] suggests how OCL (object constraint language) can help improving understandability of UML models. Similar to the notion of level of detail, the use of OCL is actually aimed at expressing more information (in a formal way) in UML models in order to improve preciseness and reduce ambiguity.

With regard to the application of level of detail in UML modeling, this paper extends the aforementioned work by proposing a measure and providing empirical evidence that confirms the relation between the level of detail in UML models and defect density. As our experiences have shown that level of detail in UML models varies considerably in practice, this study should increase the awareness of software engineers about the importance of level of detail in UML models, and should subsequently allow them to make informed decisions in dealing with the issue, especially in defining target levels of quality for UML models.

5.3 Threats to Validity

Internal Validity. The main threat to the internal validity of this study concerns inconsistency amongst inspectors in analyzing defects. As there were three persons involved in inspecting defects and calculating metrics, individual judgments of the inspectors may not always be consistent. This inconsistency will affect the amount of faulty classes and their metrics, and might subsequently lead to inconsistent results. Nevertheless, we have minimized this threat by establishing guidelines, performing joint analysis for a number of cases (to assure a uniform way of working), and by engaging in discussions in cases of doubt.

External Validity. The following factors should be considered as threats to the external validity of this study. First, project specific contexts such as project size, team size and composition, and time pressure might influence the overall quality of the final software. Hence, the use of only one case study might limit the generalizability of the results discussed in this paper. Second, the generalizability of the results might be limited to systems where the models were developed using UML CASE tools comparable to the one used in this study.

6 Conclusions and Future Work

In this paper we discuss a novel and practical approach to measure the level of detail (LoD) in UML models and describe its application to an industrial case study. We define two LoD measures based on class- and sequence diagrams respectively, and investigate the correlation between the LoD measures and defect density. The findings from the correlation analyses show a significant correlation between LoD of classes and defect density, when sequence diagram metrics are used to determine the LoD. The negative nature of the correlation implies that the higher the LoD of a class, the lower the defect density.

Future research should identify which sequence diagram LoD metrics have the most prominent correlations with defect density. This knowledge is of high importance for software modelers as a guide in choosing the most effective modeling notations in order to reduce defects in the final software. Furthermore, replications of this study using comparable data from other real software projects must be conducted to validate the generalizability of the results reported in this paper. For this purpose, a web-based tool that eases replications and collaboration has been developed. Finally, future research should take into account project specific contexts that might influence the introduction of defects in software systems.

Acknowledgments

This work was accomplished under the FINESSE (des7015) project supported by the STW (Stichting Technische Wetenschappen), the Netherlands. We thank Siu Wai Tang for his collaboration in this study and also the IPS project team for the discussions and support in providing the project data.

References

1. Chidamber, S.R., Kemerer, C.F.: A metrics suite for object oriented design. IEEE Trans. Softw. Eng. 20(6), 476–493 (1994)
2. Gyimothy, T., Ferenc, R., Siket, I.: Empirical validation of object-oriented metrics on open source software for fault prediction. IEEE Trans. Softw. Eng. 31(10), 897–910 (2005)

3. Subramanyam, R., Krishnan, M.S.: Empirical analysis of ck metrics for object-oriented design complexity: Implications for software defects. IEEE Trans. Softw. Eng. 29(4), 297–310 (2003)
4. Brito e Abreu, F., Melo, W.: Evaluating the impact of object-oriented design on software quality. In: METRICS 1996: Proceedings of the 3rd International Software Metrics Symposium. IEEE Computer Society Press, Los Alamitos (1996)
5. Janes, A., Scotto, M., Pedrycz, W., Russo, B., Stefanovic, M., Succi, G.: Identification of defect-prone classes in telecommunication software systems using design metrics. Information Sciences 176(24), 3711–3734 (2006)
6. Succi, G., Pedrycz, W., Stefanovic, M., Miller, J.: Practical assessment of the models for identification of defect-prone classes in object-oriented commercial systems using design metrics. Journal of Systems and Software 65(1), 1–12 (2003)
7. El Emam, K., Melo, W., Machado, J.C.: The prediction of faulty classes using object-oriented design metrics. Journal of Systems and Software 56(1), 63–75 (2001)
8. Basili, V.R., Briand, L.C., Melo, W.L.: A validation of object-oriented design metrics as quality indicators. IEEE Trans. Softw. Eng. 22(10), 751–761 (1996)
9. Dobing, B., Parsons, J.: How UML is used. Commun. ACM 49(5), 109–113 (2006)
10. SDMetrics: The UML design quality metrics tool, `http://www.sdmetrics.com`
11. Chillarege, R., Kao, W.L., Condit, R.G.: Defect type and its impact on the growth curve. In: Proceedings of the 13th international conference on Software engineering, pp. 246–255. IEEE Computer Society Press, Los Alamitos (1991)
12. Chillarege, R., Bhandari, I.S., Chaar, J.K., Halliday, M.J., Moebus, D.S., Ray, B.K., Wong, M.Y.: Orthogonal defect classification-a concept for in-process measurements. IEEE Transactions on Software Engineering 18(11), 943–956 (1992)
13. IEEE: IEEE standard classification for software anomalies. IEEE Std 1044-1993 (1994)
14. Lange, C.F.J., Chaudron, M.R.V., Muskens, J.: Practice: UML software architecture and design description. IEEE Software 23(2), 40–46 (2006)
15. Nugroho, A., Chaudron, M.R.V.: Managing the quality of UML models in practice. In: Rech, J., Bunse, C. (eds.) Model-Driven Software Development: Integrating Quality Assurance. Idea Group Inc. (2008)
16. Nugroho, A., Chaudron, M.R.V.: A survey into the rigor of UML use and its perceived impact on quality and productivity. In: 2nd International Symposium of Empirical Software Engineering and Measurement (2008)
17. Briand, L.C., Labiche, Y., Penta, M.D., Yan-Bondoc, H.D.: An experimental investigation of formality in UML-based development. IEEE Transactions on Software Engineering 31(10), 833–849 (2005)

An Empirical Investigation on Dynamic Modeling in Requirements Engineering

Carmine Gravino[1], Giuseppe Scanniello[2], and Genoveffa Tortora[1]

[1] Dipartimento di Matematica e Informatica, University of Salerno, Via Ponte don Melillo, I-84084 Fisciano (SA), Italy
{gravino,tortora}@unisa.it

[2] Dipartimento di Matematica e Informatica, University of Basilicata, Viale dell'Ateneo, I-85100 Potenza, Italy
giuseppe.scanniello@unibas.it

Abstract. Modeling is a fundamental activity within the requirements engineering process concerning the construction of abstract descriptions of system requirements that are amenable to interpretation and validation. In this paper we report on a controlled experiment aimed at assessing whether dynamic modeling of system requirements provides an accurate account of stakeholders' requirements. The context is constituted of second year Bachelor students in Computer Science at the University of Basilicata. The data analysis reveals that there is not significant difference in the comprehension of system requirements achieved by using or not dynamic modeling.

1 Introduction

Requirements engineering is a relevant and challenging branch of systems engineering [1], [2]. The activity most often regarded in the requirement engineering process is perhaps the requirements elicitation. Information gathered during requirements elicitation often has to be interpreted, analyzed, modeled, and validated before the requirements can be considered correctly collected and ready to be considered and implemented in a software system.

Elicited requirements are validated in the agreeing requirements activity to establish whether they provide an accurate account of stakeholder requirements [3], [1]. Requirements validation is difficult for a number of reasons. The main difficulty concerns the question of truth and what is knowable. Adapted from the problem of validating scientific knowledge, validation is the task of making sufficient empirical observations to check that an objective problem existing in the world has been captured correctly. In order to assess whether the requirements have been correctly captured, stakeholders should effectively interpret and comprehend their abstract descriptions (i.e., the models) [3].

Several modeling methods and their associated analysis techniques have been proposed in the past. Behavioral modeling is one of the widely employed modeling approaches, which often involves the modeling of dynamic or functional behavior of stakeholders and systems, both existing and required [4], [5], [3].

K. Czarnecki et al. (Eds.): MoDELS 2008, LNCS 5301, pp. 615–629, 2008.

Misunderstood requirements are generally expensive to fix later in the project lifecycles [6], [7].

In this paper we report on an empirical study aimed at assessing whether dynamic modeling provides an accurate account of stakeholder requirements. Indeed, we have conducted a controlled experiment to assess the comprehension of software requirements abstracted by using the behavioral modeling approach [3]. The experiment has been conducted within a software engineering laboratory and carried out by 24 second year students of the Bachelor program in Computer Science at the University of Basilicata. All the recruited subjects attended a Software Engineering course before conducting the experiment. The data analysis reveals that there is not significant difference in the comprehension of system requirements achieved by using or not dynamic modeling.

The remainder of the paper is organized as follows: Section 2 discusses related work, while the controlled experiment and the achieved results are presented in Sections 3 and 4, respectively. Future work and final remarks conclude the paper.

2 Background and Related Work

Software engineering is concerned with the theories, methods, and tools needed to develop software. It stretches from technical issues, such as databases and operating systems, to social and psychological issues because of the human intensive nature of software development. A critical part of the software system development is the requirements engineering process. Broadly speaking, requirements engineering concerns the discovering of the system purpose by identifying stakeholders and their needs, and documenting these in a form that is amenable to analysis, communication, and subsequent implementation [1].

The main activities within a requirement engineering process are: eliciting requirements, modeling and analyzing requirements, communicating requirements, agreeing requirements, and evolving requirements. These activities are actually interleaved, iterative, and may span the entire software systems development life cycle [3]. In the activity eliciting requirements the requirements engineer gathers information on the system to develop, and often has to interpret, analyze, model, and validate them before he/she can feel confident that a complete enough set of requirements has been collected. The construction of abstract descriptions, that are amenable to interpretation, represents the main issue of the activity modeling and analyzing requirements. In the activity communicating requirements the different stakeholders communicate about the identified system requirements. In the activity agreeing requirements all the involved stakeholders have to reach an agreement on the modeled system requirements. Finally, the evolution and the changing of system requirements are considered in the evolving requirements activity.

It is easy to recognize that the way in which requirements are documented and specified plays an important role in ensuring that they can be read, interpreted, analyzed, rewritten, evolved, and validated [5], [8]. In the past, several empirical studies have been proposed to assess the effectiveness of modeling techniques and to validate elicited requirements and models. For example, Anda *et al.* [9] analyzed a set of quality attributes for the use case models focusing on quality and understandability. In particular, they performed an exploratory study aimed at investigating three different sets of guidelines employed to construct and documenting use case models. The experiment involved undergraduate students and the results of the empirical analysis revealed that the guidelines based on templates were easier to understand. Moreover, guidelines based on templates better supported the students in constructing use case models and the quality of the produced documentation was higher. Similar to our controlled experiment, Britton *et al.* [10] reported on a study performed to investigate relationship between user preference on the UML sequence or collaboration diagrams with their accuracy in understanding information modeled using these diagrams. The context of the study was constituted of first year students in Computer Science. The study revealed that the effect of diagram type was not significant. Moreover, user preference for sequence diagram before performing the tasks was not related to significantly better performance with sequence diagrams.

Letier *et al.* [11] proposed a technique to analyze requirements-level scenarios. This technique can be used in the early phase of the software system development as it highlights the relevance of monitoring and controlling issues. In particular, they investigated the so-called input-output implied scenario, which is able to expose problematic behaviors in scenario descriptions that standard scenarios could not detect. By using several examples taken from the literature the authors showed the relevance of their approach.

To assess the models produced during the requirement engineering process different approaches can be employed [12], [3]. For example, checklist based inspection techniques can be used [13], [14]. Different checklists aimed at identifying defects in use case descriptions have been proposed and adopted in the literature. Cox *et al.* [13] performed a laboratory experiment to compare the widely employed checklists with the checklist they defined. The results of the experiment suggested that the description and quality of use cases is improved when the checklist proposed by the authors is used.

Several controlled experiments have also been conducted to assess the effectiveness of using UML in the design of software systems. For example, Torchiano [15] verified whether the use of UML object diagrams improves the comprehension of software systems. The results of this empirical investigation suggested that object diagrams can significantly improve the comprehension for certain types of systems as compared to the use of only class diagrams. The author highlighted that further analysis is needed to establish for what type of systems the use of object diagrams improves the comprehension.

Otero and Dolado [16] performed an empirical study aiming at comparing the semantic comprehension of three dynamic models of UML, namely sequence, collaborations, and state diagrams. The study revealed that generally the comprehension of dynamic models depends on the diagram type and on the complexity of the functionality. However, they also found that software design documents were more comprehensible when sequence diagrams are used to model dynamic behavior. In a subsequent study the same authors observed that the specification of the dynamic behavior using OML (Open Modeling Language) is faster to comprehend and easier to interpret than using UML [17].

Ricca *et al.* [18] presented the results of three experiments carried out to assess the effectiveness of the UML stereotypes proposed by Conallen [19] to design Web applications. The experiments involved subjects with different levels of experience and ability. The data analysis revealed that it is not possible to conclude that the use of stereotypes significantly improves the comprehension performances of the subjects. However, the analysis highlighted that ability significantly interact with the considered treatment (i.e., using or not the Conallen stereotypes). Indeed, subjects with low ability achieved significant benefits from the use of stereotypes, while subjects with high ability obtained comparable comprehension performance with or without using stereotypes. Thus, the authors concluded that the use of stereotypes reduces the gap between novice and expert software engineers. The use of stereotypes was also been analyzed by Kuzniarz *et al.* [20], who obtained results similar to Ricca *et al.* [18]. However, they did not consider and discuss the effect of different levels of ability of the involved undergraduate students.

Cruz-Lemus *et al.* [21] presented a controlled experiment on the UML statecharts. This study revealed that the use of composite states in a UML statechart improves the understandability of the diagrams when subjects had previous used them. Similar results have been obtained by Briand *et al.* [22], who established that training is required to achieve better results when UML is completed with the use of OCL (Object Constraint Language) [23]. They also observed that there was a significant interaction between ability and treatment in the case of defect detection. Reynoso *et al.* [24] showed that comprehensibility of OCL also depended on the coupling among subsystems. Differently, Arisholm *et al.* analyzed more in general the impact of UML on software maintenance [25]. The results suggested that the availability of documentation based on the UML may significantly improve the functional correctness of changes as well as the design quality when complex tasks have to be accomplished.

3 The Controlled Experiment

In this section we describe the design of the controlled experiment following the template suggested by Wohlin *et al.* [26].

3.1 Experiment Definition and Context

Analysis focuses on abstracting software system requirements. To this end, different modeling methods can be used. In this experiment, we consider the method suggested in [3], where analysis modeling is composed of: functional model, analysis object model, and dynamic model. Functional model focuses on the functionality and is based on use cases and scenarios, while analysis object model focuses on the individual concepts that will be manipulated by the system. UML class and/or object diagrams are employed to represent the identified concepts of the problem domain. Dynamic model concerns the system behavior. UML statecharts and/or sequence diagrams can be used to represent the behavior of the meaningful use cases presented in the functional models.

The controlled experiment presented in this paper aims at assessing whether dynamic models improve the comprehension of system requirements from the stakeholders' point of view. To this end, we investigated the effect of using or not the UML sequence diagrams.

The controlled experiment was conducted within a software engineering laboratory at the University of Basilicata with volunteers. In particular, 24 second year students of the Bachelor program in Computer Science. All the involved subjects attended a Software Engineering course before conducting the experiment. One of the main topics of this course is the modeling of object oriented software systems using UML. It is worth noting that the subjects also had object oriented programming experience and Web technology knowledge.

The experiment has been performed in a controlled setting, organized in two laboratory sessions. In each session, the subjects were asked to perform a task concerning the comprehension of a functional requirement of a system on which they were familiar with.

Two different modeling methods, namely DM (Dynamic Model) and NO_DM (No Dynamic Model), have been considered to perform the tasks. Subjects use functional, analysis object, and dynamic models to perform the comprehension task when the DM method is used. On the other hand, functional and analysis object models are applied to accomplish the task with the NO_DM method. It is worth noting that we have considered as functional models structured description of use cases, while the UML class diagrams have been employed to abstract analysis object models. To model the dynamic aspect of a given functionality we consider the UML sequence diagrams.

The following are the comprehension tasks we have selected:

T1. Comprehending the functional requirement "Processing an order" of an e-commerce systems, e.g., amazon.

T2. Comprehending the functional requirement "Adding a course" of a software system for the management of courses, lecturers, and students of a given University.

The complexity level of the tasks is comparable and were expected to be accomplished within 30 minutes. Further details on the tasks can be found in [27].

3.2 Hypothesis Formulation

The first goal of the experiment was to verify whether the use of dynamic models influences the comprehension of software requirements. Thus, we formulated the null hypothesis that no difference is observed using DM and NO_DM.

H_{n_0}. The use of dynamic models does not significantly support subjects in comprehending system requirements.

In case the null hypothesis can be rejected with relatively high confidence, it is possible to formulate an alternative hypothesis that typically admits a positive effect of the use of the UML sequence diagrams as comprehension support. Thus, the following is the alternative hypothesis we have considered:

H_{a_0}. The use of dynamic models significantly supports subjects in comprehending system requirements.

3.3 Selected Variables and Experiment Design

In order to properly design the controlled experiment and analyze the results, we considered the following independent variables, also called factors:

- **Method.** This variable indicates the factor on which the study is focused on, namely DM and NO_DM.
- **Task.** This variable indicates the tasks to perform (see Section 3.1), namely **T1** and **T2**.
- **Lab.** The experiment is organized in two laboratory sessions, namely **Lab 1** and **Lab 2**.

To verify the considered hypotheses we have taken into account a measure based on the comprehension of the considered requirements. As suggested in [20], [28], [29], [18] we used a questionnaire consisting of multiple choice questions to assess the comprehension of the subjects. The questions concerned several aspects of the system requirements. Each question could assume one or more correct answers. Furthermore, the number of answers was the same for each question. Details on the questionnaire can be found in [27].

Owing to the used questionnaire we were able to assess the comprehension of each subject using the measures: recall, precision, and F-measure [30]. We defined the recall and precision as follows:

$$recall_s = \frac{\sum_i |answer_{s,i} \cap correct_i|}{\sum_i |correct_i|} \%$$

$$precision_s = \frac{\sum_i |answer_{s,i} \cap correct_i|}{\sum_i |answer_{s,i}|} \%$$

where $answer_{s,i}$ is the set of answers given by the subjects s to the question i and $correct_i$ is the set of correct answers expected for the question i. Note that the measures defined above represent aggregations of the precision and recall values that have been obtained considering each question of the questionnaire. Differently from aggregate measures based on the mean of precision and recall values the adopted measures also consider the fact that subjects do not provide any answer for a given question [31], [32].

The defined precision and recall measures can be easily interpreted. In particular, the recall measure represents the percentage of expected answers that a subject correctly identified, while the precision measure shows the percentage of answers given by the subject that are actually correct. Since these measures abstract different concepts, we used an aggregate measure (i.e., F-measure [30]) to obtain a balance between them:

$$F{-}measure_s = 2 * \frac{precision_s * recall_s}{precision_s + recall_s}\%$$

To verify the defined null hypothesis, we used the following dependent variable:

- **Comprehension.** The F-measure of the precision and recall values.

Although we designed the experiment to avoid the task effect on the dependent variable, the **Task** variable has to be considered and tested to evaluate that it does not impact on the subjects' comprehension. Therefore, the treatments of the experiment are represented by the possible combinations of the factors **Method** (DM and NO_DM) and **Task** (**T1** and **T2**).

To avoid results to be biased by learning or tiring effects, each subject experienced both the factors **Method** and **Task** over the two subsequent laboratory sessions (i.e., **Lab 1** and **Lab 2**). To minimize the learning effect, we also needed subjects starting to work in **Lab 1** both with and without the dynamic model on the tasks **T1** and **T2**. Whatever the treatment was, functional models and analysis object models were always provided to the subjects. Table 1 summarizes the design of the experiments. We randomly assigned the subjects to the groups A, B, C, and D. Indeed, six were the subjects assigned to each group. When necessary we use the labels *Xi*, to refer to the subject *i* of the group X (i.e., A, B, C, or D). Subjects carried out the laboratory sessions of the experiment without interacting each other.

3.4 Preparation

The subjects attended an introductory lesson where detailed instructions on the tasks to be performed were presented. This lesson aimed at highlighting the goal of the experiment, while details on the experimental hypothesis were not provided.

Similar to the works presented in [33], [22], [18] at the end of the second laboratory session a survey questionnaire has been proposed to the subjects. This survey aimed at assessing the overall quality of the provided material, the perceived usefulness of the considered **Method** (i.e., DM and NO_DM), and the clearness of the tasks and the laboratory session goals.

The survey questionnaire is composed of ten questions (see Table 2). The answers to the questions **Q1**, **Q2**, and **Q3** are based on a five-point Likert scale [34]: from strongly agree (1) to strongly disagree (5). The questions from **Q4** to **Q7** expected answers according to a different five-point Likert scale ranging form very high (1) to very low (5). The question **Q8** aimed at investigating the **Method** (i.e., DM or NO_DM) that the subject perceived as more useful in the comprehension of the system requirements. A neutral judgment could be also expressed by the subjects. To assess the modeling method (i.e., functional model,

Table 1. Experiment design

Subjects' Group	Method	
	DM	NO_DM
A	T1, Lab 1	T2, Lab 2
B	T2, Lab 2	T1, Lab 1
C	T2, Lab 1	T1, Lab 2
D	T1, Lab 2	T2, Lab 1

Table 2. Post-experiment survey questionnaire

Id	**Question**
Q1	I had enough time to perform the tasks
Q2	The task objectives were perfectly clear to me
Q3	The tasks I performed was perfectly clear to me
Q4	Judging the difficulty of the task on the e-commerce system
Q5	Judging the difficulty of the task on the system for the management of courses, lecturers, and students
Q6	Assessing your experience level on the analysis object modeling and UML class diagrams
Q7	Assessing your experience level on the dynamic modeling and UML sequence diagrams
Q8	The method more useful to comprehend and interpret software requirements is
Q9	To comprehend and interpret software requirements I believe that the following is the more useful modeling method

the dynamic model, or the analysis object model) that the subjects perceived as more useful the question **Q9** was used.

4 Results

At the end of each laboratory sessions the questionnaires used to assess the subjects' comprehension were collected. Let us note that we also collected the post experiment survey questionnaires.

Two researchers working together analyzed the questionnaires to compute the values of precision, recall, and F-measure. Table 3 shows some descriptive statistics (i.e., median, mean, and standard deviation) - grouped by **Method** and **Task** - on the considered dependent variable.

In the following subsections we present and discuss the obtained results, analyzing the effect of the main factor (i.e., DM and NO_DM). Furthermore, we also present the results showing that the other factors (i.e., **Task** and **Lab**) do not affect the considered dependent variable. The results of the survey questionnaire

Table 3. Descriptive statistics

Task	DM			NO_DM		
	Med.	Mean	Std. Dev.	Med.	Mean	Std. Dev.
All	62.50	63.33	19.76	63.00	61.21	15.87
T1	73.00	63.75	20.50	69.00	64.67	14.16
T2	59.50	62.50	21.24	62.00	57.75	17.32

Table 4. Analysis of the influence of the factors Task and Lab

Factor	**Influence**
Method	0.689
Task	0.734
Lab	0.869
Method vs. Task	0.604
Method vs. Lab	0.689

are presented and discussed as well. Let us note that the results of the tests used here are intended as statistically significant at $\alpha = 0.05$.

4.1 Influence of Task and Lab

We analyzed the interaction between the dependent variable and the factors **Task** and **Lab** in order to verify the absence of learning or tiring effects. Due to the experiment design, we have adopted the two-way ANOVA test [35]. To apply this parametric test the following four assumptions have to be verified: the observations are independent, the scale of measurement is interval, the distribution is normal, and the variance of the observations is constant. The first and the second assumptions are easily verified due to the experiment design and the scale of measurement. On the other hand, to verify the normality of the distribution we used the Shapiro-Wilk test, while to verify the last assumption the Levene statistic test was applied.

The normality of the distributions of the dependent variable and its variance are constant as the Shapiro-Wilk test (p-value = 0.215) and the Levene statistic test revealed (p-value = 0.974 grouping by **Task** and p-value = 0.877 grouping by **Lab**), respectively. Therefore, the two-way ANOVA test can be applied on the analyzed factors.

Table 4 summarizes the results achieved by applying two-way ANOVA on the factors **Method**, **Task**, and **Lab**. The results concerning the interaction between **Method** and **Task**, and between **Method** and **Lab** are shown as well.

ANOVA revealed that there was not a significant effect on both **Task** and **Lab**. No significant interaction between **Method** and **Task** and **Method** and **Lab** was shown as well.

Table 5. Wilcoxon test results

#obs.	p-value	% of DM > NO_DM	% of DM < NO_DM	% of DM = NO_DM
48	0.260	50.00	37.50	12.50

4.2 Influence of Method

In order to test the null hypothesis $\mathbf{H}_{n_0}$ we used a paired Wilcoxon one-tailed test [36]. It was possible to use this non parametric due to the design of the experiment. We used this test to analyze differences exhibited by each subject on the **Method** variable.

This test revealed that the null hypothesis $\mathbf{H}_{n_0}$ cannot be rejected (i.e., p-value = 0.260). This means that there is not significant difference in the comprehension of system requirements achieved by using or not dynamic modeling. The test results are reported in Table 5. This table also shows the percentage of subjects that using the dynamic model achieved a better F-measure value (% of DM > NO_DM) and the percentage of subjects that without using the dynamic model achieved a better F-measure value (% of DM < NO_DM). 50% of the subjects benefit more of the dynamic models. The subjects that did not benefit from the use of the dynamic modeling are 37.5%. The remaining subjects obtained nearly the same F-measure value using or not dynamic models.

Observe that the results of the two-way ANOVA test [35] reported in Table 4 confirmed that the **Method** does not influence the system requirement comprehension.

4.3 Survey Questionnaire Results

In this section we analyzed the feedbacks that subjects provided using the post-experiment survey questionnaire. The answers provided to the questions ranging from **Q1** to **Q7** are visually summarized by the boxplots in Figure 1. We do not show the boxes regarding to the questions **Q8** and **Q9** due to the different adopted scale (see Section 3.4). However, the answer analysis of these questions are presented and discussed as well.

The analysis of the collected answers of the question **Q1** showed that the time to carry out the experiment was considered appropriate (see Figures 1). The boxes of the answers of the questions **Q2** and **Q3** revealed that the objectives and the laboratory tasks were considered clear. The subjects manifested a neutral judgment regarding the complexity of both the comprehension tasks as the boxes of the questions **Q4** and **Q5** show. The subjects asserted that their knowledge on the analysis object modeling and UML class diagrams and on the dynamic modeling and UML sequence diagrams is comparable (see the boxes of **Q6** and **Q7** in Figure 1).

Finally, the answers of the questions **Q8** and **Q9** reveal that subjects generally considered dynamic modeling and the UML sequence diagrams more useful to comprehend software requirements.

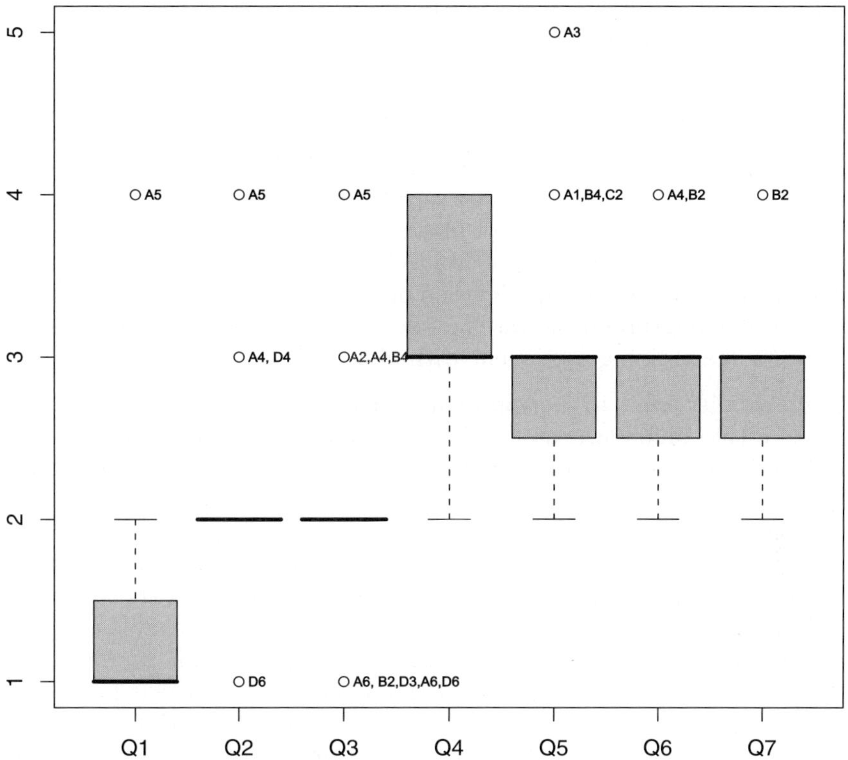

Fig. 1. Answers of the subjects

4.4 Threats to Validity

In this section we describe the threats to validity (i.e. *internal*, *construct*, *external*, and *conclusion* validity threats) that could affect the experiment presented in this paper. The *internal* validity threat is relevant in studies that try to establish a causal relationship. In particular, the presented experiment aimed at assessing whether dynamic modeling provides an accurate account of stakeholder requirements. In our experiment stakeholders are students. The key question in the internal validity threat is whether the observed differences can be attributed to the learning effect and not to other possible causes. In the experiment presented here this threat is mitigated by the design as each group worked, over the two laboratory sessions, on different tasks and with DM and NO_DM. Nevertheless, there is still the risk that, during two laboratory sessions, subjects might have learned how to improve their comprehension performances. However, the factor **Lab** does not significantly affect the comprehension performances of the subjects as shown in Section 4.1. It is worth noting that the internal validity threats has also been mitigated as the subjects in each group had similar experience with UML and software system modeling. The survey also showed that the subjects found clear everything regarding the controlled experiment.

Construct. Validity threats that may be present in this experiment were mitigated by a proper experiment design. The questionnaire used to assess the subjects' comprehension could affect the obtained results. Even the metric used to get a quantitative evaluation of the subjects' comprehension could affect the results. However, questionnaires and aggregate measures of precision and recall have been widely employed in the past [31], [18], [32]. To avoid social threats due to evaluation apprehension, students were not evaluated on the results they obtained. Moreover, subjects were not aware of the experimental hypotheses. It is important to note that the experiment has been carried out to evaluate the value of dynamic models in the comprehension of software requirements. Thus, ease of comprehension/interpretation was the sole examined criterion as it represents a key issue for maintaining agreement with all subjects.

External. Validity refers to the approximate truth of conclusions involving generalizations within different contexts. External validity threats are always present when experiments are performed with students. However, the students we considered in the study were familiar with the problem domain of the selected comprehension task. Consequently, we regard them as representative of the context where we would like to generalize the achieved results. Nevertheless, replications should be performed with different subjects in different contexts to confirm or contradict the results. In our case we selected these tasks to enable the subjects to conclude the laboratory sessions of the experiment within 30 minutes. This fact has conditioned the complexity of the models used in the experiment. We are also confident that with more complex tasks, the help of dynamic models may be more effective. Thus, we also plan to perform replications on different and more complex comprehension tasks.

Conclusion. Validity threats concern the issues that affect the ability of drawing a correct conclusion. A definition of conclusion validity could be the degree to which conclusions we reach about relationships in our data are reasonable. The conclusion validity threats were mitigated by the experiment design and by the properly selection of the population. Regarding the recruited subjects, we drew a fair sample from that population and conducted our experiment with subjects belonging to this sample. Moreover, proper tests were performed to statistically reject the null hypothesis. In cases differences were present but not significant, this was explicitly mentioned. Furthermore, the used aggregate measure allowed us to assess in an objective way the comprehension of the subjects. As the conclusion validity could be affected by the observation number, further replications on a larger dataset are required to confirm or contradict the achieved results. The survey questionnaire, mainly intended to get subjective insights, was designed using standard ways and scales [34].

5 Conclusion

In this paper we have reported on a controlled experiment aimed at assessing whether the dynamic modeling and UML sequence diagrams provide an accurate account of stakeholder requirements. Indeed, this experiment was focused on the comprehension of software requirements abstracted by using a behavioral modeling approach [4]. The context of the experiment was constituted of second year Bachelor students in Computer Science at the University of Basilicata.

The subjects judged the use of dynamic modeling more useful to comprehend and interpret software requirements as the survey questionnaire revealed (see Section 4.3). Conversely, the analysis of the factors of interest revealed that there is not significant difference in the comprehension of system requirements achieved by using or not dynamic modeling. This is the case where controlled experiments provide an insight into the difference between the perceived usefulness of a given method and the effective advantage of using it.

The achieved results can be considered relevant as the subjects are representative of the context where we would like to generalize them. Indeed, the selected subjects were familiar with object oriented programming, the UML visual notation, software system modeling, and Web technologies. Furthermore, they were also familiar with the problem domain of the functional requirements of the comprehension tasks to be performed.

Regarding the considered tasks some considerations are also due. In particular, we can assert that they were properly selected and can be considered representative as they concern actual and widely known systems. Also the complexity and size of the tasks can be judged appropriate as the subjects declared as well (see Section 4.3). However, despite the significance of the achieved results, we are going to replicate the experiment in different contexts. In particular, we plan to perform two replications: with master students and industrial subjects (i.e., analysts and practitioners). The effects of changing complexity and size of the comprehension tasks will be considered in these replications. As matter of fact, the comprehension of more complex software requirements could benefit from the use of dynamic modeling.

Acknowledgments

The authors would like to thank Michele Risi and Rocco Oliveto for the stimulating discussion and the precious suggestions.

References

1. Nuseibeh, B., Easterbrook, S.: Requirements engineering: a roadmap. In: Proceedings of the Conference on the Future of Software Engineering, pp. 35–46. ACM Press, New York (2000)
2. Finkelstein, A.: Requirements engineering: an overview. In: 2nd Asia-Pacific Software Engineering Conference (1993)
3. Jackson, M.: Software Requirements and Specifications: A Lexicon of Practice, Principles and Prejudices. Addison-Wesley, Reading (1995)
4. Bruegge, B., Dutoit, A.: Object-Oriented Software Engineering Using UML, Patterns, and Java. Prentice-Hall, Englewood Cliffs (2004)

5. Davis, A.: Software Requirements: Objects, Functions and States. Prentice-Hall, Englewood Cliffs (1993)
6. Boehm, B.W.: Software Engineering Economics. Prentice-Hall, Englewood Cliffs (1981)
7. Nakajo, T., Kume, H.: A case history analysis of software error cause-effect relationships. Transactions on Software Engineering 17(8), 830–838 (1991)
8. Wieringa, R.J.: Requirements Engineering: Frameworks forUnderstanding. Wiley, Chichester (1996)
9. Anda, B., Sjoberg, D.I., Jorgensen, M.: Quality and understandability of use case models. In: Knudsen, J.L. (ed.) ECOOP 2001. LNCS, vol. 2072, pp. 402–428. Springer, Heidelberg (2001)
10. Britton, C., Kutar, M., Anthony, S., Barker, T., Beecham, S., Wilkinson, V.: An empirical study of user preference and performance with UML diagrams. In: IEEE Symposia on Human Centric Computing Languages and Environments, pp. 31–33. IEEE Computer Society Press, Los Alamitos (2002)
11. Letier, E., Kramer, J., Uchitel, J.M.S.: Monitoring and control in scenario-based requirements analysis. In: 27th International Conference on Software Engineering, pp. 382–391. ACM Press, New York (2005)
12. Heitmeyer, C., Jeffords, R.D., Labaw, B.G.: Automated consistency checking of requirements specifications. Transaction on Software Engineerig and Methdology 5(3), 231–261 (1996)
13. Cox, K., Aurun, A., Jeffery, R.: Classification of research efforts in requirements engineering. Journal of Research and Practice in Information Technology 36(4), 211–229 (2004)
14. Fagan, M.: Design and code inspections to reduce errors in program development. IBM Systems Journal 15(3), 182–211 (1976)
15. Torchiano, M.: Empirical assessment of UML static object diagrams. In: Proceedings of the 12th International Workshop in Program Comprehension, Bari, Italy, pp. 226–229. IEEE Computer Society Press, Los Alamitos (2004)
16. Otero, C., Dolado, J.J.: An initial experimental assessment of the dynamic modelling in UML. Empirical Software Engineering 7(1), 27–47 (2002)
17. Otero, M.C., Dolado, J.J.: An empirical comparison of the dynamic modeling in OML and UML. Journal of Systems and Software 77(2), 91–102 (2005)
18. Ricca, F., Di Penta, M., Torchiano, M., Tonella, P., Ceccato, M.: The role of experience and ability in comprehension tasks supported by UML stereotypes. In: Proceedings of the 29th International Conference on Software Engineering, Minneapolis, MN, USA, pp. 375–384. IEEE Computer Society Press, Los Alamitos (2007)
19. Conallen, J.: Building Web Applications with UML. Object Technology. Addison-Wesley, Reading (1999)
20. Kuzniarz, L., Staron, M., Wholin, C.: An empirical study on using stereotypes to improve understanding on UML models. In: 2th International Workshop on Program Comprehension, Bari, Italy, pp. 14–23. IEEE Computer Society Press, Los Alamitos (2004)
21. Cruz-Lemus, J.A., Genero, M., Manso, M.E., Piattini, M.: Evaluating the effect of composite states on the understandability of UML statechart diagrams. In: ACM/IEEE 8th International Conference on Model Driven Engineering Languages and Systems, Montego Bay, Jamaica, pp. 113–125. Springer, Heidelberg (2005)
22. Briand, L., Labiche, Y., Di Penta, M., Yan-Bondoc, H.: An experimental investigation of formality in UML-based development. IEEE Transactions on Software Engineering 31(10), 833–849 (2005)

23. OMG: Object constraint language (OCL) specification, version 2.0 (2005)
24. Reynoso, L., Genero, M., Piattini, M., Manso, M.E.: Does object coupling really affect the understanding and modifying of UML expressions? In: Proceedings of ACM Symposium on Applied Computing, pp. 1721–1727. ACM Press, New York (2006)
25. Arisholm, E., Briand, L.C., Hove, S.E., Labiche, Y.: An empirical comparison of the dynamic modeling in OML and UML. Transactions on Software Engineering 32(6), 365–381 (2006)
26. Wohlin, C., Runeson, P., Host, M., Ohlsson, M.C., Regnell, B., Wesslen, A.: Experimentation in Software Engineering - An Introduction. Kluwer Academic Publishers, Dordrecht (2000)
27. Gravino, C., Scanniello, G., Tortora, G.: A controlled experiment conducted with bachelor students on dynamic modeling. Technical report, University of Salerno (2008), http://www.scienzemfn.unisa.it/scanniello/RE_Exp1/
28. Purchase, H.C., Colpoys, L., McGill, M., Carrington, D., Britton, C.: UML class diagram syntax: an empirical study of comprehension. In: Proceedings of Australian Symposium on Information Visualisation, Sydney, Australia, pp. 113–120. Australian Computer Society (2001)
29. Purchase, H.C., Wellanda, R., McGillb, M., Colpoysb, L.: Comprehension of diagram syntax: an empirical study of entity relationship notations. International Journal of Human-Computer Studies 61(2), 187–203 (2004)
30. Baeza-Yates, R., Ribeiro-Neto, B.: Modern Information Retrieval. Addison-Wesley, Reading (1999)
31. Antoniol, G., Canfora, G., Casazza, G., De Lucia, A., Merlo, E.: Recovering traceability links between code and documentation. IEEE Transactions on Software Engineering 28(10), 970–983 (2002)
32. Zimmermann, T., Weissgerber, P., Diehl, S., Zeller, A.: Mining version histories to guide software changes. IEEE Transactions on Software Engineering 31(6), 429–445 (2005)
33. Briand, L., Penta, M.D., Labiche, Y.: Assessing and improving state-based class testing: A series of experiments. Transaction on Software Engineerig 30(11), 770–793 (2004)
34. Oppenheim, A.N.: Questionnaire Design, Interviewing and Attitude Measurement. Pinter Publishers (1992)
35. Devore, J.L., Farnum, N.: Applied Statistics for Engineers and Scientists. Duxbury (1999)
36. Conover, W.J.: Practical Nonparametric Statistics, 3rd edn. Wiley, Chichester (1998)

Heterogeneous Coupled Evolution of Software Languages

Sander Vermolen and Eelco Visser

Software Engineering Research Group
Delft University of Technology, The Netherlands
s.d.vermolen@tudelft.nl, visser@acm.org

Abstract. As most software artifacts, meta-models can evolve. Their evolution requires conforming models to co-evolve along with them. Coupled evolution supports this. Its applicability is not limited to the modeling domain. Other domains are for example evolving grammars or database schemas. Existing approaches to coupled evolution focus on a single, homogeneous domain. They solve the co-evolution problems locally and repeatedly. In this paper we present a systematic, heterogeneous approach to coupled evolution. It provides an automatically derived domain specific transformation language; a means of executing transformations at the top level; a derivation of the coupled bottom level transformation; and it allows for generic abstractions from elementary transformations. The feasibility of the architecture is evaluated by applying it to data model evolution.

1 Introduction

Data models are an integral part of software development. They define the structure of data that is processed by an application and the schema of a database. Running applications produce and store data that conforms to the data model.

Due to changing requirements or maintenance, data models need to evolve. This process is known as *format evolution* [15]. As a consequence of evolution, stored data no longer conforms to the evolved data model and can thereby become useless to the evolved application. To continue using existing data, the data needs to be transformed to reflect the evolution, which is an instance of coupled evolution.

Coupled evolution does not only apply to data transformation, but is a reoccurring problem in computer science [14]. Models need to be transformed to reflect evolution in their meta-models [7,6,23]. Programs need to be transformed when the programming languages (or domain specific language) they have been written in evolves [18]. And a data model itself needs to be transformed to reflect evolution in the data modeling language (e.g. UML). We unify these scenarios by considering evolving software languages and transformation of sentences in these languages.

Current approaches to support coupled evolution of software languages are homogeneous. They solve the problem in a specific domain. They repeatedly implement the coupled evolution structure and solve problems common to coupled evolution locally. Instead, we would like a systematic approach to realize heterogeneous coupled evolution for any scenario of software language evolution.

K. Czarnecki et al. (Eds.): MoDELS 2008, LNCS 5301, pp. 630–644, 2008.

```
User {
  name    :: string
}
Web {
  admin   :: set of User
  topic   :: string
}
Page {
  content :: string
  date    :: date
  author  :: User
  web     :: Web
}
```

Fig. 1. Data model 1

```
User {
  name    :: string
}
Web {
  admin   :: set of Group
  topic   :: string
}
Page {
  content :: string
  date    :: date
  author  :: User
  web     :: Web
  topic   :: string
}
Group {
  name    :: string
  members :: set of User
}
```

Fig. 2. Data model 2

In this paper, we present two generalizations over coupled software language evolution scenarios and introduce the concept of heterogeneous coupled evolution. To enable the generalization, we present an architecture to support heterogeneous coupled evolution of software languages. We have implemented a tool to support the architecture. It generates a domain specific transformation language (DSTL) for an arbitrary software language domain. It generates an interpreter of transformations defined in the DSTL. And it supports generic abstraction from the basic transformations that are defined in the DSTL. We illustrate the architecture and tool by elaborating their application to coupled data model evolution.

The paper is structured as follows: In Section 2 we briefly introduce data model evolution and its context. In Section 3 we elaborate on coupled data evolution by defining data model transformations and deriving data transformations to reflect these. In Section 4 we generalize over the different scenarios of coupled software language evolution. In Section 5, we discuss the architecture to support heterogenous coupled evolutions. Section 6 discusses related work. Section 7 concludes.

2 Data Model Evolution

Data models describe the structure of data that is processed and stored by an application. As example application we consider a Wiki. It consists of web pages, users to edit these and webs, which are collections of pages that cover a similar topic. The corresponding data model is shown in Figure 1.

Changing requirements and maintenance cause data models to evolve along with the application they are set in, a process known as format evolution [15]. Consider for example the shift from a user-based to a group-based access control security mechanism and the addition of page topics. The new data model to support these is shown in Figure 2.

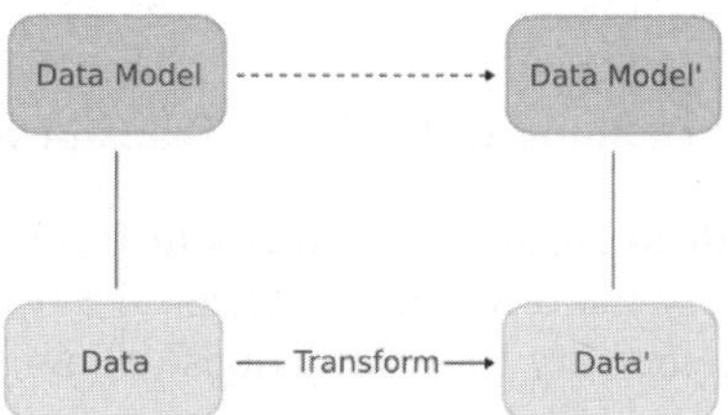

Fig. 3. Data model changes

Since the Wiki is a running application during evolution, it has stored pages, users and webs. Such data conforms to some version of the data model. To prevent the loss of data when the data model changes, the data needs to be transformed to reflect these changes. Figure 3 shows the process graphically. At the top level, we see two versions of the data model. At the bottom level we see the stored data and the transformation needed to reflect the data model change. The vertical lines indicate conformance. The dashed arrow indicates the changes applied to the data model and is usually performed manually by editing the data model. The transform arrow on the other hand requires tools for database transformations, as it is usually too much of an effort to reenter all data manually.

3 Coupled Data Evolution

When a data model evolves, stored data may no longer conform. In practice the data is usually no longer usable. To continue to use the data, we need to reflect the data model changes in a transformation of the stored data. Supporting a single data model change, requires a significant effort. Supporting data model changes in an evolution process, requires repeated data transformations. If these transformations are defined manually, this becomes costly and holds back the development process.

Coupled data evolution automates the data transformation process. It is based upon the assumption that the data model transformation and the data transformation are related. The concept of coupled data evolution is shown in Figure 4. Coupled evolution consists of two components, which are represented by the two new arrows: (1) A definition of the data model transformation (the evolve arrow) and (2) a mapping from data model transformation to data transformation (the dashed arrow). The first needs to be specified for each change of the data model, whereas the second is typically defined once for our data models.

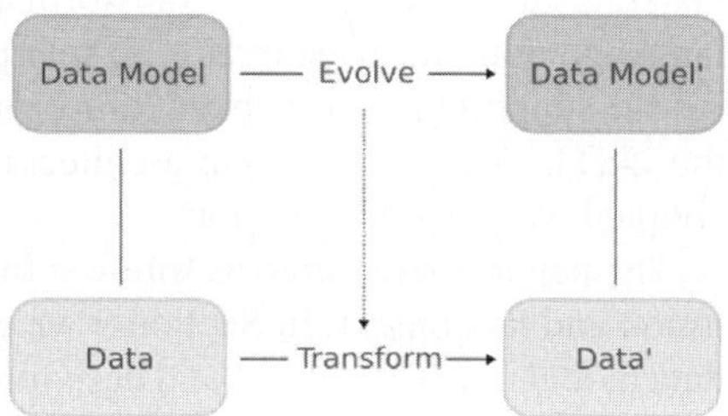

Fig. 4. Coupled data evolution

The questions that remain are: How to define the data model transformation and how to derive a data transformation. In the literature we can find various approaches to formalize both [15,2,4]. In this section, we take a closer look at the two, using the Wiki data model as a running example. We introduce a language for defining data model transformations and show a mapping that targets a broad set of databases.

3.1 Defining Data Model Transformations

We distinguish two methods to formalize transformations for coupled evolution [7]: Specify the difference between the two versions of the data model or specify a trace of elementary transformations defining how the new version is obtained from the old version. Both have advantages and disadvantages. We choose the second because it allows us to define the mapping, as we will see in the next section.

Our data models are relatively basic. They consist of entities with a name and properties. Each property has a name and a type. Entities, properties, types and names are the constructs of our data model. A fairly limited set of constructs. Consequently, the number of elementary transformations we can perform on our model (on our constructs) is fairly small. We identify:

- adding or removing entities
- changing the name of an entity
- adding or removing properties
- changing the name of a property
- substituting the type of a property
- substituting the type of a set

We define for example the addition of a new entity "Group" as follows:

```
add Group {
  name        :: string
  description :: string
  members     :: set of User   }
```

Although the addition is in itself a valid transformation, in general the elementary actions above do not have sufficient meaning on their own. One cannot change the name of an entity without knowing which entity is being referred and a substitution of a type should not only specify the new type, but also the old type that is being replaced. The transformations above are local and need a location to make them executable to a specific model.

The representation of a data model is tree-structured. The root node is the model itself. Its direct children are entities, which have in turn properties as their children and so on. We define a unique location in a data model by specifying a path from the root node. For example: "Entity *Group* - Property *members* - Type" indicates the type of the `members` collection in the `Group` entity that we have just added. In a similar way, we define locations for our transformations using the APath [13] notation, which is based on the XPath language [3]. APath expressions consist of a /-separated list of construct names. The above would be written as:

```
Entity [Id="Group"] / Property [Id="members"] / Type
```

The `[...]`-part indicates a predicate on the node that is being evaluated. If we would have written `Entity/Property/Type`, we would have got all types, of all properties, of all entities. The predicates restrict this by only allowing those with the right id's.

We define a transformation to be a combination of an APath and a local transformation. The two are separated by a ::-sign. As examples, we specify the removal of the 'description' property and the substitution of the type in a set:

```
Entity[Id="Group"] / Property[Id="description"] :: remove
Entity[Id="Web"] / Property[Id="admin"] / Type / Set / Type :: substitute with Group
```

We also need more complex transformations, such as copying properties over an association, or merging entities. Although these can be modeled as separate transformations or transformation patterns [12], we recognize them to be similar to the already defined transformations, with the addition of being able to use other data model elements as input. So copying the topic from a Web to all of its pages is similar to adding a topic property to every page, with its web topic as a source:

```
Entity[Id="Page"] / Property :: add Web/Property[Id="topic"]
```

Elementary transformations are combined by sequential composition indicated by a semi-colon. Figure 2 shows the result of applying the above transformations to the Wiki data model in Figure 1.

3.2 Deriving Data Migrations

We have defined the data models and the data model transformation. The last step is therefore to specify a 'data model transformation' to 'data transformation' mapping, as indicated by the dashed arrow in Figure 4. The implementation of the mapping depends on numerous factors, such as how the data is stored, what platform is available to execute the data transformation on and the quantity of the data. The implementation is therefore driven by the context. We have implemented the mapping using Stratego/XT [21] and a data model to Java classes mapping from the WebDSL project [22]. It maps the data model transformations as shown above to a data migration program in Java. The migration program loads objects from a database, transforms them to conform to the new data model and stores the new objects. It follows a so-called Extract-Transform-Load (ETL) process.

The migration mainly uses two libraries, namely an object to relational mapping and an object transformation library. The first library provides functionality for loading and storing Java Objects in a relational database. The migration program is based upon the Java Persistence API (JPA) [20], which provides an interface to accessing these types of libraries. Consequently, any JPA compliant library is suitable. An example of such a library is Hibernate [11]. The combination of JPA and for example Hibernate supports a large number of database systems. The second library provides functionality for transforming Java objects and managing these transformations. It supports transformations such as adding attributes, changing attribute types and changing attribute names, but due to Java restrictions, the set of transformations does not directly cover the elementary transformation set we have seen above. We have written the transformation library specifically for the mapping, but it could also be used in different settings.

In the remainder of this section, we introduce the mapping using the examples we have presented above. Although the mapping directly refers to the transformation library, we use a domain specific language (DSL) for the library to abstract away from the underlying Java and JPA details. Nevertheless, the DSL can directly be mapped onto executable Java code.

Basic concepts. The group addition, introduces most of the basic concepts. It is mapped to the following:

```
transform () to (Group) {
   EmptyObject();
   AddAttributeByValue("name", "Group Name");
   AddAttributeByValue("description", "...");
   AddAttributeByValue("members", null)
}
```

The `transform` directive defines a transformation as follows:

```
transform INPUT-TYPES to OUTPUT-TYPE
   {  TRANSFORMATION-DEFINITION  }
```

In the Group addition, `INPUT-TYPES` is empty and `OUTPUT-TYPE` is a Group. The transformation itself starts with an empty object (an object with no attributes) and subsequently adds the various attributes of Group. The `AddAttributeByValue` directive has the new attribute's name as first parameter and the attribute's value as second.

Similarly, the description removal is mapped to:

```
transform (Group) to (Group) {
   DropAttribute("description")
}
```

Annotations. In the data transformations above, we carelessly introduced values for each of the attributes (`"Group Name"`, `"..."` and `null`). These are required in a data transformation, but unknown in the data model or data model transformation. Such information can be considered to be a separate input of the mapping, yet at the same time, storing it separately from the data model transformation would be impractical.

As a solution, we allow data model transformations to be annotated. When transforming data models, these annotations can be ignored, but when looking at data transformations, annotations provide the information we were missing. Instead of writing:

```
Entity[Id="User"] :: add age :: int
```

to add an attribute age, we therefore write:

```
Entity[Id="User"] :: add age :: int        defaultValue(25)
```

Using a similar approach we specify the value of a newly added group.

Data-level computations. Copying the topic property from a web to a page is done by an attribute addition. The attribute addition by constant value we have seen above is not sufficient. We need an attribute addition by computed value here. The computation itself is a parameter to the attribute addition:

```
transform (Page) to (Page) {
  AddAttribute("topic", getWeb().getTopic() )
}
```

In Java, the computation is represented by an anonymous class.

The substitution from the previous section indicates a type substitution. At the data level this is reflected by a conversion to a value of the new (substituted) type. There are various type substitutions that have a standard value conversion. Examples are int to string, string to int, but also set of int to set of string. We have explicitly included the conversions for these substitutions in our mapping.

The substitution from the previous section is a set of User to a set of Group substitution. Such a substitution does not have a standard value conversion. To still be able to execute the data transformation, the user is required to explicitly specify the desired conversion by means of an annotation[1]. An example conversion would be to convert our set of user to a set of singleton groups in which each group holds exactly one user. This is mapped to:

```
transform (Web) to (Web) {
  AttributeSetConversion("admin", new Group( getUser().getName(), { getUser() } ) )
}
```

[1] Not by means of a parameter, as this computation only influences the data, not the data model.

Note that the name `AttributeSetConversion` indicates that the conversion (the second parameter) is applied to each of the elements in the admin set, not to the set as a whole, which would be the functionality of the `AttributeConversion` transformation.

Types. Each of the above transformations refers to types. They have a set of source types and a target type. Since the code above is directly mapped to Java, these should represent actual Java types. The final step of the mapping is therefore to construct a Java type base to support the transformations. To establish the type base, we use a Java type generator from the WebDSL project, that takes a data model as input and produces the corresponding Java classes as output. Without investigating the transformations, we generate all types for the data model before transformation as well as all types in the data model after transformation. The resulting types are stored in different Java packages to prevent name clashes.

In addition to the source and target types, we also sometimes need types half-way through the transformation (e.g. when using the attribute addition by computation). These are generated when performing the mapping.

4 Heterogeneous Coupled Transformation

When data models evolve, conforming data needs to be transformed to reflect these changes. Although a frequently reoccurring approach is to define data transformations manually, it requires a significant effort and can hold back a development or maintenance process. We have shown that it can be performed automatically. In this section we step away from the detailed look on data model transformations and take a broader look at the problem from a higher level of abstraction.

4.1 Horizontal Generalization

Recall Figure 4. It shows the outline of the coupled data evolution problem. We have looked at Object Oriented data models describing data in a data base. If we would have described our data by means of a database schema (e.g. SQL schema), we would have an evolving database schema and data that has to be transformed to reflect these changes [4,2,8], as shown in Figure 5. The problem of coupled data evolution therefore reoccurs when using a different formalism for describing our data.

Similarly, we could use XML to store our data and DTD's to describe it. Again our DTDs evolve to satisfy changing requirements and our XML data needs to be transformed to reflect these changes [15], as shown in Figure 6.

We also see the same problem reoccurring in different domains. When programming languages evolve, the programs written in it have to be migrated to the new version of the languages. The programs have to conform to the grammar of the programming languages [18] (Figure 7). Similarly, when meta-models evolve, conforming models need to be transformed to reflect the evolution [7,24,6,23,12,9].

Coupled evolution is a reoccurring phenomenon. Naming conventions for the coupled evolution problem vary in the different areas between co-evolution, two-level

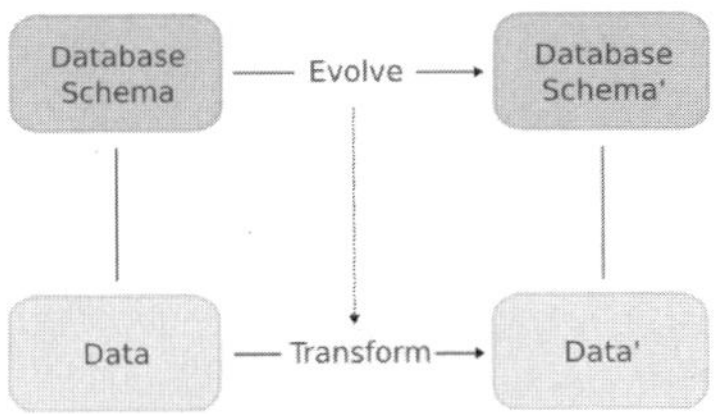

Fig. 5. Schema evolution

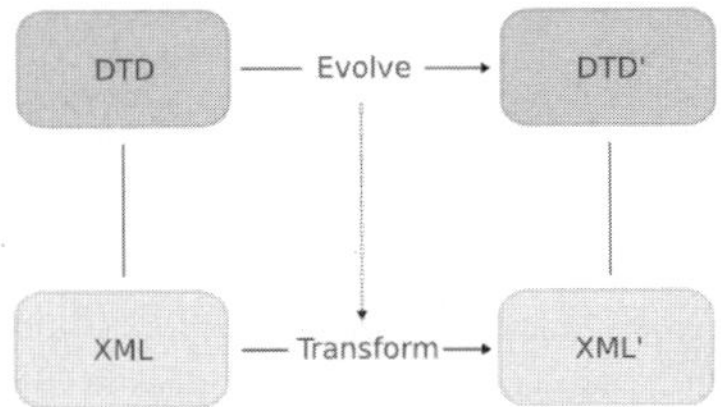

Fig. 6. DTD evolution

data transformations, coupled transformation and simply synchronization or adaptation. But they effectively address the same problem of coupled evolution. Lämmel discusses this for a subset of the above in [14], naming it the ubiquity of coupled transformation problems. Identifying the coupled evolution problem in different domains is a form of *horizontal* generalization.

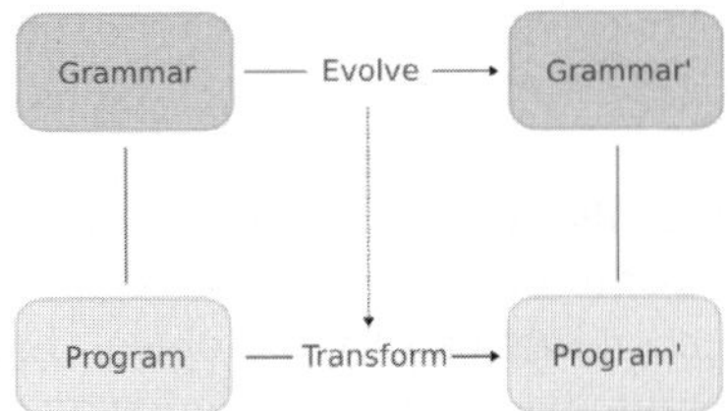

Fig. 7. Grammar evolution

4.2 Vertical Generalization

We introduced the data model language on the fly in the previous sections. We thereby implicitly defined its syntax. The syntax is formalized by the grammar found in Figure 8. It is written in SDF [**?**] format. For simplicity, it only shows the context-free production rules. The lexical syntax definitions and the start symbol (`DataM`) definition have been left out. On the left-hand-side of each production rule the construction of the specific sort is defined, on the right-hand-side the produced sort. Each of the rules are annotated, which is indicated by the `{...}` text at the end of each rule. We ignore these annotations for now.

```
Entity*              -> DataM {cons("Model")}
Id "{" Prop* "}"-> Entity{cons("Entity")}
Id "::" Type         -> Prop  {cons("Prop")}
"int"                -> Type  {cons("Int")}
"bool"               -> Type  {cons("Bool")}
Id                   -> Type  {}
"set of" Type        -> Type  {cons("Set")}
Name                 -> Id    {cons("Id")}
```

Fig. 8. Data model grammar

As data conforms to a data model, data models conform to the data model grammar. The grammar describes the structure of the data model and the data model describes the structure of the data. The data model grammar itself is rather limited. In future, it may for example be useful to add support for more attribute types, inheritance, or support for uniqueness of property values. So, in practice, the grammar is far from fixed and is itself subject to expansion and modification. No different from the data model scenario, if the grammar changes, data models that originally conformed to it are invalidated and need to be migrated along with the grammar. In other words, we have a second scenario of coupled evolution in the single context of data models. Figure 9 shows the extension with the additional evolution scenario.

We cover another conformance level by saying that also the SDF syntax may be subject to change, at which point, the grammar defined above has to be migrated along

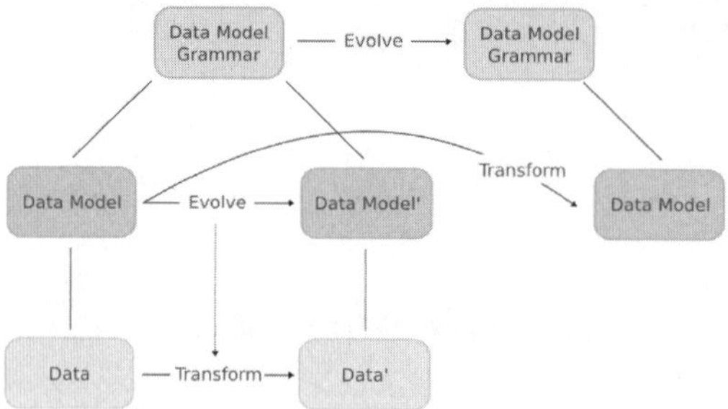

Fig. 9. Vertical generalization

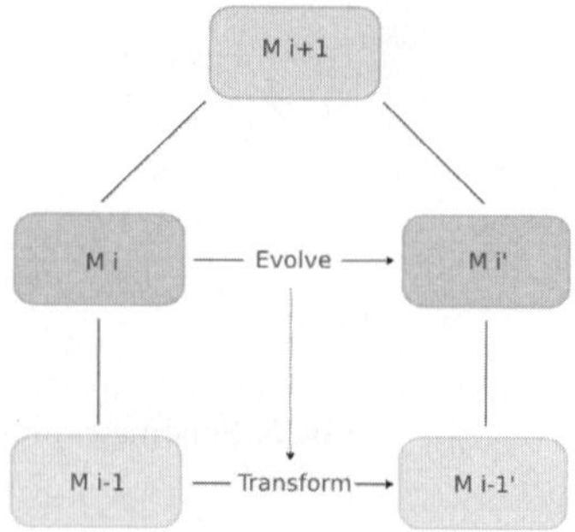

Fig. 10. Software language evolution

with the changing SDF definition. From which we see that the same coupled software transformation problem reoccurs over different conformance levels, which is a vertical generalization of the problem. In MDA [19] terms the vertical generalization can be phrased as coupled evolution on the levels M_1-M_0 (data model - data), M_2-M_1 (data model grammar - data model), M_3-M_2 (SDF - data model grammar), or even higher if M_3 is not defined in itself.

To abstract away from a specific conformance level and from specific areas of application, we will from now on use a generalized representation of the problem as shown in Figure 10. In this generalized view, we see the common aspects of coupled software language evolution:

– An evolving software language (M i)
– Software that is subject to transformation to reflect the evolving language (M i-1)
– A means to define software languages (M i+1)

For the case of data model evolution, we have automated the transformation process. To do the same in the generic case, we need a way to formalize the evolution for an arbitrary software language. Furthermore, we need a mapping from the language evolution to a concrete transformation.

5 Generic Architecture

In this section we propose and outline a generic architecture for coupled software evolution. Its goal is to reduce the manual effort involved in traditional coupled evolution. Furthermore, it structures the evolution process, increases the transformation abstraction levels and allows for common problems to be solved once instead of repeatedly.

Traditional approaches to coupled evolution are usually based on architectures similar to the one in Figure 4. The generic solution is based on the generalized and extended architecture displayed in Figure 11. The main component in the architecture is the definition of the transformation language used to formalize the evolution (named DSTL). In earlier work, the transformation language is usually fixed and considered to be an assumption of the approach. We assume it to be variable and consider it an artifact in coupled evolution.

Although the transformation language stands out most in the figure, the key concept of the architecture lies in the added arrows. The dashed arrow denotes a transformation defined by the user. The solid arrows denote automatic transformation, these do not require human interaction.

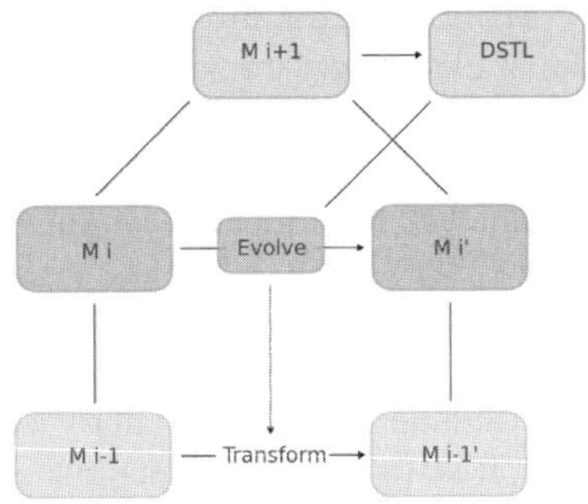

Fig. 11. Generic architecture

Input to the architecture is a coupled evolution scenario as explained in the previous section and a mapping from a top-level transformation to a bottom-level transformation. The first should come for free (either implicit or explicit), since it is merely defining what is to be evolved. Without it, the coupled evolution problem does not exist. The second is also part of most domain-specific approaches and may to that respect be reused in these specific domains.

The mapping, or dashed line in the figure, is defining a semantic link between the two levels, which is by definition sufficient to allow for coupled evolution. Since it is indirectly based upon M i+1, it is generic over any software (or model) being evolved within the same domain. We therefore have fixed mappings for the domain of data model evolution, or the domain of SDF evolution. In practice, the evolution scenario is therefore the main input, varying most frequently.

Based upon the two inputs, the architecture provides a structured approach to software language evolution, consisting of:

- Automatic derivation of a transformation language for each domain
- Automatic derivation of an interpreter for transformations in the transformation language
- Automatic software migration along a specified transformation

In practice there is a non-obvious ordering in these items, different from the ordering above. One needs the transformation language to define the mapping. Yet, since the transformation language derivation is automatic, the ordering will not be a problem in practice.

The following subsections focus on the aspects of the architecture individually.

5.1 Deriving Domain Specific Transformation Languages

The first and most central component of the architecture is a transformation language specific to the M i+1 definition. We will refer to it as the Domain Specific Transformation Language (DSTL). The transformation language cannot be generic, as we cannot construct a complete mapping from a generic language. Generic languages contain by definition concepts that are not part of the domain[2].

[2] Having a partial mapping is similar to using an implicit domain specific language. The language is defined by the domain of the mapping.

Many of the traditional transformation languages for coupled evolution define a large set of elementary transformations and an extensive mapping. In contrast to this, we focus on a transformation language that is as small as possible, but still covers all transformations. This makes defining the mapping as easy as possible. Usability of the language is achieved through abstractions. We have implemented the DSTL derivation in Stratego/XT and assume M i+1 to have been defined in SDF. The DSTL syntax is again defined in SDF.

Input to the derivation is M i+1, the software language grammar (in SDF). The derivation produces elementary transformations from the production rules in the grammar. It starts at the productions of the start symbol and traverses the grammar recursively. We distinguish different types of production rules, for which different types of elementary transformations are generated.

Lists. The top-most production rule in the data model grammar (Figure 8) defines a data model to be a list of entities:

```
Entity*         -> DataM
```

In the transformation language, the list is reflected by two list operations, namely addition and removal of entities. The syntax for these transformations is defined by the context-free productions:

```
"add" Entity    -> Transformation
"remove"        -> Transformation
```

In the same way, the addition and removal of properties are generated when considering the Entity production recursively. Furthermore, we generate transformations for optional symbols in a similar way (these are set and unset transformations).

Lexical Syntax. When a symbol is defined to be lexical, it has no more productions and can thus not be decomposed further. The recursion therefore stops and a transformation is generated to substitute its value. An example of a lexical symbol is `Name`, for which the following transformation is generated:

```
"substitute with" Name -> Transformation
```

Multiple Productions. The symbols that are considered above are either lexical, or produced by a single production. The `Type` symbol inside a property can be produced in multiple ways (`"int"`, `"bool"`, `"set of Type"`, or `Id`). Consequently, we must allow it to be substituted by one of these:

```
"substitute with" Type -> Transformation
```

We import the original data model grammar into the DSTL definition to reuse the `Type` symbol that was defined in the original grammar.

Type checking. A software language defines groups of software elements. For data models we have entities, properties, ids, but also ids inside sets, or ids inside a property. The local transformations defined above are only applicable to some of the element groups, which make up the domain of a local transformation. For example, the addition of entities can only be applied to data models and the substitution of types only to properties or sets.

We use APath expressions to indicate where a local transformation is to be applied. Each APath expression results in certain groups of software elements. To make sure a local transformation is applied within its domain, we need to verify that the APath expression to which it is connected can only result in elements that are in the domain of the local transformation, which is a form of type checking.

We have implemented type checking for any DSTL. It primarily consists of three components: A generation of domains for each of the local transformations. A (generic) type derivation for APath expressions and (generic) functionality that checks whether the result of the APath will indeed fall inside the domain of the local transformation. The type checking is complicated by the use of recursive productions: the `set of int` should fall in the same group as the set inside `set of set of int`.

Larger grammars. The presented data model grammar is small. We have used a much larger data model grammar, which was developed as part of the WebDSL project. Although the principles above can be applied to all the rules in a larger grammar, in practice, one does not want to be able to transform every group of software elements. In the small grammar, we could for example leave out the type substitution within sets if we would not be able to map it to a data transformation.

By means of annotations on the production rules of a grammar, the user can indicate which rules (and thereby what symbols) should be transformed and which should not be transformed. There are two possible annotations: A 'transform' annotation, which tells the tool to generate transformations for a production rule and a 'constant' annotation, which tells the tool to take the production rule into account by recursively generating transformations for each of the symbols on the left-hand-side (in SDF), but not generating transformations for the production rule itself. No annotation on a rule means that it is ignored during DSTL derivation.

5.2 Automated Transformation

The DSTL syntax we have defined allows us to write transformations. The next step is to execute these transformations. For this purpose, we have defined an interpreter generator. Similar to the syntax generator, it takes the software language definition as input, but instead produces an interpreter for the associated DSTL as output. The interpreter mainly consists of:

- A mapping of the elementary DSTL transformations onto generic transformations
- A generic transformations library (build on top of Stratego/XT)
- Implementation of generic DSTL constructs such as composition and abstraction
- An APath evaluation library

The first is specific for the DSTL and therefore generated. It mainly consists of production rules that denote the specific to generic mapping. These look like:

```
transform(|mmodel, path):
  AddProperty(newValue) -> <addAtLocator(|path, newValue)> mmodel
```

The last three items are generic over all DSTLs, so defined once. Their definition is in most ways straightforward and is therefore not discussed here.

6 Related Work

Coupled evolution plays a significant role in computer science and has been treated in various areas. Earlier research has primarily focused on constructing coupled evolution support for specific domains. We discuss related work in the most important domains of coupled evolution: model evolution, domain specific language evolution and schema evolution.

Coupled evolution for the meta modeling domain is introduced by Gruschko [7]. As is the case for most publications on coupled evolution for models, Gruschko models evolution using small elementary transformation steps. A classification of these steps is proposed: non-breaking changes, breaking and resolvable changes and breaking and unresolvable changes. A classification, which is frequently reused in later work and is also applicable to our work, yet not directly relevant to the proposed architecture. In his paper, Gruschko also identifies different steps in coupled evolution, although these steps are generic, they mainly consider what we have called 'the mapping' and are in that sense only applicable to a subset of what has been discussed here. The only step, which does not fall inside the scope of this mapping is a change detection, to determine the evolution steps that have occurred between two given models. If automated, the change detection may provide a useful addition to our work as it reduces the number of required inputs. Yet existing change detections are usually specific to a certain domain and are only applicable within these domains.

Wachsmuth [23] introduces a set of transformations specific to MOF [16] compliant meta models. The set is very similar to the set of elementary transformations for data models as we have introduced in Section 3.1 and which is derived automatically in our approach. Different to the transformations we have derived is their distinction between two type changes, namely generalization and restriction, yet they do not provide a specification on how these should be mapped to concrete types. Furthermore, they have transformations to support changes to inheritance and inlining of classes. Both concepts were not included in our input data model grammar and are therefore not reflected in the output. Wachsmuth proposes a mapping to model migrations implemented in QVT [17].

Similar to Wachsmuth, Herrmannsdoerfer [10] considers coupled model evolution based on small evolution steps. He focuses on the Eclipse Modeling Framework (EMF) [5], in which ECore, the meta-meta model implements a subset of MOF. In his approach, named COPE, Herrmannsdoerfer distinguishes two types of evolution steps: open and closed coupled evolution. The first is what we have named the elementary transformations and the second are transformations based upon these. In contrast to other works, this view does provide a way of abstracting from meta-model specific transformations. However, the derivation of the elementary transformations as well as the definition of these transformations are left to the user. This does not only require additional effort, it also prevents structured abstractions as are possible in our approach. Herrmannsdoerfer provides a prototypical editor based on Eclipse.

In the area of domain specific languages, Pizka et al. discuss the evolution of DSLs. They claim three obstacles in DSL development: (1) Stepwise bottom-up generalization is required, which is a special case of the evolution we have been looking at. (2) DSLs should be layered, which is specific to DSLs and not directly related to coupled evolution. (3) Automated co-evolution is required for DSLs, which is what we generically solve in our work. As we have seen in [23], Pizka's work is focused on a single domain, namely DSLs, it is limited to the discussion of a transformation definition and mapping specific to this domain.

With respect to the data variants of coupled evolution (schema evolution) and the related two-level data transformations, numerous approaches have been found to solve these problems [15,4,2,8,1]. These mainly focus on the schema to data mapping, frequently taking different types of complicating concepts into account, such as data restrictions and performance optimization. These are typically aspects that may also be solved generically, such that they can be used in any domain. In current work, we have not focused on this, but it may be interesting as future work.

7 Conclusion

In this paper, we presented two directions of generalizing coupled software language evolution scenarios and introduced the concept of heterogeneous coupled evolution. We presented an architecture to automate coupled evolution on an arbitrary software domain (e.g. programming languages, modeling or data modeling). The architecture requires as input: a coupled software evolution scenario and a mapping from software language transformations to software transformations. The outputs are: Automatic derivation of a domain specific transformation language (DSTL) to formalize the software language evolution; automatic derivation of an interpreter for transformations conforming to the DSTL; and automatic software migration along the evolving software language.

Using Stratego/XT, we have implemented a coupled evolution tool to support the architecture. It is based on software languages defined in SDF. We have succesfully applied the tool to the domain of data modeling in the web modeling language WebDSL [22], where we have used it to create a tool for automatic database migration along an evolving data model, which targets a broad set of databases.

Acknowledgments. This research was supported by NWO/JACQUARD project 638.001.610, *MoDSE: Model-Driven Software Evolution.*

References

1. Alves, T., Silva, P., Visser, J.: Constraint-aware schema transformation. In: Ninth International Workshop on Rule-Based Programming (Rule 2008) (2008)
2. Berdaguer, P., Cunha, A., Pacheco, H., Visser, J.: Coupled schema transformation and data conversion for XML and SQL. In: Hanus, M. (ed.) PADL 2007. LNCS, vol. 4354, pp. 290–304. Springer, Heidelberg (2006)
3. Clark, J., DeRose, S., et al.: XML Path Language (XPath). W3C Recommendation 16 (1999)
4. Cunha, A., Oliveira, J., Visser, J.: Type-safe two-level data transformation. In: Misra, J., Nipkow, T., Sekerinski, E. (eds.) FM 2006. LNCS, vol. 4085, pp. 284–299. Springer, Heidelberg (2006)
5. Eclipse Foundation. Eclipse Modeling Framework Project (EMF) (2008), `http://eclipse.org/emf`

6. Favre, J.: Meta-model and model co-evolution within the 3D software space. In: Evolution of Large-scale Industrial Software Applications (ELISA 2003), pp. 98–109 (2003)
7. Gruschko, B., Kolovos, D.S., Paige, R.F.: Towards synchronizing models with evolving metamodels. In: Workshop on Model-Driven Software Evolution at CSMR 2007 (2007)
8. Gupta, A., Mumick, I.S., Subrahmanian, V.S.: Maintaining views incrementally. In: International conference on management of data (SIGMOD 1993), pp. 157–166. ACM, New York (1993)
9. Hearnden, D., Lawley, M., Raymond, K.: Incremental model transformation for the evolution of model-driven systems. In: Nierstrasz, O., Whittle, J., Harel, D., Reggio, G. (eds.) MoDELS 2006. LNCS, vol. 4199, pp. 321–335. Springer, Heidelberg (2006)
10. Herrmannsdörfer, M.: Metamodels and models. Master's thesis, München University of technology, München, Germany (July 2007)
11. Hibernate. Relational persistence for Java and.NET (2008), `http://www.hibernate.org`
12. Hoßler, J., Soden, M., Eichler, H.: Coevolution of models, metamodels and transformations. In: Bab, S., Gulden, J., Noll, T., Wieczorek, T. (eds.) Models and Human Reasoning, Berlin, pp. 129–154. Wissenschaft und Technik Verlag (2005)
13. Janssen, N.: Transformation tool composition. Master's thesis, Institute of Information and Computing Sciences Utrecht University, Utrecht, The Netherlands (March 2005)
14. Lämmel, R.: Coupled Software Transformations (Extended Abstract). In: First International Workshop on Software Evolution Transformations (November 2004)
15. Lämmel, R., Lohmann, W.: Format Evolution. In: Reverse Engineering for Information Systems (RETIS 2001). books@ocg.at, vol. 155, pp. 113–134. OCG (2001)
16. Object Management Group (OMG). Meta Object Facility (MOF) Core Specification - Version 2.0 (January 2006)
17. Object Management Group (OMG). MOF QVT Final Adopted Specification (March 2007)
18. Pizka, M., Jurgens, E.: Tool-supported multi-level language evolution. In: Tomi Männistö, E.N., Raatikainen, M. (eds.) Software and Services Variability Management Workshop, Helsinki, Finland. Helsinki University of Technology Software Business and Engineering Institute Research Reports, vol. 3, pp. 48–67 (April 2007)
19. Soley, R., et al.: Model driven architecture. OMG white paper 308 (2000)
20. Sun. Java persistence api (2008), `http://java.sun.com/javaee/technologies/persistence.jsp`
21. Visser, E.: Program transformation with Stratego/XT: Rules, strategies, tools, and systems in StrategoXT-0.9. In: Lengauer, C., Batory, D., Consel, C., Odersky, M. (eds.) Domain-Specific Program Generation. LNCS, vol. 3016, pp. 216–238. Springer, Heidelberg (2004)
22. Visser, E.: WebDSL: A case study in domain-specific language engineering. In: Lammel, R., Saraiva, J., Visser, J. (eds.) GTTSE 2007. LNCS, vol. 5235. Springer, Heidelberg (2008)
23. Wachsmuth, G.: Metamodel adaptation and model co-adaptation. In: Ernst, E. (ed.) ECOOP 2007. LNCS, vol. 4609, pp. 600–624. Springer, Heidelberg (2007)
24. Xiong, Y., Liu, D., Hu, Z., Zhao, H., Takeichi, M., Mei, H.: Towards automatic model synchronization from model transformations. In: Automated Software Engineering (ASE 2007), pp. 164–173. ACM, New York (2007)

Automatability of Coupled Evolution of Metamodels and Models in Practice

Markus Herrmannsdoerfer[1], Sebastian Benz[2], and Elmar Juergens[1]

[1] Institut für Informatik
Technische Universität München
Boltzmannstr. 3, 85748 Garching b. München, Germany
{herrmama,juergens}@in.tum.de
[2] BMW Car IT GmbH
Petuelring 116, 80809 München, Germany
sebastian.benz@bmw-carit.de

Abstract. Model-based software development promises to increase productivity by offering modeling languages tailored to a problem domain. Such modeling languages are often defined by a metamodel. In consequence of changing requirements and technological progress, these modeling languages and thus their metamodels are subject to change. Manually migrating models to a new version of their metamodel is tedious, error-prone and heavily hampers cost-efficient model-based development practice. Automating model migration in response to metamodel adaptation promises to substantially reduce effort. Unfortunately, little is known about the types of changes occurring during metamodel adaptation in practice and, consequently, to which degree reconciling model migration can be automated. We analyzed the changes that occurred during the evolution history of two industrial metamodels and classified them according to their level of potential automation. Based on the results, we present a list of requirements for effective tool support for coupled evolution of metamodels and models in practice.

1 Introduction

Due to their high degree of specialization, domain-specific languages (DSLs) are a promising approach to decrease software development costs by increasing development productivity. Consequently, a variety of metamodel-based approaches for DSL construction, such as Generative Programming [1], Model-Driven Architecture [2] and Software Factories [3], have been proposed in recent years. In response, DSLs are receiving increased attention in industry. BMW Car IT for instance applies DSLs for the specification of user interfaces [4] and test case generation [5]. With the integration of DSLs into industrial development practice, their maintenance is gaining importance. Although significant work in both research and practice has been invested into tool support for the initial development of DSLs, issues related to their maintenance are still largely neglected.

One important issue in language maintenance is the need to migrate existing models in response to the adaptation of their metamodel. As all software

K. Czarnecki et al. (Eds.): MoDELS 2008, LNCS 5301, pp. 645–659, 2008.

artifacts, DSLs are subject to change. Although often neglected, even general-purpose languages are evolving because of changing requirements and technological progress [6]. Due to their close proximity to their problem domain, DSLs are even more prone to change, since many problem domains undergo continuous evolution. However, when a DSL's metamodel changes, dependent artifacts such as models, editors and interpreters may no longer obey the adapted metamodel. Among the required reconciliation efforts, migration of models is probably most challenging, since their number typically outweighs the other artifacts by far. Manually migrating models to a new version of their corresponding metamodel is costly, tedious and error-prone. In order to make cost-effective model-based software development feasible in practice, methods and tools are required to support efficient migration of models in response to changing metamodels.

We consider the evolution of a DSL as a *coupled evolution*[1] of its metamodel and models. Coupled evolution is a problem encountered in several areas of computer science [7], e.g. schema evolution, grammar evolution and format evolution. For each area, different approaches to reduce the associated effort – each with specific advantages and weaknesses – have been proposed. Recently, several approaches [8,9,10] have been transferred to the problem of metamodel evolution. Unfortunately, the requirements for effective tool support for coupled evolution of metamodels and models in practice are far from clear. On the one hand, transferability of existing approaches for e. g. schemata or grammars to the technical space of metamodels is difficult to assess: success of schema evolution approaches has been governed, amongst other things, by their ability to perform data migration in an online fashion; grammar evolution approaches have to take care to preserve the class of context free grammars that the employed parsing technology can handle – success or failure of these approaches in their respective domain can thus not immediately be transferred to metamodeling. On the other hand, and even more importantly, it is largely unknown to which degree changes occurring during language maintenance in practice can be automated. Can suitable tool support substantially reduce migration effort or are changes so domain-specific, that they defy generic solutions? Given the increasing importance of language maintenance in practice, we consider this lack of understanding a precarious situation.

To provide a better understanding of language evolution in practice, and of how much associated effort can be reduced by adequate tool support, this paper presents a study of the histories of two industrial metamodels. To the best of our knowledge, this is the first work to examine the automatability of coupled evolution of metamodels and models in practice. The main contributions are:

- a classification of metamodel adaptation and corresponding model migration operations according to their potential for automation,
- an empirical study of the evolution of two industrial metamodels with respect to this classification, and
- a substantiated list of requirements for effective tool support in practice.

[1] Throughout the paper, we use the term *coupled evolution* instead of the term *co-evolution*, as we feel it better conveys the notion of coupling.

Outline. The remainder is structured as follows: In Section 2, we provide an overview of existing approaches to coupled evolution of specifications and instances. The proposed classification of combined metamodel adaptation and model migration is presented in Section 3. In Section 4, we outline the setup and results of the study we performed on the histories of two industrial metamodels. In Section 5, we discuss the results and derive requirements for efficient tool support. We conclude and give directions for future work in Section 6.

2 Related Work

When a specification changes, potentially all existing instances have to be reconciled in order to conform to the updated version of the specification. Since this problem of *coupled evolution* affects all specification formalisms (e. g. database or document schemata, types or grammars) alike, numerous approaches for *coupled transformation* [7] of a specification and its instances have been proposed. Apart from the target specification formalism, existing approaches mainly differ in their degree of automation and expressiveness, i. e. the kinds of coupled transformations they support. In this section, we outline different classes of approaches to coupled evolution, namely schema, grammar, format and metamodel evolution, focusing on their coupled evolution capabilities rather than on idiosyncrasies of their target specification formalism.

Schema evolution – the migration of database instance data to an updated version of the database schema – has been a field of study for several decades, yielding a substantial body of research [11]. For the ORION database system, Banerjee et al. propose a fixed set of change primitives that perform coupled evolution of the schema and data [12]. While highly automated, their approach is limited to local schema restructuring. To allow for non-local changes, Ferrandina et al. propose separate languages for schema and instance data migration for the O_2 database system [13]. While more expressive, their approach does not allow for reuse of coupled transformation knowledge. In order to reuse recurring complex coupled evolutions, SERF, as proposed by Claypool et al., offers a mechanism to define arbitrary new high-level primitives [14], providing both automation, reuse of coupled transformation knowledge and expressiveness.

Grammar evolution – the migration of textual programs to changes of their underlying grammar – has been studied in the context of grammar engineering [15]. Lämmel proposes a comprehensive suite of grammar transformation operations for the incremental adaptation of context free grammars [16]. The proposed operations are based on sound, formal preservation properties that allow reasoning about the relationship between grammars before and after transformation, thus helping engineers to maintain consistency of their grammar. However, the proposed operations are not coupled since they do not take the migration of words into account. Building on Lämmel's work, Pizka and Juergens propose a tool for the evolutionary development of textual languages called Lever, which is also able to automate the migration of words [17]. Primitive grammar and word evolution operations can be invoked from within a general-purpose language to perform all kinds of coupled transformation. Similar to SERF, Lever provides a mechanism to define arbitrary new high-level primitives.

Format evolution denotes the migration of a class of documents to changes to their document schema. Lämmel and Lohmann suggest operators for format transformation, from which migrating transformations for documents are induced [18]. The suggested operators are based on Lämmel's work on grammar adaptation. Furthermore, Su et al. propose a complete, minimal and sound set of evolution primitives for formats and documents and show that they preserve validity and well-formedness of both formats and documents [19]. Even though both approaches are able to automate document migration for a fixed set of format changes, they are not able to handle arbitrary, complex migrations.

Metamodel evolution denotes the migration of models in response to changes to their metamodel. In order to reduce the effort for model migration, Sprinkle proposes a visual, graph-transformation based language for the specification of model migration [20]. Gruschko et al. envision to automatically derive a model migration from the difference between two metamodel versions [9,10]. Wachsmuth adopts ideas from grammar engineering and proposes a classification of metamodel changes based on instance preservation properties [8]. In order to automate model migration, the author plans to provide a predefined set of high-level transformations which represent the defined classes and are able to adapt the metamodel as well as to migrate models. Due to lack of reports on experience of their application, little is known on how effectively these approaches can be applied to coupled evolution of metamodels and models in practice.

In a nutshell, apart from differences between their target specification formalisms, existing approaches to coupled evolution mainly differ in the provided level of automation, expressiveness, reuse of coupled transformation knowledge and well defined preservation properties. To our best knowledge, little is known on the combination of capabilities that best supports the requirements faced during development and maintenance of metamodels and models in practice.

3 Classification

In this section, we introduce a classification that allows us to determine how far coupled evolution can be automated. Usually the metamodel is adapted manually and models are migrated at different levels of automation. The first level of automation is to encode a transformation that is able to automatically migrate a single model. A higher level of automation is achieved, if a single transformation can be used to migrate all existing models of a metamodel. When manually specifying such transformations, one discovers that they contain recurring patterns. Thus, the third level of automation corresponds to the application of generic transformations embodying such recurring patterns that automate both metamodel adaptation and model migration. In order to define the levels of automation, we introduce the notion of a coupled change. A *coupled change* is defined as a combination of an adaptation of the metamodel and the reconciling migration of the models conforming to that metamodel. Coupled changes do not comprise metamodel changes that do not require a migration of models, e. g. additive changes. In the following, we introduce the classes in combination with representative examples, working our way up from lower to higher levels of potential automation.

3.1 Running Example

We use a simple modeling language for hierarchical state machines to illustrate our classification. Figure 1 depicts the metamodel and a corresponding model in both concrete and abstract syntax.

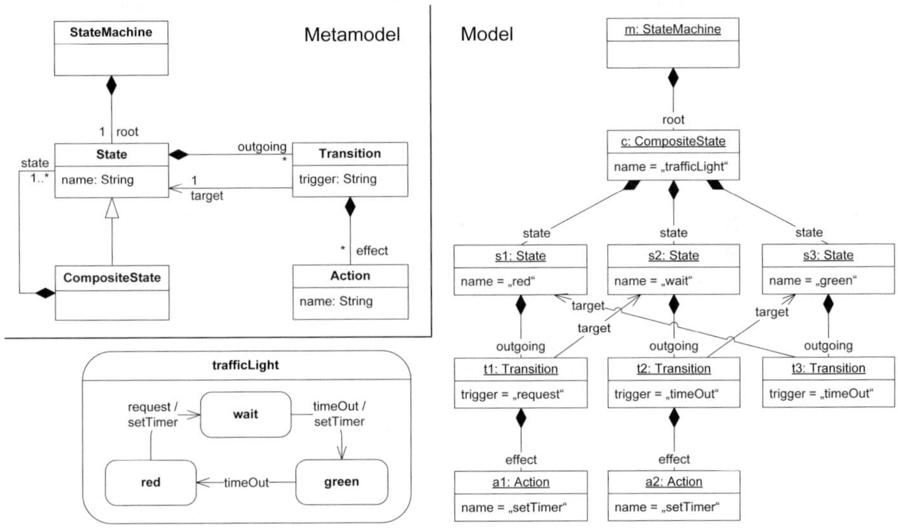

Fig. 1. State machine example

The root element of a state machine model is of type StateMachine and contains the root state. A State may be decomposed into sub states through its subclass CompositeState. A Transition has a target state and relates to its source state through the outgoing composition. Upon activation of a transition by its trigger, a sequence of Actions is performed as effect. Strings are used for state and action names and to denote triggers. The model describes the simplified behavior of a controller for a pedestrian traffic light and uses all the constructs defined by the metamodel. When the traffic light is red and a pedestrian requests a green phase, the controller transitions to wait and activates a timer (setTimer). When its timeOut occurs, the controller transitions to green and activates the timer again. When its timeOut occurs, the controller returns to state red.

3.2 Model-Specific Coupled Change

A coupled change is called *model-specific* if the migrating transformation is specific to a single model and thus cannot be reused to migrate different models of the same metamodel. This happens when the specification of a migration requires information which varies from model to model. Figure 2 depicts both metamodel and model after an example of a model-specific coupled change[2]. In the metamodel, the class Action is refined in order to group actions into specialized kinds. At the same time, the attribute name is deleted, by means of which actions were assigned a meaning before. As the class Action is itself made abstract, model elements of this type need to be migrated to a refined type in order to reestablish conformance and preserve information. As the metamodel was not precise enough to restrict the syntax of the action name, different names might be used in different models to denote the same kind of action. Therefore, model-specific information is required to be able to completely specify the migration.

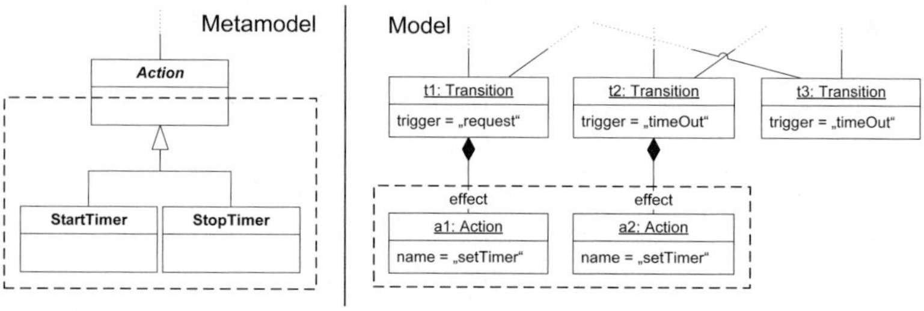

Fig. 2. Refinement of *Action*

3.3 Model-Independent, Metamodel-Specific Coupled Change

When a coupled change is not model-specific and all models of a metamodel can be automatically migrated, it is called *model-independent*. If the change is specific to the metamodel's domain, it is called *metamodel-specific*. In that case, its reuse across different metamodels makes no sense. Figure 3 depicts the impact of a metamodel-specific coupled change, which introduces a separate class for events. In the metamodel, the trigger attribute is factored out into the class Event. The state machine then administers all events and the transitions only refer to them by the trigger association. Since the attribute trigger is removed at the same time, models are no longer conforming to the modified metamodel. To readapt the model to the metamodel, an instance of Event has to be created for each distinct trigger name and to be assigned to the parent state machine. Therefore, only one event with name timeOut is created in the example and both transitions refer to it. As the migration is rather specific and therefore not likely to recur very often, it makes no sense to reuse this coupled change across metamodels.

3.4 Metamodel-Independent Coupled Change

A coupled change is called *metamodel-independent* if both metamodel adaptation and model migration do not depend on the metamodel's domain and can be

[2] For better overview, modified elements are highlighted by a dashed box.

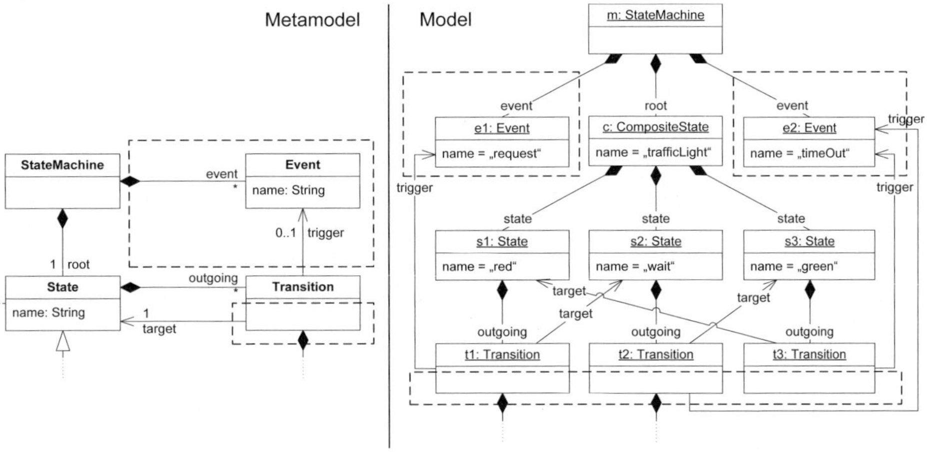

Fig. 3. Introduction of *Event*

expressed in a generic manner. If they are likely to recur in the evolution of different metamodels, it makes sense to generalize them into an operation that that can be reused to evolve other metamodels. Figure 4 depicts the impact of a metamodel-independent coupled change, which is a first step to introduce the concept of concurrent regions to the modeling language. In the metamodel, the class Region is introduced as a container of the directly contained sub states within a CompositeState. To compensate the change in a model, the migration creates a Region as child of each CompositeState and moves all directly contained sub states to the newly created Region. A possible generalization of this coupled change extracts a collection of features of one class into a new class which is accessible from the old class via a single-valued composition to the new class.

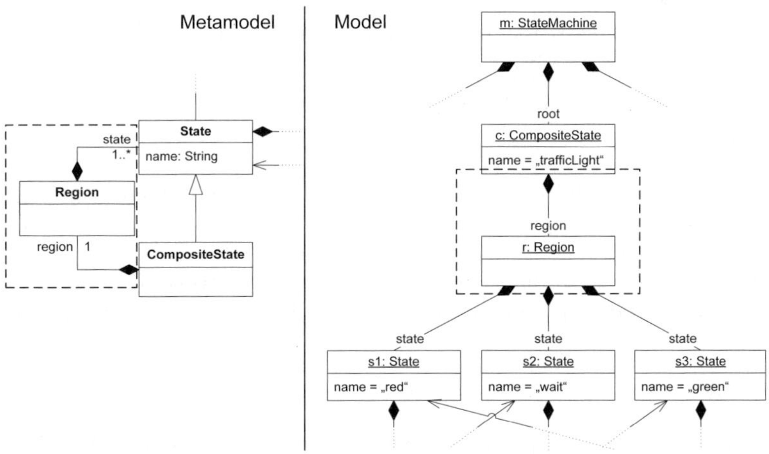

Fig. 4. Introduction of *Region*

3.5 Summary

Figure 5 depicts an overview of the classification, and is augmented by a separate class for *metamodel-only* changes which do not require a migration of the models. For each class of coupled changes, the figure indicates to which level they are specific: The higher the level on which a coupled change depends, the more can be reused and therefore automated. A model-specific coupled change can only be used for a subset of the models of a metamodel. A metamodel-specific coupled change provides automation for all models of a metamodel. A metamodel-independent coupled change can be even applied to all metamodels and their models.

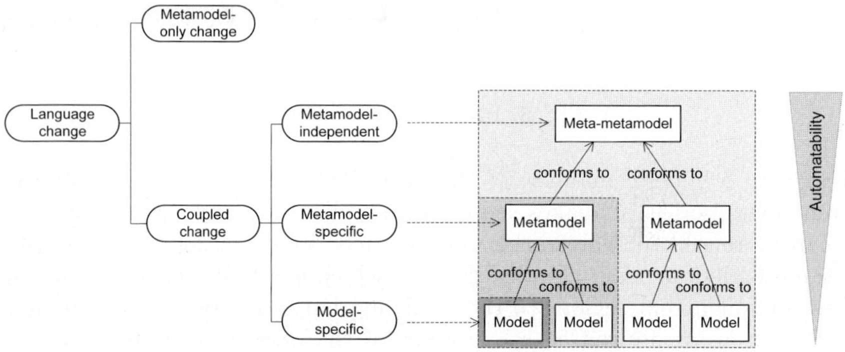

Fig. 5. Classification of coupled changes

4 Study

In order to asses the potential for automation in practice, we applied the classification to the histories of two industrial metamodels. In this section, we present the execution and the results of this study.

4.1 Goals

The study was performed to answer which fraction of language changes

- requires no model migration?
- is model-specific and thus defies automation of migration?
- is metamodel-independent and thus generalizable across metamodels?

4.2 Setup

Two industrial metamodels from BMW Car IT were chosen as input. Both metamodels were developed and maintained by several persons. FLUID (FLexible User Interface Development) is a framework for rapid prototyping of human machine interfaces in the automotive domain [4]. A metamodel defines a modeling language that enables the abstract specification of a human machine interface. An executable prototype of the human machine interface can be generated from a model written in that language. TAF-Gen (Test Automation Framework - Generator) is a framework to automatically generate test cases for human machine interfaces in the automotive domain [5]. The metamodel defines a statechart variant, a structural screen model and a test case language.

The histories of the metamodels were only available in the form of snapshots. A snapshot depicts the state of a metamodel at a particular point in time. As a consequence, further information had to be inferred to obtain the coupled changes leading from one metamodel version to the next. In order to achieve this, we performed the following steps[3]:

1. *Extraction of metamodel versions* (1 person week): Each available version of the metamodel was obtained from the revision control system used in the development of the metamodel[4].
2. *Comparison of subsequent metamodel versions* (2,5 person weeks): Since both revision control systems used are snapshot-based, they provide no information about the sequence of changes which led from one version to the following. Therefore, successive metamodel versions had to be compared in order to obtain the changes in a difference model. The difference model consists of a collection of primitive changes from one metamodel version to the next and has been determined with the help of tool support[5].
3. *Detection of coupled changes* (3 person weeks): Some primitive changes only make sense when regarded in combination with others. When an attribute is for example removed from a class and an attribute with the same name and type is added to its super class, then the two changes have to be interpreted as a compound change in order to conserve the values of the attribute in a model. Therefore, primitive changes were combined based on the information how corresponding model elements were migrated. The coupled changes between metamodel versions were documented in a table.
4. *Classification of coupled changes* (1 person week): The classification was applied to each coupled change.

4.3 Results

In this section, we present the results of the study in a compiled form. The full results are shown in Table 1 in the appendix[6]. In order to get a better impression

[3] In order to get an impression of the extent of the study, the approximate effort is mentioned in parenthesis for each step.

[4] The metamodels were specified by the Ecore metamodeling language from the Eclipse Modeling Framework (EMF, `http://www.eclipse.org/modeling/emf/`).

[5] Two prototypes now contributed to the EMF Compare tool (`http://www.eclipse.org/modeling/emft/?project=compare`) were applied.

[6] Due to a non-disclosure agreement, we cannot provide more detailed information. Informal description of the language changes are made available through our website `http://wwwbroy.in.tum.de/~herrmama/cope`

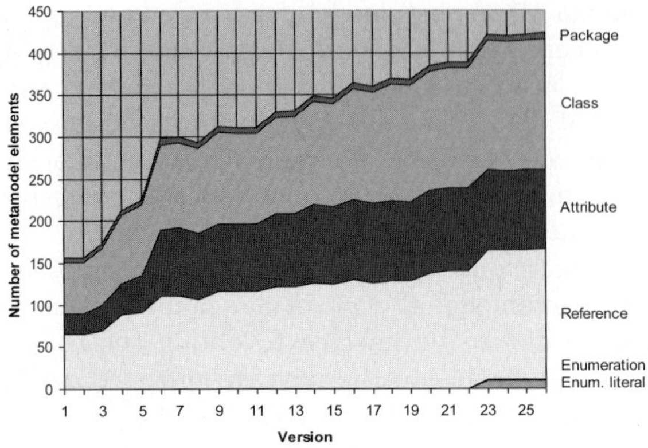

(a) Evolution in numbers

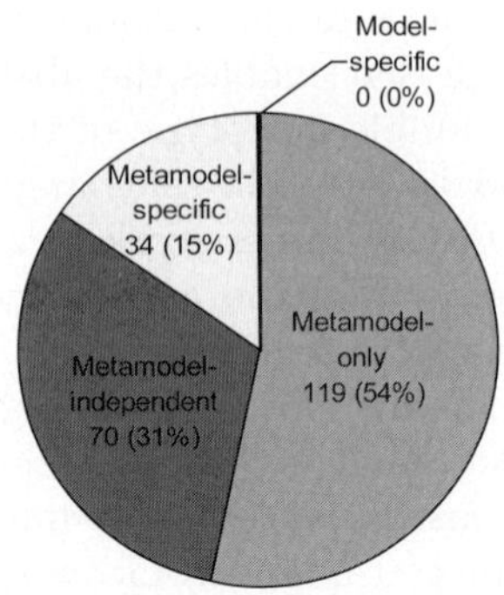

(b) Classification

Fig. 6. Evolution of FLUID metamodel

of the evolution, Figure 6(a) illustrates the number of metamodel elements for each version of the FLUID metamodel. The area is further partitioned into the different kinds of metamodel elements. The figure clearly shows the transition from an initial development phase to a maintenance phase, where the grow in number of metamodel elements slows down. Figure 6(b) shows which fraction of all language changes falls into each class. 54% of the language changes can be classified as metamodel-only. No coupled change can be classified as model-specific, 15% as metamodel-specific and 31% as metamodel-independent. Note that each language change was counted as one, even though some changes were more complex than others.

Figure 7(a) depicts the number of metamodel elements for each version of the TAF-Gen metamodel. In this case the passage from the initial development

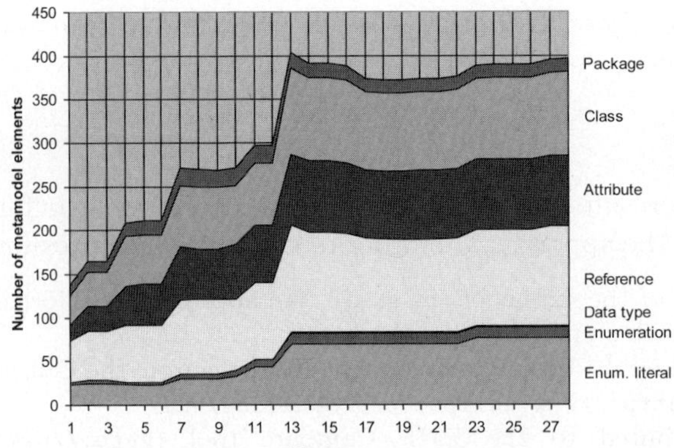

(a) Evolution in numbers

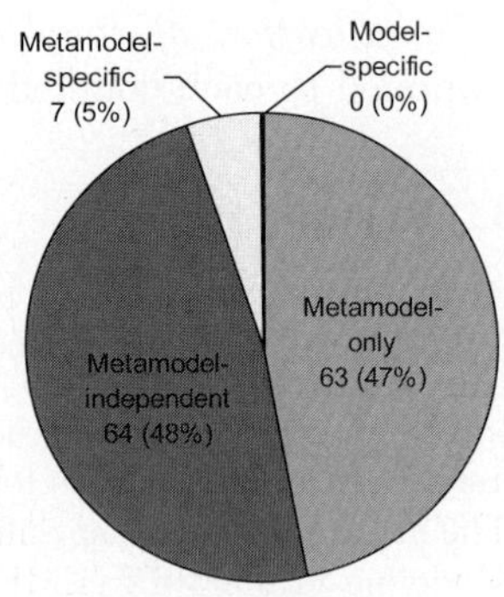

(b) Classification

Fig. 7. Evolution of TAF-Gen metamodel

phase to the maintenance phase is more distinctive and happens around version 13. Figure 7(b) illustrates the fragmentation of all encountered language changes into the four classes. 47% of the language changes have not required a migration at all. As in the history of FLUID, no coupled change is model-specific. The fraction of metamodel-independent coupled changes is even higher than in case of FLUID, amounting to 48% compared to 5% classified as metamodel-specific.

4.4 Discussion

The study showed that in practice the history of a metamodel can be split into mostly small language changes. We found out that most metamodel changes required a migration of existing models. Furthermore, snapshots from different metamodel versions are not sufficient to derive the model migration. As we have not found any model-specific coupled changes, we would have been able to specify transformations to automate migration of all models. However, model-specific coupled changes cannot be entirely excluded and we plan to further investigate them. More than two thirds of all coupled changes were classified as metamodel-independent which provides a large potential for further automation. We also found a small number of metamodel-specific coupled changes and thus the coupled evolution was a combination of both metamodel-specific and -independent coupled changes.

4.5 Threats to Validity

The result of the study suggests a high degree of potential automation for model migration. However, threats need to be mentioned which can affect the validity of the result. They are presented according to the steps of the execution to which they apply together with the measures taken to mitigate them:

1. It was assumed that committing the metamodel to the revision control system indicates a new version of the metamodel. Therefore, only the primitive changes from one commit to the next were considered to be combined. However, metamodels were sometimes committed in a premature version and hence complex changes which span several commits of the metamodel threaten the validity. Even though enacted development guidelines at BMW Car IT forbid to commit artifacts in a premature version, primitive changes of other metamodel versions were also taken into account when a migration could not be determined otherwise.
2. A prerequisite to determine the differences is the calculation of a matching between the elements of one metamodel version and those of the next. However, in the absence of unique and unchangeable element identifiers, the comparison cannot always be performed unambiguously [21]. Furthermore, the difference model leaves out changes which have been overwritten by others in the course of the evolution from one version to the next. In order to mitigate this threat, the correctness of the primitive changes was validated in close cooperation with the metamodel developers.

3. Unfortunately, models were not available for all versions of the corresponding metamodels. This poses a threat to the correct formation of coupled changes, since primitive changes were combined based on the associated migration. In order to mitigate this risk, the metamodel developers were exhaustively questioned about the correctness of the derived migration.
4. The differentiation between metamodel-specific or -independent coupled changes is not 100% sharp. Even though a generalization may be constructed for the most sophisticated changes, it is unlikely that it can be reused on any other metamodel. In order to mitigate this risk, we chose a conservative strategy: When we were not sure whether reuse makes sense, we classified such a coupled change rather metamodel-specific than metamodel-independent.

5 Requirements for Automated Coupled Evolution

Based on the results of the analysis, we discuss several requirements that an approach must fulfill in order to profit from the automation potential in practice.

Reuse of migration knowledge. In order to profit from the high number of metamodel-independent coupled changes found in the study, a practical approach needs to provide a mechanism to specify metamodel adaptation and corresponding model migration independent of a specific metamodel.

Expressive, custom migrations. As there was a non-negligible number of metamodel-specific coupled changes, the approach must be flexible enough to allow for the definition of custom metamodel adaptation and model migration. Since metamodel-specific changes can be arbitrarily complex, the formalism must be expressive enough to cover all evolution scenarios.

Modularity. In order to be able to specify the different kinds of coupled changes independently of each other, a practical approach must be modular. Modularity implies that the specification of a coupled change is not affected by the presence of any other coupled change.

History. Since models may be distributed and therefore not all models may be available during metamodel adaptation, a history is required that comprises the information to migrate the models at a later instant.

Existing approaches to automate model migration only satisfy the stated requirements to a certain degree: Sprinkle's visual language [20] does not provide a construct for the reuse of migration knowledge. Gruschko's approach [9,10] leaves open how it achieves modularity and how it deals with complex custom migrations. And it remains unclear whether Wachsmuth's high level primitives [8] are able to perform all kinds of migration scenarios. In order to fully profit from the automatablity of coupled evolution in practice, an approach is needed that fulfills all the presented requirements.

6 Conclusion

We presented a study of the evolution of two real world metamodels. Our study confirmed that metamodels evolve in practice and that most metamodel changes require a migration of existing models. The study's main goal was to determine the potential for reduction of language evolution efforts through appropriate tool support. To this end, we categorized metamodel changes according to their degree of metamodel specificity. When a change is metamodel-specific, the corresponding model migration is as well. Otherwise, the model migration can be reused to migrate models that obey to different metamodels. Our results show that there is a large potential for the reuse of coupled evolution operations, because more than two thirds of all coupled changes were not metamodel-specific. If metamodel adaptation and model migration are encapsulated into a coupled operation, it is possible to reuse the operation for the evolution of different metamodels and their models. Such reuse of already tested coupled evolution operations can reduce maintenance effort and error likelihood. Nevertheless, a third of the coupled changes were specific to the metamodel's domain and therefore required a custom model migration. A metamodel hence evolves in a sequence of *metamodel-specific* and *-independent* changes. Therefore, an approach for automated model migration must support the reuse of coupled changes as well as the definition of new metamodel-specific changes. We hope that the results of this study can provide helpful input to guide the development of effective tool-support for coupled evolution of metamodels and models in practice.

References

1. Czarnecki, K., Eisenecker, U.W.: Generative programming: methods, tools, and applications. Addison-Wesley, New York (2000)
2. Kleppe, A.G., Warmer, J., Bast, W.: MDA Explained: The Model Driven Architecture: Practice and Promise. Addison-Wesley, Boston (2003)
3. Greenfield, J., Short, K., Cook, S., Kent, S.: Software Factories: Assembling Applications with Patterns, Models, Frameworks, and Tools. Wiley, Chichester (2004)
4. Hildisch, A., Steurer, J., Stolle, R.: HMI generation for plug-in services from semantic descriptions. In: Proceedings of the 4th International Workshop on Software Engineering for Automotive Systems (SEAS), Washington, DC, USA. IEEE Computer Society, Los Alamitos (2007)
5. Benz, S.: Combining test case generation for component and integration testing. In: Proceedings of the 3rd International Workshop on Advances in Model-based Testing (A-MOST), pp. 23–33. ACM Press, New York (2007)
6. Favre, J.M.: Languages evolve too! changing the software time scale. In: Proceedings of the Eighth International Workshop on Principles of Software Evolution (IWPSE), pp. 33–44. IEEE Computer Society Press, Los Alamitos (2005)
7. Lämmel, R.: Coupled Software Transformations (Extended Abstract). In: First International Workshop on Software Evolution Transformations (2004)
8. Wachsmuth, G.: Metamodel adaptation and model co-adaptation. In: Ernst, E. (ed.) ECOOP 2007. LNCS, vol. 4609, pp. 600–624. Springer, Heidelberg (2007)
9. Becker, S., Gruschko, B., Goldschmidt, T., Koziolek, H.: A Process Model and Classification Scheme for Semi-Automatic Meta-Model Evolution. In: Proc. 1st Workshop MDD, SOA und IT-Management (MSI), GI, pp. 35–46. GiTO-Verlag (2007)

10. Gruschko, B., Kolovos, D., Paige, R.: Towards synchronizing models with evolving metamodels. In: Proceedings of the International Workshop on Model-Driven Software Evolution (2007)
11. Rahm, E., Bernstein, P.A.: An online bibliography on schema evolution. SIGMOD Rec. 35(4), 30–31 (2006)
12. Banerjee, J., Kim, W., Kim, H.J., Korth, H.F.: Semantics and implementation of schema evolution in object-oriented databases, vol. 16, pp. 311–322. ACM Press, New York (1987)
13. Ferrandina, F., Meyer, T., Zicari, R., Ferran, G., Madec, J.: Schema and database evolution in the O2 object database system. In: Proceedings of the 21th International Conference on Very Large Data Bases (VLDB), pp. 170–181. Morgan Kaufmann, San Francisco (1995)
14. Claypool, K.T., Jin, J., Rundensteiner, E.A.: SERF: schema evolution through an extensible, re-usable and flexible framework. In: Proceedings of the seventh international conference on Information and knowledge management (CIKM), pp. 314–321. ACM Press, New York (1998)
15. Klint, P., Lämmel, R., Verhoef, C.: Toward an engineering discipline for grammarware. ACM Trans. Softw. Eng. Methodol. 14(3), 331–380 (2005)
16. Lämmel, R.: Grammar testing. In: Fundamental Approaches to Software Engineering, pp. 201–216 (2001)
17. Pizka, M., Juergens, E.: Automating language evolution. In: Proceedings of the First Joint IEEE/IFIP Symposium on Theoretical Aspects of Software Engineering (TASE), Washington, DC, USA, pp. 305–315. IEEE Computer Society Press, Los Alamitos (2007)
18. Lämmel, R., Lohmann, W.: Format Evolution. In: Proceedings of the 7th International Conference on Reverse Engineering for Information Systems (RETIS), vol. 155, pp. 113–134. OCG (2001)
19. Su, H., Kramer, D., Chen, L., Claypool, K., Rundensteiner, E.A.: XEM: Managing the Evolution of XML Documents. In: Proceedings of the 11th International Workshop on research Issues in Data Engineering (RIDE), p. 103. IEEE Computer Society Press, Los Alamitos (2001)
20. Sprinkle, J., Karsai, G.: A domain-specific visual language for domain model evolution. Journal of Visual Languages and Computing 15, 291–307 (2004)
21. Robbes, R., Lanza, M.: A change-based approach to software evolution. Electron. Notes Theor. Comput. Sci. 166, 93–109 (2007)

Appendix

Table 1. Number of occurred language changes and their classification

	Metamodel evolution	Model migration	Class	FLUID	TAF-GEN	Overall
pack.	add package	no migration required	MMO	0	10	10
	move package	compensate move	MMI	0	8	8
	remove empty package	no migration required	MMO	0	4	4
enum.	add enumeration	no migration required	MMO	0	4	4
	change order of enumeration	no migration required	MMO	0	1	1
	rename enumeration literal	compensate rename	MMI	0	4	4
class	add class	no migration required	MMO	0	3	3
	add sub class	no migration required	MMO	45	2	47
	change super class	remove data of lost features	MMI	0	1	1
	move class	compensate move	MMI	5	18	23
	remove class	remove objects	MMI	1	0	1
	remove sub class	remove objects	MMI	1	0	1
	rename class	compensate rename	MMI	5	5	10
	set class abstract	migrate objects to sub classes	MMS	1	0	1
	specialize super class (optional features)	no migration required	MMO	3	1	4
attribute	add optional attribute	no migration required	MMO	15	5	20
	add required attribute	set default value	MMI	5	1	6
	change type of attribute	convert values	MMI	2	1	3
	decrease upper bound of attribute	remove superfluous values	MMS	1	0	1
	drop attribute as key of class	no migration required	MMO	6	0	6
	extend multiplicity of attribute	no migration required	MMO	5	1	6
	make attribute an key of class	guarantee uniqueness	MMS	3	0	3
	move optional attribute to super class	no migration required	MMO	1	0	1
	move required attribute to super class	set default value	MMI	1	0	1
	remove attribute	remove attribute values	MMI	11	1	12
	rename attribute	compensate rename	MMI	3	1	4
association	add optional association	no migration required	MMO	5	4	9
	add optional composition	no migration required	MMO	3	3	6
	add required composition	create objects	MMI	3	0	3
	change type of association	remove links	MMI	5	0	5
	change type of composition	migrate objects	MMS	1	0	1
	decrease upper bound of association	remove superfluous links	MMS	1	1	2
	drop persistence of association	remove links	MMI	0	1	1
	establish persistence of association	no migration required	MMO	0	1	1
	extend multiplicity of association	no migration required	MMO	14	2	16
	generalize type of association	no migration required	MMO	6	4	10
	increase lower bound of association	no migration required	MMO	2	0	2
	make assocation bidirectional	no migration required	MMO	0	3	3
	move association by association	move links accordingly	MMI	0	1	1
	move association to sub classes	no migration required	MMO	0	2	2
	move optional association to super class	no migration required	MMO	1	1	2
	remove composition	remove part objects	MMI	3	0	3
	remove cross association	remove links	MMI	1	4	5
	remove opposite association	no migration required	MMO	0	2	2
	rename association	compensate rename	MMI	7	3	10
	transform association to composition	no migration required	MMO	1	2	3
	transform composition to association	assign otherwise	MMS	22	3	25
composite	add proxy	add proxy object	MMI	0	1	1
	extract part class	add part objects	MMI	6	2	8
	extract super class	no migration required	MMO	3	1	4
	inline part class	remove object of inlined class	MMI	0	1	1
	integrate association into another	move data accordingly	MMI	4	0	4
	integrate sub class	migrate objects to super class	MMI	0	2	2
	integrate super class	no migration required	MMI	0	1	1
	merge sub classes	migrate objects to common class	MMI	1	0	1
	remove proxy	remove proxy objects	MMI	1	0	1
	replace association by key	set identifier based on links and remove links	MMI	2	0	2
	replace key by association	add links based on identifier	MMI	2	0	2
	replace inheritance by composition	add part object	MMI	0	1	1
	use part class	add part objects	MMI	1	1	2
	use super class	no migration required	MMO	1	0	1
compl.	add optional part structure	no migration required	MMO	8	7	15
	remove part structure	remove data	MMI	0	6	6
	revolution	complex migration	MMS	5	3	8
				223	**134**	**357**
		Metamodel-only	MMO	**119**	**63**	**182**
		Metamodel-independent	MMI	**70**	**64**	**134**
		Metamodel-specific	MMS	**34**	**7**	**41**
		Model-specific	MS	**0**	**0**	**0**

Enriching Reverse Engineering with Annotations

Andrea Brühlmann, Tudor Gîrba, Orla Greevy, and Oscar Nierstrasz

Software Composition Group, University of Bern, Switzerland
http://scg.unibe.ch/

Abstract. Much of the knowledge about software systems is implicit, and therefore difficult to recover by purely automated techniques. Architectural layers and the externally visible features of software systems are two examples of information that can be difficult to detect from source code alone, and that would benefit from additional human knowledge. Typical approaches to reasoning about data involve encoding an explicit meta-model and expressing analyses at that level. Due to its informal nature, however, human knowledge can be difficult to characterize up-front and integrate into such a meta-model. We propose a generic, annotation-based approach to capture such knowledge during the reverse engineering process. Annotation types can be iteratively defined, refined and transformed, without requiring a fixed meta-model to be defined in advance. We show how our approach supports reverse engineering by implementing it in a tool called Metanool and by applying it to (i) analyzing architectural layering, (ii) tracking reengineering tasks, (iii) detecting design flaws, and (iv) analyzing features.

1 Introduction

Most reverse engineering techniques focus on automatically extracting information from the source code without taking external human knowledge into consideration. More often than not however, important external information is available (*e.g.*, developer knowledge or domain specific knowledge) which would greatly enhance analyses if it could be taken into account.

Only few reverse engineering approaches integrate such external human knowledge into the analysis. For example, reflexion models have been proposed for architecture recovery by capturing developer knowledge and then manually mapping this knowledge to the source code [1,2]. Another example is provided by Intensional Views which make use of rules that encode external constraints and are checked against the actual source code [3].

In this paper we propose a generic framework based on annotations to enhance a reverse engineered model with external knowledge so that automatic analyses can take this knowledge into account. A key feature of our approach is that the types of supported annotations need not be fixed in advance. A developer can introduce new types of annotations at any time, and refine or transform the existing types in a flexible way. For example, using the reflexion model approach to analyze how a system is split into architectural layers, the reverse engineer

K. Czarnecki et al. (Eds.): MoDELS 2008, LNCS 5301, pp. 660–674, 2008.

can define the notion of a layer, instantiate this concept for the different layers that can be found in the code and then attach the specific layers to code entities.

Annotations are intended to augment reverse engineering analyses by providing additional information otherwise absent from the source code. This information is then available to refine the results of queries, visualizations, and other automated tasks.

We have built a prototype, called Metanool, that demonstrates our approach, and we have integrated it into the Moose reengineering environment [4]. Our approach is inspired by Adaptive Object-Models and it is applied in the context of reverse engineering [5]. We argue that the approach is quite general, and could be easily integrated into any reverse engineering tool or development environment based on explicit meta-models of software. We believe that such a mechanism to facilitate the incorporation of external knowledge should be an integral part of every reverse engineering tool suite.

Metanool's annotations are similar to Java annotations [6] in the sense that they are meta-described, hence can be examined by the run-time system, but the two differ in several important ways: (1) Metanool annotations can be changed at runtime, (2) they can be manipulated from the user interface, and (3) they can be attached to any object.

We have applied Metanool to a number of different experimental use cases to assess the usefulness of our approach to reverse engineering. In one experiment we used Metanool to encode manually detected architectural layers of jEdit, and then used this information to check for violations of architectural constraints. In another experiment, annotations were used to directly encode the architectural constraints themselves. In a very different use case, we used annotations to express and manage pending reverse engineering tasks. Two further use cases entailed augmenting automated design flaw detection with annotations to manually flag false negatives and false positives, and augmenting feature analysis with developer knowledge of available features. Although these experiments are only anecdotal in nature, they serve well to illustrate the usefulness of the approach.

In the next section we illustrate our approach as it is manifested by the Metanool tool. In Section 3 we outline the implementation and the meta-model of Metanool. Section 4 presents four example use cases for our approach, thus illustrating how Metanool annotations can effectively enrich the reverse engineering process. In Section 5 we compare our approach with related work, and in Section 6 we conclude with remarks on future work.

2 Metanool by Example

To provide a flavor of the reverse engineering use cases we solve, in this section we illustrate our approach by showing how to use our Metanool infrastructure to annotate a reverse engineered model of a software system. In this example, Metanool is used together with the Moose reengineering environment [4]. A model describing the static structure of jEdit [7] has been loaded into Moose, and Metanool is then used to enrich this model with external knowledge expressed by means of annotations. Here we imagine a developer identifying the architectural layers and determining which packages belong to which layer. Finally this enriched model is used to generate a report.

2.1 Adding an Annotation

Figure 1 shows the Moose Browser presenting a model of jEdit, which has been loaded by parsing the jEdit source code. The figure shows that we have selected the org.gjt.sp.jedit.gui package (or namespace) (1).

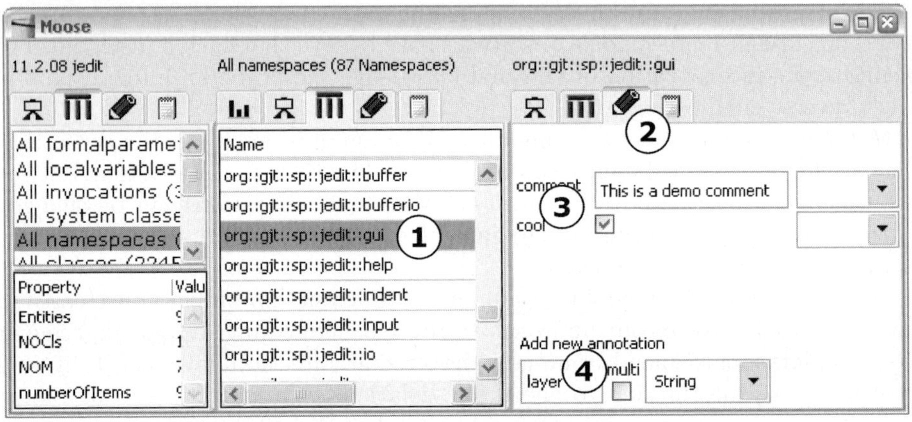

Fig. 1. A Moose model of jEdit

On the right hand side, we have the Metanool annotations tab open for this package (2). It contains the list of annotations (3). There are already two annotations called comment and cool.

To create a new annotation, we enter the name, for example layer and assign a type to it, *e.g.*, String at the bottom of the annotations tab (4). As a result, our newly created annotation appears in the annotations list, where we can edit its value (see Figure 2).The annotation is added to all elements that have the same type as the selected element (by default, the value of the annotation is nil). As a consequence, in our example, we can now edit the layer names for all namespaces.

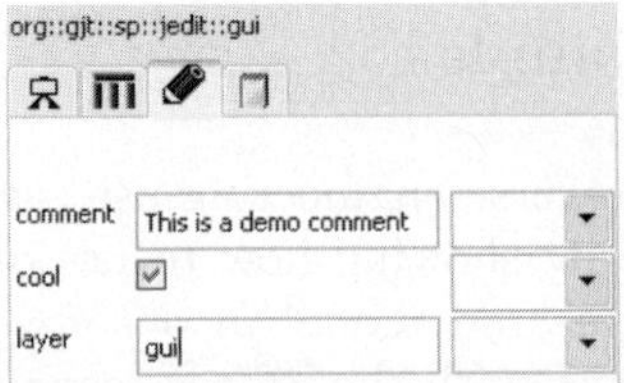

Fig. 2. A new annotation

2.2 Refining an Annotation Type

A key feature of our approach is that annotation types can be changed easily at any time, even when values have already been assigned. After annotating some of the jEdit packages, it occurs to us that usability would be improved by adding a drop down menu with the list of known layers.

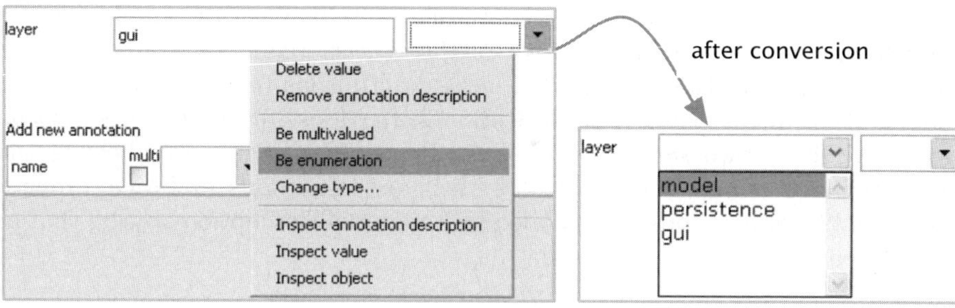

Fig. 3. Converting an annotation type to an enumeration

In this case, we choose "Be enumeration" from the menu. This searches for all layer names that are already specified and transforms the type of the annotation into an enumeration of these names.

2.3 Creating a Report

Finally, we can use the information from the annotated model to generate reports. For example, in Figure 4 we show a possible visualization that would be included in such a report. The visualization, generated using Mondrian [8], a scriptable visualization engine, shows the namespace (small squares) organized in layers. The Mondrian code to the left illustrates (in bold) how we take the 'layer' annotation into account to group the namespaces.

```
namespacesByLayers := namespaces groupedBy: [:each |
   each annotations named: 'layer'.
].

view := ViewRenderer new.

view umlPackageShapeWithLabel.
view nodes:namespacesByLayers forEach: [:eachAssociation |
   view nodes: eachAssociation.
   view horizontalLineLayout.
].
view verticalLineLayout.

view open
```

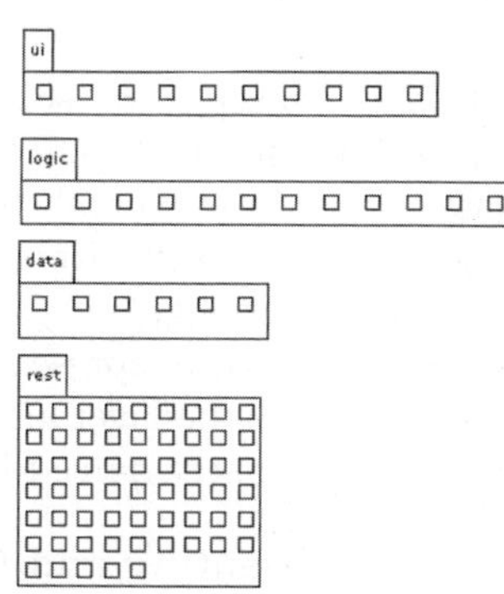

Fig. 4. Visualizing the layers with a Mondrian script

3 Metanool Meta-model and Implementation

In this section we present the meta-model that Metanool uses to represent annotations, and we outline how Metanool uses this meta-model to manage and manipulate annotations.

3.1 Metanool Meta-model

Figure 5 illustrates the annotation meta-model by means of a simple example. The example shows an small excerpt of the objects (e.g., :FAMIX.Namespace), classes (e.g., FAMIX.Namespace) and meta-descriptions (e.g., EMOF.Class) that were involved in the scenario from Section 2. In Moose, each object is attached to an EMOF meta-description [9]. We extended this model by allowing each object to have annotations, which in turn are extensions of EMOF.Property. The available annotations are encoded in AnnotationDescription objects that are attached to the meta-descriptions.

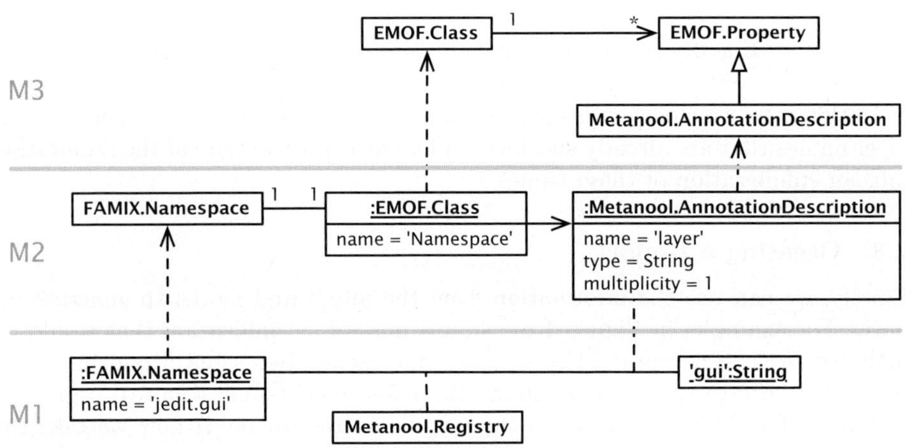

Fig. 5. Metanool core structure

In this example, we see that the jedit.gui namespace is an instance of the FAMIX.Namespace class. This class is meta-described by an instance of EMOF. Class named 'Namespace'. It has one AnnotationDescription, which specifies that annotations of FAMIX.Namespace objects may have single-valued 'layer' annotations of type String.

Annotations are represented as associated properties. In this case the 'jedit.gui' namespace has the layer annotation 'gui'. Annotation descriptions are registered in a global registry named Metanool.Registry.

3.2 Representing and Manipulating Annotations

As we have seen, each annotation has a name, a type and a multiplicity. In our implementation, the allowable types include not only all classes of the host programming language (in this case Smalltalk), but we also allow enumerations of values of a given class. In order for the annotation editor to allow users to conveniently set the values for annotations, the corresponding Smalltalk class should be extended with a dedicated GUI method. In lieu of this, values can also be set programmatically for arbitrary types.

As exemplified in Section 2.2, Metanool allows the user to modify the annotation descriptions in different ways. First of all, the type can be changed. This is, of course, not problematic when no values have been stored for this annotation. But it is useful to have this flexibility later during analysis if the structure of a human knowledge concept emerges over time. When the type needs to be changed, Metanool takes all existing values and tries to transform them to fit the newly defined type. For example, when changing a simple type to an enumeration, Metanool will create an enumeration from all existing values.

An annotation can also be transformed into an enumeration: in this case, all existing values of this annotation are collected into a set which is then defined to be the type of the annotation. The reverse operation is also possible: the new type is determined by taking the most specific common superclass of all the enumeration elements.

We also allow the multiplicity of an annotation to be modified after it has been defined. An annotation can easily be made multi-valued at any time, and almost as easily be made single-valued again. Going from multi-valued to single-valued will result in loss of information if multiple values need to be dropped. Metanool prompts the user which values to keep.

3.3 Programmatically Manipulating Annotations

Annotations can also be created and edited programmatically from the host language. The following lines show the code to create a layer annotation and edit it in Smalltalk. It also exemplifies the relations between annotation descriptions and their values:

```
layerDescription := AnnotationDescription name: 'layer' type: String.
FAMIX.Namespace annotationDescriptions add: layerDescription.

namespaceA annotations named: 'layer' put: 'ui'.
namespaceB annotations named: 'layer' put: 'data'.
```

Values can be read from annotations as follows:

```
namespaceA annotations named: 'layer'.
```

Further details of Metanool can be found in Brühlmann's Masters thesis [10].

4 Reverse Engineering with Annotations

We now illustrate the usefulness of annotations for reverse engineering by presenting four typical use cases. First, in subsection 4.1 we show how annotations can be used to check architectural constraints by encoding either the layers or the constraints themselves. Next, in subsection 4.2 we show how a specialized annotation type with its own GUI can easily be added to represent pending tasks. In subsection 4.3 we show how false negatives and false positives can be tagged as annotations to refine the results of automated design flaw detection. Finally, in subsection 4.4 we show how implicit knowledge about internal features can be used to enrich and refine the results of feature analysis.

4.1 Checking Architectural Constraints

Software companies often define a standard architecture for a set of applications. As new applications are developed or existing applications evolve, they should be checked for compliance with architectural constraints. Unfortunately architectures are typically not explicit in the source code. Packages are generally used to group classes according to their particular role or function in the system. However there may be multiple packages associated with an architectural layer, or a package may even be associated with multiple layers. In the absence of a dedicated language construct to express architectural layering, annotations provide an ideal way during analysis of a system to associate packages with layers. An analysis of the call graph can then make use of the layering annotations to check the architectural constraints [2].

We present two ways to encode layering knowledge with annotations. In the first case we number layers and annotate packages according to their layer number. In the second case we name the layers, and directly encode the desired accessibility constraints as annotations. In both cases we then visualize the packages and their access relations, coloring with red forbidden calls and with blue allowed calls.

Numbered Layers. In this use case, we took the work of Patel *et al.* who previously analyzed jEdit and classified its packages according to 14 layers [11].

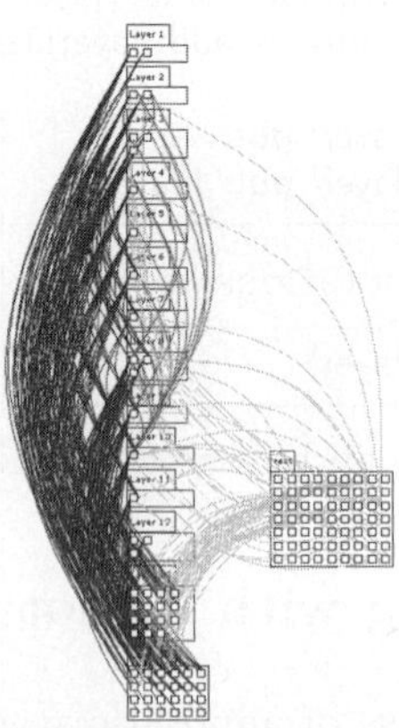

Fig. 6. jEdit in 14 layers with access violations in red

We defined a single-valued annotation description named layerNumber of type Integer and then encoded knowledge about the 14 layers by annotating each package with the layer numbers. Figure 6 shows a Mondrian visualization of the 14 layers depicting allowed calls (*i.e.* going downwards) with blue, call violation (*i.e.* going upwards) in red, and not qualified calls in gray. The code of the visualization is similar to the one from Figure 4.

Named Layers with Explicit Constraints. Another approach is to add a String annotation to each package, containing the name of its layer, *e.g.*, gui, model, persistence etc. Relations between these layers specify whether calls of components from one layer to another are allowed or forbidden. These relations are also expressed using annotations. We create two annotation descriptions and attach them to String (see Figure 7). They are multi-valued because each layer has multiple forbidden or allowed layers to access. The reason why we added it to String instead of a dedicated Layer class, is just convenience, as strings can easily be instantiated using 'quotes'.

We can again display the call relationships (see Figure 7) with a dedicated visualization that takes annotations into account. Blue calls are explicitly allowed and red calls are forbidden. Grey calls are not specified with our annotations, so they are neither allowed nor forbidden.

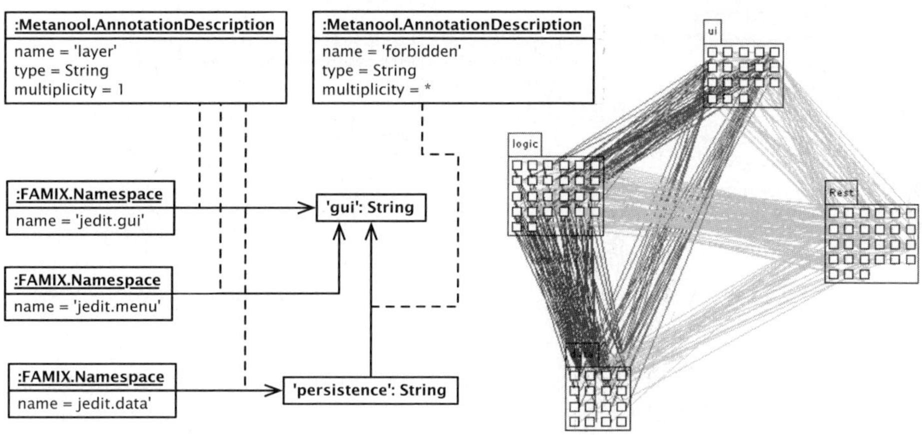

Fig. 7. Explicit constraints over named layers. The 'allowed' annotations are similar to the 'forbidden' one, and were omitted from the diagram due to space limitation.

4.2 Task Lists

In this example, tasks are added to objects and a list of all tasks is generated. This is analogous to the @ToDo annotation in Java.

Introducing a Task Type. To attach to-do tasks to elements such as classes and namespaces, we must introduce a new type: ToDo. We define the new class

ToDo with two instance variables: a String named 'task' and a Boolean named 'done'. Like this, each ToDo has a description and can be marked as done. This new type can already be used in Metanool as is, but it is better to offer a specialized GUI to make it easy to enter and update tasks. The metanoolEditPane method creates the GUI editor pane for tasks consisting of a checkbox (by adding the default edit pane for Boolean) and a text input field (by adding the default edit pane for String):

```
ToDo≫metanoolEditPane
  ↑ Form new
    addComponent: (Boolean metanoolEditPaneForProperty: 'done' of: self);
    addComponent: (String metanoolEditPaneForProperty: 'task' of: self).
```

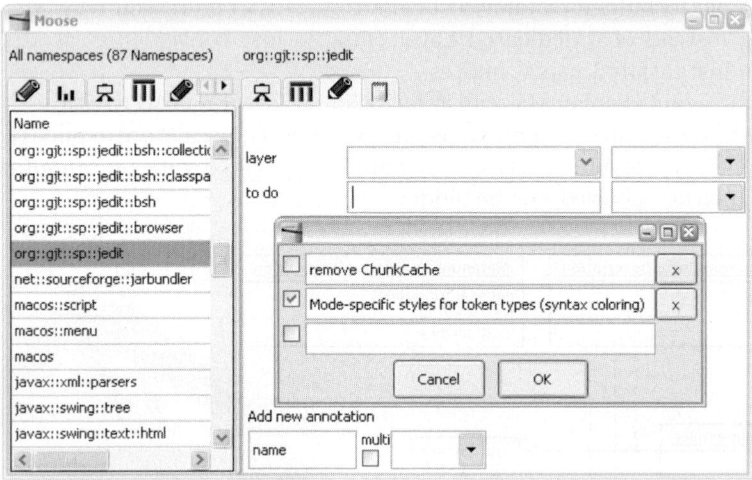

Fig. 8. A specialized GUI for multi-valued to-do annotations

Editing the Tasks. After creating the ToDo type, we add a multi-valued "to do" annotation description of type ToDo to the elements we want to annotate. Like this, every element can have as many tasks as needed (see Figure 8). We can also add the same annotation description to several elements, *e.g.*, FAMIX.Class and FAMIX.Namespace.

4.3 Detection Strategies

Detection strategies are metrics-based rules to detect candidates for common design flaws in a system, such as god classes, data classes, brain classes and other code smells [12]. Since detection strategies only detect *candidates*, manual inspection is often needed to filter out false positives. Annotations can be used to flag these false positives, and also to flag false negatives that may have been detected by other means.

Let us consider the example of detecting god classes in jEdit. First we add annotation descriptions "auto god class" and "manual god class", both of type Boolean. We set the auto god class annotation to true for all classes identified by our detection strategy. Then we manually set the annotation for all god classes we have knowledge of.

In Figure 9 we see a visualization of the jEdit class hierarchy in which all god classes are represented by large rectangles. Classes are colored black only if the manual and automatic annotations agree. False positives are shown as small pink boxes (manually refused). False negatives are shown as large red boxes (manually detected but not automatically). Grey boxes are automatically detected god classes that have not been manually rejected.

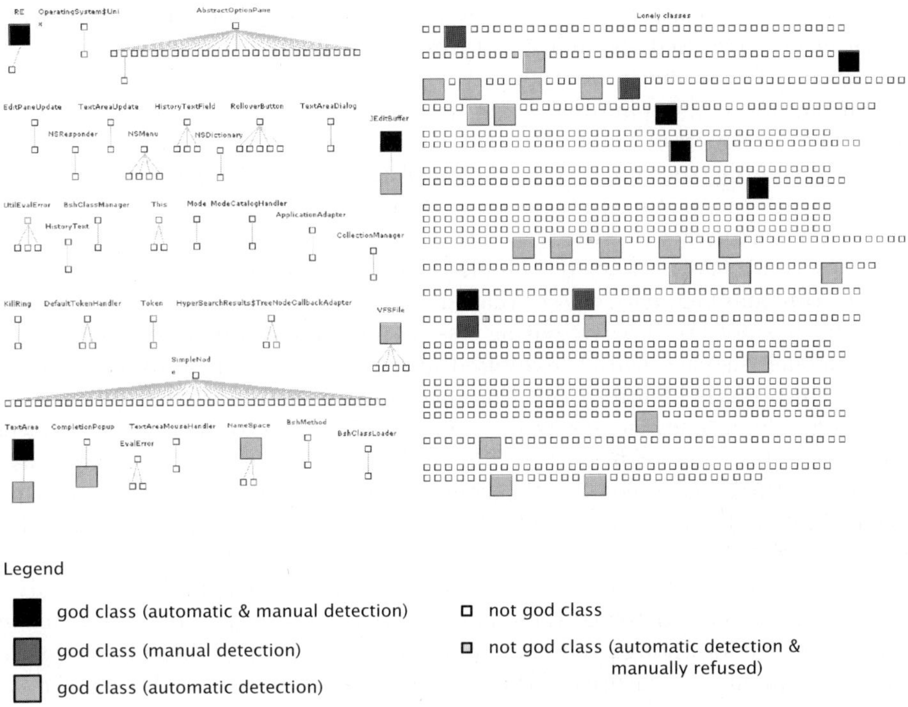

Fig. 9. Automatic and manual detection of god classes. The reason for the existence of 5 categories out of two boolean variables is that the default value is nil.

4.4 Feature Analysis

The final example shows how to use our annotations to perform and validate the results of automatic feature analysis based on dynamic analysis of traces [13].

Features are abstractions that encapsulate knowledge of a problem domain and describe units of system behavior [14]. Several researchers have identified the potential of exploiting features in reverse engineering [15,16]. Feature identification approaches (*e.g.*, *Software Reconnaissance* [17]) describe various techniques for locating which parts of the code implement a given feature. Automatic approaches to feature identification are typically based on dynamic analysis where the features are executed on an instrumented system and the traces of all message sends are captured.

We show how Metanool annotations can help to refine the results of feature analysis by taking additional developer knowledge into account. In particular, the presence of hidden features can perturb the analysis unless they are taken into account.

Feature Analysis of Moose. We performed a feature analysis on the Moose system itself with 8 specified features using a Dynamix model of Moose [14]. Then we applied the feature affinity metric to the classes based on these results to quantify which classes belong to only one feature (single feature affinity), and which classes are used for many features (ranging from low group affinity, to high group affinity and infrastructural).

Our feature analysis automatically detects three classes as being *infrastructural.* The developers of Moose deny this result. They state that one of the classes detected as infrastructural, the FamixNameResolver class, implements functionality specific to importing a Moose model from Smalltalk source code. This functionality should in fact constitute a distinct feature. Another of the three detected infrastructural classes is named UnresolvedClass in our model. The events captured for a feature may reference classes that are not present in static model of the system and thus not every participating class of a feature can be resolved to a class in the model. As each feature exhibited unresolvable classes, automatic feature analysis incorrectly identified this UnresolvedClass as an infrastructural class.

This developer knowledge reveals two important facts to the reverse engineer: Firstly, the behavior of importing Smalltalk models needs to be treated as a distinct feature, and secondly, the behavior of the executed features was not well delimited. They all used Smalltalk source code import which made the class FamixNameResolver appear as an infrastructural class.

However, we do not want to throw away the results of dynamic feature analysis just because we have detected these false positives in *feature affinity* assignment. Our feature views, though they are approximations, reveal other interesting information about the features of the Moose system. Instead we choose to refine the feature representations using annotations.

We create an annotation named feature–affinity with the enumeration type #('none' 'single feature' 'low group' 'high group' 'infrastructural'). We then annotate the classes according the their automatically computed *featureAffinity* values, but we change the value manually for the classes that have been classified wrongly. The class FamixNameResolver takes the annotation value 'single feature' instead of 'infrastructural'.

Refined Visualization. In Figure 10 we show part of the system complexity view with the classes coloured according to their feature–affinity annotation. The class MooseModel (1) is the only class that appears now as 'infrastructural' in this picture. As this class is fundamental to every feature when using

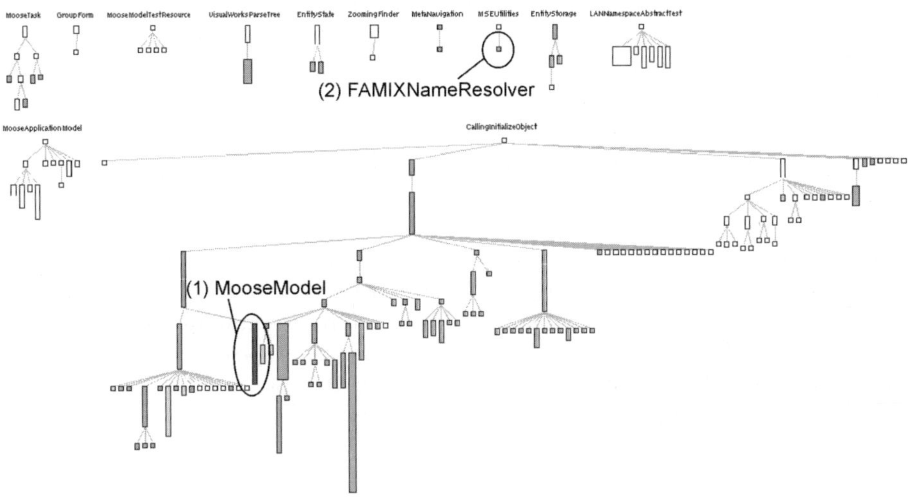

Fig. 10. The refined feature affinity values of classes

Moose, this result is closer to reality. The originally wrongly categorized class FamixNameResolver is now correctly coloured as a 'single feature' class (blue).

5 Related Work

Every programming language offers the possibility of embedding textual comments in the source code to encode external knowledge directly in the system [18,19]. Comments serve as a form of documentation and should be accessible to code analysis tools since they provide an important source of additional information. Comments, however, are unstructured and cannot easily be taken into account for further analysis. One notable exception is the use of clustering techniques to identify concepts implicit in the textual comments of source code [20].

A more advanced approach of annotating source code is offered by Java Annotations[6]. They are meta-described by instances of AnnotationTypes thus enabling run-time examination. However, as Java Annotations are source code based, they cannot be used to annotate objects as would be necessary when working with models. As with comments, the source code itself needs to be changed if a class or any other code artifact is annotated. Every time an annotation description is changed, it has to be compiled and all annotations described by this AnnotationType have to be changed manually to conform to it again. Java Annotations also do not provide specialized editors for annotating and for editing the meta-descriptions.

Adaptive Object-Models (AOM) [5,21] encode domain entities in metadata instead of classes. Thus, whenever a change is needed, the meta-model is changed which is then immediately reflected in the running code. AOMs have only been proposed to solve changing business models in applications, but they could be applicable for modeling external knowledge during reverse engineering. This solves the problem of inflexibility we have with Java annotations. Our solution is inspired by AOM in the way that not only the values but also the structure of our annotations can be changed at any time.

Annotations can also be fruitfully integrated into the runtime of a programming language. Reflectivity is a framework that extends Smalltalk with support for reflection at the sub-method level [22]. Representations of source code can be annotated at run-time for use by various tools. This has been used to perform feature analysis [23]. Instead of generating traces to be analyzed *post hoc*, objects representing the static structure of the system are annotated with feature information while features are exercised. However, as opposed to Metanool, the annotations proposed in Reflectivity are not typed thus they are less useful for modeling complex concepts.

6 Conclusions

We have presented an approach to enriching the results of reverse engineering analyses with human knowledge by means of iteratively and incrementally defined, typed annotations. Annotations are meta-described, and can therefore be analyzed and manipulated at run-time by the same reverse engineering tools that carry out analysis of unadorned source code models.

We have demonstrated our approach by presenting Metanool, a tool for defining, editing and manipulating annotations. We have also shown four concrete scenarios of our approach using Metanool in the context of the Moose reengineering environment. We have shown how annotations can be fruitfully exploited to enrich reverse engineering with information that is implicit in, or even absent from the source code, such as adherence to architectural constraints, the presence of design flaws, or the relationship between software components and system features. We have also shown how annotations can flexibly added over time, and transformed as the needed structure of the information emerges. Graphical editors can be easily added to support new types of annotations.

During the development of Metanool, several directions for further research became apparent:

- *User defined type transformation.* Changing the type of an annotation and automatically transforming all existing values to conform to the new type is a central point of our approach. A useful extension would be to allow the reverse engineer to define a transformation strategy. This would be similar to the solution featured in DabbleDB[1], and it would not only allow the user to change existing annotations to a new type without implementing the strategy up front, but also to augment the existing strategies when needed.
- *Scoping.* In Metanool, annotation descriptions are globally defined. More sophisticated scoping of annotations could be useful, especially for analysis of

[1] http://www.dabbledb.com

large systems where certain annotations types might only make sense for particular subsystems. Also, the idea of value inheritance could be interesting. With value inheritance, a child object would return the annotation value of its parent unless it has its own value.
- *Java annotations.* Java annotations could be enhanced with GUI support to provide some of the benefits of Metanool in Java source code. Lightweight reverse engineering tools could then be better supported in environments such as Eclipse [24].
- *Annotations for forward engineering.* Annotations could be integrated into code browsers in various ways to also support forward engineering. For example, source code artifacts could be tagged and categorized by annotations and then be browsed based on these categories.

Acknowledgments. We gratefully acknowledge the financial support of the Hasler Foundation for the project "Enabling the evolution of J2EE applications through reverse engineering and quality assurance" (project no. 2234) and the Swiss National Science Foundation for the project "Analyzing, capturing and taming software change" (SNF Project No. 200020-113342, Oct. 2006 - Sept. 2008). We would also want to thank Alexandre Bergel and Lukas Renggli for their comments on drafts on this paper.

References

1. Koschke, R., Simon, D.: Hierarchical reflexion models. In: Proceedings of the 10th Working Conference on Reverse Engineering (WCRE 2003), p. 36. IEEE Computer Society, Los Alamitos (2003)
2. Murphy, G., Notkin, D., Sullivan, K.: Software reflexion models: Bridging the gap between source and high-level models. In: Proceedings of SIGSOFT 1995, Third ACM SIGSOFT Symposium on the Foundations of Software Engineering, pp. 18–28. ACM Press, New York (1995)
3. Mens, K., Kellens, A., Pluquet, F., Wuyts, R.: Co-evolving code and design with intensional views — a case study. Journal of Computer Languages, Systems and Structures 32, 140–156 (2006)
4. Nierstrasz, O., Ducasse, S., Gîrba, T.: The story of Moose: an agile reengineering environment. In: Proceedings of the European Software Engineering Conference (ESEC/FSE 2005), pp. 1–10. ACM Press, New York (2005) (invited paper)
5. Yoder, J., Balaguer, F., Johnson, R.: Architecture and design of adaptive object models. In: Conference on Object-Oriented Programming Systems, Languages, and Applications (OOPSLA 2001), pp. 50–60 (2001)
6. Sun microsystems: Java annotations (2004), `http://java.sun.com/j2se/1.5.0/docs/guide/language/annotations.html`
7. jEdit web site: jEdit: a programmer's text editor (2008), `http://www.jedit.org`
8. Meyer, M., Gîrba, T., Lungu, M.: Mondrian: An agile visualization framework. In: ACM Symposium on Software Visualization (SoftVis 2006), pp. 135–144. ACM Press, New York (2006)
9. Ducasse, S., Gîrba, T.: Using Smalltalk as a reflective executable meta-language. In: Nierstrasz, O., Whittle, J., Harel, D., Reggio, G. (eds.) MoDELS 2006. LNCS, vol. 4199, pp. 604–618. Springer, Heidelberg (2006)

10. Brühlmann, A.: Enriching reverse engineering with annotations. Master's thesis, University of Bern (2008)
11. Patel, S., Dandawate, Y., Kuriakose, J.: Architecture recovery as first step in system appreciation. In: 2nd Workshop on Empirical Studies in Reverse Engineering, Politecnico di Torino (2006), `http://softeng.polito.it/events/WESRE2006/`
12. Lanza, M., Marinescu, R.: Object-Oriented Metrics in Practice. Springer, Heidelberg (2006)
13. Greevy, O., Ducasse, S.: Correlating features and code using a compact two-sided trace analysis approach. In: Proceedings of 9th European Conference on Software Maintenance and Reengineering (CSMR 2005), pp. 314–323. IEEE Computer Society, Los Alamitos (2005)
14. Greevy, O.: Enriching Reverse Engineering with Feature Analysis. PhD thesis, University of Berne (2007)
15. Eisenbarth, T., Koschke, R., Simon, D.: Locating features in source code. IEEE Computer 29, 210–224 (2003)
16. Antoniol, G., Guéhéneuc, Y.G.: Feature identification: a novel approach and a case study. In: Proceedings IEEE International Conference on Software Maintenance (ICSM 2005), pp. 357–366. IEEE Computer Society Press, Los Alamitos (2005)
17. Wilde, N., Scully, M.: Software reconnaisance: Mapping program features to code. Software Maintenance: Research and Practice 7, 49–62 (1995)
18. Gosling, J., Joy, B., Steele, G., Bracha, G.: The Java Language Specification, 3rd edn. Addison Wesley, Reading (2005)
19. Stroustrup, B., Ellis, M.A.: The Annotated C++ Reference Manual. Addison Wesley, Reading (1990)
20. Kuhn, A., Ducasse, S., Gîrba, T.: Enriching reverse engineering with semantic clustering. In: Proceedings of 12th Working Conference on Reverse Engineering (WCRE 2005), pp. 113–122. IEEE Computer Society Press, Los Alamitos (2005)
21. Yoder, J.W., Johnson, R.: The adaptive object model architectural style. In: Proceeding of The Working IEEE/IFIP Conference on Software Architecture 2002 (WICSA3 2002) (2002)
22. Denker, M., Ducasse, S., Lienhard, A., Marschall, P.: Sub-method reflection. Journal of Object Technology 6, 231–251 (2007)
23. Denker, M., Greevy, O., Nierstrasz, O.: Supporting feature analysis with runtime annotations. In: Proceedings of the 3rd International Workshop on Program Comprehension through Dynamic Analysis (PCODA 2007), Technische Universiteit Delft, pp. 29–33 (2007)
24. Murphy, K.: Findlater: How are Java software developers using the Eclipse IDE? IEEE Software (2006)

Towards a Formal Account of a Foundational Subset for Executable UML Models

Michelle L. Crane and Juergen Dingel

School of Computing, Queen's University
Kingston, Ontario, Canada
{crane,dingel}@cs.queensu.ca

Abstract. A current Request for Proposal [1] from the OMG describes the requirements for an "Executable UML Foundation". This subset of UML 2 would serve as a shared foundation for higher-level modeling concepts, such as activities, state machines, and interactions. In a sense, this subset would define a basic virtual machine for UML, allowing the execution and analysis of runtime behavior of models. Regardless of the executable subset chosen, a precise definition of execution semantics of UML actions is required. To the best of our knowledge, no formal semantics of such a subset yet exists. We present our work on clarifying the semantics and pragmatics of UML actions. In particular, we sketch a formalization of a subset of UML actions and discuss common usage scenarios for the most complex actions, identifying usage assumptions that are not explicit in the UML 2 specification.

Keywords: Executable UML, actions, activities, formal mapping, semantics, Model-driven Engineering.

1 Introduction

Early software development methods incorporating the idea of executable models include STATEMATE [2], the Shlaer-Mellor method [3] and ROOM [4]. In all of these methods, executable code is generated automatically from models of behavior. This feature makes them particularly suitable for the construction of automated testing and simulation environments and explains their popularity for the development of embedded systems where the testing of the software on a specific target system can be particularly difficult. The purpose of executable versions of the Unified Modeling Language (UML) is to make these advantages available to UML users by enabling "a chain of tools that support the construction, verification, translation, and execution of computationally complete executable models" [1].

An oft-voiced criticism of UML is its lack of a formal, unambiguous description of its semantics. While the UML 2 specification [5] is still lacking such semantics, it does offer a new three-layer semantics architecture to aid in the development of a formal semantics. This architecture provides a stratification of the description

K. Czarnecki et al. (Eds.): MoDELS 2008, LNCS 5301, pp. 675–689, 2008.

of UML models that clearly separates 'low-level' (i.e., primitive) behavioral specification mechanisms such as actions from 'high-level' (i.e., derived) mechanisms such as activities, state machines, and interactions. The Object Management Group (OMG) has published a Request for Proposal [1], soliciting a definition of an "Executable UML Foundation". This foundation would be a computationally complete and compact subset of UML, with fully specified executable semantics, which would "serve as a shared semantics foundation that would support additional semantics...covering the higher-level formalisms defined in UML."

The UML specification defines a set of "fairly low-level actions sufficient to describe behavior" [6]. UML specifically does not choose one particular action language, in order to refrain from restricting modelers to any specific paradigm. That said, the specification does declaratively define an action semantics, i.e., what actions should do, but not how they should do it. In order to provide a truly executable modeling language, any executable UML foundation must be accompanied by an action language, preferably one which has been formally specified. To the best of our knowledge, no formal semantics for any UML 2 action language yet exists.

In addition to being informal, the description of actions in UML is rather fragmented, making it difficult to discern the pragmatics of actions, that is, the practical aspects of how the constructs and features of actions may be used to achieve various objectives. For instance, the semantics and pragmatics of actions designed to initiate the execution of a behavior are complicated by the fact that UML supports different computational paradigms (e.g., object-oriented, procedural, data flow, control flow, synchronous, asynchronous, etc.).

The purpose of this paper is to report on our work to clarify the semantics and pragmatics of UML actions. In particular, we will sketch a formalization of a subset of UML actions and discuss common usage scenarios for the most complex actions. The work described in this paper is the result of our ongoing efforts to create a virtual machine for UML.

This paper is structured as follows: Section 2 lays the groundwork by introducing UML's semantic architecture and by describing the semantic domain, specifically those concepts necessary to understand the formal mapping presented in Section 3. Section 4 discusses the pragmatics of the most complicated actions—invocation actions. Related work is discussed in Section 5, while Section 6 concludes the paper.

2 Background

2.1 UML Semantic Architecture

UML is a "general-purpose visual modeling language" [6] that can be used in the analysis and design of software systems. Although well-documented, UML does not yet have a formal semantics. The abstract syntax is carefully laid out in over 1000 pages of specification, but the meaning of the syntactic elements is discussed in prose, with a smattering of Object Constraint Language (OCL) constraints.

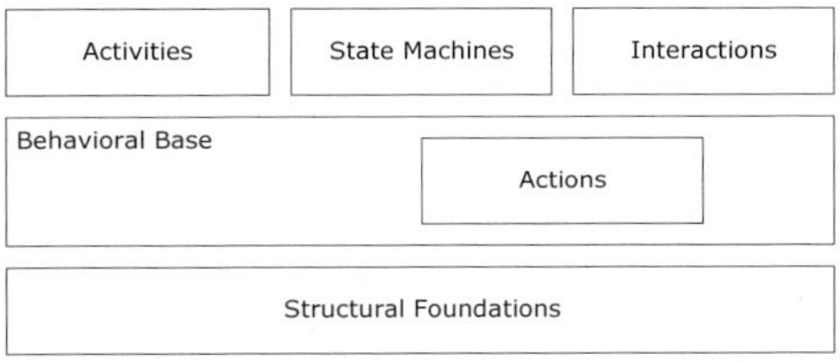

Fig. 1. The UML three-layer semantics architecture

The runtime semantics of UML is defined as a "mapping of modeling concepts into corresponding execution" [5]. This semantics is not formally defined in the UML specification. Instead, the specification outlines a three-layer semantic architecture, which "identifies key semantics areas...and how they relate to each other" [5].

This three-layer architecture is shown in Fig. 1. Each layer depends on those below it, but not vice versa. The bottom layer represents the structural foundations of UML, including concepts such as values, objects, links, messages, etc. The middle layer is the behavioral base, which contains mechanisms for individual object behavior, as well as behavior involving more than one object. More importantly, this layer also contains the description of a set of UML actions. The top layer represents different behavioral formalisms in UML, all of which rely on the behavioral base. Activities, state machines, and interactions all make use of the actions in order to express behavior; these actions are explained in terms of constructs in the structural foundation.

The key to this architecture lies in the middle layer, i.e., actions. A fundamental premise of UML behavioral semantics is the assumption that "all behavior...is ultimately caused by actions" [5]. Actions are "fundamental units of behavior" [5]. As an analogy, actions are comparable to "executable instructions in traditional programming languages" [5].

The advantage of this approach to defining the runtime semantics is the fact that once UML actions are clearly mapped to the structural foundation, it should be relatively easy to define the semantics of different behavioral formalisms.

2.2 Semantic Domain

Our formalization leverages a previously developed semantic domain called the "System Model". Generally, the meaning of a UML specification is given by "the constraints that models place on the runtime behavior of the specified system" [1]. Described in a series of three documents [7,8,9], the goal of the System Model is to allow for these constraints to be captured and collected in their purest and most general form. Therefore, the System Model description intentionally avoids the use of existing formal specification notations such as Z or Abstract State Machines and relies solely on simple mathematical concepts such as sets, relations, and functions. The System Model contains a formalization of UML's structural foundation (i.e., the bottom layer of the architecture in Fig. 1), which results in a

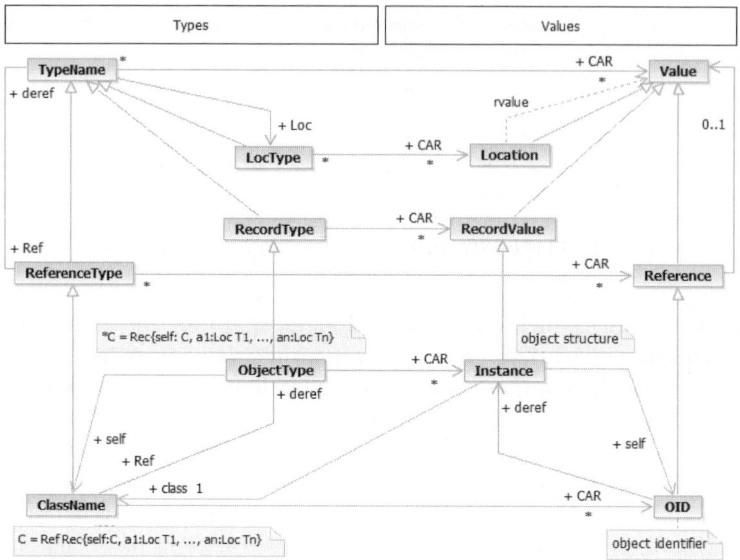

Fig. 2. Class diagram representing System Model *TypeName* and *Value* concepts. Note the symmetry between the two sides

formal notion of state. The meaning of a single behavioral diagram is captured by a (possibly timed) state machine. The meaning of a collection of behavioral UML diagrams is given by the composition of the state machines for each diagram.

The reader is encouraged to refer to the System Model documentation [7,8,9] to get a full description of all System Model concepts. In this paper, we present the essentials required to understand the formal mapping presented in Section 3.1. More precisely, we will only sketch the notion of state used in the System Model. First, a number of universes are postulated, such as *UTYPE* (type names), *UVAL* (values), *ULOC* (locations), *UVAR* (attribute and variable names), *UCLASS* (class names), *UOID* (object identifiers), *USTATE* (states), *UPC* (program counters), *UTHREAD* (threads), etc. Note that these universes encompass all UML models, all executions, and all behavioral formalisms. For example, *USTATE* is the universe of all states for all executions of all UML models, regardless of the type of behavioral formalism used, be it activities, state machines, etc. Then, types and values are organized into a type system as shown in Fig. 2. *Values*, on the right, are elements of carrier sets of *TypeNames*, on the left. A third high-level concept, *VariableName* (not shown), represents attribute and variable names. References are "pointers" to values, whereas locations can hold values and correspond to the "slots" referred to in UML's structural foundation [5]. Type names can be composed into record types. A class name is a type name, defined as a reference to a record type. On the value side, an object identifier is defined as a reference to a record value. For instance, consider the class diagram in Fig. 3(a). If we instantiate an object of type *Class_Car*, the resulting System Model universe contains the elements shown in Fig. 3(b).

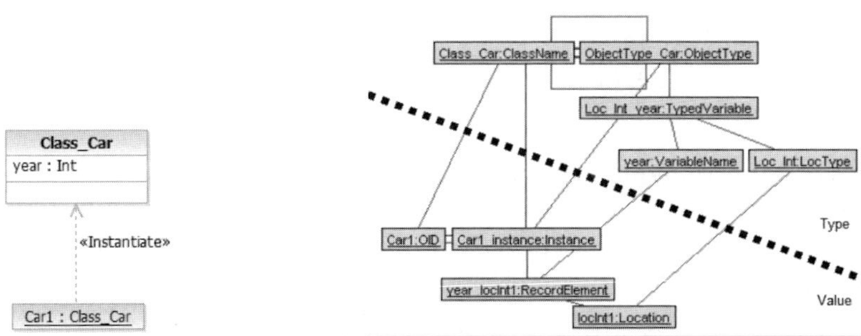

(a) Example class diagram of *Class_Car* class, with an instantiated *Class_Car* object

(b) Partial view of System Model universe consistent with the class diagram in (a). In general, elements above the dotted line represent the definition of *Class_Car*; elements below represent the definition of *Car1*

Fig. 3. Mapping from simple UML class and object to relevant System Model concepts

A state $s \in USTATE$ is defined as a triple $s = (ds, cs, es)$ where

- $ds \in DataStore$ is the data store, i.e., information about the current state of the UML model under examination. The data store (o, m) contains information about objects that currently exist in the execution ($o \subseteq UOID$), as well as mappings of those objects' attributes to values ($m \subseteq ULOC \nrightarrow UVAL$).
- $cs \in ControlStore$ is the control store, i.e., information related to the transitioning from state to state. We have added certain items to the control store description in order to allow the capture of the semantics of activity executions. The control store $(ad, pc, thr, vars)$ contains information about the activity diagrams currently being executed (one activity can call upon others), program counters ($pc \subseteq UPC$) and threads ($thr \subseteq UTHREAD$). In addition, we use the control store to store information about local variables, i.e., variables local to individual activities. The set $ad \subseteq ActivityDiagram$ is composed of individual activities, each defined by a unique identifier, a set of nodes, and a set of initial nodes. Every node is either an *ActionNode*, *ObjectNode*, or *ControlNode*; the union of these sets is the set *GraphNode*.
- $es \in EventStore$ is the event store, i.e., information related to messages, message passing, event buffers, etc. Each object has an associated event buffer.

When executing a typical imperative program, the control store's program counter would hold the address of the next instruction to be executed. However, activities are by nature concurrent executions. We have introduced the concept of $Token \subseteq UPC$ to represent control tokens[1] in the executing set of activities. Thus, pc in the control store is now the set of tokens sitting on nodes. Moreover,

[1] As of UML 2, activities have been "redesigned to use a Petri-like semantics" [5]. Specifically, the concept of token offering is a generalization of Petri net transition enablement [10]. However, complications due to the token offer semantics precludes treating activities simply as Petri nets [10,11,12].

$SchedulerThread \subseteq UTHREAD$ is used to represent the runtime threads used during activity execution.

A token $t \in Token$ is defined as a 4-tuple $t = (id, thread, sittingOn, cameFrom)$ where

- $id \in String$ is a unique identifier
- $thread \in SchedulerThread$ is the runtime thread associated with this token
- $sittingOn \in GraphNode$ is the activity node upon which this token rests
- $cameFrom \in GraphNode$ is the activity node from which this token was sent

A scheduler thread $th \in SchedulerThread$ is defined as a pair $th = (id, token)$ where

- $id \in String$ is a unique identifier
- $token \in Token$ is the token associated with this thread

$Token_s$ is the set of tokens existing in state s and $Token = \bigcup_{s \in USTATE} Token_s$. In general, $Token_s \subseteq s.cs.pc$;[2] however, when dealing with activity diagrams, tokens are the *only* program counters and thus $Token_s = s.cs.pc$. Similarly, $SchedulerThread_s \subseteq s.cs.thr$ in general and $SchedulerThread_s = s.cs.thr$ when dealing with activities.

In general, threads contain information used during the execution of certain invocation actions. For the purposes of this paper, it is enough to state that tokens and scheduler threads are uniquely paired, i.e., every token has an associated scheduler thread, and vice versa:

$$(\forall t \in Token \mid \exists! th \in SchedulerThread \mid t.thread = th \wedge th.token = t)$$
$$\wedge(\forall th \in SchedulerThread \mid \exists! t \in Token \mid th.token = t \wedge t.thread = th).$$

3 Semantics of Actions

As discussed earlier, an executing UML model is treated as a large state machine. Individual UML actions act like executable programming language statements, modifying the underlying state as they execute. Each action may have attribute and associations, which are used to provide static information to the action, e.g., the type of classifier to use with the CreateObjectAction. In addition, actions may have input and/or output pins, which are used dynamically, e.g., an output pin would hold the resulting object of the CreateObjectAction.

Activities are used to compose individual actions into larger executions. We describe activities as directed graphs; each graph node $gn \in GraphNode$ represents some concept in UML activities, e.g., an action node representing a specific UML action or a control node representing a fork, etc.

[2] Dot notation is used as shorthand for projections on particular fields of a tuple. For example, state s is defined as a tuple (ds, cs, es). The expression $s.cs$ retrieves the cs term of state s, i.e., the control store. $s.cs.pc$ retrieves the pc term of the control store, i.e., the set of program counters. This convention is used throughout the paper.

An activity can call on other activities. Executing such a set of activities consists of finding a suitable path through the directed graphs(s) corresponding to the activities. As each graph node is traversed/executed, changes are made to the underlying state. For example, executing an initial node results in the passage of control tokens to the initial node's targets. Executing an action node (a graph node representing a specific UML action) causes various changes to the state, depending on the type of the action, as well as on that action's attributes, associations and inputs. There are a total of 45 actions defined in UML, 36 of which are concrete. To date, we have formalized 22 of the concrete actions; these are listed in Table 1.

An action node $an \in ActionNode$ is an 8-tuple. For the purposes of this paper, we are interested in only four of its terms: $action \in Action$ (referring to the specific UML action represented by the node), $in, out \subseteq GraphNode$ (the sets of source nodes and target nodes of this node),[3] and $annot \subseteq Annotation$ (representing the set of annotations on this node–these provide information to populate the action's attributes and associations).

An action $a \in Action$ is defined as a 4-tuple $a = (name, inPins, outPins, attrs)$, where $name \in String$ is the name of the action, e.g., "CreateObjectAction". $inPins, outPins \subseteq String \times UVAL$ are the input and output pins, respectively. Finally, $attrs \subseteq String \times (UVAL \cup UVAR \cup UTYPE)$ is the set of attributes and associations for the action.

Information about an action's attributes, associations, and pins can be found in the UML metamodel. For example, Fig. 4 shows the UML metamodel related to the AddStructuralFeatureValueAction. Figure 5 shows a sample activity diagram making use of this action. When describing this activity, the relevant action node an would refer to action

$$a = (\text{“AddStructuralFeatureValueAction”}, \{(\text{“object”}, \mathit{Car1}), (\text{“value”}, \mathit{2005})\}, \{\}, \{(\text{“structuralFeature”}, \mathit{year})\}.$$

3.1 Sample Mapping

Using the System Model as our basic semantic domain, we formally define the semantics for the behavior of individual UML actions by clearly identifying how the underlying state $s = (ds, cs, es)$ changes as an action node representing each particular action executes. Here, we present a formal definition of the state changes for the AddStructuralFeatureValueAction, e.g., as used in the activity in Fig. 5.

Let $asfva$ be an action node representing an instance of AddStructuralFeatureValueAction. We explain the effect of executing $asfva$ by defining a function

$$[\![asfva]\!] : USTATE \rightarrow USTATE$$

such that $[\![asfva]\!](ds, cs, es)$ for $(ds, cs, es) \in USTATE$ is defined as follows:

[3] The sets in and out are the direct sources and targets of a particular node. However, token offering/passing typically occurs between action nodes only, skipping any pins or control nodes. Thus, the functions $realIn : GraphNode \rightarrow \mathcal{P}\,GraphNode$ and $realOut : GraphNode \rightarrow \mathcal{P}\,GraphNode$ are defined to find the 'true' targets of any graph node.

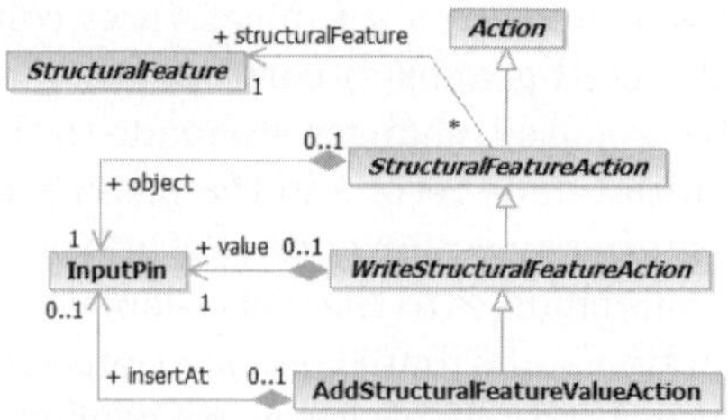

Fig. 4. UML metamodel for AddStructuralFeatureValueAction. StructuralFeature is the attribute to be modified, the "object" pin is the object to be modified and the "value" pin is the new value of the attribute. The "insertAt" pin is not used as we do not permit collections.

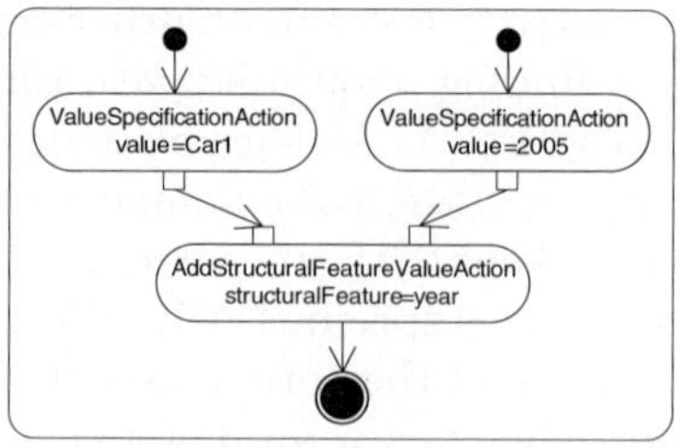

Fig. 5. Sample activity. The ValueSpecificationAction retrieves a value, e.g., the object identifier named *Car1*. The AddStructuralFeatureValueAction assigns a value to an attribute of an object. This diagram is equivalent to the pseudo-code statement `Car1.year = 2005`.

Pre-conditions. The action node *asfva* is *enabled*[4] and has been selected by the scheduler to fire.

Post-conditions. If the pre-conditions are met, then

$$[\![asfva]\!](ds, cs, es) = (ds', cs', es')$$

where

$$\begin{aligned} ds' &= setval(ds, oid, at, v) \\ cs' &= advance(cs, asfva) \\ es' &= es \end{aligned}$$

where

– $setval : DataStore \times UOID \times UVAR \times UVAL \rightarrow DataStore$ is defined as

$$setval((o, m), oid, at, v) = (o, m \oplus [*oid.at = v])$$

and

- $oid \in UOID$ is the object identifier whose attribute will be modified

$$(\text{“object”}, oid) \in asfva.action.inPins$$

- $at \in UVAR$ is the attribute to be modified

$$(\text{“structuralFeature”}, at) \in asfva.action.attrs$$

[4] The precise definition of *enabled* has been removed due to space restrictions. An action node is considered enabled if it is not stalled (due to the nature of token offers and passing), it does not represent a call action waiting for a result, it does not represent an accept action waiting for an event, and it has sufficient tokens on its incoming edges.

- $v \in UVAL$ is the new value of the attribute

$$(\text{“value”}, v) \in asfva.action.inPins$$

- $\oplus$ is an operator that extends a mapping, e.g., $f \oplus [a = b]$ extends f by mapping a to b.
- $*$ is the dereferencing operator. Recall that an object identifier *oid* is a reference to a record; $*oid$ is that record.

– $advance : ControlStore \times GraphNode \rightarrow ControlStore$ is a function defined as

$$advance((ad, pc, thr, vars), gn) = (ad, pc', thr', vars)$$

and the new set of program counters is the same as the old set, minus any tokens sitting on the currently executing node, plus a new token for each of the current node's true targets, i.e.,

$$pc' = pc \backslash removed \cup added$$

where

$$removed = \{t \in pc \mid t.sittingOn = gn\}$$

and

$$added = \{t \in Token \backslash pc \mid t.cameFrom = gn \\ \wedge \exists ! n \in gn.realOut \mid t.sittingOn = n\}$$

and all threads in the new set of threads are matched with the new set of tokens

$$th' = \{t \in SchedulerThread \mid t.token \in pc'\}.$$

3.2 Summary of Changes to State

Table 1 lists all of the currently formalized concrete actions and indicates (with Δ) those parts of the state that change as each action is executed. We have also indicated exactly which parts of the control store are affected. Those parts of the state that are merely read during an action's execution are marked with ✓.

UML actions are considered the “fundamental unit of behavior specification” [5]. For the most part, these actions can considered primitive; they are defined to perform computation or access memory, but not both [5]. These blanket statements about UML actions are supported by several observations, drawn from the table:

– The execution of any action causes, at the very minimum, an advancement in the program counters and threads of the control store.
– Several actions only cause a change to the program counters and threads of the control store; they do not affect the rest of the state. These actions are essentially ‘read’ operations, e.g., ReadVariableAction. In addition, several actions read information from the System Model at large, instead of from the data store. For instance, the ValueSpecificationAction retrieves a value from the universe; the TestIdentityAction compares two values, etc.

Table 1. Summary of state changes caused by the execution of individual UML actions. Entries marked with ✓indicate that information is read only. Entries marked with Δ indicate that information is written.

Action	*ds*	*cs*			*es*
		vars	*pc/th*	*ad*	
AcceptCallAction			Δ		Δ
AcceptEventAction			Δ		Δ
AddStructuralFeatureValueAction	Δ		Δ		
AddVariableValueAction		Δ	Δ		
CallBehaviorAction			Δ	Δ	
CallOperationAction			Δ	Δ	Δ
ClearStructuralFeatureAction	Δ		Δ		
ClearVariableAction		Δ	Δ		
CreateObjectAction	Δ		Δ		
DestroyObjectAction	Δ		Δ		Δ
ReadExtentAction	✓		Δ		
ReadIsClassifiedObjectAction			Δ		
ReadSelfAction			Δ	✓	
ReadStructuralFeatureAction	✓		Δ		
ReadVariableAction		✓	Δ		
RemoveStructuralFeatureValueAction	Δ		Δ		
RemoveVariableValueAction		Δ	Δ		
ReplyAction			Δ		Δ
SendSignalAction			Δ	✓	Δ
StartClassifierBehaviorAction			Δ	Δ	
TestIdentityAction			Δ		
ValueSpecificationAction			Δ		

- Several actions require information about their context in order to execute. These are marked with a ✓in the *ad* column. For instance, the ReadSelfAction returns the object identifier of the object that owns the activity in which the action is found. To do this, the action needs to navigate to its surrounding activity diagram, and thence to the owning object of the diagram.
- Several actions do not read information about their context, but instead modify their context, i.e., the set of activity diagrams currently being executed. For example, the CallOperationAction, CallBehaviorAction and StartClassifierBehaviorAction all refer to behavior that might be contained in a separate activity diagram. As the call is executed, the additional diagram is incorporated into the set *ad*.
- In general, most actions are 'specific' in that they modify only one part of the state. For instance, structural feature actions only modify the data store, variable actions only modify the *vars* portion of the control store, etc.
- Thus far, we have identified only two 'non-specific' actions; they affect two or more areas of the state, in addition to the advancement of program counters and threads. CallOperationAction modifies both the set of current activities *ad* (by causing the called activity to be added) and the event store *es* (by

handling a call message). DestroyObjectAction removes an object from the data store, and its attendant event buffer from the event store.
– Finally, for the most part, actions can be considered 'single-step'. By this, we imply that the action's execution causes changes to the state, and then the action need not be revisited. In contrast, a 'multi-step' action must be visited twice in order to fully complete its execution. For instance, when either the CallOperationAction or CallBehaviorAction is used synchronously, the execution of the calling action is not considered complete until the called behavior (e.g., another activity) has been completely executed. It is, however, not the case that all invocation actions are multi-step. Either of the call actions can be executed asynchronously, which means that the invoked behavior is added to the current set of activities, and then the call is considered complete. Similarly, the send/broadcast actions never wait for a reply.

4 Pragmatics of Invocation Actions

In general, the majority of UML actions are straightforward, e.g., the CreateObjectAction creates a new object identifier, the ReadVariableAction reads a variable, etc. Invocation actions, on the other hand, can be quite esoteric. There are so many actions devoted to invoking behavior in UML that it can be rather complicated to determine exactly which action to use when modeling an activity.

Table 2 lists the various actions in UML that can be used to invoke behavior. The actions are categorized according to two dimensions: whether the invocation can be considered direct or indirect, and whether the invoked behavior can be executed synchronously or asynchronously. For our purposes, an invocation is direct when the target behavior is accessed without any intermediaries, e.g., there is no message or signal to be accepted before the invoked behavior can execute. Indirect execution relies on a call message, or a transmitted signal or object, in order to request the execution of a behavior. In other words, there is the possibility that a behavior invoked indirectly will not actually execute. On the other hand, behavior invoked directly should execute, barring unforeseen circumstances. With respect to the second dimension, a behavior that is invoked synchronously must execute and terminate before the calling behavior can complete its own execution. When a caller invokes a behavior asynchronously, however, the calling behavior can continue to execute while, or even before, the invoked behavior executes.

Direct Invocation

1. CallBehaviorAction with isSynchronous = false: This action is used to invoke a behavior directly, without using message or signal passing. There is no requirement for an accept action in the targeted behavior. An asynchronous CallBehaviorAction is considered completed when its called "behavior is started, or at least ensured to be started at some point" [5, §11.3.9].
2. StartClassifierBehaviorAction: Although not technically an invocation action (it does not inherit from InvocationAction), this action "initiates the behavior

Table 2. Summary of invocation actions. While not technically an invocation action, the StartClassifierBehaviorAction is included because its function is to initiate the classifier behavior of an object.

Invocation	Asynchronous	Synchronous
Direct	1. CallBehaviorAction isSynchronous = false 2. StartClassifierBehaviorAction	3. CallBehaviorAction isSynchronous = true
Indirect	4. CallOperationAction isSynchronous = false 5. SendSignalAction 6. SendObjectAction 7. BroadcastSignalAction	8. CallOperationAction isSynchronous = true

of the classifier of the input object" [5, §11.3.46]. There are no messages or signals and the targeted object has no choice but to execute the behavior; thus, this action is a direct invocation. It is asynchronous in that the calling behavior continues execution as soon as the classifier behavior is invoked.

3. CallBehaviorAction with isSynchronous = true: When used synchronously, the CallBehaviorAction "waits until the execution of the invoked behavior completes and a result is returned on its output pin" [5, §11.3.9].

Indirect Invocation

4. CallOperationAction with isSynchronous = false: This is an indirect invocation action in that it "transmits an operation call request to the target object, where it may cause the invocation" [5, §11.3.10] of the desired behavior. When used asynchronously, the calling behavior can continue execution after the call request has been sent. On the receiving end, the AcceptEventAction is designed to be used for accepting asynchronous calls; however, the AcceptCallAction can also be used. In fact, we prefer using the AcceptCallAction so that the same target activity can be used to handle both synchronous and asynchronous calls.
5. SendSignalAction: This action creates a signal and transmits it to the target object, where it may cause the invocation of behavior [5, §11.3.45]. The calling behavior continues execution. On the receiving end, an AcceptEventAction is required.
6. SendObjectAction: Similar to the SendSignalAction, this action transmits an object to the target object, where it may invoke behavior [5, §11.3.44]. Here too, the calling behavior continues execution.
7. BroadcastSignalAction: This action is identical to the SendSignalAction, except that the signal is sent to multiple targets, where it may invoke behavior [5, §11.3.7].
8. CallOperationAction with isSynchronous = true: When used synchronously, the CallOperationAction must be accepted on the receiving end by an AcceptCallAction [5, §11.3.1], which will be linked to a ReplyAction. The ReplyAction completes the execution of the call, returning the result to the caller [5, §11.3.43], which can then terminate.

5 Related Work

The UML specification defines the *action semantics*, which describes the effects of a set of "fairly low-level actions sufficient to describe behavior" [6] but it does not define a concrete syntax for actions. Any executable UML foundation must be accompanied by an action language. We are primarily interested in formal semantics, specifically of UML actions. In order to examine the execution of actions, we use UML activities as our action language to 'glue' actions together.

Academic action languages tend to be part of tools focused on the analysis of models. OxUML is an OCL-based action language, which supports actions with side effects. The result is an executable UML, supported by a UML virtual machine [13]. [14] suggests a profile for UML that provides "complete and precise Aspect-Oriented behavior modeling" including UML's action semantics. After weaving, the complete model can be executed in order to observe the behavior of the modeled aspects. ActiveChartsIDE [15] is a plugin for Microsoft Visio with an interpreter that supports the simulation and debugging of activity diagrams.

There are several commercial tools, which support executable UML; each of these includes their own proprietary action language. xUML [16] is a subset of UML, used by Kennedy-Carter in their iUML tool, and which incorporates the Action Specification Language and permits the construction of executable models. xtUML [17] makes use of the Object Action Language, and is implemented by Mentor Graphics' BridgePoint tool suite. There is also a plugin for IBM's Rational Modeling tools that "enables the execution, debugging and testing of UML models" [18] using state machines and activities. This execution engine does not specifically support UML actions; it uses Java as an action language.

Although a requirement for an executable UML is the inclusion of some kind of action language, none of the related work presented thus far focuses on the individual UML actions. These initiatives all make use of higher-level action languages. To the best of our knowledge, none of these action languages is accompanied by a formal semantics.

Defining the semantics of UML activities is a vibrant research area; although the fact that activities substantially changed with the introduction of UML 2 narrows the field somewhat. For instance, [19] provides a semantics for an older version of UML actions, but is obsolete because pins have since been introduced. On the other hand, there has been research on defining the semantics of UML 2 activities based on several formalisms, such as Abstract State Machines [15], Petri nets [11,12] and dynamic metamodeling [20]. Other research has focused on model checking activities [21]. Unfortunately, none of this particular research supports individual UML actions.

Thus far, the OMG has been presented with one submission [22] in response to their RFP for an Executable UML Foundation. This submission defines the Foundational Subset for Executable UML (fUML) and is supported by many of the large names in modeling technologies. Our research into the semantics of actions is most closely related to this submission. In our case, we are not so much interested in producing a "compact" subset of UML. For example, we are able to support calls, and thus AcceptCallAction and ReplyAction. We also support variable actions, as well as the decision control node (with guards). Instead of decisions, fUML supports the loop and conditional nodes. Neither project supports links or associations.

6 Conclusion

We formally define the execution semantics of a subset of UML actions. This definition is expressed in terms of state changes to the global state machine that represents an executing UML model. We also discuss common usage scenarios for the most complex actions, i.e., invocation actions.

Our research has resulted in uncovering certain ambiguities and implicit assumptions about UML actions. For instance, the UML specification does not specify what should happen when the DestroyObjectAction destroys its owning object. In addition, the requirement to pair a synchronous CallOperationAction with an AcceptCallAction is not clear from the description of the former action. Finally, the fact that an asynchronous CallOperationAction should be matched by an AcceptEventAction, but could be matched by an AcceptCallAction is potentially confusing—the modeler would need to know whether the call was to be synchronous or asynchronous before creating the receiving behavior.

In addition to formally specifying the execution semantics of actions, a major contribution of our work is that we are validating the three-layer semantics hierarchy from Fig. 1. By using activities as our action language, we successfully map a higher-level behavioral formalism to actions. Then, we map these actions to the state transformers over the structural foundation, described by the System Model, a semantic domain specifically designed to capture the semantics of UML models on a maximally general level and to deal easily with collections of different kinds of UML diagrams.

Finally, this research is part of our ongoing efforts to create a virtual machine for UML. A discussion of our interpreter for actions and activities can be found at [23].

Acknowledgements

This research is supported by the Centre of Excellence for Research in Adaptive Systems (CERAS) and IBM. The authors would like to thank Bran Selic of Malina Software Corporation and Conrad Bock of the National Institute of Standards and Technology for their invaluable assistance.

References

1. Object Management Group: Semantics of a foundational subset for executable UML models. Request for Proposal ad/2005-04-02 (April 2005)
2. Harel, D., Politi, M.: Modeling Reactive Systems with Statecharts: The STATEMATE Approach. McGraw-Hill, New York (1998)

3. Shlaer, S., Mellor, S.: Object Lifecycles: Modeling the World in States. Prentice-Hall, Englewood Cliffs (1992)
4. Selic, B., Gullekson, G., Ward, P.: Real-Time Object-Oriented Modeling. Wiley, Chichester (1994)
5. Object Management Group: Unified Modeling Language: Superstructure version 2.1. Document ptc/06-01-02 (January 2006)
6. Rumbaugh, J., Jacobson, I., Booch, G.: The Unified Modeling Language Reference Manual, 2nd edn. Addison-Wesley, Reading (2005)
7. Broy, M., Cengarle, M., Rumpe, B.: Semantics of UML – Towards a System Model for UML: The Structural Data Model. Technical Report TUM-I0612, TUM (2006)
8. Broy, M., Cengarle, M., Rumpe, B.: Semantics of UML – Towards a System Model for UML: The Control Model. Technical Report TUM-I0710, TUM (2007)
9. Broy, M., Cengarle, M., Rumpe, B.: Semantics of UML – Towards a System Model for UML: The State Machine Model. Technical Report TUM-I0711, TUM (2007)
10. Bock, C.: Re: Token/offer semantics for activities. E-mail to J. Dingel (April 25, 2008)
11. Störrle, H., Hausmann, J.: Towards a formal semantics of UML 2.0 activities. In: Software Engineering. LNI, vol. 64, pp. 117–128 (2005)
12. Schattkowsky, T., Förster, A.: On the pitfalls of UML 2 activity modeling. In: Proceedings of the International Workshop on Modeling in Software Engineering (MISE), p. 8 (2007)
13. Jiang, K., Zhang, L., Miyake, S.: An executable UML with OCL-based action semantics language. In: Asia-Pacific Software Engineering Conference (APSEC), pp. 302–309 (2007)
14. Fuentes, L., Sánchez, P.: Towards executable aspect-oriented UML models. In: 10th International Workshop on Aspect-oriented Modeling (AOM), pp. 28–34. ACM Press, New York (2007)
15. Sarstedt, S., Kohlmeyer, J., Raschke, A., Schneiderhan, M., Gessenharter, D.: ActiveChartsIDE. In: ECMDA 2005 (2005)
16. Raistrick, C., Francis, P., Wright, J., Carter, C., Wilkie, I.: Model Driven Architecture with Executable UML. Cambridge University Press, Cambridge (2004)
17. Mellor, S., Balcer, M.: Executable UML: A Foundation for Model Driven Architecture. Addison-Wesley, Reading (2002)
18. Dotan, D., Kirshin, A.: Debugging and testing behavioral UML models. In: 22nd ACM SIGPLAN Conference on Object Oriented Programming Systems and Applications (OOPSLA), pp. 838–839. ACM Press, New York (2007)
19. Ober, I., Coulette, B., Gandriau, M.: Action language for the UML. In: Langages et Modèles à Objets (LMO), Hermes, pp. 277–291 (2000)
20. Engels, G., Soltenborn, C., Wehrheim, H.: Analysis of UML activities using dynamic meta modeling. In: Bonsangue, M.M., Johnsen, E.B. (eds.) FMOODS 2007. LNCS, vol. 4468, pp. 76–90. Springer, Heidelberg (2007)
21. Eshuis, R.: Symbolic model checking of UML activity diagrams. ACM Transactions on Software Engineering and Methodology (TOSEM) 15(1), 1–38 (2006)
22. Object Management Group: Semantics of a foundational subset for executable UML models. Initial Submission ad/06-05-02 (May 2006)
23. Crane, M., Dingel, J.: Towards a UML virtual machine: Implementing an interpreter for UML 2 actions and activities. In: 2008 conference of the Centre for Advanced Studies on Collaborative research (CASCON) (to appear, 2008)

A Lightweight Approach for Defining the Formal Semantics of a Modeling Language

Pierre Kelsen and Qin Ma

Laboratory for Advanced Software Systems
University of Luxembourg
6, rue Richard Coudenhove-Kalergi
L-1359 Luxembourg
{Pierre.Kelsen,Qin.Ma}@uni.lu

Abstract. To define the formal semantics of a modeling language, one normally starts from the abstract syntax and then defines the static semantics and dynamic semantics. Having a formal semantics is important for reasoning about the language but also for building tools for the language. In this paper we propose a novel approach for this task based on the Alloy language. With the help of a concrete example language, we contrast this approach with traditional methods based on formal languages, type checking, meta-modeling and operational semantics. Although both Alloy and traditional techniques yield a formal semantics of the language, the Alloy-based approach has two key advantages: a uniform notation, and immediate automatic analyzability using the Alloy analyzer. Together with the simplicity of Alloy, our approach offers the prospect of making formal definitions easier, hopefully paving the way for a wider adoption of formal techniques in the definition of modeling languages.

1 Introduction

To fully define a modeling language one needs to specify: (1) the abstract syntax (the structure of its models), (2) the concrete syntax (the actual notation presented to the user), (3) the static semantics (well-formedness rules for the models), (4) the dynamic semantics (the meaning of a model). Ideally all these elements of a modeling language are formally defined. By having a formal definition one can precisely reason about the language; by eliminating any ambiguities inherent to informal descriptions such a formal specification is also a good starting point for developing tool support.

Despite the widely recognized advantages of a formal description, modeling languages are often introduced without a full formal definition. A good example is the Unified Modeling Language [11]. This modeling language is the de facto standard modeling language in software engineering. Nevertheless the semantics of the UML is not fully formally defined. This complicates the development of UML tools and compromises their interoperability [1].

This paper focuses on the formal definition of the semantics. "formal semantics" in the title usually refers to the dynamic semantics only (see, e.g., [13]).

K. Czarnecki et al. (Eds.): MoDELS 2008, LNCS 5301, pp. 690–704, 2008.

Because the dynamic semantics intimately relates to the abstract syntax and the static semantics but is independent of the concrete syntax, we study in this paper approaches for defining abstract syntax, static semantics and dynamic semantics using a concrete example language. We first present two traditional approaches for defining abstract syntax and static semantics based on EBNF and type systems on one hand, and metamodeling on the other hand. For dynamic semantics we present one traditional approach based on operational semantics. We then propose a uniform approach for defining these aspects of a modeling language based on Alloy ([4]). Besides having a single language for this task, Alloy provides the additional benefit of providing automatic tool support for checking the correctness of semantic specifications. Automatic analysis facilitates incremental development of complex semantic descriptions by uncovering errors early. The term "lightweight" used in the title of the paper was chosen because Alloy attempts to obtain the benefits of traditional formal methods at lower cost [5].

We now discuss related work. We illustrate the Alloy-based approach for defining the formal semantics by looking at a concrete language which is a subset of the EP language, a declarative executable modeling language [6,8]. The same exercise was done for the full EP language and similar conclusions were reached ([7]). We only present one traditional approach for specifying dynamic semantics: operational semantics. For a fuller account of this approach the reader is referred to [13]. Other approaches for specifying the dynamic semantics are [10,14]: denotational semantics (map models to denotations and reason in terms of the denotations), axiomatic semantics (exploiting assertions about programs), and hybrid approaches.

Although much effort has been dedicated to establishing firm theoretical foundations for formal semantics during the last four decades, it is recognized that there is still no universally accepted formal notation for semantic description [14]. More importantly formal semantics approaches currently have limited practical use. Possible hindrances cited by Mosses (e.g., [9]) are readability and lack of tool support, which we will address with the Alloy approach.

This rest of the paper is structured as follows: in the next section we present the concrete modeling language that will be used as a running example for the remainder of the paper. In section 3 we describe traditional approaches for defining abstract syntax and static and dynamic semantics of the example language. In section 4 we do the same exercise using Alloy. We then compare in section 5 the Alloy-based approach with the traditional approaches. We close with concluding remarks in the final section.

2 Example Language

The chosen EP subset is specified by the metamodel in Figure 1. An EP *system* defines a set of *models*, each of which consists of a set of *properties* and a set of *events*. EP models play a role similar to classes in an object-oriented system. *Instances* of models exist at runtime, where the value assignment to their properties constitutes the state of the system, and events represent available operations on these instances. For simplicity, we omit primitive types, i.e., types are models and values are instances. Each valid system should have exactly one main model, considered as the entry point of a system, in the sense that the initial state of an EP system is acquired by creating an unique instance of it.

The novelty of the EP language is that behavior of events is modeled declaratively via *event edges*. Briefly, execution of an event on an instance can influence the state of a system in two ways: it can either change the value of a property of the instance using an *impact edge*, where the new value is evaluated from the expression associated with this edge; or trigger other events on some instances via *push edges*, which then proceed in a similar fashion. A push edge is a directional connection from a source event to a target event. It has a link property whose value indicates on which instance the target event will be triggered. Because each event can have *parameters*, the push edge specifies for each parameter in the target event an expression that computes the value of this parameter. (We omit details of the expression language in this paper because of the limited space; in [8] we showed that OCL is a good candidate language.)

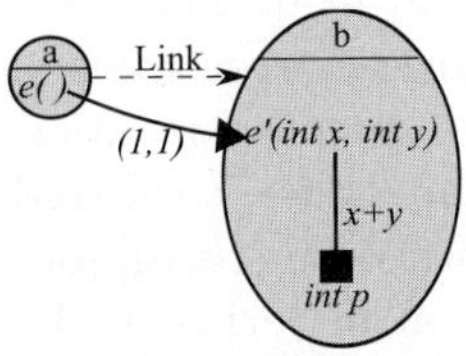

We close our informal description of the EP subset by looking at an example of two instances "a" and "b" existing at runtime and belonging to some models in which events and event edges are defined as in the graph to the left. Instance "a" has an event "*e*" with no parameters, and instance "b" has an event "*e*′" that takes two integer parameters. The triangle-headed solid arrow denotes the push edge between events; the dashed arrow labeled "Link" specifies the link of the edge which is basically a local property of "a" that points to "b". In comparison, the square-headed arrow between event "*e*′" and local property "*p*" denotes an impact edge, labeled by expression $x + y$, i.e., the sum of the two parameters of the event. In a nutshell, this example depicts the following event propagation and local property modification: (1) Execution of "*e*" on "a" would trigger execution of "*e*′" on "b" with the constant arguments 1 and 1; (2) this would in turn change the value of "*p*" of "b" to the sum of the two arguments of "*e*′", i.e., 2.

3 Traditional Approaches

3.1 Abstract Syntax and Static Semantics

3.1.1 EP Metamodel and OCL Constraints

Figure 1 defines the abstract syntax of the chosen EP subset as a meta-model and the static semantics as OCL [12] constraints. Four groups of well-formedness constraints are specified, in addition to the inherent syntax restrictions designated by the class diagram, such as compositions and multiplicities. For any valid system, the appointed *main* model should be defined in the system, and for any valid event, the set of feeding properties should all be defined in the model that also owns the event. The sanity rules for impact and push edges in

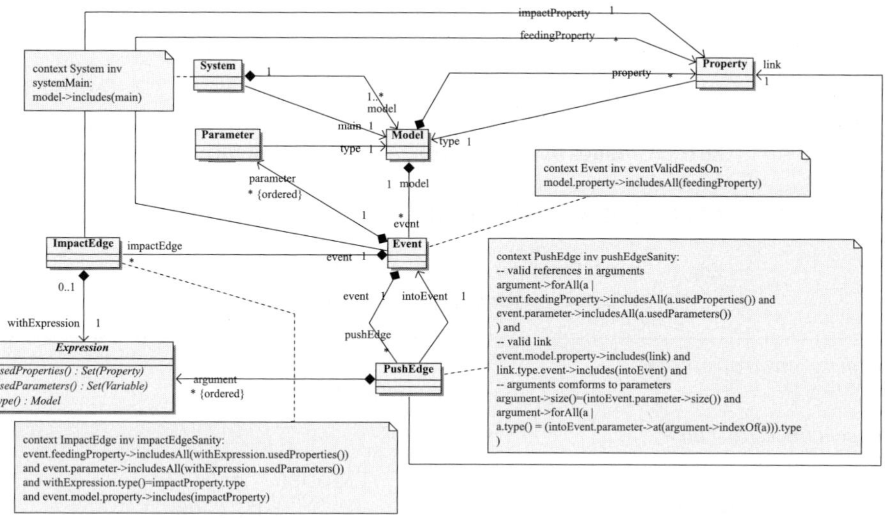

Fig. 1. EP subset meta-model with constraints in OCL

event definitions are a bit more involved. The following constraints must be satisfied in order for an impact edge to be valid: (1) the expression that specifies the new value of the impacted property should only reference properties that feed the event and event parameters; (2) the expression and the impacted property should have the same type; (3) the impacted property and the event that owns the edge should both be owned by the same model.

For a push edge to be valid, the following constraints are enforced: (1) the expressions used to compute arguments of the target event should only reference parameters of the source event or properties that feed the source event; (2) the link of the edge should point to a property, whose type, which is a model, owns the target event. (3) the sequence of arguments and the sequence of parameters of the target event should have the same size and the same type, respectively.

3.1.2 EBNF Syntax and Typing Rules

Another way to formalize the abstract syntax and the static semantics of the example language is to follow the approach usually adopted in specifying formal languages, namely via EBNF based syntax and type checking rules.

The EBNF based abstract syntax appears on top of Figure 2. Different from the EP metamodel in which all syntax entities are referred to by direct references, this approach is textual, i.e., references are via names. As a consequence, we assume the following disjoint sets of names: variable names $x \in \mathcal{X}$, where **self** is a special variable denoting the recursive "self" reference; property names $p \in \mathcal{P}$; event names $e \in \mathcal{E}$; and model names $m \in \mathcal{M}$. Moreover, we write $\overline{\mathtt{XX}}$ for a sequence of form $\mathtt{XX}_1, \ldots, \mathtt{XX}_k$. An alternative notation is $\mathtt{XX}_i{}^{1 \leq i \leq k}$, or simply $\mathtt{XX}_i{}^{i \in I}$ where I stands for the set of possible subscripts. We abbreviate a sequence of pairs as a pair of sequences, namely writing $\overline{\mathtt{XX}}\llcorner\overline{\mathtt{YY}}$ as shorthand for $\mathtt{XX}_1\llcorner\mathtt{YY}_1, \ldots, \mathtt{XX}_k\llcorner\mathtt{YY}_k$. An empty sequence is denoted by ϵ.

EBNF abstract syntax:

$\mathtt{Sys} ::= \overline{\mathtt{Mdf}}$	EP systems
$\mathtt{Mdf} ::= \textbf{model}\ m\ \{\overline{m}\ \overline{p};\ \overline{\mathtt{Edf}}\}$	Model definitions
$\mathtt{Edf} ::= \overline{p}\ \textbf{feed}\ e(\overline{m}\ \overline{x})\ \{\overline{\mathtt{Edg}}\}$	Event definitions
$\mathtt{Edg} ::= \textbf{push}\ \overline{\mathtt{Exp}}\ \textbf{into}\ e\ \textbf{via}\ p$	Push edges
$\quad\quad\quad\ \ \textbf{impact}\ p\ \textbf{with}\ \mathtt{Exp}$	Impact edges

Typing environments:

$$\Gamma ::= \epsilon \mid (x : m\restriction\overline{p}), \Gamma$$

Type checking rules:

TSystem

$$\frac{(\vdash \mathtt{Mdf}_i :: \textbf{ok})^{\,i\in I} \quad \text{Main is declared} \quad \mathtt{Mdf}_i^{\ i\in I} \text{ declare distinct model names}}{\vdash \mathtt{Mdf}_i^{\ i\in I} :: \textbf{ok}}$$

TModel

$$\frac{(\vdash^{(m,\overline{p})} \mathtt{Edf}_i :: \textbf{ok})^{\,i\in I} \quad \overline{p} \text{ distinct} \quad \mathtt{Edf}_i^{\ i\in I} \text{ declare distinct names}}{\vdash \textbf{model}\ m\ \{\overline{m}\ \overline{p}, \mathtt{Edf}_i^{\ i\in I}\} :: \textbf{ok}}$$

TEvent

$$\frac{\overline{p} \subseteq \overline{q} \qquad \overline{x} \text{ distinct} \qquad ((\overline{x} : \overline{m}) \vdash^{(m,\overline{p})} \mathtt{Edg}_i :: \textbf{ok})^{\,i\in I}}{\vdash^{(m,\overline{q})} \overline{p}\ \textbf{feed}\ e(\overline{m}\ \overline{x})\ \{\mathtt{Edg}_i^{\ i\in I}\} :: \textbf{ok}}$$

TPushEdge

$$\frac{\mathit{etype}(\mathit{ptype}(m,p),e) = m_i^{\ i\in I} \qquad (\Gamma \cup (\textbf{self} : m\restriction\overline{p}) \vdash \mathtt{Exp}_i :: m_i)^{\,i\in I}}{\Gamma \vdash^{(m,\overline{p})} \textbf{push}\ \mathtt{Exp}_i^{\ i\in I}\ \textbf{into}\ e\ \textbf{via}\ p :: \textbf{ok}}$$

TImpactEdge

$$\frac{\Gamma \cup (\textbf{self} : m\restriction\overline{p}) \vdash \mathtt{Exp} :: \mathit{ptype}(m,p)}{\Gamma \vdash^{(m,\overline{p})} \textbf{impact}\ p\ \textbf{with}\ \mathtt{Exp} :: \textbf{ok}}$$

Auxiliary definitions:

EventTypeLookUp

$$\frac{\textbf{model}\ m\ \{\overline{m_1}\ \overline{p_1}; \overline{\mathtt{Edf}}\} \in \mathtt{Sys} \quad \overline{p_2}\ \textbf{feed}\ e(\overline{m}\ \overline{x})\ \{\overline{\mathtt{Edg}}\} \in \overline{\mathtt{Edf}}}{\mathit{etype}(m,e) = \overline{m}}$$

PropertyTypeLookUp

$$\frac{\textbf{model}\ m\ \{\overline{m_1}\ \overline{p_1}, m'\ p', \overline{m_2}\ \overline{p_2}; \overline{\mathtt{Edf}}\} \in \mathtt{Sys} \qquad p' \in \overline{p}}{\mathit{ptype}(m\restriction\overline{p}, p') = m'}$$

Fig. 2. EBNF abstract syntax, typing, and auxiliary functions

Typing rules appear in the middle of Figure 2. The special type **ok** denotes well-typedness. The typing environment Γ is a finite binding from variables to types, in which the mask operation on models: $m\lceil\overline{p}$, allows us to control the visibility of properties of model m in different circumstances. Putting a mask $\overline{p}$ on m restricts only those properties of m appearing in $\overline{p}$ to be visible. A default mask is $\mathcal{P}$, which is usually omitted; it allows all properties to be visible.

Two auxiliary functions are used in typing rules, defined in the bottom of Figure 2. Function $etype(m, e)$ returns the sequence of types of the parameters of event e as defined in model m, or otherwise returns $\perp$, denoting an error during type checking. Function $ptype(m\lceil\overline{p}, p)$ returns the type of property p as defined in model m if not masked (i.e. $p \in \overline{p}$), or otherwise $\perp$.

Typing rules in principle correspond to the OCL constraints discussed in Section 3.1.1. For example, the first premise in rule TEvent corresponds to the eventValidFeedsOn invariant of Event (see Figure 1). Moreover, the enforcement of the three constraints discussed on page 693 for impact edges is distributed across typing rules as follows: (1) the typing environment in which the expression of the impact edge is typed consists of two parts: the first part is the event parameters accumulated in the second premise of rule TEvent, and the second part is the set of properties that feed the event, accumulated in the premise of rule TImpactEdge. In other words, the only possible references from the expression fall into these two categories; (2) the type of the expression is required to be the same as the type of the impacted property p, as depicted by the premise of rule TImpactEdge; (3) the ownership of model m to p is assured when computing $ptype(m, p)$, because otherwise $\perp$ will be returned.

Similarly, the sanity constraints of PushEdge are all spelled out, too, across the premises of rules TEvent and TPushEdge.

However, because of the textual nature of the approach, additional bookkeeping and name distinction premises are required, such as in rule TSystem and TModel. But we also gain from the naming facility. For example, we spare the systemMain invariant of System, because asking for a unique model defined in the system with name Main suffices to assure its ownership thanks to name scoping: in the scope of the system, name Main will always refers to the unique model in the system with name Main.

3.2 Operational Semantics

In this section we assume that the reader is familiar with operational semantics [13]. A system configuration (Λ, s) is a pair of an evaluation environment and a state. As defined on top of Figure 3, the state records the current set of instances, and the environment, binding variables to values, tells how to access these instances via variables. A value $v \in \mathcal{V}$ is either **null** denoting void, or an identity $id \in \mathcal{ID}$ denoting an instance of a certain model. Instance identities are distinct. In the state, an instance identity is bound with a pair (m, φ_m). The former denotes the model of the instance and the latter gives its evaluation. An evaluation of an instance of model m, written φ_m, is a partial function from properties to values where $\forall p \in \mathcal{P}$, $\varphi_m(p) = \perp$ (i.e. undefined) if and only if p is

Values, states, and substitutions:

$$\begin{array}{lrl}
\text{States:} & s & ::= \emptyset \mid (id : (m, \varphi_m)), s \\
\text{Values:} & v & ::= \textbf{null} \mid id \\
\text{Evaluations:} & \varphi_m : & \mathcal{P} \to \mathcal{V} \\
\text{State substitutions:} & \sigma \ : & \mathcal{ID} \times \mathcal{P} \to \mathcal{V}
\end{array}$$

Substitution application:

$$s\sigma(id).m = s(id).m$$

$$s\sigma(id).\varphi_m(p) = \begin{cases} s(id).\varphi_m(p) & \sigma(id,p) = \bot \\ \sigma(id,p) & \text{otherwise} \end{cases}$$

Evaluation environments:

$$\Lambda ::= \epsilon \mid (x : v), \Lambda$$

Expression evaluation (partial):

VARIABLE

$$\frac{\Lambda(x) = v}{\Lambda \models (x,\ s) \Downarrow (v,\ \emptyset)}$$

INSTANCECREATION

$$\frac{id \text{ fresh}}{\Lambda \models (m :: \textbf{create}(),\ s) \Downarrow (id,\ (id : (m, \phi_m)))}$$

PROPERTYCALL

$$\frac{\Lambda \models (\mathsf{Exp},\ s) \Downarrow (id,\ s_\Delta) \qquad (s \cup s_\Delta)(id).\varphi_m(p) = v}{\Lambda \models (\mathsf{Exp}.p,\ s) \Downarrow (v,\ s_\Delta)}$$

Edge evaluation:

EIMPACTEDGE

$$\frac{\Lambda \models (\mathsf{Exp},\ s) \Downarrow (v_1,\ s^1_\Delta) \qquad \Lambda \models (\textbf{self},\ s) \Downarrow (v_2,\ s^2_\Delta)}{\Lambda \models (\textbf{impact}\ p\ \textbf{with}\ \mathsf{Exp},\ s) \Downarrow (((v_2, p) : v_1),\ s^1_\Delta \cup s^2_\Delta)}$$

EPUSHEDGE

$$\frac{\Lambda \models ((\textbf{self}.p).e(\overline{\mathsf{Exp}}),\ s) \Downarrow (\sigma,\ s_\Delta)}{\Lambda \models (\textbf{push}\ \overline{\mathsf{Exp}}\ \textbf{into}\ e\ \textbf{via}\ p,\ s) \Downarrow (\sigma,\ s_\Delta)}$$

Event call evaluation:

EVENTCALL

$$\frac{\begin{array}{ll} \Lambda \models (\mathsf{Exp},\ s) \Downarrow (v,\ s_\Delta) & v \neq \textbf{null} \\ \Lambda \models (\overline{\mathsf{Exp}},\ s) \Downarrow (\overline{v},\ \overline{s_\Delta}) & \overline{p}\ \textbf{feed}\ e(\overline{m}\ \overline{x})\ \{\mathsf{Edg}_i{}^{i \in I}\} \in (s \cup s_\Delta)(v).m \\ \multicolumn{2}{l}{(\Lambda \cup (\overline{x} : \overline{v}) \cup (\textbf{self} : v) \models (\mathsf{Edg}_i,\ s \cup s_\Delta \cup \overline{s_\Delta}) \Downarrow (\sigma_i,\ s^i_\Delta))^{i \in I}} \end{array}}{\Lambda \models (\mathsf{Exp}.e(\overline{\mathsf{Exp}}),\ s) \Downarrow (\biguplus_{i \in I} \sigma_i,\ s_\Delta \cup \overline{s_\Delta} \cup (\bigcup_{i \in I} s^i_\Delta))}$$

Event invocation reduction:

EVENTINVOCATIONREDUCTION

$$\frac{\Lambda \models (\mathsf{Exp}.e(\overline{\mathsf{Exp}}),\ s) \Downarrow (\sigma,\ s_\Delta)}{(\Lambda,\ s) \xrightarrow{\mathsf{Exp}.e(\overline{\mathsf{Exp}})} (\Lambda,\ (s \cup s_\Delta)\sigma)}$$

Fig. 3. Operational semantics

not a property of m. For each model m, we assume a default evaluation for its instances, denoted by ϕ_m, in which we associate **null** to all properties defined in m. Given a state s and an instance id in it, we use $s(id).m$ to denote the model of the instance, and $s(id).\varphi_m$ the corresponding evaluation. Finally, system state substitution, denoted by σ, is a partial function from pairs of instance identities and properties to values. For a given substitution σ, $\sigma(id, p) = v$ means to change the value of p of instance id into v, and $\sigma(id, p) = \bot$ means to leave this value unchanged. As a consequence, applying the substitution to a state s, written $s\sigma$, returns a new state whose definition is also presented in Figure 3. Sometimes (for instance in rule EImpactEdge of Figure 3), we specify a substitution by directly listing the triples defined in it as: $\sigma ::= \emptyset \mid ((id, p) : v), \sigma$.

Upon initialization, the system configuration, (Λ_0, s_0), has a unique instance in s_0 of identity id where $s_0(id).m = \mathsf{Main}$ and $s_0(id).\varphi_m = \phi_{\mathsf{Main}}$ (the default evaluation of the main model), and a unique binding $(\mathsf{main} : id)$ in Λ_0. Interacting with an EP system amounts to invoking some event on some instance accessible from variable main and changing the system into a new configuration. The formal reduction relation is given at the bottom of Figure 3. Note that the evaluation environment Λ does not change after the reduction, because invoking an event as by $\mathsf{Exp}.e(\overline{\mathsf{Exp}})$ would not change the set of global variables nor their bindings. However, the set of accessible instances from variable main may still evolve, for instance by changing the value of the properties of the main instance.

Let us elaborate on the evaluation rules for event calls and edges. The judgment $\Lambda \models (\mathsf{Exp}.e(\overline{\mathsf{Exp}}), s) \Downarrow (\sigma, s_\Delta)$ means: calling event e under environment Λ and in state s evaluates to a substitution σ and a set of new instances s_Δ created during the evaluation. In rule EventCall we first evaluate the callee Exp into a value v [1], which should not be **null** in order for the calling to be meaningful, hence is an instance identity. Then, the arguments $\overline{\mathsf{Exp}_i}^{i \in I}$ are evaluated respectively. We pick up the body of the called event from the definition of $(s \cup s_\Delta)(v).m$, which effectively denotes the model of the callee, and evaluate the body, i.e. the edges, in a new evaluation environment extended with the parameters all bound to the just computed argument values, and **self** bound to the callee instance.

Evaluation judgments for edges take the form: $\Lambda \models (\mathsf{Edg}, s) \Downarrow (\sigma, s_\Delta)$. In rule EImpactEdge evaluating an impact edge would result in a substitution of form $((v_2, p) : v_1)$, which basically asks to change the value of the impacted property p on instance denoted by **self** (i.e. v_2) into the new value (i.e. v_1) computed from the expression Exp. By contrast, the result of evaluating a push edge (rule EPushEdge) is derived from recursively calling the target event on the instance denoted by the link property p of **self** within the same evaluation environment and state.

The second part in the results of evaluations, namely s_Δ, keeps track of the new instances that are created during the evaluations. As new instances can only be created in **create** expressions (rule InstanceCreation), where we have already required the freshness of identity, the accumulated s_Δ's would never conflict on identities, neither with each other nor with an instance in the original

[1] Being out of the scope of the paper, expression evaluation rules are only partially presented in Figure 3 to help readers understand the other parts.

state. Therefore, the plain set union operation suffices. By contrast, in order to keep the dynamic semantics deterministic, namely at most one modification of a property of an instance is called for during an event invocation, we use the disjoint set union, denoted by $\uplus$, when collecting the substitutions along the evaluation, to enforce disjoint domains.

Finally, in rule EventInvocationReduction, the accumulated substitutions and new instances take effect by applying to the original state and reach a new state: $(s \cup s_\Delta)\sigma$.

4 The Alloy Approach

4.1 Overview of Alloy

Alloy [4] is a language that expresses software abstractions precisely and succinctly. A system is modeled in Alloy using a set of types called *signatures.* Each signature may have a number of *fields.* Constraints may be added as *facts* to a system to express additional properties. In terms of rigor Alloy rivals traditional formal methods. Its novelty is the *Alloy Analyzer*, a tool that allows fully automatic analysis of a system; it can expose flaws early and thus encourages incremental development. Two types of analyses can be performed using the Alloy Analyzer: we can search for an instance (obtained by populating signatures with elements) satisfying a predicate and we can look for a counterexample for an assertion; both assertions and predicates are part of the Alloy model. Both types of analyses rely on the *small scope hypothesis* ([4]): only a finite subspace is searched based on the assumption that if there is an instance or a counterexample there is one of small size.

In the remainder of this section we present the Alloy models representing the syntax and semantics of the example language. To fully understand the models, the reader needs to be familiar with the Alloy language. We will, however, comment the models so that readers new to Alloy should still be able to understand the salient features of this approach.

4.2 Abstract Syntax and Static Semantics

The Alloy model given below expresses both abstract syntax and static semantics. We will explain it by comparing it to the metamodel of figure 1. Each of the eight classes in the metamodel has a corresponding signature with a similar name in the Alloy model. For instance, the *System* class is represented by the *EPSystem* signature. Associations in the metamodel are usually represented by fields of a signature: thus the field *models* in *EPSystem* corresponds to the aggregation from the *System* class to the *Model* class in the metamodel. Multiplicities on the association ends in the metamodel are normally expressed as constraints in the Alloy model. For instance, the fact that each *Model* is contained in a single *System* is expressed as the signature fact (i.e., a fact associated with each element of a signature) `{one s:EPSystem | this in s.models}` in signature *EPModel.* There are two signatures in the Alloy model that do not correspond to classes of the metamodel: the *Main* signature expresses the fact that there is a single distinguished model called *Main*: this is expressed in the metamodel by an association from *System* to *Model*. The signature *ParameterMapping* expresses the correspondence between parameters and expressions. This correspondence is expressed in the metamodel by each event having an ordered sequence of parameters and each push edge having an ordered sequence of expressions, with the assumption that these sequences are in one-to-one correspondence.

Note that we have chosen a single Alloy model to express both the abstract syntax and static semantics of the example language since both structural properties and well-formedness rules are expressed by constraints in the Alloy model and there is no natural separation between the two. We also note that the Alloy Analyzer allows the graphical presentation of the meta-model specified by an Alloy model such as the one below.

```
sig EPSystem {models: some EPModel} {one (models & Main)}
sig EPModel {properties: set Property, events: set Event}
  {one s:EPSystem | this in s.models}
sig Main extends EPModel { }

sig Property { type: EPModel } {one m:EPModel | this in m.properties}
pred Property::sameModel[p:Property] {this.~properties=p.~properties}

sig Event {feedsOn: set Property, params: set Parameter,
  edges: set PushEdge, impactEdges: set ImpactEdge}
fact { all e:Event | { e.feedsOn in (e.~events).properties
  all g:e.edges|{e.sameModel[g.link] && g.link.type=g.into.~events
  conformMapping[g.mappings, g.into.params]
  all m:g.mappings | { m.expr.usesProps in e.feedsOn &&
    m.expr.usesParams in e.params}
  all c: e.impactEdges | { e.sameModel[c.impact] &&
    c.expr.usesProps in e.feedsOn &&
    c.expr.usesParams in e.params }
      one m:EPModel | e in m.events }}}
pred Event::sameModel[p:Property] {this.~events = p.~properties}
pred Event::sameModel[e:Event] {this.~events = e.~events}

sig PushEdge {into:Event,link: Property,mappings:set ParameterMapping}
  { one e:Event | this in e.edges }
fun PushEdge::paramExpr[p:Parameter]: Expression {
  (p.(~param) & this.mappings).expr}
sig ImpactEdge {impact: Property,expr: Expression}
  {expr.type =impact.type && one e:Event | this in e.impactEdges}

sig Parameter{type: EPModel} { one e:Event | this in e.params }
sig ParameterMapping {param: Parameter,expr: Expression}
  { expr.type=param.type }
pred conformMapping(m:set ParameterMapping, x: set Parameter) {
    # m = # x && m.param = x }

sig Expression { type: EPModel, usesProps: set Property,
  usesParams: set Parameter }
```

4.3 Dynamic Semantics

To describe the dynamic semantics, we first introduce in the Alloy model below the notion of state (*State signature*) and instance (*EPInstance* signature): we note that an instance has a type (an *EPModel*) and assigns for each state to each property at most one value. The *neighbors* field of *EPInstance* comprises all instances referred to by a property of this instance in a given state. The value of a property is either null or another instance; this is expressed in the Alloy model by *Value* being an abstract signature (i.e., no element can have this type) and *EPInstance* and *NullValue* being the only concrete subsignatures (i.e., subsets) of *Value*. We abstract from the expression language using the *ExpressionValue* signature, which gives the value (*val* field) of an expression (*expr* field), given the values for the properties and parameters used by the expression (*settings* field).

The actual behavior of the system is specified in the *step* predicate. This predicate expresses the fact that state $s2$ results from state $s1$ by triggering *instance event* i. The instance event (signature *InstanceEvent*) contains the information which event is triggered on which instance and what the parameter values are for a given state. To compute the effect of the instance event, it suffices to consider all instance events (including this one) that are direct or indirect successors of this instance event via push edges. This is expressed by computing the reflexive and transitive closure of the successor relation *succ* of signature *InstanceEvent* for state $s1$. This closure is denoted by the *scope* variable in the *step* predicate (line 54). We then consider all instances having an associated instance event in the scope and restrict our attention to those instance events in the scope associated with each such instance: we denote this subset of the scope by the variable *iScope* (line 55). To express the new state $s2$, we evaluate for each property that is the target of an impact edge originating from an instance event in *iScope* the expression associated with this edge (using the *exprVal* function) and state that the value of this property in state $s2$ is equal to this value (lines 58-59). All properties not targeted by impact edges in *iScope* (lines 56-57) as well as properties of instances not in the scope (lines 60-61) have the same value in $s2$ and $s1$.

```
1   open  meta_small
2   open util/ordering[State] as SO -- ordered set of states
3   sig State { }
4   pred State::init { MainInstance::defaultVal[this] }
5   sig EPInstance extends Value {
6     type: EPModel,
7     neighbors: EPInstance -> State,
8     valuations: State -> Property -> Value }
9   { all s: State | {
10    this.reachable[s] => all p: type.properties|one this.val[p,s]
11    neighbors.s = {x: EPInstance | some p: type.properties |
12      s.valuations[p] = x } }}
13  fact {  all s: State| all y: EPInstance | all ev:Event |
14      ( y.reachable[s] && ev in y.type.events ) =>
15        some i: InstanceEvent | ( i.e =ev && i.x =y ) }
16  fun EPInstance::val [p:Property,s:State]:Value{p.(this.valuations[s])}
17  pred EPInstance::defaultVal[s: State] {
```

```
  all p: this.type.properties | this.val[p,s] = NullValue }
pred EPInstance::reachable[s: State]{
  this in MainInstance.*(neighbors.s) }
one sig MainInstance extends EPInstance { }{type = Main}

abstract sig Value{}
sig NullValue extends Value { }
sig ExpressionValue  {
  expr: Expression,
  setting: (Property + Parameter) -> lone Value,
  val: Value  }
{ setting.Value & Property = expr.usesProps
  setting.Value & Parameter = expr.usesParams }

sig InstanceEvent { e: Event, x: EPInstance,
  v: State-> Parameter -> lone Value,
  succ: InstanceEvent -> State }
{ let exprs = e.impactEdges.expr + e.edges.mappings.expr |
    all s: State | all ex:exprs | one exprVal[this,s,ex]
  e.~events = x.type
  all s: State | {s.v.Value = e.params &&
    {all j: succ.s|some g: e.edges| j.successorOf[this,s,g]} &&
    { all g: e.edges  | let v = x.val[g.link,s]|
      v != NullValue => some j: succ.s| j.successorOf[this,s,g]}}}
pred InstanceEvent::paramsOk[i:InstanceEvent, g: PushEdge, s:State] {
  all p:i.e.params | let ex = g.paramExpr[p] |
    p.(s.(i.v)) = exprVal[this, s, ex].val }
pred InstanceEvent::successorOf(i:InstanceEvent,s:State,g:PushEdge){
  g in i.e.edges && this.paramsOk[i,g,s] &&
     this.e = g.into && this.x = (i.x).val[g.link,s] }
fun InstanceEvent::exprVal[s: State,e: Expression]:ExpressionValue{
  { ev:ExpressionValue| ev.expr = e  &&
    (all p: e.usesParams  | ev.setting[p] = p.(s.(this.v))) &&
    (all p: e.usesProps  | ev.setting[p] = this.x.val[p,s]) }}

pred step[s1: State, i: InstanceEvent,  s2: State] {
  let scope = i.*(succ.s1) | {
    all y: scope.x | let iScope = (y.~x) & scope | {
      all p: y.type.properties| { p not in iScope.e.impactEdges.impact
        => y.val[p,s2] = y.val[p,s1]}
      all j: iScope | all g: j.e.impactEdges |
          y.val[g.impact,s2] = exprVal[j,s1,g.expr].val }
    all y: EPInstance-scope.x | all p: y.type.properties  |
      y.val[p,s2] = y.val[p,s1] }}
```

5 Discussion

We now compare traditional approaches presented in section 3 to the Alloy-based approach described in the last section. Comparing approaches implies selecting a set of criteria to base the comparison on. For this we need to first clarify the goal of the comparison. As mentioned already in the introduction many modeling languages are used without having a formal semantics. The main purpose of writing this paper is to remedy this state of affairs. Therefore it makes sense to look at those factors that have the greatest influence on the adoption of formal techniques for defining the semantics of a modeling language.

We focus on two properties that have an influence on the adoption of a formal notation (these have also been identified as key factors in the work of Mosses (eg.,[9])): (1) complexity of the notation and (2) analyzability of semantic specifications. Let us start with the notational complexity. For the abstract syntax and static semantics we saw two traditional approaches: EBNF and type checking on one side, and metamodeling on the other side. While both EBNF and metamodeling provide a succinct description of the abstract syntax, the static semantics description provided by the OCL constraints seems more accessible than the type checking approach: the more mathematical flavor of the latter notation and its higher density are probably an obstacle for a wide-spread adoption (see also [3]) in the modeling community, where this technique is less known. In our eyes both metamodeling and the Alloy approach have a similar notational complexity. In fact their close correspondence clearly comes out in the explanation of the Alloy approach in subsection 4.2 in terms of the metamodel.

For the dynamic semantics we presented only two options: operational semantics and the Alloy-based approach. We believe that that the difference between these two approaches is similar to the difference between type checking and Alloy for static semantics: the operational semantics has also a strong mathematical flavor with a very compact notation relying on many special symbols, while an Alloy model looks more like a module written in an object-oriented programming language. This should ease the adoption of Alloy in the modeling community.

If we now look at abstract syntax, static semantics and dynamic semantics as a whole, traditional approaches require at least two rather different notations, e.g., metamodeling and operational semantics, to specify the language while Alloy handles all three parts using a single notation. This is again points in favor of Alloy.

By analyzability, the second factor we want to consider, we mean the possibility to analyze the correctness of the specification using an automatic tool. Verifying the semantics of all but the most simple languages is a non-trivial task. If no tool support is provided for checking a formal description, our confidence in the correctness of the formal description is often not very strong. Immediate analyzability is also important if we want to support opportunistic design of semantics specifications, which seems to be the preferred way for humans to design complex objects (such as a formal semantics) [3].

For the traditional approaches some tool support is available: for instance we can check the metamodel with constraints using the USE tool [2]. Checking the operational semantics is usually done by proving manually or via proof assistants that some properties hold, or by implementing its rules in code and then testing or formally verifying the code. In addition to the drawback that both manual proof and code implementation can be error-prone, the diversity of the traditional approaches makes the effort of checking them automatically definitely higher than with Alloy since the latter one comes out of the box with a powerful tool, the Alloy analyzer.

Using this tool we can immediately check the correctness of the current (partial) specification (within the limits of the finite scope hypothesis). In our own experience this allowed us to find errors early in the writing of the formal semantics. Here are concrete examples of how the Analyzer helped us to write the formal specifications: first, the tool performed standard syntactic checks to reveal, for instance, incorrect use of signatures (e.g., accessing a field that does not exist in this signature); second, we checked the conformance of the static semantics in Alloy to the meta-model by formulating the OCL constraints as assertions in Alloy and looking for counterexamples using the Analyzer; third, we checked the dynamic semantics by "running" an example EP system (i.e., letting the Analyzer generate an instance satisfying the step predicate) and observing whether it "behaved" as expected.

6 Conclusion

Defining the formal semantics of a modeling language is important for reasoning about the language and for providing tool support (other arguments are given in [14]). Current approaches to formalizing semantics are often difficult to use in practice which may explain the introduction of many modeling languages that lack a formal semantics description.

In this paper we have presented a novel approach for the definition of the abstract syntax, the static semantics and the dynamic semantics of a modeling language based on the Alloy language. Two key advantages of the Alloy-based approach, which should be relevant for the applicability of the approach, are the low complexity of the notation (partly due to the fact that we need to deal with a single notation rather than several notation for the different aspects) and automatic analyzability.

Alloy was developed as a lightweight approach for developing software abstractions. It encourages incremental development of software models and reaps some of the benefits of traditional formal methods at a lower cost. Based on our experience documented in this paper we believe that the same features of Alloy also apply in the area of formal model semantics, thus opening the prospect of formal semantics becoming more accessible and more widely adopted in the definition of modeling languages.

The use of Alloy for specifying the formal semantics was illustrated in this paper on one concrete example. Future work should analyze for what type of modeling languages the Alloy based approach works well. Competing formal approaches such as those based on abstract state machines or conditional rewriting logic should also be compared with Alloy to examine the strength and weaknesses of each approach for different classes of modeling languages.

References

1. Broy, M., Crane, M., Dingel, J., Hartman, A., Rumpe, B., Selic, B.: 2nd UML 2 semantics symposium: Formal semantics for UML. In: Kühne, T. (ed.) MoDELS 2006. LNCS, vol. 4364, pp. 318–323. Springer, Heidelberg (2007)
2. Gogolla, M., Büttner, F., Richters, M.: USE: A UML-based specification environment for validating UML and OCL. Sci. Comput. Program 69(1-3), 27–34 (2007)
3. Green, T.R.G.: Cognitive dimensions of notations. In: Proceedings of 5th conference of the British Computer Society, Human-Computer Interaction Specialist Group on People and computers V, pp. 443–460 (1989)
4. Jackson, D.: Software Abstractions: Logic, Language, and Analysis. MIT Press, Cambridge (2006)
5. Jackson, D., Wing, J.: Lightweight formal methods. IEEE Computer 29(4), 16–30 (1996)
6. Kelsen, P.: A declarative executable model for object-based systems based on functional decomposition. In: Proceedings of the 1st International Conference on Software and Data Technologies, pp. 63–71 (2006)
7. Kelsen, P., Ma, Q.: A formal definition of the EP language. Technical Report TR-LASSY-08-03, Laboratory for Advanced Software Systems, University of Luxembourg (May 2008)
8. Kelsen, P., Pulvermueller, E., Glodt, C.: Specifying executable platform-independent models using OCL. In: ECEASST (2008)(9)
9. Mosses, P.D.: Theory and practice of action semantics. In: Proceedings of 21st Int. Symp. on Mathematical Foundations of Computer Science, pp. 37–61 (1996)
10. Mosses, P.D.: The varieties of programming language semantics. In: Proceedings of 4th International Andrei Ershov Memorial Conference on Perspectives of System Informatics, pp. 165–190 (2001)
11. OMG. Unified modeling language superstructure specification 2.0 (November 2005)
12. OMG. Object Constraint Language 2.0 (May 2006)
13. Winskel, G.: The formal semantics of programming languages: an introduction. MIT Press, Cambridge (1993)
14. Zhang, Y., Xu, B.: A survey of semantic description frameworks for programming languages. SIGPLAN Not. 39(3), 14–30 (2004)

Semantically Configurable Code Generation

Adam Prout, Joanne M. Atlee, Nancy A. Day, and Pourya Shaker

David R. Cheriton School of Computer Science
University of Waterloo, Waterloo Ontario, N2L 3G1, Canada
{aprout,jmatlee,nday,p2shaker}@uwaterloo.ca

Abstract. In model-driven engineering (MDE), software development is centred around a formal description (model) of the proposed software system, and other software artifacts are derived directly from the model. We are investigating *semantically configurable* MDE, in which specifiers are able to configure the semantics of their models. The goal of this work is to provide a modelling environment that offers flexible, configurable modelling notations, so that specifiers are better able to represent their ideas, and yet still provides the types of analysis tools and code generators normally associated with model-driven engineering. In this paper, we present a semantically configurable code-generator generator, which creates a Java-code generator for a modelling notation given the notation's semantics expressed as a set of parameter values. We are able to simulate multiple different model-based code generators, though at present the performance of our generated code is about an order of magnitude slower than that produced by commercial-grade generators.

1 Introduction

A critical aspect of model-driven engineering is keeping the modelling tools – that is, the editing environments, model analyzers, and code generators – in sync with the semantics of their respective modelling notation as the notation evolves (e.g., statecharts, UML) or as new domain-specific notations are created. Maintaining these correspondences is time-consuming. Small changes to the semantics of a notation often result in wide-spread changes to the supporting tools.

To address this problem, we are investigating the feasibility of *semantically configurable* modelling tools as a way of avoiding the problem of maintaining separate tools for separate modelling notations. Semantically configurable tools enable specifiers to create or customize their own modelling notations, and yet still have access to tools for editing, manipulating, and analyzing models in those notations. Note that our work is distinct from complementary efforts on configurable tools [9,11] that support configurability with respect to the abstract syntax of a family of notations [23], but not with respect to semantics.

In previous work, we introduced *template semantics* [21] as a way to configure semantics definitions. Template semantics structures the operational semantics of a family of modelling notations as a set of predefined templates that are instantiated with user-provided parameter values. Thus, a member of this family

K. Czarnecki et al. (Eds.): MoDELS 2008, LNCS 5301, pp. 705–720, 2008.

can be described succinctly as a set of template parameter values. The intended scope of template semantics is the family of notations whose semantics can be expressed operationally in terms of execution traces. This family includes process algebras, statecharts variants, Petri-Nets, SDL, and SCR. Because a notation's semantics can be expressed as a collection of parameters, it can be parsed, and we are starting to develop semantically parameterized tools [19].

In this paper, we present our first prototype of a semantically configurable code-generator generator (CGG) that creates Java code generators. The CGG takes a description of the notation's semantics, expressed as a set of template-semantics parameter values, and produces a code generator for that notation. Problems that we addressed in the course of this work include

- **Representing composition operators in Java:** The Java scheduler imposes an interleaving semantics on concurrent threads, whereas many model-based concurrency operators are tightly synchronized (e.g., rendezvous).
- **Resolving nondeterminism:** There are several natural sources of nondeterminism in models (e.g., selecting one of many enabled transitions to execute). While it may be appropriate to leave such nondeterminism unresolved during modelling, such nondeterminism in source code is unnatural. The transformation of a model into source code may involve decisions to eliminate nondeterminism.
- **Optimizing the generated code:** A key concern of this work is how efficient CGG-generated code can be, given that our configurable CGG that is general enough to support a family of modelling notations.

The rest of this paper is organized as follows. In Section 2, we review template semantics, which we use to configure the semantics of modelling notations. We describe our code-generator generator and the architecture of the generated code in Sections 3 and 4. In Section 5, we discuss techniques for resolving nondeterminism in the model when generating deterministic code. We evaluate our work in Section 6 by comparing the performance of our CGG-generated code to the performances of code generated by three notation-specific code generators: Rational Rose RT [15], Rhapsody [28], and SmartState [1]. We conclude the paper with discussions on related work, limitations, and future work.

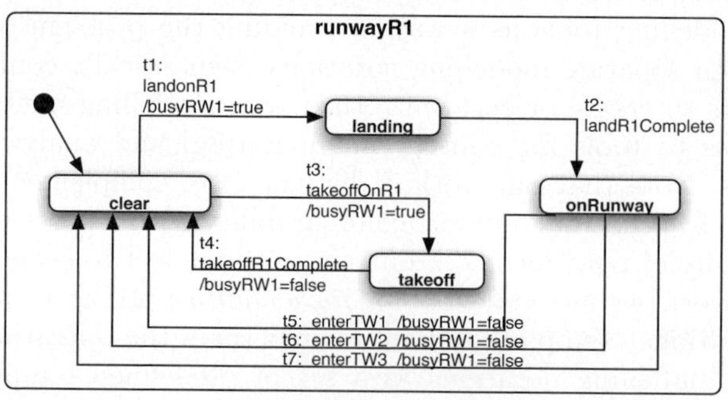

Fig. 1. Example HTS

2 Modelling Notation

In this section, we describe the syntax and configurable semantics of our modelling notation. We achieve configurability using template semantics [21].

2.1 Syntax

To accommodate a variety of modelling notations, we base the syntax of our notation on a form of extended finite-state machine that we call *hierarchical transition systems (HTS)*, which are adapted from statecharts [14]. An example HTS is shown in Figure 1. It includes control states and state hierarchy, state transitions, events, and typed variables, but not concurrency. Concurrency is achieved by composing multiple HTSs. Transitions have the following form:

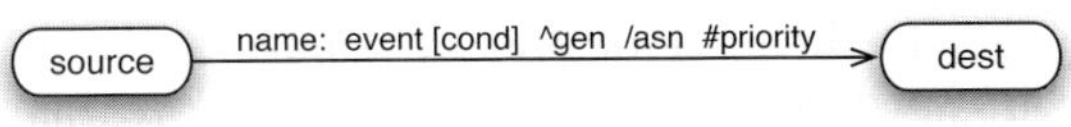

Each transition has a source state, is triggered by zero or more events, may have a guard condition (a predicate on variable values), and may have an explicit priority. If a transition executes, it leads to a destination state, may generate events, and may assign new values to variables. An HTS designates an initial state for each hierarchical state and initial variable values (not shown).

2.2 Semantic Domain

The semantics of an HTS is defined in terms of sequences of snapshots, where a *snapshot* records information about the model's execution at a discrete point in the execution. The basic snapshot elements are

CS - the set of current states
IE - the set of events to be processed
AV - the current variable-value assignments
O - the set of generated events (to be communicated to other HTSs)

In addition, the snapshot includes auxiliary elements that, for different notations, store different types of information about the HTS's execution:

CS_a - data about states, such as enabling or history states
IE_a - data about events, such as enabling or nonenabling events
I_a - data about inputs to the HTS
AV_a - data about variable values, such as old values

An execution starts with an initial snapshot of initial states and variable values. Consecutive snapshots ss_i and ss_{i+1} represent a "step" in the HTS's execution. The semantics of an HTS is the set of possible execution sequences.

2.3 Parameterized Semantics

Semantics are defined in terms of functions and relations over snapshot elements (the semantic domain). However, even though different modelling notations have

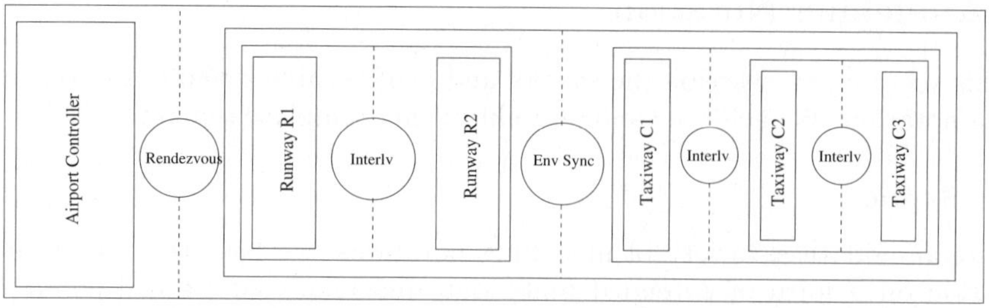

Fig. 2. Compositional Hierarchy for a Ground-Traffic Control System

many of the same language constructs and are defined over the same snapshot information, they vary in their use of that information.

In previous work, we developed a formalism called *template semantics* [21] in which semantics definitions are *parameterized*, resulting in a definition for a *family* of modelling notations. The parameters effectively represent semantic variation points. We provide two template definitions below, as examples:

$$\text{ENABLED\_TRANS}(ss, T) \equiv$$
$$\{\tau \in T | \, \mathbf{en\_states}(ss,\tau) \wedge \mathbf{en\_events}(ss,\tau) \wedge \mathbf{en\_cond}(ss,\tau)\}$$

$$\text{EXECUTE}(ss, \tau, ss') \equiv$$
$$\text{let } \langle CS', IE', AV', O', CS'_a, IE'_a, AV'_a, I'_a \rangle \equiv ss' \text{ in}$$
$$\mathbf{next\_CS}(ss,\tau,CS') \wedge \mathbf{next\_CS}_a(ss,\tau,CS'_a) \wedge \mathbf{next\_IE}(ss,\tau,IE') \wedge \mathbf{next\_IE}_a(ss,\tau,IE'_a) \wedge$$
$$\mathbf{next\_AV}(ss,\tau,AV') \wedge \mathbf{next\_AV}_a(ss,\tau,AV'_a) \wedge \mathbf{next\_O}(ss,\tau,O') \wedge \mathbf{next\_I}_a(ss,\tau,I'_a)$$

Definition ENABLED_TRANS returns the subset of transitions whose source states, triggering events, and guard conditions are all enabled in snapshot ss. Predicates **en_states, en_events,** and **en_cond** are template parameters for how the snapshot elements are used to determine the set of enabled transitions. Definition EXECUTE uses template parameters **next_X**, one for each snapshot element X, as placeholders for how the execution of a transition τ affects the individual snapshot elements.

Our template semantics has 22 parameters that represent variations on how a model's snapshot can change during execution: when inputs are sensed from the environment, how inputs update the snapshot, how the snapshot determines the set of enabled transitions, priority among transitions, how a transition's actions update the snapshot, and how conflicting assignments to variables are resolved. We do not claim to have identified a complete set of template parameters, but we do believe that the set of parameters is relatively stable.

2.4 Composition Operators

So far, we have discussed the execution of a single HTS. Composition operators specify how multiple HTSs execute concurrently and how they share information.

Our prototype supports variations of seven binary composition operators, whose operands are either HTSs or collections of previously composed HTSs.

- ***interleaving:*** At most one enabled operand executes in a step
- ***parallel:*** Both operands execute simultaneously if both are enabled. Otherwise, one or the other operand executes, if enabled.
- ***interrupt:*** Control passes between the operands via a set of interrupt transitions.
- ***sequence:*** One operand executes to completion, then the other operand executes.
- ***choice:*** One operand is chosen to execute, and only the chosen operand executes.
- ***environmental synchronization:*** The operator specifies a set of *sync events*. When a sync event occurs, descendant HTSs that have a transition enabled by the event execute simultaneously. Otherwise, the operands' executions are interleaved.
- ***rendezvous:*** The operator specifies a set of *rend events*. The operands execute simultaneously only if (1) one operand has an enabled transition that generates a rend event, and (2) the other operand has a transition that is enabled by that event. Otherwise, the operands' executions are interleaved.

Composition operators may be combined in the same model to affect different types of synchronization and communication among the model's components. We use the term *composition hierarchy* to refer to a model's composition structure, because the structure forms a binary tree (see the left side of Figure 3).

Figure 2 shows the composition hierarchy for a ground-traffic control system specified by Yavuc-Kahveci and Bultan [29]. The airport-controller component responds to airplanes' requests to take off, land, and taxi by telling them which runway or taxiway to use. The models for runways (Figure 1) and taxiways keep track of the current states of the real-world entities they represent. The runways are interleaved with each other, as are the taxiways. The environmental synchronization operator synchronizes the runways with the taxiways, so that both are aware when an airplane is at the intersection of a runway and a taxiway. The rendezvous operator synchronizes the controller and the runways to ensure that they have a shared understanding of the status of the runways.

3 CGG Architecture

We have developed a prototype code-generator generator (CGG) that is parameterized by our template parameters. The CGG produces notation-specific code generators that can transform models into representative Java programs.

The CGG source code is annotated with preprocessor directives that encapsulate the source code that is specific to each parameter value. The user provides a file that specifies the value of each template parameter. Thus, compiling the CGG source code, along with the semantics-parameter definition file, compiles only the parts of the CGG code that are associated with the specified parameter

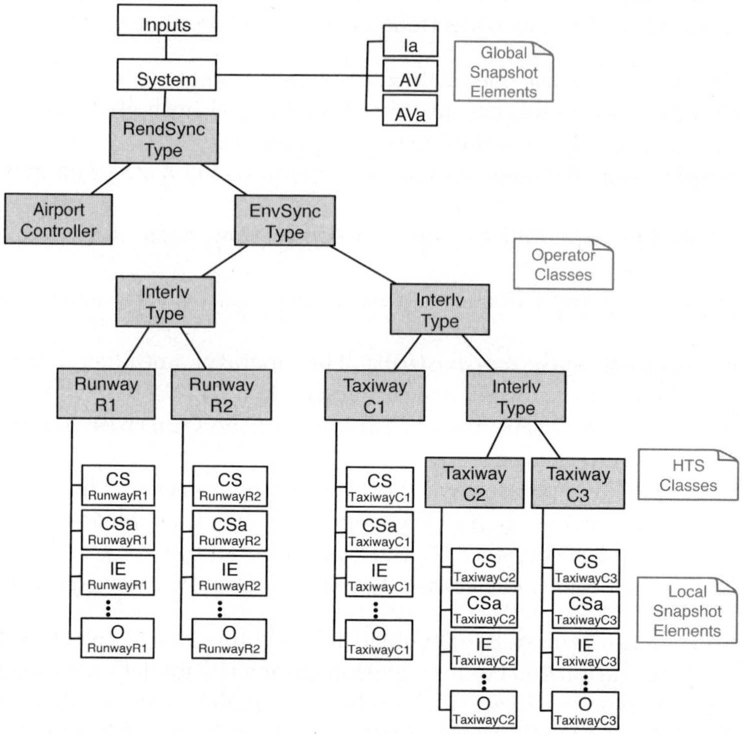

Fig. 3. Code structure for Ground Traffic Control System example. Shaded modules mimic the composition hierarchy of the model from Figure 2.

values, thereby producing a notation-specific code generator. We then execute the produced code generator on an input model, thereby generating a Java program whose executions match the model's execution traces.

Our prototype CGG supports 57 parameter values, roughly 2-5 values per parameter. We have not attempted to implement a complete set of parameter values, as this work is simply a proof of concept. In fact, we do not even claim to have identified a complete set of parameter values; we expect specifiers to devise new semantic variants as they try to model unusual problems. To that effect, we have structured the CGG program such that the preprocessor directives are highly localized, easing the task of adding support for new parameter values.

4 Generated Java Code

The generated code is a single-threaded program that controls the execution of its concurrent components via method calls. One might instead consider mapping HTSs to separate Java threads. The problem is that some composition operators require global knowledge to determine whether concurrent machines ought to execute simultaneously: for example, the environment synchronization operator needs to know about all components that have transitions enabled by some sync event. Collecting this information effectively synchronizes all of the program's threads, and the savings that would be gained from executing the HTS steps in parallel is not large enough to offset the cost of this synchronization.

The object model of the generated program for the Ground-Traffic Control System (from Figure 2) is shown in Figure 3. Each composition operator and HTS is implemented as a (shaded) Java object. Moreover, every HTS object has member variables that refer to local objects implementing local snapshot elements (CS, IE, IE_a, etc.). The snapshot elements I_a, AV, AV_a are shared, and every HTS object has references to these global objects.

The generated program simulates the "steps" of the model's possible behaviours. A step has two phases. The first phase is an enabledness check: Triggered by the sensing of input events from the environment (module Inputs in Figure 3), the System module requests information about all enabled transitions. This request is recursively passed down the composition hierarchy, with each operator class requesting information from its operands' modules. At the leaf nodes of the hierarchy, each of the HTS modules identifies its enabled transitions, store its results locally in member variables, and passes its results back to its parent node in the composition hierarchy. In turn, each operator class combines its operands' results and passes the information to its parent node, and so on until the System module receives all of the information.

In the second phase, execution decisions in the form of constraints flow from the System module down the composition hierarchy to the HTSs: (1) every operator receives execution constraints from its parent node, (2) possibly asserts additional constraints, and (3) recursively sends the cumulation of constraints to one or both of its operands. Constraints may be as specific as stipulating that a particular transition be executed or as general as requiring that some enabled transition execute. Constraints reach only the HTSs that are chosen to execute. Each chosen HTS executes a transition that satisfies its constraints and updates its snapshot.

The rest of this section describes the generated Java classes in more detail. The generated code preserves any nondeterminism in the model, which is useful for simulation and reasoning about all possible executions. In Section 5, we discuss how we produce deterministic code from nondeterministic models.

4.1 HTSs

A separate class is generated for each HTS in the input model. Figure 4 sketches the class generated for the C1Taxiway HTS from the Ground-Traffic Control System example. The Taxiway class contains a member variable for each of the HTS's snapshot elements, some of which are local objects and some of which are references to global snapshot objects. In addition, there are member variables to store information about enabled transitions.

Each HTS object is responsible for determining which of its HTS's transitions are enabled in the current snapshot and for executing the HTS's transitions. It has an IsEnabled() method that identifies the enabled transitions (shown on

```
VAR EventSnap &Ia = globalIa
VAR VarSnap &AV = globalAV
VAR VarSnap &AVa = global AVa
VAR StateSnap CS
...
VAR EventSnap O

VAR Set enabledTrans
VAR Map syncTrans, rendTrans
VAR Transition exec
```

```
1: IsEnabled(set syncEv, rendEv; bool enabled)
2: enabled = false
3: for each transition τ in HTS do
4:   if EN_STATE(τ) ∧ EN_COND(τ) ∧ EN_EVENTS(τ) then
5:     enabled = true
6:     if τ is triggered by a rendezvous event e then
7:       rendEv.add(e)
8:       rendTrans.insert(e,τ)
9:     else if τ is triggered by a sync event e then
10:      syncEv.add(e)
11:      syncTrans.insert(e,τ)
12:    else
13:      enabledTrans.add(τ)
14:    end if
15:  end if
16: end for
```

```
1: Execute(event syncEv, rendEv)
2: if rendEv is not null then
3:   exec = rendTrans.lookup(rendEv)
4: else if syncEv is not null then
5:   exec = syncTrans.lookup(syncEv)
6: else
7:   exec = top priority τ ∈ enabledTrans
8: end if
9: {update snapshot elements}
10: Ia.NEXT(exec)
11: AV.NEXT(exec)
12: AVa.NEXT(exec)
13: CS.NEXT(exec)
14: CSa.NEXT(exec)
15: IE.NEXT(exec)
16: IEa.NEXT(exec)
17: O.NEXT(exec)
```

Fig. 4. Pseudocode for Taxiway HTS. Configurable code is highlighted in SMALL CAPS.

the left in Figure 4). Much of this task is done by methods that implement the semantic parameters **en_state**, **en_event**, and **en_cond** (lines 4-5). These methods compare a transition's source state, triggering event, and guard against the contents of the snapshot objects and determine whether the transition is currently enabled. IsEnabled() also computes and stores any enabledness information that is needed by any of the composition operators in the model: in the case of Taxiway C1, if a rendezvous transition is enabled then it is stored in member variable rendTrans (lines 6-8), and if an enabled transition is triggered by a synchronization event then it is stored in syncTrans (lines 9-11). Ordinary enabled transitions are stored in member variable enabledTrans (lines 12-13). Abstract information about enabled transitions, sync events that enable transitions, and so on are passed back to the HTS's parent node via assignments to the IsEnabled() method's parameters (lines 1, 5, 7, 10).

Each HTS also has an Execute() method (shown on the right in Figure 4) that is called when the HTS is instructed to execute as part of a step. In this method, one of the enabled transitions identified by IsEnabled() is chosen for execution. Invocation may include execution constraints as parameters (line 1), in which case the transition chosen for execution must satisfy the constraints (lines 2-5). If there are no execution constraints, then the top-priority transition in enabledTrans is selected to execute (lines 6-7). In the end, the chosen transition is "executed" via inline procedures that implement the **next_X** template parameters, which in turn update all of the snapshot elements (lines 10-17).

4.2 Composition Operators

The implementations of composition operators are model independent. A class is generated for each operator type used in the model, and an object is instantiated

```
VAR bool LEnabled, REnabled
VAR operand compToExecute

1: IsEnabled(bool enabled)
2: left.IsEnabled(LEnabled)
3: right.IsEnabled(REnabled)
4: enabled = LEnabled ∨ REnabled
```

```
1: Execute()
2: if LEnabled ∧ REnabled then
3:     compToExecute = choose left or right child
4:     compToExecute.execute()
5: else if LEnabled then
6:     left.Execute()
7: else if REnabled then
8:     right.Execute()
9: end if
```

Fig. 5. Pseudocode for interleaving composition.

for each operator instance in the model. Thus, the code for our Ground-Traffic Control example includes three operator classes: rendezvous, environmental synchronization, and interleaving. The interleaving class is instantiated three times.

Each operator class has an IsEnabled() method that determines which of the operator's operands are enabled. The method for an interleaving operator is shown on the left in Figure 5. The method calls its operands' IsEnabled() methods and stores the results in member variables (L/R)Enabled (lines 2-3). The method then computes the operator's enabledness, which is *true* if either of the operands is enabled (line 4), and returns the result via its parameter (line 1). The IsEnabled() methods of other operator types have a similar implementation, differing primarily in how they determine their own enabledness (line 4) and what information they return via their parameters (line 1). For example, the IsEnabled() method of an environmental synchronization operator returns not only a flag indicating whether the operands are enabled but also the set of sync events that enable its operands' transitions.

Each operator class also has an Execute() method that conveys execution constraints to the operator and its operands. The method for an interleaving operator is shown on the right in Figure 5. If both operands are enabled, then one of the components is nondeterministically chosen to execute (lines 2-4). Otherwise, the solely enabled operand is instructed to execute (lines 5-8). One of these three cases is guaranteed to hold, because an operator's Execute() method is invoked only if the operator is enabled.

Synchronization operators have more complicated Execute() methods than described above because of the potential for execution constraints. For example, environmental synchronization's Execute() method may have an input parameter that asserts that only transitions triggered by a particular sync event can execute in the current step. If no constraint is imposed by an operator higher in the composition hierarchy, then the environmental synchronization operator might assert its own execution constraint – that only transitions triggered by one of the operator's sync events can execute in the current step. Otherwise, the operator instructs one of its enabled operands to execute without imposing additional constraints. In all cases, the operator propagates constraints via recursive calls to the operands' Execute() methods, but uses information gathered by IsEnabled() to invoke only operands whose enabled transitions satisfy the constraints.

Other Composition Operators. Our CGG also supports rendezvous, interrupt, sequence, and choice composition operators. The Java classes generated for these operators resemble that generated for the environmental synchronization operator, in that they introduce operator-specific member variables to keep track of operator-specific enabledness information, and their Execute() methods enforce execution constraints imposed by operators that are higher in the model's composition hierarchy. Note that in a model that uses multiple types of composition operators, it is not enough for each operator to keep track of just the enabledness information relevant to its own operation. Operator classes must have member variables for *all* types of enabledness information needed by *any* operator in the composition hierarchy, and all of their IsEnabled() methods must include parameters for these data. The details of how all supported composition operators are implemented can be found in [25].

4.3 Optimizations

The CGG employs a number of simple optimizations to improve the performance of the generated Java code. Some optimizations are based on the modelling notation's semantics. For example, the Java classes for unused snapshot elements are not generated. As another example, the search for enabled transitions is done in order of the transitions' priority (based on the model's composition hierarchy, the HTS's state hierarchy, and the value of the template parameters). Thus, when an enabled transition is found, no transition of lower priority is checked.

Most optimizations are model independent. For example, some computations can be statically computed or optimized, such as the determination of which HTS states are entered and exited when a transition executes. As another example, if a composition operator is associative, then consecutive applications of that operator can be compressed to a single operator with multiple operands. A flatter composition hierarchy results in a more efficient execution step because there are fewer recursive calls and less caching of enabledness information.

5 Resolving Nondeterminism

The code described in previous section simulates a model's nondeterminism. Such a semantics-preserving transformation is useful during modelling and analysis, but is not appropriate for a deployable implementation. Our CGG can either generate a nondeterministic program that completely simulates the input model or generate a deterministic program that satisfies the model's specification.

Our general strategy for resolving nondeterminism is to introduce default priorities. Because the specifier has implicitly indicated that all choices are equally valid, any default priority that we choose should be acceptable. In cases where a default priority would introduce an asymmetry that could lead to unfair executions, we rotate priority among the enabled entities:

- ***HTSs:*** simultaneously enabled transitions within an HTS, if they are not prioritized by explicit priorities on the transition labels or by the template parameter values, are "prioritized" according to the order in which they are declared.

– ***interleaving:*** the interleaving of two simultaneously enabled components is "prioritized" by alternating which component is executed when both are enabled.
– ***synchronized operations:*** simultaneously enabled synchronized transitions (enabled by simultaneous sync or rend events), if not prioritized by an explicit ordering on the events, are "prioritized" by the order in which the events are declared.
– ***synchronized operations:*** if synchronized and non-sychronized transitions are simultaneously enabled, the synchronized transitions are given higher priority, so that components do not miss the opportunity to react a synchronization event.
– ***rendezvous operations:*** if components can synchronize either by sending or receiving a rend event, the role (sender or receiver) that a component plays alternates.

6 Evaluation

We report on utility, correctness, efficiency, and limitations of our work.

6.1 Utility

Students taking a graduate course on computer-aided verification used our configurable modelling notation to specify the behaviour of elevators, an office lighting system, and a hotel-room safe. They used Express [19], a semantically configurable translator to SMV [20] that we have developed, to transform their models into representative SMV models, and then they verified their models using the SMV model checker. The students were free to choose their own modelling semantics, and only one student used a semantics that conforms to the classic semantics of some existing notation. Many specifications had a statecharts-like semantics, but used rendezvous for a critical synchronization. Other specifications had a CCS-like semantics, but used global shared variables. These observations suggest that (student) modellers are comfortable manipulating the semantics of a modelling notation as a strategy to producing a correct model.

6.2 Correctness

To assess correctness, we designed a test suite of models that exercise different parts of the CGG. The test suite covers each implemented template-semantics parameter and each composition operator at least once, and covers all pairs of composition operators. For each test case, we manually inspected the sequence of snapshots produced by the generated program's execution and checked it against the sequence of snapshots comprising the model's "execution" of the same test.

In order to test more complex composition hierarchies involving some of the more sophisticated operators, we also evaluated CGG on the ground-traffic control system that was introduced in Section 2. This example also used some nonstandard template-parameter values (e.g., an enabling event persisted until it triggered some transition). We generated the code for this model and tested it on input sequences that exercise a number of safety properties (e.g., an airplane can taxi across a runway only if the runway is not in use). We inspected the code's execution traces and verified that they conform to the model's traces.

6.3 Efficiency

To determine the cost of semantically configurable code generation, we compared our generated code to that of three commercial tools, each of which generates code for a single modelling notation. For each tool, we expressed its notation in template semantics and produced our own code generator for that notation. We then used the code generators to generate Java programs for four models: *PingPong* is an example model provided in the distribution of Rose RT. It consists of two concurrent machines that execute a simple request-reply protocol. The other models are small but typical software controllers for embedded systems: (1) An *Elevator* for a three floor building, whose components model the controller, service-request buttons, the engine, and the door and door timer. (2) A *Heater*, whose components model the controller, the furnace, and sensors in the room. (3) A hotel-room *Safebox*, whose components model a keypad for entering security codes, a display, and the status of the lock. Each of the embedded-system models is composed with an appropriate environment component that feeds input events to the system model. By forming a closed-world model of the system and its simulated environment, we are able to evaluate the performance of the generated code without having to interact with the program while it executes.

The first two studies, shown in Table 1, compare our generated code against that from two UML-based code generators: IBM's Rational Rose Realtime (Rose RT) [15] and Telelogic's Rhapsody (RH) [28]. The two tools support similar UML semantics: communication between machines is via message passing, all generated messages are sent to a single global queue[1], and only the event at the head of this queue can trigger transitions. One difference is that in Rose RT a message event triggers only one (compound) transition, whereas in RH an event can initiate a sequence of transitions.

Using CGG, we generated code generators that simulate the semantics of the Rose RT and RH code generators. We ran the code generators on all four models, and then measured the execution times of the generated programs. The results are reported in Table 1 are the average execution times over 10 runs, with each run consisting of 100000 iterations between the system and environment components in *Heater*, *Elevator*, and *Safebox*, and 500000 iterations between the Ping and Pong components in *PingPong*. All runs were performed on a 3.00Ghz Intel Pentium 4 CPU with 1GB of RAM, running Windows XP Professional Version 2002. On average, deterministic CGG generated programs (CGG-Det) took 8.8 times longer to run than Rose RT generated programs, and 1.9 times longer to run than RH generated programs. The deterministic CGG version of *PingPong*

[1] Both Rose RT and RH allow multiple event queues and allow the specifier to indicate which machines share which event queues.

Table 1. UML Comparisons (seconds)

Model	Rose RT	RH	CGG-Det
PingPong	0.5	1.3	1.2
Elevator	3.5	18.8	53.3
Heater	0.4	2.3	5.3
Safebox	1.1	3.2	4.5

Table 2. Statecharts Comparisons (seconds)

Model	SS	CGG-Det
PingPongSS	1.3	1.6
ElevatorSS	16.6	14.3
HeaterSS	3.9	2.6
SafeboxSS	6.8	6.2

performed slightly better than the RH version. Similar comparisons with nondeterministic CGG generated programs similar results. This is not surprising given that all of the models in our evaluation suite are deterministic.

We also generated a statecharts-based code generator and compared it to SmartState (SS) [1]. SS uses parallel composition and broadcasting of events. In addition, SS assumes open-world models, so we removed the environmental component from each input model and provided an application wrapper that generates environmental events for the model. The performance results are summarized in Table 2. On average, SS generated programs ran 1.2 times longer than deterministic CGG generated programs (CGG-Det). The SS generated *PingPong* program slightly outperformed the deterministic CGG generated program.

Overall, the cost of semantically configurable code generation appears to vary with the semantics chosen and the number of concurrent components. Our statecharts-based code generator performs slightly better than SS on the larger models, but not as well on the toy model *PingPong*. Our UML-based code generators are competitive with RH for models with fewer components (*PingPong*, *Heater*, *Safebox*), but less so on the larger model, *Elevator*. Rose RT significantly outperforms RH and CGG-Det on all models. We believe that with an investment in further optimizions to CGG generated code, this performance gap can be reduced. For example, when the input model does not use any of the synchronization operators, each HTS could run on its own thread and the coordination of enabledness checks and execution directives could be loosened.

7 Related Work

Most model-driven-engineering environments are centred on a single modelling notation that has a single semantics[6,28,15,27]. Configurability in such systems is geared more towards flexibility in the target language or platform [7,10] than in the modelling notation. There are a few exceptions. For example, Rational RoseRT and Rhapsody have options to choose whether event queues are associated with individual objects, groups of objects, or the whole model. Such options allow the specifier some control over the modelling notation, but are not nearly as rich as our template-semantics parameters.

Our work can be viewed as an instance of generative programming, where template semantics is a domain-specific language for describing "features" of modelling notations, and CGG is a generator for a family of model-driven code generators. What distinguishes our work from typical generative programming is that the "features" are not functional requirements or components, but instead are semantic parameters of a general-purpose behavioural modelling notation. Admittedly, preprocessor directives are a rather primitive form of generative programming, and other generative technologies could be explored [3,4,5]. However, preprocessor technology is sufficiently powerful for our needs and is stable.

Our work is also loosely related to that of compiler generators, in which a compiler is constructed directly from a language's semantics [16]. Researchers have investigated how to generate compilers from denotational semantics [2,24], operational semantics and rewrite rules [12,13], natural semantics [8], and language algebras [17]. A key disadvantage of these approaches is that one has to write a complete semantics for the notation to be compiled (a feat sometimes worthy of a research publication). In contrast, in our approach, specifying the semantics of a modelling notation is reduced to providing a collection of relatively small semantics-parameter values. The trade-off is that our CGG creates code generators only for template-semantics expressible notations – although the CGG is structured to facilitate the adding of new template-parameter values.

Meta-modeling [23] notations are more expressive than template semantics in describing modelling notations. However, their focus is on the abstract syntax of a modelling notation and not on its semantics. Model transformation technologies, such as QVT [22] and graph grammars [18], facilitate the transformation of models whose meta-models are well-defined. However, it is not clear that these technologies will help meta-model designers to create code generators for their modelling notations. Instead, the state of the art in code generation seems to be to support configurable language features [11,9], and to embed the semantics of those features in the implementation of the code generator.

8 Conclusion

In this work, we explore template semantics as a parse-able semantics description that enables semantically configurable code generation. Configurability is in the form of semantics parameters, such that the specifier is spared from having to provide a complete semantics definition. We view semantically configurable MDE as an appropriate compromise between a general-purpose, single-semantics notation that has significant tool support and a domain-specific language that has a small user base and few tools. Another potential use is to provide tool support for UML, which has a number of semantic variation points that match template semantics' variation points [26]. Our technology does not yet compete with commercial-grade code generators, but its future looks promising enough to continue investigating.

References

1. ApeSoft. Smartstate v4.1.0 (2008), http://www.smartstatestudio.com
2. Appel, A.W.: Semantics-directed code generation. In: Proc. ACM Sym. on Prin. Prog. Lang (POPL 1985), pp. 315–324. ACM Press, New York (1985)
3. Batory, D., O'Malley, S.: The design and implementation of hierarchical software systems with reusable components. ACM Trans. Soft. Eng. Meth. 1(4), 355–398 (1992)
4. Cleaveland, C.: Program Generators with XML and Java. Prentice-Hall, Englewood Cliffs (2001)
5. Czarnecki, K., Eisenecker, U.W.: Generative programming: methods, tools, and applications. ACM Press/Addison-Wesley Publishing Co., New York (2000)
6. Harel, D., et al.: STATEMATE: A working environment for the development of complex reactive systems. IEEE Trans. on Soft. Eng. 16(4), 403–414 (1990)
7. D'Ambrogio, A.: A model transformation framework for the automated building of performance models from uml models. In: Proc. Intl. Work. on Soft. and Perf (WOSP 2005), pp. 75–86. ACM Press, New York (2005)
8. Diehl, S.: Natural semantics-directed generation of compilers and abstract machines. Form. Asps. of Comp. 12(2), 71–99 (2000)
9. G.S.S., et al.: Clearwater: extensible, flexible, modular code generation. In: Proc. IEEE/ACM Intl. Conf. on Aut. Soft. Eng(ASE 2005), pp. 144–153. ACM Press, New York (2005)
10. Floch, J.: Supporting evolution and maintenance by using a flexible automatic code generator. In: Proc. Intl. Conf. on Soft. Eng (ICSE 1995), pp. 211–219. ACM Press, New York (1995)
11. Grundy, J., et al.: Generating Domain-Specific Visual Language Editors from High-level Tool Specifications. In: Auto. Soft. Eng. (ASE), pp. 25–36 (2006)
12. Hannan, J.: Operational semantics-directed compilers and machine architectures. ACM Trans. Prog. Lang. Sys. 16(4), 1215–1247 (1994)
13. Hannan, J., Miller, D.: From operational semantics to abstract machines. Math. Struct. Comp. Sci. 2(4), 415–459 (1992)
14. Harel, D.: On the formal semantics of statecharts. Symp. on Logic in Comp. Sci., 54–64 (1987)
15. IBM Rational. Rational Rose RealTime v7.0.0 (2005), http://www.ibm.com/rational
16. Jones, N.: Semantics-Directed Compiler Generation. LNCS, vol. 94. Springer, Heidelberg (1980)
17. Knaack, J.L.: An algebraic approach to language translation. PhD thesis, University of Iowa (1995)
18. Königs, A., Schürr, A.: Tool integration with triple graph grammars – a survey. Elect. Notes in Theor. Comp. Sci. 148(1), 113–150 (2006)
19. Lu, Y., Atlee, J.M., Day, N.A., Niu, J.: Mapping template semantics to SMV. In: Proc. of Auto. Soft. Eng. (ASE 2004), pp. 320–325 (2004)
20. McMillan, K.: Symbolic Model Checking: An Approach to the State Explosion Problem. Kluwer Academic Publishers, Dordrecht (1993)

21. Niu, J., Atlee, J.M., Day, N.A.: Template Semantics for Model-Based Notations. IEEE Trans. on Soft. Eng. 29(10), 866–882 (2003)
22. Object Management Group. Revised submission for MOF 2.0 Query/View/Transformation RFP, `http://www.omg.org/docs/ad/05-03-02.pdf`
23. Object Management Group. Meta Object Facility Core Specification, Formal/06-01-01 (2006)
24. Paulson, L.: A semantics-directed compiler generator. In: Proc. ACM Sym. on Prin. of Prog. Lang (POPL 1982), pp. 224–233. ACM Press, New York (1982)
25. Prout, A.: Parameterized Code Generation From Template Semantics. Master's thesis, School of Computer Science, University of Waterloo (2005)
26. Taleghani, A., Atlee, J.M.: Semantic variations among UML statemachines. In: ACM/IEEE Int. Conf. on Mod. Driven Eng. Lang. and Sys., pp. 245–259 (2006)
27. Telelogic. Telelogic TAU SDL Suite, `http://www.telelogic.com/corp/products/tau/sdl/index.cfm`
28. Telelogic. Rhapsody in J v7.1.1.0 (2007), `http://modeling.telelogic.com/products/rhapsody/index.cfm`
29. Yavuz-Kahveci, T., Bultan, T.: Specification, verification, and synthesis of concurrency control components. In: Proc. Intl. Symp. on Soft. Test. and Anal (ISSTA 2002), pp. 169–179. ACM Press, New York (2002)

Safety Hazard Identification by Misuse Cases: Experimental Comparison of Text and Diagrams

Tor Stålhane and Guttorm Sindre

Dept of Computer and Information Science, Norwegian Univ of Science and Technology (NTNU), NO-7491 Trondheim, Norway
{stalhane,sindre}@idi.ntnu.no

Abstract. In general, diagrams and text are both considered to have their advantages and disadvantages for the representation of use case models, but this is rarely investigated experimentally. This paper describes a controlled experiment where we compare safety hazard identification by means of misuse cases based on use case diagrams and textual use cases. The experiment participants found use case diagrams and textual use cases equally easy to use. In most cases those who used textual use cases were able to identify more failure modes or threats. The main reason for this seems to be that use cases encourage analysts to specifically focus on threats related to the functions mentioned in the use case, and textual use cases include more functional details than diagrams. The focus is decided by information in each use case which will thus decide the number of threats identified.

Keywords: Use cases, misuse cases, safety hazards, experiment.

1 Introduction

There is an increased use of IT both in infrastructure and in work support tools in almost every part of society. This also means that there are increasing safety hazards from failures related to the systems and to the humans that are using them. Accidents related to IT systems tend to stem more from requirements defects than from coding errors [1]. Mainstream software developers often lack safety expertise and may be unable to apply formal, heavyweight methods [2], and such methods will be even more difficult to apply in collaboration with users and other stakeholders lacking technical expertise. The involvement of these stakeholders is crucial in safety analysis, as social and technical aspects need to be considered together [3]. Better integration of formal and informal methods is one way ahead for the engineering of safe software systems [4], and similarly better integration between safety engineering and mainstream software engineering can ensure the joint participation of a wider group of stakeholders.

One technique which has been proposed to accommodate safety concerns into mainstream software engineering, is misuse cases [5]. The technique was originally proposed to capture security threats, but has also been investigated with respect to safety-related problems, for instance in [6, 7, 8]. In [9] a comparison was made between misuse cases and an adapted version of Failure Mode and Effect Analysis

K. Czarnecki et al. (Eds.): MoDELS 2008, LNCS 5301, pp. 721–735, 2008.

(FMEA) [10], starting with use case diagrams as the input. A controlled experiment was set up where participants worked on the same task, one group using misuse case diagrams, the other group using an adapted version of FMEA where failure modes would be identified per use case. The subjects that used misuse case diagrams found significantly more safety hazards than those who used FMEA. This was especially the case for hazards resulting from human error, while the results were roughly equal for technical errors. For some types of technical errors, like network outages, FMEA outperformed misuse cases.

The misuse case group in the experiment in [9] used only misuse case diagrams. It is therefore interesting to also investigate the number of hazards identified when using textual misuse cases. Hence, a new experiment was set up to perform a controlled comparison of textual misuse cases and misuse case diagrams.

The rest of the paper is structured as follows: Section 2 reviews related work. Section 3 presents the two techniques compared in the experiment. Section 4 presents the experimental design, and section 5 presents the results from the experiment. Section 6 discusses threats to validity, whereupon section 7 concludes the paper and indicates some directions for future work.

2 Related Work

To our knowledge, there are no previous experiments comparing textual / tabular (mis)use cases and (mis)use case diagrams, neither with the purpose of finding threats to a system nor more generally. Indeed, there are few controlled experiments about use cases to be found in the literature at all; for instance [11, 12, 13] which are concerned with guidelines for writing good use cases, [14] looking at the transition from use cases to class diagrams, and [15, 16, 17] investigating inspection of use cases. Looking at conceptual modeling more generally, there are experiments comparing the effectiveness of representation languages, for instance ER or EER diagrams with relational tuples, one well known example being [18]. However, one important point to note here is that the two forms of representation then compared contained the same information but were on different life-cycle levels, ER being an analysis stage language, while relational tuples belong to the design stage. The relationship between use case diagrams and textual use cases is different: both are requirements stage representations but the textual descriptions contain more information than the diagrams.

An experiment more directly targeting the comparison of diagrams versus tables and textual representations is [19], confirming claims about advantages of diagrams previously made analytically in [20]. Experiments have also found diagrams superior for presenting procedural instructions [21], which is closely related to conceptual modeling. More generally, the empirical evidence is not so consistently in favor of diagrams. As reported in [22], some experimental studies have shown advantages for diagrams, but others have shown advantages for tables, or given mixed results. One particular study also showed the outcome to be dependant on the subject group, business students solving problems more effectively with tables while engineering students solved problems more effectively with graphs [23].

3 Use Case Diagrams and Textual Use Cases

3.1 Misuse Case Diagrams

Misuse cases [5] were originally proposed for eliciting security requirements, but they have also been used for safety analysis, misuse cases then being accidents causing harm to the system [6]. The diagram of Fig. 1 shows the human operator functions related to an automated system used to keep the water level in a tank constant while delivering steam to an industrial process. This is done by filling the tank through one valve and emptying it through another valve when needed. If the pressure in the tank becomes too high, a relief valve should open automatically as the pressure exceeds the critical pressure pre-set by the operator. The operator may also manually empty the tank, for instance if the relief valve fails to work when the pressure becomes too high, or manually fill the tank if the automatic adjustment of water level does not work. A misuse case such as "Set too high pressure" may have a "threatens" relationship to one or more use cases – in this case "Set critical pressure". It is also possible that one misuse case may "aggravate" the effect of another, or that a use case may have a "mitigates" relationship to that misuse case. Such relationships are not exemplified in Figure 1.

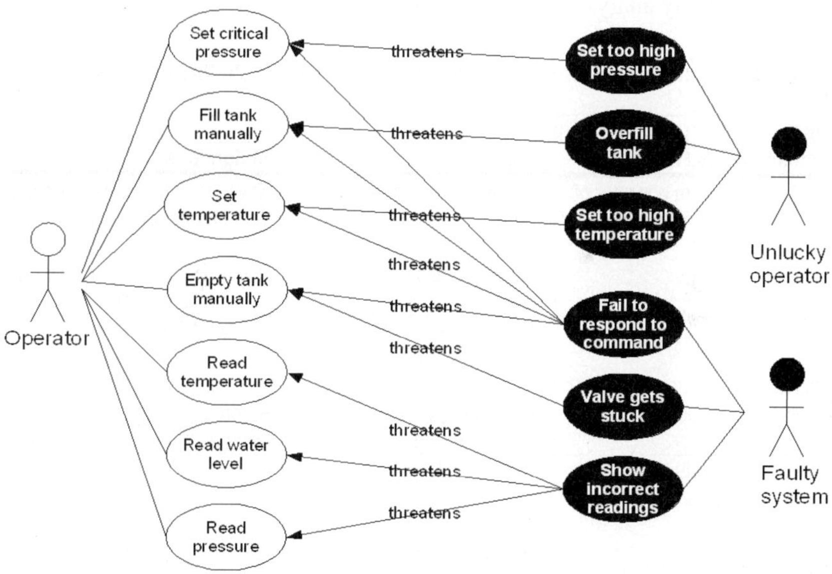

Fig. 1. Example safety-oriented misuse case diagram for a boiler tank system

An essential idea of misuse case analysis is that the representation format causes only a limited overhead if use cases are already applied in a project, which is often the case in mainstream software projects. Moreover, the informality and simplicity of the technique makes it suitable for supporting brainstorming about threats at an early stage of development. For a more complete coverage of misuse case analysis, the reader is referred to [5] and [7].

3.2 Textual Misuse Cases

Use cases [24] were originally most focussed on text, and the textual representation of a use case gives more detailed information than its diagrammatic counterpart [25]. The textual representation may make it possible to investigate threats in more detail, i.e., on the level of single use case steps instead of just looking at the entire use cases. On the other hand, since the textual use case splits up the functional requirements into a set of disjoint descriptions, it removes the possibility of seeing all functions together to get the complete picture. In addition, we remove the possibility of adding a threat to a use case by just adding a line from a previously identified threat.

There are several ways of writing textual use cases. A most basic distinction in format is between the original single-column style and the two-column style first proposed by [26], where the left column shows the user actions and the right column the system response. Similarly, textual misuse cases could also be written single-column or with 3 or 4 columns – adding a column for threats and possibly also one for mitigation options to those threats [5]. One example is shown in Table 1. Again, this example is not meant to be complete, as there may be several other threats involved even in this simple use case as well as several possible mitigations in addition to the ones suggested here. The main point is to illustrate the usage of the technique, not to present a complete safety analysis of the example system.

Table 1. A textual misuse case for the boiler example, including mitigations

U C name	Respond to over-pressure		
User actions	**Sys Response**	**Threats**	**Mitigations**
	Alarm operator of high pressure	System fails to alarm; Operator fails to notice alarm	Have two independent alarms; Test alarms regularly; Use both audio and visual cues; Alarm also outside control room
Operator gives command to empty tank		Operator fails to react (e.g., ill, unconscious) Operator gives wrong command, e.g., filling tank	Alarm backup operator Automatic sanity check, disallow filling at high pressure
	System opens valve to sewer	System fails to relay command to valve; Valve is stuck	
Operator reads pressure		Operator misreads and stops emptying too soon	Maintain alarm until situation is normal

4 Experimental Design

4.1 Research Approach

The two primary research questions for the experiment comparing textual misuse cases and misuse case diagrams were:

- RQ1 – will one technique identify more safety hazards than the other technique? If the answer is yes – is this technique uniformly better, i.e., outperforming the other one for all types of safety hazards? This will be investigated looking at the participants' answers to the modeling task provided in the experiment.
- RQ2 – is one of the techniques perceived as being better than the other one by the experiment participants? This question will be investigated by a post-task questionnaire eliciting participant opinion about the technique just tried.

RQ1 concerns the *performance* of the participants – do they perform better with one technique, or are the techniques equally effective? RQ2 concerns the *perception* of the participants – do they have a more positive opinion about one technique than the other? The null hypotheses for the experiment were as follows:

- $H1_0$: There will be no significant difference in the number of safety hazards identified by the two techniques.
- $H2_0$: There will be no significant difference in the participant opinion about the two techniques.

It seems reasonable to use hypotheses of no difference as a starting point here, rather than hypotheses going in one particular direction, as it could be quite uncertain what to expect. Some arguments point in favor of textual (mis)use cases:

- Textual use cases give more details than use case diagrams, e.g., including action paths within the use cases where the diagrams just give the use case name. There may be safety hazards related to almost every step in a use case, hence the textual variety might trigger ideas about hazards that would ignored with just a diagram as input.
- Just writing text may be quicker than drawing diagrams, as there is less need to worry about layout.

On the other hand, there are also arguments in favor of misuse case diagrams:

- In some cases, diagrams are more expressive than text [27]. Especially, when one threat is relevant in several places, the diagram makes it possible to draw it just as one node – e.g., "Select wrong patient" in a healthcare information system, and then draw a "threatens" arrow to each use case where this threat might be relevant (e.g., "Review treatment plan", "Review drug dosage", "Schedule patient for surgery", "Order test"). With textual use cases, on the other hand, the threat of selecting the wrong patient would have to be repeated in all the relevant tables.
- It could also be imagined that the increased detail of textual tables could be a disadvantage, making the analysts too focused on hazards directly related to the suggested action path, while possibly ignoring other hazards which could be imagined with the less detailed diagrams as input. In general, diagrams are sometimes considered more appealing to creativity than text or tables [28].

The data analysis for RQ1 consists of two steps (1) categorizing the failure modes into a common set for both methods and (2) use t-tests to compare the two data sets – one for the total number of failure modes identified from each method and one for the number of failure modes identified in each of the three categories primary user, system, and secondary user.

The data analysis for RQ2 is done by using the t-test on the coded scores in the usual way – using a Likert scale where strongly disagree to strongly agree is coded as 1 to 5. The questions used to answer RQ2 were based on the TAM model [29].

We have observed that there are purists who do not like to use the t-test on Likert scale data, but we are not going to repeat this discussion. Instead the reader is referred to [30] where this discussion is summed up and, hopefully, brought to an end.

4.2 Experiment Design

All the students participating in the experiment had finished a fourth semester course in software engineering based on UML. They were randomly divided into two groups, one using TMUC (Textual MisUse Case) for the analysis task and the other using DMUC (Diagram MisUse Case). Both groups solved their tasks under equal conditions - same room, same time-frame. The experiment consisted of four steps: (1) studying the four page tutorial describing the respective methods, (2) filling in the pre-experiment questionnaire, (3) performing a DMUC or TMUC analysis, with the help of the tutorial, and (4) filling in the post-experiment questionnaire. We allocated 20 minutes for studying the tutorial and completing the pre-experiment questionnaire, 50 minutes for doing the analysis and 10 minutes for completing the post-experiment questionnaire. The students were instructed to identify as many failure modes as possible. A failure mode was defined as any system event that could threaten the well-being of one or more patients. Based on our own observations, no group seemed to have problems with finishing their tasks within the allocated time frame.

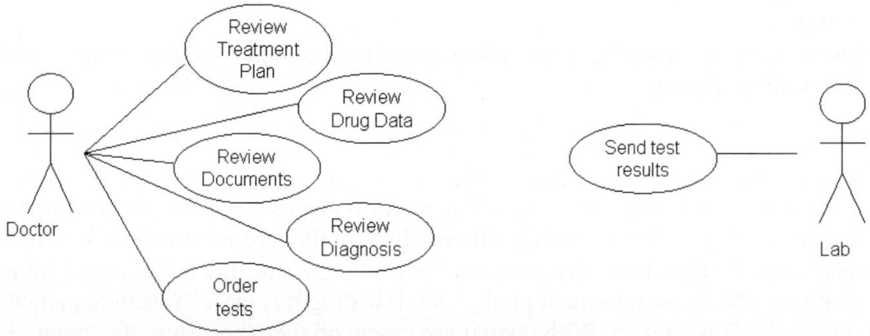

Fig. 2. The use case diagram that was input for the experiment

The use case diagram to be analyzed stems from a system for electronic patient journals and is shown in Figure 2. The doctor has five functions – he can review (i.e., read and update) the patient's treatment plan, the patient's drug data, the diagnosis and other documents, and order tests from the lab. The lab performs tests and sends test results back to the doctor.

The textual use cases for this experiment were constructed based on a pattern suggested by Heldal [31] as indicated in Figure 3. The most important concept of this pattern is that it will help the developer to focus on the two core activities (1) validate

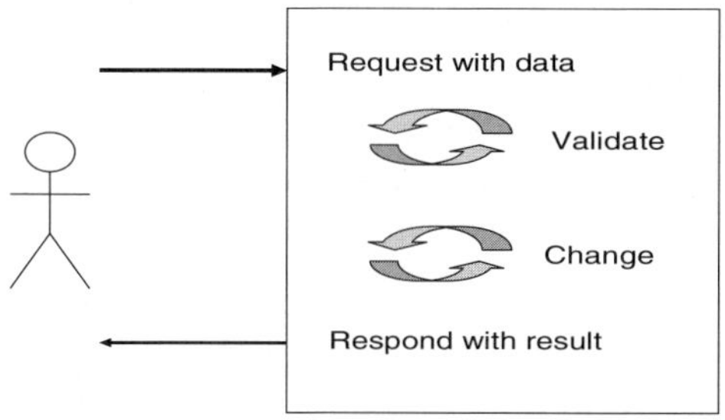

Fig. 3. Pattern for steps in textual use cases

the input and (2) change the state based on this input. An example of a textual uses case used in the experiment is shown in Table 2. The use case names and actor names are the same as the ones used in the use case diagrams.

The textual use cases will have one important advantage over the use case diagrams: they contain more information. This will hold true for all textual use cases when compared to use case diagrams. It will, a fortiori, hold in our case, where the selected textual use case pattern force us to include input checks – see steps 2 and 3 in the textual use case of Table 2.

Table 2. Example use case

Use case name	Review treatment plan
Use case actor	Doctor
User action	**System action**
1 Request treatment plan for patient X	2 Check if patient X has this doctor? 3 Check if there is a treatment plan for patient X
	4 Return requested document
5 Doctor reviews treatment plan	
Exceptional paths	
	2.1 This is not this doctor's patient 2.2 Give error message This ends the use case
	3.1 No treatment plan exists for this patient This ends the use case

5 Main Results

5.1 Identified Failure Modes

In order to compare the two methods we looked at two sets of differences: (1) the difference between the total number of failure modes and (2) the difference for each actor – doctor, lab and computer system. The results turned out as follows:

- The total system. TMUC found significantly more defects than DMUC – 11.6 vs. 10.7. $p = 0.01$ and the effect size is 0.7. Thus, we will reject hypothesis $H1_0$. The total number of failure modes was 33.

- The doctor. No difference in the number of failure modes identified
- The computer system. TMUC found significantly more failure modes than DMUC – 4.1 vs. 2.5 with a p-value of 0.01 and an effect size of 0.7. The total number of computer system failure modes was 12.
- The lab. No difference in the number of failure modes identified.

In all cases the participants in the experiment on the average found approximately one third of the possible failure modes – 6 out of 15 for the doctor use cases, 4 out of 12 for the system and 2 out of 6 for the lab use case. As should be expected, some failure modes were identified by more participants than others.

In order to study the causes of the differences between DMUC and TMUC, we used a detailed plot of the threats identified for the computer system. This plot is shown in Figure 4. The plot shows the fraction of the participants that identified each failure mode. This fraction can be interpreted as the probability of identifying a failure mode, using either DMUC or TMUC.

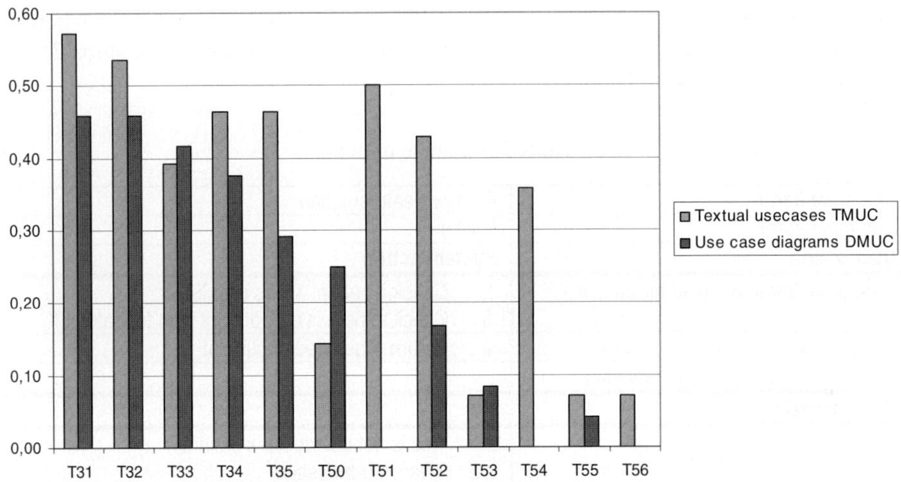

Fig. 4. The probability of identifying each failure mode

Even though the fraction of persons that identified each failure mode in the computer system is larger for TMUC than for DMUC in most of the cases, the differences are more outspoken for the failure modes in the second part of the list, e.g. T51 – "data not available", T52 – "data is lost" and T54 – "incorrect error message".

The differences between the portions of persons that identified each failure mode using TMUC and DMUC respectively for the unlucky doctor and for the faulty system are shown in fig 5 and fig 6.

When we look at the plot for the differences for each identified threat, two things become clear:

- In three out of four cases, the threat "select wrong patient" is identified significantly more often using TMUC than using DMUC. The p-values are less than or equal to 0.01 for T11, T14 and T20.

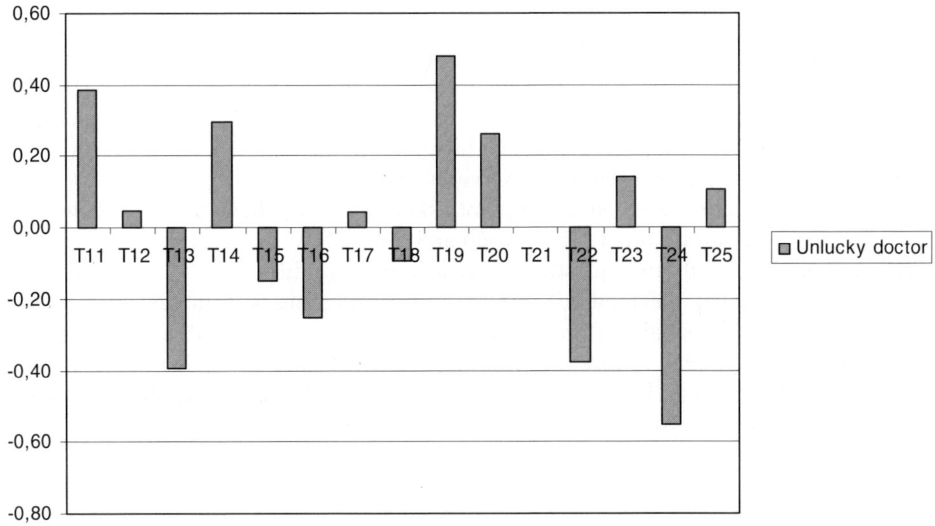

Fig. 5. Difference plot for unlucky doctor

- In three out of four cases, the threat "wrong or missing update" is identified significantly more often using DMUC than using TMUC. The p-values are in all cases less than or equal to 0.03 for T13, T16 and T22.

In fig 6 we see that TMUC is better than DMUC in all cases but one. No system related information is shown in the use case diagrams. The observation thus confirms our results when we compared DMUC and FMEA – see [27]: use case diagrams will not help the developers to identify failure modes in the underlying computer system.

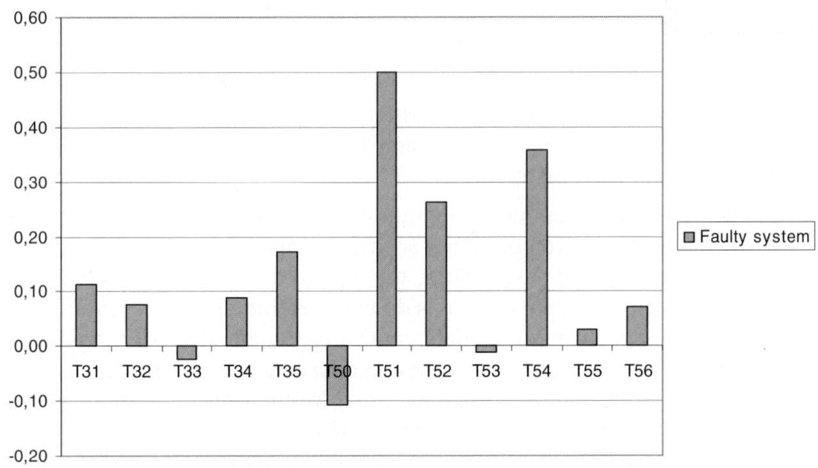

Fig. 6. Difference plot for faulty system

5.2 Learning and Using the Methods

In order to answer RQ2 – is one of the two methods DMUC and TMUC easier to use – we used the TAM model [29] with the three factors Perceived ease of use (PEOU), Perceived usefulness (PU) and Intention to use (IU) – see Fig. 7. The post-experiment questionnaire had four questions for each factor. Both the model and the questionnaire were the same as the ones used in the previous experiment

The answers were scored on a five point Likert scale. We have used t-tests to compare the scores given by the TMUC group and the DMUC group. Using a p-value of 0.10 we found that only two questions gave a significant difference – Q7 (I was never confused when using the method) and Q10 (The diagrams and tables were easy to draw). All in all, the small differences in item responses were as should be expected when there are no real differences. For PEOU we found the same score for Q1, DMUC was better than TMUC in two cases and TMUC was better than DMUC in one case. This pattern was repeated for ITU and PU.

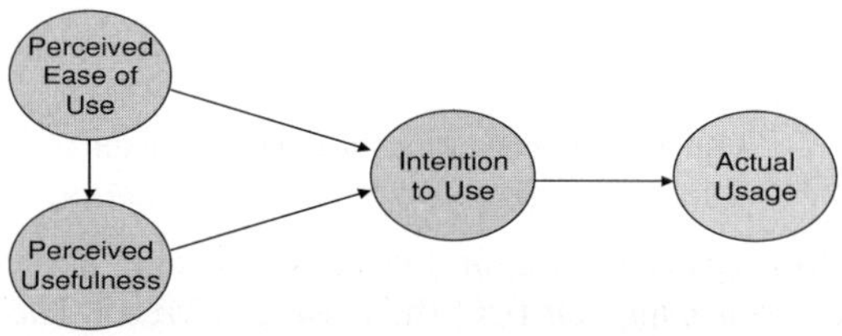

Fig. 7. The factors in the TAM model

Based on the summary above it is reasonable to claim that there is no significant difference between DMUC and TMUC, neither for perceived ease of use, nor for intention to use or perceived usefulness. We will thus accept hypothesis $H2_0$.

5.3 Discussions

We will start by restating our most important findings (1) persons using TMUC found more threats pertaining to the computer system, (2) persons using TMUC found more defects of the category "wrong patient" and (3) persons using DMUC found more defects of the category "wrong update".

For (1): the textual use cases have separate columns for system responses. This is partly due to the chosen pattern – see fig 3 – and partly due to the chosen layout of the textual use cases. Thus, the textual use cases bring the system into focus, while the use case diagrams do not even mention the system.

For (2): the textual use cases brings data control to the attention of the analyst since the selected use case pattern focuses on data control – see fig 3.

For (3): textual use cases and use case diagrams give the same amount of information concerning the review activity. For the use case diagram, however, all focus is on the review activity while for the textual use cases it is one of many others.

For both (2) and (3) and partly for (1), the explanation can be summed up in one word: "focus" and focus is again created by the information available. As we see from the textual use case example, each textual use case starts with a check for the right patient – "is this the doctor's patient?" – more information, while the use case diagrams have all their focus on the review itself – e.g. "review treatment plan". Nothing else is even mentioned.

Thus, the focus decides the outcome – a method or representation will enable the analyst to identify more threats in the areas where the method helps him to focus. If we take this a step further we should consider using something like HazOp's guide words, which are also used to focus the analysis [30]. This has already been tried in small cases studies [28, 29]. The results from our experiments indicate that in our case, the words used in the text connected to a use case play the role of guide words, although in a rather unsystematic way.

6 Threats to Validity

We will use the categories defined in [32] as a starting point for our discussion on threats to validity. We will look at each threat in a short section before giving a sum-up of our validity claims.

6.1 Conclusion Validity

Conclusion validity is concerned with our ability to draw the right conclusions about the relationship between the treatment and the outcome. An important question here is sample size. We will denote the type I error probability by α and the type II error probability by β. The following relationship holds:

$$N = \frac{4(u_{\alpha/2} + u_{\beta})^2}{ES^2} \tag{1}$$

If we use $\alpha = 0.05$ and $\beta = 0.20$, we get $N = 26/ES^2$. We have N = 52, which gives us ES = 0.7.

For the number of identified failure modes, we found an effect size of 0.7, which is large enough. For the post-experiment questions, we found only two questions that showed any statistically significant differences between DMUC and TMUC. In both cases, however, the effect size was smaller than 0.7 – 0.6 for both Q7 and Q10.

6.2 Internal Validity

Internal validity is concerned with the relationship between treatment and outcome – was it the treatment that caused the outcome? The analysis reported in section 5.1 shows that using the method DMUC or TMUC explain the difference, while factors like UML experience and use case experience did not explain the observed differences in the number of failure modes identified. Thus, we are confident that it was the difference in analysis method that caused the observed differences in the number of failure modes identified.

For the post-experiment questionnaire, there are no combinations of pre-experiment factors that can explain more than 25% of the variation in observed values for any of the post-experiment questions. The variation in experiment (DMUC vs. TMUC) can only explain the observed variations for two of these questions.

6.3 Construct Validity

Construct validity is concerned with the relationship between theory and observations – was the experiment realistic? The realism of the experiment is lacking in two ways: (1) little training with a new method and (2) the quality of the result has no influence, neither on a real product nor on the participants' working situation. However, the above-mentioned threats will influence both groups in the same way. Since we are only looking for differences between two methods and not for any absolute measure of efficiency, this should not influence our conclusions of the two methods' relative merits.

6.4 External Validity

External validity is concerned with generalization – where and when are the conclusions applicable and can we generalize from our experiments to industrial practice? The important problem here is whether we can generalize our results to the software industry. Experiments on defect detection performed by Runeson [33] found no significant difference between graduate students and professionals. As shown by [34] generalization is not a question of students vs. professional developers – it is mainly a question of level of competence. UML competence did not seem to influence the results. The only competence that could influence the results in a significant way is the domain competence – in our case competence related to hospital work and working with patient journals.

6.5 Our Claims to Validity

Based on the discussions above, we claim that there are no serious threats to validity for our conclusions on the number of identified failure modes – RQ1. For factors related to ease of use, we see problems related to conclusion validity due to the small effect sizes.

7 Conclusions and Further Work

Our main conclusions from this experiment are as follows:

- A misuse case analysis based on textual use cases will produce more failure modes than a misuse case analysis based on use case diagrams. The main reason for this is that a textual use case contains more information which is used by the experiment participants to focus the analysis.
- Usability, as defined from the TAM model, is the same for textual use cases and use case diagrams.

In order to follow up on the use of guide words in DMUC analysis, we will run a new experiment where DMUC using the use case diagrams only is compared to DMUC using use case diagrams and a set of guide words. In addition, an experiment where we compare DMUC using simple use cases to DMUC using quite elaborated use cases is already in its planning stage.

References

1. Firesmith, D.G.: Engineering Safety Requirements, Safety Constraints, and Safety-Critical Requirements. Journal of Object Technology, 3, 27–42 (2004)
2. McDermott, J., Fox, C.: Using Abuse Case Models for Security Requirements Analysis. In: 15th Annual Computer Security Applications Conference (ACSAC 1999). IEEE Computer Soceity Press, Los Alamitos (1999)
3. Leveson, N.G.: Safeware: System Safety and Computers. Addison-Wesley, Boston (1995)
4. Lutz, R.R.: Software Engineering for Safety: A Roadmap. In: Finkelstein, A. (ed.) The Future of Software Engineering, pp. 213–226. ACM Press, New York (2000)
5. Sindre, G., Opdahl, A.L.: Eliciting Security Requirements with Misuse Cases. Requirements Engineering 10, 34–44 (2005)
6. Alexander, I.F.: Initial Industrial Experience of Misuse Cases in Trade-Off Analysis. In: Pohl, K. (ed.) 10th Anniversary IEEE Joint International Requirements Engineering Conference (RE 2002), Essen, Germany, 9-13 September. IEEE, Los Alamitos (2002)
7. Alexander, I.F.: Misuse Cases, Use Cases with Hostile Intent. IEEE Software 20, 58–66 (2003)
8. Sindre, G.: A look at misuse cases for safety concerns. In: ME 2007, Geneva, Switzerland. IFIP. Springer, Heidelberg (2007)
9. Stålhane, T., Sindre, G.: A comparison of two approaches to safety analysis based on use cases. In: ER 2007, Auckland, New Zealand. LNCS. Springer, Heidelberg (2007)
10. Stamatis, D.H.: Failure Mode and Effect Analysis: FMEA from theory to execution. American Society fbor Quality (ASQ), Milwaukee, Wisconsin (1995)
11. Achour-Salinesi, C.B., Rolland, C., Maiden, N.A.M., Souveyet, C.: Guiding Use Case Authoring: Results from an Empirical Study. In: 4th International Symposium on Requirements Engineering (RE 1999), 7-11 June, pp. 36–43. IEEE, Los Alamitos (1999)
12. Cox, K., Phalp, K.: Replicating the CREWS Use Case Authoring Guidelines Experiment. Empirical Software Engineering 5, 245–267 (2000)
13. Anda, B., Sjøberg, D.I.K., Jørgensen, M.: Quality and Understandability of Use Case Models. In: Knudsen, J.L. (ed.) ECOOP 2001. LNCS, vol. 2072, pp. 402–428. Springer, Heidelberg (2001)
14. Anda, B., Sjøberg, D.I.K.: Investigating the Role of Use Cases in the Construction of Class Diagrams. Empirical Software Engineering 10, 285–309 (2005)
15. Thelin, T., Runeson, P., Regnell, B.: Usage-based reading: an experiment to guide reviewers with use cases. Information & Software Technology 43, 925–938 (2001)
16. Cox, K., Aurum, A., Jeffery, D.R.: An Experiment in Inspecting the Quality of Use Case Descriptions. Journal of Research and Practice in Information Technology 36, 211–229 (2004)
17. Bernardez, B., Genero, M., Duran, A., Toro, M.: A Controlled Experiment for Evaluating a Metric-Based Reading Technique for Requirements Inspection. In: 10th International Symposium on Software Metrics (METRICS 2004), 11-17 September, pp. 257–268. IEEE, Los Alamitos (2004)
18. Batra, D., Hoffer, J.A., Bostrom, R.P.: Comparing Representations with Relational and EER Models. Communications of the ACM 33, 126–139 (1990)

19. Cheng, P.C.-H.: Why Diagrams Are (Sometimes) Six Times Easier than Words: Benefits beyond Locational Indexing. In: Blackwell, A.F., Marriott, K., Shimojima, A. (eds.) Diagrams 2004. LNCS (LNAI), vol. 2980, pp. 242–254. Springer, Heidelberg (2004)
20. Larkin, J.H., Simon, H.A.: Why a Diagram is (Sometimes) Worth Ten Thousand Words. Cognitive Science 11 (1987)
21. Boekelder, A., Steehouder, M.: Selecting and Switching: Some Advantages of Diagrams over Tables and Lists for Presenting Instructions. IEEE Transactions on Professional Communication 41, 229–241 (1998)
22. Allmendinger, L.: Diagrams and Design Tools in Context. ACM SIGDOC Asterisk Journal of Computer Documentation 18, 25–41 (1994)
23. Coll, R.A., Coll, J.H., Thakur, G.: Graphs and tables: a four factor experiment. Communications of the ACM 37, 77–84 (1994)
24. Jacobson, I., Christerson, M., Jonsson, P., Overgaard, G.: Object-Oriented Software Engineering: A Use Case Driven Approach. Addison-Wesley, Boston (1992)
25. Cockburn, A.: Writing Effective Use Cases. Addison-Wesley, Boston (2001)
26. Wirfs-Brock, R.: Designing Scenarios: Making the Case for a Use Case Framework. The Smalltalk Report, vol. 3 (1993)
27. Bertin, J.: Semiology of Graphics: Diagrams, Networks, Maps. University of Wisconsin Press, Madison (1983)
28. Cheng, P.C.-H., Simon, H.A.: Scientific Discovery and Creative Reasoning with Diagrams. In: Smith, S., et al. (eds.) The Creative Cognition Approach, pp. 205–228. MIT Press, Cambridge (1995)
29. Davis, F.D., Bagozzi, R.P., Warshaw, P.R.: User Acceptance of Computer Technology: A Comparison of Two Theoretical Models. Management Science 35, 982–1003 (1989)
30. Tukey, J.W.: Data analysis and behavioral science or learning to bear the quantitative's man burden by shunning badmandments. In: Jones, L.W. (ed.) The Collected Works of John W. Tukey, Wadsworth, Monterey, CA, vol. III, pp. 187–389 (1986)
31. Heldal, R.: Use cases are more than System Operations. In: 2nd International Workshop on Use Case Modelling (WUsCaM-2005), Montego Bay, Jamaica, October 2-7 (2005)
32. Wohlin, C., Runeson, P., Höst, M., Ohlsson, M.C., Regnell, B., Wesslén, A.: Experimentation in Software Engineering: An Introduction. Kluwer Academic, Norwell (2000)
33. Runeson, P.: Using Students as Experiment Subjects – An Analysis on Graduate and Freshmen Student Data. In: Linkman, S. (ed.) 7th International Conference on Empirical Assessment & Evaluation in Software Engineering (EASE 2003), Keele University, Staffordshire, UK, 8-10 April, pp. 95–102 (2003)
34. Arisholm, E., Sjøberg, D.I.K.: Evaluating the Effect of a Delegated versus Centralized Control Style on the Maintainability of Object-oriented Software. IEEE Transactions on Software Engineering 30, 521–534 (2004)

Appendix A. Coded Threats

Threatens	Misuse case	Code
Review treatment plan	select wrong patient	T11
	show incorrect info	T31
	misread plan	T12
	wrong or missing update	T13
Review drug data	select wrong patient	T14
	show incorrect info	T32
	misread drug data	T15
	wrong or missing update	T16
Review docu-ments	select wrong patient	T17
	show incorrect info	T33
	misread document	T18
	wrong or missing update	T19
Review diagnosis	select wrong patient	T20
	show incorrect info	T34
	misread diagnosis	T21
	wrong or missing update	T22
Order test	Select wrong patient	T23
	Select wrong test	T24
(cont.)	Order unnecessary test	T25
	Test order not arriving	T35
Send test result	Test result not arriving	T41
	Send wrong info	T42
	Enter wrong results	T43
	Error in test performance	T44
	Fail to perform test or send res	T45
	Send test res to wrong address	T46
All	Fail to respond to command	T50
	Data not available	T51
	Data is lost	T52
	Program unavailable	T53
	Incorrect error message	T54
	Network down	T55
	Delete files	T56

Adding Dependability Analysis Capabilities to the MARTE Profile*

Simona Bernardi[1], José Merseguer[2], and Dorina C. Petriu[3]

[1] Dipartimento di Informatica, Università di Torino, Italy
bernardi@di.unito.it
[2] Departamento de Informática e Ingeniería de Sistemas,
Universidad de Zaragoza, Spain
jmerse@unizar.es
[3] Department of Systems and Computer Engineering,
Carleton University, Ottawa, Canada
petriu@sce.carleton.ca

Abstract. Dependability is a non-functional property that should be assessed early in the software lifecycle. Although several UML profiles exist for quantitative annotations of non-functional properties, none of them provides concrete capabilities for dependability analysis of UML system models. In this paper, we propose a dependability analysis and modeling profile. The objective is twofold: to reuse proposals from the literature on deriving dependability models from UML annotated specifications and to be compliant with the recently adopted MARTE profile, which provides a framework for general quantitative analysis concepts that can be specialized to a particular analysis domain. The profile definition process was done in several steps. Firstly, an in depth analysis of the literature has been carried out to collect the information requirements for the profile. Secondly, a domain model for dependability analysis was defined independently of UML. Thirdly, the domain model was mapped to UML extensions by specializing MARTE.

1 Introduction

The *dependability* of a system, as defined in [1] is the ability to avoid failures that are more frequent and more severe than acceptable. The dependability encompasses a set of non-functional properties, called *attributes* of dependability, such as: a) *availability*, the readiness for correct service; b) *reliability*, the continuity of correct service; c) *safety*, the absence of catastrophic consequences on the users and environment; d) *maintainability*, the ability to undergo modifications and repairs.

* This work has been supported by the European IST project CRUTIAL-027513 (CRitical UTility InfrastructurAL resilience), the project DPI2006-15390 of the Spanish ministry of Science and Technology, and the Discovery grant from the Natural Sciences and Engineering Research Council of Canada (NSERC).

K. Czarnecki et al. (Eds.): MoDELS 2008, LNCS 5301, pp. 736–750, 2008.

Although there are several proposals in literature on extending Unified Modeling Language (UML) models with dependability annotations, as reviewed in Sect. 3 of this paper, each covers only a subset of dependability aspects. Compared with the performance and schedulability analysis domains, which are supported by standard UML profiles such as Schedulability, Performance and Time (SPT) [2] and MARTE [3], there is no similar standard profile for the dependability analysis of UML-based models yet. Another Object Management Group standard specifying UML extensions for a variety of non-functional properties, the "Profile for Modeling Quality of Service and Fault Tolerance Characteristics and Mechanisms" (QoS&FT) [4], provides a flexible but heavy-weight mechanism to define properties such as performance, security or reliability by means of specific QoS catalogs. The annotation mechanism is supported by a two-step process, which implies catalog binding and either the creation of extra objects just for annotation purposes, or the specification of long Object Constraint Language (OCL) expressions.

The main objective of this paper is to propose a UML profile for quantitative dependability analysis of software systems modeled with UML with particular focus on the following facets of dependability: reliability, availability and safety. One of the requirements for such a profile is to reuse the best practices reported in literature, and to unify the terminology and concepts for different dependability aspects under a common dependability domain model. Another requirement is to be compliant with the recently adopted MARTE profile [3] in two ways: a) by using the Non-Functional Properties (NFP) framework and its corresponding Value Specification Language (VSL) for defining dependability-specific data types necessary for the profile definition; and b) by specializing general concepts from MARTE's generic quantitative analysis model (i.e., GQAM sub-profile) for the dependability analysis domain. This paper builds on the previous work [5], where a first attempt to extending UML with dependability analysis capabilities was proposed.

We have adopted a systematic approach for the definition of the dependability profile according to the recommendations from Selic [6] (see also Lagarde et al.[7]). Firstly we define a conceptual domain model for dependability analysis and modeling, which covers different dependability aspects, and reuses and unifies the concepts from previous work, and secondly we map the domain concepts to elements of a UML profile. The new proposed stereotypes extend either UML meta-classes or MARTE stereotypes, and the stereotype attribute definitions use dependability-specific types defined in VSL. Our work proposes a unified DAM profile, but does not discuss the different model transformation techniques for generating different dependability models (Markov chains, Fault Tree, Petri Nets, etc.). The proposed profile provides all the information necessary to produce such models, but the actual model transformations represents future work.

The paper is organized as follows: Sect. 2 gives an overview of the approach followed for the profile definition; Sect. 3 gives a brief survey of related work from literature; Sect. 4 introduces the dependability analysis (DA) conceptual model, composed of different packages that cover separate dependability aspects; Sect. 5 presents the proposed dependability profile; Sect. 6 gives an example of profile application and Sect. 7 presents the conclusions.

2 Approach Overview

This section presents the process followed to define the dependability analysis profile, in order to ensure that we produced a technically correct quality UML profile that covers the necessary concepts according to the best practices reported in literature.

Literature Review. The existing standard UML profiles for the analysis of non functional properties of software systems have been analyzed, in particular the SPT [2], QoS&FT [4] and MARTE [3]. None of them provides a comprehensive support for dependability analysis, especially from a quantitative point of view. We investigated the literature on dependability main concepts and taxonomy (e.g., Avizienis et al. [1], Leveson [8], Lyu [9,10]) as well as on standard methods used for the quantitative assessment of dependability (e.g., [11,12]). We also surveyed the works from the literature proposing dependability modeling and analysis of UML system specifications (about twenty papers). The output of this preliminary step is a checklist of information requirements that a UML profile for dependability analysis should satisfy reported in detail in [13].

Definition of Dependability Analysis (DA) Conceptual Model. We defined a DA conceptual model to represent the main dependability concepts from the literature. Its construction required several refinement steps to consider all the surveyed works. The final domain model is described in Sect. 4.

Completeness Assessment of the DA Domain Model. We verified whether all the concepts considered in the survey have been included. If a concept was not considered, we either repeated the refinement step or provided a motivation for its exclusion.

Definition of the Dependability Analysis Modeling (DAM) Profile. Using the DA conceptual model we defined: a) the DAM extensions (stereotypes and tags), and b) DAM library containing dependability specific types. The objective is to introduce a small set of stereotypes that can be easily used by the software analyst. The DAM library has been defined by importing the MARTE library and consists of basic and complex DA types.

DAM Profile Assessment. We verified whether the information requirements from [13] are satisfied. If a requirement was not met, we went back to the previous step in order to refine it.

3 Related Works

The brief survey from this section focuses on existing work from literature that provides support for the quantitative dependability analysis of UML-based designs. (A more detailed survey can be found in [13]).

Pataricza [14] extends the General Resource Modeling package of the SPT profile with the notion of faults and errors to support the analysis of the effect of local faults to the system dependability. The work includes permanent and transient faults in the resources and error propagation to estimate which fault may lead to a failure. Explicit fault injection behavioral models are also proposed to represent faults as special virtual clients.

Addouche et al. [15] define a profile for dependability analysis of real-time systems compliant with the SPT resource modeling. The UML extensions are used to derive probabilistic time automata for the verification of dependability properties via temporal logic formulas. The static model of the system is enriched with new stereotyped classes associated with resources (but has the disadvantage that new classes are introduced in the system model for dependability analysis purposes).

Bernardi et al. [16] propose a set of UML Class Diagrams structured in packages for collecting dependability and real-time requirements and properties of automated embedded systems with the use of COTS fault-tolerance (FT) mechanisms. The approach provides support for a semi-automatic derivation of dependability analysis models, such as Stochastic Petri Nets and temporal logic. In [17] is proposed a method to assess the quality of service of FT distributed systems by deriving performability models from UML+SPT models.

The most comprehensive approach so far for reliability and availability analysis of UML specifications has been proposed by Bondavalli et al. [18]. A profile for annotating software dependability properties compliant with the taxonomy and basic concepts from [1] is proposed. A model transformation process derives Timed Petri Net models via an intermediate model from the annotated UML models. The approach supports the specification of error propagation between components, as well as independent and dependent failures. It is possible to discriminate between normal and failure states and events. The main drawback of this work is the introduction of unnecessary redundant information in the UML model, as sometime the joint use of more than one stereotype is needed.

DalCin [19] proposes a UML profile for specifying dependability mechanisms, aimed at supporting the quantitative evaluation of the FT strategy effectiveness. However, the profile lacks support for modeling the interactions between dependability mechanisms and system components. Pai and Dugan [20] present a method to derive dynamic fault tree from UML system models. The method supports the modeling and analysis of sequence error propagations that lead to dependent failures, redundancies and reconfiguration activities.

The papers [21,22,23] address specifically the reliability analysis of UML-based design. D'Ambrogio et al. [21] define a transformation of UML models into fault tree models to predict the reliability of component-based software. Cortellessa and Pompei [22] propose a UML annotation for the reliability analysis of component-based systems, within the frameworks of the SPT and QoS&FT profiles. The annotations defined in [22] are used by Grassi et al. [23] where a model-driven transformation framework for the performance andreliability analysis of component-based systems is proposed. The method uses an intermediate model that acts as bridge between the annotated UML models and the analysis-oriented models. In particular, discrete time Markov process models can be derived for the computation of the service reliability.

Jürjens et al. define a safety [24] and reliability [25] check list, based on UML extension standard mechanisms, to support the identification of failure-prone components in the software design.

The approaches [26,27,28] support the safety analysis of UML-based system models. Pataricza et al. [26] use UML stereotypes to identify erroneous states and error correcting transitions in state machine diagram, integrating the normal and the faulty behavior of a system component in a single state machine. Goseva et al. [27] devise a methodology for the risk assessment of UML models at architectural level; a Markovian model is constructed to estimate the scenario risk factor from risk factors associated to software components and connectors. Hassan et al. [28] introduce a methodology for the severity analysis of software systems modeled with UML, which integrates different hazard analysis techniques (Functional Failure Analysis - FFA, Failure Modes and Effects Analysis - FMEA - and Fault Tree Analysis - FTA) to identify system level and component/connector level hazards and to evaluate the cost of failure of system execution scenarios, software components and connectors.

4 Dependability Analysis Conceptual Model

The DA conceptual model has been constructed considering the main dependability concepts from the literature as well as standard methods used for the dependability assessment. It is organized into a set of packages, as shown in Fig. 1. The top-level package includes:

- The *System Core* model. It provides a description of the system to be analyzed, according to a component-based view of the system [1,9]. The model includes also additional concepts for the description of redundancy structures that may characterize a fault tolerant system [10].
- The *Threats* model introduces the threats [1,9,8] that may affect the system at different levels as well as the relationships between the threats.
- The *Maintenance* model introduces the repair/recovery actions that are undertaken in case of repairable systems [1,10].

Figures 2,3,4, and 5 show the Class Diagrams of the DA conceptual model; the markups used for the classes will be explained in Sect. 5. The *Core* model (Fig. 2) represents the *context* for carrying out dependability analysis. Actually, it is a component-based description of the system to be analyzed that includes both structural and behavioral views. From the structural point of view, the system consists of a set of *components* that are bound together through *connectors*, i.e., logical/physical links, in order to interact. A component can be a sub-system consisting of sub-components. The structure of the system is what enables it to generate the behavior. The system delivers a set of high-level *services*, in response to user *service requests*. Each high-level service is, then, the system

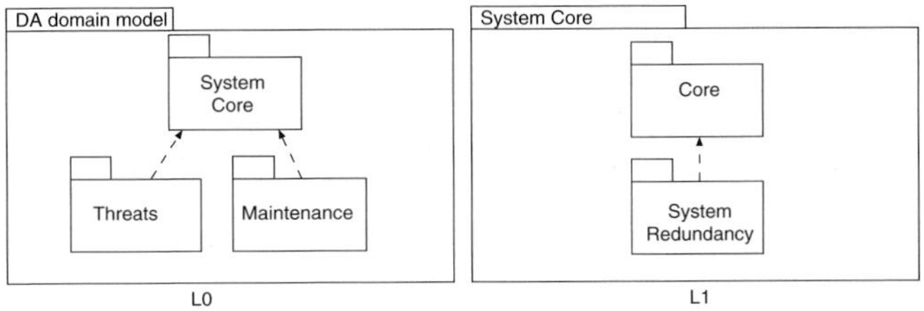

Fig. 1. Top-level package (L0), System Core package (L1)

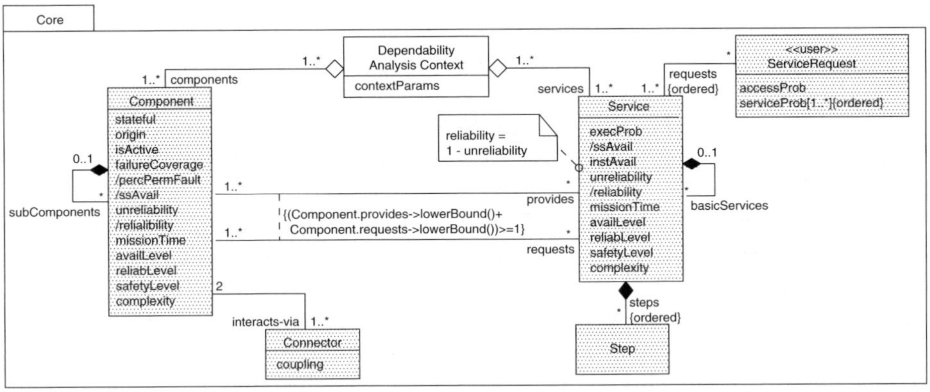

Fig. 2. Core model

behavior as perceived by its users and it is carried out by the interaction of system components, which provide and request basic services to each others. A service is implemented by a sequence of *steps* that represent component states and actions.

The *Core* model acts as a bridge between the DA concepts and the concepts introduced in MARTE for general quantitative analysis. Indeed, several classes of the *Core* model will be mapped to stereotypes that specialize the ones introduced in the GQAM profile.

Observe that some classes of the DA conceptual model have attributes that represent requirements, metrics, properties or input parameters used in dependability analysis, according to the surveyed works from literature. A detailed description of the meaning of the attributes and their types is given in [13].

A system may be characterized by redundancy structures. Software and hardware redundancy are the typical means used to increase the FT of software systems, e.g., by eliminating single points of failure. The *System Redundancy* model (Fig. 3) represents *FT components* [10], e.g., used in [18] to specify the role played by a component within a *redundant structure*. In particular, a redundant structure may consist of several *variants*, i.e, modules with different design that provide the same services, allocated over different *spares*, a *controller*, that is responsible for the co-ordination of the variants, an *adjudicator*, that either

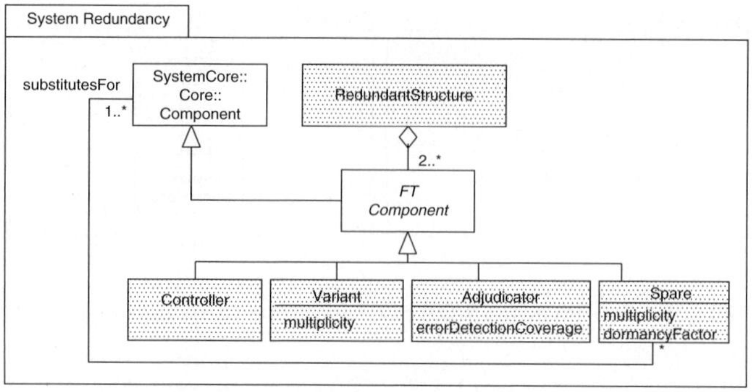

Fig. 3. System Redundancy model

looks for a consensus of two or more outputs among the variants ("N-version software" scheme) or applies an acceptance test to the variant outputs ("recovery block" scheme).

Note that it is out of scope of this work to provide a support for the modeling of FT architectures and, besides, this issue has been tackled by the QoS&FT profile [4]. Rather, the introduction of the *System Redundancy* model is motivated by the objective of providing a specific support for the quantitative dependability analysis of those FT systems characterized by redundant structures.

The *Threats* model (Fig. 4) includes the threats that may affect the system, namely the *faults, errors, failures* [1,9] and *hazards* [8]. We have introduced an abstract concept of *impairment*, that can be specialized depending of the type of analysis domain, i.e., *failure* for reliability/availability analysis and *hazard* for safety. The model represents also the cause-effect relationships between the threats and the relationships between the threats and the system core concepts. Then, a fault is the original cause of errors and impairments, and affects system components. A *fault generator* concept is added to represent a mechanism, used for example in [17,14], to inject faults in the system and to specify the max number of concurrent faults.

Errors are related to steps (i.e., states or actions) of the basic services provided by the faulty components. When an error affects an external state of a faulty component, that is the service interface of that component, then *error propagations* may occur from the faulty component to the interacting ones, via the corresponding connectors. Error propagations may be related to each others, for example they occur according to a given order [20]: the *error propagation relation* indicates the sequence of error propagations. Errors may cause impairments at different system level: 1) at service step level, then leading to *failure/hazard steps*, when the service provided by the component becomes not correct, 2) at component level, when the component is not able to provide any basic service, 3) at system level, when the impairment is perceived by the system users. Finally, multiple dependent impairments can affect a redundant structure, such as when several redundant components fail in the same mode (i.e., *common mode failures* [10]).

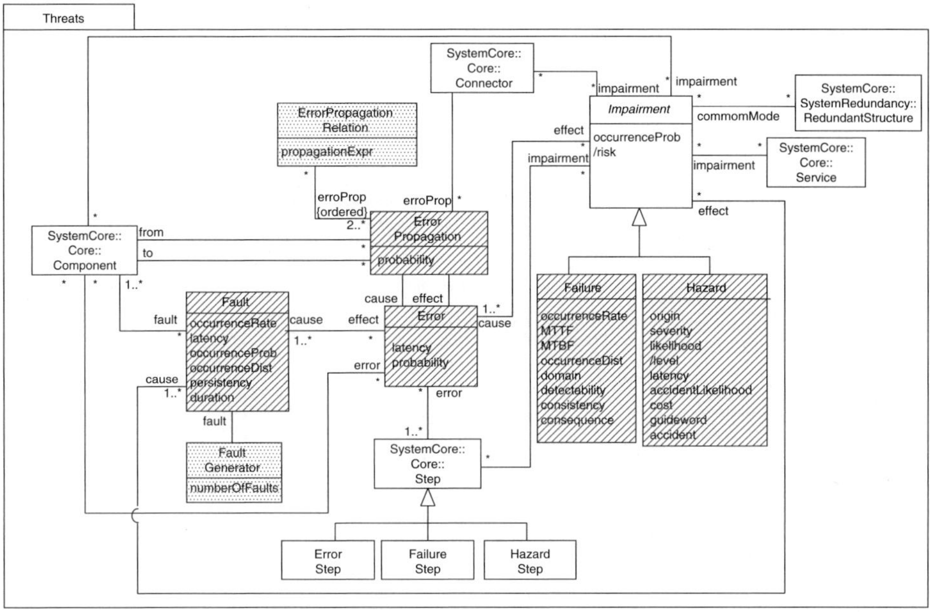

Fig. 4. Threats model

The *Maintenance* model (Fig. 5) concerns repairable systems and includes concepts that are necessary to support the evaluation of system availability, that is the *maintenance actions* undertaken to restore the system affected by threats. According to [1,10], we distinguish *repairs* of system components, that involve the participation of external agents (e.g., repairman, test equipment, etc) and *recovery* strategies, usually implemented in FT systems, that aim at transforming the system anomalous states into correct states. In particular, the reconfiguration steps imply the use of spare components [20]. The model represents the *replacement steps*, in which faulty components are replaced by spares, and the *reallocation steps*, in which software components are reallocated onto spares.

5 Dependability Analysis Modeling Profile

The process of mapping the conceptual model elements to profile elements has been an iterative process, in which each class has been examined, together with its attributes, associations and constraints, to identify the most suitable UML base concepts for it. Such activity has been carried out by following the general guidelines in [6] and by specializing the UML extensions of the MARTE profile [3].

Figure 6(a) shows an overview of the DAM profile. It consists of an UML extension package, including the set of dependability stereotypes and attributes, and of a model library, in which basic and complex dependability types associated to the attributes are defined. Most of the dependability stereotypes specialize the ones of the GQAM sub-profile of MARTE.

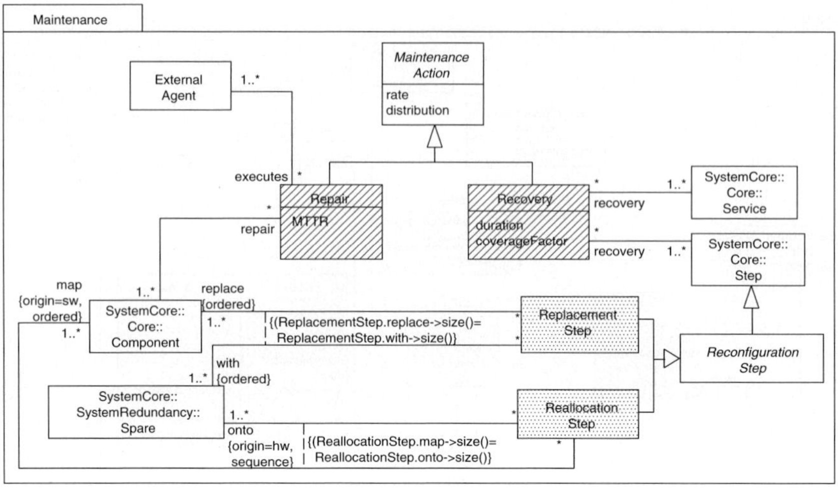

Fig. 5. Maintenance model

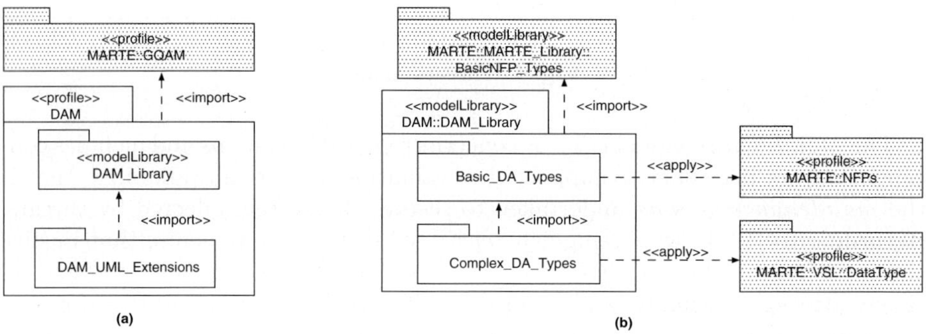

Fig. 6. (a) DAM profile and (b) DAM library

A low level view of the *DAM Library* is shown in Fig. 6(b). Complex dependability types are MARTE data-types which combine different basic NFP types, from MARTE library, and/or basic dependability types. On the other hand, basic dependability types can be either simple enumeration types (such as *CriticalLevel* used to specify a failure consequence or an hazard severity) or, in turn, specialization of basic NFP common types. An example, of the latter is the *DaFrequency*, which is a basic NFP real type, introduced to specify, e.g., a failure occurrence rate as a real value together with a failure frequency unit (e.g., 0.1^{-2} failures per hour). We have also applied the MARTE NFPs profile to define new dependability types, e.g., *DaFrequencyUnitKind* which is an enumeration type including a set of frequency units of fault/failure occurrence rates and of repair/recovery rates (see Fig. 7(c)).

The specialization of the concept of basic NFP common type allowed us to reuse several properties of the super-type that enrich the annotation capabilities

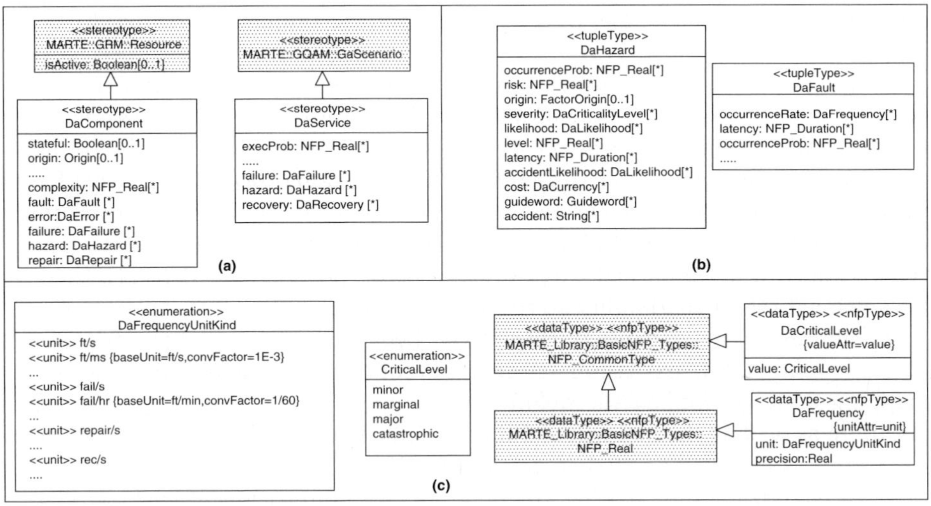

Fig. 7. (a) stereotypes, (b) complex dependability types, (c) basic dependability types

at system model level, such as the *expression* property, that supports the specification of expressions using the VSL syntax, and the *source* property that can be used to define the origin of the specification (e.g., a requirement, a metric or an input parameter).

In the DAM profile definition, we have applied several suggestions and patterns proposed in [7] that enable the creation of a profile from the conceptual model which is consistent with the UML meta-model. Moreover, we adopted the best practise of MARTE to keep track of the mapping between the conceptual model and the DAM profile. In particular, the name of each DAM extension (stereotype, complex/basic dependability type) is the name of the corresponding conceptual model element prefixed by *Da*, namely Dependability Analysis.

Domain classes are good candidates to become stereotypes but, eventually, only a subset of them have been mapped to a stereotype (i.e., the dotted classes in Figs. 2, 3, 4 and 5). Indeed, as in [7], we aimed at providing a small set of stereotypes that will be actually going to be used in practical modeling situations. Then, abstract classes, e.g., *FT Component* (Fig. 3), have not been considered in the mapping process. Nevertheless, if an abstract class carries information and it is specialized with concrete classes, such information has been considered in the mapping of the latter as well as of the concrete classes associated with the abstract class. This is the case, for example, of the abstract class *Impairment*, where its attributes have been mapped to attributes of the complex dependability types *DaFailure* and *DaHazard*. Moreover, the association-ends *impairment* have been renamed and mapped to attributes of the stereotypes *DaComponent*, *DaService* corresponding to concrete classes associated with the abstract class (compare Figs. 4 and 7(a,b)). On the other hand, the classes modeling threats and maintenance actions (i.e., classes with diagonal stripes in Figs. 4 and 5) have been defined to characterize complex dependability concepts through their attributes. Then, such classes have been mapped to complex dependability types of the DAM library (Fig. 7(b)).

Each stereotype extends either a set of UML meta-classes or MARTE stereotype. To define extension associations for a given stereotype, we have applied the general guidelines in [6], based on similarity of the semantics of the UML meta-classes and of the stereotype. To facilitate the extension process we have exploited the proposals in the surveyed literature, to identify the UML model elements annotated with the same dependability properties as the ones characterizing the stereotype. Finally, if a semantically equivalent stereotype exists in MARTE, then we have defined the dependability stereotype as a sub-stereotype of the former.

Attributes of a conceptual class have been mapped to attributes of the corresponding UML extension (stereotype/complex dependability type). This mapping activity implied the definition of a basic dependability type for each attribute as well as the definition of its multiplicity. The mapping of associations has been less trivial than that of attributes. We have often applied the *reference association* pattern of Lagarde et al.[7]. An exemplification of such pattern is given in Fig. 4, where the *Component* class is characterized by an association with the *Fault* class supported by the association-end *fault.* The latter is used to define the attribute *fault* of *DaComponent,* of complex dependability type *DaFault* (Fig. 7(a)). Observe that association multiplicities have been mapped to attribute value multiplicities.

It is worth to note that the conceptual model is characterized by several constraints written in OCL. Such constraints have been assigned to the DAM extensions and represent constraints for the use of the profile at model specification level. An excerpt of the DAM profile is depicted in Fig. 7: due to space limitation, not all the attributes are shown. The whole set of DAM extensions can be found in [13].

6 Usage of the DAM Profile

The purpose of this section is to illustrate, through an example, the usage of the DAM profile, as well as to demonstrate how an established methodology [27]

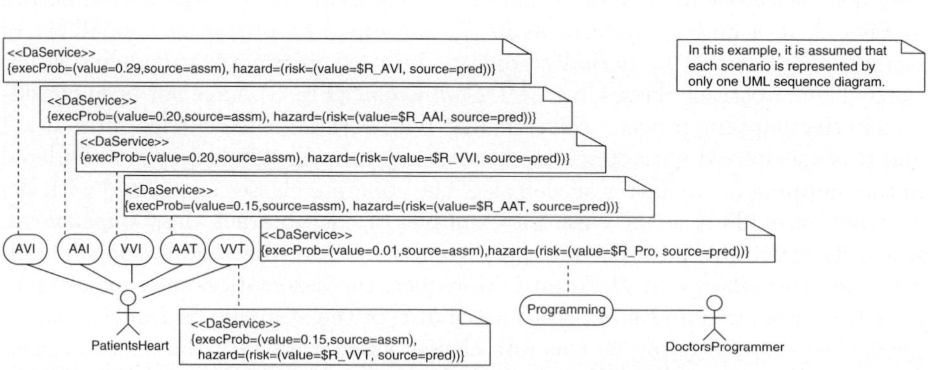

Fig. 8. Use case diagram of the pacemaker

for dependability analysis benefits from the DAM profile. The methodology for risk assessment proposed by Goseva et al. [27] introduces the safety related parameters in a tabular form, i.e., no UML extensions are provided. This section shows how these parameters can be added to a UML diagram using the DAM profile, while the methodology steps proposed in [27] (which cannot be presented here in detail due to space limitations) can still be applied.

Figure 8 depicts the use case diagram of the pacemaker example used in [27] to illustrate the methodology. Each use case (UC) is later realized as a (set of) UML sequence diagram(s) representing system *scenario(s)*. We have attached to the UCs, using the DAM profile, the original annotations that were given by the authors in the tabular form. Note that the UCs are stereotyped as *DaServices*. So, the corresponding attributes can properly describe their dependability properties. As an example, see the annotation in the AVI UC, where its execution probability `execProb`, i.e., a software requirement describing an input dependability model parameter (`source=assm`), is gathered in the UML model. Also, it can be observed how the dependability metrics to be computed in the model (i.e., the hazard risk factors) are considered as predicted values (`source=pred`). Using the VSL syntax, variable names are preceded by the $ symbol, as the $R_AVI variable.

Figure 9 shows the components and connectors that make up the pacemaker architecture[1]. In [27], the dependability input parameters *complexity and coupling* are calculated from the software functional requirements. Indeed, the *coupling* of a connector is derived from the UML SD, while the *complexity* of a component is obtained from its associated state-chart. On the other hand, the characterization of the hazards (*severity, guideword, accident*) affecting a component/connector is the result of the FMEA technique, carried out by a domain expert.

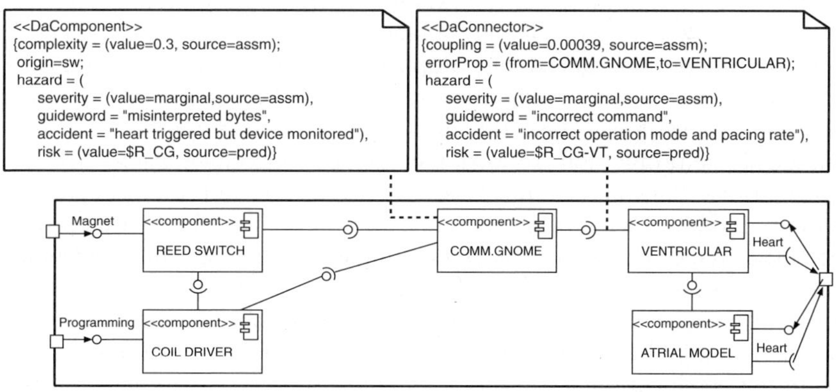

Fig. 9. The architecture of the pacemaker

For each scenario, the dependability metrics (*risk factors*) are estimated as a product of the *complexity* (*coupling*) of the component (connector) and the

[1] To avoid cluttering, only one component and one connector have been annotated.

hazard *severity* (the authors map the *marginal* severities to 0.5). The methodology ranks the critical components/connectors using such information. Moreover, considering these component (connector) risk factors together with a "control flow graph" obtained from the functional software requirements, the methodology is enabled to construct a Markov model for each scenario, where the scenario risk factor can be computed. Finally, the scenario risk factors are used to get the UCs risk factors as well as the overall system risk factor.

In conclusion, we observe that the DAM profile covers all the safety input parameters and metrics proposed in [27]. Since the DAM profile is compliant with the UML standard, it is possible now to enter all the annotations required for the Goseva methodology by using any standard UML tool. The only additional effort is the implementation of the model transformation which will take as input UML models with DAM annotations and produce as output the Markov chain model, following the approach proposed in [27].

7 Conclusion

In this paper we have proposed a profile to support dependability modeling and analysis of UML designs. The proposed profile is compliant with the standard MARTE profile, and has been built considering current dependability standards. We have defined the profile by following the approach proposed by Selic [6] and applying the patterns from Lagarde [7]. To the best of our knowledge, this is the first attempt to provide a common conceptual UML model for different dependability communities. We consider the profile as an open proposal, subject to future refinements and extensions to address particular issues in the different dependability domains (e.g., FT systems). Several reasons let us envision a great potential for our proposal. First, the existing UML-based approaches for analyzing dependability aspects of software systems surveyed in Sect. 3, can get direct benefit from the profile. Indeed, our proposal offers a common modeling support intended to covers all the information required by the existing methodologies. As an example, we have illustrated how one of these proposals [27] can take advantage of the profile. Future work includes the implementation of the model transformations that take as input UML+DAM models and produce different dependability models, by following the same approach as in the existing proposals. On the other hand, the works that focus exclusively on modeling dependability as opposed to analyzing it, can also be benefit from the profile by using its annotations or even by extending it. Among such works, there are methodologies for collecting dependability requirements, e.g. safety domain requirements in [29]; others target certification according to standard software requirements [30]; and finally, there are traditional works in dependability analysis of software systems outside the UML umbrella. In the last case, the challenge is not how to integrate the DAM profile, but rather how to integrate the UML within the respective methodology.

References

1. Avizienis, A., et al.: Basic concepts and taxonomy of dependable and secure computing. IEEE Trans. on Dependable and Secure Computing 1(1), 11–33 (2004)
2. Object Management Group: UML Profile for Schedulability, Performance and Time Specification. (January 2005) V1.1, f/05-01-02
3. Object Management Group: A UML profile for Modeling and Analysis of Real Time Embedded Systems, Beta 1. (August 2007) Adopted Spec., ptc/07-08-04
4. Object Management Group: UML Profile for Modeling Quality of Service and Fault Tolerant Characteristics and Mechanisms. (April 2008) V1.1, f/08-04-05
5. Bernardi, S., Merseguer, J.: A UML profile for dependability analysis of real-time embedded systems. In: Proc. of WOSP, February 2007, pp. 115–124. ACM, New York (2007)
6. Selic, B.: A systematic approach to domain-specific language design using UML. In: 10th IEEE Int.l Symposium on Object and Component-Oriented Real-Time Distributed Computing (ISORC 2007), pp. 2–9 (2007)
7. Lagarde, F., et al.: Improving UML profile design practices by leveraging conceptual domain models. In: 22nd Int.l Conf. on Automated Software Engineering, Atlanta (USA), November 2007, pp. 445–448. ACM, New York (2007)
8. Leveson, N.: Safeware. Addison-Wesley, Reading (1995)
9. Lyu, M.R. (ed.): Handbook of Software Reliability Engineering. IEEE Computer Society Press, Los Alamitos (1996)
10. Lyu, M.: Software Fault Tolerance. John Wiley & Sons, Ltd., Chichester (1995)
11. Commission, I.E.: IEC-60300-3-1 standard: Dependability management
12. Commission, I.E.: IEC-61508 standard: Functional Safety of Electrical/ Electronic/ Programmable Electronic safety related problems
13. Bernardi, S., Merseguer, J., Petriu, D.: An UML profile for Dependability Analysis and Modeling of Software Systems. Technical Report RR-08-05, Universidad de Zaragoza, Spain (2008), http://www.di.unito.it/~bernardi/DAMreport08.pdf
14. Pataricza, A.: From the General Resource Model to a General Fault Modelling Paradigm? In: Workshop on Critical Systems, held within UML 2000 (2000)
15. Addouche, N., Antoine, C., Montmain, J.: UML models for dependability analysis of real-time systems. In: Proc. International Conference on Systems, Man and Cybernetics, October 2004, vol. 6, pp. 5209–5214. IEEE Computer Society, Los Alamitos (2004)
16. Bernardi, S., Donatelli, S., Dondossola, G.: A class diagram framework for collecting dependability requirements in automation systems. In: Proc. of 1st Int.l Symposium on Leveraging Applications of Formal Methods, Cyprus (October 2004)
17. Bernardi, S., Merseguer, J.: QoS Assessment via Stochastic Analysis. IEEE Internet Computing, 32–42 (May-June 2006)
18. Majzik, I., Pataricza, A., Bondavalli, A.: Stochastic Dependability Analysis of System Architecture Based on UML Models. In: Architecting Dependable Systems. LNCS, vol. 2677, pp. 219–244. Springer, Heidelberg (2003)
19. Dal Cin, M.: Extending UML towards a Useful OO-Language for Modeling Dependability Features. In: Proc. of 9th Int.l Workshop on Object-Oriented Real-Time Dependable Systems, Capri Island, Italy, October 2003, pp. 325–330. IEEE Computer Society, Los Alamitos (2003)
20. Pai, G., Dugan, J.: Automatic Synthesis of Dynamic Fault Trees from UML system models. In: Proc. of 13th Int. Symposium on Software Reliability Engineering, Annapolis, MD, USA, November 2002, pp. 243–256. IEEE Computer Society, Los Alamitos (2002)

21. D'Ambrogio, A., Iazeolla, G., Mirandola, R.: A method for the prediction of software reliability. In: Proc. of the 6-th IASTED Software Engineering and Applications Conference (SEA 2002), Cambridge, MA, USA (November 2002)
22. Cortellessa, V., Pompei, A.: Towards a UML Profile for QoS: a contribution in the reliability domain. In: Proceedings of the Fourth International Workshop on Software and Performance (WOSP 2004), pp. 197–206 (January 2004)
23. Grassi, V., Mirandola, R., Sabetta, A.: Filling the gap between design and performance/reliability models of component-based systems: A model-driven approach. Journal of Systems and Software 80(4), 528–558 (2007)
24. Jürjens, J.: Developing safety-critical systems with UML. In: Stevens, P., Whittle, J., Booch, G. (eds.) UML 2003. LNCS, vol. 2863, pp. 360–372. Springer, Heidelberg (2003)
25. Jürjens, J., Wagner, S.: Component-based Development of Dependable Systems with UML. In: Atkinson, C., Bunse, C., Gross, H.-G., Peper, C. (eds.) Component-Based Software Development for Embedded Systems. LNCS, vol. 3778, pp. 320–344. Springer, Heidelberg (2005)
26. Pataricza, A., et al.: UML-based design and formal analysis of a safety-critical railway control software module. In: Tarnai, G., Schnieder, E. (eds.) Proc. of FORMS 2003, Budapest (Hungary), pp. 125–132 (May 2003)
27. Goseva-Popstojanova, K., et al.: Architectural-level risk analysis using UML. IEEE Transactions on Software Engineering 29(10), 946–960 (2003)
28. Hassan, A., Goseva-Popstojanova, K., Ammar, H.: UML Based Severity Analysis Methodology. In: Proc. of Annual Reliability and Maintainability Symposium (RAMS 2005), Alexandria, VA (January 2005)
29. Allenby, K., Kelly, T.: Deriving safety requirements using scenarios. In: 5th IEEE International Symposium on Requirements Engineering (RE 2001), pp. 228–235. IEEE Computer Society, Los Alamitos (2001)
30. Zoughbi, G., Briand, L., Labiche, Y.: A UML Profile for Developing Airworthiness-Compliant (RTCA DO-178B), Safety-Critical Software. In: Engels, G., Opdyke, B., Schmidt, D.C., Weil, F. (eds.) MODELS 2007. LNCS, vol. 4735, pp. 574–588. Springer, Heidelberg (2007)

Visual ScatterUnit: A Visual Model-Driven Testing Framework of Wireless Sensor Networks Applications

Mohammad Al Saad, Nicolai Kamenzky, and Jochen Schiller

Freie Universität Berlin
Computer Systems & Telematics
Takustr. 9, 14195 Berlin, Germany
{saad,kamenzky,schiller}@inf.fu-berlin.de

Abstract. We present a model-driven test environment called Visual ScatterUnit, which optimizes the application testing process of wireless sensor networks. Instead of having to implement the test case completely manually, the model-driven test environment allows the abstract modeling of the test process. At the same time the test case's technical implementation requirements are kept hidden from the user.

In the following a code generator is able to create the necessary test case code, which complies with technical requirements from the test case model. The test case is executed with the help of Visual ScatterUnit and the test results are subsequently visualized in the test case model's diagrams. In this way the user can easily comprehend the test run and consequently understand the cause of failure. Furthermore the test case's abstract modeling allows it to be validated, which brings with it a quality assurance for the executable test case.

1 Introduction

A WSN may consist of several hundred sensor nodes, which are independent processing units equipped with various sensors and which communicate wirelessly. WSNs can be compared to wireless ad-hoc networks, but the sensor nodes are constrained by very limited resources and suit the purpose of collecting and processing sensory data. For testing WSN applications, many common services are needed, e.g. the simulation of sensor input. To provide those services, we implemented a testing framework for our WSN platform ScatterWeb [1], [2] called Visual ScatterUnit.

In order to improve the testing process with the help of Visual ScatterUnit we studied the process in its entirety. The following activities make up the process: Choice of suitable test scenarios for the test application, development of test cases, which implement the test scenarios, running the test and analysis of the test results. During the analysis of the test results the user can have two different intentions. On the one hand he may wish to find out if a failure has occurred or not, and on the other hand he may wish to examine the test results in order to gather information on the cause of failure. This information helps in locating the fault in the application code. Overall the test case development as well as the discovery of a failure and the subsequent location of the fault should be supported.

K. Czarnecki et al. (Eds.): MoDELS 2008, LNCS 5301, pp. 751–765, 2008.

Within the course of test case development primarily the time involved for the implementation should be reduced. The reduction of time spent is very important, because an application's quality assurance demands that many test cases be implemented. In the case of fault localisation primarily the complexity of the implementation becomes a problem. As fault localisation needs exact information on the failure's course of events the test case needs to be expanded gradually, in order to provide this information. The test case expansion though is difficult, because of the complexity of its implementation. Thus the complexity needs to be reduced in order to increase the ease of modification. The aim of Visual ScatterUnit though is primarily to reduce the complexity of the test case implementation, so that the test case development and fault localisation can be as time effective as possible.

The paper is structured as follows: The next section illustrates the framework's architecture and how the architecture's components work together. In section 3 Model-Driven ScatterUnit, the framework's core, is presented. An in-depth examination of the evaluation of test case results, obtained after running the test case, can be found in section 4. The detection of a failure in the WSN leads to the question how the fault in the application code can be located. The answer can be found in section 5 where it is shown that Model-Driven ScatterUnit can be used to gradually locate the fault. This is the area, in which the model-driven approach really pays off. In section 6 the code generation process within the confines of the framework is discussed. In section 7 the case study's results are presented, before the paper is brought to a close with related work (section 8), our ongoing work (section 9) and the conclusion (section 10).

2 Architecture of the Framework

Initially we developed a test infrastructure called ScatterUnit, which allowed the automated testing of ScatterWeb applications and included component tests, tests of their integration and system tests. This test infrastructure is comparable to the JUnit for Java applications, which makes it possible to control the test run and follow the course of the test, in order to decide if the application failed or not.

Although ScatterUnit offers test automation in the desired manner, the implementation of test cases is still complex and time consuming. This is primarily because a test case must be conducted on distributed sensor nodes of the sensor network. Therefore the execution of the test case code must be coordinated, which demands code implemented especially for this purpose. In order to alleviate the user of implementing code for the coordination of test case execution, we supplemented ScatterUnit with Visual ScatterUnit, which allows the model-driven test case development. Unlike previously, where the user had to manually implement the test case code, the user can now model the course of the test run with the help of Visual ScatterUnit. Out of this test case model the code generator can then produce much of the test case code. After the user has manually implemented the missing parts he receives the necessary test case code, which can then be run with the help of ScatterUnit. Fig. 1 shows Visual ScatterUnit's architecture based on the activities, which are performed when ScatterUnit is used for the test case development:

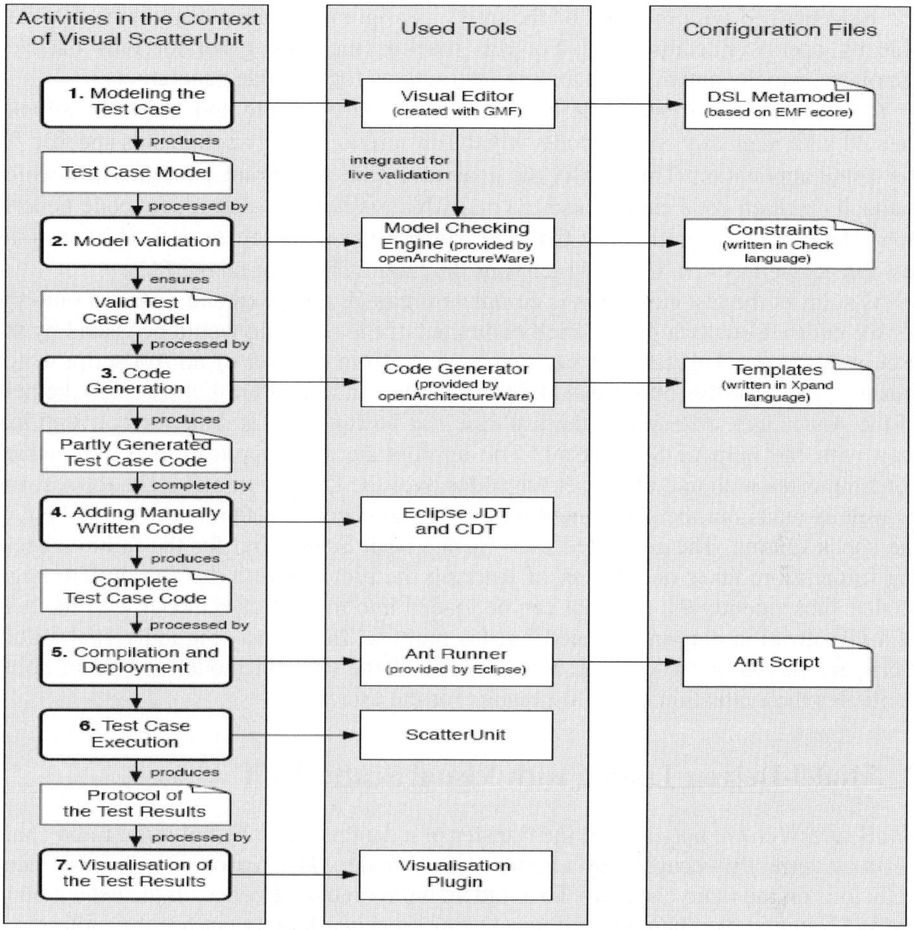

Fig. 1. Activities in the context of Visual ScatterUnit

First the user models the course of the test run with the help of a visual editor and a Domain Specific Language (DSL), which was especially created for the Visual ScatterUnit's purposes. This DSL was defined by a meta-model, which in turn was defined by an EMF [3] Ecore meta-meta-model. With the help of the Graphical Modeling Framework (GMF) we created the visual editor, which enables the test case modeling on basis of the DSL. The DSL resembles the activity diagrams of the UML notation, because it lends itself to modeling the course of the test run. During the test case modeling the model is already being validated with the help of openArchitectureWare's (oAW) [4] model checking engine. For this purpose with regard to the test case model specially written, constraints are used to evaluate. The constraints were written in the language Check [5], which is very similar to OCL. Individual constraints check for example if the model element is connected in a correct way.

Before code is generated from the test case model though, it is completely validated again just to ensure that that model is valid. If this is the case the test case code can be generated with the help of the freely configurable code generator made available by openArchitectureWare. For this purpose the code generator falls back on templates, which contain the necessary instructions for the code generation.

The generated test case code is however not yet complete and has to be supplemented with manually written code, which runs predominately commands specific for the tested application. This is why the generated code has protected regions, in which manually written code can be inserted and which is not lost after a new code generation. The user has to implement C-Code, which runs on the sensor node to control the test run, as well as Java Code, which runs the failure checking on the PC.

As soon as the test case code is complete it can be compiled and installed onto the sensor nodes. Usually a proper shell command of the makefile would be issued by the user at this stage. This task has been taken away from the user by an Ant script which was generated for this purpose, so that this script can run within Eclipse with the help of the Ant plugin. Afterwards the test case can be run. This is done the conventional way with the help of ScatterUnit. The appropriate Java application is run, which communicates with one of the sensor nodes over the COM port and starts the test run as well as reads out the subsequent protocols and checks for failures with the help of the check routine. The generated code from Visual ScatterUnit for the failure checking furthermore takes on the task of marking the protocol with the appropriate flags, so that subsequently the protocol can be loaded into the test case model with the help of a visualization plug-in designed for this purpose. In this way the individual failure alerts are shown at the corresponding points of the test run model and in so doing facilitates the evaluation of the test results for the user.

3 Model-Driven Testing with Visual ScatterUnit

For ScatterWeb we noticed that the transfer of a data packet may fail if the radio channel was currently occupied by another sensor node. (The reason may be too many collisions on the radio channel.) To avoid an unfavorable influence on the execution of the WSN application being tested, our testing framework must not use the radio channel too frequently. Thus we decided not to use a centralized but a decentralized approach [6] for our testing framework ScatterUnit, which meets the requirement to produce the least possible intrusion effect: To avoid sending commands over the radio channel each sensor node is configured with its own set of actions before the execution of a test case is started. Those actions may call a method of the application being tested, e.g. to send a data packet using the routing protocol. They may also simulate an event, e.g. to simulate sensory data input. And they may be used to start waiting for a specific event, e.g. to wait for the reception of a data packet on the radio channel. All actions which will be executed on the same sensor node are implemented by a node script which also knows when to execute them. To coordinate the actions executed on different sensor nodes, a command service is provided by ScatterUnit [7]. Sending commands for coordination is the only reason to use the radio channel for testing purposes while the test case is running. During the execution of the test case, all relevant events are logged on the sensor node where they occur. The radio channel is used to send the logs of all sensor nodes to a PC connected to the WSN only after the execution of the test case was terminated. The PC uses these logs to evaluate the behavior of the application being tested and to decide whether a failure occurred or not.

In order to be able to implement a test scenario easily we have to delegate the task to implement the code that coordinates the execution of the actions. For that we applied a model-driven approach to ScatterUnit, where we delegate this task to the code generator which generates the node scripts from a test case model whereas the test case model is a direct representation of the test scenario.

The crucial part of the model-driven approach we applied to ScatterUnit is the choice of those aspects of the test case that are to be modeled in an abstract way. We model a direct representation of the test scenario wherein the corresponding actions, their assignment to a sensor node on which they will be executed, and the order in which they are executed is modeled. Given this information, the code generator can do the job to generate the code for the node scripts. When modeling a test case with Model-Driven ScatterUnit, we start with a diagram like the one shown in Fig. 2. It depicts the course of the test scenario which tests a routing protocol. The notation is very similar to UML Activity Diagrams. It only differs regarding the activities: An activity represents a group of actions which serve a single purpose, e.g. changing the topology of the WSN. Furthermore, the interior of an activity shows which sensor nodes the represented actions are executed on. Thus, the diagram reads as follows: Once the test case is started, two activities are executed in parallel. Sensor node 1 sends the first data packet, and sensor node 4 waits for reception of that packet. After the packet has arrived, the topology of the WSN is changed. Then the second packet is sent from sensor node 1, while sensor node 4 waits for reception. If the data packet is received, the execution of the test case is terminated.

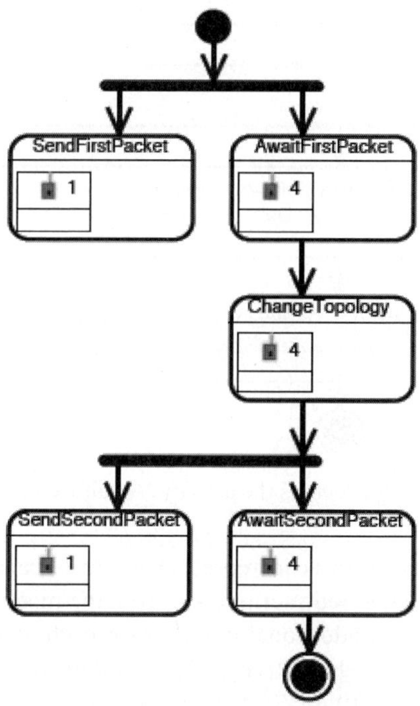

Fig. 2. Diagram that models the course of a test scenario to test a routing protocol

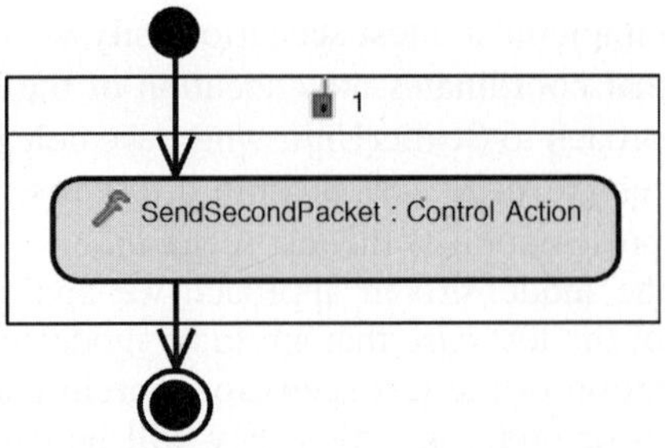

Fig. 3. Diagram that details the activity 'SendSecondPacket' in Fig. 2

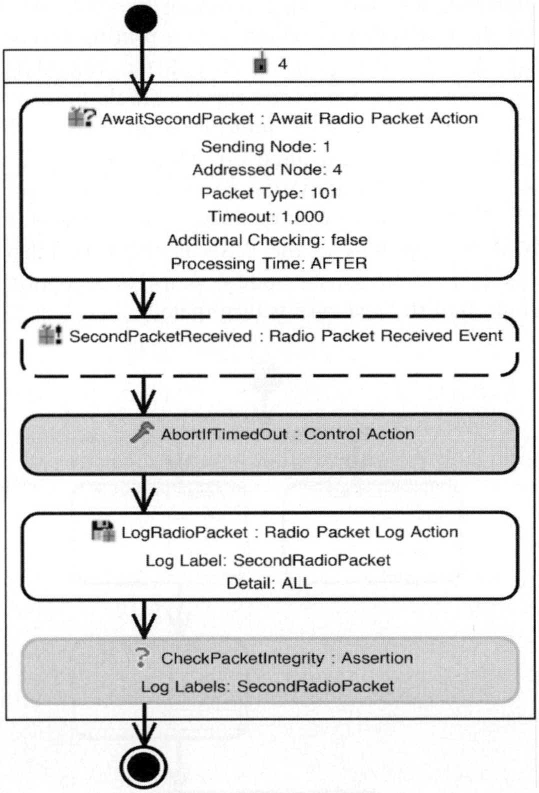

Fig. 4. Diagram that details the activity 'AwaitSecondPacket' in Fig. 2

The purpose of this diagram is to represent the test scenario in an intuitive way. But to be able to generate the node script code from the model, we have to fill in more detail. Therefore, we add an additional diagram for each activity that models the actions that are represented by the activity. Fig. 3 shows the diagram that models the actions represented by the activity `SendSecondPacket`. We actually see just one action with no further detail because manually written code will do the work. To send a data packet over the radio channel using the routing protocol – which is the application being tested – we have to prepare the data packet and call a method of the routing protocol to send the packet. This action is very specific to the application being tested. That is why this action has to be implemented manually. There would be no benefit in trying to model every action in a way that no manually written code is needed, because the work done by actions varies widely since we have a wide spectrum of WSN applications potentially being tested using ScatterUnit. Fig. 4 shows the diagram which models the actions represented by the activity `AwaitSecondPacket`:

First, the waiting service provided by ScatterUnit is asked to give a notification once the awaited data packet has been received. This notification is represented by the event `SecondPacketReceived`. Then follows the action `Abort-IfTimedOut` for which we manually implement code to abort the execution of the test case in case the data packet was not received and the waiting job timed out. (Actions which are implemented manually are indicated by a gray background). If no timeout occurred, we actually received the data packet which is logged by the action `LogRadioPacket`. Referring to this data packet by using the log label `SecondRadioPacket`, we check its integrity with the assertion `CheckPacketIntegrity`. Assertions are executed after the execution of the test case is terminated and analyze the log accumulated during the execution in order to check for failures of the application being tested. Since those assertions are application specific, they are manually implemented as well, i.e. we check if the payload of the data packet was corrupted during transmission.

The code generated from the test case model for maintaining the execution order is called infrastructure code because this code is needed in order to write a test case on the ScatterUnit platform. This technical term is used in the context of architecture-centric model-driven software development (AC-MDSD [8]), which we applied to ScatterUnit: The main purpose of code generation is to generate infrastructure code – for coordination, that is – which is required by the platform, in this case ScatterUnit. As a result, the user can focus on the design of the test scenario rather than having to spend valuable development time on writing infrastructure code which is a complex and time-consuming task. Apart from infrastructure code for coordination purposes, we also enabled the generation of infrastructure code that is needed to evaluate and analyze the test results, which is discussed in the next section.

4 Analyzing the Test Results

After the execution of a test case is terminated, we get a log of all relevant events that have been observed while the test case was running. This log is then analyzed by routines which each check for a certain failure in order to decide whether the WSN application being tested failed or not. Those routines are represented by assertions in the test case model.

To run a routine that checks for a specific failure, we have to accomplish two tasks: First, during the execution of the test case, the data must be logged that indicates the absence or the presence of the failure we look at. Second, after the execution of the test case is terminated, the corresponding log entries must be picked out of the log in order to analyze them. We log the required data by adding log actions to the test case model, i.e. the log action `LogRadioPacket`. To have the corresponding log entries right at hand when implementing a routine to check for a certain failure, log labels are used, i.e. the log action `LogRadioPacket` declares the log label `SecondRadioPacket`, which is referenced by the assertion `CheckPacket-Integrity`. Thus, we do not have to implement code for picking the required log entries out of the log, because this can be done by the code generator which processes the log labels in the test case model. Altogether we accumulate the following test results: Failures reported by assertions, a failure which is indicated by aborting the execution of the test case (e.g. by the action `AbortIfTimedOut`), and the data that has been logged by log actions. To facilitate the reading of these test results, we incorporated them into the diagrams of the test case model.

The diagram in Fig. 5 incorporates the test results indicating the failure reported by the assertion `CheckPacketIntegrity`. This failure is shown by the lightning icon in the lower left of the assertion. The tooltip of that icon prints: "The payload of the data packet was corrupted." Additionally, the icon in the lower left of the log action `LogRadioPacket` indicates the logged data.

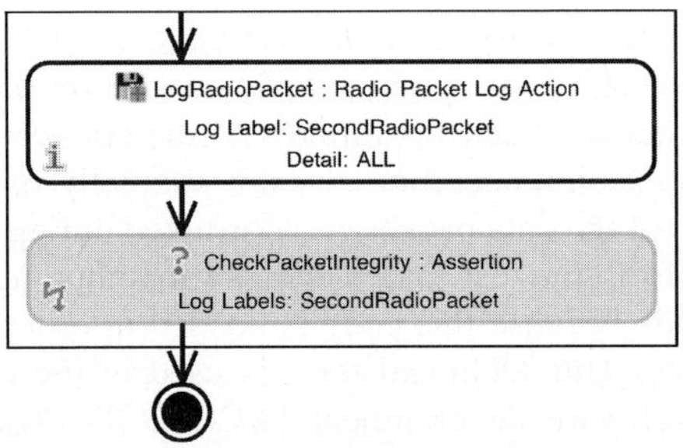

Fig. 5. Test results incorporated into the diagram by adding icons to the lower left of the actions

The tooltip of that icon prints the data of the data packet. Thus, the test results are easily accessible in the diagrams, because each piece of information is assigned to a corresponding action in the test case model. Without the incorporation of the test results, the user would have to read a textual log which is a difficult and time-consuming task. The improved readability of the test results also makes it easier and less time-consuming to use log actions to get insights on the cause of a reported failure. This is beneficial in case a bug is detected in the code of the application being tested.

5 Detecting Bugs in the Application Being Tested

After we detected a failure by executing a test case, our next step is to fix the bug within the application being tested which caused it to fail. But before we can correct the application code, we have to locate the bug. In general we do this by gradually isolating its code location until we can pinpoint the bug. The process of detecting a bug is a very demanding cognitive task where hypotheses about the cause of a failure are suggested and verified iteratively [9]. To do this, we need to gather information on the behavior of the erroneous application. Actually, information can be gathered by adding log actions to the test case model, which logs the needed information. Thus, we refine the test case model in order to get more insight on the cause of the failure reproduced by the test case. But what does the complete picture of the debugging process look like?

When using Model-Driven ScatterUnit, the task to detect a bug can be done as depicted in Fig. 6. First, we examine the test results which are incorporated into the test case diagrams. On the basis of the available information on the behavior of the application being tested, we can suggest new hypotheses on the cause of the failure. Then we refine the Test Case to be able to verify our hypotheses. After we execute the test case we examine the test results again and evaluate the correctness of our hypotheses. If we cannot pinpoint the bug yet, we refine our hypotheses or suggest new ones and iterate again. For example, we execute our test case which tests the routing protocol (see Fig. 2). When we examine the test results, we may get to know that the second data packet was not received. We suggest the hypothesis that the packet was forwarded to the wrong intermediate node. Thus, we want to know on which route it was forwarded. Thereto we refine the test case by adding additional activities to the test case model which observe on which intermediate node the data packet is forwarded (see Fig. 7).

The activities `AssertForwarding` and `AssertNoForwarding` both wait for the data packet which may be forwarded on sensor node 2 or 3. After we execute the refined test case and examine the test results we can verify our hypothesis which proves valid if a failure was reported. Since the obtained information is not sufficient to pinpoint the bug we have to refine the test case again and so on.

Model-Driven ScatterUnit eases the focused detection of bugs by incorporating the test results into the test case diagrams and by allowing to refine the test case model easily – as needed to gather information to suggest and verify hypotheses on the cause of the failure. The main benefit of the model-driven approach lies in the need to refine the test case model many times when detecting a bug: If we insert a new action into the test case, we have to alter the order of the existing actions. This involves altering the infrastructure code for coordinating the execution of the node scripts. The same applies for the infrastructure code needed to evaluate the test results.

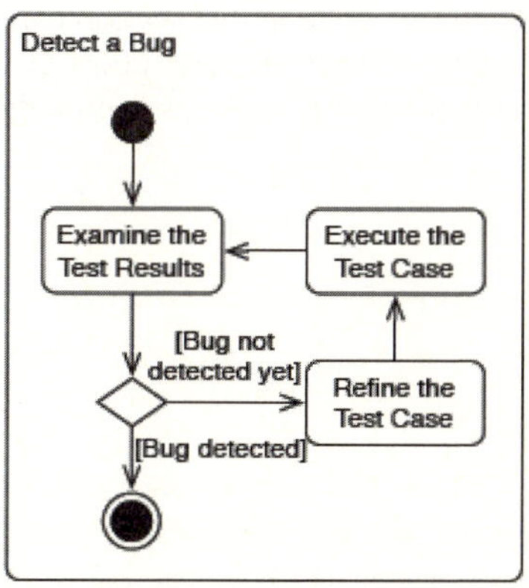

Fig. 6. The proposed debugging process

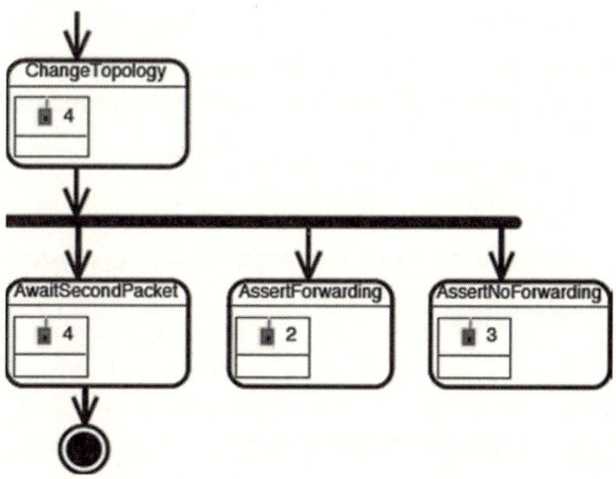

Fig. 7. Revision of the test case shown in Fig. 2 with additional activities to assert the correct forwarding of the data packet

6 The Code Generation Process

The template language XPand, which is used to give generation instructions to the oAW code generator, offers many possibilities for a comfortable code generation. There is one thing the language does not offer: the termination of the code generation. This function would be helpful, if it was established during the generation that no usable code could be generated from the model it was based on. Actually the function is missing on purpose, as it is assumed that all relevant interconnections had already been checked during the validation, so that the subsequent code generation will in any case result in usable code.

The separation of concerns, on the one hand the model validation and on the other the translation of the model into code, significantly facilitates the implementation of generation instructions. For example code is generated for a thread by traversing the activity diagram from the source vertex to the destination vertex. This procedure during the test case generation assumes that the thread diagram always consists of exactly one source vertex, one destination vertex and a certain number of instructions. Furthermore it is assumed that the diagram elements are connected in a linear succession or in other words the connections do not create any branches or circles. Only if these assumptions are conformed to, the code generation can take place. That is why the model validation checks before the code generation, whether the given test case model complies with these assumptions. If this is not the case, then the code generation is not started. Thus a thread diagram can be traversed without having to take into account the danger of creating a potential circle with connections, which would lead to infinite loop.

Generally speaking the commands of the test case have to be manually implemented, as their implementation is very dependant on the tested application. Therefore, one has to create the part, which can be generated, and then amend the remaining code regarding the instructions. If the test case code is subsequently modified and re-generated, as often shown in the example of the fault localisation, manually written code is inevitably lost, as the existing source code is overwritten. Naturally the manually written code should be maintained. In order to carry over the already manually written code to newly generated code, the oAW generator offers the possibility of using protected regions:

A region in the generated code, in which the manually written code should be inserted, is labelled in the appropriate way, so that the manually written code in this section can be buffered before re-generating the code and then inserting it into the new code in the correct section. The generated code with its manual implementation, looks as following:

```
// ControlAction InitNode1
bool bAbortTestCaseExecution = False;

/*PROTECTED REGION ID(MovingReceiverTestCase_Init_InitNode1) ENABLED START*/

DSDV_init();

/*PROTECTED REGION END*/

if (bAbortTestCaseExecution) {
    Test_abort(0);
    return;
}
```

Listing 1. Protected regions for manually written code

Manually implemented code is inserted in the correct section. Accordingly only code modifications made between such areas are maintained. The code generator still does not have any influence on the protected regions's content. Accordingly the generated code's structure has to be suitably chosen, so that it can interact with the manually implemented code. As can be seen above, the code for the test run's termination (lines 10-13) should only be executed, if it is needed by the code within the protected region. This essential interaction between the generated and the manually implemented code is made possible with the help of a Boolean variable (line 2), so that the interaction between the two code types is distinctly separated. In order to ensure the quality of both the generated code and the test case, the test case model is checked with regard to its syntactic and semantic rules in the form of constraints. This happens not only before the code of the test case model is generated, but also during the modeling of the test case and is called therefore "Live-Validation". As the model validation is run with the help of openArchitectureWare and as the visual editor was created with the help of the Graphical Modeling Framework, the components are combined with the help of the GMF2 Adapters to enable Live-Validation. For this purpose the visual editor embeds the GMF2 adapter, which allows access to the oAW's model checking engine. This is repeatedly called to validate the test case model, which is momentarily being edited, based on the constraints. Fig. 8 shows Visual ScatterUnit's Architecture regarding the Live-Validation.

For instance, the command names used in the generated code's method names are not allowed to contain any special characters, so that the code can be compiled. A large number of syntactic rules can be compiled, but the true use of model validation unfurls when checking for semantic rules. For instance as it is defined that a test case model models a course of the test case, it is therefore sensible to check (see Fig. 9), if the test case model consists of a linear sequence of commands:

```
context testcase::ControlPath
      ERROR "A control path must have one incoming link."
:
      this.incoming.size == 1;

context testcase::ControlPath
      ERROR "A control path must have at maximum one out-
going link." :
      this.outgoing.size <= 1;
```

Overall the model validation secures the quality of the executable test case and increases with it the robustness of the test case development. Furthermore the Live-Validation shows mistakes during the test case modeling, so that the user can correct them in a timely fashion.

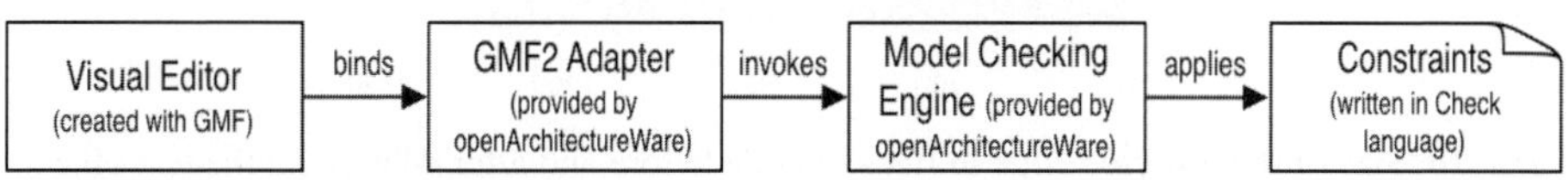

Fig. 8. Visual ScatterUnit's Architecture regarding the Live-Validation

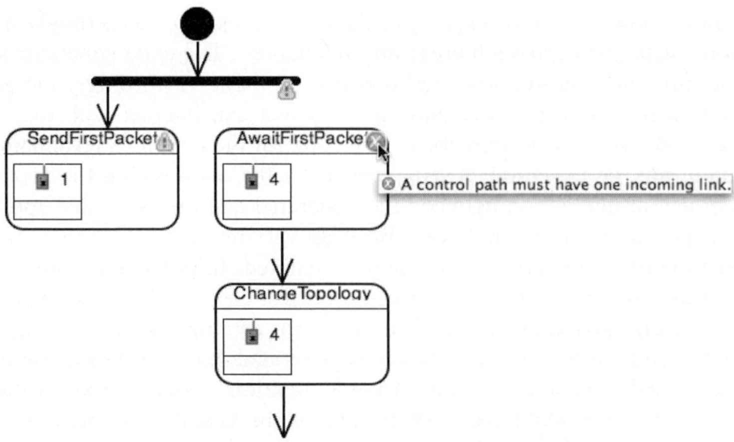

Fig. 9. Live-Validation detected a control path with no predecessor

7 Case Study

One person tested an implementation of the DSDV routing protocol by applying the test case shown in fig. 2. It took him half an hour to model the test case, add manually written code, and execute it. Fig. 10 indicates in the row before that only 5% of the test case code had to be written manually. The first execution of the test case unveiled that the routing protocol failed to send the first packet. Thus the person – who was unfamiliar with the actual implementation of the routing protocol – proceeded by using the procedure to detect bugs proposed in this paper (see Fig. 6). That took nine hours until the test case was executed without reporting a failure. Altogether he found four bugs. Two of them caused a non-deterministic behavior of the routing protocol and therefore were hard to detect. Fig. 10 shows that the size of the test case grew by nearly 60% whereas the size of the manually written code remained small. If one calculates the effort needed for the construction of a test case model, which is marginal, into the equation, then one receives a powerful test case implementation with little effort. A further advantage results by virtue of the large portion of generated code: The generated portion of the code is used mainly for the coordination of the test case execution. This code ensures that the actions are executed in the correct order. This sequence can be modeled in the test case model in a clear and understandable manner, so that bugs during the sequence modeling are unlikely.

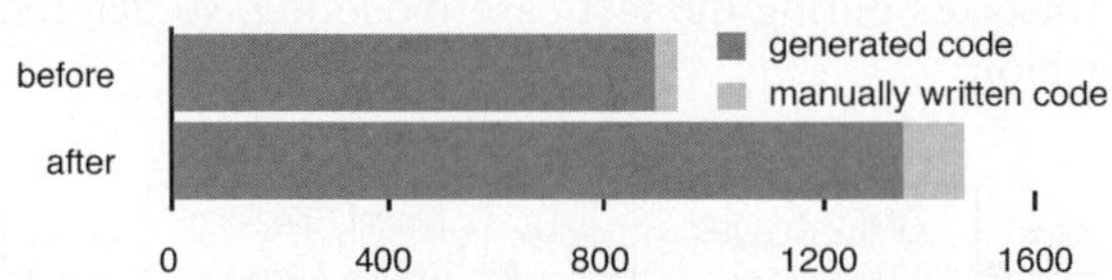

Fig. 10. Size of the test case code in lines of code before and after debugging the test object

However if the same code had been written manually, then a bug would be more probable. Such a bug results in the test case being defect, which is highly undesirable. This is why the use of a model-driven test environment gives a certain robustness against bugs made during the development of the test case. The model validation also makes a large contribution towards robustness by discovering certain bugs early on, which, if manually implemented, would only be discovered very late in the process.

8 Related Work

MoteLab [10], developed at Harvard University, is a web based test environment for sensor network consisting of a web interface, a database, a logger and a so-called job daemon. The user can use the test environment by registering a job. Within a job some of the network's nodes are then assigned tasks, which the user needs for test purposes. TWIST [11], developed at the TU Berlin, is a testbed for WSNs, which is also based entirely on open source components. It offers several helpful features including node configuration, network-wide programming and further complex features like power supply control of nodes. However for the use of TWIST so-called super nodes as communication interface/layer between the testbed and the WSN are necessary. Thereby every super node is connected with a corresponding USB2.0 HUB. Then the normal WSN nodes can be connected via cable with any such HUB, whereby the connection or rather communication can be achieved. The increase in hardware requirements and wiring worsens the system's scalability and costs in terms of the test process.

SeNeTs [12] is also a related testing infrastructure for WSN Applications. A base station sends commands to the nodes in the network – e.g. to initiate sending the data packet – and the nodes send information on all relevant events back to the base station, i.e. where the route the data packet took is reconstructed. We cannot afford to establish a resource-demanding communication between a base station and the sensor nodes as SeNeTs does. To avoid an unfavorable influence on the execution of the WSN application being tested, our testing framework must not use the radio channel too frequently. Thus we decided not to use a centralized but a decentralized approach as discussed in section four.

None of the above mentioned works support an automated test process for WSN applications. This is why our framework is novel, as it combines the model-driven paradigm with a visual test process. Other model-driven projects for WSN, like [13], [14], confine themselves either to simulation or programming of WSN applications. A visual automated test process with just in time model validation has not yet come into consideration.

9 Ongoing Work

We did not consider before that the sensor nodes participating in a test scenario may run different instances of the WSN application being tested. For example, we may want to test a WSN application with the purpose of collecting sensory data over a long period of time. Not all sensor nodes may have storage to save the data. Thus, we need two different application instances: One for sensor nodes that do not have storage and therefore transmit the collected data to a neighboring sensor node with storage available. And one application instance for sensor nodes with storage available which stores the received data. The runtime for the first application instance must provide drivers for the sensors, and the runtime for the second one must provide storage access.

ScatterFactory [15] is a tool we developed to configure the runtime of each application instance in a model-driven manner. ScatterFactory produces a complete, model-driven, architecture centric, generative infrastructure beginning from an essential MOF conformed meta-meta model all the way to the generating of C-Code for a MSP430- processor on our sensor boards. The ScatterFactory framework was completed with additional components like assistants or flash-components for the automatic deployment of generated artifacts in an existing network. The goal is the furthermost automated and standardized production of software system families for the ScatterWeb sensor boards.

In a diagram, the different runtimes – consisting of hardware drivers, libraries, etc. – are tailored to the needs of the application. We integrated ScatterFactory with Model-Driven Visual ScatterUnit to consider the different application instances in the context of a test case. Therefore, each sensor node specified in the test case model is associated with an application instance, which in particular allows that test cases are able to be reused within software families. Without a doubt the modeled associations between application instances and test cases increases the productivity of the testing process, because the user no longer has to concern himself that the sensor node's required software, consisting of node script, application instance and libraries, is assembled with the right combination.

The integration of both tools is an example of our ongoing research to create tools [16], [17] that support the development of WSN applications on our WSN-platform ScatterWeb. A screencast of Visual ScatterUnit can be found in [18].

10 Conclusion

Considering how the execution of the node scripts is coordinated, the task to distribute the actions of a test scenario among the node scripts and to coordinate their execution can be delegated to the code generator. Due to this task delegation, the test case implementation process becomes more efficient. The benefits become apparent during the proposed visual and automated debugging process in Visual ScatterUnit: When refining the test case model iteratively, the person writing the test case would have to rewrite the infrastructure code of the test case many times if the model-driven approach was not applied. Since the code generator can rewrite the infrastructure code automatically, significant time for refining the test case is saved.

To sum up, several tasks of implementing a test case and detecting a bug are delegated to the code generator. This is beneficial because these tasks are complex and time-consuming. Rather than performing these tasks himself, the user who tests a WSN application can concentrate on more important matters: Regarding the implementation that is the design of the test scenario; in case of the detection of a bug, that is the decision on an appropriate refinement of the test case to verify a hypothesis.

A contribution that could be of general interest is our approach to incorporate the test results into formal models in the context of the Model-Driven paradigm. In so doing models are enhanced with the results of the test process, a method which is practical in other domains as well.

References

1. ScatterWeb, http://scatterweb.mi.fu-berlin.de
2. Schiller, J., Liers, A., Ritter, H.: Scatterweb: A wireless sensornet platform for research and teaching. Computer Communications 28, 1545–1551 (2005)
3. GMF, http://www.eclipse.org/gmf
4. OAW, http://www.openarchitectureware.org
5. Check language, http://www.eclipse.org/gmt/oaw/doc/4.1/r30_checkReference.pdf
6. Ulrich, A.W., Zimmerer, P., Chrobok-Diening, G.: Test architectures for testing distributed systems. In: Proc. of Quality Week (1999)
7. Rafiq, O., Cacciari, L.: Coordination algorithm for distributed testing. The Journal of Supercomputing 24, 203–211 (2003)
8. Stahl, T., Voelter, M.: Model-Driven Software Development: Technology, Engineering, Management. Wiley, Chichester (2006)
9. Xu, S., Rajlich, V.: Cognitive process during program debugging. In: Proc. of the Third IEEE International Conference on Cognitive Informatics (ICCI 2004), pp. 176–182 (2004)
10. Werner-Allen, G., Swieskowski, P., Welsh, M.: MoteLab: A wireless sensor network testbed. In: Proc. of the Forth International Conference. Information Processing in Sensor Networks (IPSN 2005) (2005)
11. Handziski, V., Köpke, A., Willig, A., Wolisz, A.: TWIST: A Scalable and Reconfigurable Testbed for Wireless Indoor Experiments with Sensor Networks. In: Proc. of the Second International Workshop on. Multi-hop Ad Hoc Networks (REALMAN 2006) (2006)
12. Blumenthal, J., Handy, M., Timmermann, D.: SeNeTs – test and validation environment for applications in large-scale wireless sensor networks. In: Proc. of the 2nd IEEE International Conference on Industrial Informatics, pp. 69–73 (2004)
13. Sadilek, D.A.: Prototyping Domain-Specific Languages for Wireless Sensor Networks. In: Proc. of the 4th Int. Workshop on Software Language Engineering (ATEM 2007) (2007)
14. Losilla, F., Vicente-Chicote, C., Álvarez, B., Iborra, A., Sánchez, P.: Wireless Sensor Network Application Development: An Architecture-Centric MDE Approach. In: Oquendo, F. (ed.) ECSA 2007. LNCS, vol. 4758, pp. 179–194. Springer, Heidelberg (2007)
15. Al Saad, M., Hentrich, B., Schiller, J.: Scatterfactory: An Architecture Centric Framework for Wireless Sensor Networks. In: Proc. of the International Conference on New Technologies, Mobility and Security, pp. 12–31. Springer, Heidelberg (2007)
16. Al Saad, M., Ding, J., Schiller, J.: Scattereditor: An Eclipse Based Tool for Programming, Testing and Managing Wireless Sensor Networks. In: Proc. of the International Conference on Sensor Technologies and Applications, pp. 59–68. IEEE Computer Soceity Press, Los Alamitos (2007)
17. Al Saad, M., Leszek, M., Schiller, J.: Scatterplug: A Plug-in Oriented Framework for Prototyping, Programming and Teaching Wireless Sensor Networks. In: Proc. of the 2nd Int. Conference on Systems and Networks Communications, pp. 37–46. IEEE Computer Soceity Press, Los Alamitos (2007)
18. http://page.mi.fu-berlin.de/saad/ScatterClipse/Video_VisualScatterUnit/VisualScatterUnit.htm

Aspect-Oriented Model Weaving Beyond Model Composition and Model Transformation*

Pablo Sánchez[1], Lidia Fuentes[1], Dominik Stein[2], Stefan Hanenberg[2], and Rainer Unland[2]

[1] Universidad de Málaga
{pablo,lff}@lcc.uma.es
[2] Universität Duisburg-Essen
{dominik.stein,stefan.hanenberg,
rainer.unland}@icb.uni-due.de

Abstract. Research in Aspect-Oriented Software Development (AOSD) has brought up powerful abstractions in order to specify under which conditions an aspect affects the base software. So far, Model-Driven Development (MDD) approaches to AOSD have mostly concentrated on the weaving process and, as a result, they have come up with manifold ways to compose aspect models and base models. All too often, however, the approaches disregard the benefits that the aspect-oriented abstractions can bring to software development, though. This paper discusses the implications that such negligence has on the specification of aspect-oriented models in MDD. Furthermore, it presents a weaver that is able to cope with sophisticated join point selection abstractions, as they are known from many aspect-oriented programming languages, and which go far beyond the selection capabilities provided by current model weavers. By means of this weaver, models can realize both a higher separation of concerns as well as a higher level of abstraction.

1 Introduction

Aspect-Oriented Modeling (AOM) basically entails the modeling of base and aspectual entities and the definition of a process for weaving or composing them. Different approaches for defining aspects at the modeling level and different weaving processes have been proposed recently, most of them relying on Model-Driven Development (MDD) technologies [11, 19, 12, 9]. One of the goals of MDD is the systematic use of models, where models are refined by means of automatic model transformations until a running system is obtained. Model transformations are often used to add certain infrastructure elements such as persistence or distribution to a base or business model. These infrastructure elements are usually considered to represent aspectual entities.

Therefore, at first glance, aspect-oriented weaving could be seen as a special case of model-to-model transformation. Examples of approaches that follow this idea are

* This work has been partially supported by MCYT Project TIN2005-09405-C02-01 and EC Grants IST-2-004349-NOE AOSD and IST-033710 AMPLE.

K. Czarnecki et al. (Eds.): MoDELS 2008, LNCS 5301, pp. 766–781, 2008.

MATA [11] or xWeave [9], among others. In these approaches, an aspect is considered as a kind of graph transformation rule, where the pointcut plays the role of Left-Hand Side (LHS) pattern, and the advice the role of Right-Hand Side (RHS) pattern. This has allowed a smooth transition of aspect-oriented concepts from the implementation level to the design level, and has permitted developers to use the mechanisms of model-driven techniques to solve inherent problems of aspect-oriented technologies. For instance, Critical Pair Analysis (CPA) of graph-transformation languages can be applied to detect conflicts caused by aspect interactions [11]. Thus, MDD and AOM seem to be similar technologies pursuing similar goals.

Nevertheless, an extensive body of research in aspect-orientation is concerned with finding suitable mechanisms for specifying the conditions under which an aspect must be executed, i.e. the specification of pointcuts. Examples of these advances are Data-flow Pointcuts [13], Path Expression Pointcuts [2], Tracematches [1], among others (e.g. [10, 17]). A thorough analysis of the approaches that combine MDD and AOM reveals that they rarely consider these kinds of mechanisms for defining expressive join point selections at the modeling level. As a consequence, more advanced pointcuts which express more sophisticated join point selections can not be easily modeled in these approaches: The designer needs to explicitly split these kinds of pointcuts into several subaspects, where each one implements just a small fragment of the pointcut. This can lead to scalability and maintenance problems.

This paper presents a novel aspect-oriented model weaver that overcomes these consequences by recognizing and adopting the advancements of aspect-oriented research regarding the specification of complex pointcuts. Complex pointcuts can be expressed at the modeling level using Join Point Designation Diagrams (JPDDs; [21, 20]). JPDDs have been presented in the aspect-oriented community as a powerful modeling notation for sophisticated join point selections. Our aspect-oriented model weaver accepts a JPDD model as input and automatically generates a set of model transformations which add the JPDD semantics to the base model.

The striking benefit of this approach is that the input models turn out to be more concise, and focus on the actual problem (i.e. are more "problem-oriented"). This is because the abstractions provided by JPDDs effectively hide away much of the weaving complexity, which is automatically generated by the aspect-oriented model weaver. This is why we consider aspect-oriented weaving to go beyond conventional model transformations and model composition: It allows developers to specify transformation rules at a higher level of abstraction.

The remainder of this paper is structured as follows: Section 2 describes the motivation for the paper. Section 3 explains how dynamic join point selections can be modeled with JPDDs. Section 4 describes how JPDD can be woven to executable UML models. Section 5 outlines why the proposed approach solves the problem. Section 6 comments on related work and Section 7 concludes the paper.

2 Problem Statement

In this section, we illustrate the drawbacks that a lack of suitable abstractions for expressing dynamic join point selections can have on the specification of aspect-oriented models. Firstly, we describe the motivating example which is used throughout this paper, and which is used to identify the shortcomings of current AOM approaches. Finally, we outline our solution, which is described with more detail in the subsequent sections.

2.1 An Online Book Store System

Let us consider an online shop[1] which – in conjuction with a local bank – issues credit cards. Let us also assume the marketing department has designed a seasonal offer for promoting credit cards. During the check out process, an advertisement is displayed to customers, offering a 10% rebate if they apply for a new credit card. This rebate shall be granted only if a customer applies for the credit card during the check out process at the moment when the advertisement is shown. If the customer applies for a new Credit Card before or after the checkout process (without reading the advertisement), the marketing department argues that the customer would have applied for the credit card anyway and no special "teaser" or promotion is needed. Also, the rebate shall only be granted on immediate purchases with that newly issued credit card (i.e. on the items contained in the shopping cart at checkout time).

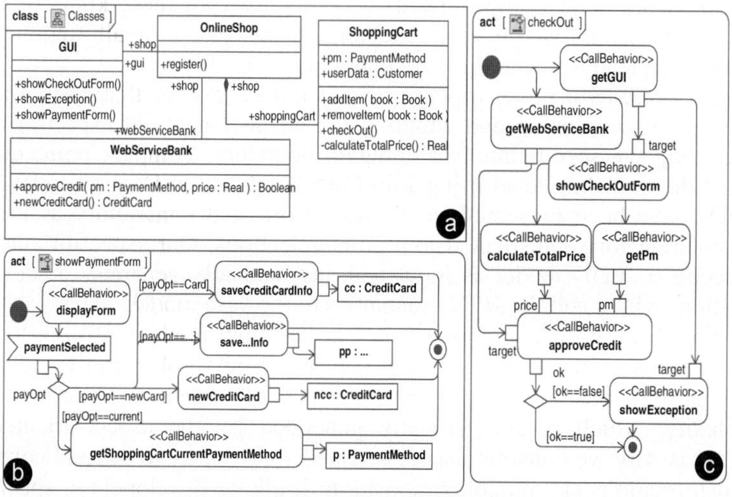

Fig. 1. (a) class diagram of the Online Book Store, (b) activity diagram of method `showPaymentForm`, (c) activity diagram of method `checkOut`.

Business rules like this have been identified to be a case for aspect-orientation [4, 18]. Moreover, this is a temporary modification, or volatile requirement [16], which will be removed again as soon as the promotion period ends. So, we decide to handle this business rule with help of an aspect.

Fig. 1 (top left) shows part of the class diagram for the application we are going to consider in the following. Basically, the model has an `OnlineShop` class which maintains `ShoppingCart` objects to store customers' orders. It has a `GUI` class, which encapsulates the logic for interacting with the user; and a `WebServiceBank`

[1] This example is based on an example presented in [15] and [6].

class that supplies credit cards and charges them. The detailed behavior of each method is described using UML activities and actions.

Fig. 1 (right) depicts the detailed behavior of the `checkOut` method. First, the `showCheckOutForm` method of the `GUI` class is invoked. This method collects some data from the customer, such as the payment method to be used for this purchase. To do so, the `showPaymentForm` method is invoked, depicted in Fig. 1 (left bottom). In that method, the user can choose from multiple payment methods, which are then stored (by the `showCheckOutForm` method) in the `pm` attribute of the `ShoppingCart`. The `checkOut` method obtains that `pm` object from the `ShoppingCart`, the total price is calculated and the `approveCredit` operation of the `WebServiceBank` is invoked. If the bank confirms the charge, the check out ends sucessfully; otherwise a message communicating the incident is shown to the user.

In the next subsection we show the complexity of adding the business rule to this model using current transformation-based AOM approaches.

2.2 Modeling the Business Rule with Transformation-Based AOM Technologies

An aspect that applies a discount to the total price of the shopping cart before requesting an `approveCredit` can be easily modeled using a model transformation-based AOM approach. Using an ad-hoc notation inspired in MATA [11], it could be expressed as depicted in Fig. 2. The model snippet on the left plays the role of pointcut and the model snippet on the right the role of advice. According to the semantics, whenever the pattern on the left is found in the model, it is replaced by the model snippet on the right, in a similar way to graph-transformation rules.

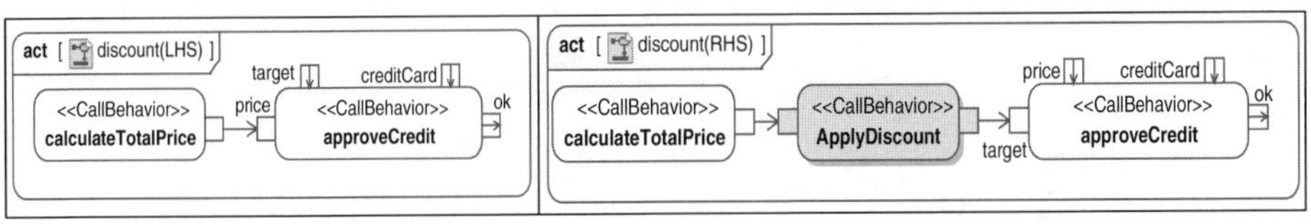

Fig. 2. Simple aspect for adding a discount to the Online Book Store

However, an aspect as depicted in Fig. 2 is not enough for modeling the business rule described in the previous section. The challenge of realizing this business rule is to ensure that the customer has applied for the credit card at the right time. Hence, before granting the 10% discount, it needs to be checked: (1) the customer has applied for a new credit card during the check out process; and (2) the newly obtained credit card must be used to pay for the current purchase. These constraints can not be easily checked using model transformation-based aspects, because they need to use some information that is not available until runtime.

An ad-hoc solution would be to set/unset flags to indicate if these dynamic conditions are satisfied. We show in Fig. 3 the set of model transformations/aspects that need to be specified for realizing the business rule. We show only the advice parts, with the modifications shown with gray background. The pointcut parts would be similar (without the modifications).

First, we need to modify the `checkOut` method so that it sets/unsets a flag at the beginning/end of its execution which indicates that it is currently being executed (Fig. 3, top). This flag is evaluated by means of another model transformation, which controls whether or not the customer has completed the request of a new credit card. This is achieved by modifying the `showPaymentForm` method for setting a `discountEnabled` flag (Fig. 3, middle (a)). Furthermore, this method needs to be modified so that the newly issued credit card is also stored – in order to verify that this card is used later on to pay for the purchase (Fig. 3, middle (b)). Then, before applying the discount, we need to check whether the `newCreditCard` method has been called previously (by evaluating the `discountEnabled` flag) and also if the credit card being used for payment is the newly created credit card (Fig. 3, bottom (a)). Finally, we need to modify the `checkOut` procedure again for unsetting the `discountEnabled` flag once the check out process has ended (Fig. 3, bottom (b)). Otherwise, the discount would apply for a future purchase, as well.

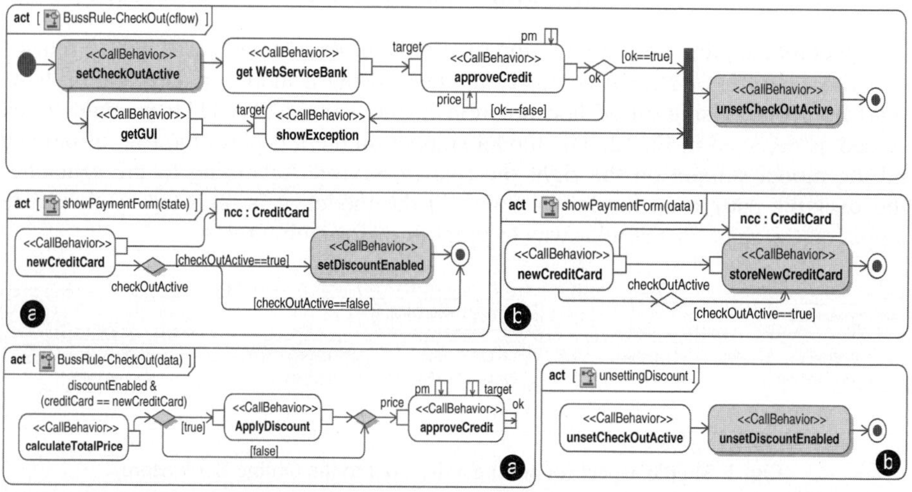

Fig. 3. Realizing the business rule with conventional model transformation approaches[2]

2.3 Conclusion So Far...

Summarizing, in order to model the business rule with transformation-based AOM approaches, multiple transformation steps must be carried out, which are concerned with selecting the points in the base model (called *join point shadows* in aspect-oriented terminology [14]) at which the dynamic constraints of the pointcut need to be evaluated. Furthermore, additional transformation steps are needed to select those points in the base model at which the information required for that evaluation is collected. As already shown, each transformation step would be encapsulated in an

[2] Some (but not all) of these transformations could be aggregated to a single one; the problem of maintaining flags and temporary data remains, though.

aspect/model transformation rule. It should be noticed however that when considering each individual transformation step separately nothing indicates that they belong to a logically related set of transformations. As a result, it is hard to recognize the meaning of a transformation step when it is considered in isolation (e.g. it is hard to understand why it is necessary to activate a flag upon entering the `checkOut` method and why it needs to be deactivated again upon its termination).

Thus, with transformation-based approaches, the designer would need to deal with a set of tangled and highly coupled aspects/model transformation rules, which might be hard to understand, maintain and evolve. For instance, a slight modification in the business rule would imply a review and update of the complex chain of flag setting and unsetting described previously. What designers would like to have, though, are suitable abstractions that permit them to abstract such details, and instead concentrate on the modeling of the actual concern, i.e. a business rule in this case.

3 Modeling Dynamic Join Point Selections

The weaver which is presented in this paper (see next section) uses Join Point Designation Diagrams (JPDDs; [21, 20]). JPDDs have been introduced as a general method of expressing queries on software artifacts. As such, they provide sophisticated abstractions that can be used to solve the problem outlined in the previous section.

JPDDs are accepted as input by our aspect-oriented model weaver, which processes it, generates and executes all the modifications/transformations that are required for weaving the JPDD into the base model. The basic idea is that the aspect-oriented model weaver automatically generates a set of model transformations as described previously. These generated model transformations would monitor control flow conditions, constraints on data, and so forth, as specified by the JPDD. Hence, the designer is not forced to manually create the complex chain of model transformations previously described. Instead, these transformations would be generated automatically by the weaver, which then applies them to the base model generating the woven model. As usual in aspect-orientation, the designer does not need to deal with the woven model. In the case where s/he would need to change something, s/he would do it on the JPDD or on the base model, and afterwards the aspect-oriented model would be rewoven. Thus, all the details about setting and unsetting flags would be hidden from the designer, who can then work at a higher abstraction level.

3.1 Join Point Designation Diagrams (JPDDs)

In this section, we will give a brief introduction to JPDDs. While doing so, we focus on the very necessary details of JPDDs which are necessary to understand the remainder of the text. A more in-depth description of JPDDs can be found at [21].

JPDDs are a Profile to UML which can be used to specify queries on UML models. JPDDs also provide a diagrammatic notation based on the symbols of the UML. This diagrammatic notation helps to render queries expressed by means of JPDDs. Fig. 4 shows an overview of the new symbols introduced by JPDDs.

The first JPDD-specific means are so-called identifiers, which are used to designate particular elements within a JPDD (e.g. `<?cc>` or `<?price>`): Identifiers (enclosed in angle brackets and preceded by a question mark) may be used to denote that two elements in different parts of the JPDD are supposed to represent the same entity (e.g. `<?cc>`), as well as to list elements in the output parameter box of a JPDD (e.g. `<?price>`). The output parameter box of a JPDD denotes those elements that can be referred to and/or modified (e.g. by an aspect-oriented advice). The output parameter box of a JPDD is located in its bottom right corner (as illustrated in the bottom right corner of Fig. 4). Apart form that, deviation means can be used to relax the selection criteria of a JPDD. For example, indirect relationships can be used in order to denote that two elements may be indirectly related to each other by a path (e.g. along the call graph (—//—▶)) as opposed to being immediate neighbors. A multiplicity attached to the indirection symbol of such relationships may restrict the number of edges that may/must be traversed along that path. Furthermore, deviations of element names may be specified with help of regular expressions. For example, it may be specified that the sender of a method is of arbitrary type (see sender of `newCreditCard` in Fig. 4). Moreover, a special dot-dot-wildcard (`..`) may be used to abstract from an arbitrary number of parameters in a parameter list (see `newCreditCard` operation in Fig. 4).

3.2 Modeling the Motivating Business Rule with JPDDs

Having introduced the novel means of JPDDs to express queries on software artifact, we now come back to the motivating example and illustrate how JPDDs can be used to render the dynamic selection constraints of the sample business rule in an abstract, localized and declarative way.

The JPDD shown in Fig. 4 designates all invocations of method `approveCredit` (called from instances of class `ShoppingCart` on instances of class `WebServiceBank`) to be the points in the base system at which aspectual modifications may take place, i.e. an advice must be executed. That method invocation is given an identifier (`<?jp>`), which is added to the output parameter box of the JPDD in the bottom right corner. That way, before this method is sent, the `applyDiscount` advice is executed[3]. Apart from the

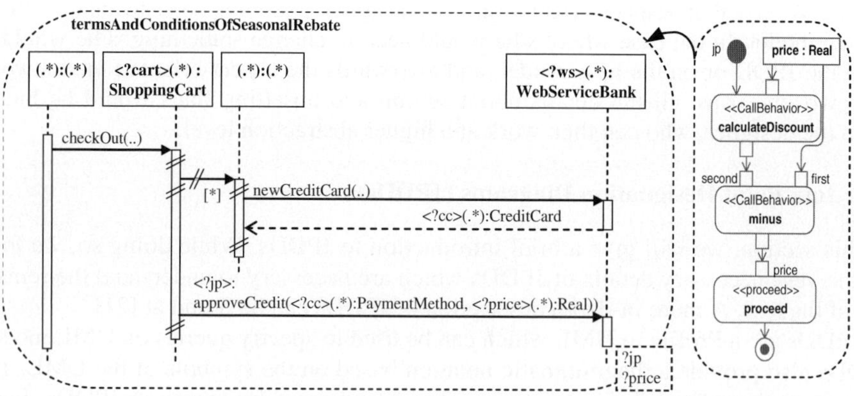

Fig. 4. Modelling the dynamic selection criteria of the business rule in a localized way

[3] Advices are modelled according to the AOEM Profile [6].

method invocation itself, one of its parameters (namely, the second one) is given an identifier (<?price>), too, and is added to the output parameter box of the JPDD, too. That parameter refers to the total price of the shopping cart, i.e. the amount the customer needs to pay. That data is passed to the advice in order to apply the 10% rebate (in case prerequisites are met).

The prerequisites are specified by the remaining methods in the JPDD. The JPDD specifies that method `approveCredit` must be invoked from within the execution of a method `checkOut` (invoked on instances of class `ShoppingCart`). Unlike the method `approveCredit`, which is required to have exactly two parameters (one of type `CreditCard` and one of type `Real`), the number (and types) of parameters of the `checkOut` method are considered irrelevant. This is denoted by the dot-dot-wildcard (`..`) in the parameter list of this method. Furthermore, the `approveCredit` method must be invoked after the completion of the `newCreditCard` method. That `newCreditCard` method must be invoked on instances of class `WebServiceBank` and may take an arbitrary number of parameters of arbitrary type. Apart from that, the `newCreditCard` method must be called in the control flow of the `checkout` method. This means that the `checkOut` method must still be active (i.e. must be on the call stack), while method `newCreditCard` is called (and completed). This is denoted by the indirect message symbol (-//-►). Finally, the object being returned by the `newCreditCard` method has to be of type `CreditCard`, and it must be the same object as the one being passed to the `approveCredit` method as its first parameter. This is denoted by assigning the same identifier (<?cc>) to both the return value of the `newCreditCard` method and the first parameter of the `approveCredit` method.

4 Aspect-Oriented Weaving: Generation and Execution of Multiple Model Transformations

Once an aspect-oriented model has been constructed, we need to compose or weave it, converting the model into plain UML, in order to be able to do the following things: (1) we might want to pass this model to a code generator for plain UML models, which generates non aspect-oriented code from it; (2) we might want to execute and simulate this model for testing purposes in a tool for debugging plain UML models, such as Pópulo [7]. This latter option will allow us in particular to check whether the selection criteria modeled by a JPDD meet the requirements expressed by the business rule, simply by executing the model and observing how it behaves. In this section, we present a novel aspect-oriented model weaver, named Almazara, which is able to compose JPDDs with the primary model generating plain UML as a result.

4.1 General Overview

Unlike other aspect-oriented approaches, the weaving process presented in this paper is not based on directly matching a JPDD to the primary model and replacing the matched model snippet with the advice. Here, the weaving process first executes a special model transformation which accepts a JPDD as input, processes it, and generates a *set* of model transformations. The generated model transformations are responsible for: (1) finding potential join points in the application model; (2) collecting all runtime information that is necessary to evaluate the dynamic join point selection constraints; (3) ensuring that the dynamic constraints are satisfied before executing the advice at the matched join points.

In general, there are three dynamic conditions that can be expressed using a JPDD:

(1) *Controlflow constraints*: The join point must occur in the execution flow of a certain method. For instance, in the example shown in Fig. 4, the `newCreditCard` method must occur within the execution flow of the `checkOut` method.
(2) *State-based constraints*: A specific event must have occured before reaching the join point. For instance, in Fig. 4, before the `approveCredit` message is reached, the `newCreditCard` method must have been invoked (and ended) in order to trigger the advice.
(3) *Dataflow constraints*: Some objects involved in different parts of the interaction must be identical in order to satisfy the JPDD. For instance, in Fig. 4, the `CreditCard` object returned by the `newCreditCard` operation must be identical to the first argument of the `approveCredit` method.

The main assumption of our weaver is that all logic which must be introduced into the application model for checking dynamic conditions can be specified abstractly as a set of template model transformations. For instance, Fig. 5, shows a simplification of one model transformation template, namely the one for monitoring control flow constraints, specified in the terms of a graph-based model transformation. It specifies that if a parameterized method, named `$method$`, is involved in a control flow condition, a parameterized flag, called `$method$Active`, which indicates that this method is active, must be set just before the method starts. In the same way, this flag must be disabled just before the method terminates.

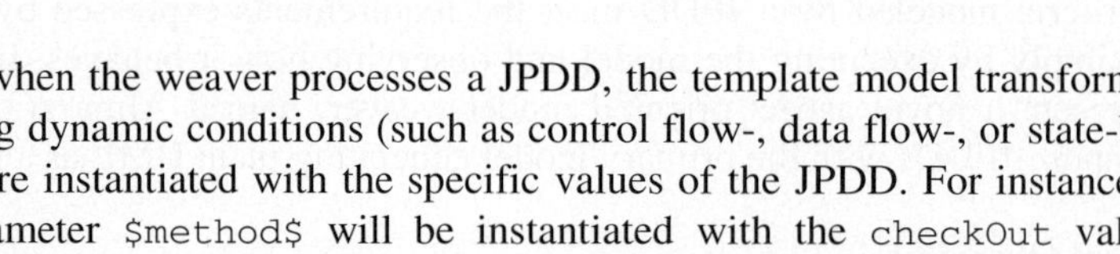

Fig. 5. Template transformation for monitoring control flows

Thus, when the weaver processes a JPDD, the template model transformations for monitoring dynamic conditions (such as control flow-, data flow-, or state-based constraints) are instantiated with the specific values of the JPDD. For instance, the template parameter `$method$` will be instantiated with the `checkOut` value, which would generate a model transformation for introducing activities that enable and disable the `checkOutActive` flag at the beginning and the end of the `checkOut` method. (Of course, this flag has to be introduced first by an instance of a (different) template model transformation which performs structural changes that are needed to monitor control flow conditions.)

The next section describes our aspect-oriented model weaver in greater detail.

4.2 The Almazara Aspect-Oriented Model Weaver

Fig. 6 shows a high-level overview of the aspect-oriented model weaving process. Almazara accepts as input the application model, the advice model and the JPDD model. It produces as output the woven model, which is a plain UML 2.0 model. In Fig. 6, transformations with text in italics are the transformations that constitute the Almazara model weaver. These transformations generate as output a set of model transformations, by instantiating templates as depicted in Fig. 5. These generated transformations implement the model weaving process for a specific JPDD.

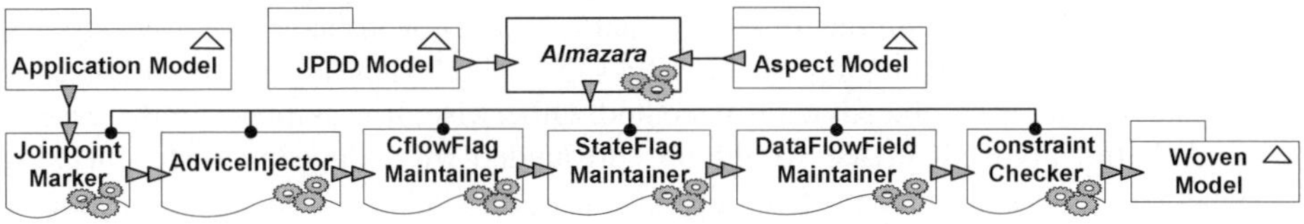

Fig. 6. Chain of transformations executed by the Almazara aspect-oriented model weaver

As commented in the previous section, the aspect-oriented model weaver initially executes the Almazara model transformations (see box *Almazara* in Fig. 6) which process the JPDD model and the advice model, and generates a set of model transformations from them. These transformations are described as follows:

(1) The *JoinPointMarkers* search for potentially selected join points, e.g. all actions with metatype `CallOperation` that satisfy the structural constraints of the JPDD, i.e. the caller type, the receiver type and the signature of the message must conform to the JPDD. These potentially selected join points are marked as `selectedJoinpoint`. The transformation also performs some structural changes to the model. It adds a class with the name of the JPDD, subfixed with `JPDD`. This class contains the flags that serve to monitor dynamic conditions. Furthermore, it serves as a container for storing the objects that appear in the JPDD and that are needed to check data flow constraints. For the example, in the case of the JPDD shown in Fig. 4, a class `termsAndConditionsOfSeasonalRebateJPDD` would be created. This class would contain a `checkOutActive` flag, a `newCreditCardExecuted` flag, an attribute `cc` of type `CreditCard` and an attribute `cart` of type `ShoppingCart`. This class also contains all the logic for setting/unsetting these flags and for storing/maintaining the attributes.

(2) A call to the advice is injected at the selected join points by the *AdviceInjectors*. The generated transformation would be similar to the transformation displayed in Fig. 2. The advice injector also takes care of inserting the call to the advice at the right place (e.g. before, after, around, or even in parallel with the selected join point). How this is accomplished is beyond of the scope of this paper (the focus of this paper is on weaving dynamic selection constrained expressed with JPDDs). We refer the interested reader to our previous work [6].

(3) The templates for control flow conditions are instantiated and applied by the *CflowFlagMaintainers*. These templates are similar to the one described in Fig. 5. They basically add actions at the beginning and at the end of methods involved in control flow constraints for setting/unsetting the appropriate flags.

(4) The templates for state-based conditions are instantiated and applied by the *StateFlagMaintainers*. These templates look out for actions that conform to messages that appear in the JPDD. At the end of these operations, the template inserts actions for activating the flag that indicates that the operation has been executed and terminated, i.e. that the requested state has been reached.

(5) Then, data flow templates are instantiated and applied to the models by means of *DataflowFieldMaintainers*. These templates look out for actions that produce data that is of relevance according to the JPDD. The template pushes the relevant data to the respective fields of the JPDD class.

(6) Finally, the *ConstraintCheckers* enclose all of the generated pieces which depend on some dynamic conditions in conditional regions. For instance, the advice is enclosed in a conditional region which checks that all relevant flags of the JPDD class are set to true. If so, the advice is executed. Otherwise, it is skipped. In the case of Fig. 4, the invoked advice would be surrounded by a decision node checking whether the first argument of the `approveCredit` call is equal to the `cc` object, which has been stored in the `termsAndConditionsOfSeasonalRebateJPDD` object after the `newCreditCard` operation. If this is the case, the behavior of the advice is executed; if not, the intercepted join point is executed without being influenced by the advice. Moreover, the methods maintaining the relevant runtime information may be enclosed in conditional regions, too. This is necessary whenever the preservation of one piece of runtime information depends on the value of other runtime information. For example, according to Fig. 4, the result of the `newCreditCard` operation must only be stored in the `cc` object if the `checkOutActive` flag is set to true. Otherwise, the `cc` object should be left undefined.

The ConstraintCheckers are probably the most essential generated model transformations of the Almazara weaving process. In contrast to the other kinds of transformations (i.e. JoinPointMarkers, AdviceInjectors, and the different Maintainers), which basically perform simple modifications of the base application model, such as introducing join point markers or inserting calls to the JPDD class (generated by the JoinPointMarker), the ConstraintCheckers take care of ensuring that the dynamic conditions of the JPDD are properly satisfied.

In summary, the Almazara aspect-model weaving process is composed of a large and elaborate chain of model transformations that involves a large number of scattered changes at several parts of the application model. This is necessary in order to evaluate at model execution time if the dynamic selection constraints specified by the JPDD are satisfied or not. The ultimate advantage of this approach is that this process is carried out automatically. As a consequence, designers are freed from contemplating, and manually specifying, each single transformation needed to collect all relevant information at the right places. Furthermore, they are not concerned with investigating, and manually specifying, how the collected information needs to be combined in order to decide whether or not the advice needs be executed.

5 Discussion

With help of Almazara – the aspect-oriented weaver presented in this paper – the modeling of the business rule presented in the problem statement can be strictly separated into (a) the modeling of the application constraints and (b) the modeling of the aspectual action that needs to be performed (see Fig. 4, section 3.2). Developers do not need to contemplate which data needs to be collected at what points in the base program (and how and where it needs to be stored, etc.), so that in the end the applicability constraints of the business rules can be evaluated. As a result, developers do not need to reconsider all those steps once the business rule needs to be modified. For example, if – after one week – the marketing department has opted for removing the requirement that the newly created credit card must be used for paying. With conventional model transformation techniques, designers would need to inspect each single transformation rule in order to assert whether it needs to be adapted or not. With JPDDs and Almazara, the designer would simply adapt the selection constraints in the JPDD, and have Almazara reweave the rule.

Furthermore, we can use the notation that more appropriately renders the designers conceptual view on the selection criteria as expressed in the JPDD. S/he is not restricted to using the same notation which is used to model the base system and/or the aspectual adaptation (see [20] for a detailed discussion on the benefits of using different notation for rendering pointcuts). Almazara will take care of mapping the concepts used in the JPDD (e.g. a sequence diagram, in this case) to the concepts used in the base system and the aspectual adaptation (e.g. activity diagrams, in this case).

The template-driven transformation approach realized in Almazara leads to a very straightforward adaptation chain of the application model. It must be noted though that this approach may sometimes lead to unnecessary storage of runtime information or superfluous constraint checks. This may be the case if, for example, some relevant runtime information could be deduced from other runtime information that has been previously gathered and stored. In these cases, the woven model leaves room for optimizations.

The aim of Almazara is not to generate optimized models/code, though. Rather, the goal is to sustain the design of aspects in a MDD way, in particular by permitting their simulation, debugging and testing. For the latter, the woven models can to be executed by an UML execution engine, such as Pópulo [7]. With Almazara and Pópulo, aspect-oriented UML models with sophisticated dynamics selection constraints expressed by means of JPDDs can be thoroughly tested and debugged in order to ensure if the designed aspects behave as intended[4].

In conclusion, the approach presented in this paper improves the situation of dealing with dynamic selection constraints. It permits designers to develop software at a higher level of abstraction, by providing appropriate selection abstractions. It is the provision of these selection abstractions and the automatic mapping onto conventional model transformations in which we consider aspect-oriented weaving to go beyond conventional model transformations and model composition. Only with help of such abstractions, designers can exploit the full benefits of aspect-orientation at the modeling level. Moreover, with JPDDs and Almazara, developers can now design aspects which resort to sophisticated dynamic join point selection constraints, and are able to test and debug them to see if their aspects behave as intended.

6 Related Work

The approach presented in this paper is related to other MDD approaches and techniques that aim to encapsulate "crosscutting concerns" (i.e. concerns which are

[4] In fact, Pópulo has been used to ensure the correctness of Almazara itself.

otherwise scattered across the software). These approaches include MATA [11], Role Models [8], xWeave [9], Kompose [19], Semantic Weaving of Scenarios [12] or Ker-Theme [3], amongst others. These approaches and techniques are comparable to the approach presented in this paper in that it is generally possible to use them to express and enforce dynamic selection constraints in one or the other manner. However, in contrast to the approach presented in this paper, developers are forced to manually collect all information required to evaluate these constraints from various places in the base model. These approaches do not provide suitable abstractions by means of which developers could specify these selection constraints in a declarative way, and have a weaver take care of the actual realization.

Further differences are that Role Models [8] and Kompose [19] require that aspect models are manually instantiated for each and every join point first, before they can be actually merged with the base models. The approach presented in this paper allows developers to declare the relevant and necessary characteristics of all join points at which an aspect should take effect, and then have the weaver automatically find all points in the base model which meet these characteristics.

MATA [11] and the Motorola WEAVR [5] permit the specification of state-based join point selections – similar to the approach presented here. As such, they improve over many currently available aspect-oriented programming languages and permit the specification of a substantial set of advanced aspects. However, the approach presented in this paper goes further in that it permits the specification of control flow- and data flow-based join point selections. While control flow-based join point selections may be simulated with help of the state-based join point selection means provided by MATA and WEAVR, the specification of data flow-based join point selections is practically impossible and requires extra means in order to be acheived.

Finally, model transformations with MATA [11], xWeave [9] or KerTheme [3] can only be accomplished if all models, i.e. the base model, the advice model and the pointcut model are specified in the same notation (e.g. sequence diagrams or state machines). In our approach, the weaver can take of mapping the concepts used to specify the join point selections (and, later on, the concepts used to specify the aspectual enhancements) onto the concepts used to specify the base model. As a result, developers can always use the notation which is conceptually most suitable to express their intententions (cf. [20] for a more detailed discussion).

7 Conclusions

In this paper, we have presented a novel model weaver for aspect-oriented models. The unique feature of this model weaver is that it is able to (statically) weave aspects that are supposed to affect a given base system only under certain (dynamic) conditions. We have identified the particular characteristics of these conditions to be (a) that they cannot be evaluated before runtime, and (b) that the information needed for their evaluation cannot be gathered from the local[5] context of the particular program element which is supposed to be affected by the aspect. We have identified existing MDD approaches as incapable to cope with such constraints. We have exemplified the severe consequences that this incapacity means to the model-driven software de-

[5] See [2] for further information on the term "local information".

veloper, and we have shown how these consequences conflict with the original aim of MDD "to develop software at a higher level of abstraction".

We have used Join Point Designation Diagrams (JPDDs; [21, 20]) as a means to overcome the problem. JPDDs have been presented as a way of representing join point selections in AOSD. In particular, JPDDs provide abstractions for representing dynamic (selection) constraints. By means of these abstractions, the model weaving approach presented in this paper brings forth the substantial advances of aspect-oriented research to the MDD domain: Developers are able to specify the selection criteria of their join point selections in a localized and declarative way. Thus, they are freed from manually identifying all points in the program at which they have to gather relevant information, just to be able to evaluate them in the dynamic selection constraints at later points in the program.

The rise in the level of abstraction – brought forth by the combined use of JPDDs and the novel model weaver presented in this paper – is in keeping with the very spirit of MDD, which aims at providing more abstract, or more "problem-oriented", ways to develop software: The approach presented in this paper hides the specific details of weaving dynamic selection constraints in a base system. As such, it represents a significant improvement over current MDD approaches which require software developers to do this manually. We consider this improvement (i.e. the provision of problem-oriented abstractions) to be a particular characteristic of aspect-oriented weaving, which distinguishes it from conventional ways of model transformation and model composition.

It is important to note that the problem pointed out by this paper is the greater, the more information needs to be gathered from different places of the base program. If all information is locally[5] available at the point at which the aspect needs to take affect, the benefits of the approach presented in this paper are at their minimum (in comparison to model transformations specified with conventional MDD approaches).

One possible workaround for the problem outlined in this paper is to refactor a given base system so that all relevant information is available in one place, and then use conventional model transformation techniques to perform the aspectual modifications. Usually however, such refactorings lead to the scattering of other information which is possibly needed by another aspectual modification, and which thus would just shift the problem to another location. This is the immediate consequence of a phenomenon which [22] refers to as the *Tyranny of the Dominant Decomposition*.

Trying to overcome this problem, extensive research has been conducted in the field of AOSD, focussing on the provision of suitable abstractions to express dynamic selection constraints. Manifold selection abstractions have already been presented (cf. [1, 2, 10, 13, 17]). We consider the (ongoing) high research activity in this field to indicate a highly relevant problem. Therefore, we expect that abstractions for dynamic selection constraints will likewise have a strong impact on the domain of MDD.

One reason for the improvements yielded by the approach presented in this paper is that JPDDs permit designers to render join point selection constraints in a different notation than the one used to specify the base program. The use of a different notation permits developers to use the most appropriate abstractions for rendering the conceptual intent of a join point selections (cf. [20]). The sample pointcut presented in this paper, for instance, focuses on control flow. Sequence diagrams are targeted towards the representation of control flow. They are rarely used to specify the behavior of a software system, though. With the help of the approach presented in this paper, developers can benefit from the conceptual abstractions provided by JPDDs when specifying dynamic selection constraints. The model weaver then takes care of translating them into the notation used for the base system.

References

[1] Allan, C., Avgustinov, P., Christensen, A.S., Hendren, L.J., Kuzins, S., Lhoták, O., de Moor, O., Sereni, D., Sittampalam, G., Tibble, J.: Adding trace matching with free variables to AspectJ. In: Proc. of OOPSLA 2005, San Diego, CA, pp. 345–364 (October 2005)

[2] Al-Mansari, M., Hanenberg, S.: Path Expression Pointcuts: Abstracting over Non-Local Object Relationships in Aspect-Oriented Languages. In: Proc. of NODe 2006, Erfurt, Germany. LNI P-88, pp. 81–96 (September 2006)

[3] Barais, O., Klein, J., Baudry, B., Jackson, A., Clarke, S.: Composing Multi-view Aspect Models. In: Proc. of ICCBSS 2008, Madrid, Spain, pp. 43–52 (February 2008)

[4] Cibrán, M.A., D'Hondt, M.: A Slice of MDE with AOP: Transforming High-Level Business Rules to Aspects. In: Nierstrasz, O., Whittle, J., Harel, D., Reggio, G. (eds.) MoDELS 2006. LNCS, vol. 4199. Springer, Heidelberg (2006)

[5] Cottenier, T., van den Berg, A., Elrad, T.: The Motorola WEAVR: Model Weaving in a Large Industrial Context. In: AOSD 2007, Industry Track, Vancouver, BC (March 2007)

[6] Fuentes, L., Sánchez, P.: Designing and Weaving Aspect-Oriented Executable UML Models. JOT, Special Issue: Aspect-Oriented Modeling 6(7), 109–136

[7] Fuentes, L., Manrique, J., Sánchez, P.: Pópulo: A Tool for Debugging UML Models. In: Proc. of ICSE 2008, Companion Volume, Leipzig, Germany, pp. 955–956 (May 2008)

[8] Georg, G., France, R.B.: UML Aspect Specification Using Role Models. In: Bellahsène, Z., Patel, D., Rolland, C. (eds.) OOIS 2002. LNCS, vol. 2425, pp. 186–191. Springer, Heidelberg (2002)

[9] Groher, I., Voelter, M.: XWeave: Models and Aspects in Concert. In: AOM Workshop, AOSD 2007, Vancouver, BC (March 2007)

[10] Gybels, K., Brichau, J.: Arranging language features for more robust pattern-based crosscuts. In: Proc. of AOSD 2003, Boston, MA, pp. 60–69 (March 2003)

[11] Jayaraman, P.K., Whittle, J., Elkhodary, A.M., Gomaa, H.: Model Composition in Product Lines and Feature Interaction Detection Using Critical Pair Analysis. In: Engels, G., Opdyke, B., Schmidt, D.C., Weil, F. (eds.) MODELS 2007. LNCS, vol. 4735, pp. 151–165. Springer, Heidelberg (2007)

[12] Klein, J., Hélouët, L., Jézéquel, J.M.: Semantic-based Weaving of Scenarios. In: Proc. of AOSD 2005, Bonn, Germany, pp. 27–38 (March 2006)

[13] Masuhara, H., Kawauchi, K.: Dataflow Pointcut in Aspect-Oriented Programming. In: Ohori, A. (ed.) APLAS 2003. LNCS, vol. 2895, pp. 105–121. Springer, Heidelberg (2003)

[14] Masuhara, H., Kiczales, G., Dutchyn, C.: A Compilation and Optimization Model for Aspect-Oriented Programs. In: Hedin, G. (ed.) CC 2003. LNCS, vol. 2622, pp. 46–60. Springer, Heidelberg (2003)

[15] Mellor, S., Balcer, M.: Executable UML: A Foundation for Model Driven Architecture. Addison-Wesley Professional, Reading (March 2002)

[16] Moreira, A., Araújo, J., Whittle, J.: Modeling volatile concerns as aspects. In: Dubois, E., Pohl, K. (eds.) CAiSE 2006. LNCS, vol. 4001, pp. 544–558. Springer, Heidelberg (2006)

[17] Ostermann, K., Mezini, M., Bockisch, C.: Expressive Pointcuts for Increased Modularity. In: Proc. of ECOOP 2005, Glasgow, Scotland, pp. 214–240 (July 2005)
[18] Pohl, C., Charif, A., Gilani, W., Göbel, S., Grammel, B., Lochmann, H., Rummler, A., Spriestersbach, A.: Adopting AOSD in Business Application Engineering. In: Proc. of AOSD 2008, Industry Track, Brussels, Belgium, pp. 11–21 (March-April 2008)
[19] Reddy, Y.R., Ghosh, S., France, R.B., Straw, G., Bieman, J.M., McEachen, N., Song, E., Georg, G.: Directives for Composing Aspect-Oriented Design Class Models. In: Rashid, A., Akşit, M. (eds.) Transactions on Aspect-Oriented Software Development I. LNCS, vol. 3880, pp. 75–105. Springer, Heidelberg (2006)
[20] Stein, D., Hanenberg, S., Unland, R.: Expressing Different Conceptual Models of Join Point Selections in Aspect-Oriented Design. In: Proc. of AOSD 2006, Bonn, Germany, pp. 15–26 (March 2006)
[21] Stein, D., Hanenberg, S., Unland, R.: Query Models. In: Baar, T., Strohmeier, A., Moreira, A., Mellor, S.J. (eds.) UML 2004. LNCS, vol. 3273. Springer, Heidelberg (2004)
[22] Tarr, P., Ossher, H., Sutton, S.M., Harrison, W.: N Degrees of Separation: Multi-Dimensional Separation of Concerns. In: Filman, R.E., Elrad, T., Clarke, S., Akşit, M. (eds.) Aspect-Oriented Software Development, pp. 37–61. Addison-Wesley, Reading (2005)

An Aspect-Oriented and Model-Driven Approach for Managing Dynamic Variability*

Brice Morin[1], Franck Fleurey[2], Nelly Bencomo[3],
Jean-Marc Jézéquel[1], Arnor Solberg[2], Vegard Dehlen[2], and Gordon Blair[3]

[1] IRISA/INRIA Rennes, Equipe Triskell, Campus de Beaulieu, 35042 Rennes Cedex, France
[2] SINTEF, Oslo, Norway
[3] Computing department, InfoLab21, Lancaster University, LA1 4WA, United Kingdom

Abstract. Constructing and executing distributed systems that can adapt to their operating context in order to sustain provided services and the service qualities are complex tasks. Managing adaptation of multiple, interacting services is particularly difficult since these services tend to be distributed across the system, interdependent and sometimes tangled with other services. Furthermore, the exponential growth of the number of potential system configurations derived from the variabilities of each service need to be handled. Current practices of writing low-level reconfiguration scripts as part of the system code to handle run time adaptation are both error prone and time consuming and make adaptive systems difficult to validate and evolve. In this paper, we propose to combine model driven and aspect oriented techniques to better cope with the complexities of adaptive systems construction and execution, and to handle the problem of exponential growth of the number of possible configurations. Combining these techniques allows us to use high level domain abstractions, simplify the representation of variants and limit the problem pertaining to the combinatorial explosion of possible configurations. In our approach we also use models at runtime to generate the adaptation logic by comparing the current configuration of the system to a composed model representing the configuration we want to reach.

1 Introduction

Context aware software systems that can automatically adapt to changes in their environments play increasingly vital roles in society's infrastructures. The demand for adaptive systems appears in many application domains, ranging from crisis management applications such as disaster and power management, to entertainment and business applications such as mobile interactive gaming, tourist guiding and business collaborations.

However, constructing and executing adaptive systems are highly complex tasks facing several challenges. Adaptive software systems are typically deployed on distributed platforms consisting of heterogeneous computing devices. The target platforms for a single system can range from computer networks of any size to small portable devices, such as phones or PDAs. Furthermore, a system is composed of components with variable configurations that might have dependency relationships that need to be resolved during adaptation; thus, compounding the complexity. Better techniques for taming the

* This work was partially funded by the DiVA project (EU FP7 STREP).

K. Czarnecki et al. (Eds.): MoDELS 2008, LNCS 5301, pp. 782–796, 2008.

complexity of adaptive software during development are needed. Another challenge in adaptive system construction and execution is the issue of combinatorial explosion. Adaptive systems are often developed by defining several variation points, which represents points in the software where different variants of the implementation might be chosen to derive the final system configuration. Resolving these variation points leads to an exponential growth in the number of possible system configurations. This presents a major problem, since reasoning on a huge number of configurations to find the best possible configuration for the current context becomes too time consuming when considering the often strict requirements to response times these systems face.

Abstraction is the most fundamental principle applied in software engineering to encounter a continuously wider range of problems and increasing complexity [21]. In Model Driven Engineering (MDE), abstractions and transformations between levels are used to manage complexity. For example, the Model Driven Architecture (MDA) specifies three abstraction levels; a Computation Independent Model (CIM) describes the environment and specifies requirements; a Platform Independent Model (PIM) describes the parts that do not change from one platform to another; and a Platform Specific Model (PSM) includes descriptions of platform dependent parts. Another principle that are commonly applied in software engineering to handle complexity are separation of concern. Aspect Oriented Modeling (AOM) approaches provides advanced mechanisms for separation of concern such as mechanisms for encapsulating crosscutting features and for composing crosscutting features to form integrated models [9,13,14,15].

In this paper we present a new approach where we address challenges in adaptive system construction and execution by combining certain aspect-oriented and model-driven techniques. In particular we use:

- Aspect-Oriented Modeling techniques in order to tackle the issue of the combinatorial explosion of variants. AOM allows us to encapsulate distinct variation points into aspects which are separated from the base model of the system's functionality. Then, distinct aspects might be composed into the base model in order to obtain different configurations. This approach allows us to reason on a limited and linearly increasing number of aspects, thus avoiding the problem of combinatorial explosion seen in other approaches.
- Model-Driven techniques to automate and improve the creation of the reconfiguration script needed to make the running system evolve from one configuration to another. Currently the adaptation logic of adaptive middleware relies on the execution of low-level and hand-written reconfiguration scripts, which specify all the possible transitions between the configurations. As these scripts decide how systems - possibly critical to safety - are manipulated at runtime, they require rigorous validation. Such a process is both time consuming and, even worse, prone to human errors. Instead of manually writing these scripts, we apply model driven techniques to generate them by analyzing the different variants of the system. In addition we apply model driven principles to provide models at run time for managing the execution of the adaptation at a more abstract level. This enable us to provide abstractions fine-tuned towards the adaptation task, reducing complexity. Furthermore, it makes our approach applicable on many execution platforms since our models at runtime is provided as platform independent models.

The remainder of this paper is organized as follows. Section 2 introduces a running example and presents some background. Section 3 presents our methodology for managing dynamic variability. Section 4 details our approach using the running example. Section 5 presents related works and Section 6 provides our conclusion.

2 Motivating Example

This section presents a brief background on management and support for variability in the context of dynamic adaptive systems, based on [1,2]. We next discuss the limitations of this approach and the solutions we propose. The discussion is in the context of mobile computing environments applications which need to dynamically discover services from a wide range of options that may be unknown during design. Such kind of applications propose a simple yet powerful motivating example of systems that need support for dynamic variability.

Traditionally, variability management has focused on variability that is solved at pre-delivery time, i.e. from requirements to deployment. However, adaptive systems exhibit degrees of variability that depend on runtime fluctuations in their contexts. This kind of variability is called dynamic variability or runtime variability [1]. Reflective and adaptive middleware platforms offer powerful mechanisms to achieve dynamic variability to enable adaptation at runtime. These mechanisms allow programmers to hard-code reconfiguration scripts to dynamically transform one component-based configuration into another.

2.1 Dynamic Service Discovery for Mobile Applications

Mobile applications need to dynamically adapt according to changes in their operating contexts. Mobile devices such as PDAs, mobiles, or laptops are capable of detecting and notify the user about new available services according to his/her preferences. The complexity arises from the fact that mobile adaptive applications are expected to support unanticipated variants associated with user preferences and properties of operating contexts that inevitably will arise during execution. Furthermore, different designs for service discovery protocols (SDPs) have been proposed. Hence, it may not be possible to completely specify at design time user preferences, properties associated with the contexts, or which protocols will be used to advertise services in a given context execution.

Flores *et al.* presents in [8] a solution to overcome the challenges posed by heterogeneous service discovery protocols. The solution offers a common core architecture that individual discovery protocols follow. Using the final architecture, discovery protocols can be implemented and dynamically plugged into the middleware platform. Using this solution, the service discovery interaction platform from our example can take different roles that individual protocols could assume:

-**User Agent (*UA*)** to discover services on behalf of clients,
-**Service Agent (*SA*)** to advertise services, and,
-**Directory Agent (*DA*)** to support a service directory where *SA*s register their services and *UA*s send their service requests. A DA also announces positive matches of requests against advertisements.

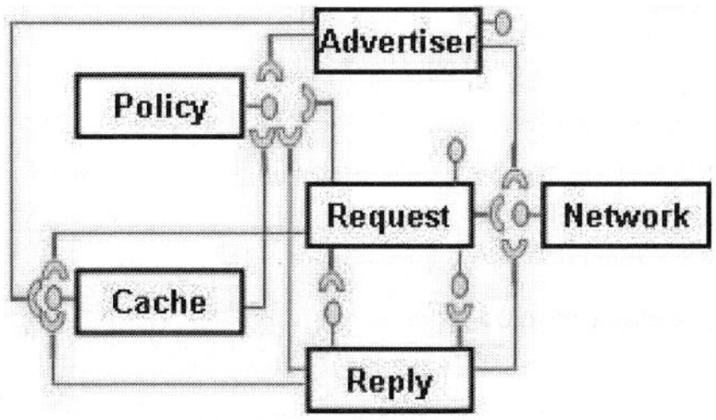

Fig. 1. Architecture of the Service Discovery Application

Depending on the required functionality, participating nodes might be required to support 1,2, or the 3 roles at any time. The common architecture, which is shown in Figure 1, has six components:

-Advertiser Component: used by *SA*s to advertise its services and by *DA*s to process incoming service advertisements storing them in cache. This component also deals with the maintenance of a directory overlay network.

-Request Component: used by *UA* and *DA*s to generate service requests.

-Reply Component: used by *UA*s and *DA*s to generate service replies.

-Cache Component: for common utility tasks such as management of temporary data, service advertisements, and location of neighboring directories.

-Policy Component: this component stores and deals with user preferences, application needs and/or inclusive context requirements.

-Network Component: for the transmission of messages.

Network, *Cache* and *Policies* components will always be present in any valid configuration. The other three components and their bindings will be part of the configuration or not, depending on the roles the protocol might perform (i.e. *SA*, *UA*, or *DA*).

In [1,2], authors complement the solution shown above targeting the development of adaptive systems. This approach uses the Genie toolkit [2], to design stable runtime configurations, as well as the possible triggers that initiate the reconfigurations. In the case of the example above, the UA, SA, and DA are the possible configurations to be used by any specific SDP. At the end of the process, a state-machine model is produced where each state represents a configuration and each transition represents a conditional reconfiguration that transforms the source configuration into the target configuration. Essentially, this state machine model drives the execution of the system. Using the Genie toolkit and the state machine model, designers can automatically generate XML files that represent the adaptation policies associated to transitions. Such policies can dynamically be introduced to change the behavior of the system during execution. Figure 2 illustrates the state machine model for the dynamic service discovery application and an example of a generated adaptation policy associated with the arc (pointed by the arrow from the top arc of the model to the generated policy).

2.2 Limitations of Existing Approaches

The approach described in [1,2] presents several limitations. First, the possible system configurations need to be enumerated and fully specified. Secondly, the generated

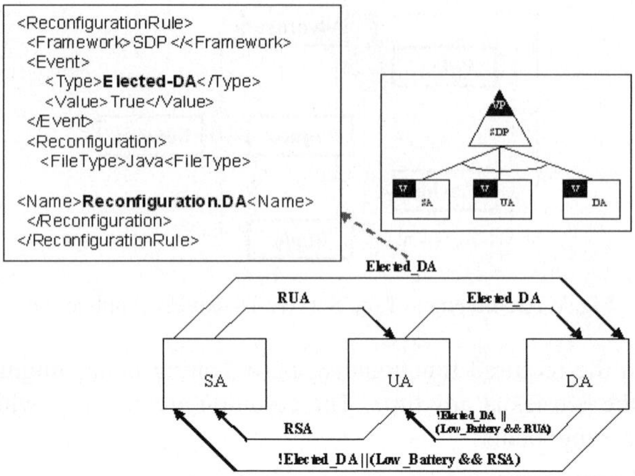

Fig. 2. Variants and transitions for the service discovery application

policies mainly specify the trigger events and which reconfiguration scripts have to be loaded to adapt the system from one state mode (i.e. agent role) to another. These scripts are currently hand-written using the API offered by the underlying execution platform. Finally, each state mode represents the whole system, in a given configuration. This is not enough in some cases. For example, in the case of the dynamic service discovery application described above, there is another variability dimension associated with the specific protocol to use such as ALLIA, GSD, SSD, SLP [8]. Each of these protocols has its own terms and rules. Therefore, in order to get a service agent and a user agent understanding each other, they need to use the same protocol. Taking into account different protocols increments the number of configurations and rules needed.

2.3 Contributions

The contribution of our proposed approach is twofold. Firstly, we argue that the reconfiguration scripts described above can also be inferred from the models, by comparing the target configuration with the current configuration, for each transition that may be triggered during runtime. The results of this comparison will allow the dynamic generation of the corresponding reconfiguration, i.e. the identification of the components that should be added or deleted. This solution is possible as we proposed to keep a reference model that represents the current system and the possible modified model that is the result of the required adaptation. This will be detailed in the next sections. Secondly, using Genie, each state mode represents the whole system as one configuration per domain (in the example above the service discovery domain). As discussed above, this is not enough in some cases. Considering the complete enumeration of configurations for different variability dimensions, such as different protocol, may be an unmanageable task. In the following sections we will show how Aspect-Oriented Modeling techniques allow the separation and composition of different views of the system reducing complexity during the development.

3 Overview of the Approach

The common practices in component-based dynamically adaptive systems (DAS) are to handle dynamic adaptation at the code level. The adaptation rules and the transformations that have to be performed on the running system are hard-coded and mixed with the code of the application [3,5,8]. This approach makes adaptive systems very difficult to understand, validate and evolve.

The idea of the approach we propose in this paper is to combine model driven and aspect-oriented techniques to handle the complexities of adaptive system construction and execution. Models cope with complexity through abstractions and are used both to specify the dynamic variability at design time and to manage run time adaptations. Aspect oriented techniques are utilized to model the adaptation concerns separately from the other aspects of the system. By utilizing model based abstractions and advanced separation of concerns in this way the adaptation becomes easier to design and understand, possible to validate and allows to easily evolve the adaptation policies even at runtime.

Figure 3 presents the conceptual model of the proposed approach. From a methodological perspective the approach is divided in two phases; design time and runtime.

At design-time, the application base and variant architecture models are designed and the adaptation model is built. At runtime, the adaptation model is processed to produce the system configuration that should be executed. The following paragraphs details the steps of Figure 3.

Because the potential number of configurations for an adaptive system grows exponentially with the number of variation points, a main objective of the approach is to model adaptive systems without having to enumerate all their possible configurations statically. To achieve this objective, an application is modeled using a base model which contains the common functionalities and a set of variant models which can be composed with this base model. The variant models capture the variability of the adaptive

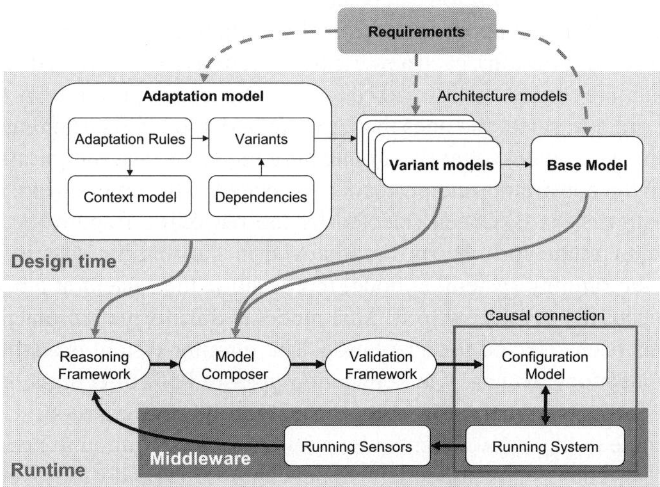

Fig. 3. Conceptual model of the approach

application. The actual configurations of the application are built at runtime by selecting and composing appropriate variants. An adaptation model specifies which variant have to be selected depending on the context of the running application.

The adaptation model is central to the approach as it captures all the information about the dynamic variability and adaptation of the adaptive system. It is built from the requirements of the system, refined during design and used at runtime to manage adaptation. It is made of four main elements:

- **Variants.** This part of the model makes references to all the available variability for the application. Depending on the complexity of the system, it can be a simple list of variants, a data structure like a hierarchy or a complex feature model.
- **Dependencies.** The dependencies specify constraints on variants that can be used in a configuration. For example, the use of a particular functionality (variant model) might require or exclude others. These constraints reduce the total number of configurations by rejecting invalid configurations.
- **Context model.** The context model is a minimal representation of the environment of the adaptive application to support the definition of adaptation rules. We only consider elements of the environment relevant for expressing adaptation rules. These elements are updated by sensors deployed on the running system.
- **Adaptation rules.** These rules specify how the system should adapt to its environment. In practice these rules are relations between the values provided by the sensors and the variants that should be used.

During runtime appropriate configurations of the application have to be built from the base and variant models. To select the appropriate configuration, the reasoning framework processes the adaptation model and makes a decision based on the current context. The output of the reasoning framework is one or more options that match the adaptation rules and satisfies the dependency constraints. For each of these options the complete model of the corresponding configuration can be built at runtime using model composition.

Because the idea of the approach is to build configurations on demand rather than enumerating all configurations, each new configuration has to be validated at runtime. The role of the validation framework is to process the configuration proposed by the reasoning framework in order to select the ones that are safe to deploy in the running system. The validation framework checks that the architecture model of the configuration is correct with respect to the constraints and protocols associated to the components it contains.

Once a configuration has been selected by the reasoning framework and checked by the validation framework, it can be deployed in the running system. To ease the adaptation of the running system, a model representing the system at a higher level of abstraction is causally connected to it. This model is transformed to match the configuration that has been selected for adaptation. The running system is adapted thanks to the causal connection. Because the connection goes in both directions, it also allows checking that the system is actually running the required configuration.

From a change to the environment quite a few steps are required to be able to safely adapt the system. These steps (especially model composition and validation) can require some time to execute and thus delay the actual adaptation. In practice, this issue is tackled by keeping track of the configurations that are validated and registering them for reuse. In extreme cases where predictable fast adaptation is required, a set of predefined configuration can be specified, built and validated in advance.

4 Managing the Combinatorial Explosion of Configurations

The service discovery application described in section 2 has two different variability dimensions: the functionality and the discovery protocols. There are three variants for the functionality: UA, SA and DA (= UA and SA). Four variants of the protocols (ALLIA, GSD, SSD and SLP) can be supported separately or not. This leads to 45 configurations (2^4-1 protocols and 3 functionalities) and potentially 1980 (45x44) different reconfigurations. However, in the example of the service discovery application, the two variability dimensions and their aspects are independent and triggered by distinct events. Thus, it is possible to manage all the reconfigurations with 12 scripts, for respectively adding and removing each aspects.

4.1 Using AOM to Represent the Variability

To avoid the combinatorial explosion, we propose to model the variants instead of the configurations. This way, the number of models to be defined grows linearly with the variability. The configurations can then be built by automatically combining the variants. In practice this is achieved using Aspect-Oriented Modeling techniques for architecture models. The application commonalities, i.e. the architecture elements which are part of all configurations, are captured in a single base model. All the variants are then defined as aspect models to be woven in the base model. From a particular selection of variants, the corresponding configuration can be built automatically by weaving the corresponding aspect models into the base model.

The specific AOM technique we use is the SMARTADAPTERS approach [14,15]. SMARTADAPTERS has formerly been applied to Java programs and UML class diagrams [14]. More recently, we have generalized this approach to any domain metamodel [15]. SMARTADAPTERS automatically generates domain-specific AOM frameworks using an input domain-metamodel. In this paper, the domain metamodel we use is a generic component model representing the main concepts needed to describe the topology of running systems: components, binding, ports, *etc.*

In SMARTADAPTERS, an aspect is composed of three parts:*i)* a graft model, representing **what** we want to weave, *ii)* an interface model, representing **where** we want to weave the aspect and *iii)* a composition protocol specifying **how** to weave the graft model into the interface model. The graft model is a model fragment representing a given concern. The interface model is a model fragment parameterized by roles allowing the interface model to be matched in different base models. Finally, the composition protocol is described by model transformation primitives that manipulate elements from the graft and the interface models.

4.2 Application to the Service Discovery Example

For handling the functionalities of the service discovery, the application is separated into a base model and two aspects. The base model contains the common components: *Policy*, *Cache* and *Network*.

The first aspect corresponds to the user agent (UA) role and is illustrated in the left part of Figure 4. The graft model contains all the components and bindings needed to realize the functionality of the UA role. The interface model contains all the base components needed to integrate the graft model: *Policy*, *Cache* and *Network*. The composition protocol, represented by the interconnecting lines, specifies how to weave the graft model into the interface model. It consists in binding components of the graft model to components of the interface model, and vice-versa. Similarly, the second aspect corresponds to the service agent (SA) role and is illustrated in the right part of Figure 4.

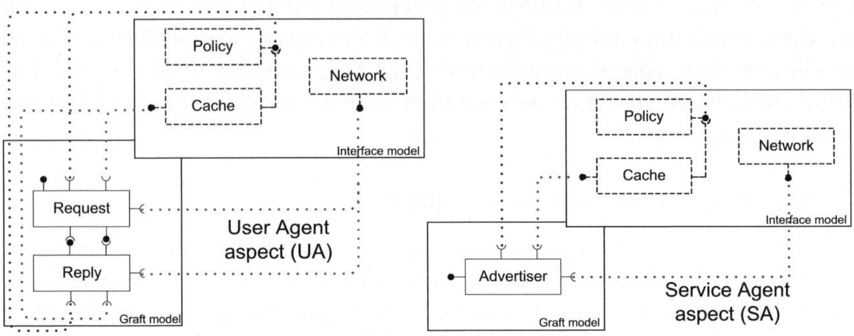

Fig. 4. User Agent and Service Agent aspect

These two aspects allow building the three functional configurations of the service discovery application. Note that these two aspects use the same interface model. Weaving only the User Agent aspect leads to the User Agent configuration, weaving only the Service Agent aspect leads to the Service Agent configuration and weaving both aspects leads to the Discovery Agent configuration.

We have illustrated the approach using the variability on the functionalities of the application but the variability on the discovery protocols is handled similarly. Four aspects have to be defined for each of the four protocols and these aspects have to be woven alternatively to build the corresponding configurations. As a result, the complete service discovery application is modeled using a base model and 6 aspects instead of the 45 models and/or the 12 scripts needed to specify all the configurations.

4.3 Discussion

Even with the simple example we described, our approach allows reducing by 50% the number of artifacts (aspects or scripts) required to describe the variability of the application. If the whole configuration models are required, (*e.g.*, for validation purpose) we reduce by 86% the number of models (6 aspects and 45 configurations) needed to describe the whole space of configurations. The important property is that the number of models grows linearly with the variability instead of exponentially when all configurations have to be described. It is interesting to also notice that the aspect models are smaller and simpler models than complete configuration models, as they focus on a single concern.

A consequence of the approach is that the adaptation rules do not have to select one specific configuration but sets of variants to include or exclude. In the service discovery example, if the adaptation is specified by a state machine the adaptation rules for the functionalities have to be duplicated for each discovery protocol. Using the proposed approach the adaptation rules for functionalities and network protocols can be defined separately since these two variability dimensions are independent.

In practice, engineers are used to state machines to represent and check adaptation policies. The proposed technique uses aspects and more generic rules which might be more difficult to understand and verify. This is especially true if there are complex interactions between the variability dimensions and variants. To overcome this limitation, the adaptation state machine of the application can be build automatically (completely or partially) from the specification of the variants and the adaptation rules. This gives an opportunity to the designer to check on his usual representation that the aspects and rules yield the expected adaptation.

In this paper, we use the SmartAdapters [14] approach that proposes mechanisms for checking aspects [16]. However, the approach proposed in this paper is not dependent from any specific AOM approach. For example, we could use MATA [13] that proposes to detect aspect interactions based on the graph theory.

5 Generating the Adaptation

In this section, we present our model-driven causal connection responsible for reflecting changes from the model to the platform, and vice-versa. We illustrate our proposition on the service discovery application and discuss the advantages and limitations of our approach.

5.1 Using MDE to Generate the Adaptation Logic

A key characteristic of adaptive systems is their ability to automatically adapt a running application. Our solution adopts a model-driven approach to runtime adaptation by using models at runtime, where the runtime model is connected to the executing system by a causal connection. This causal connection allows us to manage the executing system by manipulating its model. Our approach is similar to how reflection/reflective platforms work, however, using higher level models adds the benefit of remaining platform independent.

Figure 5 presents our approach to runtime adaptation and details the causal connection depicted in Figure 3. A reference model is generated using reflection over the running system, representing the current running configuration. This reference model conforms to our core metamodel for representing component-based running systems. This metamodel contains the core concepts needed to represent a component-based configuration at runtime and is independent of any specific execution platform. The reference model is updated using listeners that observe the architectural reconfigurations of the running system, which allows us to update the model without instantiating it from scratch.

Adaptations are triggered by an adaptation need, usually caused by a context change. In our approach, a reasoning framework decides on a set of aspects according to the new context, and a new configuration the application should adapt to is created by weaving these aspects. It is also possible to create a new configuration by a model transformation or manually by modeling the modified model in a graphical editor.

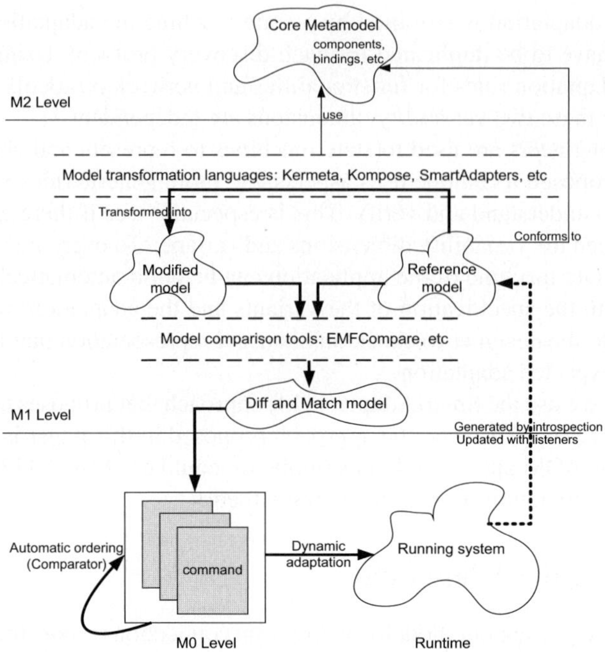

Fig. 5. Model-Driven adaptation at runtime

Once the new configuration is created, it is compared with the reference model (representing the existing configuration). In the current implementation of our tool, we use EMF Compare in order to compare models. It produces a diff and a match model that specifies the differences and the similarities between the models. Note that this model comparison makes our approach independent from any particular transformation language. We browse both diff and match models to analyze the relevant changes between the reference model and the new configuration. During this analysis, we instantiate some reconfiguration commands, responsible for adding and/or removing bindings and/or components, etc. These commands are ordered according to their priority. Indeed, the way the model is transformed does not really matter, provided that the modified model still conforms to the metamodel after transformation whereas the running application should be adapted rigorously. In the final step, the ordered sequence of commands is executed by the platform in order to actually adapt the running system.

As a verification step we check that the new reference model (which is automatically derived through reflection) is identical to the configuration model we wanted to reach. This is an important step as it allows us to verify that all the adaptation commands have been executed successfully.

5.2 Application to the Service Discovery Example

Let us assume that due to a context change, the application is to be adapted from the currently running User Agent configuration to the Service Agent configuration

(Figures 5, 2 and 4). Looking at Figure 5, the former corresponds to the reference model while the latter corresponds to the new configuration. The model comparison detects several changes between these two configurations: *i)* the *Reply* and *Request*, as well as their bindings, have been deleted; *ii)* the *Advertiser* component is introduced into the runtime architecture and connected to the *Cache*, *Policy* and *Network* components. Based on this information, we automatically instantiate a set of reconfiguration commands in order to adapt the system at runtime. As an example, Listing 1.1 presents a reconfiguration script that was generated for the Fractal platform [3]. This script is written in FScript [6], a language that abstracts the Fractal API.

Listing 1.1. UA to SA reconfiguration script expressed in FScript [6]

```
action reconfigureUAtoSA(root, Request, Reply, Advertiser){
  stop($Request);
  stop($Reply);
  // Remove the Request component
  unbind($Request/interface::network);
  unbind($Request/interface::cache);
  unbind($Request/interface::policy);
  unbind($Request/interface::reply);
  remove($root, $Request);
  // Remove the Reply component
  unbind($Reply/interface::network);
  unbind($Reply/interface::cache);
  unbind($Reply/interface::policy);
  unbind($Reply/interface::request);
  remove($root, $Reply);
  // Add the Advertiser component
  add($root, $Advertiser)
  bind($Advertiser/interface::network);
  bind($Advertiser/interface::cache);
  bind($Advertiser/interface::policy);
  start($Advertiser);
}
```

5.3 Discussion

Our approach of using causally connected models during runtime for dynamic reconfiguration has several advantages. First and foremost, we allow automatic generation of reconfiguration scripts instead of having to write them by hand. In our example reconfiguration example from the previous sub-section, 17 operations are needed to reconfigure the application, as shown in Listing 1.1. These operations have to be ordered correctly to produce a consistent script. Our model-driven approach, based on model comparison, allows us to automatically compute and order the reconfiguration operations. Given that the transformations generating the reconfiguration scripts have undergone rigorous testing, these scripts will produce less errors than humans - thus increasing safety. In the service discovery application, we generate 6 scripts to handle the variability on the functionalities (one for each transition in Figure 2).

Second, we remain independent from any model transformation language. The model comparison allows us to be totally disconnected from any tools for manipulating models. Third, we validate target configurations before actually adapting the running system, by checking static constraints and simulating the models [4] for example using Kermeta [17]. It improves the confidence of runtime adaptation, especially when the underlying execution platform is not transactional and does not offer support for rolling back to the previous consistent configuration. In fact, our causal link is strongly synchronized from the running system to the model and delayed from the model to the running system. Finally, our approach can be mapped to different reflective execution platforms. For example, we can monitor and adapt Fractal [3] and OpenCOM [5] systems using the same kind of models.

While using a causally connected model to manipulate the running system has many benefits, it also has a cost. Response times are often important for adaptive systems, and calculating the diff model and automatically generating the reconfiguration scripts from it takes more time than simply executing predefined scripts. A possible solution to that problem is to pre-generate the critical scripts before the system execution. This way, the adaptation can be performed very quickly and the causaly conected model can be updated afterwards. Another solution to avoid model comparison would be to directly connect a particular model transformation language (*e.g.* SmartAdapters) to our causal link. This language would instantiate reconfiguration commands during model transformation and execute these commands after transformation. However, this would make our approach specific to a given model transformation language, while remaining independent from the execution platform.

6 Related Works

Recent middleware platforms like Fractal [3] or OpenCOM [5] propose ways to adapt a system at runtime, inspired by the work by Oreizy *et al.* [18] ten years ago. These approaches do not really propose to manage variability at runtime but propose mechanisms to reconfigure a system at runtime. We propose to map our causal link to any of these platforms. Our metamodel can be seen as a dynamic ADL to describe the running system. We can use any (aspect-oriented) model transformation languages to manipulate the reference model. We are not limited to an ad-hoc imperative reconfiguration language. Our causal link automatically computes the adaptation logic by comparing the reference model to a modified model.

Many mechanisms for runtime variability management have been proposed. They are mainly focused on exchange of runtime entities using parametrization, inheritance, and preprocessor directives [10,19,20]. Our approach is more coarse-grained and uses architecture based models for the management of whole sets of components, their connections and semantics [1]. We can adapt running system via high level transformation languages and graphical editors.

Of particular relevance to our work is MADAM/MUSIC [7,12] which uses the adaptation capabilities offered by middleware platforms, and treats dynamically adaptive systems as dynamic software product lines [11] with the corresponding support for variability management. The main variability mechanism consists in loading different implementations for each component type (primitive or composite) of the architecture.

By decomposing the system into a base model and several aspects, we reduce the complexity related to the representation of variation points and their selection. We automatically compute safe reconfiguration scripts to adapt the system from the reference model to a target configuration. Finally our approach is generic: it can be mapped to different execution platforms whereas MADAM is limited to mobile computing applications, and we can use different model transformation languages to modify the reference model *e.g.* AOM languages like SmartAdapters [14,15], MATA [13] or Kompose [9].

Wolfinger et al. [22] demonstrates the benefits of the integration of an existing product line engineering tool suite with a plug-in platform for enterprise software. As in our case, automatic runtime adaptation and reconfiguration are achieved by using the knowledge documented in variability models. Our differences exist mainly because of the different aims of each approach. Their work focuses on enterprise software while our work covers the domains grid, mobile computing, and embedded systems. While variability decisions in [22] are user-centered our variability decisions, based on the Genie approach [1] are environment-centered.

7 Conclusion and Future Works

In this paper we have presented a novel combination of Model-Driven Engineering (MDE) and Aspect-Oriented Modeling (AOM) to support dynamic variability. AOM allows us to focus on variability dimensions with no need to consider the whole configuration. By composing aspects, it is possible to produce a wide range of configuration models, while managing the combinatorial explosion of variants. Using a MDE approach, we use these configuration models to generate the adaptation logic needed to adapt the running system from one runtime configuration to another, instead of writing it by hand.

In future works, we plan to extend our core metamodel and monitor interesting properties of the running system, such as QoS-related properties, resource consumption, etc. This will allow us to develop a reasoning framework that will automatically select and weave the most adapted aspects. Another perspective is to pre-compile the most useful reconfiguration scripts. For the moment, our causal link computes these scripts at runtime. However, compiling the scripts implies that the model is not yet synchronized with the running system and consequently we do not know which components and bindings to adapt. Languages like FPath [6] may help us in retrieving the component we want to adapt at runtime.

References

1. Bencomo, N., Blair, G., Flores, C., Sawyer, P.: Reflective Component-based Technologies to Support Dynamic Variability. In: VaMoS 2008: 2nd Int. Workshop on Variability Modeling of Software-intensive Systems, Essen, Germany (January 2008)
2. Bencomo, N., Grace, P., Flores, C., Hughes, D., Blair, G.: Genie: Supporting the model driven development of reflective, component-based adaptive systems. In: ICSE 2008 - Formal Research Demonstrations Track (2008)
3. Bruneton, E., Coupaye, T., Leclercq, M., Quéma, V., Stefani, J.B.: The FRACTAL Component Model and its Support in Java. Software Practice and Experience, Special Issue on Experiences with Auto-adaptive and Reconfigurable Systems 36(11-12), 1257–1284 (2006)

4. Chauvel, F., Barais, O., Jézéquel, J.M., Borne, I.: A Model-Driven Process for Self-Adaptive Software. In: ERTS 2008: 4th European Congress on Embedded Real Time Software, Toulouse, France (2008)
5. Coulson, G., Blair, G., Grace, P., Joolia, A., Lee, K., Ueyama, J.: A Component Model for Building Systems Software. In: SEA 2004: IASTED Software Engineering and Applications, Cambridge MA, USA (November 2004)
6. David, P.C., Ledoux, T.: Safe Dynamic Reconfigurations of Fractal Architectures with FScript. In: Proceeding of Fractal CBSE Workshop, ECOOP 2006, Nantes, France (2006)
7. Floch, J., Hallsteinsen, S., Stav, E., Eliassen, F., Lund, K., Gjorven, E.: Using architecture models for runtime adaptability. Software IEEE 23(2), 62–70 (2006)
8. Flores-Cortés, C.A., Blair, G., Grace, P.: An Adaptive Middleware to Overcome Service Discovery Heterogeneity in Mobile Ad-hoc Environments. IEEE Dist. Systems Online (2007)
9. France, R., Fleurey, F., Reddy, R., Baudry, B., Ghosh, S.: Providing Support for Model Composition in Metamodels. In: EDOC 2007: 11th Int. Enterprise Computing Conf. (2007)
10. Goedicke, M., Köllmann, C., Zdun, U.: Designing runtime variation points in product line architectures: three cases. Science of Computer Programming Special Issue: Software variability management 53(3), 353–380 (2004)
11. Hallsteinsen, S., Hinchey, M., Park, S., Schmid, K.: Dynamic Software Product Lines. IEEE Computer 41(4) (April 2008)
12. Hallsteinsen, S., Stav, E., Solberg, A., Floch, J.: Using product line techniques to build adaptive systems. In: SPLC 2006: 10th Int. Software Product Line Conf., Washington, DC, USA, pp. 141–150. IEEE Computer Society, Los Alamitos (2006)
13. Jayaraman, P.K., Whittle, J., Elkhodary, A.M., Gomaa, H.: Model Composition in Product Lines and Feature Interaction Detection Using Critical Pair Analysis. In: MoDELS 2007: 10th Int. Conf. on Model Driven Engineering Languages and Systems, Nashville, USA (October 2007)
14. Lahire, P., Morin, B., Vanwormhoudt, G., Gaignard, A., Barais, O., Jézéquel, J.M.: Introducing Variability into Aspect-Oriented Modeling Approaches. In: MoDELS 2007: 10th Int. Conf. on Model Driven Engineering Languages and Systems, Nashville, USA (October 2007)
15. Morin, B., Barais, O., Jézéquel, J.M.: Weaving Aspect Configurations for Managing System Variability. In: VaMoS 2008: 2nd Int. Workshop on Variability Modelling of Software-intensive Systems, Essen, Germany (January 2008)
16. Morin, B., Vanwormhoudt, G., Lahire, P., Gaignard, A., Barais, O., Jézéquel, J.M.: Managing Variability Complexity in Aspect-Oriented Modeling. In: Czarnecki, K., et al. (eds.) MoDELS 2008. LNCS, vol. 5301, pp. 797–812. Springer, Heidelberg (2008)
17. Muller, P.A., Fleurey, F., Jézéquel, J.M.: Weaving Executability into Object-Oriented Metalanguages. In: Briand, L.C., Williams, C. (eds.) MoDELS 2005. LNCS, vol. 3713, pp. 264–278. Springer, Heidelberg (2005)
18. Oreizy, P., Medvidovic, N., Taylor, R.N.: Architecture-Based Runtime Software Evolution. In: ICSE 1998: 20th Int. Conf. on Software Engineering, Washington, DC, USA (1998)
19. Posnak, E., Lavender, G.: An adaptive framework for developing multimedia. Communications ACM 40(10), 43–47 (1997)
20. Svahnbergel, M., van Gurp, J., Bosch, J.: A taxonomy of variability realization techniques. Software: Practice and Experience 35(8), 705–754 (2005)
21. Tamai, T.: Abstraction orientated property of software and its relation to patentability. Information & Software Technology 40(5-6), 253–257 (1998)
22. Wolfinger, R., Reiter, S., Dhungana, D., Grunbacher, P., Prahofer, H.: Supporting runtime system adaptation through product line engineering and plug-in techniques. In: ICCBSS 2008: 7th Int. Conf. on Composition-Based Software Systems, pp. 21–30 (2008)

Managing Variability Complexity in Aspect-Oriented Modeling*

Brice Morin[1], Gilles Vanwormhoudt[2], Philippe Lahire[3], Alban Gaignard[3], Olivier Barais[1], and Jean-Marc Jézéquel[1]

[1] IRISA/INRIA/Rennes1, Equipe Triskell, F-35042 Rennes Cedex
[2] Institut Telecom / LIFL, Université de Lille 1, F-59655 Villeneuve d'Ascq Cedex
[3] I3S Nice-Sophia Antipolis, Equipe Rainbow, F-06903 Sophia-Antipolis Cedex

Abstract. Aspect-Oriented Modeling (AOM) approaches propose to model reusable aspects that can be applied to different systems at the model level. To improve reusability, several contributions have pointed out the needs of variability in the AOM approaches. Nevertheless, the support of variability makes the aspect design more complex and the introduction of several dimensions of variability (advice, pointcut and weaving) creates a combinatorial explosion of variants and a risk of inconsistency in the aspect model. As the integration of an aspect model may be a complex task, the AOM framework has to be a support for the designer to ensure the consistency of the resulting model. This paper presents an approach describing how to ensure that an aspect model with variability can be safely integrated into an existing model. Verification includes static checking of aspect model consistency and dynamic checking through testing with a focus on the parts of the model that are impacted by the aspect.

1 Introduction

Model-driven engineering (MDE) involves the development and evolution of complex models. To manage this complexity, models are usually decomposed in several smaller models. Different criteria can be considered for decomposition: a concern-driven decomposition (e.g. aspect-oriented modeling AOM), decomposition according to views (e.g. UML proposes several views to build a model), an object-oriented decomposition (where packages can provide a manageable unit for modeling), etc. Once a large model is decomposed into smaller models that can be managed, it becomes possible to work on these models. They can be discussed, refined, checked or simulated. To improve reusability, several contributions, as our previous work called SmartAdapters [7], have pointed out the needs of variability support in the modeling approaches and introduce variability mechanisms into an aspect-oriented modeling approach.

Nevertheless, if the support of variability improves reusability, it makes at the same time the model design more complex. For example, in the context

* This work was partially funded by the DiVA project (EU FP7 STREP).

K. Czarnecki et al. (Eds.): MoDELS 2008, LNCS 5301, pp. 797–812, 2008.

of aspect-oriented modeling in which each model represents one concern of the system, the introduction of several dimensions of variability into the advice, the pointcut and the weaving creates a combinatorial explosion of variants and a risk of inconsistency in the aspect model. As the interaction between an aspect model and the existing base model may be itself complex, it is essential that the AOM provider ensures the consistency of the AO model.

In this paper, we present how to ensure that an aspect model with variability can be safely integrated into an existing base model. The verifications include static verifications that check coherence properties on the aspect model and dynamic verifications through testing that focus on the parts of the base model that are affected by the aspect model. As a result of these verifications, aspect models can be provided as a commodity, such that a software architect can confidently apply an aspect model obtained from a third-party designer.

The remainder of this paper is organized as follows. In Section 2, we present a short overview of SmartAdapters, the AOM approach chosen as a basis of this work and we motivate our work through the presentation of samples of design errors linked to the variability support in an AOM approach. Section 3 presents an overview of the checking process performed on the aspect model in order to improve the designer confidence. Sections 4 and 5 detail two main steps of this process: the static analysis and the testing phase. Section 6 illustrates how the design errors presented in section 2 are detected thanks to this process. Finally, Section 7 presents related works and Section 8 concludes and points out future works.

2 Background and Motivating Examples

SmartAdapters is an AOM approach that has formerly been applied to the domain of Java programs [8] and UML class diagrams. More recently, it has been generalized to any domain meta-model [11]. In the remainder of this paper, we will focus on class diagrams but the ideas described in this paper may be generalized to any domain.

In the SmartAdapters approach, an aspect is composed of three parts: *i)* a graft model, representing *what* we want to weave, *ii)* an interface model, representing *where* we want to weave the aspect and *iii)* a composition protocol specifying *how* to weave the graft model into the interface model. The graft model is a model fragment representing a given concern. The interface model is a model fragment parameterized by roles enabling the interface model to be matched in different base models [15]. Finally, the composition protocol is described by model transformation primitives that manipulate elements from the graft and the interface models.

In [7] we extended SmartAdapters with the addition of variability constructs to both composition protocol (*how*) and interface model (*where*). We have adopted concepts introduced by Software Product Lines (SPL) [22] such as alternatives and variants, options, and constraints. An *alternative* in the composition protocol indicates that there exist several possible ways to compose a part of the graft model into the interface model. An *option*, either in the composition protocol or

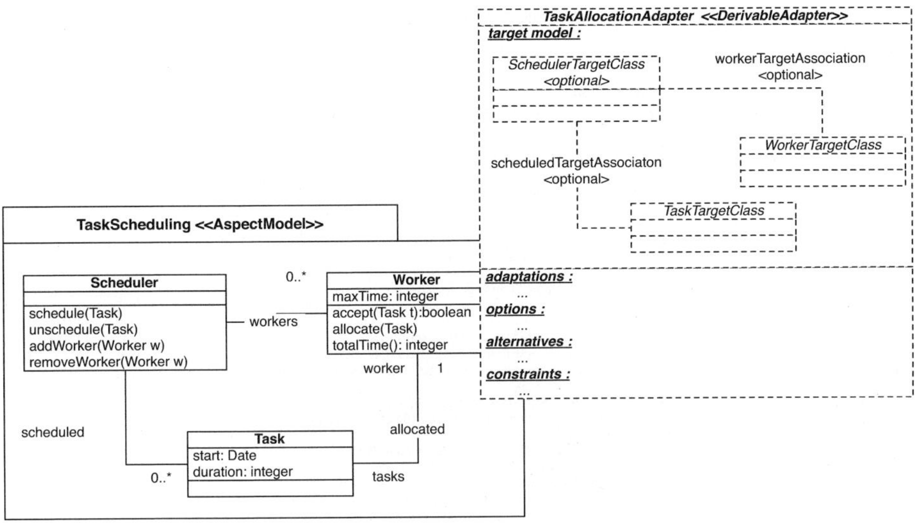

Fig. 1. The task allocation aspect

in the interface model, indicates non-mandatory elements. In the protocol, an optional adaptation might be realized or not. In the interface model optional elements may be bound or not at composition time. The resulting aspect family (i.e. all the aspects we can obtain by derivation), may not be consistent. We propose to add *constraints* in the protocol in order to maintain its integrity.

To illustrate the SMARTADAPTERS approach with variability, we introduce an aspect that aims at allocating tasks to workers, according to their skills and working load. Figure 1 depicts this aspect. Its graft model contains a *Scheduler* class that manages workers described by the *Worker* class and allocates tasks described by the *Task* class. Its interface model, illustrated in top right part of Figure 1, declares that three classes related by associations, some being optional, must be present in a base model to apply this aspect. The composition protocol that describes the different ways to compose this aspect is illustrated in Figure 2.

This protocol proposes to integrate elements (e.g. classes and associations) of the task allocation aspect into a base model either by merging, inheritance or insertion. To this end, it introduces several alternatives. The first alternative called *TaskWorkInsertion* deals with the integration of features provided by classes *Worker* and *Task*. This alternative contains two variants corresponding respectively to the choice between inheriting from these classes or merging their features into *WorkerTarget* and *TaskTarget* classes. A variant may contain several adaptations and options. Implicitly this means that these elements are dependent on each others. In the example, *Worker* and *Task* classes as well as their associations are integrated together in a consistent way.

The second alternative called *SchedulerInsertion* is related to the integration of the *Scheduler* class. This alternative consists of choosing between merging

```
TaskScheduling <<CompositionProtocol>>
adaptations :
options :
alternatives :
  TaskWorkerInsertion [VInheritanceTW] {
      - insertTask : inherit class Task in TaskTarget
      - insertWorker : inherit class Worker in WorkerTarget
      - insertAssoc: introduce association allocated (Task, Worker)
  } or else [VMergingTW] {
      - insertTask: merge class Task in TaskTarget
      - insertWorker: merge class Worker in TaskTarget
      - insertAssoc: introduce association allocated (TaskTarget, WorkerTarget)
  }

  SchedulerInsertion [VIntroductionSched] {
      - insertScheduler : introduce class Scheduler
  } or else [VMergingSched] {
      - insertScheduler : merge class Scheduler in SchedulerTarget
  }

  SchedulerAssociationsInsertion [VIntroductionTWMerge] {
      - insertAssoc1: introduce association workers (Scheduler, WorkerTarget)
      - insertAssoc2: introduce association scheduled (Scheduler, TaskTarget)
  } or else [VIntroductionTWInheritance] {
      - insertAssoc1: introduce association workers (Scheduler, Worker)
      - insertAssoc2: introduce association scheduled (Scheduler, Task)
  } or else [VMappingTWMerge] {
      - insertAssoc1: merge association workers (Scheduler, Worker) with
                      workersTarget (SchedulerTarget, WorkerTarget)
      - insertAssoc2: merge association scheduled (Scheduler, Task) with
                      scheduledTarget (SchedulerTarget, TaskTarget)
      - option renameAssoc1: rename association workers
      - option renameAssoc2: rename association scheduled
  }
constraints :
    VMappingTWMerge implies VMergingSched
    VMergingTW excludes VIntroductionTWInheritance
```

Fig. 2. Composition protocol of the Task Allocation aspect

its features to an existing class of the base model or inserting the class as new. For this second variant, recall that the class is declared optional in the interface model and therefore does not require a binding.

Next, the composition protocol addresses the two associations between the *Scheduler*, the *Worker* and *Task* classes. To manage these associations, the composition protocol declares an alternative with three variants called *VIntroductionTWMerge*, *VIntroductionTWInheritance* and *VMappingTWMerge*. The first two alternatives deal with the case where the associations do not exist in the base model and must be inserted. In this case, two variants are proposed to consider the ways to insert both *Worker* and *Task* classes: the first variant corresponds to the inheritance version whereas the second variant deals with the merging one. As we can see through this example, an alternative may depend on the choice made for another one. The third variant assumes that both associations exist in the base model and provide the adaptation to map them. This variant also gives the capacity to rename each association. Each renaming adaptation (*renameAssoc1*, *renameAssoc2*) is an example of optional adaptation included in a variant.

The choice of the variants and options is realized during the derivation step that produces an aspect with no variability, depending on the choices of the user. For the previous example, we may decide to select variants in order to insert the Scheduler class in combination with the inheritance of Task and Worker and the introduction of association between Scheduler, Task and Worker. After derivation, the resulting aspect can be composed with a base model by specifying

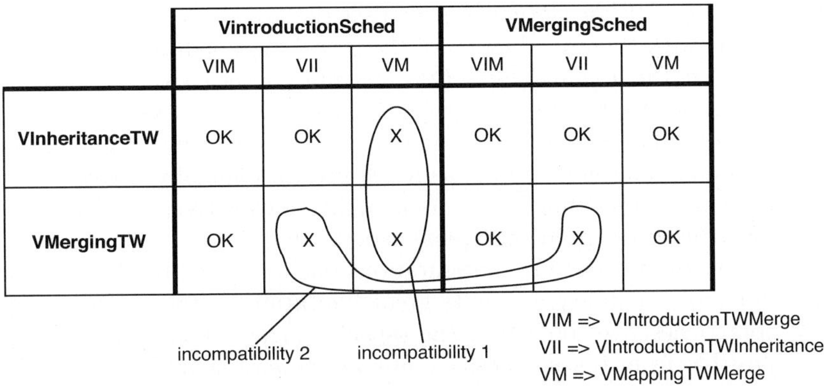

Fig. 3. All variant combinations of the TaskScheduling aspect

a binding that associates each interface model element to a model element of the base model. This binding implicitly contextualizes the primitives planned in the composition protocol with concrete elements.

The table given in Figure 3 summarizes all possible combinations of variants for this previous aspect and indicates if the corresponding combination is consistent. An inconsistent combination means that the adaptations resulting from the selected variants are incompatible. There may be several reasons why variants are incompatible : *i)* a variant depend on elements introduced by other variants not selected in the derivation, *ii)* a variant introduces elements that prevent other selected variant to be applied and, *iii)* combined variants break the conformance with the meta-model or invalidate user-level constraints. In case of the previous aspect, we identify two main incompatibilities corresponding respectively to cases i) and ii):

Incomp. between VIntroductionScheduler and VMappingTWMerge:
The insertion of the *Scheduler* class into the base model excludes the mapping of the associations between *Scheduler*, *Task* and *Worker* with any existing ones. This incompatibility exists regardless if these last two classes are introduced by inheritance or by merging.

Incomp. between VMergingTW and VIntroductionTWInheritance:
The merging of *Task* and *Worker* with existing classes of the base model is incompatible with the introduction of the associations dedicated to the inheritance version.

In order to deal with these incompatibilities, the previous protocol defines one dependency constraint and one mutual exclusion constraint. These constraints restrict the number of possible combinations of variant to consistent ones. The dependency constraint between *VMappingTWMerge* and *VMergingSched* ensures that the variant to map existing associations between *Scheduler*, *Task* and *Worker* classes can only be selected if the first class is integrated by merging, e.g. the *VMergingSched* variant. The mutual exclusion constraint between *VMergingTW* and *VIntroductionTWInheritance* implies that the merging of *Task* and *Worker* is incompatible with the introduction of the association dedicated to the inheritance version, i.e. the *VIntroductionTWInheritance* alternative.

A constraint is an essential construct to ensure the consistency of a family and increase its reliability. However, defining these constraints manually might be time-consuming and not optimal as it requires to manually derive the whole family. The constraints defined by a user might be over (resp. under)-specified leading to a reduced (resp. inconsistent) aspect family.

This need to test all possible configurations (as illustrated by the table of our example) hinders scalability and puts great limitation on the use of variability in AOM approaches. We think that the aspect designer should be alleviated as much as possible from these repetitive operations and should benefit from an automatic support that generates and tests all configurations without designer intervention. Such support should provide feedback at design time about the configurations of variants that cause conflicts so that the aspect designer is able to ensure the consistency of its protocol by introducing all necessary constraints. In the following, we present our solution to provide this automatic support in the context of our AOM approach.

3 Checking Aspect Family Consistency

We propose a systematic approach for analyzing and assessing the consistency of aspect models with variability [7,11]. Our approach generates, analyzes and tests all the possible variants of the aspect family. The complexity of managing all the members of a product line may be time and resource consuming in the case of real SPL. However, an aspect model can be seen as a micro software product line focusing on a given concern and does not aim at representing a whole application. Thus, the number of possible variants for each variable aspect model is reasonable[1].

Our proposed process, shown in Figure 4, starts with a variable aspect. It is composed of three sequential steps which are performed for all possible variants of the variable aspect:

Step 1: Producing a variant of the aspect family: This step produces an aspect model without variability corresponding to a test case for the analysis. The produced aspect model is computed by selecting a configuration of options and variants among the ones defined by the variable aspect: its composition protocol (resp. interface model) only contains elements defined (resp. used) by the selected variants and options. For instance, applying this step in the context of our example consists of constructing an aspect model corresponding to one cell of the table shown in Figure 3.

Step 2: Static analysis of produced aspect: This step takes the produced aspect model as input and performs a static analysis that checks various

[1] However we should study approaches related to testing coverage like [3,9] in order to propose a more realistic solution being a trade off between coverage and testing cost.

properties of consistency on each part of the aspect (graft model, interface Model, composition protocol). If the aspect is detected to be inconsistent, the process stops and the following step is not performed.

Step 3: Testing aspect composition: In this step, the produced aspect is tested for validation by applying its composition protocol to a generated base model. This base model is automatically built from the content of the interface model to ensure that the base model elements respect all its structural constraints. The binding of the aspect model is computed to match each interface model element to the corresponding base model element. If the composition raised an error, a variant is inconsistent.

At the end of the process, a report is generated that specifies all variant configurations that have been tested. For the ones that have failed, explanations about which checking step (step 2 or 3) fails and a detailed diagnostic is provided. This report allows the aspect designer to identify and understand precisely the issues and fix them by changing or extending parts of the aspect model. After the changes, the effects on the aspect model can be tested again by re-running the previous process. The analysis process can be repeated until the test of the variable aspect model is error-free.

4 Aspect Model Static Analysis

In this section, we address *i)* the consistency of the models involved in the description of the aspect model (Section 4.1), *ii)* the consistency of the composition protocol (Section 4.3). To achieve the latter we propose in Section 4.2 an approach allowing an accurate description of the composition protocol semantics.

4.1 Well-Formed Rules of an Aspect Model

Given an aspect model, SmartAdapters first checks that its various elements are syntactically correct and respect the Well-Formedness Rules.

Graft model and Interface model. Both the graft model and the interface model are designed using the concepts defined in our domain meta-model which is very similar to MOF (in fact we use EMF/ECore[2] which is dedicated to the design of class diagrams). Unlike base models, graft and interface only represent model fragments. However, we statically check that model elements are well-typed e.g. all association ends are correctly typed and an object cannot be contained by two model elements.

Adaptations. Several features of the composition language have been designed to prevent the designer from expressing unsafe composition. For example, the association in SmartAdapters is based on the linking of two references (*Ereference* in the ECore meta-model) in two classes. When the designer specifies

[2] See *http://www.eclipse.org/modeling/emf/*

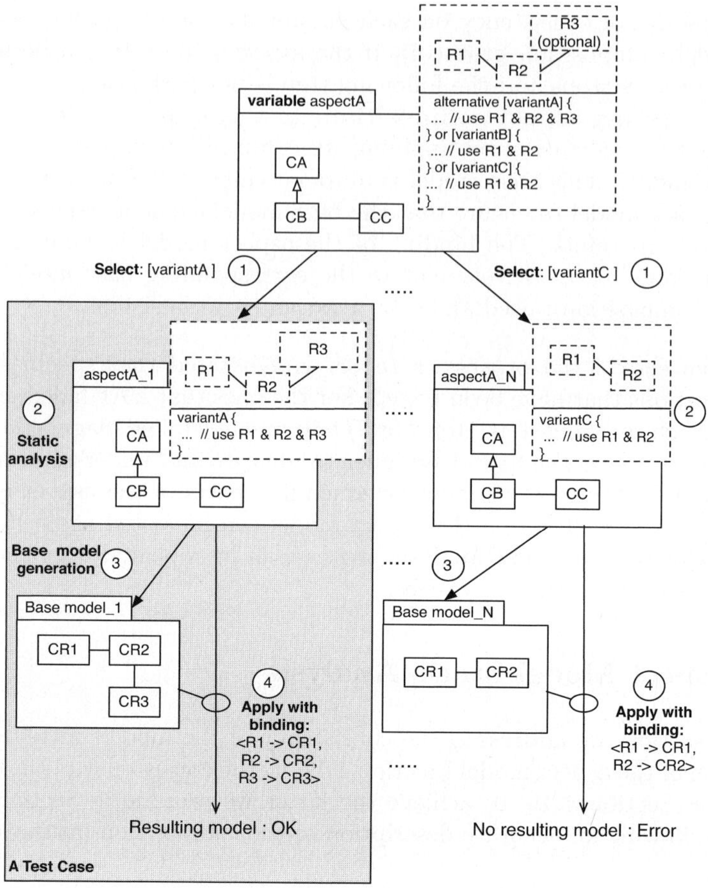

Fig. 4. Overall analysis process

that he wants to set one of the references, SmartAdapters modifies the related association end automatically, relieving the designer of the burden of setting the opposite reference of an association, and then reducing the size of the transformation specification. The SmartAdapters model also requires that each model element is linked through a composition relationship (i.e. the containment property is set in EMF) to at most one model element. The composition protocol enforces this constraint by automatically removing the element of the containment property in the container when the designer changes the container of a model element.

4.2 Adapter Specification Language Semantics

To perform this static analysis, we propose to express our aspect models with a lower level composition language that has a clear operational semantics. We distinguish two types of model composition: basic primitives and merging. We propose to define the semantics of these composition operators in the remainder of this section. This composition language allows us to reason about an aspect before actually weaving it into a particular base model.

An Action Language for Manipulating Models. Basic composition primitives are simple operations on model elements and can easily be implemented with an action language such as Kermeta [12]. The language proposes basic operators on model elements (create, update, delete) and properties (get, set, add, remove). It supports associations and provides loop and condition statements. A full description of the semantics of this language is provided in [19].

The graft model, the interface model and the composition protocol are described with the primitives of this action language. Figure 5 shows an excerpt of the graft model of the task scheduling aspect defined with this action language features. *EClass* and *Ereference* are two meta-classes of ECore allowing to define a class and an object reference. *eReferences* is a property of the meta-class *EClass* which contains all the object references of one class. Lines *01* and *02* show the creation of the classes *Task* and *Worker* and lines *03* and *04* describe the association-end *allocated* connecting these two classes.

```
....
01 CREATE {Eclass,Worker}: creation of class Worker
02 CREATE {Eclass,Task}: creation of class Task
03 CREATE{Ereference,allocated}: creation of reference "allocated" between classes Worker and Task
04 ADD_REF{eReferences,Worker,allocated}: association of reference "allocated" to property eReferences of class Worker
...
```

Fig. 5. Extract of the graft model description with our language [19]

All the basic adaptations provided by SmartAdapters (e.g. adding a super class, adding a parameter in an operation) can be expressed using these low level primitives. For example, the adaptation for adding a super class A to a class B is expressed with our action language by: $\text{ADD\_REF}_{eSuperTypes,A,B}$ where A is the class to be added as parent and B the class to which A should be added as parent. *eSuperTypes* is the property contained in the metaclass "Eclass" that allows to record the super types of a class. A and B are instances of the metaclass *Eclass* and had been already created as shown in Figure 5.

High-Level Model Composition Operator. The composition of model elements can be also performed through a merging operator, which is a symmetric 1 to 1 composition operator (it involves exactly two input models). It is an operator that combines two model elements representing different views on the same concept (in both input models) into a new (or into an updated version of a) model element that represents the merge of those views.

SmartAdapters Models (SAM) composition involves the unification of common elements in the SAM being merged. The composition of two SAMs is based on a merge operator with a parametric semantics proposed in previous work [1]. The characteristic of this merge operator is the fact that it provides a default merge behavior when no conflicts exist between SAMs to be merged. The default behavior defines directives which include: "the members of two classes with the same identifier should be unified into one composite class with this identifier". The conflict detection is based on the following mechanism. First, two elements that have the same identifier are detected. When two model elements have the same identifier, they become possible candidates for being merged. Next, the signatures of these elements are compared in order to check if there is a strict equivalence between them. When the signatures of two matching elements are not equal, a conflict is detected. In [1], we define the signatures for each model element and all possible conflicts. The designer can extend the merge semantics in registering a plugin (conflict fixer) in order to customize the semantics of *merge*.

4.3 Composition Protocol Analysis

The language described in a previous section allows us to benefit from *i)* a description of the model element creation (See Figure 5) and *ii)* a clear semantics of the adaptations. We first propose to analyze each composition protocol *a priori*, before actually weaving the aspect into any model. Each composition protocol is an ordered sequence of adaptations. An example of adaptation described with our action language is presented in Section 4.2 for one type of adaptation. We propose to raise some errors when the composition protocol may produce inconsistencies in the woven model. In order to ease the analysis of composition protocols, we consider *canonical* composition protocols.

Definition 1 (Canonical composition protocol). *A canonical composition protocol is composed of adaptations that all actually have an effect. It does not contain antagonist adaptations (e.g. adding/deleting the same element) nor neutral adaptations (e.g. adding several times the same element in a set).*

A non-canonical protocol will be considered as an error. A report specifying which adaptations are antagonists is generated in order to help the designer in refactoring his aspect.

Definition 2 (Impact). *The impact of a canonical composition protocol on a property p of an object obj is a value $\Delta_{p,obj} \in \mathbb{Z}$ computed as follows:*

$$\Delta_{p,obj} = \#ADD\_{}^{*}{}_{p,anyInstance,obj} - \#DEL\_{}^{*}{}_{p,anyInstance,obj}$$

Less formally, it quantifies the increase or decrease of the size of the property.

Based on the above definitions, we can perform a static analysis of a composition protocol, independently from any base model where it may be applied. We define and formalize a set of rules:

- **1)** $\exists$ CREATE$_{anyMeta,instance}$ $\wedge$ $\exists$ ADD_REF$_{anyPrty,instance,anyTarget}$ $\Rightarrow$ $\exists$ ADD_CONTAIN$_{anyPrty,instance,anyTarget}$[3]

[3] ADD/DEL_CONTAIN [19] enable to set/unset the containment property mentioned in Section 4.

This rule detects the dangling references that refer to elements that are not present in the resulting model.
- **2)** $\forall$ obj : Object, p : Property $\in$ obj
  $\Delta_{p,obj} \leq$ p.upper - p.lower
  This rule detects if the composition of the aspect respects the cardinality defined in the meta-model.
- **3)** $\exists$ DEL_CONTAIN$_{p,obj,any} \Rightarrow \neg\exists$ obj',p' | obj $\in$ obj'.p'
  This rule raises a warning specifying that a model element is removed from the resulting model and may lead to some dangling references.

Rules **1** and **2** allow to detect some inconsistencies before actually weaving the aspect into a particular base model. We now propose to use the knowledge provided by the base model to describe some model-specific rules that are checked before weaving. In the following rules, we denote *base(obj)* of the base model element associated to the interface model element *obj* and *base(obj).p.size* the actual size of the property *p* of the base model element bound to *obj*.

- **4)** $\forall$ obj : Object, p : Property $\in$ obj
  base(obj).p.size - p.lower $\leq \Delta_{p,obj} \leq$ p.upper - base(obj).p.size
  This rule refines rule **2** with the knowledge provided by the base model and verifies that the cardinality defined in the metamodel will be respected by the resulting model.
- **5)** $\exists$ DEL_CONTAIN$_{p,obj,any} \Rightarrow \neg\exists$ obj',p' | base(obj) $\in$ obj'.p'
  This rule refines rule **2** with the knowledge provided by the base model and verifies that no dangling references will be produced after weaving.

5 Validating an Aspect Model through Testing

5.1 Overview

The static analysis step can detect some errors but others are not detected through the static analysis due to the lack of information in the interface model. The last step of the process is a testing approach. In this case, we consider the aspect model with variability as a system to check. Each derived aspect model (see Section 3) can be seen as a test case for the system. The oracle is composed of two kinds of assertion:

1. Could we perform the composition? If the composition raised an error before the end, we are in the case of an inconsistent aspect model. It generally means that some constraints are missing to correctly handle the variation points of the aspect model.
2. Does the resulting model conform to its meta-model and respect its well-formedness rules ?

The last point in the testing process consists of obtaining the test data. From the interface model, we generate a set of base models. The derived aspect model will be woven into each of the generated base models.

For each kind of error, the SmartAdapters framework gives a diagnostic that explains why the test case fails. In the first case, it gives the diagnostic to explain which adaptation cannot be executed and why. In the second case, it gives which global invariant is not respected. The designer should then analyze precisely the generated variant and the generated base model to understand the issue.

5.2 Generating a Set of Base Model

We automatically generate a set of base models in order to validate composition protocols. Generating base models from scratch may be resource and time-consuming. But, we are only interested in base models where the derived aspect model may be applied, i.e. where the interface model matches. In other words, models that do not integrate the interface model are not interesting for validating our composition protocols. We propose to use the approach of Sen *et al.* [18,17] to produce a set of base models that completes the interface model in order to respect all the explicit and implicit constraints defined in the meta-model.

The base models that are used as test data for model composition are mainly constrained by the interface model that defines a set of constraints on the required base model. Thus, in order to automatically generate base models for testing it is necessary to interpret both structural information and invariants defined in the interface model (see [15]) into a consistent set of information that can be used for model synthesis. In our approach, we use the Cartier tools [17] based on the first-order relational logic language Alloy to transform interface models into constraints. Once solved, these constraints lead to a selection of qualified base models from the input domain of the model composition.

For each composition protocol, we generate a report that specifies the percentage of woven models meeting the oracle criteria defined in Section 5.1. This report can be used by the designer to validate and invalidate some variants of the composition protocol. Note that this report does not prove that the composition is totally safe.

6 Assessments

In section 2 we introduce a task scheduling aspect that contains variability. In Figure 3, we identified four cases where the derived aspects does not make sense. In this section, we give a quick look on how these cases could be automatically identified by our verification process. Due to a lack of space, we detail only two of the four problematic cases identified in Figure 3: Entry 2.1 and Entry 2.2.

6.1 VMergingTW x VIntroductionSched x VIntroductionTWInheritance

The derived aspect corresponding to this case is illustrated in Figure 3 (Entry 2.1). The *Task* and *Worker* classes are respectively introduced by merging into the *TaskTarget* and *WorkerTarget* classes. An association is introduced between those two merged classes. Note that our merge modifies the existing classes[4], so the association is properly introduced. The *Scheduler* class is then

[4] "Merge a into b" modifies b with features from a.

introduced. Whether the *SchedulerBase* class is present or not in the interface model, the *Scheduler* class can be introduced. The introduction of the associations *worker* and *scheduled* is problematic. Indeed, only one extremity class of each association has been introduced. In other words, we refer to elements outside of the resulting model. This problem is detected by two violations of the rule **1**:

- $\exists$ CREATE$_{class,Worker}$ $\wedge$ $\exists$ ADD_REF$_{referenceType,worker,Worker}$ $\Rightarrow$ $\exists$ ADD_CONTAIN$_{_,_,Worker}$
  The *Worker* class will not be introduced into the base model but the *worker* association will refer to it.
- $\exists$ CREATE$_{class,Task}$ $\wedge$ $\exists$ ADD_REF$_{referenceType,scheduled,Task}$ $\Rightarrow$ $\exists$ ADD_CONTAIN$_{_,_,Task}$
  The *Task* class will not be introduced into the base model but the *worker* association will refer to it.

6.2 VMergingTW x VMergingSched x VIntroductionTWInheritance

The derived aspect associated to this combination of alternative (Entry 2.2 in Figure 3) leads to the violation of the same rules. Moreover, the two extremities of both associations (*worker* and *scheduled*) are not present in the resulting model because the *Scheduler* class is introduced by merging it into the *SchedulerTarget* class. Thus, it cannot be referred to.

We have shown in this section how the static analysis of the derived aspects can determine before weaving two problematic cases. The detection of these problems early in the design of an aspect model allows the designer to identify that it misses constraints to forbid these configurations during the derivation. The three kinds of checking: WFR (Section 4.1), static analysis through partial evaluation (Sections 4.2-4.3), and test (Section 5) create a modular verification process allowing the designer to incrementally validate his aspect model. For example, if an error is detecting by static analysis, it is not necessary to perform the testing phase.

7 Related Work and Discussion

Ensuring software correctness is an important issue and this is amplified in the case of software product lines [14,20]. One of the main concerns for correctness in product lines is about the methods to be used in order to limit the number of tests to be performed for a family of products. Two issues are especially considered: the increase of work for the programmer and the time spent to perform them [3,9]. These contributions mainly introduce formal methods in order to exploit the commonalities of a software family in order to achieve these issues. They rely on SAT solver [4] or more generally on model-checking [6] techniques in order to verify those tests.

Because the domain engineering is handled in the early phases of the software development process, approaches requies test modeling - for example - on use-cases [13], activity diagrams [16], feature models [4,10,16,21], OCL [4] or on a combination of these formalisms. It is interesting to mention that application engineering deals more with source code testing and that tests related to domain engineering can be addressed also later on during product line evolution.

When the product line is built from legacy systems, the main idea is to generalize tests made for existing applications [5]. On the contrary, when the product line is built first approaches favor the design of generic tests [6,16] enabling to produce tests for the applications which are derived from the product line.

It is worth noting that the "product" which is foreseen in our approach is the composition protocol associated to a graft model. The complexity which is expected for such a product line can not be compared with the one addressed by [3,9] so that, trying to reduce the number of tests to be performed is not an issue. Moreover, the operations supported by our product line correspond to a small set of adaptations whose semantics is precisely defined (see Section 4.2) so that most of the tests could be generated. Because a composition protocol relies on a business model, our approach deals with model-testing but not source-code testing.

When dealing with tests relating to the domain engineering phase, some of the interesting issues are dealing with the kind of tests to be performed. Possible ones are: *i)* to check that the derived products do not break any rules of the meta-model that is used to describe the product family [4], *ii)* to ensure that the product derivation ensures the variability constraints [2,16], *iii)* to control that there is no more functionality than those used by the derived applications [16] and, *iv)* to check the consistency of the product line that is designed.

Most approaches are dealing with testing the conformance of applications with a product line but very few consider the issue of building a consistent product line (point *iv*). Our approach intends to provide an homogeneous process to guide and control the derivation process even if our contribution mainly focuses on point *iv*. According to this last issue, we should mention contributions such as [4] which relies on OCL constraint specification or [10] which provides advanced tests. The tests proposed by [10] deal with *i)* realizability (are there non-realizable product line members?); *ii)* internal competition (are there identical feature combinations?), *iii)* commonality between realizable product line members and *vi)* dead variants or features in the derived product. Like our approach, these approaches are not dedicated to a specific product line.

8 Conclusion and Future Work

SmartAdapters promotes the design of reusable business models that can be woven according to the needs of application architects. In our approach these reusable models are composed of: a graft model (the business description), an interface model (the required entities from base models) and a composition protocol (how to compose the graft model into the interface model) independent from the base model. Because there exists a wide range of base models for a given domain, the way we compose our reusable models should really be flexible in order to fit to the various contexts of reuse. To achieve this issue we designed our composition protocol as a product line [7] but its underlying variability mechanisms create a combinatorial explosion of variants and a risk of inconsistency in the aspect model.

Consequently, it is necessary to provide not only the aspect description but also the verification process that comes with it: like software engineering, model engineering requires validation. To ensure the consistency of the models obtained after weaving an aspect, it is mandatory to ensure the consistency of the aspect model, that is to say to perform a deep analysis on *i)* the set of derived composition protocols and *ii)* the involved models (graft and interface). This work has proposed a checking process that achieves static analysis and consistency tests of aspect models with variability. It relies on clear semantics of both the domain and the composition protocol thanks to an action language and generative features. This checking process aims at ensuring that the aspect designer did not forget any of the constraints driving its variability.

In future works, we plan to extend our approach in order to provide an integrated environment dedicated to the control and the guidance of the user during the derivation process. We also plan to add the capability to attach domain constraints to an aspect model that will act as post-conditions of the model compositions. Our approach is not currently supporting the detection of faults in the pointcut definition but we intend to show that domain constraints contribute to address this issue. Lastly, we plan to study more sophisticated strategies for the generation of base models in order to get tests which validate an aspect model on contexts closer to what may be found in industrial case-studies.

References

1. Barais, O., Klein, J., Baudry, B., Jackson, A., Clarke, S.: Composing Multi-View Aspect Models. In: 7th IEEE International Conference on Composition-Based Software Systems (ICCBSS), Madrid, Spain (Febuary 2008)
2. Bertolino, A., Fantechi, A., Gnesi, S., Lami, G.: Product Line Use Cases: Scenario-based Specification and Testing of Requirements. In: Software Product Lines, pp. 425–445. Springer, Heidelberg (2006)
3. Cohen, M.B., Dwyer, M.B., Shi, J.: Coverage and Adequacy in Software Product Line Testing. In: ROSATEA 2006: ISSTA 2006 workshop on Role of software architecture for testing and analysis, pp. 53–63. ACM Press, New York (2006)
4. Czarnecki, K., Pietroszek, K.: Verifying Feature-Based Model Templates Against Well-Formedness OCL Constraints. In: GPCE 2006: Proceedings of the 6th Int. Conf. on Generative Programming and Component Engineering, pp. 211–220. ACM Press, New York (2006)
5. Geppert, B., Li, J.J., Rößler, F., Weiss, D.M.: Towards Generating Acceptance Tests for Product Lines. In: Bosch, J., Krueger, C. (eds.) ICOIN 2004 and ICSR 2004. LNCS, vol. 3107, pp. 35–48. Springer, Heidelberg (2004)
6. Kishi, T., Noda, N., Katayama, T.: Design Verification for Product Line Development. In: Obbink, H., Pohl, K. (eds.) SPLC 2005. LNCS, vol. 3714, pp. 150–161. Springer, Heidelberg (2005)

7. Lahire, P., Morin, B., Vanwormhoudt, G., Gaignard, A., Barais, O., Jézéquel, J.M.: Introducing Variability into Aspect-Oriented Modeling Approaches. In: Engels, G., Opdyke, B., Schmidt, D.C., Weil, F. (eds.) MODELS 2007. LNCS, vol. 4735, pp. 498–513. Springer, Heidelberg (2007)
8. Lahire, P., Quintian, L.: New Perspective To Improve Reusability in Object-Oriented Languages. Journal Of Object Technology (JOT) 5(1), 117–138 (2006)
9. Mannion, M., Cámara, J.: Theorem Proving for Product Line Model Verification. In: van der Linden, F.J. (ed.) PFE 2003. LNCS, vol. 3014, pp. 211–224. Springer, Heidelberg (2004)
10. Metzger, A., Heymans, P., Pohl, K., Schobbens, P.-Y., Saval, G.: Disambiguating the Documentation of Variability in Software Product Lines: A Separation of Concerns, Formalization and Automated Analysis. In: RE 2007: 15th Int. Conf. on Requirements Engineering, Delhi, October 2007, pp. 243–253. IEEE Computer Society, Los Alamitos (2007)
11. Morin, B., Barais, O., Jézéquel, J.M.: Weaving Aspect Configurations for Managing System Variability. In: VaMoS 2008: 2nd International Workshop on Variability Modelling of Software-intensive Systems, Essen, Germany (2008)
12. Muller, P.A., Fleurey, F., Jézéquel, J.M.: Weaving Executability into Object-Oriented Meta-languages. In: Briand, L.C., Williams, C. (eds.) MoDELS 2005. LNCS, vol. 3713. Springer, Heidelberg (2005)
13. Nebut, C., Fleurey, F., Le Traon, Y., Jézéquel, J.M.: A Requirement-Based Approach to Test Product Families. In: van der Linden, F.J. (ed.) PFE 2003. LNCS, vol. 3014, pp. 198–210. Springer, Heidelberg (2004)
14. Pohl, K., Metzger, A.: Software Product Line Testing. Commun. ACM 49(12), 78–81 (2006)
15. Ramos, R., Barais, O., Jézéquel, J.M.: Matching Model Snippets. In: Engels, G., Opdyke, B., Schmidt, D.C., Weil, F. (eds.) MODELS 2007. LNCS, vol. 4735, pp. 121–135. Springer, Heidelberg (2007)
16. Reuys, A., Reis, S., Kamsties, E., Pohl, K.: The ScenTED Method for Testing Software Product Lines. In: Software Product Lines, pp. 479–520. Springer, Heidelberg (2006)
17. Sen, S., Baudry, B., Mottu, J.-M.: On Combining Multi-formalism Knowledge to Select Models for Model Transformation Testing. In: ICST 2008: 1st Int. Conf. on Software Testing Verification and Validation, Lillehammer, Norway (April 2008)
18. Sen, S., Baudry, B., Precup, D.: Partial Model Completion in Model Driven Engineering using Constraint Logic Programming. In: Int. Conf. on Appl. of Declarative Programming and Knowledge Management, Wurzburg, Germany (October 2007)
19. SmartAdapters action language semantics (2008), http://www.irisa.fr/triskell/perso_pro/obarais/pmwiki.php?n=Research.SmartAdapters
20. Svahnberg, M., Bosch, J.: Issues Concerning Variability in Software Product Lines. In: van der Linden, F.J. (ed.) IW-SAPF 2000. LNCS, vol. 1951, pp. 146–157. Springer, Heidelberg (2000)
21. Thaker, S., Batory, D., Kitchin, D., Cook, W.: Safe Composition of Product Lines. In: GPCE 2007: 6th Int. Conf. on Generative Programming and Component Engineering, pp. 95–104. ACM, New York (2007)
22. Ziadi, T., Jézéquel, J.M.: Product Line Engineering with the UML: Products Derivation. In: Software Product Lines, pp. 557–588. Springer, Heidelberg (2006)

Mapping the UML2 Semantics of Associations to a Java Code Generation Model

Dominik Gessenharter

Ulm University, Institute of Software Engineering
and Compiler Construction, D-89069 Ulm, Germany
Dominik.Gessenharter@uni-ulm.de

Abstract. It is state of the art to provide UML modeling by means of class diagrams and code generation from there. But whereas drawing diagrams is most often well supported, code generation is limited in scope. Association classes, multiplicities, aggregation and composition are not correctly or not at all processed by most code generators. One reason may be that the UML semantics is not formally defined in the UML specification. As a result of that, associations are usually transformed into code by using properties of the same type as the associated classes or corresponding typed sets. This approach must fail although the UML2 Superstructure Specification considers association ends owned by a class to be equal to a property of the owning class. In this paper, we describe why associations should be implemented as classes when generating code from class diagrams.

Keywords: UML, Associations, Code Generation, Java.

1 Introduction

OMG's Model Driven Architecture [18] is an approach to a Model Driven Development (MDD) process using the Unified Modeling Language (UML). MDD concentrates on models, whereas code is generated from there. Only the quality of a model should influence the code's quality, i. e. a highly detailed model covering all aspects of an application should result in automatically generated code with no necessity for adaptations. This ambition requires good code generation tools. But most code-generators produce code that does not cover all the elements of the input model.

This situation is problematic: Models are the result of the analysis and design phases and must conform to all requirements of a system and therefore, generated code should cover the entire semantics of the model. Otherwise, the conformance of the code to the model remains in the sole responsibility of the developer. This entails more lines of hand-written code and is error prone. Furthermore, the verification of a model is invalidated. Generated code should enforce all constraints to be always held, as it is the case in modern database systems, where foreign key definitions allow to define the rejection of the deletion of a dataset if it would result in a violation of the underlying ER-Model.

K. Czarnecki et al. (Eds.): MoDELS 2008, LNCS 5301, pp. 813–827, 2008.

With regard to associations, both the UML specification [21] and code generation should be improved. We contribute to both in the following way:

- We shortly introduce the specification [21] of associations in Sect. 2 and show its shortcomings.
- An evaluation of some code generators reveals, that only the code pattern discussed in Sect. 3 is used for the implementation of associations.
- In Sect. 4 we point out, why this pattern is invalid and how it relates to deficiencies of the UML specification [21].
- In Sect. 5, we discuss how another approach of translating associations considers the characteristics of associations that are explained in Sect. 2.

The context of this work is the ACTIVECHARTS project [23], which requires a code generator for static structure modeled in UML 2 class diagrams. It is based on the UML 2.1.2 Superstructure Specification [21]. Keywords of the UML as well as class or instance names are written in *italics*. Instances of classes are named with the class name in lowercase letters.

2 Associations at a Glance

In this section, we describe the concept of an association. We concentrate on binary associations unless otherwise stated.

2.1 Elements of Associations

> "An association specifies a semantic relationship that can occur between typed instances. It has at least two ends represented by properties, each of which is connected to the type of the end. (...) Each end represents participation of instances of the classifier connected to the end in links of the association." [21, p. 39]

An association end may be adorned with a role name, a multiplicity, a property string, a navigability and a visibility modifier. It may be owned by the association itself or by the classifier connected to the opposite end of the association.

The UML provides no means of defining a uni-directional association. Relating a class A to a class B entails that both classes are related to each other and associations therefore cannot be uni-directional.

> "An association describes a set of tuples whose values refer to typed instances. An instance of an association is called a link." [21, p. 39]

However, the UML specification is general enough to allow both uni-directional and bi-directional links. We write a bi-directional link for an association L between classes A and B as $(a \leftrightarrow b)_L$, a uni-directional link from a to b as $(a \rightarrow b)_L$. For brevity, the index $_L$ will be omitted when no confusion is possible. A reference on b held by a (in Java) is denoted by $a \rightarrow_{ref} b$.

Note that uni-directional links are not contradictory to bi-directional associations. A bi-directional association may be implemented by two uni-directional links as long as they are consistent as defined in the following section.

2.2 Consistency of Associations

A tuple (a, b) in an association L can be represented by a bi-directional link $(a \leftrightarrow b)$ or two uni-directional links $(a \rightarrow b)$ and $(b \rightarrow a)$. Note that the roles of a and b may be chosen arbitrarily, but must be kept consistent for a given association.

The consistency of unidirectional links for an association is assured when $\forall a : A, b : B : (a \rightarrow b) \Leftrightarrow (b \rightarrow a)$ holds.

2.3 Multiplicities at Association Ends

An essential feature of associations are multiplicities at association ends.

> "A multiplicity is a definition of an inclusive interval of non-negative integers beginning with a lower bound and ending with a (possibly infinite) upper bound." [21, p. 94]

Multiplicities are used to determine how many instances of the associated classes can or must be linked at a time.

2.4 Ownership of Association Ends

The UML specification defines that an association end may be owned by the association itself or by a member end class.

Association ends are properties. Owning an association end means that the property becomes a structural element of the owning classifier, and consequently, part of the object's state. Therefore, adding or removing a link will have an impact on the object's state in cases where the end is owned by a class. For ends owned by associations, the same rules hold, but the impact is on the association.

The relation between the objects remains unaffected, but a directive where to store links at runtime is made. Links may not appear in objects of classes, that do not own the corresponding association end. So far, a correlation between ownership of association ends and implementation of links (in particular where links are to be stored) as suggested by Diskin and Dingel [8] is even mandatory.

2.5 Navigability of Association Ends

> "Navigability means instances participating in links at runtime (instance of an association) can be accessed efficiently from instances participating in links at the other ends of the association." [21, p. 41]

An association end is navigable when it is either a *navigableOwnedEnd* of the association or an *ownedAttribute* of an end class. Otherwise, it is not navigable [21, p. 39]. The specification does not claim that a non-navigable end must not be accessed by opposite ends. It rather states that it may or may not. Accordingly it is not necessary to store links directed in a non-navigable direction of an association, however, it is not invalid to store them either. For an association between A and B navigable from A to B, a link $a : A \rightarrow b : B$ is sufficient.

An informal convention whereby non-navigable ends are assumed to be owned by the association whereas navigable ends are assumed to be owned by the classifier at the opposite end is deprecated [21, p.43], but we find a dependency when having a look at the inversion. A non-navigable end must be owned by the association. If owned by the class via *ownedAttribute*, it is navigable.

2.6 Visibility of Association Ends

The visibility "determines where the NamedElement appears within different Namespaces within the overall model, and its accessibility" [21, p.98]

The specification allows to define a non-navigable end as public. Such an end must be owned by the association (because it is non-navigable) but may be accessed. However, a non-navigable end not necessarily grants access to the opposite classifier. The effect of accessibility to a non-navigable end is unclear.

2.7 Aggregation Types of Association Ends

An association end has an *aggregationType* which may have one of the values *none*, *shared* or *composite*. The values *shared* and *composite* may only appear in binary associations and indicate a whole/part relationship. Aggregation is transitive and may not be modeled in a cyclic way. An association end with *aggregationType composite*

> "indicates that the property is aggregated compositely, i. e., the composite object has responsibility for the existence and storage of the composed objects (parts)." [21, p. 39]

This implies that the deletion of the composite entails the deletion of all of its current parts.

2.8 Piecing it Together

The specification states that "aggregation type, navigability, and end ownership are orthogonal concepts," [21, p. 43]. However, the concepts are not independent since an association end owned by a class via *ownedAttribute* implies that this association end is navigable.

Being non-navigable implies that the association end is owned by the association via *ownedEnd* and must not be included in the subset *navigableOwnedEnd*.

The specification does not define where links are to be stored. This implies that parts of links may not be stored at all if these parts are derivable from other information. Diskin and Dingel [8] give a detailed discussion about that.

Figure 1 shows an association that is navigable from A to B. An instance $b : B$ does not need any information about which instances $a_i : A$ it is related to. This information is derivable from the references stored in each a_i. As these links may be implemented in code by a static `map<A,List<B>>`, accessible through the class A, the multiplicity constraint of the A-end can be satisfied. Each instance $b : B$ must not be contained in more than 10 lists, i. e. be referenced by more than 10 $a_i : A$.

Fig. 1. An association navigable from A to B

3 Code Generation – State of the Art

We evaluated Altova umodel [3], ARTiSAN Studio [4], Borland Together [5], ChangeVIsion Jude Professional [6], Gentleware Apollo [14], IBM Rational Software Architect [16], No Magic MagicDraw [19], Sparx System Enterprise Architect [24] and Visual Paradigm for UML [27], which are linked in the UML vendor directory [26] as well as EMF [9], Fujaba [11], Gentleware Poseidon [15] and Telelogic Rhapsody [25]. Code generation from UML class diagrams is supported by all these tools, but the level of compliance to the UML specification varies considerably. Having a closer look at associations, some insufficiencies become evident.

3.1 Common Implementation of Associations

All evaluated tools generate code for associations by using attributes in the member end classes. In the case of a binary association, each class obtains an attribute that can store a reference to the opposite class.

3.2 Multiplicities at Association Ends

Except from Together [5], MagicDraw [19] and Enterprise Architect [24], upper bounds of multiplicities are rudimentarily implemented. If it is greater than 1, the attribute representing the association end is of a collection type. Thus, only two states are identified, namely an upper bound that equals to 1 or one of a higher value. None of the tools rejects a new link if the upper bound is violated. Looking at lower bounds, the situation is even worse. They are completely omitted. A compliant mapping of a lower bound to source code is more difficult than that of an upper bound. Nevertheless, it is possible (see Akehurst et al. [2]).

3.3 Ownership of Association Ends

Only umodel [3] and MagicDraw [19] allow modeling the ownership of association ends. However, all tools treat associations as if the association ends were owned by the member end classes. This implies that non-navigable ends become navigable, but the specification does not force non-navigable ends to be not accessible. Because "(...) an association end owned by a class is also an attribute" [21, p. 45], the above outlined policy of association implementation is no contradiction to the specification. Developers probably will not miss the feature of modeling ownership, as it is not even discussed in most UML books that address developers like UML2.0 - Das umfassende Handbuch [17] or UML 2 glasklar [22].

3.4 Navigability of Association Ends

The lack of ownership representation in code leads to associations that are navigable in both ways. It is common to omit the generation of an attribute in a member end class if the opposite end is non-navigable. It is assumed that an association where all ends are non-navigable will never appear in a model.

This assumption is problematic because non-navigable associations might be useful in combination with association classes and therefore should be allowed and translated to code.

By omitting the generation of an attribute, the ownership of a non-navigable association end is considered (see Sect 2.5) as it is no feature of the classifier.

3.5 Visibility of Association Ends

The visibility of association ends is taken over to the generated attribute representing the association end. As non-navigable ends are not implemented in code, visibility for those ends is not taken into account. Thus, all implemented association ends are supplied with the intended visibility.

Because a non-navigable end is not necessarily accessible, a visibility modifier is not needed. We consider public visibility of an inaccessible feature useless.

3.6 Consistency of Associations

Many tools just provide the static structure for associations, i. e. the attribute generation in the member end classes. When using those tools, managing the association remains in the scope of the developers' work.

However, Fujaba [11], Rhapsody [25] and EMF [9] generate code that allows to add or remove instances from associations. These tools even implement the consistency of associations:Whenever an instance a is referenced by an instance b (i. e. $b \rightarrow_{ref} a$), the instance b calls a generated method in a passing itself as a parameter. The instance a then obtains a reference to b ($a \rightarrow_{ref} b$) [10].

3.7 Aggregation and Composition

The situation regarding code generation for aggregate associations is staggering. The evaluated tools do not consider the difference between "plain" associations and aggregations or compositions. A more detailed evaluation of the tools will be published in a forthcoming paper. Akehurst et al. [2] evaluated a selection of more tools describing nearly the same situation in 2006. As far as we know, the situation has not substantially changed. In this regard, the modeling facilities of the current tools allow the violation of UML semantics like having a part included in multiple composites at a time. Probably, the reason for this is that a composite cannot be implemented by the standard association implementation. A discussion of this issue is given in Sect 5.5.

3.8 Summary of State-of-the-Art Code Generators

The coverage of code generation ranges from preparing associations by generating adequate attribute definitions to sophisticated mechanisms that manage association consistency at runtime.

However, as we will see in the following section, many deficiencies remain in the common patterns of generated code for associations.

4 Why Do Common Code Generation Methods Fail?

There are two reasons why code generation as described in the previous section fails. The first is that a mutual update of references requires association ends to be visible to the opposite end, the second is that if for non-navigable ends no attribute is generated in a member class, information of multiplicities may be left out.

4.1 The Informally Defined Set of Links

The specification gives an informal definition of the set of tuples as follows:

> "For an association with N ends, choose any N-1 ends and associate specific instances with those ends. Then the collection of links of the association that refer to these specific instances will identify a collection of instances at the other end. The multiplicity of the association end constrains the size of this collection." [21, p. 40]

Fig. 2. A binary association

A formalization of the cited definition is given by Diskin and Dingel [8]. The association shown in Fig. 2 defines tuples (a_i, b_j) and for each arbitrarily chosen $a : A$, there must exist at least m and at most n tuples, for each arbitrarily chosen $b : B$, at least s and at most t tuples must exist.

4.2 Implementation of Links by the Use of References

In general, a single reference cannot implement a link. However, two references do as long as the following condition holds:

$\forall\ a_i : A \leftrightarrow b_j : B\ \exists\ a_i \rightarrow_{ref} b_j\ \wedge\ \exists\ b_j \rightarrow_{ref} a_i$

This condition requires a mutual update of both references if a link is changed.

4.3 Dependency between Navigability and Visibility

Navigability requires efficient access to the opposite side of an association. In case of a binary association with both ends navigable and owned by the member end classes, both classifiers can access each other. The use of references as described above suffices.

Fig. 3. An association with two navigable ends, each of which has the *VisibilityKind* public

A mechanism for satisfying the condition formulated in Sect. 4.2 is described in [10]. It is based on the idea introduced in Sect 3.6. The code generated for class *A* and the association in Fig. 3 looks like Listing 1, class *B* may be implemented analogously. EMF [9], Fujaba [11] and Rhapsody [25] implement this pattern.

```
public class A{
    private B b;
    public boolean setB (B value){
        if (this.b == value) return false;
        B oldValue = this.b;
        this.b = value;
        if (oldValue != null)
            oldValue.setA (null);
        if (value != null)
            value.setA (this);
        return true;
    }
    public B getB () { return this.b; }
}
```

Listing 1. Implementation of mutual updates for links of an association

A problem is that if one (or both) association end(s) is (are) of private visibility, one (or both) side(s) must not be allowed to update the links at the opposite end [13]. The implementation of Fujaba [11] generates non-compilable code when modeling an association with all ends defined private. EMF [9] and Rhapsody [25] violate the visibility and define the attributes as public. It must be considered that the Ecore-model of EMF [9] relates to the MOF [20] (see [1]) and not to the UML [21]. In the Essential MOF (EMOF) that only slightly differs from the Ecore, associations are not defined. It is only possible to link a property to another property called the *opposite*. EMF [9] thus implements the Ecore-model correctly. However, tools claiming to be UML compliant must implement associations, but all evaluated tools except from Fujaba [11] and Rhapsody [25] do not generate code for associations as specified by the UML (see [21]) but in the style of the MOF (see [20]).

In general, the problem can be formulated as follows:

Note 1. If an association is navigable in more than one direction, the *visibility* of the navigable ends must allow the connected classifier to access this end.

4.4 Attributes, Associations and Links

As described in Sect 3.4, navigability is implemented by the suppression of attribute generation for non-navigable ends. This technique follows a transformation of notations (which we term $\mathbf{T_1}$) defined in the specification as follows:

> "The attribute notation can be used for an association end owned by a class, because an association end owned by a class is also an attribute. This notation may be used in conjunction with the line-arrow notation to make it perfectly clear that the attribute is also an association end." [21, p. 45]

Instead of *"may be used"*, it should rather state *"can only be used* in conjunction with (...)". A proper application of this transformation is discussed by Crane et al. [7], where classes are enriched by attributes instead of replacing associations.

An analogous transformation from the attribute to the association notation (which we term $\mathbf{T_2}$) is stated as follows:

> "An attribute may also be shown using association notation, with no adornments at the tail of the arrow (...)" [21, p. 56].

The item *"with no adornments"* inhibits the explicit definition of multiplicities and navigability which leads to a multiplicity of [1..1] and an undefined navigability. $\mathbf{T_2}$ is supposed to be the inverse to $\mathbf{T_1}$ (for which we write $\mathbf{T_1^{-1}}$ and $\mathbf{T_2} = \mathbf{T_1^{-1}}$ must hold).

Note 2. In general, an association end owned by an end class is not equal to a property. It is strongly required that the information about the association of which the property is an end is not lost even if the opposite end is not navigable.

Note 3. The limitations forced for transformation of an attribute to an association must be forced analogously for a transformation vice versa.

4.5 Links Defined by Attributes

Figure 4 shows two class diagrams. $\mathbf{T_1}$ allows the transformation from the left to the right diagram, $\mathbf{T_2}$ allows the inversion. The multiplicity of the *A*-end of the association is equal to the default of a multiplicity element 1, because a multiplicity for this end cannot be modeled using the attribute notation. This entails that every instance $b_i : B$ must be linked to an instance $a_j : A$ and $\forall i_1, i_2 : i_1 \neq i_2 \leftrightarrow j_1 \neq j_2 \wedge i_1 = i_2 \leftrightarrow j_1 = j_2$. Furthermore, we can see that an instance $b : B$ must not be referenced by more than one instance $a : A$ at a time. This is much more restrictive than the common view of attributes and the way all code generators we evaluated generate code or implementors would write it.

Having a look at the metamodel, we consider the underlying models of the two diagrams not to be identical. An association has at least two ends, each of

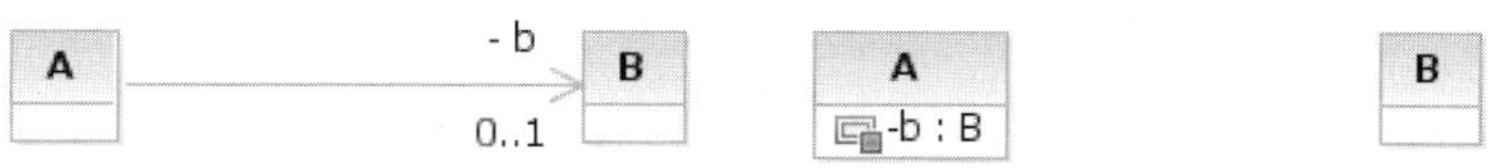

Fig. 4. Attribute notation vs. association notation

which is a *Property*, a subtype of *MultiplicityElement*. An attribute is a *Property*, too, but there is no second *MultiplicityElement* contained in the model.

Note 4. Association notation and attribute notation are defined to be exchangeable. This analogy does not reflect the difference between the concepts on the meta-level.

Modeling a reference from A to B with no restrictions about how many references to B may exist at a time cannot be achieved by an attribute but only by means of an association with appropriate multiplicities. On that issue, the semantics of the specification might be seen as unnatural and we assume that this semantics is not intended by the specification.

5 A Mapping of the UML Semantics to Java Code

This section discusses concepts that can be used to overcome the deficiencies outlined in the previous sections. It addresses the issue of extending currently used code generation patterns and presents a promising alternative pattern.

5.1 Extending State-of-the-Art Code Generation

Code generation of EMF [9], Fujaba [11] and Rhapsody [25] is missing consideration of multiplicities, ownership and orthogonality of navigability and visibility. With little effort, checking bounds of multiplicities can be implemented as discussed by Akehurst et al. [2]. As ownership and the conflict between mutual updates and visibility is not addressed there, we suggest the use of separate code classes for associations as it is described in the Complete MOF (CMOF) part of the MOF specification [20] and give a Java implementation for it.

5.2 Using a Separate Code Class for an Association

Note 1 of Sect. 4.3 is a limitation to the use of associations. To overcome this limitation, associations could be translated to classes of their own right. Two alternatives are possible: storing all links in a separate object or creating an object for each link (see Fig. 5). We prefer the second idea because a link is an instance of an association which is a classifier and hence has its own identity.

Note that figure 5 is intended to illustrate the code pattern used to translate the model shown in figure 2, but not to be seen as a transformation of that model. Generating a class for an association is a straight-forward implementation of a link that is defined as a tuple of values by the UML specification. Accordingly, we term instances $ab : AB$ links and the references to instances $a : A$ and $b : B$ the values of a link.

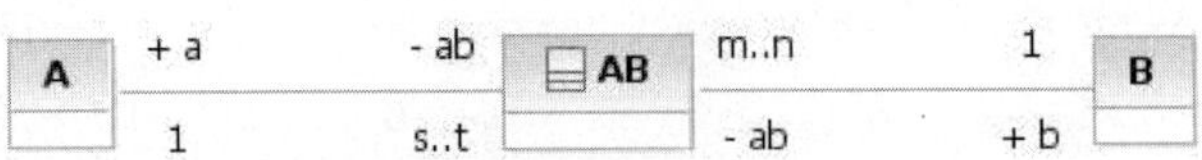

Fig. 5. Association representation by one object per link

Implementing Ownership. An association end that is owned by a member end class is a structural feature of that class. We assume the *b*-end of Fig. 2 to be owned by *A*, the *a*-end to be a *navigableOwnedEnd* of the association *AB*. Listing 2 is an implementation of *A* and uses a list of links (line 4) as an implementation of the *b*-end.

Listing 3 is an implementation of the class *B*. Note that no links are stored within that class. The implementation of the association uses a static map that contains a list of links for each instance of *B* that is associated with one or more instances of *A* (see listing 4, line 5).

```
1  public class A implements ABEnd{
2    private int upper = 2, lower = 0;
3    private B b = null;
4    private List<AB> links = new Vector<AB>();
5    public void addB(B value) throws Exception{
6      b = value;
7      AB.getLink(this);     }
8    public void take(AB link) throws Exception{ link.setB(b); }
9    public void notifyRelation(AB link){ links.add(link); }
10   public boolean canAcceptLink(AB link){ return (links.size()<upper); }
11 }
```

Listing 2. Implementation of a class *A* of Fig. 2

```
1  public class B implements ABnavigableOwnedEnd{
2    private A a = null;
3    public void take(AB link) throws Exception{ link.setA(a); }
4    public void addA(A value) throws Exception{
5      a = value;
6      AB.getLink(this);     }
7  }
```

Listing 3. Implementation of a class *B* of Fig. 2

Implementing Navigability. Listings 2, 3 and 4 implement navigable ends. If the *a*-end is not navigable, the implementation of class *B* may be reduced to an empty class. The implementation of the association may be shortened as the method `getLink` (lines 31 to 35) is no longer needed. Even links for associations with both ends being non-navigable are possible. However, the question arises which element should be responsible for creating, accessing and removing links.

Implementing Visibility. For an association end that is private, access methods to the corresponding set of links must be defined private (see listing 2 line 5 and listing 3 line 4).

Furthermore, it must be assured that links are only created by instances of the classes participating in the association. This can easily be achieved by passing references to only those types. The required code for this is an application of the visitor pattern [12] and implemented in listing 4 by the `getLink` methods and the `take` methods in the associated classes. The interfaces of listing 5 are needed to guarantee that the associated classifiers allow the passing of the link.

```
1  public class AB{
2    private A a;
3    private B b;
4    int lowerB = 0, upperB = 3;
5    private static HashMap<B, Vector<A>> as = new HashMap<B, Vector<A>>();
6    private AB() {}
7    public A getA() { return a; }
8    public B getB() { return b; }
9
10   public void setA(A a) throws Exception{
11     if(a.canAcceptLink(this)) this.a = a;
12     else throw new Exception(
13       "Violation of upper bound for association end a.");  }
14
15   public void setB(B b) throws Exception{
16     if (!as.containsKey(b)) as.put(b, new Vector<A>());
17     if (as.get(b).size() == upperB) throw new Exception(
18       "Violation of upper bound for association end b.");
19     else this.b = b;   }
20
21   public static void getLink(ABEnd r) throws Exception{
22     if(r instanceof A){
23       AB link = new AB();
24       r.take(link);
25       link.setA((A)r);
26       link.getA().notifyRelation(link);
27       as.get(link.getB()).add(link.getA());     }
28   }
29   public static void getLink(ABnavigableOwnedEnd r) throws Exception{
30     if(r instanceof B){
31       AB link = new AB();
32       r.take(link);
33       link.setB((B)r);
34       link.getA().notifyRelation(link);
35       as.get(link.getB()).add(link.getA()); }
36   }
37 }
```

Listing 4. Implementation of an association owning one of both ends

```
public interface ABnavigableOwnedEnd {
  public void take(AB link) throws Exception;
}
public interface ABEnd extends ABnavigableOwnedEnd{
  public void notifyRelation(AB link);
  public boolean canAcceptLink(AB Link);
}
```

Listing 5. Interfaces required for classes participating in associations

Implementing Consistency of Associations. By passing an instance when invoking the `getLink` method, it is assured that only this instance gets a reference to the link and that it is referenced by the link. The second value of a link is set by the invoking instance. After both values of a link are set, the referenced instances are notified and can store a reference to the link. For removing links, a similar pattern can be used. For lack of space, we give no listing for that.

Implementing Upper and Lower Bound Checks. Checking upper and lower bounds must be done by the owning elements of the association ends. In listing 2, the `canAcceptLink` method in line 10 checks the upper bound, in listing 4 line 18, this is done for a non navigable end when setting the value of a link. Lower bounds must be checked when links are removed in a similar way as it is done when adding links. If all ends of an association have a lower bound greater than 0, a factory pattern [12] can be used for the creation of instances. A factory makes complex object structures unavailable before all links are set and thus ensures that no inconsistent state is revealed to other instances.

Updating References. Consider a 1 to 1 association between classes X and Y and the situation that $x_1 : X$ is associated to $y_1 : Y$ and $x_2 : X$ to $y_2 : Y$. To update the references so that x_1 references y_2 and x_2 references y_1, it must be possible to temporarily violate multiplicities. This issue relates to ACID-transactions of database systems with a special focus on isolation. A mechanism for deferring multiplicity checks and hiding temporarily inconsistent states is most likely possible but not yet considered.

5.3 Implementing Association Classes

For the implementation of an association class, its attributes and operations have to be added to the implementation of the association. A constructor with parameters for supplying association ends with instances could be added as well.

5.4 Making Orthogonal Concepts Independent

By using implementation classes for associations, orthogonal concepts of the model refer to independent parts of the generated code. Visibility of an association end corresponds to the visibility of access methods in the member end class, navigability is integrated in the consideration of ownership which is itself implemented by storing links within that element that owns the association end.

5.5 Implementing Aggregation and Composition

The semantic impact of aggregation is little. It just indicates, that an instance is part of another instance, representing the whole whereas a composition entails that the whole is responsible for the lifetime of its parts.

Java uses a garbage collector that removes unreachable objects. As long as a part is contained in the composite, both the part and the whole are referenced by a link and either both or none of them are removed. This effect runs contrary to lifetime control in the way that the parts may prevent the composite from being destroyed. If an element representing the whole of a composite is no longer referenced by an instance not participating in the composition, it should be removed by the garbage collector. Akehurst et al. [2] consider the use of Java weak references but discard it because this mechanism does not assuredly prevent access to deleted parts. An alternative implementation is given but a drawback of this is that objects are marked inaccessible while links persist.

For the proposed code pattern, a simple idea is applicable: Links are always accessible, either directly by the referenced instances or indirectly by the association. If the whole of a composition is to be deleted, the values of links referencing its parts must be set to `null` if the links are not an instance of the composition itself. If neither the whole nor its parts are referenced by a property of another class, both stay linked but become unreachable from anywhere else and may be removed by the garbage collector. An unsolved problem is that destroying links may violate multiplicities of associated classes.

6 Discussion and Related Work

This paper shows shortcomings of the UML specification concerning relations between associations and attributes as well as dependencies between concepts that are actually designed to be orthogonal.

A straight forward implementation for associations is to use references to the opposite class in each class participating the association. We agree to this implementation if all ends are defined as public, but in general, this code pattern is not sufficient [13]. Akehurst et al. [2] and Génova et al. [13] discuss this technique of association implementation. Unfortunately, visibility is not considered by Akehurst et al. [2] and therefore, an alternative code pattern is not required. Furthermore, it is stated that navigable ends must be owned by the classifier whereas non-navigable ends must be owned by the association. Our work differs from Akehurst et al. [2] by considering visibility and by considering that a navigable association end can be owned by the association. However, Akehurst et al. [2] discuss other characteristics like e. g. qualified associations.

Génova et al. [13] consider visibility and state that associations with both ends defined private cannot be managed because synchronizing references is not possible. Using an implementation class for an association is discussed and discarded, because it is assumed that it does not solve the problem either, since it involves auxiliary classes that cannot provide access to the methods for managing the association to some classes excluding all other classes [13]. Unlike Génova et al. [13], we show how to provide access to links to only some classes by combining the visitor pattern [12] and implementation classes for associations.

A detailed examination of the proposed code pattern with regard to n-ary associations, association classes and specialization of associations as well as a systematic evaluation of tools and code generators will be covered by forthcoming publications. An Eclipse-based implementation of the proposed code generation pattern for ActiveCharts [23] is currently under development.

References

1. The Eclipse Modeling Framework (EMF) Overview (June 16, 2005), `http://help.eclipse.org/ganymede/index.jsp?topic=/org.eclipse.emf.doc/references/overview/EMF.html`
2. Akehurst, D., Howells, G., McDonald-Maier, K.: Implementing associations: UML 2.0 to Java 5. In: Software and Systems Modeling (SoSyM), vol. 6(1), pp. 3-35(33). Springer, Heidelberg (2007)
3. Altova Inc. ALTOVA umodel 2008, Enterprise Edition, Version 2008, rel. 2 (2008), `http://www.altova.com/products/umodel/uml_tool.html`

4. ARTiSAN Studio (Version 6.1.21) (2006), `http://www.artisansw.com/`
5. Borland Software Corporation. Borland Together 2007, Service Pack 1, Version 1.0.0 (2008), `http://www.borland.com/us/products/together/index.html`
6. ChangeVIsion Inc. Jude Professional 5.2.1,Model Version:27 (2008), `http://jude.change-vision.com/jude-web/index.html`
7. Crane, M.L., Dingel, J., Diskin, Z.: Class Diagramms: Abstract Syntax and Mapping to System Model (Draft - Version 1.7), School of Computing, Queen's University, Kingston, Ontario, Canada (2006)
8. Diskin, Z., Dingel, J.: Mappings, maps and tables: Towards formal semantics for associations in uml2. In: Nierstrasz, O., Whittle, J., Harel, D., Reggio, G. (eds.) MoDELS 2006. LNCS, vol. 4199, pp. 230–244. Springer, Heidelberg (2006)
9. Eclipse Foundation. Eclipse Modeling Framework (2008), `http://www.eclipse.org/emf/`
10. Fujaba Associations Specification (2005),`http://www.se.eecs.uni-kassel.de/fujabawiki/index.php/Fujaba_Associations_Specification`
11. Fujaba Development Group. Fujaba Tool Suite 4.3.2 (2007), `http://www.fujaba.de/`
12. Gamma, E., Helm, R., Johnson, P., Vlissides, J.: Design Patterns: Elements of Reusable Object-Oriented Software. Addison-Wesley, Reading (2003)
13. Génova, G., Llorens, J., del Castillo, C.R.: Mapping UML Associations into Java Code. Journal of Object Technology 2(5), 135–162 (2003)
14. Gentleware AG. Apollo for Eclipse, Version 3.0 (2008), `http://www.gentleware.de/`
15. Gentleware AG. Poseidon for UML Professional Edition 6.0.2-0 (2008), `http://www.gentleware.com/apollo.html`
16. IBM Corp. IBM Rational Software Architect, Version 7.0.0 (2008), `http://www-306.ibm.com/software/awdtools/architect/swarchitect/index.html`
17. Kecher, C.: UML 2.0 - Das umfassende Handbuch. Galileo Computing, Bonn (2006)
18. Object Management Group, MDA Guide 1.0.1, Document 03-06-01 (2003)
19. No Magic Inc. MagicDraw UML 15.5 EAP beta 1 (2008), `http://www.magicdraw.com`
20. Object Management Group. Meta Object Facility (MOF) Core Specification, Document formal/06-01-01 (2006)
21. Object Management Group. UML 2.1.1 Superstructure Specification, Document formal/2007-02-05 (2007)
22. Rupp, C., Hahn, J., Zengler, B., Queins, S.: UML 2 glasklar. Hanser, München Wien (2007)
23. Sarstedt, S., Gessenharter, D., Kohlmeyer, J., Raschke, A., Schneiderhan, M.: ActiveChartsIDE – An integrated Software Development Environment comprising a component for Simulating UML 2 Activity Charts. In: The 2005 European Simulation and Modelling Conference (ESM 2005) (2005)
24. Sparx Systems. Enterprise Architect,Version 7.1.829 (Build: 829)(2008), `http://www.sparxsystems.com/products/ea.html`
25. Telelogic. Rhapsody 7.2 (2008), `http://www.telelogic.com/products/rhapsody/`
26. UML Vendor Directory (2008), `http://uml-directory.omg.org/vendor/list.html/`
27. Visual Paradigm for UML, Enterprise Edition, Version 6.1 (2007), `http://www.visual-paradigm.com/product/vpuml/`

Meaningful Composite Structures
On the Semantics of Ports in UML2

Arnaud Cuccuru, Sébastien Gérard, and Ansgar Radermacher

CEA LIST, Boîte 65, Gif-sur-Yvette, F-91191 France
{arnaud.cuccuru,sebastien.gerard,ansgar.radermacher}@cea.fr

Abstract. UML2 composite structures are a natural solution for the basic modeling issues associated with component-oriented approaches. They provide mechanisms for defining reusable "pieces" of design, which are well-encapsulated through explicit interaction ports. While intuitive in principle, the semantics of request propagation across ports may cause semantic ambiguities if the composition mechanisms are not used consistently, thus leading to meaningless composite structures (that cannot be safely reused within the context of a particular environment). To ensure consistent usage, this article proposes an empirical study that provides an intuitive description of composite structure semantics focusing on request propagations across ports. It supplements this description by highlighting cases conducive to semantic ambiguities and offers practical solutions and a rationale for building composite structures that avoid them. Among possible solutions, the opportuneness of encapsulating explicit behaviors in ports is discussed.

1 Introduction

In the Unified Modeling Language version 2 (UML2) [8], the Class concept (which originated from the Object-Oriented paradigm) now also proposes natural solutions for certain basic modeling issues associated with component-oriented approaches: defining reusable "pieces" of design, exposing the functionalities they provide to/require from their intended environments, through explicit interaction ports that afford a better encapsulation (i.e. "environment-free" description) of their internal structures and behaviors. The term "Composite Structure" is generally used to refer to this extended form of classes[1].

The ports of a composite structure basically act as "relay" objects between the internals of the composite structure and its environment. When a functionality request is emitted by the environment, the targeted port is in charge of propagating (or delegating) the request to the composite structure internals, which handle the request and realize the expected functionality. Similarly, when

[1] The expression "Composite Structure" is more precisely used for the UML2 metamodel package in which the Class metaclass is extended to support composition mechanisms. The expression "Composite Structure" will refer in this article to this extended form of Class.

K. Czarnecki et al. (Eds.): MoDELS 2008, LNCS 5301, pp. 828–842, 2008.

a functionality request is emitted by the composite structure internals, the targeted port is in charge of forwarding the request to the environment, which must properly handle the emitted request. More generally, it can be said that port semantics is driven by a kind of "request propagation process".

While this propagation process is in principle quite intuitive, it may generate multiple semantic ambiguities if the proposed composition mechanisms are not used properly. Our experience of various European or national projects such as COMPARE [9], MERCED [10] or more recently Flex-eWare[2] (all concerning UML-based and component-oriented approaches for Real-Time Embedded Middleware) have shown that the boundaries of port semantics are not well perceived by users. The latter often go too far in interpreting composition mechanisms, and this leads to meaningless composite structures with potential semantic ambiguities. To avoid such situations, our article proposes an empirical study of port semantics and clearly sets bounds for the request propagation process, by defining the points at which semantic ambiguities appear. The study also provides practical advice and rules for building composite structures that avoid or solve semantic ambiguity problems.

Section 2 below considers propagation semantics for ports with provided interfaces. Using this description, we then propose representative solutions for avoiding semantic ambiguities. Section 3 does the same for ports with required interfaces. In section 4, we highlight the modeling potential offered by the UML2 metamodel with regard to encapsulating explicit behaviors into ports. We first discuss the port and connector typing mechanisms, to show how behavior encapsulation is actually made possible. Then, we put the mechanisms into practice for the explicit resolution of a particular semantic variation point, and provide guidelines for the resolution of the other semantic ambiguities identified in sections 2 and 3. Section 5 briefly describes related works. Section 6 then concludes the article and sets guidelines for future research.

2 Realization of Provided Interfaces

To be considered meaningful, a composite structure must truly realize the functionalities it provides. This is the minimum requirement for a composite structure to be safely used in the context of a particular environment. The way functionalities are realized depends heavily on the "nature" of the ports (which may be "behavioral" or "non-behavioral"[3]) through which functionalities are provided, as each kind of port carries its own delegation semantics. These delegation semantics and their potential ambiguities are discussed below and various feasible solutions are suggested for avoiding them. For each kind of port, several modeling variants for describing ambiguity-free composite structures are illustrated in a single diagram.

---

[2] http://www.flex-eware.org/

[3] For the Port metaclass of the UML2 metamodel, the fact that a port is a behavioral or a non-behavioral port is captured by the `isBehavior:Boolean=False` metaattribute.

2.1 Non-Behavioral Ports

The delegation semantics of non-behavioral ports with provided interfaces is informally illustrated in the activity diagram depicted by Fig. 1[4]. In the case of a non-behavioral port, the requests emitted by the environment and targeted to this port (step 1 of Fig. 1) are actually forwarded to the corresponding parts (or ports of these parts) of the owning composite structure through explicit "delegation" connectors (steps 2.a and 3.a of Fig. 1). The term "delegation" refers to the connectors used to relate ports of a composite structure to some of its corresponding parts (or ports of these parts). For the composite structure to be properly described, the parts (or ports of parts) targeted by delegation connectors must be able to handle the propagated requests, which either results in another request delegation (if the connector targets a non-behavioral port) or triggers a response behavior (if the connector targets a behavioral port) as illustrated by step 4 of Fig. 1, with a recursive definition of the delegation process. Two semantic ambiguities are identified in the UML2 superstructure [8]. They concern the case of conflicting ends of delegation connectors (SVP.1 in Fig. 1) and that of partial delegation (Message lost.1).

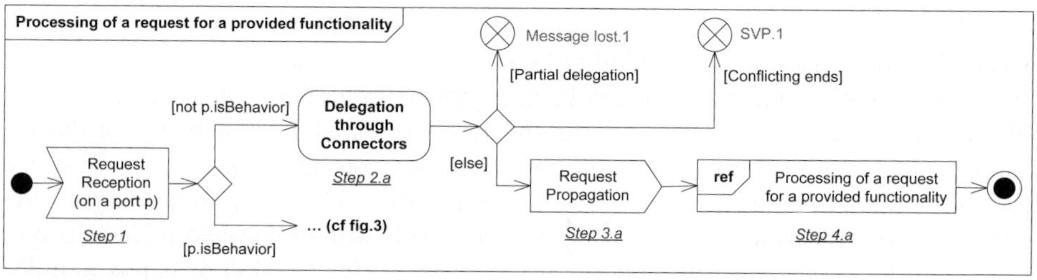

Fig. 1. Delegation Semantics of a "Provided Functionality" Request Received on a Non-Behavioral Port

Conflicting ends of delegation connectors (SVP.1). When a non-behavioral port provides several interfaces, the fact that the ends targeted by its delegation connectors are "non-conflicting" is essential. To unambiguously identify the connector through which the request must be delegated, the opposite ends of the connectors (i.e. the parts or the ports of these parts) must be distinguishable in terms of the interfaces they actually realize. If several ends realize a common interface (i.e. the ends are conflicting), it is a semantic variation point whether requests (for behavioral features of the common interface) are forwarded across only one connector or all connectors. In variants 1 (with delegation connectors to parts) and 2 (with delegation connectors to ports of parts) as shown in Fig. 2, the ends are not conflicting, as each provides an interface (or, more generally, a set of interfaces) that is not provided by any other end. In our example (and

[4] This activity provides a partial view of the delegation semantics of ports with provided interfaces. The remaining part is shown in Fig. 3, and describes the case where `p.isBehavior` (i.e. the delegation semantics in the case of behavioral port).

for both variants), it means that: 1) if a request for a behavioral feature of `Pull` arrives at `pn`, it will unambiguously flow across the delegation connector leading to `pr:Prod` (`pr.p` in variant 2); and 2) if a request for a behavioral feature of `Notify` arrives at `pn`, it will unambiguously flow across the delegation connector leading to `nt:Notifier` (`nt.n` in variant 2). Indeed, the two parts (or ports of these parts) are clearly distinguishable in terms of provided interfaces. Note that in variant 1, the realization relationships between `Prod` and `Pull` and between `Notifier` and `Notify` are mandatory to allow determination of the interfaces actually provided by the targeted end (i.e. the interfaces they realize), and thus to identify through which connector a request arriving at `pn` must be propagated.

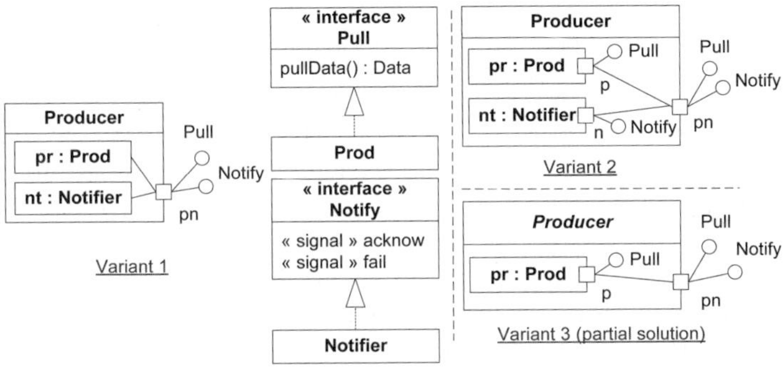

Fig. 2. Meaningful Variations in the Context of Non-Behavioral Ports

Partial delegation (Message lost.1). Another possible variation is described as variant 3 in Fig. 2. This is the case where some provided functionalities are not realized by the ends targeted by the delegation connectors, i.e. there is only partial delegation of provided functionalities. Port `pn` of `Producer` then provides two interfaces, `Pull` and `Notify`, whereas the delegation connector expressed from `pn` targets `pr.p`, which realizes only the `Pull` interface. In this case, requests for `Notify` functionalities are lost at `pn` (as stated by the UML2 specification), and `Producer` can be considered underspecified. To avoid this unexpected situation, there is a good methodological rule that calls for a composite structure embedding non-behavioral ports with partial delegations to be abstract (in order to capture the fact that it is partially specified and not directly instantiable). This assumes that other composite structures will make it "concrete", by carrying a generalization relationship with this abstract composite structure, and completing or refining the set of delegation connectors.

Let's now take a look at what happens for interfaces provided by behavioral ports.

2.2 Behavioral Ports

The delegation semantics of behavioral ports with provided interfaces is informally captured in the activity diagram depicted by Fig. 3. In the case of a behavioral port, the requests received at this port (step 1 of Fig. 3) are directly forwarded to the classifier behavior of the owning composite structure (step 2.b and 3.b of Fig. 3). This classifier behavior specifies the behavior of the composite structure itself. In one way or another, this behavior should account for such requests (step 4.b of Fig. 3), in order to actually realize the expected functionalities.

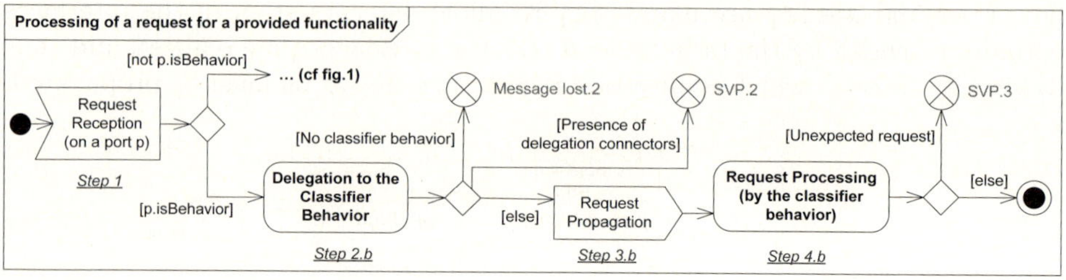

Fig. 3. Delegation Semantics of a "Provided Functionality" Request Received on a Behavioral-Port

In variants 1 and 2 of Fig. 4, the state machines actually represent possible classifier behaviors of each `Producer` variant. Note that the UML2 metamodel does not impose the use of state machines to describe classifier behaviors, i.e. other kinds of behavior such as Activities can also be used. Our example relies on state machine, since this is common behavior description practice. The classifier behaviors illustrate the fact that the triggers associated with transitions are based on requests for behavioral features (i.e. provided functionalities) declared in the interfaces provided by the behavioral ports. Each transition specifies the behavior to be executed in response to request events[5], in order to realize the functionality expected by the environment. In variant 1, where `Producer` contains several parts, response behaviors would typically be captured through behavioral feature invocations sent to one of these parts (or one of the ports of these parts). In variant 2, where `Producer` contains no parts, response behaviors would typically be captured through direct behavior invocations, or through invocation of behavioral features of `Producer` (as illustrated in Fig. 4 variant 2). In both variants, note that the $'from' < port\_name >$ notation[6] (`"from pn"` in variant 1, and `"from p"` in variant 2) enables specification of triggers related to particular ports of the context composite structure, implying that the response behavior should be fired only if the event (i.e., the request occurrence) identified by the trigger actually occurs on the specified ports. In practice, this modeling artifact enables several ports to expose the same provided interface. Different response behaviors can then be triggered according to the port on which the request is received.

[5] In the context of a statemachine, response behaviors can also be captured as Entry/Do/Exit activities of each state.

[6] This notation has a counterpart in the metamodel, which is the `port:Port[*]` property of the Trigger metaclass.

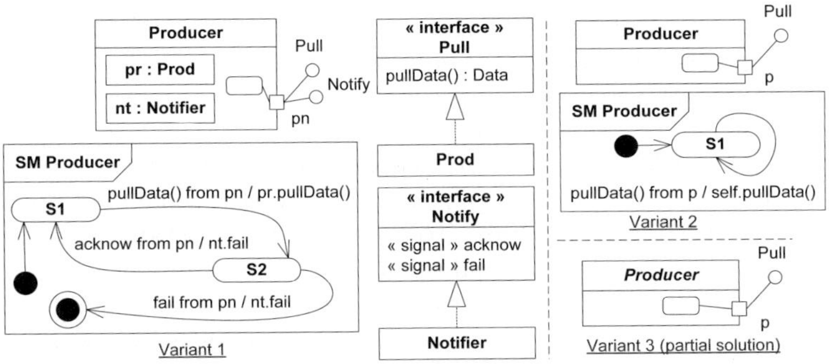

Fig. 4. Meaningful Variations in the Context of Behavioral Ports

Three semantic ambiguities related to propagation of requests received on a behavioral-port are identified in the superstructure [8]. These concern the presence of delegation connectors (SVP.2 in Fig. 3), the occurrence of requests not expected by the classifier behavior of the owning composite structure (SVP.3) and the absence of classifier behavior (Message lost.2).

Delegation connectors on behavioral ports (SVP.2). The UML2 metamodel does not preclude definition of delegation connectors from behavioral ports, although, normally, requests made to such ports are directly forwarded to the classifier behavior of the owning composite structure. The meaning of delegation connectors in this context can thus be considered as a semantic variation point (though this is not explicitly stated in the UML specification). There are, however, reasonable interpretations for such usage, e.g. that only a subset of functionalities is delegated to the classifier behavior, with the remaining functionalities delegated to parts (or ports of parts) via the delegation connectors (thereby mixing semantics of behavioral ports with those of non-behavioral ports). As such cases are not defined in standard UML, rules should be explicitly captured in a specific user-defined profile.

Unexpected requests (SVP.3). In UML2, many semantic variation points are related to behaviors. Providing a detailed discussion for each would fall outside the scope of this paper. One of them, however, has a significant impact on the way an unambiguous composite structure is defined in cases where some of its provided functionalities are exposed on a behavioral port: the consequence of a request event occurrence for which no reactions are planned in the classifier behavior is a semantic variation point. To avoid this semantic variation point, the obvious solution is to only define classifier behaviors that account for all kinds of request events likely to occur for the owning composite structures, that is, for each behavioral feature of each provided interface exposed on its behavioral ports (this is the case for variants 1 and 2 in Fig. 4). Alternatively, we note several reasonable interpretations for unexpected request events, such as implicit and direct invocation (invocation not passing through the classifier behavior) of behavioral features of the owning composite structure. Such interpretation are, however, beyond the scope of standard UML semantics and thus should be explicitly captured in a specific profile.

Absence of classifier behavior (Message lost.2). When a composite structure embeds no classifier behavior, requests arriving at a behavioral port are lost (as stated by the UML specification). To avoid this unexpectable situation, there is an easily applicable methodological rule (i.e. one not imposed by UML) as follows: a composite structure without classifier behavior but with behavioral ports should be "abstract". Said rule assumes that this composite structure is made "‘concrete" by other composite structures (composite structures that actually own a classifier behavior and have a generalization relationship with the abstract composite structure[7]). This is actually the case for `Producer` in variant 3 of Fig. 4 (where the solution is, however, partial, since the composite structures that make `Producer` concrete are not represented).

The next section focuses on how a composite structure can properly use functionalities exposed on the required interfaces of its ports.

3 Use of Required Interfaces

To properly realize its provided functionalities, a composite structure may interact with its environment, by either sending signals or calling operations. Ports with required interfaces enable capture of functionalities that a composite structure expects from the environment in which it is used and clearly identify the interaction points through which requests for the required functionality are emitted. The activity diagram of Fig. 5 informally describes the propagation semantics of a request emitted through such a port.

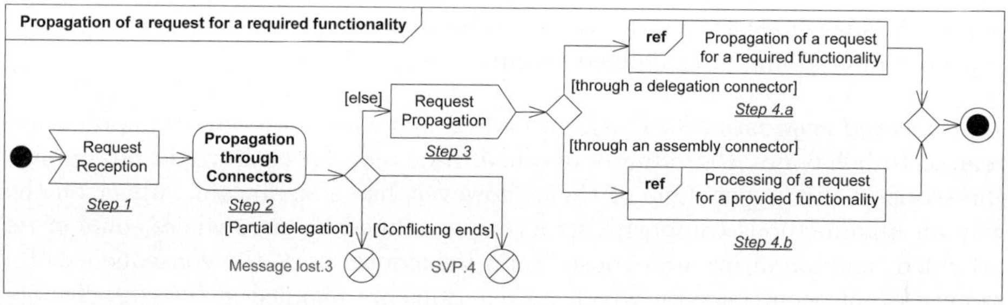

Fig. 5. Propagation Semantics of a "Required Functionality" Request Received on a Port with Required Interfaces

A request emitted from composite structure internals, either through a delegation connector or directly by the classifier of the owning composite structure, targeted at this port (step 1 of Fig. 5) is propagated to the environment through

[7] Readers interested in composite structure inheritance should refer to [1].

connectors (steps 2 and 3). In the propagation process, the situation varies according to the kind of connector (delegation or assembly connector). In the case of a delegation, the propagation semantics is similar to what is described above for ports with provided interfaces, except that the request propagation takes place in the opposite direction. The request is emitted from the internals - parts or ports of these parts - and propagated to the ports on the owning composite structure, which are recursively in charge of forwarding it to the environment through either another delegation connector or an assembly connector (as captured by steps 4.a and 4.b of Fig. 5).

The situation differs slightly for an assembly connector. Such connectors are designed to relate elements (parts or ports of parts) at the same level in a same composite structure. To ensure consistent use, a constraint defined in the UML2 metamodel imposes that what is required at one end of an assembly connector must also be provided at the other. More specifically, an assembly connector relates a port with a given required interface to a port with a compatible provided interface. Therefore, when a request is propagated on such a connector, the process described in the previous section (to treat a request for a provided functionality) goes into action (as illustrated by step 4.b of Fig. 5), so that the request emitted by a composite structure through one of its ports is actually handled by a an element targeted by the connector.

Two semantic ambiguities relating to this propagation semantics are identified in the superstructure [8]. They concern cases where ends targeted by the delegation or assembly connectors are conflicting (SVP.4 in Fig. 5), and where the assembly or delegation connectors are only partially specified (Message lost.3).

Conflicting ends on delegation or assembly connectors (SVP.4). In the same way as for connectors from ports with provided interfaces, the delegation semantics is only unambiguous if the delegation connectors target non-conflicting ports (ports clearly distinguishable in terms of the interfaces they require). Otherwise, it is a semantic variation whether the request is propagated on only one or on all delegation connectors. Variant 1 shown in Fig. 6 actually avoids this semantic variation point. This is because `Consumer` contains a part with delegation

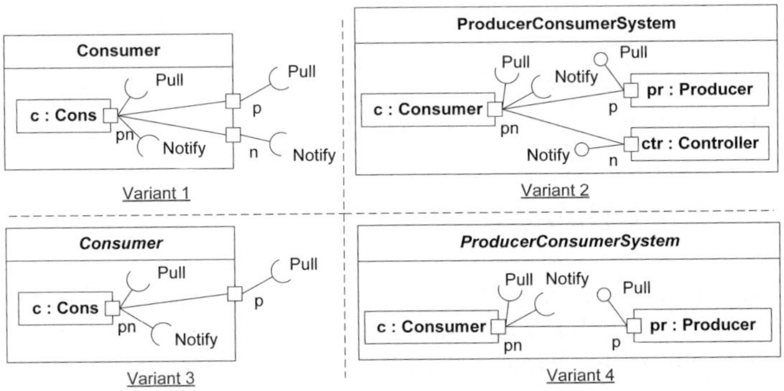

Fig. 6. Meaningful Variations in the Context of Ports with Required Interfaces

connectors targeting the `p` and `n` ports, whereby `p` requires the `Pull` interface, and `n` the `Notify` interface. When a request is emitted from said part, the delegation connector through which the request must be propagated can be unambiguously selected. In variant 2 of Fig. 6, the remarks just made about non-conflicting ends and delegation semantics remain valid, except that here assembly connectors are used. This variant also avoids the semantic variation point, by using assembly connectors to relate `c.pn` (which requires the `Pull` and `Notify` interfaces) to elements that are not conflicting in terms of required interfaces (`pr.p` and `ctr.n`).

Partial delegation or assembly (Message lost.3). When a request emitted on a port (from the internals of the owning composite structure) cannot be propagated due to the absence of eligible delegation or assembly connectors, the request is lost. In other words, the delegation or assembly connectors expressed from the port target ends that do not cover all interfacesrequired by the source port, and a request corresponding to an interface that is not covered cannot be propagated. In this case, the owning composite structure can be considered "underspecified" and should be abstract, assuming that concrete composite structures (inheriting from it) will complete or refine the set of delegation and assembly connectors so that each port with required interfaces is actually connected to other ports able to propagate or handle the request emitted from it. In Fig. 6, the `Consumer` abstract composite structure of variant 3 follows this simple rule. It therefore avoids the ambiguity that may arise from partial delegation of functionalities required by the `cn` port (no delegation connector targets a port requiring the `Notify` interface) in a case where `Consumer` would otherwise be concrete. In variant 4 of Fig. 6, the same rule is applied to the abstract `ProducerConsumerSystem`, except that in this case, a partial assembly is used as an example. The `Notify` interface, required by `c.pn`, is not in fact provided by the port targeted by its assembly connector.

We have now provided an intuitive description of request propagation semantics across ports (from both the provided and required sides), highlighted any semantic ambiguities as may appear and proposed reasonable methodological solutions for avoiding them. The most daring readers may themselves wish to confront these semantic issues and solve them. Specific user-defined UML profiles arguably provide an efficient solution. Another potentially powerful means for addressing these issues is to use the leeway left by the UML2 metamodel for encapsulating explicit behaviors in ports. The purpose of the next section is to show how such explicit behaviors can be seamlessly integrated.

4 Explicit Port Behaviors

The usual way to eliminate UML semantic variation points (or ambiguities) is to define specific profiles. For example, for the "conflicting ends" semantic variation point, we could define a profile that captures a particular delegation scheme and thus dispels ambiguity. It is nevertheless possible to elaborate on composite structure models to make port delegation behaviors explicit, instead of keeping them implicit through profile definition. This possibility relies on the typing mechanisms of ports and connectors, described in the section below. Based on this description, we then show how to properly perform encapsulation and we illustrate the process for resolution of the "conflicting ends" semantic variation point, in the case of non-behavioral ports (SVP.1 in Fig. 1). We finally discuss the complementarity of profiles and explicit behaviors.

4.1 Port and Connector Typing

One fundamental characteristic of port typing is captured by the UML2 metamodel as follows: The provided/required interfaces of a port are derived properties of the Port metaclass. From the user point of view, this means that it is not possible to directly specify on the port which interfaces are provided and/or required. These interfaces are in fact "computed" (i.e., derived) according to a derivation rule, actually based on the type of the port[8] (as illustrated in Fig. 7).

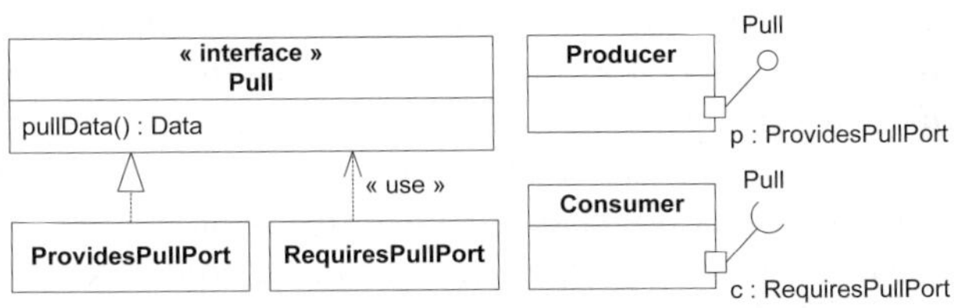

Fig. 7. Exposition of Provided/Required Interfaces on Ports

This rule states that the set of interfaces provided by a port is derived from the set of interfaces realized by its type (or the superclasses of this type)[9]. In Fig. 7, port `p` of the `Producer` composite structure is typed by `ProvidesPullPort` (a class realizing the `Pull` interface), which implies that the set of interfaces provided by `p` only contains `Pull`. Concerning required interfaces, the derivation rule similarly states that the set of required interfaces exposed by a port is derived from the set of interfaces used by its type. Based on the rule, we deduce that port `c` of `Consumer` in Fig. 7 only requires the `Pull` interface. This is because the `RequiresPullPort` class (used to type `c`), only carries one usage relationship, i.e. with the `Pull` interface. More generally, to expose several provided/required interfaces on a port[10], several realization/usage relationships (between types of ports and interfaces to be exposed) must be defined.

[8] In the UML2 metamodel, Port is an indirect subclass of *TypedElement*, implying that a port can be typed.

[9] More precisely, the class used to type the port carries realization relationships with these interfaces. Note that a variant of the derivation rule also states that when a port is directly typed by an interface, this interface is the only interface provided by the port.

[10] A given port can expose both required and provided interfaces, and a given interface can be both required and provided by the same port.

From a purely syntactic standpoint, the interface exposure mechanism implies that the only kind of Type that can reasonablly be used to type ports is Class (where Class and Type denote the corresponding UML2 metaclasses). This *de facto* rule is not imposed by a particular constraint of the UML2 metamodel (Port is just a kind of TypedElement), but instead by the absence of interface derivation rules for other kinds of Type. For example, no derivation rules are defined for PrimitiveType[11], even though typing a port by `Integer`, for example, would probably make sense in application domains where dataflow-oriented communications are considered.

From a semantic standpoint, the fact that classes are used to type ports raises numerous questions about the potential "complexity" of these classes. For instance, a perceptive reader may wonder whether such classes embed explicit classifier behaviors. If so, how could a classifier behavior properly account for the context of any particular port typed by a given behaviored class? Regarding the first question, the UML superstructure [8] (p.181) states that *"[an explicit classifier behavior (of a port type)] allows elaborate specification of the communication over a port. For example, it may describe that communication is filtered, modified in some way, or routed to other parts depending on its contents as specified by the classifier that types the port"*. Regarding the second question (related to the proper integration of the port type and its underlying behavior), the connector typing mechanism described in the UML2 metamodel eases this integration.

In UML2, a connector can be typed by an association. This association must however be specified between types that are compatible with the type of the connector ends. In [1], Conrad Bock thus describes connectors as "associations in context". Intuitively, it means that the connected ends (i.e. ports or parts), which play "roles" in the context of a given composite structure, also play the roles specified by the association used to type the connector. As a consequence, a given class (used to type a port) could encapsulate a classifier behavior based on the roles of these associations in order to capture particular propagation or delegation schemes.

Even though this possibility has been identified in [8] and [1], no practical guidelines for putting it into action have thus far been given. Such practical aspects are considered in the following section, which describes the encapsulation of a routing behavior that explicitly eliminates the "conflicting ends" semantic variation point (SVP.1 in Fig. 1, discussed in section 2.1), for non-behavioral ports with provided interfaces.

4.2 Eliminating the "Conflicting Ends" SVP

It is not always possible, in modeling a composite structure, to avoid conflicting parts. It may sometimes even be desirable to have them, if their conflicts reflect the reality of the system to be modeled. We have already explained, however, that from both the provided side (with non-behavioral ports) and the required

[11] Except if we consider that a PrimitiveType can have realization relationships with some interfaces. The meaning of "realization" is however not clear in this context.

side, selecting the connector through which a request is propagated is a semantic variation point when the opposite ends (i.e. parts or ports of parts) are conflicting in terms of provided/required functionalities.

An explicit resolution for the "Conflicting Ends" semantic variation point (in the context of non-behavioral ports) is proposed in Fig. 8. It is based on the port and connector typing mechanisms described in section 4.1. In the example, the `Provides` association is expressed between `ProvidesPullPort` (which is used to type port `p` of `Producer`) and `Pull` (provided by port `p` of the `Prod` composite structure, used to type `pr1` and `pr2`). According to the connector typing mechanism (and the type compatibility rule), this association can be used to type the connectors expressed between `Producer.p` and ports `pr1.p` and `pr2.p`. It implies that `pr1.p` and `pr2.p`, which play particular roles in the context of `Producer`, also play the `providers` role in the context of the `Provides` association (specified between `ProvidesPullPort` and `Pull`).

The classifier behavior of `ProvidesPullPort` specifies explicit `pullData()` delegations. Each reception of a request for `pullData()` is indeed propagated to a `Pull` object contained in the `providers:Pull[1..*]` collection. The target `Pull` object is selected via a local operation call to `selectNextProvider()`, which embeds a particular selection policy. In the context of `Producer` where delegation connectors from `p` are typed by the `Provides` association, it intuitively means that requests arriving at `p` will be alternatively forwarded to `pr1.p` and `pr2.p` (with respect to the selection policy described in the behavior of `ProvidesPullPort`). In other words, the "conflicting ends" semantic variation point has been explicitly eliminated.

The same mechanisms can be put into practice to address the other semantic ambiguities described in sections 2 and 3. The general principle is just that classes used to type ports only needs to have associations with elements to which requests must be propagated (where the corresponding roles may be played by

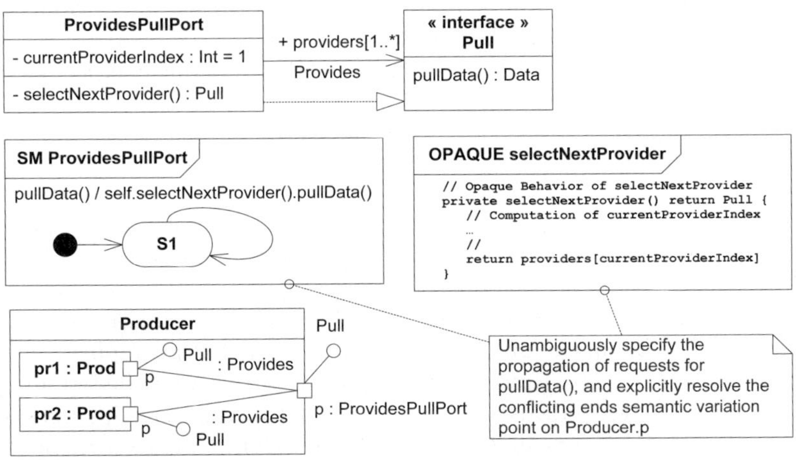

Fig. 8. Eliminating the "Conficting Ends" SVP through Explicit Port Behaviors

parts, ports of parts or composite structures owning the behavioral ports typed by these classes), and a classifier behavior capturing the appropriate response behavior (i.e. either an appropriate delegation scheme or a default behavior to be executed when a request cannot be propagated).

4.3 Explicit Port Behaviors vs. Profiles

We have presented the use of explicit port behaviors as an alternative to profiles. In our "conflicting ends" example, a profile could also be defined, with a stereotype of Port for capturing in a declarative way particular delegation policies. An argument in support of explicit behaviors is related to the ongoing standard on executable UML semantics [7]. The offshoot of this standard should be an executable semantics description (in operational style) for a UML subset. This subset contains the mechanisms we have put into action for explicit behaviors (i.e. objects communicating by either sending signals or calling operations), so that explicit behaviors could almost directly benefit from the execution semantics provided by this standard (except for the semantics of high-level behavioral description formalisms such as state machines).

Care must be exercised, however, in defining explicit classifier behaviors on port types. In the superstructure, when the classifier behavior is not explicit, it is implicitly constrained by UML semantics about ports: the behavior only propagates requests, for behavioral ports (delegation to classifier behavior of the owning composite structure), non-behavioral ports (delegation to parts via the specified connectors) and ports with required interfaces (propagation via assembly or delegation connectors). The explicit classifier behavior we describe in Fig. 8 respect these principles. It just selects the ends to which the requests must be delegated, propagating the requests "as they come", without any modification. However, it is technically possible to describe behaviors that go far beyond request propagation and default semantics of ports, such as a default behavior execution when a request cannot be propagated. In this case, the combined usage of a profile is encouraged to highlight the fact that ports behave in a way that differs slightly from standard UML semantics, while remaining compatible with it.

5 Related Works

Very few in-depth studies of UML2 composite structures have been published. The reference "tutorial" in this area is probably the article from Conrad Bock [1], which explains in didactic fashion conceptual relationships between the usual class models and composite structure models (and their complementarity). It also addresses instantiation and run-time issues, along with composite structure inheritance. The article by Haugen and al. [5] can be recommended as additional reading, since it likewise deals with issues related to relationships between behavioral models and composite structures. The present article can be seen as a useful adjunct to these two papers, for two reasons: it provides practical and easy-to-apply advice for avoiding semantic ambiguities, by clearly delineating the limits of port semantics (i.e. the points at which ambiguities may appear or interpretations may go too far, and those where profiles must be defined); and it provides practical solutions (not previously available) to possibilities identified in both the UML superstructure specification [8] and Bock's article [1] for the classifier behaviors of port types.

An article by Oliver and Luukkala [6] provides an interesting survey, which shows that the way users interpret composite structures sometimes goes far beyond the intended meaning of composition mechanisms, and concludes that this divergence is probably due to the vagueness of composite structure semantics and a lack of examples for using them. Bruel and Ober [2] basically conclude their article with the same observations. We hope that the examples, advice and rationales we have described here are sufficiently didactic and representative to avoid such confusions in the future.

6 Conclusion

Composite structures are probably one of the major improvements of UML version 2 (as compared to earlier versions). By enhancing the usual classes with composition mechanisms, they have significantly broadened the scope of application domains or methodologies potentially covered by the language. This enhancement is however useless if semantics of composition mechanisms (and their limits) are not well understood, that is, if people see in composite structures something other than what they really are. We hope that the material we have provided here on the propagation semantics of ports and how to avoid or dispel their ambiguities (as a supplement to work quoted in section 5), will contribute to this global understanding.

Among the solutions discussed in this article, that of encapsulating explicit classifier behaviors into port types is truly innovative: no similar solution has been proposed to date. We have illustrated its use in dealing the "conflicting ends" semantic variation point, by focusing on non-behavioral ports with provided interfaces. One of the roads we are currently exploring is to generalize this approach by providing broader design patterns, studying its applicability for more general purposes than the resolution of semantic ambiguities.

Still other research is concerned with implementation-related issues, and more specifically validation of composite structure implementations with respect to the semantics of their models. Our current focus is on symbolic conformance testing [4]. Interesting results concerning applicability to component-based models have already been published in [3], but further work will be necessary to adapt our findings to the particular semantics of UML composite structures. The basic principle of symbolic conformance testing is to compare execution traces of real implementations to execution traces produced from their models (and their underlying formal semantics). Such comparison can determine whether an implementation satisfies a given conformance relationship with its model. Note that request propagation semantics informally described in this article basically represent an abstraction of these execution traces.

Acknowledgment. We would like to thank Francois Lagarde and Chokri Mraidha for their useful feedbacks during the writing of this article.

References

1. Bock, C.: UML 2 Composition Model. Journal of Object Technology 3(10), 47–73 (2004)
2. Bruel, J.-M., Ober, I.: Components modeling in UML 2. Studia Jurnal 1, 79–90 (2006)
3. Faivre, A., Gaston, C., Le Gall, P.: Symbolic Model Based Testing for Component Oriented Systems. In: Petrenko, A., Veanes, M., Tretmans, J., Grieskamp, W. (eds.) TestCom/FATES 2007. LNCS, vol. 4581, pp. 90–106. Springer, Heidelberg (2007)
4. Gaston, C., Le Gall, P., Rapin, N., Touil, A.: Symbolic execution techniques for test purpose definition. In: Uyar, M.Ü., Duale, A.Y., Fecko, M.A. (eds.) TestCom 2006. LNCS, vol. 3964, pp. 1–18. Springer, Heidelberg (2006)
5. Haugen, O., Moller-Pedersen, B., Weigert, T.: UML for Real. In: Lavagno, L., Martin, G., Selic, B. (eds.) Structural Modeling with UML 2.0: Classes, Interactions and State Machines, pp. 53–76. Kluwer Academic Publishers, Dordrecht (2004)
6. Oliver, I., Luukkala, V.: On UML's Composite Structure Diagram. In: Fifth Workshop on System Analysis and Modelling (SAM), Kaiserslautern, Germany (June 2006)
7. OMG. Semantics of a Foundational Subset for Executable UML Models RFP (2005)
8. OMG. Unified Modeling Language: Superstructure version 2.1.2 (November 2007)
9. Robert, S., Radermacher, A., Seignole, V., Gérard, S., Watine, V., Terrier, F.: Enhancing Interaction Support in the CORBA Component Model. In: Rettberg, A., Zanella, M.C., Rammig, F.J. (eds.) From Specification to Embedded Systems Application. IFIP TC10 Working Conference: International Embedded Systems Symposium (IESS). Springer, Heidelberg (2005)
10. Robin, P., Robert, S., Sall, M., Berthier, S.: Market Enabler for Retarget-able COTS Components in Embedded Domain. In: Proceedings of the Embedded Real-Time Software (ERTS), Toulouse, France, SIA (French automotive engineers society) (2006)

A Systematic Approach to Connectors in a Multi-level Modeling Environment

Matthias Gutheil, Bastian Kennel, and Colin Atkinson

Chair of Software Technology, University Mannheim
A5, 6 B 68131 Mannheim, Germany
{Matthias.Gutheil,Bastian.Kennel,
Colin.Atkinson}@informatik.uni-mannheim.de

Abstract. The advantage of supporting a uniform modeling approach across multiple, logical (or ontological) instantiation levels has been well documented in the literature. However, the published approaches for achieving this have focused on making it possible for classes and objects to be treated uniformly across multiple instantiation levels, but have neglected the problems involved in doing the same thing for "connectors" (i.e. concepts rendered as edges in graph based depiction of models rather than nodes). On closer examination, this turns out to be a significant problem, because without an effective strategy for modeling connectors in a uniform way, multi-level modeling as a whole is not possible. In this paper we describe the problems arising from the way in which connectors (e.g. associations, links, generalizations etc.) are currently supported in mainstream modeling languages such as the UML and why they are incompatible with multi-level modeling. We then define three fundamental connector rendering and representation principles that rectify the identified problems.

Keywords: Metamodeling, Multi-Level Modeling, Connector, Association.

1 Introduction

The value of organizing a modeling infrastructure in terms of multiple classification (i.e. instantiation) levels is now more or less universally accepted. The UML, the most widely known and used modeling language, has been underpinned by a four level "model" hierarchy throughout its 10 year history, and metamodeling - the modeling of type models - is now a commonly used term in the software engineering lexicon. Even tools that appear to operate across only two levels, such as domain specific modeling tools like MetaEdit [15] and GMF[11], in fact do so within the bounds of an implicit multi-level framework since models created using them are generally translated to another technology space where their instances can be supported. In other words, although individual tools may only cover two adjacent levels directly, tools dealing with different pairs of levels are invariably used in combination to cover a multi-level space [2].

Although the value of multiple model levels is widely accepted, however, there is no general consensus on how many levels are needed, what their relationship should be and how they should be organized. By virtue of the UML's popularity, the linear,

K. Czarnecki et al. (Eds.): MoDELS 2008, LNCS 5301, pp. 843–857, 2008.

four-level infrastructure of the OMG is the default approach, but even this has not had a stable organization during its 10 year history. The original four level modeling framework of UML1.0 assumed that there were four true classification levels, in which objects – instances of classes at M_1 – occupied the bottom level M_0. However, the four level infrastructure of UML 2 [17] is based on a radically different interpretation of the bottom two levels in which the M_0 level is regarded as being the "real world" outside the modeling space, and M_1 is regarded as the location of models of instances (so called instance specifications) as well as normal classes. A range of different modeling infrastructure proposals have been put forward over the years ranging from highly organized, recursively nested architectures [1] to loosely organized, free style architectures such as ConceptBase [12].

One approach, outlined in a series of papers by Atkinson and Kühne's from 1997 to 2005 (e.g. [3], [4], [5]) is the so called Orthogonal Classification architecture (OCA). This approach is based on the idea of distinguishing two orthogonal classification dimensions [7], [3], [8] and fits roughly between the two extremes represented by the approaches described above. By allowing an arbitrary number of logical classification levels to be defined by the user, but nevertheless organizing them according to the principles of strictness [4], the approach manages to combine conceptual soundness with ease-of-use. Despite its benefits, however, to our knowledge no tool has yet been built from the ground up to support multi-level modeling based on the OCA. Kühne and Schreiber [14] have built a programming environment that supports multiple classification levels in the context of Java programming, while others such [9],[10], [13] have built modeling environments that support the notion of separate instantiation dimensions. However, these tools do not apply the rules of strictness to organize the logical metalevels.

To fill this vacuum, and explore the efficacy of these ideas, we are building an OCA-based, multi-level modeling tool based on the principles and concepts outlined by Atkinson and Kühne. However, during the course of this work we realized that the set of OCA ingredients published to date do not cope with all the fundamental issues that need to be addressed – they are necessary but not sufficient for multi-level modeling. More specifically, we realized that when describing principles of multi-level modeling based on the OCA, previous papers have focused on model elements that are rendered as nodes in graphical depictions of models and have neglected model elements that are rendered as edges. In effect, they have assumed that the solutions devised for nodes also automatically accommodate the representation and visualization of connectors. However, our investigations have shown that this is not the case and that additional principles are needed to effectively support connectors (i.e. model elements typically rendered as edges in graphical depictions of models).

In section 2 we first review the key principles of OCA-based, multi-level modeling as published in the literature, and in section 3 we describe how one would intuitively like connectors to be accommodated within such a modeling environment from a user point of view. In section 4 we describe the shortcomings of the UML's approach to the representation and rendering of connectors, and then in section 5 we describes our solution which defines three new principles to be followed in the realization of a multi-level modeling environment. Section 6 then concludes with some observations about the strengths and weaknesses of the approach and some closing remarks.

2 Multi-level Modeling Based-on the OCA

One of the key goals of a multi-level modeling environment is to provide a general purpose modeling language that is both "level-aware" and "level-agnostic". The language needs to be "level-aware" in that it enforces rules related to strict metamodeling and allows users to access and influence level information related to model elements. The language needs to be "level agnostic" in that it can be used in the same way across an arbitrary number of logical levels, and provides a uniform, level independent way of representing a given concept. In this section we briefly describe the key principles and concepts outlined by Atkinson and Kühne to support such an approach [3].

OCA

The orthogonal classification architecture defines the basic conceptual infrastructure in which multi-level modeling takes place. It is based on the principle that there should be two distinct, "orthogonal" classification dimensions, each organized according to the principles of strict metamodeling (i.e. only instanceOf relationships can cross level boundaries). One dimension, referred to as the linguistic dimension, deals with the form of user models and how they are internally represented. The other, the ontological dimension, deals with the semantic content of user models and what properties of the subject domain they are intended to capture. A user defined model element exists in each dimension, and thus has two distinct classifications – one linguistic and one ontological, as shown in Fig 1.

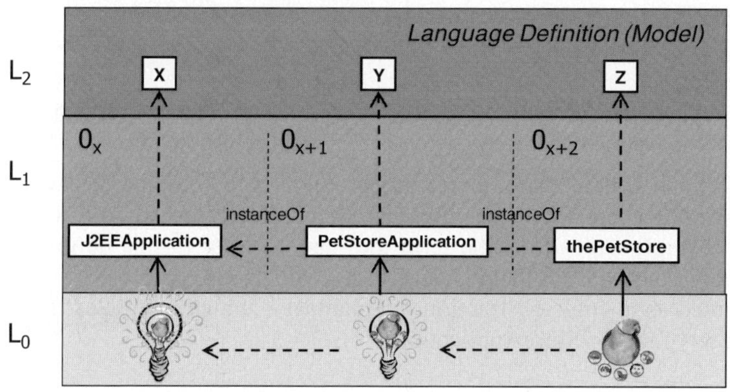

Fig. 1. Orthogonal Classification Architecture

One of the key consequences of this architecture is that a single model, from the traditional linguistic point of view (that is the whole L_1 level in Fig 1) can contain model elements at different logical (or ontological) levels of classification with logical instanceOf relationships between them.

Clabjects

When a user model only includes two ontological levels, each model element can play either the role of a type or the role of an instance but not both. However, as soon as there are more than two ontological levels, the elements in the middle level play two roles – they are instances of the ontological level above and types for the ontological level below. This is illustrated on the left hand side of Fig. 1 which shows how the notion of PetStoreApplication can be seen from two view-points. The upper part (in the ellipse) represents the object view of PetStoreApplication, when seen as an instance of J2EEApplication, while the lower part represents the class view of PetStoreApplication, when seen as the type of the object thePetStore.

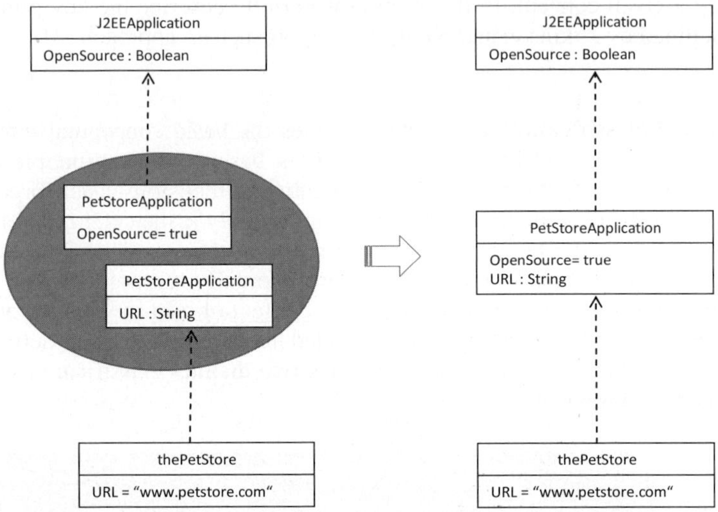

Fig. 2. Integrating Type and Instance Facets through Clabjects

Atkinson and Kühne's solution to this problem is to combine the two views into a single unified concept which has the dual facets of a type and an instance but is depicted as a single entity [5]. The term they use to refer to this notion is "clabject". This is shown on the right hand side of Fig. 1 which shows how PetStoreApplication is represented as a single abstraction – a clabject – which integrates the type and instance facets of the PetStoreApplication.

Deep Instantiation

Often, in the real world, concepts influence more than just their immediate instances. For example, the ContainerPersistence attribute of the class ApplicationServer in Fig. 3 is an attribute which is not only derived by its instances such as JBossServer but also by instances of its instances such as swtJBossServer. Thus the ContainerPersistence attribute is in a sense being carried over more than one classification level. Atkinson and Kühne propose to support the modeling of such situations through "deep instantiation" [5] which introduces the notion of potency to represent the endurance of a model element or its properties over instantiation steps. Instantiation always lowers the potency of a model element and property by one. Thus a model element or property of potency 0 behaves like an object or a slot, while a model element or property of potency 1 behaves like a class or an attribute. However, potencies of 2 or greater give rise to totally new kinds of model elements which endure over more than one instantiation step. In Fig. 2 potency is shown as a small superscript after the name of the affected element. Thus, ApplicationServer is a clabject of potency 2, and can be instantiated twice. JBossServer, as an instance of ApplicationServer, has a potency of 1 and swtJBossServer, as an instance of JBossServer has a potency of 0 and cannot be further instantiated.

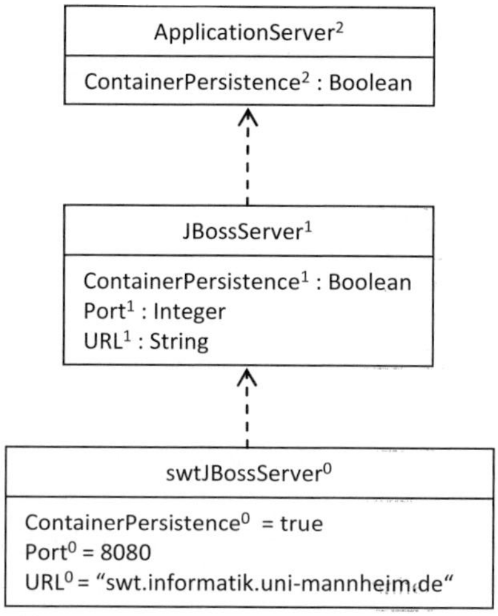

Fig. 3. Deep Instantiation through potency

3 Connectors in a Multi-level Environment

Once the notions of clabjects and deep instantiation (with its associated concepts) have been defined, the handling of relationships between clabjects in a multi-level, modeling environment appears to be fairly straightforward. As Fig. 3 (and many similar diagrams in papers by Atkinson and Kühne) illustrates, one would also like deep instantiation to apply to relationships between clabjects so that they can be instantiated many times and have an influence beyond the classification level immediately below. The example models the notion of a runsOn relationship between J2EEApplication an ApplicationServer, which is reflected in a runsOn relationship between their instances, such as PetStoreApplication and JBossServer, which in turn is reflected in a runsOn Relationship between their instances.

By the same reasoning applied at the beginning of this section leading to the notion of clabjects, if we view the relationships in Fig. 3 from a UML perspective, (i.e. if we view the top runsOn relationship as an association, the bottom runsOn relationship as a link, and the middle one as both) we once again encounter the dual facet issue, but for relationships rather than "nodal" clabjects of the kind described previously. Applying the same solution philosophy as before, in a uniform multi-level approach it is desirable to integrate a relationship with these two facets into a single unified concept.

Resisting the temptation to create a hybrid term from "association" and "link"[1] analogous to clabject from "class" and "object", we introduce the general term "connector" to represent the notion of a level-agnostic relationship between nodal clabjects in a model. This is also motivated by the desire to have a term that include all kinds of relationships that appear in models, some of which may not have dual facets, like generalization relationships, dependencies and instanceOf relationships.

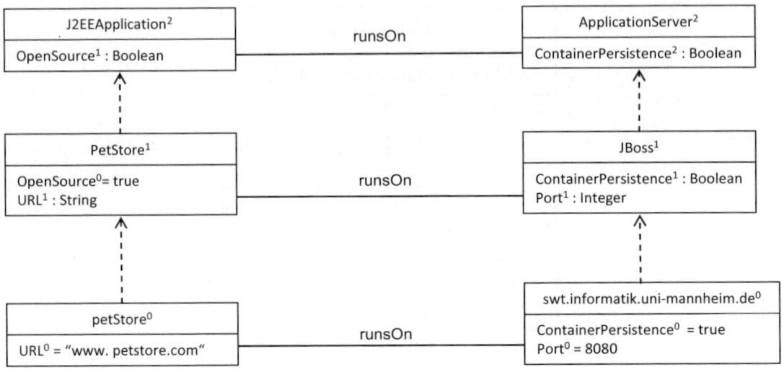

Fig. 4. Multi-level modeling with connectors

Although the intended mode of usage and visualization of connectors in a multi level environment is clear from Fig. 3, providing a clean and conceptually sound realization raises some fundamental issues which have not been addressed in the literature to date. These relate both to the internal representation of connectors - that is the internal, tool representation of connectors as defined in the linguistic (meta) model (in L_1 of the OCA), and to the visualization (i.e. rendering) of such connectors in a multi-level diagram. To provide the motivation and context for our proposals, in the next section we discuss the shortcomings of the UML's strategy for representing and rendering connectors, both from a normal UML modeling point of view, and from the point of view of adapting the UML approach to the multi-level approach.

4 Connectors in the UML

The most general and widely used connectors in UML class diagrams are associations. Links – instances of associations – are used much less frequently. Various special forms of associations exist such as aggregation and composition. UML class diagrams also support two other fundamental connectors between nodal model elements - generalizations and dependencies - each based on a different representation strategy.

Associations and Links

Associations have a nontrivial internal representation which is comprehensively documented in the UML metamodel and specification. As illustrated in Fig. 4, a

[1] Especially since there does not appear to be any combination that flows off the tongue like "clabject". "lissociation" or "assink" do not have the right resonance.

(binary) association is represented internally by three elements, one – an instance of the metaclass Association – representing the association itself, and the other two – instances of the metaclass Property, representing the participation of one attached classifier in the association. These are traditionally called "association ends".

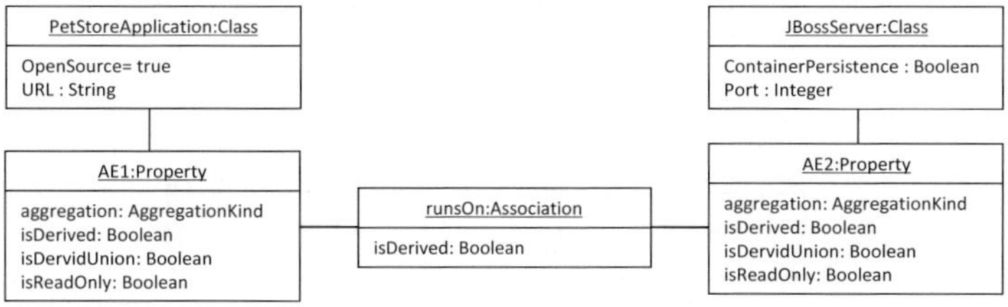

Fig. 5. Internal representation of a UML association

The internal representation of links is less well defined in the UML specification, but page 84 of the UML Superstructure specification states that -

"An instance specification whose classifier is an association represents a link and is shown using the same notation as for an association, but the solid path or paths connect instance specifications rather than classifiers." [18]

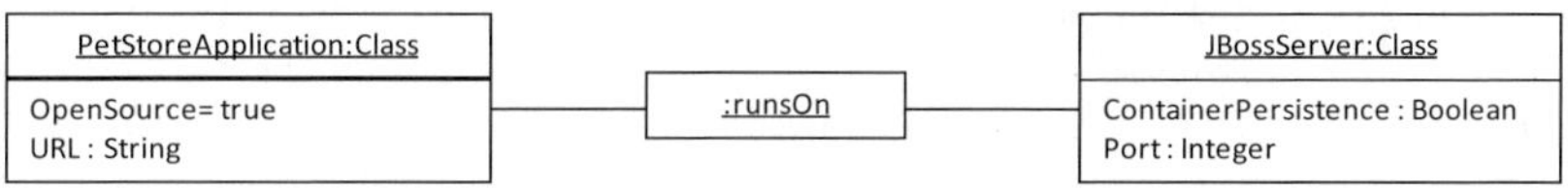

Fig. 6. Internal Representation of a UML link

This definition implies that a link is represented by one and only one internal model element rather than three, as shown in Fig. 5.This seems to be the approach adopted in most of the UML tools (e.g. MagicDraw [16]) that we investigated. An important consequence of this is that since the representations of UML associations and links are different they cannot be used at the same time to represent a dual-faceted connector in a multi-level modeling environment.

The UML specification also provides a good example of the modeling difficulties caused by UML's current strategy for representing associations/links, and the advantages that a coherent approach would bring. In the UML, deployment diagrams are used to show how components are mapped to nodes representing physical processing elements in a network. Since Node is a special form of model element with a special symbol, Node is defined as a specialization of Class in the UML metamodel. To allow users to indicate which nodes are connected together, the UML makes it possible for users to define CommunicationPath associations between Node classes (see middle level of Fig 7). The intent is to allow users to create object diagrams that show specific instances of AppServer and DBServer with specific CommunicationPaths links between them (see bottom level of Fig. 7).

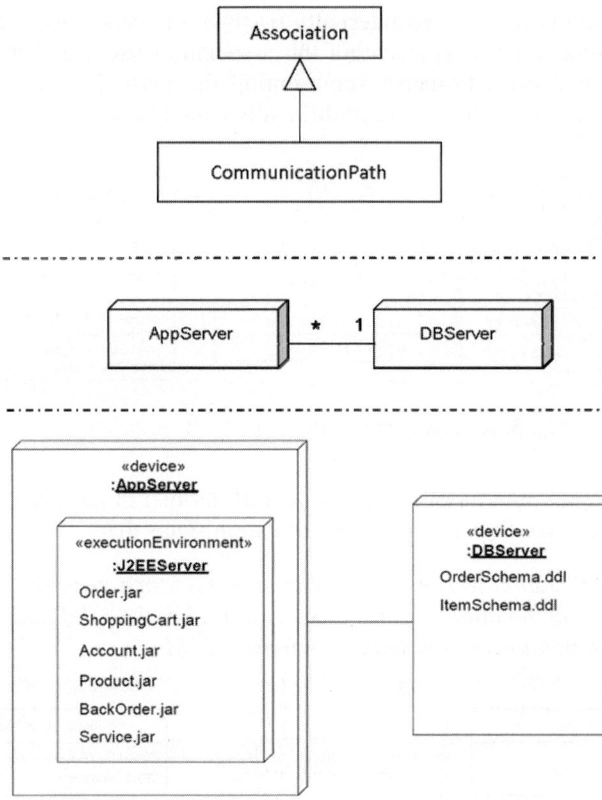

Fig. 7. Two Node Types with a CommunicationPath [18, from Figs. 10.3, 10.14 and 10.17]

This situation corresponds almost exactly to the J2EEApplication scenario illustrated in Fig. 3. However, because the UML does not allow instances of associations to be associations, in the UML metamodel the meta-level connector (Commnication-Path) has to be represented as a normal metaclass that specializes Association rather than as a connector as a user would intuitively expect (see top level of Fig. 7). The only way to ensure that the appropriate kinds of model elements can be related by the special domain association is to use OCL to constrain the classifiers that can be connected by a CommunicationPath. The corresponding constraint in the UML specification is

```
self.endType->forAll (t | t.oclIsKindOf(DeploymentTarget))
```

where Node, Property and InstanceSpecification are all specializations of DeploymentTarget (figure 10.4 of the UML Superstructure [18]). The counterintuitive nature of this way of defining meta connectors in the UML is evidenced by the fact that this constraint does not in fact have the desired effect. The motivation for using DeploymentTarget in the constraint (rather than Node) is to capture the fact that instances of Nodes (InstanceSpecifications) can participate in CommunciationPath relationships as well as Nodes themselves. However, the constraint not only allows all InstanceSpecifications to participate in such relationships, it also allows Nodes (i.e. type) to have CommunciationPath connectors to Node objects (i.e. instances).

Generalization and Dependencies

The other two fundamental kinds of connectors in UML class diagrams are Dependencies and Generalizations both of which are internally stored as a single model element according to the UML specification. However, their visual reprsentations can differ widely. Generalizations are always rendered as an arrow with a hollow head pointing to the general element. However the rendering of dependencies, depends on how many elements it connects. If a dependency has *"a set of elements for the client or the supplier"* [18, page 62] it is drawn as multiple arrows.

The consequence of these widely different definitions of connectors in UML class diagrams is that there is no consistent mapping pattern between the internal representation, the semantics and the external rendering of connectors. Class and Object, on the other hand, are almost always represented and rendered by a single model element[2].

5 Connector Representation and Rendering Principles

Based on the observations described in the previous section, we believe that to fully support multi-level modeling in an OCA environment, connectors need to be represented (for internal storage) and rendered (for external visualization) according to the following fundamental principles. These principles essentially govern how the ingredients of OCA-based multi-level modeling outlined in section 2 should be applied to connectors.

Principle 1: Uni-element Connector Representation

The lack of consistency in the way that the UML defines connectors is not only incompatible with their level agnostic representation and rendering, it also means that there is no natural relationship between the way models are stored and depicted. Moreover, as the discussion in section 4 indicates, it leads to confusion and error, even by experts such as the authors of the UML specification.

The first principle addresses this problem by requiring that all connectors be represented by one and only one model element. This ensures that all connectors are represented in the same way, and if the model element is a clabject it provides a natural way of capturing the type and instance facets of a dual facetted connector. Fig. 7, below, shows how the connectors in Fig. 3 would be internally represented using this approach.

This shows that all the information usually associated with connectors in languages like the UML (roles names, multiplicities, directionality etc.) can be captured as fields within the representing element.

[2] The exception is when classes are directly rendered within other classes, such as for example when a port is rendered within a connector (i.e. on the side of a component).

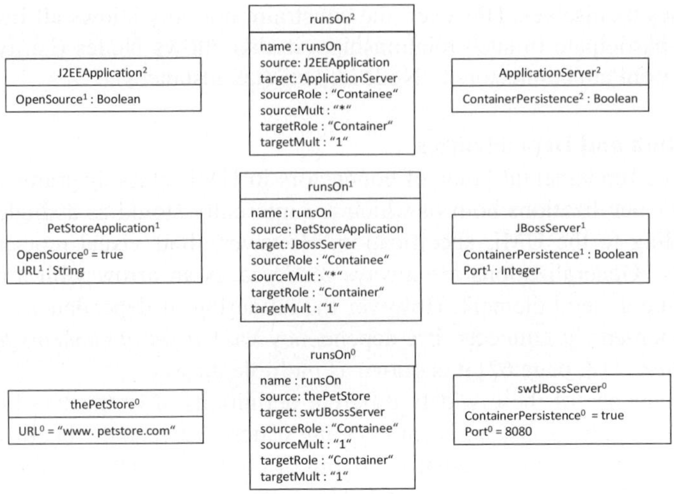

Fig. 8. Uni-element representation of Connectors

Principle 2: Multi Form Connector Rendering

We have deliberately left all lines (i.e. edges) out of the Fig. 7 because this picture is intended to convey only the internal representation. However, to be realizable in a way that matches current rendering conventions, principle 1 needs to be accompanied by a suitable approach for depicting connectors. We address this need through the notion of multi-form rendering.

Since connectors are invariably rendered using some combination of lines in modern modeling languages (indeed, this is of course the very meaning of connector in a visual sense), we need a strategy to assign lines to the single model element that represents a connector according to principle 1. A naive way to do this would be to simply say that a connector is always rendered as a single line in a way that resembles the traditional UML rendering of association and links etc. But then it would never be possible for a user to view the model element representing the connector as a normal nodal model element with its full complement of attributes.

Alternatively, one could render the connector model element using the usual rectangular notation for model elements, and in addition draw two lines connecting them to their source and target elements as shown in Fig. 8 below[3]. However, this not only diverges from normal rendering conventions, it also has the problem that the connectors are then essentially behaving like nodes (normal model elements) in the diagram, and the questions arises as to how the two lines connecting them to their source and target should be interpreted and represented. Are they connectors in their own right, and if so do they have their own model elements to represent them? The infinite regression implied clearly indicates that they cannot be regarded as connectors. But then what are they?

[3] We are limiting the discussion to binary connectors for simplicity, but the discussion applies to high order connectors in the same way.

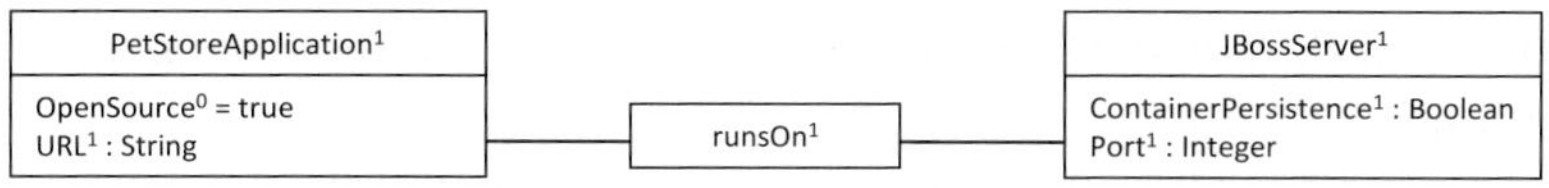

Fig. 9. Usual rectangle Connector Rendering

The solution we propose essentially aims to find a balance between these two approaches. The principle is that all (binary3) connectors are always rendered in the form of a nodal symbol plus two lines (as in the second approach), with the proviso that the node can take multiple forms, one of which can be "visually insignificant". By "visually insignificant" we mean that the model element can be rendered as little more than a dot which, although visible, gives the overall construction the visible appearance of an edge. This "dotted" form is used to render the top runsOn connector in Fig. 9. The fully elaborated form, on the hand, is used to render the middle runsOn connector. Furthermore, to illustrate that there can be multiple nodal symbols assigned to a connector, a domain specific symbol is used to render the bottom runsOn connector.

All rendering forms exist simultaneously in the sense that they are stored in the repository and can be called up at any time. The user can toggle between the different forms at will depending on which form best suits his or her purpose at a particular point in time (e.g. entering data, preparing the model for depiction in a document). Many tools support the ability to open mini forms to add data to model elements but this is usually done in an ad hoc way and is not part of language or the inherent rendering mechanism.

The application of this principle avoids the regression problem because all connectors are always implemented as a nodal symbol plus two primitive "element reference" lines (e.g. arrows). Thus, there is never any chance of confusion between a fully fledged connector and the source/ target element reference lines that form part of its rendering. This principle is not only simple for users to remember and to use, it is also simple for tools to implement. The element reference lines pointing to the source and target elements can have the usual arrowheads used to render the special connector forms recognized in the UML (e.g. white triangular arrowhead for generalization).

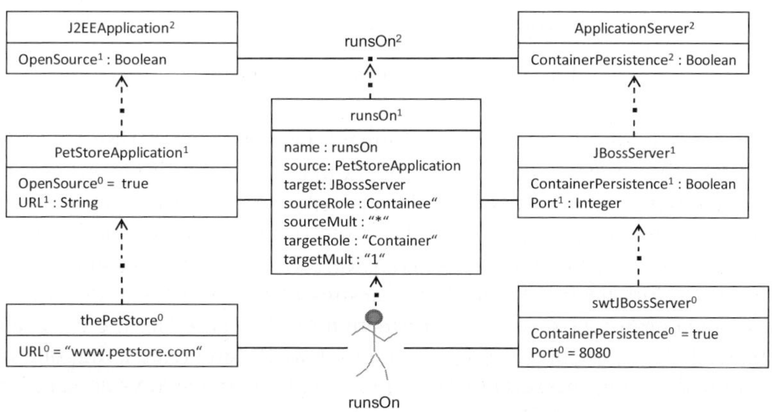

Fig. 10. Dotted Connector Rendering

Principle 3: Exclusive and Mandatory Connector-Based Rendering of Relationships

The final principle deals with another source of confusion that often occurs with the rendering of models in infrastructures like the UML. Although the previous principle explains how connectors are rendered, it does not address the issue of when they need to be rendered (i.e. should they be rendered in all circumstances) and whether there are any other forms of information in models that can be rendered as lines (i.e. edges). There is certainly a lot of information within the normal (non connector) model elements that could potentially be rendered as edges. For example, every node has information about its classifier that could easily be rendered as an InstanceOf arrow. But allowing any conceptual relationship stored in the model repository to be rendered as edges at will (without actually being connectors in the sense described above), detracts from the clear rendering metaphor established by the previous two principles, and makes the management of model visualizations much more of an ad hoc activity. For this reason, we add a third principle to the previous two which essentially requires that (a) only connectors can be rendered using lines and (b) all connectors must be rendered using lines.

The first of these requirements is made more palatable for the user by ensuring that the multi-level modeling language has a concrete syntax (i.e. a visualization approach) that allows internal relationship information to be captured in the nodes of a rendered model without the use of lines. The UML has a well known example of such a mechanism – the extension of a class or object name with a colon followed by another class name to indicate the former's type. Fig. 10 shows other symbolic conventions that we use to show all the information in the internal representation of model elements such as the level (subscript) and the potency (superscript) as well as the super class of the class (as suggested in [5]). The level is only shown for the clabject, because all fields of a clabject have the same level as the clabject.

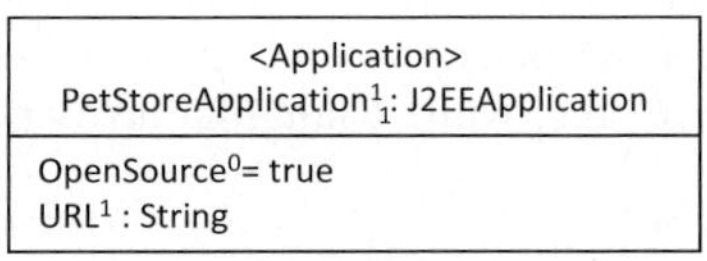

Fig. 11. Rendering without Connectors

The practicality of the second requirement becomes more obvious when one realizes that in the future "views" (e.g. diagrams) will increasingly be generated on demand from other models by automated transformations. In other words, new temporary models will be generated "on the fly" from central repositories for the specific purpose of rendering particular views. Transformation engines can thus generate the necessary connectors needed to meets the desires of the user for a specific diagram, but within the central repository the information used to generate the connector need not be changed. Thus, as shown in Fig. 9, if a user wishes to create a diagram in which instanceOf relationships are actually rendered visually using arrows he needs to direct the tool to generate a new "view" model containing the appropriate connectors which are then rendered using the collapsed (dotted) form. In the context of such transformation based modeling tools, there is no point in having any model element in a "view" model which is not rendered. In other words, either a model is rendered in full (e.g. it is a view) or not at all (e.g. it is a central model).

6 Conclusion

Although the principles outlined in this paper may at first appear relatively simple, and designed to address relatively minor issue related to representation and rendering details, in fact their overall cumulative effect is quite profound.

First, they plug a gap in OCA based, multi-level modeling by explaining how connectors can be consistently brought into the multi-level modeling paradigm in the way envisaged by Atkinson and Kühne [5]. The direct modeling benefits for the user are twofold: (a) as illustrated in Fig 10, meta-level connectors whose instances also have a type facet can be modeled using the same basic (edge) metaphor used for connectors at other levels (as opposed to the counterintuitive and error prone use of metaclasses and OCL constraints discussed in section 4), and (b), connectors can have explicit connectors of their own, including generalization and instanceOf connectors as shown in Fig 10. Although associations are redefinable elements in the UML, displaying generalization relationships between associations has never been a widely accepted practice in UML modeling. In effect, the approach turns connectors into "first class citizens" with all the rights and capabilities of node-rendered model elements. From a UML perspective one might say that the approach treats every relationship as an association class, but without the clumsy UML notation.

Second, by allowing users to model connectors in a much more natural and intuitive way, regardless of which ontological model level they belong to, the approach helps reduce the artificial complexity in models [6] which in turn reduces the risk of errors and misunderstandings. An example of unnecessary (artificial) complexity caused by the UML's current way of handling connectors is the forced use of node-rendered classes to visualize meta-connectors. As pointed out in section 4, even the experts who specified the UML were unable to use this approach correctly when defining how CommunicationsPaths should be used. By reducing the inbuilt impedance to capturing domain concepts in a modeling language, the multi-level modeling approach in general, and the connector representation principles in particular, enhance the fidelity and communicative ability of models (which, after all, is their fundamental purpose).

Third, by defining a consistent and uniform strategy for representing and rendering all connectors, and making this strategy an extension of the basic "one element – one symbol" principle that is used for model elements traditionally rendered as nodes (e.g. class, objects etc.) the approach ensures that there is a single and a natural interpretation of a model as a graph. This is not the case in UML modeling where the relationship between the internal representation of connectors as nodes and edges is unsystematic, and the representation of dual-faceted connectors is ambiguous. In a multi-level model based on these principles, however, there is always one interpretation of the model as a graph and this is always reflected naturally in the rendering. For example, the model in Fig.10 is interpreted as a graph with 15 nodes and 18 edges.

This property of models is of fundamental importance for the definition of meaningful graph-based metrics on models (for example to capture their quality).

There are of course also disadvantages to the approach but we believe them to be relatively minor. First, the idea that relationships between abstractions are always to be thought of as first class entities with their own nodes is an unfamiliar one for UML modelers and will require some adjustment. However, thinking of relationships as edges rather than as nodes in a graph-based model has not always been the norm. For example, in Entity-Relationship diagrams which are still used to depict relational data models, relationships have always been represented in the way advocated by our principles – namely as a nodal symbol (a diamond) connected to the related entities by edges. The "trick" of allowing the connector node symbol to be rendered in a "visually insignificant" way as a dot provides a convenient way of allowing users to develop models with the traditional look and feel of UML, but in the systematic, "graph-faithful" way described above.

Second, the idea of requiring all connectors in a model, indeed all the model elements within a model, to be rendered whenever a diagram is generated from a model is a foreign notion to many tool vendors, and will require changes to the way future tools are implemented. However, we believe that as model transformation becomes ubiquitous, the natural way to support the rendering of a model in different ways is to generate different "view models" from them on-the-fly. The choice of what model elements are to appear in a diagram is then made during this transformation process (i.e. the creation of the view model from the basic model) rather than in the rendering process, which can then obviously be performed according to the "every model element is rendered" principle. For the end user there is no difference.

The principles outlined in this paper are independent of the particular repository technology and rendering engine used. We are currently working on a prototype built on top of EMF using the GMF rendering engine, but many other implementation platforms are possible. For space reasons, in this paper we have focused on binary connectors, but the principles naturally scale up to accommodate higher order connectors as well.

References

1. Álvarez, J.M., Evans, A., Sammut, P.: MML and the Metamodel Architecture. In: Workshop on Transformations in UML (WTUML 2001) (2001)
2. Atkinson, C., Kühne, T.: Concepts for Comparing Modeling Tool Architectures. In: ACM/IEEE 8th International Conference on Model Driven Engineering Languages and Systems, MoDELS / UML 2005, Montego Bay, Jamaica, October 2–7 (2005)
3. Atkinson, C., Kühne, T.: Model-Driven Development: A Metamodeling Foundation. IEEE Software (September/October 2003)
4. Atkinson, C., Kühne, T.: Rearchitecting the UML Infrastructure. ACM journal Transactions on Modeling and Computer Simulation 12(4) (2002)
5. Atkinson, C., Kühne, T.: The Essence of Multilevel Metamodeling. In: Gogolla, M., Kobryn, C. (eds.) UML 2001. LNCS, vol. 2185, pp. 19–33. Springer, Heidelberg (2001)
6. Atkinson, C., Kühne, T.: Reducing accidental complexity in domain models. Software and Systems Modeling (2007)

7. Bézivin, J., Lemesle, R.: ntology-Based Layered Semantics for Precise OA&D Modeling. In: Proceedings of the Workshops on Object-Oriented Technology, June 09-13, pp. 151–154 (1997)
8. Gašević, D., Kaviani, N., Hatala, M.: On Metamodeling in Megamodels. In: Duval, E., Klamma, R., Wolpers, M. (eds.) EC-TEL 2007. LNCS, vol. 4753, pp. 91–105. Springer, Heidelberg (2007)
9. Gogolla, M., Favre, J.-M., Büttner, F.: On Squeezing M0, M1, M2, and M3 into a Single Object Diagram. In: Proc. MoDELS 2005 Workshop Tool Support for OCL and Related Formalisms (2005)
10. Gonzalez-Perez, C., Henderson-Sellers, B.: A powertype-based metamodelling framework. Software and System Modeling 5(1), 72–90 (2006)
11. Graphical Modeling Framework (2008), `http://www.eclipse.org/modeling/gmf`
12. Jarke, M., Gallersdörfer, R., Jeusfeld, M.A., Staudt, M., Eherer, S.: ConceptBase - a deductive object base for meta data management. Journal of Intelligent Information Systems, Special Issue on Advances in Deductive Object-Oriented Databases 4(2), 167–192 (1995)
13. Korthaus, A., Gitzel, R.: The Role of Metamodeling in Model-Driven Development. In: Proceedings of the 8th World Multi-Conference on Systemics, Cybernetics and Informatics (SCI 2004), Orlando, Florida, USA, July 18-21, 2004. Information Systems, Technologies and Applications: I, IIIS, vol. IV (2004)
14. Kühne, T., Schreiber, D.: Can Programming be Liberated from the Two-Level Style? — Multi-Level Programming with DeepJava. In: ACM SIGPLAN International Conference on Object-Oriented Programming, Systems, Languages and Applications: OOPSLA 2007, Montréal, Canada, October 21–25 (2007)
15. MetaEdit+ Tool (2008), `http://www.metacase.com`
16. No Magic Inc., MagicDraw Tool, `http://www.magicdraw.com/`
17. OMG UML 2.1.2 Infrastructure Specification, Object Management Group (OMG), Tech. Rep. (November 2007)
18. OMG UML 2.1.2 Superstructure Specification, Object Management Group (OMG), Tech. Rep. (November 2007)

Model-Based Quality Assurance of Automotive Software*

Jan Jürjens[1], Daniel Reiß[2], and David Trachtenherz[3]

[1] The Open University, UK
[2] Elektrobit Group Ltd, Germany
[3] Techische Universität München, Germany

Abstract. Software in embedded (e.g. automotive) systems requires a high level of reliability. Model-based development techniques are increasingly used to reach this goal, but so far there is relatively little published knowledge on the comparative benefits in using different assurance techniques. We investigate different and potentially complementary model-based software quality assurance methods (namely simulation and white-box testing vs. model-checking) at the hand of an application to the software component of a door control unit. We draw conclusions with regards to suitable application use cases.

1 Introduction

Software plays an increasingly important role in embedded systems. This applies in particular to the automotive sector, characterized by strict safety requirements to components of a motor vehicle (see [4,15,6,17] for background). The constantly growing portion of software, the short development cycles and the rising complexity of software in the automobile represent high challenges to the car manufacturers, together with the limited computer resources available on the embedded components which have to be kept as cheap as possible because of the high sales numbers in this domain. This factors require an intensive use of quality assurance measures to ensure a high level of reliability, quality, and safety. Modern development procedures such as modelling and quality assurance using graphical description methods are increasingly used towards achieving this goal. Unfortunately, despite the high amount of attention that these techniques receive in the software development community, there does not seem to be much published knowledge available which would compare the effectiveness of the different and potentially complementary approaches when applied to the kind of software used in embedded and in particular automotive systems, in particular when it comes to a leading edge approach such as model-checking.

One goal of this work is to address this knowledge gap with an experience report on a field study which had the goal to compare conventional software quality assurance methods (specifically, testing) with one of the recently developed assurance approaches

* This work was performed partly when the first and second authors were at TU Munich and the third at BMW. Contact: http://www.jurjens.de/jan

K. Czarnecki et al. (Eds.): MoDELS 2008, LNCS 5301, pp. 858–873, 2008.

(specifically, model-checking). The field study took place in the context of the automobile industry. The target of the field study was the development of a door controller unit based on a publically available textual specification [13]. The components for the door lock, the window lifter and the light control described in this specification were modelled in two CASE tools, the commercially distributed tool ASCET (which offers extensive test assistance), and the research prototype AutoFOCUS (which comes with innovative quality assurance plug-ins like model-checkers). For each of the two models constructed within these tools, different quality assurance techniques (white-box testing for ASCET and model-checking for AutoFOCUS) were applied. We then evaluated the outcomes and compared the two approaches with the goal to investigate the relative advantages and disadvantages in using them, wrt. their effectiveness in finding errors and the required time efforts. We also discuss possibilities for a complementary use.

Case study Door Control Unit: We evaluated the software quality assurance methods in the context of the development of the software component of an electronic door controller unit from [13]. This example was selected on the basis that it is representative for a specification in the automotive domain, with a particular emphasis on functionality (rather than requirements on base level software). According to the specification a door controller unit (DCU) is installed in each front door. Both electronic controller units are connected via the CAN bus and hence to the other electronic control units and intelligent sensors of the electronic comfort system. The DCUs are responsible for the settings of the front seats and the side-view mirrors, the management of user settings, the interior lighting, window lifter and the central locking system. This work concentrated on the functionality of the last three components. Error protection mechanism and on-board diagnosis were not in scope of this work. Fig. 1 gives an overview over the window lifter module as part of the door control unit. *Dispatcher* distributes the incoming signals to the concerned components over the connected communication channels[1]. *CAN_Front* and *CAN_Back* process signals for the CAN bus. *Request_Front* and *Request_Back* process signals from the local peripherals of the door control unit. The result is passed to the engine controls *FrontMotor* and *BackMotor*.

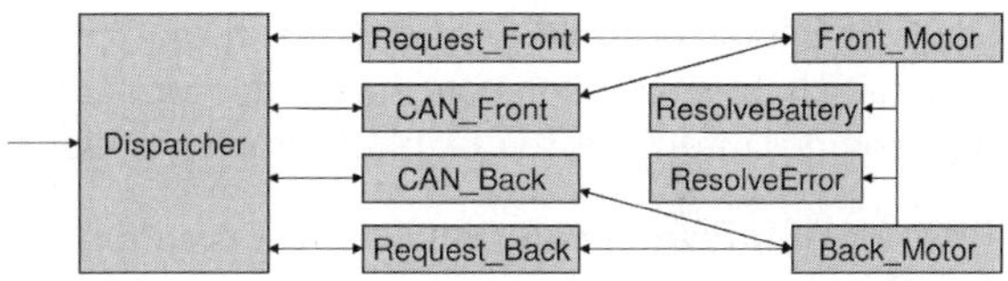

Fig. 1. DCU component *Windows* – Overview

Properties under test: Only functional errors in the model or implementation were in scope of our investigations (and thus the errors were found after the modelling resp. code generation phase). More specifically, we focussed on those properties that could be expressed as state reachability properties. Errors in or misinterpretations of the original specification were not included in the error count (but they did have an impact on the time effort needed for the modelling phase). Data collection was performed by the person who undertook the study (the second author).

[1] A "channel" is a communication link between two modules.

2 Application in ASCET

The ASCET tool chain provided by the ETAS Group is used by automobile manufacturers and suppliers in the automotive industry. It supports an integrated software development process according to the V-Model. In conjunction with ASCET, additional tools are used to apply the desired conventional testing methods with code coverage. Within the case study, we used the tool CTE XL to graphically specify test cases in form of a matrix. They could then be exported and converted into an appropriate format to be executed in ASCET. On the other hand we measured the code coverage of the test cases using the testing framework "Test RealTime" provided by IBM Rational.

3 Application in AutoFOCUS

The CASE tool AutoFOCUS is a freely available system development tool developed at TU Munich. It is based on concepts of the formal description methodology FOCUS [5] and provides interfaces to QA plug-ins such as the SMV model-checker.

Testing: AutoFOCUS can simulate the execution of a model in discrete time steps. The data flow between components and the computations of the individual components of a system and their underlying state machines (modelled as State Transition Diagrams / STDs) can be visualized in a simulator. For every time step input test data can be manually specified. Using the Validas code generator one can also generate code and then apply conventional testing methods to the generated code. Since the code is generated in a canonical way it is straightforward to transfer bug fixes back to the model.

Model-Checking: Due to the state explosion problem, we only verified components with less than ten State Transition Diagrams using SMV. The time effort to check a property varied in general between two and ten minutes for each check depending on the complexity of the components. Logical errors could thus be determined and excluded easily without interrupting the development process of the modules for too long.

Example Crush Guard: We discuss the use of model-checking on a property of the crush guard for the front window. As mentioned, the complete DCU model was not processed by the model-checker at once. Hence a modular approach was chosen to show the crush guard's correctness for the whole system: The model was divided up from a functional point of view and structured hierarchically. The goal was to minimize mutual dependencies and interface dependencies so that each block could be viewed as a "black box". The significant component *FrontMotor* is located in the *Windows*-component. The interface of this component consists of the following inputs:

- *Bottom_Front*: registers if the window pane resides at the lower block
- *MovingSensor_Front*: registers the movement of the pane
- *Top_Front*: registers if the window pane resides at the upper block
- *Battery_Front*: registers the current battery voltage
- *MotorFront*: registers a command request of the component *Request_Front*

```
1.  []((
2.       (Val(MC_FrontMotor.Front_Motor)==F_MOTOR_Up) &&
3.          () ((Val(MC_FrontMotor.Front_Motor)==F_MOTOR_Up) &&
4.            () ((Val(MC_FrontMotor.Front_Motor)==F_MOTOR_Up) &&
5.              () ((Val(MC_FrontMotor.Front_Motor)==F_MOTOR_Up) &&
6.                () ((Val(MC_FrontMotor.Front_Motor)==F_MOTOR_Up) &&
7.                  () ((Val(MC_FrontMotor.Front_Motor)==F_MOTOR_Up)
8.                       && not(is_Msg(MC_FrontMotor.Top_Front))
9.                       && not(is_Msg(MC_FrontMotor.MovingSensor_Front)))))))
10.   ) => (
11.     (()(()(()(()(()(()(
12.       ( (Val(MC_FrontMotor.Front_Motor)==F_MOTOR_Down)
13.         $Until
14.         ( (not(is_Msg(MC_FrontMotor.Bottom_Front)) &&
15.            not(is_Msg(MC_FrontMotor.MovingSensor_Front)))
16.           || (Val(MC_FrontMotor.Bottom_Front)==F_UNTEN_Bottom))
17.       ) || (
18.         (Val(MC_FrontMotor.Front_Motor)==F_MOTOR_Down) &&
19.           () ((Val(MC_FrontMotor.Front_Motor)==F_MOTOR_Down) &&
...           ... // 6 identical lines with NEXT operator omitted for sake of brevity
26.                         () ((Val(MC_FrontMotor.Front_Motor)==F_MOTOR_Down) &&
27.                           () (Val(MC_FrontMotor.Front_Motor)==F_MOTOR_Down)
28.   ))))))))) ))))))) ))
```

Fig. 2. LTL formula

The outputs are the following:

- *Front_Motor*: controls the voltage of the window lifter motor
- *Front_Out_ERROR_WIN*: signals an error
- *FrontLowWin*: signals low battery voltage

Using model-checking, the following property could be verified for *FrontMotor* for all system states, following the DCU specification:
If the motor is on for at least the length of the startup-time (which is the time needed for the window pane to start moving) and a blockage of the window pane is registered after the expiry of this time then move the window down until:

- *the lower block is reached,*
- *the 3-second-timeout occurs or*
- *the window movement is blocked (e.g. due to a mechanical malfunction).*

The corresponding LTL formula is shown in Fig. 2 (line numbers were added for referencing the lines). In detail, the lines in the formula mean the following:

Line 1: For all system states the lines 2 to 28 apply.
Line 2 to 7: The activation of the motor occurs at least for 6 system ticks (abstraction of startup time).
Line 8 to 9: After startup, the window is at the upper block and does not move.
Line 10: If a blockage is registered (line 2 to 9) then react (line 11 to 28).
Line 11: The reaction follows at the point in time after registering the blockage.
Line 12 to 15: Move down the window (line 12) until (line 13) the window blocks (line 14 to 15) or the lower block is reached (line 16),
Line 17 to 27: or 10 system ticks have passed (abstraction of 3-seconds-timeout).

The LTL formula accesses neither subcomponents nor internal channels of *FrontMotor* but only the external interface. Thus the formulated property describes a black-box property of *FrontMotor*. The processing of a signal input in the component *FrontMotor* needs some time in form of global time ticks. Thereby messages can internally pass through a pipeline[2] of subcomponents. Hence some system ticks are needed before a result is available on the output channels. When setting up a formula in AutoFOCUS this pipelining effect is also considered. For a given property (e.g. "if X applies, then Y arises") the temporal delay must be expressed. The time delay becomes manifest in the change of the formula ("if X applies Y results in 2 system ticks"). Implementing these technical details results in increased formula size. Furthermore small improvements of the model can lead to great changes of the formula. On the other hand, the AutoFOCUS-model can also be modified to get a simpler and clearer formula. E.g., to avoid pipelines, a component network can be combined into a single STD.

Note that getting the LTL to correctly formalize the requirement one wants to verify is non-trivial. Since the original requirement is itself not formal, it is not possible to prove that the LTL formula is correct, but one can only increase confidence in it by inspection and simulation. In particular it can happen that the verification fails because the LTL formula is incorrect. This means that if the verification fails, both the model and the LTL formula have to be checked and any of them may need to be corrected.

4 Evaluation

4.1 Evaluation of the Tools

To compare the tools AutoFOCUS and ASCET, one should keep in mind that they were developed against different backgrounds: AutoFOCUS is supposed to be as generally applicable as possible, while ASCET is more aligned to the development of electronic control units and specialized for use in the automotive domain. Also the influence of the market and the manpower of the corresponding companies differs. Therefore the following sections concentrate on the comparison of the principles behind the two tools and the applied verification methods. It is also emphasized that some restrictions in AutoFOCUS were only imposed by the constraints of model-checking, e.g. due to the state space explosion problem. The time needed for constructing the LTL formalization of the requirements to be verified is not included in the effort discussed above.

Modelling: The AutoFOCUS notation is relatively simple compared to other modelling tools such as ASCET. This results in a simpler semantics which is more easily accessible for formal verification. The approach is also relatively general: Application areas of AutoFOCUS are not limited to embedded systems in the automobile industry. However, it also makes it more difficult to deeply integrate concepts of the automotive domain, such as:

- Scheduling in OSEK using tasks and processes
- Mapping of the data types which are supported on the target hardware

[2] With "pipeline" we mean a chain of channels each leading to a communication delay.

– Distinction of program code and data fields in memory (e.g. for future replacement of configuration data)

Thus AutoFOCUS is primarily suitable for the description of the abstract logic of a function. The embedding into the hardware context and the precise modelling of the above mentioned concepts should not be attempted using AutoFOCUS, since this would significantly increase the size and complexity of the model (and lead to problems with model-checking because of the state explosion problem). Also the pipeline effect of the signal processing flow and associated synchronization problems due to the parallel computation of the component network get more complex with an increasing model size. In ASCET the synchronisation of the individual components also plays an important role. There a sequential processing flow is supported by the use of process and task scheduling concepts. On the level of the component behaviour, in AutoFOCUS the selection of state machine transitions with the same priority takes place indeterministically, so the user has to enforce determinism explicitly by assigning appropriate preconditions and priorities. In ASCET the computations in STDs are deterministic because different transition priorities are mandatory. The modelling of time-controlled behaviour in AutoFOCUS requires the discretisation of time because of the global system ticks. Timer components can be realized in AutoFOCUS using integer variables. The resolution of a timeout interval is determined by a number of ticks. In ASCET time values are directly declared in the model. Restrictions in AutoFOCUS arise due to the state explosion problem when using model-checking. A limitation of the number of computation steps and of the integer values is necessary. Hence AutoFOCUS in combination with model-checking is well suited for event-controlled systems without temporal conditions.

Temporal effort for the modelling: The simple AutoFOCUS notation can be learned within a day due to its simplicity (as was demonstrated in the case-study since the user did not have any prior knowledge of the AutoFOCUS notation). The modelling of the components for the central door lock and the window lifter took place in three weeks for each. The interior light component was modelled in one week. The difficulty was in the correct interpretation and conversion of the textual specification. In particular, the time effort for constructing the AutoFOCUS model includes the effort for clarifying any unclear issues with the original specification. Further additional corrections of basic errors and the bug fixes for synchronization problems required a complex restructuring. The time effort was also a result of the restrictive notation and the missing possibility to copy whole component hierarchies. This drawback is being resolved in the ongoing development of AutoFOCUS. The need for copying hierarchies could also be avoided if the complete model was known in advance and requirements were fixed. But in practice this assumption usually does not hold since requirements can change during the development phase and a model is constructed successively during the development phase. Another week had to be invested for restructuring the *Windows* component to make it suitable for model-checking with respect to the state space explosion problem.

ASCET required a longer phase of one week to get familiar with the modelling elements. The reason for this is the vast variety of modelling elements with association to concepts of the automotive domain. The main problems concerning the interpretation of the DCU specification were already discovered due to the modelling in AutoFOCUS. Thus the time to create the model of each component in ASCET took about half

Table 1. Time effort

	ASCET	AutoFOCUS (Incl. spec.)
Training	1 week	1 day
Modelling: door lock	1.5 weeks	3 weeks
Modelling: window lifter	1.5 weeks	3 weeks
Modelling: interior light	0.5 weeks	1 week

Table 2. Number of errors found

	ASCET	AutoFOCUS
Experiment / simulation	10	5
Model-checking	-	5
White-box tests	5	-

the time as in AutoFOCUS. Also the liberal description languages and modelling elements facilitated the modelling. The structure of the model in AutoFOCUS was reused in ASCET and brought into a more compact form. The application of the test procedures led only to small bug fixes. The logical concept remained stable.

Table 1 gives the time effort spent for the modelling in both tools. Note that the time effort for AutoFOCUS also included the preliminary work on the specification that did not need to be repeated for ASCET, so these effort values are not meant to be used to draw any conclusions about the relative ease of using the two tools but just to give an idea about the size of the case-study that was performed. Unfortunately it is difficult to determine in a reliable way which fragment of the time effort needed for constructing the AutoFOCUS specification was needed to understand the specification, because these two activities cannot be separated when constructing a first model of a specification (because many clarification questions about the specification only arise while working on the model). Therefore, we do not attempt to adjust the data given in Table 1 to account for this difference. However, we estimate that the conversion and interpretation of the specification constituted nearly half of the time used for modelling in AutoFOCUS (and this was not repeated in ASCET since one could benefit of the experience previously acquired when building the model in AutoFOCUS). Thus one may hypothesize that in fact approximately the same time effort was necessary for the modelling in both tools (apart from adaptations for model-checking that became necessary in addition).

4.2 Evaluation and Comparison of the Quality Assurance Methods

Both testing and model-checking were tool-supported and used automation available in the tools (in particular producing input data in CTE XL and exporting them for testing, as well as automated model and property export from AutoFOCUS for model-checking). Thus we believe the experimental arrangements for both methodologies to be fairly comparable. The errors found when comparing the two quality assurance approaches can be considered to originate from modelling resp. code generation and to be independent of possible misinterpretations of specification: Both models as well as their quality assurance were performed based on the same interpretation of the system requirements specification. Thus the quality assurance for the two models reflected the same specification interpretation as implemented in the models and just determined whether the implementation was correct with respect to this interpretation of the specification. Therefore the comparison results should not be influenced by possible misinterpretations of specification. Validation of the requirements specification is out of scope of this paper, as the focus of this work lies on comparing different approaches to quality assurance.

Error Finding: Table 2 compares the number of bugs found using both tools. It lists the bugs which were uncovered after the completion of the modelling of the components by applying the testing methods. Furthermore it must be noted that for the listed bugs the simulation always preceded model-checking and white-box testing. Hence the majority of the bugs listed were already found during the simulation.

The errors could be classified as follows:

- errors in interpreting the specification
- specification errors (e.g. incorrect timing information)
- oversights (e.g. forgetting a transition)
- conceptual errors (specification correctly interpreted but incorrectly transformed to design)
- obscure errors (only occurring under obscure side conditions, e.g. race conditions, sporadic errors or timing errors, e.g. due to pipeline effects)

In ASCET discrepancies with the DCU specification were found by simulating the model. These errors were due to a wrong implementation: For example setting the wrong priority for a transition of a state machine or forgetting to reinitialize the trigger of a transition. There were also deadlocks or incorrect transition preconditions which led to a wrong state machine behaviour. In the code generation phase, omitted cases in case distinctions can be detected. Missing initializations or type errors should already be detected by the tool during the modelling phase and thus were not relevant for our study. White-box testing with code coverage analysis detected the remaining bugs like careless errors (e.g. transmission of a wrong message value) or unreachable code due to missing transition preconditions, or errors originating on the conceptual level (unless these were caught earlier if they lead to incompatible interfaces).

In AutoFOCUS the simulator was quite helpful in order to expose basic errors (e.g. wrong prioritization of transitions). Bugs which were hard to detect (e.g. concerning pipeline synchronization and boundary conditions) could easily be found by the model-checker. We did not notice any errors that would have been introduced by changing the model in order to make it amenable to model-checking (although in larger projects involving more people this could certainly be expected). However, some kinds of errors (e.g. pipeline synchronization for time-triggered communication) were due to the time-triggered communication semantics of the AutoFOCUS modelling notation, while other errors (e.g. boundary conditions and incorrect prioritization of transitions) occurred for both modelling techniques. Such bugs would take an substantially longer time to be found using conventional testing methods because of the difficulty in determining the corresponding test input data.

Some errors were found with both approaches. For example, states that will not be reached (e.g. because of a missing transition or a wrong transition priority) can be found using simulation or testing by transversing the relevant transition path, or using model-checking against a suitable reachability property. Conversely, showing that a certain state will *not* be reached can be easier using model-checking because it ensures that all possible paths are investigated.

Note that in principle, all errors found using model-checking could also be found using automated testing because at least theoretically it would usually be thinkable to achieve a complete test value coverage (i.e. to test every possible sequence of input

```
[](((Val(MC_FrontMotor.Front_Motor)==F_MOTOR_Up) &&
     () ((Val(MC_FrontMotor.Front_Motor)==F_MOTOR_Up) &&
       () ((Val(MC_FrontMotor.Front_Motor)==F_MOTOR_Up) &&
         () ((Val(MC_FrontMotor.Front_Motor)==F_MOTOR_Up) &&
           () ((Val(MC_FrontMotor.Front_Motor)==F_MOTOR_Up) &&
             () (((Val(MC_FrontMotor.Front_Motor)==F_MOTOR_Up)
                  && not(is_Msg(MC_FrontMotor.Top_Front))
                  && not(is_Msg(MC_FrontMotor.MovingSensor_Front))) &&
               ()((Val(MC_FrontMotor.Front_Motor)==F_MOTOR_Up)
                  && not(is_Msg(MC_FrontMotor.Top_Front))
                  && not(is_Msg(MC_FrontMotor.MovingSensor_Front)))))))
  ) => ( (()(()(()(()(()(()( Val(MC_FrontMotor.Front_Motor)==F_MOTOR_Down ))))))))
```

Fig. 3. LTL formula for *FrontMotor*

values and every possible sequence of assignments to local variables). In practice, a complete test value coverage is usually not feasible given the available time and money. However, this means that one cannot characterize errors that can be found using model-checkers but not using automated testing on a logical level, but this always depends on the practical application situation (in particular economic aspects).

Example: As an example one can consider the component *FrontMotor* responsible for driving the window pane motor. Its subcomponent *DispatchCommand* handles the current state of the pane movement. *DispatchCommand* is connected to a further subcomponent *UpError* responsible for detection of a window jam condition. The LTL-formula in Fig. 3 has to be verified for *FrontMotor*. It can be interpreted in the same way as shown for the LTL-formula in Fig. 2 and tells that a window jam has to be acted on. Since external signals are forwarded by other subcomponents until they reach *DispatchCommand* the jam condition has to be checked twice after the startup time (pipelining effect). But this also imposes a synchronization problem as it could be shown by a counter example of the SMV model-checker: A certain signal input sequence leads to a window jam signal which will not be processed - the window pane continues moving up instead of down. The reason for this is a reset input signal for *DispatchCommand* which overlaps the jam input signal and is followed by a window close input signal.

Neither in AutoFocus nor in ASCET did bugs occur due to a wrong interpretation of the textual DCU specification. Inconsistencies in the specification (e.g. different interpretations of the values for the CAN message *ZV_SCHL_X* in different sections in the document) were resolved before implementing the corresponding functionality.

Intellectual effort: The main effort for testing in ASCET was particularly the interpretation of the test case output and checking its consistency regarding the DCU specification. Generally it is possible to reduce this effort with an increasing degree of automation. The difficulty here lies in the collection of dependencies between the requirements and their transformation into a computable form. There seems to be so far no tool which automatically transforms requirements from a textual form into a machine processable one without human interaction. The existence of a specification on a formal basis would support this process.

Model-checking for AutoFocus models was used to examine properties for small component networks. Since the knowledge of the internal structure of the components was available (white-box assumption), simple properties (e.g. absence of deadlocks) could already be formulated and checked during the development phase. The reason

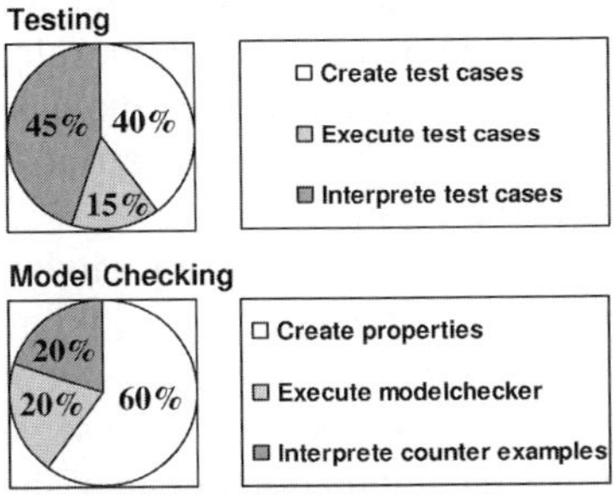

Fig. 4. Time distribution

Table 3. Found bugs in relation to time effort

Procedure	Time effort (hours)	Number of bugs
Experiment (ASCET)	24	10
Simulation (AutoFOCUS)	24	5
Model-checking	80	5
White-box testing	56	5

for an error found by model-checking could be either a bug in the model, an error due to the interpretation of the specification, or an error in the specification. The difficulty in model-checking is the formulation of correct properties which are consistent with the specification. One is forced to closely inspect the specification to avoid introducing consistency errors. The formulation of properties without any knowledge of the internal data flow of a component (black-box assumption) is difficult in AutoFOCUS. For example, time delays can be expressed by concatenating NEXT-operators according to the time discretization in AutoFOCUS. The resulting properties are generally complex due to internal interactions and pipeline effects. With increasing complexity of the formula it is also often hard to convince oneself of the correctness of the formalization of the property itself. However, the added redundancy forced by formalizing the verification properties allows one to find errors that may be undetected by straightforward testing. Where possible, both approaches should be used both in parallel to the development itself by the developers (model-checking for an incremental development of model, and unit testing for quick feedback on the ongoing development), but also by an independent QA group (who may have additional specific expertise in applying them, and a different motivation and point of view that facilitates finding different kinds of errors).

Time effort: Nearly the entire time for conventional testing was spent on creating test cases to get a good code coverage and for the interpretation of the test case outputs. This part could be reduced if appropriate automation tools are available, for example automated oracles on the basis of state invariants. For model-checking nearly the whole time had been spent to formulate the properties in accordance to the model. A run of the model-checker to show or contradict a property for small components with a small state space lasted not more than five minutes on average. However, such a relatively short time cannot always be assumed. Depending on the model size several hours or days can be spent. Thus a compromise has to be made between model accuracy and the time effort, depending on the assurance level needed. Fig. 4 shows the estimated effort distribution within the testing and model-checking activities.

When building the model an alternation of model-checking and resulting model changes will sum up the time effort spent for model-checking. So even if one model-checking pass lasts only some minutes the overall amount of time could be considerable. If the existence of a bug was shown by the model-checker its localization also takes some time. A counter-example must be executed and interpreted which can be an intuitive task without automation. It is possible to accelerate this process by bounded model-checking. Apart from the runtime of the model-checker bounded model-checking will also reduce the length of the counter example. Table 3 sets in relationship the time effort for each quality assurance method and the number of bugs found. Again it is noted that simulation preceded model-checking and white-box testing.

In the context of this case study the same number of bugs were found by model-checking as for code coverage testing. However it must be noted that the errors found by model-checking were essentially of logical nature: For example when the result of a parallel computation of components had to reach a receiving component at the same time tick, the model-checker could simply tell the user if the computation of one of the preceding components delayed and failed to deliver its result in time. Mainly synchronization errors in a component network were detected easily by model-checking.

Careless errors like having forgotten to specify a channel, priority or using an incorrect data type were also in the scope of the bugs found by model-checking but most errors of this type were found in AutoFOCUS by static interface checking and simulation (preceding the model-checking). In ASCET testing with code coverage and simulation detected mainly careless errors (e.g. using the wrong priority of a transition). Here the amount of synchronization errors was smaller since ASCET does not use global time ticks where some signal has to reach a component at an exact point in time. Errors of logical nature were deadlocks due to missing preconditions of transitions.

The relative amount of time needed for finding a particular bug in comparison between testing and model-checking depends on the error at hand: Simple errors can be quickly found using simulation (and would take more effort to be found using model-checking because there one first needs to formalize the relevant requirement in LTL), while intricate errors can be found more quickly and reliably using model-checking. Testing is thus best for quickly ruling out a large number of simple errors, while model-checking is best for reliably ruling out certain intricate errors. Typical examples for this observation are the following:

- State machine dead-locks because a transition priority is defined incorrectly. Found using the ASCET simulator. Time effort: few minutes.
- Data arrives in the wrong order at a module because of the pipelining effect. Found using the AutoFOCUS simular. Time effort: few minutes.
- Race condition causes a window to continue closing although the sensor has recognized that it is blocking. Found with model-checking using AutoFOCUS. Time effort 1-2 days (to determine and formalize the relevant property in LTL).

5 General Comparison of the Two Methodologies

From the mere testing point of view, more bugs are found the more successful the tests are (although of course in a larger context, it is rather that the more successful the development is the fewer errors are found during testing). The probability to find errors increases with the number and meaningfulness of the test cases. Many large test cases in the CTE-Tool lead to large matrices which do not really contribute to the clarity of the interpretation. It is generally not possible to get a 100% input coverage. The number and time of possible test cases is limited in practice.

The same applies to model-checking: Generally it is not possible to prove a 100% correctness of a model under all circumstances. Only the correctness of the specifically formulated properties can be proven. The coverage of the model thus depends on the number of properties that were investigated. Ideally for each requirement of the specification the appropriate property is proven. For safety reasons also the corresponding negated form of requirements should be investigated (and shown not to hold) to avoid system failures due to incorrect usage. Thus also for model-checking revealing a bug in a complex system is simpler than the proof of its overall correctness. And even showing the correctness of a property is relativized by the following possible problems:

- Initially defined assumptions do not hold (e.g. due to hardware problems)
- The textual specification is erroneous or its interpretation incorrect.
- The proof system is incorrect (e.g. due to programming bugs).

If quality assurance is performed by the developers of the software themselves, model-checking has the advantage that it forces the users to think in a way that is much different from the writing of the software, because they have to create the model and the formalized of the property under investigation. In comparison to that, conventional testing, when performed by the developers themselves, is much closer to the programming itself. For example, the code may have actually been constructed with a certain set of test cases in mind, so that it by construction it will satisfy these test cases, but may not satisfy others then, which however the developer may then not think of.

In practice, model-checking generally requires a significant effort when applied to complex projects. A simplification of the model as had to be done for the DCU in AutoFocus to reduce the state space would pose additional problems in practice. The developers are usually concerned with problems of control systems and hardware problems and normally do not have the time to cope with the theoretical challenging of model checking due to a short production schedule. Forcing modelling guidelines to achieve a model-checkable system by default would impair usability. Therefore, similar to the necessity of separate testing groups for conventional testing verification, specialists should accompany the development process of complex projects when model-checking is used.

Nowadays, much of the software of electronic control units is written in a conventional programming language like C (also in systems supporting AUTOSAR (see http://www.autosar.org for more information). It includes the basic software modules (e.g. operating system and diagnosis) with their hardware dependent functionality (communication bus and microcontroller interface). The use of models is more popular only on the higher application layers. It is however often difficult to provide an abstract interface to these by hiding hardware aspects (e.g. interrupts, workarounds for hardware bugs). In AUTOSAR, one tries to cope with this situation using a layered approach including a virtual function bus and a run-time environment.

Limitations for model-based development and model-checking in embedded (in particular automotive) systems in practice thus include the following:

- Limitations of computing power or time.
- Only software components of limited complexity can be abstracted sufficiently to become model-checkable.

- Model-based approaches work well only on high levels of abstraction: Time dependencies and interrupts which occur in the base software are hard to formalize in the model without compromising its usability and the feasbility of its model-checking.
- Memory constraints do not allow generating arbitrarily complex code (unless optimized for space).
- Lack of existing experiences in practice.
- Ongoing developments in model-checking research which make it difficult for practitioners to keep track.

6 Related Work

Only few case-studies on testing or model-checking automotive or more generally embedded software are published. [16] reports on a case study of an automotive network controller to assess different test suites in terms of error detection, model coverage, and implementation coverage, where the suites were generated automatically or manually in various ways. Automatically and manually derived model-based test suites detected significantly more requirements errors than hand-crafted test suites directly derived from the requirements. [11] appears to conclude that the significant progress in terms of productivity and quality made in recent years in automotive software development has been achieved without direct usage of formal methods. This raises the question whether further improvements could be reached *with* the use of formal methods (to some extent suggested by our case-study, although we did not aim to perform a full empirical study on this). A comparative description of ASCET, AutoFOCUS and further CASE tools can be found in [18], with a focus on methodology. There has not been much work comparing formal verification and traditional quality assurance so far. [1] compares directed testing, random testing and model-checking, but treated hardware verification rather than embedded software. [3] gives a detailed study on the usage of testing, runtime analysis, model checking and static analysis techniques for NASA Rover Software, although design model verification was not considered. [12] reports on a controlled experiment that investigates the impact of using statecharts for testing class clusters that exhibit a state-dependent behaviour. [7,14] report on experiences on UML model analysis, but do not consider model-based testing. [2] presents an assessment framework for symmetrical comparison and evaluation of testing and formal analysis with respect to debugging and more specifically bug detection. Other experience reports on software verification include [8] (on using automated theorem provers) and [9] (on tool-supported inspections).

7 Conclusion

We performed a field study in the automotive domain to compare traditional testing with model-checking. We implemented an industrial specification in two different model-based development tools. We performed quality assurance using simulation in both tools, testing in ASCET, and model-checking in AutoFOCUS. We evaluated the number and type of errors that were found and compared the effort and the effectiveness of the quality assurance methods. An interesting result is the effort distribution within each of

Table 4. Conventional testing vs. model-checking

Testing	Modelchecking
Examines a physical or concrete system	Examines an abstract model
In-the-loop-tests take place in an environment near to the real one	Cheap and early verification (without setting up complex in-the-loop-test environments)
No proof of correctness of properties possible	Proof of correctness of properties possible
Uses often many, superficial test cases	Uses selected user specific properties

the two methods: while in the case of testing the evaluation of the test results required the largest part of the effort needed, in the case of model-checking the formulation of properties to be checked turned out to be most time-consuming. Note that it was not our goal to compare ASCET and AutoFOCUS regarding the relative effort they require compared to each other (in particular, the two modelling phases were performed subsequently which means that the second modelling task using AutoFOCUS may have been facilitated by insights gained during the first using ASCET). The presented comparison does not aim to be complete or statistically significant as we did not perform a comprehensive empirical study with a high number of experiment participants. The result is thus mostly a qualitative assessment of the effort and results of traditional and formal verification. Our outcome was that model-checking needs some more time effort compared with testing, but was worth the effort because some types of errors could rather be found by model-checking than by testing, especially errors that developers may not look out for specifically during testing (such as synchronization error or boundary conditions). A combination of both methods might be optimal because both of them have their strengths in finding different types of errors.

Table 4 compares general aspects of the examined quality assurance methods. We could show that there exists no overall winner and that each verification methods has its own specialties: One deficit of the model-checking method is the problem of the state space explosion. However, model-checkers are still subject to ongoing improvements, and at least in the case of event-controlled systems at a higher abstraction level, they are already applicable. Regarding automotive applications, the use of formal verification techniques should not mean the absence of conventional test procedures. Rather, formal verification provides complementary quality assurance techniques which could lead to synergy effects if applied along with conventional testing methods. For example, a base model for successive development steps and test procedures could be created by providing verified models for generating test cases for Back-to-Back tests. Note that "complementary" here does not necessarily mean that certain errors can be found *only* with one of the two techniques (except of course errors that cannot be found using model-checking because that works on a higher level of abstraction). Instead, it means that to detect large classes of simple errors, testing is more time-effective, while model-checking is more effective to find specific classes of particularly intricate errors.

Although some of the results that were found during the case-study may confirm existing intuitions (e.g. that model-checking may find additional bugs but takes more time to learn than testing), we are not aware of any other literature comparing model-checking and model-based testing, in particular not regarding embedded or automotive software. Although we target our discussion e.g. in Sect. 5 mostly to the automotive domain, we believe that it generalizes to other embedded domains that are both safety-critical (which justifies the use of sophisticated assurance techniques such as model-checking) and at the same time are characterized by large product numbers (forcing hardware cost reduction and therefore optimized code) as well as a relatively short development cycle (which presents time pressure in the development).

Lessons learned regarding the experimental setup include that it may have been beneficial to have the two QA techniques applied by two different users in parallel, rather than by the same sequentially. Disadvantages would however include that this will be comparable only if the two users have the same expertise, and that this would significantly increase the effort needed for performing the experiment. Since the person performing the study did not have any prior knowledge in the two tools that were used, we however believe the experiment to be repeatable by others.

Details of experimental results omitted for space reasons can be found at [10].

Acknowledgements. Constructive feedback from the anonymous referees that led to a significant improvement in the presentation of the paper is gratefully acknowledged.

References

1. Bartley, M.G., Galpin, D., Blackmore, T.: A Comparison of Three Verification Techniques. In: DAC, pp. 819–823. ACM, New York (2002)
2. Bradbury, J.S., Cordy, J.R., Dingel, J.: An empirical framework for comparing effectiveness of testing and property-based formal analysis. In: PASTE, pp. 2–5 (2005)
3. Brat, G., Drusinsky, D., Giannakopoulou, D., et al.: Experimental Evaluation of Verification and Validation Tools on Martian Rover Software. Formal Methods in System Design 25(2-3), 167–198 (2004)
4. Broy, M.: Challenges in automotive software engineering. In: ICSE, pp. 33–42. ACM, New York (2006)
5. Broy, M., Stolen, K.: Specification and Development of Interactive Systems. Springer, Heidelberg (2001)
6. Cheng, B., Houdek, F., Kawana, S. (eds.): Workshop on Automotive Requirements Engineering (AuRE). IEEE, Los Alamitos (2006)
7. Cheng, B.H.C., Stephenson, R., Berenbach, B.: Lessons learned from automated analysis of industrial UML class models (an experience report). In: MoDELS, pp. 324–338 (2005)
8. Denney, E., Fischer, B., Schumann, J.: An empirical evaluation of automated theorem provers in software certification. Int. J. on Artif. Intell. Tools 15(1), 81–108 (2006)
9. Halling, M., Biffl, S., Grünbacher, P.: An experiment family to investigate the defect detection effect of tool-support for requirements inspection. In: IEEE METRICS, pp. 278–285 (2003)
10. Jürjens, J., Reiss, D., Trachtenherz, D.: Model-based quality assurance of automotive software: Experimental data (April 2008), `http://mcs.open.ac.uk/jj2924/publications/experiments/autoqa`
11. Kropf, T.: Software bugs seen from an industrial perspective or can formal methods help on automotive software development? In: Damm, W., Hermanns, H. (eds.) CAV 2007. LNCS, vol. 4590. Springer, Heidelberg (2007)
12. Mouchawrab, S., Briand, L.C., Labiche, Y.: Assessing, comparing, and combining statechart-based testing and structural testing: An experiment. In: ESEM, pp. 41–50 (2007)
13. Paech, B., Houdek, F.: The door controller unit – an example specification. Technical Report 002.02/D, Fraunhofer IESE (2002)

14. Pilskalns, O., Andrews, A.A., Knight, A., Ghosh, S., France, R.B.: Testing UML designs. Information & Software Technology 49(8), 892–912 (2007)
15. Pretschner, A., Broy, M., Krüger, I., Stauner, T.: Software engineering for automotive systems: A roadmap. In: ICSE, Future of Softw. Engin., pp. 33–42. ACM, New York (2007)
16. Pretschner, A., Prenninger, W., Wagner, S., Kühnel, C., Baumgartner, M., Sostawa, B., Zölch, R., Stauner, T.: One evaluation of model-based testing and its automation. In: ICSE, pp. 392–401. ACM, New York (2005)
17. Pretschner, A., Salzmann, C., Schätz, B., Stauner, T.: ICSE Workshop on Software Engineering for Automotive Systems. In: ICSE Companion, p. 146. IEEE, Los Alamitos (2007)
18. Schätz, B., Hain, T., Houdek, F., Prenninger, W., Rappl, M., Romberg, J., Slotosch, O., Strecker, M., Wißpeintner, A.: CASE Tools for Embedded Systems. Technical Report I0309, TU Munich (2003)

Ontology Guided Evolution of Complex Embedded Systems Projects in the Direction of MDA

Lars Pareto[1], Miroslaw Staron[1], and Peter Eriksson[2]

[1] IT University of Göteborg, 412 96 Göteborg, Sweden
{lars.pareto,miroslaw.staron}@ituniv.se
[2] Ericsson Software Research, Ericsson AB, Sweden
peter.r.eriksson@ericsson.com

Abstract. Implementation of MDA in large, product developing organizations involves changing processes, practices, tools, and communication infrastructures. The paper presents a case study, in which modeling related needs of a unit within Ericsson were compared to features of current and envisioned MDA tools, using qualitative methods. The paper's main contribution is an ontology defining areas and sub-areas of improvement associated with the introduction of MDA in complex embedded systems projects. The ontology is grounded in interviews with senior modellers at Ericsson and in survey publications from within the field of MDA. It identifies 26 improvement areas concerned with model content, modeling activities, and the management of modeling projects. The ontology has been presented to stakeholders within the unit studied, with positive feedback: appreciated were its groundedness, traceability, holistic scope, and potential as platform and checklist for several recurrent analysis and communication tasks related to software process improvement within Ericsson.

1 Introduction

To implement MDA in a large organization with products on the market is, in many senses, a wicked problem [1]: required changes are plentiful and interrelated; data on which to base estimates of costs, benefits and risks are scarce; the implementation target is moving. Yet, many companies realize that their future software development requires better utilization of modeling technologies—they are just unsure about the path.

The purpose of this paper is to support organisations in this situation—large, product developing companies that strive to increase their use of modeling in the direction of the MDA vision, but whose decision making regarding this stutter because of too many risks and constraints.

The paper approaches this problem from the perspective of practicing software engineers in commercial, complex embedded systems projects, already using UML for informal modeling. Our view of such projects is captured by the conceptual framework in Fig. 1: we view software as produced by engineers in specialized roles (Requirement engineer, etc.), who are steered by processes (defining who should produce what when for whom), and who communicate under the constraints of a communications infrastructure (consisting of model repositories and tools); the project is steered by business goals (such as reducing the time to market for new products) and subject

K. Czarnecki et al. (Eds.): MoDELS 2008, LNCS 5301, pp. 874–888, 2008.

to business constraints (such as bounds on development costs). We view project improvement as the matter of engineering features of internal processes and infrastructure towards several requirement sources (needs of every role, business goals, and business constraints), utilizing features of modeling technologies and process frameworks developed outside the project. By complex embedded system we mean a large, special purpose, real-time, multiple processor, computer system that is part of a larger, technical system.

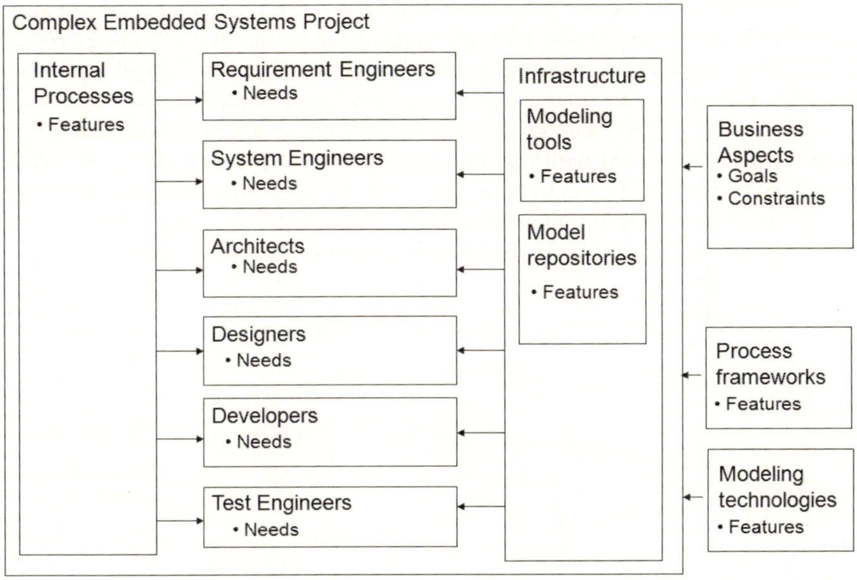

Fig. 1. Improvement variables in complex embedded systems projects

The research question addressed in this paper is which improvement areas projects of this kind face when implementing MDA. Put precisely: which areas of improvement do requirement engineers, system engineers, architects, designers, developers, and test engineers, developing and maintaining complex embedded systems, need to be concerned with when proceeding from informal UML-based software development to MDA? By MDA, we mean the use of domain specific UML dialects and model transformations for specification and realization of software. (Stahl [2] gives an overview.)

The paper addresses this question by an exploratory, holistic, single case, case study [3]. The unit of study is a subproject within Ericsson developing embedded software for a constituent part of a mobile-communications-network product. The main outcome of the study is an ontology defining improvement areas associated with the introduction of MDA in complex embedded systems projects.

The paper is organised as follows: we describe our research design (Sec. 2), our case (Sec. 3), our study of this case (Sec. 4–5), the ontology resulting from this study (Sec. 6), and the use of it in process evolution (Sec. 7); we discuss limitations of our study (Sec. 8), and related work (Sec. 9); finally, we summarize or findings and draw conclusions about the approach (Sec. 10).

2 Research Design

Our epistemological position is interpretative research [4]; our research strategy is qualitative research [5]; our data analysis method is grounded theory in the tradition of Strauss [6]. The research design is outline in Fig. 2. Data collection has proceeded by *semi-structured interviews* and selection of written sources from within the modeling research community. Data analysis techniques used are *open coding* (conceptualization of data sources using descriptive codes), *categorization* (grouping of codes with commonalities into categories), and *axial coding* (relating categories to subcategories). Our application of these techniques has been guided by *technology roadmapping* [7] (that emphasizes the modeling of needs and technological options in a common framework). The analysis outcome is a simple, informal ontology with inclusion hierarchy [8] (also known as a taxonomy) characterizing areas and sub-areas of improvement associated with the introduction of MDA in complex embedded systems projects. Analytic generalization [3] has been used to obtain an ontology presumably useful for complex embedded systems projects in general. The ontology's validity relies on the grounded approach and feedback from practitioners.

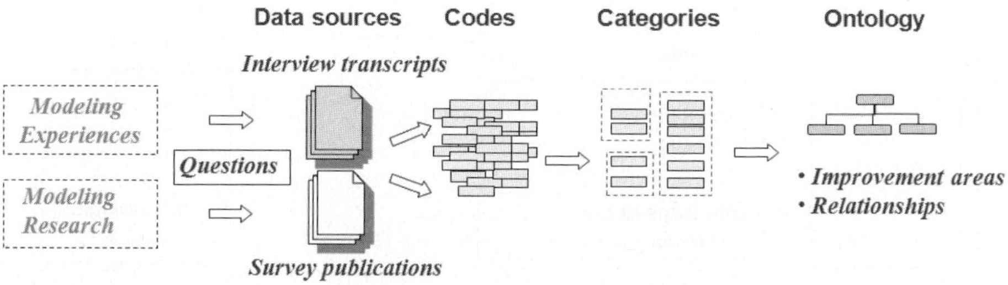

Fig. 2. Research design

Research has been collaborative [9], and involved three Ericsson insiders (a senior technical specialist, a software architect, and a project manager), and two outsiders (one software engineering researcher with a background in stereotype-based language customization, and another with a background in software quality and programming language semantics). Insiders have facilitated the study, defined the problem, set the scope, selected informants, and given recurring feedback on the study's development; outsiders have designed the study, conducted data collection and analysis, framed the study, and communicated the results.

Our choice of a single case case-study is partly due to the revelatory nature [3] of our research question (we seek to elicit areas of software process improvement in a certain situation, rather to confirm or refute an hypothesis), and partly due to our use of enquiry based qualitative research (which is limited to small samples): distributing available resources over the study of several cases had been at the cost of penetration of individual level needs and inconsistent with our choice of method.

The particular unit was chosen because the Ericsson insiders were familiar with, and had a direct stake in improving this unit: this improves the quality of sampling, the data analysis, and eases the validation results (compared to the choice of some unfamiliar unit).

3 The Case and Its Context

Ericsson has a long tradition in model driven development: the use of software models with associated semantics dates back to 1967, with the AKE switch, first delivered in 1971, built using such [10]. Ericsson contributed to development of SDL [11] during the 70s, and applied SDL extensively during the 80s; use case based modeling was pioneered by Ericsson in the 80s [12]; in the 90s, Ericsson was an early adopter of RUP [13]; today, MDD plays a central role in several Ericsson product lines, and model based software engineering is recognized as a prioritized area of improvement.

The project, to which the unit belongs, uses UML for requirements modelling, system design, systems architecture work, software architecture-work, detailed software design, and software implementation. Other notations are also used: requirement engineers also use textual use cases and supplementary requirements specifications; hardware designers use block diagrams, and Mealy/Moore state machines (of their trade). Where UML is used, it is often complemented with text based notations, e.g., for signal and protocol specification, and with informal text-based specification documents for aspects not easily expressed in standard UML, e.g., non-functional requirements or configurations.

The unit operates in the following technical context: it develops the software part of a subsystem; the software runs on in-house developed, multi-processor hardware (involving digital signal processors, field programmable gate arrays, and ordinary processors); it is subject to real-time constraints (response time, throughput, and space bounds), compatibility constraints (RTOSes and in-house developed platforms), and special run-time requirements (monitoring, configuration, upgrading, and rollbacks).

The project has a conventional line organisation. The unit itself has approximately 100 engineers situated on a single location; the whole project is much larger and distributed over several locations. The unit is divided into six sub-units: two responsible for software specification, three for software implementation and maintenance, and one for integration and validation.

4 The Unit's Needs

4.1 Interviews with Engineers

Informants were selected by the insiders, using the following criteria: the scope of their experience should be wide; they should have worked with model driven development in their daily work, they should understand model driven development from the perspective of several roles (and those of architects and designers in particular).

The enquiries were semi-structured interviews revolving around the following set of questions:

> What, do you think, Ericsson hopes to achieve by model driven development? Do you believe in this for Ericsson as a whole / for your project / for your role? What improvements of your project do you spontaneously associate with model driven developments? Which deteriorations do you associate? Is there some slave-work / double work, do you think, that could be automated/eliminated? Do you see

any obviously inefficient practices that ought to be improvable? What's your view on the use of modelling for the activities in this list: requirements work, architecture work, detailed design, estimation, function testing, subsystem testing, documentation work, maintenance, code generation, configuration/run-time-use, change request handling, defect handling? How could modelling be used in the near future? Do you have any vision for your own, work/for the work of others? Are you aware of any modelling success stories inside or outside Ericsson?

Questions were designed to, in an non-leading way, bring out the personal attitude and perceived goals of model driven development, to trigger an open-ended exploration of the informants perceived own needs, those of others, and company objectives. To avoid discussions on the differences between MDA and model driven development, questions purposely referred to the latter. The need for MDA was probed for indirectly, through questions to reveal a need for automation.

Interviews lasted 1-2h each, and the resulting transcriptions amounted to 60 pages of 10 pt, singly spaced text files. A summary of the interviews is given in Table 1. In addition to the interview transcripts (S_1,...,S_4), notes from a preparatory meeting, in which four designers discussed what to bring forward in an upcoming meeting with a tool vendor, was added as a supplementary data sources for needs (S_5).

4.2 Interpretation of Interviews

Interview transcripts were coded in search for *needs*—a concept prevalent in technology roadmapping—in a broad sense: we included *direct needs* expressed by the informants themselves and *indirect needs* inferred from their descriptions of situations or problems; in addition to *unsatisfied needs,* we included *satisfied needs*, not to be overlooked in process change; we included *realistic needs* whose satisfaction seemed plausible as well as *wishful needs* whose satisfaction seemed to require advances beyond state of the art. The scope of the identified needs was model based software engineering and management, which is a larger scope than MDA technologies, but necessary to consider when implementing MDA.

To make the set of needs intellectually manageable and to facilitate communication of our results to non-analysts within Ericsson, interpretation was subject to the following principles, which emerged during the interpretation: each need should be (1) abstract enough to fit on a single line, but (2) concrete enough to suggest a specific improvement (or a set of specific improvements); (3) needs shall be *distinct*, by which we mean that all passages in the data sources referring to the same phenomenon are represented by a single need; (4) unless 2 is violated, similar needs should be coalesced into one more abstract needs; (5) needs that apply to several roles should be generalized into such.

We illustrate the interpretation process and these principles through the need
Subsystem level cohesion analysis

which is the analysts interpretation of the following two passages of text (in their contexts):

"It's like, should I introduce a new component, or should I put the function into this old one"

"we really tried to understand the problem [...] to avoid the solution from being too scattered"

This need is indirect: from a particular work situation, the analyst has recognized that engineers are concerned with component cohesion, concluded that analytic tools for reasoning about cohesion would be helpful, and phrased this as a need; later, the phenomenon has reappeared in a slightly different work context, similar enough to be an instance of the same need (possibly along with other needs). The need is unsatisfied: the unit's engineers do not use tools for cohesion analysis in their daily work. The need is realistic: several theories and tools for cohesion analysis of models are available.

Further, the need satisfies principles 1–5: it is short, it points into a concrete domain, i.e., model quality metrics, it represents several instances of the phenomenon in the text, and it entails needs of architects and designers. The need could be further improved with respect to principle 5 by removing the restriction to subsystem level, as cohesion analysis is a likely concern at the system and implementation levels too.

In all, 269 distinct needs were identified in 36254 words originating from 7 engineers in 3 roles, at system (S) and subsystem (SS) level. The number of inferred needs and examples of needs for each data source are given in Table 1. (Some needs were mentioned by several informants, and one informant represented in two data sources, which is why summing columns 3 and 5 results in larger numbers than those above.)

Table 1. Some of the Unit's needs and the underlying data sources

<table>
<tr><td>S_1</td><td>May 14, 2007</td><td>Architect (SS)</td><td>14 588 words; 20 pages</td><td>143 needs</td></tr>
<tr><td colspan="5">Subsystem design- and implementation models shall be distinct. E-sketching using UML. UML for use case analysis. UML for reverse engineering. UML for refactoring. OO framework design supported by workflow. Deployment modeling. Implementation modeling should be optional. …</td></tr>
<tr><td>S_2</td><td>May 16, 2007</td><td>System Eng (SS)</td><td>8 297 words; 11 pages</td><td>67 needs</td></tr>
<tr><td colspan="5">Open formats for models. Tool integration flexible. Vendor independence. Documentation globally searchable. Documentation should be structured for large information volumes. Baseline handling for reading users should be simple. Requirements tracing from model. Model oriented description at system level. Text search into model database should be global. ...</td></tr>
<tr><td>S_3</td><td>May 16, 2007</td><td>Developer (SS)</td><td>11 994 words; 17 pages</td><td>85 needs</td></tr>
<tr><td colspan="5">Subsystem level analysis modelling. Subsystem level cohesion analysis. Subsystem level architecture knowledge among designers. Analysis modeling and implementation modeling shall be distinct.
Education in work-task specific modelling. Clear separation between specification and white box interface synchronization.</td></tr>
<tr><td>S_4</td><td>July 7, 2007</td><td>Architect (S,SS)</td><td>845 words; 2 pages</td><td>18 needs</td></tr>
<tr><td colspan="5">Better definition which elements are in diagrams. Overview mechanisms for complex models. Links between information in legacy elements and system model. Improved inspections of models. Guidelines for managing documentation update. Auto-generation of documents from design models. Guidelines for model walkthroughs. Specifications written at the same level of abstraction. Single point of adding information in model. System model is the primary source of information. ...</td></tr>
<tr><td>S_5</td><td>April 27, 2007</td><td>1 Sys., 3 Dev. (SS)</td><td>510 words, 8 pages</td><td>22 Needs</td></tr>
<tr><td colspan="5">Better definition which elements are in diagrams. Overview mechanisms for complex models. Links between information in legacy elements and system model. Improved inspections of models. Guidelines for managing documentation update. Auto-generation of documents from design models. Guidelines for model walkthroughs. Specifications written at the same level of abstraction. Single point of adding information in model. System model is the primary source of information. Requirements modeling using deployment diagrams. System model is the primary source of information. Align legacy documents and new tooling. ...</td></tr>
</table>

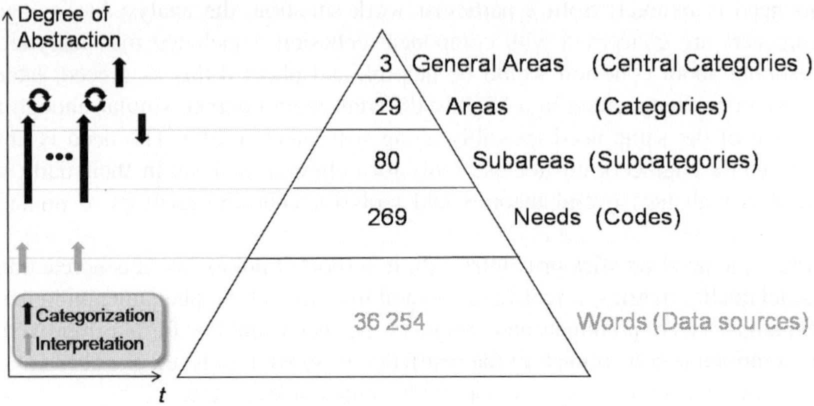

Fig. 3. Categorization process (left) and outcome (right)

4.3 Categorization of Needs

The categorization of the needs was iterative, incremental, and interleaved with the interpretation of needs and the categorization of features (left part of Fig. 3): codes resulting from an initial interpretation of the transcripts (leftmost grey arrow) were grouped into areas of improvement (leftmost black arrow) and named; categories were then restructured and renamed (leftmost circulation-symbol) for consistency with those emerging from the analysis of the survey publication, which was conducted in parallel; categorisation and restructuring were repeated several times, when new data sources were interpreted or old data sources re-interpreted.

To make the category system suited for process improvement work (i.e., comprehensible, credible, maintainable, and usable) categorization was subject to the following principles: (1) categories should have concrete, suggestive names capturing the underlying phenomena (rather than abstract names capturing too much); (2) categories should be given meaning by characterizing definitions along with traceable connection to the underlying data sources; (3) categories should be coarse enough to allow quick classification of needs; (4) within categories, sub-categories should be used to group elements with closer relationships to each other; (5) categories should be general enough to serve as containers for both needs and features (thereby making needs and features easier to compare); (6) deep-hierarchies should be used sparingly (as an overuse makes category system difficult to comprehend and maintain); (7) categories should be role centric (to make the responsibility for satisfying needs more clear).

The categorization process involved (in addition to the grouping of needs and introduction of names and characterizing definitions) coalescing, subdividing, widening, narrowing, and renaming categories; it involved re-categorization and renaming of codes to better realize interpretation and categorization principles.

The process eventually resulted in the ontology outlined in the right part of Fig. 3 (and which is further described in Section 6). Improvement areas are found at four levels of abstraction: 3 general areas, 26 areas, 80 subareas, and 269 needs.

5 Features of MDA Technologies and Processes

5.1 Literature Search

The literature study addressed the following main question:

Which are the features of current and envisioned MDA processes and tools?

Sampling was restricted to survey publications; these were selected to cover both technical and managerial aspects from the perspectives of modeling researchers, modellers in industry, and suppliers of modeling tools. An overview of the publications used in our analysis is given in Table 2.

5.2 Interpretation of Survey Publications

Interpretation of survey publications used the following principles: (1-5) principles similar to the five used in the interpretation of transcripts; (6) process features with no other distinct phenomena than the use of a technology feature, should be implicitly defined by the latter; (7) process and technology features should not be kept apart. We motivate 6 by the following example of two possible features:

"Automated model metrics is used" (Process feature)
"Automated model metrics" (Technology feature)

Any technology feature has an obvious corresponding process feature, whose presence would clutter the ontology through redundance. We motivate 7 by the following process feature:

"Software product lines" (Process feature and technology feature)

This feature comes with certain commitments to both process (configuration is done by compilers rather than people) and technology (feature diagrams, connected to model to model transformations, and composition infrastructure in certain ways), thus it is a compact carrier of both concerns. Encouraging analysts to view all codes from both angles gives a more compact representation better coverage, and quicker classification compared to keeping process and technology features apart.

Interpretation of the survey publications, along these principles, resulted in 214 features, some of which are given in Table 2.

Table 2. Process- and technology features and the underlying data sources

<table>
<tr><td>S_6</td><td>MDD practices within Mototorola [14]</td><td>39 features</td></tr>
<tr><td colspan="3">Data reuse between design and testing activities. Testing by co-simulation. Automatic test generation. Automatic code generation. Standardized and non-proprietary modeling languages....</td></tr>
<tr><td>S_7</td><td>MDD research roadmap [15]</td><td>61 features</td></tr>
<tr><td colspan="3">Models describe the system at multiple levels of abstraction. Formal semantics. Generation of configuration files. Synchronization transformation (Model-Code). Verification by simulation modelling. ...</td></tr>
<tr><td>$S_{8\text{-}10}$</td><td>Modelware Metrics, Projects, Frameworks [16-21]</td><td>69 features</td></tr>
<tr><td colspan="3">Maturity levels definition. Models used for production of documentation. Platform independent and platform specific models separate. Generation of implementation infrastructure....</td></tr>
<tr><td>S_{11}</td><td>MDD technologies and tools [2]</td><td>30 features</td></tr>
<tr><td colspan="3">Aspect models. Bidirectional transformation. Code and document generation automated. Config. by feature models. Domain specific modeling. M2C weaving. ...</td></tr>
</table>

5.3 Categorization of Features

Categorization of features followed the same steps as, and was interleaved with, the categorization of needs. Initially, separate category system were maintained, but during the course of analysis the two were merged, for the following reasons: there was a large overlap in concepts; a common system eliminated the task of relating the two system and that of keeping them consistent; viewing needs and feature as members of the same category had analytic power (it enabled the analyses describe in Section 7.2, and simplified identification of sub-categories).

6 Ontology of MDA Implementation Improvement Areas

6.1 General Areas and Areas

The ontology is a hierarchy, in which general areas and areas form a tree, but in which sub-areas crosscut (technically a graph). Each node consists of a *name* and *characterizing definition* and is associated with a subset of all features and needs. There is a strict inclusion order: any need or feature that belongs to a sub-area also belongs to the ancestors of this node. The topmost two levels of the ontology, the general areas and areas, are given in Table 3 on next page: the three general areas

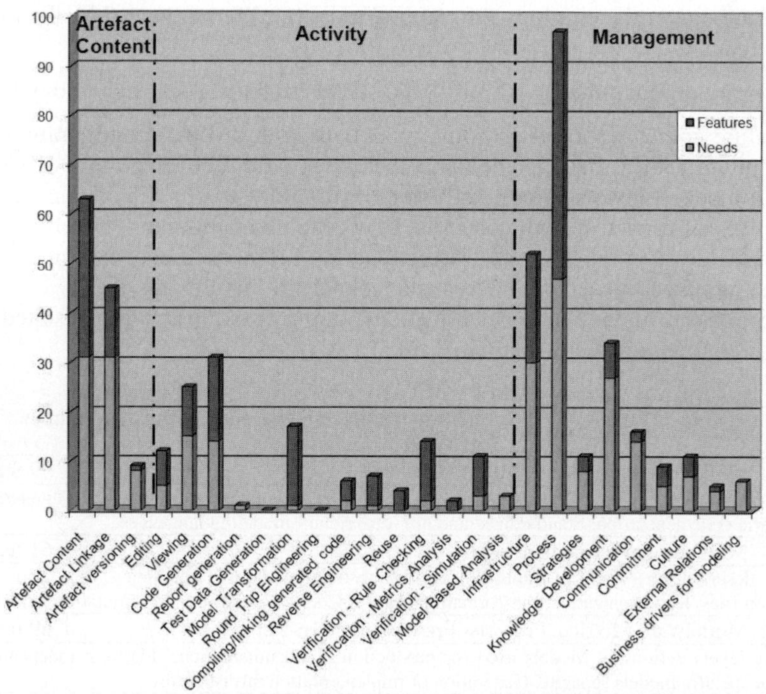

Fig. 4. Histogram showing the distribution of the needs and features over modeling areas

(Content, Activity, Management) are subdivided into 26 areas (Artefact content, etc.) each with a characterizing definition of the areas *concern*. The number of needs and features associated with each of these areas are given by the histogram in Fig. 4: the area *Artefact Content* contains 31 needs and 32 features, etc.

Table 3. Improvement areas when implementing MDA in complex embedded systems projects

Content *Information in models*	**Activity** *Operations on models*	**Management** *Socio-technical aspects of modeling*
Artefact content *The syntax and semantics of the artefact kinds, and their use.*	**Editing** *Reading, writing, modifying models.*	**Infrastructure** *Servers and tools for producing using/sharing/reusing/distributing/archiving models/artifacts and the integration of these.*
Artefact linkage *How artefacts (models, code, interface files, scripts, metamodels, ...) at different levels of modeling (requirements level, system level, subsystem level, implementation level) in different activities (specification, implementation, testing, documentation) should be linked.*	**Viewing** *Navigating and searching own models and those of others.*	**Process** *Who should produce what model when for whom.*
Artefact versioning *Information related to the evolution of models.*	**Code generation** *Automatic production of programming code in text based languages from models.*	**Strategies** *Tactics for introducing, executing, and optimizing the use of modeling.*
	Report Generation *Automatic production of documentation, and specifications from models.*	**Knowledge development** *Education (in tools, practices, abstract thinking) and internal knowledge transfer (of technologies, architectural principles, design rules).*
	Test Data Generation *Automatic generation of test scripts or test data from models.*	**Communication** *Exchange of information between roles.*
	Model Transformation *Automatic transformation of models from one kind or use to another kind or use.*	**Commitment** *Managers and engineers engagement in the introduction and improvement of modeling.*
	Round Trip Engineering *Co-existing manual development of models and code.*	**Culture** *Relative values of artefacts, roles, and tasks among managers and engineers.*
	Compiling/linking/tracing code *Integration of models with their target system incarnations.*	**External Relations** *The technology suppliers' responsiveness to organization's needs; negotiation position.*
	Reverse Engineering *Creation of model from source code.*	**Business drivers** *Economical incentives for using model driven development instead of something else.*
	Reuse *Libraries of models and patterns.*	
	Verification - rule checking *Well-formedness of models wrt. rules.*	
	Verification - metrics analysis *Computation of model metrics.*	
	Verification – simulation *Off-line execution of models.*	
	Model based analysis *Use of models to reason about the system built or the project building it.*	

Subareas

The third level of the ontology, the subareas, is given in Table 4 for the general area Content:

Table 4. Improvement subareas for the artefact-content, -linkage, and -versioning areas

Content		
Artefact Content	**Artefact Linkage**	**Artefact Versioning**
Artefact Kinds *The type of diagrams used (class-, sequence-, timing-, etc.).*	**Connectivity/ integration** *How diagrams are attached to each other by the infrastructure.*	**Conflict avoidance/resol.** *Detecting and handling concurrent changes in models.*
Abstraction *The levels of abstraction at which the diagrams are used; whether abstraction is respected.*	**Separation of Concerns** *The degree to which aspect views are distinguished in models.*	**Change book-keeping** *Versioning information, e.g., tags, branches, log appears.*
Annotation *Information not intrinsically part of the diagram (e.g., links and author tags).*	**Consistency** *Syntactic consistency across diagrams with respect to names and structure.*	**Change impact analysis** *Detecting which artefacts in which branches would be affected by a change to one.*
Modeling Areas *What are diagrams are used for (e.g., code generation, design).*	**Principality** *The recognition of some linked artefacts as authorative.*	**Baseline handling** *Annotation of artefacts as belonging to baselines, and retrieval of such.*
Modeling Tasks *Specific tasks that require specific content.*	**Pollution reduction** *Stopping lower level concepts from leaking into higher level models.*	**Access** *Ease with which artefacts may be obtained from own repositories and those of other groups.*
Artefact Semantics *Precision in and variability of meaning.*	**Propagation** *Changes to one model automatically causing updates in other.*	**Branch & Merge** *Forking, synchronizing tracks; bringing tracks together.*
Conventions *The uphold of good common modeling practices.*	**Isolation** *The ability to restructure two linked models at one end only.*	**Volatility** *The recognition of some artefacts as temporary throwaways.*
Customization *Degree to which diagram-types can be adapted to company specific needs.*	**Model-Code Interfacing** *Embedding of models in code, and the embedding of code in models.*	**Reuse** *The distinction of artefacts as general/special, shared/project-specific and stable/changeful.*
Degree of modelling *Degree to which modeling is put to use in a certain area (informal, formal, executable, complete, incomplete).*	**Access** *Ease with which artefacts developed by other groups may be obtained /updated.*	**Granularity** *Scope of syntactic units that are versioned (Model tree, Diagram, Single Transition).*
	Cohesion *The degree to which related parts are held together.*	**Isolation** *Repository structure constraining the artefact structure.*
	Linkage visibility *Whether, how, and where links appear in user interfaces.*	

7 Ontology Guided Evolution

Our main use of the ontology has been in the context of technology roadmapping.

7.1 Technology Roadmapping

Technology roadmapping [7] is a technique widely used in industry for technology strategy work. By a combination of analytical and collaborative activities, a time-based chart comprising a number of layers representing both commercial and technological perspectives—a *roadmap*—is built and maintained. Our exploration of technology roadmapping focussed on its analytical activities and relied on the ontology in the following ways.

A roadmap was obtained by (1) categorization of needs and features along the temporal dimensions in Table 5, and (2) by presenting needs and features in a matrix display [22] with categories of Table 3 as rows, and those of Table 5 as columns.

Table 5. Temporal Categories used in Roadmapping

Done *Needs already satisfied within unit.* 67 needs	**Piloted/planned** *Needs soon to be satisfied.* 34 needs	**Vision within WoW** *Needs whose solutions are compatible with present WoW.* 107 needs	**Vision beyond WoW** *Needs whose solutions require major changes of present ways of working.* 59 needs
Mature/straightforward *Features available in shelfware / books or whose implementation is standard.* 100 features	**Emerging** *Features of technologies / processes with early adopters in ind.* 26 features	**Researched** *Features of technologies / processes that have gained use in the research community.* 66 features	**Vision** *Features that are visions even to researchers.* 34 features

7.2 Ontology Based Analyses

We used the ontology in two analysis tasks associated with roadmapping: establishment of linkages [7] between needs and features, i.e., a relation defining which needs are are supported by which features; identification of gaps [7] in sets of features and needs, i.e., missing needs and features that would be present in an ideal roadmap.

Both linkages and gaps were established by crosswise comparison of needs and features and incremental definition of a relation x isSupportedBy y, stating, for example, that "feature selection tool support" isSupportedBy "software product lines". *Linkages* are the needs-feature pairs $\langle x,y \rangle$ associated by this relation. *Gaps in features* manifest themselves as needs not linked to a feature, e.g., in our set of needs and features, the need "fine grained version control" is not linked to a supporting feature, which points out a potential gap in the feature set. *Gaps in needs* manifest themselves as features not linked to a need, e.g., the feature "instance modelling of signals", which has proved valuable in contexts similar to that of the unit, did not support any need, thus pointed out a potential gap in the set of needs.

Notice that what this detects are *potential gaps* in needs: it may well be that a feature is not needed; features solving a certain need may not have been invented yet. To turn potential gaps into actual ones is always a matter of additional data collection and interpretation.

7.3 Feedback from the Unit

The ontology has been presented to participants in, and closely related to, the unit at 7 occasions (Jun 06, Jun 18, Dec 13, Feb 20, Mar 14, April 11, April 22) in oral form (workshops, seminars, presentations, status meetings) and in written forms (posters, spreadsheets, slides), sometimes as categories sometimes in roadmap form.

The general feedback is that the approach is interesting and promising and that strategy work at this level of detail would be a valuable supplement: inquiries and qualitative data analysis is already used for improvement work, but not to this extent; particularly appreciated was that needs and features are anchored in data sources, and that the knowledge database is common, shared, and updateable.

Several work situations that could benefit from having an ontology were recognized by the unit: engineers and managers could quickly get ideas about what is on the market and what people would like to see in their processes; engineers and managers communicating with tool vendors would have a checklist of requirement areas and specific requirements to point at; process engineers could use the areas to subdivide and coordinate process improvement efforts; technology boards would have a good starting point for their analyses; engineers would find it easier to relate to technology strategy work. The approach was found promising not only for introduction of MDA, but software process improvement work in general.

Naturally, there was also critique: acute needs that engineers face every day (such as better layout-editors) tend to dominate over the long-term needs (such as better separation of concern in models); the sheer size of the roadmap made it difficult to comprehend; needs were too plentiful and detailed to guide improvement work; it was not obvious how an ongoing analysis activity at this level of technical detail would fit in the present organization; some unsatisfied identified were already satisfied in other units; the needs model was incomplete with respect to the project as a whole; needs were not ranked according to benefits to the organisations (some would lead to really big savings); to be really useful, a roadmap should also contain strategic information telling what to improve next.

8 Threats to Validity

Our research design is sensitive to following sources of errors, many of which are intrinsic to interpretative, case study research: (e_1) both needs and features are dynamic entities, i.e., the ontology is an interpretation of a snapshot of a situation that will change; (e_2) needs-related sampling is restricted to 7 out of 100 engineers, so the characterization of needs is hardly complete; (e_3) feature-related sampling is restricted to survey publications, thus recent advancements may not be represented; (e_4) the needs are influenced by the conceptions of the informants, and (e_5) the analysts; (e_6) the features are influenced by the conceptions of the analysts, and (e_7) the authors of the survey publications; (e_8) sampling and interpretation may be consciously or unconsciously biased to researcher concerns; (e_9) analytic generalization from a single project within a single unit may yield an ontology incomplete with respect to improvement areas of other projects, and (e_{10}) yield areas associated with the unit studied rather than complex embedded systems projects in general.

The following precautions have been taken to reduce the effect of these sources: for e_1, abstraction has been used (in the formulation of needs, features, and areas) to eliminate conceptual details not likely to withstand time; for e_2 we have chosen informants with long experience in modelling, a wide perspective of the problems, and complementary views; for e_3, we only chose (at the time) recent survey publications; for e_4, we used open questioning from many perspectives and interpretation in search for indirectly expressed needs; for $e_{2\text{-}3}$ we developed a method to detect gaps in roadmaps; for $e_{5\text{-}6}$, needs, features, areas, and their relationships have been incrementally modelled using a qualitative data analysis tools and a common case study database shared by all analysts; analysts have met in four half-day sessions to discuss and revise concepts; concepts have been put to test in three analysis tasks; for $e_{7\text{-}8}$ emerging concepts have been presented to the unit, and the feedback taken into account. To handle $e_{9\text{-}10}$ requires a multiple case study, which is future work.

As for the validity of our approach: we have handled the critique of the roadmap by positioning the use of our ontology in software process improvement work as a well-developed starting points for recurring, organization specific ontology develop-pment in a changing world, rather than a universal ontology carved in stone; to investigate whether recurring ontology development is a cost effective complement to present process improvement activities is future work.

9 Related Work

The use of knowledge modeling techniques in software process improvement work is standard (see [23] for an overview), as is the use of ontologies for knowledge modeling [24]. We are not aware of any ontologies that give an empirically grounded holistic characterization of the improvement areas associated with introduction of MDA: Lange identifies 8 areas of activities supported by UML modeling tools [20] (which have been included in our ontology), but does not cover model content and managerial aspects; Störrle identifies 6 general areas and 18 specific operations of models [25], but does not characterize managerial and content aspects.

10 Summary and Conclusions

We have identified needs and features of concern to requirement engineers, system engineers, architects, designers, developers, and test engineers, proceeding from informal UML-based software development to MDA in the context of complex embedded systems development within Ericsson (Table 1–2). We have categorized the needs and features found to obtain a simple, informal ontology that defines improvement areas and subareas concerned with model content, modeling activities, and the management of modeling projects (Table 3-4). We have exemplified how the ontology may be used for roadmapping (Sec. 7.1), and defined methods to detect gaps in knowledge about features and needs (Sec. 7.2). We have identified 4 specific work situations within Ericsson that would benefit from using the ontology (Sec. 7.3). We have assessed the validity of the ontology for practical use (Sec 8.) and found it to be relevant and potentially useful. This, and experiences of ontology- driven and roadmap driven improvement work in other fields, allow us to conclude that, with the provided ontology, analysis methods, and underlying roadmap strategy at hand, MDA introduction in complex embedded systems projects becomes easier than in the absence of these aids.

Future work includes refining categories to reduce conceptual overlap, testing the ontology in actual software process improvement work, incorporating needs and features relevant to other units and organizations, and studying the cost effectiveness of the approach.

Acknowledgments. This work has been supported by Ericsson Software Research through Ericsson's Software Architecture and Quality Centre (SAQC).

References

1. Churchman, C.W.: Wicked problems. Management Science 14(4), 141–142 (1967)
2. Stahl, T., Völter, M.: Model-driven software development: technology, engineerig,management. Wiley, Chichester (2006)
3. Yin, R.K.: Case study research: design and methods. Sage Publications, ThousandOaks (2003)
4. Walsham, G.: Interpretive case studies in IS research: nature and method. Eur. J.Inf. Systs. 4(2), 74–81 (1995)
5. Wohlin, C., Höst, M., Henningsson, K.: Empirical research methods in softwareengineering. In: Empirical methods and studies in software engineering. LNCS,vol. 2765. Springer, Heidelberg (2003)
6. Strauss, A., Corbin, J.: Basics of qualitative research: techniques and procedures for developing grounded theory. Sage Publications, Thousand Oaks (1998)
7. Phaal, R., et al.: Technology roadmapping –a planning framework for evolution and revolution. Technological forecasting and social change 71, 5–26 (2003)
8. van Rees, R.: Clarity in the usage of the terms ontology, taxonomy and classification. In: CIB workgroup 78 conference, Auckland, Australia (2003)
9. Adler, N., Shani, A.B., Styhre, A.: Collaborative research in organizations. Sage Publications, Thousand Oaks (2004)
10. Jacobson, I.: Object oriented software engineering: a use case driven approach. Addison-Wesley, Reading (1992)
11. Rockstrom, A.S.: SDL-CCITT specification and description language. IEEE Transactionson communications 30(6), 1310–1318 (1982)
12. Jacobson, I.: Object-oriented development in an industrial environment. ACM SIGPLAN Notices 22(12), 183–191 (1987)
13. Börjesson, A.: Making software process improvement happen, Doctoral dissertationIT University of Gothenburg (2006)
14. Baker, P., Loh, S., Weil, F.: Model-driven engineering in a large industrial context -a Motorola case study. In: Briand, L.C., Williams, C. (eds.) MoDELS 2005. LNCS,vol. 3713, pp. 476–491. Springer, Heidelberg (2005)
15. France, R., Rumpe, B.: Model-driven development of complex software: a research roadmap. In: 29th Int. conf. on software engineering, Minneapolis, USA (2007)
16. FP6-IP 511731 MODELWARE D1.1-2 QoS Support in MODELWARE (2006)
17. FP6-IP 511731 MODELWARE D2.2 MDD Engineering Metrics Definition (2006)
18. FP6-IP 511731 MODELWARE D2.3 MDD Maturity Levels Definition (2006)
19. FP6-IP 511731 MODELWARE D2.5 MDD Engineering Metrics Baseline (2006)
20. FP6-IP 511731 MODELWARE D2.6 MDD Maturity Model (2006)
21. FP6-IP 511731 MODELWARE D2.8 MDD Process Framework (2006)
22. Miles, M.B., Huberman, A.M.: Qualitative data analysis. SAGE Publications, Thousand Oaks (1994)
23. Komi-Sirviö: Development and evaluation of software process improvement methods. Doctoral dissertation University of Ooulu (2004)
24. Djurić, D., Gašević, D., Devedžić, V.: Ontology modeling and MDA. Journal of bject Technology 4(1), 109–128 (2005)
25. Störrle, H.: A PROLOG-based Approach to Representing and Querying UML Models. n: Workshop on Visual Languages and Logic (VLL), Coeur d'Al`ene, Idaho, USA (2007)

General Mode Controller for Software on Artificial Satellite with Model-Based Validation Tool

Toshihiro Obata and Teiichiro Inoue

Mitsubihi Electric Corporation Kamakura Works,
325 Kamimachiya Kamakura Kanagawa 247-8520 Japan
Obata.Toshihiro@dp.MitsubishiElectric.co.jp

Abstract. High quality and flexibility are strongly required for embedded software on artificial satellites. High quality is very important because any single halt is not allowed over 15 years operation period without any significant maintenance. Flexibility is also important to adapt customer requirements which may vary after operation experiences. A quick and reliable way to modify the software functions is required. The model-based approach will contribute to solve this problem. Mitsubishi Electric Corporation, one of the representing artificial satellite suppliers in Japan, is now implementing a General Mode Controller on on-board software of satellites. We noticed functions related to modes and sequences are often required to modify from previous projects. The General Mode Controller can modify them in a reliable way by changing control parameters without modifying source code. The control parameters are verified by using a model-based tool, Matlab Simulink and Stateflow, to enable quick and low risk modifications.

Keywords: Mode controller, embedded system, high quality, flexibility, Simulink, Stateflow.

1 Introduction

Software of an artificial satellite on-board computer must keep working without a single halt and major maintenance for 15 years in space. It is very difficult to update the software, that may impose a risk of software malfunction, and eventually satellite loss. So the reliability of software is the most important issue. Standardization of software was encouraged because it is an easy and an efficient way to satisfy the required reliability.

The situation of the satellite on-board software has changed. A main purpose of space development was previously a technology development. It is now gradually changing to governmental and commercial services. This means a balance of requirements for software is also changing. Previously the reliability was the most important requirement, but now flexibility to the customer request are more important than before as well as quick and low cost development. Standardization of software only cannot be the best way any more to satisfy those current requirements. Model-based approach can be one of the solutions.

An analysis of software modifications on previous projects has done to improve a current modification process. It reveals one of frequently modified functions is a

K. Czarnecki et al. (Eds.): MoDELS 2008, LNCS 5301, pp. 889–895, 2008.

modification on mode related functions. A model for the mode related functions are generalized like Fig. 1. Typical modifications of mode related functions are from simple modifications like:

- Modification of a telemetry when modes are changed
- Addition of a task in a task sequence executed during a specific mode

to more complex modifications like:

- Addition of a set of a mode and task sequence
- Addition of a new condition for a mode transition

Flexibility will be limited because modifications on the source code need cost and time, even if the modifications are simple.

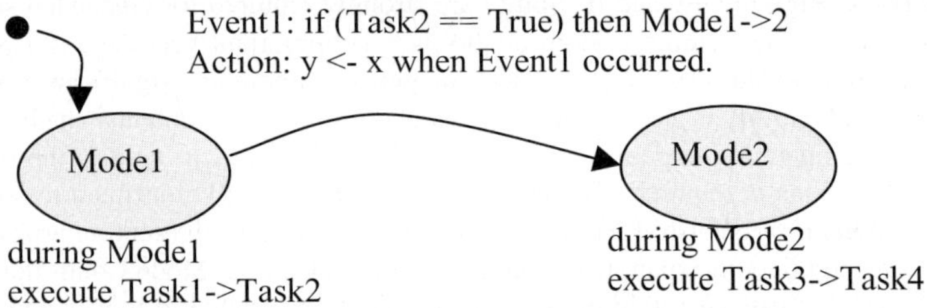

Fig. 1. Generic Model for Mode Related Functions

Model-based approach is one of effective methods to achieve quick, high quality and flexible software implementation. Especially automated source code generation tool like Real Time Workshop of Simulink is highly useful for the purpose. However automated source code generation is seemed to be premature for the software on satellites. There is a necessity to modify the software of satellites on orbit. By-passing the modules to replace with modified ones and overwriting specific variables on RAM are usually used for the modifications on software. The automated code generation does not easily fit to these methods, because each module needs some special codes for these methods and a RAM image must be managed.

The other way is to implement a model-based function in the embedded software and control its behavior by changing parameters (ex. variables and constants). The quick and flexible modifications are possible, because a model-based tool like Simulink and Stateflow can be applicable for quick, flexible design and verification of the software behavior. Changing the behavior by the parameters is also efficient, because it does not affect any source codes whose modifications are cost consuming. Moreover the satellite has Telecommands as a common test and operation method to change the parameters. It is very convenient, because both of suppliers and customers can modify functions during any phase using standard test and operation facilities.

2 General Mode Controller (GMC)

The goal of General Mode Controller (GMC) is to provide a support environment for an easy installation and modification of mode transition functions that is often modified in each satellite program. GMC behaves as same as Stateflow and its mode transition behavior can be controlled by parameters for flexibility. However functions are simpler than Stateflow to fit to the embedded software on satellites. Basic concepts are the followings (Fig. 2):

- Quick function implementation from state model into embedded software
- High quality by minimizing code modification for new functions
- Flexibility achieved by changing control parameters

GMC has three elements: Task DB, Control Parameters and GMC Engine (Fig. 3). The Task Database contains atoms of 'Tasks' like:

- Algebraic function
- Data check
- Timer

These Tasks are something like a block in a Simulink. A specific sequence of Tasks is called during a specific 'Mode'. The sequence of Tasks can generate 'Event' to make a transition of Modes. When the transition of Modes occurs, a specific 'Action' is called. Each Action executes a specific sequence of Tasks.

Control Parameters define

- The sequence of Tasks executed during Mode
- The set of Mode transitions and Events
- The Action generated when the Mode transitions happened
- The sequence of Tasks executed when the specific Action happened

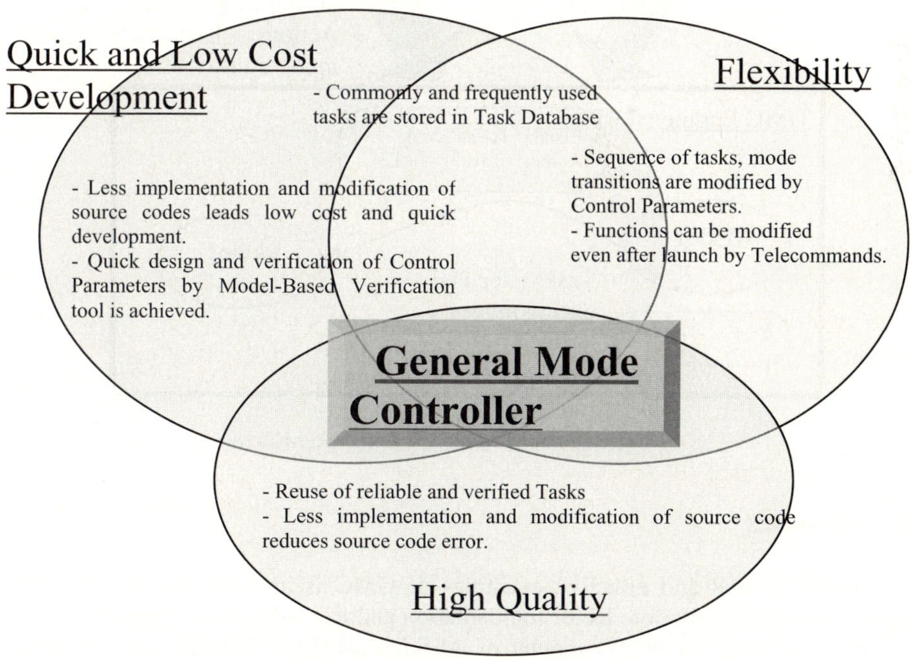

Fig. 2. Concept of General Mode Controller (GMC)

GMC Engine acts like the Stateflow and controls Mode transitions, generation of Actions, execution of Tasks in accordance with Modes and Actions. The similarity of behavior between GMC Engine and a model-based tool like Stateflow enables quick function implementation, because the model-based tool can verify the software behavior.

Task Database is expected to raise reuse rate of source codes and decrease modification cost. Analysis of modifications of the software on satellites shows that majority of modifications are minor and simple like adding a wait timer. Modifications with GMC can be simple. It is changing one of Control Parameters to reuse a Task like a timer Task from Task Database to the Task sequence. If there is no timer Task in Task Database, it will be implemented, tested and added in Task Database, but other source codes are kept as it was and not need to be verified. This makes reduction of modification cost.

A validation of Control Parameters is one of important issues for GMC to achieve quick and high quality modifications with flexibility. The model-based tool can also help it during the verification of the behavior.

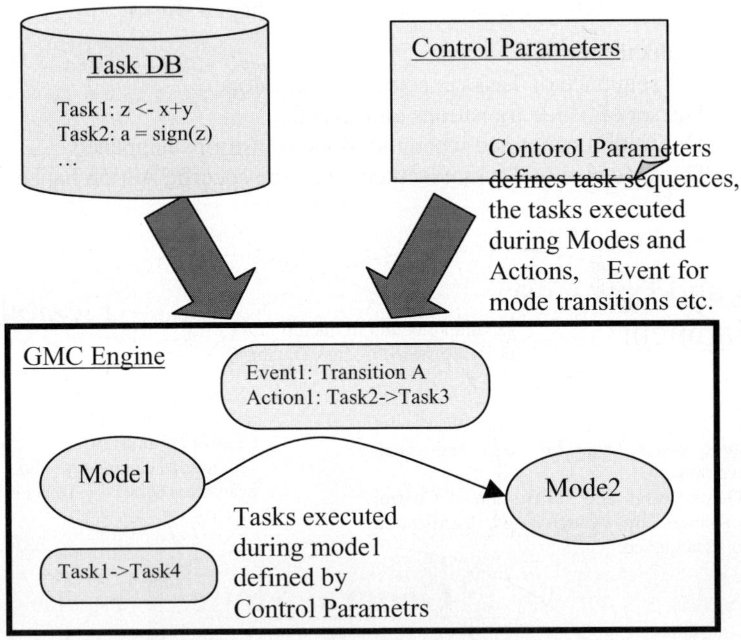

Fig. 3. General Mode Controller (GMC)

3 Examples

One of the typical and effective examples of GMC is an error handling function, called FDIR. FDIR (Failure Detection, Isolation and Reconfiguration) function is very important for an embedded computer of artificial satellites. It is because that only a single function loss may derive loss of power from solar battery or communication link with a ground station. Both of them have a possibility to cause a complete loss of satellite. So, all the indispensable functions must keep working without a frequent human operation. That is why automatic FDIR is necessary.

The FDIR function can be generalized as a transition between 2 modes, 'Pre-failure detection' and 'Post-failure detection'. Therefore, the FDIR function can be supported by GMC concept. Moreover the flexibility of GMC is suitable for the FDIR implementation. The requirements for FDIR are tends to be frequently modified, because the FDIR function has a close relationship with a design and an operation of a satellite that are different for a each satellite.

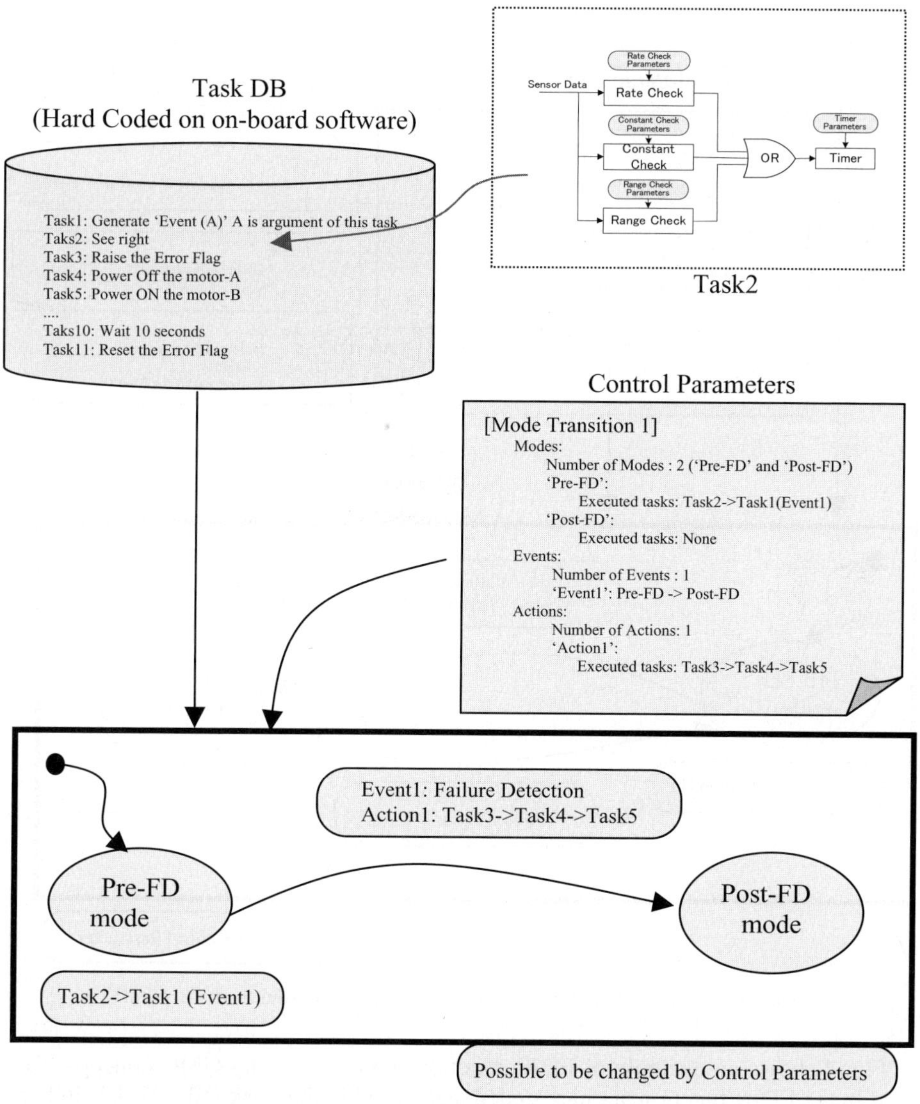

Fig. 4. Example of General Mode Controller (Original)

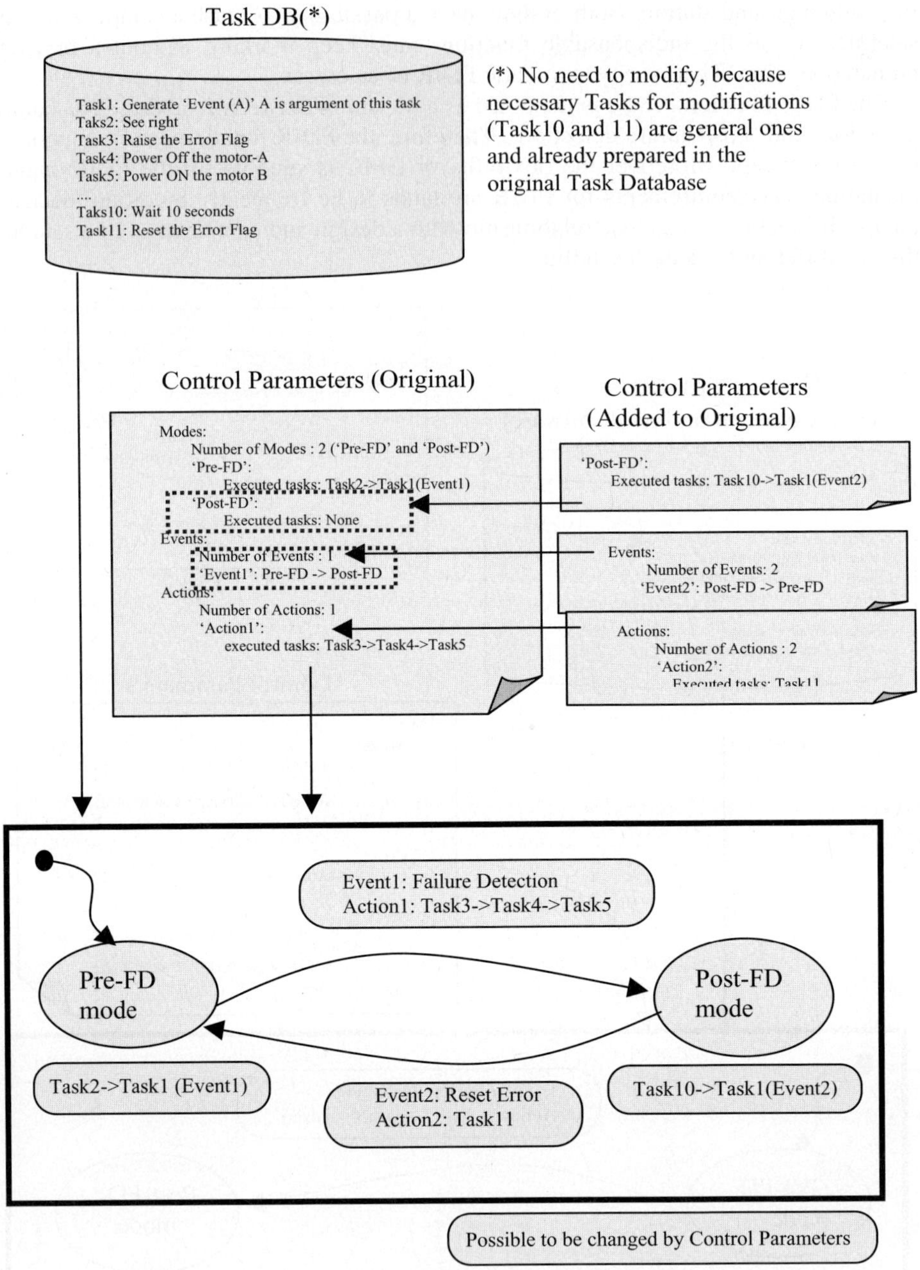

Fig. 5. Example of General Mode Controller (Modified from Original)

Fig. 4 shows an example of FDIR function implemented by GMC concept. Tasks used in the FDIR function are hard coded and stored in the Task DB. 'Task2' in Fig. 4 shows an example of tasks, which is one of a popular function of failure detection of signal data. There are 2 modes implemented in this example, 'Pre-FD (Failure Detection)' mode and 'Post-FD' mode. Control Parameters define the sequence of Tasks executed during each mode. 'Task1' is executed after 'Task2' during 'Pre-FD' mode and when the result of 'Task2' is 'True', Task1 generate 'Event1'. Then the transition from 'Pre-FD' mode to 'Post-FD' mode happens and the 'Action1' that is the sequence of 'Task3', 'Task4' and 'Task5' is executed. 'Task1' and 'Task2' are Tasks to detect failures of a signal and 'Action1' is the Tasks to isolate and reconfigure the failures detected. The sequence of Tasks executed in specific Modes and Actions are specified by 'Control Parameters'.

Fig. 5 shows how easily GMC accommodate a modification of requirement for this FDIR. The required modification is assumed that the Tasks shall be added during 'Post-FD' that may generate 'Event2' to transfer 'Post-FD' to 'Pre-FD'. This is a typical FDIR requirement, that is, "after the isolation and reconfiguration of the failure, the system must return in the normal operation". Adding a few Control Parameters makes easy modification to satisfy the additional requirements. Added 'Control Parameters' adds the sequence of Tasks executed during 'Post-FD' mode, 'Event2' and defines 'Action2'. There is no modifications on source code for this modification.

The Control Parameters to modify functions can be set in ROM during the implementation and the test phase of the software, or sent to the software by Telecommand during a normal operation of satellite in orbit. This means GMC can achieve flexible modifications at the same quality and cost during any phase in the life cycle of satellites. It is definitely one of the benefits for a software development of satellites.

4 Conclusions

The software of satellite on-board computer has restrictions about updating or modifying its functions. However General Mode Controller (GMC) can contribute to quick, low cost and flexible implementation of new functions or modifications with high quality. GMC supports modifications of mode transitions, which is often required for each satellite development program. Modifications can be done in a simple and effective way by using a standard function of satellites, Telecommands during design, test and also operation phase using a standard facility. Model-based tool like Simlink and Stateflow supports to verify the behavior of GMC.

To enrich the benefit of GMC, a customized model-based tool to represent a behavior of GMC will be required. This tool enables quicker translation of state models to GMC and quicker validation of Control Parameters.

Reference

1. Broenink, J.F., Groothuis, M.A., Visser, P.M., Orlic, B.: A Model-Driven Approach to Embedded Control System Implementation. In: WMC 2007(2007)

Workshops at MODELS 2008

Michel R.V. Chaudron

Leiden Institute of Advanced Computer Science
Leiden University, Netherlands
chaudron@liacs.nl

1 Introduction

The MODELS conference organizes a number of workshops as co-located events. Workshops provide the opportunity for a small group of people to exchange recent or preliminary results and to conductintensive discussions on a particular topic. They complement the main conference and are generally very well appreciated by attendees.

The selection committee that reviewed the proposals was formed by the following researchers:

Workshop Selection Committee

Chair: Michel R.V. Chaudron, University of Leiden, Netherlands
Holger Giese, Hasso-Plattner-Institut, Germany
Jochen Küster, IBM Zurich Research Laboratory, Switserland
Henri Muccini, University of L'Aquila, Italy
Hans Vangheluwe, McGill University, Canada

For this 2008 edition, it has been decided to host 12 one-day satellite events, during the first days of the conference. The workshops that were selected are detailed in the following section. The topics of the workshops suggest the following trends in research in model-based software development:

- Integration the modelling of extra-functional properties together with traditional functionality-oriented modeling of structure and behaviour. This is witnessed by workshops on security, adaptivity and self-management (models@runtime), and non-functional properties in domain-specific languages.
- The assessment of the impact of model-driven development. This is witnessed by the workshops on Empirical Studies in Model Driven Engineering and Quality in Modeling.
- The study of model-driven development for specific application domains, such as healthcare, web-systems, embedded systems.
- Maturing of tools and development techniques through workshops on co-evolution and consistency management as well as on OCL tools.

K. Czarnecki et al. (Eds.): MoDELS 2008, LNCS 5301, pp. 896–905, 2008.

Among the selected workshops, some have been held in previous edition of the conference, and some are new to the conference. This novelty is important to the conference because it shows that the area of model-driven development still opens up new questions and areas of research.

In the next section follows a brief overview of each of the workshops. Each workshop publishes its program online and we encourage you to also consult the Satellite Events Proceedings that is expected to be published after the workshops have taken place and that will contain highlights of each workshops. This can be a summary written by their organizers and/or improved versions of the best two papers of each workshops. We hope that this will provide a good idea of the workshops discussions and results.

2 Detailed List of Workshops

W1: Challenges in Model Driven Software Engineering

Organizers: Ragnhild vd Straeten (Vrije Universiteit Brussel), Tom Mens (Université de Mons-Hainaut), and Stefan van Baelen (K.U.Leuven, Belgium)

Abstract: The state of research and practice of model-driven engineering has significantly progressed over the last decade. Nevertheless, there are still many open problems and shortcomings of current-day model-driven software engineering. Therefore, during this workshop we raise the question of how to proceed next, and we want to identify the future challenges in the field of MDE. This workshop aims to be the place to disseminate new and revolutionary ideas, to discuss future challenges, and to encourage new ways of thinking in the field of MDE.

Consider to submit the challenges you feel are important, or to submit your revolutionary ideas or your new ways of thinking about MDE. The workshop seeks original research statements. Papers with a long term vision, providing revolutionary new ideas and "grand challenges" in model-driven software engineering are particularly welcomed.

URL: `http://ssel.vub.ac.be/ChaMDE0`

W2: Model-Driven Web Engineering

Organizers: Nora Koch (Ludwig-Maximilians-Universität München and irquent GmbH, Germany), Antonio Vallecillo (Universidad de Malaga, Spain), and Geert-Jan Houben (Technische Universiteit Delft, The Netherlands)

Abstract: The MDWE'2008 workshop aims at providing a discussion forum where researchers and practitioners on model-driven development of Web applications can meet, disseminate and exchange ideas and problems, identify some of the key issues related to these topics, and explore together possible solutions and future works.

Web Engineering is a specific domain in which Model-Driven Software Development (MDSD) can be successfully applied. Existing model-based Web engineering approaches already provide excellent methods and tools for the design and development of most kinds of Web applications. They address different concerns using separate models (navigation, presentation, workflows, etc.) and come with model compilers that produce most of the application's Web pages and logic based on these models. However, most of these Web Engineering proposals do not fully exploit all the potential benefits of MDSD, such as complete platform independence, metamodeling, and model transformations.

Recently, the MDA initiative has introduced a new approach for organizing the design of an application into different models so portability, interoperability, and reusability can be obtained through architectural separation of concerns. MDA covers a wide spectrum of topics and issues (MOF-based metamodels, UML profiles, model transformations, modeling languages and tools, etc.). In another camp, Software Factories provide concepts and resources for the model-based design of complex applications. At the same time, we see a trend towards the incorporation of emerging technologies like the Semantic Web and (Semantic) Web Rule Languages, which aim at fostering application interoperability, especially with the advent of the Web 2.0 and its related technologies and richer applications. However, the effective integration of all these new techniques with the already existing model-based Web Engineering approaches is still unresolved.

The main goal of this workshop is to offer a forum to exchange experiences and ideas related to model-driven software development (MDSD) in the Web Engineering field.

URL: `http://mdwe2008.pst.ifi.lmu.de`

W3: Model-Based Design of Trustworthy Health Information Systems

Organizers: Ruth Breu (University of Innsbruck, Austria) and Janos Sztipanovits (Vanderbilt University, USA)

Abstract: The objective of the workshop is to discuss model-based methods for the design of Health Information Systems (HIS) offering a revolutionary new way for the interaction between medical patients and Health Care Providers. While other information-intensive industries have developed and deployed standards-based, secure information infrastructures, healthcare has been characterized as a "trillion dollar cottage industry" that is still dependent upon paper records and fragmented, error-prone approaches to service delivery. The primary concern is security and privacy that needs to be organically integrated into HIS architectures.

The workshop intends to bring computer scientists, medical experts, and legal policy experts together to discuss research results in the development and application of model-based methods for representing, analyzing and integrating, architectures, privacy and security policies, computer security mechanisms, web authentication, and human factors engineering. A central focus of the discussions will be a Design Platform, which will provide a suite of modeling languages, modeling tools, model verification tools and model-based generators for building HIS, integrating HIS with Electronic Medical Record systems and the business processes of providers.

URL: `http://qe-informatik.uibk.ac.at/mothis2008`

W4: Model Based Architecting and Construction of Embedded Systems

Organizers: Iulian Ober (University of Toulouse, France), Stefan Van Baelen (K.U.Leuven, Belgium), Susanne Graf (VERIMAG, France), Mamoun Filali (CNRS IRIT, France), Thomas Weigert (Missouri S&T, USA), and Sébastien Gérard (CEA, France)

Abstract: The development of embedded systems with real-time and other types of critical constraints raises distinctive problems. In particular, the development teams have to handle very specific architectural choices, as well as various types of critical non-functional constraints (related to real-time deadlines and to platform parameters like energy consumption, memory footprint, etc.). In this context, the last few years have seen an increased interest in using model-driven engineering (MDE) techniques. Such techniques are interesting for two main reasons: (1) they allow for capturing dedicated architectural and non-functional information in precise (preferably formal) domain-specific models, and (2) they provide the premise for a layered construction of systems, in which the (platform independent) functional aspects can be kept separated from architectural and non-functional (platform specific) aspects, after which they can be combined more or less automatically via model transfor! mations to obtain the final system.

The objective of this workshop is to bring together researchers and practitioners interested in modelbased software engineering for real-time embedded systems. We are seeking contributions relating to this subject at different levels, from modelling languages and semantics to concrete application experiments, from model analysis techniques to model-based implementation and deployment. Given the criticality of the application domain, we particularly focus on model-based approaches yielding efficient and provably correct designs. Concerning models and languages, we welcome contributions presenting novel modelling approaches as well as contributions evaluating existing ones. We target in particular Architecture description languages (ADLs), Domain specific design and implementation languages, Languages for capturing non-functional constraints, and Component languages and system description languages.

URL: `http://www.artist-embedded.org/artist/ACES-MB-08.html`

W5: Transforming and Weaving Ontologies and Model Driven Engineering

Organizers: Fernando Silva Parreiras, Jeff Z. Pan (University of Aberdeen, U.K.), Uwe Aßmann (Dresden University of Technology, Germany), and Jakob Henriksson (Dresden University of Technology, Germany)

Abstract: The interest in integrating Ontologies and Software Engineering has gained more attention with commercial and scientific initiatives. The Semantic Web Best Practice and Deployment Working Group (SWBPD) in W3C included a Software Engineering Task Force (SETF) to explore how Semantic Web and Software Engineering can cooperate. The Object Management Group (OMG) has an Ontology Platform Special Interest Group (PSIG) aiming at formalizing semantics in software by knowledge representation and related technologies. The concrete results of such initiatives are the specification of the OMG Ontology Definition Metamodel, the OWL 1.1 Metamodel, the introduction to Ontology Driven Architectures and a Semantic Web Primer for Object-Oriented Software Developers.

Nevertheless, many questions come to light, as Model Driven Engineering (MDE) or Model Driven Architecture (MDA) spreads. Disciplines like model transformation and domain specific languages become essential in order to support different kinds of models in a model driven environment. Understanding the role of OWL/RDFS ontologies in these fields is crucial to leverage the development of such disciplines. Thus, we highlight the following open questions: How can the scientific and technical results around OWL/RDFS ontologies, ontology languages and their corresponding reasoning technologies be used fruitfully in Model Driven Engineering (MDE) or Model Driven Architecture (MDA)? What is the role of OWL/RDFS ontologies in supporting model transformation? How can OWL/RDFS ontologies improve designing domain specific languages? Are current query languages able to query both kinds of models?

URL: `http://isweb.uni-koblenz.de/events/TWOMDE2008`

W6: Empirical Studies of Model Driven Engineering

Organizers: Bente Anda (Simula Research Laboratory, Norway), Erik Arisholm (Simula Research Laboratory, Norway), and Lionel Briand (Simula Research Laboratory, Norway)

Abstract: *Motivation.* It is often difficult to rigorously evaluate Model-Driven Engineering (MDE) technologies. In particular, the challenges associated with the involvement of human subjects and organizations in empirical studies of MDE need to be tacked. The choice of research method (experiments/case studies/action research) also entails important tradeoffs with regards to the applicability and validity of results and needs careful consideration. The aim of this workshop is to discuss ways in which proposed model-driven engineering (MDE) technologies should be evaluated, with a specific emphasis on how to plan, conduct, analyze and report the results of empirical studies. The emphasis will be on empirical studies involving human users, since MDE technologies are typically expected to be used by software engineers to improve various quality aspects of software systems and the productivity of software development.

Goals. Research challenges that are of particular importance in the context of MDE evaluations will be discussed. Topics include: What are the main obstacles and potential remedies when performing empirical studies of MDE? What are the relative strengths and weaknesses of controlled experiments in laboratory and field settings, industrial case studies and action research in the context of MDE evaluation? How should we deal with the unavoidable tradeoffs between realism (to ensure that the results are applicable to "real" development contexts) and control (to ensure trustworthiness in the cause/effect-relationships being claimed on the basis of the empirical data)? The goal of the workshop is to pave the way for the development of a MDE-specific framework for empirical evaluation of MDE technologies, or at least provide a minimum standard for evaluation that published work in the MDE community should abide by.

URL: `http://www.simula.no/~erika/ESMDE`

W7: Quality in Modeling

Organizers: Jean-Louis Sourrouille (INSA Lyon, France), Miroslaw Staron (IT University of Goteborg, Sweden), Ludwik Kuzniarz (BTH, Sweden), Mohagheghi Parastoo (SINTEF ICT, Norway), and Lars Pareto (Chalmers University, Gotenborg, Sweden)

Abstract: Quality assessment and assurance constitute an important part of software engineering. The issues of software quality management are widely researched and approached from multiple perspectives and viewpoints. The introduction of a new paradigm in software development—namely Model Driven Development (MDD) and its variations (e.g., MDA [Model Driven Architecture], MDE [Model Driven Engineering], MBD [Model Based Development], MIC [Model Integrated Computing]—raises new challenges in software quality management, and as such should be given a special attention. In particular, the issues of early quality assessment, based on models at a high abstraction level, and building (or customizing the existing) prediction models for software quality based on model metrics are of central importance for the software engineering community.

The goal of this workshop is to gather researchers and practitioners interested in the emerging issues of quality in the context of Model Driven Development. In the long run, the aim of this workshop is to raise knowledge about Quality in Modeling to a similar level than knowledge about quality in usual development contexts. In the short run, the objective is to continue discussions on various aspects of model quality as well as to draw conclusions about a common quality model.

URL: `http://www.ituniv.se/~miroslaw/qim08`

W8: Non-functional System Properties in Domain Specific Modeling Languages

Organizers: Marko Boskovic (University of Oldenburg, Germany), Dragan Gašević (Athabasca University, Canada), Claus Pahl (Dublin City University, Ireland), Bernhard Schätz (Technische Universität München, Germany)

Abstract: *Description.* The NFPinDSML 2008 workshop brings together researchers and practitioners from communities dedicated to non-functional properties of software systems and researches from language engineering to study the principles of integration of various non-functional system properties and language engineering in order to further expand principles of reasoning about non-functional properties of software systems in Domain Specific Modeling Languages, and model-driven engineering in general.

Relevance. For the engineering of systems of a particular domain, Domain Specific Modeling Languages (DSML) - domain-oriented modeling languages developed for solving specific classes of problems related to such a domain - are becoming a common-place in software and system engineering. While DSML are mostly dedicated to functional requirements, often they do not address non-functional system properties (e.g. availability, reliability, security, performance, timeliness, efficiency, etc.). Non-functional system properties are recognized as at least as important as functional properties and have to be addressed during the design of systems. Non-functional properties of interest vary from domain to domain. Furthermore, there is different understanding of what are non-functional, and functional properties from domain to domain (e.g. timing and reliability properties are considered functional in the domain of embedded systems, and that is not the case in information systems). Finally, because of different relations, intrinsic-when one non-functional attribute affects another, or extrinsic-when a value of a non-functional property is behaving in opposing way to value of another, analysis of non-functional properties can be single and multi-dimensional.

As till now, the study of engineering DSMLs and analysis of non-functional properties of software systems lack common principles. For this reason the workshop tries to gather a forum discussing issues of integration of non-functional system properties estimation and evaluation in the context of software system engineering with DSMLs. Because of the significant variety of languages and their application, the synergic use is a complex task that requires join efforts of different communities.

Scope. The central question this workshop is the study of common principles of Domain Specific Language Engineering, and analysis of non-functional properties. The typical NFPinDSML 2008 paper studies Domain Specific Modeling Language concepts, non-functional system properties and annotation, computation and evaluation of non-functional properties of the final software product as a characteristic of a language.

URL: `http://planet-mde.org/nfpindsml`

W9: Modeling Security

Organizers: Jon Whittle (Lancaster University, UK), Jan Jürjens (Open University, UK), Bashar Nusheibeh (Open University, UK), and Glen Dobson (Lancaster University, UK)

Abstract: *Description.* Ensuring computer security is one of the key challenges in making modern systems safe, reliable and dependable. Sophisticated types of attacks require a holistic view of a system's vulnerabilities and necessitate security analysis techniques that take into account all phases of development. In other words, there is a pressing need for systematic methods for analysing and assessing the security of system models, where models here are interpreted broadly to include requirements, architecture and design, as well as organizational and business models.

Aims. This workshop aims to bring together practitioners and researchers in both software and system modeling and security to transfer ideas, foster new collaborations, and define a research agenda for secure modeling of software-intensive systems. Through technical presentations and directed discussions, the workshop will deliver a document outlining research challenges for the community, which will act to inspire future research and to summarize state-of-the-art work in this area.

URL: `http://www.comp.lancs.ac.uk/modsec`

W10: Models@run.time

Organizers: Nelly Bencomo (Lancaster University, UK), Gordon Blair (Lancaster University, UK), Robert France (Colorado State University, USA), Freddy Munoz (INRIA, France), and Cedric Jeanneret (Universitat Zurich, Switzerland)

Abstract: *Motivation.* We are witnessing the emergence of new classes of application that are highly complex, inevitably distributed, and operate in heterogeneous and rapidly changing environments. These systems are required to be adaptable, flexible, reconfigurable and, increasingly, self-managing. Such characteristics make systems more prone to failure when executing and thus the development and study of appropriate mechanisms for runtime validation and monitoring is needed.

Goal. The goal of this workshop is to look at issues related to developing model-driven approaches to monitoring and managing the execution of systems. This theme and its treatment requires the bringing together of a variety of communities including researchers working on model-driven software development, software architectures, reflection (including for example architectural reflection), and autonomic and self healing systems. Discussions in the workshop will address questions such as: What should a runtime model look like? How can the models be maintained at runtime? What are the best approaches to follow when developing runtime models?

URL: `http://www.comp.lancs.ac.uk/~bencomo/MRT`

W11: Model Co-evolution and Consistency Management

Organizers: Alfonso Pierantonio (University of L'Aquila, Italy), Dirk Deridder (Vrije Universiteit Brussel, Belgium), Pierre-Yves Schobbens (University of Namur, Belgium), and Jeff Gray (University of Alabama at Birmingham, USA)

Abstract: A core task in MDE is the manipulation and transformation of models. Thus, model co-evolution and consistency management become crucial activities to cope with the natural changes of any software system. In fact, there is an increasing need for more disciplined techniques and engineering tools to support a wide range of model evolution activities, including model differencing, model comparison, model refactoring, model inconsistency management, model versioning and merging, and co-evolution of models.

Recently, a number of works devoted to the detection of differences between models has emerged to foster enhanced model management practices. The exploitation of differences is an appropriate solution for version management, because in general the complete system model is far larger than the modifications that occur from one version to another. Apart from these works, further research is required to address the rest of the model evolution activities (refactoring, inconsistency management, versioning, etc.). Moreover, the different dimensions of evolution make the problem intrinsically difficult because modifications can reflect coherent adaptations of correlated artifacts at several layers of the metamodeling architecture. For example, some well-formed rules can be invalidated when a metamodel evolves. The same happens with the associated model transformations. Furthermore, model adaptations should be propagated to artifacts interconnected by means of model transformations. ! Finally, evolution of model transformations should be reflected in both source and target models.

URL: `http://www.info.fundp.ac.be/mccm`

W12: OCL Tools: From Implementation to Evaluation and Comparison

Organizers: Jordi Cabot (Open University of Catalonia, Spain), Martin Gogolla (University of Bremen, Germany), and Pieter Van Gorp (University of Antwerp, Belgium)

Abstract: In recent years, MDA and associated MDE methodologies, approaches and languages (like QVT) emphasized the role that OCL has to play in MDE development. Moreover, the modeling community is continuously pushing forward the OCL, far beyond its initial requirements as a precise modeling language complementing UML specifications. Now, OCL is used in quite different applications domains (e.g., domain-specific languages, web semantics) and for various purposes (e.g., model verification and validation, code-generation, test-driven development, transformations). To be successful, all these new OCL applications, extensions and usages require new OCL tools that support them.

This workshop aims to look specifically at how to develop, apply, evaluate and compare all kinds of OCL-related tools. The workshop will bring together OCL practitioners and OCL tool builders (from both academy and industry) in order to evaluate today's state-of-the-practice. In particular, the workshop will focus the discussion on how to evaluate, compare and select the right OCL tools for a given purpose, how to deal with the expressiveness and complexity of the language and how to tackle its ambiguous or underdefined issues from a practical point of view.

URL: `http://www.fots.ua.ac.be/events/ocl2008`

Educators Symposium at MODELS 2008

Michał Śmiałek

Warsaw University of Technology,
Warsaw, Poland
smialek@iem.pw.edu.pl

Abstract. Model-driven engineering is becoming increasingly popular in software development projects as it raises level of abstraction, thus improving our ability to handle complex systems. In many academic and industrial centers, software modeling has already been introduced into their curricula. Despite this, it seems that education does not yet support the modeling paradigm well enough thus limiting its acceptance as a mature method of developing software systems. The goal of this symposium was to find ways to change this situation. Specifically, the symposium sought ways of showing benefits of modeling in a way that is pedagogically effective and attractive to the students. It also tried to make recommendations for placing the modeling courses in the overall software development educational path, which should include not only UML fundamentals but also a demonstration of the importance and place of modeling in the overall path from business (environment) to software products.

1 Introduction

Modeling is an important part of any software development effort, even if the developers do not realize that they are in fact doing modeling by eg. scribbling quick diagrams on whiteboards. It allows developers to abstract over complex problems and create "visual maps" of the "territory" covered by the resulting programs. However, usually, models are used only informally to support programming with additional (often hand-written) "visual notes". Although it is fairly widespread, the approach of using models in a systematic way which includes automatic model transformation and code generation has not yet got through to industry to the degree which would satisfy the advocates of the approach. This might be caused by lack of high quality, pedagogically effective MDE courses. Assuming we are convinced ourselves, we need to convince the students – prospective software engineers – that MDE gives significant benefits over other approaches. The students need to experience these benefits and gain appreciation leading to usage of MDE in their day-to-day business. Convincing the students of MDE is not easy, as it is usually treated as a "nice to have" feature within a software engineering project. We should thus discuss ways to convince people within the project teams to treat the model-driven approach as a "must have" that introduces additional, necessary level of abstraction thus

K. Czarnecki et al. (Eds.): MoDELS 2008, LNCS 5301, pp. 906–907, 2008.

leveraging understanding of complex systems. We need to convince students who normally use eg. only Java IDEs that they also need modelling plug-ins which would not only give a visual map of their Java programs but also allow for better organization of the path from user requirements to code.

2 Organization, Selection and Thematic Areas

The symposium was organized around three types of submissions: full papers, short position papers and informal teaching technique descriptions. Formal submissions resulted in classical paper presentations and associated discussion. Informal submissions resulted in "tricks and tips" sessions where several educational artifacts were presented and discussed. From the submitted formal papers only 8 could be selected, and a thorough review process was needed. The selected paper submissions formed three thematic groups: teaching model semantics, tool support for teaching models and modeling course concepts.

Within the first area, there were presented approaches to show to the students that modeling (specifically in UML) is more than just drawing nice (meaning also: syntactically correct) diagrams. Within the proposed courses, the role of modeling language semantics is presented to the students. This is important, as only presenting model semantics in a pedagogically effective way can supply the students with arguments for using models in practice. The second group of papers stresses the role of tools that support teaching. This does not only pertain to the obvious role of CASE tools. Novel approaches use tools to give certain pedagogical feedback on the models created by students. While creating their models within CASE tools, students receive instant comments that help in improving their modeling style. Such tools relieve the teachers and help in organizing courses with many attendants. They can also help in preparing fair and transparent criteria for assessing models created by many students. The final group of presentations treated new course ideas. This includes ideas on how to cope with large "volumes" of students (up to 1000 per course) and approaches which bring the modeling theory closer to practice by introducing project assignments that emulate real life in a software development organization.

The symposium concluded with discussion in groups formed around the above three thematic areas. The discussion concentrated on finding more effective ways to promote the MDE paradigm through software modeling education. The detailed results of this discussion can be found on the symposium web page: http://www.iem.pw.edu.pl/edusymp08/

Acknowledgement

I would like to thank all the members of the Program Committee for their help in selecting the most relevant papers which highly contributed to the symposium's success. I would also like to thank them for valuable comments which resulted in improving this summary text.

Doctoral Symposium at MODELS 2008

Alexander Pretschner

Information Security, ETH Zürich, Switzerland
pretscha@inf.ethz.ch

The doctoral symposium solicited submissions on research-in-progress that is meant to lead to a PhD dissertation. The goal of the symposium is to provide doctoral students with independent constructive criticism

- by written reviews of three members of the program committee; and
- by discussing their work with senior scientists and other doctoral students.

Regardless of whether or not the submission is accepted for presentation, students would hence benefit from submitting to the symposium.

Submissions were required to describe research - and intended research - from any area of model-based development in any activity of the development process. Students were asked to precisely state the problem, the (intended) solution, and the (intended) contributions, including pointers to relevant related work. The described research should have been concrete enough as to allow for its assessment. It should, however, also have been premature enough as to allow the doctoral students to incorporate the comments received from the reviewers and the audience before submitting the thesis (i.e., approximately in the 2nd to 3rd year, depending on the system).

In contrast to contributions to the main conference track, submissions to the doctoral symposium were explicitly allowed to concentrate on the overall goals of the doctoral thesis rather than on single technical results.

24 papers from 14 countries were submitted. The program committee judged the submissions w.r.t. originality and precision of the problem statement, solution description, and the contributions. Ideas and mere statements of intent were not deemed sufficient for acceptance. The program committee also assessed whether or not the (intended) contributions appeared realistic.

In alphabetical order of the first author, the following contributions were accepted:

1. Michael Felderer: *A Framework for Model–Based Quality Assurance of Service Oriented Systems*
2. Elina Kalnina: *DSL tool development with transformations and static mappings*
3. Georgia Kapitsaki and Iakovos Venieris: *Model-Driven development of Context-aware Web Applications based on a Context Management Architecture*
4. An Phung-Khac: *A Model-driven Architecture- based Approach to Adaptable and Evolvable Distributed Collaborations*

K. Czarnecki et al. (Eds.): MoDELS 2008, LNCS 5301, pp. 908–909, 2008.

5. Sergejs Rikacovs and Janis Barzdins: *Towards a seed transformation language and its implementation*
6. Victor Sanchez, Jose Luis Roda, Adolfo Sánchez-Barbudo Herrera and Antonio Estévez: *Using a Virtual-Machine Strategy to Enhance Model Transformation Experiences*
7. Antoine Wiedemann: *Relational Database Modeling*
8. Andres Yie: *Multi-step Concern Transformation*

Pietro Colombo's contribution on *A SysML-based approach to requirements analysis of real-time systems* would have been accepted but was considered too close to the end of the thesis — feedback provided at the symposium seemed unlikely to influence the results.

Each paper was reviewed by at least three reviewers. The doctoral symposium is the result of the constructive work of the program committee:

- Benoît Baudry, INRIA Rennes, France
- Ruth Breu, University of Innsbruck, Austria
- Betty Cheng, Michigan State University, USA
- Jürgen Dingel, Queen's University, Kingston, Canada
- Gregor Engels, University of Paderborn, Germany
- Robert France, Colorado State University, USA
- Ulrich Frank, University of Duisburg-Essen, Germany
- Sudipto Ghosh, Colorado State University, USA
- Mats Heimdahl, University of Minnesota, USA
- Jean-Marc Jézéquel, INRIA Rennes, France
- Jochen Küster, IBM Research Zurich, Switzerland
- Yves Le Traon, TELECOM Bretagne, Rennes, France
- Tom Mens, University of Mons-Hainaut, Belgium
- Pieter Mosterman, The MathWorks, USA
- Henry Muccini, University of L'Aquila, Italy
- Claudia Pons, University of La Plata, Argentinia
- Alexander Pretschner, ETH Zürich, Switzerland
- Miroslaw Staron, University of Göteborg, Sweden
- Friedrich Steimann, Fernuniversität Hagen, Germany

IBM generously sponsors a best paper award that will be awarded during the symposium.

The organizer would like to express his gratitude to all students who submitted their work, to the members of the program committee, to IBM for sponsoring the award, to Claudia Pons for sharing her experiences from last year's symposium, and to the organizers of the main conference, Ileana Ober and Jean-Michel Bruel.

Tutorials at MODELS 2008

Xavier Blanc

UPMC
Université Pierre et Marie Curie
75006 Paris, France
Xavier.Blanc@lip6.fr

1 Introduction

Model-driven engineering (MDE) is used frequently for complex systems development in various domains. Although the UML has played a large role in software modeling in both academia and industry, other languages and systems are also used. The 2008 edition of MODELS tutorials covered a wide range of domains in which MDE is applied, including semantic web, real-time distributed and embedded systems, web services, and security.

The selection committee reviewing the proposals was formed by the following researchers:

- Colin Atkinson, University of Mannheim, Germany;
- Xavier Blanc, University Pierre et Marie Curie, France (chair);
- Jeff Gray, University of Alabama at Birmingham, USA;
- Tom Mens, University of Mons-Hainaut, Belgium; and
- Jacques Robin, Universidade Federal de Pernambuco, Brazil.

The committee selected nine tutorials which are detailed in the following section.

2 Detailed List of Tutorials

T1: Aspect-Oriented Modeling

Presenters: Jon Whittle, Joaõ Araújo, Ana Moreira

Abstract: ModelAspects are concerns whose representation is scattered across multiple software artefacts. If not handled properly, they lead to the problems of concern scattering (a single concern is represented in many different places) and concern tangling (a single artefact represents multiple concerns). Aspects are now fairly well understood at the programming level but at the modeling level, despite a plethora of proposals, there is not yet any real consensus on the best approach.This tutorial will survey the most promising approaches to aspect-oriented modeling and will therefore give attendees an ideal introduction into the world of aspect-oriented modeling. Rather than

K. Czarnecki et al. (Eds.): MoDELS 2008, LNCS 5301, pp. 910–915, 2008.

trying to cover all approaches, the tutorial will present representative examples of the major ideas that have influenced the field. The tutorial will, therefore, provide an immersive introduction into this exciting area in a way that succinctly characterizes the major achievements so far as well as the major challenges yet to be overcome. The tutorial will be highly interactive and will be based on a variety of teaching methods, including lectures and hands-on exercises. In particular, one concrete example will be tackled by the participants using multiple approaches so that attendees get a very real sense of the advantages and disadvantages of the different methods.

T2: Model-to-Model Transformation with ATL

Presenters: Frédéric Jouault, Brahim-Khalil Loukil, William Piers

Abstract: Modeling technologies help design software systems by offering the possibility to represent their different parts (e.g., user interface, class structure) more adequately as models defined in Domain- Specific Languages (DSLs). This contrasts with the traditional way of encoding all the functionality of a large system using a single General Purpose Language like Java. However, for the system to actually run, code has to be generated from these higher-level models. Model-to-Model (M2M) transformation is one of the key techniques that are used to achieve this result. The ATL tools provided in the M2M Eclipse.org modeling project make it possible for developers to use this technique in practice. These tools are to model-to-model transformation what JDT (Java Development Tools) are to Java development. This tutorial presents the ATL language and its toolbox, which consist of: an editor with syntax highlighting, and content assist; a speed-optimized execution engine; and a debugger. Three different transformation examples will be presented and implemented in ATL. The presentation will be performed by model-to-model transformation experts, among who is the architect of ATL, who designed the language and created the initial implementation (now further developed by contributors from the Eclipse.org community).

T3: Model-Based vs. Code-Based Verification for Critical Systems

Presenters: Jan Jurjens

Abstract: An important missing link in the model-based development of critical systems is finding a practical way to establish correspondence between a software design and its implementation. This tutorial presents work towards a solution to this problem for the case of crypto-based implementations in Java (such as crypto protocols). Given a textual specification of a crypto-based system and its implementation, we show how one can construct a precise and compact specification using the security extension UMLsec of the Unified Modeling Language (UML), which is based on a formal semantics defined using Abstract State Machines (ASMs). This formal model can then be automatically and formally verified against the security goals using automated theorem provers for first-order logic. In a second step, one can then make sure that the implementation correctly implements the specification by making use of techniques such as model-checking, run-time verification, and security testing. Our approach is supported by a tool available as open-source. As a running example for the tutorial, we use the open-source Java implementation Jessie of the SSL protocol. We will also explain how to apply the approach to the Java Secure Sockets Extension library recently made open-source by Sun.

T4: Product-Line Modeling and Automation with Eclipse

Presenters: Jules White, Egon Wuchner

Abstract: A core activity in developing a Software Product-Line (SPL) is the documentation of product variability. Product variability dictates the rules governing how an application can be retargeted to different requirement sets. Typically, product variability is captured in models, such as feature models. Once models are built that document SPL variability, tool support can be developed to help SPL engineers configure individual SPL variants. Often, complex automation may be needed to help choose good or optimal settings for the SPL's points of variability. Developing these modeling tools and automation mechanisms is challenging. This tutorial introduces Eclipse-based modeling technologies that can be used to help reduce the cost of building model-based SPL configuration tools. Furthermore, the tutorial covers different Eclipse frameworks that can be used to build constraint-based automation mechanisms into SPL modeling tools for Eclipse. Finally, the tutorial provides an introduction on how these automation mechanisms can be used to help derive optimal variants and product/application configurations for a requirement set.

T5: Model-Driven Engineering for Continuous System Integration of Large-Scale Component-Based Systems

Presenters: Dr. Aniruddha S. Gokhale, James H. Hill

Abstract: Large-scale component-based systems usually require multiple years of development effort to realize a production system. Ensuring the production system meets its performance requirements is hard due to the serialized phasing development process — where functionally correct infrastructure and application components are developed in different phases but do not meet performance requirements when integrated with each other — and unforeseen software contention issues (e.g., performance anti-patterns) that arise when the system is deployed. System execution modeling tools play a vital role in addressing this challenge. Model-driven engineering (MDE) techniques coupled with SEM tools provide intuitive abstractions to system developers for expressing system structure and behavior. Emulation and analysis frameworks associated with SEM tools enable execution and evaluation of a system under development on the target architecture. For system developers, this capability can provide early understanding of system performance and locate performance problems before they become too hard to find. Moreover, the process can be applied continuously throughout the development lifecycle. This tutorial will illustrate these features for component-based large-scale systems using the CUTS MDE-SEM tool suite. A number of case studies and short demonstrations will be used to illustrate the challenges and the solutions provided by continuous system integration using SEM tools.

T6: Effective Model Driven Engineering Patterns Principles and Practices in Action

Presenters: Bruce Trask, Angel Roman

Abstract: Model Driven Engineering (MDE) brings together multiple technologies and critical innovations and formalizes them into the next wave of software development methods. This tutorial will cover the basic patterns principles and practices of MDE. The three main MDE categories include the development of Domain Specific Languages (DSL), Domain Specific Editors (including Domain Specific Visual Languages) and, Domain Specific Transformation Engines or Generators. Expressed in terms of language development technology, these mirror the development of the Abstract Syntax, Concrete Syntax and Semantics of a new Domain Specific Language. This tutorial will cover the basic effective patterns, principles and practices for developing these MDE software artifacts. The tutorial will show how to apply these concepts as effective means with which to both raise levels of abstraction and domain specificity and thus increase power and value of tools and languages that allow developers to tackle the complexities of today's software systems. It will also show how to effectively leverage abstraction without sacrificing the ability to robustly and precisely refine these abstractions to solve real world problems. Additionally, this tutorial will cover the exact details of how to leverage the Eclipse Modeling Framework (EMF), the Eclipse Graphical Editor Framework (GEF), and the Eclipse Graphical Modeling Framework (GMF), to support the development of these three areas. These three frameworks provide a unique and integrated platform in which to learn the basics of Model Driven Engineering in full application not just in theory. Conversely, Model Driven Engineering provides an effective context in which to learn how to apply the power of these integrated Eclipse Frameworks developed to support MDE.

T7: Model Driven Language Engineering

Presenters: Jean-Marc Jezequel, Franck Fleurey

Abstract: In many domains such as aerospace and automotive industries, engineers rely on Domain Specic Modeling Languages (DSML) to solve the complex issues of engineering safety critical software. Traditional Language Engineering starts with the grammar of a language to produce a variety of tools for processing programs expressed in this language. Recently however, many new languages tend to be first defined through metamodels, i.e. models describing their abstract syntax. Relying on well tooled standards such as E-MOF, this approach makes it possible to readily benefit from a set of tools such as reflexive editors, or XML serialization of models. This tutorial aims at showing how Model Driven Engineering can easily complement these on-the-shelf tools to obtain a complete environment for such a language, including interpreter, compiler, pretty-printer and customizable editors. We illustrate the conceptual simplicity and elegance of this approach using the running example of the well known LOGO programming language, developed within the Kermeta environment.

T8: Analyzing UML/OCL Models Wit HOL-OCL

Presenters: Achim D. Brucker, Burkhart Wolff

Abstract: In this tutorial, we present the theorem proving environment HOL-OCL. The HOL-OCL system (http://www.brucker.ch/projects/hol-ocl/) is an interactive proof environment for UML/acsocl specifications that is integrated in a Model-driven Engineering (MDE) framework. HOL-OCL allows to reason over UML class models annotated with OCL specifications. Thus, HOL-OCL strengthens a crucial part of the UML to an object-oriented formal method. HOL-OCL provides several derived proof calculi that allow for formal derivations of validity of UML/OCL formulae. These formulae arise naturally when checking the consistency of class models, when formally refining abstract models to more concrete ones or when discharging side-conditions from model-transformations.

T9: Model-Based Development of Service-Oriented Architectures (SOA)

Presenters: Gregor Engels

Abstract: Service-oriented architectures (SOA) are promoted as the final answer to the long standing demand to bridge the gap between business needs and IT-solutions. Like object-orientation has been advocated as the overall structuring principle in the 90s, service-orientation is nowadays discussed as the magic bullet to align business requirements with software applications. As it is typical for any hype approach, a commonly agreed understanding of the basic principles and notions for service-oriented concepts is still missing. This leads often to misunderstandings and communication problems in IT-projects and, thus, jeopardizes the success of migration projects where existing architectures are advanced towards service-oriented architectures. The tutorial aims at clarifying the understanding of basic principles, notions, languages as well as methods of a service-oriented approach. In particular, it is explained how modelling languages like UML may be used within a structured development method for a service-oriented design of an application landscape. All introduced concepts are related to existing knowledge on software architectures, architectural styles, and architecture frameworks. Presented concrete methodical guidelines have been derived from successful industrial IT-projects and are related to Quasar Enterprise, the service-oriented development approach of sd&m AG, Munich (Germany).

Panels at MODELS 2008

Sudipto Ghosh

Department of Computer Sience
Colorado State University
Fort Collins CO 80523
ghosh@cs.colostate.edu

Panel 1: Addressing the Challenges of Multi-modeling for Domain-Specific Modeling Languages

Chair: Doug Schmidt, Vanderbilt University, USA

Domain-specific modeling languages (DSMLs) are designed to provide precise abstractions of domain-specific constructs. Models for complex systems typically do not fit neatly within a single domain, however. Moreover, capturing all important aspects of such a system requires developing multiple models using different DSMLs. This panel will explore key challenges and promising solutions associated with combining DSML models into multi-models. Example challenges discussed in the panel include (but are not limited to):

– Capturing multi-model interdependencies. Interdependencies between models, identified by a sharing or exchange of data between the models are rarely made explicit. As the number of models, the complexity of their interaction, and/or the size of the system being modeled increases, it becomes hard to keep track of model interdependencies. It is even harder to track and analyze the implications of these dependencies, both of which are necessary and challenging aspects of the multi-model integration.
– Maintaining multi-model consistency. In a consistent multi-model, there can be no unpropagated model changes, i.e., when a model in a consistent multi-model is modified, changes to the model must be propagated correctly to dependent models. Such changes may propagate through the entire set of models in the multi-model and even back to the original model itself. Not until the propagated changes converge so that no more change propagation is necessary, can we say that the multi-model is again consistent. To reach multi-model consistency, model changes must be propagated in order, with respect to their interdependencies. It is hard, however, to determine such an ordering when the dependencies are cyclic. Moreover, even if a suitable ordering of change propagation can be determined, it is hard to assess if the models will converge.
– Semantic precision of inter-model data exchange. The fact that models are interdependent necessitates that they share or exchange data. The semantics of the data must be precisely known and understood by all models

K. Czarnecki et al. (Eds.): MoDELS 2008, LNCS 5301, pp. 916–917, 2008.

participating in the exchange. Achieving this precision is challenging given multiple models, expressed in different DSMLs. Moreover, even if a syntactically correct representation of data in one model is imported into another model in the same language, there is no guarantee that the data is interpreted correctly with respect to the semantics of that data. This problem is exacerbated when data is exchanged between models specified in different DSMLs. While syntactic transformation between languages may be possible and even potentially automatable, ensuring and/or preserving semantic correctness remains challenging.

Candidate panel participants include:

– Trip Denton, Lockheed Martin Advanced Technology Labs
– Edward A. Lee, University of California at Berkeley
– Jose Meseguer, University of Illinois at Urbana-Champaign
– Douglas C. Schmidt, Vanderbilt University

Panel 2: Past and Future of MDD

Chairs: Robert France, Colorado State University, Fort Collins, USA

In this panel, a selected set of experts in the MDD research and practice arena will give their personal perspectives on what they perceive as major MDD accomplishments and challenges. Some trace the genesis of MDD to the work on object-oriented modeling (OOM) in the late eighties which led to the Object Management Group's work on defining and promoting MDA standards in the late nineties. Others go further back and recognize the pioneering work of researchers in the Computer-Aided Software Engineering (CASE) and the formal specification communities as contributing to the foundation for MDD. No matter how far back you go, it is evident that there is a significant body of MDD work and experience out there. Now is as good a time as any to reflect on what has been accomplished and what challenges remain to be tackled.

The panelists have diverse MDD-related backgrounds and thus one can expect to hear a variety of perspectives on the past and future of MDD (panelists are listed in alphabetical order in the following): Grady Booch is one of the early pioneers of OOM methods and an early architect of the UML standard, Patrick Farail has significant experience and expertise related to the use of MDD techniques on complex systems, Jeff Kramer is the author of many seminal papers on formally modeling software architectures and on software abstraction, Bran Selic has led UML-related standardization groups at the OMG and has played a key role in launching initiatives around formalizing the UML and modeling complex systems, and Richard Soley is the CEO of OMG and is one of the key driving forces behind the MDA initiative.

Author Index

Printing: Mercedes-Druck, Berlin
Binding: Stein+Lehmann, Berlin